MW01079151

# The Encyclopedia of Jewish Values

*The*
# ENCYCLOPEDIA
*of*
# JEWISH VALUES

## · Nachum Amsel ·

URIM PUBLICATIONS
Jerusalem · New York

*The Encyclopedia of Jewish Values*

by Nachum Amsel

Copyright © 2015 Nachum Amsel

Typeset by Ariel Walden

Printed in Israel

First Edition

ISBN 978-965-524-163-1

Urim Publications, P.O. Box 52287
Jerusalem 9152102 Israel

www.UrimPublications.com

Library of Congress Cataloging-in-Publication Data

Amsel, Nachum, author.
The encyclopedia of Jewish values / Nachum Amsel. – First Edition.
   pages cm
ISBN 978-965-524-163-1 (hardback)
1. Jewish ethics. 2. Jewish way of life. 3. Judaism–21st century.
4. Judaism–Doctrines. 5. Judaism and social problems.  I. Title.
BJ1285.2.A52 2015
296.3'603–dc23
2014050117

To Judy,

My *Eshet Chayil*,

My Life Partner

and true love,

Who exemplifies the very best of Jewish Values

# CONTENTS

## · CONTENTS ·

# INTRODUCTION

**M**ORE THAN EVER, PEOPLE TODAY ARE SEARCHING FOR ANSWERS, A set of values to help guide their lives and use as a compass for moral actions on a day-to-day basis. Many thinking people have concluded that the evolving values of Western society today do not provide the ethics and moral code that they are searching for. Judaism's values, which according to Jewish tradition are God-given and do not change with each generation as society changes, have already given mankind many basic ethical principles that today are considered universal morals. This volume comes to explain the details and ethics regarding a wide range of Jewish values, how Jewish law reflects the normative principles of Jewish morality, and how these principles are applied and translate into daily living in the twenty-first century. The values espoused in this book can provide an anchor for identifying right and wrong in one's life and which will allow any person, Jew or non-Jew, to find meaning in his or her daily endeavors.

In an age in which many ethical systems seem relativistic, changing and non-responsive to the needs of the times, this volume will demonstrate to the reader that normative traditional Judaism indeed has a response to every moral question of today, based upon principles that have not changed since Mount Sinai. Sometimes, the underlying value or response to a given ethical dilemma is not easy to uncover, but, as the Mishna says, if you search hard enough, the Jewish value will be found, since everything meaningful and good can already be found in Judaism.[1] Even ritual precepts of Judaism can offer underlying values, ethics, and morality that will lead to a meaningful life. Thus, the topics in this work are not limited to man-to-man commandments, but include a discussion of the man-to-God commandments as well.

Why an entire volume about morals and ethics? Why is this topic especially crucial for the Jew, not only for those searching for meaning and guidance in life, but for every person alive? It is the improvement of one's moral character and ethical behavior that is

---

1. Mishna *Avot* 5:22

the essential goal of all of Judaism according to Rabbi Eliyahu Kremer, known as the Vilna Gaon. If a person does not constantly better his or her moral values and ethical behavior, he says, then why bother living at all?[2]

This book is intended for the layman and the reader who is not necessarily knowledgeable about Judaism; Hebrew terms are explained or translated. At the same time, this work is also intended for the Torah scholar, and therefore, much effort and care has been expended to include each and every source's quote within each chapter in English and at the end of the work in the original Hebrew. Those that can understand the original sources are urged to study them for themselves and reach their own conclusions. Each chapter is written as an independent unit, which the reader can read in any order or preference he or she desires. This is a similar format to an earlier work by this author, where seventy different chapters and topics were presented ("The Jewish Encyclopedia of Moral and Ethical Issues", Jason Aronson). The reader will also notice that many statements, thoughts, and sources overlap from chapter to chapter. This is not accidental. Judaism is a complete unity[3] whose parts are enmeshed with one another and cannot always be separated into neat, specific categories.[4] Just as an orchestra is made up of many different instruments, and a symphony played properly must combine many of these instruments simultaneously, so too, Judaism's ideas and sources combine in various harmonies to help explain numerous concepts. Overlap is necessary and part of the fabric of Jewish thought.

It is *not* the purpose of this book to be a comprehensive and complete presentation of each topic, but rather a general Jewish overview in a few pages so that the reader can "taste" and then see the greatness of Judaism.[5] The Midrash says that it is preferable, at first, to speak in general terms when learning Torah.[6] Therefore, the reader should not conclude that the general overview contained in a few pages is exhaustive in nature.

The title of the book, "The Encyclopedia of Jewish Values" is a bit presumptuous. These forty topics and the 71 issues in the previous volume certainly do not cover all of Jewish values. Another three volumes with new topics will hopefully follow this one, and nearly the entire gamut of Jewish values subjects will have then been discussed.

## JUDAISM IS NOT A RELIGION, BUT, RATHER A WAY OF LIFE

The reader who delves into these pages will quickly realize that Judaism does not merely relate rituals, as do other classic religions, but rather is a way of life that affects every aspect of daily living. Thus, King Solomon states that a person can come to "know God" through

---

2. *Even Shlaima* 1:2
3. Psalms 19:8
4. *Megillah* 13a
5. Psalms 34:9
6. Midrash, *Sifra, Ha'azinu* 306

every pursuit and every action in life.[7] Therefore, every deed of every day can become transformed into a "Jewish" action if it is done for the right reasons and based on the proper motivation. Maimonides clearly says this and emphasizes that each of man's actions, from walking, eating, concluding a business deal, and even sleeping can and should be done with a moral and godly purpose.[8]

Rabbi Judah Loew, known as the Maharal, speaks of the three relationships in a person's life and how these are affected by all of an individual's actions – that of man to himself, that of man to God, and that of man to his fellow man.[9] These three relationships are all impacted by each person's thoughts, values, and actions. And while each specific activity usually affects one of the three relationships more than the others, inevitably that activity also impacts the other relationships as well. In a similar manner, Jewish tradition believes that the performance of each one of the commandments has an impact on all 613 commandments.[10] It is for this reason too that a Jew does not repeat the daily blessing recited for Torah learning each time he or she learns Torah during the day, since the Jew's mind is supposed to be connected somehow to Judaism all day through all one's actions. Thus, the wording of the blessing is "to be involved" with words of Torah, and not simply "to learn Torah."[11]

## JEWISH THOUGHTS AND VALUES ARE NOT MONOLITHIC

Since Judaism is more than three thousand years old and contains thousands of recognized volumes and sources to draw upon, there is never one monolithic Jewish opinion on any one issue. Therefore, a careful attempt has been made to find the *normative* view in each chapter, and to bring the sources that reflect that view. Undoubtedly there will be those who disagree with some of the viewpoints taken by the author and some of the decisions as to what is considered normative and what is not. An attempt has been made to find the view and ideas favored by most Rabbis today, as well as those of previous generations. However, Jewish action codified in Jewish law is considered reflective of a normative Jewish value.

But Jewish values differ markedly from Jewish law in this one respect. Despite the disputes in Jewish law that can be found on virtually every one of the thousands of pages of the Talmud, when it came to codifying Jewish law, the entire Jewish people agreed in the sixteenth century to accept *Shulchan Aruch* as The *Code of Jewish Law*. Even with greatly divergent customs between Sephardic and Ashkenazic Jews, the Rabbis at that time realized that it is was crucial to come together in one volume, and thus, the Ashkenazic

---

7. Proverbs 3:6
8. Maimonides, *Hilchot De'ot* 3:2
9. Maharal, *Derech Hashem* 1, p. 25
10. Prayer recited before many commandments such as *Tzitzit* (fringes), Sukkah, and the Four Species
11. Blessing recited each day in morning prayers

rulings of Rabbi Moshe Isserles were woven into the very fabric of the text of the rulings of Rabbi Yosef Caro, who was of Sephardic descent. One book contained the "final" Jewish law (at the time) that guided the Jew how to behave in every situation.

But when it comes to Jewish thought, there is no one book that encompasses *the* correct Jewish view on any issue. Nor should there be. Unlike Jewish law, i.e., Jewish actions, when it was necessary to come to a consensus in order to form a generally unified Jewish practice, Jewish thought *always* permitted various viewpoints. This is even alluded to in the Torah itself. The Torah, on two separate occasions, tells us that when the Jewish people originally accepted the Torah and said, "We will do it." This acceptance of practicing the Torah was said by the Jews in unison, as a totally unified people. But a few verses later, when the acceptance by the Jewish people of the Torah practice *and its ideas* is recorded as, "We will do it and we will understand it," there the unity and the words "*Yachdov*" – "unified" and "*Kol Echad*" – "one voice," are conspicuously missing.[12] From the very beginning, Jews understood that there could not be unanimity when it comes to Jewish thought. There is no one "right" idea or monolithic value concerning Jewish beliefs and outlook on life. Thus, referring to the joy gained from understanding of Jewish or Torah life, King Solomon wrote that the *paths* of Torah are pleasant, not the one singular path, but paths in plural, because there are many ways to understand the Torah and Judaism properly and legitimately.

Maimonides makes this same point in his Mishna commentary.[13] He states that unlike Jewish law, which necessarily must come to one conclusion and follow one practice, when it comes to Jewish thought, one need not rule like any one of the various opinions. Judaism makes room for more than one attitude within the structure of traditional Judaism. Within the framework of Jewish tradition, there can be more than one proper path when it comes to philosophical ideas, ethics, and beliefs.

The reader will find that the term "Judaism" has often been used in this book to describe the normative Jewish view. As explained above, this term certainly does not imply that every Judaic source agrees with this particular view, nor does it imply that this opinion reflects the gamut of Jewish thought. It is a clumsy term of convenience used for explaining the normative Jewish view, as the author understands it. Wherever possible, the sources brought to support the viewpoint espoused will be of an earlier era, such as references of Biblical and Talmudic times, rather than more modern sources. The codifiers of Jewish law have often been cited to verify that the view and value expressed has been accepted as normative. The reader who wishes to do so is encouraged to study each of the sources in the original Hebrew, in the back end of this volume.

The author has had many teachers and *Rabbeim* over the years and has drawn from

---

12. Exodus 19:8, 24:3, 24:7
13. Maimonides commentary on Mishna *Sanhedrin* 10:3

them all. Unfortunately, he has not been blessed with a good enough memory to recall each and every teacher, each and every class, and which teacher taught which ideas. Therefore each of his teachers cannot be given his or her proper credit in this book, and for that he apologizes. However, there are a number of great, outstanding scholars upon whose written and audio *Shiurim* (classes) he has consciously drawn upon to complete this work. When a certain chapter has extensively used the ideas of one or two master teachers, their contribution has been cited in the chapter itself.

Therefore, I wish to acknowledge my Rebbe, Rabbi Joseph Soloveitchik, *zt"l*, whose ideas and classes have inspired most of my other teachers as well as myself. In a similar manner, I was privileged to study with Professor Nechama Leibowitz, *zt"l*, who helped me clarify many ideas in this book. In addition, this volume could not have become a reality without the *Shiurim* and ideas of Rabbi Shlomo Aviner, Rabbi Benjamin Blech, Rabbi J. David Bleich, Rabbi Mordechai Elon,[14] Rabbi Hershel Schachter, Rabbi Yissocher Frand, Rabbi Dr. Norman Lamm, Rabbi Dr. Aharon Rakeffet, Rabbi Jonathan Sacks, Rabbi Dr. Moshe Tendler, and Rabbi Berel Wein.

I especially thank my in-laws, Max and Jenny Weil, *Ad Meah v'Esrim*, who show my family their support in so many ways each day, and who were especially generous in helping this *sefer* become a reality.

I thank my long-time friend, Tzvi Mauer, publisher of Urim, for guiding me through this project. I also thank Michal Alatin, project coordinator at Urim, and Sharon Meyer for helping me resolve many delicate issues concerning this book. Raquel Kampf, my editor, helped make my original words look better. My very special wife, Judy, to whom this book is dedicated, has not only been an inspiration, but has tolerated many lonely hours as I toiled in research and writing these chapters. I truly appreciate her patience. Finally, I thank Hashem-God, who has given me the opportunity to share my ideas and the ideas of Jewish greats from the past and present generations.

— Nachum Amsel

Tevet 5775

January 2015

---

14. See *Chagiga* 15b

# The
# ENCYCLOPEDIA
## of
# JEWISH VALUES

# ALTERNATIVE MEDICINE IN JUDAISM

CCORDING TO MOST REPORTS, more than 50% of people with illnesses today seek out medications and physicians that are not conventional. These include medicines that are called "alternative," "complementary," integrative," or "holistic," and the unorthodox therapies include acupuncture, naturopathy, chiropractic, herbal remedies, homeopathy, metabolic therapies, amulets, crystals, touch therapy, and vitamin and mineral therapies. Specifically in treating cancer, many patients are willing to try unproven methods and cures in addition to conventional therapy.

Judaism has a long recorded history of individuals who have used non-conventional approaches to cure disease. How does Judaism view these therapies? Could there possibly be any problem from a Jewish perspective in trying them if no harm comes to the patient? If these methods prove successful in reducing pain and symptoms, would there be any objection from the medical community or the Rabbis? Judaism has much to say about these questions and about other methods of alternative medicine that have very practical implications for today.

Before we can discuss non-conventional medicines, however, we must first understand the normative Jewish attitude towards medicine and doctors in general, and define what makes certain medicines "alternative" from a Jewish perspective. (For an expanded discussion about doctors, see the chapter "Jewish Attitudes to Doctors and Visiting the Sick.")

## THE OBLIGATION OF A JEW TO BE HEALTHY AND HEALED

One of the 613 Torah commandments incumbent upon every Jew is to be healthy and protect oneself from harm. The Torah tells us to guard ourselves from sickness and anything that may bring harm to the body, and the Talmud equates sustaining even a single human life with the infinite value of an entire world.[1] Therefore, every Jew has a special obligation to do whatever it takes to remain healthy. This appears to include taking any medications that would bring someone back to health as well as protect the body from becoming ill in the first place. The Talmud understands this principle to be the logical way to live one's life and even asks why a verse is necessary.[2] When a person is sick, he or she should call a doctor, says the Talmud. The Torah specifically tells us that a sick person should be healed by a doctor.[3] Maimonides seems to indicate that just as a doctor has an obligation to heal a patient (see below), so too, a patient has an obligation to try to protect his or her health and prevent sickness.[4] In a different context, Maimonides emphasizes a Jew's obligation to strive to be healthy, explaining that someone who is not healthy cannot fulfill his mission on earth to serve God properly.[5] Furthermore, in building a Jewish community, there are certain rudimentary elements that must be present, even in the case of the smallest Jewish population living together. In addition to a synagogue and a teacher, every Jewish community must have at least one doctor.

## DEFINING CONVENTIONAL AND ALTERNATIVE MEDICINE IN JUDAISM

The fact that doctors hold an important place in Jewish communities does not negate the fundamental Jewish belief that all healing does not come about due to any medicine or a particular doctor, but only through God. God is

---

1. Deuteronomy 4:15, *Sanhedrin* 27a
2. *Bava Kama* 46b
3. Exodus 21:19
4. Maimonides commentary on Mishna *Nedarim* 4:4
5. Maimonides, *Hilchot De'ot* 3:3, 4:23

called "your doctor" in Scripture[6] in order to highlight Judaism's core belief that everything comes from God, including the healing that is derived from medicines and the advice of doctors. In fact, traditional Jews pray three times daily for God to relieve their illnesses without placing their faith on doctors or medicines.[7] Thus in Judaism, prayer is no less an effective "medicine" to achieve healing than any physical pill or treatment. If prayer is a recognized and legitimate Jewish "medicine," it becomes increasingly difficult to define specifically what conventional medicine is and what constitutes alternative medicine from a Jewish perspective. Since all healing comes from God anyway, what difference does it make if the medicine is officially sanctioned by licensed doctors or not? If we define medicine as "anything that is used to cure, halt, or prevent disease or ease symptoms," then how does Judaism differentiate between conventional and alternative medicines?

Perhaps we can define conventional medicine as constituting only those remedies whose modus operandi, i.e., how they work to heal the body, scientists and doctors can understand precisely, while alternative medicines are those treatments whose ability to heal is not well understood. But if this were the major distinction between the two forms of medicine, then many common remedies like Statin (which is used to lower cholesterol), as well as Lithium and Tylenol, which are examples of medicines that doctors still do not know *exactly* how they work, would have be classified as alternative medicines! Perhapsconventional medicines are simply those which are approved by the FDA (Federal Drug Administration) and which licensed doctors are permitted to use, while alternative medicines have not been approved. However, this distinction is also a fuzzy and artificial one, since many new medicines and practices used by doctors around the world were originally not sanctioned and authorized for years until official approval came after testing, and now they are recognized as conventional medicine. Thus today's "alternative" medicine may actually be tomorrow's conventional medicine. Therefore, simply defining the term "alternative medicine" is indeed difficult. From a Jewish perspective as well, it is a challenge to define what is "conventional" and what is "alternative" as they both seem to work in healing ailments. Yet, as we will see later on, for purposes of Jewish law we will indeed have to make this distinction at some point.

## THE NEED FOR DOCTORS FROM A JEWISH PERSPECTIVE

If God indeed does all of the healing, why have doctors at all? Why not simply pray to God every time someone is sick, and God will either answer the prayer and heal the patient or not? This philosophically sound argument is the actual practice of some religious groups such as Christian Scientists and Jehovah Witnesses who shun doctors and rely only on God for healing. This theological question was also asked by the Talmud,[8] and it answers that had God not sanctioned doctors with a specific verse permitting them to practice medicine,[9] perhaps Judaism also would not have permitted doctors to heal as this would have been a realm left exclusively to the Almighty. In fact, several well-known commentaries write that in an ideal world, Jews would indeed behave like these Christian groups and not need doctors.[10] People who were ill would go to the prophets, not doctors, for healing, since all sickness is derived from our misdeeds and God's consequent non-protection, and therefore only God can ultimately cure any malady. However, since most people today are not on the high spiritual level required to be healed directly by God, people require doctors for healing, and God specifically desires doctors

---

6. Exodus 15:26
7. Tenth blessing of the daily *Shmoneh Esreh*

8. *Bava Kama* 85a
9. Exodus 21:19
10. *Turei Zahav* 1, on *Shulchan Aruch, Yoreh De'ah* 336, based on Nachmanides' commentary on Leviticus 26:11

to be part of the process of treatment. In the same sense it is similar to man's obligation to help poor people. One could simply ask that if God wanted to eliminate poverty, He could see to it that poor people were given adequate funds to live. But just as God put poor people in the world specifically with the intention that Jews (and others) should give them money to remove their poverty, God also desires that qualified physicians be part of the process of healing. Since traditional Judaism believes that it is God who causes most sickness, so too, God intentionally has physicians in the world to heal much of that sickness.

Therefore, anyone with the necessary knowledge (or a physician's license) is now not only permitted to treat the sick, but is *obligated* to heal, since a Jew may not stand by while someone else is hurting and can be helped. There is also another commandment to return to someone anything that was lost by him, and health is considered something that a doctor can return to his or her patient.[11] After the Torah "allows" doctors to heal and help God, Nachmanides and others say it is an obligation and commandment for doctors to be part of God's process of helping.[12] Thus, the Talmud naturally assumes that a sick person should go to a physician to be healed, and it says that when someone is bitten by a snake, his first response should be to go to a doctor.[13] *The Code of Jewish Law* thus rules that it is not only "allowed" for a Jew to be a doctor, but it is an obligation to heal – so much so that if a doctor refuses to treat a patient, it is as if that doctor is guilty of murder.[14] Thus, physicians are needed for their role in the process of healing, but Judaism (and observant doctors) nevertheless believes that all healing comes from God.

## DEFINING CONVENTIONAL DOCTORS, MEDICINE & ALTERNATIVE MEDICINE IN JUDAISM

In discussing doctors, *Shulchan Aruch* adds that the doctor who is obligated to heal in Judaism is only someone who is officially recognized by a Jewish court as having specific expertise in healing (there were no licenses for doctors in the 1500s).[15] Thus, *Shulchan Aruch* mandates that Jews only go to doctors who are approved by the Jewish community (through the courts) as conventional doctors prescribing conventional medicines. He then adds that those people who claim to be doctors, but who are not recognized by the Jewish courts and their communities and who then administer medicines (which might be called alternative medicine), run the risk of being sued and must pay damages if their non-conventional remedies do not work or cause additional sickness. However, a recognized conventional doctor in the Jewish community who acts in good faith cannot be sued and is not obligated to pay damages if his remedy does not work or if he or she causes further sickness. (This explains the double verb in the Torah verse "Heal, you shall be healed," mentioned earlier in footnote number 3, to emphasize that recognized doctors should try to heal and cannot be held responsible for lack of success if they treated in good faith.)

It is important to note that even conventional doctors who are recognized by the courts are not deemed to be omniscient and infallible in their medical expertise. Already in the 1300s, Rivash said that the Torah and its ideas trump all the knowledge of doctors and not the other way around.[16] A nineteenth-century Rabbi was much more practical. He writes that the most important aspect in evaluating the effectiveness of a doctor is experience and examination of the results.[17] If a medication

---

11. Leviticus 19:16, Deuteronomy 22:1-2
12. Nachmanides, *Torat Ha'adam* 6
13. *Yoma* 83b
14. *Shulchan Aruch, Yoreh De'ah* 336:1

15. *Shulchan Aruch, Yoreh De'ah* 336:1
16. *Responsa Rivash* 447
17. *Responsa Chatam Sofer*, Section 2, *Yoreh De'ah* 45

works, is effective in lessening symptoms, or accomplishes healing, then that is evidence that the medicine and doctor are effective. He does not distinguish between conventional and alternative medicines in this regard. *If it works, it is valid.*

The Rabbis also recognized that the science of medicine is constantly changing and is fluid both in terms of knowledge and remedies. Thus, a doctor in any era can heal based only on the knowledge that is available in that time period. Just as the Torah says that we must consult the Rabbis "in that generation" for Jewish law, so too we must consult and rely on only the reputable doctors we have in each generation. On this verse, the Talmud asks, "Can we ask other Rabbis who are not from the generation?"[18] It answers that the Torah is teaching us that we must rely on those leaders (and hence, doctors) that we have, whom God provided for us, realizing that they may be fallible. Therefore, though today's alternative medicine may indeed turn out to be the next generation's conventional medications, we can only use the valid knowledge that we currently have and the doctors recognized today as the "experts," even with all their fallibilities. As Rav Kook, the Chief Rabbi of Israel who lived in the twentieth century wrote: "Which human being is bold enough to claim that he understands how the physical and spiritual forces of a human being work, as well as all the forces in the world that affect the human body?"[19]

Because they recognized that doctors are not omniscient and perfect in their abilities to heal, the Rabbis often trusted the instincts of a patient more than doctors, even when these instincts and feelings were contraindicated by the physicians or when they disagreed with the therapy and prescriptions recommended by the doctors. Therefore, in the 1500s Rabbi David ben Zimra ruled that if a patient wanted to eat a certain food that the doctor said would hurt him or her, we listen to the patient, based on the verse in Proverbs that

the heart of a person understands the soul/body best.[20] Similarly, Jewish law rules that if a sick person feels that he or she has to eat on Yom Kippur (to alleviate pain or symptoms), even if a hundred doctors say that eating is not necessary or even that, in their estimation, this food will cause the patient further damage, we allow the patient to eat on Yom Kippur and violate the Torah's prohibition.[21] Thus, we clearly see that Judaism does not view even conventional doctors as all-knowing in their treatments or flawless in their medical practice. On the other hand, when it comes to possible life-threatening situations that would violate Shabbat, when two doctors disagree or even when the patient disagrees with the doctor, we always follow the more lenient view that tends towards saving life even if it violates the Shabbat.[22] This again points to the uncertainty in the field of medicine (which still exists today). It is recognized in Judaism that doctors often disagree on a specific course of treatment or medication, and that a doctor's belief in following a certain medical path cannot always be trusted. The passage further says that sometimes we follow the patient's wishes and violate Shabbat simply to make the patient feel better (such as putting out the light so that the patient can sleep if he or she requests it, even when the doctors specifically indicate it will have no medical benefit), since Judaism recognizes that the psychological state of the patient often influences his or her medical state.

## ALTERNATIVE MEDICINE AND PRACTICES THAT ARE FORBIDDEN IN JUDAISM

In the Torah, there were many "experts" who claimed that they could cure disease and sickness using ways and methods that did not involve standard medical practices. What all of these practices had in common was that these

---

18. Deuteronomy 26:3, *Rosh Hashana* 25b
19. *Olat Re'iyah* 1:290

20. *Responsa Radbaz* 4:66, Proverbs 14:10
21. Maimonides, *Hilchot Shevitat He'asor* 2:8, *Shulchan Aruch, Orach Chaim* 618:3 and Magen Avraham commentary
22. *Shulchan Aruch, Orach Chaim* 328:10-11

individuals believed they possessed a power to heal that came from someplace other than God. Therefore, all these "alternative therapies" (as outlined in the Torah), which are based on a belief in other powers such as idols, are forbidden. Although we no longer have the same deep desire to worship idols today, Judaism still believes that anytime some other power than God is claimed to be involved, that practice is forbidden. Thus, healing by using witchcraft is forbidden in the Torah, as is the healing of a wizard, relying on omens, astrology, (stick) divination, mediums, or illusions to provide a cure.[23]

The Talmud and later commentaries define precisely the nature of each of these practices for medical cures, which are forbidden by the Torah but which were very common in earlier eras. For example, the Talmud argues about the exact nature of a *Me'onen*, which, believe it or not, was very popular then as a provider of cures that people believed in.[24] Some used witchcraft, others used astrological calculations, and still others created illusions that were complete fakes. But all attributed their "curative powers" to other forces than God, and that is why all of these methods are forbidden to be used by Jews. Another Talmudic passage talks about the use of demons and sorcery to cure sickness.[25] Some "healers" claimed to help others by using "ventriloquism" to contact the dead, in which parts of the body other than the mouth spoke, and these are also forbidden.[26] This included those "experts" who spoke from joints in their bodies or put a bone in their mouths to speak to the dead, soothsayers who used skulls or spent the night in a cemetery to call up the dead, etc. And yet, when Rabbi Chanina and Rabbi Oshia used the *Book of Creation* (*Sefer Yetzira*) to actually create a calf (and eat it) each Shabbat, this was permitted. Why? Although they used

"alternative methods," they did not believe in or use forces other than God.[27]

Some occult practices were indeed used by Rabbis and Jewish leaders who summoned otherworldly forces, a phenomenon we cannot fathom today. The Talmud recounts that when King David dug pits, a force emerged from the netherworld that would have submerged the planet had King David not sung the fifteen psalms (Songs of Ascent) to prevent this from happening.[28] That same passage speaks about writing God's special (ineffable) name on a shard of clay, which would cause that destructive force to subside. The Talmud accepts these forces, which we cannot understand today, as real and impacting the world.

There seems to be some disagreement among later commentaries about whether the reason not to allow all of these occult practices in healing is that they call upon powers other than God, or simply because they are utter nonsense that has no effect at all in healing. Maimonides clearly says that all of these practices are mere foolishness that unlearned Jews sometimes believe in, but are forbidden nonetheless.[29] *Sefer HaChinuch* agrees with this approach, calling these practices falsehoods that can sway Jews away from true belief in God.[30]

When it comes to Jewish law, *Shulchan Aruch* certainly decries and forbids these practices in general, but when it involves actual medical emergencies, he sometimes allows these practices for various legitimate and/or questionable reasons.[31] Therefore, after he forbids all kinds of remedies using occult practices, three paragraphs later he states that if a person was bitten by a snake, that person is permitted to use incantations to try to help the wound even on Shabbat. Why? If the person will relax by thinking that this helps (as mentioned above), it is permitted even though it does not help in reality.[32] But within one paragraph he

---

23. Exodus 25:17, Leviticus 20:27, Deuteronomy 18:9-12
24. *Sanhedrin* 65b with Rashi commentary
25. *Sanhedrin* 67b
26. Mishna *Sanhedrin* 7:7

27. *Sanhedrin* 65b
28. *Sukkah* 53b
29. Maimonides, *Hilchot Ovdai Kochavim* 11:16
30. *Sefer HaChinuch*, Mitzvah 249
31. *Shulchan Aruch, Yoreh De'ah* 189:3
32. *Shulchan Aruch, Yoreh De'ah* 189: 6

writes two diametrically opposed statements.[33] First he says that anyone who pronounces incantations over a wound and then spits and reads a verse from the Torah loses his share in the World to Come for that forbidden act. Afterwards he says that if it is a case in which a person's life is in danger, everything of this nature is permitted. Thus, while he forbids the actions, he does give some credence to their medical value if he permits them when there is a possible loss of life. But then again, in the next paragraph he writes that for a child who was hurt, it is forbidden to read Torah verses to make him healthier or to place a Torah scroll over the child to heal him.[34] Thus, the ambivalence in the use of these "alternative medical practices" is evident even within Jewish law.

## UNTESTED ALTERNATIVE MEDICINES THAT ARE PERMITTED IN JUDAISM

In the Torah we see that Moses used an unconventional cure to heal the people suffering from a plague. When Jews began dying in some kind of epidemic as a result of their sins, Moses and Aaron took incense and placed it on the Altar, which immediately stopped the plague in which 14,700 Jews died.[35] Therefore, we already see in the Torah that sometimes unexplainable but sanctioned cures, which we might today call "alternative medicine," alleviates a desperate medical condition.

The Mishna discusses the use of certain "alternative medicines" popular in Mishnaic times, and there is a fundamental argument between Rabbi Meir and the rest of the Sages about their use.[36] In order to prevent illness, many thought that carrying or wearing the egg of a certain type of locust, a fox's tooth, or a nail from the coffin of a convict would keep a person healthy. All of these do not fall under the forbidden laws of the occult mentioned above in the Torah, but are merely practices

that were popular in the time of the Mishna. Rabbi Meir permitted people to have these for medical reasons, while the Sages forbade these practices as "the ways of Amorites," i.e., forbidden practices or customs of non-Jews. The Talmud then makes a statement that is the basic guide to how Judaism views alternative medicines and their use. It says that if these practices are effective in keeping people healthy or healing sickness, then they are not considered "ways of Amorites" and are permitted. However, if these strange practices are not effective, then they are considered "Amorite practices" that are forbidden.[37] Therefore, we see that any alterative medical practices that yield verifiable results to improve health or minimize sickness are permitted in Judaism, as long as they do not violate any Jewish laws. The Talmud goes on to list actions that were permitted at that time and that were forbidden as "Amorite practices."[38] To the twenty-first-century eye, all of these look strange and ineffective. Yet apparently, some of these treatments did work to minimize pain and sickness and were therefore permitted by the Rabbis, and they are permitted in Judaism today as well. These strange practices (which we might consider "nonsense" by today's standards) also bothered Maimonides, the world-renown scientist who lived about a thousand years after the Mishna was written. He explains that although these "medications" seem strange to us, they indeed proved effective at that time and were therefore allowed and even encouraged to be used.[39] Perhaps this also explains why Shulchan Aruch, cited above, permitted a certain incantation that healed the person bitten by the snake in a life-threatening situation. If it worked, then it was permitted.

Based on the above, today's alternative medicines would be permitted in Judaism if all three of these conditions are present: (a) they heal pain or sickness or prevent sickness in a verifiable, consistent manner, (b) they do

---

33. *Shulchan Aruch, Yoreh De'ah* 189:8
34. *Shulchan Aruch, Yoreh De'ah* 189:9
35. Numbers 17:14-14
36. Mishna *Shabbat* 6:10

---

37. *Shabbat* 67a
38. *Shabbat* 67a
39. Maimonides, *Guide for the Perplexed* 3:37

not cause any additional pain or damage to the body, and (c) they do not violate other Jewish laws.

## AMULETS

Since the earliest times, man has tried to protect himself from misfortune through the use of objects that he considers holy or otherwise potent. One of the ways of doing this was to keep the object close by frequently wearing it as an article of clothing or as an ornament. The use of inscription as a means of warding off evil spirits stems from a belief in the holiness and power of words. Jews also frequently used amulets and they are often mentioned in Talmudic literature. There were two kinds of amulets used by Jews: one made from roots and one with words inside.[40]

Jews apparently used amulets throughout the ages in order to maintain their health and ward off evil, and this practice was sanctioned by the Rabbis. The Tosefta distinguishes between two kinds of amulets – those "proven" to be effective and those of questionable effectiveness – and says that those proven effective (three times or more) could be used even on Shabbat.[41] However, one had to be careful while wearing an amulet on Shabbat as an ornament lest it appear like jewelry, which was forbidden. This sentiment was also echoed both in the Babylonian Talmud[42] and the Jerusalem Talmud.[43] The Talmud even inquires whether amulets have holiness and debates the issue, as the implication of holiness would determine whether they are permitted in the bathroom and whether one tries to save them from a fire.[44]

Post-Talmudic authorities debated the efficacy of amulets. Rashba, who lived in the thirteenth century, allowed the manufacture and use of amulets as long as they were proven to work and did not violate any of the specific "Amorite ways" listed in the Tosefta.[45] Maimonides, who lived around the time of the Rashba, seems to be conflicted about this issue. In one place he strongly condemns the practice, especially the adding of words and incantations to *Mezuzot* in order to further protect homes from evil.[46] (This practice seemed to negate the belief in the efficacy of the Biblically mandated *Mezuzot* to do so.) On the other hand, Maimonides follows the Talmud passage that says that once proven effective three times, an amulet is considered a "professional amulet" and may even be used on Shabbat to heal a patient whose sickness is not life-threatening.[47] Maimonides thus recognizes that amulets may be used even on Shabbat, providing their effectiveness was previously proven.[48] *Shulchan Aruch* also shows ambivalence concerning amulets by on the one hand permitting the use of an amulet (only as a preventative for sickness, and not as medication for healing a sick person), but on the other hand stating that amulets with words or verses in them are forbidden.[49]

In modern times, the Kabbalistic movement and some Sephardic communities have made the use of amulets very popular up until today. However, many of the Ashkenazi Rabbis take a dim view of amulets as mere "magic" that may or may not have any effectiveness. Like the use of alternative medicine in Judaism, amulets would certainly be permitted to either prevent or cure sickness under the same conditions: (a) the user does not believe that any other power than God is alleviating or preventing the medical condition, (b) Jewish laws are not violated (we will discuss below when certain laws of Shabbat can or cannot be violated regarding amulets), and (c) they cause no harm to the person.

---

40. *Shabbat* 61a
41. Tosefta *Shabbat* 4:9
42. *Shabbat* 61a
43. Jerusalem Talmud, Shabbat 36a
44. *Shabbat* 61b

45. *Responsa Rashba*, 1:167
46. Maimonides, *Hilchot Tefillin* 5:4
47. *Shabbat* 61a
48. Maimonides, *Hilchot Shabbat* 19:14
49. *Shulchan Aruch, Yoreh De'ah* 189:12

## AYIN HARA – EVIL EYE

Any person who knows Yiddish, or even just a few Yiddish expressions, is familiar with the expression "*K'neiyna Hara*" (or a similar pronunciation of that expression), which is used whenever speaking about something good or that one is proud of. These words actually are "*K'neged Ayin Hara*" – which are intended to be used against or to prevent the evil eye. Even people who do not believe in the occult or amulets use this expression regularly. While it is not strictly speaking of "alternative medicine," fighting off the evil eye seems to be something very mainstream to Judaism and is regarded as keeping Jews healthy and joyous. What exactly is it? How does it work? And how do Jews prevent it from harming them?

This concept is much more prevalent in Judaism than one might think. There are two narratives in the Torah that involve the concept of *Ayin Hara*. When the ten sons of Jacob went down to Egypt to buy food during the famine, Rashi explains that Jacob commanded each brother to enter Egypt through a separate entrance. What was his purpose in saying this? So that the evil eye should not be cast upon them, which might have occurred were they to enter together.[50] This explanation is based on the Midrash that says that because they were especially strong and attractive, the bothers should not gather in one place lest the *Ayin Hara* be cast upon them.[51] When Bilaam tried to curse the Jewish people and he gazed at them, Rashi says he tried to cast the evil eye upon them.[52] The mystical book, the *Zohar*, explains that Bilaam had this special power of being able to cast the evil eye upon people and cause them harm.[53] What does this signify? How does the evil eye, or *Ayin Hara*, work?

When the Mishna in *Ethics of the Fathers* explains that a person should have the quality of an *Ayin Tova* – a good eye, and not an *Ayin Hara* – an evil eye, this usually signifies that a person should be generous and not stingy in how he treats and gives to others.[54] Rabbeinu Yonah explains that this element of stinginess is derived when someone is jealous of the good that others have.[55] When the jealous person has this *Ayin Hara*, or evil eye feeling against another person's success, this causes Heaven to take away the good from the person who feels jealous, but it also sometimes results in *the removal of the bountiful gifts that the other person enjoys*. But why and how does it work that jealousy can cause harm to a person who did nothing wrong?

Apparently when people are judged on Rosh Hashana, when their worldly goods and other benefits for that year are determined, they are judged with mercy. When someone "casts an evil eye" on someone else through jealousy, it causes Heaven to "take a second look" at this person and judge him or her again, but this time more objectively. If the person is not deserving of the gifts he or she enjoys, it is possible that Heaven will decide at that point to remove some or all of these intended gifts. That is why Jacob made sure that his handsome and strong sons should not stand together in one place. Perhaps Heaven would see this gathering and question whether Jacob deserves such a large and blessed family. Bilaam tried to cause God to judge the Jewish people once again in a stricter manner, but he failed. Today, Jews use the expression "*K'neiyna Hara*" whenever they express pride in something or a special gift from God. That, in effect, signifies that Jews are asking God not to look again at their situation and judge them more harshly. Thus, Jews should not do anything that will draw attention to themselves and cause God to "take a second look" at them. So, for example, when people ask how many grandchildren or great-grandchildren one has, some people refuse to answer with a specific number, in order not to invite the *Ayin Hara* and so that God will not re-judge them and consider taking away one of those children or

---

50. Genesis 42:5 with Rashi commentary
51. Midrash, *Beraishit Rabbah* 91:6
52. Numbers 24:2 with Rashi commentary
53. *Zohar* 1:68b

54. Mishna *Avot* 2:11
55. Rabbeinu Yonah commentary on Mishna *Avot* 2:11

great-grandchildren. The same is true when speaking about a person's wealth or anything else that is good in a person's life. A Jew should simply not call attention to any benefits in his or her life.

Now we can understand the numerous examples of *Ayin Hara* described in the Talmud. For example, a person should not stand in the middle of a friend's field when the crops are in full growth, because he may admire the bounty of his friend and that can bring the evil eye, says Rashi.[56] In another passage, the Talmud says that when the Land of Israel was divided into portions for the different tribes and some Jews did not get any or enough land (for legitimate reasons), they should not have complained, because it would have brought the *Ayin Hara* – i.e., it might have caused God to take away land from others who did receive a more favorable portion.[57] In another passage it says that a Jew trading in business as a wholesaler will have difficulty increasing his sales because he deals with such large quantities that he calls attention to himself, and the evil eye is upon this person.[58]

This idea of *Ayin Hara* is so ubiquitous in Judaism that in their daily morning prayer, one of the things Sephardic Jews ask of God is to ensure that the evil eye does not touch them.[59] This idea also impacts Jewish law. Even though there is technically nothing forbidden in the practice, *Shulchan Aruch* rules that two brothers should not be called to the Torah one after the other and that a son should not directly follow his father for an *Aliya* (honor of being called) to the Torah and vice versa, because this will draw the evil eye.[60] What does it signify? By drawing attention to a large and blessed family, it may induce the *Ayin Hara*. For the same reason, a parent should not name two children with the same name, as it may

draw the *Ayin Hara* and cause God to rejudge the family.[61] Similarly, two grooms celebrating their weddings in the synagogue on the same Shabbat should make only one special blessing for grooms (together), instead of two separate blessings.[62]

What about today? We have seen that the evil eye in Judaism is much more than an "old wives' tale" and is part of mainstream Jewish law. But do we really have to worry each moment and in each of our actions about inviting the evil eye and God's harsh judgment that will cause us great pain? Rabbi Ovadiah Yosef was asked about two brothers marrying two sisters, which Rabbi Yehuda HaChasid said is forbidden because it draws attention to the families and to the evil eye. Rabbi Yosef answered that because many Rabbis in the Talmud and even later married the sister of the brother's wife and nothing happened to them, one need not worry about the evil eye in this specific case. He adds that today, the impact and worry about the *Ayin Hara* is far less than in the past. If the *Ayin Hara* does bother you, however, you should be careful not to do anything that would invite it to call attention to you. But if you are not bothered by this, then you need not worry about the *Ayin Hara* today.[63] Rabbi Moshe Feinstein wrote something similar.[64] You should, in general, worry about the potential effects of the evil eye, but not too much. And if you are not bothered by it, it cannot have an effect upon you.

## WHEN AND IF ALTERNATIVE MEDICINE CAN BE USED EVEN IF VIOLATING JEWISH LAW

Until now, we have discussed the permissibility of using alternative medicines in Judaism when no Jewish law is violated in the process. However, if the only way to use a certain alternative medicine means that a Jew has to violate Halacha-Jewish Law, would that alternative

56. *Bava Batra* 2b with Rashi commentary
57. *Bava Batra* 118a
58. *Pesachim* 50b
59. Sephardic prayer book, daily prayer following the morning blessings
60. *Shulchan Aruch, Orach Chaim* 141:6 with *Mishna Berurah* commentary

61. *Pitchai Teshuva, Yoreh De'ah* 116
62. *Shulchan Aruch, Orach Chaim* 62:3
63. *Responsa Yabia Omer*, Section 4, *Even Ha'ezer* 10
64. *Responsa Igrot Moshe, Even Ha'ezer* 3:26

treatment still be permitted? Does its medicinal value override Jewish law because saving a patient's life or healing a sickness is paramount and generally overrides other Jewish laws? Or perhaps, since this treatment is essentially untested, can it be used only as long as other Jewish laws are not desecrated and no harm comes to the patient? As is often the case in Judaism, there is an argument among the Rabbis about this issue.

The Mishna discusses a case in which someone was bitten by a rabid dog (this is before the era of tetanus shots) and the only remedy was to feed him the liver of that dog, which clearly is not kosher and a violation of Jewish law. Is it permitted or not permitted to feed the patient this non-kosher food to heal the sick person? The *Tanna Kama* (first opinion in the Mishna) says that it is forbidden to do so, but Rabbi Matya permits it.[65] Rashi explains that according to the first opinion, even though some doctors may use this as treatment, the dog's liver is not a *Refuah Gemura*, a proven and effective medication – i.e., it may work sometimes, but not always.[66] Rabbi Matya argues and says that this treatment is indeed a proven and tested remedy for this particular disease. On this Mishna, Maharam ben Chaviv asks the obvious question: Since we know that one may violate even the laws of Shabbat, a very serious sin, in order to save lives, why would the first Rabbi in the Mishna not allow this treatment when a life is possibly in danger? He answers that this treatment with a dog's liver has no effect at all and has no medical value whatsoever.[67] Therefore, it is forbidden to use this as a medicine because it violates Jewish law and it will never save lives or benefit anyone.

Maimonides agrees with this assessment and says that Jewish law does not follow Rabbi Matya because this treatment does not help medically, but only helps as an unproven and mystical treatment (or alternative medicine).[68]

One may only violate Jewish law for a proven medical treatment that has been tested and found effective. Thus Jewish laws of *Kashrut* (a food's status as kosher) and Shabbat may not be violated for this unproven, alternative medicine. Radbaz then asks: How is it that we may violate any Jewish law when even the remotest chance of saving a life is involved, but may not use this experimental or alternative medicine which may, in some fashion, help save the bitten (or sick) person? He answers that we have to separate between a doubt regarding the saving of a life and a doubt regarding the medicine's effectiveness at all.[69] Indeed, it is permitted to use any proven medicine and violate Jewish law when there is even the remotest chance of saving a life, but a doubt regarding the efficacy of the medicine itself never allows a Jew to violate Torah law on the outside chance it might work this time. Tiferet Yisrael agrees with this assessment,[70] and in the codes of Jewish law, both Rabbi Isserles and Magen Avraham clearly state that the medication must be proven to be effective in order for it to be used in violation of Jewish law.[71]

But there seems to be another side to the story and another opinion in Jewish law. Rashba stresses that because of the possible danger to life, even an untested amulet may be used to heal, and one may even write on Shabbat for this untested amulet since possible loss of life is involved.[72] Thus, Rashba argues with Maimonides and with the above premise, and says that when the illness is that serious, even untested and unproven alternative medication may be used if it showed some effectiveness in the past. When it comes to saving human life almost anything (including violating Shabbat) may be done to save it. Pri Megadim agrees with Rashba and questions how the Rema could have said that alternative medicines that are unproven cannot be used when a person is very sick. He concludes that

---

65. Mishna *Yoma* 8:6
66. Rashi commentary on Mishna *Yoma* 8:6
67. *Tosafot Yom HaKippurim, Yoma* 83a
68. Maimonides commentary on the Mishna *Yoma* 8:6

69. *Responsa Radbaz* 5:153
70. Tiferet Yisrael on Mishna *Yoma* 8:6
71. Rema, *Shulchan Aruch, Yoreh De'ah* 155:3, Magen Avraham on *Shulchan Aruch, Orach Chaim* 328
72. *Responsa Rashba* 4:245

Rema's prohibition must have been referring to a sick person who is not in any danger of loss of life. But for a truly sick person, Shabbat and other Jewish laws may indeed be violated with an experimental or mystical medication.[73]

The later authorities and Rabbis have basically echoed one of these two positions regarding actual cases that have been presented recently. On one side is Maimonides who says that unproven medicines and alternative treatments are forbidden when their use violates Shabbat, since they have not been vetted medically and their effectiveness is questionable. Thus, one may not violate Shabbat or any other Torah law in order to use them. On the other side are Rashba and Nachmanides who say that one may use any medical treatment, including alternative medicine, and even violate Shabbat and other Torah laws when a sick person's life may possibly be in danger. In the 1700s Rabbi Yosef David Azulai was asked about a person who wrote an amulet on Shabbat to help save someone's life.[74] Although he is sympathetic to the situation and does bring down those Rabbis who permit such an action, he believes like Maimonides that using unproven and mystical medications while violating Shabbat is not permitted even when a sick person's life may be in danger. Rabbi Moshe Sofer takes the opposite view regarding a Kohen (Priest) who is ill and would become ritually impure, which is a Torah violation, if he takes an amulet to heal himself. Since possible loss of life hangs in the balance, in this case of doubt we rely on those who are more lenient, and he therefore allows the practice.[75]

Rabbi Shlomo Kluger (early 1800s) was asked if a person could violate the Shabbat by writing a note (Kvitel) and traveling by vehicle to a great Tzadik (righteous man) in the next city, who would pray on behalf of a sick person to recover from his sickness.[76] Since Rabbi Kluger sides with the opinion of Maimonides, he forbids the violation of Shabbat for this alternative option of prayer by a righteous man. He does, however, allow a non-Jew to do the writing and travelling on Shabbat so that this righteous man can pray for the deathly sick individual in time. Another Rabbi who lived in the 1800s, Rabbi Nathanson, similarly allows a non-Jew to send a telegram on Shabbat for the righteous Tzadik to pray on behalf of the sick person.[77]

Rabbi Wosner, a contemporary Rabbi, was asked about violating the laws of Passover for using homeopathic medicines containing Chametz on Passover, which is essentially a variation of the same question we have been dealing with until now. He summarizes both sides of the question, and then says that until a specific medicine – conventional or alternative – is proven effective for a particular medical problem, it would be forbidden to violate Jewish law in order to use it.[78] Finally, another contemporary Rabbi, Rabbi Ovadiah Yosef, was asked simply if one is allowed to violate Shabbat with alternative medicine in order to save the life of a sick person. As is his wont, Rabbi Yosef brings down every opinion on the issue. In the end, he says that since there are strong opinions on each side of the argument, as demonstrated above, and we are left in doubt over which is correct, we side with the more lenient opinion when dealing with matters of life and death. Therefore, he permits the violation of Shabbat to administer the alternative medicine.

---

73. Pri Megadim on Shulchan Aruch, Orach Chaim 328
74. Responsa Birkei Yosef, Orach Chaim 301:6
75. Responsa Chatam Sofer, Section 2, Yoreh De'ah 339
76. Responsa U'vacharta Bachaim 87
77. Responsa Shoel Umaishiv (Tlitaa) 1:194
78. Responsa Shevet HaLevi 5:55

# ANGER IN JUDAISM

ALTHOUGH ANGER IS A UNIVERSAL human emotion, it is nevertheless a very unusual sensation and reaction to something that upsets us. There are many variables involved when people get angry, including *how* angry they get or how long they stay angry after experiencing a threatening, hurtful, or unexpected situation. The definition of anger is "a strong feeling of displeasure and belligerence aroused by a wrong." It is an emotion related to one's psychological interpretation of having been offended, wronged or denied something that was expected, and it is characterized by a tendency to react through retaliation. Anger as a normal emotion involves a strong, uncomfortable, and emotional response to a perceived provocation. The external expression of anger can be found in facial expressions, body language, physiological responses, and at times, in acts of aggression.

Anger is unusual in that some people can control it while others cannot, and everyone expresses his or her anger differently. Sometimes it seems that anger only makes things worse. So why do people get angry? How much control over this emotion do we really have? Why do reactions vary so widely between people or even day to day within the same person? What are the benefits and drawbacks of expressing ourselves and being or getting angry? We will attempt to address some of these questions as we discover the Jewish attitude towards anger through the traditional sources, since the Torah and Rabbis have much to say about anger.

## SOME OF THE CHARACTERISTICS AND ATTITUDES TOWARDS ANGER

The Mishna recognizes that everyone can get angry at some point, but strongly advises that an individual should strive to be very slow to

anger and not get angry often.[1] One of the commentaries specifically says that this emotion is part of human nature, but it is a very bad trait and feeling.[2] Therefore, a person should try to work on himself or herself and only express this emotion by rarely letting it come to the surface. In the Talmud, three different Rabbis show the negative effects of expressing anger. One Rabbi says that when an individual is angry, even God's presence would not have any impact on that person. Another opinion is that at the moment of anger an individual forgets whatever he or she has learned about proper behavior and acts like a fool. The third and harshest view is that anger proves to everyone that the angry person's sins are more numerous than his or her merits as a human being and as a Jew.[3]

A different Talmudic passage states that a person who acts upon his or her anger, such as tearing things or smashing objects, is equated with an idol worshipper. "Why?" asks the Talmud. Because this individual becomes a slave to his passion and his evil desires, and is no longer in control of himself.[4] Rabbi Moshe Chaim Luzzato explains this and says that when a person is so full of rage, his fury controls him and he would destroy the world at that moment if he could. His or her brain and good inclination become powerless to fight against the negative emotion.[5] The Talmud itself explains the comparison between anger and worshipping an idol, saying that when a person blindly follows his anger, he gives it power and thereby negates God's power, which is the very definition of idol worship.[6] By falling prey to uncontrolled anger, a human

---

1. Mishna *Avot* 2:10
2. Rabbeinu Yonah commentary on Mishna *Avot* 2:10
3. *Nedarim* 22b
4. *Shabbat* 105b
5. *Mesilat Yesharim*, chapter 11
6. *Shabbat* 105b

being allows the evil inclination to triumph and gain power over his or her actions. Lest we think that this emotion and its power to control a person's response to adversity is referring only to weak, immoral, and unlearned people, the Talmud reminds us that God intentionally installs a greater evil inclination in the greatest people, i.e., the higher the moral potential of a person, the greater is the capacity of his or her evil inclination and desire to do evil.[7] Thus, an outstanding, ethical, and learned individual has a *greater* potential for anger, not a lesser one, and has to work even harder than ordinary people to overcome this natural desire. The mystical *Zohar* says that a person who acts upon his anger is intentionally ignoring his soul as he lets a "strange god" take possession of him. And just as one is supposed to shun an idol worshipper, one should shun an individual who is in a state of anger.[8] Rabbi Yehuda HaChasid agrees with this approach and prohibits others from looking at or interacting with the angry person while he or she is angry.[9]

Maimonides summarizes various Talmudic passages and shows all the deleterious effects of someone who displays his or her anger. He says that the angry person appears to be worshipping a different "god" loses his learning and wisdom at the moment of anger (if he is a prophet, he loses his prophecy), and loses his quality of life itself. Therefore, Maimonides strongly recommends that a person should constantly work on himself not to feel anger and not to react to those things that normally would generate anger. In this way, he becomes a righteous individual by accepting personal attacks without responding at all. In addition, he should strive to react to suffering with joy.[10] Nevertheless, the Torah clearly says that a person should not hate another person "in his heart," to which the commentaries (such as Nachmanides) explain that if a person feels

wronged and angry, he or she should not harbor that anger and hate inwardly, but rather confront the person (in a courteous manner) asking the offender to explain his or her behavior and letting the person know why one feels wronged.[11] This will ultimately engender more love, peace, and understanding, and remove anger (see chapter "Hatred in Judaism" for an expanded discussion of this issue). Thus, in this case we see that, if done in a civil manner, it is good for a person to express his or her feelings of anger to the one who is the object of that anger, and it is beneficial not to deny or hold these feelings inside of oneself. The Torah then understands that it is sometimes better to express one's angry feelings, but not in an angry way, if the goal is to dissipate them. That is why the Mishna, in describing four types of people, says that the best kind of person is someone who takes a very long time to become angry and then dissipates that anger quickly (and the worst is the opposite – someone who is very easily angered, who takes a very long time to calm down and forget his anger).[12] Thus, in Judaism, a person is judged by his or her reaction to anger and how he or she displays or does not display it, and not by the feeling itself.

How can a person learn not to display feelings of anger? Maimonides says regarding all of life's values and behaviors that to reach a desired character trait and right a flawed value, one needs to go to the opposite extreme for a period of time.[13] Therefore in this case, a person should practice ultimate patience in all parts of life and not react to any situation that would normally make him or her angry. This will train the individual not to display anger each time an incident arises that would normally make the person angry.

Rabbi Ilai said that the true feelings of a person are revealed in three situations: when a money transaction is involved, when he is full

---

7. *Sukkah* 52a
8. *Zohar* 2:182a
9. *Sefer Chasidim* 1126
10. Maimonides, *Hilchot De'ot* 2:3

11. Leviticus 19:17 with Nachmanides commentary
12. Mishna *Avot* 5:11
13. Maimonides, Introduction to *Shmoneh Perakim*, chapter 4

of liquor, and when he is angry. Therefore, one should strive to avoid these situations completely, but if this is not possible, he should at least not be in such a situation when others are present.[14] A later Jewish philosopher writes that anger causes a person to "paint himself into a corner" and never admit a mistake or the truth when he or she is wrong even later on, after the anger subsides.[15] Another Talmudic passage is the source of Maimonides' statement quoted above about becoming righteous by not reacting to anger.[16] A person should try to teach himself not to respond whenever he or she is insulted or humiliated, and certainly never do the insulting or humiliating. In addition, an individual should work on himself or herself to accept all situations of suffering with joy. If a person can do this, God calls this person a true hero, courageous (see chapter, "Heroes"), and beloved to God. The Talmud echoes this idea when it says that anger that leads to strife is like a hole made by a rush of water that keeps getting wider and wider, or like the planks of a wooden bridge that grow stronger and harder with each passing day. In order to not let a small argument and minor anger between two people seethe and get much worse, a person should train himself to ignore one hundred negative statements that bother him or put him down.[17]

The classic Jewish work that explains how to build up Jewish character and values, *Mesilat Yesharim*, describes the different types of anger.[18] All types are bad for a person, but some are worse than others. The worst is the anger described above when the emotions and actions completely take over a person. There is another kind of angry person – not as extreme – who does not let everything bother him or her, but when something does, this individual explodes with anger. A lesser degree of anger is found in the person who can ignore almost

everything, but when he or she does get angry, he or she reacts strongly in a small way rather than loudly and boisterously. On the other hand, he or she also keeps this feeling inside for a long time. The least anger is the case of a person who rarely gets angry, and when he or she does, he or she displays anger for only a minute and then lets it go. Even a teacher and a parent who have to punish a child (more about these specific cases below) should never do so out of anger. In short, all anger, however mild, is negative. In summing up not only Rabbi Luzzato, but also all that has been written above, Rabbi Yeshaya HaLevi Horowitz (1558-1630) simply says that all anger is bad for a person and there is no evil in the world as bad as this particular character trait.[19]

## ANGER IN THE BIBLE

The very first man-to-man sin in the world was the act of murder caused by anger. Both Cain and Abel brought sacrifices to God. When God favored Abel's over Cain's, Cain became very angry, so much so that he killed his brother.[20] This set the pattern for anger and angry reactions until today. Therefore, we see from the very beginning of history how pernicious this character trait is. It causes man to say and do things that are irrational and for which he may later be sorry but cannot undo. The Midrash states that it was the anger between people in the time of Noah that caused bitter fighting between them, which led to the ever-present stealing that sealed the fate of all mankind and resulted in God's destruction of all people in the world (except for Noah's family).[21] Thus, like in Noah's time, sometimes anger that starts small can grow into something very big and dangerous with unimaginable negative consequences.

Yet we see that God Himself gets angry several times in the Torah when the Jewish people sin, abrogate their promises, or complain

14. *Eiruvin* 65b
15. "The Gate of Anger," chapter 12 in *Orchot Tzaddikim*
16. *Gittin* 36b
17. *Sanhedrin* 7a
18. *Mesilat Yesharim*, chapter 11

19. Shelah Hakadosh, *Gate of Letter* 200
20. Genesis 4:5
21. Midrash, *Beraishit Rabbah* 31:2

needlessly. When the Jewish people worship the Golden Calf, God is so angry that He threatens to destroy the people and build another Jewish people with Moses alone as their forebear.[22] Moses prays to God and argues logically that he should not destroy the people, and God relents. How are we to understand God's anger? Can we say that God "lost it" and should not have gotten angry as we said about man above? The truth of the matter is precisely the opposite: Since God does not have any real "emotions," God is by definition all good, and since the purpose of the Torah (as well as the very meaning of the word) is to teach the Jewish people, we can learn from this incident that it is indeed sometimes legitimate to get angry, as long as it is a detached anger and not overly emotional. Thus for a parent, like God, who is referred to as a parent of the Jewish people[23] and legitimately gets angry with the Jewish people, so too, it is proper at certain times and in certain situations to get angry with his or her own child. When the people disobey Him by worshipping a golden statue a mere forty days after hearing God at Mount Sinai and committing their allegiance to Him, it is indeed the proper place to be angry. Moses apparently learns the lesson. Moses, the father figure and leader of the Jewish people, does not react when God tells him that the people sinned but simply prays to save them.[24] But after hearing and seeing God get angry, Moses imitates God and becomes angry with the people for their sin when he descends the mountain and sees the Golden Calf.[25] Almost every time Moses gets angry with the Jewish people the Torah seems to justify this anger, because, being a leader, his anger was due to the immoral actions of the people. However, one Midrash castigates Moses for becoming angry in a situation when it is inappropriate to do so.[26] (Another time, when Moses got angry

by hitting the rock to get water, according to Maimonides, he is punished by being denied entrance into the land of Israel.[27])

In speaking about a future time in which God predicts that the Jewish people will abrogate the Covenant and sin again and again, God uses the verb for anger three separate times in different forms in reference to expelling the Jews from the land of Israel as punishment for idol worship and other sins.[28] Yet there are times when a leader (parent or teacher) should not get angry at the people (or child). Nevertheless, it is appropriate in certain situations for a leader, a parent, or a teacher to become angry (exactly when and how will be discussed below).

## CAN ANGER BE POSITIVE AND GOOD?

Normally, we assume that anger is one of a human being's negative emotions like hatred, sadness, depression, or anxiety. The brain usually reflects the gamut of these emotions, with brain activity for positive emotions heightened on the right side of the brain, while for negative emotions brain activity is heightened on the left side. But recent studies have shown an anomaly. Anger, which is supposed to be a negative emotion, engenders more activity on the right side of the brain than the left, indicating that it is a positive emotion.[29] How can this be? Can anger, indeed, be a positive reaction? After all the negative comments and sources about the Jewish view of anger, can Judaism also find a positive side to anger as well? This discussion about anger as positive or negative, believe it or not, took place long ago in Talmudic times.

On Shabbat a Jew does not commit a Torah violation (as opposed to a Rabbinically forbidden edict) unless the action is a positive one. Therefore, someone who destroys something

---

22. Exodus 32:7-11
23. Deuteronomy 14:1, blessing before *Shema* of the morning prayers
24. Exodus 32:7-11
25. Exodus 19-20
26. *Berachot* 63b

27. Maimonides, Introduction to *Shmoneh Perakim*, chapter 4
28. Deuteronomy 29:23-27
29. "The Bright Side of Anger – It Motivates Others," *Time*, December 15, 2010

simply to destroy it is NOT guilty of a Torah prohibition, because nothing positive results. But if he destroys in order to build something upon it or of there is any other positive purpose about this action, it *is* a Torah violation of Shabbat. The Mishna says that a person who tears clothes out of anger or because he or she is so upset after hearing news that a loved one has died, has not violated the Shabbat.[30] Since there is no positive action in getting angry in this manner, tearing clothes out of anger (a violent reaction) is *not* a Torah prohibition on Shabbat and is permitted. However, the Talmud brings a contradictory statement that violence (tearing) as a result of anger on Shabbat *is* a transgression of the Torah (i.e., because it *is* a positive action).[31] This opinion states then, that anger is a positive reaction. The Talmud resolves this contradiction by stating three different principles.

One aspect of anger is that getting angry and a resultant violent action are actually positive because they calm down a person's feelings. An opposing view about anger, noted above, is that anger leads to idol worship, because an angry person loses control just as in the ecstasy of idol worship a person may also lose control. Finally, the Talmud says that if a husband *intentionally* feigns anger and *looks* angry in order to teach his family an important moral lesson, then this is indeed a positive act. But it is not permitted (in this view) to actually get angry. Thus, two reasons are cited as positive outcomes of getting angry. Maimonides cites *all* of these views in his writings (both the positive and negative).

After Maimonides cites all three possibilities, he then writes as his final ruling in Jewish law – as the final Halacha – that a violent reaction due to anger *is* a positive act, since it calms one's feelings of anger and is thus blameworthy according to the Torah on Shabbat (according to the argument explained above).[32] Rashi, on that same Talmud passage, argues

with Maimonides and says that anger can never have a positive outcome because getting angry then becomes habitual and overcomes a person's desire to control it and do good actions.[33] Thus, we have an argument both in the Talmud and between Rashi and Maimonides whether there can be any positive outcomes from getting angry.

Maimonides also cites the second reason from the Talmud and rules that another positive outcome of getting angry is when it is feigned in order to teach a lesson to one's family,[34] much like God's getting angry at the Jewish people in the Torah (more about this will be discussed below). Thus we can indeed have positive aspects of getting angry. But let us not forget that it was Maimonides who also wrote (right before and after these comments about positive feigned anger with the family) that anger is a horrible trait to have, and it is so bad that it may even be the exception to his golden mean rule of finding the middle ground with every character trait.[35] He also writes that angry person is like an idol worshipper, loses his wisdom, etc. Therefore, it is clear that overall Maimonides does not advocate getting angry. But nevertheless, he does find some positive aspects in the act of getting angry.

The question arises of why getting angry at one's family would be permitted, even if it is feigned. Won't this teach a family that it is "good" to sometimes get angry? One answer comes from the passage that says that if a person can prevent his home (i.e., his family) from doing a sin and does nothing about it, then he is as guilty as if he himself actually did that sin.[36] Therefore, if the only way to prevent something immoral or illegal from taking place within one's family is to "fake" anger, then it is permitted. This sin of not doing something to prevent others from sinning is so severe that the Talmud says that the only time in history when God reversed a positive decree against certain righteous people was when the angels

---

30. Mishna *Shabbat* 13:3
31. *Shabbat* 105b
32. Maimonides, *Hilchot Shabbat* 8:8

33. Rashi commentary on *Shabbat* 105b
34. Maimonides, *Hilchot De'ot* 2:3
35. Maimonides, *Hilchot De'ot* 2:3
36. *Shabbat* 54b

pointed out that these righteous people could have prevented wicked people from sinning and they did nothing.[37] God agreed with the angels and changed the reward of these righteous people to punishment. (A negative heavenly decree can easily be reversed if the people it is directed against repent.)

The mystical *Zohar* cites another instance when it is proper and positive to get angry.[38] When Torah scholars and Rabbis get angry over secular or personal matters, the *Zohar* says it is totally improper. But when the anger is for the purpose of defending the honor of the Torah and Judaism if it is being mocked or violated, then that anger is proper and positive. Both God and Moses demonstrated anger in the Torah to teach us that in instances such as these, it is indeed proper to get angry – not to respond to a personal insult, but to defend the Torah and the principles of Judaism. Of course, this "leniency" only applies to Torah scholars, as other Jews might use this "loophole" to become angry in many situations in which it is improper to do so.

Another positive aspect of getting angry comes from the Torah itself, from a source previously cited. It is far better and more positive to let the anger out rather than to harbor it inside and let it seethe and fester. Thus, a Jew is not permitted to hate a person in his heart, but should confront the person in as nice and non-angry fashion as possible, as discussed above.[39]

Finally, Maimonides, who was careful and exact in every word he wrote, does write that sometimes – if the issue is a very grave and large one – it *is* proper to get angry, but only once in a while, so that this emotion never becomes habitual.[40]

## ADDITIONAL REASONS NOT TO GET ANGRY

Besides all the damage getting angry can do one's personality and relationships cited above, there are several more specific rationales why a person should do everything to avoid getting angry.

Even though in rare instances we saw that it is proper to get angry at one's family when they are doing wrong, repeated anger by either parent will alienate one's children and that person's end will be either actual hell or his family making his life seem like hell.[41] Thus, another passage recommends that a parent or spouse should never get offended, no matter how angry the comments or actions may make this person feel or want to react.[42] The Talmud gives an example of an observant family that got so upset with a father who continually got angry and made them cringe in his presence that they wanted to feed him sinful food, namely, meat cut off from a live animal.[43] *Orchot Tzaddikim* says that a parent who gets angry often and causes his or her family acute fear is responsible if they react and do something foolish, sinful, or immoral (like feeding him improper meat).[44]

Another person who should especially avoid getting angry is a teacher. The Mishna already says that an angry person cannot be an effective teacher.[45] Elijah the prophet said that the Torah could not properly be explained by a teacher who is angry and that he (Elijah) would never appear to such a person.[46] *Orchot Tzaddikim* explains why this is so. He says that students who are afraid that their teacher will get angry will stop themselves from asking important questions. In addition, an angry teacher does not have the patience to repeat and explain something or explain an idea in

---

37. *Shabbat* 55a
38. *Zohar* 2:182a
39. Leviticus 19:17
40. Maimonides, *Hilchot De'ot* 1:4

41. *Derech Eretz Zuta*, chapter 3
42. *Kallah Rabbati*, chapter 5
43. *Gittin* 7a
44. "The Gate of Anger," chapter 12 in *Orchot Tzaddikim*
45. Mishna *Avot* 2:5
46. *Kallah Rabbati*, chapter 5

the depth that may be required. Students also will not argue with an angry teacher, even when it is proper and within the subject matter.[47] But the Talmud does say that a student who learns to be quiet (and not answer back) when a teacher gets angry will merit understanding the greatest intricacies in Judaism in the fields of the laws of money matters and life and death.[48]

Another benefit of not becoming angry has affected all of Jewish history and Jewish law, when it was decided that in arguments between the House of Hillel and the House of Shammai, Jewish law follows the House of Hillel and not the House of Shammai. This is not because they had greater intellectual arguments, but rather because the House of Hillel never became angry.[49] They followed the teachings of their leader Hillel, who never showed anger, even when pesky non-Jews made outrageous demands. When they confronted Shammai, he threw them out, but Hillel accepted them.[50] *Netivot Olam* explains the connection between anger and Jewish law. He says that since Shammai and his followers were more hot-tempered than Hillel and his followers, Jewish law should follow only Rabbis who can maintain an even keel in life and in judgment.[51]

There are many other reasons why individuals should try to suppress their anger as much as possible. A person who does not get angry will sin significantly less than someone who is prone to anger.[52] There are three groups of people who God especially favors and loves: those who never get angry, those who never get drunk, and those who are modest and do not show off their talents.[53] God also loves three other groups of people (whose traits are much more difficult for us to achieve today): those who are insulted (but do not respond in

anger) and never do the insulting, those who are humiliated but do not humiliate, and those who accept suffering in joy, not anger.[54] One of the three groups of people whose life is not a "real life" (i.e., not worth living) is the group that is characterized by anger.[55] Angry people can never truly better themselves since other people will not try to tell them how to improve (out of fear of inciting anger).[56] Even if an angry person is admonished for poor or immoral behavior, he or she will simply get angry and not accept the words of advice that are meant to help, not hurt. Similarly, *Orchot Tzaddikim* says that an angry person will argue more with his or her acquaintances than other individuals, which will eventually bring jealousy and hatred.[57] Finally, an angry person will never be liked by others because the uncontrolled anger is a serious impediment to the development of any relationship, and even if the easily angered person is observant and full of Torah and good deeds, no one will want to learn from this person or imitate him or her.[58]

## THE TORAH SCHOLAR AND ANGER

There is a special relationship between the Torah scholar and the character trait of anger. We saw above that it is proper for the Torah scholar to get angry to protect and defend the Torah, but never for a personal reason.[59] There are many times, though, when a Torah scholar should go out of his way not to get angry.

King Solomon informed us that the words and reproof of a Torah scholar will be heard and internalized better if they are said sweetly, without any anger.[60] Maimonides reiterates this as a matter of Jewish law and says that a Torah scholar should never scream like

---

47. "The Gate of Anger," chapter 12 in *Orchot Tzaddikim*
48. *Berachot* 63b
49. *Eiruvin* 13b
50. *Shabbat* 31a
51. "Anger," chapter 1 in *Netivot Olam*
52. *Berachot* 29b
53. *Pesachim* 113b

54. *Shabbat* 88b
55. *Pesachim* 113b
56. "The Gate of Anger," chapter 12 in *Orchot Tzaddikim*
57. "The Gate of Anger," chapter 12 in *Orchot Tzaddikim*
58. "The Gate of Anger," chapter 12 in *Orchot Tzaddikim*
59. *Zohar* 2:182a
60. *Ecclesiastes* 9:16

an animal when he speaks or even raises his voice, because such behavior (as opposed to using quiet, sweet words) will only distance his audience.[61] The Talmud has sympathy and understanding for the Torah scholar who gets angry because of the Torah he learns and gives over.[62] The Torah is like fire and can make someone emotional. Nevertheless, the Torah scholar should still train himself to transmit the fiery words of Torah in a non-angry and gentle manner.

The first Lubavitcher Rebbe went even further and said that at the moment of anger, the Torah scholar actually loses his belief in God, since a believer could not of his own free will choose to get so angry.[63] The Midrash says that because of anger, Moses forgot Jewish law on three separate occasions.[64] Therefore, because an angry person will forget his wisdom, *Orchot Tzaddikim* says that someone who is prone to anger can never and will never attain the status of a Torah scholar in the first place.[65] Rabbi Chaim Vital, the foremost student of the Arizal, explains that because anger causes a scholar to lose some of his learning, his Rebbe and teacher, the Ari, was extremely careful never to get angry. He explains that some sins affect different parts of the body, but anger affects every part of the body. Since one's entire spirituality actually exists within the body, all the previous spiritual buildup that a scholar has achieved until then will be lost and has to be "rebooted." Thus, a Torah scholar who gets angry, even if he is pious in all other areas, will destroy all the spirituality he has accomplished.[66]

Another reason that a Torah scholar should not get angry and thereby sin comes from the Talmud. If his anger causes people to speak about him in a negative way, and to become ashamed of him because of his anger, then these actions cause a *Chilul Hashem*, a

desecration of God's name, and not a *Kiddush Hashem*, a sanctification of God's name.[67] And even when this person is permitted to reprove another person who is sinning, it should be done in a warm and loving manner without anger.[68] Perhaps now we can understand the response of one of the greatest Talmudic scholars of the last two centuries, Rabbi Yosef Shalom Elyashiv, who lived until the age of 102 (and died in 2012). When asked the reason for his longevity, he repeatedly said that "in his entire life, he never once got angry." Those who knew him well attested to the veracity of this statement.

## THE UNIQUENESS OF THE TRAIT OF ANGER

After defining, discussing, and analyzing the trait of anger, we find something surprising and unique about this trait. When the Mishna describes the trait of anger, it enumerates four types of people: those easily angered and slowly pacified (the worst), those easily angered and easily pacified, those slowly angered but slowly pacified, and those slowly angered but easily pacified (the best). The last person is called a *Chasid*, someone who goes beyond what is required.[69] (See the chapter entitled "Is Being Good the Most Important Thing in Judaism?" for an expansion of this theme.) The highest level of the trait, the one that goes beyond normal expectations, is a person who is slowly angered. But there is no fifth category listed – the person who *never* gets angry at all (like the one-in-a-million Rabbi Elyashiv). That is because Judaism and the Mishna understand that it is virtually impossible for a person never to get angry. How one expresses that anger is a different matter. (Perhaps that is what Rabbi Elyashiv meant – that he never responded to provocation by showing anger he felt inside.) Unlike other feelings or values, this emotion will inevitably be present within

---

61. Maimonides, *Hilchot De'ot* 5:7
62. *Ta'anit* 4a with Rashi commentary
63. Tanya, *Igrot HaKodesh*, chapter 25
64. Midrash, *Sifri, Matot* 5, *Vayikra Rabbah* 13
65. "The Gate of Anger," chapter 12 in *Orchot Tzaddikim*
66. Rabbi Chaim Vital, *Sha'ar HaRuach* 8b

67. *Yoma* 86a
68. *Sefer HaChinuch*, Mitzvah 338
69. Mishna *Avot* 5:11

every person. Knowing this, it is the job of every Jew to work on this nasty trait that will be experienced at various times in his or her life and try to sublimate it or use it for positive purposes. Perhaps that is why Maimonides listed anger as one of the very few traits in a human being for which it is not proper to find "the golden mean," a middle path, but rather to keep it to one extreme side, i.e., try to eradicate it completely.[70] He understood how every person feels this emotion and that each person has to work on himself or herself not to react to or act on this emotion. As Rabbi Horowitz referred to it, anger is the worst of all the character traits in man.[71]

---

70. Maimonides, *Hilchot De'ot* 2:3
71. Shela Hakadosh, Gate 200

# BIRTHDAYS IN JUDAISM

A BIRTHDAY, THE DAY A PERSON celebrates the anniversary of his or her birth into the world, is commemorated in almost every culture often with a party, gifts, or other rites of passage. Although the actual birth of a child and the thirteenth birthday (for a boy, twelfth for a girl) are certainly causes for great joy in Judaism, the yearly celebration of one's birthday is not found mentioned as part of standard Jewish practice and rituals in traditional Judaism. What is the view about celebrating yearly birthdays in Judaism? Is it allowed? Is it encouraged? Or is it forbidden? What are the reasons behind the traditional Jewish response in this area? Did any famous Rabbis celebrate their birthdays? If yes, how were their birthdays celebrated "Jewishly"? If not, why not? This chapter will examine the sources that will help answer these and other questions about birthdays.

## BIRTHDAYS MENTIONED IN CLASSIC JEWISH SOURCES

The only birthday celebration mentioned in the Torah is the birthday of Pharaoh, which indirectly caused Joseph to be saved from jail (after two years).[1] This happened because Pharaoh's chief butler was reinstated on this day, and he later remembered Joseph and mentioned him to Pharaoh as an interpreter of dreams. However, since the only birthday commemoration mentioned in Scripture is that of a non-Jewish enemy of the Jewish people, this would seem to indicate that such a celebration is not a particularly Jewish idea. But in explaining Pharaoh's celebration, Rashi defines exactly what a birthday is and how it was celebrated then,[2] and Rabbi Naftali Tzvi Yehudah Berlin's commentary explains

birthdays as a joyous day for the celebrant in which others try to bring him or her delight.[3]

Curiously, another commentary, the Ibn Ezra, says that the king's birthday is "*like* the day he was born," and not the day of birth itself. According to him, it marked the anniversary of the day that the king ascended to the kingship and was celebrated as the king's birthday. The Ibn Ezra also says the king would call together all his servants (perhaps for a celebration) and would give *them* gifts.[4] The idea that birthdays were celebrated on an anniversary and not on the exact date of a person's birth is not only referred to regarding Pharaoh and kings. Rashi, in an unusual explanation, states that this is how all birthdays were celebrated by the Jews in the desert after they left Egypt.[5] In order to answer the apparent quandary about the counting of Jewish males (between the ages of 20-60) in the desert, which was precisely 603,550 both times even though the countings happened several months apart,[6] Rashi points out that in that miraculous generation no one died and that everyone's birthday was celebrated on the first day of Tishrei, the birthday of the world. In other words, anyone born during that year would automatically become one year older only on the first day of the month of Tishrei, and at that time every member of the Jewish people, therefore, celebrated his or her Jewish birthday on the anniversary of the birthday of the world. Since each counting in the desert took place "between" two Tishreis (in the month of Tammuz right after the sin of the Golden Calf when each Jewish male adult donated a half a shekel, and then again in Nisan after the Tabernacle was erected), no Jewish person turned twenty or turned sixty-one in the interim.

---

1. Genesis 40:20
2. Rashi commentary on Genesis 40:20

3. *Ha'amek Davar* commentary on Genesis 40:20
4. Ibn Ezra commentary on Genesis 40:12
5. Rashi commentary on Exodus 30:16, with *Siftei Chachamim* commentary on Rashi
6. Exodus 38:26, Numbers 2:32

The other references to the day of birth or birthdays in Scripture are not particularly flattering or celebratory. Ezekiel compares the Jewish people to a newborn on its day of birth, covered in blood and unattractive.[7] King David describes the Jewish people as the child of God born on a particular day.[8] Jeremiah curses the day he was born (for all he has suffered) and says that this day will not be blessed, and Job also curses his day of birth.[9] King Solomon makes light of birthdays, declaring that the day of death is far better than the day of birth.[10] The Midrash explains the reason for this statement, indicating that King Solomon is logically correct. Why is the day of a person's birth celebrated? After all, it is a day when, at the time, no one knows what, if anything, this infant will accomplish worthwhile during his or her lifetime. Rather, the day of death should be celebrated because that is when the world can take stock of a person's lifetime accomplishments.[11] The Midrash compares celebrating birthdays to the foolish custom of people at the docks who cheer a ship that leaves port full of people and cargo. But when the ship ends its voyage, very few people, if any, are there to greet her. This is illogical. Why should the ship leaving be cheered when no one knows if it will accomplish its mission or achieve anything? Like the day of death, the day the ship docks should be far more celebrated and cheered than the day the ship leaves port at the beginning of its journey.

There is one Mishna that seems to celebrate and mark the achievements of a person as part of the Jewish life cycle. On a child's fifth birthday, he or she should begin to study a Torah text. On the tenth birthday, the Mishna should be studied for the first time. On his thirteenth birthday, a boy begins to do Mitzvot (that he is responsible for, while for a girl this begins at age twelve). On the fifteenth birthday, Talmud should begin. The eighteenth birthday is for marriage. The thirtieth birthday represents the height of strength, the fortieth represents intelligence, the sixtieth wisdom, etc.[12] While it is not clear whether the dates are simply the general year or the very first day of that year (i.e., the person's birthday), the idea of these milestones as birthday celebrations has certainly been adopted as the basis of the Bar and Bat Mitzvah celebrations, which do indeed begin on the Jewish birthday of the boy and girl. Therefore, it is logical to assume that the Mishna intended that these other life events should commence on one's birthday as well.

## THE DATE OF BIRTH IS A PROPITIOUS TIME IN JUDAISM

King Solomon states that there is a special time for birth in Judaism and a special time for death.[13] Just as Jews commemorate the special day of death, it is logical that they should also commemorate the day of birth. But what does this verse signify when it says that the day of birth is a special time? Is there anything special about the day a person is born? The Talmud, Midrash, and later sources seem to think so.

The Talmud and Midrash explain how the Amalekites had the audacity to fight the Jewish people when they knew that God protected the Jews and had saved them from the Egyptians. The Amalekites were very intelligent. They had the tradition that on a person's birthday, a human being has special protection and special luck.[14] Thus, they chose as soldiers only Amalekite people who had a birthday on the day they fought the Jews. And indeed, for a time the Amalekites did prevail, until the Jews prayed to God. There is an explanation involving birthdays that relates to Haman, who was very careful about "choosing" the date (through a lottery, the *Pur*) for when to fight and destroy the Jewish people. When the lottery (finally) fell on the month of Adar, Haman was very happy since on the

7. Ezekiel 16:4
8. Psalms 2:7
9. Jeremiah 16:4, Job 3:1
10. Ecclesiastes 7:1
11. Midrash, *Shemot Rabbah* 48:1

12. Mishna *Avot* 5:21
13. Ecclesiastes 3:2
14. Jerusalem Talmud, *Rosh Hashana* 17b; Midrash *Yalkut Shimoni, Habakkuk* 247:564

seventh day of that month Moses died, which he considered a good omen for killing Jews. What Haman did not know, says the Talmud, was that Moses was also born on the seventh of Adar, which was clearly a propitious time for the Jewish people.[15]

The Talmud also says "*Ein Mazal l'Yisrael,*"[16] which is commonly mistranslated to mean, "The Jews have no luck." What this statement really signifies is that the fate of the Jewish people, unlike other nations in the world, is not tied to any star or "timing." While this is true for the Jewish people as a whole, it seems that the Talmud does believe that the occasion of an individual's birthday is indeed a good time that brings fortune to the person and even to the Jewish people. The Talmud says that when Rabbi Elazar ben Azariah was appointed as the head of the Sanhedrin at the age of eighteen, his beard miraculously turned while overnight, making him look seventy years old, with the wisdom and experience of an older man and not a youngster. The Rabbis then took Rabbi Elazar and his opinions more seriously. One commentary explains that this miracle occurred exactly on his eighteenth birthday because birthdays are a propitious time for every person, and this day should be celebrated.[17]

Even the birthdays of the Patriarchs, who had died long before, were considered important enough that the dates of the dedication of both the Tabernacle and the Holy Temple were postponed only because of this reason. One Midrash says that the building of the Tabernacle was completed on the first day of the month of Adar but the entire Jewish people let the Tabernacle stay dormant and it was not dedicated or used until one month later, the first of Nisan, because that was the birthday of Isaac.[18] Another Midrash states that the dedication of the Holy Temple was delayed until the month of Tishrei because it was in

that month that Abraham was born.[19] The Talmud even specifies that the moment of birth gives each human being certain proclivities and personality traits.[20] This does not necessarily determine a person's future, especially in the moral sense, but it does give a person specific tendencies. Thus, for example, it states that if a person is born under the planetary influence of Mars (the red planet), a person will be a shedder of blood. When the Talmud asks if this means he or she will be a murderer, it answers that this is only one possibility. Other possibilities include a ritual slaughterer, a *Mohel* (one who performs ritual circumcision), or a surgeon, all of whom also "shed blood" in their noble professions.

As mentioned above regarding Haman, the day of death is generally considered a bad omen and the day of birth a good omen. Therefore, in an effort to minimize the sadness and depression caused by the death of a great sage, the Talmud lists the various great Rabbis whose birthday (the day they were born) coincided with the deaths of other great Rabbis.[21] This is not only a statement about the continuity of the Torah and oral traditions from one generation to the next, but also a statement of comfort in times of sadness – that the joy of birth minimized the sadness of death. Thus, Rabbi Judah the Prince was born on the day that Rabbi Akiva died. Rabbi Judah was born the day that Rabbi Judah the Prince died. Rava was born the day that Rabbi Judah died, etc.

This same idea was stressed on the saddest day of the Jewish year, Tisha B'av, not the day of the death of one person, but the "death" of the Holy Temple and a way of life for Jews. It was on that day, the destruction of the First Holy Temple, that the Messiah was born (which has to be understood, but is too detailed for this context).[22] Another Midrash says that Tisha B'av is not a day of sadness, but rather a day of joy because Menachem

---

15. *Megillah* 13b
16. *Shabbat* 156a
17. *Berachot* 28a with Ben Yehoyada commentary
18. *Midrash Tanchuma* 11

19. Midrash, *Pesikta Rabbati* 6:4
20. *Shabbat* 156a
21. *Kiddushin* 72b, *Yoma* 38b
22. Midrash, *Agadat Bereishit* 68

(another name of Messiah) was born.[23] It was for this reason that, according to many commentaries, Jeremiah, the prophet of the Temple's destruction, called Tisha B'av a holiday.[24] The "holiday" aspect of this sad day is reflected in the omitting of the Tachanun prayer in the service and other joyous customs practiced by certain individuals on Tisha B'av after the Mincha (afternoon prayer) service – all because of the "birthday" of Messiah.[25] Rabbi Moshe Isserles, certainly not a mystic, codifies as Jewish law (still practiced in many Yeshivot today) that the beginning of learning for a year or long time period should take place on Rosh Chodesh, the first day of the Jewish month.[26] Why? It is the moon's "birthday" each month and a propitious time to learn Torah.

The one actual birthday celebration mentioned in the Talmud is that of Rabbi Yosef, who threw himself a birthday party when he turned sixty.[27] When questioned why he celebrated this particular birthday, he answered that this is the year that he can no longer die from *Karet*, the punishment of an early death. But, other than the fact that the age of sixty was considered to be a very old age at that time, is there anything significant about this year as signifying the end of the possibility of an early death? Perhaps if the "ideal" age for a Jew is to die at the age of 120, getting to the age of sixty signifies that a person has achieved more than half of that age. In the same vein, the Talmud says that if a person has passed more than half of his or her years without sin, then that person will never sin for the rest of his or her life.[28] In some Jewish circumstances, more than half is considered equal to the whole.[29]

## NON-JEWISH AND PAGAN ORIGINS OF BIRTHDAY CELEBRATIONS

Academics have differing views of the origin of birthday celebrations, but all of the opinions have one thing in common: Birthday rituals and parties are derived from pagan beliefs and as a tribute to their gods. One explanation involved the Greek belief that every person had a protective spirit who watched over him or her in life, a sort of guardian angel. The birthday cake was offered to this protective god, the lighted tapers represented an altar to that god, and these candles are endowed with a special magic to grant wishes.[30] Another explanation involved the moon god Arteis, and her birthday took place on the sixth day of each month. The round cake represented the full moon and the candles represented the light that emanated from the moon. Still others say that the Greeks took their birthday rituals from the Egyptians. Whichever theory is correct, the question must be asked: If this is indeed the origin of the birthday celebration, then what is the implication for traditional Jews? May Jews, then, celebrate their birthdays at all?

Part of being Jewish is remaining distinctively Jewish in beliefs and actions. Therefore, the Torah forbids imitating the customs of foreign cultures.[31] The Mishna also associates birthday celebrations with non-Jewish kings who worshipped idols, and therefore forbids Jews to make a celebration on the day the king celebrates his birthday.[32] After much discussion in the Talmudic and post-Talmudic period about the precise implications of the *Averah/sin*, the *Code of Jewish Law* rules that any custom that was entirely pagan or idol-worshipping in origin is forbidden to Jews, even if the custom is no longer even religious today (like celebrating Halloween, for example). Similarly, if the original reason for the ritual or custom is unknown, then it is similarly forbidden (since

---

23. Midrash, *Esther Rabbah, Peticha* 11
24. Lamentations 1:15
25. *Beit Yosef* commentary on *Tur, Orach Chaim* 554
26. Rema on *Shulchan Aruch, Yoreh De'ah* 179:2
27. *Mo'ed Katan* 28a
28. *Yoma* 38b
29. *Nazir* 42a, *Shulchan Aruch, Yoreh De'ah* 95:2

30. Ralph and Adelin Linton, *The Lore of Birthdays* (New York, 1952)
31. Leviticus 18:3
32. Mishna *Avodah Zara* 1:3 with Rashi and Rabbeinu Chananael commentaries

it might have had pagan origins). However, if the custom has legitimacy in and of its own, without pagan ideas, then even if non-Jews originated the particular practice, it is not forbidden to Jews (like hairstyles today or wearing a suit).[33] Would this Jewish law forbid or permit celebration of birthdays today by Jews?

Although the specific rituals may have been pagan in origin, the celebration of the birth of something or someone is not unique to idol worshippers (as was demonstrated above in sources and will be expanded upon below). Thus the idea of celebrating a birthday in and of itself is not pagan in origin and would be permitted from that perspective. However, the specific rituals that are associated with birthday celebration may be questionable. The use of a cake, even a round cake, does not necessarily signify the pagan origin, as many celebrations involve the baking of cakes (and a round cake is simply the standard, not due to the shape of the moon). However, the use of candles, (especially the blowing out of candles) and attaching magical powers for wishes to these candles is certainly questionable from a Jewish perspective. Therefore, one modern Rabbi forbids the use the candles in Jewish birthday celebrations.[34] Specifically, Jews are never supposed to blow out candles, since King Solomon has taught that a candle represents a human life that should never be extinguished by blowing it out.[35]

## BIRTHDAYS ARE TRULY SPECIAL IN JUDAISM, BUT WHY?

The day of birth is indeed special in Judaism. But rather than acknowledge this unusual event once a year, Judaism, in a certain sense, acknowledges a person's day of birth each and every day of life! Since Judaism believes that sleep is the equivalent of one-sixtieth of death, each time that a person sleeps, he or she dies

in a symbolic sense. It is for that reason that when a Jew wakes up each morning, his very first words should be *"Modeh Ani"* – "I am grateful," an acknowledgement and appreciation that life has been restored (from this dead person) and he or she is "born anew." It is also for that reason that a few paragraphs later, the traditional Jew prays to God and thanks Him that his or her soul given to them today by God comes with a "clean slate" (by virtue of that rebirth).[36]

Although traditional Judaism and Jewish sources do not contain a discussion of the birth of each individual, one central idea of Judaism is the birthday of the world, which is celebrated as the holiday of Rosh Hashana.[37] During the celebration of the birthday of the world, Jews acknowledge God as the source of all, and God chooses to evaluate His creation. Just as the world is evaluated on the celebration of its birthday, it is logical that each person should also celebrate his or her own individual birth on its anniversary, acknowledging God and doing a self-evaluation. In fact, according to one opinion, the first day of Tishrei is not the birth of the world, but the birth of man, and that is the reason for the holiday and celebration – the birthday of mankind (as the beginning of Creation of the world was six days earlier).[38]

The significance of a birthday – both of the world and of man – was so important to the Rabbis that they tried to find a connection between the birthday of the world and the birthdays of the Forefathers, Abraham, Isaac, and Jacob. According to the opinion that the world was created in the month of Nisan, the Forefathers were also born in that month, but according to the opinion that the world was created in the month of Tishrei, the Forefathers were born in Tishrei as well. In fact, the Talmud goes out of its way to find significant

---

33. *Shulchan Aruch, Yoreh De'ah* 178
34. Rabbi Avrohom Blumenkrantz, "The Laws of Pesach" (2002), p. 206
35. *Kaf HaChaim* (Palagi) 31:25, Proverbs 20:27

36. *Berachot* 57b, Daily morning prayer
37. Abarbanel commentary on Exodus 12:2, *Shulchan Aruch* 592:1, Rosh Hashana prayer book (*Machzor*), *Shofar* blowing service
38. Midrash, *Devarim Rabbah* 1:13

Jewish events in history to correspond to the birthday of the world.[39]

It is not only the birth of the world that has significance in Judaism. In every culture, including Judaism, there is great meaning attached to the birth of that nation. And there are many parallels between the celebration of the birthday of a people and the celebration of an individual's birthday. It is no accident, therefore, that the very first Mitzvah given to the Jewish people was to establish a Jewish calendar, whereby the counting would commence on the birthday of the Jewish people.[40] One modern commentary states that it is very natural and important to commemorate all significant events in life by remembering them on the anniversary that they took place (like a birthday). That is why Rosh Hashana (the birth of the world/mankind) is significant for the Jew, as is the beginning of Nisan (the birth of the Jewish nation after the Exodus). And even the weekly lighting of the Havdalah candle on Saturday night is a weekly commemoration of God's creation of the world (since the beginning of any day of the year as well as the first day of Creation, Sunday, begins at night in Jewish thought), and the very first element created by God in the world was light.[41]

In fact, the word "nation" came into English from the Old French word "nacion," which, in turn, originates from the Latin word "nation" (nātĭō), literally meaning "that which has been born." This idea is derived from the sources as well. Hosea describes the "Day of the King" which compares the anniversary of the king's rise to power with the birth of a human being.[42] Ezekiel compares the birth of a nation to the birth of a baby, in the way a baby is now more independent of its mother after birth, according to one commentary.[43] Rabbi Tzadok compares the birth of a baby to the Exodus from Egypt and the birth of the Jewish nation

that underwent great "pangs of labor" to become a Jewish people.[44]

## BIRTH AND DEATH ON THE SAME DATE AND THE SIGNIFICANCE OF THAT DATE

For all human beings, their date of birth is significant. However, for the truly righteous, states the Talmud, God intentionally allows them to complete their year of living, to the day, before they die. Therefore, the truly righteous die on the same date as their birth (according to the Jewish calendar).[45] We saw this above with regard to Moses. It was also true of King David, who was born and died on Shavuot,[46] Rabbi Shimon bar Yochai,[47] and countless other righteous individuals.

Even for those who do not merit death on the same date as their birth, the day of birth itself gives special merit to each individual. The idea of making wishes and God granting those wishes on a person's birthday is already alluded to by King David, as he immediately follows the words "day of birth" with "ask Me and I will give to you" in the Psalms. This clearly indicates that the day of birth is indeed "special."[48] According to Chidah, the "Mazal" on the day of one's birth (see above) is extremely strong and healthy, indicating it is a special time.[49] One Midrash says that because people are so grateful that they completed an entire year of living (i.e., reached their birthday), they are very happy and it is very appropriate to make a party.[50] Rabbi Ephraim Greenblatt describes the various celebrations in Jewish history on the birth of certain children, including Isaac and Moses, and then says it is appropriate to celebrate one's birthday.[51] Rav Tzadok writes that even though at a baby's birth one does not know the future and what will become of the

---

39. Rosh Hashana 10b
40. Exodus 12:2 with Nachmanides commentary
41. Ha'amek Davar commentary on Exodus 12:2
42. Hosea 7:5 with Metzudat David commentary
43. Ezekiel 16:4 with Malbim commentary

44. Pri Tzadik, "Et HaOchel" 14
45. Rosh Hashana 11a
46. Sha'arei Teshuva, Orach Chaim 494
47. Pri Tzadik, Lag B'omer 1
48. Psalms 2:7-8 with Radak commentary
49. Sefer Chomat Anach, Kohelet 10, Job 3
50. Midrash, Sechel Tov 40:20
51. Revevot Ephraim 4:240

infant, each human being has a certain innate holiness that will eventually be revealed, and therefore it is appropriate to celebrate one's birthdays.[52]

## WHY SHOULD AND SHOULDN'T JEWS CELEBRATE BIRTHDAYS TODAY?

Despite the positive statements about birthday celebrations in Judaism mentioned above, numerous Rabbis and other sources are vehemently opposed to the celebration of birthdays by Jews. One Talmudic source gives a philosophical reason. Beit Shammai and Beit Hillel argued for two and a half years about whether it would have been better or worse if man had not been created. The final conclusion is that it would have better if man had *not* been created, and therefore, it would have been preferred if each human being had not been born. (It is beyond the scope of this volume to explain the deeper meaning of this concept.)[53] Thus, based on this statement, there is no positive reason to celebrate an individual's birth or the anniversary of that birth, namely, one's birthday. Another argument against commemorating birthdays was alluded to above. If it was, in ancient times, non-Jewish pagans who instituted birthday celebrations, why then should Jews celebrate their birthdays? Furthermore, since birthday celebrations are not mentioned anywhere (except for one lone Talmudic reference) in all classic Jewish sources, then this ritual is obviously not something Jewish and should not be practiced today.[54]

Another Rabbi explained why birthday celebrations are inappropriate for Jews, but are nevertheless quite proper for non-Jews. Since Jews have been given so many commandments (613) and can more easily fail than succeed in fulfilling them, it is better for a Jew not to have been created – the odds against him succeeding are very high. Thus, celebrating the day of birth is not appropriate. But for non-Jews who have to fulfill only seven commandments (of Noah) to achieve the World to Come, it is far easier to succeed, and thus for them, a day of birth is an event to be celebrated.[55] In 1889 in the city of Kovno, the people wanted to make a joyous celebration for their Rabbi, Rabbi Isaac Elchanan Spektor, on his fiftieth anniversary as Rabbi of the city. Not only did he decline, but he stated that this type of celebration or any birthday commemoration is forbidden for Jews. His son said that this practice was just copying non-Jews, as monkeys copy what they see without any understanding.[56] Rabbi Eliyahu David Rabinovits-Te'omim, known as Ha-Aderet, (1843-1905) concurs and he "cursed" those who wished him a "happy birthday."[57] He used some of the same arguments cited above, as well as the Midrash comparing the day of birth, before a person accomplishes anything, to the foolish celebratory sending off of a ship, when in reality the coming in of the ship or the death at the end of a person's life should truly be celebrated for their accomplishments.[58]

## WHY SHOULD JEWS CELEBRATE BIRTHDAYS TODAY?

On the other hand, many contemporary Rabbis, as well as leading Rabbis from the previous generations, have disagreed with the above analysis, and openly encouraged Jews to celebrate their birthdays in the right way and for the right reasons. Rabbi Chaim Dovid HaLevi (1924-1988), who was the Chief Rabbi of Tel Aviv, writes that in modern times there is no prohibition for Jews to celebrate their birthdays in a family context, since it is logical to be appreciative to God for extending one's life for one more year.[59] In previous generations, when idol worship was connected to this ritual, it is understandable that there might have

---

52. *Yisrael Kedoshim* 8
53. *Eiruvin* 13b
54. *Otzar Kol Minhagei Yeshurun*, p. 60

55. *Sefer HaKatan Vehilchotav* 24:1
56. *Otzar Kol Minhagei Yeshurun*, p. 60
57. *Tefillat David*, p. 204
58. Midrash, *Shemot Rabbah* 48a
59. *Responsa Asei Lecha Rav* 3:21

been objections, but that is no longer the case today. A birthday party with a Mitzvah meal and words of Torah turns this ritual into a holy event. The contemporary Rabbi Ovadiah Yosef (1920-2013) permits all birthday celebrations as long as the purpose is to honor God and the festive meal is a Mitzvah meal with words of Torah.[60] He further adds that the famous Ben Ish Chai (1834-1909) was in favor of a yearly birthday celebration. Rabbi Moses Feinstein discouraged a public observance of birthdays in the synagogue, but certainly permitted birthday rituals in one's home.[61] Many other Rabbis also encouraged or permitted Jews to celebrate their birthdays, and several prominent Rabbis actually celebrated their birthdays publicly in various ways. It should be understood that all birthday celebrations mentioned refer to the date of a person's birth on the Jewish calendar, not the secular calendar.

## WHICH GREAT RABBIS CELEBRATED JEWISH BIRTHDAYS?

In the Lublin Yeshiva in 1931, all the students signed a "birthday wish" to their Rosh Yeshiva (Head of the Academy), Rabbi Meir Shapira, and the entire Yeshiva gathered for this purpose. Thereafter, every year on the seventh of Adar, the Rabbi's birthday (as well as the birthday of Moses), the administration of the Yeshiva found an "excuse" to organize a gathering of all the students on this date in order to intentionally honor the birthday of their Rosh Yeshiva. This practice of celebrating Rabbi Shapira's birthday continued even after he died.[62] In a similar manner, when the prominent Jerusalem Rabbis gathered in 1906 to honor the accomplishments of the Chief Rabbi, Rabbi Shmuel Salant, they intentionally timed the gathering to coincide with the Rabbi's ninetieth birthday, and his birthday was publicly celebrated by all. (According to one eyewitness, Rabbi Chaim Berlin brought

the "birthday boy" a cake with good wishes written in Hebrew.)[63]

One of the most interesting heads of a Yeshiva who was outspoken about the issue of birthdays is Rabbi Abraham Schreiber, known as the Ketav Sofer (1815-1872). Based on a phrase in the Torah that God will "fill your days," Rabbi Schreiber writes that a Jew is obligated to count his or her days (i.e., commemorate birthdays) and count how many years have passed, in order to be diligent in the service of God and to prepare for the Next World.[64] One source states that on his birthday each year, the seventh of Tishrei, Rabbi Schreiber would learn with his students and complete the Written Torah.[65] But another source, reported by one of Rabbi Schreiber's students, states that when that student awoke early on the Rabbi's birthday and visited him early in the morning, Rabbi Schreiber was reciting the Psalms and crying non-stop. When asked why he was crying, Rabbi Schreiber replied that on this day, his birthday, he would take stock of his life and would always come up "short" because he felt he never reached his potential. But, the student continued, the idea of the commemoration of one's birthday was crucial in giving thanks to God for the length of one's life, and this birthday celebration was even more important than prayer for a guarantee that life would continue until the next year.[66]

In addition to these Rabbis, it has been reported (orally) that in his later years, Rabbi Yisrael Meir Kagan (1932-1933), known as the Chafetz Chaim, celebrated his birthday in order to publicize the rewards of refraining for Lashon Hara, evil speech. It was well known in Chabad Chassidut that birthdays are special and should be celebrated. Rabbi Menachem Mendel Schneerson (1902-1994) commemorated his birthday publicly each year, and it became a Lubavitcher custom to compose a song in honor of this occasion with words taken

---

60. Responsa Yabia Omer, Orach Chaim 6:29
61. Responsa Igrot Moshe, Orach Chaim 1:104, 4:36
62. Sefer Yeshivat Chachmei Lublin, pp. 101-102

63. Otzar HaChesed Keren Shmuel, p. 36
64. Exodus 23:25-26 with Ketav Sofer commentary
65. Minhagei Chatam Sofer 7:14
66. Responsa Kinyan Torah BeHalacha 3:21, Toldot Arugat HaBosem, p. 298

from the psalm whose number corresponded to his birthday year (words from Psalm 72 on his seventy-second birthday, for example).

## WHAT IS A "JEWISH" BIRTHDAY CELEBRATION?

What constitutes a uniquely Jewish ritual in celebrating birthdays? The Rabbis mentioned above certainly did not make themselves a birthday cake and blow out the candles. What, then, did they do to celebrate their birthdays? How should a believing Jew today make his or her birthday celebration "special" and "Jewish"?

Rabbi Moshe Chagiz, who lived in the 1700s, encourages every Jew to take a new fruit or piece of clothing on his or her birthday and recite the *Shehechiyanu* blessing on it, having in mind also the birthday, since this blessing thanks God for reaching this moment in time. And from the age of seventy, a special festive meal should be eaten each year on one's birthday, especially if the person is a Torah sage.[67] Similarly, Rabbi Yair Bachrach (1638-1701) seems to say that the *Shehechiyanu* blessing may be recited outright for someone celebrating his seventieth birthday, but an accompanying meal may not be obligatory. Therefore, it is preferable to include words of Torah at the feast, which turns any meal into a *Seudat Mitzvah*, a Jewish ritual meal.[68] This sentiment is also echoed by Rabbi Yosef MiBagdad, who says that the birthday boy or girl should have the birthday in mind when reciting the *Shehechiyanu* blessing on a new fruit or new clothing.[69]

Rabbi Hillel Posek adds that since each Jew already has special favor on his or her birthday, this day should be dedicated completely to God, in an effort to annul any evil decrees against that person. In addition, since there is a general Jewish concept to perform a commandment as early as possible, the commandment to become more spiritual and dedicate oneself to God should be undertaken at the earliest possible time in each person's year and the very first moments of that person's year – on his or her birthday.[70] One modern Rabbi gives several other possible suggestions and customs for celebrating a Jewish birthday.[71] One suggestion is that the birthday person should complete a Talmud tractate or the Written Torah, as we saw above with Ktav Sofer (Rabbi Schreiber). Tiferet Yisrael told his children that after he died they should begin the practice each year of writing birthday wishes to each sibling. (Perhaps this was the first birthday card.) Another custom for a "Jewish" birthday should be to give extra *Tzedaka* (charity) on this day. It became a custom by Rabbis in Jerusalem to honor a great Rabbi by sending a donation to a worthwhile cause on his birthday. The amount of charity would be the specific number of that birthday in *Tzedaka* (ninety dollars on his ninetieth birthday, for example). They did this for both Rabbi Salant and Rabbi Sonnenfeld.

The book of Chabad customs brings down a number of distinctly Jewish birthday practices.[72] It mentions giving the birthday man an *Aliya* to the Torah either on the day of his birthday or the Shabbat beforehand (if the Torah is not read on the birthday), a custom that is practiced in many Jewish communities today. It also mentions giving extra *Tzedaka* on one's birthday, learning extra Torah on this day, taking time for introspection and self-analysis of the past and commit to changes for the future, as Rabbi Schreiber (above) did, on one's birthday. In 1988, Rabbi Schneerson inaugurated a "Jewish Birthday Campaign" and asked that each birthday person utilize this most special day in life to its utmost. It should become a day to recommit to the mission that God entrusted to each Jew, by bettering and sanctifying oneself and the world around us.

---

67. *Leket HaKemach* 131
68. *Responsa Chavot Yair* 70
69. Ben Ish chai, *Parshat Rosh* 17
70. *Responsa Hillel Omer* 139
71. *Sefer HaKatan Vehilchotav* 24:1
72. *Sefer Minhagim Shel Chabad*, "Inyanim Shonim," p. 81

# CAPITAL PUNISHMENT IN JUDAISM

THE MORALITY AND ETHICS OF CAP-
ital punishment, i.e., the death penalty
for murder, has been greatly discussed
in the past few years, especially in the United
States, where it was ruled illegal for a short
time (between 1972-1976), but where its legality is now decided by each state. Thirty-three
states currently allow it and seventeen do not.
Several prominent states abolished the death
penalty only recently, such as New York in
2007 and Connecticut in 2012, so the debate
rages on. Internationally, of the 194 United
Nations member countries, 98 have abolished
capital punishment completely, and another
49 nations still have it "on the books" but have
not implemented it in the last few years. As
the debate about the ethics and morality of
such a punishment continues in the world, it
is important to understand the Jewish view on
this subject, and to show that this is an ancient
Jewish ethical discussion that has continued
throughout the ages. In Israel, the question of
the death penalty for terrorists has been re-
vived after the recent exchange of many killer
terrorists for Gilad Schalit in 2012, which resulted in Arab terrorists becoming less afraid
of being apprehended for murdering Israelis,
since they count on being freed in a future
exchange for another captured Israeli soldier.
Capital punishment for terrorists would eliminate this assumption. *Is this sufficient reason to
institute the death penalty for captured terrorists
who are known to have committed horrendous
acts of murder against civilians?* What then
is the traditional Jewish view on the death
penalty?

## THE RATIONALE AND CAPITAL
## PUNISHMENT IN THE TORAH

What is the rationale for killing a human being who kills someone else? The traditional
arguments in favor of capital punishment for
an act of murder are threefold. The first is

deterrence. When those who may potentially
commit murder know that the punishment
upon being caught is death this may prevent
many potential killers from carrying out the
act. The second is retribution or justice. If a
person takes the life of a human being, the logical punishment for such an act is to lose his
or her own life. This is the most "fair" punishment for murder. It also provides a feeling of
justice and closure for the family of the victim,
who suffer the most when a relative is brutally
murdered. The third argument is safety – i.e.,
it is important to keep a murderer away from
an innocent population since this person
may murder again. However, this argument is
negated if a policy of imprisonment without
the possibility of parole for murderers exists,
because it is an alternative punishment to the
death penalty that addresses this concern. But
if we look at the Torah, Judaism offers a fourth
rationale for capital punishment.

Even before the Torah addresses capital
punishment for crimes and sins in an all-Jew-
ish society, the Torah makes it clear that even
for non-Jews the punishment for murder is
death. When speaking to Noah, God says that
he who sheds blood, i.e., the person who murders, should die as a result of his crime.[1] But
then the Torah gives a specific reason for this
punishment: man was created in the image of
God. Thus, in addition to the other rationales
for capital punishment, the Torah says that because every person has a piece of God within
him or her, if a person takes the life of another
human being (who also had a piece of God
within), that person forfeits his or her "image
of God" and is no longer worthy to be called
a human being with God's image. It is for this
reason that the Torah says he does not deserve
to live.

But the Torah, which later on describes
a Jewish society that does not distinguish

---

1. Genesis 6:9

46

between man-to-man and man-to-God crimes/sins, lists numerous other sins whose punishment is also the death penalty. In addition to murder, the death penalty is listed for striking one's parent, kidnapping, bestiality, violating Shabbat, idol worship, adultery, homosexual behavior, and cursing God.[2] All these sins are heinous from a Jewish perspective, and the seriousness of their punishment attests to that. However, it would be foolish to form the Jewish view of capital punishment based on these verses alone. Why is this so?

According to Jewish tradition, the corpus of Oral Law was given along with the Written Torah at the very same time, in order to render the barebones legal system of Torah verses into a working Jewish society of law for everyday living. Therefore, if we examine the details of capital punishment along with the details of its oral laws, we will discover that it was almost impossible to actually punish a perpetrator of any of these crimes or sins with the death penalty. For example, while the Torah says that a court needs two witnesses to convict a murderer,[3] it does not set down the conditions or details about those witnesses or what they saw. The details of all the conditions that need to occur, which are specified in the Oral Law, make it almost impossible to actually convict a murderer or perpetrator of any of the sins mentioned above.

The Talmud in tractates *Sanhedrin* and *Makkot* discusses the specific elements and conditions of all that must occur in order to convict a murderer in a Jewish court. For example, the two witnesses have to be adult Jewish men who keep the commandments, know the Oral Law fairly well, and have legitimate professions. Both witnesses must have been able to see each other at the time of the act or sin. The witnesses must be able to speak clearly, without any speech impediment or hearing deficit. They are invalidated if they are related to the accused or to each other. In addition, the witnesses have to give a warning to the

person right before the sin, saying that the sin he or she is about to commit is a capital offense. If the warning is not delivered within approximately ten seconds before the sin/crime, it is not valid. In that short time period after the warning, the sinner has to respond that he or she is familiar with the punishment, is going to commit the crime/sin anyway, and then begin to act immediately thereafter.

In court, the following conditions must also be present: The judges have to examine each witness separately, and if even one point of their evidence is contradictory (even the eye color of the sinner), the witnesses' testimony is not admitted. Of the twenty-three Jewish judges in a capital case, a simple majority vote of twelve to eleven is not enough to convict (it needs to be at least thirteen to ten) and if all twenty-three unanimously vote to convict, the sinner goes free (based on the logic that if at least one judge cannot find something exculpatory about the accused, then there is something wrong with the court). Thus, it would be nearly impossible to satisfy each and every one of these conditions. While the punishment of death for sins or crimes is clearly stated in order to show the severity of each sin or act, and while the person who commits such crimes may indeed *deserve* to be killed, in practice, Judaism and Jewish courts could almost never actually convict and put someone to death.

## THE AMBIVALENCE ABOUT THE DEATH PENALTY IN THE TALMUD

After showing the vast difference between the Torah's verses about the death penalty and the ability to actually carry out such a sentence, we also see that the Rabbis in the Talmud were conflicted about this practice. In one Mishna alone, some of the greatest Rabbis in the history of Judaism argued about the morality of the death penalty.[4] One opinion is that any Jewish court that puts to death one sinner in seven years is considered a bloody court. Rabbi Eliezer disagreed and says that

---

2. Exodus 21:12, 15-17, 31:14, Leviticus 20:2, 10, 13, 24:16
3. Deuteronomy 17:6

4. Mishna *Makkot* 1:10

one death penalty in seventy years renders it a bloody court. Rabbi Tarfon and Rabbi Akiva say that had they been in the Sanhedrin judging capital crimes, no one would have *ever* been put to death. But then, Rabbi Shimon, who was on a par with these other Rabbis, answers them all and implies that capital punishment *should* indeed be used on a regular basis in order to deter murders. "If Judaism were to follow your ideas," he tells the other Rabbis, "you would be actively causing more people to murder innocents." Thus, we can see the battle about this issue right within the Mishna. On the one hand, the extreme sensitivity to life – all life, even that of a murderer – compels some Rabbis not to put him to death. On the other hand, that very sensitivity to life of innocents leads Rabbi Shimon to conclude that having no death penalty in practice will cause a lack of deterrence, and will lead to a proliferation of murder by Jews.

This ambivalence about capital punishment (between showing mercy for the murderer by a Jewish court vs. the need to deter others from murdering) continues in the period after the Mishna, as is evident from a number of statements in the Talmud, in the Midrash, and in Jewish law. Various conflicting passages show the two views. On the one hand, the Midrash states that Judaism should not adopt (today's) liberal view not to kill a murderer, simply because by killing him, the victim will not be brought back to life.[5] But another Mishna states that two of the conditions of being a judge on capital cases are that each judge must be married with children and not be too old. The reason for these conditions, explain the commentaries, is that someone who never had any children will not have the required mercy to know what it feels like to put someone's child to death, and someone too old may have forgotten how to be merciful with children.[6] Maimonides quotes these two conditions as part of Jewish law.[7]

## SOLVING THE PROBLEM WITHIN JEWISH LAW

In the latter years of the period under Roman rule, the incidence of murders in the Jewish community apparently proliferated greatly. The Rabbis, the majority of whom were already averse to putting convicted killers to death, did not want to continue the practice at all. Changing Jewish law regarding capital punishment was out of the question, as Jewish law could not be altered or amended simply because a problem arose or conditions changed. So the leading Rabbis of the Sanhedrin, the Jewish high court, needed to find a solution within Jewish law. The Torah states that when a convicted murderer was taken out to die, part of Jewish law was that the location of where the convicted murderer had to be taken from, i.e., the Sanhedrin, had to be next the Altar in the Temple.[8] Because of this verse, it was a law that the Sanhedrin could only meet to decide capital (and therefore all) cases in the *Lishkat haGazit*, the chamber within the Temple next to the Altar, where the Jewish high court sat.[9] Then, the Talmud tells us that when murders proliferated under Roman rule, forty years before the destruction of the Second Temple (around 30 CE),[10] the Rabbis decided to abandon the home of the Sanhedrin in the Temple because it was forbidden to judge capital cases outside the Temple.[11] In this way, the Rabbis avoided having to try capital cases without having to change previously established Jewish law. This also shows us their rationale for the death penalty (in addition to the reasoning cited above based on the Torah verse). The death penalty was only effective as long as it provided a deterrence to minimize people's incentive to commit murder. Once murder became so common in the land of Israel under Roman rule, there was no point in continuing the death penalty, since the deterrence was no longer effective. It was then that the Rabbis

---

5. Midrash, *Sifri, Shoftim* 44
6. Mishna *Horayot* 1:4, with Tosafot Yom Tov and Maimonides commentaries
7. Maimonides, *Hilchot Sanhedrin* 2:3

8. Exodus 21:14
9. Midrash, *Mechilta* on Exodus 21:14
10. *Avodah Zara* 8b
11. *Sanhedrin* 52b

decided to move their court in order to avoid capital punishment altogether.

Once there was no Sanhedrin in the Temple or no Temple at all, no Jewish court was even allowed to pronounce a death sentence for a capital crime. When Imarata, the daughter of a Kohen (Priest), committed adultery, Rabbi Chama pronounced a death sentence upon her, even though it was after the Temple's destruction. Rabbi Yosef and all the Talmudic Rabbis castigated Rabbi Chama because it was a well-known Jewish law that when there is no Kohen serving in the Temple or no Temple at all, capital punishment as the penalty for those sins outlined in the Torah is forbidden.

## THE DEATH PENALTY FOR NON-CAPITAL CRIMES IN JUDAISM

Although the death penalty was very rarely used to begin with and the era of the Jewish court using the penalty for capital sins in the Torah formally came to a close when the Sanhedrin moved outside of the Temple (and finally with the Temple's destruction), there is another set of instances when Jewish courts may use the death penalty, although not on a regular basis. When Judaism itself and the system of Jewish law are being threatened, Jewish law allows Jewish courts to pronounce the death penalty for sins and crimes that normally do not incur the punishment of death. This is permitted simply in order to demonstrate to the people the importance of upholding Jewish law and the power of the court. But this can be done only on a one-time or very sporadic basis.

Thus, during the Greek period, when many Jews were attracted to Hellenism and began abandoning traditional Judaism and observance of the details of Rabbinic law, the Rabbis made an example of one person who was caught riding a horse on Shabbat, which was forbidden by the Rabbis as a fence around the Torah law in order not to come to tear off leaves from a tree. (A person riding a horse may easily do this and therefore the Rabbis forbid riding a horse in any place on Shabbat,

even in the desert where there are no trees.) When this person intentionally defied the Rabbis and rode a horse on Shabbat, the Jewish court ruled the death penalty for him, even though this act normally would result in the maximum punishment of lashes. Why? They wanted to demonstrate to the people the severity of ignoring Rabbinic law.[12] But this specific death penalty was enacted for this purpose and as a one-time legislation. Maimonides cites this example from the Talmud and rules that any Jewish court overseeing the laws of a Jewish/religious community has this right to enact the death penalty in order to establish the primacy of Torah law, but only as a one-time pronouncement.[13] Similarly, elsewhere Maimonides rules that if a murderer who had escaped the official death sentence because of the myriad of technicalities cited above, seemed to be flaunting the fact that they he literally "gotten away with murder," the king has the authority to pronounce the death sentence upon this individual, as does the Jewish court, if they felt it was necessary in a particular situation.[14]

## THE DEATH PENALTY AFTER THE TALMUDIC PERIOD

If the death penalty was generally forbidden after the Temple's destruction, then what happened in those rare instances when Jews committed murder in the Jewish community? During the period of the Gaonim (approximately 550-1000 CE), this question arose numerous times. Rabbi Nutrani Gaon (800s) was asked what should happen to someone who is guilty of a capital crime or sin, now that capital punishment is banned.[15] He answers that since his punishment should have been death, the Jewish court cannot give him lashes as a Torah punishment, which is a lesser punishment than that which he deserves. However, he can be given Rabbinic lashes (a slightly

---

12. *Sanhedrin* 46a
13. Maimonides, *Hilchot Sanhedrin* 24:4
14. Maimonides, *Hilchot Sanhedrin* 2:4
15. *Teshuvot Rav Nutrani Gaon, Choshen Mishpat* 375

different punishment than Torah lashes in terms of its number and other details), and this person is excommunicated from the Jewish community, which means that no one can speak to or have dealings with him or her (at a time period when moving out of the community was almost impossible and conversion was not an option). Thus, the punishment of excommunication from the Jewish community was severe indeed.

About one hundred years later (during the 900s), Rabbi Sherira Gaon was asked the same question about a sinner.[16] He writes that the Jewish community cannot punish this person physically at all. However, one may not have anything to do with this person, one may not pray with him or look at him, and he may never testify in a Jewish court. In a later period, during the Middle Ages, it was apparently known that in certain circumstances, the local court did administer the death penalty,[17] not as an "official" punishment but as a one-time act to warn the community about the severity of the sin, as seen in the Talmud and Maimonides (above). When a Jew informed on other Jews to the government, it usually meant certain death for those Jews. This is one example of the kind of sin that would engender the death penalty in some cities by certain Jewish courts during various periods.

During the Middle Ages, Rashba (1250-1310) was asked what should be done with a Jew who was pardoned by the king (because of "connections" or a payoff) even though he killed another Jew.[18] Rashba states what we already know – that the Jewish court cannot officially put this person to death. However, he gives them permission to do almost anything short of killing this murderer. He permits a Jewish court to give him lashes or even to cut off one limb. They can excommunicate him or remove him from the community (and other surrounding communities would also know what he did and comply with the ban as well).

They could even put him in jail and feed him only a little bit of food. Maimonides similarly states that since it is forbidden to kill him, the most a court can do is excommunicate him, give him lashes, or incarcerate him.[19]

## THE PHILOSOPHICAL AND PRACTICAL DEBATE CONTINUES UNTIL TODAY

The ambivalence about capital punishment can be seen by examining the words of one Rabbi, Maimonides, who seems to state both sides of the argument in two separate passages. In one place, he says that if a killer cannot be killed because of a technicality, but you are sure that "he did it," you can put this person in jail and feed him little food until he gets sick and even dies. He adds that although the Torah listed numerous sins that incur the death penalty (like adultery and idol worship), he is only speaking about the sin and crime of murder, which is so much worse than any other crime or sin. God will take care of the man-to-God "capital crimes" like violation of Shabbat and idol worship, but a murderer is so heinous that he is called completely evil, and any of the commandments he has fulfilled during rest of his life can never outweigh this one act.[20] But in another passage, Maimonides speaks about the necessity of being absolutely sure in a Jewish court that a crime was committed before any punishment is allowed. Thus, even if the circumstantial evidence is overwhelming, a Jew may not be punished until his or her guilt is definitively ascertained. Maimonides cites the noted case of a Jew who is chasing his enemy with a knife and they both go into a house, then the one being chased is then found dead and the chaser, who is covered in blood, is standing over him with a bloody knife. All this circumstantial evidence is still not enough to convict the chaser as a murderer in a Jewish court unless there is a witness who actually saw the murder take place. (This is based on

---

16. Rav Sherirah Gaon, *Takanot HaGeonim*, chapter 12
17. *Takanot HaGeonim*, chapter 12, p. 106
18. *Responsa Rashba*, 349

---

19. Maimonides commentary on the Mishna *Chulin* 1:2
20. Maimonides, *Hilchot Rotze'ach* 4:8-9

the Talmudic discussion in *Sanhedrin* 37b of an identical case that says it is possible the chased person accidentally tripped and fell on the knife and the chaser then pulled it out of him.) However, Maimonides states that "it is better to let 1000 killers go free than to kill one innocent person."[21] All of these laws show both sides of the capital punishment issue and the attitude towards murderers all within the point of view of one great Jewish scholar, as well as his genuine attitude toward the court system in general and in regard to capital punishment in particular.

The experiences of Rabbeinu Asher (1250-1327) are particularly noteworthy, because he was a famous Ashkenazic Rabbi and decisor of Jewish law who at the age of fifty-three was forced to run away from Germany due to anti-Semitism. He wound up as a Jewish community leader in Spain. He thus witnessed first-hand the practices of both Ashkenaz and Sephard communities. Concerning capital punishment, he writes that he was very puzzled when he came to Spain and saw that the Jewish courts there actually administered the punishment of death, even though the Sanhedrin and Temple no longer existed. When he inquired about this from the local Jewish judges, he was told that if they did not try, convict, and execute Jewish murders, then the local non-Jewish government threatened to do so and they would certainly kill many more Jews. Thus, they actually instituted this practice in order to save the lives of countless Jews. Rabbeinu Asher concludes that although he never approved of this practice, he also never stepped in as the leader of the community to ban capital punishment from the Jewish courts in Spain.[22]

This debate did not subside in the twentieth century either. Rabbi Moshe Feinstein, recognized as the leading Torah authority on Jewish law in the USA and possibly the entire Jewish world during the latter half of the twentieth

century, was asked by an American government official about the Jewish attitude towards capital punishment (when the debate was raging in the courts and in state legislatures). He responded by demonstrating the importance of every Jewish life in Judaism, which has infinite value, and then traces the history of capital punishment in Talmudic times, as mentioned above. Rabbi Feinstein explains that only the Jewish high court could administer the death penalty, because they had the wisdom and sensitivity to know when to kill a person for committing murder and when not to. But since we have no Temple and no Jewish high court, there is no capital punishment today. He concluded by pointing out that this holds true when murderers are not common and murders are rare occurrences. However, when people do not value human life and they kill in a barbaric manner, perhaps capital punishment is necessary as a deterrent.[23] In the same time period, Rabbi Aharon Soloveitchik, another noted authority in Jewish law in the United States, was asked the very same question by the Orthodox Union, and he sent a letter in which he states that "[I]t is irresponsible and unfair to submit a statement in favor of capital punishment in the name of Orthodox Jewry. In my humble opinion, from a Halachik point of view, every Jew should be opposed to capital punishment. It is true . . . that the Torah recognizes capital punishment. However, the Torah delegates the authority to mete out capital punishment only to the Sanhedrin, not to anyone else. Even the Sanhedrin are [sic] not able to mete out capital punishment if there is no Beis Hamikdash (Temple)."[24] Two noted Rabbis, with the same tradition, still differ on the use of the death penalty when murder is very common in society. The debate continues.

In the State of Israel today, the laws of capital punishment are clearly part of the country's statutes. Although Israel's court system

---

21. Maimonides, *Sefer HaMitzvot*, negative Mitzvah 290

22. *Responsa Rosh* 17:8

---

23. *Responsa Igrot Moshe*, Choshen Mishpat 2:68

24. Diament, Nathan J. "Judaism and the Death Penalty: Of Two Minds but One Heart. " *Tradition* 38:1 2004, p. 78, Letter from Rabbi Ahron Soloveitchik to David Luchins at the Orthodox Union, 1970s

generally does not operate according to strict Jewish law and although hundreds or possibly thousands of Arab murderers of Jews have been tried and convicted over the years (with most still sitting in Israeli jails), the State of Israel has executed only one person in its entire existence of close to seventy years – the mass murderer of Jews during the Holocaust, Adolf Eichman. This policy seems to mirror the opinion of Rabbi Eliezer (cited above) about a Jewish court that kills once in seventy years.

# CLONING OF HUMAN BEINGS

THE CONCEPT OF HUMAN CLONING is not only a great technical scientific development, but is an issue wrought with emotion, ethics, major consequences for the future, and possibilities that only a short time ago were written about only in science fiction books. To decipher all the controversies and then try to formulate a Jewish approach is quite difficult, since technology changes almost daily, and also because humanity is only at the very first stages of the idea of cloning. Although no one has yet cloned a human being, the fact that animals have been cloned demonstrates that the day when people will be cloned is not far off.

What exactly is human cloning? In layman, non-scientific jargon, it is simply the artificial process of making a genetic twin of a person. This is accomplished by introducing nuclear material of a human cell into a fertilized or unfertilized egg in order to create a person with duplicate DNA, an exact replica of that individual. Until now, this process still involves taking the fertilized cell and inserting it into a woman's womb who will then give birth nine months later, through the normal birth process. But one day in the future it may be possible to clone human beings without this gestation process or birth at all, and "duplicate" an adult as another adult, not an infant.

Before discussing the Jewish views, there are a number of moral issues involved in cloning humans. There is a general fear that with gene manipulation, a technology that already exists, it will be possible to clone many human beings who have super strength, super IQs, and create an "army" of soldiers that will pose a danger to any society where evil people control such clones. Because of such fears, the Human Cloning Prohibition Act of 2009 makes the cloning of human beings unlawful in the United States, as it is deemed unethical and immoral. On the other hand, the potential for cloning and gene manipulation also opens wondrous opportunities and possibilities in the not-too-distant future. Some variations on cloning technology are already used in biotechnology labs and these techniques will eventually allow, among other things, the creation of cloned herds of sheep and cows that produce medicines in their milk. Researchers also hope that one day the ability to clone adult human cells will make it possible to "grow" new hearts, livers, and nerve cells of each human being. The cloning of foods and animals could end the possibility of famine in the world. Through cloning and gene manipulation, people might be able to insure that their offspring will be devoid of genetic diseases. A child with cancer in need of a bone marrow transplant would always be able to find a donor – himself or herself – as part of the cloning process. Lost limbs by any person might be easily replaced with cloned parts of each human being. These are just a few examples and a few possibilities that may become real within the next fifty years.

Thus, while there is a great potential evil unleashed in such a technology, there is a great potential goodness that may save many lives and make every human life qualitatively better. Where would Judaism stand on this game-changing technology? Should it be pursued or not? What are the other potential Jewish issues involved in this new process? For example, what would be the status of the cloned human being vis-à-vis the original donor? Would the clone be an offspring of the donor or a sibling (with the same DNA, like an identical twin)? Would such a person have human status in every way, such as being counted for a *Minyan* or inheritance? Would killing such a clone be considered murder in Judaism?

## MAN'S ROLE TO CREATE IN THE WORLD

While the concept of cloning in the laboratory is a new phenomenon, as with any new technology, Judaism tries to find precedents within Jewish law and tradition in order to form a normative attitude and approach. Although the science may be new, Judaism's sources and concepts demonstrate a fundamental Jewish approach that gives guidance concerning this or any new scientific breakthrough, as it has for many years in the past whenever a new invention or technology was introduced. As the Mishna tells us, although it may be challenging, if we search hard enough, anything can be found within Judaism.[1] Surprisingly, quite a lot has already been written recently about the cloning of human beings, and similar issues have been discussed by Rabbis in the past.

The basic, fundamental, and philosophical question that Jewish authorities have asked themselves is if cloning another human being falls into the human realm, or if such technology should be left only to God. When God created man in His image,[2] we understand that this trait of each human cannot signify that man resembles God physically, since God has no physicality. Many have understood the godliness in man's ability to create in the world, just as God creates in the world. It is that ability to do something new that makes man godly, unlike any other creature created by God. This concept seems to encourage all types of creativity by man, including all scientific breakthroughs such as cloning. Furthermore, God gave all human beings the mandate to "capture the world," which, according to Nachmanides, mandates that man should use all his knowledge and all things physical in the world to benefit mankind in any way that man sees fit.[3]

Furthermore, the idea that man creates new creations in the world seems to be a fundamentally Jewish idea. The word *"Melacha"* is used in only three contexts in the Torah. The first is what God did in the first six days of the world – Creation itself. The second context is by Shabbat, when God tells man to create for six days of the week (a commandment according to some commentaries, not merely a recommendation), but not to create on Shabbat. Finally, the entire building of the *Mishkan*, the Tabernacle, repeatedly uses the word *"Melacha,"* indicating that this structure is a mini-world created by the Jewish people as a means of coming closer to God.[4] The fact that man is supposed to create in the world seems to give him carte blanche to develop any and all technologies that will advance mankind, including cloning. King David may have been referring to this concept when he wrote that the realm above, the heavens, belong to God, while the realm below, the earth, was given by God to man.[5]

## LIMITING MAN'S ROLE TO CREATE

Early on, mankind already demonstrated that his ability to create in the world was not always used for the proper purpose and goals. After man developed a new technology to create bricks in order to be used as building material, which meant that mud could now be hardened, man was no longer limited to living near caves and mountainous areas that forced him to make houses from rocks. But instead of using this expertise to spread out and build cities, the Torah tells us that the first use of this technology was to build a tower in the sky to try to reach and challenge God. For this misuse of technology, man was punished.[6]

Although man was given the ability and general mandate to create in the world, we will see that there were limits and specific areas , limiting his ability to create, according to some opinions. The obligation to observe commandments is certainly mandatory for traditional Jews, irrespective of the reasons behind those commandments. However, this obligation did not stop the commentaries from speculating regarding the philosophical reasons for some of the commandments. One such commandment is the prohibition of mixing seeds from

---

1. Mishna *Avot* 5:22
2. Genesis 1:27
3. Genesis 1:28 with Nachmanides commentary

4. Genesis 2:2-3, Exodus 20:9-10, 31:2-3, 36:1
5. Psalms 116:27
6. Genesis 11:1-3, 8

different species and planting them together, mating different species of animals to create a hybrid, and mixing linen and wool in the same garment.[7] While Rashi states that these are commandments without logical reason, Nachmanides disagrees. He believes that God is telling man that there are limits to his ability and mandate to create and tamper with God's creation. Man may not make hybrids of plants and animals, because that kind of creation is beyond man's scope. Man can create in the world, but not create new species or new creations. Ibn Ezra also states that this prohibition limits man's ability to mix species in his creation.[8] These opinions seem to prohibit man's ability to manipulate genes or to even attempt cloning human beings, as this should remain in God's realm, not man's.

Rabbi Samson Raphael Hirsch also indicates that God wishes to limit man's ability to create through the prohibition of *Shatnez*, mixing wool and linen. He says that wool represents the kingdom of animals (the source of wool) while linen represents the kingdom of plants (the source of linen).[9] Man may not mix them, in order to show symbolically that man may not interfere in the creation of any species or change of any creation by God. Thus, cloning would be a realm beyond man's mandate to create in the world.

Since, according to the Talmud, there are three equal parts in the creation of each human being – God, the father and the mother – it would seem to be immoral to create a human being or clone a person without the specific consent of all three partners, including God's, which has not yet been given.[10] It seems from these commentaries that God does not give permission to man to create new human beings in an unnatural manner not prescribed by the Torah. Similarly, because each human being is unique, unlike any other person in existence, with each being worth the value of an entire

world,[11] creating a clone that is not unique, but rather a mere duplicate of someone else, may be problematic in Judaism. God seems to especially say through Isaiah that it is only His (God's) purview to create new worlds and new creations, not man's.[12] And the idea of creating life from non-life, which some call "resurrection," seems to be God's purview alone, and not man's, another reason for precluding him from tampering with creation by attempting to clone human beings.[13]

## MAN MUST GO BEYOND AND CREATE EVEN MORE

Until now, we have shown only one side of the argument regarding man's role in the world. There are an equal number of Rabbis and sources that demonstrate the other trend in Judaism: that there are no limits to man's abilities to create and expand his horizons. These will show all the reasons why man should and must develop human cloning.

The Talmud explains that when he was created on Friday, the sixth day of Creation, man wanted to create two new creations, but waited until after Shabbat to do so. Urged on by God, man created fire on Saturday night and also took two animals of different species and then created a hybrid animal.[14] This demonstrates man's unique ability to create, as fire is certainly a uniquely human creation. Just as God created light on the first day of Creation, man created fire exactly one week later. But what about man's ability to create a new species? Is not that forbidden according the source learned above regarding the mixing of two species of plants or animals? Maharal explains that man's mandate is to expand his horizons and create as much as possible, as symbolized by the creation of fire. Part of that mandate is also to create new species with animals. The fact that the Torah later forbade this for Jews does not abrogate the duty of man as a species

7. Leviticus 19:19
8. Nachmanides and Ibn Ezra commentaries on Leviticus 19:19
9. Hirsch commentary on Leviticus 19:19
10. *Kiddushin* 30b

11. *Sanhedrin* 37a
12. Isaiah 65:17, 66:22
13. Isaiah 26:19
14. *Pesachim* 54a

to continue to expand upon God's creation (there are other specific reasons why creating hybrids is forbidden only to Jews, according to Maharal).[15] Thus, the creation of new species, which is not only forbidden, but encouraged by the Maharal, would seem to indicate that the next step in creating, human cloning would be encouraged by God.

Rabbi Israel Lipschitz, who wrote a nineteenth century Mishna commentary, says categorically that any part of life or any action in the world regarding which no specific prohibition is actually stated, should be practiced and tried without hesitation.[16] This attitude and philosophy is in direct opposition to some of the opinions above that limit man's role in the world. Since there is no specific prohibition against human cloning, Rabbi Lipschitz would not only permit it, but would even encourage it. This attitude seems to be based on a Talmudic passage. The verse in *Isaiah* says that the only aspect differentiating man from God is that man sins and God does not.[17] Based on this notion, the Talmud states that if not for the sins of man, human beings would have been able to create worlds. Thus, rather than limit creation to God alone, this passage tells us that God would have wanted man to create worlds and other creations, but it was his transgressions that prevented him from doing so.[18] The idea, then, of man creating new creations, including people, is something to that is not only in the purview of mankind, but actually encouraged by God.

Another Talmudic passage states that in the future Messianic times, God will create trees that yield cakes and plants that produce linen garments, without the help of man. Currently, man is needed to take God's creations and turn them into usable foods and clothing, but that will change in the future. On this passage, Rabbi Yosef Dov Soloveitchik (1820-1892) explains that until the future Messianic times, man must remain God's partner in Creation.

God created the seed, but man must work the ground and help that seed grow.[19] After it yields wheat, then only man's effort – through a long process of extracting the kernel, turning the kernels into flour, and then baking the flour – will yield bread. Therefore, until Messianic times, God is telling man that He only begins the process of developing the world, but it is up to man to continue what God begins and take it to the next step, expanding the horizons of the world through man's actions. This is supported by the Midrash that explains that God intentionally created all male babies uncircumcised, in order to allow man to complete God's creation as He intended it. God intentionally limited Himself in Creation to allow man to expand on what He began.[20]

In explaining the forbidden laws of Shabbat, one nineteenth century commentary explains that for six days man is supposed to be creative and expand and embellish the world. It is only on Shabbat that it is forbidden.[21] Rabbi Joseph Soloveitchik (1903-1993), the namesake of the Beit HaLevi quoted above, echoes this sentiment. He explains that man is obligated to imitate God and create in the world, writing in one article, "We have steadily maintained that involvement in the creative scheme of things is mandatory. Involvement with the rest of mankind in the cosmic confrontation . . . First, as we have mentioned previously, we, created in the image of God, are charged with responsibility for the great confrontation of man and the cosmos."[22] In another article, Rabbi Soloveitchik echoes the same idea: "Man reaching for the distant stars is acting in harmony with his nature which was created, willed, and directed by his Maker. It is a manifestation of obedience to rather than rebellion against God."[23] There are those who have deduced from the words of another twentieth

---

15. Maharal, *Be'er Hagolah* 39
16. Tiferet Yisrael commentary on Mishna *Yadayim* 4:3
17. Isaiah 59:2
18. *Sanhedrin* 65b with Rashi commentary

19. *Shabbat* 30b with Beit HaLevi commentary
20. Midrash, *Beraishit Rabbah* 46:3
21. *Ketav VeKabbalah* commentary on Exodus 20:10
22. Rabbi Joseph Soloveitchik, "Confrontation." *Tradition*, vol. VI:2, p. 20
23. Rabbi Joseph Soloveitchik, "Lonely Man of Faith." *Tradition*, vol. VI:2, p. 15

century Rabbi (and distant relative of Rabbi Soloveitchik), Moshe Feinstein, a similar view. When he writes about doctors, he says that it is counterintuitive to allow doctors to heal, as this seems to go against the mandate of God as doctor of the world (see the chapter "Alternative Medicine in Judaism" for a discussion of this moral issue). Yet, that is precisely what God desires.[24] In the same way, claim some contemporary Rabbis, even though it seems counterintuitive for man to create through cloning and to imitate God, this is God's desire nonetheless. Thus, it is clear that according to all these opinions, the cloning of humans, while fraught with difficult Jewish and ethical dilemmas, is within the purview of man.

In addition to the specifics of human cloning, there are overarching themes and sources pushing man to advance human civilization through the scientific breakthroughs of human cloning. One of the first questions that God will ask every human being after death is, "Did you involve yourself with procreation?"[25] Since it does not say specifically "Did you procreate?" but, rather, "Did you involve yourself . . . ," some commentaries view this as a general obligation of each person to try to bring as many children into the world as possible. One of the main purposes of human cloning is to increase the human population. In addition, there is a very provocative statement in the mystical book of *Zohar*, that states that in the 600th year of the sixth millennium, God will open the gates of wisdom, as man makes "preparations" for the seventh thousandth year (400 years later), which implies that then will be the time of the Messiah.[26] This year referred to corresponds to 1840 in the Gregorian (secular) calendar, and it says that at that time, enhanced scientific exploration will commence, which is approximately the date that major scientific breakthroughs in most spheres began to occur. Rabbi Moshe Chaim Luzzato comments on this *Zohar* passage and says that

a scientific tidal wave will commence in the 600th year (1840), just as the tidal wave of water commenced in the 600th year of Noah's life.[27] Scientific knowledge and inventions will proliferate, and these are encouraged by God. This passage also seems to support the notion of human cloning as a positive and desired step for mankind.

Some of the very verses that were quoted above to demonstrate the idea of limiting Creation to God alone can also be used to encourage creation and inventiveness by man. Since man is supposed to imitate God's ways,[28] one of the ways man should imitate God is by being a creator like God. Thus, when it says that Creation is God's purview,[29] rather than limiting creation to God's realm, perhaps this implies that man should imitate this aspect of God. And when it says that God will make the non-living come to life,[30] perhaps it implies that man should attempt to do the same through human cloning.

Therefore, we see two distinct overall approaches in traditional Judaism towards man's obligation to advance his scientific knowledge and inventiveness, specifically in the realm of creating new forms of life. One says that this one area should remain beyond human endeavor, while the other places no limit on man's ability to advance the world and science, even to the point of human cloning.

## PRECEDENTS IN JEWISH TRADITION TO MAN CREATING HUMAN BEINGS

The Talmud records that Rava actually created a human being by using a combination of letters from the *Sefer Yetzira*, the *Book of Creation* (a mystical book about Jewish letters and Creation). He showed the created being to Rabbi Zera. Rabbi Zera spoke to this man, but the man did not answer. Rabbi Zera said that "you are not real, and you should return to the dust." He then "killed" that being. The Talmud then

---

24. *Responsa Igrot Moshe, Orach Chaim* 3:90
25. *Shabbat* 31a
26. *Zohar* I:117a

27. Kelach, *Pitchei Chochma*, Introduction
28. *Sotah* 14a
29. Isaiah 65:17, 66:22
30. Isaiah 26:19

continues and says that Rabbi Chanina and Rabbi Oshiya used to study the *Sefer Yetzira* every Shabbat eve, and as a result, created a calf each Shabbat and ate it in honor of the Shabbat.[31] This Talmudic passage shows us that man has been able to create human beings in the past, albeit only great sages. There is no condemnation for such a practice mentioned anywhere, suggesting that the idea of a human being creating another man is acceptable. This would answer those who object to humans creating a clone from a human cell, which is even less miraculous than the creations mentioned in the Talmud. In fact, in a different place, Rashi comments that because these Rabbis used the *Book of Creation* as their source and not witchcraft, it was acceptable.[32] Thus, if the creation of a human clone or a human is accomplished with the spirit of God and not by attributing it to another power, then it seems to be laudable.

Rabbeinu Bechaye discusses exactly how is a human being is defined, and he says that every human being is made up of three parts, one part of plant attributes, one part of animal attributes, and one part of uniquely human attributes.[33] A complete human must have thought, speech, and action. The man created by Rava lacked some of the uniquely human attributes such as speech, and therefore was not fully human. A clone, on the other hand, lacks nothing, no different from any other human being, and thus the question is if the clone is considered a full human being or not (discussed below).

Rabbi Jacob Emden, who lived in the 1700's, after the legend and rumors of the Golem of Prague had spread, discusses the creation of Rava and attributes many of the attributes later ascribed to the "Golem" to this creation in the Talmud.[34] The being created by Rava acted like a servant and its power came from the letters on its forehead. It could not talk, but became more powerful each and every day. Because of the fear that it might kill, the letters were removed from its forehead and the being "died," and instantly became a pile of dust. Maharsha echoes some of the same sentiments and says that the lack of speech is what made this being not human, as speech is the essence of being human,[35] as explained by Targum Onkelos.[36] A normal human clone, however, would have every faculty that all other human beings possess, including speech.

## ETHICAL AND OTHER LIMITS TO HUMAN CLONING

In addition to the general argument to limit man's abilities when it comes to creating new human beings, there are other specific objections in Jewish thought that might preclude mankind from proceeding in the development of human cloning.

As noted above, Rashi described the legitimate creation of a human being when the manner in which it was created was legitimate. One of the sins mentioned in the Torah is the prohibition of witches and witchcraft, which is so heinous in Judaism that the penalty for its practice is death.[37] Why such a severe punishment for obvious chicanery? The Talmud explains that the concept of a witch, by definition, denies the legitimacy of God's power and attributes all actions and successes to a power other than God.[38] Thus, according to the Torah, witchcraft is abhorrent to the Jews, for the same reason that idol worship is so objectionable in Judaism: it gives ultimate power in the universe to something other than God. This is echoed by the explanation of this prohibition in *Sefer HaChinuch*.[39] Therefore, if man attributes the success of human cloning to any other power, including himself or science, without credit to God, then this would violate the spirit and possibly the letter of Jewish law.

31. *Sanhedrin* 65b with Rashi commentary
32. Rashi commentary on *Sanhedrin* 67b, s.v. *"iski"*
33. Rabbeinu Bechaye, *Kad ViKemach*, "Reshut" and commentary on Genesis 2:7
34. Rabbi Jacob Emden, *Megilat Sefer*, p. 4
35. Maharsha commentary on *Berachot* 10a
36. Genesis 2:7 with Onkelos commentary
37. Exodus 22:17
38. *Sanhedrin* 67b
39. *Sefer HaChinuch*, Mitzvah 62

Thus, as long as the cloning process or any other human creation is within the spirit of God's guidance, this might not present a problem. But as soon as this technology is lauded as an alternative to God, this would violate Jewish thought.

Another potential problem with this specific technology may be a passage from the Talmud that states that there are three specific "keys" (areas) that God wishes to remain in His realm and not be given over to human beings: the "key" of rain, the "key" of childbirth, and the "key" of resurrection.[40] If the secrets of childbirth and resurrection (creating man from the "dust" of the earth) are to be reserved only for God, then human cloning may violate this prohibition. Cloning man certainly involves the process of birth, and the creation of a person from a cell of DNA may also violate the "key" of Resurrection.

Another objection to human cloning may come from the Midrash and Talmudic passages that inform us that God intentionally limited Himself in the act of Creation.[41] Perhaps through this act God is informing man to imitate His ways in this particular area as well. Even though man *can* perform human cloning (in the future), he should limit his ability to create in this area, imitating God, Who limited His ability in the initial Creation. This notion has ramifications in actual Jewish law. There were times, says Maimonides, when the Rabbis and Rabbinic courts enacted laws not because the Torah demanded it, but in order to protect Judaism itself when new situations arose to threaten it.[42] Perhaps the issues that human cloning will raise are so thorny and difficult that the Rabbis will decide it is preferable not to enter the sphere entirely, rather than open the Pandora's box that human cloning will inevitably bring along with it. For example, will the human clone be considered a full human being regarding murder if it is killed? Will a male clone be counted

for a *Minyan* even though it was not "born" like other Jews? Will it have to wait thirteen years after the cloning in order to be counted? Will a clone inherit from a relative? How will its relatives be defined? Who are its parents, legally? It is for these reasons that the great authority, Rabbi Yosef Shalom Elyashiv, was against cloning human beings: It violates the "spirit of the Torah."[43] In fact, one such "sticky" problem is actually discussed in the Mishna, concerning two people who have identical genes but are not related to each other according to Jewish law. This is the situation of identical twin sisters whose mother converted, and the daughters converted with her. Since a convert has no legal relatives, those two sisters are not legally related, even though they have identical genes.[44]

Another potential problem is still a very long way off technologically, but could eventually happen. If the day comes when human cloning does not take the form of a baby that must grow up, but rather the technology is developed to clone an adult human being directly as an adult, then no one would ever have to die. As soon as a person became old, he or she would simply clone himself or herself and continue to live forever, with the same genes and possibly the same memories. Would a world without death be a good phenomenon? This issue and the challenge of trying to overcome the death process and remain alive, has intrigued man for generations. Essentially, cloning is merely the next logical step in delaying death. Medical science has been very successful in pushing the average lifespan further and further back. (In 1900 it was 45 years, in 2000 it was close to 80 years.) This is the next logical progression. Is that what God desires for mankind? Of course, every person might seem to want to live forever. And yet, in one city where there was no death, the city of Luz, the Talmud tells us that after a long while,

---

40. *Ta'anit* 2a
41. Midrash, *Beraishit Rabbah* 46:3, *Chagiga* 12a
42. Maimonides, *Hilchot Mamrim* 2:3, 5

43. "Cloning and Its Challenges," Torah U'Madda Journal, vol. 9, 200, p. 195 and p. 187, footnote 2 (in an oral communication to Dr. Yoel Jakobovitz and Dr. Abraham S. Abraham)
44. Mishna *Yevamot* 12:2 with Rashi commentary

people seemed to get bored with life, and they just went out of the city in order to die.[45]

Thus, the issues raised by human cloning are certainly numerous and very complicated. The question is whether the great benefits outweigh the challenges, and whether the secular world and Jewish authorities are up to handling these challenges.

REPRODUCTION WITHOUT SEX

Until now, we have assumed that all human cloning involved placing the cloned cell in a woman's womb where it would gestate for nine months like any "normal" fetus before being born, the same way as other human beings come into this world. But what if a human clone could be produced without having to go through pregnancy, either as a baby clone or as an adult? Would that change matters from a Jewish perspective?

Many Jewish sources refer to and define human beings as "those born to a [human] mother," as in Scripture, the Talmud, and the Midrash.[46] Would a person who is not born from the womb also be considered human? Some might argue that the very first human being in history, Adam, was created by God without nine months in the womb and without a mother, but was nevertheless was called human in all his characteristics and was considered a full human being. Some may claim, therefore, that a human clone born in a laboratory would lack the basic definition of humanity because it was not born from a mother's womb. The commandment given to Adam and Eve about having children specifically mentions the union of a man and a woman in order to produce a child.[47] Would lacking that aspect of the process invalidate a child's humanity? Meiri, who lived in the thirteenth century, already discusses this issue and claims that asexual reproduction is part of natural life and is not considered witchcraft.[48] Thus, according

to him, a human being born in the laboratory would still be considered fully human.

Thus, the question remains according to those who disagree with the Meiri. If the human clone created in a laboratory is not human, how would or should this creature be classified? There are numerous Talmudic and post-Talmudic discussions of creatures that performed human tasks but that are not classified as human, while other creatures performing similar tasks are indeed called human. This is one more area that will entangle the Rabbis (as well as the general populace) with moral discussions when human cloning becomes a reality.

After all is said and done, the fundamental disagreement about the issue of human cloning, even before it becomes a reality, continues among leading Rabbis and observant Jewish doctors. Because of the possible dangers and difficulties this technology may engender, numerous Rabbis and doctors have come out against proceeding further in exploring this technology. Other Rabbis, enamored by the potential benefits that such scientific advances will bring mankind, endorse this new technology. Those who seem to be or have explicitly come out against human cloning include Rabbi Yisrael Meir Lau (past chief Rabbi of Israel), Dr. Eitan Fiorino, Dr. Abraham S. Abraham, Rabbi Emanuel Jacobovits, *zt"l*, (past chief Rabbi of Great Britain), and Rabbi Yosef Shalom Elyashiv, *zt"l*. On the other hand, many other Rabbis and doctors of note would seem to heartily approve of human cloning, including Dr. Pinchas Lipner, Dr. Fred Rosner, Rabbi Dr. Moshe Tendler,[49] Rabbi Michael Broyde, Dr. Abraham Steinberg, and Rabbi Joseph Soloveitchik, *zt"l*. As in all Rabbinic arguments, only in the future when the majority of Rabbis and traditional Jews weigh in, will a consensus develop and this question will finally be able to be decided one way or the other. The implications in either direction are great indeed.

---

45. *Sotah* 46b
46. Job 14:1, 15:14; *Yoma* 85b; *Nidah* 13a; Midrash, *Vayikra Rabbah* 35:2
47. Genesis 2:24 with Rashi commentary
48. *Beit HaBechira* commentary on *Sanhedrin* 67b

---

49. Rabbi Dr. Moses Tendler, "Letter to the Editor," *New York Times*, December 12, 1997

# COLLATERAL DAMAGE: UNAVOIDABLE CIVILIAN CAUSALITIES

IT IS AN UNFORTUNATE TRUISM OF modern life, especially in the last few years, that virtually all over the world terrorism is a major component of each and every war. Conventional wars used to be fought on a battlefield between armies in uniform (often in an officially designated area), but that kind of warfare is virtually a thing of the past. Each time a passenger enters an airport and goes through its elaborate security checks, it is an acknowledgement that the threat of terrorism is a part of life. Therefore, when actual combat fighting involves terrorists, the circumstances, facts, and conditions of war have drastically changed. The battleground is now often in civilian neighborhoods, and the goals of each battle and war are also different than before. One "new" aspect of such warfare is the element of collateral damage – i.e., the unavoidable deaths of civilians in the midst of battle. This chapter will discuss what Judaism has to say about such situations and how to resolve the inherent dilemma of fighting terrorists who are located within civilian populations.

In order to make the dilemma more real and practical, let us describe a scenario based on actual circumstances faced by soldiers past and present. The same dilemma exists today in different contexts in various wars involving countries all over the world, but the most well-known and most frequent examples involve Palestinian terrorists who intentionally hide and live among the Palestinian civilian populations. Regarding a known terrorist who has killed many Israelis in the past, Israeli intelligence has confirmed that he plans to blow up a bus of Israeli civilians within the next twenty-four hours. The man is hiding in Gaza City, in an apartment known to the Israeli army, but is located in a building with ten other apartments that are filled with innocent women and children. The Israeli army is cognizant of exactly where he is hiding. However, in order eliminate the imminent terrorist threat he presents (since he will almost certainly kill many Israelis the next day), the army will necessarily have to kill between ten to fifteen women and children. Should they take the lives of these innocent people in Gaza in order to assassinate the terrorist and destroy the threat to the civilian Israeli population? (This essay is not intended as a political discussion, but rather is designed to illustrate the Jewish view regarding this moral dilemma. If some readers have a visceral reaction regarding the killing of civilian Arabs, they may substitute with the families of multinational forces and observers, foreigners living in the apartment house, rather than Palestinian Arabs.)

If killing fifteen civilians is indeed justified in order to eradicate this terrorist threat, then what if the situation required killing fifty people in that apartment complex? What if it might cost one hundred lives? If killing fifteen civilians, however, is considered immoral and does not justify killing the terrorist, then would killing five innocents be considered moral? One? Can innocent residents legitimately be "sacrificed" in order to slay a terrorist and prevent him from killing civilians? Are there reasons to allow this collateral damage? What are the reasons to allow the terrorist to live (so that Israeli soldiers will not kill innocent people in Gaza) even though that terrorist will almost certainly kill innocent people in the future?

Once the hiding place of the terrorist from Gaza is clearly identified (the specific apartment in the housing complex), the General Chief of Staff of the army of the Prime Minister can give the order to kill this terrorist any time he deems it warranted. He may decide to use a few bombs from a ship offshore, a drone (unmanned plane) or a helicopter (at no risk to Israeli lives) that will fire on that apartment house and kill the terrorist, thereby abolishing the threat from the bomb explosion scheduled for the next day on a bus in Jerusalem. However, there is often great hesitation in killing this man who has murdered many innocent Israelis in the past and will shortly kill again, because innocent people in that apartment house will have to die in the process. Why the hesitation? If the terrorist is not killed now, more lives will be lost the next day. Does the larger number of lives potentially lost the next day justify killing the civilians now in the apartment? Does it matter that these innocents to be killed along with the terrorist are not Jewish, while the innocents who would be killed in the bus the next day would be Jewish? If the Israeli army knowingly risks the lives of civilians in order to kill the terrorist and eliminate the threat, is that any different from all terrorists whose purpose is to intentionally kill innocent people?

Since this is such a new phenomenon in modern warfare, are there traditional Jewish sources that discuss this issue at all? Is there a normative Jewish view about how to resolve this painful dilemma in which innocent people necessarily will have to die one way or the other? Is the idea of fighting a terrorist enemy equivalent to fighting a conventional war? Amazingly, Jewish tradition has discussed this issue long before the concept of "terrorist" and the expression "collateral damage" were even invented.

## SENSITIVITY & PRECEDENT IN JUDAISM FOR PREVENTING CIVILIAN CASUALTIES

Even though in ancient times there were no suicide bombers or terrorists as we know them today, nevertheless there are sources in Judaism that can speak to this issue, and the moral dilemma of possibly having to kill innocents while fighting in a war has been found in actual incidents already discussed or alluded to in the Bible. It begins with the very first Jew in history and the very first war ever fought by a Jew. Immediately after Abraham was victorious in his war against the Four Kings, which

freed his kidnapped nephew Lot, God appears to Abraham and tells him that Abraham's reward will be great. Rashi explains why God felt it necessary to reassure Abraham.[1] Abraham was worried that he had "used up" any rewards due him because he might have killed people during the war, says Rashi, and God reassures Abraham that he need not be afraid of this. The Midrash explains in greater detail specifically what Abraham was afraid of. Abraham was not fearful that he had killed the warriors that opposed him. Rather, says the Midrash, Abraham was afraid that he might have inadvertently killed civilians who may have been righteous, and for this immoral act, his rewards would be "used up." God tells Abraham that every person he killed was like a thorn – i.e., was destined and deserved to die. Thus, no innocent civilians were killed in the war. But the fact that Abraham was worried about this possibility already shows a precedent of Jewish concern for civilians who might accidentally be killed as part of war.[2] One super-commentary on Rashi explains Rashi's words in a similar manner. Abraham was not worried about killing the evil enemy in war, and he was even proud that he eliminated this threat. But maybe a few people who died were righteous, and Abraham was willing to forgo any personal reward due him as long as he would not be punished for killing these innocent civilians.[3] Thus, Abraham felt that he deserved to be punished for killing innocent people in the course of battle, even if this was not intentional.

An analogous emotion was expressed by Abraham's grandson, Jacob, when he was faced with a similar emotion and situation. When confronted with the possibility of fighting his brother, Esau, along with Esau's entourage, the verse states that Jacob felt two emotions: he was both fearful and distressed. Answering why the verse uses both verbs, Rashi explains that Jacob was not only distressed that he may be killed (since he might be found unworthy

---

1. Genesis 15:1 with Rashi commentary
2. Midrash, *Beraishit Rabbah* 44:4
3. Levush Ora commentary on Rashi commentary on Genesis 15:1

to continue living), but was also distressed that he might kill innocent people during the confrontation.[4] Rashi's super-commentary, Siftai Chachamim, explains Rashi's words in greater detail: Jacob had no fear of killing Esau or anyone who had come to kill him (since this killing would be legitimate self-defense). However, Jacob was afraid that there were innocents within Esau's camp who had no intention of harming Jacob or his family. Jacob was afraid that he might kill them in the "confusion of war."[5] (It is interesting to note that the modern expression, "the fog of war" may have originated or have been derived from this commentary, which was published in the 1700s.) Thus, we see another Torah precedent legitimately worrying about collateral damage, supporting the view that says that soldiers should not bomb that apartment building in order to kill the terrorist.

An even more explicit reference regarding Jewish understanding of the issue of collateral damage is the action of King Saul, who was commanded to kill all the Amalekites. When he approached the city that mostly contained Amalekites but also some people from the Kenite tribe, he warned the Kenites to leave city immediately so that they would not be killed accidentally during the battle.[6] Here, too, we see Jewish sensitivity to collateral damage. Unfortunately, this course of action is not available to resolve our dilemma, since a public warning, like King Saul's, to the innocent residents of that apartment house would also alert the terrorist to flee among the civilians, helping him escape injury. What cannot be inferred from Saul's incident, however, is what would have happened if the Kenites had refused to leave. Would King Saul have refrained from attacking the Amalekites, knowing innocents would inevitably be killed? And even if he would have attacked the Amalekites knowing some Kenites might be killed, we can distinguish between that case and our case because

the Kenites were forewarned and consciously chose to stay nevertheless. That could change the equation of what is morally permitted and forbidden. Thus, in our situation, in which the innocents *cannot* be warned, we can still ask what the proper Jewish course of action should be.

In another Torah narrative, we may be able to infer that Moses himself was sensitive to the needless killing of innocents, even in wars mandated in order to capture the land of Israel. After numerous wars in the desert against various nations, the Torah records that the Jewish people offered peace to the nation of Sichon if the Sichonites would simply let the Jewish people pass through their land unharmed. When they refused, the Jews battled with them and defeated them. But nowhere did God ever command Moses to first offer them peace.[7] Elsewhere the Torah itself says that it was Moses' own idea to offer peace as an alternative to war.[8] Why did Moses do it? The Midrash alludes to one possible reason. It says Moses believed there were among Sichon those innocents who had not sinned, and it was apparently for this reason that Moses decided to offer this specific nation the possibility of peace (which they refused).[9] Thus, in order to avoid killing non-sinners, Moses preferred a peaceful alternative. The Midrash goes on to say that Moses "taught" God this concept, and it is for this reason that God later on in the Torah commands Moses (and all Jewish leaders) to always first offer peace to the enemy before going to war.[10] It is possible that the reason behind this tactic is to avoid killing innocent people during warfare.

There is one more allusion to Jewish sensitivity to collateral damage in the Bible. In the last book of narrative, Chronicles, which reviews Jewish history up until that point, King David writes that the reason that he was not allowed to build the Holy Temple is that he shed blood in wars. The Radak explains that this

4. Genesis 32:7 with Rashi commentary
5. Siftei Chachamim commentary on Rashi commentary on Genesis 32:7
6. Samuel I 15:5-6

7. Numbers 21:21-23 with Rashi commentary
8. Deuteronomy 2:26-27 with Rashi commentary
9. *Midrash Tanchuma* 96:3
10. Deuteronomy 20:10-16

specifically refers to acts of collateral damage, the innocent lives that had to be taken by King David in the course of war.[11] Thus, according to a modern Rabbi explaining this verse and commentary, while this action of killing civilians was sometimes necessary as part of waging war, Judaism did not attach enough guilt to this deed to actively punish King David for this necessary action, but rather denied him the merit of building the Holy Temple, which is the symbol of peace and atonement.[12]

## JEWISH LAW ALSO SEEMS TO BE SENSITIVE TO COLLATERAL DAMAGE

In the section of Midrash that discussed Jewish law, Sifri describes proper Jewish behavior in times of war. In addition to the prohibition to intentionally defeat the enemy by tactics of starvation (unless they resist all peace overtures), it is also forbidden to kill the women and children in war, the "innocents."[13] Thus, even in an obligatory war, a Jewish army should be sensitive not to cause collateral damage, whenever possible. It should be noted that this was written at a time when every other army in the world killed innocents indiscriminately, including women and children in the course of war, unless they were later "saved" for slave labor or other future (generally nefarious) uses by the soldiers.

In accordance with the verses quoted above, Jewish law mandates that when fighting a conventional war, the Jews must first publicly declare their intentions to fight by sending public letters to the enemy.[14] This allows the innocent civilians and those who do not want to fight to escape the battle scene. Unfortunately, as noted above, this tactic could not possibly be used in our situation, since the element of surprise is a prerequisite for killing the terrorist. As soon as the Israeli army would warn the

residents of an apartment house that it intends to kill the terrorist living there and that they should therefore leave the place, the element of surprise would be lost, and the terrorist would be able to escape along with the others.

When fighting a Jewish war, Jewish law also forbids an army from completely surrounding the enemy.[15] One of the reasons for this is to allow any civilians and those that do not want to fight to leave the camp or escape the city, thus preventing the bloodshed of innocent lives. Even when there is a Torah Mitzvah to completely destroy a city of idol worshippers by burning the city – including all lives and all booty – according to the simple reading of the text, Nachmanides says that innocent women and children may not be killed (although not all opinions agree).[16] Although this principle of not killing innocent people during a war seems obvious by twenty-first century standards, the massacres that took place in Sudan and before that in Rawanda just a few years ago demonstrate that many nations even today do not abide by or practice this principle. At the time Nachmanides lived, and certainly in Torah times, *no army* observed these ethics in war except for the Jewish people. Similarly, Maimonides rules that in the course of any non-obligatory war, a Jewish army may not kill innocent women and children.[17]

## INNOCENT BYSTANDERS AS THE OBSTACLE TO KILLING THE TERRORIST

Preserving innocent life is so crucial in Jewish thought that Jewish law allows, or rather demands, that a Jewish onlooker kill a potential murderer who is about to commit a murder of an innocent person. The would-be killer is called a *Rodef*, a pursuer, and the Torah allows this special law in this particular circumstance – i.e., in order to save the life of an innocent intended victim. But even in this situation, when

---

11. Chronicles I 22:8 with Radak commentary
12. Rabbi Asher Weiss, *Minchat Asher* on Deuteronomy 32:6
13. Midrash, *Sifri, Shoftim* 56-57
14. Maimonides, *Hilchot Melachim* 6:5

15. Maimonides, *Hilchot Melachim* 6:7
16. Deuteronomy 13:9 with Nachmanides commentary
17. Maimonides, *Hilchot Melachim* 6:5

killing this murderer is mandated, Jewish law also demands that if the Jew can stop such a person (the *Rodef*) by maiming him and not killing him, the person must take only this action. Failing to maim that person, and killing him instead, turns that Jewish onlooker into a murderer.[18] Thus, the principle in Judaism that is established here is that even when it is clearly permitted to kill, if the killing can nevertheless be avoided, even for a criminal and murderer, it is the only correct course of action. This seems to imply that Jews avoid any and all murder, even the murder of criminals, but certainly of innocents, whenever possible. This idea is codified by Maimonides as normative Jewish law.[19]

On the other hand, what happens when the innocent child himself or herself is the obstacle that causes the murder of other people? For example, what happens when children are unknowingly armed and dangerous, or someone gave them a bomb and they are walking toward an innocent group of people, about to kill them? Or if the child has a gun and he is morally unaware of right and wrong, but begins shooting this "toy" which kills people and is about to kill more? Does Jewish law allow the killing of this (morally) "innocent" child who unintentionally is now placed in the role of a *Rodef*, a murderer about to kill an innocent person, even if he or she is not morally culpable and is unaware of the meaning of his or her actions? May that child be killed in order to prevent the deaths of other innocent people, in the same manner that an intentional murderer may or must be stopped? How far does this Jewish law extend in preventing the deaths of innocents? Is there a rationale or justification for killing children in order to stop them from killing others? Maimonides rules that there is. The same Maimonides who ruled that innocents may be protected by killing the pursuer also rules that it is permitted or even obligatory to kill this child, even though he or she is morally unaware of right and wrong

and is not legally culpable.[20] The fact that the child will kill innocent people mandates that this child be stopped – preferably by maiming rather than killing. Thus, even an innocent child, unaware of the damage he is about to cause, can also be considered a *Rodef*. This law is also codified by Rabbi Yosef Caro in *Shulchan Aruch*, his *Code of Jewish Law*.[21]

From the perspective of one Jewish authority, the terrorist is considered a *Rodef*. He is a pursuer who is about to kill innocent people and he may be stopped even if doing so necessitates killing him. Similarly, he continues, even the children in the apartment building may also be considered pursuers who are preventing the elimination of terror, namely, killing that terrorist. Therefore, logically a Jew would be permitted or even obligated to kill such a child (who is preventing the death of the terrorist) in order to avoid the deaths of other innocents. Rabbi Shaul Yisraeli (a twentieth century Rabbi) specifically compares the innocent child armed with a bomb to the innocent child in the apartment complex who is living next door to the terrorist. In both cases, the child, through no moral fault of his or her own, is standing between the killing or rescuing of the lives of other innocent people. If the child with the bomb does nothing, that bomb will explode and kill innocent people, and that is why it is permitted to kill that child before the bomb explodes. So too, writes Rabbi Yisraeli, just by living in the adjacent apartment without doing anything, that child is preventing the army from killing the terrorist. And just as it is permitted (or even obligatory) to kill the morally innocent child with the bomb or gun in order to save innocent lives and prevent further bloodshed, so too it is permitted or mandated to kill the innocent child along with the terrorist in the apartment complex for the purpose of preventing the killing of more innocent people.[22]

Rabbi Yisraeli buttresses his argument by

---

18. *Sanhedrin* 74a
19. Maimonides, *Hilchot Rotze'ach* 1:7, 13

20. Maimonides, *Hilchot Rotze'ach* 1:6
21. *Shulchan Aruch, Chosen Mishpat* 425:1
22. *Responsa Amud Hayemini* 16:4

using another section of Maimonides' code to prove the same point. There, the case involves an overloaded boat with too much cargo that is about to sink, and Maimonides rules that if a man throws some of the cargo overboard (in order to prevent the boat from sinking), that man need not reimburse the owner of the cargo. Maimonides explains that this cargo itself, though inanimate, is classified in the category of a *Rodef* because it threatens the boat, the other cargo, and also passengers' lives. Thus, it can justifiably be eliminated without the need to assume culpability.[23] Rabbi Yisraeli claims that children in the apartment complex are no worse than that inanimate cargo. If cargo that has no thoughts or conscience at all can still be considered a *Rodef*, children who stand in the way of killing a terrorist can also be killed, and they would also be considered pursuers, like the cargo.[24] Maimonides' philosophical rival, Ra'avad, strongly disagrees with Maimonides, claiming that an inanimate object cannot be categorized a *Rodef* that threatens the lives of innocents.[25] Therefore, Ra'avad might also disagree with the logic applied to the case of innocent children that pose a threat to other lives. He may argue with Maimonides and *Shulchan Aruch*, claiming that innocent children should also not be considered pursuers, and thus it would be forbidden in our case to kill the children along with the terrorist, even though they stand in the way of other innocents dying.

Consequently, the underlying question concerning this argument might actually be: is there a difference between the child pursuing to kill someone and the cargo on the ship? In other words, when the child is actively pursuing to kill, everyone agrees that you may and must kill this child as a *Rodef*. However, when that same child is doing nothing but merely sitting in his home passively, though he is concurrently preventing a soldier from killing a terrorist, we must ask: is this similar to the child actively pursuing other innocents or not?

Maimonides seems to feel it *is* the same and thus you may throw over the cargo in order to save the boat or kill the child, while the Ra'avad says that the cargo or anything inanimate or passive may never be considered a *Rodef*.

### ARE THE CIVILIANS IN THE APARTMENT HOUSE ACTUALLY INNOCENT?

Until now, the assumption has been that the women and children in the adjacent apartments to the terrorist in Gaza have either been innocent Arabs or foreigners not connected to the terrorist in any way. But is that truly the case in reality? Are these Arab children and women really so innocent to begin with? Some military experts claim that the children and all others in the area certainly *know* that the terrorist is living among them. The terrorist is often considered a hero in the community and is treated like a celebrity. (This is not the same as the situation that occurred in Southern Lebanon in the summer of 2006, when some Hezbollah fighters took over civilian Lebanese homes at gunpoint in order to be able to fire Katyushas at Israeli civilians in Northern Israel, with the specific intention of being surrounded by civilians as protection. If the terrorist in Gaza is somehow forcing these women and children to live in that apartment in order to provide protection for him, that is a completely different scenario, and the hostages would be considered wholly innocent.) If it is true that the Arab women and children admire the terrorist, does this make them complicit in protecting this terrorist from the enemy, knowing that the Israelis will not intentionally kill children? Are these people, then, no longer considered collateral damage, but rather willing collaborators?

This question of "who is really innocent" came to light in an actual incident in Gaza on November 17, 2000. On that particular day, the Israeli army did warn the residents to leave a particular apartment house, since they would soon blow up the building that contained a

---

23. Maimonides, *Hilchot Chovel U'Mazik* 8:125
24. *Responsa Amud Hayemini* 16:4
25. Ra'avad commentary on Maimonides, *Hilchot Melachim* 9:14

terrorist – which is our specific scenario (acting like King Saul and the Kenites). But rather than simply leaving, as instructed by the Israeli army, in order to prevent the bloodshed of "innocent" lives and collateral damage, these residents called their friends and neighbors and together they formed a human shield, allowing the terrorist to escape unharmed, as the Israeli army (who would not shoot at all the civilians protecting the terrorist) had to just stand by helplessly and watch.

Maimonides shows a scenario and rationale by which intentionally killing these women and children is valid in Jewish law when he describes the story in the Torah regarding Shechem, who kidnapped and raped Dina, the daughter of Jacob.[26] Maimonides states that when the Torah describes Dina's bothers, Simeon and Levi, who murdered all the residents of the city (including "innocents"), they were justified by Jewish law! Why? These townspeople knew full well that their leader, Shechem, was committing these horrendous crimes. They were obligated to subdue an attempt to convict Shechem for his actions, as one of the Seven Noahide laws. When they did not do so and let his crime stand, they were now considered as guilty as Shechem was, and they too deserved death, according to the Noahide laws. Thus, if the women and children admire the terrorist and knowingly protect him, then they would not be considered innocent civilians and collateral damage if killed, but willing collaborators.

## THE CONFLICT AGAINST TERRORISTS: IS THIS LEGALLY A WAR?

The correct moral action in addressing this entire question of fighting terrorists may hinge on the status of this conflagration. If the Israeli army is fighting individual terrorists, even under the general umbrella of the Hamas organization, then many of the laws and reactions explained above may be appropriate. But if

the terrorist in question has the status of an actual soldier as part of an army fighting a war against the State of Israel, then the appropriate reaction and his status may be quite different. For example, Rabbi Naftali Tzvi Yehuda Berlin, in his commentary to the Torah, states that in a time of legal war against Israel, many of the concepts governing Judaism are changed, and it may be appropriate to kill people (even innocents) when it is not normally permitted to do so. He says that in the time of war, the rules are different and that innocent people *may* be killed if necessary to defeat the enemy.[27] That is why the verses in Ecclesiastes say in one verse that "there is an appropriate time (and reaction) for war," and "an appropriate time (and reaction) to hate."[28]

This idea also helps us understand how Maimonides could rule that Simeon and Levi were justified in killing all the people in the city of Shechem when, in reality, only their leaders actually kidnapped and raped their sister Dina (as mentioned above). Nachmanides takes strong issue with Maimonides and states that Simeon and Levi were wholly unjustified in killing the entire townspeople for the heinous acts of their leaders.[29] Wherein rests the argument between Maimonide and Nachmanides? In his Torah commentary, Maharal helps resolve the argument. He explains that if Simeon and Levi were reacting to individuals who kidnapped and raped their sister, then they were not justified in killing the entire city's people (the approach of Nachmanides-Ramban). But if this was a war between two peoples, between the Jewish nation and the tribe of people living in Shechem, then in war it is totally justified to kill the people in the entire town, even if they are civilians, as a means in defeating the enemy (the approach of Maimonides-Rambam).[30] In Judaism, the laws of war are distinct from those governing personal or collective self-defense. If, then, the fight against the terrorist has a status of war, in the new twenty-first century

---

26. Maimonides, *Hilchot Melachim* 9:14

27. Genesis 9:5 with *Ha'amek Davar* commentary
28. Ecclesiastes 3:8
29. Nachmanides commentary on Genesis 34:13, 49:5
30. Gur Aryeh commentary on Genesis 34:13

definition of modern conflagration between nations, then that alone may justify killing the civilians in the apartment building in an effort to eliminate the terrorist. This act becomes morally acceptable in the context of war if it is unavoidable as the only means to defeat the enemy.

This idea – that in war it is moral to kill civilians as a means of defeating the enemy – has been practiced for years. In the twentieth century alone, the Allied Powers blockaded the civilians of the Central Powers during World War I as a means to force them into submission through starvation. The Allies in World War II bombed civilian cities in Germany as a tactic to wreak havoc and fear as a means to more quickly defeat the enemy. The use of the atomic bombs by the United States against the Japanese cities of Nagasaki and Hiroshima in 1945 intentionally killed thousands of civilians in order to end the war earlier and prevent future casualties of US soldiers. The idea that conflict with terrorists is not considered actual war changed dramatically on September 11, 2001, with the attack on the Twin Towers. However, many years prior to this tragedy, the State of Israel viewed the terrorist Arabs who vowed to destroy the State of Israel as a formal enemy army.

Other modern commentaries agree with the analysis of Maharal. Rabbi Zalman Sorotzkin (1880-1966) writes that since the war between Jacob's family and the town of Shechem was indeed a war between nations, Simeon and Levi were fully justified in killing the entire population of Shechem as a means of defeating the enemy.[31] This is also the view of Rabbi Shaul Yisraeli,[32] as well as the opinion of the contemporary Rabbi Herschel Schachter, who writes that Israel is engaged in war with the terrorists, and it is therefore legitimate to kill civilians in this context if necessary.[33]

## PUTTING ISRAELI SOLDIERS AT RISK TO AVOID CIVILIAN CASUALTIES

In this context of an actual war, the issue of soldier casualties must also be addressed. Often, soldiers' lives are put at risk when trying to save the lives of innocent civilians. Chief Rabbi Avraham Shapira (1911-2007) was specifically asked if civilians of the enemy may be killed if this action will save the lives or minimize the deaths of Israeli soldiers.[34] He answered that as long as there is no direct danger of the lives of Israeli soldiers, it is forbidden to kill or harm any civilians of the enemy. But if sparing the lives of enemy civilians will directly result in the deaths of Israeli soldiers, then it is permitted to kill civilians (in the context of war), rather than lose the lives of one's soldiers. As mentioned above, this policy was standard practice on both sides in World War I and World War II. This is also the view of Rabbi Yisraeli in the context of war.[35] Rabbi J. David Bleich agrees and states that there is no source that demonstrates that danger to civilian lives is a factor in the context of a military operation of war.[36]

On the other hand, there are several contemporary Rabbis who express a special sensitivity for enemy civilians and civilian death, even in the context of war. Rabbi Dov Lior, Rabbi of Kiryat Arba-Chevron, writes that even during wartime, mercy should be shown toward the enemy civilian population, in the proper Torah context.[37] In non-war situations, there is no justification whatsoever for killing the civilian population. Nevertheless, he, too, writes that the lives of Israeli soldiers take precedence over the lives of the civilian enemy. Rabbi Aharon Lichtenstein, Rosh Yeshiva of Yeshivat Har Etzion, writes that King David fought obligatory wars and yet was censured for killing civilians during these wars (by not being able to build the Temple, as noted

---

31. Oznayim LeTorah commentary on Genesis 34:25
32. *Responsa Amud Hayemini* 16:2
33. *Ikvai Tzon* 32:3

34. *Techumin* 4:182
35. *Responsa Amud Hayemini* 16:5:1
36. Rabbi J. David Bleich, "Preemptive War in Jewish Law," *Contemporary Halachik Problems* 3:276-277
37. *Techumin* 4:186

above). Therefore, even in the context of war, compassion must be demonstrated concerning the lives of the enemy civilian population whenever possible.[38] Although he too cannot demarcate exactly how and where, Rabbi Yitzchak Blau also believes that consideration for the lives of civilians and collateral damage must also be a factor in determining the actions of soldiers, even in the context of war.[39]

This general sentiment, that sometimes the lives of innocents have to be sacrificed in the context of war, is reflected in other Jewish sources as well. The Talmud states that to retrieve the cabbage from the ground, sometimes in order to detach the thorn (of the cabbage), part of the cabbage itself has to removed and sacrificed.[40] Though this is not the optimal desired outcome, it is often inevitable. Similarly, occasionally the deaths of innocent civilians are necessary in order to defeat the enemy, be it a traditional army or an army of terrorists. Thus, the Talmud even allows the sacrificing of one's *own* civilian population, if that is what it takes to be victorious in war and survive as a nation. The Talmud says that up to one sixth of one's civilian population may be sacrificed (16%!), if there is no other choice, in order to achieve ultimate victory.[41] Therefore, when the choice is the nation's defeat vs. harming one's own population, even allowing the death of some of one's own civilians is permitted. Sometimes the killing of the civilians of the enemy and collateral damage is mandated in order to achieve the same goal.

## THE FOURTH GENEVA CONVENTION AND JEWISH THOUGHT

The Fourth Geneva Treaty of 1949 was drawn up in particular because the number of civilian casualties in World War II surpassed the number of soldiers killed in action. This treaty forbids any harming of non-combatants, i.e., civilians, in the course of war in all situations. There are currently 194 countries that signed the 1949 Geneva Conventions, including the State of Israel, making it illegal for Israel to kill civilians in wartime. If the outcome of the above discussion indeed permits the killing of civilians in certain circumstances from a Jewish perspective, including our specific case when the killing of innocents is necessary as the only way to stop a terrorist from killing more innocents in the future (which the Fourth Geneva Convention never even imagined as a scenario when it was written), then what would the Jewish perspective be in such a situation? Would it be permitted to violate such a convention that Israel signed if it seems to run counter to Jewish law or Jewish thought in specific situations?

It is interesting to note that this question already arose long ago in Jewish history, and it has been clearly answered. Must the Jewish people abide by a "bad treaty" that it has signed? When the Jewish people first entered the land of Israel under the guidance of Joshua, they were quite successful in their battles to conquer the land. Afraid of being conquered, the tribe of Gibeonites, residents of the land, posed as foreign nationals from a faraway land and requested a treaty with the Jewish people in order to avoid their conquest by the Jews in the land of Israel. The Jews, unaware of the actual place of residence of the Gibeonites, signed such a peace treaty with them. When it was later discovered by the Jews that they had been completely duped into signing the treaty and the conditions outlined were not the reality, many Jews wanted to violate the treaty in order to destroy and conquer the Gibeonites. It was then that Joshua ruled that the signed treaty must be upheld, even though it was signed under false pretenses.[42] Even an immoral treaty signed due to intentional deception must be abided by, since the word of the Jewish nation must be upheld. The reasons to uphold the treaty might have included the

---

38. *Techumin* 4:185
39. Rabbi Yitzchak Blau, "Biblical Narratives and the Status of Enemy Civilians in Wartime," *Tradition* 39:4:25-26, pp. 25-26
40. *Bava Kama* 92a with Rashi commentary
41. *Shavuot* 35b with Tosafot commentary

---

42. Joshua 9:3-18

desecration of God's name in the eyes of other nations (who would witness that the Jews had violated a signed treaty), or there might be many other reasons. But the principle was established. Once the Jewish nation signs a treaty, even if it is an immoral treaty that was signed due to hidden facts, the treaty must be upheld. This concept was adopted into normative Jewish law by Maimonides.[43]

Therefore, it seems that in Jewish thought and according to Jewish law, the Israeli army would have to uphold the Fourth Geneva Convention because the country signed it, and can never touch any civilians in any war scenario, even though parts of this agreement run counter to normative Jewish thought. It seems, then, that it may be forbidden by Jewish law to violate the treaty, even though not killing civilians in our case would result in the deaths of innocent Israelis or even soldiers. And this is despite the fact that the enemy terrorists are not signatories and certainly do not observe any of the Geneva Conventions in their fight against Israel.

However, there is one caveat to the conventions and laws signed by nations of the world that also applies to the laws within each nation, which Jews are supposed to abide by (as long as they do not contradict Jewish law). The Jewish people and individual Jews are bound by the laws as they are *practiced* in day-to-day reality, and not as laws that are merely *written* or "on the books." Therefore, if a certain law is ignored in practice by all or nearly all, then Jews need not observe it. For example, if speeding tickets in a 55-miles-per-hour zone are only issued for violators driving 63 miles and above, then it is permitted in Jewish law for Jews to drive up to 62 miles per hour even though the secular law, normally obligatory upon Jews as well, states 55 miles per hour as the limit.[44] In the same manner, almost no nation that has fought a war since 1949 has fully honored this proviso of the Geneva Convention, i.e.,

sparing civilians, even when their solders are put in harm's way as a result. If that is the case, then although the treaty is signed by Israel and 193 other countries and is clearly "on the books," Jewish law would permit its violation if other nations regularly violate this aspect of the treaty and if violation of the treaty does not run counter to normative Jewish thought. On that basis, from a Jewish perspective, the Israeli army would certainly be permitted to harm or even kill civilians, if Jewish law and Jewish thought mandated this course of action in certain situations.

## THE POLICY OF THE ISRAELI ARMY REGARDING THIS MORAL ISSUE

Based on the above analysis, most Rabbis would probably permit the killing of the civilians in Gaza if that were the only way to eliminate an imminent terrorist threat and kill the terrorist. Nevertheless, that is *not* the practiced policy of the Israeli army. Even when the army is aware of a known and wanted terrorist in an apartment complex, it does not bomb that apartment, since this bombing will necessitate the deaths of innocent civilians. Rather, the army patiently waits for the terrorist to exit the building and enters his automobile (for as long as it takes). Then it immediately bombs the car. The passengers of the car are also usually killed, under the assumption that anyone entering the car with this person is not an innocent civilian.

In addition, despite the rulings of almost every Rabbi that the lives of the Israeli soldiers take precedence over the deaths of civilians, the practice of the Israeli army is not to bomb civilians in order to save the lives of Jewish soldiers (as many other armies regularly do in other conflicts around the world). Therefore in 2002, following a string of suicide bombings killing hundreds of Israelis, capped by the Pesach bombing in the Park Hotel in Netanya on March 27, Israel launched a counter offensive, Operation Defensive Shield, in the Palestinian towns, in order to root out these suicide bombers. One of the hotbeds of terror and bombers

---

43. Maimonides, *Hilchot Melachim* 6:5
44. Rabbi Chaim Jachter, "Gray Matter," vol. 3, 2008, p. 217, footnote 7

was the city of Jenin, which the Israeli army entered (without any journalists or press). This Battle of Jenin took place from April 1 to April 11, 2002. Rather than carpet bomb the entire Jenin camp in one fell swoop in order to kill all the known terrorists living among the civilians, thereby avoiding all Israeli casualties of its soldiers, the Israeli army went into the town slowly and methodically, house to house, day after day, in search of terrorists. Although the Palestinians initially claimed a massacre had taken place, this was proved false. In the end, the reported number of Palestinian deaths was fifty-six, while the corresponding number of Israeli losses was thirty-three soldiers. Most of the Palestinians who died were gunmen who had booby-trapped the area in order to inflict casualties on the Israelis. In addition, the Israeli army did in fact take other measures in Jenin in order to keep civilian casualties to a minimum by warning all non-combatants to leave the area of action, for example.

Similar tactics were employed in the summer of 2006 in order to root out Hezbollah fighters shooting Katyusha rockets at Israeli civilians from Lebanese homes. Rather than bomb all the homes from the air, knowing that many civilians lived in these homes (and were forced to remain there by Hezbollah gunpoint), the Israeli army tried to kill the Hezbollah fighters in house-to-house combat, which resulted in many casualties for Israeli soldiers. Many similar scenarios were reported in the fighting in Gaza during Operation Protective Egde in the summer of 2014.

Finally, the Israeli army did something amazing in Gaza that was never before seen in war, in 2008, 2012, and again in 2014, in order to help minimize civilian casualties. While the tactic of dropping leaflets from planes has been used for many years in the past in order to warn civilians to leave target areas, the Israeli army actually phoned and sent text messages to each Palestinian family in Gaza before bombing sites where rocket launchers were hidden among civilians. This gave time for those civilians to flee and avoid injury, thereby minimizing unnecessary civilian casualties.

# COMPETITION IN JEWISH THOUGHT

I**N JULY OF 2002, THE FINAL RESULT** of the annual baseball All-Star Game that went into extra innings was a 7-7 tie. Because almost all the pitchers had been already used as the game went beyond the nine-inning minimum, the Commissioner of Baseball, Bud Selig, declared the game a tie, rather than waiting until a winner emerged and possibly risk injury to some of the players. The fans in the ballpark screamed "Refund!" and people all around the United States were outraged and frustrated. Later Mr. Selig apologized and regretted his decision. Why were the fans so upset? Apparently, the vast majority of people, generally speaking, demand to see a victor and a loser in any contest. They relish the idea of competition and cannot tolerate a tie in a competitive sport like baseball, and, as some believe, in all other areas of life as well. To many people, everything in life is a competition, and there must always be a winner and a loser. There can be no ties in sports or in life.

The verb "to compete" is defined as "to strive against another or others to attain a goal, such as an advantage or a victory." Thomas Hobbes and other philosophers argue that it is basic to human nature to constantly race against everyone, on every level and in every activity, in order to attain anything in our world. Some people are very much in favor of this competitive spirit, pointing out that it is a strong motivator for people to do and to accomplish. But there are those who have the divergent view and are opposed to the idea of competition as much as possible. They believe that whenever there is competition, the self-esteem of participants who fail to achieve the top score is often damaged, and the pressure to win is constant. Where does Judaism stand on the idea of competition as a way of determining outcomes in life, who is "better," or who attains a particular goal? Is competition an inherently good value, a proper perspective in which to perceive and behave in life, or is it an

inherently bad concept? Can there be some contexts in which competition is good and others in which it is evil? Should Jews always attempt to avoid competition completely and arrive at a compromise in the situations that life presents? This chapter will examine these and other questions through the sources.

## COMPETITION IN THE TORAH

Even before man was created, the Torah already alludes to competition in this world, as amplified by the Rabbis. A verse in the Torah says that on the fourth day of Creation, two large luminaries were created, the sun and the moon, and then the verse states that the larger luminary, the sun, ruled during the day, while the moon ruled the night. Rashi asks: If the verse calls them both large, how could the moon be referred to as small later in that same verse? He answers that originally there was a competition between the sun and the moon for dominance of the world. They contended about which would provide more light for the earth. Since there cannot be two equal rulers and "winners" in this competition, Rashi says that the moon was made smaller and "moved" to the night. God even "compensated" the moon for this and gave it the stars.[1] The Midrash, the origin of Rashi's commentary, further explains that both the sun and moon, in competition mode, each said, "I am greater than you." In order to maintain peace, God made the moon smaller.[2] Yet another Midrash explains that after its "demotion" and losing the competition, the moon did not want to obey God and become smaller, claiming that "it is not fair." God admitted to the moon that its claim was legitimate and, as "compensation" for its diminishment (and losing the "competition"), declared that a special sacrifice will be

---

1. Genesis 1:16 with Rashi commentary
2. Midrash, *Pirkei DeRabbi Eliezer* 5

brought each month at the beginning of the lunar month (Rosh Chodesh) to honor the moon for its diminution. Thus, competition existed in the world even before the first human being was created on the sixth day.[3]

The next competition alluded to in the Torah is that between the serpent and Adam, the first man. Before its sin, the serpent was erect, tall, and able to speak, according to the Midrash. It vied for the affection of Eve and, as part of its sin, competed with Adam for Eve's love and even attempted to kill Adam in order to marry Eve.[4] Thus, later authorities depict the serpent as the symbol of the evil inclination within man, when he is filled with haughtiness, jealousy, competition, and speaking evil about others.[5] Therefore, competition was present from the very beginning of history, even when only one man and one woman lived on the earth.

This continued into the next generation between the very first two brothers in the world, Cain and Abel. One commentary describes the entire episode of the sacrifices of Cain and Abel (which led to Cain slaying Abel) as a competition between the two for the affection and approval of God.[6] The Midrash also depicts the relationship of Cain and Abel as competitive, but gives three different underlying reasons for this rivalry.[7] The first explanation is that they were arguing over possessions: Cain claimed all the land in the world for himself and Abel claimed all the objects in the world as his own. But then Cain told Abel to get off of "his" land, and Abel told Cain to give him back "his" clothing that Cain was wearing. They argued and Cain killed Abel. Rabbi Joshua disagrees. He says that they split the land and possessions amicably, but they were actually competing and arguing about whose property would contain the Holy Temple. Each claimed the Temple site for himself, they argued and Cain killed Abel. Yehuda bar

Ami says they were arguing about and competing with each other over Eve or the twin sister of Cain and Abel who was also born to Eve, as both Cain and Abel wanted to take her as their wives, until Cain killed Abel. A modern commentary has explained this Midrash to exemplify all competitions in human history, the prototype of what leaders and nations have always fought over and competed for: land/possessions, religion, and sex.

The next story describing competition in the Torah occurred when the shepherds of Lot vied for ascendancy over Abraham's shepherds. Abraham saw that no compromise or resolution to this competition was possible, and he therefore sent away Lot and his shepherds, who then settled in Sodom.[8] In the following generation, there was another sibling rivalry and competition between the children of Abraham – Isaac and Yishmael – a rivalry that continues today through their descendants, the Jewish people and the Arabs. When Sara perceived that Hagar, Yishmael's mother, was vying for the inheritance of Abraham, and that Yishmael was a bad influence upon Isaac, Sara banned Hagar and Yishmael from their home, which God told Abraham to agree to.[9] The *Zohar* and Midrash say that Yishmael, as the Arab nation, never abandoned his desire and claim for the land of Israel, which his nation did receive later in history for a period of years, and this competition between the two brothers and nations will continue even into the times of Messiah, when the Jewish people will emerge triumphant.[10] When Yishmael thought that Isaac would be sacrificed by Abraham, another Midrash states that Yishmael also competed with Abraham's servant, Eliezer, for the inheritance of Abraham.[11]

In fact, the entire book of Genesis can be viewed as a competition between brothers. In each succeeding generation, the results of that competition became less harmful. In the first generation, the result of the competition

---

3. Midrash, *Pirkei DeRabbi Eliezer* 3
4. Midrash, *Beraishit Rabbah* 20:5
5. *Ye'arot Devash* 1:11
6. Abarbanel commentary on Genesis 4:1-8
7. Midrash, *Beraishit Rabbah* 22:7

8. Genesis 13:5-11; Midrash, *Pesikta Rabbati* 3
9. Genesis 21:8-12
10. Zohar II:32a; Midrash, *Yalkut Shimoni* 6:45
11. Midrash, *Pirkei DeRabbi Eliezer* 30

was the death of Abel. In the generation of Abraham's sons, the result was banishment of Yishmael. In the competition between the sons of Isaac, Jacob and Esau fought for the inheritance through the blessings, but then Jacob had to leave his home in fear for his life. After twenty years the brothers then met and reconciled. In the next generation, the sons of Jacob competed for their view of the Jewish future with their brother Joseph, and in jealousy due to this competition and Jacob favoring Joseph, they sold Joseph as a slave to Egypt. Many years later, the brothers not only reconciled, but were also remorseful about their actions, and the entire family lived together in harmony for many years. In the final "competition" between brothers in the book of Genesis, in blessing the sons of Joseph, Jacob chose one grandson, Ephraim, over his older brother Menasheh, to receive the first blessing. Unlike the previous generations, however, we never see any rivalry, discontentment, or bitterness between these two brothers, and they continued to love each other despite this competition that Ephraim "won." In addition to the fact that all the brothers competed in Genesis, a very interesting truth emerges. At that time, as well as in certain contexts even today (such as the monarchy in England), the older sibling was always presumed to be the "winner," and he inherited his father's mantle. But in each story described in the Torah, Judaism is clearly teaching us that blood lines and predetermination do not decide the winner of the competition in advance. The competition is always fair and the more deserving competitor is victorious. In fact, in each of the stories, it is the younger brother who consistently is the winner and hero, and not the older brother, who is the presumed winner.

Despite the unity of Jacob's family, the rivalry and competition between the tribes did not diminish later in the desert. When Moses wished to appoint seventy new Judges to be the Sanhedrin, the highest Jewish court, he was fearful that if he appointed even one more judge from one tribe (six) while some of the other tribes have one judge fewer (five), those

tribes would be angry at Moses and feel like losers of the competition. Since with exactly seventy judges not all of the twelve tribes could receive six judges (two tribes would necessarily have five), Moses was forced to conduct a lottery so that the competition would be minimized and the appointment of judges would seem equitable to all, and not a decision by Moses, which would anger the less enfranchised tribes.[12] Similarly, in deciding which tribe would permanently receive which part of the land of Israel, there was great competition as well. God was aware of this competition and thus instructed Moses to conduct a lottery to determine not only which tribe would receive which section of land, but also which family within each tribe would receive which parcel of property.[13]

Another competition took place in the Torah between the firstborn sons in the desert. Originally, the firstborn Jewish males were supposed to serve God in the Temple, but after they participated in the sin of the Golden Calf and the Levites did not, the holiness was to be "transferred" from the firstborn sons to the Levites. In a public ceremony, the 22,000 Levites were to line up opposite all the firstborn sons and this symbolic exchange would then take place. But there were 22,273 firstborns. The "extra" 273 sons could be redeemed not by a Levite, but rather through five silver coins.[14] But the Talmud says that none of the firstborn sons wanted to be redeemed by coins and all vied to be redeemed by a living Levite. Thus, once again Moses was forced to conduct another lottery (with 22,273 pieces of paper – on 22,000 it was written "Levite" and on 273 it was written "five coins"), in order to assure that this competition was fair.[15]

Even within the same tribe, we see that there was rivalry and competition in the Torah. The holy Levites, after they were chosen for service in the Tabernacle, competed for the

12. *Sanhedrin* 17a
13. Numbers 26:55-56; Midrash, *Yalkut Shimoni, Beraishit* 22:98
14. Numbers 3:11-13, 44-51
15. *Sanhedrin* 17a

most prestigious job with the greatest reward – carrying the Holy Ark. By doing this, they ignored the holy task of carrying the other utensils.[16] Therefore, God was forced to assign specific tasks for each of the Levite families, and the family of Kehat carried the Holy Ark,[17] which did not sit well with the other Levites. Later on, a disgruntled member of the Levite tribe, Korach, led a rebellion against Moses and he was joined by members of the tribe of Reuven, the eldest tribe, who also felt they had lost in the competition for leadership when Moses was chosen to lead. As the oldest son of Jacob, this tribe felt that Jewish leadership was rightfully theirs. Korach claimed that he wanted equality for everyone with no leaders, but he actually wanted to be the High Priest and felt that he had lost the competition to become the *Nasi*, the leader of the tribe of Levi, which he thought was due him because of seniority.[18]

Later on in Jewish history, some viewed the entire story of Chanukah as a competition between the traditional Jews and the Hellenists, a competition for the hearts, minds, and souls of the masses of Jewish people.[19]

## NON-COMPETITION IN THE TORAH

After all the sibling rivalries and competitions between brothers in the book of Genesis, the very next story of siblings in the Torah shows the opposite situation. After the very peaceful resolution in Genesis between Menashe and Ephraim, the leadership of the Jewish people would come from one very prestigious family – the children of the leader Amram and his wife, Yocheved, the daughter of Levi. Rather than vie and compete, all three children helped each other out and demonstrated harmony in assuming their leadership roles. Miriam established her leadership credentials in her willingness to defy the king and risk her life by not killing Jewish babies as she was ordered

(according to the view that Miriam was Puah, the midwife in the Torah). Then, as a big sister, she again risked her life as her baby brother Moses was sent in a basket along the Nile to be found by Pharaoh's daughter, and Miriam then came forth to say that her mother would nurse the infant. After leaving Egypt when the Jewish people were saved by God from the Egyptians at the Sea of Reeds, it was Miriam who led the women in song.[20] Despite being the eldest (and possibly the most worthy, based on past acts), we see that Miriam had no difficulty "losing" when the mantle of leadership of the Jewish people was given to the youngest sibling, Moses.

The middle child, Aaron, also demonstrated leadership ability. When Moses was hesitant to accept the leadership and was concerned about his ability to speak publicly, God assigned his brother Aaron as his spokesperson. Moses was concerned that Aaron might be jealous that Moses was selected for leadership over him, but God assured Moses that this was not the case, and the Torah records that Aaron was actually happy for Moses and not jealous at all.[21] Since all three siblings did indeed lead the Jewish people in different ways, all were rewarded with significant legacies. Moses has the status of a king, Aaron was the Kohen Gadol, the High Priest, as were his descendants, and Miriam was rewarded with both wisdom and the kingship for the Davidic dynasty and therefore the Messiah himself (through her husband, who was from the tribe of Judah).[22] Miriam was held in such high regard that the entire nation did not travel and waited for her until her seven-day punishment was completed.[23] That particular blemish on Miriam involved the one time that a sense of competition emerged between these three siblings – Miriam, Aaron, and Moses. When Moses was forced to separate from his wife,

---

16. Midrash, *Bamidbar Rabbah* 5:1, 9
17. Numbers 4:15, 16-17
18. Numbers 16:1-3 with Rashi commentary
19. *Sefer HaToda'a*, chapter 11

20. Exodus 1:15-20, 2:1-7, 15: 20-21 with Rashi commentary
21. Exodus 4:14 with Rashi and Rabbeinu Bechaye commentaries
22. *Midrash Tanchuma, Vayakhel* 5, *Shemot Rabbah* 1:17
23. Deuteronomy 24:9; Midrash, *Sifri, Ki Tetze* 65

Tzipporah, because he was always with God, Miriam remarked to Aaron that they (Aaron and Miriam) were also prophets, and they did not have to separate from their spouses. For this one "competitive" and disparaging remark, Miriam, who was held to a higher standard than most, was punished with the plague of *Tzaraat*, leprosy-like symptoms, for seven days, and she remained outside the camp.[24] Despite the negative remark about him by his sister, it was Moses that prayed for Miriam's recuperation, and this prayer apparently helped to limit Miriam's punishment to seven days.

Perhaps the greatest display of the negation of competition in the Torah is not obvious from the text itself and is only brought to light by piecing together the remarks of the commentaries. The competition to donate the materials needed for building the Tabernacle (especially after the sin of the Golden Calf) had been very spirited. The people all rushed to donate. Rashi explains that the *Nesi'im*, the leaders of each tribe, intentionally waited until the people would finish bringing their donations, thinking that they would "top" the people by donating whatever that was missing.[25] However, the masses brought so much and so quickly that Moses had to actually tell them to stop, and the *Nesi'im* were left with nothing to bring.[26] Thus, Moses told them that each tribal leader would bring his own set of sacrifices during the twelve days of the dedication of the Tabernacle. The competition between the tribal leaders was on! The first *Nasi*, prince, to bring a sacrifice on the first day, the eminent Nachshon, was a proven leader within the leadership tribe of Judah, and he brought a silver dish and silver bowl, both filled with fine flour and oil, a spoon made of gold full of incense, a bull, ram, and lamb as burnt offerings, a kid goat as a sin offering, and two oxen, five rams, five goats and five lambs as peace offerings.[27] This was quite a display and quite an offering.

Now everyone was waiting for the next day's offering to see what the next leader would bring in his natural effort to try to top what Nachshon had contributed. Who was to be second in line after Nachshon? The Midrash, after citing the initial story about how the *Nesi'im* missed out in the original donations (the basis of Rashi's commentary), explains that there was great competition between the *Nesi'im* to be second, and Netanel was chosen by God to bring his sacrifice on the second day because he was a great Torah scholar, as the entire tribe of Yissachar was known as Torah scholars.[28] Another Midrash affirms that Netanel was not only smart in Torah learning, but altogether very intelligent.[29] This is very important to know because of Netanel's decision of what to bring. In fact, one commentary states that Netanel gave advice to all the other tribes about what was the proper sacrifice to bring.[30] What precisely did Netanel do and what did he bring as his sacrifice?

Instead of joining the competition of what today has become known as the "Bar Mitzvah syndrome" mentality, where Jews often try to outdo each other in how special, unique, and expensive their *Simcha* (celebration) will be, Netanel, with his Torah and innate wisdom, decided to bring the identical sacrifices brought by Nachshon, down to the last detail.[31] This way, he set the tone for the *Nesi'im* that followed during the next ten days. After two identical sacrifices one day after the next, each *Nasi* then fell in line and also brought the exact same sacrifice as the leaders from the first two days. Thus, Netanel created a situation in which the potential competition between these leaders was eliminated. Netanel's special "sacrifice" and advice are alluded to in Rashi. Rashi says that the verse says "he sacrificed" twice – only by his offering – in order to teach us that not only was he more deserving than the others because of his vast Torah scholarship, but also because he gave special

---

24. Numbers 12:1-3, 9-13, 15
25. Rashi commentary on Numbers 12:3
26. Exodus 36:5-7
27. Numbers 7:12-17

28. *Midrash Tanchuma, Naso* 14
29. Midrash, *Beraishit Rabbah* 72:5
30. Ba'al HaTurim commentary on Numbers 7:18
31. Numbers 7:18-19

advice to all the princes of each tribe to bring the sacrifices specifically in this manner (the same has he did, imitating the first offering of Nachshon).[32] These twelve sacrifices, brought in a non-competitive spirit, taught the entire Jewish people that there need not be the normal competition between tribes, and that everyone could work together without the need to be the "best" and outdo the other tribes. In fact, when these leaders brought all the sacrifices to the Tabernacle, the Torah records that the sacrifices were brought all together, not in twelve separate wagons, but together in six wagons with two sacrifices in each wagon.[33]

## WHAT, THEN, IS THE JEWISH ATTITUDE TOWARDS COMPETITION?

There is no direct discussion in the ancient sources about the concept of competition per se. And one must assume that the use of the modern Hebrew word for competition, "*Tacharut*," when used often in early sources, had the same connotation then as it does today (although we cannot be certain). But there are numerous comments about this idea in both ancient and modern traditions. Chazon Ish of the twentieth century states that every person naturally loves the idea of competition, especially as a mental test of wills, or what we would call "brain-teasers." He also says that any form of competition is desirable by human beings, including competitions between friends, competitions between one group and another group in a society, and even the competition between generations, when the younger generation tries to outdo previous generation. This is a natural drive within each person.[34]

In earlier traditional sources, however, the term for competition is usually associated with the negative traits of jealousy and hatred, and it is depicted as a trait to be avoided. Thus, the Midrash says that *Tacharut*, competition, is not a good trait to possess, as it stands in opposition to the desired trait of peace between people. Since competition between angels does not exist, when the angels above see people competing, the angels will accuse them of not fulfilling the Torah.[35] In fact, Rashi states that the natural outgrowth of jealousy is competition.[36] Rabbi Joseph Albo refers to the trait of competition as evil.[37] Rabbi Shimon stated that the reason God gave the Jewish people the laws about courts even before He gave them all the Torah laws, is that the laws of the court, if followed properly, would encourage peace and discourage competition.[38] In the fourteenth century, *Sefer HaChinuch* explained that the reason for the Torah's prohibition for the king to have too many wives (and presumably this explains the common Jewish practice of why every Jewish man should have only one wife) is that with more than one wife, the competition between these ladies for the husband's favor will be so great that it will cause great damage.[39]

In order to avoid competition between Jews, the Rabbis enacted several edicts as part of established Jewish practice. The Talmud records that there used to be a competition regarding the fruit baskets that were brought to the homes of mourners. The wealthy people went out of their way to give the fruit in silver and gold baskets, which the poor could not afford, and they gave fruit in baskets of peeled willow wigs. Since poor people were embarrassed by this practice, the Rabbis enacted that this competition had to be eliminated, and from that point on, only peeled willow twigs were allowed for all fruit baskets for mourners.[40] In the same vein, the mourners themselves used to compete to serve their guests in their house of mourning by offering drinks in the finest glasses, and the poor mourners could not

---

32. Rashi commentary on Numbers 7:19
33. Numbers 7:3
34. Chazon Ish, *Sefer Emunah U'bitachon* 5:1

35. Midrash, *Shir HaShirim Rabbah* 8:17
36. Rashi commentary on *Shabbat* 152b
37. *Sefer HaIkaraim* 2:28
38. Exodus 15:25; Midrash, *Mechilta, Mishpatim Nezikin* 1
39. *Sefer HaChinuch*, Mitzvah 501
40. *Mo'ed Katan* 27a

compete with this and felt embarrassed. The Rabbis then enacted an edict that all glasses served at a mourner's home had to be plain and cheap, regardless of the level of wealth of the mourner. In a similar manner, the Talmud goes on to record several more enactments that eliminated the competition between poor and rich Jews. The Jerusalem Talmud records that for a certain time period there was competition between mourners about how they would dress at a funeral, as the custom was for the mourners to pass between two rows of people after the burial. The wealthier mourners would "show off" their fine clothing. The Rabbis then changed this practice so that the people would pass before the mourners (in order that there would be no "parade of the mourners") until after a time the competition between mourners ceased and the original custom was reinstated.[41] Today, the custom is indeed for the mourners to pass between the two rows of people.

Maimonides calls the very desire for competition a sin that requires repentance, even without any specific action. And these sins involving emotions, continues Maimonides, are worse than sins of action, since the emotions take hold of the entire person.[42] Another Medieval commentary states that competition originates from man's evil inclination, and since an angel does not have an evil inclination, but rather only an inclination to please God, there can be no competition between angels.[43] The Midrash highlights this idea and states that if in the heavens there is peace between angels due to lack of competition, how much more so do human beings need to make peace between themselves and eliminate the concept of competition.[44] Rabbeinu Bechaya records this specific idea as well.[45] Rabbi Yonatan Eibshutz in the 1700's echoed this idea when he said that the Rabbis chose to end the *Shmoneh*

*Esreh* prayer with the final blessing about peace because Jews should pray to eliminate disagreements, hatred, jealousy, and competition between themselves and rather should strive to achieve peace. This is the very purpose of the commandment to "love thy neighbor as thyself."[46]

Although we do not know or fully understand what the Next World will be or feel like, the Talmud states that it will be a spiritual world without eating or drinking and also devoid of competition.[47] Maimonides states that in this world as well, during Messianic times, there will be no competition between people.[48]

## GOOD COMPETITION

From all of the above sources, it seems that from the Jewish perspective, all competition is something truly evil and to be avoided. But it that true? Are Jews supposed to quash all of their natural feelings to compete, or are they supposed to channel these feelings to something positive? Is it possible to compete and still have feelings of compassion without jealousy towards others? If people can attain peace with others, should they still feel guilty about desiring to compete? We will see that even within Judaism, there are positive aspects of competition, regarding which it is desirable to compete.

In certain aspects of Jewish life competition is encouraged. Each day, as every Kohen-Priest in the Temple desired to be the one who would do the first service of the removal of the ashes on the Altar, they conducted an actual running competition: Two Kohanim raced up the ramp to the Altar in order to see who would get to the Altar first. The winner would be given the coveted honor of preforming the removal of the ashes.[49] Therefore, we see that when it is for a positive purpose and goal, competition is indeed not only allowed, but also encouraged in Judaism, even in the Temple itself. However,

---

41. Jerusalem Talmud *Berachot* 25a
42. Maimonides, *Hilchot Teshuva* 7:3
43. Rabbeinu Bechaye commentary on Exodus 4:24
44. Midrash, *Vayikra Rabbah* 9:9
45. Rabbeinu Bechaye commentary on Deuteronomy 16:18

46. *Ye'arot Devash* 1:1
47. *Berachot* 17a
48. Maimonides, *Hilchot Melachim* 12:4-5
49. Mishna *Yoma* 2:1

if the result will make the loser feel badly or will hurt or embarrass someone, it is not permitted. Thus, in the same Temple, one of the requirements of bringing the *Bikurim*, the first fruits, by every Jew, was to recite a few Torah verses as part of the ceremony. When all Jews could read Hebrew, this was no problem, and there was healthy competition over who could recite these Hebrew words "the best." But once some Jews did not know how to read Hebrew properly, this competition turned into an embarrassment for them. Thus, the Mishna records that the Rabbis decided to appoint one permanent reader who would read the verses for all, not only to eliminate the competition but also to eliminate embarrassment. (This is the same reasoning today for why a reader of the Torah reads for all men called up, even for those called up who know how to read.) Likewise, as noted above, unfair competition between the rich and poor had to be eliminated. Thus, when there was a competition to see who would bring the nicest baskets of *Bikurim*, the poor would be embarrassed by the rich Jews, and then the Rabbis had to eliminate this form of competition.[50]

Although he speaks specifically about jealousy, Rabbeinu Yonah actually writes about two kinds of competition: the good kind and the bad kind.[51] If a person is jealous of the good accomplishments of a friend, and it causes the friend to become angry and frustrated, this prompts the bad type of competition. But if the jealousy causes this onlooker to compete in a way that imitates the success and accomplishments of the other individual, and it betters him or her as a result, this becomes good competition. The Midrash makes an astounding statement that can only be understood in this light. It says that without jealousy, the world could not possibly survive because then no one would marry or build a home.[52] What this Midrash is telling us is that it is the jealousy of another person (whether it is about

another's wife or his home) that provokes an individual to equal or better the other person's accomplishments. If he consequently tries to find a better wife or build a better home, this form of jealousy and competition is very positive, because it helps the world function better. In other words, if a person's competitiveness is inner-directed, bringing someone to hate an opponent, and the goal is to beat the other person at any cost, then no victory will be truly satisfying and morally legitimate. But if the other person's attainment pushes a person's competitive spirit outward – i.e., to do better and become better in order to maximize one's abilities – then this competition is good. *Orchot Tzadikim* demonstrates this idea when he says that hatred based on a specific situation is tolerable, such as hatred for a person who stole from you, since if the situation changes (i.e., the stolen object is returned), the hatred dissipates. But hatred due to jealousy (i.e., the bad form of competition) can never be corrected.[53]

In a sports competition, this idea can be summarized as the difference between hating one's opponent and not hating one's opponent, but competing just as strongly. Bad competition involves hating the opponent in order to defeat him or her. Good competition recognizes that the opponent is doing his or her best, and there is no animosity as you try to do your best and defeat the opposition. One prime example of good competition is an event that took place in April 2008 in the northwest of the United States at a women's college softball league. Sara Tucholsky played softball for Western Oregon University, and she had never hit a home run in high school or college. On April 26, 2008, her opponent was Central Washington University. After Sara hit her first home run over the fence, she began to run the bases, but a misstep resulted in a torn knee ligament and she couldn't continue. The umpire mistakenly ruled that a team member couldn't run in her place or assist her around the bases. What, then, could be done? A member of the opposing team, first baseman

50. Mishna *Bikurim* 3:7-8
51. Rabbeinu Yonah commentary on Mishna *Avot* 4:21
52. *Midrash Tehilim*, Psalm 37

53. "Gate of Jealousy," chapter 14 in *Orchot Tzadikim*,

Mallory Holtman, the career home run leader in the Great Northwest Athletic Conference, asked the umpire if she and her teammates could help Sara run the bases. He said they could, and Mallory and shortstop Liz Wallace carried her around the field as she gently tapped her uninjured leg on each base. If they had not helped Sara, the home run would not have counted against their own team. This act of kindness shows the good kind of competition, through which playing one's hardest to win does not signify hating the opponent.

One specific area in which Judaism encourages competition is in Torah learning. Jealousy of someone's success in Torah learning is a positive reaction if it will encourage the jealous person to learn more Torah. The Midrash, for this reason, calls jealousy of Torah learning a good thing.[54] For the same reason, the Talmud says that it is a positive development to have a second teacher who is competing with the first in teaching Torah, because this will improve each teacher's performance and more Torah will be learned as a result.[55] So it is with two Talmud scholars in the same neighborhood or city who argue with each other. The Talmud compares these two men to two pieces of iron that, when rubbed together, each one becomes sharper,[56] as the verse says that each piece of iron will be sharper as a result.[57] For the same reason, it is forbidden to stop a second teacher from setting up a Torah class in the same alley or neighborhood as the first (although if they would be in different profession this would be forbidden).[58] Two teachers competing against each other leads to a qualitative and quantitative advantage for the Torah that is being taught, which is the ultimate goal in teaching Torah. For this reason, a second Jewish school may be set up in any area, even it competes with the first. Similarly,

two Torah study partners should argue with each other in learning, but not compete and hate each other.[59]

The entire Talmud can be seen as a competition between various Rabbis to "win" and have their viewpoint become normative Jewish law, based on how they convince others to accept their logic. On nearly every page of almost 2,500 Talmudic (Babylonian) pages, arguments are recorded competing for the "truth" on many subjects. But if the spirit of this competition is right and proper, then all struggles and intellectual combat are left in the halls of the house of study. This is most aptly demonstrated by the two main and most famous groups of competitors in their day, the House of Shammai and the House of Hillel, who argued vociferously on behalf of their viewpoints. Nonetheless, says the Talmud, after all of the arguments and disagreements, not only did these two groups of Jews socialize, but it was also common for the men and women from the Houses of Shammai and Hillel to marry one another.[60] Even though they even disagreed about certain points of law regarding marriage itself, this did not prevent them for marrying one another since they left their rivalries in the *Beit Midrash*, the house of study.

Another area of natural competition in the world is the ongoing rivalry between the Jewish people and the nations of the world that takes place in each generation. The Midrash states that this competition is good because it keeps the Jews apart from the non-Jewish world so that Jews will not learn from them and their non-Jewish ways.[61] The Talmud speaks of this eternal competition as an ongoing struggle, with one loser and one winner that change from generation to generation.[62] The competition between Jerusalem (the Jewish people) and Caesar (Rome, the non-Jewish powers) is so fierce, says the Talmud, that there must always be one winner and one loser

54. *Tanna Debai Eliyahu* 19:2
55. *Bava Batra* 21a
56. *Ta'anit* 7a
57. *Proverbs* 27:17
58. *Bava Batra* 22a

59. *Pele Yo'etz* on "*Chavrutah*"
60. *Yevamot* 14a
61. *Midrash, Batei Midrashot*, section 2; *Temura Hashalem* 5
62. *Megillah* 6a

in each generation. Sometimes Jerusalem will be on top and the Caesar will be down, while at other times Caesar will be victorious and Jerusalem the loser. But it will never happen that both Jerusalem and Caesar will both be up at the same time or down at the same time.

Another area where competition is encouraged in Jewish thought is in the marketplace, as long as the competition is fair. Thus, a competitor can set up a rival shop, according to must Talmudic opinions, because the second seller can legitimately claim, "You sell in your store and I will sell in my store."[63] Similarly, although there is a disagreement between various opinions if one seller can legally give away free samples in order to lure in new customers,[64] the Rabbis say that the person who does this is "remembered for good" because, as Rashi explains, in the end the consumer will benefit – as long as the competition remains equitable.[65] Thus, the *Code of Jewish Law* rules that a seller can indeed give away free samples to gain an advantage, as long as this option is also open to the competition.[66]

## IMPROPER COMPETITION

Although there are certain contexts in which competition is encouraged in Judaism, there are also other situations when competition is utterly discouraged. One of these is within the family structure. The Mishna makes a general statement that in the Jewish home there should be no competition at all, as the goal there is to create an atmosphere of peace rather than a competitive atmosphere.[67] Maimonides concretizes this general statement by saying that a parent should never favor or treat any child differently from the rest, since this will cause competition and jealousy between the children, as demonstrated in the Torah by how Jacob favored Joseph, with disastrous results.[68]

Making children compete for the attention or affection of a parent is a sure-fire recipe for adversity.

A nineteenth-century Jewish thinker, Rabbi Eliezer Papo, writes that competition in which the focus is exclusively on winning and defeating one's opponent, whether in sports or in life, is not a Jewish trait, and it delays the coming of the Messiah.[69] He says that this form of competition between Jews – specifically Torah scholars – creates hatred because the lust for winning is so great that all other Jewish values fall by the wayside. The desire to win at all costs clouds a person's judgment and values, even that of a Talmud scholar. This is the opposite of the view and behavior of the Houses of Shammai and Hillel discussed above. Rabbi Moshe Chaim Luzzato agrees with this principle regarding the wrong way to compete. He states that if a person is so focused on doing a Mitzvah properly and better than anyone else, this could lead to battles, desecration of God's name, and a clouding of one's judgment and values. He mentions the situation described above in which the Levites all competed to carry the Holy Ark because of its greater reward and prestige, and in the process ignored all the other vessels of the Tabernacle, creating a desecration of God's name.[70] Rabbi Karelitz added another factor in describing proper and improper competition. He says that if a person has true faith in God, he will not be bothered by competition (in business, life, or sports), even when the opponent appears to be winning. Like the girls on that softball team, Rabbi Karelitz writes that if a person attempts to help one's opponent in a competition (while not necessarily giving up or letting the person win) rather than always trying to crush him or her, this will create a sanctification of God's name.[71] God will help those who have trust in Him and do not try to defeat an opponent at all costs, neglecting interpersonal ethics and values.

63. *Bava Batra* 21b
64. *Bava Metzia* 60a
65. Rashi commentary on *Bava Metzia* 60a
66. *Shulchan Aruch, Choshen Mishpat* 228:18
67. Mishna, *Avot DeRabbi Natan* 28:3
68. Maimonides, *Hilchot Nachalot* 6:13

69. *Pele Yo'etz* on "Nitzuach"
70. *Mesilat Yesharim*, chapter 20
71. *Chazon Ish, Emunah U'bitachon* 2:5

## COMPROMISE OR COMPETE?

Generally, most people think of compromise as a means of achieving peace between two competitors. But in Judaism, as demonstrated above, the goal is to achieve this peace even within competition. In that case, is it preferable in Judaism to compromise, with each side somewhat giving in, in order to eliminate competition completely and arrive at a mutually agreeable solution? Or perhaps, the competition mode is preferred if peace between the opponents can be maintained? On this question, we find two "competing" opinions.

Rabbi Eliezer clearly prohibits compromise in a situation that there is natural competition, and he calls anyone who compromises in such a case a sinner.[72] But then he says that there are two models in Judaism. The Moses model competes to the end and never gives in concerning matters of Jewish law, always attempting to demonstrate the correctness of his opinion. But the model of Aaron the High Priest is that of an individual seeking peace between two competing parties as the highest value, and this model would always prefer compromise over one winner and one loser. Rashi explains that before the competition would begin in a courtroom between the litigants, Aaron the High Priest would try to get the two parties to agree on a compromising solution.[73] Therefore, both approaches, that of Moses and that of Aaron, competing versus compromising, are evident and valid in normative Judaism.

These two views can also be seen elsewhere in the Talmud. In one tractate, Rabbi Yochanan says we always follow the view of he who compromises.[74] But another statement in another tractate says that the third compromising opinion between two divergent views should never hold sway.[75] Maharal explains that the path of Aaron is to show people that their views are not absolute and that people must be willing to bend their views. Hillel, who was flexible in his views, follows the path of Aaron. But Hillel's rival, Shammai, followed the philosophy of "sticking to your guns" when a person feels that he or she is correct, and not compromising.[76] Maimonides rules regarding the importance of compromise. He says that before the two litigants begin to compete in the courtroom, it is a Mitzvah, a commandment, for the judge to try to get them to compromise, which would be the ideal. This process can and should be conducted until final judgment is pronounced. However, continues Maimonides, once there is a winner and loser in the case – i.e., after the final judgment is decided – then it is forbidden for the judge or anyone else to try to get the parties to compromise.[77] Therefore, we see from the words of Maimonides that he too believes compromise has its place and competition has its place, even in the courtroom. *Shulchan Aruch* rules according to Maimonides, quoting him almost word for word.[78]

Finally, the classic case is brought in which two boats or two camels coming from opposite directions into a narrow area are competing for the same tight passageway. (This represents a situation in which there can be only one winner.) They are approaching from opposite directions and each wants to pass through first. If they try to enter at the same time, both boats will sink or both camels will fall. Who wins? Who gets the right of passage first? The Talmud says (and Maimonides and *Shulchan Aruch* rule this way as well) that if one boat or camel is fully loaded with cargo and the other is not, the loaded boat or camel takes precedence. If, as they approach the narrow passageway, one boat or camel is clearly closer to the passage, then that one takes precedence.[79] But if both of the boats or both camels are either loaded or not loaded with cargo and both are equidistant from the passageway, which takes

---

72. *Sanhedrin* 6b
73. Rashi commentary on *Sanhedrin* 6b, s.v. "Aval"
74. *Berachot* 43a
75. *Chulin* 137a

76. Maharal, *Derech Chaim* 1:15
77. Maimonides, *Hilchot Sanhedrin* 22:4
78. *Shulchan Aruch, Choshen Mishpat* 12:2
79. *Sanhedrin* 32b; Maimonides, *Hilchot Rotze'ach* 13:12; *Shulchan Aruch, Choshen Mishpat* 272:14

precedence? Who wins? In that case, says the Talmud, they must make a compromise and the boat or camel that yields is paid by the other one for its extra waiting time. Here, once again, we see that both approaches – the "winner/loser" competition and the compromise – are suggested. But in this situation, unlike previously, first an attempt is made to find a winner, and only after no winner can be determined (in order to decide who will go first), only then is a compromise sought. Thus, both approaches of competition and compromise are legitimate within traditional Judaism when dealing with difficult situations between two parties, depending on the context.

# CONCEIVING TO ABORT FOR STEM CELLS AND OTHER STEM CELL ISSUES

THE DEVELOPMENTS IN STEM CELL research are among the most promising, yet controversial, technological breakthroughs of our generation. Most cells in the human body are differentiated and, if they have the ability to divide at all, they can form only cells that are similar to themselves. However, stem cells have the unique property of being able to divide while maintaining their "universal" characteristics, and they can eventually become any specialized cell of the human body. If scientists are able to manipulate the conditions controlling cellular differentiation, they might eventually be able to create replacement cells and organs, and even cure illnesses such as diabetes, Alzheimer's disease, and Parkinson's disease. In 2011, doctors were able to improve heart function and reverse tissue damage in heart failure patients using stem cells taken from the patients' own heart tissue. Embryonic stem cell therapy has shown promise in curing certain kinds of blindness. Quadriplegics and scientists hope that in the not-too-distant future, stem cells will help cure paralysis. The ultimate promise of stem cell technology would be to produce a person's own replacement limbs and save dying people by replacing a vital organ formed from the person's own stem cells.

As the technology evolves, Rabbinic authorities continually address the new ramifications in Jewish law. What is Jewish law's perspective on stem cell research, and what could be the possible objections to such research? There is little argument that the use of stem cells derived from adult somatic tissue poses few ethical problems. Rather, it is the issues and concerns raised by stem cell research that involve the use of in vitro fertilized eggs which have not yet been implanted in a woman, as well as the use of tissue from aborted fetuses that may be immoral. As is common with new scientific developments, the technology often leaps ahead of the discussion of relevant ethical issues. This chapter will present one actual dilemma, and then discuss the overall question of using stem cells derived from fertilized eggs.

## ONE DILEMMA INVOLVING STEM CELLS

Stem cells derived from an aborted fetus that are then injected into the brain have already shown to be effective in limiting and sometimes even curing the symptoms of Parkinson's disease, a very debilitative condition caused when the brain stops producing the neurotransmitter called dopamine. The most obvious symptoms are movement-related, which include shaking, rigidity, slowness of movement, and difficulty walking. Later, cognitive problems may arise, with dementia commonly occurring in the advanced stages of the disease. Consider this hypothetical case: A man has this disease, but due to his medical history, a hospital denies him treatment with stem cells to limit or eliminate the effects of the Parkinson's. He and his wife decide to conceive a fetus for the express purpose of aborting it during the fourth month of pregnancy and using the cells of that aborted fetus to inject into the husband's brain. They go to another hospital to do the abortion and inject the stem cells. The husband and wife claim that without this treatment, not only will the symptoms increase, but the husband will die within a year. Should the hospital agree to this procedure if it can eliminate the symptoms and save the husband's life? In the non-Jewish world there are many ethical issues that need to be resolved before a hospital will consent to such treatment, including the common standard that donors and recipients of treatment are usually unknown to each other. But what are the Jewish implications of such a dilemma?

## RESOLVING THE DILEMMA THROUGH JEWISH SOURCES SHOWING JEWISH VALUES

A moral dilemma involves two conflicting ethical values. In this case, it is the life or health of the husband on one side, and the life of a fetus on the other side. Where does Judaism stand on each of these issues?

A fundamental Jewish concept gleaned from several chapters in this volume is that there is no higher priority in Judaism than the value of life. If the man's life is indeed in danger, then Maimonides (and normative Jewish law) rules that a Jew can violate every one of the commandments in the Torah, except for the three cardinal sins (adultery, idol worship, and murder) in order to save a human life – any human life, even a sick one.[1] This is based on the verse that commands a Jew to stay alive in order to observe the commandments.[2] The Talmud interprets this command to signify that it is preferable to violate one commandment like Shabbat in order to keep many more Sabbaths in the future, and uses the Torah phrase, "You shall live by them," to deduce that you shall not die by them (i.e., the commandments).[3]

On the other hand, any commandment (like saving a life) that comes about through sin is considered tainted, and one may not perform a commandment if the means to fulfilling that commandment is a sin (like stealing a *Lulav* in order to fulfill the commandment to shake it on Sukkot, for example).[4] This concept is codified in Jewish law,[5] and thus, one may not violate one commandment by committing a sin as the means to do another commandment. Therefore, if it is a sin to have an abortion, it seems that it would be forbidden to commit this sin in order to save a life. This concept seems to contradict the previously mentioned passages from Talmud and Jewish laws, which say that saving a life is the highest value and even by committing a sin, would be allowed or even mandatory. Which is it? Since the Rabbis clearly place saving a life at the top of the list of Jewish priorities, in this and other cases where life is at stake, even if a Jew sins and violates 610 of the 613 commandments in the Torah, it is permitted (and required) to save his or her life.

However, one of the three sins that are prohibited to violate in order to save a life is murder. If an unborn child is considered a human life in Judaism, then it is clearly forbidden to murder that fetus, a human life, in order to save the parent, another human life. How do Judaism and Jewish law view that four-month-old fetus?

## THE STATUS OF A FETUS IN JUDAISM

There are numerous sources that seem to be in conflict with regard to answering the question of whether or not the fetus is considered a human life and, therefore, if an abortion is the equivalent of murder. A simple reading of the Torah verse involving a pregnant woman whose fetus was accidentally killed in a dispute between two people shows that a fetus is considered to be personal property rather than human life.[6] In that case, when the loss of the fetus was caused accidentally, the Torah merely tells the culpable person to pay damages based on a certain formula of the value of the fetus. There is not even any hint of murder or immoral behavior, and payment for damages is all that is required. If the fetus were considered mere property of the mother, then it certainly would be permitted to get pregnant in order to save the life of the father of the fetus. However, other sources make the status of that fetus much more complicated.

In commanding Noah (and hence all non-Jews in future generations) not to murder, the wording of the verse is very strange. The verse states, "He who sheds the blood of man that is within a man, his blood shall be shed as well,

---

1. Maimonides, *Hilchot Yesodai HaTorah* 5:1-2
2. Leviticus 18:5
3. *Yoma* 85b
4. *Sukkah* 30a
5. *Mishna Berurah* on *Shulchan Orach, Orach Chaim* 10:31

6. Exodus 21:22

because man was created in God's image." In analyzing the literal meaning of the words "man that is within a man" the Talmud concludes that this refers to a fetus, since this is literally a man within another human – i.e., the mother.[7] Therefore, according to this passage, any abortion is equal to murder, and the fetus is considered to be a human being. In Jewish law, Maimonides rules this way for a non-Jew, and therefore a non-Jew who performs an abortion is considered a murderer.[8] Thus, if the parents were non-Jews, even if the father would probably die if denied the stem cells, it would be prohibited to "murder" the fetus and perform the abortion in order to save his life. But what is the case for Jews? How does Judaism view that fetus regarding the instance of Jews?

In a famous Mishna that mirrors our dilemma in a number of ways, it says that if a fetus threatens the life of the mother and a Jew must choose between aborting the fetus and letting the mother die, then clearly one aborts the fetus in order that the mother may live. But once the baby's head (or most of its body) emerges into the world, that baby has the same status as the mother, and one may not kill the minute-old baby in order to save the mother.[9] It is clear from this Mishna that the status of the fetus is that of a potential life, but not an actual life. And since one may abort the fetus in order to save the mother, it stands to reason that one may abort it to save the father who is in danger of dying as well, which brings us to our dilemma. However, the status of a "potential life," while clearly not the same as an actual life, shows the ambivalence of Judaism in how it views the fetus in the womb. Several other Jewish laws reflect this inconsistency.

THE AMBIVALENCE IN JUDAISM ABOUT THE STATUS OF THE FETUS

Two separate statements on the very same page of the Talmud show contradictory rulings about the status of the potential child in the mother's womb. On one side of the page, it states that if a pregnant mother who is close to delivery is sentenced to death, one does not wait until she gives birth, but rather the fetus dies within the mother. Moreover, it says that the fetus should be killed with a death blow even before the mother is put to death because the inevitable blood and unpleasantness that will emerge after her death (due to the live fetus inside) would cause much more embarrassment to her, so killing the fetus before her death would better preserve her dignity.[10] This ruling clearly shows that the fetus is not considered a life, and one does not even try to save the fetus of a mother that is about to be put to death. On the other side of the same page, however, the Talmud states that when a pregnant mother dies on the operating table on Shabbat, there is an obligation to violate the Shabbat in order to save her fetus.[11] Since violation of the Shabbat is only permitted when actual life is at stake, this passage clearly rules that the status of this fetus is like any other human life, regarding which, violation of the Shabbat laws is obligatory in order to save. These are two radical statements at opposite ends of the spectrum about the status of the fetus. Tosafot rules that we do indeed violate the Shabbat to save any fetus because it is considered a "danger to life" and it is treated, in this respect, like a full human being.[12] (See more about this below.)

So which is it then? Does the "potential life" status of the fetus mean that it is treated like an actual life and thus, abortion to save the father's life would be prohibited? Or does a "potential life" suggest just that – i.e., potential – and the fetus has no legal status or rights until it is born? This remains a question, as later authorities differ on this issue (which will be discussed at greater length below), and although there are some aspects of actual life in a fetus, it can never supersede an actual life. Therefore,

---

7. Genesis 9:6, *Sanhedrin* 40b
8. Maimonides, *Hilchot Melachim* 1:4
9. *Mishna Ohalot* 7:6

10. *Arachin* 7a
11. *Arachin* 7b
12. Tosafot commentary on *Nidah* 44, s.v. "Mihu"

if the fetus or its stem cells are needed to save a life, whether the mother's (as in the Mishna) or the father's, as in our dilemma, there is no question that any measure short of murdering an actual living person would be permitted and obligatory. In our dilemma, if the father's life were indeed in danger, the abortion would be permitted in order to retrieve the stem cells. However, most doctors today agree that Parkinson's disease is *never* a life-threatening condition. Although the person will live in pain or without the ability to function, this disease does not end or even shorten the life of the person who is unfortunately stricken with it. The question arises that if the stem cells from the abortion can *cure* the disease although the father's life is never at stake, would it still be permitted?

## ABORTING A FETUS IN ORDER TO HEAL A SICK PERSON

Although a very noble goal, would Judaism permit a woman to get pregnant in order to cure her husband's Parkinson's disease by aborting and inserting the stem cells of the fetus into his brain? Many sources show why this would be a problem from a Jewish perspective.

In addition to the obligation mentioned at the beginning of Creation for man to be fruitful and multiply, Isaiah also mentions that the general purpose of Creation is to populate the earth.[13] Therefore, the only "permission" to go through the painful (and sometimes life-threatening) process of pregnancy is for the sole purpose of populating the world – i.e., having children. If that is not the purpose of the pregnancy, then such an act would never be permitted in the first place. Thus Rabbi Moses Feinstein even forbids marital relations, and all the more so pregnancy, if not for the express purpose and possibility of having children.[14] In several other responsa, Rabbi Feinstein gives other reasons to forbid what the couple was trying to do to cure the hus-

band's disease. In one place he says that every abortion is considered murder, even for a Jew (not only for a non-Jew, as Maimonides ruled above).[15] However, this murder or abortion is sanctioned and permitted only when the mother's life is at stake. But in any other circumstance, such as our dilemma, it would be forbidden to abort because it is considered murder. Rabbi Feinstein also writes that since every birth and every abortion put a woman in a possible life-threatening situation, it is even forbidden to intentionally move up the birth date (unless medically mandated), because the only reason to allow the woman to enter into this life-threatening situation in the first place is to give birth, and only if it comes naturally. But to force it (or perform an abortion, which subjects the woman to similar risks) is forbidden.[16] He also says that even an abortion within the first forty days, which is permitted by some authorities (see below), is forbidden.[17] That ruling would certainly forbid abortion in our dilemma (where the husband's life is not directly threatened), which takes place well after forty days.

## TALMUDIC PRECEDENTS FOR OUR DILEMMA

Are there any cases in the Talmud or Rabbinic literature that are similar to the dilemma presented above, in which a couple wants to perform an abortion in order to create a positive outcome?

The Talmud discusses the situation where a *Yavam*, a Levir, married his sister-in-law whose husband (his brother) died without children.[18] This is a Torah Mitzvah-commandment (Deuteronomy 25:5-6), commanded by God in order to have a child to keep the memory of the dead brother alive. However what happens if, after the wedding to her former brother-in-law, it is discovered that the woman had actually been impregnated (before the death

---

13. Genesis 1:28, Isaiah 45:18
14. *Responsa Igrot Moshe, Even Ha'ezer* 1:71

15. *Responsa Igrot Moshe, Choshen Mishpat* 2:69
16. *Responsa Igrot Moshe, Yoreh De'ah* 2:74
17. *Responsa Igrot Moshe, Choshen Mishpat* 2:69
18. *Yevamot* 35b

and the wedding) by the husband who died? If the baby is then allowed to be born, both the wife and new husband would be guilty of a sin, since this unique commandment (the exception to the usual prohibition in Jewish law to marry a brother-in-law even after the death of his brother) applies only to a childless sister-in-law. Therefore, it seems logical that the woman should have an abortion, in order to prevent a sin from taking place. (As long as she does not give birth, there is no violation.) This seems to be a case that is somewhat parallel to the dilemma of aborting the fetus in order to give the stem cells to the sick husband: In both cases there appears to be to be a valid reason in Jewish law to permit an abortion (in order to prevent a sin or to heal the Parkinson's sickness, which is also a positive commandment). What does the Talmud rule? An abortion in the case of the pregnant woman whose husband died is forbidden, even though it will result in sin. The woman may not abort. She should give birth, and then both the father and mother need to bring a sin offering as atonement (even though neither intentionally sinned). Therefore, we see that the Talmud does not permit an abortion, even when there seems to be valid grounds to have one.

A similar case involves a married woman who was a sinning adulteress and is pregnant as a result, but now regrets her past sins (of adultery) and does *Teshuva*-repentance. By giving birth, she will bring an illicit *Mamzer*-bastard into the world, which is also a sin. This sin could be prevented by having an abortion. Is it permitted? Although some authorities, notably Rabbi Jacob Emden (1698-1776),[19] permit an abortion in this case because of the shame and damage to the family, most authorities forbid it for the reasons Rabbi Feinstein stated above. As Rabbi Joseph Babad (1800-1874) explains, the only reason to allow relations between a man and woman is to produce children. If that is not the goal, as in this case, then taking any action associated with the fetus is forbidden.[20] Therefore, in all cases, having an abortion for a good ulterior motive would be forbidden, as in our dilemma.

There is further explanation for forbidding such an abortion. The Talmud says that there are three partners in the creation of every baby: the father, the mother, and God.[21] If all three partners need to give permission in order to abort (even for a very great motive), then even if two of the three partners have agreed, as in our case when the husband and wife agree but God dissents, any abortion would be forbidden, no matter how great the purpose.

Based on everything written above, Rabbi Bakshi-Doron, former Sephardi Chief Rabbi of Israel, brings an almost identical case to our dilemma related specifically to stem cells – i.e., a woman intentionally gets pregnant in order to abort and use the stem cells of the fetus to cure a diseased person. He writes (like Rabbi Babad above) that all births involve danger. If there were no Mitzvah attached to the birth process (i.e., having children), then it would be forbidden in Judaism.[22] Thus, any pregnancy that is not explicitly intended for the purpose of having children is not permitted in Judaism. Therefore he concludes that a pregnancy intentionally formed (by a Jewish couple) in order to terminate the fetus and use it for stem cells is forbidden.

In summation, an abortion performed in order to use the stem cells to save a life (a case that has never actually occurred yet in reality), would be permitted. But to terminate a fetus and use the stem cells to heal a sickness would be forbidden in Jewish law.

THE JEWISH LAW STATUS OF PRE-EMBRYOS NEEDED FOR STEM CELL RESEARCH

Taking stem cells from adults to use for research or to actually inject into human beings to help cure sickness presents absolutely no

---

19. *Responsa Ya'avetz* 1:43

20. *Minchat Chinuch*, Mitzvah 1
21. *Kiddushin* 30b
22. *Techumin*, vol. 15, pp. 311-315

problem from a Jewish perspective. Unfortunately, the most effective stem cells come from fetuses (discussed above) or from pre-embryos. What are pre-embryos?

In vitro fertilization (IVF) involves extracting immature eggs (oocytes) from a woman's ovaries, combining those eggs with nutrients, obtaining sperm from a donor, fertilizing the egg in the laboratory dish, and then transplanting the fertilized ovum into the woman's uterus. If all goes well, the embryo will implant and a pregnancy will ensue and be detectable within ten to fourteen days after the transfer. Over five million IVF babies have been born in this manner. "Pre-embryo" is the term often used for a fertilized ovum that has not yet been transferred into a uterus because the typical IVF procedure extracts multiple oocytes to raise the probability of successful fertilization. These pre-embryos may be cryopreserved (frozen) for future use in another reproductive cycle, donated to other infertile couples, or used for experimentation and research such as stem cells. What is the Jewish status of the pre-embryos or fertilized eggs that are no longer needed by the couple to achieve conception of a fetus? If they are considered human beings since life begins at conception, they may only be used for impregnation. But we saw above that fetuses within the womb are considered a "potential life" but not an actual life. Then what would be the status of pre-embryos even prior to their placement in the womb according to Jewish law?

In another context (speaking about the status of a golem, a human-like creature created by man), Rabbi Tzi Hirsch Ashkenazi (1658-1718) rules that a fetus (and a human being) is only called such if it has entered into the mother's womb.[23] The implication of this ruling from the eighteenth century, long before the invention of in vitro fertilization procedures, is that anything that has not yet entered the mother's womb – i.e., a pre-embryo – is not considered a fetus or a human being in any way, and would not be subject to the prohibition

preventing its destruction and use for anything else besides developing a viable fetus. It would thus be permitted to use stem cells from the pre-embryo. Another argument permitting its use was alluded to above – the many Jewish sources which differentiate between a fetus prior to forty days and one after forty days. Why and how? The Talmud discusses the divorced daughter of a Kohen-Priest who is allowed to once again eat the holy *Terumah*-first grain, which is permitted only to a Kohen and his family. Once the daughter is divorced, she can immediately eat the *Terumah* again. But the Talmud questions this, since she may be pregnant from her divorced husband and thus would be ineligible to eat the *Terumah*.[24] Rabbi Chisda states that until the first forty days it is not considered an actual pregnancy, and the Jewish status of such a fetus is that it is considered "only water." Maimonides explains the reason for this, saying that full formation of the fetus does not take place until forty days.[25] (It is interesting to note that this statement was written over 700 years before today's scientists have determined that babies become fully formed at about six weeks, or forty-two days). If this is the accepted ruling, then any fetus prior to forty days would have a different status, and certainly pre-embryos, which are not yet placed in the womb, would not have the status of a fetus. Thus, they are fully permitted to be used for stem cells.

## THE CONTROVERSIAL STATUS OF THE FETUS BEFORE FORTY DAYS

As noted above, some sources have said that we violate the Shabbat in order to save a fetus in danger. An ancient Jewish law book (from the 800s) rules this way, and makes no distinction between the first forty days of gestation and the rest of the pregnancy.[26] Therefore, since violation of Shabbat is permitted only in order to possibly save a life, logically any

---

23. *Responsa Chacham Tzvi*, 93

24. *Yevamot* 69b
25. Maimonides, *Hilchot Issuri Biah* 10:1
26. *Sefer Halachot Gedolot* 13

fetus that would be saved on Shabbat must be considered a potential life from its very early formation, even the pre-embryonic stage, which would preclude discarding it or using it for stem cell research. A later authority, Rabbeinu Asher, brings both sides of the argument, but seems to agree that we do violate Shabbat to save a fetus.[27] This view also seems to forbid destroying the fetus at any stage, even in the pre-embryo stage.

Since *Shulchan Aruch* rules in the same fashion,[28] as does Rabbi Yechiel Michel Epstein (1829-1908),[29] a noted Jewish law authority from the nineteenth century, and Rabbi Waldenberg from the twentieth century,[30] it seems clear that since saving a fetus (at any stage) is the equivalent of saving a life, destroying a fetus (at any stage) would be the equivalent of destroying a life and thus forbidden, even for pre-embryos. However, a more modern Rabbinic authority, Rabbi Yechiel Yaakov Weinberg (1884-1966), differentiates between the two concepts. He writes that a Jewish woman *is* permitted to have an abortion prior to the fortieth day of gestation, even though the obligation to save the life of a fetus would be in full force.[31] The reason is that you save a fetus for what it will become – a full life – not because of what it is at this moment. Therefore, using pre-embryos for their stem cells, which are certainly considered before the fortieth day, would be completely permitted according to him. Another modern decider of Jewish law also rules that abortion is permitted before the fortieth day, which would allow pre-embryos to be used for stem cell research.[32]

## ACTUAL JEWISH RULINGS TODAY ABOUT THE STATUS OF PRE-EMBRYOS

In our time, there are a number of Rabbis who have ruled specifically about pre-embryos, so that nowadays one need not merely infer from the words of earlier Rabbis. Rabbi Shmuel Wosner was asked if pre-embryos may be discarded completely (and certainly if they can be used for general benefits and stem cell research).[33] Using all the sources noted above, he claims that although Shabbat is violated for an actual fetus, and this in no way contradicts the permissibility of considering a fetus before forty days as "mere water," pre-embryos do not deserve this protection on Shabbat since they were never implanted into the woman. Therefore, he clearly allows the destruction of pre-embryos and their use for stem cells. One of the greatest Halachik decisors of the twentieth and twenty-first centuries, Rabbi Shalom Yosef Elyashiv, was asked if pre-embryos could be inspected for life-threatening diseases before being implanted into the mother. He allowed this and then allowed the diseased pre-embryos to be discarded, unlike the situation of a sick fetus in the womb, which cannot be aborted.[34] Thus, he too agrees that the pre-embryo is not a fetus and he would allow it to be used for stem cell research and other use.

In 2001, when President George H. Bush was trying to decide whether to allow or disallow stem cells from pre-embryos to be used for research in the United States, the Orthodox Jewish community was asked to weigh in with its opinion on this matter from a Jewish law perspective. The Union of Orthodox Jewish Congregations and the Rabbinical Council of America sent an official letter to the President of the United States, which unequivocally

---

27. Rosh on *Yoma* 8:13
28. *Shulchan Aruch, Orach Chaim* 330:5
29. *Aruch HaShulchan, Orach Chaim* 610:1
30. *Responsa Tzitz Eliezer*, 11:43
31. *Responsa Sridei Eish* 3:127
32. *Responsa Torat Chesed, Even Ha'ezer* 42:33

33. *Responsa Shevet HaLevi* 5:47
34. Personal communication, January 9, 2001 with Dr. A. Steinberg, as quoted by Fred Rosner, MD in "*Embryonic Stem Cell Research In Jewish Law*" in the *Journal of Halacha and Contemporary Society*, vol. 43, p. 58, footnote 18

and clearly states that pre-embryos may indeed be used for stem cell research, with certain provisos.[35] Since this research may lead to life-saving technologies, expert Rabbis in Jewish law allow it. Even though Jewish life is the highest Jewish value, the isolated fertilized egg (pre-embryo) does not enjoy the status of a person or a life. Only pre-embryos that were created as a result of the IVF procedure and that would otherwise be discarded can be used. However, it would be forbidden in Jewish law to create a pre-embryo merely for the sake of stem cell research, (which might lead to the dilemma discussed at the beginning of this chapter).

One of the leading authorities on technology and Jewish law, Rabbi Moses David Tendler, testified before the National Advisory Bioethics Advisory Commission. It was there that he stated the position reflected above that prior to forty days and prior to implantation in to the mother's womb, the fetus does not have the status of a human being. However, its destruction for no legitimate reason at all is forbidden, since it violates the prohibition of "wasting human seed" (which echoes the position of his father-in-law, Rabbi Moses Feinstein, discussed above).[36] Later on, however, Rabbi Dr. Tendler, in emphasizing the moral obligation to save human life, clearly permits and urges research using stem cells, which will result in cures and save lives, even if pre-embryos must be used to facilitate such research.[37]

Therefore, it is clear that most if not all of contemporary experts on Jewish law do not treat a pre-embryo as equivalent to a fetus in the first forty days, and would allow it be destroyed or used for stem cell research. It is hoped that the results of such research will yield breakthroughs and technologies that will save many human lives, which is the highest priority in Jewish law.

35. Letter of Orthodox Union about Stem Cell Research, July 6, 2001

36. Testimony of Rabbi Moshe David Tendler to National Bioethics Advisory Commission, *Stem Cell Research and Therapy: A Judeo-Biblical Perspective.* Ethical Issues in Human Stem Cell Research, vol. III: Religious Perspectives, September 1999, p. H-4.

37. Testimony of Rabbi Moshe David Tendler to National Bioethics Advisory Commission, *Stem Cell Research and Therapy: A Judeo-Biblical Perspective* Ethical Issues in Human Stem Cell Research, vol. III: Religious Perspectives, September 1999, p. 4.

# DIFFERENCES BETWEEN MAN AND ANIMAL

AS A SPECIES, THE HUMAN BEING clearly dominates the world and is superior to all animals. But if we try to analyze how and why man is superior to animals, it is not so easily explained.

For example, some might believe that man is physically stronger than all the animals. But that is clearly not so. In the case of mammals, the leopard is much stronger than man, as it can pull seven times the force of an adult human being and preys on animals up to ten times its size. Pound for pound, the rhino beetle is the strongest animal in the world, as it can carry 847 times its body weight (equal to a man lifting a 65 ton tank). Yet no one views these animals as dominant on the planet.

Some people mistakenly believe that the human being is the fastest animal on the planet. But that proposition is also clearly false. The fastest man can run 100 meters in less than 10 seconds. Even if this speed were sustainable, it is 36 kilometers or less than 23 miles per hour. The cheetah can travel over longer distances at 72 miles per hour. The fastest human swimmer can swim at a pace of 5 miles per hour over the course of 100 meters, while the air fish swims at 109 kilometers or 68 miles per hour. Similarly, the human record for a high jumper is less than 9 feet, which is less than one and a half times the size of a human. But a flea can jump 150 times its own height. Clearly, physical strength does not separate man from animal.

Some mammals have brains the size of human beings' brains. Many animals can communicate with each other, just as man communicates with his kind. In fact, the similarities between man and animal seem to be greater than any differences.

What then makes man superior to animals? How *is* the human being similar to animals and how is he different? What does Judaism believe about the similarities and differences between man and animal?

## HOW MAN AND ANIMAL ARE THE SAME

If we look only at the words of Ecclesiastes, then Judaism seems to believe that there are absolutely no differences between man and animal, and that man, indeed, is *not* superior to the animals. The verse says, "For the fate of men and the fate of beasts – they all have the same fate. As one dies, so dies the other, and they all have the same spirit. Man has no superiority over the beast, for all is futile."[1] Thus, man and animal suffer the same fate in life and there *are* no differences between man and animal. If we examine the species of Homo Sapiens and those of other animals, we do find many similarities between them.

We might think that man is unique in that he gives much attention and time to his family. Yet many animals also care about and protect their families (through the mothers, not the fathers). Man might be considered unique in that he builds in the world. But many animals also build structures, such as the beaver, which build dams. Ants build structures that, relative to their size, are many times higher than the tallest skyscrapers in the world.

There are certain basic qualities that are common to man and every animal, actually every living organism. These are spelled out in the Talmud.[2] To survive, every living organism, plant and animal, must ingest nourishment in order to grow and continue to live. Every living creature has this survival instinct. Similarly, all animals and plants, as well as humans, must produce offspring, or the species will perish. Finally, all organisms dispel waste that is not needed by the body. The Midrash adds one more obvious quality that is common between man and all animals: Each organism is

---

1. Ecclesiastes 3:19
2. *Chagiga* 16a

destined to eventually die.[3] In speaking about mammals, one twentieth-century Rabbi describes the comparison between man and animal. He says that the general structure of the bodies of each species is similar.[4] (Today we know that the many of the aspects of the anatomy of a rat is very similar to the anatomy of a human being, and hearts of pigs have been transplanted into humans). Mammals have many or all of the five senses that man has, and they usually have a male and a female, with the female reproducing and caring for the young. One medieval commentary says that the mobility of many animals and human beings is similar.[5] Animals and man usually choose what is (immediately) beneficial to them, and they both run from pain and death. Some animals can be so close in structure and actions to humans that the *Code of Jewish Law* had to rule that ritual slaughter by a monkey is not valid for kosher meat, demonstrating that monkeys are certainly capable of performing ritual slaughter.[6]

Clearly, there are many common denominators between man and animal. And yet, man is clearly different, despite the verse in Ecclesiastes mentioned above. How specifically is man different from animals? In which particular ways is the human special and in which is he the same as animal?

## MAN IS AN AMALGAM OF BOTH ANIMAL AND GODLY COMPONENTS

Unlike the rest of creation, man is created in "the image of God."[7] This makes him qualitatively different from all other creatures. The qualities that make him uniquely human will be discussed below. On the other hand, when the creation of man is described elsewhere,[8] it is clear that man is made from two components: the earth as well as the soul he received

from God. Both components make man what he is – his animal/earth side, along with his godly side. And each side continually struggles for supremacy.

Perhaps this dual quality of man can best be seen in the two stories of Creation in the first two chapters of Genesis. When man's creation is first described, the human being is the last creation of a continuum that begins on the first day of Creation.[9] On the sixth day, all of the animals are created, and man is but the last of these creations. This demonstrates that man is an integral part of nature, part of the animal kingdom and the same as all other creations, as he has much in common with them. But in the next chapter, the Torah speaks about Creation and mentions just one creature that God created – that creation is man.[10] Thus, man seems to be unique, the very purpose of Creation itself, and its central focus. *Both* descriptions are correct, and man struggles daily with each part of his nature.

Two consecutive verses in Psalms seem to point to this duality. The first verse says that man is "nothing," so insignificant when compared to God. The very next verse says that man is a little lower than the angels, and the subsequent verses tell us that God gave man dominion over all the other creatures of the world.[11] Thus, sometimes man is described as just another animal and nothing special. But sometimes he is special, holy, and Godly. The Midrash highlights this duality and explains that when man is worthy, when he uses his "Godly" component, he is called the "first" or the focus of God's creation. If he is unworthy, using his animal side, God will remind him that he is last of the creations, because even the mosquito was created before man, and in that sense is more important than man.[12] Rabbi Moshe Chaim Luzzato describes this struggle that occurs within every human being,

---

3. Midrash, *Beraishit Rabbah* 8:11
4. Chazon Ish, *Emunah U'bitachon* 1:7
5. Ramban commentary on Genesis 1:29
6. *Shulchan Aruch, Yoreh De'ah* 2:11
7. Genesis 1:27
8. Genesis 2:7

9. Genesis 1:24-27
10. Genesis 2:4-8
11. Psalms 8:5-6
12. Midrash, *Vayikra Rabbah* 14:1

between man's body and his animalistic urges, and man's brain with its loftier spiritual urges.[13]

## HOW IS MAN UNIQUE?

Because man was given a spark of godliness (*Tzelem Elokim*), this causes him to be different from all other creations of God, and thus remain unique in several significant ways. We will describe nine of them here.

1. *Only man feels shame and embarrassment.*
   Every animal in the world was born naked and remains naked for its entire life. It never thinks of itself as naked, and is never clothed (unless it is in a circus or the pet of an overzealous owner). An adult man, on the other hand, feels embarrassed about his nakedness, from the time after the first sin of Adam and Eve, when God had to clothe them after they felt embarrassed.[14] Man does not even think of animals as naked, but (most) naked people immediately call attention to themselves and are highly ashamed to be seen in public. In a similar manner, all animals feel no shame in relieving themselves in public or in front of other people. They are not embarrassed by this act. No sane human being would ever relieve himself or herself in public without feeling shame. According to the Midrash, the feeling of shame was given by God to man in order to distinguish him from all other creations.[15]

2. *Man's ability to communicate is unique.* Although animals can often communicate nonverbally and some animals can even be taught sign language, no animal can speak in the manner of man or express complex ideas. When man was created and became a unique "living being" after "God blew into his nostrils the soul of life" this unique living being, according to Onkelos' commentary, was differentiated from animals by his ability to speak.[16] The Talmud and Midrash make note

of this unique aspect of man.[17] Man's ability to speak also includes, by extension, his ability to write, to record his own history, and to analyze himself. No other creature is capable of any of these attributes.

3. *Because man can think and make decisions for himself, he has free will.* Animals are programmed from birth, and thus, their choices are limited. Animals are not capable of moral choices, and thus receive no reward for "doing the right thing" or punishment for acting immorally. Every human being faces many moral choices each day. Even though the Torah "commands" man to commit many moral acts or commandments, at the very end of the Torah, the Torah itself proclaims that man retains the right to reject God and these Commandments, and choose between right and wrong.[18] Of course, he will be rewarded or punished accordingly. This free choice and free will is described by Maimonides in detail.[19] It matters not with what tendencies and personality traits a human is born. He retains the ability to go on a moral or immoral path, regardless of his environment or past history.

4. *Man has dignity.* The verse specifically states that man possesses dignity, while the beasts do not.[20] Dignity, or self-respect or self-esteem, is the flip side of shame. It is such an important concept, that the Talmud states that one is permitted to violate a (negative) Torah injunction in order to maintain a person's dignity.[21] This is more than a suggestion or demonstration of the importance of maintaining a person's dignity. It is codified into Jewish law by Maimonides[22] and *Shulchan Aruch*.[23]

5. *Man seeks meaning.* No animal questions why it exists or its purpose in life. Man constantly looks for meaning and purpose. Just as God is purposeful, man is purposeful as well. When describing man, the Talmud calls him

---

13. *Derech Hashem* 3:4
14. Genesis 2:25, 3:6-7 (Why man did not feel embarrassed before the sin is a discussion beyond the scope of this essay.)
15. *Otzar Hamidrashim*, "Ma'asim" 9
16. Genesis 2:7 with Onkelos commentary

17. *Chagiga* 16a; *Midrash Tanchuma*, Emor 15; *Otzar Hamidrashim*, "Ma'asim" 9
18. Deuteronomy 30:15-19
19. Maimonides, *Hilchot Teshuva* 5:1
20. Psalms 49:21
21. *Berachot* 19a
22. Maimonides, *Hilchot Shabbat* 26:23
23. *Shulchan Aruch, Orach Chaim* 13:3

*Ma'ave*, which according to some translates as "a seeker."[24] Man seeks to go beyond himself and find purpose in his life and actions. An animal, on the other hand, does not question its purpose for existence.

6. *Man is a creator.* Just as God worked during the six days of Creation and then rested on the seventh, so too, man is commanded to do so.[25] This is an acknowledgement that man also has the ability to create, and his creativity could be the essence of the "image of God" that was given to man. More than creating ideas and concepts, man also creates new things in the physical world every day. These creations that man brings to the world make life easier or free up time. Even the most intelligent animal cannot create the most basic of man's creations – fire. (This may be the reason that the first ritual of the week is the lighting of fire for Havdalah after Shabbat. Man does a creative human activity forbidden on Shabbat that is similar to God's first creation on the first day, i.e., the creation of light). In comparing man's qualities to those of angels, in contrast to those of animals, the Midrash says that man can see straight ahead, but animals can only see from the side.[26] Since this is not to be understood in a physical sense (many animals can physically see straight ahead), perhaps the meaning is that man can see things in the natural world and thus create, while animals do not have this quality.

7. *Man can influence the spiritual realms.* According to some opinions, man who is a spiritual being, can impact the higher spiritual worlds.[27] While this mystical idea is not universally accepted, praying to God is something that is unique to man and is commanded by God for man to do.[28] Whether man can "change God's mind" or change himself to influence God's decisions, man certainly has some influence on the spiritual world.

8. *God has Divine Providence for each person. For animals, Divine Providence is only for an entire species.* One of the basic beliefs of Judaism is that since man has a divine spark, God has a relationship with each person, and He knows and cares about each human being. This is codified by Maimonides in his Thirteen Principles, which are found in the prayer book.[29] Maimonides also explains that God has no specific relationship with any animal and is not involved in each instance of interaction between animals. Rather, God insures the survival of the species and cares about each species as a whole, but unlike in the case of man, He is not concerned with any one animal.[30]

9. *There is afterlife for man, but none for animals.* When Judaism speaks about a World to Come, it is a world reserved for human begins alone. (In Judaism, there is no doggie heaven). Since man is spiritual because of the Godliness within him, his soul continues on to the Next World upon his body's demise in this world. Maimonides explains that a person's portion in the World to Come is proportional to the *Mitzvot*, the commandments, a person has done in this world.[31] A purely evil person will lose his entire portion. But animals never get any portion. *Sefer Chasidim* also explains that while a human's soul cannot die, an animal's soul perishes along with its death in this world.[32] This view is echoed by Rashi[33] and the Midrash that states that while an animal that dies goes to a final resting place, people are judged for their actions in this world, and a determination is then made about what will happen with them next.[34]

24. *Bava Kama* 3b
25. Exodus 20:9-10
26. Midrash, *Beraishit Rabbah* 8:11
27. *Nefesh HaChaim*, gate 1:3
28. Deuteronomy 11:13, *Ta'anit* 2a

29. Principle 10 of the Thirteen principles of Maimonides, found in the *siddur* after the morning prayers
30. Maimonides, *Guide for the Perplexed*, Section II, 17
31. Maimonides, *Hilchot Teshuva* 8:1
32. *Sefer Chasidim* 1131
33. Rashi commentary on Ecclesiastes 3:21
34. Midrash, *Eliyahu Zuta* 24:1

A DEEPER UNDERSTANDING OF
THE FUNDAMENTAL DIFFERENCE
BETWEEN MAN AND ANIMAL

In order to understand the fundamental difference between human beings and animals
on a deeper level, Maharal writes we must first
analyze the names of each. In Hebrew, the holy
tongue, words can have far deeper meanings
than simple descriptions.[35] The Hebrew word
for animal, "*Behema,*" can be broken down into
two words, "*Ba*" and "*Ma,*" which translate
"there is something (already) within it." Thus,
the Maharal goes on to explain that an animal
is born completely formed. All of its instincts
and tendencies already exist at birth. It is no
wonder that most animals can move unas-
sisted within a few hours or days after birth.
But man is different, says the Maharal.[36] His
Hebrew name in the Torah is "*Adam,*" which
comes from "*Adama,*" the earth, from which
he was formed. And man, in some ways, is
like the earth. One the day before a rainstorm
(after planting) and the day after the rain, the
earth looks the same. Everything is going on
underneath. Only months later are the results
of the planting, rain, and effort revealed in
something tangible. So it is with man. The human being is born with great potential. How
that potential becomes a reality takes a very
long time. Therefore, it takes many years for
man to develop and leave his parents to be
on his own. It is for this reason that after the
animals were created, God said that "it was
good"[37] because the result of the creation of
animals, completely developed at birth, could
already be seen as good. And while it is true
that He called Creation as a whole "good,"[38]
after man's creation we do not find that God
said "it was good,"[39] because at that point it
was not yet good. The reason for this is that
the creation of man was one of potential, and
man could turn out good or not good. Since

man has the potential to perfect or destroy, his
creation alone cannot signify completion of
purpose.

This fundamental difference between man
and animal also helps answer questions about
some laws of ritual impurity. Touching a dead
animal causes ritual impurity for a person for
one day until nightfall.[40] But an animal can
never make anything else ritually impure as
long as it is alive, as it says "whoever touches
them when they are dead, shall be unclean
until evening" (Leviticus 11:31). But a human
being can sometimes cause ritual impurity
even while alive. For example, childbirth, the
very act of giving life, makes a woman ritually
impure for 7 or 14 days.[41] This is the antithesis
of the law and logic concerning animals. Why
is there a difference between man and animals
in ritual purity and impurity?

When man or animal fulfills its potential
or purpose, it is in consonance with its basic
nature. The life of an animal is such that as long
as it is alive, its purpose is fulfilled. Every minute of its life it is actualizing its potential and
fulfilling its reason for existence. Therefore,
an animal can only become ritually impure
when its purpose no longer exists, i.e., upon
its death. If the animal still has a purpose even
after death, then it does not become ritually
impure when touched. Thus, kosher animals
(those with split hooves that chew their cud)
that are ritually slaughtered and continue to
have a purpose for human beings as food or
a sacrifice, do not become ritually impure.[42]

But why does a woman become impure
at that great moment of giving life, which
seems to be the antithesis of ritual impurity?
Perhaps this question can be answered by understanding another anomaly regarding the
mother giving birth. The Torah tells us that
after her time of impurity, the mother brings
a sin offering and receives atonement.[43] What
possible sin could the mother have committed
in giving birth that requires a sin offering and

---

35. Maharal, *Drush al HaTorah* 11
36. Maharal, *Tiferet Yisrael* 3
37. Genesis 1:25
38. Genesis 1:31
39. Genesis 1:26-27

40. Leviticus 11:24-26, 31, 39
41. Leviticus 12:2-6
42. Maimonides, *Hilchot Avot HaTumot* 1:2
43. Leviticus 12:6-7

atonement? Although there are many answers to this question, Rabbeinu Bechaya reminds us that the first mention of childbirth in the Torah was connected to the first sin, when Eve ate the forbidden fruit and gave it to Adam.[44] Her punishment was a childbirth filled with travail.[45] Thus, every birth reminds us of a time that man did not fulfill his potential, and the sin offering tries to repair that first sin, whose consequences are seen in the case of each childbirth. Since man is not completed at birth and has not yet fulfilled his potential, he can become ritually impure in life and can render others ritually impure as well.

An outstanding contemporary Rabbi has captured how man should be regarded as different from an animal in analyzing one Torah verse.[46] The verse uses three different words for the types of animals to be sacrificed: "*Behema*," an animal, "*Bakar*," cattle, and "*Tzon*" flock. Each of these represents an aspect of life common to both man and animal. "*Behema*," as noted above, represents the animal born with instincts to live and survive. Man, too, has instincts. But if man uses all of his efforts merely to survive, like an animal, this person has not distinguished himself as a human being. "*Bakar*," cattle, is a word that reminds us of "*Boker*," the dawn, when light breaks through the night. *Bakar* has the ability to break through barriers by stampeding

without recognizing boundaries. The human being who acts like *Bakar* and does not respect boundaries – boundaries between pure and impure, between holy and profane – has not risen above the animal. Finally, the *Tzon*, the flock, has a "flock mentality," acting a certain way because every other animal is doing so, without any individuality. The human who constantly gives in to peer pressure and does not think for himself or herself has not risen above the animal either.[47]

Ultimately, what makes man unique and distinguished from animals comes down to the human soul and brain, and how he uses both. The rest of his body is not qualitatively different than the body of an animal. The Jerusalem Talmud has an interesting discussion about a creature that is half man and half animal, and tries to analyze whether this creature is to be considered human or animal according to Jewish law. In the final analysis, the Talmud rules that we go after the head (containing the brain and soul). If the head is that of a man, even if the rest of the body is an animal, then we rule that this creature is a human. Conversely, if the creature's head is that of an animal, even if his body is completely human, even if it can read the Torah (!), we rule that it is an animal.[48] Ultimately, it is the brain and the soul, contained the head, that is the key to the difference between man and animal.

---

44. Rabbeinu Bechaya commentary on Leviticus 12:7
45. Genesis 3:16
46. Leviticus 1:2

47. Rabbi Lord Jonathan Sacks, former Chief Rabbi of England, *Covenant and Conversation, Vayikra* 5771
48. Jerusalem Talmud, *Nidah* 10a

# DOCTORS AND VISITING THE SICK – THE JEWISH VIEW

As the life span of human beings has generally been dramatically increasing in the twentieth and twenty-first centuries, most people tend to suffer more illnesses over a lifetime than their ancestors did in previous generations. In addition, whereas in generations past most bedridden people were confined to the home, where visits by friends and community members were a common occurrence, today almost all seriously ill people are sent to a hospital. Visiting someone in the hospital is much more daunting, uncomfortable, and inconvenient than visiting a sick person in his or her home. How do these realties affect the Mitzvah-commandment to visit the sick? Additionally, in the age of new medical technology and breakthroughs, as well as revised health care attitudes and health maintenance organizations (HMOs), how does Judaism view the role of the doctor in the current century? This chapter will show that the myriad of sources from Jewish tradition, some of which are thousands of years old, addressing these and other questions facing society today.

## THE PHILOSOPHICAL ISSUE: WHY ARE DOCTORS ALLOWED TO HEAL?

Prior to discussing the commandment of visiting the sick, it is first important to investigate those who heal the sick – doctors – from a Jewish perspective. This important issue has been analyzed elsewhere in this volume (see the chapter "Alternative Medicine,"), but here we will expand this discussion in the specific context of examining the doctor's role in society from a Jewish perspective. There is an essential existential dilemma: If Jews believe that events and many experiences in their lives come directly from God (including sickness), then what right does man have to interfere with the desires of God (for a person to suffer through sickness) and take away that malady

and pain? It is for this reason that many religions actually forbid physicians from treating the ill (Christian Scientists, for example). The Rabbis discuss this issue and marshal sources on both sides of this moral question. On the one hand, it is very clear in Jewish thought that sickness comes directly from God, often as a reaction to immoral actions by man. That is why God promises a life of health without sickness for those that follow in God's ways.[1] King David said that God, not doctors, protects an individual from sickness and keeps a person alive,[2] and each weekday traditional Jews pray to God three times a day, as the ultimate doctor and healer, to remove any and all sicknesses.[3] How then are doctors ever allowed to step in and heal according to Jewish thought? Where is the logic?

Since the Torah itself discusses paying doctor bills as part of restitution for damages, the Talmud cites this verse as "permission" for doctors to heal.[4] But how does it work? Since God knows that doctors exist and have the ability to heal in society, when He brings sickness upon an individual, God *wants* that doctor to administer medicine and heal the patient. Therefore, if a person contracts an illness that would normally take three weeks to heal without medicine, and the doctor can eliminate the malady in a week, then God intentionally wanted the person to be ill for a week, not three weeks. In this way, the physician actually partners with God in healing human beings. But even as the doctor prescribes treatment, Jews believe that the healing still comes from God – through the doctor.[5]

This idea, although agreed upon in normative Judaism by most Jewish thinkers, is not necessarily the ideal. Nachmanides, himself

---

1. Exodus 15:26
2. Psalms 41:2-3
3. Eighth blessing of the daily *Shmoneh Esreh*
4. Exodus 21:19, *Berachot* 60a
5. *Chovot Halevavot*, chapter 4

a physician, believes that if people were on a higher spiritual plane, doctors would be unnecessary, as Jews would go only to prophets to heal diseases that came about because of spiritual imperfections. Alas, as people are no longer on that lofty plane today, continues Nachmanides, they are allowed to go to doctors and should go to heal themselves.[6] *Turei Zahav* echoes this approach and stresses that all healing comes from God, but He works through the natural means of doctors.[7] A twentieth century leading Rabbi also stressed this idea, writing that a person may not rely on a miracle from God to be healed without medicine, since almost no one today is on such a high spiritual level. Rather, a Jew should rely on the healing of a doctor in today's non-perfect, immoral world.[8] And yet, based on this idea, not all commentaries believe that all maladies must be treated by doctors. Ibn Ezra, for instance, wrote that this practice of going to doctors rather than directly to God applies only to external illness that can be seen on one's body. Internal illness is still the realm of God, since the inner core of the person remains only in the spiritual realm.[9] In a similar vein, Tosafot writes that man's realm and the ability of doctors to heal are limited to damage to the body that came from another human being. However, illness that came directly from God (and not man) must be healed directly by God and not through a doctor.[10] Rabbi Yitzchak Arama (fifteenth century) states that even while the doctor is administering medicine and treatment, a Jew is obligated to direct his or her thoughts and prayers to God, who is actually doing the healing.[11] Needless to say, the normative Jewish view today is that a Jew turns to a doctor to heal every illness, even though Jewish thought still believes that all healing

ultimately comes from God. After citing these other views, Rabbi Moses Feinstein of the twentieth century clearly states the normative Jewish viewpoint explained above regarding how doctors work in tandem with God: God is fully aware of man's most modern capabilities to heal when He brings the sickness to an individual, and God wants man to use the full range of cutting-edge medical knowledge in order to heal each sickness as quickly as possible.[12]

## OBLIGATION OF A DOCTOR TO HEAL IN JUDAISM

After establishing that a doctor is *allowed* to heal, even though all sickness and healing ultimately comes from God, how do we know that a doctor is *obligated* to do so if he or she has the knowledge required to help sick people? In addition to the verse cited above that doctors' bills must be paid, there is a general obligation upon every Jew to help anyone in trouble. Thus, one verse prohibits a Jews from standing by and doing nothing when someone's life is in danger, and another verse obligates a person to return any lost object that once belonged to someone. (In Judaism this is an obligation, not a mere good deed.[13]) This obligation to help anyone in danger was codified into Jewish law, and it requires a Jew to help anyone in a life-threatening situation or even in ordinary trouble.[14] Thus, doctors would be obligated to heal any sick person based on this general obligation, since they have the knowledge to save people who are in trouble – i.e., those who are ill.

However, the specific obligation of doctors to heal is also mentioned overtly. In his commentary to the Mishna, Maimonides, who was also a physician, writes that a doctor is obligated to heal any sick person if he or she is able to do so, as this is a requirement that falls under the obligation of "returning a lost

---

6. Nachmanides commentary to Leviticus 26:11
7. Taz commentary on *Shulchan Aruch, Yoreh De'ah* 336:1
8. *Responsa Tzitz Eliezer* 11:14, no. 3
9. Ibn Ezra and Rabbeinu Bechaye commentaries to Exodus 21:19
10. Tosafot commentary on *Bava Kama* 85a, s.v. "Shenitnah"
11. Akeidat Yitzchak commentary, *Vayishlach*, gate 26

12. *Responsa Igrot Moshe, Orach Chaim* 3:90
13. Leviticus 19:16, Deuteronomy 22:2
14. *Shulchan Aruch, Choshen Mishpat* 426:1

object," reasoning that a person's health was lost and the doctor returns it to the patient.[15] For this and other reasons, the *Code of Jewish Law* states that once the permission is given to doctors to heal, as discussed above, it is now a Mitzvah, a commandment to do so[16]. Taz explains how *Shulchan Aruch* can say that a doctor has permission to heal and then also say it is an obligation. He reiterates that in the ideal world, doctors would not be unnecessary, but now that they are needed because people are on a lower moral level and cannot rely solely on God, the doctors are obligated to heal, since that is what God currently desires.[17]

However, there are some caveats in Jewish law regarding what kind of doctors are allowed to heal, which practices are allowed, which are forbidden, etc. *Shulchan Aruch* lists some of these.[18] A doctor must be a recognized expert in medicine in order to practice, or what we would today call a licensed practitioner. He or she may not treat a patient if a doctor with more knowledge and experience is present to heal the patient in a more effective way. If a doctor does not yield to the best physician present and decides to heal a very sick patient anyway, that doctor may be guilty of murder if the patient dies. If an unlicensed physician treats someone without obtaining the permission of a Jewish court of Rabbis (which is equivalent to a license), that doctor is obligated to pay all the damages a patient may suffer needlessly as a result of the doctor's negligent treatment. However, if a licensed doctor makes an unintended error, he or she cannot be sued, but God will punish that person. According to Jewish law, a doctor may *not* take an exorbitant fee for services, claiming that it pays in part for all the years of training or for the extensive knowledge that he or she has accumulated. A doctor who says that he or she is

licensed or an expert in a particular field does not need to bring witnesses to attest to this fact, and is believed.[19] If, in an effort to save money, the person who damaged another individual says that he will heal the injured party himself, or that he knows a doctor that will give his services without charge, we do not listen to this person who did the damage, but rather, we bring in a paid doctor to heal the injured party.[20]

One very strange and misunderstood Mishnaic statement is indeed unusual, but understanding it will shed further light on the proper behavior of doctors. The Mishna states that "the best doctors are in hell," or "the best doctors should go to hell."[21] What does this statement signify, especially in light of the previous sources stating that a doctor who saves a life is fulfilling a Torah commandment and the well-known Jewish concept that he who saves a single life it is as if he saved and entire world?[22] Many explanations have been offered for this difficult statement. Rashi and Tosafot Yom Tov explain that this refers to doctors who are so proficient medically that they are unafraid of any sickness and even of death, and believe that their skills can succeed no matter what God desires as the outcome. They also do not treat the poor who are ill.[23] Rabbeinu Nissim believes that this statement refers to doctors who either are not licensed or who have a license but are just not careful in how they deal with patients, and many die due to their negligence.[24] Rabbi Yosef Chaim from Bagdad, who lived in the 1800s, believes that this statement refers to incompetent doctors who are afraid to try powerful, effective medicine in difficult cases, since there is a risk involved with treating aggressively and not properly. All of these explanations describe

---

15. Maimonides commentary to the Mishna *Nedarim* 4:4
16. *Shulchan Aruch, Yoreh De'ah* 336:1
17. Taz commentary on *Shulchan Aruch, Yoreh De'ah* 336:1
18. *Shulchan Aruch, Yoreh De'ah* 336:1-2

19. *Shulchan Aruch, Orach Chaim* 301:26
20. Maimonides, *Hilchot Chovel U'Mazik* 2:18; *Shulchan Aruch, Choshen Mishpat* 420:21
21. Mishna *Kiddushin* 4:14
22. Mishna *Sanhedrin* 4:5
23. Rashi and Tosafot Yom Tov commentaries on *Kiddushin* 4:14
24. Rabbeinu Nissim commentary on *Kiddushin* 4:14

doctors that do not medically behave in a proper "Jewish" manner.[25]

## OBLIGATION IN JUDAISM TO SEEK A DOCTOR FOR HEALING

There is a general prohibition in Jewish law, which is the very last ruling in all of *Shulchan Aruch*, that a Jew is forbidden to place himself or herself in any dangerous situation.[26] This would prohibit any Jew who is sick from neglecting his or her health by not seeking a physician for treatment. The Talmud says that Shabbat may be violated when someone is bitten by a snake and calls upon a doctor from a different city (who has to violate the Shabbat prohibition not to travel outside a city for more than 2,000 cubits).[27] Rabbi Zutra allowed a doctor to treat an infected eye on Shabbat, despite the violation of the laws of Shabbat.[28] Samuel Yarchina was the physician of Rabbi Judah. When Rabbi Judah contracted an eye disease, Samuel tried several remedies to heal this great Jewish community leader, but they all caused Rabbi Judah greater pain. Eventually, Samuel found a cure that was painless.[29] A doctor is integral to and necessary for every Jewish community to exist and thrive. The Talmud lists ten components of communal life that are absolutely necessary before a Talmud scholar is permitted to move there. Among these, including a synagogue, teacher, and public bathroom, is the need for a doctor in each community.[30] Maimonides codifies this Talmudic passage, but changes the order of the ten components and places the doctor first, indicating that this is the most crucial aspect needed for any Jewish community, even before a synagogue and a teacher (since these do not save lives daily).[31]

Maimonides also lists the obligation to stay healthy as part of Jewish law. (See chapter, "Sports," for an expansion of this theme). He says that preventing sickness (as well as having a doctor treat a Jew when sick) is part of Jewish law. A Jew cannot live his or her life in a Jewish manner and worship God properly if he or she is ill.[32] The obligation to heal oneself is so fundamental that if we suspect that someone does not want to be healed, we can even prevent this person from receiving monies dedicated to his healing. Thus, if a person who was injured tells the person who injured him to pay him the doctor's fees directly and then he will heal himself without a doctor, Jewish law says that the person who did the damage need not pay him this money for healing, as we suspect that he may never actually heal himself, which is forbidden.[33] Therefore, we see that it is clearly prohibited for any person who is injured or sick to attempt to heal himself or herself. Similarly, Rabbi Eliezer Waldenberg ruled in the twentieth century that anyone who is injured or ill must go to a doctor to be healed, since not going to a doctor will place the person in real danger.[34]

## PRAYING FOR A SICK INDIVIDUAL – AS A REMEDY

Judaism, as well as most religions, believes in prayer to God as a means of attaining what a person desires, including health. The philosophical question is: Should a person pray for recovery of someone else if a doctor is already treating that person? Perhaps prayer to God shows lack of faith in that doctor. Or perhaps prayer is supposed to be a substitute for a doctor entirely. Where does Judaism stand on prayer for recovery from sickness, when a person is being treated by a doctor at the same time?

Prayer in Judaism, at any time for any reason, is generally acceptable and desired by God. Even in the direst situations, when there

---

25. Ben Yehoyada commentary on *Kiddushin* 4:14
26. *Shulchan Aruch, Choshen Mishpat* 427:10
27. *Yoma* 83b
28. *Avodah Zara* 28b
29. *Bava Metzia* 85b
30. *Sanhedrin* 17b
31. Maimonides, *Hilchot De'ot* 4:23

32. Maimonides, *Hilchot De'ot* 3:3
33. *Shulchan Aruch, Choshen Mishpat* 420:21
34. *Responsa Tzitz Eliezer* 11:14, no. 3

seems to be no way out or no hope, the Talmud says that a person should always pray.[35] Prayer that asks God to heal someone from sickness is something desirable in Judaism and can be found numerous times in the Jewish Bible. King Avimelech, who took Sara to his palace thinking she was Abraham's sister, was afflicted with a disease. God told Avimelech in a dream to return Sara to her husband Abraham, and Abraham will pray for his recovery.[36] King David's child became sick, and then King David prayed for his recovery and also fasted.[37] After the son of the Shunamite woman died, Elisha prayed to God for his revival and was then answered by God.[38] King Hezekiah was so ill that he was at death's doorstep. He prayed for his own recovery, God answered him, and he became well.[39] Thus, prayer to be healed from sickness is something very natural and desirable in Judaism.

Rabbi Yitzchak advises Jews to pray to God when they are healthy as well, that they should not become ill. Why? When a person is ill, he or she is automatically judged and must prove worthy of being returned to health. The passage says that when a person is stricken with any malady, he should feel as if he is on trial for his life and pray to God. Repentance and good deeds will save him. But even if 999 angels argue for this person's punishment, as long as one angel argues for this person's innocence, he will be healed.[40] The Talmud also records an incident whereby Rabbi Chanina ate an onion with a snake inside, and he became so ill that he was about to die. His Rabbinic colleagues prayed for his recovery, saying that they needed him for his Torah learning and teaching, and then he recovered.[41]

Rabbi Elazar said that prayer is more effective and desirable than even good deeds, since Moses, despite his numerous good deeds, was denied entry into the Land of Israel. He could not merit even seeing the Land until he prayed to God and was able to see the entire Land from the top of one mountain.[42] Rabbi Chanina ben Dosa was so gifted at prayer for the sick that after he prayed, he would announce who would recover from the illness and who would die. He explained that if a particular prayer went smoothly, he knew that this person would recover.[43] Maimonides ruled that an integral part of the commandment to visit the sick, to be discussed in detail below, was for the visitor to pray for the recovery of the person who is ill.[44] The Rema in *Code of Jewish Law* further ruled that if someone visited the sick person but did not also pray for this person's recovery, then the visitor has not fulfilled the commandment to visit the sick.[45] It is clear from all of the sources, as well as these rulings in Jewish law, that prayer is an integral part of the process of healing, even if the person is being treated by a doctor, visited by friends, or is involved in any other actions that hasten healing. Prayer also has the power to heal, even while medical treatments are being administered to the person who is ill. That is why Rabbi Moses Feinstein also rules that even today, prayer is a necessary component to healing the sick and fulfilling the commandment to visit them, and that a great Torah scholar who prays for a sick person is more helpful than any other Jew praying for that person's recovery.[46]

## COMMANDMENT TO VISIT THE SICK – THE BASIS AND OBLIGATION

Why visit the sick? Is it a nice thing to do? Visiting the sick is not specifically mentioned as one of the 613 commandments in the Torah, and yet the concept is found in all traditional Jewish sources throughout the ages. What is the basis of the obligation for a Jew to visit the sick? How does a Jew specifically fulfill this

35. *Berachot* 10a
36. Genesis 20:6-7
37. Samuel II 12:15-16
38. Kings II 4:32-33
39. Chronicles II 32:24
40. *Shabbat* 32a
41. *Eiruvin* 29b

42. *Berachot* 32b
43. *Berachot* 34b
44. Maimonides, *Hilchot Avel* 14:6
45. Rema on *Shulchan Aruch, Yoreh De'ah* 335:4
46. Responsa *Igrot Moshe, Yoreh De'ah* 4:51

commandment? What should the procedure and protocol be when visiting a sick person?

At the very beginning of the Torah, it states that the human being was created in the image of God.[47] Since God does not have a physical image, there are many interpretations of what this verse signifies. But it is clear that more than any other creature, man has the ability to imitate God's greatness and uniqueness through his actions. In fact, imitating God by following in His ways seems to be a prime directive of the Torah.[48] Imitating Godly activities complement keeping the Torah's commandments.[49] How does a Jew, who is merely human, follow in God's footsteps when God is purely spiritual? One way to follow God is to imitate the "actions" of God in the Torah, says the Talmud. Thus, just as God visited the sick (visiting Abraham in Genesis 18:1), so too should each Jew visit the sick.[50] Another Talmudic passage derives this commandment from a different verse (Exodus 18:20).[51] The Midrash also uses this same verse to derive this Mitzvah-commandment, but stresses that it is inferred from the words "they shall go" in the verse, indicating that part of the commandment is to walk to visit the sick person.[52] Another Talmudic passage draws this commandment from yet another verse (Numbers 16:29).[53]

The Mishna states that anyone who fulfills the commandment to visit the sick and visits or comforts mourners brings goodness to the world.[54] One notable book listing the commandments bases this obligation of visiting the sick as part of the requirement of each Jew to imitate God's ways.[55] Maimonides lists this obligation of visiting the sick as one of the commandments received by Moses from God that is not written in the Torah, but passed on to the Jewish people orally.[56] But in another one of his works, Maimonides describes the commandment to visit the sick as Rabbinic in origin, under the all-encompassing concept of "Love your neighbor as yourself" and the obligation of each Jew to do kind acts.[57] Since people generally want to be visited when they are ill, Jews should comply with their wishes. *Tur* cites many of the Talmudic sources and verses cited above as the basis of this commandment, but then adds that visiting the sick is a "great Mitzvah," a phrase he only uses four other times in his entire four-set volume of Jewish law.[58] Thus, it is clear that visiting the sick, despite not being mentioned specifically in the Torah as a commandment, is an extremely important obligation for any Jew who wishes to follow Jewish law.

This unique Mitzvah of visiting the sick is so special and so important that the rewards for its fulfillment are numerous. Rav lists the "compensation" for visiting the sick as (1) avoiding *Gehinom* (hell), (2) gaining God's protection from enemies and keeping the person alive, (3) obtaining God's protection from acceding to one's evil inclination, (4) being saved from suffering and, (5) gaining everyone's respect and being honored by all.[59] Rabbi Yehudah bar Shila states (according to the teachings of Rabbi Yochanan) that visiting the sick is one of the six special commandments in Judaism. Moreover, its reward is received in both this world and the next world.[60] This passage was deemed so important that it was placed in the morning prayers recited each day by traditional Jews. Thus, although not a Torah obligation, this commandment is one of the most important in all of Judaism. Why is this so?

---

47. Genesis 1:27
48. Deuteronomy 28:9
49. Deuteronomy 13:5
50. *Sotah* 14a
51. *Bava Metzia* 30b
52. Midrash, *Mechilta* of Rabbi Yishmael, Amalek 2
53. *Nedarim* 39b
54. *Avot DeRabbi Natan* 30:1
55. *Sefer Mitzvot Gedolot*, positive Mitzvah 8

56. Maimonides, *Sefer HaMitzvot*, Shoresh 1:2
57. Maimonides, *Hilchot Avel* 14:1
58. *Tur, Yoreh De'ah* 335
59. *Nedarim* 40a
60. *Shabbat* 127a

## WHY IS IT SO IMPORTANT TO VISIT THE SICK?

What makes this commandment so special, so much more "important" than many others actually written in the Torah? One main reason is that by visiting the patient, the visitor has the ability to help the ill person become healthier! One Talmudic passage ascribes this ability only to the sick person's friends – that by his or her visiting, one sixtieth of the illness will be removed.[61] Another passage also states this power of a visit to a sick person but does not limit it to the ill person's peers. Rather, this applies to anyone who visits the sick. The passage then asks if sixty people were to visit a sick individual, would he or she be completely healed? The answer is that each person can only take away one sixtieth of the person's current sickness. So the tenth person who visits that individual can only remove one sixtieth of the malady that remains after nine have already removed one sixtieth of the malady when they visited.[62] Now we can understand why this commandment is indeed so important in Jewish thought. Just as every doctor has an obligation to heal a person who is ill because this can often extend life, as explained above, *any* person can function in some small way as a doctor with the power to heal by removing some of the sickness of the patient through a visit to him or her. Therefore, while a doctor can heal through his or her special skills, each person can help heal a patient just by paying a visit and exhibiting concern. Thus, it is clear why every Jew has a special obligation to visit patients who are ill and help them get better through the visit. That same Talmudic passage stresses that a person can even visit one hundred times each day.

This statement, that a visitor can remove some of the patient's illness, might have seemed absurd in the past. But recent studies have clearly shown that the mood of a sick person, both good and bad, affects his or her

medical condition.[63] Patients who are depressed take much longer to heal than others with the same symptoms who are optimistic and full of cheer. Therefore, if a visit can cheer up a sick person even a little, that person's medical condition may indeed improve as a result. The famous editor, Norman Cousins, proved this when he became a patient with a life-threatening illness. He reasoned that if he laughed repeatedly, his sickness (and its symptoms) would decrease in severity as his mood improved. Against doctors' orders, he repeatedly watched many comedy movies and his condition indeed improved due to what is now legitimately called "Laugh Therapy." He lived another twenty-eight years after first being diagnosed with his critical illness.

Thus, the Talmudic statement does not seem so far-fetched now. Visiting the sick, especially by friends and loved ones, can indeed help a person to heal faster. In fact, Rabbi Akiva admonished his colleagues for not visiting a student who was ill. After Rabbi Akiva visited with the student, the student felt that Rabbi Akiva's visit caused him to recover from his symptoms. Afterwards, Rabbi Akiva stated that anyone who does not visit a sick person is the equivalent of a murderer. Rav Dimi reinforced this idea when he said that anyone who visits a sick person causes him or her to live longer, and anyone who does not visit causes an ill person to die earlier.[64] The Midrash also states that visiting the sick removes one sixtieth of a person's sickness, while not visiting the sick (when one could have done so) adds another sixtieth to that person's sickness.[65] These are not to be taken as hyperbolic statements, as Maimonides codifies this concept into

---

63. "Impact of Emotional Reactions on Patients' Recovery from Physical Illness: Implications for the Medical Social Workers," J. K. Mojoyinola, Department of Social Work, Faculty of Education, University of Ibadan, Ibadan, Nigeria
*Joint Commission on Quality and Safety*, vol. 9, no. 12 (December 2003). "Addressing Patients' Emotional and Spiritual Needs", Paul Alexander Clark, M.P.A., Maxwell Drain, M.A., Mary P. Malone, M.S., J.D.
64. *Nedarim* 40a
65. *Midrash Socher Tov, Tehillim* 41

---

61. *Bava Metzia* 30b
62. *Nedarim* 39b

normative Jewish law and he indeed equates someone who does not visit the sick with a murderer, similar to a doctor that refuses to treat a sick patient.[66] Therefore, everyone has the potential to be a doctor in part, with regard to his or her ability to somewhat heal an individual who is sick, and the obligation to visit the sick in order to heal them is no less than the obligation of a doctor to heal any individual who is ill.

## JEWISH ETIQUETTE AND JEWISH LAW IN VISITING THE SICK PERSON

Judaism and Jewish law show an amazing sensitivity towards the needs of the sick, as well as the psychology of both the patient and the person trying to fulfill this important commandment to visit the sick individual. These ancient sources will guide the Jew to understanding the proper "etiquette" of a proper Jewish visit to a sick patient.

There is a statement in the Talmud, which is surprisingly repeated by all the Jewish law authorities of Maimonides, *Tur*, and *Shulchan Aruch* almost word for word, that conveys a profound understanding of the sick person and the visitors. It says that it is forbidden to visit a person who is sick with an illness of the stomach, the eye, or the head, because in all of these cases, it is difficult and embarrassing for this patient, who truly does not want visitors to see him or her in these circumstances.[67] This teaches us that the visit is not for the benefit of the visitor or to fulfill a commandment, but it must be for the benefit of the sick person. If the patient is embarrassed by his or her appearance (or by the need to constantly go to the bathroom), visitors will not be welcomed by the patient, and the visit should therefore not be undertaken at all. This also teaches us that the visitor should always behave in a manner that will demonstrate a desire to benefit the patient and make him or her feel

good about the visit, as only this kind of visit will remove one sixtieth of the sickness. In the same vein, therefore, the visitor must be sensitive to other needs of the patient. For example, some patients simply may not want visitors, even if they do not suffer from the maladies mentioned above. In that case, one should not visit. A phone conversation with the patient should always take place prior the visit in order to determine if the patient is up to having visitors or to determine when to visit, since at the time that doctors are making rounds or taking tests, it would be inconvenient to visit. Rabbi Yechiel Michel Epstein summarizes this concept by writing that the essence of this commandment is to be sensitive to the needs of the sick person and do whatever will benefit him or her.[68]

As part of this goal of trying to make a patient feel better psychologically, a visitor should always practice a simple but effective gesture: knocking before entering the hospital room. Every adult is used to some privacy and some control over his or her life. Entering a hospital room takes away much of that person's control. Just as no one would never enter a sick person's home or room without knocking first, so too, a knock at the patient's door in the hospital gives that patient a bit of dignity and control to decide when and if the visitor can enter. This is especially true if the curtain is drawn.

The Talmud says and Maimonides codifies that a sick person should never be told about another sick friend or relative who has died, because this will cause the patient to be very uncomfortable, especially considering his or her condition.[69] This also provides an insight into what kinds of conversations are permitted or forbidden with an individual who is ill. We should never discuss topics that will cause a patient distress, like announcing someone's death. Similarly, criticizing the doctors or the care of the nurses will only diminish the confidence of the patient in the care that he or she

---

66. Maimonides, *Hilchot Avel* 14:4
67. *Nedarim* 41a; Maimonides, *Hilchot Avel* 15:5; *Tur* and *Shulchan Aruch, Yoreh De'ah* 335:8

68. *Aruch HaShulchan, Yoreh De'ah* 335:3
69. *Mo'ed Katan* 26b; Maimonides, *Hilchot Avel* 8:4

is receiving, and should therefore be avoided. Inquiring about the details of the illness may bring some patients distress and should then be avoided, but other patients love to speak about their sickness. A visitor should listen to the patient for cues about what he or she wishes to speak about. Patients generally do not want to hear about others that the visitor knows who had the same illness, or hear a personal description of a different illness that the visitor once suffered from. A joke, story, or anything that will bring a smile to the patient is encouraged. Asking the patient about his or her interests or family usually causes the sick individual to perk up. *Aruch HaShulchan* says that a visitor must be both sensitive and wise in knowing what to speak about and what to avoid.[70]

Maimonides writes and *Shulchan Aruch* codifies that the visitor in a hospital room should never stand over the patient while the patient is in bed.[71] This makes a patient feel uncomfortable, as the visitor is literally and figuratively talking down to the patient while hovering. Rather, the visitor should sit on a chair at eye level with the patient.

Maimonides and *Shulchan Aruch* also list other considerations that are subjective, depending on the individual patient and the particular situation.[72] For example, they rule that a great person, like a great Rabbi or Head of Yeshiva, both of whom are very busy, should take time to visit the sick, even to visit a child who is ill. It is also appropriate for a person to visit several times a day if that will bring cheer to the sick person. If it is clear that the patient has an illness that will continue for an extensive period, one should generally not visit during the first three days. If a sick person takes a turn for the worse and may be near death, the visitor should not delay and should

see the patient immediately. Finally, one should not visit a patient early in the morning, during the first three hours of the day, as the doctors are usually busy with the patient during this time. (It seems that this practice has not changed much since the Middle Ages.)

Judaism is sensitive to the general needs of the entire community. Thus, part of the fulfillment of this commandment is a Mitzvah to visit non Jews as well.[73] There are many sick people in every hospital who have no family and few friends, or people who are often afraid to visit. Therefore, a Jew should visit other patients in the hospital, both Jews and non-Jews, whom they do not even know, as this act will often cheer up these individuals even with an unannounced visit. (Of course, if a person sees that a visit from a stranger makes the patient uncomfortable, then he or she should leave quickly and tactfully.)

Although Maimonides mentions it, *Shulchan Aruch* expands upon the specifics of the prayers that are a necessary part of the fulfillment of the command to visit the sick. He writes that the visitor (if he or she knows both Hebrew and English) can pray in any language to God while he or she is in front of the sick person, but should pray only in Hebrew after the visit on behalf of the patient.[74] Public prayer for the sick in the synagogue is appropriate, even on Shabbat, and most synagogues today publicly recite a prayer for the sick whenever the Torah is read while it is removed from the ark for Torah reading. The reason for this is that even if the individual sick person is not worthy, by praying for all of the sick people in the community and the Jewish nation, there is a better chance that God will bring healing to this individual as well. So too, in the merit of the Torah, the prayers might be answered more positively and more quickly.

70. *Aruch HaShulchan, Yoreh De'ah* 335:4
71. Maimonides, *Hilchot Avel* 14:6; *Shulchan Aruch, Yoreh De'ah* 335:3
72. Maimonides, *Hilchot Avel* 14:4-5; *Shulchan Aruch, Yoreh De'ah* 335:1, 2, 4

73. Maimonides, *Hilchot Avel* 8:4, 14:12; *Shulchan Aruch, Yoreh De'ah* 335:9
74. *Shulchan Aruch, Yoreh De'ah* 335:5-6

## MODERN ISSUES REGARDING VISITING THE SICK

Until two hundred years ago in most Jewish communities, nearly all of one's friends and extended family lived in the same town, with all homes within walking distance of each other. Visiting a sick person, who was usually in bed at home and not in a hospital, was a relatively simple matter, and everyone who wished to do so could fulfill this Mitzvah rather easily. Today, however, a sick friend often stays in a hospital that is very far away. Sometimes close friends live in a different city or country, as do many family members. For such people, if an actual visit to them is extremely difficult or impractical, can this important commandment of visiting the sick be fulfilled by other communication, and not only by an in-person visit?

Rabbi Moses Feinstein was asked about fulfilling this commandment by telephone.[75] He answered that since the entire commandment involves more than simply speaking to the sick individual, one cannot really perform this commandment via the telephone. If there is absolutely no alternative, then of course a telephone conversation is better than no communication at all with the sick person, but the commandment has not been satisfied completely. He mentions that when Moses first heard that the people worshipped the Golden Calf, he did not smash the first tablets until he actually *saw* the people worshipping. So too, there is something visceral about being in the same room with the sick person and seeing him or her that cannot be duplicated by telephone or mere verbal communication. Rabbi Ovadiah Yosef gives a similar response, reminding us that the original verse from which this commandment was learned is "they will go." It does not say, "they will talk," since actually going to the person is a key component of the commandment, and one cannot compare seeing to hearing.[76] Furthermore, a person is only fully motivated to pray for a sick individual after he or she actually sees the patient. Thus, speaking on the telephone is not sufficient. Rabbi Mordechai Breisch adds that, for the same reason, sending a letter or even sending someone else as an emissary to the sick person to take one's place is not sufficient to fulfill this commandment. Since the presence of God (*Shechina*) is above the sick person's head, that cannot be experienced by a call, email, or a letter.[77] All of these responses are based on the Talmudic passage that implies that asking about someone's health in the street (without a visit) is not the same as actually visiting the individual who is ill, and one has not fulfilled the commandment by merely asking about the sick person.[78]

In a very unusual and prescient responsum in 1956, Rabbi Yitzchak Weiss discusses not only visiting the sick via telephone, but also the possibility of doing this Mitzvah via a television screen through which people can speak to each other. At that time, interactive television, Skype and Face Time was not even a dream, and neither was video conferencing. Yet Rabbi Weiss spoke about this question nonetheless.[79] Regarding the telephone, Rabbi Weiss says that if a visitor sees the patient the first time in person, then it is perfectly legitimate after that to fulfill the commandment subsequently by telephone, even up to one hundred times, as it says in the Talmud. Regarding television, if the two people see each other and converse, Rabbi Weiss seems to say that this is close enough to actually visiting the person, and thus one could fulfill this commandment through video conferencing.

---

75. *Responsa Igrot Moshe, Yoreh De'ah* 1:223

76. *Responsa Yechave Da'at* 3:83
77. *Responsa Chelkat Yaakov, Yoreh De'ah* 2:188
78. *Nedarim* 38b-39a
79. *Responsa Minchat Yitzchak* 2:84, no. 10

# DOWNLOADING FILMS AND SONGS, COPYING SOFTWARE: COPYRIGHT IN JUDAISM

**B**EFORE THE DEBUT OF MANY HOL-lywood films in movie theaters, a trailer is shown of an ordinary person going into a store and stealing an item. The viewer is asked: "You would not do this," i.e., steal an item or a movie from a store, "then why do this?" The trailer then shows someone down-loading a film from the Internet. This is consid-ered theft in American law and a legal prohibi-tion in most countries, yet millions of people download songs and films for free from the In-ternet and think nothing of it. Many people do not consider it a crime to copy software rather than purchase it. But companies lose tens of billions of dollars each year as a result of these actions and are very angry about their loss of revenue. What does Jewish law say about this issue, in which many normally law-abiding citizens are involved? Is it somehow all right because "everyone is doing it"? Is intellectual property considered the same as actual prop-erty in Judaism?

## OWNERSHIP IN JUDAISM

Scripture tells us that the world and everything in it belongs to God.[1] Therefore, in a literal sense, no human can own anything in the world. At the very moment that He designates the Jewish people for a special relationship with Him, God tells us that the entire world belongs to Him.[2] One of the reasons, says God, that land in a Jewish society in Israel cannot be sold in perpetuity is that the land belongs to God.[3] In fact, there is no Hebrew verb at all for ownership, indicating that ownership in the world is not a Jewish concept. There-fore, the sentence "I own this item" cannot

be translated into Hebrew. And yet, there is a mandate not to steal from your neighbor's goods.[4] How can there be a concept of stealing if God owns everything?

The Scripture does indeed say that God gives worldly goods to us, but we must real-ize that all comes from Him.[5] Thus, while it is clear that although God owns everything in the ultimate sense, He gives us the use of things in our possession. Though we do not have full ownership of worldly goods since they are God's, we do have full "rights" and we can buy things in a symbolic action called *Kinyan* (i.e., picking up an item), when we are given something by another "owner" or when we pay money to acquire it. This gives us the right to use an item in any way we choose (as long as we do not harm anyone with it), including the right to give it away, sell it, and even destroy it if there is a valid reason. Thus, Jews have certain rights over physical goods. The Mishna says that Jews should give every-thing to God since everything really belongs to Him.[6] What does that signify? One com-mentary explains that those items that Jews have rights over, including their bodies, should be used for God's sake and benefit, like giving *Tzedaka* (charity) for example, since in the ul-timate sense everything does belong to God.[7] However, this also clearly implies that there are things that are for human beings to use. This refers to all physical items in the world. But what about ideas? Can these belong to a person as well? Specifically, can Torah ideas be said to belong to a person? What about things we create that did not exist before? Do human beings have "rights" to these?

---

1. Psalms 24:1
2. Exodus 19:5
3. Leviticus 25:23

4. Leviticus 19:11
5. Chronicles I 29:14
6. Mishna *Avot* 3:7
7. Rabbeinu Ovadia Bartenura commentary on Mishna *Avot* 3:7

## MAN CREATING NEW THINGS

There is a general rule in Jewish life to try to imitate God and God's ways in the Torah, since He is the symbol of perfection.[8] This usually refers to the values that God represents and demonstrates in the Torah, like generosity and helping other human beings. But if we take this concept one step further, if we as human beings are indeed to imitate God and everything about Him, then the very first thing that God did in the Torah was to create the world.[9] One of God's characteristics that we say every day in prayer is that God is the Creator who continues to create in the world (present tense).[10] Thus, just as we are obligated to say that "He helps the downtrodden, so should we," this mandate also includes man's obligation to create, just as God created. (See the chapter on "Cloning" for a discussion in depth of this concept.)

This idea of man's obligation to create in the world is not just a good idea or an extrapolation. The word in the Torah usually mistranslated as "work" is "*Melacha*" (i.e., the activities that are forbidden on Shabbat). But this word is used in only three contexts in the entire Torah – regarding Creation by God, what is forbidden for man to do on Shabbat, and the building of the *Mishkan*, the Tabernacle.[11] Thus, what God did to create the world is *Melacha*. But right before the Torah forbids Jews to do *Melacha* on Shabbat, it says that man *must* do *Melacha* during the other six days.[12] (According to many commentaries, this is a command rather than only a dispensation allowing man to do this kind of activity.) If so, man is *commanded* to create, to invent, and to come up with new ideas and new inventions in the world, just like God.

Although there are many explanations regarding the meaning of the expression that man is created in God's image,[13] it certainly cannot refer to man's physical characteristics, as God has no physical features. According to come commentaries, this unique quality signifies man's ability to create, just as God creates.[14] That is why observant Jews create fire as the very first action during the week, in the Havdalah service following Shabbat. Just as God created light as His first creation on the first day of the week,[15] man imitates God by creating fire. More than any other human act, making a fire demonstrates man's creativity, as no animal or other creature in the world can create a fire. Only man is obligated to create in this world. It is clear that the physical objects he creates belong exclusively to him and he has rights over them. However, can he likewise claim ownership of the new ideas he creates, specifically new Torah ideas, and can they be protected like physical creations are, with the prohibition of stealing applying to these as well?

There is one passage in the Mishna that seems to debate this very idea. In the Temple, there were families who had the unique ability to perform certain services and activities more expertly than anyone else.[16] The Garmu family, for example, knew how to make the *Lechem HaPanim*, the bread for display, better than anyone else, with a secret recipe. Similarly, only the Avtinas family could properly make the incense used in the Temple service. Hygros had the unique ability to compose music, and the Ben Kamtzar family had a unique writing ability for the Temple service. When the Rabbis wanted these families to reveal their secret formulas, their "copyrighted" unique ideas, each family refused. The Talmud seems to say that the Rabbis were angry with these families for not sharing their creations. They even used the verse quoted above, that everything belongs to God, so that they would share.[17] (This verse may also be referring to

---

8. *Sotah* 14a
9. Genesis 1:1
10. Daily morning prayer, beginning of the *Shema* blessings
11. Genesis 2:2, Exodus 20:10, Exodus 36:4-5
12. Exodus 20:9
13. Genesis 1:27
14. *Nefesh HaChaim* 1:3
15. Genesis 1:3-5
16. Mishna *Yoma* 3:11
17. *Yoma* 38a

the fact that all of their creations were used in the service of God.) Based on this Talmudic passage, we may surmise that the Rabbis expected people to share their "copyrighted" ideas and creations, while the creators did not wish to. At the end of the passage, all of the families explained that the reason they were reluctant to share their knowledge was that they feared their recipes would fall into the wrong hands and be used for idol worship. This is a proper and noble reason not to want to share. Thus, there is no conclusive proof from these incidents in the Talmud whether original ideas, "intellectual property," can be protected in Judaism, like actual property is protected, or not.

## TORAH IDEAS IN JUDAISM – CAN WE USE THOSE OF OTHERS?

When Jeremiah reminds us not to become haughty in our personal achievements because all of our success comes from God, he includes three spheres of success in life: wisdom, strength, and wealth.[18] Thus, it seems that just as wealth is not ultimately ours, our wisdom or ideas also do not belong to us. On the other hand, just as it would be forbidden to steal someone's wealth, it should be forbidden to steal someone's ideas. And yet, several passages in the Talmud seem to say the opposite.

If a Jew wishes to take someone else's Torah idea and use it by quoting it to others, the Mishna seems to permit this, as long as he or she gives full credit to the originator of the idea.[19] This is based on the story of Purim, when Esther told King Achashverosh about the plot to kill him, and attributed this knowledge to Mordechai and not to herself.[20] It seems then that as long as a person does not misrepresent the ideas as his own, he or she can freely take someone else's ideas and use them. This is not just a wise practice or good character concept suggested by the *Ethics of the Fathers*, but it is brought down in Jewish

law that whoever uses someone else's ideas without attribution is guilty of sin and can be punished for this infraction.[21] The Tosefta calls someone who uses another's ideas as his own a thief, and though he or she may merit the study of Torah as a result, that person still remains a thief.[22]

These ideas are a very worthy discussion about character and integrity in general. However, if a person stands to lose financially because others took his Torah ideas, does that make a difference?

## FINANCIAL RISK IN SPREADING TORAH IDEAS

The original historical precedent of stealing someone's Torah ideas did not involve the actual ideas of the person himself, but the cost of publishing those ideas. Maimonides had written his *Mishne Torah*, a fourteen-volume book of Jewish law, 300 years before Rabbi Meir ben Isaac Katzenellenbogen, chief Rabbi of Padua, Italy, wished to publish this work on the newly invented printing press. Though the work did not now belong to anyone, it was very expensive to set up the typeset and publish the books. As a result, the books were published in partnership with the Italian publisher Eluzi Bragadin in 1550. This enraged the very wealthy Marc Antonio Giustiniani who at the time was the exclusive printer of Hebrew books in Venice. (He had forced out another printer and could not come to terms with Rabbi Katzenellenbogen about this work.) In order to bankrupt Rabbi Katzenellenbogen and Bragadin, Giustiniani published the same *Mishne Torah* and charged a much cheaper price. This prompted Rabbi Katzenellenbogen to contact Rabbi Moshe Isserles, the leading Rabbi of Jewish law at the time, and ask for a ruling about whether the rival, non-Jewish printer could legally print the same work right after he had done so. Rabbi Isserles, known as Rema, issued a responsum forbidding any

---

18. Jeremiah 9:22-23
19. Mishna *Avot* 6:6
20. Esther 2:22

21. *Magen Avraham, Orach Chaim* 156:2
22. Tosefta *Bava Kama* 7:3

Jew from buying the *Mishne Torah* printed by Giustiniani.[23]

Therefore, we can conclude that when financial loss is involved for taking someone else's ideas, there is a responsibility not to duplicate the work of the first person to publish these ideas. It became standard practice after this incident to obtain the *Haskama*, or approbation, of a noted Rabbi when publishing any work with Torah ideas, which would limit the time anyone else could print the same work, either for ten or twenty-five years (not like today's *Haskama* for a book, which shows that the Rabbi approves of the content). In addition, it was understood that if all the books in the original printing were sold, then the ban to publish this book would be lifted as well, even if less than ten years had elapsed, since the publisher undoubtedly made a profit and recouped all of his outlay and risk. All traditional Jews respected the *Haskama* of the Rabbis in the books, and would refrain from publishing the same book printed by a rival publisher. In effect, it limited other publishers from even attempting to publish the same volumes.

However, this issue deals only with the financial risk of publishers and the ideas and works of Rabbis who lived long ago. What about the new books that contemporary Rabbis print? Would they need a Rabbi to issue a ban to prevent others from taking their ideas, or would these ideas be forbidden on their own as theft?

## IS INTELLECTUAL PROPERTY EQUIVALENT TO ACTUAL PROPERTY IN JUDAISM?

The basic and main question is this: Is intellectual property considered equivalent to physical property or not? While the Western world has debated this issue for many years, what is the Jewish view? Is stealing someone's ideas, creative thoughts, or published book considered actual theft, or is it somehow different? Is there a difference between using someone's

Torah ideas and using someone's creation that is not a Torah lesson? Since there is a general commandment to learn and spread Torah, and there is a tradition that everything "new" that is learned today in Torah is actually "old" and was already shown and given to Moses,[24] perhaps there is a different ruling for Torah ideas that are copied, as opposed to other creative ideas and books? What do the sources tell us?

This topic has been discussed at length and two distinct views have emerged. The majority view of Rabbinical authorities is that intellectual property is considered like all other property. Thus, its theft is the equivalent to stealing any other physical property. Another (minority view) is that intellectual property does not belong to the individual who created it. However, copying it is still forbidden for a variety of reasons, and Jewish laws protect unfair competition, which will be explained below. The implications of each view and the differences between these views are manifold.

## THE MAJORITY OPINION

According to most decisors of Jewish law, intellectual property is considered actual property. Thus, all the laws prohibiting stealing also apply to taking copyrighted material and copying or downloading it without permission from or payment to the owner. This would include the copying of software, MP3 songs, and films from the Internet. Rabbi Yaakov Cohen, a modern writer, summarized all of the opinions in his 1999 book *Emek Hamishpat*. In it, Rabbi Cohen points out that the following great Rabbis categorized using any copyrighted material (or material that says "All rights reserved") without permission, as stealing: Maharam Schick, Naftali Tzvi Yehuda Berlin, Malbim, Sdei Chemed, Rabbi Shimon Shkop, and Chofetz Chaim. He clearly says that although there are four different categories and definitions of ownership (based on different opinions), all agree that from the perspective of Jewish law, every person has

---

23. *Responsa of the Rema, 10*

24. *Megillah 19b, Kol Eliyahu on Agadot Shas*

full rights and ownership on anything he or she creates.[25]

One Jewish law decisor from the nineteenth century, Rabbi Shaul Yosef Nathanson (1810-1875) writes that the rights of an author who wrote a book never cease, even if a Rabbi wrote that the *Haskama* to last only for twenty-five years. He goes on to show other reasons that copying someone else's work is actual stealing.[26]

But now we have to define what is considered classical stealing in Jewish law. If the one a person is copying from does not even know his or her efforts are being copied, is it still forbidden? What if many others are also doing it and no one is getting caught? If the owner will not lose a sale from copying, would it then be permitted?

## DEFINING STEALING AND ITS CONSEQUENCES IN JUDAISM

How can we define stealing in Judaism? At its most basic level, we should define stealing in Judaism as taking something that belongs to someone else if you know the owner will mind. If you know that the owner will not mind that you take it (like a pen from a hotel room, for example, or a one-dollar bill or anything without an identifiable sign in the middle of a crowd), then it would not be considered stealing. What if you are not sure if the owner will mind or not? It remains prohibited unless the finder or taker is sure the owner will not mind.

What if the owner is not even aware of the theft? The Talmud discusses the case in which the theft takes place before the owner finds out: would it be considered "*Ye'ush*," "giving up" on the item (or not minding), since when he later finds out he will not mind about its loss and/or he will give up on its recovery? The Talmud has two conflicting opinions in this case,[27] but both Maimonides[28] and *Biur*

*Halacha*[29] rule that it is still forbidden because an owner does not "give up" on his possessions, even when he is unaware of theft. In any case, when there is a copyright sign or an item says "All Rights Reserved," this is a clear indication that the owner does mind about protecting his ownership. If you ask any Hollywood studio president or CEO of a software company whether or not they mind if their product is copied, they would say that they certainly do mind. Therefore, copying goes against their will and is considered stealing.

The value of an item does not affect the question of stealing because taking even one penny's worth of something is still regarded as stealing in the eyes of Judaism. Even if a person merely wants to use the software or film for a short time and then "gave it back" it is still forbidden. The prohibition even includes making a commitment to yourself that you will pay for it later because when you take it without paying for an object now, it is still stealing from a Jewish perspective.[30]

How serious is the sin of stealing (or robbery) in Judaism? Much more serious than one would imagine. The *Tur* says that robbery is tantamount to murder![31] One of the *Tur's* commentaries discusses whether the thief is guilty of killing himself or killing the owner of the property he stole![32] The Talmud states that the people who lived in Noah's time were guilty of "every sin in the book," but were only punished to be killed through the flood when they stole and robbed.[33] Proverbs asserts that greedy people (who act on that feeling) take away their own lives.[34] One commentary (based on a discussion of this verse in the Talmud) explains the verse and says that God actually takes away the thief's life twice: once for the emotional and other type of pain he or she causes the owner for the loss, and once for denying God (because a person who believes

25. *Emek HaMishpat*, chapter 4
26. *Responsa Sho'el U'maishiv* 1:40
27. *Bava Metzia* 21b
28. Maimonides, *Hilchot Gezaila VeAvaida* 14:5

29. *Biur Halacha* on *Shulchan Aruch, Orach Chaim* 769
30. Maimonides, *Hilchot Genaiva* 1:1-3
31. *Tur, Choshen Mishpat* 359:1
32. Sm"a commentary on *Tur, Choshen Mishpat* 359:9
33. *Sanhedrin* 120a
34. Proverbs 1:19

in a God that is just and that distributes His wealth fairly would not be tempted to steal from others).[35] While Judaism differentiates philosophically between a thief (who takes at night without the owner knowing) and a robber (who takes something at gunpoint), the ultimate sin and prohibition is the same for both acts.[36] Buying or taking from a thief is also prohibited.[37] Therefore, in Judaism, copying from a pirated copy or a copy of a copy is just as forbidden as taking the original.

## THE MINORITY OPINION

There are a few Rabbis who believed that an idea *cannot* be owned, and thus copying intellectual property or books is not stealing per se. Nevertheless, they forbade the practice of copying for different reasons in Jewish law. A main proponent of this view of copyright law in the nineteenth century was Chatam Sofer, who spells out different reasons to forbid copying books and someone's original text, but does not consider this actual theft.[38] Rabbi Banet, a contemporary of Chatam Sofer who argued with him about some of the details of this issue, also says that copying material is forbidden, but not because of theft. He says that many non-observant Jews do not care that the Rabbis banned copying a book for ten or twenty-five years, and since many of the publishers are not Jewish, they also do not care.[39]

If it is not considered stealing, then why is copying forbidden? The first reason given is that if secular law prohibits copying, then Jewish law must follow secular law (in areas that do not conflict with Jewish law). This principle is discussed many times in the sources and is brought down as Jewish law in numerous places by *Shulchan Aruch*.[40] Thus,

if a country has laws against copyrighting and downloading, which most countries today do, this is be prohibited by Jewish law as well (even in Israel, where this principle is not always applied, but in this case almost all Rabbis agree it does apply).

The second reason is the prohibition of encroaching on someone else's business, which is forbidden in Judaism, based on a Torah verse.[41] Chatam Sofer specifically says that anyone who will cause others to lose money as a result of copyright infringement and copying anything owned by someone else is guilty of this sin.[42] (It is estimated that the recording and film industries lose billions of dollars a year because people download songs and films for free instead of paying for them.) The third reason is what is called in legal terms "accepted practice law." Whenever there is a legitimate agreement among the people of a city or in a particular industry, this is regarded as binding in Jewish law.[43] Since copyright infringement is agreed upon by most law-enforcing countries, this agreement, even if not official law, is binding in Jewish law.

A fourth and novel reason to forbid copyright infringement is put forth by a contemporary Israeli Rabbi of note, Rabbi Zalman Nechemia Goldberg.[44] The Talmud already establishes that Rabbi Meir said that if during the sale, an owner makes a stipulation and the buyer agrees, the buyer may not violate that part of the agreement even after the sale.[45] This idea has also been incorporated into Jewish law. Thus, if a seller of a house stipulates that he wants to retain a small portion of a home in the agreement, it is his right to do so.[46] And even if something is not stipulated in the agreement, but it is logical from the terms of the sale, then that (non-written) stipulation is also valid.[47]

35. Rabbeinu Yonah commentary on Proverbs 1:19 and *Bava Kama* 119a
36. Maimonides, *Hilchot Gezaila* 1:1-3
37. Maimonides, *Hilchot Gezaila* 5:1-2
38. *Responsa of Chatam Sofer*, Section 5, *Choshen Mishpat* 41
39. *Responsa Parshat Mordechai, Choshen Mishpat* 7-8
40. *Shulchan Aruch, Orach Chaim* 55:11, *Choshen Mishpat* 369:6; Rema, *Yoreh De'ah* 165:1, *Choshen*

*Mishpat* 207:115, 236:9
41. *Deuteronomy* 19:14
42. *Responsa of Chatam Sofer*, Section 5, *Choshen Mishpat* 79
43. *Rema, Shulchan Aruch, Choshen Mishpat* 37:22
44. *Techumin*, vol. 7, pp. 369-381
45. *Bava Metzia* 78a
46. *Shulchan Aruch, Choshen Mishpat* 214:8
47. *Shulchan Aruch, Choshen Mishpat* 212:3

Therefore, says Rabbi Goldberg, every time a movie is sold on a disc or a song is sold on a computer, there is an unwritten stipulation by the owner: "You have bought the rights to play this song or watch this film, but not the rights to make a copy." This is a valid concept in Jewish law. The reasons to prohibit copying in this minority opinion are summarized by a contemporary Halacha (Jewish law) decisor, Rabbi Nachum Menashe Weisfish.[48]

The main contemporary proponents of this minority view today are Rabbi Shlomo Zalman Auerbach, Chazon Ish, and Rabbi Vozner.[49] Even though according to both the majority and minority opinions it is forbidden to copy copyrighted material, there are some major differences between the two. For example, according to the majority opinion, the prohibition is Biblical, while according to the minority opinion the prohibition is "only" Rabbinic. (Most prohibitions in Jewish law today are Rabbinic.) Another difference is that if copying or downloading copyrighted material is actually stealing, then the ownership is inherited by the children of the creator. If it is only prohibited for the other reasons, it is not forbidden after the death of the owners (not necessarily the songwriters, but the company that owns the song). In any event, there is an overall, all-encompassing verse and mandate in Judaism to do the right thing in every situation.[50] Even if it is technically permitted to copy in certain situations, it should not be done because it causes the owner anguish.

## IS COPYING TORAH CLASSES OR BOOKS DIFFERENT?

It is clear from the above discussion that copyrighted material may not be copied without the author's permission. But if this prohibition will infringe, limit, or prevent Torah learning,

is it then permitted to make copies of Torah classes, Torah books, etc.?

Already in early medieval times, Rabbi Alfasi was asked: if a student who stole a friend's notes of a Torah class may copy them (by hand) as a condition before returning them (this was before the printing press had been invented)? Rabbi Alfasi answered that copying is forbidden because it is stealing, and therefore is classified as a Mitzvah (Torah learning) that came through a sin (which is forbidden).[51] Rema ruled that it is forbidden to even read someone else's Jewish books without permission, and certainly to copy them. However, he adds that a Torah scholar who does not have this particular book may indeed read and even copy part of the book (for his Torah needs) if the owner is not around to be asked permission.[52] This is because it is assumed that anyone would gladly lend a book to a Torah scholar for his personal use. Since Rabbi Alfasi lived in the 1100s, when books and written manuscripts of many books were very difficult to find, the Rema, who lived in the sixteenth century, adds that if a wealthy individual possesses books that are not available anywhere else in the city, the Jewish court can force this man to make them available for Torah learning, as long as the owner is compensated for any depreciation of the value of the books when they are repeatedly used.

Beit Yitzchak was asked a question that relates to the various opinions discussed above. If a person finds an original Torah manuscript and copies it during the lifetime of the author, then wishes to print it after the author dies, can the children of the author prevent its publishing or not? Beit Yitzchak holds like the majority opinion – namely, it would be forbidden to publish this Torah work without the permission of the author's children.[53] A contemporary Rabbi was asked about a school that could not afford to buy all the books needed for Torah classes, as often many books are

48. *Mishnat Zechut HaYotzer*, chapter 5 (translated into English by Feldheim, "Copyright in Jewish Law" 2010)
49. *Mishnat Zechut HaYotzer*, chapter 18
50. Deuteronomy 6:18

51. *Responsa of the Rif* 133
52. Rema, *Shulchan Aruch, Choshen Mishpat* 292:20
53. *Responsa Beit Yitzchak, Yoreh De'ah* 5:72

needed to teach one class of students. In that case, is it permitted to photocopy sections of Torah books in order to produce source sheets for the students in the school? Rabbi Vozner answered that it would be permitted to do so unless the publisher wrote in the book that all copying, even small sections, is forbidden. If not, one could copy sections and even a complete article, as long as it remained in the classroom.[54] This is similar to US copyright law, which allows up to two pages or 10% of a work to be copied for the classroom, and only for one time use. If the material is used repeatedly, then the teacher has to buy the book.

## DOWNLOADING SONGS & FILMS FROM THE INTERNET – WHAT TODAY'S RABBIS SAY

Although he died before the digital age, Rabbi Moshe Feinstein (1895-1986) wrote a landmark decision with regard to copying audiotapes, which applies to digital music and films as well.[55] A tape of a professional song (or film) cannot be copied unless permission is received from the owner. However, regarding a public Torah class that anyone could have taped to begin with (for free), it is permissible to tape that class (and copy the tape) without asking permission. Of course, if the Rabbi giving the class announces that taping is forbidden (or if it is well known that tapes of the class will be sold commercially), then taping such a class would be forbidden. On the other hand, if it is a classroom situation and a student wants to tape the class simply to review the lesson (and not share it with anyone else), it would be permitted.

As mentioned above, Rabbi Nachum Menashe Weisfish wrote an entire volume about this issue after carefully reviewing all the sources and consulting with the great Rabbis and deciders of Jewish law in our generation. Here are his conclusions regarding

downloading songs or films (from the Internet or elsewhere) for free:[56]

1. If the original is copyrighted by law or has the words "All rights reserved," it is forbidden from the Torah to copy or download the item, according to all opinions. It is clearly stealing. Even a copy of a copy, even for private use only, is forbidden.

2. According to the majority opinion (cited above), even a very small loss to the publisher due to copying would be forbidden. According to the minority opinion, if the very small loss would be only to the singer or writer, then copying may be permitted for private use. (However, very few songs or films today are owned by the writer or singer.)

3. According to the majority opinion, a Jew cannot download even a poor quality of the original or even part of a song of film. But according to the minority opinion, these may be permitted. (In the digital age, however, unlike the video age of copying, subsequent copies do not lose quality.)

## COPYING SOFTWARE WITHOUT PAYING – WHAT TODAY'S RABBIS SAY

Generally, software is more expensive to purchase than a film and may often cost more to develop than a film or a song. This higher cost gives added incentive for unscrupulous people to copy, even though it may sometimes be harder to protect the code that unlocks the software. What is the specific Torah view about copying software programs for free?

In a computer magazine for observant Jewish families, two contemporary Rabbis published the following statement in 1999:[57]

"We confirm in this statement that any company that sells CDs and similar items, and writes on the CD: 'This product is for private use only. Any reproduction, even for private use or for others, even not for any financial profit, is strictly forbidden.' This is

---

54. *Responsa Shevet Levi*, vol. 4, *Choshen Mishpat* 202
55. *Responsa Igrot Moshe, Orach Chaim* 4:40, section 19
56. *Mishnat Zechut HaYotzer*, chapter 13
57. Computer Monthly for the Jewish Home 5:1, Kislev 5759 (1999), p. 27

valid according to Jewish law, according to all opinions. It is forbidden to copy this product for personal use or for others, even not for profit. Similarly, it is forbidden to copy from those who copied an original disk and those that made a copy of a copy, etc. Anyone who buys from them is considered to be in the category of he who assists in the commission of a crime/sin. Rabbi Moshe Shaul Klein, Rabbi Yehuda Silman."

Rabbi Nachum Menashe Weisfish has a chapter in his book specifically about the laws and details of copying software, and he includes:[58]

1. If the creator of the software forbade at purchase the copying of the product or made this a condition of sale, then according to all opinions it is forbidden from the Torah for any purchaser or seller to copy the product, and it is considered theft. And another person cannot use the disc that was copied by others.

2. One may not copy a disk for other computers (in the home) without having the original disk. Even according to the minority opinion, copying a computer disk is forbidden.

3. If the code on a program was broken and everyone can copy it at will, then there are those who say that it is permitted to copy that disk because there is no hope that the owners will sell another copy of that program.

4. One may not even copy an old version of the program. Some say that if the company is no longer selling that version of the program, it is permitted to copy it.

5. It is within the rights of the creator of a program to limit the use of each disk sold to one computer, even in the same home.

Rabbi Yosef Shalom Elyashiv (1910-2012), one of the greatest recognized decisors of Jewish law in his time, answered specific questions regarding the copying of software. Among the points he made were:[59]

1. Stealing intellectual property is like stealing all other property and is theft according to the Torah (majority opinion).

2. The owner of software and intellectual property retains the rights over his creation indefinitely, longer than the 50 years allowed by secular law.

3. It makes no difference if the owner (of the film, software, song, etc.) is Jewish, non-Jewish, or an apostate. Copying and violating copyright is forbidden.

4. Even if everyone else is copying or downloading for free and no one is enforcing the law, it is still forbidden to copy or download copyrighted items, even for personal use – as long as the item is copyrighted or it is stated that "All rights [are] reserved." This is Jewish law, even if only a very small percentage of the people actually comply.

---

58. *Mishnat Zechut HaYotzer*, chapter 14

59. *Mishnat Zechut HaYotzer*, chapter 18

# GUN CONTROL – THE JEWISH VIEW

THE NUMEROUS SHOOTINGS OF many innocent people in the past few years, which have occurred in public places such as schools and movie theaters, have caused renewed debate and attempts at legislation regarding prevention or limitation of gun ownership, popularly known as "gun control." This issue is especially acute in the United States, where the Second Amendment to the United States Constitution, "the right of the people to keep and bear arms," gives each citizen the legal right to protect himself, even with guns obtained legally and quite easily. In 2008 and again in 2010, the Supreme Court of the United States issued two landmark decisions officially establishing that the Second Amendment protects an individual's right to possess a firearm, unconnected to service in a militia, and to use that arm for traditionally lawful purposes, such as self-defense within the home. Therefore, the percentage of US citizens who own handguns and the actual number of legal guns in the United States far exceeds the number in any other country in the world. However, this law and protection also makes it far easier for deranged people to obtain guns and kill blameless individuals for no logical reason at all. As more and more guiltless people are being shot publicly for no apparent reason, many US citizens and legislators are seeking to limit the guns that people can legally obtain. They also want to legislate closer scrutiny for obtaining a firearm, thereby limiting the damage and deaths that a single gun can cause, in order to minimize such incidents in the future. Where does Judaism stand on this issue? Since traditional Jewish sources were all written before handguns were invented, can Judaism possibly have a view on this and related issues?

Because Judaism is not merely a religion, but also a way of life, many of the issues related to gun control have indeed been addressed by Rabbis and by Jewish law in the distant past.

As with any modern issue, Judaism's principles, established hundreds or thousands of years ago, are still as valid today as they were then, since human nature has not changed. These concepts may clearly and decisively be applied to our discussion of gun control and help develop the normative Jewish view on this important and timely issue. The sources of the past have certainly dealt in general with the issues of weapons, safety, and self-protection, the right to protect one's property, and using weapons for sport. These and other topics will be presented and analyzed from a Jewish perspective.

## PROTECTION AND SAFETY

Self-protection and survival are basic instincts and needs for every species. It is certainly part of human nature as well. But this idea is also one of the 613 commandments in the Torah. The Torah commands a Jew to protect himself or herself,[1] and repeats this warning a few verses later.[2] Specifically, when it comes saving oneself from danger, the Talmud is very sensitive to this requirement, as it states that the possibility of danger sometimes supersedes observing Jewish law.[3] Amazingly, this concept is quoted in the Code of Jewish Law, the essential book of Jewish law, written by Rabbi Yosef Caro.[4] But it states that God also promises to protect man from all evil (possibly referring only to the very righteous.)[5] How does this promise reconcile with the requirement for each Jew to protect himself or herself? Since Judaism is a religion about actions, laws, and details, and not just concepts and thoughts, let us explore how Judaism, in another Torah law, puts these ideas into practice.

---

1. Deuteronomy 4:9
2. Deuteronomy 4:16
3. *Chulin* 10a
4. *Shulchan Aruch, Orach Chaim* 183:2
5. Psalms 121:7

The Torah mandates that a Jew protect his or her home – not with guns, but with a fence that must be placed surrounding a (straight) roof which will prevent family members and strangers from accidentally falling off and killing themselves.[6] Rashi defines this fence as something that protects the occupants inside, and even if a person falls accidentally, he or she probably "had it coming" as retribution for some other sin. Nevertheless, each Jew has a responsibility to see that this does not happen.[7] Thus, just as a gun is bought to protect one's home and family, like the fence, the owner of the home must be careful to also protect others in his home, even sinners, from coming to unnecessary harm. Rabbeinu Bechaye expands this concept to mandate that each person must guard himself and others in his home from any type danger that may come. While this may allow for the purchase of a gun as protection in the twenty-first century, it also places a responsibility for the safety of that gun upon any homeowner who owns one – i.e., that it does no accidental harm to anyone in the house.[8] Shulchan Aruch codifies this idea into law, requiring anyone who owns a home to minimize danger within and maximize safety on the premises, including putting a fence around or covering a pit with or without water in it, in order to prevent accidents.[9] In this same vein, some states today have passed a law that an owner of a swimming pool must put a fence around it in order to protect not only invited guests and household members, but also trespassers – "sinners" who come illegally at night onto the property and who may unknowingly fall into the pool and drown. Thus, the safety of a home is a prime principle in Judaism, mandated by Jewish law.

The Talmud expands upon this obligation of a person who owns a home. Not only must any stationary, permanent obstacle that is part of the structure of the house be protected, but even protecting a non-stationary object (like a gun) or anything located in the house that may pose a danger is also the responsibility of the homeowner. Thus, it is forbidden for a Jew to leave around the house a dangerous dog or a faulty ladder, unprotected, as a possible danger.[10] This would be analogous to leaving a gun lying around the house and not in a special safe (under lock and key). Judaism also prohibits endangering others even outside the home, as it forbids placing a stumbling block before a blind person, which is interpreted by all the commentaries not only in the physical sense but also metaphorically.[11] Therefore, it is forbidden to endanger anyone else, and maximum safety must be ensured. Why the Jewish stress on safety? Judaism is a religion of peace and tries to ensure peaceful living, says the Talmud.[12]

## THE RIGHT OF SELF-PROTECTION IN JUDAISM

In general, Judaism does not allow an individual Jew to take the law into his or her own hands and execute justice for criminals. For instance, there is the situation where a person witnesses, along with many judges, a clear-cut murder – the case in which the perpetrator will certainly be convicted, according to all logic and the opinions of those witnessing this act, and at the time it is easily within the power of a witness to kill that murderer right then and there (thus avoiding a long trial and possibility that the criminal could be freed on a technicality). Nevertheless, it is still forbidden to take justice into one's own hands according to Jewish thought and kill that murderer on the spot. That killer must, nevertheless, be given over the police and brought to trial like any other criminal.[13] However, there are some instances in which this situation is impossible, and an individual is forced to take the law into

---

6. Deuteronomy 22:8
7. Rashi commentary on Deuteronomy 22:8
8. Rabbeinu Bechaye commentary on Deuteronomy 22:8
9. Shulchan Aruch, Choshen Mishpat 427:7
10. Bava Kama 15b
11. Leviticus 19:14
12. Gittin 59b
13. Maimonides, Sefer HaMitzvot, negative Mitzvah 292

his or her own hands. The classic case is that of the intruder, the thief who attempts to rob one's home at night. In that situation, there is usually not enough time to call the police before the thief robs the house, or worse, harms the occupants. May a Jew prepare for this situation by purchasing a weapon? May a Jew take preventative action to eliminate the danger by using this gun against the intruder?

The Torah describes just such a case. If the thief is found breaking into a home at night, the Torah says that if a Jew kills that thief, he or she is blameless.[14] This seems to give legal authority for purchasing a weapon in advance in order to kill an intruder who may break into a home. But why is this so? By what legal authority can the owner of the home become both judge and jury in one fell swoop and kill this thief, without the legal system first determining that this man is a (potential) murderer who may be stopped with a gun? Rashi, in his commentary on this verse, gives us a clear explanation. Killing this intruder, says Rashi, is not considered murder because the Torah creates a special ruling in this case. This person, intent on murdering the occupants of the house, already has the legal status of a "dead man" (equal to a legally convicted murderer) that may legally be killed, since he will certainly kill the occupants if he is confronted. Thus, it is lawful to kill such a person by any means necessary.[15] But how do we know that this person is indeed a murderer, even in potential? Maybe he came only to steal some objects, but if he were to be challenged by the residents of the home, he would run away? The Talmud responds to this question by explaining that a typical thief knows that most homeowners, if the owners face him, will not simply give up their possessions. Thus, the thief who knows this in advance generally comes armed and is prepared to kill the inhabitants if confronted.[16]

Based on this verse and the Talmudic discussion, the Talmud establishes the legality of

the principle of self-defense – if someone is coming to kill you, you may kill him first.[17] In addition, God's command to the Jews to attack the Midianites who attacked the Jewish people in the desert[18] is also a basis for the concept of self-defense.[19]

However, this principle of self-defense and the right to kill an intruder are predicated on the assumption that the thief is indeed a potential and likely murderer and will kill the inhabitants if confronted. What happens when the homeowner knows that the thief is not at all interested in confrontation and has absolutely no desire to harm the inhabitants, but only wants to steal, and will run out of the house if someone wakes up? The continuation of the Torah in the next verse speaks of this situation. It says that if "the sun shines" on the homeowner and he then kills the intruder, then the homeowner is guilty of murder.[20] What does the sun shining signify? The Talmud discusses this subject by framing the question: "Does the sun only shine on the homeowner? It shines on everyone!"[21] It answers that the phrase about the sun shining means that it is "as clear as day" to the homeowner. What is so clear? If it is evident that the thief will not kill or harm the people in the house, then the owner who pulls out a gun and kills the thief is indeed guilty of murder. Therefore, use of a gun or any weapon to harm or kill the intruder must be justified. Similarly, the Midrash says that the sun is the symbol of warmth and peace. Thus, if the sun is shining and it is clear that the thief is no threat to life, it is forbidden to kill that thief, and the resident of the home who does so is considered a murderer.[22]

But how can the head of the house know in advance the specific intentions of the thief? One explanation is the situation in which the thief is the father of the occupant of the house. The Talmudic passage quoted above

---

14. Exodus 22:1
15. Rashi commentary on Exodus 22:1
16. *Sanhedrin* 72a

17. *Yoma* 85b
18. Numbers 25:16-18
19. *Midrash Tanchuma, Pinchas* 3
20. Exodus 22:2
21. *Sanhedrin* 72a
22. Midrash, *Mechilta, Nezikin* 6

states that children who hate their parents may both steal from and even kill a father or mother. But the opposite is not true. While a father might resort to stealing from one's child, he would never murder him or her. Thus, if the thief is the father, it is certain that the homeowner need not resort to using his gun to protect himself. Maimonides codifies this idea and adds that if the thief is on the way out of the home when the owner sees him, clearly with no intent to harm the occupants, it is forbidden to shoot and kill that thief who is no longer a threat to the lives of the people he stole from.[23]

## THE JEWISH ATTITUDE TOWARDS WEAPONS

Before a discussion of gun control in Jewish thought can be explored in detail, it is important to first discuss how Judaism views guns and weapons in general. Are these simply a part of everyday living in every society where there are criminals? Are they desirable or undesirable? A necessary evil or part of every ideal society?

Weapons first appear in the Torah at the very beginning of Creation after Adam and Eve sinned, with the flaming sword that protected the Garden of Eden and the Tree of Life, preventing man from re-entering.[24] This first divine weapon then, was intended to protect property, like a gun in a home, but for defensive purposes only. A few generations later, as society developed implements and tools for working the land and musical instruments, one person, Tuval Kayin, forged sharp instruments out of bronze and iron, which Rashi says were weapons made for murderers to kill people.[25] Thus, the first human weapons were made in order to hurt individuals and kill human beings, not essentially different from the guns and other weapons that are manufactured to kill people today. Needless to say, the Rabbis

did not look upon this invention as a positive development for mankind. Nachmanides expands on this story and says that Lemech, the great-great-grandson of Cain, was very smart and inventive.[26] He had three sons and he taught each one a unique skill and new trade in the world. His oldest son perfected how to herd animals, the middle son perfected musical instruments, and the youngest son, Tuval Kayin, perfected weapon making. When Lemech's wives were afraid that Lemech would be punished for introducing weapons into the world, especially for his son who was named after the first murderer in the world, Kayin (Cain), Lemech, according to Nachmanides, gave the answer that is still given today by manufacturers of weapons who do not want to assume any responsibility for deaths and destruction that takes place as a result of using these weapons. He said, "The weapons do not kill people. People kill people." As is the case today, this argument did not hold water with most people or with God.

Later in the Torah, when the Jewish people left Egypt, it says that the Jews left "Chamushim."[27] The word that has many explanations, but one translation is that they left armed with weapons. In fact, this is the explanation of the Ibn Ezra, the Rashbam, and Rabbeinu Bechaye.[28] The Jews knew they would be fighting battles in the desert and to conquer the land of Israel, and therefore needed weapons for these wars. Based on these explanations, weapons were a "necessary evil" for the Jewish people, and were needed to accomplish the national task to defeat the enemy (on the occasions when God did not do so by Himself miraculously, as by the Red Sea, the Sea of Reeds). Though the Jews relied on God as well, they also had to fight other nations by natural means, using the weapons of the day, says Rabbeinu Bechaye. In fact, King David attributes to God not only his successes in wars, but also considers God his teacher to become an expert

---

23. Maimonides, *Hilchot Genaiva* 9:10-11
24. Genesis 3:24
25. Genesis 4:22 with Rashi commentary

26. Nachmanides commentary on Genesis 4:23
27. Exodus 13:18
28. Ibn Ezra, Rashbam and Rabbeinu Bechaye commentaries on Exodus 13:18

in using weapons for his many battles.[29] Thus, Judaism clearly recognizes the need of weapons on the battlefield as a necessary part of life.

And yet, Judaism makes a clear distinction between "religion and state" when it comes to weapons. Weapons are indeed necessary, but they remain an "evil" and must never be used in any realm considered "religious" or holy. Thus, already in the Torah, God forbids the building of the Holy Altar using any metal implement (it was built miraculously with a special Shamir worm that cut stone).[30] Why? Rashi explains that the symbol of the Holy Altar is to extend human life, while metal, representing weapons, diminishes life. One cannot be used to build the other. *Bechor Shor* similarly states that since metal and weapons represent hurting man, the opposite of holiness, the Altar, the symbol of holiness, could not be built with metal.[31] It is clear, then, that while Judaism recognizes the need for weapons in the context of war, they are only a necessary tool for engaging in battle and not something to be proud of or admired. The ultimate goal for weapons, in the famous verse in Isaiah, is to make them totally unnecessary and hope for the time when the metal from weapons will be melted down to be used for farm tools.[32]

The separation between weapons and holiness that begun with the Altar, i.e., "religion and state", continues with the Jewish law that forbids any weapon to be brought into a House of Study, which is already seen in Talmudic times.[33] Similar to the building of the Altar, the author of *Shulchan Aruch* forbids a Jew to enter the synagogue with a knife, because the synagogue symbolizes lengthening life, while the knife represents shortening of life.[34] Then *Shulchan Aruch* codifies this Jewish law in his code.[35] When discussing the prohibition of carrying on Shabbat, the Mishna questions

whether wearing the artifacts made of weapons is considered carrying or not, much like some soldiers carry and wear souvenirs of war today. Rabbi Eliezer considers wearing parts of weapons to be like jewelry and thus permits them to be worn on Shabbat. The Rabbis vehemently disagree and state that these are considered a disgrace, and are forbidden to wear not only on Shabbat but during the rest of the week as well.[36] *Shulchan Aruch* codifies the opinion of the Rabbis and rules that any wearing of weapons is not attractive, forbidden on Shabbat, and even a disgrace.[37] This Jewish law demonstrates the normative view of weapons in Judaism.

Even other kinds of weapons, those not used in the battlefield but nonetheless dangerous, are discouraged in Judaism. A wild dog was already used in Talmudic times (and still today) as a weapon to protect one's home. Even though this is not a weapon of war, it is still considered a weapon (more about this below), and its use is discouraged as a "weapon" to protect one's home. The Talmud says that a wild dog used as weapon in a home minimizes kindness in the home.[38] Maharsha explains that even the rumor of a vicious dog in a person's home will discourage guests from entering and poor people from coming around, thus minimizing social interaction and good will for this family.[39]

For many years, the issue of bringing weapons into a synagogue or a *Beit Midrash*, a House of Learning, was not a very practical one, since few Jews carried weapons to begin with, there was no Jewish army, and there was no concept of observant Jews with weapons coming into the synagogue. However, with more and more Israeli soldiers today emerging from observant homes, the question of a solider coming from the army base with a gun directly to the synagogue is a very real one today. Rabbi Ovadiah Yosef was asked this question, knowing that it is not permitted for a solider

---

29. Samuel II 22:35
30. Exodus 20:21-22
31. Rashi and Bechor Shor commentaries on Exodus 20:22
32. Isaiah 2:4
33. Sanhedrin 82a
34. *Beit Yosef* commentary on *Tur, Orach Chaim* 151
35. *Shulchan Aruch, Orach Chaim* 151:6

36. Mishna *Shabbat* 6:4
37. *Shulchan Aruch, Orach Chaim* 301:7
38. *Shabbat* 63a
39. Maharsha commentary on *Shabbat* 63a

in uniform to part with his gun. What should this solider do when he wants to pray? Rabbi Yosef answers that since the soldier must have his weapon with him at all times, the soldier should try to cover it up in the synagogue as much as possible, so that it cannot be seen by others. But if this is impossible, as in the case of a rifle, and for security reasons the weapon must be brought into the synagogue, then he permits it.[40]

## JEWISH GUN CONTROL IN ANCIENT TIMES AND TODAY

Although there were no handguns in ancient times, people (including Jews) used other means and other "weapons" as a way of protecting their homes. Certain wild animals were kept in one's home and used as a means of scaring and warding off trespassers, robbers, or even murderers. The Mishna has a disagreement about the lion, the bear, the leopard, and the panther. The majority opinion is that these animals are always dangerous and cannot be controlled, so they cannot be kept in a home as a "weapon" of protection, while Rabbi Eliezer says that these animals can be tamed in certain situations.[41] If they are indeed untamable, these animals are unacceptable as "pets" in a home and any damage they cause to an outsider or attacker would be the responsibility of the homeowner. Rabbi Eliezer believes that these animals can be tamed, as they are in the circus, and are therefore able to protect one's home. All agree that a snake can never be tamed and would be a liability, forbidden to be kept in any home. How do the Sages rule? Although there is a minor opinion that the wild animals can indeed be tamed, both Maimonides and *Shulchan Aruch* rule that these animals may not be used in a home as a weapon, as they are too dangerous for home protection.[42] Therefore, we see that Judaism believes that some weapons have too great

a risk factor to be used as protection in the home. While it is anyone's guess precisely how this translates into which weapons of today are similarly perilous, undoubtedly assault rifles and machine guns would be considered inherently hazardous, like these wild animals, and for that reason unsuited for home protection.

Which weapons are acceptable for home protection? There was one type of city that was an unusual "experiment" for people with a proclivity for using weapons. While cold-blooded murderers would immediately go to jail and be punished after the trial in a Jewish society, there is a different Jewish law for those who killed "accidentally" – i.e., a person who killed someone with a weapon, when the death might have been prevented with a bit more care and sensitivity. These people who killed accidentally would be forced to live in one of six cities of the Levites that were called "Cities of Refuge."[43] But the majority of inhabitants were Levites and were not murderers. There had to be mostly regular, upstanding, law-abiding Levites, as well as elderly people, in order for the accidental murderers to live in a society of "regular" people. Moving away from family and friends for a time period was their punishment (until the High Priest died, when they would return home).[44]

In these cities of refuge, there were arguments about which weapons were permitted for a person to have and which were forbidden. Rabbi Nechuniah said no weapons at all were permitted in these cities, in order to avoid tempting these accidental killers to use weapons and possibly kill again. The Rabbis understood that a total ban on weapons was not feasible or practical, since weapons can always be smuggled in (as is done in today's societies). Thus, the Rabbis permitted some weapons. However, both the Rabbis and Rabbi Nechuniah agreed that weapons that were traps for animals, such as ropes, should not be left about and openly displayed in the city itself. Why? The relatives of the victims of these

---

40. *Responsa Yechave Da'at* 5:18
41. Mishna *Bava Kama* 1:4
42. Maimonides, *Hilchot Nizkei Mamon* 1:6; *Shulchan Aruch, Choshen Mishpat* 389:8

43. Numbers 35:9-13
44. Maimonides, *Hilchot Rotze'ach* 7:4-6

accidental murderers were always on the look-out to kill these people who murdered their loved ones accidentally, in order to get some sense of revenge and closure, and indeed, they were legally permitted to kill these murderers if the murderers left the city of refuge. But both the Rabbis and Rabbi Nechuniah feared that if traps were left open in this city, this would attract the relatives to enter the city surreptitiously and use the traps against the accidental murderers.[45] These relatives would not be so brazen as to bring in their own weapons into these cities and kill the accidental murderers, but if they saw weapons of opportunity lying around, they would not hesitate to use them against those who killed their relatives. Thus, we see that when weapons of opportunity are left around, they add to the potential dangers of a society and increase killings. One commentary adds that the reason that other kinds of weapons were not a threat in the cities of refuge was that the relatives would never kill these people inside the city limits with regular weapons. But with ropes and traps left around in public areas, these relatives might try to kill these people in a way that would look like an accidental death, so that the relatives would never be caught and charged with murder.[46] The lessons learned from this law is that in situations in which murder is more likely to take place, no weapons should be left around, and that weapons should not get into the hands of those who are more likely to use them.

Although no handguns were around then to use for protection, the equivalent to guns at the time were wild dogs, used as protection from home invaders. People kept wild dogs on their property to scare away thieves and murderers. Much can be learned and derived about gun control today from how Jews were permitted or forbidden to keep wild dogs then (as well as today). The Talmud says that wild dogs could be kept in one's home near the frontier (for the purposes of biting and harming thieves and murderers in areas where their intrusion is more likely), on the condition that they were tied up securely during the day and only let out on the property at night when people were sleeping.[47] This indicates to us today that even when a weapon of protection is permitted, it is must be safeguarded and be eliminated as a danger to others, except at times when theft is more likely. The same Talmudic passage also informs us that tame animals such as domesticated dogs, cats, and tamed monkeys were permitted in the home in order to keep the house clean from rodents and other small animals. Domesticated livestock was forbidden to be kept in homes in cities the land of Israel because of limited living space, but was permitted outside of Israel or in the deserts of the land of Israel.

Another passage shows that some feared wild dogs even if they were chained (like today), since the dogs scared people even while tied down, and once such a dog barked so loudly that it caused a pregnant woman to miscarry.[48] Evidently, even secured weapons had their detractors then. When ruling in normative Jewish law, *Shulchan Aruch* follows the basic rulings of the Talmud, but not only demands that a wild dog be tied down, but it must be tied down with a metal chain and can never be untied, except in frontier areas where there is real danger of theft and murder.[49] The implications for the twenty-first century are that a gun must be kept in a very secure place, and it is only permitted where the chance of theft and murder is very likely. This is not the standard law concerning where and when a gun is permitted in the United States today.

Rabbi Meir Eisenstadt (1670-1744) limited the permissibility of weapons even further, by writing that wild dogs were permitted for protection from intruders only in areas where large groups of Jews lived and needed protection. But in areas where only a few Jews lived, wild dogs would be forbidden.[50] In the eighteenth century, Rabbi Yaakov Emden

---

45. *Makkot* 10a
46. *Sia'ch Yitzchak* on *Makkot* 10a

47. *Bava Kama* 79b with Rashi commentary
48. *Bava Kama* 83a
49. *Shulchan Aruch, Choshen Mishpat* 409:1,3
50. *Responsa Panim Meirot* 2:133

permitted such wild dogs only in areas where the danger was real, and further limited the use of these dogs to one per household.[51] The implication for today is clear: If there is no real danger of break-in or theft, guns for protection would not permitted, and even in dangerous areas, only one gun per household is allowed. The contemporary Rabbi Pinchas Zvichi rules that that if a person fears burglary, then the chained dog should be visible by day, but a clear sign must be posted about a vicious dog on the premises. Then the dog can be let out into the courtyard at night. But if there is legitimate fear of an attack, then the dog can be kept unchained at all times, provided that safeguards are taken to prevent it from harming innocent people.[52]

## GUN CONTROL IN TWO COUNTRIES: UNITED STATES AND ISRAEL

After the massacres of adults and children in schools in America, some "experts" in the United States have made the argument that the USA needs to implement a policy about guns similar to the one in Israel, where there is a guard in every school, placed there in order to prevent weapons from entering and being used in a possible attack. Since a plethora of guns exist in both countries, the situations seem to be very similar, they say. But even a cursory analysis shows that in each country the attitudes towards civilian weapons differ radically.

Because Israel has a citizen army, guns can be seen almost everywhere, as soldiers riding on buses and coming home for the weekend carry their weapons. But these are army-issued weapons, quite different from the guns owned by citizens that are the subject of this discussion. In addition, no attack on an Israeli school or in a public area has ever been made by a deranged lone gunman who killed civilians, as has occurred recently in other countries. Mass attacks on civilians in Israel are always in the

guise of a national attack by Arabs (sometimes a single Arab terrorist) who are usually part of an organization bent on destroying Israel (such as the 1974 attack in Ma'alot, where twenty-two schoolchildren were murdered). Thus, the purpose and goals of these attacks in Israel are very different from those in the United States. The way these Arab killers procure illegal weapons to carry out their attacks (and the weapons themselves) are also very different. Let us instead compare apples to apples by investigating the laws of each country and the process to legally obtain a handgun, as well as the number of legally obtained guns in each country.

In the United States, the obtaining of a weapon by a civilian is seen as a national right, as explained above. In Israel, obtaining a weapon by a civilian is seen as a privilege. Therefore, the sum total of weapons in the hands of Israeli non-soldiers is 170,000 out of a population of seven million (2.5% of the population, or one in every thirty people). In the United States, there are about 315 million legally purchased handguns in the hands of civilians, the same number of American citizens (or 100% of the population, or one gun for every person). In Israel, 80% of the people who apply for a handgun for protection are turned down. In most states in the United States, if a person buys a handgun from a private dealer (which is very easy to do), then the buyer does not even need a license and no background check is required! In Israel, automatic weapons are banned for private ownership, and it is very rare that any one person is authorized to own more than one gun. In the United States, this is not the case. In Israel, applicants must undergo police screening and medical exams, in part to determine their mental status, before obtaining a license to own a gun. In addition, to own a gun in Israel, a need must be shown, such as living in a settlement surrounded by a hostile Arab population. In the United States, no such rigorous conditions exist as a prerequisite to purchase a gun and no legitimate need for the gun must ever be demonstrated. Thus, the difference between these two countries

---

51. *Responsa Shei'lat Ya'avetz* 1:17
52. *Responsa Ateret Paz* 1:3, *Choshen Mishpat* 8

and societies in this area is vast, and the much lower homicide rate in Israel can at least partially be attributed to the difficulty in acquiring guns.

## PROVIDING GUNS TO OTHER PEOPLE

Already in Mishnaic times the Rabbis forbid selling wild animals to non-Jews because of the damage that these animals can cause to innocent people. (Non-Jewish idol worshippers at that time were always suspected of immoral behavior, since they did not subscribe to a code of ethics.)[53] The Talmud also forbids selling these people weapons of any kind because they will undoubtedly misuse them and hurt people with them.[54] Rabbi Nachman says that Jews cannot even sell to middlemen – Jewish arms dealers who may sell to non-Jews, who will then misuse the weapons. Rabbi Dimi says that it is forbidden to sell weapons to unscrupulous and criminal Jews who may use them for nefarious ends.[55] All of these ideas are codified into normative Jewish law by Maimonides.[56] Thus, it is clear from all of these statements that a Jew is forbidden to give or sell a weapon of any kind to any individual who may use it for harm or worse. The Jewish need to determine that the buyer of any weapon in the twenty-first century is a mentally stable non-criminal and a responsible person is evident through the sources. The argument that, "I am only selling the guns. It is my business and not my job to care what happens to them afterwards," does not hold water in Jewish thought.

## USING GUNS FOR HUNTING OR AS SPORT

One of the main reasons that the National Rifle Association insists on not limiting the sale of guns is that they are not only bought for protection of one's home (that would never require more than a handgun), but the guns are also needed for sport and for hunting. Thus, a very large percentage of gun sales in the United States and around the world are for this purpose as well. What is the Jewish view of hunting and using guns for sport?

The Torah speaks of hunting animals or fowl.[57] The use of the world "*Tzayid*" clearly signifies hunting, which seems to be permitted in Judaism. But the Torah context of hunting is very different from the concept of hunting in the modern sense. First, in the verse itself, as explained by the commentaries, the "hunt" is for food that is kosher, which will then be eaten by the hunter, and it especially refers to the hunting of geese and wild chickens.[58] Thus, there is no Jewish term for hunting merely for sport. Similarly, when the Mishna uses this term, "hunting," it never refers to a gun, knife, or weapon to be used to kill the animal, but rather to trapping the animal while it is still alive, especially since killing the animal with any weapon would render it non-kosher for eating.[59] Therefore, there is no concept of hunting for sport or killing any animal with a weapon in Judaism.

This concept is codified in Jewish law. *Shulchan Aruch* rules that it is forbidden on Shabbat to "hunt" even a deer (a kosher animal) that is old, blind, sick, or damaged. Rema adds that hunting with trained dogs is not only forbidden on Shabbat, but is prohibited even during the week, since it is a frivolous, non-Jewish activity.[60] Why is hunting forbidden? Rema, in another of his books, explains that hunting is forbidden, whether the purpose is for "fun" or to sell the prey.[61] This is the occupation of the evil Eisav, which shows a quality of cruelty in preying on animals and killing God's creations. When man curtails life as sport or for fun, it is the opposite of his purpose in life, which is to

---

53. Mishna *Avodah Zara* 1:7
54. *Avodah Zara* 15b
55. *Avodah Zara* 15b
56. Maimonides, *Hilchot Avodah Zara* 9:8

57. Leviticus 17:13
58. Rishi Mizrachi and Gur Aryeh commentaries on Leviticus 17:13
59. Mishna *Beitza* 3:1-2
60. Shulchan Aruch, Orach Chaim 316:2
61. *Darchei Teshuva, Yoreh De'ah* 117:44

enhance and expand the world. Not only is Eisav depicted as the classic hunter, but another evil leader, Nimrod, is also called a hunter in the Torah and is viewed very unfavorably in Jewish thought.[62] *Sefer HaChinuch* forbids hunting as part of the prohibition of needlessly causing pain to animals.[63] Hunting also violates the general spirit of Judaism, which is to promote peace in the world.[64]

The most famous discourse on the Jewish opposition to hunting is a responsum of Rabbi Yechezkel Landau (1713-1793). In it Rabbi Landau reviews all the reasons presented above to prohibit hunting. He adds that it is forbidden for a Jew to hunt because part of hunting for sport involves putting oneself in danger in the forest or jungle, which is forbidden. He concludes that the entire activity is disgusting, cruel, and dangerous, and is utterly forbidden for all Jews.[65]

---

62. Genesis 25:27
63. *Sefer HaChinuch*, Mitzvah 550
64. *Gittin* 59b

65. *Responsa Noda BeYehudah Mahadura Tennina, Yoreh De'ah* 10

# HATRED IN JUDAISM

EVERY THINKING PERSON SHOULD agree that hatred is an emotion that not only hurts people in general, but also damages many individuals who are the object of this emotion. Yet hate is such a powerful feeling that it often guides the actions of many people and even the actions of nations. It seems very natural to hate and wish to harm someone who has wronged you. Should a person always fight that emotion, or should he sometimes give in to it? Does Judaism advocate avoiding hatred in all situations or is it permitted to hate someone in certain circumstances? Or rather, should a person love *everyone* and hate no one? Is that really a Jewish idea?

## WHERE AND WHY JUDAISM OPPOSES HATRED

There are many sources pointing out the strong antagonism of Judaism to the emotion of hatred. These sources flow from the Torah, the Tanach (Scripture), the Talmud, and the Midrash. The Torah specifically says that one may not hate a brother (fellow Jew) in one's heart.[1] The verse in Obadiah admonishes the Jew for rejoicing when a particular enemy is fallen.[2] Another verse also says that one may not be joyous when his enemy is defeated, lest God get angry.[3] This concept of not being happy when an enemy falls is codified in the Mishna by Shmuel Hakatan.[4]

The idea of hatred was so distasteful to the Jew that the Talmud records that the Second Temple was destroyed because of unfounded hatred among Jews *even though they performed Mitzvot-commandments, and were also kind people.*[5] Furthermore, it also says in that passage that since we know that the First Temple

was destroyed because Jews violated the three cardinal sins of Judaism – adultery, murder, and idolatry (the only three of the 613 *Mitzvot* that one must rather die for rather than perform at gunpoint) – this teaches us that he who hates needlessly, *it is as if he has violated all three cardinal sins combined*! Other commentators have taken this Talmudic statement one step further. In view of the fact that the length of the Diaspora following the destruction of the First Temple lasted only seventy years but the length of the Diaspora following the destruction of the Second Temple has lasted more than 1900 years and is still continuing, we can further see the even greater severity of the sin of hating compared to the three sins of adultery, murder and idolatry.

The very essence of Judaism itself involves the avoidance of hatred. When Hillel was asked by the non-Jew to tell him the entire essence of Judaism while standing on one foot, Hillel replied that you should not do unto others what is *hateful* to you. The rest is commentary. Now, go learn.[6] Thus, the essence of Judaism, according to Hillel, is not to act in a hateful manner. (It is interesting to note that this statement was stated in the negative rather than the positive – to love one's neighbor – as is stated in the Torah verse, because God does not mandate an emotion such as love. But God *does* demand actions towards others that are not hateful.) *Sefer HaChinuch* calls this trait of hatred the ugliest of all human traits.[7] The Mishna says that the emotion of hatred can remove a person from the world.[8] We see that the Rabbis were so afraid of the emotion of hatred that they asked only Shmuel Hakatan, the epitome of the person who could not hate (and composer of the Mishna about not hating one's enemy) to compose the nineteenth

---

1. Leviticus 19:17
2. Obadiah 1:12
3. Proverbs 24:17-18
4. *Avot* 4:19
5. *Yoma* 9b

6. *Shabbat* 31a
7. *Sefer HaChinuch*, Mitzvah 238
8. *Avot* 2:11

blessing in the Silent Prayer against talebearers and informers.[9] It would be too easy for most people to write this blessing with a bit of hatred. The Rabbis, therefore, asked Shmuel Hakatan, who could not hate, to compose this blessing.

The first Jewish Diaspora in Egypt as well as Jewish slavery came about, according to the Talmud, only because of hatred.[10] The hatred of the brothers for Joseph caused them to sell him and eventually bring the Jews down to Egypt. The very definition of a Jewish hero is not measured in terms of physical prowess. According to the *Avot DeRabbi Natan*, the ultimate Jewish hero is he who can turn one's enemy into a friend – i.e., convert hared into love (see chapter "Heroes" for an expansion of this theme).[11] Maimonides informs us that the Torah attempted to eradicate feelings of hatred by commanding every Jew to help unload the burden on the back of an animal belonging to his enemy.[12] In this way it is hoped that both parties will come to eliminate any feelings of hatred.[13]

After the defeat of the great enemy of the Jews, Pharaoh and the wicked Egyptians who had mercilessly killed Jewish babies, who were drowned in the sea, the angels wished to rejoice and sing praises. God admonishes them by saying, "My handiwork (My creations, the Egyptians) are drowning and you wish to sing praise and be happy?"[14] This shows that God and the Jews themselves should not hate even the worst enemies of the Jews. It also shows *why* one cannot hate anyone. The most evil person is still a creation of God, containing the image of God within. Thus, rejoicing at the death of any creation of God diminishes God. Therefore, on Passover it is the Jewish custom to remove ten drops from the wine cup when recounting the Ten Plagues, which killed many wicked Egyptians. Similarly, during the last six days of Passover, the entire *Hallel* (praise of God) prayer is not recited, but two paragraphs are omitted in deference to the Egyptians, creations of God who died.

## DEFINITION OF THE SIN OF HATRED

Defining the specific sin of hatred is much more difficult than simply stating to Jews, "do not hate." First, in general Judaism does not define sinning as merely feeling an emotion, such as hatred. Usually (but not always) a sin requires an action or refraining from an action that is driven by a feeling. In addition, we will see that there is a fundamental disagreement about what precisely constitutes the sin of hatred from a Jewish perspective.

The Mishna simply states that hatred is defined as disliking an individual so much that it causes a Jew to refrain from speaking to that person for a minimum of three days as a result of that animosity or antagonism towards him or her.[15] A fifteenth century Rabbi does not attach a specific action to hatred, but says that this emotion is a sin when it causes several other actions that violate Jewish law, including slanderous speech, revenge, lying, etc.[16] A contemporary Rabbi, Rabbi Yitzchak Silver, defines this sin as lack of communication with the object of one's loathing for a minimum of three days, like the Talmud. Then he adds that this person would be forbidden to sit on a Jewish court and judge the object of his scorn. He continues and states that even though this Jew feels hated, it is forbidden in Jewish law to return that hatred to the other person.[17]

The specific argument about the sin of hate, however, is based on a close reading of the Torah text prohibiting hatred of another Jew. The verse says, "You may not hate your brother in your heart."[18] The implication is that it is only in your heart that it is forbidden to hate. The Talmud in fact states that only hatred in one's heart violates this particular sin, implying that

---

9. *Berachot* 28b
10. *Megillah* 16a
11. *Avot DeRabbi Natan* 23
12. Maimonides, *Hilchot Rotze'ach* 13:13
13. Exodus 23:5
14. *Sanhedrin* 39b

15. Mishna *Sanhedrin* 3:5
16. "The Gate of Hatred," chapter 6 in *Orchot Tzadikim*
17. *Mishpitei Hashalom* 2:8, 10, 12
18. Leviticus 19:17

if the animosity is stated openly, then the sin is not violated.[19] Describing the classic example of hate in the Torah narrative, it states that Joseph's brothers hated him and could not speak in peace with him.[20] On this last phrase, Rashi comments that although they were wrong in hating him, at least this hatred was out in the open and they were not hypocritical by keeping hate in their hearts while outwardly feigning friendliness.[21] That would be far worse than openly showing one's hatred. Like the Talmud, the Midrash also states that only hatred in one's heart (privately), and not expressed hate, is forbidden by the Torah.[22]

Maimonides specifically says that if a person informs someone that he hates him or her, he or she has not violated the prohibition of hatred (although other sins may have been committed).[23] Later on, in a different volume, Maimonides rules that if a Jew does not keep anger in his or her heart, there is no violation of the sin of hatred, even if he or she takes action as a result of the hatred, and hits or damages the person of scorn.[24] He then states that the continuation of the Torah verse about not hating, which is to reprove and admonish a sinner, is actually connected to the prohibition of hatred. If you hate someone, you should tell the person why you hate him or her and what this person has done wrong, says Maimonides. *Sefer HaChinuch* continues this theme and also says that openly stating one's hate removes any violation of the sin of hatred, which must take place only in one's heart to be a Torah violation.[25] However, by announcing his hate, the person does violate the prohibition of taking revenge and does not fulfill the Mitzvah-commandment of "loving one's fellow neighbor as oneself." That is why Abraham openly admonished King Avimelech when his servants

had stolen from Abraham.[26] According to tradition, Abraham observed the entire Torah, so he knew that the prohibition of hatred was to keep that antipathy within his heart. Thus, he told Avimelech about his feelings and explained why he felt that way.

On the other hand, Nachmanides disagrees with this approach. He makes no distinction between hatred that is kept in one's heart and hatred that is expressed openly.[27] Rabbi Yaakov Kenievsky, known as the Steipler Gaon (1899-1985), points out the difference between Maimonides and Nachmanides (and *Sefer Yerai'im*), which is that according to Nachmanides, even if a Jew expresses his or her anger, the command is still violated.[28] Rabbi Yisrael Meir Kagan (known as the Chofetz Chaim) states that it is far better for a person to declare his anger openly rather than act hypocritically.[29] He then says that the sin is defined like Maimonides and *Sefer HaChinuch*, and not like Nachmanides. Rav Silver brings all of the opinions discussed above, but then explains that it makes no difference practically if one keeps the hatred within or not. If a Jew expresses his hatred, even though he has not violated one sin of hatred, he still is committing other sins, as noted above. In addition, every act of hatred (whether expressed or not) is always a failure to fulfill the Mitzvah of loving one's fellow Jews.[30]

The Sheiltot, as explained by Rabbi Naftali Tzvi Yehuda Berlin in his commentary,[31] as well as another modern Rabbi,[32] have a different interpretation of why the Torah speaks about "hating in one's heart." The Torah is trying to teach us that *not only* is a Jew guilty of hatred if he or she acts upon the hatred, but even if the hatred is kept silent within one's heart, that person is *still* guilty of this sin. Fi-

19. Erchin 16b
20. Genesis 34:4
21. Rashi commentary on Genesis 34:4
22. Midrash, *Yalkut Shimoni*, Leviticus 19, 613
23. Maimonides, *Sefer HaMitzvot*, negative Mitzvah 302
24. Maimonides, *Hilchot De'ot* 6:5-6
25. *Sefer HaChinuch*, Mitzvah 338

26. Genesis 21:25
27. Maimonides commentary on Leviticus 19:17-18
28. *Kehilot Yaakov*, Erchin 4
29. Chafetz Chaim, *Hilchot Lashon Hara*, Introduction with *Be'er Mayim Chaim* commentary
30. *Mishpitei HaShalom* 2:7, 5
31. *Ha'amek She'elah* on Sheiltot 27
32. Rabbi Asher Weiss, *Torah HaAdam Le'adam*, Kovetz 3, p. 71

nally, there is a fourth interpretation of the nature of this sin. The Meiri argues that a Jew is not guilty of sin until he or she acts upon it. Therefore, hatred is one's heart is not a sin unless a specific action comes about as a result.[33] Rabbi Asher Weiss expands upon this interpretation, but then says that this is a novel approach that is not held by anyone else.[34]

## WHY DO PEOPLE HATE OTHERS?

Why is it so common for human beings to tend to hate each other? By understanding what drives people to hate, maybe a person can overcome that feeling and eventually minimize it or make it disappear. Orchot Tzadikim gives many reasons and motivations why, in the course of life, individuals are resentful of others and hate them.[35] When a person feels wronged monetarily, it often results in hate. A human being naturally hates anyone who has physically assaulted him or her. Hatred is also naturally directed at anyone who embarrasses an individual or slandered him or her. Although it is extremely difficult, a Jew who is the object of such pain should resist the natural urge to hate the person who caused that pain. That is the essence of this commandment. Orchot Tzadikim further says that even a failure to do a favor for someone or lend money in a time of need may also bring about hate. Sometimes even a positive act can result in hate. When a person receives a gift, but the gift is inadequate or far less than expected, it can result in feeling hatred for the gift giver. There is also a far worse source of hate: jealousy. Hating someone who does something good for others or "better than me" is also quite common.

Rabbi Silver expands upon jealousy as a source of hatred, and says that competition between two individuals can also cause this emotion (see the chapters "Jealousy" and "Competition" for an expansion of these themes). In addition, when people argue

about what is right and wrong or other moral issues, their diametrically opposed opinions often bring about hostility towards those that disagree. Especially when it comes to differences in political views or lifestyles, great animosity can be engendered.[36] Rabbi Papo adds that petty differences among family members also often bring out feelings of loathing. Any time a person's honor has been damaged, it can result in feelings of enmity, as can feelings of jealousy.[37] In a different place, Pele Yoetz says that sometimes seeing a person going down the wrong path in life can engender feelings of antagonism towards that person.[38]

What then should a person do when he wants to hate someone, as the Torah forbids hating? How can he or she be around this person and see the object of his or her hatred on a regular basis, and not display this emotion? The Rabbis, based on the precedent of Abraham, give us one possible remedy. When Abraham saw that his nephew Lot and Lot's shepherds were acting in an immoral and despicable manner (by stealing the grazing land of others), in order not to come to the forbidden emotion of hate over these actions, Abraham asked Lot to depart from him and gave him the choice of the best land. Thus, by choosing to avoid any further contact with these people, Abraham rid himself of his ill feelings before those feelings could turn into actual hatred.[39]

## WHEN HATING IS PERMITTED

Having shown Judaism's antipathy toward hatred, there are numerous other Jewish sources that seem to permit hatred in certain circumstances. Once these sources are presented, it is important to demonstrate where and when Judaism permits and where and when it forbids hatred. The very same book of Proverbs that said not to rejoice when an enemy falls also says that when the wicked are eliminated one

---

33. Meiri commentary on Yoma 85a
34. Rabbi Asher Weiss, Torah HaAdam Le'adam, Kovetz 3, p. 71
35. "The Gate of Hatred," chapter 6 in Orchot Tzadikim
36. Mishpitei HaShalom 2:8, 10, 12
37. Pele Yo'etz on "Ahavat Re'im"
38. Pele Yo'etz on "Sinah"
39. Genesis 13:5-12

*should* be happy.[40] Ecclesiastes says that there *is* a proper time to hate.[41] The Talmud says that it is permitted to call an arrogant person an "evil person" and one is even permitted to hate him,[42] based on the verse in Ecclesiastes.[43] The Psalms say that God *does* hate the enemies of the Jews.[44] A Talmudic quotation also declares that one may hate the sinner.[45] The logic of the Talmud is that the Torah acknowledges that a person has enemies. Therefore, one is permitted to hate, if the Torah itself speaks of enemies, whose animal one is still commanded to unload. When the great Rava became ill, it was announced that now his enemies could rejoice.[46]

All of these sources seem to fly in the face of the previously cited sources, which showed Judaism's repulsion to the emotion of hatred. How can the two views be reconciled, if at all? When is it allowable to hate and when is it wrong? There seem to be two specific groups of people that Judaism seems to consider legitimate objects of hatred, under certain circumstances. One target group is one's enemies. It appears that one may indeed hate those people who try to destroy the Jews – e.g., Haman, Hitler, Ahmadinejad, etc. But how can this hatred be permitted when the verse in Proverbs and later in the Mishna says, "You may not rejoice when your enemy falls"? *At the very moment* that one's enemies fall, one may not rejoice. But afterwards (and before), one may indeed hate them and what they stood for.

Why is it that Jews are not supposed to be happy at the time of the death of their enemy? As with the angels who were instructed by God not to rejoice when the enemy of the Jews, the Egyptians, drowned in the sea, these enemies are still human beings created in God's image. For that part of them that is destroyed, one cannot rejoice when they die. Afterwards, one

certainly can be happy that these people are no longer around to destroy the Jewish people. This concept is reflected in a situation in which the killer or sinner is to be hanged by a Jewish court. Although this person was evil, Judaism does not permit the community to let the body hang publicly for more than a few hours,[47] based on a clear verse in the Torah.[48] Here too, says the Talmud, since this evil person is still created in the image of God and is a reflection of that image, shaming him even after death is forbidden. And after all, the Jewish community does celebrate the downfall of Haman and the defeat of the Egyptians. Part of the Purim and Passover holidays certainly include being happy that the enemy is defeated. Hating an enemy, especially during time of war, is part of warfare. When Ecclesiastes says "a time to hate,"[49] the Midrash clearly explains that this refers to an enemy during time of war.[50] In addition, according to one opinion in the Talmud, when the verse and Mishna recorded that one may not rejoice at the downfall of an enemy, it refers only to a Jewish enemy, but regarding a non-Jewish enemy one *may rejoice* (even though this seems to contradict the earlier reference, that God did not allow the angels to sing praises when the Egyptians died).[51] Although it may not be logical, says the Talmud, there are times when one *should* hate an enemy such as Amalek, for example.[52]

The second category of people one is apparently permitted to hate is true Jewish sinners. The Talmud says that one may hate a Jew who is so evil that, after thoroughly knowing how serious a sin is, he still sins repeatedly.[53] This is the enemy referred to in the Torah whose animal you must help, and this is thus codified by Maimonides.[54] Chinuch also says that it is a Mitzvah-commandment to hate sinners after they have been admonished for their sins

40. Proverbs 11:10
41. Ecclesiastes 3:8
42. *Ta'anit* 7b
43. Ecclesiastes 8:1
44. Psalms 139:21-22
45 *Pesachim* 113b
46. *Berachot* 55b

47. *Sanhedrin* 46b
48. Deuteronomy 21:22-23
49. Ecclesiastes 3:8
50. Midrash, *Kohelet Rabbah* 3:10
51. *Megillah* 16a
52. *Yoma* 22b
53. *Pesachim* 113a
54. Maimonides, *Hilchot Rotze'ach* 13:14

many times but did not change their ways.[55] However, before the reader gets the idea that one may hate Jews today, Maimonides immediately specifies a modification to when one is allowed to hate – *only for the purpose of getting this sinner to repent.* From the tenor of Maimonides and the positive feelings towards every Jew he expresses in that same paragraph, it is clear that if one will not affect repentance upon a Jewish sinner, *then one may not hate.* (This is the case of almost all sinners today.) In addition, Rabbi Yeshayahu Karelitz, who lived in the twentieth century, says there is no Mitzvah to hate Jews today and no Mitzvah to even rebuke sinners today.[56] Thus, this category of hate is *not* applicable today.

There are other categories and types of individuals that it seems proper to hate. The Talmud describes three types of individuals that God hates (and by extension, we, who are supposed to imitate God's ways, should also hate):[57] 1) a person who is a hypocrite (who speaks one way but feels differently in his heart), 2) a person who has knowledge to exonerate someone in a court of law, but refuses to testify, and 3) a person who sees someone commit a terrible sin but cannot testify, since the testimony of one person has no validity in a Jewish court. Although nothing can legally be done to this person, it is permitted to hate him or her for this action.

Another type of individual who may be hated is a person who tries to uproot Judaism and its values through his or her actions. The Torah speaks about this person in the parlance of the time, for what was common then – he who tries to get others to worship idols. This Jew may be hated and is not subject to the obligation to "love every Jew as oneself."[58] Maimonides codifies this Jewish law regarding anyone who tries to uproot Judaism, and says that not only is a Jew not obligated to love this person (as every other Jew), but he or she

may even hate this person.[59] Chinuch stresses the "importance" of hating such an individual even more than Maimonides does.[60] Chafetz Chaim brings as examples of this idea two individuals in the Torah, Datan and Aviram, who continually tried to undermine Moses and the Jewish people.[61]

## PRACTICAL QUESTIONS REGARDING JEWISH HATRED TODAY

As noted above, there are sometimes people in the Jewish community who are hated for legitimate reasons. Often, this legitimate animosity has caused real problems and questions regarding certain aspects of Jewish life. We will examine three of these situations.

The cantor's role in a synagogue (see chapter, "Music") is not to entertain and not even simply to lead the services, but in essence, the *Chazan*, the cantor, functions as the community's representative to God. If one person in the community has animosity towards the cantor and legitimately hates him, can this hatred prevent the cantor from leading the services, as the cantor cannot legitimately represent all of the people – in this case, not the person who hates him? Unfortunately, this is a question that has been asked in Jewish communities for many hundreds of years. Rema in *Shulchan Aruch* (in the 1500s) rules that this one individual can indeed prevent a cantor from representing the entire community, but only if it is before the cantor is appointed.[62] Rabbi Yisrael Meir Kagan, in his twentieth century book of Jewish law, expands on this idea.[63] He explains that since the prayers take the place of the public offerings in the Holy Temple, having a cantor not representing every individual in the congregation might invalidate the entire "offering" to God. After the cantor has been

---

55. *Sefer HaChinuch*, Mitzvah 338
56. Chazon Ish on Maimonides, *Hilchot Shechita* 2:16
57. *Pesachim* 113b with Rashi commentary
58. Deuteronomy 13:7-9 with Rashi commentary

59. Maimonides, *Sefer HaMitzvot*, negative Mitzvah 17-18
60. *Sefer HaChinuch*, Mitzvot 457-458
61. Chafetz Chaim, *Be'er Mayim Chaim* 9
62. Rema, *Shulchan Aruch*, *Orach Chaim* 53:19
63. *Mishna Berurah* commentary on *Shulchan Aruch*, *Orach Chaim* 53:19

appointed, however, one individual's legitimate hatred cannot remove the cantor. Only if the majority of the congregation wishes to remove this person can they do so. However, that cantor must receive his entire promised salary. This situation only applies to a cantor who represents the community to God. A Rabbi or noted teacher in the same situation cannot be removed.

Another situation in which a hated person involves a Mitzvah is the in regard to the obligation to visit the sick. Can someone who hates an individual legitimately visit that person when he is ill? Is he obligated to do so? It is possible that he wishes to make peace with that person before the individual dies. This question is also discussed at length. Although Rabbi Moshe Isserles brings some minority views that it is permitted, he rules that it should not be done. He reasons that others (or the sick person) may interpret the visit in the wrong manner, believing that the visitor is "gloating" over the condition of the sick individual and is happy that this person who was hated is now ill. Therefore, it is best not to visit.[64]

The same question is discussed regarding visiting an individual mourning a parent during the seven-day *Shiva* period of mourning for a close relative, when there is an obligation to go to be with him or her. Unlike visiting the sick, the purpose of comforting the mourners is more complicated. Rabbi Moshe Feinstein explains that there is a double commandment when visiting a *Shiva* house. There is comfort provided for the relatives of the person who died, the mourners, but also comfort and respect for the actual person who died.[65] If the animosity was between the potential visitor and the actual person who died, Rabbi Reisman writes it is then certainly legitimate to visit the mourners, since the person who died is no longer affected by the hatred, and the visit will be taken as a gesture of reconciliation. However, if the hatred is towards the mourners themselves, then while it is true that visiting them might also honor the departed parent, the mourners may interpret the visit as "gloating" over their loss. Thus, for this reason it would be improper to visit this *Shiva* house. However, it is always advisable to try to reconcile with anyone who hates another individual. If the visitor knows for certain that his or her visit will help reconcile the hatred, then a visit is indeed in order.[66]

---

64. *Shulchan Aruch, Yoreh De'ah* 338:2 with *Siftei Kohen* commentary

65. *Responsa Igrot Moshe, Orach Chaim* 4, 40:11
66. *Ratz Katzvi, Yerach Eitanim* 11:2-3

# HEROES IN JEWISH THOUGHT

THE CRISIS OF LEADERSHIP IN BOTH the Jewish and non-Jewish worlds is at all all-time high. Many people in leadership roles, including presidents, prime ministers, mayors, CEOs, Rabbis, and teachers have been found to engage in immoral or illegal activities. Some individuals who many people thought were their heroes often turn out to be anything but, as they engage in self-centered behaviors. In the Jewish community, some of those leaders whom Jews previously respected have been accused or convicted of crimes or improper behavior. In addition, search committees in the Jewish community that try to replace retiring leaders take longer and longer to find candidates worthy of the leadership positions. There are fewer and fewer Rabbis today whom everyone looks up to and acknowledges as true leaders. Why is this occurring specifically now? What is the definition of a true hero and true leader in Judaism? Perhaps after defining what authentic Jewish heroism and leadership are through the sources, we may begin to choose different kinds of leaders for today.

## DEFINING A JEWISH HERO

A hero in Western society is generally defined as "a man of distinguished courage or ability, admired for his brave deeds and noble qualities." We know of many heroes who have performed various heroic actions. Yet if we were to ask today's youth who *their* heroes are, whom they want to be like, the overwhelming majority (in survey after survey) answers athletes, actors, and pop singers. The values of most of these individuals (while there certainly are exceptions in every field) do not usually represent the best of Western society's values and certainly not Jewish values. What then is the Jewish definition of a hero, and how is this definition the same as or different from that of society at large? What

makes a hero become a uniquely Jewish hero?

The closest words for the terms "hero" and "heroism" in Hebrew and in the Bible are "*Gibor*" and "*Gevura*." However, if we examine the use of this word in the Bible, we will see that it is rarely used in the sense of heroism, and it sometimes has a negative reference. For example, the very first time the word "*Gibor*" appears in Scripture is in describing Nimrod, who is regarded as evil in Jewish thought.[1] The Torah says that he was the first *Gibor* twice, referring to his hunting skills. One commentary describes Nimrod in a positive light, as the person who showed courage in hunting and then taught humanity how to hunt animals.[2] Rashi, on the other hand, says that Nimrod "hunted people" and used his cunning to rebel against God.[3]

Other personalities described as *Gibor* in the Bible are depicted in a more positive light, but once again, only to describe physical prowess. Gidon, one of the exemplary Judges, is called a *Gibor*.[4] On the other hand, Yiftach, whose character was somewhat questionable, is described as both a son of a prostitute and a *Gibor*.[5] This indicates that they were physically strong men, but says nothing about their character. In addition to his other traits, Saul, the first king of Israel, is also called a *Gibor*.[6] Saul's successor, King David, is usually thought of as a non-imposing figure physically, especially when we think of his encounter with Goliath. He did not "look" like a king (see Samuel I, chapter 16), as he was the last person Samuel and his family believed would be selected by God as king. Yet David is called a *Gibor* as a warrior, in the same verse that he is described as a musician and a man of

---

1. Genesis 10:8-9
2. Ibn Ezra commentary on Genesis 10:8
3. Rashi commentary on Genesis 10:8-9
4. Judges 6:11-12
5. Judges 11:1
6. Samuel I 14:52

war.[7] Some commentaries explain that this verse may be using "*Gibor*" not to describe his physical prowess, but his mental abilities in devising strategy and his great personal courage (David became a general after his conquest of mighty Goliath).[8] The evil Yerovam, who split the Kingdom of the Jewish people into two, is also described as a *Gibor* in war, a clear reference to physical strength and certainly not to heroism.[9]

Later, Jeremiah warns people not to feel self-important and haughty due to their attainments of wisdom, strength, courage, and wealth, but rather to realize that these accomplishments all come from God.[10] Clearly, the quality of a *Gibor* referred to by these verses is primarily that of physical strength, and not necessarily a characteristic to be admired or that is heroic. But then, after all these amoral references to human beings as *Gibor*, we find that God Himself is described a *Gibor*, first in the Torah itself,[11] and then repeatedly by Jeremiah[12] and King David in Psalms.[13] Obviously, this description cannot be referring to physical strength, since God has no physicality. What then does this term signify and how does it relate to our original question about heroism in the Jewish sense?

## A CHANGE IN THE MEANING OF *GIBOR* AND *GEVURA*

Until now, we have seen that all references in the Scripture to "*Gibor*" and "*Gevurah*" indicate physical prowess. Even when referring to God, it seems to describe God's acts of might and power in the world. But then something changed. The Talmud informs us that because the Jewish people were suffering mightily at the hands of non-Jewish kings and countries, Daniel actually removed the term "*Gibor*,"

referring to God, from the prayer service, as God's power and might were no longer readily evident in the world.[14] Later, the Men of the Great Assembly reinstated the word as they redefined the concept. In Judaism, the term "*Gibor*" no longer signifies physical strength and might. Rather, it indicates inner strength and the ability to hold back one's natural tendencies and to instead behave courageously from within. By withholding His anger with the non-Jewish nations that were persecuting His people, the Jews, God demonstrated *Gevurah*, inner strength and courage. This, then, is the definition of Jewish heroism. All references to "*Gibor*" in Judaism after the Men of the Great Assembly seem to use this definition of heroism.

Since Jews are commanded to imitate God's ways and values,[15] it becomes a positive Jewish value to be like God, to overcome one's natural tendencies and inclinations, and hold oneself back from doing the wrong thing. Jewish heroism, then, is defined as a quality of inner strength that is accomplished privately. It is distinguished from the usual concept of the "flashy" hero performing acts in public. Thus, when the Mishna asks what true heroism and true courage are, it answers, "He who overcomes his natural desires."[16] This is Jewish heroism.

In a related idea demonstrating the importance of the privacy of Jewish heroism, the Talmud tells the story of a Jewish hero, Mar Ukva, who used to anonymously leave coins each day at a poor man's house in order not to embarrass him and to prevent him from revealing the identity of his supporter. One day the man was curious who his benefactor was, so he stayed near the door. As Mar Ukva was approaching the poor man's house from a distance, he noticed the poor man at the door and he knew he had to hide himself. However, the only available hiding place was a furnace. Mar Ukva jumped into the furnace and stayed

---

7. Samuel I 16:18
8. Radak and Ralbag commentaries
9. Kings I 11:28
10. Jeremiah 9:22-23
11. Deuteronomy 10:17
12. Jeremiah 20:11, 32:18
13. Psalms 24:8, 78:65

14. *Yoma* 69b
15. *Sotah* 14a
16. Mishna *Avot* 4:1

there until the man left. He chose to burn himself rather than cause this man any embarrassment.[17] This incident displays true Jewish heroism – an act of goodness done privately. In a similar manner, the ten Rabbis who were tortured and killed by the Romans because they refused to refrain from teaching Torah when the Romans banned the learning of Torah, are called in the prayers *"Giborai Ko'ach"* – "heroes of strength."[18] Their inner strength and values – their heroism – compelled them to teach Torah even if it meant risking their lives.

Therefore, the Western definition of a hero and the Jewish definition of "hero," although somewhat related, are in reality quite different. Perhaps this difference can be highlighted by which group of Jews is viewed as true heroes in the Holocaust. In the non-Jewish world, people point to the individual Jews who physically rebelled against the Nazis in the Warsaw Ghetto, holding off the Nazi army for nearly six weeks, longer than the entire Polish army managed to do. The millions who were murdered in the gas chambers are sometimes looked upon negatively as "sheep going to the slaughter." But based on our new definition of a Jewish hero, it is the Jews who died with the *Shema* prayer on their lips, who never abandoned their dignity and faith despite the apparent logic in doing so, who are considered the real Jewish heroes of the Holocaust.

Another example depicting the difference between the Western concept of hero and the Jewish concept of hero can be seen through two different incidents. On January 15, 2009, Captain Chelsey Sullinger was flying his US Airways plane when it became damaged. Despite the personal peril involved, he safely landed the plane in the Hudson River, saving all 150 passengers aboard. While this certainly was a heroic act, even by Jewish standards (saving even a single life in Judaism is an act deserving of the highest merit), Jewish lore often describes heroism in a different form.

Rabbi Israel Salanter (1810-1883), the Rabbi of his community, did not show up at his synagogue one Yom Kippur night. All of the people were worried, and after the services they searched for him. They found him in the small home of a single mother who wanted to pray in the synagogue so much that she foolishly left her sleeping baby alone. On the way to synagogue, Rabbi Yisrael heard the crying baby, investigated, and realized the situation. He chose to babysit and miss Yom Kippur services rather than leave the helpless child alone. Even though Rabbi Salanter certainly wanted to pray in the synagogue, especially on Yom Kippur, he overcame his desire to do so in order to do what he believed was more important. This is an example of Jewish heroism.

No matter what the definition of a hero is, one eternal question remains: are heroes (or leaders, for that matter) born that way, or does the situation make them act in a heroic manner? There are many ordinary people or even scoundrels who are not considered heroes or leaders, but when a unique situation presents itself, they step up and act heroically like a true leader. (Consider Oskar Schindler and similar stories during the Holocaust, for example). Were these people heroic to begin with and they only needed a situation to demonstrate what was already inside of them, or did they become heroes only once a specific situation arose? This question is debated in the in the Talmud,[19] and has never been resolved.

## WHO WOULD BE CONSIDERED JEWISH HEROES TODAY?

Despite the general definition of a Jewish hero described above (which makes anyone who retains this quality a hero of sorts) are there any specific kinds of people that Jews should aspire to imitate? Are there role models that Jews should look up to as heroes and try to be like?

Although there is no specific list, perhaps two sources can help give us direction. In

---

17. *Ketuvot 67b*
18. *"Arzei HaLevanon"* – "Cedars of Lebanon" lamentation in the Tisha B'av service

---

19. *Erchin 17a*

one blessing that traditional Jews recite three times daily, we pray to God to be with and like a group of people ("set our lot with them").[20] Who are these people that we aspire to be in their company and to emulate? They are the "the righteous, the pious, the elders, . . . the remnant of the Scribes, the righteous converts . . ." What exactly is special about each type of "hero" who is described in this blessing?

A righteous individual, a *Tzadik* in Judaism, is not someone who is a "great guy" or holy. "*Tzadik*" comes from the word "*Tzedek*," which connotes doing the right or proper thing in each situation.[21] Knowing what the Torah and Jewish law demand of a Jew in each situation and not deviating from the proper action is what makes a person a *Tzadik*. A pious person (*Chasid*) is an individual who goes beyond the letter of the law and also demonstrates extra kindness. An elder in Judaism is not someone who is old. Rather, it is a person who has acquired wisdom.[22] A young person with wisdom can be called a *Zaken*, an elder.

What is a "remnant of the Scribes"? The Scribes used to write down all practices and transmit the tradition. The remnant is the last person of a generation who remembers what it "used to be like" when Jews observed certain customs. This person is the link to the previous generations and the one who passes down the tradition correctly to keep the chain of Jewish traditions and customs preserved. Finally, the righteous convert is to be admired because he or she sought truth and rejected an entire lifestyle, community, values, and family in order to convert to Judaism and embrace a Jewish way of life. Therefore, this person is also a hero to be admired.

There is another source that further identifies the "best" people in the Jewish community, the heroes to seek out. In searching for the perfect spouse (in Talmudic times the man chose his wife usually based on the qualities of the father or the family), the Talmud tells us which values and qualities to look for. The first choice for a spouse is to be [the daughter of] a *Talmid Chacham*, someone imbued with the wisdom of Torah. If that person cannot be found, then one should marry [the daughter of] a great man of the generation, which refers to a leader of the community. If not available, then marry [the daughter of] a head of a synagogue (perhaps the president). If this category is also unavailable, then marry [the daughter of] a *Gabbai*, someone who is responsible for distributing *Tzedaka* (charity) monies to the needy of the community. Finally, one may otherwise seek to marry [the daughter of] a teacher of Torah.[23] Although these would certainly not be the heroes one would think of in classic Western culture (and some may say these categories do not adequately portray the Jewish perspective either), the Talmud seems to declare that these five role models may also be considered heroes in the Jewish community.

---

20. Thirteenth blessing of the daily *Shmoneh Esreh* ("*Al HaTzadkim*")
21. Leviticus 19:36, Deuteronomy 16:20
22. *Kiddushin* 32b

23. *Pesachim* 49b

# HOMOSEXUALITY AND HOMOSEXUALS IN TRADITIONAL JUDAISM

I N THE PAST TWENTY FIVE YEARS, HO-
mosexuality and the homosexual lifestyle
have gradually become accepted in most
circles of Western culture, while steadfastly
remaining eeschewed in non-Western societ
ies. This phenomenon is a radical departure
from how homosexuals and lesbians were
viewed by virtually all societies less than fifty
years ago, and it remains a very sensitive moral
issue, with financial, political, and societal
implications.

In the last decade, a new subgroup has
emerged – "Orthodox gays." Many consider
this term to be oxymoronic. How does traditional Judaism respond to this lifestyle which
everyone feels passionate about? What do
the sources specifically tell us about both
homosexuality and homosexuals? Can someone have a gay lifestyle and still claim to be
Orthodox? Can the traditional view of homosexuality be altered, based on the practice and
values of a given society? Traditional Judaism
has much to say about these issues, and the
sources, taken as a whole, are not as cut-and-
dried as most people would assume.

## THE CLASSIC TORAH VIEW OF
HOMOSEXUALITY

The Torah clearly states its views about the act
of homosexuality. Homosexuality, i.e., two
men having sexual relations, is unmistakably
prohibited.[1] The act is twice called a *"To'aiva,"*
an "abomination" and it is such a severe sin
that it merits the death penalty in a Jewish
court system.[2] If not for the fact that homosexuality is prevalent and accepted in Western
society today, there would be little controversy
about this Torah sin. It is clearly forbidden and
never condoned anywhere in the Torah.

The very context of the prohibition gives us
an indication of the severity of the homosexual
act.[3] It is couched between the prohibitions
of child sacrifice (to an idol) and bestiality
(sexual relations with an animal). In almost
every culture in the twenty-first century, these
two acts are considered abhorrent, repugnant,
and contrary to society's values. This attitude
seems to reflect the Torah's attitude towards
the act of homosexuality. It is only because
homosexuality is relatively widespread and
condoned by so many people today, a relatively new phenomenon, that it appears that
the Torah is "out of step" with the real world.
"Live and let live" concerning all sexual unions
is a consensus that emerged only in the latter
part of the twentieth century. This apparent
conflict raises an important issue that has clear
ramifications and will be discussed below.

Although it is not specifically mentioned
in the Torah, lesbianism was regarded by the
Rabbis in the same manner as homosexuality – i.e., as an unnatural sexual bond.[4] They
clearly forbade it in Jewish law as a Rabbinic
violation without the classical punishment
for sin (because no classical intercourse takes
place),[5] but did suggest Rabbinic flogging as
a punishment. The *Code of Jewish Law* adopts
this view as well.[6]

Because of the severity of the sin, in the past,
many Jewish homosexuals feared a severe reaction by the Jewish community and by their own
families if they "came out of the closet." Some
even feared traditional parents who would
sit *Shiva* (the traditional seven day mourning
ritual for the death of close relatives) upon
hearing that their child is a homosexual, much
like the classic response to intermarriage. And
yet, after the initial shock, many traditional

---

1. Leviticus 18:22
2. Leviticus 20:23

3. Leviticus 18:21-23
4. Midrash, *Sifra, Acharei Mot* 8:8
5. Maimonides, *Hilchot Issurei Bi'ah* 21:8
6. *Shulchan Aruch, Even Ha'ezer* 20:2

parents today often take a more sympathetic attitude towards homosexual children. Which reaction is the "proper" one for observant Jews, given the Torah's straightforward attitude and stated prohibitions? What do the sources and Rabbinic authorities tell us? We will examine these practical issues below, after we analyze the deeper understanding of the sin in through classic texts.

## THE CONTEXT AND REASONS FOR THE TORAH VIEW OF HOMOSEXUALITY

The Torah calls homosexuality a "*To'aiva*." What exactly does this term signify? Almost every English translation of the Bible translates "*To'aiva*" as "abomination." But can there be any other translations of this word? Usually, the Rabbis do not explain the meaning of the Torah's words in the Talmud. And the traditional meaning of abomination seems reasonably clear – it is abhorrent to God. But in this case, the Talmud does offer a specific explanation of this word that is quite different from the traditional understanding. Based on a play on the Hebrew words, the Talmud says that in the act of homosexuality, the person is "straying." [7] What exactly does this mean?

The commentaries on the Talmudic passage say that by abandoning heterosexual relations, the person is straying from one of his prime goals in life – to procreate and populate the earth.[8] This Talmudic explanation does not seem to reflect the "abhorrence" that the word "*To'aiva*" implies in the simple meaning that is understood by most regarding the Jewish view of homosexuality. Thus, the Talmudic explanation of why homosexuality is prohibited in the Torah is because of "straying," i.e., failure to populate the earth. Chinuch explains that any "wasting of seed" on homosexual relations is preventing procreation and inhabiting the earth, the prime directive of man.[9] This "prime

directive" is echoed by Isaiah in describing the purpose of creation – for the world "to be inhabited."[10]

If this explanation does not point to the "abhorrence" of the homosexual relationship, but rather to the violation of man's purpose on earth and of core Torah values, then this new understanding is the true reason for the prohibition of homosexuality. If legitimate, then this analysis should also be valid if we compare it to other sins in the Torah that are also called a "*To'aiva*," for which there are numerous other references. By examining each one, we may be able to ascertain what they all have in common.

## WHAT OTHER SINS IN THE TORAH ARE CALLED "*TO'AIVA*" – "ABOMINATION"?

Desiring and then worshipping idols of the nations that the Jews conquer is considered a *To'aiva*.[11] Eating non-kosher foods is also called a *To'aiva*.[12] There is a general statement that *all* of the customs of the Canaanite nations are considered to be *To'aiva*.[13] This is followed by some examples (noted above), including child sacrifice to their gods and using a seer or "magician" to contact the dead or predict the future.[14] The Torah again uses the term "*To'aiva*" regarding these acts, and tells us that God says it is *because* these nations did all of these acts of *To'aiva* that God is letting the Jewish people vanquish them.[15] One paragraph later, the Torah records nine verses in which God reiterates these sins, including homosexuality.[16] These verses begin with the prohibition of child sacrifice, stating that the purpose of the prohibition is in order not to defile God's name. Then the verses mention "*To'aiva*" four separate times in describing how these sins pollute the Land of Israel. The verses

---

7. *Nedarim* 51a
8. *Genesis* 1:28
9. *Sefer HaChinuch*, Mitzvah 209

10. Isaiah 45:18
11. Deuteronomy 7:25-26
12. Deuteronomy 14:3
13. Deuteronomy 18:9
14. Deuteronomy 18:10-11
15. Deuteronomy 18:12
16. Deuteronomy 18:21-29

end by stating that this land will "vomit" out anyone who commits these sins, whether the inhabitants are non-Jews or Jews, and that the sinners will be punished.

What do all of these acts have in common? These do not seem to be particularly "abominable" acts that are abhorrent to the senses (the common understanding of "To'aiva"). Rather, all of these sins seem to be pagan customs derived from non-Jewish values basic to those societies whose morality is antithetical to Judaism. God emphatically warns the Jewish people not to learn these customs or follow these values. There is also a general prohibition in addition to the prohibition of these specific sins.[17] These sins, then, violate core Jewish values, highlighting To'aiva as the straying from the Jewish mission, as explained earlier in the Talmud. Based on this new explanation and the context of the sin, homosexuality, also considered a To'aiva, can be understood to be a societal value and sin that is alien to Judaism and Jewish values, which should not be imitated or "learned" from the societies in which the Jews have lived or which they have conquered.

## HOMOSEXUAL ACTS AND THEIR CONSEQUENCES IN THE TORAH

Several incidents of homosexuality in the Scripture, as elucidated by the Talmud and Midrash, help amplify this understanding of the homosexual act, and also clarify the overall Torah attitude towards homosexuality. Although not expressed explicitly in the Torah, the Rabbis understood that, according to the Torah,[18] Potiphar bought the Hebrew, Joseph, specifically for homosexual purposes.[19] This is significant, as it clearly implies that homosexuality was prevalent in Egypt at that time. Thus, when the Torah (later on) commands Jews not to imitate the ways of the Egyptians (and Canaanites), this prohibition could also include the practice of homosexuality that was commonly found in these societies. This in fact is the Rabbinical source prohibiting lesbianism, as mentioned above.

One of the explanations for the cause of the Flood and God's dissatisfaction with the world[20] is the widespread homosexual activity at that time. According to the commentaries, each species "corrupted its way," i.e., had improper sexual relationships.[21] Man and other species regularly engaged in bestiality (sexual relations with other species) and homosexuality. It was for this reason that God destroyed the world, showing that these practices are antithetical to God's vision for man and society's development. After the Flood, Noah became drunk and Canaan, his grandson, entered his tent and committed a sin with him.[22] According to one Talmudic opinion, Canaan forced Noah to engage in a homosexual act and this is why Canaan was cursed as a result.[23] Later, in the society of Sodom, the Torah says that the townspeople demanded that the strangers be given to them in order "that they shall know them."[24] Rashi explains that they wanted the men for homosexual purposes,[25] based on the previous uses of the verb "knowing" in the Torah as being associated with the sexual act.[26] This was apparently common practice in that society, and hence this is the origin of the term "sodomy." This common practice in Sodom is one of the main reasons that the city was destroyed very soon thereafter.

All of these Torah examples have in common the fact that homosexual activity was common in these cultures and that God disapproved. Consequently, some of these societies were eventually destroyed. This, once again, shows that Jews may not engage in such activity and imitate the mores of these foreign societies.

17. Leviticus 18:3
18. Genesis 39:1
19. *Sotah* 13b

20. Genesis 6:12-13
21. Rashi, Chizkuni, and Mizrachi commentaries on Genesis 6:12
22. Genesis 9:22-24
23. *Sanhedrin* 70a
24. Genesis 19:5
25. Rashi commentary on Genesis 19:5
26. Genesis 4:1

## HOW JUDAISM SEEMS TO VIEW THE ORIGIN OF HOMOSEXUAL BEHAVIOR

There has been some controversy about the nature of homosexuality – if it is a totally inborn and genetic phenomenon or if it is a learned or societal behavior, or a combination of both. Many doctors and scientists today claim that homosexuality is inborn and not a learned behavior, and the American Medical Association (AMA) seems to reflect this view in how it classifies homosexual behavior. However, based on certain recent studies and the fact that a number of homosexuals have "learned" to become heterosexuals, some today argue that homosexuality is a learned behavior that is dependent on one's environment. The fact that the rate of homosexual activity increases drastically in all-male populations or societies (such as prisons or all-male dormitories) also seems to indicate that homosexuality is, at least in part, a societal or learned behavior.

Based on the sources above and the normative Halacha (to be discussed below), the Torah seems to view homosexuality as a societal or behavioral phenomenon, and not an inborn proclivity. It is for this reason that the Torah commands Jews to stay away from the practices of those societies where homosexuality is common. All "foreign" aspects of those societies are detested by God and Judaism, as these are not holy acts and would not be tolerated in the Holy land of Israel (no matter who commits them). God destroyed those societies in which homosexual activity was common (i.e., Noah's antediluvian society, Sodom, Egypt). Jewish law in practice seems to reflect this view.

## HOW CHANGING HOMOSEXUAL PRACTICES AMONG JEWS AFFECTED JEWISH LAW

Although these two acts are viewed very differently in the modern world, the Mishna, like the Torah, links the sexual acts of homosexuality

and bestiality.[27] One minority view is that the Rabbis were worried that a single man may commit both of the sins, and thus a man is prohibited from being alone with either an animal or another man. This is similar to the prohibition for a Jewish man not to be alone with a woman, for the same fear that the natural sexual urges will take over and an illicit act may be committed.[28] However, the majority opinion in that Mishna is that Jews are *not* suspected of bestiality and homosexual behavior, and therefore, a man *can* remain alone with an animal or another man. This shows that although there was one opinion that Jews were cognizant of natural sexual urges to other men and to beasts, the majority view was that we need not fear this natural urge, and that homosexuality was *not* prevalent in the Jewish community in Talmudic times. (This should not be viewed as a "cover" by the Rabbis to protect the reputations of some Jews, since if these acts were indeed found in the community, the Rabbis would not have hesitated to forbid men from being alone with other men.) In addition, we find almost no responsa literature in the 500 years following the Talmud discussing the issue of homosexuality, indicating that it was not a prevalent issue. While Jews were not hesitant to discuss and ask Jewish law questions about many other illicit and "abhorrent" behaviors and sins, homosexuality was not one of them.

Maimonides, who lived in the twelfth century, also ruled like the majority opinion in the Talmud - i.e., that Jewish males were not suspected of homosexual behavior (or bestiality). He does add, however, that those Jews who *do* refrain from being alone with a man or an animal are to be praised.[29] Thus, in Spain and in Egypt of the twelfth century, homosexual activity was still not a prevalent activity found among the Jews. However, this norm seems to have changed in the time of Rabbi Yosef Caro, the author of *Shulchan Aruch*.[30] He first quotes Maimonides word for word, but then

---

27. *Kiddushin* 4:19
28. Maimonides, *Hilchot Isurei Bi'ah* 22:1
29. Maimonides, *Hilchot Issurei Bi'ah* 22:2
30. *Shulchan Aruch, Even Ha'ezer* 24:1

adds that as in "these" (his) times there is great licentiousness, two men should not be alone together (or sleep in the same bed). We see from these words two important concepts. First, that in the sixteenth century in the land of Israel, there seemed to be substantial homosexual activity among Jews. Second, Jewish law recognizes that homosexuality is a function of individual societies, and it responds to this societal change with changes in Jewish law.

However, two centuries later, a commentary on *Shulchan Aruch*, Rabbi Sirkis (the Bach) writes that he does not understand these words of *Shulchan Aruch* because he cannot find any homosexual activity in his community. Therefore, he does not agree with (or apply) this particular Jewish law to his community, and he permits two males to be alone together.[31] A more modern Jewish law authority who lived in the nineteenth century first echoes the words of Maimonides and Rabbi Sirkis, but then in a prescient manner adds that "if there will be a society (in the future) whereby licentiousness will be common, then it will be forbidden for two men to remain alone (in a locked room) and certainly forbidden to sleep in one bed." Today, given the more widespread homosexual activity in general society and also (plausibly, no doubt) in the Jewish community in Western countries, perhaps the Halacha would now revert to the time of *Shulchan Aruch* and it would be prohibited for two men to be alone or share the same bed.

## THE TRADITIONAL JEWISH VIEW OF HOMOSEXUALS

Judaism clearly separates between the desire to sin and the sin itself. In every realm of life, Judaism recognizes that Jews, as normal human beings, have desires to commit sins. The premise of the concept of the inner battle between the good inclination and the bad inclination is based on man's normal desire to sin, as alluded

to in the Torah.[32] It is only because of the great natural desire that the Torah prohibits every Jewish man from being alone with a woman (the commandment of *Yichud*, as cited above). Similarly, because the Torah recognizes the normal desire among men to have homosexual activity, in certain societies Jewish law prohibits two men from being alone together (as discussed above). But although it is natural to have certain sexual feelings, the Torah says clearly that it is forbidden to *act* upon those desires.[33] Thus, while many sexual desires may be normal and not prohibited, *acting upon those desires* violates Jewish principles and Jewish law, whether they are between man and man or man and (a forbidden) woman.

For example, while it may be normal for a heterosexual married man to desire a beautiful married woman who is not his wife, *acting* upon this desire violates the seventh of the Ten Commandments. Similarly, while the Torah may understand homosexual desire, acting upon it is forbidden. Therefore, the Midrash specifically says concerning all prohibitions in the Torah that a Jew's attitude should *not* be, "I have no desire for that which is forbidden (pork or even another man)," but a Jew should rather say, "What can I do, since God has commanded me not to act upon these desires."[34] Every society, even secular society, demands that some sexual desires be held in check, and regulates man's acting upon his sexual desires. Judaism regulates illicit sexual activity as well and thus prohibits man to act on his illicit homosexual desire.

## JUDAISM ABHORS THE SIN BUT NOT THE SINNER

The first Lubavitcher Rebbe writes that Jews can hate the sin, but also must continue to love the sinner.[35] This is consistent with the normative Jewish view. Thus, while Jews may abhor the sin of homosexuality, they must continue

---

31. *Bayit Chadash* commentary on the *Tur*, *Even Ha'ezer* 24

32. Genesis 9:21
33. Numbers 15:39
34. Midrash, *Yalkut Shimoni*, *Vayikra* 20
35. *Tanya*, chapter 32

to love the homosexual, despite his sinning behavior. Jews should not and cannot reject people as Jews and as individuals because of a particular sin. Those who violate the Shabbat, for example, (who are also guilty of the death penalty in the Torah) are not thrown out of the Jewish community or denied the ability to pray in the synagogue. Similarly, homosexuals who have sinned with acts of homosexuality may not be thrown out of the Jewish community or shunned.

Since *everyone* has committed *some* sin,[36] Jews would have to expel everyone from the synagogue if we excommunicated all sinners. For example, if Jews were to eject from the synagogue or deny membership to anyone guilty of the sin of gossip, then Jewish communities would have no *Minyan* (religious quorum) in almost any synagogue in the world, due to lack of people. And yet, this sin of gossip is referred to as the most severe sin of all, equal to the three cardinal sins of Judaism combined![37] Since in practice Jews do not judge sinners and sins – i.e., which sin is a more severe and which a less severe sin – all Jews are permitted to remain in the community as long as they want to be Jews and a part of the community. This idea is expressed in the Talmud when it says that a Jew remains a Jew even after he sins.[38]

There is a difference, however, in how Judaism looks at two types of homosexuals, even though they committed the very same act. Judaism distinguishes between two kinds of general sinners. First, there is the Jew who tries to observe *Mitzvot*-commandments, but because of urges, he or she cannot hold himself for herself back and sins even though he or she knows it is wrong. This is called a sinner *L'tai'avon*, due to urges. There is a second kind of sinner, who can easily overcome his or her desires, but sins (often publicly) because he or she wants to demonstrate his or her loathing for Judaism

and Jewish practice. This is called a Sinner *L'hachis*, to infuriate (others). Rabbi Meir of Rothenberg, whose teaching is brought down in Jewish law, distinguishes between these two types of Jewish sinners.[39] Judaism views the first kind of sinner as any other Jew (in reacting to his death, for example), but shuns the second kind of sinner, who chooses not to be part of the community. Thus, the homosexual who is part of the community and is contrite about his homosexual activity but cannot help himself, is certainly welcomed in to the Jewish community, as most of the community is unaware of his private sexual practices. But the homosexual who takes pride in his sin and does not care who knows about it (or leads the gay parade) is saying by his actions that he defies the Torah and its laws proudly. This person is a sinner *L'hachis* and is looked upon very differently by the Torah community, as he chooses to exclude himself.

There are other Jewish homosexuals who desire and choose to "be with their own" and form "gay congregations" and communities exclusively for Jewish homosexuals. This is *not* the Jewish way. Each Jewish community should be made up of a diversity of Jews. The Hebrew word for community, Tzibbur, is an acronym for three groups: *Tzadikim, Benonim, and Risha'im*, or righteous, "middle of the roaders," and sinners.[40] Thus, every Jewish community is and should be made up of diverse people of all moralities. This is also the symbolic concept obligating every Jew to hold the Four Species together on Sukkot (each species representing a different level of morality, a different kind of Jew),[41] and is also represented in the words recited immediately prior to *Kol Nidrei* on Yom Kippur, when we ask the sinners to be part of the congregation and pray for forgiveness with everyone else.[42] The Mishna specifically says that it is not proper to

---

36. Ecclesiastes 7:20
37. Maimonides, *Hilchot De'ot* 7:3
38. *Sanhedrin* 44a

39. *Tur, Yoreh De'ah* 340
40. Rabbi Menachem Mendel of Shklov, *Mishnat Chasidim*, p. 253
41. Midrash, *Vayikra Rabbah* 30:12
42. Words recited on Yom Kippur eve immediately prior to the *Kol Nidre* prayer

separate from the general Jewish community and from your own Jewish community.[43]

## CONTEMPORARY VIEWS (WITHIN HALACHA) ABOUT HOMOSEXUALITY AND HOMOSEXUALS

The views of three contemporary scholars reflect the ideas and concepts discussed above. Rabbi Shmuel Boteach has lectured to many non-Jewish and gay audiences and has also written about this subject at length. Rabbi Boteach states that homosexuality cannot be a deviance, since by definition, sexual deviance is an oxymoron.[44] Since sex is instinctive, an instinct cannot be deviant. God expressed a preference for heterosexuality and mandated that only this type of sexual activity is permitted for human beings. Since the Torah has defined Western morality (and has preserved it for thousands of years), its viewpoint needs to be taken seriously.

Rabbi Aaron Feldman from Baltimore, Rosh Yeshiva of the Ner Israel Yeshiva and a noted Rabbi in the Charedi sector, has come under some criticism for his views on this subject. Rabbi Feldman has written that non-practicing homosexuals have an important role to contribute in Jewish life. He also said that a Jew is judged by his actions and not his orientation. Only actions are prohibited, not proclivities. Controlling behavior, though difficult, is what the Torah asks. Judaism regards homosexual activity negatively, but does not condemn the homosexual.[45]

Dennis Prager has also written and spoken extensively on the Jewish view of homosexuality.[46] He writes that Judaism does not look down on homosexual love. Only homosexual intercourse is prohibited. In Judaism, Jews are simply sexual and are not classified by their sexual preference. Prager notes that the Torah has done more to civilize the world than any other book in history. Therefore, if the Torah makes a proclamation (against homosexuality), it should be taken seriously by the world. In this area, the Torah is not ambiguous, and modern values cannot be reconciled with the Torah, as it can in many other areas. Although it prohibits *Melacha*-creative activity on Shabbat, the Torah does not make a *moral* statement about the Shabbat and its violation. But in regard to homosexuality, the Torah says it is a *To'aiva*, an abomination, and thus expresses great repugnance. This is clearly unambiguous.

---

43. Mishna *Avot* 2:4
44. Rabbi Shmuley Boteach, "My Jewish Perspective on Homosexuality," *Wall Street Journal*, October 15, 2010

45. Rabbi Aharon Feldman, "A Letter to a Homosexual Baal Teshuva," *Jerusalem Letter*, 1, no. 5 (March 24, 1998)
46. Dennis Prager, "Judaism's Sexual Revolution: Why Judaism (and then Christianity) Rejected Homosexuality," *Crisis Magazine*, 11, no. 8 (September 1993)

# HOW TZEDAKA-CHARITY IS DIFFERENT FROM ALL COMMANDMENTS

O F THE 613 IN JUDAISM, THE MITZ-vah of *Tzedaka*-charity, is unique in certain attributes, Jewish law, and other anomalies connected with it. This makes *Tzedaka* the most unusual of all of the commandments. Three of the remarkable aspects of *Tzedaka* will be examined in this chapter.

## PERFORMING A MITZVAH-COMMANDMENT FOR AN ULTERIOR MOTIVE

In describing the verse instructing the Jew to give ten percent of produce to the poor, the Torah repeats in the verse the verb for tithing: "*Aser Ta'aser.*"[1] The Talmud often gives a deeper explanation when any "unnecessary" addition or repetition of a word occurs in a verse. On this verse, the Talmud states that one should tithe to the poor *for the purpose* of becoming rich.[2] Since the letters of tithing and wealth are identical (*Ayin, Shin/Sin, Resh*), the verse can then be read, "Tithe so that you can attain wealth." This seems to imply that one's motivation in giving charity in Judaism is not to please God or follow His commands, but rather, in order that God reward monetarily the person fulfilling this commandment, and he receive back from God much more than was donated. This notion seems to contradict the overarching attitude towards serving God and performing commandments: a person should act as a servant (to God) without expectation of reward.[3] And yet, the Talmud clearly says that one's motivation in giving *Tzedaka* can be for material gain and expected wealth.

The idea of ulterior motives in giving *Tzedaka* becomes even more pronounced in God's own words to the people through the prophet Malachi.[4] God tells the Jews that if they bring the tithe, they can test God through this act and God promises that great wealth will follow. Thus, the verse actually encourages Jews to test God in performing this Mitzvah. Based on this unusual verse, the Talmud states in several places that if a person conditions his *Tzedaka* donation upon God's response that his son will be cured of serious sickness and live, or upon his achieving the World to Come, then this person is considered a fully righteous individual.[5] This implies that a person can withhold giving the promised charity until one's son is healed and if the son's health does not improve, a person's promise to give *Tzedaka* is no longer obligatory. If a person were to condition performance of any other Mitzvah based on this kind of "deal" with God, it would be considered improper, blasphemous, and contrary to Jewish law. For example, if a man were to say "I will only put on Tefillin after God makes me a rich man," or a woman were to say "I will keep the Shabbat only once God gives me five healthy children," that would be considered heretical! And yet, with regard to the singular commandment of *Tzedaka*, that is not only acceptable, but the person is considered wholly righteous! It is totally legitimate, for example, to condition giving *Tzedaka* to an institution only if the building will be named in memory of one's parents. Why should this be so? The very notion of "commandment" is based on the notion that God commands and Jews obey, without questioning, without demanding, and without making any contract or exchange. How can we then understand this unusual notion in the case of *Tzedaka*? What makes giving charity so different from all other commandments that allows its performance to be conditional and violate the general princi-

---

1. Deuteronomy 14:22
2. *Ta'anit* 9a
3. Mishna *Avot* 1:3

4. Malachi 3:10
5. *Rosh Hashana* 4a, *Bava Batra* 10b, *Pesachim* 8a

ple of "serving the Master without expecting reward"?

The Rabbis and commentaries have struggled to try to explain why conditional charity in Judaism is permitted and even welcomed, while conditional performance of any other Mitzvah is forbidden. But before any explanations are attempted, it is important to point out that the power of *Tzedaka* is a stronger cosmic and spiritual force than any other Mitzvah.

## THE POWER OF TZEDAKA AS A COSMIC FORCE

In describing the ten strongest "forces" in the world, Rabbi Judah goes through each one, such as the hardness of a rock, but also then describes another force that is stronger and overcomes the first force.[6] Thus, iron can cut the rock, fire can melt iron, water quenches the fire, etc. Near the end of the list, he mentions the force of death, which overcomes everything that is living. But the most powerful force in the world, says Rabbi Judah, is *Tzedaka*, charity. Only *Tzedaka* can overcome that most powerful force of death, as it says two separate times in Proverbs[7] that *Tzedaka* can save a person from death. Concerning no other commandment does it say in Scripture that its performance will protect a person from the decree of death. Thus, the verses and Talmud already hint that the act of *Tzedaka* is quite extraordinary and inherently different from all other commandments and actions in the world.

## SEVERAL REASONS WHY AND HOW TZEDAKA IS DIFFERENT FROM ALL OTHER COMMANDMENTS

Various explanations have tried to elucidate a rationale for why conditional *Tzedaka* is acceptable, permitted, and even encouraged in Judaism:

1. The Satmar Rebbe compares the Jew accumulating wealth in this world to the worker in the field that produces fruits.[8] The Torah permits the worker to eat from those fruits that he is picking, as long as the worker is working and remains in the field.[9] Maimonides requires as part of Jewish law that the owner give food to his worker while performing this task.[10] But this Jewish law does not apply to a worker performing any other task in the field (such as fence building) or after a particular task is complete. The Jew in the physical world, says the Satmar Rebbe, is similarly, working for God in "His field" (the world) to accumulate funds in order to give some of them to *Tzedaka*. As long as the Jew is engaged in this work, he too is permitted to use these *Tzedaka* funds for his own benefit – i.e., he can receive something for giving them away, just as the worker can use what he is picking for his benefit. Thus, a Jew can "control" these earned charity funds by making conditions for how they are spent.

2. God promises to always take care of the downtrodden in society, and at the same time, commands Jews to help the downtrodden and give to them.[11] Therefore, the act of giving *Tzedaka* fulfills both obligations at the same time – God's and each Jew's. Since this is the only Mitzvah which accomplishes both goals in the same act, *Tzedaka* is unique, and God allows Jews to make giving conditional.

3. Judaism is a lifestyle that is supposed to be pleasant and not painful.[12] God understands how difficult it is to work in this world, to acquire funds, and to provide for one's family's needs, saying that this task is more difficult than childbirth, more difficult than bringing the ultimate salvation, and just as difficult as God splitting the Sea of Reeds.[13] To ask someone to then part with some of this money (even though everything belongs

---

6. *Bava Batra* 10b
7. Proverbs 10:2, 11:4

8. Quoted in "Priorities in Tzedaka," Rabbi Moshe Goldberger, 2007, pp. 41-42
9. Deuteronomy 23:25
10. Maimonides, *Hilchot Sechirut* 12:1
11. Exodus 22:21-22, Deuteronomy 24;19, Deuteronomy 15;11
12. Proverbs 3;17
13. *Pesachim* 118a

to God ultimately in any case) can be a very painful commandment. Thus, to ease the pain, God allows a person to make the giving of these accumulated funds to others conditional.

4. It is true that the Talmud cites the person who gives *Tzedaka* conditionally as being righteous, and the verse in Malachi seems to approve of testing God in this area. However, this concept is not brought down in Jewish law in the classic books of Halacha. Perhaps, then, this act is not encouraged in practice. If we look at the two specific conditions that are approved in the Talmud for giving *Tzedaka* conditionally – "my son will live" and "I will attain the World to Come" – these both involve life and death situations. Perhaps conditional *Tzedaka* is permitted only when life itself is at stake, in the same manner that all commandments may be violated in order to save a life (except for three).[14]

5. The Talmud tells us that helping the poor and downtrodden is in the spiritual DNA of each Jew (which is evidenced by the high percentage Jews giving charity today, even those who are not necessarily observant, and also by Jewish involvement in many organizations helping the downtrodden).[15] Rashi states that because of this predisposition of Jews, even when the stated condition by the potential giver is not fulfilled, the Jew still wishes to give that *Tzedaka* in any case and will donate the funds.[16] The Talmud also seems to make this distinction between Jews who would ultimately give the *Tzedaka* in any case, and some non-Jews who would use permitted conditional charity giving merely to obtain riches.[17]

6. In a similar vein, Meiri says that in a situation in which the stated provision for giving is not fulfilled, many Jews view this as God denying them because they are not worthy, and would then give the *Tzedaka* in any event.[18]

7. P'nai Yehoshua explains that the specific language in the Talmud describes the person who gives conditionally as "righteous," but does not use the word "pious" (*Chasid*) to describe this person. That is because although it might be within a person's *right* to give conditionally, it is *not* the proper Jewish way of giving *Tzedaka*.[19]

8. Rabbi Yechezkel Landau distinguishes between the Mitzvah of *Tzedaka* and every other Mitzvah in the Torah. Concerning all other actions, the intent (to perform that deed for God) is crucial and an important part of the commandment. But with charity, the intention is not truly important. The only thing that really counts is that the poor person is helped. Thus, intention, while it is an extra benefit, is not necessary in the case of *Tzedaka*, as long as the money gets to the needy individual. Therefore, even if given on condition, the Mitzvah is fulfilled, as long as the act is completed.[20]

With all of the above explanations trying to rationalize how and why *Tzedaka* is different in regard to testing the Almighty, the Chinuch, a post-Talmudic commentary, reiterates that it is forbidden to test God in one's actions in this world. He then continues to state categorically that the one exception to this rule is *Tzedaka*, regarding which one's giving can indeed be provisional upon God's compliance with a certain condition the giver specifies. While Chinuch gives several reasons for this exception (many of them cited above), he clearly permits this behavior for this Mitzvah.[21]

Given all the above arguments, sources, and statements, Jewish law follows the Chinuch, even though this idea remains counterintuitive to the system of commandments. *Tzedaka* is an extremely powerful force in the world, writes *Shulchan Aruch*. And while it is generally forbidden to test God and do a Mitzvah conditionally, Rema states that the tithing for

14. *Kesef Mishne* on Maimonides, *Hilchot Tefillin*, chapter 10
15. *Yevamot* 79a
16. Rashi commentary on *Rosh Hashana* 4a, s.v. "kahn beYisrael"
17. *Bava Batra* 10b

18. Meiri commentary on *Rosh Hashana* 4a
19. Pnai Yehoshua commentary on *Rosh Hashana* 4a
20. *Derushai Tzelach, Ahavat Tziyon*, tenth address
21. *Sefer HaChinuch*, Mitzvah 424

*Tzedaka* is the one area where a Jew can test God and give conditionally.[22]

## PRIORITIES IN TZEDAKA

In virtually every other area in which the Jew is mandated to give something from his or her possessions, each Jew has the flexibility in choosing which individual to give to. For example, regarding the gifts of produce that went the Kohen-Priest or Levite, each Jew could decide which Kohen or Levite to give it to.[23] Similarly, concerning fines that went to the Kohen in the Temple, the offending Jew could decide which specific Kohen to give to.[24] When an Israelite brought a sacrifice to the Temple, and certain parts of the animal were forbidden to be eaten by the Israelite, but permitted to the Kohen, the person who brought the sacrifice decided which Kohen would receive those parts of the animal due to him.[25]

Even regarding the poor in ancient times, dispersement of what we today would call "*Tzedaka*-charity" was relatively straightforward. In an agrarian society, The Torah mandates that one corner of the field be set aside for the poor, and produce that was dropped or forgotten in the field had to be left for the poor people to collect on their own, usually at night, in order not to publically embarrass them.[26] Even when dispersal was done during the day, there were set times for the poor to come to each field, and all of the poor gathered and collected the produce at one time together.[27] In those years when there was an additional tithe given to the poor (years one, two, four, and five of the seven year cycle), the poor gathered and divided the produce among them (if received in the field). If given from the home, the owner could decide which poor person to

give the produce to.[28] It was a simple and very orderly system of *Tzedaka*.

Today, on the other hand, we no longer speak about distributing produce to the poor. Rather, we give money. Since we have much more disposable income, the system has changed radically, making the giving of *Tzedaka* one of the most difficult commandments to fulfill properly. The laws about whom to give, which institution gets Jewish *Tzedaka* first, or which group of poor people has precedence, can confuse even a Torah scholar. The sources within Jewish law seem contradictory, unlike most other areas of Halacha.

The amount that should be given seems straightforward. The *Code of Jewish Law* rules that a certain small amount once a year fulfills the bare minimum, but it is considered miserly.[29] An average Jew gives ten percent of his or her income after basic living expenses. The maximum one may give its twenty percent. However, knowing exactly how to disperse the funds and to whom, seems very confusing, making it a very difficultcommandment to fulfill.

## NUMEROUS STATEMENTS IN JEWISH LAW ABOUT THE "MOST IMPORTANT" TZEDAKA

Part of the confusion about how to properly satisfy the obligation to donate funds in the Jewish community is that there are numerous statements in Jewish law, each stating that "this cause" or "this institution" is the most important and takes priority over everything else in the distribution of *Tzedaka*. They are:

1. Both Maimonides and *Shulchan Aruch* state that the *most important* Mitzvah in apportioning charity funds is to redeem those who were kidnapped.[30] This takes precedence over the hungry poor. Moreover, even if money was collected for a specific holy purpose – while normally it is not permitted to use this money

---

22. *Shulchan Aruch, Yoreh De'ah* 247:4
23. Bartenura commentary on Mishna *Demai* 6:3
24. Bartenura commentary on Mishna *Challah* 1:9
25. Tosefta *Pe'ah* 2:13; *Shulchan Aruch, Yoreh De'ah* 61:28
26. Leviticus 23:22, Deuteronomy 24:19
27. Maimonides, *Hilchot Matnot Aniyim* 2:17

28. Maimonides, *Hilchot Matnot Aniyim* 6:7, 9, 10, 12
29. *Shulchan Aruch, Yoreh De'ah* 249:1
30. Maimonides, *Hilchot Matnot Aniyim* 8:10; *Shulchan Aruch, Yoreh De'ah* 252:1

for other purposes – one can divert these funds to redeem captives without first asking the donors.

2. The *most important Tzedaka*, states *Shulchan Aruch* in a different place, is to donate funds to poor single girls so that they can have enough money to get married.[31]

3. In the next paragraph, the same *Shulchan Aruch* states that some believe that donating to the community synagogue is more important than poor girls and is *the greatest reason for giving charity* in the Jewish community.[32]

4. Then *Shulchan Aruch* quotes another opinion that says that donating money to enable poor boys to learn Torah is *the highest form of Tzedaka*,[33]

5. OR, continues *Shulchan Aruch*, donating to the poor who are sick is *the highest Tzedaka*.[34]

So we are left wondering which need is indeed the most pressing. If a person has limited funds for *Tzedaka* donations, which cause takes precedence above all others – redeeming captives or supporting the synagogue, poor girls needing to get married or poor boys needing to learn Torah? Or is the most essential need to donate to sick poor people so that they can regain their health (since there were no hospitals or medical insurance in Talmudic times or when *Shulchan Aruch* was written)?

In order to answer these questions, we have to introduce additional factors that are also "important" and take precedence in giving *Tzedaka*, which may at first confuse the reader even more. However, only then will we be able to resolve the conflicting needs and determine a hierarchy of giving *Tzedaka* monies in Jewish law.

### YOU AND YOUR FAMILY COME FIRST

The verse speaks about when poverty exists "within you" or "within your community."[35]

Based on this verse and the Talmudic discussion, Rema in the *Code of Jewish Law* rules that you come first.[36] If you are poor, then you come before anyone else and you give to yourself first, in order to escape poverty. *Mishna Berurah* commentary, however, is quick to add that it is forbidden to rationalize in this area and be lenient with your own needs in order to give yourself more funds than you are actually entitled to.[37] You are only permitted to give yourself enough funds for subsistence and to remove yourself from abject poverty before you are obligated to begin giving to others.

If any person extends his or her hand to receive charity, even a non-Jew, unless a Jew is certain that this person is a fake and not actually poor, the Jew must give this person some small amount at the minimum.[38] Even if a Jew possess relatively little for himself or herself, he or she must never turn away a person putting out his or her hand for charity.[39] Since, according to strict Jewish law, a parent's obligation to feed one's children ends at the age of six (at that time most young children worked and earned income), paying for one's children's food and Torah learning fulfills the *Tzedaka* obligation.[40] This is based on the Talmudic passage that speaks about some *Tzedaka* that is fulfilled day and night,[41] which Rashi explains refers to children, who need to be taken care of and have their needs paid for at every moment.[42] Then *Shulchan Aruch* continues with a list of priorities in giving *Tzedaka*. One's relatives come before other people in need. This is followed by the poor of one's community, which takes precedence over the poor of other communities. However, the poor of the Land of Israel are of equal status with the poor of your community.[43]

---

31. *Shulchan Aruch, Yoreh De'ah* 249:15
32. *Shulchan Aruch, Yoreh De'ah* 249:16
33. *Shulchan Aruch, Yoreh De'ah* 249:16
34. *Shulchan Aruch, Yoreh De'ah* 249:16
35. Deuteronomy 15:7

36. Rema on *Shulchan Aruch, Yoreh De'ah* 61:28
37. *Mishna Berurah* commentary on *Shulchan Aruch, Orach Chaim* 156:2
38. *Tur, Yoreh De'ah* 251.
39. Rema on *Shulchan Aruch, Yoreh De'ah* 249:4
40. *Shulchan Aruch, Yoreh De'ah* 251:3
41. *Ketuvot* 50a
42. Rashi commentary on *Ketuvot* 50a
43. *Shulchan Aruch, Yoreh De'ah* 251:3

## MAN VS. WOMAN

The Mishna states that, if everything else is equal, a man takes precedence over a woman when it comes to life and returning lost objects, while a woman takes precedence over a man when it comes to clothing needs and the redeeming of a captive.[44] And yet, elsewhere the Talmud states that when it comes to needy orphans, the woman always takes precedence over a man because a man can more easily obtain employment and secure funds.[45] Sefer Be'er Sheva resolves the apparent contradiction and says that in both areas of food and clothing, a woman always takes precedence over a man if their situation is equal.[46]

## DIFFERENT TYPES OF TZEDAKA AND DISTINCTIONS WITHIN THE DIFFERENT TYPES

Until now, we have been comparing "apples" and "oranges." While it is true that all the cases above are situations in the Jewish community that require monetary donations to resolve them, there is little similarity between a captive whose life is in danger and the needs of a synagogue, which are both different from a poor person needing funds in order to live. Thus, say the Rabbis, we must first separate between categories that require community or personal funds, but may not even be considered Tzedaka in the technical sense, and then define which need indeed takes precedence. Then we must analyze, differentiate, and determine who takes precedence within each category (such as poverty) and determine precedence (relatives, men, and women, etc.).

First and foremost, says Chochmat Adam, we must differentiate between situations when life is in danger or potential danger.[47] This need always comes before anything else. This may include the need to pay a tax to the ruthless king (in a society where failure to pay

taxes would result in death), taking care of a sick poor person who may die, and certainly redeeming a captive, whose life is always considered in danger (see chapter "Redeeming Captives"). Beit Yosef (author of Shulchan Aruch) states that taking care of the synagogue (which was and often still is the main center of Jewish life in the community) takes precedence over all Tzedaka needs for the poor, but may be referring to life and death situations there as well.[48]

## WHAT TO DO WITH CONFLICTS IN PRIORITIES

Rav Moshe Shternbuch was asked about a particular case involving legitimate contributions: giving money for a couple to get married or giving funds to a Yeshiva so that it can teach Torah. He then says that it is important to examine the details of each case individually, as there can be vast differences within each category and even within the obligation to help a bride and groom. There is a big difference, for example, between a bride who does not even have any money to pay for the simplest wedding dress and food for guests at the wedding, and a couple who needs money to purchase a three-room apartment, rather than a two or one-room apartment. Similarly, there is a vast difference between the needs of a Yeshiva that is trying to build a new wing and another Yeshiva that cannot pay teachers' salaries and may have to close. Thus, determining precedence, even within categories, depends on how dire the situation is in each case. He then quotes Vilna Gaon on the verse "You shall not close your hand to the poor."[49] When a person closes his or her hand and looks at one's fingers, they all appear to be the same length. It is only when the hand is opened that a person realizes that each finger is of a different length. Thus, the Torah is telling us not to close our hands to the poor and see each situation as equal. Rather, we are obligated to open our

---

44. *Horayot* 3:7
45. *Ketuvot* 67a
46. *Sefer Be'er Sheva* commentary to *Horayot* 13a
47. *Chochmat Adam* 145:8

48. *Beit Yosef* on *Tur, Yoreh De'ah* 149
49. *Deuteronomy* 15:7

hands and see that each finger, situation, is of different length, need, and then we will be able to determine if the situation of the couple who wants to get married is more dire than the situation of the Yeshiva or vice versa. If, after careful examination, the two situations seem identical in need, says Rav Shternbuch, then the Torah needs of the many come before the needs of the individual couple.[50]

Rabbi Moshe Feinstein was asked a similar question.[51] A person's relative can afford to get married but needs money to then sit and learn Torah for a year or two after marriage. At the same time, a poor person needs money for food and sustenance now, but it is not a matter of life and death. Does the small financial need of the relative take precedence over the more immediate need of the poor person who is a stranger? Rabbi Feinstein determines that the financial hardships do not have to be identical in order to favor the relative. Since the financial needs of a relative come before the needs of a poor stranger, even if the needs of the stranger are more dire (but not life-threatening), the general rule is that a relative takes precedence stands.

It is clear that even when the general rules of precedence of Tzedaka are laid out, when a specific case arises, doubt or conflict, a Rabbi should be consulted to determine the correct thing to do according to Judaism.

## FINAL PRIORITIES ACCORDING TO ONE MODERN DECISOR

Rabbi Asher Weiss discusses each category outlined above and each priority at length, and then tries to simplify the process by outlining a clear list of rules regarding priorities in giving. He first analyzes all of the statements and categories quoted above as "the most important Tzedaka." He concludes that supporting Torah learning takes precedence over supporting poor that are sick. But supporting the poor person who is sick takes precedence over

supporting the synagogue, which takes precedence over supporting the poor in general.[52]

Rabbi Weiss then lists the six categories of Tzedaka support in order of importance:

1. *Anything that involves possible loss of life is the first priority.* This includes sick poor people who may die and captives who need to be redeemed.

2. *Supporting the learning of Torah is the next priority.* This includes supporting a *Beit Midrash*, a house of Jewish learning, and buying any needed Torah books. (Undoubtedly, he would include in this category the recent phenomenon of the tuition crisis whereby many observant parents today cannot afford to send their children to Yeshivot-Day Schools. Donations to enable these students to be enrolled in day schools would be included in this priority.)

3. *Poor who are ill are the next priority.* This includes not only medical expenses, but also all other expenses necessary to get them back to health.

4. *Building and maintaining a synagogue is the next priority.* However, Rabbi Weiss mentions that the Vilna Gaon and others disagreed with this priority.

5. *Marrying off orphans.* He says that with the enormous expenses today for a wedding and beginning a family, this priority may apply to any poor that cannot afford to get married.

6. *Sustaining the poor of the Jewish people.* The priority and order of precedence within this category should be followed according the hierarchy outlined by *Shulchan Aruch* as explained above.

## GIVING TZEDAKA TO THE POOR ON PURIM

There is indeed another very strange aspect of giving *Tzedaka.* Even though there is a commandment to give to the poor the entire year, on Purim day (the fourteenth of Adar, or the fifteenth of Adar in Jerusalem) there is a special commandment to give to the poor. This

---

50. *Responsa Teshuvot Vehanhagot* I:567
51. *Responsa Igrot Moshe, Yoreh De'ah* I: 144

52. *Minchat Asher, Parshat Re'ah* 21

is indeed a very strange Mitzvah. We find no other commandment regarding which there is a general commandment to do it all year long, and then an identical, additional commandment to perform on one specific day of the year. While we know that *Matzah* is specific to Pesach, and *Lulav* is specific to Sukkot, honoring one's mother and father is a year-round, everyday commandment. Thus, in Judaism, there is no additional Mother's Day or Father's Day to honor one's parents on one specific day. Yet it seems that this is indeed the case with *Tzedaka*. In addition to the everyday Mitzvah, there is a specific commandment to give to the poor on Purim! Why would the Rabbis add an identical Mitzvah, an identical action, again on Purim day? And then we must query: is the Mitzvah on Purim indeed identical in all its laws and *Halachot* to the Mitzvah of giving to the needy the rest of the year? And if this a *not* a Mitzvah of *Tzedaka* on Purim, what else could it be?

The Megillah itself describes the custom to give gifts to the poor on Purim.[53] The Talmud quantifies the obligation as two gifts to two poor people.[54] This is codified in Jewish law – i.e., two gifts must be given to two poor people.[55] The question is if this Mitzvah is unique to Purim and separate from the general commandment to give *Tzedaka*, or if it is an additional obligation of charity. What could be the difference?

There could be several important distinctions. If this Purim commandment is part of the general commandment to give *Tzedaka*, then while a poor person is also obligated to give *Tzedaka* from that which was given to him,[56] this poor person may do it but once a year, on any day of the year. He would not have to do this on Purim. However, if this were a commandment that is part of the Purim Mitzvot and not related to *Tzedaka* per se, then the poor person would also have to give something to another poor person on this day.

Similarly, if this Purim Mitzvah were part of *Tzedaka*, then all of the laws related to *Tzedaka* (the priorities regarding who receives it, for example, as cited above) would be in force. But if this is a unique Purim Mitzvah, then the recipients and priorities may be different from those of "normal" *Tzedaka*. So which is it, a commandment of *Tzedaka* or a unique Purim commandment?

Maimonides seems to leave no doubt. He states that the purpose of giving monies to the poor on Purim is specifically to make joyous the heart of the poor, as well as orphans, widows, and converts.[57] Thus, the funds they receive will add to their Purim joy. This is clearly not related to the general commandments to give funds to the needy, but rather, a unique Purim Mitzvah.

Shiblei HaLeket, on the other hand, clearly states that the funds given to the poor on Purim are considered part of the commandment of *Tzedaka*.[58] But clearly, his view is in the minority.

The Jerusalem Talmud says that unlike the recipients of *Tzedaka* the rest of the year, one need not examine closely the specific situation and need of the poor person you give to on Purim.[59] Rather, anyone who puts out his or her hand to take money on Purim should be immediately given. Ritva elucidates this passage and says that the laws of priorities of *Tzedaka* that apply all year to the giving to the poor do not apply on Purim, and that this is not a Mitzvah of *Tzedaka*, but rather a commandment to make the poor happy on Purim.[60] The *Code of Jewish Law* reflects this attitude as well and states that a Jew is supposed to give to anyone who extends his or her hand on Purim, even to a non-Jew (where this is the local custom).[61] Clearly, Jewish law and all of these opinions demonstrate that giving to the poor on Purim is a special Mitzvah not connected to usual *Tzedaka*.

---

53. Esther 9:22
54. *Megillah* 7a
55. *Shulchan Aruch, Orach Chaim* 694:1
56. *Shulchan Aruch, Yoreh De'ah* 248:1

57. Maimonides, *Hilchot Megillah* 2:16-17
58. *Shiblei HaLeket* 202
59. Jerusalem Talmud, *Megillah* 5a
60. Ritva commentary on (Babylonian) *Megillah* 7a
61. *Shulchan Aruch, Orach Chaim* 694:3

It is for this reason that Bayit Chadash writes that a poor person must also fulfill this Mitzvah specifically on Purim day. Even though the rest of the year the poor person fulfills his *Tzedaka* Mitzvah by giving to another poor person just once a year, since this practice on Purim is not related to *Tzedaka*, the indigent must also perform this Mitzvah specifically on Purim day.[62]

This view is also echoed by *Turei Zahav*.[63]

Therefore, while it may seem that giving money to the poor on Purim is a fulfillment of *Tzedaka-charity*, similar to the rest of the year, the overwhelming majority of commentaries view this act as a unique Mitzvah to make the poor happy on Purim, and the normal rules of *Tzedaka* do not apply.

---

62. Bach on *Tur, Orach Chaim* 694:1

63. Taz on *Shulchan Aruch* 694:1

# IS BEING GOOD THE MOST IMPORTANT THING IN JUDAISM?

ROM A VERY YOUNG AGE, PARENTS teach their child to be a "good boy" or "good girl." Everyone usually aspires to be a good person and almost every individual, according to studies that have been conducted, thinks of himself or herself as a "basically good person." We all basically want to do "the right thing" in every situation and help others when possible. Yet, when these acts of goodness are pitted against other values that are highly regarded by society, such as amassing money, attaining success and power, having fun or other, similar values, goodness and acting ethically often take a back seat and fade from the forefront of priorities. How important is goodness in Judaism? As in every society, within Judaism there are competing Jewish values, such as Torah learning and performing Mitzvot-commandments, rituals, and beliefs. How does "goodness" and proper behavior towards others stack up in the hierarchy of Jewish values? How much of a Jewish priority is being a good person and how important a goal is it for each Jew to attain?

## IN JUDAISM, ACTING MORALLY AND HELPING OTHERS IS THE HIGHEST VALUE

Judaism, as will be shown through numerous sources, places caring about others and acting benevolently towards other people as the absolute highest priority of the religion. From Scripture to the Talmud to the Midrash and beyond, the value of behaving ethically towards other human beings describes the essence of being Jewish. For example, when declaring which one principle epitomizes Judaism, Rabbi Akiva states it is the verse, known to many: "You shall love your neighbor as yourself."[1] He mentions nothing about God,

beliefs, or man-to-God Mitzvot-commandments in describing the essence of Judaism. Rather, only good behavior towards one's fellow man. In a similar vein, Hillel was forced to encapsulate all of Judaism to the potential convert standing on one foot. Hillel stated essentially the same thing as Rabbi Akiva, except he couched the idea in a more negative but practical manner: "Do not do to your neighbor what you would not want to have done to you."[2] He continues and says that all the rest of Judaism is only commentary based upon this one essential principle and that the convert should now go learn all of the Torah.

The Torah itself also emphasizes this concept. It tells us not merely to attain it, but to run after and pursue righteousness (sometimes mistranslated as "justice").[3] This is commonly understood to signify that each Jew should insure that he or she should do the right thing in every situation, i.e., specifically between man and his fellow man. The Torah emphasizes the importance of this notion in the verse in two different ways: it repeats the word "righteousness" twice and it also tells us to run after this concept. In no other place in the Torah (and in only one instance in Psalms, about pursuing peace) does God use the term "run after it" concerning any other Mitzvah-commandment. Jews are not commanded to run after keeping Kosher or run after eating Matzah on Passover. Only with regard to treating others in the right manner must one actively pursue this goal. The prophet Micah also informs us exactly what God wants from each Jew: to do justice and kindness as one walks modestly with God. According to the commentaries, this refers only to those commandments that

---

1. Jerusalem Talmud, *Nedarim* 30b

2. *Shabbat* 31a
3. Deuteronomy 16:20

pertain to our goodness and how well we treat our fellow man.[4]

In addition to the many individual commandments mandating proper behavior between Jews and others, there is one overarching commandment, a general Mitzvah that covers all man-to-man situations not specifically enumerated in the rest of the Torah. This Mitzvah "to keep the straight path and do what is right" is given so that the Jew is aware at all times, in every situation, that Jewish behavior mandates doing what is good and right.[5] In another verse commanding the Jew to do the "straight and right thing,"[6] the Midrash explains that this refers specifically to how a Jew behaves towards others in business, and then states that any Jew who treats others properly in commerce, it is as if that person has fulfilled the entire Torah.[7]

Just as proper behavior to others is the most important aspect of Judaism and of life in general, the lack of this behavior can bring disastrous results. The people in Noah's generation, for example, committed many horrible sins, but the destruction of the entire world through the flood came about only when the people began stealing from each other en masse.[8] The great Vilna Gaon states the importance of goodness in simple terms. He says that the essential purpose of life is to constantly improve one's character and act morally towards others.[9] If not, what is the purpose of living? Another way to evaluate Judaism's hierarchy of values is to see how a person will be judged after one's life in this world is completed. The Talmud declares that a Jew will be asked a series of questions to assess his or her life.[10] The *very first* question a person will be asked after death will not be about Yom Kippur, proper feeling in prayer, or even about belief in God.

The first question will be, "Were you honest in your business dealings?"

As generations of Jews began to decline morally after the Sinai experience, King David advised that Jews should concentrate on eleven specific virtues, all of them between man and man.[11] That Talmudic passage continues and explains that as time passed, moral decline increased. The prophet Micah streamlined the focus from eleven Jewish principles down to three areas: to judge truthfully, to do acts of kindness, and to perform the Mitzvot without ostentation before others. Seeing yet a further decline, the prophet Jeremiah encouraged the people to focus on just two aspects: to do justice and to give *Tzedaka*-charity. All of the prophets stressed what the quintessential element of Judaism entails – behaving ethically with others. This quality of kindness is so crucial to Judaism that the Midrash says that anyone who denies the importance of kindness denies the entire Torah.[12]

## ROLE MODELS FOR JEWS

In pointing to nearly every admirable individual both in the Scripture and in the Talmud, the role models of Jewish life were based almost solely on how they interacted with other human beings, and not on how they interacted with God. The very first Jew, Abraham, is singled out for being special because he would teach his children (and they would in turn teach their children, until today) about kindness and the importance of justice and righteousness.[13] This verse is placed in the Torah right before Abraham argues with God about the five cities of evil people (including Sodom) that God was about destroy, when Abraham convinced God not to destroy them if there were only ten righteous men living in the cities. And Abraham had never even met any of the people in these cities who would shortly die! Almost every other leadership figure in

4. Micah 6:8 with Ibn Ezra commentary
5. Deuteronomy 6:18 with Nachmanides commentary
6. Exodus 15:26
7. Midrash, *Mechilta, Beshalach* 1
8. *Sanhedrin* 120a
9. *Even Shlaima* 1:2
10. *Shabbat* 31a

11. *Makkot* 24a
12. Midrash, *Yalkut Shimoni*, Samuel I 25:134; *Midrash Shmuel* 23:8
13. Genesis 18:19

the Torah is also described in terms of man-to-man kindness, and not piety to God. Moses, known as Moshe Rabbeinu, Moses our teacher, is never lauded in the Torah about his vast Jewish knowledge or great teaching abilities. Rather, he is praised for his unique kindness and sense of justice, even for people he did not know and even for non-Jews (Exodus 2:11-19). This characteristic of kindness is present in almost every Torah leader, including Judah, Miriam, Yocheved, the new Elders and others.

This idea and its importance in Judaism have been passed down until today. Chofetz Chaim, who lived in the twentieth century, writes that the path referred to in the above verse by Abraham, is the path of kindness that has guided every Jew since his time.[14] This echoes the Talmudic passage that states that the verse in Exodus declared the path of the Jewish people signifies kindness.[15] One of the great Torah luminaries who died only about a hundred years ago, Rabbi Chaim Soloveitchik, developed a new and unique way of how to learn Talmud with a methodology called the "Brisker" method. He was a Torah genius. Nevertheless, the words written on his grave mention neither his Torah greatness nor his genius. Rather, they merely state "Master of Kindness."

## GOD AS A ROLE MODEL

When the Torah commands the Jews to follow the ways of God, the Talmud asks how it is possible for a man of flesh and blood to be like the Creator of the universe. It answers that Jews are commanded to imitate God's characteristics.[16] Which characteristics of God are we meant to imitate? The answer is that we should perform His acts of kindness that show caring about other people, such as giving clothing to those that lack clothes, visiting the sick, and comforting the mourner. Later on that same Talmudic page it says that the

beginning of the Torah has the story of God's kindness to man (when God gave clothing to undeserving Adam and Eve) and also at the end of the Torah is an instance of God's kindness to a man (when God buried Moses), implying that everything in between these two stories should also be connected to kindness, as this is the essence of God and the Torah.[17] Thus, the Torah teaches us (the word "Torah" technically translates as "that which teaches us") to follow God's lead and be kind always.

In the weekday Shmoneh Esreh, the Silent Prayer, traditional Jews recite three times daily that God's ongoing kindness to all human beings in the world every day, all the time, is lauded.[18] In the first blessing, God is described as a God who grants great kindnesses constantly, and in the second blessing, God is described in many ways, but in particular as One who sustains the world economically, lifts up those who have fallen, heals the sick, and frees those who are bound. Chofetz Chaim summarizes all of the above ideas and urges the Jew to imitate God by practicing these traits shown to man by God.[19]

## ADDITIONAL INSIGHTS ABOUT THE CENTRALITY OF GOODNESS IN JUDAISM

Besides the sources brought above, many other sources confirm that being moral and acting with kindness and goodness towards others are the central themes of Judaism. Yet too many Jews and non-Jews do not see nor practice Judaism in this way. And even fewer internalize these ideas and translate them into daily action (though there are some great and noble people who are the exceptions). Thus, it is important to stress how crucial and significant this behavior is for the practicing Jew.

In Prophets, when God condemned the Jewish people, He almost never condemned them about a lack of ritual behavior (except

---

14. Ahavat Chesed, "Introduction," 2
15. Bava Kama 100a
16. Deuteronomy 13:5, 28:9, Sotah 14a
17. Sotah 14a
18. First and second blessings of the daily Shmoneh Esreh
19. Shemirat HaLashon 1:7

for idol worship), but always complained about their lack of ethical behavior towards one another. This included the lack of helping the poor, lack of justice, lying, and stealing.[20] When King David asks who can enter the tent of God and who can remain and reside on the mountain of God, he outlines a plan how to get there and stay there. The next verses outline the major characteristics and traits that a person needs in order to do this – all of which are acts between man and man – walking uprightly (being honest), doing what is right, speaking only the truth, not doing evil and shameful acts to one's fellow man, not embarrassing others, not swearing falsely, giving people interest-free loans, and not accepting any bribes. He who does all of these will never be moved from his place, says King David.[21]

Even though all Mitzvot are to be treated with equal importance, in the morning blessings several commandments are enumerated either because they have no upper limit or because their reward is given both in this world and the next world.[22] Only two of these commandments are on both lists, indicating that these are the "top two" of Jewish commandments. One is Torah learning and the other is showing kindness towards others. It is interesting to note that of the eight commandments specified as so important that their reward is both in this world and the next world, six are between man and man, requiring kindness, and only two are between man and God (i.e., coming early to prayer and Torah learning).

When the Torah commands the Jew to do the right and good thing in all situations (mentioned above), one commentary says that this refers specifically to acts of kindness, and these actions will bring goodness to the world and a blessing to the person performing these actions.[23] If we look again carefully at that central verse commanding the Jew to treat all people like he would want to be treated, we see that the verse ends with the words "I am God."[24] Why end the most man-to-man verse in the Torah with "I am God"? God is teaching us that every action between men is also an action between man and God. Why and how is this so? Just as a man shows honor to an artist by admiring his painting or respecting his work, by treating a human being with honor, Jews also show respect to the "Artist," the Creator of that human being – God. Thus, every act towards man also brings with it respect for God, the Artist, and transforms it into a man-to-God act as well. One contemporary thinker compared how Jews treat each other to the treatment between siblings, because God is called the Father of the Jewish people (and of all people, for that matter) and Jews are His children.[25] What would any parent prefer experiencing: a child who shows love and devotion to the parent exclusively, or two siblings who show love and devotion to each other? Just as any normal parent would certainly prefer the latter, God also prefers for Jews to demonstrate love for one another, even more than love for Him. This idea seems to be echoed by King Solomon when he tells us that God prefers justice and *Tzedaka* (charity) between men over man's sacrifices to God, and the Rabbis reiterate this idea as well in the Talmud.[26]

Apparently, how Jews behave towards each other will help them endure until the Messiah arrives. One prophet predicts[27] that the only Jews who will survive the onslaught of Jewish history and endure the test of assimilation and antisemitism will be those Jews who do not hurt their fellow Jews, who do not speak lies and deceive one another, and who feed those that are hungry.

---

20. Amos 2:7, 5:7, Micah 2:2, 6:10-11, Jeremiah 9:4, 7:9, 5:2, 22:13
21. Psalm 15
22. Daily morning prayer service, morning blessings at the beginning of the service
23. *Ha'amek Davar* commentary on Deuteronomy 6:18
24. Leviticus 19:18
25. Malachi 2:10
26. Proverbs 21:3, *Sukkah* 49b
27. Zephaniah 3:13

## WHY SHOULD JEWS BE GOOD TO ONE ANOTHER?

The baseball manager Leo Durocher once famously remarked, "Nice guys finish last." That certainly does not seem to be an incentive to be good. Does Judaism believe that being good results in hardships, as Mr. Durocher believed? Aside from the commandments to be good and the strong emphasis in Judaism for Jews to be full of goodness, are there are other practical reasons or benefits to being good on a regular basis and to live one's life in this manner?

A man, if he is normal, seeks to maximize his pleasure in the world. Normally, one thinks of pleasure as the satisfying of one's physical desires. However, the Mishna states that the real pleasures in life are not in this world, but in the next world.[28] In fact, the words of that Mishna are very explicit: If we were to take all the physical pleasures experienced by every human being in the history of the world and add them up, they would not equal one minute of spiritual pleasure in the Next World. So the goal of every normal person who seeks maximum pleasure (non-Jews can also attain the next world in Jewish thought) should be to strive to get to the next world and maximize his or her "portion" of pleasure there in order to receive the most pleasure possible.

But how does a person get to the Next World? The Sages tell us that one cannot get there through the accumulation of money, gold, or diamonds. These are worthless in the next world. The two precious commodities there are the Torah learning and acts of goodness that were attained in this world.[29] Logically then, to receive maximum pleasure, a person in this world should spend maximum time in these two pursuits. Every Mitzvah a person performs in this world is "paid to his or her account" in the next world.[30] The Midrash even describes the scene that everyone will experience after death when standing at the gates of Heaven. The person will be asked, "What did you do in this world?" If he or she says, "I fed the hungry," that person will be let in straight away. Similarly, if the person says that he or she gave clothing to the needy, that person will be immediately let in. The same holds true for those who helped orphans, gave Tzedaka, or performed any acts of goodness on a regular basis. It is interesting that the ritual commandments like Shabbat or keeping Kosher are not mentioned as a prerequisite for entry or for this unique pleasure.[31] Another Midrash implies the same notion when it says that acts of goodness draw a person closer to the presence of God, while acts lacking goodness are "ugly" and distance a person from God's presence.[32]

Another reason to be good is to achieve another kind of reward. In general, the Torah never states a specific reward for a specific Jewish act or Mitzvah. The exception to that rule is found in only three places, which promise long life as a reward for doing these actions (either long life in this world, the next world, or both).[33] What are the three actions and what do they have in common? The first is honoring one's parents. The second is sending away the mother bird before taking her eggs, which Maimonides explains, trains a person to have mercy on all animals and human beings as well. The third is being honest in business. All three require acts of goodness between men that involve justice, kindness, and doing the right thing. Therefore, to attain long life, a person should be a good person who does good acts on a daily basis.

The idea of long life (be it in this world or the Next World) is not only about years. Everyone naturally wants immortality, to continue to live beyond life, even though everyone dies. But by doing good acts, people *can* attain immortality. How? Rashi explains that the Torah mentions the death of the evil

---

28. Mishna *Avot* 4:17
29. Mishna *Avot* 6:9
30. *Sotah* 3b
31. *Midrash Tehilim* 118:17
32. Midrash, *Tana Debai Eliyahu Rabbah*, 18
33. Exodus 20:12; Deuteronomy 22:6-7, 25:15; Maimonides, *Guide for the Perplexed* 3:48

Terach, Abraham's father, long before he actually died in order to teach us that an evil person who contributes nothing to this world is considered dead even when he is physically still alive. But Rashi continues and explains that the opposite is also true. If we are good parents, our ideas, ideals, and values live on after us through our children.[34] But when the Torah first describes Noah and says, "These are his children," instead of listing his three sons, the Torah then says that Noah was a righteous person. Rashi answers the obvious question and says that for righteous people, their acts of goodness are like their children. Why? Like children, the actions of the righteous live on after a person dies. That is why Rashi states that the righteous are called alive even after they die.[35] Thus, immortality can indeed be achieved by doing righteous acts that affect people. The impact of these acts continues long after the person dies physically, which helps immortalize a person and continues his or her influence forever. Chofetz Chaim enhances this concept when he says that one strong act of kindness can impact not only one person, but can continue to have impact from generation to generation until the end of time.[36] Therefore, by being good, a person has the potential to affect thousands or even tens of thousands of individuals for the better and change the world positively forever.

Another advantage of doing something good is that sometimes a person can get credit (in Judaism) for a good act even when he or she had no intention to do goodness. Therefore, if a person lost money in a public place (so that there can be no expectation of return to its owner) and a poor person happens to pick it up, the original owner gets credit as if he or she actually gave the money to *Tzedaka*-charity.[37] There is yet another advantage of being good. The prophet Isaiah promises that if enough people act with justice and *Tzedaka*, they can together then influence God to bring

the redemption.[38] Of course, just the knowledge and good feeling attained after a person has helped someone is sometimes enough to motivate people to do and to be good. But all of these other "Jewish" reasons provide an added incentive to do acts of goodness on a regular basis.

## WHEN GOODNESS CONFLICTS WITH OTHER JEWISH ACTIONS, WHICH WINS OUT?

There are many important values in any system of law, in every society, and in every religion. Judaism is no different in this respect. In any society or system, it is when these values come into conflict with each other that we can determine which are indeed the most important. This entire volume deals with extremely important Jewish values that every Jew should highly respect, such as Torah study, fulfilling commandments, etc. What happens when Jews have to choose between being a good person and other positive Jewish values? For example, in Christianity, while being a good person is important, an overall belief in the religion's teachings is far more important and fundamental. Which values are the most important in the hierarchy of Jewish actions and Jewish thought?

Even when in conflict with other important values in Judaism, being good and helping other people seems to "win out." The most profound example of this idea occurs in the Torah. Abraham is ill following his circumcision at age 99, but despite his weakness, he longs for strangers to visit him so that he can help them because that is his nature. God sends three angels disguised as people, while at the same time God Himself visits Abraham, teaching the world the importance of visiting the sick. In most religions, this "together time" alone with God would be considered the highest ideal possible. Yet, when the strangers arrive, Abraham asks God to wait for him, while

---

34. Rashi commentary on Genesis 11:32
35. Rashi commentary on Genesis 6:9
36. *Shemirat HaLashon* 1:7
37. Midrash, *Yalkut Shimoni* 937

38. Isaiah 56:1

he (Abraham) takes care of these guests![39] Abraham felt that helping strangers was *more important* than togetherness with God! And Abraham is praised for this act, as he teaches the principle that inviting guests is indeed more important that being with God, according to the Midrash.[40] This concept – that inviting strangers is even more important than a private audience with the Almighty – is not only a Midrashic suggestion, but is brought down as part of normative Jewish law, both in the Sephardic[41] and Ashkenazic[42] traditions.

Another apparent "conflict" between two fundamental issues occurs in the two stories described in the Torah portion of *Noach*. The first involves the sinning of the people as they committed unspeakable sins among themselves, resulting in the flood and the destruction of the world. The second, at the end of the Torah reading (Genesis 11:1-1), describes a generation that rebelled against God and challenged Him for superiority in the world. Their punishment was the sudden emergence of seventy languages, which confused everyone and stifled the project. Rashi cites both stories and both punishments and asks: It seems that the generation of the Tower of Babel committed the far more egregious sin of challenging God (rather than the man-to-man sins culminating in stealing, by the generation of the flood). Why then was the generation of the flood destroyed, while the Babel generation was merely "slapped on the wrist" and allowed to live? Rashi answers that even though their sin was far worse, the Babel generation demonstrated unity and caring for each other as they challenged God.[43] The generation of the flood always fought with each other, and there is no hope to build a society once that occurs. While it is true that the Babel generation sinned and was misguided, a society that can unite has the hope of building for the

future and correcting its mistakes. This may also explain why Abraham sent his servant Eliezer back to his homeland to find a wife for his son Isaac. Since at that time everyone was not Jewish, what difference did it make if Isaac married a local Canaanite girl or a woman from Mesopotamia? The answer may be that Abraham witnessed the debauchery and deceit of the people of Canaan, in the city of Sodom, and later, in his dealings with Ephron when he tried to buy a burial plot. In his homeland, on the other hand, despite the idol worship, there were basically good people who dealt properly with each other. He preferred a daughter-in-law from this society to help build the Jewish people over the wicked locals of Canaan who dealt treacherously with each other. In fact, it was the quality of goodness towards strangers that led Eliezer to select Rebecca to be Isaac's wife.

Another area of discord involves the conflict when a ritual commandment comes into conflict with a command to be good, specifically to oneself – i.e., to preserve one's own dignity. If preserving dignity would violate a Torah or Rabbinic commandment, which takes precedence? Once again, the Talmud and Jewish law state that it is preferable to violate a commandment as long as one's dignity is preserved.[44] The classic case involves a Kohen-Priest who is commanded not to be in a house where a dead body lies, in order not to become ritually impure. Such a person must leave the house immediately if a corpse is inside. But what should the Kohen do if he is sleeping without clothing and then wakes up to discover the body? Technically, he must leave the house immediately once he becomes aware of the dead body, even without his clothing. However, Jewish law says that he may violate this Jewish law by remaining with the dead body in order to preserve his dignity, and he may dress before leaving the house.

There is another instance, described by the prophet, when a man wishes to act piously

---

39. Genesis 18:3 with Rashi commentary
40. Midrash, *Yalkut Shimoni* 18:82
41. *Kaf HaChaim* 5:6
42. Rema, *Shulchan Aruch, Orach Chaim* 33:1 with *Mishna Berurah* commentary 8
43. Rashi commentary on Genesis 11:9

44. *Berachot* 19b; Maimonides, *Hilchot Shabbat* 26:23; *Shulchan Aruch, Yoreh De'ah* 372:1

and adopts a fast to demonstrate that piety. If however, he ignores the needs of the poor, God says that he prefers that the person not fast, but instead he should feed the hungry and give clothing to whoever needs clothes.[45] Similarly, God tells the person who thinks he can "fix" bad ethical behavior with ritual acts and prayer that he is mistaken.[46] Based on the verse in Hosea in which God states that He desires kindness and not sacrifices, the Midrash says that God would rather see people helping other people than receive all the sacrifices that were brought to the First Temple by King Solomon.[47]

A *Tzadik*, a righteous person, is a Jew who is careful in every detail of observance of the commandments. But regarding someone the prophet calls a "good *Tzadik*," the Talmud asks if there can be someone who is a "bad *Tzadik*" and another who is a "good *Tzadik*." It answers that someone who is especially careful in those commandments between man and God is indeed righteous, but a person who is especially vigilant in the details of the man-to-man commandments as well is called a "good *Tzadik*."[48] Thus, we see again and again the higher priority for goodness in Judaism, even when in conflict with other values and commandments.

## IF GOODNESS IS SO IMPORTANT, HOW CAN "OBSERVANT" JEWS EVER NOT BE GOOD?

After establishing the principle of goodness as the highest priority in Judaism, how is it possible for anyone who wants to observe God's commandments not to be a good person every day, all the time? And how can it be that basically good people sometimes act in a way that hurts others?

In order to maintain man's free will, God intentionally implanted in all human beings both the good inclination and the inclination to do evil. But both tendencies are not equal within

each person. Left unchecked, the Torah seems to say that the evil inclination will win out every time.[49] However, shouldn't a person born with good tendencies be able to overcome his evil side and do kind acts? The Talmud answers by saying that God made sure that the opposite is true: The more righteous a person is, the greater his or her evil inclination.[50] Therefore, it is even more difficult for naturally good people to actually do good things. The Talmud continues and says that each day, the propensity for evil wins out most of the time. Therefore, it is quite understandable that even though people *know* what is the right thing to do, actually doing it while battling the evil inclination is quite difficult. God does promise, however, that while man necessarily sins in this world, in the World to Come God will remove the evil inclination, and then man will only do what is right.[51]

## NOT DOING EVIL DOES NOT MAKE AN INDIVIDUAL INTO A GOOD PERSON

In survey after survey, individuals are asked if he or she is "a good person," and more than 95% of the respondents respond that they think of themselves as basically good. Even though they may regularly lie and not help others in need, they still believe they are good. How is that possible? This phenomenon occurs because most people tend to believe that as long as they do not do anything truly evil and do not commit a major crime, they are good. Does that concur with the Jewish definition of goodness?

King David outlines the formula for Jewish goodness, saying that it is a two-step process. First a person has to reject and desist from doing all evil actions, but that is not enough. After rejecting evil, the person must actively do moral acts and help others. Only then is that individual considered to be a good person.[52]

---

45. Isaiah 58:5-7
46. Isaiah 1:15
47. Hosea 6:6; Midrash, *Yalkut Shimoni* 522
48. Isaiah 3:10, *Kiddushin* 40a

49. Genesis 6:5, 8:21
50. *Sukkah* 52a
51. *Midrash Tanchuma, Vayikra* 6
52. Psalms 34:13, 15

This is also reflected in the Mishna, which says that if the person does nothing to help or hurt others ("what is mine is mine, what is yours is yours"), at most he is considered a mediocre person, but certainly not a good person.[53] Another opinion equates this person with the evil values of Sodom. Thus, doing no evil is certainly not enough to be considered good in Judaism.

In actuality, doing nothing is more than just being "neutral" in Jewish thought. In the twentieth century, Edmund Burke stated that, "All that is necessary for the triumph of evil is that a few good men do nothing." But long before Burke, the Torah and Jewish law considered it a sin to do nothing when anyone in need can be helped.[54] In fact, Judaism is the only legal system in the world in which a person can be punished and it is considered a crime if he or she does nothing when in a situation to stop evil actions. Thus, from the Jewish perspective, not being a bad person does not render an individual a good human being.

## UNIQUELY JEWISH TRAITS OF GOODNESS

Until now, we have generally defined goodness as "helping others in need." However, we have already seen several scriptural terms describing goodness, and not all are exactly the same. For example, in the verse described above, commanding each Jew to do justice and kindness, one commentary defines "*Mishpat*-justice as "not doing to someone what you would not want to have done to you," and "*Chesed*-kindness, as "doing your utmost to help out anyone in need in every situation."[55] What are the specific traits that define Jewish goodness?

The Talmud makes a statement that seems very provocative by twenty-first century standards. It says that any person who is merciful must be a Jew from the seed of Abraham.[56]

This sounds racist. Does the statement imply that there are no non-Jews in the world who are merciful, or that every Jew in the world is merciful? Of course this is not the case. Then what does it signify?

As seen above through all of the sources, goodness in all its forms is an extremely important value to God. When God saw that Abraham possessed this and other values that he would pass down to his children, God selected Abraham to begin the Jewish nation. This teaching inculcated the values of goodness into the Jewish people, so much so that it became part of their spiritual DNA. Do other people have this trait? Of course they do. But *every* Jew has the potential for mercy and goodness. The Jew is predisposed and expected to act in this manner. Perhaps this explains why Jews tend to be involved, way out of proportion to their numbers, in so many causes helping make the world a better place or in giving a much higher percentage of *Tzedaka* than other groups. Rabbi Moshe Chaim Luzzato says that the tendencies of each nation were established very early in history and became part of each nation's culture.[57] This seems to also explain why Maimonides states that giving *Tzedaka* is part of the traditions established by Abraham and passed down to his children.[58] Sefat Emet also makes the point that there is something unique that Abraham passed down which is spiritually inside every Jew.[59]

There is another reason that Jews have developed a special sensitivity to be good. The experience of suffering in Egypt acted like a spiritual refinery, says God, as explained by Rashi.[60] As Jews suffered so much for so long due to the evil of their oppressors, they developed a loathing towards doing evil to others, and they especially help underdogs who suffer as they did. This idea is also reflected in the words of Isaiah when he describes that this process is also part of the reason God chose

53. Mishna *Avot* 5:10
54. Leviticus 19:16; *Shulchan Aruch, Choshen Mishpat* 426:1
55. Micah 6:8 with Ibn Ezra commentary
56. *Beitza* 32b

57. *Derech Hashem* 2:4
58. Maimonides, *Hilchot Matnot Aniyim* 10:1; Genesis 18:19
59. *Sefat Emet, Lech Lecha* 5635
60. Deuteronomy 4:20 with Rashi commentary

the Jewish people to be His nation.[61] If that is true, then which other traits (that lead to goodness) do Jews have spiritually ingrained within them, in addition to those described above?

Jews have more of a sense of shame than other people, according to the Talmud.[62] Another passage says that Jews have three distinctive values or traits: mercy, bashfulness, and kindness.[63] (This does not mean that anyone who has these traits is Jewish, as many non-Jews possess all three traits. But Jews are spiritually predisposed to them.) Jeremiah cites three terms, which God demonstrates and Jews are supposed to imitate: *Chesed* – kindness, *Mishpat* – justice, and *Tzedaka* – charity.[64] Interestingly, one decisor of Jewish law explains the reason that a blessing is not recited on all commandments involving goodness and man-to-man actions. He clarifies that since the actions of goodness that both Jews and non-Jews do are identical, even though the Jews may be doing them because of God's command (as stated in the text of blessings on commandments), no blessing is recited. An onlooker would not be able to know that the motivation for the Jew's action was purely due to the Mitzvah, the commandment to do so.[65]

Just as there are different traits that comprise Jewish goodness, there are different types of Jewish personalities that describe good Jews. One type is the *Tzadik*-righteous Person, and the other is the *Chasid*-kind person (not to be confused with the Chassidim of today, who are part of a movement that was founded in the eighteenth century, thousands of years after the Torah was given). Both are full of goodness. Since Jews are commanded to imitate God and His ways, God is described as both a *Tzadik* and a *Chasid*.[66] The goal of every Jew is to be both a *Tzadik* and a *Chasid*, says

the Midrash.[67] What exactly is the difference between a *Tzadik* and a *Chasid*, between *Tzedaka*-charity, and *Chesed*-kindness?

Maimonides explains that *Chesed* is something that is done for a person that is undeserved or beyond the norm.[68] Thus, a *Chasid* is someone who goes way beyond the letter of the law in every way, whether by helping others or in his own piety. *Tzedek* is justice, which implies exactitude to uphold the law and do everything that is right and correct. Thus a *Tzadik* follows the law to the letter and helps everyone equally, based on what is required by Jewish law. The Midrash implies that everyone should aspire to become a *Tzadik*, and that everyone has the potential to attain this status, regardless of his background.[69] The Mishna shows many examples of people called a *Chasid*, who demonstrate outstanding character traits that go beyond the expected norm in goodness and helping others.[70] The Talmud gives an example of a person who legally took out Shabbat goods from a burning house where the owner had renounced ownership, yet after Shabbat this person returned the items to the owner. He is called a *Chasid*.[71] Ulla was castigated in one instance because he merely did what Jewish law required of him. (see chapter, "Going Beyond the Letter of the Law" for a full discussion of this issue.) Since he was known to be a *Chasid*, he was expected to go beyond what the law required and do even more.[72] Maimonides reinforces this idea in defining a *Chasid*.[73] Rabbi Yisrael Meir Kagan rules that although both are great men, when "push comes to shove," a *Chasid* is regarded as greater than a *Tzadik*. Why? In the end, it is the *Chasid* who helps others more than the *Tzadik*. And since that is the most important aspect of Judaism, the *Chasid* is considered the greater Jew.[74] This distinction between these

61. Isaiah 48:10
62. *Nedarim* 20a
63. *Yevamot* 79a
64. Jeremiah 9:22-23
65. *Aruch HaShulchan, Choshen Mishpat* 427:10
66. Psalms 145:17, Jeremiah 3:12

67. Midrash, *Sifri, Eikev* 49
68. Maimonides, *Guide for the Perplexed* 1:53
69. *Midrash Tehilim* 146
70. Mishna *Avot* 5:10, 11, 13
71. *Shabbat* 120a
72. Jerusalem Talmud, *Terumot* 47a
73. Maimonides commentary on Mishna *Avot* 5:7, 6:1
74. *Shemirat Halashon* 1:7

two legitimate and praiseworthy role models, the *Tzadik* and the *Chasid*, was so pronounced in Jewish thought that one authority actually ruled that in the same way it was customary in some communities not to bury a righteous Jew next to a sinning Jew, so too, a *Chasid* should not be buried next to a *Tzadik*.[75]

Although these two different personalities, *Tzadik* and *Chasid*, epitomize the Jewish values of justice and kindness or love, in the end, as we saw in the verse above (Micah 6:8) and in the Midrash, God wishes for each Jew to do both "justice" *and* "love of kindness," in other words, to combine both of these values, because both are necessary in order to achieve goodness in relating to one's fellow man. This is because kindness (or love) alone, without justice, eventually leads to rivalry, which may even lead to hatred. And justice alone without kindness and love is devoid of the humanizing forces of compassion and mercy. Thus, to achieve true goodness and God's ethical ideal of a Jew's role in this world, Jews need to strive to attain both of these qualities.

---

75. *Or Zarua, Hilchot Aveilut* 422:4

# JEALOUSY

EALOUSY IS DEFINED BY THE DICTIO-
nary as "feeling resentment against someone because of his or her success or advantages." Judaism has much to say about this
feeling and about the sin of acting upon this
emotion in a specific manner. Surprisingly,
many Jewish sources point to some positive
aspects of jealousy as well.

## HOW JEALOUSY CAN DESTROY A
## PERSON

A recent Jewish commentary (nineteenth century), who organized a book describing Jewish
concepts in detail, explained jealousy as a very
poor character flaw that is driven by man's evil
inclination. When a person strives to succeed in any field and sees another individual
achieve the success that he or she craves, jealousy drives this person to anguish, and creates
a desire to besmirch the successful individual.[1]
This feeling can remove any joy from the life of
the person experiencing jealousy.

Many verses in Jewish Scripture describe
this terrible character flaw. Proverbs describes
the jealous person as full of constant rage,[2] a
feeling much more severe than cruelty and
anger.[3] Song of Songs compares jealousy to a
form of "hell."[4] This character flaw makes one's
bones rot[5] and can even kill a person, say other
verses.[6] Jealousy can also cause a person to lose
his or her share in the World to Come.[7]

The declarations in these verses are not
mere predictions and ideas. Specific individuals in the Torah, some even great and righteous
people, have demonstrated the enormous
damage that jealousy can cause in the world.

The very first and second sins in the history
of man came about because of jealousy. The
Talmud explains that the serpent became jealous of Adam and how man was being treated
by God, and this led him to entice Eve to eat
from the forbidden fruit.[8] The very first murder in this world also came about because of
jealousy, when Cain was jealous of his brother
Abel, after God accepted Abel's offering and
not his own. The jealousy caused an inner rage
that led Cain to then kill Abel.[9] The Torah also
tells us that Jacob's sons were jealous of their
brother Joseph,[10] which not only led to the
sale of Joseph and his slavery in Egypt, but
also, according to Rabbi Joshua,[11] led to retribution of the famous ten Rabbis who were
tortured and then murdered by the Romans,
much later in Jewish history.[12] The Rabbis discuss how painful and terrible were the results
of jealousy among several personalities in the
Bible.[13] These included Esau and Jacob, Saul
and David.

When Eldad and Medad started prophesy-
ing in the camp, Joshua was jealous on behalf
of his mentor and teacher Moses, thinking that
the gift of prophecy was reserved for Moses exclusively or for whomever Moses designated.[14]
Moses was surprised by Joshua's reaction and
asked, "Are you jealous on my behalf? That all
the Jews would be able to prophesy like these
two." Moses, the humblest man in the Torah,
was never jealous of anyone's success. Moses
despised jealousy so much that the Rabbis
tell us that Moses said that he preferred dying
one hundred times, rather than feeling one

---

1. *Pele Yo'etz* on "Jealousy"
2. Proverbs 6:34
3. Proverbs 27:4
4. Song of Songs 8:6
5. Proverbs 14:30
6. Job 5:2
7. Ecclesiastes 9:6

8. *Sanhedrin* 59b
9. Genesis 4:4-5, 8
10. Genesis 37:11
11. *Midrash Mishlei* 1:19
12. How and why this works and how it is "fair" that
 a rabbi suffers for the sins of their ancestors, is
 beyond the scope of this essay.
13. Midrash, *Shir Hashirim Rabbah* 8:7
14. Numbers 11:28-29

emotion of jealousy.[15] On the other hand, the word "jealous" occurs four separate times in the discussion of the suspected unfaithful wife, the *Sotah*.[16] The husband is jealous of his wife's lover, whom he suspects had sexual relations with his wife. The offering that she must bring is called the "*Mincha* of jealousy," and the summation of the portion is called the "Torah of jealousies."

Rabbi Elazar Hakapar points out that jealousy is one of three negative character traits that can remove a person from this world, either due to his anguish or as a punishment.[17] The Rabbis say that jealousy actually tears up a person inside (makes a person's bones rot), while a non-jealous person will never suffer this fate.[18] As much as this trait is undesirable in Judaism, the Rabbis also recognized that it is a common emotion, even among Rabbis themselves. The Talmud thus declares that if two Rabbinic scholars live in the same city but do not get along in Torah law due to jealousy, one should die and the other should be exiled.[19] Another passage says that this jealousy among Rabbis also causes Divine displeasure.[20]

## PREVENTING JEALOUSY

Knowing how easy it is for a person to become jealous and the damage it can cause, one should anticipate certain situations in advance and take action, whenever possible, to prevent any person from becoming jealous. The Talmud explains that when God asked Moses to gather seventy new elders/judges, Moses realized that if he merely selected the seventy best people in his estimation, this would certainly cause jealousy among the twelve tribes, as some tribes would necessarily receive more elders/judges and some fewer (seventy is not evenly divided into twelve). What did he do?

He selected six from each tribe (seventy-two) and then held a lottery in which seventy slips of paper were marked "judge" and two were left blank. Thus, the two tribes who were eventually left with five judges could not blame Moses or become jealous because their tribe now had fewer judges.[21] In a similar manner, the Rabbis admonish every parent to treat all children exactly the same and not to favor any one child over the others by bestowing an extra gift to the favored child, as this will certainly lead to jealousy, just as it did when Jacob favored Joseph over all of his sons.[22] Similarly, Rabbi Nehemiah declared that Achashverosh treated all his guests equally at his banquet (and not according to their standing), in order to prevent jealousy among the participants.[23]

## WHY PEOPLE SHOULD NOT BE JEALOUS

Although the emotion of jealousy is common and "normal," logically, a God-fearing person should never become jealous of someone else's good fortune. The Mishna says that one of the reasons that God created each individual in a unique manner with different characteristics was to prevent jealousy.[24] If everyone were created literally equal in all ways, and then some people received more desirable attributes while others received less, then everyone who received less would most likely and legitimately become jealous. But since, in fact, people have unique physical traits, different talents, singular personalities, and diverse goals in life, reasonable people should *not* be jealous of each other. Especially if a person believes in God, a God that gives every individual specifically what is right and needed for that unique person, then "desiring" something more for oneself or comparing one's achievements and accomplishments to that of another, different person, is pointless and demonstrates a lack of trust in God's judgment. Since all people or all

15. Midrash, *Devarim Rabbah* 9:9
16. Numbers 5:14-15, 29
17. Mishna *Avot* 4:21
18. *Shabbat* 10a
19. *Sotah* 49a
20. *Ta'anit* 8a

21. *Sanhedrin* 17a
22. *Shabbat* 10b
23. *Megillah* 12a
24. *Avot DeRabbi Natan* 4:6

Jews are compared to one body, then it is similarly pointless for one part of the body to be "jealous" of another part of the body because it is larger, or receives more oxygen or blood than a different part of the body.[25] Thus, for a God-fearing individual, jealousy of another person is illogical.

Even though Aaron displayed many leadership qualities, upon hearing that his brother Moses was chosen to be the leader of the Jewish people, the Talmud says he was happy for Moses rather than jealous of his younger brother.[26] For this selfless feeling, Aaron was rewarded to become the High Priest, with the holy breastplate placed upon his heart. Just as the Rabbis tell us that no parent or teacher begrudges or is jealous of a child or student who exceeds the parent's or teacher's achievements, so too, all people should be happy when all others they know succeed in life and reach their potential.[27]

## POSITIVE JEALOUSY

It would seem from all the above words that feelings of jealousy are to be avoided at all costs, as they inevitably lead to inner discontent and can destroy a person. Nevertheless, the sages tell us that sometimes jealousy can be something very positive and useful. If an individual recognizes jealous feelings and uses them to build himself up rather than direct the feeling towards the other person, this emotion can indeed be very positive.[28] Thus, if a person sees the achievements of a friend and analyzes *why* that person achieved what he or she did, and then uses that achievement as motivation to better himself or herself, this jealousy is turned outward and becomes a motivator to help a person succeed more. Therefore, intellectual jealousy among Rabbis is permitted in order to increase Jewish wisdom.[29] The Midrash explains that if not for this kind of

jealousy – i.e., using others' achievements to motivate to accomplish more – the world as we know it would fall apart.[30] Fewer people would be motivated to build homes, marry, and achieve more in life. Proverbs tells us not to envy sinners, but rather to be jealous of those that fear the Lord.[31] The commentaries explain that a person should not be jealous of any success of evildoers. Rather, they should envy the accomplishments of the righteous and then try to emulate them.

When Rachel saw that her sister had given birth to many children while she remained barren, the Torah says that Rachel was jealous of her sister.[32] But she used that jealousy to improve her own deeds and eventually merit to having children.[33] Based on this Biblical story, the Talmud makes a general statement that childless women are usually jealous of friends who have children.[34] How one uses this jealousy (positively or negatively) is up to each individual.

## HOW COULD GOD BE JEALOUS?

Whether jealousy is a positive or negative trait, it would hardly be imaginable as an attribute of God Almighty. And yet, in the Ten Commandments[35], it states that the Lord is a jealous God, concerning those who forsake Him and worship idols. The Torah repeats this concept of a jealous God numerous times.[36] How can we possibly understand this concept? Even if we can comprehend that the Almighty could have base emotions like jealousy, why would or should God be jealous of stones that people foolishly worship? How do the classical commentaries understand this idea?

Rabban Gamliel was asked this very question by a non-Jewish philosopher: We can understand that someone, even God, could be

---

25. *Pele Yo'etz* on "Jealousy"
26. *Shabbat* 139a
27. *Sanhedrin* 105b
28. *Pele Yo'etz* on "Jealousy"
29. *Bava Batra* 21a
30. *Midrash Tehilim* 37a
31. Proverbs 23:17
32. Genesis 30:1
33. Midrash, *Beraishit Rabbah* 71:6
34. *Megillah* 13a
35. Exodus 20:5
36. Exodus 34:14; Deuteronomy 5:9, 6:14-15

jealous of something that is better than Him or has worth. But how could God be jealous of meaningless idols? Rabban Gamliel answers that if a son names his dog the same name as his father, the father is jealous of his son.[37] How could the son equate his father with a dog? So too, God is jealous of the Jewish people who foolishly call stones and wood by the same name, God, as the Almighty. Another Midrash explains that since (at the time) the urge to worship idols was so great, God wanted to give extra reward to those Jews who resisted the urge to worship idols, and thus used the terminology of jealousy to make their reward higher. Other explanations compare God's love for the Jewish people as being so strong that He is "jealous" when any Jew forsakes Him for an idol.[38] (It is clear that the Torah spoke in anthropomorphic terms in order to help us act and possibly understand, as God does not really "feel" any of the emotions of love or jealousy.[39]) God's relationship with the Jewish people is thus compared to that of a scorned lover,[40] much like the Sotah and her jealous husband mentioned above.[41] One commentator notes that the only time in the entire Bible that God is referred to as jealous is in the context of idol worship, to demonstrate that special husband-wife relationship between the Jewish people and God.[42]

ZEALOUS AND JEALOUS –
CONNECTED OR NOT?

The word zealous is defined in the dictionary as "filled with or inspired by intense enthusiasm or zeal; ardent; fervent." But the term zealot is also somewhat negatively defined as "fanatical or extreme adherent to a cause, especially a religious one." In Biblical Hebrew, the same word is used for both jealousy and zealotry (Kana). In fact, the Greek origin for both words jealous and zealous is "Zelotes," which connotes "emulation, admirer, or follower." Are these two concepts connected? And if so, how?

One commentary explains that zealousness is another form of positive jealousy – jealousy for God, in which the zealot will defend God's name and honor whenever it is threatened.[43] Pinchas is called a zealot by God,[44] as he is praised by the Almighty for killing two people who publicly worshipped idols, thereby desecrating God's name. Their actions brought about a plague upon the followers of the idol worship, while Pinchas' deed stopped the plague after 24,000 people were killed, and he is rewarded by God. Elijah is also called a zealot when he confronted the idol worshippers in his time.[45] Moses, too, was called a zealot by the sages, when he gathered the Levites to smite the 3,000 idol worshippers of the Golden Calf.[46] Like the jealousy describing God, it seems that zealotry of behalf of in the Bible relates exclusively to idol worship.

However, we also see that the commentators did not wholeheartedly support the notion of zealotry. Elijah seems to be castigated by God for being "too" zealous. In addition to the perpetual priesthood for all his descendants, Pinchas is given the gift of "Brit Shalom-Covenant of Peace." One modern commentary explains what this reward actually was and suggests that this quality of zealousness for God by Pinchas was appropriate in that particular instance, but only as a one-time act.[47] God was afraid that Pinchas might become emboldened by this action and use zealotry again in subsequent activities. God, therefore, changed the personality of Pinchas to make him a peaceful man (Covenant of Peace), never to use the trait of zealousness again. Thus, while zealousness and zealotry may be appropriate in certain situations, it is not positive if it is an ongoing character trait. Later on in the Torah, when

37. Midrash, Mechilta 6
38. Midrash, Devarim Rabbah 2:18
39. Berachot 31b
40. Midrash Tanchuma 94:6
41. Numbers 5:14
42. Rabbeinu Bechaya on Exodus 20:5

43. Pele Yo'etz on "Jealousy"
44. Numbers 25:11-13
45. Kings I 19:10-14
46. Midrash, Pesikta Rabbati 4:3
47. Ha'amek Davar on Numbers 25:12

God commands the Jewish people to utterly destroy a city whose Jewish population was worshipping idols[48] – an act of zealotry on behalf of God – the "reward" these destroyers received was the gift of mercy and peace from God, to insure that this would be a one-time action only.[49]

## JEALOUSY AS A PUNISHABLE SIN: "THOU SHALL NOT COVET"

While jealousy is an emotion mentioned in the sources, it is not one of the 613 commandments and prohibitions enumerated in the Torah. However, acting upon the feeling of envy and jealousy, or doing more than simply feeling jealous *is* mentioned prominently in the Torah, in the Ten Commandments: "Thou shall not covet." What is the difference between jealousy and coveting? It seems that a person is jealous only of another person (generally not a good emotion unless channeled properly, but not a sin either). But when a person covets a specific item belonging to that person, then it is a sin. What exactly is the sin of coveting? How "big" is this particular sin in the larger scheme of things?

## COVETING IS ONE OF THE WORST SINS IN THE TORAH

The Vilna Gaon states that coveting is so severe that every other sin in Judaism is ultimately derived from the sin of "Thou shall not covet."[50] The Midrash draws a parallel between the laws and ideas in Leviticus 19 (stated before the entire Jewish people) and the Ten Commandments.[51] It then compares the prohibition of not coveting to the Mitzvah of loving one's neighbor, which is then called the central principle of the Torah.[52] Thus, by implication, it seems that not coveting would be the central prohibition in the Torah. One

later commentary, in fact, says that since the prohibition of coveting is placed as the final commandment in the Ten Commandments, it encompasses them all.[53]

One of the three fundamental characteristics of Abraham and his descendants, says the Mishna, is a "good eye," which is explained[54] as being satisfied with what one has and not desiring or coveting the objects of anyone else.[55] One medieval Rabbi says that desiring a specific object of one's neighbor not only damages the person who desires the object, but even hurts the owner of that object.[56] Another medieval commentator states, in effect, the converse: A person who refrains from coveting any of his or her neighbor's objects, will come to never harm any individual.[57]

What then is the specific prohibition of coveting? Must a person take an action, or can he be guilty of this sin merely for thinking or feeling an emotion? Is there any time or situation when coveting is permitted?

## DEFINING THE PROHIBITION OF COVETING

The Torah repeats the Ten Commandments in the book of Deuteronomy. In the book of Exodus, the tenth commandment reads, "You shall not covet your neighbor's house. You shall not covet your neighbor's wife, nor his manservant, nor his maidservant, nor his ox, nor his donkey, nor any thing that is your neighbor's."[58] The Hebrew verb prohibiting coveting is "*Lo Tachmod.*" In Deuteronomy, however, a second verb is added with other slight changes: "You shall not desire your neighbor's wife, nor shall you covet your neighbor's house, his field, or his manservant, or his maidservant, his ox, or his donkey, or any thing that is your neighbor's."[59] The additional verb, "do not desire"

48. Deuteronomy 13:13-17
49. Deuteronomy 13:18
50. Gaon of Vilna, *Even Shlaima*, chapter 3
51. Midrash, *Vayikra Rabbah* 24:5
52. Midrash, *Beraishit Rabbah* 24:7

53. *Pele Yo'etz* on "*Chemdah*"
54. Bartenura commentary on Mishna *Avot* 5:19
55. Mishna *Avot* 5:19
56. Rabbeinu Yonah commentary on Mishna *Avot* 5:19
57. Ramban commentary on Exodus 20:3
58. Exodus 20:14
59. Deuteronomy 5:18

("*Lo Titave*"), is the subject of debate among the commentaries.

Some Jewish law authorities see both verbs as identical and make no distinction between the laws in Exodus and in Deuteronomy.[60] Rashi agrees with this interpretation.[61] However, the vast majority and normative Jewish approach is to divide this prohibition into two distinct categories.[62] One prohibition, merely desiring your neighbor's object, is prohibited under *Lo Titave*, without requiring any action to take place. Coveting, on the other hand, requires a distinct action to be taken in order to be guilty of the sin. But how could a Jew be guilty of a sin for a mere emotion, which may beyond his control? Maimonides indeed points out that merely desiring the object is not enough to be guilty of "do not desire" ("*Lo Titave*"). A person must actually plot and scheme how he will obtain the object (without doing any action) to be guilty of this prohibition.[63] Thus, while this sin does not involve any actual action, it does require much more than a mere base emotion. The *Code of Jewish Law, Shulchan Aruch*, agrees with Maimonides. One can sin without an action, but to be guilty a person must do more than simply desire. He must also use his brain to devise a means to buy or obtain the object.[64]

The second prohibition of coveting is more clear-cut. The Midrash states that in order to be guilty of sin, a person must act upon his desire to obtain his neighbor's wife, his house, or any object belonging to him.[65] What action renders one guilty of coveting? *Tur* seems to say that merely talking about obtaining the object is enough to make a person guilty.[66] Maimonides believes that a person must take a concrete action to obtain the object, by approaching the neighbor and repeatedly annoying him or her to give or sell it when the neighbor is reluctant to do so. If the neighbor actually does give it or sell it, only then is the person guilty of the sin of coveting. *Shulchan Aruch* reflects the view of Maimonides, which has become normative Jewish law: Until the neighbor (reluctantly) gives or sells the object after badgering, a person is not guilty of "thou shall not covet."[67] Rabbi Eliezer Papo, a later commentary (1785-1825), sums up the two prohibitions succinctly: "Anyone who desires and then attempts to obtain his neighbor's object as a gift or by purchasing it, violates 'Thou shall not covet.' And even if he does not attempt to buy it, but merely thinks about ways to get the object into his possession, he has violated the prohibition of 'Thou shall not desire.'"[68]

## WHEN IT IS PERMITTED TO COVET

Only tangible objects that can be bought and sold are subject to the prohibition of "Thou shall not covet." Thus, the *Zohar* states that is it is permitted to be jealous and covet the Torah learning of another individual without violating any prohibitions.[69] While certain commandments are not subject to this prohibition, coveting other objects of a Mitzvah can violate it. For example, coveting the *Shofar* or *Lulav* of a neighbor, and then trying to obtain it *would* be prohibited, since these are objects that are bought and sold, even though their purpose is for a Mitzvah and holiness.[70] Rabbeinu Bechaya even claims that a Jew even receives reward for coveting a neighbor's non-tangible Mitzvot.[71] Chofetz Chaim writes that this prohibition does not apply to giving *Tzedaka*-charity, and one may continually badger a wealthy neighbor to give *Tzedaka*.[72]

60. Semag, Mitzvah 158
61. Rashi commentary on Deuteronomy 5:18
62. Zohar 3:261
63. Maimonides, *Hilchot Gezaila* 1:10
64. Shulchan Aruch, Chosen Mishpat 359:10-11
65. Midrash, Mechilta, HaChodesh 8
66. Tur, Choshen Mishpat 371

67. *Shulchan Aruch, Chosen Mishpat* 359:10
68. *Pele Yo'etz* on "*Chemdah*"
69. *Zohar, Yitro* 2:93
70. *Responsa Betzail Chochma* 3:43
71. Rabbeinu Bechaya commentary on Exodus 20:14
72. *Shemirat Halashon*, Section II, end of the book, #4

## DOES THIS PROHIBITION APPLY IN ALL (NON-MITZVAH) SITUATIONS?

Some authorities believe that the prohibition to covet applies even to minute, almost worthless objects as well.[73] There is a debate whether the object must be one that is hard to obtain or if it also applies even to objects that can be purchased in any store. Logically, if the object can be purchased anywhere, then a person will not feel specific envy, and thus will not desire or covet his neighbor's object. He can simply go and buy the object for himself whenever he wants. Nevertheless, a Talmudic passage claims that this prohibition applies even to easy-to-purchase objects and even to money itself.[74] But most of the later authorities restrict this prohibition to items that are hard to find and that one can only obtain from that neighbor.[75]

The prohibition to covet need not apply only to a tangible object. One can be guilty of envying (and then acting upon that feeling) the standing or the position that someone obtained, such as High Priesthood, presidency, or even a promotion.[76] On the other hand, if a tangible item is already for sale, badgering the owner to lower the price in order to buy the object would *not* be considered a violation of the prohibition.[77] But approaching a neighbor, who has no interest in selling the object, and constantly offering more money to entice the neighbor to sell, would clearly be a violation of the sin.[78] Pressuring a neighbor to give the item that a person desires, even as a gift, also violates *Lo Tachmod*.[79] This prohibition is not limited to Jews, but is forbidden to non-Jews as well.[80] The reverse situation is also forbidden: A person, desirous of his neighbor's money, may not parade his unique object on his front lawn in order to entice the neighbor to become jealous and try to obtain the object.[81]

In the final analysis, the Talmud promises that a person who spends his time trying to obtain that which is not his, will, in the end, forfeit that which he already has.[82] The result for any person will be similar to the result of the first act of jealousy by the serpent, which thought he could obtain everything he wanted and rule over all the other animals, but in the end the serpent is the most cursed of the animals. So too will be the fate of those who think they can profit and gain through their jealousy and desire.[83]

---

73. Minchat Chinuch, Mitzvah 38 claims "*Lo Tachmod*" applies to objects worth less than a Perutah (penny)
74. *Kalah Rabbati* 6
75. Rabbi Aryeh Tzvi Fromer, *Responsa Eretz Tzvi* 4
76. *Sotah* 9a with Rashi and Meiri commentaries

77. *Responsa Shevet Kehati* 3:329
78. *Sefer Charedim* 21:2-5
79. *Sha'arei Teshuva* 3:43, *Responsa Eretz Tzvi* 3:6
80. *Sefer HaChinuch* 416
81. *Sefer Chasidim* 99
82. *Sotah* 9a
83. *Sefer HaMitzvot HaKatan* 19

# JERUSALEM – ITS MEANING FOR THE JEWISH PEOPLE

Most experts agree that the city of Jerusalem has no special strategic value or terrain that makes it a desirable location for an occupying army. Neither does Jerusalem possess many natural resources that would attract a large population to relocate there, nor is it located near any major waterway or trade route. Normally, one or more of these qualities is a prerequisite for making a city a major center and an attractive place for people to live. And yet, more wars have been fought to occupy or retain Jerusalem than any other city in history. Why? Without any physical advantages making this city special, why is it so desirable and important to so many people? What makes Jerusalem unique for nearly all the major religions?

Christians believe that Jesus was brought to Jerusalem as a child to be "presented" at the Temple. They also believe that Jesus preached in Jerusalem and that the Last Supper, his trial, crucifixion, and resurrection, took place in Jerusalem. Islam considers Jerusalem it third holiest city, even though Jerusalem is never mentioned in the Koran. Moslems believe that Muhammad visited the city on a nocturnal journey in 610, while he prayed and visited heaven. Jerusalem was the first qibla (direction of prayer) for Muslims, and the Al-Aqsa Mosque in Jerusalem was designated for pilgrimage.

But for the Jews, in contrast, Jerusalem is the center of their universe, their focal point. By understanding what Jerusalem means for the Jew and why, perhaps we may be able to discover underlying paradigms and concepts for idyllic Jewish living and creating an ideal Jewish society.

## IMPORTANCE OF JERUSALEM FOR JEWS

Each time a traditional Jew prays the central Amidah prayer anywhere in the world, three times daily, he or she is required by Jewish law to face Jerusalem.[1] One of the nineteen blessings in the weekday Amidah, or Shmoneh Esreh, beseeches God to return to His city, Jerusalem, reside there forever, and eventually rebuild the Temple.[2] Every time a Jew recites the prayer of Grace following a meal, Jerusalem is the central focus of one of the four blessings, asking for God's mercy upon the city and the rebuilding of the Temple.[3] Even after eating a cookie or certain fruits, or drinking wine, Jewish law requires a blessing that mentions Jerusalem.[4] On the holiest day of the year, the Kohen Gadol-High Priest, made a special blessing for the city of Jerusalem,[5] which Jews today repeat every Shabbat, asking God for mercy on the city because it is the source of our Jewish life.[6] At a Jewish wedding, the Seven Blessings are an integral part of the ceremony. One of these blessings beseeches God to bring joy to the city of Jerusalem through the ingathering of Jews from all over the world.[7]

While mentioning Jerusalem at times of his greatest joy, a Jew also must remind himself or herself that no joy can be complete and total as long as the city of Jerusalem lies bereft of its true spirituality and central jewel, the Temple. Thus, at the most joyous moment of marriage, a groom often places ashes upon his forehead as a symbol of mourning, and then the traditional glass is broken, symbolizing the destruction of the Temple.[8] Another great time of joy occurs when a person buys a home, usually the largest single purchase of a lifetime. Because of the mourning over Jerusalem, traditional Jews

---

1. *Shulchan Aruch, Orach Chaim* 94:1
2. Fourteenth blessing of the weekday *Shmoneh Esreh*
3. Third blessing of *Birkat HaMazon* (Grace after Meals)
4. *Al Hamichya* blessing
5. *Sotah* 41a
6. Blessings after the Haftorah
7. Fourth blessing of the *Sheva Berachot* (Seven Wedding Blessings)
8. *Shulchan Aruch, Even Ha'ezer*, 65:3

leave one small corner of the house barren, unpainted, indicating that no joy in life can be complete as long as the Temple is in ruins.[9]

Even in times of greatest sorrow, when mourning a relative, the city of Jerusalem is also prominently remembered. The traditional words of comfort one expresses to a mourner are, "May God comfort you among the mourners of the city of Jerusalem,"[10] equating the personal tragedy and loss with the national tragedy and loss of the Temple and Jerusalem.[11] The Rabbis tried to enact several additional laws that would remind a Jew each day about the status of Jerusalem, establishing daily mourning customs to remind Jews of life without the Temple, but these were never adopted en masse by the people. For example, the Rabbis forbade eating meat and drinking wine (two primary rituals performed in the Temple) on any day in which a Jew visits Jerusalem in its destruction, without a rebuilt Temple.[12] But when some Rabbis also tried to ban wine and meat altogether for the same reason, this ban never was not enacted because this restriction would have been beyond the ability of the majority of Jews to observe.[13] In the same passage, the Rabbis legislated that a family should leave out one course of each cooked meal in remembrance of Jerusalem, and a woman should leave off one ornament of her numerous items of jewelry when dressing up for the same reason. While these customs did not "take," the custom about leaving one square of the wall opposite the entrance to a house unadorned did become normative Jewish practice.

which God created the world.[14] The "rock" in the Dome of the Rock that the Muslims built on the site of the Temple is based on the Jewish tradition that the foundation stone, *Even Shtiyah,* located in front of the Temple Ark, was the place from which God created the world.[15] This is the place where, according to tradition, Adam brought the first sacrifices to God,[16] Cain and Abel brought their sacrifices (which led to Abel's murder by Cain),[17] and Noah brought his sacrifice following the great flood.[18] This is also the place where Abraham was willing to sacrifice his son Isaac at God's command.[19] That mountain, the Temple Mount, the mountain to where God directed Abraham, was first called Mount Moriah in Genesis, and was the place that King Solomon knew he should build the Temple.[20]

Because of this unique location and all of the events that occurred at this place, the entire city of Jerusalem is infused with holiness – so much so that the city of Jerusalem is called the connecting point between the two worlds, this physical world and physical Jerusalem, with the heavenly world and the heavenly Jerusalem.[21] Thus, there is a parallel, ethereal Jerusalem, which is hovering above and in some ways mirrors the physical Jerusalem below. From the time the Temple was built, the city of Jerusalem became God's "residence" on earth, and, according to tradition, it will be so once again when the Temple is rebuilt.[22] Therefore, it is not only the Temple that is holy or the Temple Mount, which houses the Temple, that possessed holiness, but the entire city of Jerusalem possesses holiness.[23]

## WHAT MAKES THIS CITY SO SPECIAL? WHY IS THE TEMPLE LOCATED HERE?

In Jewish tradition, Jerusalem is literally the very center of the universe, the place from

9. *Shulchan Aruch, Orach Chaim* 560:1
10. *Responsa Igrot Moshe, Orach Chaim* 5:20
11. Rabbi Moshe Shternbuch, *Chachma VaDa'at* on Genesis 42:28
12. *Tosefta Nedarim* 1:4
13. *Bava Batra* 60b

14. *Midrash Tanchuma, Kedoshim* 10
15. Midrash, *Bamidbar Rabbah* 12:4; *Midrash Tanchuma, Pikudei* 3
16. Maimonides, *Hilchot Beit HaBechira* 2:2
17. Genesis 4:1-5, 8
18. Genesis 8:20
19. Genesis 22:1-5, 14-18
20. Chronicles II 3:1
21. Psalms 122:3 with Rashi commentary
22. Maimonides, *Hilchot Beit HaBechira* 1:3-4
23. Maimonides, *Hilchot Beit HaBechira* 7:14

## THE NAMES OF THE CITY IN THE SCRIPTURE BUT NOT IN THE TORAH

The city of Jerusalem is not mentioned even once in the Koran, but it is mentioned 669 separate times in Jewish Scripture (Tanach). But none of these of verses about Jerusalem are mentioned specifically in the Torah, only in the later books of Jewish Scripture. Why not? Although the city's specialness and holiness was indeed transmitted orally to Jewish leaders through the generations, Maimonides gives several explanations why the name was not written down specifically in the Torah.[24] First, if the nations of the world had known in advance that Jerusalem was the holiest city of the Jewish people (through its proclamation in the Torah), those other nations would have fought desperately never to allow the Jews to conquer this city and proclaim it as their capital. Second, the non-Jewish religions of the time would have taken that Jewish holiness and intentionally used the city of Jerusalem for their own idol worship (which is what happened in later times), something that would be an anathema to Jews. In addition, non-Jews might have purposely razed the city and destroyed it, simply to prevent the Jewish people from ever using it as their holy city and capital. Finally, the sibling rivalry between the Jewish tribes might have caused each tribe to claim Jerusalem for itself, in its territory. Thus, God intentionally never mentioned the name of the city in the Torah, before the Jews conquered Jerusalem, but merely called it "the place where I will choose to put My name."

The first allusion to the city of Jerusalem in the Torah is in Genesis, when it says that Malki Tzedek was king of the city called Shalem.[25] One early commentary says that this was the city of Jerusalem.[26] The next mention of this place is Mount Moriah, described above, where the binding of Isaac by Abraham took

place. After this event, Abraham calls this place "*Adonai Yireh*-God will see," because in this place God will be seen.[27] Rashi comments on this verse that this will be the place in the future where God will choose His Divine Presence to reside and where the people will bring future sacrifices as well.[28] Apparently, before it was conquered by the Jews, Jerusalem under Jebusite rule was divided into two cities, the western part called *Jeru* (Yere) and the eastern part called *Salem* (Shalem). The Midrash explains that today's name of Jerusalem is made up of the combination of the original name of the city, "Shalem," given by Shem son of Noah, indicating completeness or perfection, and "Yireh," the name given by Abraham, to become "*Yireh Shalem*," – the place where completion or perfection will be seen, "Yerushalayim."[29]

Later on, Scripture refers to the city of Jerusalem by other names. It was called "The Holy City" by Isaiah and Nehemiah.[30] Isaiah and Daniel also referred to the city of Jerusalem when they called it "The Holy Mountain."[31] Zachariah called it "The City of Truth"[32] and King David, who captured the city and lived there as king, called Jerusalem "The City of God."[33] King David also describes Jerusalem as Mount Zion and the "City of the King" that is both beautiful and joyous.[34]

## HOW THE CITY OF JERUSALEM IS REFERRED TO BY THE RABBIS

In the post-scriptural era, the Rabbis also referred to Jerusalem and described it with numerous designations. When God told the Jews that they would eventually come to the place of "rest and inheritance,"[35] the Rabbis described Jerusalem as either "the place of rest" for the

---

24. Maimonides, *Guide for the Perplexed* 3:45
25. Genesis 14:18
26. *Targum Onkelos* commentary on Genesis 14:18

27. Genesis 22:14
28. Rashi commentary on Genesis 22:14
29. Midrash, *Beraishit Rabbah* 56:10
30. Isaiah 48:2, Nehemiah 11:1
31. Isaiah 27:13, Daniel 9:16
32. Zachariah 8:3
33. Psalms 46:5
34. Psalms 48:3
35. Deuteronomy 12:9

Jewish people or "the place of inheritance" or both.[36] The Talmud simply calls Jerusalem "the City," as someone living in the suburbs today would refer to "going to the city" and everyone understands the designation to refer to their main center.[37] The Mishna refers to Jerusalem as "the place within the walls" because Jerusalem was one of the few walled cities from the time of Joshua, and many special Jewish laws applied to Jerusalem as long as a person was located within its walls.[38] By inference, the Talmud refers to Jerusalem as the "City of Prophets."[39] When a prophet gave his name and his city, all knew he was from the city he cited. When he gave only his name, all knew he came from Jerusalem.

## TO WHOM DOES THIS CITY OF JERUSALEM BELONG?

Of course, Jerusalem belongs to the Jewish people, as God promised it in the Torah, either as the city of "rest" or "inheritance," referred to in the verse cited above. But within the Jewish people, to which tribe or tribes did this city really belong? We know that every inch of the land of Israel was divided among the twelve tribes. To which tribes did the city belong?

There is one opinion that the city was indeed divided between the tribes of Judah and Benjamin, with the Temple area in the section of Benjamin. But the other opinion is that this is the one place in Israel that was never apportioned to the tribes, because Jerusalem is a unique city in that it belongs to all the tribes equally (similar to Washington DC, but not an exact parallel). It is this second position that seems to be accepted, which affects Jewish law in a number of ways.[40] For example, because the city did not belong to any one tribe, all of the city's expenses, according to the Mishna, were taken and paid for from the Temple's

treasury.[41] Maimonides finds a parallel between the four camps in the desert and the four layers of holiness in Jerusalem leading up to the Temple itself.[42] But the city of Jerusalem parallels the camp of the Israelites because, like the Israelite camp, the city belongs to the entire people.

## THE UNIQUE LAWS THAT PERTAIN TO THIS UNIQUE CITY

Because Jerusalem was so distinctive, many special laws were enacted and maintained to demonstrate that Jerusalem is unique. In a certain sense, these laws show us what the ideal Jewish city should look like and how it should be taken care of.

Since Jerusalem was holy and certain sacrifices could be eaten only within the city walls, Maimonides outlines numerous laws and procedures to maintain Jerusalem as the holy city.[43] When someone died, burial had to be immediate, in order not to have the corpse remaining overnight in the city. Since the city of Jerusalem belonged to the entire Jewish people, it was forbidden to take money or rent from lodgers, especially when the entire people came to the city for the Jewish holidays three times a year. These lodgers, after all, were technically part owners in the city. (The Rabbis worked out a system whereby the people living in Jerusalem did not lose money.) At that time, no cemeteries were allowed in the city proper, except for graves of the family of King David and Chulda the prophetess. Certain plants and fruits could not be planted in the city because they would give off a foul odor, and the scent of the holy city had to remain sweet. In the same vein, no garbage heaps could be located in the city proper. No smokestacks were permitted in Jerusalem in order that there should be no air pollution and smoke in the city.

Because Jerusalem is considered a city that belongs to all Jews and is holier than any

36. *Zevachim* 119a
37. *Sanhedrin* 2a with Rashi commentary
38. Mishna *Kelim* 1:8
39. *Megillah* 15a
40. *Megillah* 26a

41. Mishna *Shekalim* 4:2
42. Maimonides, *Hilchot Beit HaBechira* 7:11
43. Maimonides, *Hilchot Beit HaBechira* 7:14

other city, a husband or wife could legally force his or her spouse to move to Jerusalem from any other city in Israel (in the same way that a spouse could force his or her partner to move to the Land of Israel against his or her will from the Diaspora). If the spouse refused, this was considered grounds for divorce, and the side that refused would forfeit the money promised in the *Ketuba* (dowry).[44] In the same manner, no spouse could force his or her partner to leave the city of Jerusalem or the Land of Israel.[45] Both Maimonides[46] and *Tur*[47] cite these Talmudic cases as normative Jewish law.

The Jerusalem Talmud states that in the Jerusalem of Talmudic times there were 460 synagogues, but tied to each synagogue was its own (equivalent to today's) elementary school and high school.[48] Unlike any other city then (and some cities even today), the streets of Jerusalem were cleaned daily.[49] Rashi states that the reason for the cleaning was to remove the dirt that might accumulate upon the feet (which was not permitted in the Temple),[50] while Tosafot explains the reason was to clear away all dead bugs and rodents that might impurify people, which was forbidden in Jerusalem.[51] In addition, while certain types of daily activities were permitted to be performed in other cities on Chol Hamo'ed, the intermediate days of the festivals, all such activity was mandated by the Rabbis as forbidden in Jerusalem on these days.[52] In order not to create any sadness in the city of Jerusalem, an accounting station was set up outside the city in order for people who had to settle accounts to do so outside the city, so that feelings of anger or disappointment would not be felt inside the city itself.[53]

## SPECIAL CUSTOMS BY ITS RESIDENTS THAT MADE JERUSALEM UNIQUE

There are certain customs and stringencies that the people who lived in Jerusalem took upon themselves, as they recognized that better behavior and a higher level of spirituality were required in the holy city.

While everyone in the rest of the world slept on Yom Kippur night, with Jews preparing for a day of prayer and repentance, the leaders and prominent people of Jerusalem stayed up all night to ensure that the Kohen Gadol would not fall asleep,[54] which would have been a violation of Jewish law.[55] On Sukkot, these noble people would bind their *Lulavim*, palm branches, with gold strands to hold it together,[56] unlike the customary strands from the *Lulav* itself that people use today. The entire population of Jerusalem observed a very unusual pattern of ritual behavior regarding the Four Species, in that all daily activities were performed with the *Lulav* and *Etrog* in hand (unlike the custom today, which is to take the Four Species only during the *Hallel* and *Hoshanot* prayers in the synagogue).[57] They would walk around the city with Four Species in hand, walk to the synagogue, say the *Shema* and *Amidah* prayers – all with the *Lulav* and *Etrog* in hand. They would put these on the side only for Torah reading and the priestly blessing. They even went to visit the sick, comforted a mourner in his home, and learned Torah with *Lulav* and *Etrog* in hand.

There is another interesting custom that was adopted only by the "special" people who lived in Jerusalem and which has also been adopted by many Jews today: to honor the Torah scroll by following it from the Ark to the place the Torah is read, and then again by walking behind the Torah as it is returned to the Ark.[58]

Some have heard of the following customs

---

44. *Ketuvot* 110a
45. Jerusalem Talmud, *Ketuvot* 22a
46. Maimonides, *Hilchot Ishut* 13:20
47. *Tur, Even Ha'ezer* 85
48. Jerusalem Talmud, *Ketuvot* 67b
49. *Bava Metzia* 26a
50. Rashi commentary on *Bava Metzia* 26a
51. Tosafot on *Bava Metzia* 26a
52. *Mo'ed Katan* 11a
53. Midrash, *Shemot Rabbah* 52:5

---

54. *Yoma* 19b with Rashi commentary
55. Mishna *Yoma* 1:7
56. *Sukkah* 37a
57. *Sukkah* 41a
58. *Soferim* 12:14

that were performed only by the single ladies of Jerusalem on the afternoons of Yom Kippur and the fifteenth of the month of Av (Tu B'av).[59] These young women would borrow white clothes from each other so that none of the single men could know who was wealthy and who was poor. They would go out into the fields in the white clothes and ask the single men to choose a bride, not based upon beauty and looks, but based on family and values. Unlike in other cities where each family decided when children should begin fasting on Yom Kippur (before the mandatory fast at the age of majority, thirteen for boys and twelve for girls), all the children of Jerusalem who reached the age of eleven would fast for half a day.[60] At age twelve they would all fast the entire day and then each child would pass before each elderly person in Jerusalem and receive a blessing. Then the parents would take the children directly to the synagogue in order to inspire them to keep the commandments properly.

Another custom unique to Jerusalem was for the benefit of the poor and the guests who came to the city on the Jewish festivals three times a year. Rather than merely give out leftover food to feed the poor or guests, which was an undignified way to provide them with meals (ask anyone who has had to wait on line at a soup kitchen or for food stamps), the residents of Jerusalem would put a special napkin on their doors, indicating that anyone who wished to could come and dine with the family. When the napkin was removed, it was a sign that the time of dining was over. In this way, people felt that they received their food as welcomed guests, rather than as a handout.[61]

Jerusalem was also the site of other unique customs that benefitted people in need. A place was set up in the city called the "Stone of Claims" in an era when Internet message boards were not available. Anyone who lost an item went to this place, as did anyone who found a lost object. The "finder" would stand up on the stone and announce what was found. If the owner supplied proper signs indicating the object was his, he claimed it.[62] Similarly, based on a verse[63] that the Midrash[64] explains refers to Jerusalem, two chambers of secret gifts were established in the city.[65] People who no longer needed any items in the house donated them to one chamber, and those unfortunate people who did not possess many needed objects could come and take what they needed from that chamber. The second chamber worked in the same manner, but involved money. People of means could leave money for the poor, and the poor took only the minimum they required to survive. Amazingly, there were never any reported cases of gouging of these chambers, that thieves robbed everything in the chamber or that one poor person hoarded all its contents.

Finally, Rabbi Eliezer says that King Solomon saw many charitable people of Jerusalem, and he built two gates of the city – one for these generous people and the other for the downtrodden and those in need of help, such as grooms, mourners, and those who were ostracized. On Shabbat, all of these groups would go up to the Temple and sit between these two gates, as the generous people helped out all those in need. Later, after the Temple was destroyed, these same people would gather at the back of the synagogue where the practice continued. The mourners would receive a special blessing and then would say the Mourner's Kaddish prayer.[66] This may be the origin of the practice of mourners saying this prayer together, and in some congregations today, it may be the reason this recitation always takes place at the back of the synagogue.

---

59. *Ta'anit* 26b
60. *Soferim* 18:5
61. *Bava Batra* 93b
62. *Bava Metzia* 28b
63. *Deuteronomy* 15:10
64. *Midrash, Sifri, Re'eh* 64
65. *Mishna Shekalim* 5:6
66. *Soferim* 19:12

## CHARACTERISTICS OF THE CITY THAT RENDER JERUSALEM SPECIAL

There are numerous statements made by the Rabbis that indicate particular attributes about Jerusalem that make it special and different from other places in the world.

Concerning the verse cited above that Jerusalem "binds together" various elements (Psalms 122:3), one interpretation is that this is the city which unites people and creates peace between all Jews.[67] While this is certainly not the case today, in general, it may have been true once and will hopefully become the reality once again in the future. The Midrash explains that because of its special holiness, anyone who prays in Jerusalem, it is as if he or she is praying directly before the throne of God.[68] Although beauty is generally held to be in the eye of the beholder, the Talmud declares that 90% of the physical beauty in the world was given to the city of Jerusalem.[69] While some may disagree, many today, in fact, see Jerusalem as the most or one of the most beautiful cities in the world. Similarly, the Talmud tells us that he who did not see Jerusalem of old in its splendor, never saw a desirable city.[70]

Jerusalem is constantly referred to as "The Holy City," both today and in the Talmud.[71] Because of this holiness, until the First Temple was destroyed, there were ten supernatural miracles that constantly took place in the city of Jerusalem.[72] While these may not be considered grandiose by today's standards of supernatural miracles, they certainly defied the laws of nature. For example, despite no refrigeration in a Middle Eastern climate and the thousands of pounds of meat slaughtered daily in the Temple, there was never a foul odor emanating from all of this raw meat in the city. No flies ever gathered around this raw meat either. On the contrary, there was always a pleasant fragrance in the entire city, emanating from the *Kitoret* spices that were brought as a sacrifice.[73] This fragrance was so powerful that women in the city did not need to wear perfume. Furthermore, a fire never broke out in the city, nor did a snake ever bite anyone in Jerusalem. On the three Jewish festivals when more than a million people must have descended upon the city, no one ever had to sleep on the street without a bed, and there was always ample room to pray and bow. Another Midrash echoes this sentiment when it says that just as many rivers emptying into the sea never totally fill the sea, the city of Jerusalem never felt full, despite the fact that all adult Jews in the land of Israel came for the Pesach, Shavuot, and Sukkot holidays.[74]

## HOW WILL JERUSALEM BE BUILT IN THE FUTURE?

While the entire political world, both inside and outside of Israel, continuously debates how and if the city of Jerusalem should be divided, they are referring to a vertical division between east and west part of the city. However, Judaism has always spoken about a different kind of division of Jerusalem, a horizontal division, between Jerusalem above and Jerusalem below. This is significant because God vowed that He would not return to the perfect heavenly Jerusalem until He first returns to the improved and a spiritually superior earthly Jerusalem.[75] And today, as the building of each new apartment in the city of Jerusalem engenders world reaction and often elicits condemnation, and as the Knesset (Israeli Parliament) often deliberates where and how to build in Jerusalem, the Talmud long ago discussed this question and gives guidance about the proper way to build in Jerusalem.

The verses in Isaiah speak about the afflicted who are not comforted.[76] The Midrash explains that this refers to the Jews living in

---

67. Jerusalem Talmud, *Chagiga* 26a
68. *Midrash Tehilim* 91:7
69. *Kiddushin* 49b
70. *Sukkah* 51b
71. *Berachot* 9b, *Beitza* 14b, *Tamid* 27b
72. *Avot DeRabbi Natan* 35:1, *Yoma* 21a

73. *Yoma* 39b
74. Midrash, *Kohelet Rabbah* 1:20
75. *Midrash Tehilim* 122:4
76. Isaiah 54:11-13

the Diaspora who are frustrated because they cannot build in Jerusalem. God responds and says that He will direct the Jews how to build in Jerusalem and comfort them (by carefully reading the words in the next verses).[77]

Those verses in Isaiah say that "I will lay your stones with fair colors and lay your foundations with sapphires. And I will make *Shimshotayich* (your windows) of *Kadkode*, and your gates of beryl, and your borders of precious stones." The verses conclude "And all your children shall be taught of the Lord and great shall be the peace of your children." On this last verse, the Talmud says that we should not read "*Banayich*-children," but rather, "*Bonayich*-builders."[78] Thus the key to the building in Jerusalem is related to the stones that are described in these verses. What are they telling us?

## WHICH STONE WILL BUILD JERUSALEM?

The Talmud discusses and argues about the meanings and names of the stones and the unusual words in the verses. When discussing the strange stone of *Kadkode*, the description is very odd. The phrase "*Kadkode Shimoshtayich*" is a gateway or a window that provides light (from the word "*Shemesh*-sun"). The argument in the Talmud is between two angels, Gavriel and Michael, or between two Rabbis, about the definition of the word "*Kadkode*." One says it is the stone *Shoham*-onyx, and one says it is the stone *Yashfe*-jade. What are these stones? In the fourth row of the twelve stones located on the *Choshen*-breastplate of the Kohen Gadol, these are the last two stones.[79] Then the Talmud says the name "*Kadkode*" in the verse signifies "*Kedain Ukedain*" – that both explanations are correct. God rules that Jerusalem will be built from both stones.[80] What is the underlying idea of this argument? Why is it significant that this is an argument between two angels, which is almost never found the

in the Talmud? If this argument took place in Talmudic times, then how could it be that the prophet Isaiah wrote the word "*Kadkode*" (i.e., both opinions are correct) even before the argument took place? What, then, is the secret to understanding this passage and the means by which Jerusalem should be built?

Rashbam explains that "*Shimshotayich*" actually signifies the walls of Jerusalem.[81] The argument, then, was which stones would be used to build the walls of Jerusalem in the future. And Rashbam then says that even from earlier times in the period of Isaiah, the question was asked about how Jerusalem should be built – with which stone – and this was Isaiah's prophecy: There will be arguments in the future about how Jerusalem will be built, but it will be built according to all of the opinions together. But what is the underlying argument and the significance of the stones?

The stones in the breastplate were set up according order of the twelve tribes. The *Shoham*-onyx, the eleventh stone in the breastplate, is the stone of Joseph, and the twelfth stone, *Yashfe*, jade, was the stone of Benjamin. The underlying concepts of these particular tribes relate to the building of Jerusalem. Maharsha enlightens us and says the fourth row containing these stones symbolizes the redemption.[82] The argument is about which concept, which stone, will light Jerusalem and be the foundation of its building. First there will be the building by the Messiah of Joseph and then the light of the city of Jerusalem will shine, which is in the section of Benjamin (according to one opinion cited above). This is "*Kedain U'kedain*." Both aspects are necessary to build Jerusalem.

The concepts of Joseph and Benjamin are two diametrically opposite systems. Both are children of Rachel, but Joseph always symbolizes the one who provides physical sustenance to the Jews (and to the Egyptians).[83] Joseph argues that the redemption comes about because of the building up of nationhood as

77. *Midrash Tehilim* 53:2
78. *Berachot* 64a
79. Exodus 28:17-20
80. *Bava Batra* 75a

81. Rashbam commentary on *Bava Batra* 75a
82. Maharsha commentary on *Bava Batra* 75a
83. Genesis 47:12, 41:57

well as physical building, and initially through Egypt and Shechem. Benjamin, on the other hand, the only son of Jacob born in Israel and who never bowed to Eisav, is known as "*Yedid Adonai*-the beloved of the Lord,"[84] symbolizing pure holiness and spirituality. (See the chapter, "Judaism: A Religion or a Nation?" for a fuller discussion of these two philosophies.) Thus, the argument rages then and today about how Jerusalem will be built – from the material, bricks, and mortar symbolized by Joseph, or spiritually, symbolized by Benjamin and by the Messiah of David when he will build the Holy Temple. (The Davidic Messiah actually has both components, as he fights wars and also builds the Temple.)

The builders will argue about how Jerusalem is to be built. Both sides seem to be mutually exclusive. The argument takes place by the angels, arguing about the Jerusalem above, but also by actual Rabbis, arguing about the Jerusalem below. And both Jerusalems have to be built properly for God to return to either city.[85] The final decision is that Jerusalem will be built according to *both* concepts together, according to *all* opinions, with any one vision of building alone insufficient. And whoever does not understand that both Messiahs (Joseph and David) are necessary does not understand how to build Jerusalem. Joseph's materialism, nationality, culture, must be the basis, but Benjamin's (*ben David's*) spirituality must be there as well, in the lead. The light that comes from this combination, *Shimshotayich*, is the essential vision of the Jewish people that originated at Sinai, that Jews must be both a kingdom of priests *and* a holy nation.[86]

This struggle between these two visions, the two sides vying to build Jerusalem, is demonstrated in another passage in the guise of two kings.[87] God appears to King Yerovam and says, "You, Me, and King David will walk together in the Garden of Eden." Yerovam, who is descended from Joseph, was previously responsible for the material needs of the country before he split the kingdom. He was a man of action, of nationhood, like his great-great-grandfather Joseph. Yerovam sets up his kingdom specifically in Shechem,[88] the very place that Joseph is sold by his brothers and the place where Joseph is buried, which his descendants inherit.[89] God wishes to reunite the two kingdoms, demonstrating that it is impossible to have a true Jewish kingdom, a Jewish nation in which God will walk among the Jewish people, without both components united. Yerovam responds by asking, "Who will ultimately be at the head?" When God answers that it must be *Ben Yishai* (King David) at the head, Yerovam refuses God's offer, and the opportunity is lost. Only when the Jewish people realize that both the foundation of Joseph is needed, combined with the spirituality of Benjamin, will Jerusalem be rebuilt properly and only then the final Messiah of David will follow the Messiah of Joseph.

There is a story of a non-Jewish tourist who came to the Kotel, the Western Wall, looked at it, and commented to the Jew next to him, a Jerusalem resident who spoke English: "I have visited China, and their Great Wall is far more impressive than this." The Jew then responded and asked, "Maybe so. But did anyone ever kiss that wall?" For the Jew, the Western Wall and the city of Jerusalem are much more than a landmark, a tourist site, or even a home. It is part of his body, part of his soul. There is no other nation that feels this way about any other city in the world. No other people equates forgetting one's city with losing one's tongue and losing the ability to speak, just as no other nation equates losing its capital city with losing one's limb, one's right hand.[90] And no other religion completes two of its most sacred rituals, Yom Kippur and the Pesach Seder, thinking only about a far-off city (for most), Jerusalem, as each Jew pronounces the words "Next year in Jerusalem."

---

84. Deuteronomy 33;12
85. *Midrash Tehilim* 122:4
86. Exodus 19:6
87. *Sanhedrin* 102a

88. Kings II 12:25
89. Genesis 48:22
90. Psalms 137:5-6

# JEWISH AND SECULAR DATES, NAMES, AND LANGUAGE

THROUGHOUT MOST OF JEWISH HIStory, the Jews have lived in the Diaspora. However, unlike almost every other nation exiled from its homeland, the Jews found a way to maintain their identity and culture while adopting from the indigenous culture as well. This included three specific areas of Jewish culture that not only demonstrate Jewish values, but also raise interesting questions in Jewish law. For example, for the last two thousand years the Jewish people have kept their own calendar while simultaneously using the non-Jewish calendar. In a similar manner, Jews kept their uniquely Jewish names but also adopted names from their host countries. Due to the influence of the surrounding culture, the Hebrew language morphed into unique Jewish languages such as Yiddish and Ladino. This chapter will discuss how the Jews blended their native and adopted cultures and how important it is in Judaism to maintain the aforementioned three aspects of Jewish culture.

## THE JEWISH AND SECULAR CALENDARS

One of the special features of every culture, country, or religion is the establishment of its own calendar. A few years ago, when Israel changed its calendar to Daylight Savings Time earlier than most counties (because of Pesach considerations), the Palestinians insisted on keeping Standard Time as a demonstration that it is an independent political entity. They did this, even though it created havoc for them, since the Palestinians are inextricably tied to the schedules of Israel (and use Israeli currency, electricity, etc.). This also explains why Israel, a secular country, insists on imprinting its coins with the Jewish year (5700+ years), instead of using the secular year that is found on most coins in the world.

Therefore, it is not surprising that the very first Mitzvah given to the Jewish people while they were still in Egypt was to establish a Jewish calendar.[1] Though the traditional understanding of this commandment was to proclaim the new moon each month, Nachmanides understands this verse to command the Jewish people to count the months from Nisan (fifteen days before Passover), with that month as the first month of the year, in order to always remember the Exodus from Egypt.[2] Thus, the Torah is telling the Jewish people not to give names to the months, but rather to count each month with a number (just like each day of the month is numbered). But we know that there are indeed names for each Jewish month, such as Nisan, Iyar, Sivan, etc. How can the months have names, if the commandment specifically says not to name the months, but to call them by numbers according to their distance from the month in which the exodus occurred?

Nachmanides continues and states that the names of the Jewish months are derived from the Diaspora after the Jews were exiled to Babylonia, and these Babylonian names became the norm when the Jews returned to the Land of Israel after the seventy years of exile. (The name of the month of Elul is still used in Turkey today, for example.) In a different place, Nachmanides explains that the reason the Rabbis allowed these names to be used in the Jewish calendar is to recognize God and His role in the Jews' return to the Holy Land after the Babylonian exile, around the year 536 BCE.[3] The original commandment of counting the months by number was still in place, as was the importance of recognizing the Egyptian Exodus, but the names of these Babylonian months are used until today. What exactly did Nachmanides intend when he wrote that although the names of the months are used, the Mitzvah is still intact? There is much disagree-

---

1. Exodus 12:1-2
2. Nachmanides commentary on Exodus 12:2
3. *Derashot* of Nachmanides for Rosh Hashana

ment by later Rabbis about what his intention was, which has implications for Jews using the calendar today.

Rabbi Albo's interpretation of Nachmanides' intention was that once the Jews returned from Babylonia, the new Babylonian names of the months replaced the previous number-ing of the months, in order to acknowledge the redemption of the Jews' return.[4] While Abarbanel agrees with this general idea, he says that both systems – names and numbers – were used simultaneously when the Jews re-turned from exile, because it cannot be that a Torah commandment was simply replaced or that the Jews stopped observing it.[5] Another explanation is that the Aramaic names of the months were already given to the Jewish peo-ple at Sinai, along with the commandment to count months by numbers, but they were not actually used until the Jews returned to the land of Israel from Babylonia.[6] In any event, most commentaries rule that the obligation to count the months from Nisan and the Egyp-tian Exodus is still in effect, but calling the months according to their Babylonians names does not violate this obligation.

THE SECULAR YEAR

Among non-Jews, the commonly used year in enumerating every date associated with the Ju-lian or Gregorian calendars, such as 2015, may be problematic from a Jewish perspective. The year used to be written followed by the letters AD, which stands for "Anno Domini," Latin for "the year of our Lord" (or "after death" in English). Likewise, any reference before the year 1 was written as BC, to signify "before Christ." These letters following the year were always rejected by Jews, who substitute them for BCE (Before the Common Era) before the year 1, and for CE (Common Era) for subse-quent years. Nevertheless, since the numbers themselves relate to the year before or after the

god of Christianity's birth, is it permissible for Jews to write this year today or even to say this year each time the date is mentioned? Is it acknowledging the legitimacy of Jesus as a god? Should not the year always be referred to as 5775, the year that Jews (solely) believe represents the years from Creation?

Rabbi Moses Sofer acknowledges that when Jews live in the Diaspora, they have to deal with the non-Jewish world and its dates on a regular basis. Nevertheless, he says that using the secular year as a designation in the calendar, rather than the Jewish year, is for-bidden by Jews, as it seems to acknowledge a non-Jewish god.[7] His student, Maharam Shick, is even more forceful when he writes that using the secular year to denote the date violates a Biblical prohibition of mentioning another god. Maharam mentions this specifically in the context of monuments at gravesites that use the secular date as well as the Jewish date to denote the day of death, which he says is forbidden.[8] Is using the secular year in record-ing any date, even in a letter to a friend, in fact forbidden to Jews?

Rabbi Ovadiah Yosef, a modern decisor, takes issue with Maharam and Chatam Sofer. He says that the common year used by non-Jews is not at all connected with the year of the birth or death of Jesus. Even though the Christians may think so, Rabbi Yosef proves from numerous Jewish sources that, accord-ing to Jewish tradition, Jesus lived much ear-lier. Therefore, any mention of 2015 is not truly connected to him and is completely permitted. He does add that it is not proper to use the secular dates on monuments of Jewish graves in any case, even though this is not strictly for-bidden.[9] Rabbi Waldenberg agrees in principle with Rabbi Yosef, especially when it comes to writing letters or checks. He recommends a practice found in some religious circles in Israel today when writing the secular date. Af-ter the year they write "Leminyanam," which

---

4. Sefer HaIkaraim 3:16
5. Abarbanel commentary on Exodus 12
6. Bnai Yissachar, "Ma'amarei Chodesh Nisan" 1

7. Chatam Sofer, "Drasha for 7th of Av," 5570
8. Responsa Maharam Shick, Yoreh De'ah 171; Exodus 23:13
9. Responsa Yabia Omer, Yoreh De'ah 3:9

means "according to their count," making it clear that this is not the Jewish year.[10] Rabbi Stern, another contemporary Rabbi, writes that since "everyone" knows that the year is a reference to Jesus, one should avoid writing it on checks or letters, despite the fact that this is not strictly forbidden. He suggests writing "80" or "980" on a check instead of "1980," for example, and says that the check will never come back for an incorrect year if this is done.[11] This practice will avoid the problem. Finally, Rabbi Sternbuch sees nothing wrong with writing the non-Jewish date with the year, and cites Rabbis from centuries ago who adopted this practice in their letters. He says that even in the Yeshiva of Brisk, Rabbi Chaim Soloveitchik paid his staff at the beginning of the secular month and not at the beginning of the Jewish month.[12] Indeed, there are almost no Jewish institutions in the world today, even in Israel, that disburse payment to their staffs at the beginning of the Jewish month. Thus, using the non-Jewish month and year is an ongoing regular practice in the business world and sometimes cannot be avoided. However, wherever possible, Jews should try to use the Jewish date – i.e., the Jewish month and year. Thus, for example, since Israel is the only country where checks written using the Jewish date are recognized as legal, checks there *should* be written with the Jewish date and not the secular date. Each time a Jew writes the Jewish date, he or she is fulfilling the Torah commandment as understood by Nachmanides.

WRITING NON-JEWISH MONTHS

After discussing the problem of writing the non-Jewish year, the Rabbis also discuss writing the non-Jewish months. Two problems are explained. First, if the months are written by a number (i.e., "8.4" for August 4th), this directly negates the original Mitzvah, according to Nachmanides, to make Nisan the first month of the year instead of January. The problem with writing the names of the months is that many of them originate from pagan gods of the Roman Empire. The origin of January is the Roman god of beginnings and endings, Janus. February is derived either from the old-Italian god Februus or from februa, signifying the festivals of purification celebrated in Rome during this month. March is named after the Roman god of war, Mars. May probably comes from Maiesta, the Roman goddess of honor and reverence, and June from Juno, a Roman goddess, the protector and special counselor of the state. Therefore, the names of these months may be problematic from a Jewish standpoint.

Because of the first problem, Rabbi Yosef writes that on Jewish wedding invitations, if the family wants to write the non-Jewish date in addition to the Jewish date, it is preferable to write the name of the month rather than the number, in order to avoid counting the months from any other starting point other than Nisan, according to Exodus 12:2, as discussed above.[13] Rabbi Waldenberg takes Rabbi Yosef to task for this position, since he says that naming the months which have origins in Roman gods is far worse and therefore, writing the numbers is surely preferable to writing the names of the secular months.[14] However, Rabbi Stern agrees with Rabbi Yosef and says while a Jew is permitted to write the names of the month on a check, he or she should not write the numbers of the month beginning from January because for the Jew, the eleventh month is Shevat and not November.[15]

THE DAYS OF THE WEEK

Just as the months of the year have special historical and religious significance for Jews, so too, the days of the week represent a religious concept of no less importance. The Midrash says that the way Jews count the days of the

---

10. *Responsa Tzitz Eliezer 8:8*
11. *Responsa Be'er Moshe 8:18-19*
12. *Responsa Teshuvot Vehanhagot, Choshen Mishpat* 1:830

13. *Responsa Yalkut Yosef, Sova Semachot 1:1:36*
14. *Responsa Tzitz Eliezer 8:8*
15. *Responsa Be'er Moshe 8:18*

week is different from the way non-Jews do it.[16] Why and how is this so? Nachmanides explains the verse "Remember the Sabbath to keep it holy,"[17] implies that each day of the week is not called by a specific name, like Monday, Tuesday, Wednesday, etc. Rather, each day is referred to by its relationship to Shabbat. Thus, Sunday is the first day of the week towards Shabbat and is called "Day One," Monday is the second day towards Shabbat and is called "Day Two," etc. Nachmanides expands on this theme elsewhere and emphasizes that there are no names of the days of the Jewish week, just numbers counting the days towards Shabbat.[18]

What is the religious and cultural significance of counting the days of the week as numbers rather than names? Just as counting the months of the year by number (from Nisan) points to and reminds Jews of a seminal event in Jewish history, the Exodus, counting the day of the week according to numbers towards Shabbat also reminds Jews of a another seminal event in the history of the world, Creation. Shabbat and the seven-day week itself remind people that God created the world in seven days. Thus, by counting each day towards Shabbat, Jews reaffirm their belief in God as Creator of the world. In the ideal Jewish community, as pointed out by Rabbi Moshe Sofer, both the days of the week and the months of the year in the Jewish calendar are represented by numbers that highlight the two foundations of Jewish belief in God – that of the Creation of the world and that of Divine Providence through the Exodus from Egypt.[19] It is interesting that the secular State of Israel adopted this religious concept for its daily calendar. In every Hebrew calendar printed today in Israel, no names of the days of the week are written, rather, Sunday is called the first day (*Yom Rishon*), Monday is called the second day (*Yom Sheni*), etc. Only Shabbat has a proper name and not a number. Thus, every Israeli today is

fulfilling this commandment according to Nachmanides by making the Shabbat holy each time he or she calls the days of the week by their numbers and not by a name.

But what about all the non-Israeli Jews, both observant and non-observant, who call the days of the week by their traditional names (in English) of Monday, Tuesday, Wednesday, etc.? Are they violating Jewish law by doing this? One contemporary Rabbi asks this question and answers that according to the Satmar Rebbe, when a traditional Jew recites the psalm of the day each morning, designated for each day of the week, the words right before each day's paragraph begin with (on Sunday) "Today is the first day that the Levites used to recite in the Temple" (on Monday it says "second day," and so on towards Shabbat).[20] These words alone, recited by every praying Jew, are enough to designate the day as a day towards Shabbat and fulfill the commandment of making the Shabbat holy, as understood by Nachmanides. But Rabbi Stern is doubtful whether this answers the question sufficiently, and he questions if it is permitted to name the days of the week as used in common English parlance. Rabbi Shlomo Zalman Auerbach cites an old Israeli custom supporting the Satmar Rebbe – i.e., that pious Jews used to recite the verse in Exodus, "Remember the Shabbat and Keep it Holy," right before they said the psalm of the day each morning.[21] However, Rabbi Abraham Danzig rules that indeed each Jew should call each day of the week by its number, and reciting the psalm of the day is not enough according to him.[22]

In addition to the problems of not fulfilling the commandments to make the Shabbat holy, each day in the English calendar is named for a specific pagan god. Sunday is the day of the sun god. Monday is the day of the moon god. Tuesday is named for the god "Tiw," a one-handed god associated with single combat and pledges in Norse mythology and also attested

16. Midrash, *Mechilta, Parshat HaChodesh* 7
17. Exodus 20:8 with Nachmanides commentary
18. Derashot of Ramban for Rosh Hashana
19. *Torat Moshe* on Parshat Bo

20. *Responsa Be'er Moshe* 8:18
21. *Halichot Shlomo, Hilchot Tefillah* 11:14
22. *Chaye Adam*, Section 2 1:1

prominently in wider Germanic paganism (thus "Tiw's day"). Wednesday is named for the Germanic god Wodan, a prominent god of the Anglo-Saxons ("Wodan's day"). Thursday is named for the Norse god known in modern English as Thor. Friday is the day of the Norse goddess Fríge, the Norse name for the planet Venus was Friggjarstjarna, "Frigg's star." (Venus was the Roman goddess of beauty, love, and sex.) Saturday is Saturn's day. (The Roman god Saturn was associated with the Titan Cronus, father of Zeus and many Olympians.)

Nevertheless, it is still common practice by many observant Jews to refer to the days of the week according to these names and not by their numbers, as mandated by Nachmanides.

## SECULAR AND JEWISH NAMES

A name for a newborn child is usually a designation that parents may think about for a long time, or maybe only fleetingly, before making a decision that affects the child forever. In traditional Judaism we will see that the name of a person (or thing) has great significance.

The Hebrew name of a person is used exclusively for calling a person to the Torah. Certain prayers, such as the memorial prayer or the prayer for the sick, also use only the Hebrew name (along with the Hebrew name of the person's father, or the mother in case the prayer is for the sick). Legal documents, such as a *Ketuba* (marriage contract) or a *Get* (divorce document), must use the person's Hebrew name.

In the Jewish community, Hebrew names started to compete with names from other languages in the Talmudic period, 200 BCE to 500 CE, when many Jews gave their children Aramaic, Greek, or Roman names. Later, during medieval times in Eastern Europe, it became customary for Jewish parents to give their children two names – a secular name for use in the non-Jewish world and a Hebrew name for religious purposes. This practice continues today in certain circles. Although in Israel and among more observant families the practice today is to give a Hebrew name

only, many English-speaking Jews continue to give their children both English and Hebrew names. Often the two names start with the same-sounding letter, like "*Bet*" in Hebrew and "b" in English. But names are far more than a designation in Judaism. How important is a person's name, specifically his or her Jewish name? Most Jews in the world use their secular name in everyday living. How important is using one's Hebrew name in Judaism each day?

## THE IMPORTANCE OF A NAME IN JUDAISM

In Judaism, names have always been far more significant than a mere designation of a person or thing. One of the very first acts recorded in the Torah is that the first man, Adam, gave names to all the animals and birds.[23] Why is this act so important that it is recorded in the Torah? The Midrash explains that one of the aspects of wisdom that God bestowed upon the first man was that he had the ability to call each beast and bird by the name that best described each species.[24] A later commentary understands this idea more deeply to signify that this trait was part of man's resemblance to God, showing he understood the nature of each animal so well that he could choose the names perfectly suited to each species, with the name actually describing the essence of each animal.[25] Thus, in Hebrew, an object's name should and often does reflect the essence of that object, animal, or even person.

Sometimes, a person's name indeed describes the person's essence and he or she becomes the person designated by his or her name. For example, one person in the Torah, Naval (which means "a despicable person"), actually became a despicable person, and the prophet says that his name described his essence.[26] Noah was named that way because his father wanted him to be a comfort to the world that was in pain. (The Hebrew word "*Noach*"

---

23. Genesis 20:2
24. Midrash, *Yalkut Shimoni*, Kings I 247
25. Rabbeinu Bechaye commentary on Genesis 2:19
26. Samuel I 20:25

signifies comfort and rest.) Noah did become that person, according to Rashi, because he invented an agricultural implement that enabled a starving world to more easily obtain food (easing the curse upon Adam for his sin). Others explain that Noah brought peace, comfort, and calm to the world by his actions in saving the human race from total destruction (for their sins) through the flood.[27] Later on in the Torah, the man responsible for planning, building, and erecting the Tabernacle knew exactly what God wanted and how to do it because his name was also his essence: "*Bezalel*" translates as "created in the image/shadow of God."[28] When God wanted to explain the essence of God and His message to the Jewish people in freeing them from Egyptian bondage, Moses asked God, "What is Your name?"[29] Not only man's essence, but even God's essence, is revealed through a name.

Judaism believes that the name of a person is so crucial that it can change and sometimes help determine a person's personality and future. In fact, the Talmud states that a person's name impacts upon his future life.[30] There is a Talmudic story describing Rabbi Meir as "one who understood the meaning of names."[31] When he and other Rabbis went to an inn, Rabbi Meir realized that the innkeeper's name revealed that he was an immoral person. When everyone else put money in the safe at the inn, Rabbi Meir did not. The next day, the innkeeper denied having received any of the money. Since the name often defines a person, the Midrash states that parents should be very careful in choosing a specific name to match the essence of the baby because the name could determine if the child will grow up to be moral or immoral.[32]

The mystical Arizal says that his student Rabbi Chaim Vital stated that whenever Jewish parents name their baby, it is not their decision alone. The name is predetermined on high, and God actually helps the parents choose the name for the baby.[33] In another place, he expresses the same idea and says that at a baby boy's *Brit Milah*, circumcision, the soul of the baby is already named, and God actually causes the parents to agree and give him that name.[34] This is one reason that it is a custom among Ashkenazim to name their children after deceased relatives who had noble character traits, in the hope that the baby will grow to emulate his or her namesake and take on his or her character.

## JEWISH NAMES REDEEMED THE JEWISH PEOPLE

When the Jews were slaves in Egypt, they had no Mitzvot-commandments, to perform. (The one commandment previously given, circumcision, was no longer observed at that time.) Without commandments, how did the Jewish people remain Jewish? What did they do in Egypt to show that they were worthy to be redeemed and become the Jewish people, the nation of God? The Midrash says that they kept using their distinctive Jewish names (as well as their distinctive Jewish language and clothing). Thus, Jewish identity was preserved, even without a Jewish lifestyle, simply by keeping and using one's Jewish name (and language and clothing).[35] Another Midrash describes this act of using Jewish (and not Egyptian) names as an ethical characteristic of the Jewish people. A parallel to today can easily be drawn: Even those Jews who do not keep a Jewish lifestyle can remain distinctively "Jewish" by using their Jewish names. The Maharal explains that their uniquely Jewish names kept the Jews from assimilating into Egyptian society and losing their Jewishness.[36] Another commentary points out that the Hebrew name for the book of Exodus in the Torah is actually "*Shemot*," "Names," because it was their names that

27. Genesis 5:29 with Rashi and Seforno commentaries
28. Alshich commentary on Exodus 35:30-33
29. Exodus 3:13 with Nachmanides commentary
30. *Berachot* 7b
31. *Yoma* 83a
32. *Midrash Tanchuma, Ha'azinu* 7

33. *Sha'ar Hagilgulim*, chapter 35.
34. *Likutim Gilgulim, Sod Chibur Hakever*
35. Midrash, *Vayikra Rabbah* 32:5
36. Maharal, *Gevurot Hashem* 43

made the Jewish people deserving of the Exodus.[37] Early on in Egypt, Joseph understood this principle and put it into action. Pharaoh had given Joseph a special Egyptian name demonstrating his rank as royalty of Egypt.[38] Yet nowhere in the Torah do we see that Joseph ever used this non-Jewish name, and once he revealed to all that he was a Hebrew, he was called in the Torah (and apparently called himself) only Joseph, the Jewish name given to him by his mother and later taken on by so many Jewish "Josephs" throughout the millennia.

## OTHER IMPORTANT ASPECTS OF THE POWER OF A JEWISH NAME

Rabbi Moshe Shick lived in the 1800s, when assimilation by Jews was running rampant. He writes that it is forbidden to abandon one's Jewish name and be called by a secular name, as this will lead to abandonment of one's Judaism and will violate an aspect of the commandment to remain distinguishable from non-Jews.[39] Almost all of those who heeded his call remained Jewish. Rabbi Moshe Feinstein, who lived through most of the cultural turmoil of the Jewish people in the twentieth century, writes that giving a baby a secular name is something disgraceful, even if it is the name of a deceased relative who only had a secular name.[40] It is preferable to choose a Jewish name of someone in Jewish history or even someone alive today who is truly a hero in the Jewish sense.

As has been mentioned, the power of a Jewish name is so strong that the Talmud states that changing one's name can alter the fate and future of a person.[41] That is the basis on which people often officially change or add a Jewish name of a relative who is very ill. A person's name has unlimited power. This is why King Solomon said that a good name is superior to great oil (i.e., great riches).[42] Rashi explains that riches have a limited shelf life and value, while a person's good name is eternal and lasts into the next world (as well as in this world, when people talk about this good person, even after his or her death).[43] The opposite is also true concerning people with a "bad name," says the Talmud.[44] No one wants to remember these people or name their children after them. Therefore a person's name will help determine the person's path in life and will help make up that person's essence. And a Jewish name will help keep a person Jewish.

## SECULAR LANGUAGE AND JEWISH LANGUAGE, HEBREW

Every culture and society needs its own language. Thus, Hebrew is the language of the Jewish people. But for the Jew, Hebrew is much more than a means of communication. The language is called holy, and the words themselves represent ideas and values that are uniquely Jewish. What makes Hebrew so special? Why is it so important for Jews to use this language today?

In the verse that commands every parent to teach his or her child Judaism and the Torah,[45] the Midrash states that from the moment a child can speak, a parent must teach the child Torah, and a parent must also teach the child to speak Hebrew. If a parent fails in either of these two obligations and the child does not learn either Torah or Hebrew, it is as if this parent has buried this child (since the next verse speaks about living in the land, and living [surviving] is conditional upon the child learning Hebrew and the Torah).[46] This daunting statement is not merely an isolated Midrash. The most famous Torah commentator, Rashi, makes a similar pronouncement explaining the verse,[47] and the Tosefta in the

37. Exodus 1:1 with *Tur* commentary
38. Genesis 41:45
39. Maharam Shick, *Yoreh De'ah* 169
40. *Responsa Igrot Moshe, Orach Chaim* 4:66
41. *Rosh Hashana* 16b
42. Ecclesiastes 7:1
43. Rashi commentary on Ecclesiastes 7:1
44. *Yoma* 38b
45. Deuteronomy 11:19
46. Midrash, *Sifri, Eikev* 10
47. Rashi commentary on Deuteronomy 11:19

Talmud also echoes the same idea.[48] What is it about learning of Hebrew that is so important that failure to do so is equated with death?

The first clue to answer this question comes from Nachmanides. When the Torah calls the coins donated by the people for the Tabernacle *Shekel haKodesh*," "holy money,"[49] Nachmanides not only clarifies why the money was called holy, but also why Hebrew is called holy.[50] He explains that this was the language in which the holy Torah was written, the language the prophets spoke to the Jewish people, and the language that God spoke to the entire Jewish nation at Mount Sinai. In addition, all the names of God and of the greats in the Torah were given in this special language. The Mishna calls this language the very building blocks of creation, as God created the world with ten "pronouncements" or "words" in Hebrew.[51] The names of each species (see above) were given in this language describing the essence of each, according to the Midrash, which echoes the idea that the world was created using this language.[52] Rashi reminds us that before the Tower of Babel was built and the punishment from God was a division into seventy languages, every person on earth spoke only Hebrew.[53] In addition to echoing these ideas, Rabbeinu Bechaye adds that certain commandments can be performed using only the Hebrew language.[54]

That which makes Hebrew so special goes beyond the factors mentioned above. We know that every language reflects, to a certain degree, the culture in which it is found. (Thus, there are thirty-eight different words describing snow in the Inuit language spoken by Eskimos.) The same is true for Hebrew, as the language itself demonstrates the values of the Jewish people. Thus, Maimonides says that there are no explicit references to sexuality or sexual organs in Biblical Hebrew.[55] In Modern Hebrew, most curses are borrowed from Arabic, since classical Hebrew does not contain curse words. In a similar fashion, there is no word for "fun" in Hebrew, since this is not a Jewish concept. The common word for "fun" is "*Kef*," an Arabic word. So too, there is no verb in Hebrew for ownership (e.g., there is no equivalent to "I own this chair"), demonstrating the Jewish value that everything essentially belongs to God. (See chapter, "Copyright in Judaism.") Rabbi Judah Halevi also says that only Hebrew words can capture the essence of people and objects.[56]

ADDITIONAL REASONS FOR AND BENEFITS FROM SPEAKING HEBREW

Commenting upon the Mishna that says we cannot know which Mitzvot are truly the "easy" ones and which are the "difficult" ones or their rewards, Maimonides explains that speaking Hebrew seems like an easy commandment to fulfill.[57] But it is actually a very crucial commandment that is equal to the commandments of *Tzitzit* (which is compared to observing all 613 commandments combined) and Passover, with great reward for speaking it.

The Jerusalem Talmud lists those things that will guarantee the World to Come for a Jew.[58] While living in the Land of Israel, eating food in spiritual purity, and reciting the *Shema* prayer twice daily seem like logical requirements, it also lists speaking Hebrew as one of the requirements for entrance. This list is echoed by Rabbi Meir in a different passage, where it says that only a Jew who does all of these actions will guarantee his place in the World to Come.[59] Another source quotes Rabbi Eibshutz, who says that speaking only Hebrew brings the redemption of the Jewish people closer.[60] Rabbi Yehuda HaChasid

48. Tosefta *Chagiga* 1:3
49. Exodus 30:12-13
50. Nachmanides commentary on Exodus 30:12
51. Mishna *Avot* 5:1 with Rabbi Ovadiah Mebartenurah commentary
52. Midrash, *Yalkut Shimoni, Beraishit* 2:247
53. Genesis 11:1 with Rashi commentary
54. Rabbeinu Bechaye commentary on Exodus 30:13

55. Maimonides, *Guide for the Perplexed* 3:8
56. *Kuzari*, chapter 4
57. Mishna *Avot* 2:1 with Maimonides commentary
58. Jerusalem Talmud, *Shabbat* 9a
59. Jerusalem Talmud, *Shekalim* 14b
60. *Otzrot HaMussar*, "Sha'ar Dibbur U'shetika" 52

lists an additional benefit to speaking (or not speaking) the Hebrew language.[61] When a very old man was asked how he attained such longevity, he said it is because he spoke Hebrew in every place during this life except in the bathroom. Even though it is permitted to speak about non-holy things in Hebrew in the bathroom, he truly saw Hebrew as the "holy tongue" and refused to speak it there. He was convinced that he had attained an extremely long life in the merit of this stringency that he took upon himself.

## ADDITIONAL REASONS WHY THE HEBREW LANGUAGE IS SPECIAL

The mystical book, the *Zohar,* treats Hebrew as so holy that it says a person is not even allowed to speak it in private unless there is a *Minyan* (quorum of ten adult male Jews) present, like anything holy in prayer that requires a *Minyan*.[62] Although Jewish law does not agree with this statement, it shows how special this language is and how it is essentially different from any other language in the world. A Talmud commentary[63] states that a Jew does not fulfill his obligation to learn Torah unless it is learned in Hebrew. Although it is not generally practiced outside the Land of Israel today, a seventeenth century Rabbi, Bezalel Ashkenazi, held that this was part of Jewish law: holy learning should be done only in the holy language. Rabbi Yeshaya Halevi Horowitz, who also lived around that time, is quoted as saying that on Shabbat, only Hebrew should be spoken.[64] Thus, the holy day should be resonant with the sound of the holy tongue. Another Talmudic commentary shows that in leading the Jews out to war, the Kohen-Priest designated for this purpose was obligated to speak to the Jewish people only in Hebrew.[65] Maimonides, in explaining the obligation to

hear and also understand the Torah reading, says that a translator would explain the reading to the congregation after each verse was read by the Torah reader, since at that time most Jews did not understand Hebrew. However, he also says that the translator had to wait for the reader to complete the verse because there was an obligation for the congregation to hear the Torah reading in the original Hebrew, even if they did not understand a word of it.[66]

## PRAYING IN HEBREW

Prayer is the one activity regarding which understanding and having a special feeling is crucial to fulfilling one's obligation. Therefore, a Jew is permitted to pray in any language that he or she understands.[67] But this applies only to public prayer, not private prayer, which must be in Hebrew according to many opinions. Regarding this idea, a twentieth century Rabbi adds that prayer in Hebrew is always preferred by God.[68] He also says that non-Hebrew prayer can occur on a one-time basis, but it would be improper to have congregations pray in other languages regularly, since this would cause Hebrew to be forgotten. To emphasize that this is something that cannot be allowed to happen, he compares forgetting the Hebrew language to the Jewish people forgetting Jerusalem. The same author elsewhere explains the reason why prayer should be in Hebrew. He says that there are many hidden attributes and virtues within the Hebrew language, and since this was the language that the Rabbis used to compose the prayers, many of the hidden meanings even the combinations of Hebrew letters are lost when a person prays in a language other than Hebrew.[69] Even if we do not have the proper intention for these and other meanings in prayer, the fact that the prayer itself is in Hebrew endows it with the

---

61. *Sefer Chasidim* 994
62. *Zohar,* Exodus 132b
63. *Shitah Mekubetzet* commentary on *Berachot* 13, s.v. "*Laima Kesavar*"
64. *Igrot HaGra,* Introduction, p. 49
65. Benayahu ben Yehoyada commentary on *Sotah* 42a

66. Maimonides, *Hilchot Tefillah* 12:11
67. *Shulchan Aruch, Orach Chaim* 101:4
68. *Mishna Berurah* on *Shulchan Aruch, Orach Chaim* 101:4
69. *Biur Halacha* on *Shulchan Aruch, Orach Chaim* 101:4

power and holiness to rise directly to God and be heard with all the right intentions.

## EVEN SECULAR WORDS IN HEBREW ARE SPECIAL

An eighteenth century Rabbi, Eliezer Papo, states that even secular words spoken in Hebrew have some holiness, and within each letter and combination of letters there are deep secrets and concepts.[70] Thus, according to him, millions of non-observant Israelis are fulfilling a holy task each time they speak in their daily lives. This seemingly mystical idea has found its way into normative Jewish law. In the *Code of Jewish Law*, Rabbi Moshe Isserles discusses which books are permitted and which are forbidden to be read on Shabbat.[71] Generally, Jewish content books (such as those relating to Torah) are permitted, while secular books are forbidden. But in an amazing statement, he rules that secular books written in Hebrew are permitted to be read on Shabbat! The *Mishna Berurah* explains the reason for this extraordinary ruling.[72] He says that because the language itself has holiness and one can learn some Torah concepts from the language even when it is devoid of Torah content, it is permitted to read non-Torah works, as well as secular correspondences, written in Hebrew.

This unusual idea can be found in another place in Jewish law as well. The idea of "swearing on the Bible" in court has its origins in Jewish law. Generally, a Jew can swear without holding a book. But if a Jew swears in the name of any other powers besides God, the oath is invalid in a Jewish court. Similarly, if a Jew swears on any non-holy book, the oath is not valid in a Jewish court. However, Rema rules that if a secular book is written in Hebrew, the oath is considered valid simply because it is written in Hebrew, the holy language![73]

## SPEAKING HEBREW RETAINS JEWISH IDENTITY

As discussed above, when the Jews were in Egypt and devoid of commandments, there were four things they did to retain their Jewish identity. The first was that they retained their Jewish names, as was expounded upon above. But another act that kept them from assimilating was that they retained their own unique language (Hebrew).[74] One codifier of Jewish law, in fact, ruled that the way to remain distinct and fulfill the Mitzvah to remain different is by not speaking the same language as the non-Jewish indigenous population (in addition to having different clothing and customs).[75] The Jews by and large did this throughout the centuries, even if their language was not purely Hebrew. European Jews combined German and Hebrew, morphing it into Yiddish, which was written with Hebrew letters. Sephardic Jews did something similar with Spanish and created Ladino. But the basis was always Hebrew.

In fact, when the Rabbis initially tried to enact laws to keep Jews separate and prevent intermarriage with non-Jews, they wanted to pass a series of laws to ensure non-assimilation and Jewish survival. Some laws were indeed passed, such as the prohibition to drink wine touched by a non-Jew. Today, some Jews also only eat food and bread that was cooked by Jews. These examples are brought in the Jerusalem Talmud, where it is mentioned that in order to maintain Jewish identity, there was an attempt to enact a law that Jews were forbidden from speaking any language other than Hebrew.[76] This was not passed into Jewish law and today it is permitted for Jews to speak all languages. Nevertheless, those Jews that spoke only Hebrew, even if non-observant, retained a much higher sense of Jewish identity than the Jews who did not. Rabbi Moshe Feinstein,

---

70. *Pele Yo'etz* on "La'az"
71. Rema, *Shulchan Aruch, Orach Chaim* 307:16
72. *Mishna Berurah* 63 on *Shulchan Aruch, Orach Chaim* 307:16
73. Rema, *Shulchan Aruch, Yoreh De'ah* 237:6

74. Midrash, *Vayikra Rabbah* 32:5
75. *Sefer Mitzvot Gedolot*, negative Mitzvah 50
76. Jerusalem Talmud, *Shabbat* 9b

who lived in the twentieth century, confirms that all languages are indeed permitted to be spoken by Jews today, but he strongly suggests that Jews speak Hebrew whenever possible.[77] Another Rabbi ruled and commented that at the time of the final redemption, all Jews will indeed speak Hebrew.[78] Even the non-Jews, who will not speak completely in Hebrew, will use many Hebrew words and expressions in their languages at that time.

---

77. *Responsa Igrot Moshe, Even Ha'ezer* 3:35

78. *Responsa Divrei Yetziv, Yoreh De'ah* 52

# JUDAISM – A RELIGION OR A NATION?

J UDAISM HAS EXISTED FOR CLOSE TO four thousand years. Any attempt to define precisely what it is and what it is not, is fraught with some controversy and imprecision, as this concept means so many different things to so many different people, today as well as in the past. Any definition will necessarily be too simplistic and will lack the nuances associated with Judaism. Nevertheless, there has been an ongoing argument throughout history, as we shall see, as to what is fundamentally Judaism. Is Judaism at its essence a religion, or is Judaism at its essence a nation or a people? This chapter will attempt to understand the implications of this essential difference in the way people view Judaism, in an attempt to discover its true basis, according to the traditional understanding through the sources.

Any religion is defined (by Webster's Dictionary) as "the belief in and the service and worship of a superhuman controlling power such as God" or "an organized collection of belief system, cultural system, and world view that relates humanity to spirituality and sometimes, to moral values." Another definition of religion is "a set of beliefs concerning the cause, nature, and purpose of the universe, usually involving devotional and ritual observances." According to any of these definitions (or any other definition of religion), Judaism certainly qualifies and can be defined as a religion. On the other hand, a nation is defined as "a large aggregate of people united by common descent, history, culture, or language, inhabiting a particular country or territory". Based on this definition, Judaism is certainly a nation as well. So which is it? Is Judaism more a religion or is Judaism more a nation?

To complicate the question, there are basic elements of Judaism that can easily qualify as both of these concepts and make no sense if Judaism is exclusively defined as one or the other. A person born in a country (a nation like the United States, for example) is automatically considered a citizen of his native land in most countries around the world, even if that person knows nothing about his or her place of birth. In contrast, nearly all religions require an active acceptance of that religion in order to be considered a member of it. Yet in Judaism, someone born a Jew remains a Jew, even if he or she does not believe in God and practices nothing religious. This points to Judaism as a nation. And like any naturalized citizen of almost every country, a person needs to master a basic understanding about that country (as well as other requirements) in order to become a citizen. In Judaism too, someone who is not born Jewish needs to master some aspects of Judaism in order to become a Jew in a special ceremony. But in Judaism, all of the knowledge needed to convert is religious in nature, with nothing about the national character or history of Judaism, and the entrance ceremony is purely a religious ritual. In another anomaly, no other religion has its own country, a homeland as a central tenet of belief. There is no country called Episcopalia or Protestan. And yet, the Land of Israel for the Jew was holy long before the State of Israel was created. The Land of Israel for the Jews is far more important than other countries are for displaced citizens from those countries. After four or five generations away from their country, ethnic Germans or ethnic Italians do not feel the same connection to their country of origin that Jews feel towards the Land of Israel, even after one hundred generations removed from the land. The Torah not only speaks about the rituals, the religious aspects of Judaism, but it also speaks about the technical borders of the Land of Israel, its government, tax system, and other very prominent features of nationhood. On the other hand, every nation has a law book, but no other nation kisses its law book, the Torah, as the Jews do. And no nation has a law that a person should recite a blessing after going to the bathroom, as Judaism does. The political leader of the Jewish people, the king, must write his own Torah and take it with him to each battle in order to insure that he, like everyone else who is Jewish, observes the entire Torah, including its rituals, thereby submitting himself to God just as any other Jew.[1] No other country has this requirement, and almost no nation subjects its supreme leader to the very same rules and laws as every other citizen. No nation has ever continued to exist for thousands of years after it was exiled from its land and was forced to live as a minority among a dominant surrounding culture – except for the Jews. The list of contradictions and anomalies goes on and on.

There are many more examples that demonstrate that Judaism is clearly both a religion *and* a nation. The question for this discussion is which aspect is more dominant and more important. The answer will depend on who is responding to the question. The secular soldier from Tel Aviv considers himself or herself a full Jew because he or she believes that Judaism, at its core, is a nation or people, with its own unique culture, language, land, and history. The Chasid living in Brooklyn considers himself a full Jew because he observes every Jewish law and ritual, and because for him, Judaism at its essence is a religion. This chapter will examine, through the sources, which aspect of Judaism is more dominant. Is Judaism, at its core, a religion or is it a nation or people?

## JUDAISM FIRST AND FOREMOST IS A FAMILY

Before the question that has been posed can be examined in depth, it is important to acknowledge that Judaism is essentially a family, even before it is a religion or a nation. The dominant name for the Jewish people throughout the entire Torah is *Bnai Yisrael*, the children of Israel. Since Yisrael-Israel was the name later given to Jacob by God, the name of the people translates as the "family of Jacob." The Jewish people are called "the family of Jacob/Israel" three hundred and ninety-four different times just in the Torah itself. No other major religion in the world contains in its moniker the name of a family. But Judaism, at is essence, is a family. Why is this so? When was the Jewish nation referred to as "the children of Israel" for the first time?

Except for one technical reference, the very first time that the sons of Jacob were called "the children of Israel" was right after the Torah referred to them for the first time as "the brothers of Joseph."[2] Why, asks Rashi, did the Torah depict these men as Joseph's brothers *now*, when they had been his brothers for thirty-nine years and they had not seen Joseph for twenty-two years? He answers that this is the first time that they had ever felt like true brothers to Joseph, as they were now remorseful when they recalled their sin of hating him and selling him to Egypt, and they wanted to find him and free him in Egypt.[3] Thus, this is the first moment in Jewish history when this family, the Jewish family, was truly united. It was only then that they were called by the Torah "the children of Israel," indicating that the essence of the Jewish people is the feeling of harmony that a truly united family feels.

This concept of unity continued as the Jews came down to Egypt. The very first verse of the book of Exodus describes that *Bnai Yisrael* came to Egypt, each person with his family, totally united.[4] But then something catastrophic happened to break apart the Jewish family. When Pharaoh forced the Jews into slavery and then threatened to kill every Jewish baby boy, the unity of the Jewish family in Egypt disintegrated. This phenomenon is exemplified by Amram, who married Yocheved, daughter of Levi, one of the leading families of the Jews. After Pharaoh's edict, he separated from her, afraid to have any more children who would then be killed. Undoubtedly many other families did the same, which broke apart

---

1. Deuteronomy 17:18-19

2. Genesis 42:3-5
3. Rashi commentary on Genesis 42:3-5
4. Exodus 1:1

the family structure of the Jewish people. But unlike those other families, now divided, their young daughter Miriam convinced her parents Amram and Yocheved to reunite.[5] It was this reunification of the family which resulted in the subsequent birth of Moses, which in turn symbolized and began the redemption of the Jewish people from Egypt.

The reunification of the Jewish family was a pre-condition of nationhood and of Judaism, a necessary step before the redemption from Egypt could take place. After suffering many plagues, Pharaoh finally asked Moses who was intended to leave Egypt to worship to God, and Moses said that both the elders and the children would go jointly. Moses understood that without families worshipping together, the redemption would not come. Pharaoh also understood the power of the united family and therefore only permitted the elders to go, leaving the children behind. When Moses heard Pharaoh's condition that families would be divided, it was unacceptable to him and he refused Pharaoh's offer.[6]

In order to insure that the Jewish family was truly unified, God commanded the Jewish people to take the Egyptian god, the lamb, and eat it as a united family, on what became the night of the Seder in Egypt. And if there were too few people in the nuclear family to finish the lamb, then they had to invite their neighbors – usually the extended family of grandparents and siblings – to join them and eat the lamb together.[7] God also commanded the Jewish people to perform another ritual act to symbolize the unity of the Jewish family. In each Jewish home (which is the symbol of family), they were to place the blood of that lamb on the doorposts as a sign that this was a unified Jewish family.[8] Only then, after each Jewish family came together, could the Jews leave Egypt.

Even after the Jews left Egypt, the family unit was still paramount in building the nation.

When God counted the Jewish people in the desert, they had to be counted by Moses as families.[9] But why was it so crucial to building the Jewish nation and religion that the family unit had to be so together? Why is this togetherness an essential element of Judaism? It is clear that in order for the Jewish people to survive and thrive, every Jew had to think of every other Jew as a member of his or her family. Just as any family member would do almost anything to help any other family member, every Jew is tied to every other Jew in the same way.[10] So too, the Midrash compares the Jewish people to one sheep. If part of the sheep is in pain, the entire sheep suffers. Similarly, all Jews are considered to be in "one boat." When one person drills a hole in one part of the boat, everyone on board is affected. So it is with the Jewish people.[11] When one hand holding a knife accidentally cuts the other hand, the cut hand is not angry at the other hand. So too, the Jewish people should avoid getting angry at each other as they are all part of one body.[12] This is the symbol of the united family as the building block of Judaism. This concept has been put into practice by Jews for thousands of years, until today. American Jews, who had never met a Russian Jew, nevertheless worked tirelessly to free the Jews of the Soviet Union in the 1960s through the 1980s. Why? Every Jew is like a family member. In 1991 the Israeli government airlifted 14,000 Ethiopian Jews to Israel and the Israelis welcomed them with open arms. Why? These Jews were family. When Gilad Shalit, an Israeli soldier, was held captive by Hamas for five years, Jews around the world all felt as if he were their own son or brother. The examples go on and on.

Thus, before we analyze the other components of Judaism, the first building block is that of family.

---

5. Exodus 2:1 with Rashi commentary
6. Exodus 10:10-11
7. Exodus 12:3-4
8. Exodus 12:7

9. Numbers 1:2
10. *Shavuot* 39a; *Shulchan Aruch, Choshen Mishpat* 87:20
11. Midrash, *Vayikra Rabbah* 4:6
12. Jerusalem Talmud, *Nedarim* 30a

## PESACH AND SHAVUOT – SYMBOLS OF NATION AND RELIGION?

Clearly, both components exist within Judaism – both the religious aspects and national aspects. It would be very easy to demonstrate that Judaism believes in both principles of religion and nationalism, by explaining Pesach as the holiday when the Jewish people became free politically as a people, the symbol of national or peoplehood aspect of Judaism. The holiday of Shavuot, on the other hand, when the Jewish people received the Torah, symbolizes the religious or spiritual aspect of Judaism. But further investigation shows that these symbols are not so clear-cut. In fact, both the national and religious components exist within each of these holidays.

It is true that on the surface it indeed seems that Pesach is the ideal holiday to represent the nationalistic aspiration of Judaism. The Jews were freed from bondage and became a people politically, culturally, and historically. They experienced independence for the first time in defying the Egyptians by taking the Paschal lamb. They walked out of Egypt on their own terms. And yet, Pesach also symbolizes the religious aspect of Judaism. It was God's specific religious commandments that the Jews observed in taking the Paschal sacrifice. And it was God who destroyed the Egyptian firstborn sons, which allowed the Jews to achieve that freedom. But even from the very beginning, freedom from Egyptian bondage was not only about nationalistic aspirations. In his initial meeting with Moses, God explains the purpose of achieving freedom from Egypt: in order to serve God on this mountain, Mount Sinai.[13] Therefore, the nationalistic freedom achieved on Passover was always directed toward devotion to God and the religious aspect of Judaism. Similarly, on Shavuot, which should symbolize the unique religious aspect of Judaism through the giving of the Torah, God tells the Jewish people right before He pronounced the Ten Commandments: you,

the Jewish people, will be My nation among all nations.[14] Thus, at the moment of highest spirituality, when Judaism became a religion, God speaks about the unique nationhood of the Jewish people. In fact, the two holidays are intertwined in the words of Ezekiel. When he refers to Passover, he calls it the holiday of Shavuot. Rashi explains that since the countdown to Shavuot begins on Pesach (with the counting of the *Omer*), Ezekiel depicts Passover as the beginning of the holiday of Shavuot.[15]

## PESACH SEDER SHOWS THAT BOTH COMPONENTS ARE EQUALLY IMPORTANT

In trying to discover the dominant component of Judaism, we shall see that both are equally necessary, and that Judaism itself cannot exist with only one and not the other. There are certain subtle aspects of Pesach and, more specifically, the Passover Seder, which demonstrate that both the religious and national aspects of Judaism are crucial, and both are needed to form what we today call Judaism. Ultimately, Judaism must be an amalgam of both nationhood and religion.

When trying to formulate the Hagaddah that is read on Passover night, the Rabbis debated the structure and content. In order for each Jew to "experience" both slavery and freedom and see himself as if he personally went out of Egypt, which is one of the requirements of the Hagaddah,[16] the Rabbis agreed that the first part of the Hagaddah must describe the disgrace and defamation of the Jewish people, and only later would describe the glory and the praise. While they also agreed about the text of the latter part of the Hagaddah describing the praise, there was a disagreement about what was considered the shame, the defamation, of the Jewish people. Rav said it was that the origins of the Jewish people, before

---

13. Exodus 3:12

14. Exodus 19:5
15. Ezekiel 45:21 with Rashi commentary
16. Text of the Passover Haggadah right before the drinking of the second cup of wine

Abraham, when they were idol worshippers. Shmuel said that the defamation of the Jewish people was that they were slaves to Pharaoh.[17] What is the underlying argument between Rav and Shmuel? It is possible that these two Torah giants were arguing about the definition of the essence of Judaism, our very discussion. Rav saw Judaism at its core to be a religion, and therefore, the defamation had to be religious in nature: the Jews were descended from idol worshippers. Shmuel, on the other hand, believed that Judaism at is core was its peoplehood, the nationalistic component. Thus, the height of the nation's defamation was to become a slave people to another country, Egypt.

These two positions and differences are clear. But what is interesting is that the later Rabbis, when finalizing the text of the Haggadah, did not choose one view over the other. They insisted that *both* components, which are both defamations of the Jewish people, should be included in Seder night. They wanted to teach us that both components are necessary in Judaism – the religious aspect espoused by Rav and the nationhood aspect espoused by Shmuel.

This idea is repeated in another strange but innocuous custom of the Seder night. First articulated in the Talmud,[18] *Shulchan Aruch* rules that while a Jew may converse, interrupt, and even eat between the first and second of the four cups of wine at the Seder, as well as between the second and third cups, it is forbidden to interrupt in any manner between the third and fourth cups of wine on Seder night.[19] Why? What is the difference between this cup of wine and this part of the Seder and the rest of the evening? While there may be some technical reasons for this Jewish law, the Rabbis perhaps were trying to teach the Jewish people a concept on a deeper, philosophical, or symbolic plane as well. What do the cups of wine at the Seder symbolize? While there may be several answers to this question, the most popular is the response of the Midrash, which states that each cup of wine represents one of the four stages of redemption outlined by God in the Torah:[20] 1) "I will bring you out from under the burdens of the Egyptians," 2) "I will rid you from their slavery," 3) "I will redeem you with an outstretched arm," and 4) "I will take you to me for a people, and I will be to you a God."[21]

If indeed each cup of wine represents each stage of the redemption from Egypt, then we may have an answer to our question. It is clear that the third stage of redemption promised by God is the actual Exodus from Egypt, when the Jewish people became a nation, a free people. The fourth stage of God taking the Jewish people and being their God refers to the revelation on Mount Sinai that took place on the holiday of Shavuot, the religious essence of Judaism. While no one would think that the first or second stage (easing the burden of slavery and then stopping the work completely) would be enough to achieve true redemption and freedom, some might think that the third stage, political freedom, leaving Egypt, would be sufficient to achieve Jewish deliverance. The fourth component, the religious experience with God, might not be necessary to establish Judaism. Therefore, the Rabbis were not worried about "interrupting" or stopping after achieving the first or second stage or redemption, and thus permitted conversations and interruptions between the first and second, as well as between the second and third cups of wine. But they were indeed concerned that some Jews might think that political freedom or nationhood, the third stage, is enough to be a Jew. Therefore, they said that once this stage is achieved, one may not stop or interrupt until the fourth stage of religious Judaism, symbolized by the fourth cup of wine, is also achieved. Through this law, the Rabbis were declaring that one may not separate or create a wedge between the national component of Judaism and its religious component. Both

---

17. *Pesachim* 116a
18. *Pesachim* 108a
19. *Shulchan Aruch, Orach Chaim* 479:1

20. Midrash, *Bereishit Rabbah* 68:5
21. Exodus 6:6-8

are necessary to mold Judaism in the Exodus experience and again today, as Jews relive that experience on Seder night.

## OTHER JEWISH CUSTOMS AND LAWS REFLECT THIS SAME IDEA

This very same lesson eerily repeats itself in another Jewish law that seems totally unrelated. As we approach Passover, beginning two weeks before Purim, there are four special Sabbaths that are distinguished by special readings of the Torah: *Shabbat Shekalim, Shabbat Zachor, Shabbat Parah*, and *Shabbat HaChodesh*. While these four Torah portions must be read in order each year, the precise Shabbat in which these special portions are read differs slightly, depending on that year's calendar. But the Rabbis ruled that while there may be an "open" Shabbat between the first and second of these special portions (when no special reading takes place), or between the second and third of these special portions, there may not be an "interruption" or open Shabbat between the third and fourth of these special Sabbaths and readings.[22] This sounds very much like the Jewish law regarding the wine cups at the Seder. What is the connection?

The third of the four special Sabbaths, Parshat *Parah*, describes the laws of the Red Heifer, the need for ritually impure Jews to become ritually pure before Passover. The seven-day process involves the sprinkling of water from the ashes of the Red Heifer. This law is known as the *"Chok* (ritual) without explanation" in the Torah since its laws seem bizarre, without any rationale.[23] This Mitzvah that existed only in Temple times is *the* symbol of the purely religious component of Judaism. The fourth special Shabbat is *Parshat HaChodesh*, the commandment for the Jewish people to set up their own calendar, the very first commandment the Jews received as a people in Egypt.[24] Since every nation establishes its own calendar, this commandment represents the essence of the peoplehood of Judaism, its national aspect. Thus, the two vital components of Judaism, the religion symbolized by the Red Heifer and the nationhood represented by the commandment to set up a Jewish calendar, cannot be separated – not by a Shabbat in between and not by any reasoning by Jews that Judaism can exist with only one and not the other. That is the deeper meaning behind this Jewish law regarding the reading of these four special Shabbat portions.

This theme of not creating a *Hefsek*, a separation, between the religious and nationalistic aspects of Judaism is a concept that seems to repeat itself again and again. As mentioned above, the counting of the *Omer* begins on Pesach, which symbolizes, in the main, the national aspect of Judaism, and it is completed on Shavuot, which symbolizes, in the main, the religious aspect of Judaism. Thus, the consecutive nightly count connecting these two symbols and the two holidays represents that connection between these two ideas of nationhood and religion within Judaism, and the importance of never breaking that connection. That is why Jewish law, once again, forbids any severing of this vital connection. If a Jew forgets to count the *Omer* linking these two parts of Judaism for just one day, then that connection is indeed broken, and the commandment of counting of the *Omer* cannot be fulfilled.[25] In a philosophical sense, we see this idea every weekday as well. There are two different parts to the commandment of putting on Tefillin by Jewish men each morning, one on the arm and one on the head. The arm, representing the action of the Jew, stands for the physical part of Judaism, including a nation with an army, a government, police, and policies put into practice. The head Tefillin, on the other hand, represents the intellectual and spiritual aspects of Judaism, the religious component. Once again, Jewish law mandates that both of these aspects remain equal and connected together as one, in order to symbolize the totality of Judaism.

22. Jerusalem Talmud, *Megillah* 25b
23. Numbers 19:1-12
24. Exodus 12:1-2

25. *Shulchan Aruch, Orach Chaim* 489:8

Therefore, it is the very same words written in each box of the Tefillin, showing the equality of the two, and it is forbidden to sever the tie between these two parts of the commandment by interrupting between the donning of the Tefillin worn on the arm and then the Tefillin worn on the head.[26]

## BOTH COMPONENTS HAVE ALWAYS BEEN PRESENT IN JUDAISM

These two elements have always been both intrinsic and necessary to Judaism, although this concept is often misunderstood by non-Jews and even Jews. For many years, other faiths and other peoples have used the phrase pronounced by God, "Let My people go," when speaking about national aspirations. But the people uttering these words who yearned for peoplehood always forgot to look up the original text in the Torah. The words "Let My people go" in the Torah are *always* followed by the words "so that they can serve Me."[27] Therefore, God is clearly saying that nationalism is indeed important in Judaism, as long as it is followed by service to God, the core religious component of Judaism. Similarly, when God chose the Jewish people to be "His" people right before the Torah was given, he clearly defined what Judaism must become: a kingdom of priests and a holy nation.[28] Normally, priests are associated exclusively with the religious realm, and a kingdom is part of the political or nationalistic realm. Yet here, God says that Judaism must combine the political concept of a kingdom with the spiritual concept of priests. The very next phrase in the verse projects the same idea. Holiness is usually left to the realm of the religious, while nationhood is usually left to the physical, non-holy aspects of life. Yet God said that Judaism must combine the two and become a holy nation. When Ruth, the ultimate convert to

Judaism and great-grandmother of King David, described the essence Judaism, she uttered just four Hebrew words: "*Ameich Ami v'Elokayich Elokai,*" "your nation is my nation, and your God is my God."[29] This encapsulates the essence of Judaism, and one aspect without the other is not truly Jewish.

These two concepts have always vied with each other from the very beginning, even before the Torah was given. The battle for leadership among the Jewish people began with two sons of Jacob, each with different visions of what Judaism should be. Joseph was the economic provider of food and other physical needs, the ruler of Egypt who represented nationhood, government, and the economy.[30] He believed in a Judaism that was dominated by the physical needs of the people, the cultural and historic components. Judah, on the other hand, was the man sent by Jacob to establish the house of Jewish study in Egypt, representing the spiritual side of Judaism.[31] They fought their entire lives for their beliefs in what Judaism should be, not realizing that both were necessary in equal parts to become the Judaism we know today. And this battle continued throughout history through the descendants of these two leaders. Joseph was given the city of Shechem as an inheritance,[32] and it was the descendants of Joseph who broke away from Jerusalem to form the monarchy of Israel, stressing the nationalistic aspects of Judaism. Where did Jeroboam, the king of Israel establish his capital? It was in the city of Shechem, the place of his ancestor Joseph.[33] The descendants of Judah continued to rule from Jerusalem, thus continuing the spilt between these two factions and two different philosophies of what Judaism should be. And this division and argument did not stop then. Even in the future this split will continue, as there will be the first Messiah, a descendant of Joseph, before the Messiah, a descendant

---

26. *Shulchan Aruch, Orach Chaim* 25:9
27. Exodus 7:16, 7:26, 9:1, 9:13
28. Exodus 19:6

29. Ruth 1:16
30. Genesis 47:12
31. Genesis 46:28 with Rashi commentary
32. Genesis 48:22
33. Kings I 12:25

of Judah, will emerge and bring the final redemption.[34]

Even though both components are of equal weight in Judaism, there can be only one ultimate leader. On his deathbed, Jacob had two choose between his two sons to lead the Jewish people, and he chose Judah over Joseph, even though Joseph had demonstrated his leadership skills for many years.[35] Later on in history, says the Midrash, God tried to reconcile these two components through two leaders, King Jerobam and King David, representing each philosophy, and God promised to walk together with both leaders. But when Jeroboam asked who would ultimately lead, God replied that it had to be Judah and that is why Jeroboam balked, thus keeping the two sides separated and delaying the coming of the Messiah.[36] It is clear, then, that only when the advocates of each core element of Judaism realize that they must unite and join together to form the totality of Judaism, only then will the Messiah come.

## THE ORDER OF FIRST NATIONALITY AND THEN RELIGION IN JUDAISM

Although it is clear that both the religious and national elements are needed to form Judaism and that they are of equal value, there is one thing that is incontrovertible: the order of these two aspects of Judaism. The national component must *always* come before the religious component. This was true at the very founding of Judaism, it is still true today, and it will be true in the future as well. Each time both components have been mentioned, it is always the nationhood aspect preceding the religious aspect.

Thus, the leadership of Joseph in Egypt came before the leadership of Judah. The holiday of Pesach and the political freedom of the Jewish people had to come before the holiday of Shavuot when Judaism became a

religion as well. The people had to "go" and leave Egypt before they could worship God on Mount Sinai. When Ruth described the essence of Judaism in its two parts, the nationhood preceded the religious aspect. Even in the Haggadah, the Rabbis placed "We were slaves in Egypt" before "Our ancestors were idol worshippers." (The one exception to this rule, *Parshat Parah* preceding *Parshat Hachodesh*, can be explained, but it is too detailed for this volume.)

This was not only true in ancient times, but is true today as well. The founding of the State of Israel in 1948, the political nationhood of the Jewish people, had to precede the liberation of Jerusalem and the site of the Holy Temple in the Six Day War in 1967, the greatest religious event in modern times. Even the dates of these two events on the Jewish calendar and the order of their celebrations (the fifth of Iyar and the twenty-eighth of Iyar, respectively) follows the pattern, with Israel's Independence Day celebrated before *Yom Yerushalayim*, Jerusalem Day.

In the future, this order must be preserved as well. As demonstrated above, first the Messiah of Joseph, the national component, will arrive before the Messiah of David, the religious component, who will then combine both aspects. Even the actions of the Messiah himself preserve this order. Maimonides explains that first the Messiah will fight wars and defeat all enemies and only then will rebuild the Holy Temple. He will return Jews to the land of Israel and establish Jewish courts and only then bring sacrifices to the Temple.[37] The weekday *Shmoneh Esreh*, the Silent Prayer, recited for thousands of years by millions of Jews, also depicts an order of events in which the physical, national elements come first, and only then come the religious elements. Thus, the fourteenth blessing first speaks about the rebuilding of Jerusalem. Then in the fifteenth blessing, the Messiah will come and only then

---

34. *Sukkah* 52a, b
35. Genesis 49:8-10
36. *Sanhedrin* 102a

37. Maimonides, *Hilchot Melachim* 11:4, 1

in blessing seventeen will the service in the Holy Temple be restored.[38]

Clearly then, the peoplehood of Judaism must always precede religious Judaism, but only when both are truly united equally – when all Jews realize that true Judaism needs both principles – will the Messiah be ready to come and actualize a time when Judaism will be lived to its fullest and intended perfection.

---

38. Fourteenth, fifteenth, and seventeenth blessings of the weekday *Shmoneh Esreh*

# JUDGING FAVORABLY IN JUDAISM

PART OF THE NATURE OF HUMAN beings is the tendency to constantly analyze everyday situations that occur in their lives – tens or even hundreds of them – like a super-fast computer, instantaneously examining many factors regarding other people's actions and then making snap judgments about what is taking place. As part of this process, people often automatically judge whether any given action by others is moral or immoral, right or wrong. Usually, if the individuals are people that we know, like, or respect, we tend to give them the "benefit of the doubt" when looking at any moral situation that could be judged in more than one manner. For those we do not particularly like or do not know, we tend to judge more harshly, even when the deduction about whether something they do is right or wrong, moral or immoral, seems evenly balanced. Regarding such everyday occasions, Judaism has a special moral imperative in almost all situations to "judge others favorably" and extend the benefit of the doubt to others by believing that they are doing the "right thing," even when we do not know the people personally. The details, reasons, and the parameters of this Jewish law will be explained below.

## THE GENERAL MITZVAH AND OBLIGATION TO JUDGE SOMEONE FAVORABLY

The verse in the Torah requires every Jew to judge all coreligionists justly.[1] While this usually refers to the commandment for Jewish judges to be impartial regarding any case between two Jewish litigants, it also commands each Jew to judge every person favorably in any non-legal situation or court. Thus, if there are two ways of viewing a person's actions or activity – one that it is moral and the other that it is immoral – there is a special imperative to choose to view it as a moral or "correct" action, accompanied by the right motives, rather than the opposite. The Mishna tells us to judge each person ( Jew or non-Jew) favorably,[2] while the Talmud based on this verse says to judge every Jew favorably in all situations.[3] Another Midrash uses this verse to prove that every person (not only Jews) should be judged favorably.[4] A different Mishna discusses another related issue, but the essence of the dictum in that Mishna boils down to the same or a similar concept. It says there that someone cannot judge anyone else until he or she has "lived in that person's shoes" – i.e., has experienced his exact circumstances in life.[5] Since no one can ever know or fully comprehend each of the all-encompassing factors and circumstances that have transpired in someone else's life, the Mishna, in effect, is instructing every Jew to judge every other person's actions favorably. The wording in Hebrew of our original Mishna also seems to support this idea. It does not simply say to judge each person (*Adam*) favorably. Rather, it states that we must judge the entire person (*Ha'adam*) favorably. It has been suggested that the use of this wording is to tell us that if a person looks at the *entire* individual – i.e., *all* of the factors involved in each act, then they will we be able to find something positive within each individual to change their perspective of what they might have at first considered negative motives or immoral actions. By searching for any possible positive explanation, human beings can and will be able to consider mitigating circumstances and see something positive within each questionable activity.

Rabbi Judah Chasid (twelfth century) also stresses the importance of judging people

---

1. Leviticus 19:15

2. Mishna *Avot* 1:6
3. *Shavuot* 30a
4. Midrash, *Sifra*, *Kedoshim* 4:4
5. Mishna *Avot* 2:4

favorably whenever possible.[6] Rabbi Moshe Coucy, in his thirteenth century *Book of Commandments*, considers this specific obligation as one of the 613 commandments of the Torah.[7] Maimonides also lists the obligation to judge everyone favorably in his *Book of Commandments*,[8] but then in his book of Jewish law, Maimonides states that this obligation to judge favorably is limited only to a Talmudic scholar who evaluates the actions of people, and thus, it does not apply to every Jew.[9] Rabbi Yisrael Meir Kagan (the Chofetz Chaim) resolves this apparent contradiction by saying that while some authorities list this obligation as a formal Torah Mitzvah (such as *Semak*, Rabbeinu Yonah, and others), Maimonides in his *Book of Commandments* writes this as only a suggestion and a moral act of good will, but not as an actual commandment.[10] A Talmudic scholar, however, *would* be obligated by the Torah to judge everyone favorably as a commandment and not merely as an act of moral good will. Whether a formal commandment, or a Torah or Rabbinic obligation, all of the Rabbis seem to agree that in almost all situations (as explained in detail below), a Jew should choose to see every act of every person in a positive, rather than a negative, light and attribute good intentions to each individual.

## THE IMPORTANCE OF JUDGING SOMEONE FAVORABLY

In addition to the commandment itself (for which a traditional Jew needs no reason or justification to obey God's desire), there are numerous other benefits for each person who goes through life judging every action of others for good, as a positive rather than a negative act, when both assessments are possible. The first reason to act in this manner is a very selfish one. The Midrash promises that if Jews judge the action of others favorably, then their own actions will be ascribed as favorable and good by God when He assesses their moral behavior.[11] Another reason to consider all possible actions by others as positive is that it will bring special reward to one who is judging. There are very few commandments in Judaism which the Rabbis say are so important that the reward for them will be given both in this world (the "interest") and the Next World (the "principle"). One of the commandments that can receive such reward is the act of judging others favorably.[12]

Another natural benefit to cultivating a generally positive attitude towards others and their behavior is the greater friendship and camaraderie that will be created among human beings. If people always attribute positive motives to others, then they will come to think better of them. *Sefer HaChinuch* explains that if everyone behaved and thought in this manner, there would be far less enmity between people, which would in turn bring much more peace and harmony between individuals.[13] This is also the opinion of Rashi, who says that peace between people is a natural outgrowth of judging people favorably.[14]

Yet another benefit of such a general viewpoint towards others is that it will bring a person closer to God. Rabbi Yisrael Meir Kagan believes that people who take this approach to the actions of others will ascribe few or no sins to other individuals, but will view their own actions and sins more harshly, causing them to repent and become more spiritual.[15] Another very practical reason to adopt this approach to life (and the manner in which people assess the behavior of others) is to avoid committing an actual sin for which there is a severe punishment. The Talmud rules that anyone who wrongly finds fault with someone else who is legitimately guilt free, is then punished with

6. *Sefer Chasidim* 31
7. *Sefer Mitzvot Gadol*, positive Mitzvah 106
8. Maimonides, *Sefer HaMitzvot*, positive Mitzvah 177
9. Maimonides, *Hilchot De'ot* 5:7
10. Chofetz Chaim, *Be'er Mayim Chaim*, "Introduction"
11. Midrash, *Yalkut Shimoni, Vayikra* 19, 611
12. *Shabbat* 127a
13. *Sefer HaChinuch*, Mitzvah 235
14. Rashi commentary on *Shabbat* 127a
15. *Sefer Mitzvot Katan*, 223

corporal (physical) punishment upon one's body.[16]

A side benefit of this attitude is that it will help other people indirectly. How Jews look at the actions of another person will directly influence how God looks upon that person as well. Each time Jews judge others positively, their behavior (in God's eyes), will also be looked upon more favorably.[17]

THREE STAGES IN JUDGING PEOPLE AND SITUATIONS, AND POSSIBLE PITFALLS

Whether people are conscious of it or not, the human brain is constantly assessing situations and making judgments that influence their actions. This occurs thousands of times a day, from the simple task of being aware of a red light and therefore choosing not to enter an intersection, to more complex situations that confront each person on a daily basis. Many of the actions regarding others involve their moral choices that people's brains automatically choose to assess and conclude as being moral or good behavior, or as immoral or bad behavior. If they understand the factors that contribute to such assessments, then human beings can consciously train themselves to come to more positive and favorable conclusions about the activities of others, which Judaism and the Torah desire.

There are three distinct phases that take place in each judgment and assessment of an action performed by another person. The first is the gathering of the details and the facts of what is actually taking place. The second is the weighing of those details, which may demonstrate a moral or immoral component (some which are amoral). Finally, based on the above, there is that "final" assessment of the overall action, deciding whether it is right or wrong, favorable or unfavorable. Very often an action has no moral component at all or an action is so overwhelmingly immoral that there is little

room to "judge" and decide whether or not it is moral. But this chapter discusses those many situations that leave open the possibility that a person's actions could be viewed either way, as favorable or unfavorable.

Knowing all of the above can help train a person to judge actions more accurately and also more favorably. Just as actual judges in court must try to correctly ascertain all of the facts and details in each case, it is important that each person carefully review the facts in his or her mind in any given situation that occurs in daily life. Did I miss something? Did I understand all the facts involved? Did I correctly see and understand all the subtle movements of the person in this situation to be sure that I have the all the facts that can be available to me? For example, it seems that an acquaintance has taken an object that the person "knows" belongs to someone else, and the first reaction is, "He is a thief." But a closer examination of the facts shows that the object looks very much like the one that belongs to that friend, but it is in fact not exactly the same object, meaning that it does not belong to that friend at all. Human eyes and ears sometimes play tricks on each of us, and what people think, see, and hear is not actually what occurred. Being aware of this helps people ascertain the facts of a situation more accurately.

Each person should consciously explore the many possible motives that might have drawn someone to perform a particular action. Both the negative and positive motives should be explored in one's mind, and one should not jump to the first and most logical conclusion. For example, if a person is late to a meeting, most people will usually ascribe reasons that put the other person at fault: he or she is inconsiderate about other people's time, he or she is disorganized, etc. But first all possibilities should be explored in assessing reasons for the lateness. Unexpected traffic due to an accident or a police chase may have been the cause. Perhaps the person was feeling ill, which caused the delay. Maybe the individual's cell phone was stolen, preventing that person from contacting the person to explain the

---

16. *Yoma* 19b
17. *Pele Yo'etz* on "*Sanaigoria*"

delay. For every negative or accusatory reason to indict an individual for his or her actions, it is possible to think of many more reasons that exempt the person from poor or wrong behavior. It is obligatory, under this commandment, to explore every possible alternative reason for why this behavior occurred.

Finally, there is the judgment itself. After concluding that there are five possible legitimate explanations why a certain behavior or action took place, but ten illegitimate reasons ascribing guilt to the person who behaved in this manner, the Torah wants Jews to choose and conclude that it was the more moral and legitimate reasons for the behavior, even when the evidence and simple logic point to the more immoral or illegitimate reasons. This is what the actual Mitzvah-commandment is all about – judging favorably and concluding that the person was not at fault, even when this explanation is the less logical and less reasonable one.

How can a person train himself or herself to look at each situation in this new and more sensitive way? One of the main ways to condition oneself to actively do all of the above was suggested by Rabbi Alexander Ziskind.[18] He says that each time a person is faced with a situation in which another person seems to be doing something immoral or illegal, that individual should think to himself or herself and say the following words (verbally or in the mind): "I am hereby ready and willing to fulfill the positive commandment to judge people properly, and I will try to find some positive reason why this action or speech took place." Then the person should proceed carefully with the three-step process outlined above.

## MISTAKES AND DANGERS IN JUDGING OR NOT JUDGING SOMEONE FAVORABLY

There are a number of common mistakes or pitfalls in misjudging the situations or the actions or speech of other people. Before any

conclusions are reached, each person should first ascertain the following:

1. *Make sure the identity of the person in question is correct.* Many people, especially from afar, look very similar. Sometimes we can think it is a certain person doing this action, but it turns out to be a stranger we do not even know.

2. *What an individual hears about a person, it may not always be accurate.* Others tell someone that this person did something wrong (usually on a subjective basis). People make mistakes in telling over the "facts." Before conclusions are drawn, it is important to find out what actually transpired and not base one's conclusion solely on the details someone related what happened.

3. *Mistakes in the media.* Sometimes details about the action are reported in the press, but they turn out to be inaccurate. Before attributing blame on a person, first ascertain that what is claimed about this person is actually true.

4. *Mistaken memory.* Sometimes people rely on their memories to form the basis of a judgment about another person. But memories are not always 100% accurate. For example, people can become angry with a person who did not return an object that was loaned to him or her. The owners get angry and upset. But it turns out, quite often, that the object was returned, and they simply forgot.

5. *Circumstantial evidence.* It "seems" like something happened in a certain way, based on circumstantial evidence. But that is not proof in a Jewish court and it should not be used to "convict" someone in one's mind either. If there is an alternative way to explain the facts, even if it is less logical, that should be the basis for the (positive) conclusion people reach.

6. *Incomplete knowledge of Jewish law.* People often believe someone is violating a particular Jewish law without any real expertise in this area. No one should judge the actions of a Jew who is violating a Jewish law until he or she goes back and checks exactly what the law is in all its details and parameters. Often, people can get it wrong and ascribe sin to

---

18. *Sefer Shoresh V'haAvodah* 1:8

someone who is acting perfectly legitimately and following proper Jewish practice.

## REGARDING A RIGHTEOUS PERSON OR TALMUD SCHOLAR

If the person who seems to be sinning is a well-known righteous person or an outstanding Talmudic scholar, it is certainly obligatory for people to say to themselves that if there is a way of explaining his actions without ascribing sin or immorality, they should do so as part of this Mitzvah (just as we people think positively regarding any other person). But the Midrash and Talmud tell us to go even further in the case of a Talmudic scholar or righteous individual. In a situation in which there is absolutely no possible alternative explanation that legitimizes a certain behavior, and the action of this particular person is completely immoral and sinful, the Midrash says that people should indeed conclude that this person sinned, as was shown above.[19] However, because of this person's good reputation, they should take into account that the next day this person must certainly have repented for the sin. The Talmud says that imputing evil to one's righteous teacher, even when the facts seem to support this conclusion, is the equivalent of imputing evil to God Himself.[20] Jews should believe that there must be a legitimate explanation for this righteous person's behavior that we just did not think of. (Of course, if this happens more than once or on a regular basis, this person would no longer be considered a righteous person, and then the above statements would not apply.)

Maimonides states that if the person who seems to be sinning is righteous, even if overwhelming logic tells you to impugn this person as immoral, and there is only a small implausible explanation (with even less than a 5% chance) that justifies the action, one is supposed to ascribe that highly improbable motive, no matter how illogical, because of

this person's past stellar behavior.[21] This is the definition of falsely suspecting a "kosher person." Thus, for example, if a noted Rabbi is riding in his car on Shabbat afternoon in the middle of the street, a Jew is obligated to say that he is probably feeling very ill and is on his way to a hospital, even if he appears to be in perfect health. Rabbeinu Yonah similarly describes how a Jew should react to the apparently immoral behavior of a righteous person and should attribute only good behavior to a seemingly immoral act.[22] The Talmud describes a story in which a great Rabbi withheld wages from a worker who was expecting to be paid on the day before Yom Kippur after having worked for three years. The worker did not suspect this Rabbi of any wrongdoing (as most people would certainly have done), despite all the apparently lame excuses the Rabbi offered. After Sukkot, when the worker was finally paid, the Rabbi showed that all the implausible excuses he had offered were indeed legitimate and the worker was rewarded for not suspecting the Rabbi of any wrongdoing.[23]

## REGARDING AN AVERAGE PERSON OR SOMEONE YOU DO NOT KNOW

Regarding the seemingly improper behavior or speech of someone whom you do not know or someone who appears "average" – i.e., he or she has both sins and good deeds, some indiscretions but many moral acts – it seems that this kind of person is the "prime candidate" for whom this commandment was designed. If a particular behavior can be interpreted to be either moral or immoral, and the chances of each are about fifty-fifty, then this commandment says that this person *must* be given the benefit of the doubt, and each Jew is obligated to ascribe only proper motives for such a person's behavior. This is precisely how Rabbi Ovadiah MeBartenura describes this commandment.[24] Rabbeinu Yonah agrees with his

---

19. *Midrash Tehilim* 125
20. *Sanhedrin* 110a

21. Maimonides commentary on Mishna *Avot* 1:6
22. Rabbeinu Yonah commentary on Mishna *Avot* 1:6
23. *Shabbat* 127b
24. Rabbi Ovadiah M'Bartenura commentary on

assessment and adds that even if this situation seems to point a little more to the evil side than fifty-fifty (such as fifty-five to forty-five), a Jew is still obligated to judge the situation favorably.[25] Maimonides agrees regarding the unknown person (about whom it is not yet known whether he or she is basically a good person or an evil person).[26] One must also judge his or her questionable actions favorably.

This preponderance of opinion has been passed down to the great Rabbis of the twentieth century as well. Rabbi Hutner speaks about the "average" person who has some sins and some positive behaviors that has to be "given the benefit of the doubt" when a particular situation can be judged either as moral or immoral.[27] The famed thinker, Rabbi Yisrael Meir Kagan (known as the Chofetz Chaim), who stressed the laws of morality and ethical behavior, concurs. He says for the average person who has both sins and good deeds, it is obligatory to judge this person's actions favorably whenever they can be interpreted in either direction.[28] But he goes on to say that this commandment is obligatory only if it is known that the person is "average." However, if the person is unknown to you, it is a "good and proper deed" to judge this person's actions favorably (when they can be interpreted both morally and immorally), but not an absolute Torah commandment to do so.[29] Finally, Rabbi Kagan says that these judgments should not take place only regarding man-to-man activities, but also concerning man-to-God actions as well. Even if the person was more evil than good, but not so evil that he is a chronic sinner, one still should judge this person's actions favorably whenever there is room to interpret the behavior as moral or immoral.[30]

### REGARDING A CHRONIC SINNER OR EVIL PERSON

Despite all that was written above about this commandment and the obligation to judge favorably, when it comes to a truly evil person whose actions are by and large immoral, this obligation no longer exists (according to most opinions). Yet, when Rav Ashi met one of the most evil Kings in Jewish history, Menashe, in a dream, the first thing he did was to ask Menashe to explain why he committed so many acts of idol worship.[31] Rav Ashi did not automatically pre-judge Menashe's actions as immoral, even though he was known to be evil, but first wanted to hear from Menashe an explanation that might exonerate him. Nevertheless, Jewish law says that Jews may indeed judge unfavorably a known evil person. Rabbi Ovadiah says clearly that it is permitted to view an essentially evil person's action as immoral, implying that this is so even when the actions could also be interpreted as moral as well.[32] Why is this so?

King Solomon already informed us that when a basically evil person seems to be doing something good, we should not believe him.[33] Proverbs also says that a righteous person can recognize the cunning ways of someone who is evil, implying that any good that an evil person seems to be doing is sometimes feigned.[34] The classic example of this can be found in the Torah when Laban, the father of Rachel, whom Jacob had just met at the well, ran out to kiss and hug his long lost relative. Rashi explains Laban's intentions behind each seemingly positive action towards Jacob as a means to find and take any jewels that Jacob might have been hiding on his person.[35]

Once a person or group of people have established for themselves a well-deserved reputation as evildoers, it is very difficult to

---

Mishna *Avot* 1:6

25. Rabbeinu Yonah commentary on Mishna *Avot* 1:6
26. Maimonides commentary on Mishna *Avot* 1:6
27. *Pachad Yitzchak*, "Igrot U'ketavim," 38
28. Chofetz Chaim, *Hilchot Lashon Hara*, "Introduction"
29. Chofetz Chaim, *Be'er Mayim Chaim*, "Introduction"
30. Chofetz Chaim, *Issurei Lashon Hara* 3:7

31. *Sanhedrin* 102b
32. Rabbi Ovadiah M'Bartenura commentary on Mishna *Avot* 1:6
33. Proverbs 26:25
34. Proverbs 21:12
35. Genesis 29:13 with Rashi commentary

undo this characterization and judge their actions favorably, no matter how good they later appear. This sad fact occurred during Temple times with no less an important office than the High Priest, which for a while was occupied by many Sadducees who did not respect or follow some of the Jewish laws set down by the Rabbis. Thus, when the Rabbis had to insure that the High Priest was properly prepared for the intricate Yom Kippur Temple service, and that he had the proper motives, they were forced to make every High Priest swear that he would follow the minute details of the service to the letter.[36] The Talmud says that when this oath was administered, both the Rabbis and the (Kosher) High Priest used to cry, since the Rabbis automatically impugned the integrity of this High Priest, especially regarding the ceremony involving the incense.[37] The fact that the Rabbis were forced to assume that this previously pristine individual was guilty (due to past experience) also made them cry, since it seemed to go against the principle of judging people favorably.[38] But they were nonetheless forced to do so in order to protect the service of Yom Kippur.

Therefore, when an individual has displayed overwhelming tendencies towards evil in the past, even an act that can now be interpreted as either moral or immoral may be viewed for this person as immoral.[39] Chofetz Chaim, however, *allows* a person to judge this evil person's action as moral in the case that it can be viewed either way, even though the person doing the judging is not obligated to do so.[40] He adds that this evil person should not be publicly embarrassed by exposing his immoral action. *Tur* rules that in a courtroom, where both people must be treated equally in each case, if one litigant is known to be evil, then both should be looked upon as evil by the judge. But once the trial is completed, both should be regarded as righteous and judged favorably thereafter.[41] Rabbeinu Yonah, however, believes that if most of a person's actions are immoral, then his actions may indeed be seen as evil, even if there is a possibility of seeing a particular action as moral (or immoral).[42]

On the other hand, both Maimonides[43] and Rabbi Yosef Caro[44] remind us that we cannot jump to conclusions in judging any situation, based on incomplete substantiation (even though it is our natural tendency to do so). Circumstantial evidence in Judaism, no matter how damaging it looks, cannot automatically make a person guilty of an immoral action, a sin, or a crime.

EXAMPLES AND SCENARIOS IN EVERYDAY LIFE

There are numerous everyday interactions with people in which many or even most individuals tend to judge the situation in one particular manner, ascribing immoral motives to the actions of certain human beings. By pointing out these daily occurrences, it may help readers break this natural habit built up over a lifetime and assist them in fulfilling the Mitzvah and obligation to judge others favorably.

1.  *Spouses.* A husband or a wife came home late without calling first, forgot a birthday gift, or consistently does not use his or her time efficiently. Rather than castigating or prejudging one's husband or wife, people should tell themselves that *the cell phone might have been lost or out of range, the person tried to buy a gift but could not find one that was adequate, or that the person is trying to improve himself daily, but cannot yet do so.*

2.  *Parents and Children.* When a child does not do what a parent requested, the parent could automatically respond negatively and judge unfavorably. Rather, *the parent should tell himself or herself that the child forgot, got distracted, and will do it soon.* Similarly, *a parent*

---

36. Mishna *Yoma* 1:5
37. *Yoma* 19b
38. Rashi commentary on *Yoma* 19b
39. Rabbeinu Yonah commentary on Mishna *Avot* 1:6
40. Chofetz Chaim, *Issurei Lashon Hara* 3:7

41. *Tur, Choshen Mishpat* 17
42. *Sha'arei Teshuva* 3:218
43. Maimonides, *Hilchot Chovel U'Mazik* 5:4
44. *Shulchan Aruch, Choshen Mishpat* 90:6

*should realize how difficult it is for a child to keep his or her room clean.* If an adult child chooses a different custom or practice than that of the parent, the parents should not get angry, but say to themselves that *had they lived in their child's generation, perhaps they too would have adopted this custom.*

3. *Siblings.* Brothers and sisters often ascribe immoral motives to the actions of their siblings. For instance, he "specifically" did this "to me" to hurt me, when this is not usually the case. He or she made me angry, was insensitive, or made noise in a shared room. It is obligatory to judge these actions favorably, whenever possible.

4. *Friends.* He or she did not greet me with a smile. *Perhaps he or she is not feeling well.* Someone told me that this supposed "friend" said this terrible thing about me. *Do not believe it until the proof is conclusive.* My best friend did not tell me the most important news of the year about himself or herself, and I had to hear it from someone else. *Perhaps this person forgot or something suddenly came up before he or she could speak to you.*

5. *Neighbors.* They make noise at night and seem so insensitive. *Perhaps they are not aware of how much the sound carries, or their work schedule does not allow them to sleep late at night.* They throw garbage into a common yard or shared area. *Perhaps they were not the ones who threw the garbage.*

6. *Teacher-Student.* The teacher seems to favor other students, and not me, by calling on them more often. *Perhaps he or she has his or her reasons.* The student does not give the teacher the proper respect. *Perhaps he or she picked up these bad habits from his or her parents.*

7. *Roommates.* He or she makes noise while I am trying to sleep. *Perhaps this insensitivity stems from the home, or he or she can sleep through anything and assumes I can as well.* He or she does not keep the room tidy and takes my things without asking. *It could be the way this person was brought up at home and he or she is only continuing habits that are practiced there.*

8. *Workplace.* The boss asks a worker to put in extra time for no extra pay. *Perhaps the*

budget is tight and he or she is under pressure to complete a project. The employee is lazy and slacks off at work for a boss. *The boss should think that perhaps this person is really trying his or her best and this is their top ability.*

9. *Store.* The store did not open on time. *Perhaps the owner had personal problems at home or there was unusual traffic.* The salesperson said he or she would get an item for a customer, but never returned. *Perhaps he or she forgot, got distracted by something in the store, or the boss needed this person for an emergency.* Prices for a certain item of merchandise are way too high. *Perhaps the customer made a mistake in what he or she thought were the prices listed in other stores for the same item.*

## OTHER WAYS TO JUDGE FAVORABLY

In addition to judging the actions of our fellow man favorably (except for known evil people), there are others who should be judged favorably in their actions as well. The first is in regard to the actions of God Himself. Moses castigated the Jewish people for impugning the motives of God in bringing them out of Egypt.[45] The people said that the only reason God took them out of Egypt was because He hated the Jewish people and wanted them to be destroyed by the Emorites. For not judging God "favorably," these Jews were punished. On the other hand, part of Rabbi Akiva's greatness was that he judged God and His actions towards people in a favorable manner, no matter how bad the situation seemed. In a famous story, Rabbi Akiva wanted to stay at the inn, accompanied by his donkey, chicken, and torch, and at every step of the way it seemed that God was "against" Rabbi Akiva.[46] And yet, Rabbi Akiva never lost hope that everything that was happening was for a positive reason, controlled by God. First, he could not find any room in any "motel" to stay at, so he had to sleep in the fields outside of town. A strong gust of wind blew out his fire, so he

---

45. Deuteronomy 1:27
46. Berachot 60b

was in complete darkness. Then a weasel ate his chicken and a lion then ate his donkey. At each step of the way, Rabbi Akiva blessed God and attributed positive reasons to everything that occurred, despite the fact that each action seemed to place Rabbi Akiva in a more desperate situation. The next morning, Rabbi Akiva awoke and saw that robbers had invaded the town and killed its inhabitants. If the robbers had seen his light or heard his chicken or donkey, they would have spotted Rabbi Akiva and killed him as well. So too, Nachum Ish Gamzu would always judge God favorably and say, "*Gam Zu LeTova*" – "This too is for good," for everything that happened in his life, even though his arms and legs were amputated at one point.[47] This attitude and obligation to judge God favorably are not mere stories in the Talmud, but are brought down in Jewish law as an obligation for every Jew in Jewish law in the way that Jews must view life and view God.[48]

Another group of people that each person must judge favorably is themselves! A person may not view himself or herself as totally evil, but should always try to judge himself or herself favorably.[49] Maimonides explains this Jewish law to signify that we may not exaggerate one's faults, but rather, we must try to see the good in his or her behavior as well.[50] Rabbeinu Yonah begins one of his philosophical works with a call for awareness about every Jew's obligation to introspect and see all the good in himself or herself. While trying to constantly improve one's moral character, a person should never lose sight of all the goodness within and should therefore judge himself or herself favorably.[51]

47. *Ta'anit* 21a

48. *Shulchan Aruch, Orach Chaim* 230:5
49. Mishna *Avot* 2:13
50. Maimonides commentary on Mishna *Avot* 2:13
51. Rabbeinu Yonah, *Sha'arei Avoda*, "Introduction"

# LAND OF ISRAEL AND THE JEWISH PEOPLE

HERE HAS BEEN AN ONGOING DE-
bate between religious and non-religious Jews as to whether Judaism
is more of a religion or more a nation (see
chapter, "Judaism: Religion or Nationality?").
A corollary question is about who is a "better" Jew. Is it the non-religious Israeli living in
the Land of Israel, fighting and ready to die
for the country, or the observant Jew living
outside the land who complies with each detail in *Shulchan Aruch-Code of Jewish Law*? Of
course each group will claim that they are the
"better" Jews and will give many arguments to
support its case. Many of the arguments will
not only be about the essence of Judaism, but
also about the essence of the land of Israel for
the Jew. This chapter will examine, through
various sources, that special connection for the
Jew to the land of Israel and what it has meant
to Jewish tradition since Judaism's inception.

For those religious Jews living outside
the Land of Israel, it is not difficult to claim,
through sources, that Judaism is incomplete
without the Land of Israel. Whether there is
a Torah obligation or Rabbinic obligation to
living the land of Israel today, the primacy of
living a Jewish life in the land should be the
focus of Judaism in all areas of Jewish behavior.
How do we know this to be true?

## LEARNING TORAH

There is no better or more appropriate place
to learn Torah than in the Land of Israel.[1] The
Talmud says that if a Jew does not mention
the concept of Torah while saying the blessing
about the land in the Grace after Meals, then
the blessing must be repeated, because one
cannot have one concept without the other.[2]
Another statement says that leaving the land
of Israel is the greatest example of *Bitul Torah*,

taking away time from Torah learning, because
leaving the land of Israel *automatically* implies
a person will learn less Torah.[3]

## PRAYER

The sources make the centrality of holiness in
the city of Jerusalem quite clear (see chapter,
"The Value of Jerusalem to the Jew"), especially for prayer, because the remnant of the
Temple, the Western Wall, the holiest place on
earth for the Jew, is located in that city. Sources
maintain that even today, the presence of God
is by the Western Wall.[4] But even before the
Temple was built on that spot, Jerusalem possessed holiness. That is why the Temple, the
place of communication with God through
sacrifice and prayer, could *only* be built in
Jerusalem.[5] And the holiness of the land, by
extension, comes from the holiness of this city,
whose holiness is derived from this one holiest
spot on earth.[6]

Long before the Temple was built, the place
of the Temple had been used as a place to pray
to God. According to Maimonides, it is the
place where Cain and Abel brought the first
sacrifices to God in human history.[7] Mount
Moriah is also the traditional place of the
binding of Isaac, where Abraham was willing
to sacrifice his son upon God's command. Jacob prayed the traditional evening prayer there
for the first time,[8] and it was also the place of
Jacob's holy dream, in which the angels were
going up and down a ladder from heaven. The
physical land of Israel was later formally connected to the Jewish people in a special law, as
Jews were instructed to come to the Temple for

1. Midrash, *Vayikrah Rabbah* 13:5
2. Jerusalem Talmud, *Berachot* 11b

3. *Chagigah* 5b
4. Midrash, *Shemot Rabbah* 2:2
5. Midrash, *Vayikra Rabbah* 13
6. Mishna *Kelim* 1:6
7. Maimonides, *Hilchot Beit HaBechira* 2:2
8. Rashi commentary on Genesis 28:11, based on *Chul-lin* 91

holidays. It states that if a Jew did not own land in Israel, he could not fulfill the Mitzvah, the commandment, to come to the Temple three times a year on each Jewish holiday.[9] This is based on an allusion in a Torah verse.[10]

## THE PLACE TO FULFILL COMMANDMENTS

Although most pious Jews in the Diaspora would never think of their observance today as anything but fulfilling the Torah's wishes to the maximum, according to the Midrash there is no obligation *at all* to keep the Mitzvot-commandments outside the Land of Israel.[11] However, the Rabbis instituted that they be kept in the Diaspora only so that the Jewish people should not forget how to keep the commandments. Thus, when they return to the land, they will know what to do! (It should be pointed out that Jewish law in practice *does* obligate Diaspora Jews to keep the commandments outside the land, despite this Midrash.) The dying request of Moses, never fulfilled by God, was to enter the land.[12] Why was it so important to Moses to enter Israel? Only in order to be able to fulfill more commandments there.[13] There is something special about performance of the Mitzvot in Israel, and there are many commandments that cannot possibly be observed anywhere *except* in the Land of Israel, such as all of the commandments relating to growing food on the land.

## PLACE OF GOD

God has no physical form and technically does not exist in any one place, but exists in all places at the same time. Nevertheless, the holiness of the Land of Israel makes it a special place of God and the place for man to best relate to Him. This concept is basic to the Jewish understanding of any holy place, be it a synagogue or the Temple Mount. The Rabbis have made numerous references to the holiness of the Land of Israel in the way that each Jew relates to God. There are some very harsh statements about those who do *not* live in the Land of Israel. For example, it says that living outside the Land of Israel is like having no God at all.[14] Therefore, continues the passage, it is preferable for a Jew to live in a non-Jewish part of Israel, completely surrounded by non-Jews, than to live in a totally observant neighborhood outside the land of Israel. In this philosophic book, the *Kuzari*, Rabbi Judah Halevi seems to say that of all the nations, only the Jews flourish in the Land of Israel, because of their devotion to God, and the Jews outside the land will not flourish as they do in the land of Israel.[15]

Clearly, the Land of Israel is more than a place for the religious Jews to live. A full and complete Jewish religious life is impossible outside of the land, and the Judaism of Israel is tied inexorably to the Land of Israel.

## RELIGIOUS COMPONENT OF THE LAND

Many of the non-observant Jews in Israel believe that the land is special in that it provides a homeland for the Jewish people, but there is nothing intrinsic about the land itself that makes it special. This is *not* the traditional Jewish approach. There *is* something unique about this land that make it respond differently from any other soil in the world. According to the Torah, it is the only land in the world that responds physically to moral behavior. Twice each day, the Jews recite the second paragraph of *Shema*, which states that if the Jewish people observe the commandments and behave morally, the land will respond by having enough rain and producing enough crops.[16] If the Jews stray from God, they will be forced to leave the

9. *Pesachim* 8b
10. Deuteronomy 16:7
11. Midrash, *Sifri, Eikev*, quoted by Rashi commentary on Deuteronomy 11:18
12. Deuteronomy 4:1
13. *Sotah* 14a

14. *Ketuvot* 110b
15. *Kuzari*, 2:11-12
16. Deuteronomy 13:18

land. This same idea is repeated many times in the Torah, including in the beginning of the portion of *Bechukotai*, where it says that the reward for keeping the Torah's statutes will be proper rain in its time and enough crops to eat until one is satiated.[17] Therefore, the quantity and quality of crops the Land of Israel will produce depend on the behavior of its inhabitants.

This idea is echoed in a different context when it says that the land will "vomit" out its inhabitants if they act in an abominable manner (referring to improper sexual behavior).[18] Although people normally associate Divine Providence of God is in relation to people, when it comes to the land of Israel, God declares that there is clear Divine Providence on a daily basis.[19] He watches the land constantly from the beginning until the end of the year, seeking the land out. It is clear, then, that the Land of Israel, from a Jewish perspective, is truly unique and cannot be looked upon as "just another piece of earth."

The Land of Israel is also linked to the Jewish people in other ways in addition to the Mitzvot-commandments. The very first words uttered by God to the very first Jew (Abraham) were to leave his homeland and come to live in the Land of Israel.[20] The repeated promise by God to Abraham contained only two themes: producing a large a nation and keeping the land forever.[21] In the Torah, God did not speak to Abraham at all about learning Torah, observing Shabbat, keeping kosher or any other Mitzvah-commandment (except circumcision). These two promises, of a large nation and the Land of Israel, were passed down to Isaac[22] and then to Jacob.[23] Therefore, the Jewish claim to the land today is based on that promise of God to Abraham, Isaac, Jacob – the Jewish people are to inherit the land forever. Without a belief in this promise, the Arabs

cannot be faulted in claiming that the Jews in the 1800s decided to take over "their" land. While Jews do not expect Arabs to believe their claim simply because it says so in the Torah, Jews themselves who do not believe in Judaism as a religion cannot justify the Jewish claim for the land of Israel *for themselves*. Just because Jews once lived there does not justify their having the land today. But if they believe in the Torah and God's promise to the Jews to give them the land "forever," their claim has some validity.

Thus, the land was the focus of Judaism from the very first words uttered to Abraham continuing through today. The very first comment of Rashi in Scripture stresses that the purpose of entire first book of the Torah is to justify the Jewish claim to the Land of Israel,[24] since only if God created the world and made the promise to the forefathers could the Jews justify conquering Israel after their enslavement in Egypt and then again in the twentieth century. And, lest any nation or any non-observant Jew think that the land lost its focus after the Jews were exiled nearly two thousand years ago, Jewish religious practice *kept* the land of Israel as the central focus since the Temple's destruction until the present day. Each day, the emphasis of all prayer three times a day, is today and always has been the land of Israel. It is the conscious direction of Israel and the Temple that a Jew always faces while praying, no matter where on earth the Jew may be.

The Talmud says that *every* activity of the Jew should have some reminder that the Jews do not have the land or the Temple.[25] Therefore, each time a Jew eats a festive meal, he or she should omit an hors d'oeuvre as a reminder that the Jews do not have the land or the Temple. Each time a woman wears her jewelry, she should not wear one piece as a reminder that the Jews do not have the land or the Temple. While these two particular customs have not been adapted in practice by Jews, the customs mentioned in the rest of that Talmudic passage

---

17. Leviticus 26:3-5
18. Leviticus 18:25
19. Deuteronomy 11:12
20. Genesis 12:1
21. Genesis 13:15-17
22. Genesis 26:3-4
23. Genesis 28:13-14

24. Rashi commentary on Genesis 1:1
25. *Bava Batra* 60b

have been practiced by Jews for hundreds of years, since Talmudic times. At the happiest moments of life, the Jew reminds himself or herself about the lack of the Temple and the homeland. At the moment when a Jew makes his most expensive life purchase, when a home is dedicated, a cornerstone is traditionally not painted for the same reason. At the happiest moment of a person's life, usually the wedding day, the ceremony is not completed without the bride and groom reminding everyone present that the destruction of the Temple and the lack of a homeland still cause Jews pain, by sprinkling ashes on the forehead (today we also symbolically break a glass for the same purpose). At the saddest moments in life as well, the Jew also does not forget the land. The traditional phrase of comfort to the mourner is, "May you be comforted with all the other mourners of Zion and Jerusalem." The pain of the loss of a close relative is compared to the national pain of the Jewish people who have lost the land. Therefore, the land has always been and continues to be today the focus of Judaism. Without a belief in Judaism as a religion demonstrated by all religious customs, the validity of claims that Israel is the land of the Jewish people is missing.

Returning to the original question, then, it is clear that both the national and religious components are integral elements of Judaism. There cannot be a religion called Judaism without the land as an integral part of it, just as there cannot be a nation of Jews without the Torah as a basis. One without the other is incomplete and indefensible Jewishly. Ties to the land can only be justified through God and the Torah, and God's concept of Judaism is incomplete with Mitzvot observance alone. To be complete, the Jew needs both. Ruth uttered a phrase that reflects both these concepts: "Your people is my people and your God is my God."[26]

The Midrash tells us that there are four Jewish concepts called "inheritance" in the scriptures: the Land of Israel, the people of Israel, the Torah, and the Temple. Only when the three are tied together will fourth come. Only then, when Israel, the people, and the Torah are bound and united together, will the fourth inheritance, the Third Temple, be rebuilt. [27]

---

26. Ruth 1:16
27. Midrash, *Mechilta, Beshalach 10*

# LOTTERIES, GAMBLING, AND BUYING LOTTERY
## TICKETS – THE JEWISH VIEW

DRAWING LOTS IN ORDER TO DE-
termine one's fate, playing games of
chance for profit, and buying lot-
tery tickets in order to win big prizes are all
phenomena found in today's society. But one
should not think that purchasing a Powerball
lottery ticket with a potential payout of half
a billion dollars is unique to and invented by
our contemporary civilization, as these trends
can be found in virtually every society over
the past 2,500 years. Lotteries can be found
in the Torah, and Jewish society used the
lottery or lots to determine many aspects of
traditional Jewish life. Judaism has much to say
about gambling and other games of chance in
which betting is required. How, indeed, does
Judaism view the drawing of lots to determine
one's actions? Should these methods be used
in life decisions today as well? Is it ever ethical
in Judaism to gamble for money? Is it permissible to purchase a legal lottery ticket, and does
this purchase depend upon where and how the
money will be used by the company organiz-
ing the lottery?

## THE USE OF LOTTERIES IN
SCRIPTURE

The drawing of lots to determine future outcomes can be seen numerous times in the
Torah and in the Prophets. In fact, without
a lottery, the Jewish people in Temple times
could not have received God's atonement for
their sins. Part of the very essence of the Yom
Kippur Temple service, mandated by God,
was to take two identical goats and then draw
lots in order to determine which goat would
be offered on the Altar and which goat would
be put to death in the desert (representing the
sins of the Jewish people).[1] The importance
of the lottery aspect in this ritual is stressed by

using the word for lottery (*Goral*) three times
in the verse. Similarly, the determination for
all of time as to which areas in the Land of Israel would belong to which tribe (except the
Levites who received forty-eight cities and no
land for agriculture) was through a system of
lots.[2] Once again, the Torah stresses this concept by repeating the word "*Goral*–lottery" in
consecutive verses. (Some commentaries explain that these were actually two lotteries, one
for the general land that each tribe received
and one for the land that each family obtained
within each tribe.) Apparently, by using both
a system of drawing lots on pieces of paper
and the breastplate of the Kohen Gadol, the
High Priest (whose letters would light up miraculously from God), the system of lots was
confirmed and indisputable.

Each week a different group of Kohanim-
Priests, and Levites would perform the service in the Tabernacle or Temple. In order to
decide which Priest or Levite would perform
which task, a lottery was held. It apparently
did not matter which Kohen-Priest or Levi
was more "worthy" or more gifted (musically,
for example). The lottery alone determined
who performed which service.[3] When one Jew
sinned by taking the forbidden booty from the
captured city of Jericho, which resulted in a
defeat in the next battle for the city of Ai, the
guilty party did not step forward and confess
his sin. Rather than simply tell Joshua who the
guilty party was, God ordered that a lottery
be set up, and the people filed by, one by one,
until the guilty person, Achan, was discovered
and punished.[4] Later on, in order to decide
which men from all of the other tribes would
fight the Benjamites after they sinned in Geva,
a lottery was used to determine who would

---

1. Leviticus 16:8

2. Numbers 26:55-56
3. Chronicles I 25:8 with Metzudat David commentary
4. Joshua 7:14-20

take part in the battle.[5] In a similar manner to finding the sinner Achan, King Saul wanted to find the sinner before battling the Philistines. The lottery fell upon his son, Jonathan, who then confessed his sin.[6]

We see that even non-Jews drew lots to determine events in the Bible. The non-Jews in Jonah's boat were convinced that it was the sins of someone in the boat that caused the great storm to come, which was about to capsize the boat and kill all of the people within. To determine who was at fault they drew lots, which fell upon Jonah, whose sin was indeed the cause of the storm.[7] In the most famous casting of lots in the Bible, the wicked Haman drew lots to decide which day of the year to do battle with and destroy the Jewish people (the thirteenth of Adar).[8] In fact, the name of the holiday itself became "Purim," the Persian word for lots. Therefore, the use of a lottery to determine the truth or how to act in the future was very significant in Scripture.

The Talmud describes two other lotteries used by the Jews in the desert, which are merely alluded to in the Torah text.[9] When Moses had to replace the original seventy elders who died (see Numbers, chapter 11 and Rashi's commentary on verse 16), he knew that merely selecting the most worthy people would be very tricky politically, since mathematically some tribes would be left with five elders, while all of the rest would have six. He solved the problem by selecting exactly six worthy people from each of the twelve tribes, and arranging seventy-two pieces of paper to represent them. On seventy were written the word "elder," and two were left blank. Thus, the seventy elders were selected by a lottery system. In a similar manner, 273 firstborn (non-Levite) individuals had to be redeemed by five silver coins. Originally, after being saved from the final plague in Egypt, the firstborn Jews "belonged" to God, and were destined to serve God in the Tabernacle and

Temple. But when they too participated in the sin of the Golden Calf (and the Levites did not), the Levites were given the task of serving God instead. A ceremony was necessary to make the "switch" between the Levites and the firstborns. Since there were 22,000 Levites and 22,273 firstborns that needed to be redeemed, only 273 firstborns needed to be "bought back" by God through the five silver pieces. (The ceremony of the redemption of the firstborn is still carried out today on the thirtieth day after the birth of Jewish firstborn males.) But every firstborn in the desert preferred to be redeemed by an actual Levite and not by the silver. Thus, Moses arranged 22,000 pieces of paper with the word "Levite" and 273 pieces of paper with the words "five pieces of silver" written on them. A lottery was conducted in order to determine who would be redeemed by a person and who would be redeemed by money, thereby avoiding any argument.

## LOTTERIES IN THE PERFORMANCE OF JEWISH RITUALS AND JEWISH LAW

We referenced above that in the Temple, the various services by the Kohanim and Levites were determined by lottery. But the Mishna explains that originally this was not the case.[10] Originally every Kohen, Priest, would volunteer for each position and everything was orderly. But then, as there were more Priests than the coveted services, the Priests used to race for each service. (If there were a tie, they would use "finger games" as a tiebreaker.) As competition for the "best" services became fiercer, there was once a time when two Priests ran up the ramp to remove the ashes (the first service of the day) and one was knocked off the ramp. From that day onwards, a lottery was set up to determine who would perform which service, no matter who came first or who was more worthy. Thus, the lottery was actually used as a safety device, in order to prevent mayhem and a desecration of God's name. In

---

5. Judges 20:5-13
6. Samuel I 14:41-46
7. Jonah 1:4-7
8. Esther 3:7, 9:24-26
9. *Sanhedrin* 17a

10. Mishna *Yoma* 2:2-3

fact, the Talmud elaborates on the need for the lottery by explaining that one time, two priests ran for a certain service and one of the priests took out a knife and stabbed the other priest, who was ahead, in order to prevent him from performing that service.[11]

In another area of Jewish law, when a father died and left land to his two sons, a lottery would be used in order to determine which son would inherit what land, according to the Talmud.[12] Maimonides explains this Jewish law in greater detail, saying when and why a lottery would be used – once again to insure that everything was fair and to prevent fighting among the brothers.[13] He explains that when all of the land was exactly equal, both in quality and position, then it made no difference as to which brother would get what section of land, and lots were not necessary. However, when one piece of land was more desirable or in a more favorable position (e.g., closer to the river), even if they were actually of equal value, then it would not be "fair" to give that land to one brother or the other. Since both desired that portion, lots were used to decide which brother would receive which parcel of land. The commentaries on Maimonides explain that the lottery did not legally give the land to each brother and that it would have to be legally acquired by living on it or performing an act that showed possession. The lottery merely settled any possible dispute. Others say that the lottery actually established Jewish law equivalent to taking possession of the land.[14]

In another interesting Jewish law, the Mishna states that at the Shabbat meal, a parent may conduct a lottery with his children in order to determine which child should receive a particular portion of food.[15] This is permissible when the size of each portion is the same, but the quality may differ, and the purpose is

to avoid jealousy among the siblings if the parent were to simply give a different portion to each child at his or her discretion. (If the father or mother were to give portions arbitrarily, it might appear to the children that he or she had favorites.) This lottery may not be held at weekday meals since it may lead to gambling. And it is only with family that this is permitted, since everyone can accept the results in good faith. *Shulchan Aruch* incorporates this concept into normative Jewish law.[16]

A final interesting Jewish practice involving a lottery took place in the synagogue right before the prayer service. Magen Avraham describes this lottery in synagogues when the practice was that only one person would recite the *Kaddish* prayer for the entire congregation, specifically on the anniversary of the death of a parent (*Yahrtzeit*).[17] If more than one person wanted this "honor," they used an intricate lottery system to determine who would say the *Kaddish*. Perhaps that is why it is almost the universal custom today that all mourners as well as all who have a *Yahrtzeit* recite the *Kaddish* together, in order to avoid having to choose just one representative.

## SIGNIFICANCE OF LOTS IN JEWISH THOUGHT

Now that we have seen that lots and "chance" drawings can be used in normative Jewish life, how are we to understand how this works? Is God telling us that it really makes no difference and whatever happens just happens? Or are we saying that God intervenes in each lottery and causes the events or the lots to work out in the certain specific manner that He wants it to occur? And if it is the latter, then why do we not use a lottery in more circumstances in daily Jewish existence?

The classic understanding of a lottery is that it is not random. Rather, it is a direct decree from God. King Solomon implied that every

11. *Yoma* 23a
12. *Bava Batra* 106b
13. Maimonides, *Hilchot Shechainim* 12:1-2
14. Lechem Mishna commentary on Maimonides, *Hilchot Shechainim* 2:11
15. Mishna *Shabbat* 23:2 with Tiferet Yisrael commentary

16. *Shulchan Aruch, Orach Chaim* 322:6
17. Magen Avraham commentary on *Shulchan Aruch, Orach Chaim* 132:2

result of a lottery is an express pronouncement from God.[18] Rashi, in commenting on the lottery that was used to divide the land of Israel, says that the lottery system was *Ru'ach haKodesh* – the holy spirit of God, i.e., a manner in which God communicated with the Jewish people.[19] One modern Rabbinic leader writes that the results from a lottery are equated to His pronouncing the results Himself, and he quotes an early source that says that anyone who does not follow the results of a lottery, it is as if that person had violated the entire Ten Commandments.[20] Thus, we see that Judaism takes the lottery very seriously and interprets the results as a divine message. But we will see below that while this idea about the lottery may have been true in the distant past, it may not hold true regarding every lottery and its results today.

## WHEN SHOULD LOTS BE USED IN JEWISH LIFE TODAY AND WHEN IS IT FORBIDDEN?

Based on the above, that Judaism sanctions the results and God communicates through all lotteries, Jews should be using lotteries in their daily lives much more often. It would certainly relieve doubts about what constitutes right and wrong actions in daily life. And yet, there seems to be strong resistance to using lotteries, especially to determine future events. When, then, are lotteries encouraged in Judaism and when are they forbidden and why?

The ambivalence about using lotteries can be seen in the apparently conflicting words of one Middle Ages Rabbi, Judah HaChasid. First he says that if a situation at sea exists similar to that of Jonah and it is clear that (a) all the other boats are sailing along without any problems, (b) only your boat is experiencing a storm, and (c) logically, the storm must have come because of the sinful actions of someone on the boat, then it is permitted to have a lottery in order to determine who is guilty and who should be expelled from the boat.[21] Even so, the other people on the boat should not actually throw the person off. Instead, they should convince the person to jump off himself or put him onto a device that can float in the sea. But then just a few chapters later, the same author describes an almost identical situation, and there says that lotteries are forbidden, both in monetary cases and certainly in life and death situations.[22] He says that while lotteries could be relied upon in the times of the prophets, today lotteries should not be used at all. He concludes that when using lots in monetary cases, all the items in the lottery must be identical, as were the goats in the lottery used in the Temple on Yom Kippur. Thus, we see that Rabbi Judah both advocated using lotteries under very specific conditions but also forbade using them in other circumstances.

On the other hand, Rabbi Yair Bachrach (1638-1701) states that a lottery is perfectly legitimate, as was seen from all the examples in the Bible mentioned above, and that the results of a lottery, if done correctly, come directly from God.[23] A more modern Rabbi brings all of the conflicting sources discussed above and then seems to say that if the lottery is conducted properly, it has validity even today, but likewise, if it is not conducted according the "rules" of a Jewish lottery, the results are invalid.[24] From where does this conflict arise? It seems clear-cut that in Biblical times, Judaism advocated and legitimized the use of a lottery. Where does the resistance to drawing lots arise from today?

*The Code of Jewish Law*, authored by Rabbi Yosef Caro, states that it is forbidden for a Jew to try to determine the future by using astrology or lots.[25] Rabbi Caro, in a different book of his, explains that the origin of this Jewish law is from the Midrash.[26] Apparently, Rabbi Caro

---

18. Proverbs 16:33
19. Rashi commentary on Numbers 26:54
20. *Responsa Yabia Omer*, section 6, *Choshen Mishpat* 4
21. *Sefer Chasidim* 679
22. *Sefer Chasidim* 701
23. *Responsa Chavot Yair* 61
24. *Responsa Sdei Chemed* 8:14
25. *Shulchan Aruch, Yoreh De'ah* 179:1
26. *Beit Yosef* commentary on *Tur, Yoreh De'ah* 179

equates using a lottery to determine future events not only with astrology, but also with witchcraft and other forbidden Jewish practices (see chapter, "Alternative Medicine"). The verse mentioned as proof is, "You shall be complete with the Lord your God."[27] This indicates, according to Rashi, that one should rely only on God, and not try to determine any future event by any means. Rather, one must accept whatever God doles out for him or her. *Shulchan Aruch* was averse to using lots in any situation relating to determining the future, equating this process with astrology. (However, he allowed lots regarding giving Shabbat food to children and dividing a deceased parents' land among their heirs, as noted above.) Therefore, based on this line of thinking, many later Rabbis banned the concept and the practical application of drawing lots to determine future events.

Rabbi Ovadia Yosef, a leading Rabbinic leader of the twentieth and twenty-first centuries, forbade using lots in our times.[28] He says that it is questionable whether they can be used even in money matters, but they certainly cannot be used in any situation in which human life is at stake. He specifically forbids a community from using lots to choose its chief Rabbi, even if both candidates for the position agree to the process. Yet, the Pitchei Teshuva (1813-1868) writes that in the classic case in which terrorists capture a group of Jews and threaten to kill all of them unless the group gives them one person to be killed, they are allowed to draw lots to determine which person should be given over to the terrorists.[29] Rabbi Avraham Karelitz (1878-1953) strongly disagrees and takes the Pitchei Teshuva to task. He says that if a lottery were a permitted solution, then the original Tosefta that discussed this very issue would have offered this solution as a legitimate option, but it did not. He says this potential solution was not mentioned

there because it is forbidden to draw lots in this situation.[30]

Minchat Asher, another twenty-first century authority, brings many of the above-mentioned sources, and then rules that lots may not be used in order to determine or predict any future outcomes, but may be used in some limited monetary situations.[31] Another modern Rabbi rules that lots are forbidden based on the edict of Rabbi Shlomo Kluger (1785-1869) that all lotteries are forbidden, even to determine who will say the *Kaddish* prayer, certainly with regard to sickness issues, and even regarding found objects.[32] He does, however, permit a lottery in the limited situation in which only two possibilities exist, in order to determine if something belongs to this or that person. He then explains this situation that a person writes on one piece of paper, "Do it," on the other paper it says, "Do not do it," and the person wants to use these to decide whether or not he or she should do a particular action. He specifically forbids this and says that this is exactly what *Shulchan Aruch* forbade. All in all, most modern Rabbis shun the use of lots, and those who permit it only allow it in very limited circumstances.

## USING VERSES AND THE SYSTEM OF THE VILNA GAON

Although lotteries have been discouraged, the use of verses from Scripture to determine events seems to be totally legitimate and sanctioned by the Rabbis. The Talmud records that Rabbi Chisda knew what would happen in the future based on a verse that a young child quoted.[33] Similarly, Rabbi Yochanan used verses quoted by young children as a sign to predict the future.[34] The Midrash explains that when Mordechai met Haman, after Haman had secured the right to destroy the Jewish people, Mordechai asked his young students

---

27. Deuteronomy 18:13 and Rashi commentary
28. *Responsa Yabia Omer*, section 6, *Choshen Mishpat* 4
29. Pitchei Teshuva commentary on *Shulchan Aruch*, *Yoreh De'ah* 157:13

30. Chazon Ish, *Hilchot Avodah Zara* 68
31. *Responsa Minchat Asher*, section 4, *Bamidbar* 72
32. *Kovetz Tel Talpiyot*, Pesach 5767
33. *Gittin* 68a
34. *Chullin* 95b

to quote various verses, and each student recited a verse indicating to Mordechai that he should not be afraid because the Jews would eventually triumph, as God was with them.[35] This clearly gladdened Mordechai. Thus, the use of verses by little children was already relied upon in ancient times.

What is behind this idea that the verses of young children have validity for predicting the future? Both *Turei Zahav*[36] and *Siftei Kohen* commentaries[37] claim that the recitation of these verses by children indicates a small element of prophecy within them. Thus, the use of verses already had validation and Jewish legitimacy.

Based on this idea and the opinions of other Rabbis, one modern Rabbi writes that it is perfectly legitimate to use the Torah as a source of determining what should be a person's future action.[38] Since the Torah is the heart of the Jewish people, when a person does not know what to do, it is valid from a Jewish perspective to open up one's "heart," the Torah, and wherever the verse falls out, it can be used to tell a person how to behave in the situation confronting him or her. Rabbi Stern describes the actual cases in which famous Rabbis of the twentieth century used this methodology to determine how to act or behave when an important decision confronted them.[39] Rabbi Yisrael Meir HaKohen, known as the Chofetz Chaim (1838-1933), would fast all day before consulting Scripture, in order to determine to which cities to travel in order to collect monies for his Yeshiva in Radin, Belarus. He used an intricate "scriptural lottery" devised by the Vilna Gaon (1720-1797) and considered the results as prophecy from God. Similarly, Rabbi Zev Halevi "Velvel" Soloveitchik (1886-1959) used the lottery of the Vilna Gaon during World War II to decide whether to travel to the land of Israel or to the United States.

The same question was faced by Rabbi Aaron Kotler (1891-1962) when the great Rabbi Moses Feinstein (1895-1986) arranged for him to come to the United States in 1941 in the middle of the Holocaust. Still, Rabbi Kotler was unsure whether to travel to the land of Israel or America. He employed the lottery method of the Vilna Gaon, and the verse that emerged was, "The Lord said to Aaron, 'Go into the wilderness to meet Moses'" (Exodus 4:27). God told Aaron (Aaron Kotler) to go to Moses (Rabbi Moses Feinstein) in the spiritual desert that was then the United States. Rabbi Kotler went and two years later established the Lakewood Yeshiva, the largest Yeshiva in the US today and one of the largest Yeshivot in the world. One of the most famous uses of this system to determine the "facts" occurred in 1951, three years after thirty-five brave people had been murdered by the Arabs in 1948, in the fall of Gush Etzion. Twelve of the bodies were unrecognizable. Rabbi Aryeh Levin, under the direction of Rabbi Tzvi Pesach Frank, Chief Rabbi of Jerusalem, used this Vilna Gaon lottery system and verse after verse pointed to the identification of each of the twelve previously unidentified bodies, who were then properly identified and buried.[40]

## GAMBLING IN JUDAISM

The use of lots and lotteries is certainly a form of gambling with the future. Gambling is generally defined as betting on an uncertain outcome in a contest, playing a game of chance for a stake, or taking a risk in the hope of gaining an advantage or a benefit. Usually gambling is associated with any game of chance when money is wagered. However, if lots can be used to determine realities, then perhaps it is also legitimate to use pieces of paper called cards in order to determine winners and losers. What about gambling through dice? Finally, what about an actual lottery, a game of lotto,

---

35. Midrash, *Esther Rabbah* 7:13
36. *Turei Zahav* commentary on *Shulchan Aruch, Yoreh De'ah* 179:3
37. *Siftei Kohen* commentary on *Shulchan Aruch, Yoreh De'ah* 179:5
38. *Kovetz Tel Talpiyot*, Pesach 5767
39. *Gedolai Hadorot*, Rabbi Yechiel Michel Stern, p. 253

40. *Otzar Yediot Hashalem*, p. 585

in which one winner wins many millions of dollars? Are any or all of these legitimate in Judaism? Why or why not?

Although the judge Samson wagered with the Philistines that he would best them in a riddle,[41] gambling is generally looked upon as something very negative in Judaism. The Mishna states that any Jew who wagers with dice (i.e., gambles) is invalidated from testifying in a Jewish court, implying that the act is that of a sinner.[42] Although no reason is given in the Mishna, there are two opinions in the Talmud for the reason behind this Jewish law.[43] Rami Bar Chama explains that all gambling is forbidden under the concept of *Asmachata*, an unintended transaction. As explained by Rashi, since each of the parties that gamble believe they are going to win the wager, the inevitable loser never actually agrees to forfeit the money, and thus the winner's taking of the money is a form of theft.[44] Therefore, thieves and gamblers cannot testify in a Jewish court. Rabbi Sheshet disagrees, however. He believes that full-time gamblers do nothing to enhance the world and remain unproductive members of society, and *that* is their sin. The difference between the two opinions is that, according to Rabbi Sheshet, if a person has a legitimate occupation and only occasionally gambles, he is not violating any Jewish law and would be able to testify.

The majority of later authorities in Jewish law agree with Rabbi Sheshet. Thus, Maimonides forbids all full-time gamblers from testifying.[45] *Tur* outlines many different kinds of games of chance, but concludes that as long as a person contributes to society with another profession, occasional gambling is not forbidden.[46] Although Rabbi Moshe Isserles does bring Rami bar Chama's explanation as a possible option, in the end both he and the *Shulchan Aruch* agree with Rabbi Sheshet's

opinion.[47] Therefore, gambling in Jewish law is not forbidden, as long as it is done occasionally and the person has a different full-time occupation. However, one twentieth-century Rabbi seems to forbid any gambling and apparently uses the reasoning of Rami bar Chama in the Talmud for his opinion.[48]

## THE ADDICTION OF GAMBLING IN JUDAISM

Even though gambling is technically permitted in Jewish law, long ago the Rabbis recognized the compulsion and potential addiction of gambling and wrote much about it. Already in the thirteenth century, Rabbi Yehudah HaChasid warned that Jews should not have compassion on those that do not have compassion upon themselves, including those who waste money by gambling.[49] He says that when gamblers ask not to be embarrassed, it is nevertheless better to embarrass them in order to get them to stop gambling. Rabbi Yehoshua Boaz writes that his teacher, Rabbi Yitzchak Alfasi, used to have mercy on gamblers and tried to find ways to release compulsive gamblers from their vows not to gamble. Realizing that this is an addiction and people are psychologically weak, Rabbi Alfasi searched for ways to annul their vows.[50] A twentieth-century author wrote about gambling compulsion in Jewish communities throughout the ages.[51] He says that although many communities forbade gambling during the year, on holidays such as Chanukah, Purim, and the intermediate days of Passover, it was permitted. The Jewish community in the city of Bologna, Italy enacted laws for the Jews in that city from 1416 to 1418. Among the laws was a prohibition against gambling since it was so prevalent and addictive.

---

41. Judges 14:12-13
42. Mishna *Sanhedrin* 3:3
43. *Sanhedrin* 24b
44. Rashi commentary on *Sanhedrin* 24b
45. Maimonides, *Hilchot Eidut* 10:4
46. Tur, *Choshen Mishpat* 34

47. Rema, *Shulchan Aruch, Choshen Mishpat* 207:13; *Shulchan Aruch, Choshen Mishpat* 370:3
48. *Mishna Berurah* commentary on *Shulchan Aruch, Orach Chaim* 322, s.v. 22
49. *Sefer Chasidim* 1026
50. *Shiltei Giborim* commentary on Mordechai commentary on *Shavuot* 29a
51. "Gambling in the Synagogue," Leo Landman, *Tradition* 10:1, 1968, p. 77

Rabbi Eliezer Papo (1786-1827) writes about gamblers that they lose days and nights on end gambling, just as they lose their money.[52] He says that some even lose their lives, in addition to all of their money, and others resort to stealing from their families to keep up their addiction, to the point that these families have no money left for food. These previously religious gamblers forsake all religious practice, and as gambling takes over their lives, they gamble at times that they normally would be eating or sleeping. A modern Rabbi in Jerusalem was asked about a Jew in Singapore who was so addicted to gambling that when he ran out of money, he put up his wife as a stake to his non-Jewish competitor, and then he lost![53] The gentile took the wife as compensation, and she had children by him. A question was asked regarding whether the children that resulted from the Jewish woman's forced union with this non-Jew could be considered legitimate Jews and part of the Jewish community. The article goes on to point out the dangers of compulsive gambling to both the Jewish and non-Jewish worlds. In England, from 1895 to 1907, for example, a study showed that there were 156 suicides and 719 thefts directly related to gambling. Thus, although to a lesser degree than in the non-Jewish community, compulsive gambling has been an issue in the Jewish community for many hundreds of years.

## PLAYING THE LOTTO OR OTHER LEGAL LOTTERIES

Today, in many countries there is a government-sponsored lotto, which means that a person can buy a lottery ticket for the equivalent of one or two dollars, with the potential winnings amounting to an equivalent of a hundred million dollars or more. The government often uses the revenue to pay for its expenditures, including (as in Israel) the building of educational institutions. Is playing such a game, which is legally sponsored by the government, permitted in Judaism, and is it ethical? Or, is it actually no better than illegal gambling? Several Rabbis have dealt with this issue and some have argued that this is not the same as gambling for money, since the potential winnings are never seen in advance, and the *Asmachta* concept is not relevant.

Rabbi Ovadia Yosef, a contemporary Rabbi and Jewish law authority recognized by all Torah-observant Jews (including those of non-Sephardic origins), has discussed the issue at length.[54] After bringing all of the opinions and many of the sources quoted above, he rules that a Sephardic Jew who follows *Shulchan Aruch* may not purchase a lottery ticket today, while an Ashkenazi Jew who follows Rema may indeed play the lottery. A contemporary Ashkenazi authority, Rabbi Moshe Shternbuch, discusses the same question and concludes that it is perfectly legitimate for all Jews to buy lottery tickets and play the lotto games.[55]

---

52. *Pele Yo'etz* on "*Sechok*"
53. Sinai, *Journal for Torah and Literature*, vol. 28, Yaakov Bazak, p. 116

54. *Responsa Yabia Omer*, section 7, *Choshen Mishpat* 6
55. *Responsa Teshuvot Vehanhagot* 4:311

# LYING – WHEN IS IT PERMITTED IN JUDAISM?

ACCORDING TO THE ESTIMATES OF some experts, every human being says a lie to, misleads, or deceives others (or even himself) on an average of nearly two hundred times each day in some form! Some of these deceptions are intentional, while others are unknown to the person, who is not cognizant that he or she is perpetrating a deception. Lying has become such an accepted part of Western culture that people often think nothing of saying an untruth. For example, when people say, "Wait a second," or, "I will be back in a minute," few people are conscious that they are lying when they do not keep to the promised times. Even a recorded company message saying, "A representative will be right with you," is often a lie for callers who have to wait up to fifteen minutes on the phone. Most people do not think that these words are even considered lies or untruths, but rather a mere exaggeration, just as some people think nothing of telling a relative who takes a call, "Tell them I am not home." Most of these daily lies do not cause any real harm or damage. Does this imply that saying untrue words in these circumstances is acceptable? Is it permissible to lie when a statement does not cause pain or hurt to others and the person speaking the words benefits from the untruth? Is telling someone causally, "I will call you," at the end of a social gathering acceptable when the person has no intention of further contact with that individual? It is clear that at any awards dinner, when the loser says, "It is an honor just to be nominated," few people believe that statement to actually be true, and yet it is repeated at countless ceremonies. The same can be said of the universal expression, "You look great," when it is clear that the receiver of the compliment does not truly look special. Everyone does it. Does that make it appropriate?

Aristotle and Emanuel Kant had quite a different view of lying from today's norm. They believed that all lies were morally wrong, no matter how small and how inconsequential. Kant called telling the truth a "categorical imperative" and said that any deception was morally wrong, even to lie to a murderer, even to save a life. Plato disagreed and believed that some lies are acceptable. So the question remains until today: Is it always unethical to lie? Or, are some lies morally acceptable? What does Judaism believe about this crucial question that has practical consequences in our daily lives? Does Judaism sanction some lies or not? We will examine this issue through the prism of Jewish sources and discover that although lying is forbidden in Judaism, there are indeed some Jewish values that are of a higher value than telling the truth. What are those values and how do they play out in the daily life of the Jew?

## THE IMPORTANCE OF NOT LYING

The centrality of the concept of truth in Judaism has been discussed elsewhere (see the chapter, "Truth and Lying" in *The Jewish Encyclopedia of Moral and Ethical Issues*, written by this author), where the idea of truth in Judaism is analyzed in depth. The importance of telling the absolute truth, especially in a Jewish courtroom, was discussed and will not be reiterated here. However, the general importance of not lying as a Jew will be emphasized here through additional sources.

Based on a Torah verse, the Talmud declares that lying in all business activities is forbidden, i.e., that your "yes" should really be a yes, and your "no" should truly be a no.[1] A sixteenth century Rabbi writes that telling the truth and not lying in a Jew's everyday routine in an actual Mitzvah, a commandment.[2] The Talmud describes four groups of people who are denied the Divine Presence, and one of them

---

1. Leviticus 19:36, *Bava Metzia* 49a
2. *Sefer Charedim, Mitzvot Asei Bipeh,* 26

is people who lie regularly.[3] By using one extra letter, the Torah teaches us to be exact in our words and never lie, even in small and obvious matters. Regarding a house that was suspected of being ritually impure (that had to be validated by a Kohen-Priest to make it official), a Rabbi seeing the home would initially say, "It appears to have ritual impurity," even though it was clear to that Rabbi that the home was impure. However, since it could not become officially ritually impure until the Kohen said so, the Rabbis added the extra letter *Kaf* signifying "it appears," in order not to tell even a mild untruth.[4] Maimonides especially warns Torah scholars to be extremely careful in their words, and never even hint at an untruth.[5] Rabbi Yisrael Meir Kagan (known as Chafetz Chaim), who became famous for the way he taught Jews how not to misuse their words, says that a Jew who lies is subject to lose all of his or her possessions as well as other harsh punishments, as the sin of lying encompasses many severe sins in Judaism.[6] A person who habitually lies, says the Talmud, will never be taken seriously or be believed, even when he or she tells the absolute truth.[7] The prophet Isaiah implies that once a person's lips are impurified by repeated lying, even the truth will then come out as lies.[8] On this verse, Chafetz Chaim points out that the impurity of lying stays with the Jew longer than any other type of impurity in Jewish law, especially regarding the impurity related to the head of a human being.[9]

The prevalence of lying did not begin in the twenty-first century, and not even in the twentieth century. Already in the thirteenth century, Rabbeinu Yonah wrote in detail about nine different categories of lying and liars. Some of these (categories of) lies were very benign and of no benefit even to the liar,

while other kinds of liars virtually destroy their own lives as well as the lives of many others.[10] Rabbi Eliezer Papo (1786-1827) also describes people that habitually lie, so much so that they convince themselves that their lies are actually true. These people "automatically" continue to lie, even when it is of no benefit to them. He also says that the evil inclination convinces these people that they will continually prosper whenever they lie, but when they are found out, these liars suffer greatly both at the hands of other human beings and at the hand of God. Furthermore, Jews who lie cause a great desecration of God's name after they are exposed. (See the chapter, "Madoff, Other Scandals and Greed," for an expansion of this theme.) A Jew should never promise something if unsure that he or she can keep that promise, and should be very careful before letting any words "escape" his or her mouth in case they will be false. Finally, this same Rabbi brings a Midrash that everything had to enter Noah's Ark in groups of two. When falsehood wanted to come into the ark, it had to find a companion, and it found the concept of "damage" willing to accompany it. They united and from that point onward, each benefitted the other. Falsehoods and lying caused great damage, and damage brought on more lying.[11] Rabbi Moshe Chaim Luzzato calls lying a sickness that envelops an individual, but then he differentiates between different types and degrees of lying.[12]

There is, however, one Talmudic source that seems to follow the philosophy of Aristotle and Kant – that all lies, no matter how small or benign, are immoral and forbidden. This was the rule in the legendary city of Kushta, where everyone always told the truth and no one ever died. Then one day a visitor came seeking to speak to a man's wife. Since she was in the middle of washing her hair, he thought it would not be proper etiquette to tell the visitor what his wife was actually doing. Therefore, he that said his wife was not home. Soon afterwards,

3. *Sotah* 42a
4. Leviticus 14:35 with Rashi and Gur Aryeh commentaries
5. Maimonides, *Hilchot De'ot* 5:7, 13
6. *Sefat Tamim*, chapter 2
7. *Sanhedrin* 89b
8. Isaiah 6:5
9. *Kavod Shamayim* 2:6

10. *Sha'arei Teshuva*, "*Sha'ar Shlishi*," 178-186
11. *Pele Yo'etz* on "*Emet*"
12. *Mesilat Yesharim*, "*Midat Hanekiut*," 11

both of his sons died as a result. The towns-people thereafter forced this man to leave the town.[13] The question, then, is if this source about the city of Kushta is representative of a legitimate Jewish view, or is it one aberrant Midrash that conflicts with normative Judaism? The rest of this chapter will show that Judaism generally does not uphold this viewpoint, and life in Kushta is not how people should really live. Lying, under certain conditions, is not only permitted in Judaism, but is actually encouraged when other Jewish values come into conflict with telling the truth. Which Jewish values supersede telling the truth, and when is lying permitted or even required in Judaism? This chapter will examine this question in detail.

## LYING TO PREVENT DANGER TO HUMAN LIFE

It has already been established elsewhere in this volume that one of the highest values in Judaism, if not the highest value, is preservation of human life. Therefore, if a Jew has to violate 610 of the 613 Mitzvot-commandments, in order to save a life even in remote danger, he or she should do so.[14] Among these 610 is the commandment to tell the truth. Therefore, if a Jew must lie to save his or her life, one not only has permission to do so, but *must* lie in such a situation. This Jewish law, of course, runs counter to the "categorical imperative" of Emanuel Kant mentioned above, and shows that there are other values higher than telling the truth in Judaism.

Long before Jewish law was even formally established, we can see many examples in the Jewish Bible that emphasize that lying is permitted in order to save one's life. The very first Jew, Abraham, lied when he perceived that his life might be in danger when he went to Egypt. He did this because he knew that it was quite common for the king to take any beautiful woman for himself, and Abraham,

therefore, worried that Sara would be taken by that Pharaoh, as she was exceedingly beautiful. Thus, he said that he was Sara's brother, and not her husband.[15] For a similar reason, David deceived the people when he went to the land of Gat to hide from King Saul, who was chasing him in order to kill him. People there saw David and wanted to bring this fugitive to King Achish (who would then turn him over to King Saul to be killed). Thus, David pretended (a form of lying) to be insane and acted crazy,[16] thereby deflecting any suspicion that he could actually be the famous David. Two of the Bible's heroines, Shifra and Puah, risked their lives by defying Pharaoh after he told them to kill all the male Jewish babies, which they refused to do. When Pharaoh questioned them, they could not possibly tell him the truth about having saved the babies (and continue to live), so they lied to him, saying that the Jewish mothers gave birth to their babies before they arrived at the scene.[17]

During war, a time of life and death decisions, it is perfectly legitimate to lie to one's enemy. Sisra, the Philistine general, did not know that Yael was Jewish when she invited him into her tent. She said she would give him water, but she gave him warm milk instead, which made him sleepy, and she then killed him.[18] The Talmud states a general rule that it is permitted to "modify the truth" for the sake of peace,[19] but based on the three Biblical examples and proofs it cites for this rule, it seems that the peace referred to in the Talmud is life itself. One instance of lying cited for the sake of peace occurred after Jacob died, and his sons were afraid that Joseph would now take revenge upon them and kill them for selling him to Egypt many years earlier.[20] Therefore, they lied and said that their father Jacob had told them before he died that Joseph should not take revenge upon them. (If Jacob had

---

13. *Sanhedrin* 97a
14. Maimonides, *Hilchot Yesodai HaTorah* 5:1-2

15. Genesis 12:10-13
16. Samuel I 21:11-15
17. Exodus 1:16-19
18. Judges 4:17-21
19. *Yevamot* 65b
20. Genesis 50:15

actually known about the sale and felt this way, he would have told Joseph directly.)[21] Thus, the brothers lied to save themselves from possible death. Similarly, the prophet Samuel was afraid that if Saul were to find out to that he was going to anoint David as king to replace Saul, King Saul would kill Samuel on the spot. After asking God what to do, God told Samuel to tell Saul that he was bringing a sacrifice in that area (which he also did), which would deceive Saul, as Samuel's main mission was actually to anoint David.[22] Thus, God told Samuel to deceive Saul in order to save his own life. Finally, the Talmud says that God actually lied when repeating to Abraham the words of Sara. When Sara heard the news that she would give birth to a baby (at the age of 90), she laughed and questioned how this could be when her husband was so old (100 years old).[23] When God told the story over to Abraham, however, God said that Sara had asked how she could give birth to a baby when *she* was so old.[24] According to some commentaries, God changed Sara's statement because He felt that if God told Abraham Sara's words precisely, Abraham might have gotten angry and not wanted to have the baby. In doing so, he would have endangered the future of not only this child's potential life, but the entire Jewish people. Thus, in a way, this lie by God was also perpetrated in order to preserve life.

The Talmud brings a case of a man who was invited to another man's house and suspected the man was about to kill him. When the meal was served, the guest remarked that this food tasted like the meal that the king had served him. When the host heard that his guest knew the king, he refrained from killing him.[25] Actually, the man lied about knowing the king, but this bluff saved his life. This is another example of permitted lying in order to save one's life. When Rabbi Elazar was brought before the Roman authorities, accused of learning Torah and stealing, he answered their series of questions by lying, which eventually saved his life.[26] Therefore, it is clear that when there is a choice between loss of life and telling the truth, a Jew should always lie in order to preserve life.

## THE "WHITE LIE" TO MAINTAIN PEACE – BUT WITH SPECIFIC CONDITIONS

It is very common in Western society to hear many "white lies," which society seems to believe is not unethical. What does Judaism believe? A "white lie" could be defined as a fib or a trivial, diplomatic, or well-intentioned untruth. It also may be characterized as a minor, harmless, or unimportant lie, especially one uttered in the interests of tact or politeness. Would such a lie be permitted in Judaism? While there is consensus in Judaism that lying is certainly permitted to save a life, there is little agreement by Jewish thinkers about when and where the "white lie" is valid.

Rabbi Eliezer of Metz in the 1100s writes that any lie regarding in which no harm will come as a result is not forbidden in Judaism.[27] He bases his belief on the famous Talmud passage in *Ketuvot*, in which the House of Shammai and the House of Hillel argue about how to describe a Jewish bride.[28] In order to fulfill the commandment to bring joy to the bride and groom, how should Jews dance and address the bride? Should the Jews at the wedding say that the bride is beautiful when she clearly is not attractive, or should they refrain from such a characterization? Beit (the House of) Shammai says that no mention of any bride's beauty should ever be uttered (since it would be terribly insulting to characterize some of the brides as beautiful and say nothing about those that are not beautiful), and thus, it is forbidden to lie and say a bride is beautiful when she is clearly not. Beit Hillel says that every bride should be characterized as beautiful. Beit

21. Genesis 50:16-17
22. Samuel I 16:2-5
23. Genesis 18:12
24. Genesis 18:13
25. *Sotah* 41a

26. *Avodah Zara* 17b
27. *Sefer Yerai'im*, p. 8, 245
28. *Ketuvot* 16a with Rashi and Tosafot commentaries

Hillel asks Beit Shammai about the situation in which a wife buys a dress she likes (that cannot be returned) and asks her husband how he likes the dress (which is clearly nothing special). Should the husband lie and say the dress is beautiful? In this situation, even Beit Shammai agrees with Beit Hillel it is permitted to lie and say the dress is beautiful, because telling the wife the truth would only result in unnecessary friction, while praising the dress will cause no harm. Beit Hillel says the same logic applies to the bride. From this Talmudic passage, it seems that it is permissible to tell a "white lie" in Judaism in order to make someone feel better, when no practical harm will come of the lie. An almost identical Talmudic passage says that Beit Hillel agrees that it is not a lie to say that the bride is beautiful since she is beautiful to her husband at that moment, or is a beautiful person "inside." Beit Shammai disagrees, but Hillel goes on to declare that unlike lying in business, the most important value here is maintaining good will and peace, as we saw that even God lied in order to maintain peace between Abraham and Sara.[29] From the perspective of Jewish law, *Shulchan Aruch* rules like Beit Hillel and we do indeed "lie" and say to *every* bride that she is beautiful.[30] What are the practical implications of this in everyday life and the ethical values of when lying is permitted?

The commentaries explain when and why this kind of lying is permitted. Rabbi Shmuel Strashun (1794-1872) wrote that since the dress bought by the wife cannot be returned, there is no practical benefit in telling the truth, as she is stuck with the dress anyway.[31] *Orchot Tzadikim* (fifteenth century) stresses that a person who modifies the truth, but derives no benefit for himself and causes no harm to others is *still* forbidden from doing so (as it can often lead to habitual lying that has dire consequences), but this act is not punishable in and of itself.[32] Rabbeinu Yonah seems to say

that if the only intention of the "white lie" was to make the person feel better and it causes no one harm, then it is permitted, as maintaining family peace is of a higher value than truth.[33]

Rabbi Yehuda Chasid adds an important caveat. The "white lie" is only permitted regarding past events (i.e., the dress was already bought and cannot be returned, or the bride is already married). But if it affects anything in the future, then even a "white lie" is not permitted. Therefore, he says, if a person is asked by a friend to lend him money, and the person does not want to make the loan because he fears that the loan will not be repaid by the friend, it is forbidden to lie in this situation and say, "I do not have the money," when he does indeed have the funds (or to say any other untruth), even though lying will keep the peace and maintain the friendship. The loan is about a future event and regarding the future, one may never lie at all.[34] Other commentaries agree with this approach and explain that regarding past events a "white lie" will not turn a person into a habitual liar. However, if a person begins to lie about the future, even by saying a "white lie," then this person will begin to lie in many more circumstances.[35]

In the end, though, the achievement of peace, when no one is hurt in the process, seems to take precedence over telling the truth. Aaron, the High Priest, appears to be universally praised for bringing together two people who had been arguing, telling each one that the other person was really sorry but just too embarrassed to say so. This is a clear lie, and yet the outcome of peace between the two people is achieved through this lie and seems to be permitted and praised.[36] One Talmud commentary states the numerical value of "*Sheker,*" "lie" in Hebrew, is the same numerical value as "*Derech Shalom,*" "way of Peace" in Hebrew, indicating that a lie needed in order to achieve peace is permitted.[37] The idea that

29. *Kallah*, chapter 10
30. *Shulchan Aruch, Even Ha'ezer* 65:1
31. Reshash commentary on *Ketuvot* 17a
32. *Orchot Tzadikim, Sha'ar* 22

33. *Sha'arei Teshuva, Sha'ar* 3:181
34. *Sefer Chasidim* 426
35. *Sefer Ta'amei Haminhagim*, p. 560
36. *Avot DeRabbi Natan* 12
37. *Ben Yehoyada* commentary on *Yevamot* 65b

a "white lie" is permitted in Judaism is also re-flected in normative Jewish law by both Rabbi Abraham Gumbiner (1637-1682) in his Jewish law commentary, *Magen Avraham*,[38] as well as by Rabbi Yisrael Meir Kagan (1838-1933) in his *Mishna Berurah*.[39]

A contemporary Rabbi stresses that such "white lies" are only permitted when no one loses, peace is achieved, and the person lying is not a habitual liar who loves to play fast and is loose with the truth. But in any situation in which the lie benefits anyone in any tangible way, causes a person a loss, does not achieve peace, or helps turn a person into a regular liar, then that lie is forbidden. He also con-firms that only a "white lie" said to achieve peace about a past action is permitted since it remains only words, quoting Onkelos' com-mentary. But once a lie affects the future, the words transform into an action that is clearly forbidden.[40] Both Rabbi Yitzchak Alfasi (1013-1103) and Rabbi Shmuel Eidels (1555-1631) re-mark that since the Talmudic passage quoted earlier states that one is not only permitted to change words to achieve peace but *commanded* to do so (it is a Mitzvah), this shows us that the value of achieving peace supersedes the value of telling the truth in Judaism.[41]

## LYING TO AN EVIL PERSON

There is an additional principle in Judaism that lying is permitted to a person who is evil, who will surely try to harm you or someone else. This idea is evident in Judaism, even though it flies in the face of one of the fundamental principles of Emanuel Kant, who specifically said that even lying to an evil person is im-moral. Based on a verse in Isaiah, The Talmud, long before Kant, clearly permitted deceiving and even lying to someone who is out to hurt

others and do evil.[42] The Mishna says that a Jew may even swear falsely to a representative of an evil or deceitful king, or anyone who is habitually dishonest.[43] The example given is regarding farmers, who are permitted to say or even swear to potential robbers that their produce already belongs to the king in order to prevent the robbers from stealing it. A Jew can also lie in order to avoid paying taxes levied only against Jews. One may even flatter a per-son by saying that he is a "servant of fire," im-plying servitude to a certain person or the Per-sian king, when the Jew actually has in mind that he is a servant of God, who is also called fire.[44] It is even permitted to lie in order to right a past wrong, in certain circumstances. If a person stole from you, and you say to his wife that her husband told you to tell her to "give me two wallets," that is permissible as a way of returning the stolen money, although her husband never actually told you anything.[45] *Shulchan Aruch* rules that it is sometimes per-mitted to lie as a means of protecting oneself from unscrupulous people in negotiations.[46]

## LYING TO PREVENT EMBARRASSMENT, ESPECIALLY OF A TORAH SCHOLAR

Many people justify lying in order to avoid personal embarrassment. Regarding a Torah scholar, Judaism believes this to be permis-sible as well. The Talmud states that in three specific areas a Torah scholar may not tell the truth – all to avoid embarrassment or appear-ing haughty.[47] What are these circumstances when lying by a Torah scholar is permitted? If a Jew asks a Torah scholar if he is familiar with the details of a certain tractate of the Tal-mud or if he is currently learning a particular passage, the scholar may answer "no" even though he is very familiar with every aspect of

---

38. *Magen Avraham* on *Shulchan Aruch*, *Orach Chaim* 156
39. *Mishna Berurah* on *Shulchan Aruch*, *Orach Chaim* 156
40. Niv Sefatayim, *Hilchot Issurei Sheker* 2:15
41. Rif commentary on *Bava Metzia* 23b, Maharsha commentary on *Yevamot* 65b

42. *Sotah* 41b
43. Mishna *Nedarim* 3:4
44. *Nedarim* 62b
45. *Yoma* 83b
46. *Shulchan Aruch*, *Choshen Mishpat* 33:5
47. *Bava Metzia* 23b with Tosafot commentary

that Talmudic book. The reason is threefold. If the Rabbi answers truthfully, then when he is not familiar with a particular tractate, the Jews will then say that the Rabbi knows this tractate but not that tractate. By answering "no" to all such questions, the questioner will never discover which tractates the Torah scholar knows and does not know, avoiding needless embarrassment. A second reason is to avoid seeming haughty by answering "yes," which appears to "show off" his Torah knowledge. A third reason is that the scholar may not want to be questioned at that particular time concerning that passage or his Talmudic knowledge. The second circumstance regarding questions a Torah scholar does not have to answer is readily understandable: if someone asks a Torah scholar how often he has marital relations with his wife, he may avoid a specific answer or not tell the truth. This violation of privacy allows that Torah scholar to lie. In a similar manner, if the Torah scholar is asked which hotel he is residing at, he may avoid the answer or give the wrong information. The reason is that he may not want many people visiting him there unannounced. The protection of the privacy of the Torah scholar (in all three cases) is labeled by Tosafot as "the path of peace" – i.e., in order to keep relations peaceful, the Torah scholar may refrain from saying the truth. Maimonides codifies this idea into Jewish law, but says it refers only to a veteran, a noted Torah scholar who would never lie in any other circumstance (and probably is bothered greatly by many questions).[48] Rabbi Moshe Isserles describes the three particular situations a bit differently from those outlined by Maimonides and the Talmud when *Shulchan Aruch* brings this concept as Jewish law, but the principle is maintained.[49]

In the same vein, we learn that under certain circumstances, it is permitted to lie to a sick person and tell him or her that the illness is not terminal even if it is – if the person is sure that the truth will only make that same individual feel much worse psychologically and may even affect the patient's physical condition. (The concept about when to tell the truth to patients and when one may lie is a long and complicated ethical discussion in and of itself, which is beyond the scope of this volume.) The prophet Elisha lied to the King of Aram by not indicating that his illness was terminal.[50] The very modest Shmuel Hakatan lied to avoid causing someone embarrassment: Rabban Gamliel had invited seven scholars to a particular meeting, but when he noticed that there were eight people in the room, he asked who had not been invited. Shmuel Hakatan lied and said that he had not been invited and excused himself, even though he had indeed been invited. He wanted to avoid embarrassing the young scholar who had invited himself to the meeting.[51]

Rabbi Yehoshua ben Chanina lied in order to avoid criticizing the bad cooking of his hostess. Instead of saying that the food was much too salty to eat, he said that he had eaten earlier in the day and was no longer hungry.[52] When criticizing the people for intermarrying with non-Jews, the prophet Ezra said that "we" sinned to God, including himself in the sin, even though his wife was clearly Jewish. He did not want to overemphasize the sin and embarrass the people by pointing out that it was only they who had sinned.[53] This concept is brought down in Jewish law even in day-to-day issues in our times. A contemporary Jewish law expert, Rabbi Shmuel Vozner, deals with a similar case. He discusses the situation in a synagogue that is collecting funds for a Torah scholar who is in a great financial need, but does not wish for anyone to know about his predicament. To avoid embarrassment, they ask if it is permissible to lie and tell the congregation that the funds are being collected for a poor bride who needs money to get married. In the end, Rabbi Vozner rules that it is permitted to falsify the goal of the *Tzedaka*-charity

---

48. Maimonides, *Hilchot Gezaila VeAvaida* 14:13
49. *Shulchan Aruch, Choshen Mishpat* 262:21

50. Kings II 8:7-10
51. *Sanhedrin* 11a
52. *Eiruvin* 53b
53. Ezra 10:1-2 with Malbim commentary

funds, if the congregation has collected in the past for poor brides as well.[54]

## LYING IN A MANNER THAT HAS SOME TRUTH WITHIN IT

Even in the certain situations in which the Rabbis gave permission for Jews to lie, it is important to minimize the lying as much as possible. That is why the Talmud said that you may "*Leshanot*" ("change") the truth to achieve peace, and did not even use the word "*Lishaker*" ("lie"). Whenever possible, there should be some truth in any untruth that is spoken. Thus, for example, in the Talmudic passage, when the prophet Samuel was instructed by God to tell King Saul that he was going to bring a sacrifice (and not anoint David to be king), in the end Samuel did actually bring a sacrifice. Meiri points out that since he did bring a sacrifice as well, even though it was not his prime objective, Samuel did not really lie to Saul.[55] Regarding the same passage, another commentary also says that if a statement can be understood in two possible ways, and the listener understands it in the "wrong" manner (in a situation that it is permitted to lie), then that kind of statement is preferable to an out-and-out lie.[56] He gives the example of Abraham declaring that Sara was his sister. This too was not an outright lie as we know that Sara was Abraham's niece.[57] In many languages, including Hebrew, the word for niece or nephew is a form of the word for brother or sister (after all, a niece or nephew is the child of a sibling). Thus, when Abraham said Sara was his sister, it was not an absolute lie.

In the passage above that says that Jews are permitted or obligated to tell all brides that they are beautiful,[58] the beauty may refer to inner beauty or, as mentioned above, the intended meaning can be that for that groom on the wedding night, she really is beautiful. Thus,

"a beautiful bride" is also not a complete lie. The Talmud recalls the story of Rabbi Eliezer who was arrested for heresy, i.e., practicing Judaism. When the non-Jewish court asked Rabbi Eliezer how he could believe in such a foolish thing called Judaism, Rabbi Eliezer answered, "The judge is correct." Rabbi Eliezer was referring to God, the Judge who is always correct. But the judge in the court (mistakenly) believed that Rabbi Eliezer was referring to him, and on that basis pardoned him.[59] Thus, a statement that can be interpreted two ways with some truth to it is the preferred type of lie. Rava said that a Torah scholar was permitted to say, "I am a worshipper of fire, and therefore, will not pay the poll tax." Apparently, this tax was levied upon Jews, but not upon Persians who worshipped fire, and thus the Torah scholar who said this was excused from the tax. But this scholar was actually referring to God, Who is also referred to as fire, unbeknownst to the Persian tax collector.[60] This type of lie is then permitted. The double meaning does not allow a lie to be spoken in the first place, but when it is allowed anyway, a lie with one possible true meaning is always preferred. Thus, a modern Rabbi rules that if the only way to achieve peace (for past events that will not harm anyone) is by lying, one should nevertheless try to lie in a way that can be interpreted in two manners, with one way being the truth. Furthermore, even a Jew who is permitted to lie in a specific circumstance should always try to limit the words of untruth as much as possible.[61]

## OTHER CIRCUMSTANCES WHEN IT IS PERMITTED TO LIE IN JUDAISM

There are other circumstances that permit a Jew to lie in specific instances. Thus, Rabbi Nachum Yavrov explains that in order to keep a commandment or avoid committing a sin, a Jew may sometimes tell an untruth. He further

54. *Responsa Shevet Levi*, section 2, *Yoreh De'ah* 119
55. Meiri commentary on *Yevamot* 65b
56. Aruch LeNair commentary on *Yevamot* 65b
57. Genesis 11:29 with Rashi commentary
58. *Ketuvot* 16b

59. *Avodah Zara* 16b
60. *Nedarim* 62b, Deuteronomy 4:24
61. *Niv Sefatayim*, *Hilchot Issurei Sheker* 2:9-10

says that if a lie will deflect attention away from a person as being very pious, it is possible to lie. He gives the example of a person who has taken upon himself to fast when most Jews do not fast in similar circumstances. When asked if he is fasting, this Jew may lie and say he or she is not fasting, in order not to call attention about piety to himself or herself.[62] These rulings are borne out by certain stories in the Midrash and Jewish law.

A Jew is supposed to say the Grace After Meals in the place where he or she ate the meal.[63] When Rabbah accidentally left the place where he ate before reciting the blessing, he told an untruth to others to in order to get himself back to the place that he ate so that he could then recite the blessing.[64] (If he had told the truth, it might have seemed like he was making himself out to be righteous.) When the sons of Rabbi Meir passed away on Shabbat, each time Rabbi Meir inquired about them, his wife Beruria (a Torah scholar in her own right) lied about what happened and told him different stories about the boys, gradually hinting to Rabbi Meir that they had died.[65] She did this in order not to interrupt his Shabbat experience and not to shock him too suddenly about the deaths. Elijah made himself out to be poorer than Rabbi Akiva (even though he was not), in order to make Rabbi Akiva feel better about himself.[66]

The scenario in which a Jew who is pious should lie in order not to reveal to others that he or she has taken upon himself or herself an "extra" fast is specifically stated as Jewish law by *Shulchan Aruch*, *Magen Avraham*, and *Mishna Berurah*.[67] Another type of lie or untruth that is permitted is an exaggeration in certain circumstances. To make a point, the prophet said that *all* of the people were behind Solomon, when it was not literally all of the

Jewish people.[68] Similarly, it is permitted to exaggerate about a person's good traits, but not lie, when it comes to a eulogy. It is even a Mitzvah-commandment to do so, in order to bring people to tears and create the proper mood of the funeral, but not to exaggerate too much.[69]

## BUT NEVER TEACH CHILDREN TO LIE

There is one area (in addition to the Jewish courtroom) in which any form of lying or even exaggeration is clearly prohibited, and that is in dealing with one's children. This is part of the Mitzvah of educating children, who often see the world as black and white. Thus, all lying is forbidden in their presence for the purpose of educating them properly.

A story in the Talmud speaks about Rav, who had a despicable wife who tormented him. Whenever Rav requested lentil soup, she purposely gave him pea soup in order to displease him. Likewise, when he requested pea soup, she purposely gave him lentil soup. Chiya, Rav's son (who would grow up to be a Talmud scholar), was pained by what his mother was doing. Thus, when Rav asked Chiya to tell his mother to cook pea soup, Chiya purposely lied and told his mother that his father had requested lentil soup, so that his father would get what he truly desired. Eventually, when Rav figured out what was going on (since he was surprised that his wife was suddenly being nice to him and preparing the soup that he requested), Rav told Chiya to stop the lying. Even though he was smart and understood the situation, it was morally wrong to lie and wrong for Rav to let his son lie, no matter how good the intentions.[70] A child who lies for the right reasons may grow up to lie for the wrong reasons.

Similarly, regarding a child using a parent's *Lulav*, Jewish law states that a child can

62. Niv Sefatayim, *Hilchot Issurei Sheker* 3
63. Maimonides, *Hilchot Berachot* 4:1
64. *Berachot* 53b
65. Midrash, *Yalkut Shimoni* 31a
66. *Nedarim* 50a
67. *Shulchan Aruch, Orach Chaim* 656:6 with *Magen Avraham* and *Mishna Berurah* commentaries

68. Kings I 1:40, Chulin 90b
69. *Shulchan Aruch, Yoreh De'ah* 344:1
70. *Yevamot* 63a

acquire an object legally, but cannot then give it to someone else. Thus, Rabbi Zeira said that a parent should not give the *Lulav* to a child to use on the *Yom Tov*-festival and then get it back again for the parent to use it the next day. When the child figures out the Jewish law, that child will understand that the parent never intended to give it as a gift to the child in the first place, and was really lying to the child all the time by doing this.[71] Then Rabbi Zeira warns all parents and gives them stern advice to which many parents today are still not sensitive: Never promise a child something and then not deliver. The child will learn that it is permissible to lie, and thereby the parent will be committing a sin.[72]

---

71. *Sukkah* 46b with Arch LeNair commentary
72. *Sukkah* 46b

# MUSIC IN JUDAISM

USIC AFFECTS MOST PEOPLE
profoundly. Music that touches
us affects our emotions and mood,
and enhances our feelings. Studies have shown
that music even affects the fetus of a pregnant
mother, and that the effects often remain later
in life.[1] The idea of music's effect on the fetus
was already known thousands of years ago, as
the sages said that even in the womb, the fetus sings a type of music.[2] The combination
of lyrics and music can sometimes change our
attitudes. For the religious person, music is the
language of the soul. Since music is connected
to the spirit of man, every religion has its own
unique melodies and compositions. How
does Judaism view music? How does music
continue to impact Judaism and Jews today?

## ALL OF JUDAISM IS AFFECTED BY MUSIC

Music is present in and impacts all aspects
of Jewish religious life, even today. In prayer,
the specific melodies of each prayer service
set the particular mood for each particular
service. These melodies are called the *Nusach*,
and the *Nusach* for the daily morning prayer
differs from the daily afternoon prayer, which
differs from the evening prayer. The mood and
music of each service is intentionally different
and is represented by each prayer service's
unique *Nusach*. Certain parts of the prayer are
required to be sung in melody.[3] Shabbat has its
own unique *Nusach*, as do the Jewish holidays.
The Rabbis emphasize that the melodies of
Shabbat should be different from the melodies
of the weekday prayer.[4] The regal atmosphere
and seriousness of the Days of Awe can be felt
by the particular *Nusach* of Rosh Hashana
and Yom Kippur. The month that contains

many Jewish holidays is named Tishrei, which
according to one opinion, is derived from the
Hebrew word "*shira*" – "song," and the name of
the holiday of Pesach, according to one opinion, is derived from the two Hebrew words "*Pe*"
and "*Sach*" – "the mouth speaks/sings."[5]

Another example concerns the prayer
announcing the new moon and upcoming
month. Some have the custom that the melody in this particular prayer should be sad in
announcing Rosh Chodesh Av, to reflect the
mood of this particular month.[6] Thus, Jews do
not recite prayer, but they actually sing it.

Central to Jewish life, along with prayer, is
Torah learning. Even here, specifically when
learning Talmud, there is a specific sing-song
chant in the way the Talmud is read and
studied. Anyone who has entered the classic
*Beit Midrash* has heard the melodies of Jewish learning. The Rabbis of the Middle Ages
brought down that a specific melody was
learned for reciting the Talmud before it was
written down, in order to remember it better.[7]
Shelah writes that those sections of the prayer
service that come from the Talmud should be
sung in the "melody specific to the reading of
the Mishna."[8] Thus, the Talmud is not only
learned, it is chanted.

Jewish Scripture also has its unique melodies. The Torah must be read with the specific
melody called the *Trop*, indicated by the music
notes found in most *Chumashim*-Torah texts,
today. The Talmud frowns upon anyone who
does not read the Torah publicly in the synagogue with the correct musical notes,[9] and
the Rabbis rule that if the wrong notes are
recited (in many cases), one has not fulfilled

---

1. Dr. Alexandra Lamont, University of Leicester, 2001
2. *Sotah* 30b
3. *Tur, Orach Chaim* 51
4. Rabbi Chaim Palagi, *Kaf HaChaim* 28:24

5. *Likutei Maharan, Mahdura Kama* 49
6. *Eliyahu Rabba, Orach Chaim* 284
7. *Tosafot* on *Megillah* 32a, s.v. "*V'hashone*"
8. Cited by *Mishna Berurah* and *Be'er Haitaiv* on *Shulchan Aruch, Orach Chaim* 50
9. *Megillah* 32a

the obligation of reading the Torah in the synagogue.[10] The Haftorah, words of the prophets read each Shabbat after the Torah reading, has a different melody than that of the Torah. Each Megillah read on different holidays has its own melody, reflecting the atmosphere and mood of that holiday. So, for example, the sadness of the Temple's destruction can be heard in the sad melody of the *Eicha* Megillah reading on Tisha B'av night and again in the Tisha B'av Haftorah the next day. *Megillat Esther* has a happy melody, reflecting the joyous nature of the holiday and the final outcome of the story. (In fact, it is customary to read the sad parts of *Megillat Esther* to the melody of *Eicha* read on Tisha B'av.)

According to Rabbi Yonah, adding Jewish song to any regular meal can turn that meal into a *Seudat Mitzvah*, a repast of holiness.[11] Thus, music is an integral part of all of Jewish religious life.

## THE IMPORTANCE OF MUSIC IN JUDAISM

Music is not only vital to Judaism and Jewish life today, but it was central to the Creation and the continuation of the world. The verse says that "the heavens declare the glory of God, and the firmament proclaims His handiwork."[12] In explaining this verse, the Rabbis clarify that the form of this declaration is through daily music of the heavens and the earth, which sing to God, and that without this daily song, God would not have created the world at all.[13] And this Midrash goes on to say that all of the rivers, mountains, and all parts of nature sing to God daily. Rabbi Nachman takes this idea one step further and says that each blade of grass and each animal has its own particular melody that it sings.[14] Another Midrash explains that God prefers the song of man to the song of angels, because the angels sing to God on a

regular basis, the same time each day, while man sings out to God spontaneously.[15] In fact the very first song sung by the Jewish people to God was the Song of the Sea following their miraculous salvation by God from the Egyptian armies.[16] Rashi explains that this song was completely spontaneous.[17] According to one source, this song was the first time that man ever sang to God, despite all the previous interactions of God with man in the Torah.[18] In fact, one opinion writes that if not for the daily song of human beings to God, He would not have created the world to begin with.[19] Another opinion is that the entire purpose of creation itself was for music and song.[20]

Song in the Temple was so crucial that atonement could not be achieved for a sacrifice in the Temple unless song accompanied it.[21] Similarly, any sacrifice brought to the Temple that lacked the song to accompany it, was invalidated because of that.[22] In fact, the highest form of service to God, according to the Talmud, is music and song.[23] The *Zohar* explains that the Levites, who sang in the Temple, were called Levites because they joined together ("*Nelavim*") in unison to sing to God.[24] One who sings to God in this world is assured that he or she will sing to God in the Next World as well.[25]

The central book of Judaism, the Torah itself, is called a song, *Shira*.[26] Rabbi Naftali Tzvi Yehuda Berlin explains why the Torah is referred to by this term. He states that every song has lyrics and feelings that are implied beneath the surface and not plainly stated. So too, the Torah's main ideas and deeper concepts are not found in the plain text, but must be understood on a hidden, more subtle level,

10. *Mishna Berurah, Orach Chaim* 142:4
11. *Sha'arei Teshuva, Hilchot Megillah* 791
12. Psalms 19:2
13. Midrash, *Otzar HaMidrashim*, Rabbi Akiva 4
14. *Likutei Maharan, Mahdura Batra* 63

15. Midrash, *Otzar Hamidrashim*, Kedusha 7
16. Exodus 14:31-15:1
17. Rashi commentary on Exodus 15:1
18. Midrash, *Shemot Rabbah* 23:4
19. Midrash, *Otzar HaMidrashim*, Rabbi Akiva 6
20. Midrash, *Otiyot Rabbi Akiva* 1
21. *Erchin* 11a
22. Midrash, *Bamidbar Rabbah* 6:10
23. *Erchin* 11a
24. *Zohar* II:19a
25. Ben Yehoyada commentary on *Sanhedrin* 91b
26. Deuteronomy 31:19

like a song. Ideas in the Torah, like in a song, are often intentionally elusive and implied, and not openly written.[27] Perhaps, in addition, just as a song has many levels of understanding, the Torah is intended to be understood on many levels. And just as a song contains many feelings and moods within it and varies from person to person, so too, the Torah generates different feelings and moods for different people. Finally, just as a song inspires people, deeply moving them to action and change, so too, the Torah is meant to inspire individuals to act and to change.

## MUSIC IN THE BIBLE

At the very beginning of human history, in the first few hundred years after the creation of man, the Torah tells us that music and musical instruments were already developed and part of the culture of human beings.[28] Singing in praise of God as a reaction to victory attributed to Him is fairly common in the Bible. Not only did the Jews sing at the Sea (as mentioned above), but the Jewish people also sang after the miracle of the well that provided them with water, life's sustenance, in the desert.[29] When the Jews were victorious over the feared and more powerful Canaanites, the prophetess Deborah and the general Barak spontaneously sang in praise after the victory.[30]

We also see numerous times in Scripture when the playing of music inspired a prophet to feel God's presence and prophesy. When Elisha the prophet wanted to connect with God, he took a musician to play for him, and then God did indeed appear to him.[31] A group of prophets were inspired to prophecy when music was produced from a combination of the instruments that included the lute, tambourine, flute, and harp.[32] King David designated several people to become musicians and

play the harps, lutes, and cymbals.[33] Similarly, when King Saul felt that God's presence had left him, he summoned a young harpist to play music in order to inspire him and regain his connection with God.[34] The musician who inspired King Saul was none other than young David the harpist, son of Yishai, who later became King David.

Over the last 3,000 years, King David, as a musician, has inspired millions or possibly billions of people with his musical compositions. Today, in Modern Hebrew, the word for music and the word for poetry is identical – *Shira*. One might think that the famous words of David, the Psalms, were composed only as poetry, as it is mostly recited today. But it is clear from the Psalms themselves (the basis for most of Jewish prayer) and from King David's background, that these 150 paragraphs were composed as songs, not poetry. The introduction to many of the Psalms connotes musical pieces. The term "*Mizmor*," translated today as simply "psalm," actually indicates a melody and occurs in fifty-eight different Psalms. The term "*Lamnatze'ach*" begins fifty-three different Psalms, and is translated as either "to the chief musician" or "for the conductor." Some form of the Hebrew word *Shir*, song, occurs in forty-three Psalms and is often the first word, indicating that the paragraph should be sung. Thus, the entire Psalms was undoubtedly composed as songs to be sung or music pieces to be played. Moreover, the Bible calls King David the "sweet singer of Israel,"[35] in addition to giving recognition to his skill as a harpist.

One Midrash explains that many famous people in the Torah wanted to sing to God, but because of King David's outstanding voice and musical abilities, they held back and let David later sing their words to God.[36] Targum Yonatan disagrees with this Midrash, and says that ten figures in the Bible actually sang to God prior to King David.[37] These songs to God be-

---

27. *Ha'amek Davar*, "Introduction to Genesis"
28. Genesis 4:21
29. Numbers 21:17
30. Judges 5:1
31. Kings II 3:14-15
32. Samuel I 10:5-6

33. Chronicles I 25:1
34. Samuel I 16:14-23
35. Samuel II 23:1
36. Midrash, *Shir HaShirim Rabbah* 4:5
37. *Targum Yonatan*, "Introduction to *Shir HaShirim*"

gan with Adam, the first man, continued with Moses (mentioned above), Joshua after the battle in Givon when the sun stood still,[38] and the prophetess Chana.[39] King Solomon, King David's son, also sang to God. The final song, says Targum Yonatan, will be sung when all of the Jews return to Israel from the Diaspora, as mentioned in Isaiah.[40]

## MUSICAL INSTRUMENTS IN JUDAISM

At the very beginning of human development, musical instruments were already created and used.[41] Musical instruments always seemed to accompany Jewish singing. In describing the scene of the Song of the Sea, King David depicts the people singing, followed by those playing the musical instruments, as the word *Shira* indicates singing with one's mouth,[42] and *Nagen* indicates playing musical instruments.[43] Musical instruments played properly seem to inspire everyone. The Talmud describes the harp of David that was above his bed, which played by itself every night at midnight. This inspired King David to learn Torah all night.[44] One commentary compares the letters of the Hebrew word *Kinor* (harp, violin, or lute) to God giving light to the world, rearranging the Hebrew letters of this instrument to twenty-six (*Kaf* and *Vav*) as the numerical value of God's ineffable name, and *Ner*, light.[45] Thus, the playing of this instrument was through the Divine spirit.

The most prominent mention of musical instruments in Jewish ritual could be witnessed and heard at the daily sacrifices in the Temple and at the annual *Simchat Beit HaSho'eva*, the water ceremony that took place on Sukkot in the Temple area. The Mishna tells us that the sounds of the musical instruments in the

Temple were so loud that people in Jericho not only heard the Levites singing, but they also heard the clanging of the cymbals, the sounds of the flutes, and the sound of the *Shofar* and trumpets blowing.[46] Which instruments were actually present in the Temple each day?

Maimonides writes that although the number of Levites singing in the Temple was unlimited (the minimum was twelve), there were twelve different instruments in the Temple, and the musician positions were not limited to Levites or Kohanim, but they had to be distinguished individuals. He also stresses that *shira* is music produced vocally, but the number of instruments varied widely. There would be 2-6 lyres, 2-12 flutes, 2-120 trumpets, and a minimum of 9 harps, without any upper limit. Yet, there would be only one cymbal.[47] With all of these instruments, the melody would only be played by a single (cane reed) flute, as this instrument produced a pleasant sound.[48] The instruments in the Temple service were so important that a maestro had to be appointed to supervise and coordinate this activity.[49]

The sound of the trumpet in the notes that we normally associate on Rosh Hashana with the *Shofar*, was sounded each day in the Temple with the *Chatzotzra*-trumpet.[50] At least twenty-one of the sounds of *Tekiah-Teruah-Tekiah* were sounded each day, and on special holidays up to forty-eight of these sounds were heard. These included three at the opening of the Temple gates each morning, nine during the daily morning sacrifice, and nine during the daily afternoon sacrifice.

The musical instruments and the mood of the once-a-year Sukkot celebration were quite different from the daily sacrifice. The Mishna describes the scene. Men of piety danced juggling torches, as the flutes played and torches were behind them in this night procession. Harps, lyres, cymbals, and trumpets were among the many instruments that

---

38. Joshua 14;13
39. Samuel I 2:1
40. Isaiah 30:29
41. Genesis 4:21
42. Psalms 68:26
43. Malbim commentary on Psalms 68:26
44. *Berachot* 3b
45. Ben Yehoyada commentary on *Berachot* 3b

46. Mishna *Tamid* 3:8
47. Maimonides, *Hilchot Kli Mikdash* 3:3-4
48. Maimonides, *Hilchot Kli Mikdash* 3:5
49. *Shekalim* 5:1
50. Mishna *Sukkah* 5:5

accompanied the dancing, as the Levites stood on the fifteen steps of the Temple courtyard. As the procession finished at dawn, two Kohanim, each with a trumpet in his hand, sounded the notes of *Tekiah*, *Teruah* and then *Tekiah* again four separate times.[51]

## WHICH IS THE ESSENCE OF JEWISH MUSIC – INSTRUMENTS OR SINGING?

Having seen the importance of both singing and musical instruments in the Temple as well as in all aspects of Jewish life, the question arises: Which is paramount – the voices singing or the playing of the musical instruments that accompany the daily service? Is the essence of Jewish music the instruments or the voices? This question is actually debated in the Talmud.[52] Rabbi Yossi believes that the instruments are the main musical component of the Temple service, while the Rabbis believe the singing is the most important factor. This argument has tangible implications in Jewish law. Anything that is connected to the daily Temple service may violate the Shabbat. Normally, musical instruments would not be permitted to be played on Shabbat. However if Rabbi Yossi is correct, they would play the instruments in the Temple on Shabbat, since they are essential to the service, while if the Rabbis are correct, only singing would be permitted on Shabbat. Maimonides seems to rule as a compromise position between both opinions. Generally, the musical instruments were not permitted on Shabbat, indicating that the vocal singing is more important. But the lone flute that played the melody *was* permitted on Shabbat and festivals, even though it violated the Shabbat, indicating that this instrument was essential to the music.[53]

Musical instruments in Judaism are more than simply the means to produce a sound. The instruments themselves often have symbolic and moral concepts within them. For example, the Midrash says that the harp used by King David (in addition to playing by itself at night) had seven strings specifically.[54] The seven strings represent natural law that we live by and that King David lived by. For example, in Judaism there is the seven-day weekly cycle, seven-week cycles, and seven-year cycles, representing the system of nature. Within this cycle of nature are also the seven notes of the musical scale. But in the future, says the Midrash, the harp in the Temple will have eight strings, which symbolizes the supernatural or what goes beyond nature. Thus circumcision is on the eighth day, because its performance changes the nature of how the baby boy was born. So too, the miracle of Chanukah was eight days, indicating its "beyond-nature" aspects. The Third Temple will have aspects that go beyond natural law, represented by the eight-string harp.

## MUSIC IN JEWISH PRAYER

Although we noted above the importance of music as part of each Jewish prayer service, there are some specific issues relating to Jewish prayer and music.

It is logical that music must be an integral part of prayer. Since, according to one opinion today's prayer takes the place of the daily sacrifices in the Temple,[55] and because we saw above that a daily sacrifice without song is invalid,[56] then music certainly should be an integral part of our prayers in the synagogue. The person who leads the prayer service today is called the *Chazan*, the *Shliach Tzibbur*, the cantor. A Rabbi in the Middle Ages writes that if a person who is blessed with a great singing voice chooses not to use it to be a cantor and sing to God, it is preferable that such a person (who deprives God of his gift) to not have been born. However, if this person does use

---

51. Mishna *Sukkah* 5:1, 4
52. *Sukkah* 50b
53. Maimonides, *Hilchot Kli Mikdash* 3;6

54. Midrash, *Bamidbar Rabbah* 15:11
55. *Berachot* 26b
56. Midrash, *Bamidbar Rabbah* 6:10

his voice for holiness and prayer, he is to be praised.[57]

An entire chapter in the *Code of Jewish Law* is devoted to cantors – who are worthy to be a *Chazan*, who is not worthy, and other related issues.[58] Clearly, being an upstanding individual with outstanding character is a more important criterion in selecting a cantor than his having a great singing voice.[59] Concerning the cantor who has a great voice and chooses to lengthen the service with his singing, *Shulchan Aruch* writes that if the purpose of singing so many of the melodies is due to the spiritual joy in his heart and the desire to praise God, then he should be allowed to continue, as he is performing a great deed. But if the cantor is singing only to hear his own voice and enhance his ego, then that kind of prayer is despised. Kaf HaChaim says that a great Rabbi who used to complain that the cantor sang too long in the synagogue was punished in the World to Come, while the simple Jew who sang these melodies in the synagogue was brought with great honor directly to the Garden of Eden.[60]

## NON-JEWISH MELODIES IN THE SYNAGOGUE

Throughout the ages, there has been controversy as to whether it is proper to use non-Jewish melodies in the prayer service. On the one hand, if the music is superior and helps people to be inspired by the prayers and feel closer to God, it should be allowed. On the other hand, if the source is non-Jewish, how could it be used in the synagogue? There has been much controversy about this question.

Hundreds of years ago, Rabbi Yehuda Chasid forbade a cantor from singing non-Jewish songs.[61] Rabbi Alfasi, who also lived in the Middle Ages, similarly rules that a cantor who sings Arabic and/or inappropriate melodies

must immediately be removed.[62] It is clear that if the origin of the melodies is religious but non-Jewish in origin, then they may not be used in the synagogue.[63] However, if the origin is purely secular, there remains an ongoing debate even today between the great decisors of the twentieth and twenty-first centuries. Rabbi Eliezer Waldenberg forbids using non-Jewish music as part of the Jewish service, claiming that it is similar to the sons of Aaron who brought a "foreign" fire into the Holy of the Holies.[64] However, Rabbi Ovadiah Yosef (and others) sees nothing wrong with combining holy words with secular songs in the synagogue if it enhances the prayer service and feeling of those who pray.[65]

## THE BANNING OF MUSIC BY THE RABBIS

At some point in Jewish history, the Rabbis decreed a ban on listening to music. Why? If music is such an integral part of Judaism, why ban it? Apparently, specifically because music is such a powerful force upon a person's mood and feelings, both positive and negative, the Rabbis felt that music after the occurrence of certain events was not appropriate. Let us investigate the reasons behind the ban of music for Jews.

The Mishna states that after the Sanhedrin, the great court, disappeared, the Rabbis banned music in places where people partied.[66] Why specifically then? The Jerusalem Talmud explains that as long as the *Sanhedrin* could exert some control over the people, the Rabbis were not afraid that the wrong kind of music would lead to debauchery.[67] But now, music would lead to the wrong kinds of celebration, based on the verse in Hosea.[68] Music was still permitted for certain professions, but

57. *Sefer Chasidim* 768
58. *Shulchan Aruch, Orach Chaim* 53
59. *Shulchan Aruch, Orach Chaim* 53:4–5
60. Rabbi Chaim Palagi, *Kaf HaChaim* 28:5
61. *Sefer Chasidim* 768

62. *Responsa Rif* 281
63. *Responsa Igrot Moshe, Yoreh De'ah* II:55, 111
64. *Responsa Tzitz Eliezer* 13:12
65. *Yechave Da'at* II:5
66. Mishna *Sotah* 9:11
67. Jerusalem Talmud, *Sotah* 45a
68. Hosea 9:1

not for others.[69] Rashi explains that music was permitted in those professions that used it to assist in their work and improve their pace.[70] Thus, it seems that music that had a purpose would be permitted, whether to improve work or for a Mitzvah, such as at a Jewish wedding.

However, both the *Tur*[71] and Maimonides[72] later give a different reason for banning music: the destruction of the Temple, which indicates the ban of music is a form of mourning. If that were the true reason behind the ban, then all music, even at Jewish weddings, would now be forbidden as a symbol of mourning, until the Temple is rebuilt. How does the *Code of Jewish Law* rule? As is his wont, *Shulchan Aruch* sides with Maimonides and seems to ban music in *all* circumstances because of the Temple's destruction.[73] However, Rema, who was the decisor for Ashkenazic Jewry, writes there that for any holy purpose, which would include weddings or celebrating Jewish holidays, music is permitted.

What is the status of Jewish music today? (A discussion of non-Jewish secular music today is beyond the scope of this book.) In view of the ban on music, can and should there be Chassidic music concerts where observant singers use words from Scripture? What about recorded music or listening to the radio? There are some more modern Ashkenazic Rabbis, even those who lived in the twentieth century,[74] who rule that it is proper to ban all music in all circumstances (like *Shulchan Aruch* does).[75] Yet, almost all Rabbis permit live music at weddings and Bar Mitzvahs, where the celebration is for a Jewish purpose only. Rabbi Moshe Feinstein permitted listening to secular music, although he cautions that a spiritual person should not listen to this music. However, music for Jewish purposes or for a Mitzvah-commandment is clearly permitted.[76] Chelkat Yaakov writes that since the ban was never declared for music heard on the radio (radios did not exist at that time), listening to music on the radio is permitted.[77] This would also apply to recorded music. Rabbi Waldenberg also allows all recorded music to be heard.[78] One modern Rabbi rules that all music is permitted today, as long as the content of the words is not improper.[79] No less an authority than Rabbi Shlomo Zalman Auerbach ruled that a Jew may listen to classical music, even during the *Omer* period of mourning.[80] It is important to understand and remind ourselves that until recent times – except for the case of a Jewish wedding – all live music that was played in communities was usually for occasions that encouraged forbidden revelry. And all music until about a hundred years ago was live music. With the advent of the radio, phonograph, and MP3s of today, listening to music has become a more private, rather than public, experience. Thus, there seems to be a consensus that if live music is played for *Simcha*-Jewish joy, Mitzvah, or to enhance Judaism, it is permitted.

There is one more rather strange custom regarding Jewish music that should be discussed. In some religious circles, there is a custom specific to Jerusalem that only one instrument (or no instrument at all, but only a drum and a singer) may be used at a Jewish wedding. What is the origin of such a custom and why is it not universally accepted today? Most observant Jews assume that since the Temple's destruction occurred in Jerusalem itself, this is an ancient custom that is a stringency of the general ban on live music. But this assumption is incorrect. The specific ban on live music in Jerusalem began in the 1860s, and was instituted with an oral decree (intentionally never written down) by Rabbi Meir Auerbach, the

---

69. *Sotah* 48a
70. Rashi commentary on *Sotah* 48a
71. *Tur, Orach Chaim* 560
72. Maimonides, *Hilchot Ta'anit* 5:14
73. *Shulchan Aruch, Orach Chaim* 560:3
74. *Chayei Adam* 137:3, *Mishna Berurah* on *Shulchan Aruch* 570:13
75. *Aruch HaShulchan, Orach Chaim* 560:7

76. *Responsa Igrot Moshe, Orach Chaim* I:166
77. *Responsa Chelkat Yaakov* I:62 (section 2)
78. *Responsa Tzitz Eliezer* 15:33 (section 3)
79. *Asei Lecha Rav* 3:4
80. *Responsa Halichot Shlomo, Sefirat HaOmer* 14, note 22

Kalisher Rav (author of the *Imrei Bina*) who moved to Jerusalem.[81] After a terrible cholera outbreak in Jerusalem in 1865, Rabbi Auerbach instituted this ban, assuming the cholera was some kind of Divine warning. He was supported by Rabbi Yehoshua Leib Diskin. Many in Jerusalem never accepted this total ban on music, and Rabbi Shalom Elyashiv believes the ban only applies to weddings that take place in the Old City itself, while others disagree. Thus today, there are some communities that still abide by this total ban of music at Jerusalem weddings, while others do not feel bound by it.

81. All this information is culled from the *Journal of Halacha and Contemporary Society*, vol. 14, pp. 22-24, footnote 13

# PAIN IN JUDAISM

WE LIVE TODAY IN A SOCIETY that is more intolerant to physical pain than any other society or time period in human history. In the past, most people learned to live with physical discomfort and pain. However, our threshold for sustaining soreness and hurt is far less than our ancestors' was, and sufferers today are willing to pay enormous sums to alleviate even minor pain. In fact, the "pain relief" industry is so large in the United States that it is estimated that consumers purchase more than $2.6 billion worth of pills each year for over-the-counter pain relief medicines, and another $14 billion for prescriptions that assuage physical suffering. Why do human beings suffer pain to begin with? Can pain ever be something positive, or must it always be a negative experience? What is the overall Jewish attitude towards pain? Is there a proper "Jewish" way to react to pain and suffering? Does Jewish law recognize pain as an exemption for certain precepts and Jewish actions? Is psychological pain considered the same as physical pain in Judaism? This chapter will attempt to answer these and other questions through traditional sources.

## THE MANY WORDS FOR PAIN IN JUDAISM

It is a well-known doctrine that the number of words that exist in a language for a particular concept reveals the significance of that concept in a society's culture. The most famous example is the more than thirty words for "snow" in the Eskimo (Aleut, Inuit) language, because this concept is so crucial to that environment. In fact, the Sami people, who live in the Arctic area that includes parts of northern Sweden, Norway, Finland, and Russia, are reported to have approximately 180 snow and ice-related words, and as many as 1,000 different words for reindeer! The many different words for God in Hebrew (more than fifteen) show how

important this concept is in Jewish thought. Regarding the subject of pain, there are eleven different words in ancient classical books in Hebrew to describe different kinds of pain. This shows a particular sensitivity in Judaism towards physical pain and suffering. How this special sensitivity to pain affects Jewish law and Jewish life will be shown below. What are these different words for pain in Jewish sources?

One Hebrew word for pain and suffering that comes from the Torah is "*Yisurim,*" which is translated as pain that comes through punishment or "chastisement."[1] The Modern Hebrew word for pain, "*Ke'ev,*" also comes from the Torah and is translated as "in pain" or "sore."[2] The Modern Hebrew verb for "(to) suffer" is "*Lisbol.*" It can also be found in Genesis, where it is translated as "to bear."[3] This word is used repeatedly in other places in the Scripture.[4] Another word for pain is "*Sigfa,*" and is explained by Rashi as suffering due to a famine, or extreme hot or cold weather.[5] The word "*Inui*" is translated alternatively as "submission" or "affliction," and it is used in the context of how slaves were treated.[6] But this word "*Inui*" is also related to the suffering and affliction of the body on a fast day such as Yom Kippur.[7] The Talmud uses the word "*Michoosh,*" which Rashi explains as a mild pain that comes and goes, as opposed to "*Ke'ev,*" which is more intense, such as the pain from a toothache.[8] Other references to pain in the Talmud are "*Shmarda,*" which is translated as "sore" (such as a sore eye), "*Daitza,*" translated as pricking, and "*Kidcha,*" translated as

1. Leviticus 26:18, 26
2. Genesis 34:25
3. Genesis 49:15
4. Isaiah 46:7, 53:4
5. Rashi commentary on *Bava Metzia* 93b s.v. "*Sigfa*"
6. Genesis 16:9, Exodus 1:12
7. Leviticus 23:29, Psalms 35:13
8. *Shabbat* 11a with Rashi commentary

"inflammation."[9] "*Mazor*" in the Bible is translated as "wound,"[10] but in Modern Hebrew this word actually signifies a type of medicine.

## THE GENERAL JEWISH VIEW OF PAIN AND SUFFERING

Unlike some religions, Judaism does not view pain as something that is generally positive or "part of the religious experience." The Talmud describes three kinds of people whose life is not really a life, and one of them is a person who feels pain all over his or her body at all times.[11] It is therefore legitimate in Jewish thought to actively try to eliminate one's pain. Each day in the daily silent prayer, traditional Jews ask God to remove sorrow (caused by physical pain) and groaning (caused by psychological pain).[12] In addition to this petition that is recited three times each day, Jews also ask God to remove their enemies, plague, the sword (set out against them), famine, and sorrow (from pain) during the evening prayer.[13] A Jew is permitted to ask a non-Jew to desecrate some Shabbat laws in order to help ameliorate a (mildly) sick person's pain. However, there are limits as to what a Jew is permitted to do in order to eliminate his or her pain.[14] If a Jew is in very great pain or will even die as a result of sickness, and the doctors declare that the only way to remove the pain and save his life is for him commit adultery with a particular married woman to whom he is attracted, the Talmud says that it is forbidden to so even if he will die, since it violates one the of the three cardinal sins of Judaism.[15] Maimonides codifies this concept into Jewish law, but also says that violating any other Torah commandments besides this one is certainly permitted if it will save the person's life.[16]

It is clearly forbidden for a Jew to cause someone else pain by physically striking another him or her. *Shulchan Aruch* derives this law from a criminal who sinned, and whose punishment by the Jewish court is lashes.[17] The Torah says that if this criminal receives even one more lash than is due him, the Jewish court's representative who strikes him violates a Torah law of causing someone unnecessary pain.[18] If this is true for a sinner who is already found guilty of a crime and receives corporal punishment, how much more it a sin to cause anyone else unnecessary pain? The prohibition of causing anyone any unnecessary pain is taken so seriously in Judaism that a twentieth century authority in Jewish law ruled that doctors who are first-year residents may not give patients any injections or put any needles into the bodies of their patients. Since they are not yet experts in these procedures, they will inevitably cause these patients more pain than is necessary since the shots given by veteran hospital workers will naturally be less painful, and it is therefore forbidden in Jewish law.[19] Similarly, Rabbi Dovid ben Zimra, who lived in the sixteenth century, rules that if a Jew sees someone suffering while carrying a heavy physical load, that Jew is obligated to help the person by lightening the load and alleviating that person's pain. He who hesitates and does not help relieve that person's pain is guilty of several sins.[20] Rabbi Judah Chasid writes that anyone who causes any unnecessary pain to another human being will be punished. And even causing unnecessary pain to an animal by putting a load on it that is too large or heavy or by striking it is forbidden, and that person is punished. If humans treat others with compassion, God will treat them with compassion.[21]

9. *Avodah Zara* 28b with Rash commentary
10. Hosea 5:13, *Sanhedrin* 92b
11. *Beitza* 32b
12. Twelfth blessing of the daily *Shmoneh Esreh*
13. "*Hashkiveinu*" prayer after *Shema* in the evening service
14. *Shulchan Aruch, Orach Chaim* 328:17
15. *Sanhedrin* 75a
16. Maimonides, *Hilchot Yesodai HaTorah* 5:6

17. *Shulchan Aruch, Choshen Mishpat* 420:1
18. Deuteronomy 25:3; Maimonides, *Hilchot Sanhedrin* 16:12
19. *Responsa Tzitz Eliezer* 14:35
20. *Responsa Radvaz* 728
21. *Sefer Chasidim* 666

## WHY DOES THE HUMAN BEING SUFFER PAIN?

Why does God cause human beings to suffer pain at all? Much natural pain can be beneficial and a gift to each human being. Imagine if a person did not feel pain when he or she put his or her hand in a fire. That person's hand would burn up and be lost before the person realized what had happened. Pangs of hunger alert a person that his or her body needs to consume food. The body's physical pain and suffering is often similar to a signal going off in a car, indicating that something is broken and must be repaired in that car or body. Without the pain to signal that something is not working properly, people would not know they are ill and need to be treated. In the same way, God also brings pain to human beings for the spiritual sins they commit, and lets them know that their souls also have to be "fixed" and mended. But each person must try to understand this signal and respond accordingly. Therefore, the Talmud says that suffering sometimes comes about because of sin.[22] *Sefer Chasidim* describes a scenario in which it is clear that in an entire crowd only one person suffers, either on a boat, in the desert, or other situations, and the possessions of everyone else were saved except this one particular person's. In that situation, it is obvious that the pain (physical or psychological) was intended for that particular person. It signals that either this pain is an indication that the person sinned, or it could be a form of punishment or wake-up call. Alternatively, the pain could act as atonement for that person's past sins.[23]

## PAYING FOR CAUSING PHYSICAL PAIN TO OTHERS

In recent years, American juries made headlines by awarding large amounts of money to people who suffered relatively minor pain, such as the case of a person who bought steaming hot coffee in a fast-food chain, spilled it on himself, and was awarded millions of dollars by the jury as a result. Judaism has always displayed a special sensitivity to pain and suffering caused by other human beings. Thousands of years ago, Judaism's system of compensation for damages always included recompense for pain and suffering. The five categories of damages payment in Jewish law, which are determined by a Jewish court when someone causes physical harm to another person are: (1) *Nezek* – Paying for permanent damage to the body (according to how much less a person is now physically worth), (2) *Tza'ar* – Paying for pain, (3) *Ripui* – Paying doctor bills, (4) *Shevet* – Unemployment benefits, i.e., the amount of a low paying job while the person is healing and cannot work in his or her profession, and (5) *Boshet* – payment for embarrassment. Depending on how the damage was done, where, and to whom, this is a subjective amount for each situation. Even if the only damage done was that of pain, it is still sufficient in Jewish law to compel the person who caused the pain to pay.[24] This ancient system clearly shows a type of sophistication far beyond what exists today in the court systems in most countries.

How does the court measure payment for pain inflicted? Maimonides states that it this is a subjective amount, differing for each person. There are some poor people who would be willing to endure much pain in order to earn a small amount of money, while other more wealthy people would not tolerate any pain even in exchange for all the money in the world. Thus, the amount paid for pain suffered in damages is subjective, depending on each individual's makeup. Maimonides concludes that the amount is equivalent to how much one would have paid to suffer the same physical loss (of a limb, for example) through non-painful drugs, rather than through a painful cut or beating by another human being. That is the amount a Jew is paid for "pain" in a Jewish court.[25] *Shulchan Aruch* quotes Maimonides

---

22. *Shabbat* 55a
23. *Sefer Chasidim* 164

24. Maimonides, *Hilchot Chovel U'Mazik* 1:1, 7
25. Maimonides, *Hilchot Chovel U'Mazik* 2:9-10

in his *Code of Jewish Law*, but Rabbi Isserles adds that if the damage was only pain, then the court determines that if the king had decreed that this person's fingernails should be burned (or something similar), how much would this person have paid to escape this pain.[26]

## WHICH IS PREFERABLE: A LIFE WITH PAIN AND SUFFERING OR DEATH?

As science progresses and more and more sick people can be kept alive for longer periods of time, this question becomes more practical and relevant for many individuals. Is a life with pain preferable to death in the Jewish view, or is death a better alternative than continued existence full of suffering? One might think that this determination would or should be the decision of each sick person or human being in pain, to decide for himself or herself the answer to this important question, and whether to act or not act upon that decision. But Judaism does not leave it up to each individual person to decide this important question. That is because, unlike the popular notion that "It is my body and I can do with it as I please," which is indeed the law in most countries, Judaism believes that one's body belongs only to God, Who lends it to each person to use and not abuse.[27] Then God takes back a person's body when he or she dies. Thus, Jews who follow Jewish law cannot decide for themselves about their bodies, and they are forbidden from intentionally harming their bodies (which belong to God). They also may not end their lives, because suicide is a sin for removing what is not theirs to begin with. What then is the Jewish view about this issue? Is it indeed preferable to stay alive with pain, or rather, to die?

The answer comes from an improbable situation discussed in the Talmud. A *Sotah* is a woman suspected of adultery whose possible sin cannot be proven. In Temple times, Jewish law compelled this suspected woman to drink special waters given by the Priest in the Temple, and if she were guilty, she would immediately die. But if she was innocent and had committed no sin, then nothing would happen to her, and she would go back to her husband. The Talmud, however, adds that if this *Sotah* was indeed guilty of adultery, but she *also* was very learned in Torah (and in this aspect she was righteous), rather than die immediately, she would suffer in great pain for one or two or three years (depending on how much Torah she had learned) and *then* she would die.[28] We see from this unusual situation that because of her merits of Torah learning, this woman would live in pain rather than die immediately. Therefore, it is clear that Judaism sees living in great pain as a better situation than instant death. Maimonides codifies this law and explains that the pain that this woman would suffer rather than die immediately came because she was deemed more worthy than any other *Sotah*.[29]

## LEGITIMATE JEWISH REACTIONS TO PAIN

We saw above that Jewish law requires each Jew to try to alleviate someone else's pain, if at all possible. But what if relieving that pain involves committing a sin such as violating the Shabbat? Is the need to mitigate pain more important in Judaism than the need to properly observe the Shabbat and keep it holy? As with most Jewish law questions, the answer is that "it depends on the circumstances." It depends on the level of pain and sickness of the Jew. Taking pills on Shabbat was generally prohibited because the Rabbis said that taking a pill might bring some Jews to actually make the pill itself, which is forbidden. Thus, in normal circumstances it would be a violation of Shabbat to take or to give someone a pill. If the pain is mild – i.e., the person can walk around and function normally – then it would be forbidden to violate the Shabbat, even Rabbinically,

---

26. *Shulchan Aruch, Choshen Mishpat* 420:16
27. Maimonides, *Hilchot Rozte'ach* 1:4

28. *Sotah* 20a
29. Maimonides, *Hilchot Sotah* 3:20

in order to relieve that minor pain. However, if a person is very sick, something that may even lead to a life-threatening situation, then in that condition, it is a Mitzvah-commandment, to violate any and all aspects of Shabbat in order to alleviate that person's pain and help him or her. He who does this quicker, says Rabbi Yosef Caro, is praised more. And he who stops to even ask the question of whether helping such a person is permitted, is equated with a murderer![30]

Therefore, the situation regarding the two extremes of a Jew who is in pain or sick on Shabbat is clear. But there is a middle situation, which is probably more common than the other two: the Jew who is in great pain and is sick, but is not deathly ill and is in no danger of entering a life-threatening situation. Can and should the Shabbat be violated for such a person? *Shulchan Aruch* rules that for such an individual, who is sick enough to be in bed or whose entire body is hurting but not in any real danger, it is permitted to ask a non-Jew to violate a Sabbath law (which is normally prohibited) to help this person. And some rule that even a Jew may violate a Rabbinic law in this case, but not a Torah law.[31] Therefore, we see that Judaism is so sensitive to pain that certain prohibitions may be violated in order to relieve it. Furthermore, Jews should help others in pain, but only if the pain is somewhat serious may a Jew be permitted to violate Shabbat.

This is the Jewish reaction regarding Shabbat observance while helping others in pain. What about the person himself during the rest of the week? If a Jew is in pain (and no tablets or painkillers seem to be alleviating that pain), what should he or she do as a Jew to help eliminate that pain? The Talmud gives one course of action: learn Torah. He who learns Torah properly should see all pain vanish.[32] On that same Talmudic page, the Rabbis give Jews other alternatives on how to alleviate pain through non-medical means. Because it is possible that God is sending a person that pain and suffering as a punishment or as a wake-up call, first that person should do an introspection of his or her moral actions and improve them. If that does not work and a person honestly concluded that all or most of his or her actions are indeed moral, then a Jew should look at how much time was wasted idly by not learning Torah.[33] Rabbeinu Yonah has another solution not only to alleviate pain, but to also prevent pain in the future. He says a Jew must actively do certain specific commandments that protect a Jew from pain and suffering. These include giving to *Tzedaka* (charity), generally helping others in need, visiting the sick, helping bury the dead, comforting the mourners, and creating extra joy for a bride and groom. In addition, if a Jew normally learns one chapter of Torah a day, it should be doubled to two chapters daily (i.e., double one's current output). These actions will ward off any physical pain, according to Rabbeinu Yonah.[34]

Maimonides seems to take a different tack. Although we cannot explain the reason for the pain, we should nevertheless embrace it and accept it as something that we need because it was sent by God. That is why when a person suffers in this world (hearing bad news or other kinds of suffering), the blessing on accepting God's judgment, even without understanding why, must be recited with *joy*, because a Jew believes that suffering is ultimately for the person's benefit.[35] People who look back on this pain years later will often be able to see the good that emerged from the painful experience. Similarly, Chafetz Chaim says that all pain, even that inflicted upon an individual intentionally by other human beings, ultimately comes from God and has a legitimate purpose.[36] Chinuch seems to say that pain is a punishment for sin from God, and that Jews should recognize this fact and

30. *Shulchan Aruch, Orach Chaim* 328:1-2
31. *Shulchan Aruch, Orach Chaim* 328:17
32. *Berachot* 5a

33. *Berachot* 5a
34. *Sha'arei Teshuva,* Sha'ar Revi'i 11
35. Maimonides, *Hilchot Berachot* 10:3; *Tur, Orach Chaim* 222:2-3
36. Chafetz Chaim, *Shem Olam* 3

not repeat the actions that brought about the pain.[37] We learn this idea from the actions and reactions of King David when other people brought pain upon him. Rather than react to these people and take revenge, he said that perhaps this was a message from God and that he would therefore not retaliate against these people.[38]

The Midrash gives four legitimate ways to react to pain, each modeled after a different personality in Scripture who suffered. Job rebelled against his pain. Abraham laughed when experiencing pain. Hezekiah saw his pain as an opportunity to come closer to God. King David reacted by feeling fortunate that the pain was sent by God, and he asked for even more pain and suffering to be sent![39]

## IS PRAYER A PROPER JEWISH REACTION TO PAIN?

Is it legitimate to turn to God when suffering and ask through prayer that the pain cease? It seems that this is indeed a valid Jewish approach to minimizing or removing one's pain. The Talmud records that Rava used to pray to God, beseeching Him to help him not to sin in the future and to eliminate the pain and suffering for his past sins.[40] Rabbi Judah Chasid says that first a person needs to recognize that the ultimate source of pain is not from a malady of the body or even due to another person's decision to harm that individual. Rather, all pain is a wake-up call from God and punishment for past sins. Only then is it permissible to turn to God and pray for Him to remove all of one's pain.[41]

There is a story in the Talmud about Rabbi Judah's handmaiden, who was very learned and pious. When she saw that Rabbi Judah was very ill and in pain and the Rabbis were praying constantly that he not die, she ascended the roof and turned to God with this message:

it is clear that the angels above are praying for Rabbi Judah to die (and join them) and the Rabbis below are praying that he live (so that there is a standoff). She begged God to please favor the Rabbis and let him continue to live. Later on, when she saw how much pain Rabbi Judah was in and how much he suffered, she prayed to God to let the angels "win" and let Rabbi Judah die. When nothing changed, she then threw a jar to the ground from the roof. The loud noise it produced when it shattered caused the Rabbis to become startled and stop praying for a moment. At that moment Rabbi Judah died.[42] Thus, it seems legitimate that although a Jew may not actively do anything to end one's life filled with pain (as noted above with the *Sotah*), a person *is* permitted to turn to God to ask God to end the pain and suffering with death. Based on this passage, Rabbeinu Nissim in fact rules that it is perfectly legitimate for a Jew to pray for his or another person's death, in order to end that individual's suffering and pain.[43]

## POSITIVE ASPECTS OF PAIN

As noted above, physical pain serves as an alarm to the person himself and to physicians that something is wrong and must be treated. In the same way, Judaism also views pain as a mental alarm that something is morally wrong with the person, and that whatever it is must be corrected. This is reflected in the words of King Solomon, who compared the soul to the collapse of a building due to shoddy construction and idle hands that cause a leak.[44] The person is like that house that will "suffer" because of poor behavior.

Some people see pain as a test of their resolve to overcome its effects and accept the pain with joy and smiles (like serious training in a health club). Thus it was Rabbi Akiva, the man who always saw the joy in situations when things looked bleak to others, who was

---

37. *Sefer HaChinuch*, Mitzvah 241
38. Samuel II 16:10-12 with Ralbag commentary
39. *Midrash Tehilim* 26:2
40. *Berachot* 17a
41. *Sefer Chasidim* 751

42. *Ketuvot* 104a
43. Ran commentary on *Nedarim* 40a
44. Ecclesiastes 10:18

smiling when the Romans were torturing his body with iron pitchforks. He saw this entire scenario as a test to determine if he truly loved God with all his soul, as the verse requires. Knowing he "passed the test," Rabbi Akiva died happy, even as he suffered great pain.[45]

There seems to be a basic disagreement in the Talmud about whether pain can be seen as something positive from God or if it should always be detested. One opinion sees pain and suffering as "sufferings of love" (in order to reward the righteous in greater measure in the World to Come), while another opinion detests both the pain and any reward it may bring.[46] In another passage, the school of Rabbi Yishmael believed that if a person can go forty days without suffering any physical pain at all, it is a sign that this person is automatically destined for the World to Come. Thus, they believed that pain is something to be avoided. But in the Land of Israel, they disagreed. A world without pain is a demonstration by God that he does not really care to rehabilitate this particular person, because he or she is beyond rehabilitation. Thus, this person who had no suffering in this world is destined for an afterlife filled with only pain and suffering.[47]

## IS PSYCHOLOGICAL PAIN CONSIDERED LEGITIMATE PAIN IN JUDAISM?

Until now, we have discussed physical pain and Judaism's reaction to it. But is psychological pain, which is subjective and hard to measure, also considered legitimate pain in Jewish thought? Are Jewish laws affected by psychological pain as well? We will see that Judaism understood this kind of pain even before the word "psychology" was invented and has always been sensitive to the non-physical pain that people suffer.

There is a Talmudic story about the great Choni, the most pious and famous person in his generation, who, like the popular children's story about Rip van Winkle, fell asleep for seventy years. When he awoke and no one recognized him, he became distraught. He sought out his friends and Torah learning partners, only to discover that they all were dead. He was in so much anguish that he cried out, "Either my friends or death" – i.e., he would prefer death to a life without companionship. God answered his prayers and he died.[48] Thus, we see that psychological anguish is quite legitimate in Judaism and is recognized as true pain. As mentioned above, when a person has any illness that may result in a life-threatening situation, all Shabbat laws may be violated for this individual. A woman who gives birth is considered to be in this situation – both during labor and the post-partum period – and if she asks for anything, the Shabbat must be violated even if it necessitates turning on a light on Shabbat. *Shulchan Aruch* adds that if this woman is blind and she asks for the light to be turned on for her, we *still* turn on the light if she demands it, even though it is clear that she does not need nor can benefit from the light.[49] But the psychological pain of not having the light on (even though it has no effect on her other than merely uplifting her mood to know that it is turned on) is a legitimate enough reason to violate the Shabbat in this case.

There is a famous story in Scripture about Elijah bringing a little boy who died back to life, whose mother had obviously been distraught.[50] Tosafot asks: how was it that Elijah was permitted to do this? He was a Kohen-Priest who is forbidden to have any contact with the dead. Tosafot answers that since it was a matter of life and death, the violation of this law by Elijah was permitted.[51] More than six hundred years later, Rabbi Moshe Feinstein asks on this Tosafot commentary: How could it be a matter of life and death? If

---

45. *Berachot* 61b
46. *Berachot* 5b
47. *Erchin* 16b
48. *Ta'anit* 23a
49. *Shulchan Aruch, Orach Chaim* 330:1
50. *Kings I* 17:21-24
51. Tosafot commentary on *Bava Metzia* 114b, s.v. "*Amar*"

the boy was already dead, there was no danger of someone dying (the definition of "life and death" that permits violation of Jewish law)? He answers that Tosafot was referring to the *mother*, not the child. She was in so much emotional pain that she might have died as a result. It was for this reason that Elijah allowed himself to violate the prohibition and revive the boy.[52] Thus in Jewish law, emotional pain is certainly a legitimate reason to act.

The legitimacy of psychological pain also affects the violation of the Shabbat in a different way. Normally, one may violate the Shabbat, as pointed out above, in order to save a human being, but not to save property. However, one modern Rabbinic law authority permitted a Jew to put out a fire and violate the Shabbat when his entire house was burning. He ruled that this individual was so emotionally distraught watching all his possessions being destroyed in the fire, that this would cause him to become truly ill (even life-threateningly so), and thus he permitted this action on Shabbat.[53] Similarly, it is normally forbidden to injure someone else on Shabbat, and it is certainly forbidden to kill anyone on Shabbat (in addition to the overall prohibition of murder). However, if someone is coming to rob a Jew's house (who observes Shabbat) and the Jew can kill this intruder, it is permitted for the Jew to kill the robber and violate the Shabbat rather than watch him take all of his or her possessions. The psychological pain of having to witness this scene and do nothing justifies violating Shabbat and killing the intruder.[54]

The Talmud permits a man to scrape off scabs on his flesh, which is normally forbidden as an act of beautifying oneself that is permitted only to women. But if the person is in psychological pain due to having ugly scabs on his body, it is permitted for him to violate this Jewish law.[55] For the same reason, it is normally forbidden for a man to pick out

and remove the gray hairs among the dark ones from his hair, or to dye his graying hair, as this is considered a "dress of a woman" and not normally permitted for a Jewish a man.[56] However, if a young man is prematurely graying and this causes him great embarrassment and emotional pain, Rabbi Shlomo Zalman Auerbach permits this person to violate this law and dye his hair.[57]

Psychological pain is even recognized in a Jewish courtroom. Jewish law mandates that as soon as the evidence and testimonies are presented, a Jewish judge should rule immediately. Why? Failure to do so causes unnecessary psychological pain to the plaintiffs, because they worry about the verdict. Therefore, a judge cannot delay his ruling.[58] It is also forbidden for one Jew to intentionally cause another Jew any psychological pain. (See chapters, "Propping Oneself Up" and "Putting Others Down" for a deeper analysis of this concept.) Thus, it is forbidden by Jewish law to remind a convert or a *Ba'al Teshuva*, a Jew returning to observance, of his or her sins of the past since this will cause the person unnecessary anguish.[59]

## IS EMBARRASSMENT CONSIDERED LEGITIMATE PAIN IN JUDAISM?

It is forbidden for a Jew to embarrass anyone. Judaism sees this as a grave sin that causes great pain, even greater pain than physical pain. Thus, we see in the Torah that Tamar, the righteous woman in the story, was prepared to die rather than embarrass her father-in-law, Judah, who would have had to admit that he had slept with (what he believed was) a harlot.[60] Based on this story, Rabbi Yochanan ruled that it is preferable for a Jew to throw himself or herself into a fire rather than publicly embarrass

---

52. *Responsa Igrot Moshe, Yoreh De'ah* 2:174
53. *Nishmat Avraham* 5:39, footnote 1
54. *Shemirat Shabbat Kehilchata*, chapter 32, footnote 174
55. *Shabbat* 50b with Rashi commentary
56. *Shulchan Aruch, Yoreh De'ah* 182:6
57. *Nishmat Avraham* 5:69, footnote 1
58. *Shulchan Aruch, Choshen Mishpat* 17:11
59. *Bava Metzia* 58b; Maimonides, *Hilchot Mechira* 14:13
60. *Genesis* 38:24-27

an individual.[61] Chinuch calls the pain that comes from embarrassment the greatest pain of all.[62]

Even when punishing a sinner in a Jewish court, Judaism is sensitive to the embarrassment of the sinner. Therefore, the person who is designated to administer the lashes to the sinner must have a demeanor that is weak and not strong, in order not to embarrass the sinner. And if in the course of the lashes, the sinner begins to urinate or defecate, the punishment must cease immediately in order not to embarrass this sinner and cause him undue psychological pain.[63] Therefore, it is clear that embarrassment is a form of pain that should be avoided whenever possible.

## SHOULD A JEW ENDURE PAIN TO PERFORM A MITZVAH?

Are pain and suffering legitimate reasons to excuse a Jew from performing the commandments? The answer seems to vary, depending upon the particular commandment. For example, the essence of the commandment itself on Yom Kippur is fasting, which will require certain pain and suffering for most Jews, as the Torah itself specifies and King David amplifies that a Jew *should* feel *Inui*, pain, on this day.[64] On the other hand, for other commandments, such as the Mitzvah to live in a Sukkah during the seven days of the Sukkot holiday, a Jew is *totally* excused if he or she feels the slightest pain or discomfort due to the Sukkah. The Talmud specifies that any slight sickness and pain at all or any discomfort due to weather, are valid reasons for exemption from performing this commandment.[65] Maimonides rules that if discomfort or pain is enough to break concentration while wearing Tefillin during prayers, then that Jewish man is exempt from this Mitzvah.[66] Rabbi Dovid ben Zimra ex-

tends this to other positive commandments as well, where discomfort, pain, or sickness are regarded as legitimate reasons for exemption.[67]

On the other hand, if a person's particular body makeup causes him or her pains when the person fulfills a particular commandment, the Rabbis discuss whether this Jew is nevertheless obligated fulfill the commandment that will necessarily bring pain. Most of these discussions are related to food consumption requirements and most specifically to the Seder night on Passover. Should a Jew allergic to wine have to drink the four cups? *Shulchan Aruch* and *Mishna Berurah* conclude that indeed this Jew *must* drink the wine, even if it affects him or her negatively, but only if it will not actually make the person sick enough to force him or her to lie down.[68] Fortunately today, a Jew can drink kosher grape juice instead, which was not available in the time of Rabbi Yosef Caro. Similarly, for people allergic to wheat (if eating any wheat products causes a harsh reaction), the Rabbis ruled this person must nevertheless eat Matzah on Seder night. Fortunately today, some Matzah is intentionally made from non-wheat grains (of the five acceptable grains for Matzah) to alleviate this problem. The Rabbis also ask if a person who suffers great pain from eating the bitter herbs must still eat them to fulfill this commandment. They rule that part of this commandment is to indeed feel slight pain to remember the bitterness of the Egyptian slavery, but each Jew may select from the array of acceptable bitter herbs, the one that is least painful to him or her.[69] Rabbi Asher Weiss, a contemporary expert in Jewish law, summarizes all opinions and says that a Jew need not be in so much pain that he or she becomes bedridden by performing a positive commandment. In addition, any Jewish action that will endanger any part of the body exempts a Jew from that action.[70] Another

---

61. *Sotah* 10b
62. *Sefer HaChinuch*, Mitzvah 2409
63. Maimonides, *Hilchot Sanhedrin* 16:9, 17:5
64. Leviticus 23:29, Psalms 35:13
65. *Sukkah* 26a; Maimonides, *Hilchot Sukkah* 6:2
66. Maimonides, *Hilchot Tefillin* 4:13

67. *Responsa Radvaz* 3:435, 2:687
68. *Shulchan Aruch, Orach Chaim* 472:10, *Mishna Berurah* no. 35
69. *Mishna Berurah* commentary on *Shulchan Aruch, Orach Chaim* 473, no. 43
70. *Minchat Asher, Beraishit* 39

expert in Jewish medical ethics, Rabbi Moshe Hershler, concurs with this view about pain and doing Mitzvot-commandments.[71]

It is interesting that on Shabbat there is a specific commandment to have "pleasure," which is reflected through eating. Therefore, *Shulchan Aruch* rules a Jew should normally have more meat and other tasty foods on Shabbat. However, if eating meat or any food causes a person pain or lack of pleasure, then it is preferable that the individual fasts, since for this particular person, fasting constitutes his or her "pleasure." Similarly, Rabbi Isserles rules that if a person is in psychological pain on Shabbat and crying alleviates that person's pain, then this Jew is permitted to cry on Shabbat, something that would normally be forbidden.[72]

## IS SEEKING PAIN FOR DEPRIVATION LEGITIMATE FOR JEWISH REASONS?

If a Jew intentionally seeks to deprive himself or herself and inflict some kind of pain or suffering as a means of coming closer to God, is that permitted in Judaism? This issue has been a long and ongoing debate that is found in the Talmud and continues until today. Samuel in the Talmud says a person who deprives himself of food and takes on private fasts in order to feel more spiritual and closer to God is called a sinner. He follows the view of Rabbi Elazar Hakafar who says that a *Nazir*, a person who voluntarily deprives himself of wine and other permitted activities (haircuts and ritual impurity), is a sinner that the Torah nevertheless permits (he brings a sin offering when he completes the Nazirite period), because he denied himself pleasures of this world.[73] Rabbi Yossi also agrees that a Jew should not take on extra fast days for himself.[74] On the other hand, on the same Talmudic page that discusses the Nazirite, Rabbi Elazar vehemently disagrees with Rabbi Elazar Hakafar (two different Rabbi

Elazars), and says that a Nazirite is called holy in the Torah and is therefore praiseworthy. Moreover, the person who denies himself or herself more pleasures in life is more praiseworthy.[75] These two opinions represent opposite ends of the spectrum about the concept of suffering pain in order to come closer to God. This debate continues throughout Jewish history in each era, including the Middle Ages, the conceptual battle between Mitnagdim and Chasidim (beginning in the eighteenth century), and up until the present day.

However, regarding one great Rabbi, we see that he himself brings both opinions. On the one hand, Maimonides calls the Nazirite a sinner who follows the wrong path in life by denying himself life's pleasures and bringing upon himself unnecessary pain.[76] But the very same Maimonides later on admires the Nazirite as a holy person and praises him, comparing the Nazirite to a prophet![77] How can the same Rabbi both condemn and praise the Nazirite? Apparently, Maimonides was speaking and teaching all Jews about two different models, two distinct ideal paths of life for a Jew. One path is that of a *Tzadik*, a righteous person, who follows all of the details of Jewish law precisely, without deviating or extending one iota beyond the precise path. This is the path of a *Tzadik*, which condemns going beyond the specific requirement in any direction and comes close to God by following the details of Jewish law. On the other hand, Maimonides also defines the path of the *Chasid* (not to be confused with today's Chassidut which did not exist in the time of Maimonides), who goes beyond what is required and tries to come close to God by going beyond the letter of the Law. Maimonides defines a "*Chasid*" as he who goes way beyond the letter of the law in observance.[78] This model tries to do anything and everything beyond what is required, in order

71. *Halacha U'refuah*, "Terufot U'refuot B'Shabbat" 8:4
72. *Shulchan Aruch, Orach Chaim* 250:2, 288:2
73. *Ta'anit* 11a
74. *Ta'anit* 22b
75. *Ta'anit* 11a
76. Maimonides, *Hilchot De'ot* 6:14
77. Maimonides, *Hilchot Nazir* 10:15
78. Mishna *Avot* 6:1 with Maimonides commentary; Maimonides, Introduction to *Shmoneh Perakim*, chapter 4

to become a better Jew. This would include the *Nazir* model that is praised by Maimonides. Both models and paths are alluded to in Psalms, as King David calls God both a *Tzadik*, righteous, and *Chasid*, pious,[79] and Maimonides, in explaining the obligation of each Jew to imitate God, cites both the model of imitating God as the *Tzadik* and imitating God as the *Chasid*.[80] *Shulchan Aruch* seems to cite both paths as well, when ruling on the issue of whether or not a Jew should intentionally put himself or herself in a situation of pain and suffering in order to come closer to God. He writes that if a Jew can easily fast without too much pain (and is "built" for suffering pain for a higher purpose), then he is called holy. But if fasting will impede this Jew's health (showing that this path is not for this person) and he or she will suffer greatly but persists in his or her fast, this individual is called a sinner.[81]

Whichever path each Jew chooses, there are limits, however. All of the Rabbis seem to agree that a worker may not fast or put himself or herself in pain even if he or she desires to do so, since it will adversely affect and reduce his or her output, and thus hurt the employer.[82] Similarly, regarding a Torah scholar, Rabbi Yosef Caro rules that he should not fast voluntarily, since the fast will affect his productivity as a Torah scholar, and is therefore prohibited. However, if the entire Jewish community is fasting, then the Torah scholar may also fast in order not to separate himself from the community. For the same reason, a Jewish teacher, who needs to be fully effective in the classroom, is prohibited from fasting voluntarily.[83] It seems, therefore, that the debate about which path is ideal for a Jew and whether a Jew should intentionally incur pain and suffering for spiritual reasons, is essentially unresolved. But it is clear that even when a Jew is permitted to suffer some pain in performing Jewish acts that will bring him or her closer to God, the pain must be minimal and never debilitating.

---

79. Psalms 145:17
80. Maimonides, *Sefer HaMitzvot*, Mitzvah 8
81. *Shulchan Aruch, Orach Chaim* 571:1

82. Tosefta *Bava Metzia* 8:2
83. *Shulchan Aruch, Orach Chaim* 571:1

I N THE PAST FEW YEARS, THE SITUA-
tion has unfortunately played itself out
many times in many countries. Kidnapping people for ransom has been on increase
around the world. The State of Israel has suffered more than most, especially in the drawn
out and sometimes public negotiations in releasing Gilad Shalit, an Israeli soldier captured
by Hamas in 2011. The details may change a
bit, but the basic dilemma facing each country is the same, time and time again. One such
scenario: A terrorist organization dedicated to
the destruction of the State of Israel kidnaps a
civilian Israeli Jewish woman. To secure her
safe return, Hamas demands in exchange the
release of 500 Hamas members currently in
Israelis jails or 100 million dollars (that we
know will be used to further Hamas terror activities). Assuming there are no other viable
alternatives to securing her release, should the
ransom be paid or not?

This chapter will attempt to discuss the
issues and ethics related to securing or not
securing the release of this kidnapped woman.
What is the right action to take from the Jewish
perspective? What is the value in Judaism of
redeeming kidnapped victims? What exactly
are the two sides of this emotional conflict,
which often tear a nation and families apart?
When does Judaism allow or not allow a ransom to be paid? Even though this seems to be
a twenty-first century issue, traditional Jewish sources show that this dilemma has been
around for thousands of years, and Judaism
has much to say about how to resolve it.

## HOW IMPORTANT IS IT TO HELP ANY JEW IN DANGER?

The Torah obligation for a Jew to help anyone
in trouble is clear and has been discussed elsewhere in this volume. The basis of this law is
the Torah verse prohibiting a Jew from standing idly by when another person is in danger

– any danger.[1] Unlike the values of other dem-
ocratic societies, Judaism *does* pronounce an
individual "guilty" if a person merely stands
around and does nothing when in a situation
and position to help someone in dire need.[2]
Based on this Jewish concept, today's Israel is
the only country in the world that has an actual law obligating *any* person to get involved
and help someone in danger (not merely professionals like a doctor in an emergency room
who notices abuse in a patient or an off-duty
lifeguard who sees someone drowning). A
person, then, can be prosecuted for not doing
anything and not helping when a person in
danger could have been be saved.

Although the obligation to assist is a general
Torah obligation, it also directly affects Jewish
thinking and the responsibility regarding the
kidnapped victim. If Jews really can do something to help or influence the victim's return,
then they cannot "hide" behind the concept
that "it's the government's problem and the
decision of the politicians." Even if people can
only influence their elected officials to act or
react, then this verse demands that they cannot stand idly by and do nothing about the
situation.

A kidnapped victim's life is always considered in danger. Jewish law states that even if
there is a small doubt if a person's life is in
actual danger, a Jew must violate Shabbat
and do everything in his or her power to save
someone, even if the actual chance of saving
the person is very remote.[3] This would also apply to a kidnapped victim. The Talmud states
that every life is equal to the infinite value of
the entire world,[4] which also obligates a Jew to
save the kidnapped person if possible. Based
on these sources, logic therefore demands
that the ransom – whether it requires money

---

1. Leviticus 19:16
2. *Shulchan Aruch, Choshen Mishpat* 426:1
3. *Shulchan Aruch, Orach Chaim* 329:3
4. *Sanhedrin* 37a

or releasing jailed Hamas members – should be paid to free this captured individual. At first glance, it seems that this action should be the proper response, even if the freed terrorists will later commit terror acts in the future or if the paid money is used to help kill people, since the life saved now is a definite factor, while the potential future acts of terror may or may not actually occur.[5] (This concept will be amplified in detail below.)

## THE SPECIFIC OBLIGATION TO REDEEM CAPTIVES

Until now, we have discussed the obligation to the kidnapped victim under the general rubric of helping others in trouble. But Judaism has much to say about the specific obligation vis-à-vis kidnapped people. Maimonides quotes seven specific Mitzvot-commandments that apply to this situation, obligating the Jew to save a kidnapped person (six from the Torah and one from the *Ketuvim*-Biblical Writings).[6] Maimonides also uses the phrase that this Mitzvah-commandment of redeeming hostages is both "a great Mitzvah," and in similar but somewhat different words, "an important Mitzvah" and that no other Mitzvah supersedes it. He does not write this about any other commandment in the Torah! This indicates how important and essential this obligation is. Maimonides also uses the specific phrase, "he who ignores" redeeming the captive, the same phraseology discussed above regarding "doing nothing" and "do not stand idly by." He also assumes that every kidnapped victim's life is in danger and Jews must act accordingly.

Thus, based on the words of Maimonides, it seems that there can be no question that Jews must do *anything and everything to save this* person whose life is in danger now, whether it be by returning potential terrorists (who may or may not commit future murders, versus the immediate danger for this woman), or by giving them money that can be used for terror

activities. *Shulchan Aruch* reiterates the words of Maimonides and adds some of his own, continuing the theme showing how special and important this particular commandment is. He also calls this obligation a "great Mitzvah."[7]

In addition to quoting many of the words of Maimonides, *Shulchan Aruch* also pens another Jewish law proving that the Mitzvah to redeem captives is indeed different from and more important than any other Mitzvah in the Torah. Normally, it is forbidden to divert money donated specifically to build a synagogue to use for any other worthy cause, such as feeding the poor or another Mitzvah (unless one receives specific permission from the donor to change the recipient of the funds). But the Mitzvah of redeeming captives is the one exception in all of Jewish law, which allows the diversion of funds (without asking the donors) in order to redeem captives, even if the funds were collected for any other holy purposes.[8] Thus, the importance of redeeming hostages places it in a separate and higher category, and shows that the phrases about "important Mitzvah" or "great Mitzvah" are not just expressions, but have definite implications in Jewish law, as this commandment seems to supersede every other Mitzvah vis-à-vis using designated funds.

*Shulchan Aruch* then goes even further than Maimonides and equates delaying the redeeming of hostages (when one is able to do so) to *murder*.[9] This shows us another dimension of this Mitzvah – that the time pressure to redeem hostages as soon as possible is also a crucial factor in Jewish law. Even a small delay for a hostage may indeed be the difference between life and death. *Shulchan Aruch* is also telling us that even if a person does eventually redeem a hostage, that person can still be culpable, if he or she could have accomplished this Mitzvah earlier.

Thus, every source presented until now points to the overwhelming obligation and

---

5. *Ketuvot* 12b
6. Maimonides, *Hilchot Matnot Aniyim* 8:10

7. *Shulchan Aruch, Yoreh De'ah* 252:2
8. *Shulchan Aruch, Yoreh De'ah* 252:1
9. *Shulchan Aruch, Yoreh De'ah* 252:3

urgency to "do whatever it takes," without reservation, to pay the ransom and redeem the woman hostage in our scenario. But then comes the next Halacha-Jewish law in *Shulchan Aruch* and completely negates everything we have shown until now.

## WHY HOSTAGES SHOULD NOT BE REDEEMED IN JEWISH LAW

After all of the sources showing how important it is to redeem hostages, *Shulchan Aruch*, in the very next paragraph, essentially says that is it forbidden to redeem hostages – i.e., the maximum one can pay is "the amount that the kidnapped victim is worth," which is a very insignificant amount (the value of the body of a servant, perhaps a few hundred dollars) that no kidnapper would accept or want in exchange.[10] What could this possibly signify, in light of all the previous sources stating the opposite concept?

The *Shulchan Aruch* was certainly aware that kidnapping was (and continues to be today) a "business," and each time a ransom is paid, it encourages those same kidnappers (and other kidnappers) to continue their crime with new victims or repeated kidnappings of the same person. However if the kidnappers knew in advance that there would be no chance that the ransom would be paid (or only a very small amount would be), then kidnapping in that society would virtually cease. That is why Maharam (Rav Meir of Rothenberg), who was seized for ransom by a Duke in Lombardy in 1286, refused to allow himself to be ransomed. Although the Jews in his community collected the exorbitant ransom money demanded, the Maharam did not to allow them to pay it: he died seven years later in a dungeon. He used the same rationale that *Shulchan Aruch* later adopted. If the greatest Rabbi could not be ransomed, all future kidnappers would hesitate to kidnap *any* Jew for ransom. It would not be worth the trouble or risk if little or no ransom were to be paid.

Hamas and any of the other terrorist organizations of today make the very same calculation. Each time an exorbitant ransom is indeed paid by the Israeli government and a hostage is then released, numerous terrorist organizations immediately and inevitably make new proclamations about future kidnappings, and often follow through on their threats.

What is the concept of the amount of "the money that he is worth" mentioned as the maximum ransom that can be paid, and how much money are we talking about? There is a minority opinion of Radvaz that this concept means the going rate of kidnapped victims (i.e., that we can pay a large sum, as long as the money paid for a Jew is not more that the "going rate" for a non-Jewish kidnapped victim).[11] But the majority opinion is that "the money he is worth" is the value (already mentioned in the Torah) for the physical work of a servant or slave, and it is a relatively small amount (not more than a few hundred dollars).[12] In those days, it was not uncommon for a kidnapped victim to be sold as a slave. Thus, the small amount of ransom permitted was intentionally low in order to discourage future kidnappings.

So the dilemma in Jewish law itself is almost palpable. On the one hand, Jews are to do everything to save the life of the victim because of the highest value of human life. On the other hand, by saving that life and paying ransom, Jews are encouraging future kidnappings and potentially putting many other lives in danger. This was the dilemma faced by the Rabbis at the time of the Talmud, during the time of *Shulchan Aruch*, and even today. Which value and whose needs (the individual victim's or society's) come first in the case posed above and in every kidnapping case? On the one hand, everyone's heart goes out to the kidnapped victims and their families, but on the other hand, a society cannot repeatedly give in to terrorists who will then be emboldened to continue kidnapping, which will lead to even higher ransoms demanded (the

---

10. *Shulchan Aruch, Yoreh De'ah* 252:4

11. *Responsa Radvaz*, 1:40
12. *Responsa Maharam* 25

release of captured terrorists or money to fund terror), subsequently leading to even more kidnappings. This cycle and ethical conflict is palpable within all the prior sources shown above, even in *Shulchan Aruch-Code of Jewish Law*, pressuring Jews to pay the ransom and do it as quickly as possible to free the hostage. And then the same *Shulchan Aruch* suddenly says "no" – do not pay the ransom.

*Shulchan Aruch* even shows his ambivalence by adding in that very same Halacha-Jewish law that an individual person *can* indeed redeem himself for *as much as he wants and needs to pay* in order to free himself.[13] This shows the great desire to free a hostage, as long as the hostage takers will understand that it is the individual, and not the public, who supported this ransom and raised this large sum. This unusual act by an individual will not necessarily encourage future terrorists to kidnap just anyone.

What is the basis in Jewish law for the ambivalence of *Shulchan Aruch*? How do these laws translate into what Jews are supposed to do today in the twenty-first century? Does it make a difference if the kidnappers are terrorists who vow to destroy the Jewish people? Does it make a difference if the negotiations are with the Israeli government rather than with private individuals?

## THE TALMUDIC BASIS OF THE CONFLICT AND RULINGS OF SHULCHAN ARUCH

*Shulchan Aruch* bases his objection to paying a large sum to the kidnappers on the Mishna that gives two opinions of why a large sum may not be paid to the kidnappers. The first Rabbi in the Mishna says that the reason why one may not pay ransom is *Tikun Olam* (improving the world), while Rabbi Shimon ben Gamliel states that the reason is "the enacted rule of kidnapping."[14] But what do these ideas signify exactly, and how do they affect our discussion

and explain our problem about whether to pay or not to pay?

The Talmud asks the question about the definition of and differences between these two concepts.[15] *Tikun Olam* signifies that if the exorbitant ransom is paid, then this will encourage other kidnappers or the same kidnappers to kidnap the same person again and again. (Apparently then, like today, it was relatively easy to kidnap someone.) Thus, by not paying an exorbitant ransom the "world will be improved" by limiting the number of overall kidnappings in the future. Rabbi Shimon ben Galmliel's worry ("the enacted rule of kidnapping") is to try to prevent the ill treatment of hostages. If more than one hostage is kidnapped and a large amount is spent for one hostage, but little or nothing is offered for a second hostage, then all the wrath of the kidnappers will be suffered by the second hostage. Thus, it is better to pay nothing or very little for any hostage in order to protect the welfare of all hostages. The Talmud then asks in which case these two reasons would make a real difference, and it answers that when there is only one hostage taken, the reason of Rabbi Shimon ben Gamliel would not come into play at all. Most of the later authorities (as we saw in *Shulchan Aruch*) adopt the first reason in the Mishna – pay little in order to prevent future kidnappings.

But in the Talmud, we already see the tension between the pain over the capture of a loved one and the logical policy of not giving in to terrorists or kidnappers. Immediately after explaining the reason why we cannot give in to kidnappers and pay them large ransoms, the Talmud states that when Levi ben Darga's daughter was kidnapped, he paid an exceedingly high price to redeem her, contrary to what the Mishna and Gemara just stated. Although the Talmud questions this act since it was against its policy and Jewish law regarding kidnapping, we do not specifically see that the Gemara scolded Levi ben Darga for his act, and it did not conclude that he was wrong to

---

13. *Shulchan Aruch, Yoreh De'ah* 252:4
14. *Mishna Gittin* 4:6

15. *Gittin* 45a

do what he did. Apparently, Jewish law even in the Talmud's time understood and was sensitive to the feelings of pain of a father and his need to save his daughter's life.

The Talmud brings another case in which a wife is kidnapped and the fear is that she will be repeatedly kidnapped after the ransom is paid by her husband, until all of the husband's money runs out. The Gemara struggles between the emotional forces pushing for a husband to redeem his wife again and again each time she is kidnapped, and the logic pushing a husband not to redeem her at all and not to give in to the pressure (which would minimize repeated capture and perhaps even secure her release if the kidnappers realized no ransom would be paid for her). The Gemara concludes that the first time the wife is kidnapped, the husband should give into the kidnappers' demands and pay the ransom (as they will probably kill her if he never pays, and perhaps they will not kidnap her again). The Gemara says that he *may* redeem her if they do kidnap her again, but he is not obligated to, because his funds will run out and they may kidnap her again and eventually kill her.[16] What is the logic of this law? Unlike the limitations placed upon the amount of ransom paid for others, a man's wife seems to be in a separate category. Since by Jewish law a person's spouse is equated to the person himself or herself,[17] it is permissible to pay as much as needed to redeem one's spouse, just as we learned above that it is permissible to pay as much as needed to redeem oneself with one's own funds. However, the Talmud is also speaking logically here (and not telling a husband that if he loves his wife more, then he may redeem her more than one time). If a husband continually pays the ransom demand for repeated capture of his wife, all of his funds will eventually be depleted. Thus, the Talmud gives him the option and suggests only paying in full the first time

the wife is kidnapped, hoping the kidnapping will stop thereafter.

## THIS CONFLICT CONTINUES TODAY

This next section we will try to develop an approach to understanding the logic of kidnapping today, which will also help us understand this Jewish law and what Jews should do in today's hostage situations brought about by terrorists. This may also help clear up the seemingly contradictory statements in the Jewish law espoused to this point. This understanding will also be helpful in trying to comprehend the Israeli government's radical changed response to kidnappings by terrorists. For the first thirty-five years of the existence of the State of Israel, the official policy of the Israeli government was never to negotiate with terrorists and hijackers. Everyone understood this approach, as this was cited in *Shulchan Aruch* above in not paying exorbitant ransoms. If the Israelis had given in and let Arab criminal prisoners free in exchange for hostages, then it would have only encouraged terrorists to continue to kidnap more Israelis. But this policy changed in 1985.

Long before Gilad Shalit, the solider in the Israel Defense Forces who was captured on June 26, 2006 and was traded for one thousand Arab terrorists on October 18, 2011, the most famous prisoner swap in the history of the State of Israel took place between Israel and the PLO on May 21, 1985. It was known as the Jibril Deal, because among the 1,150 terrorist prisoners freed by Israel was Fatah terrorist Ahmed Jibril. In exchange, Israel received three soldiers, live prisoners of war: Hezi Shai, who had been captured in the battle of Sultan Yaaqub during the Peace for Galilee War nearly three years earlier, Yosef Grof and Nissim Salem, captured in Lebanon in September 1982.

There have been several times, thereafter, when Israel has indeed returned many jailed members of terrorist organizations, even for the remains of kidnapped soldiers who had died. This policy change seems to run counter to the Jewish law cited above (not that the

---

16. *Ketuvot* 52a
17. *Berachot* 24a; *Shulchan Aruch, Even Ha'ezer* 78:2; *Mishna Berurah on Shulchan Aruch, Orach Chaim* 366:1

Israeli government always follows Jewish law) and Jewish values.

Why did Israel change its policy and decide to "give in" to terrorist demands? Is there any justification in Jewish law for this "revised" policy?

## DIFFERENCES BETWEEN VALUES OF THE COMMUNITY & INDIVIDUAL

Based on a class taught by Rabbi Dr. Moshe Tendler, we will attempt to discover a new outlook to resolve our issue, both in the case of the kidnapped person described at the outset and the "revised" policy of the Israeli government.

The Mishna discusses a number of situations involving values, dilemmas, and dire choices regarding two communities in distress. If there are two towns, one with enough water for its own drinking needs (Town A) and the other town without any water for its drinking needs (Town B), everyone agrees that Town A need not give its drinking water to Town B in order for Town B to survive, because giving Town B water would put its own citizens in mortal danger in order to save the citizens of the other town. This follows the general principle and Jewish value that "saving my life comes before saving your life" first enumerated by Rabbi Akiva[18] and then followed by both the early codes of Jewish law[19] as well as the later codes.[20] Similarly, if both towns have enough water for drinking, and Town A has, in addition, enough water for its laundry needs, while Town B has enough water for drinking but not laundry, Town A need not give its laundry water to Town B. But the dilemma arises when Town A has enough water for both drinking and laundry needs and Town B does not even have enough water for drinking.

If Town A has enough water for both drinking and laundry, and Town B needs water to drink for its very survival, logic and basic Jewish values about saving a life seem to dictate

that Town A give its laundry water to Town B. This is indeed the opinion of the *Tanna Kamma*, the first opinion in the Mishna. But Rabbi Yossi disagrees and says that Town A should *not* give its laundry water to Town B, even if Town B's citizens will die as a result. He specifically says that Town A's laundry needs comes before the lives of the people Town B.[21] How can this be so?

Furthermore, the *Sheiltot* of Hai Gaon says that Jewish law in this case follows Rabbi Yossi and not Tanna Kamma (whose opinion is usually followed in an argument between the two).[22] What is the logic? How can saving lives in one place be secondary to laundry needs in another place? After all the sources learned above about the importance of saving lives, how can *Sheiltot* rule according to Rabbi Yossi and essentially "kill" the people in Town B?

*Ha'amek She'aila* commentary on the *Sheiltot* (authored by Rav Naftali Tzvi Yehuda Berlin, the Netziv) writes that analyzing the needs of the community is evaluated differently from analyzing the needs of the individual. He says that the case of the towns with the laundry water seems identical to the more famous argument of Ben Petura and Rabbi Akiva of two people walking in the desert and one has a canteen with enough water to keep one person alive, and both need it to survive. In that case, although Ben Petura says the water should be split between them, Jewish law follows Rabbi Akiva's opinion that the owner of the canteen has first claim and should not give it away, citing the "my life comes before your life" principle outlined above.[23] Netziv and almost all other Rabbis rule according to Rabbi Akiva, i.e., that you should keep your canteen and not share it because your life takes precedence. But then the Netziv asks: What is the logic of Ben Petura? It seems to make no sense to split the water and allow both to die!

Netziv explains Ben Petura's logic and says that Ben Petura was looking at the long-range

---

18. *Bava Metzia* 62[1]
19. *Tur, Yoreh De'ah* 251
20. *Pri Megadim* on *Shulchan Aruch, Orach Chaim* 72; *Chochmat Adam* 145

21. *Nedarim* 80b
22. *Sheiltot* of Hai Gaon, *Parshat Re'eh*, 147, s.v. "Beram Tzarich"
23. *Bava Metzia* 62a

picture. If they both shared the canteen, then both would stay alive a little longer and maybe tomorrow someone would come along and rescue them both. Rabbi Akiva looked only at the situation as it is right now before us, and on that basis he ruled that the owner of the canteen should keep it and live. While we rule like Rabbi Akiva in the case of the individual (looking at the case only in terms of the present situation), Netziv says that we *do* rule like Ben Petura when it comes to the community, and as a community we are obligated to look at the long-range situation.[24]

What would eventually happen to Town A if it gave its laundry water to Town B and did not do any laundry? Eventually, in a few months' time, without any water to do laundry, disease would become rampant in Town A. Then people would surely die in Town A or move away, destroying the town in either case. Because of this long-term view, Rabbi Yossi rules that Town A keeps its laundry water, in order to save itself and its citizens in the long run, even if people in Town B will die earlier due to thirst. And that is why *Sheiltot* rules according to Rabbi Yossi, since Town A's long-term needs come before Town B's short-term or long-term needs. Based on this new understanding of the difference between the individual's needs (immediate issue and resolution) and the community's needs (long-range view), we can now resolve and understand the rulings regarding most or all of our issues in the kidnapping case.

When *Shulchan Aruch* wrote that the individual can do everything and pay anything in order to save himself (quoted above), he was referring to the immediate problem of saving his life as a kidnapped victim and that individual's need. From a short-term perspective, the individual is permitted and is actually obligated to do everything in his or her power to resolve the current situation and redeem himself or his loved one. He is not concerned (nor should he be concerned) with the long-term impact of such an act. The community, however, must be concerned with the long-range

impact of paying the ransom. Besides causing repeated kidnappings, paying the ransom repeatedly could also deplete the entire wealth of the community, as kidnapping could become a regular activity. Therefore, the long-term needs of the community are served by *not* paying the ransom, which will stop kidnappers from capturing individuals and prevent future deaths (since kidnappers will know in advance that the community will not pay ransom). In that same Jewish law about the individual's right to spend as much as it takes in order to save himself, *Shulchan Aruch* writes immediately thereafter that Jews (as a community) cannot pay more than "his value as a laborer" (i.e., a few hundred dollars), but this law limiting the ransom that is paid is addressed to the community.[25] Thus, the individual's needs are served best by paying the high ransom now and doing anything and everything to save himself or a loved one who is kidnapped. But the community's needs are served best by paying very little or nothing to redeem any captive. That is also why *Shulchan Aruch* later says that a father should do everything to redeem a child, and every person should do everything to redeem a captured relative – this is done on an individual basis.[26]

Without mentioning the case of the two towns, Rabbi Eliezer Waldenberg, in his *Tzitz Eliezer,* comes to the same conclusion about community needs being different from private needs.[27] He explains that normally (from an individual standpoint) we would reason and rule that no soldier may ever endanger himself to go into a war zone since a Jew may not place himself in mortal danger. But this is a Jewish law related to an individual. Since the soldier is representing the community, whose long term needs are not about this particular soldier, but the greater good of its citizens long term, a government may indeed send a soldier to a war zone (this is similar to policemen and firemen who put themselves in danger every day),

---

24. *Ha'amek She'eilah* commentary on *Sheiltot* 147

25. *Shulchan Aruch, Yoreh De'ah* 252:4
26. *Shulchan Aruch, Yoreh De'ah* 252:12
27. *Responsa Tzitz Eliezer* 13:100

since its long-term needs of the community are served by these actions. In his responsa, Rabbi Kook also agrees and states specifically that Jewish laws and the values of a community are different from the Jewish laws and values of an individual.[28]

This same concept helps us understand other similar policies and Jewish laws. In that same section in which he writes about hostages, right after stating that the community cannot pay more than a minimal amount but an individual can pay as much as he needs to, *Shulchan Aruch* states that the community *can* and *should* pay the full ransom for a *Talmid Chacham*-Torah scholar, or a potential *Talmid Chacham*.[29] What is the logic? Assuming that this person is the greatest Torah authority in the community, the public must pay his ransom, since losing him would severely damage the long-term Torah needs of the community. And thus, full ransom should be paid for this particular person, even if it will encourage future kidnappings. This payment serves the long-term needs of the community.

It is interesting that in this, *Shulchan Aruch* thus ruled *against* the actions of Maharam of Rothenberg, who was undoubtedly the greatest Torah sage of his generation and of his community, but nevertheless refused to let himself be ransomed. Perhaps Maharam, knowing his particular community in Germany, believed that the Torah future of the community would not be in grave danger without him, but the threat of multiple kidnappings posed a greater risk to the future of his community.

This will also help us understand the logic of the Israeli government in giving back many terrorists in order to obtain captured live soldiers. When the Israelis gave back hundreds of criminals and terrorists in Israeli jails in exchange for a few captured Israeli soldiers, they were strongly criticized, as people feared this would lead to an increase in immediate terrorism, which it did. However, some of the generals of the army explained at the time

that this action served the long-term needs of the State of Israel, not the short term. The act of returning many terrorists to free a soldier who was held hostage, both in 1985 and in 2011, showed every soldier in the Israeli army that the government will do *anything* to get back its captured soldiers, even giving back known terrorists. This value – that soldiers know that no matter what, the government will do anything to save them – is an important concept for the Israeli army and for each soldier. The long-term effect of this knowledge is that since every soldier is aware of the lengths to which the government will go on his behalf, this will encourage the Israeli soldier to fight harder and be more loyal and effective. This long-term need *may* supersede the short-term harm terrorists may cause. Only a general who knows the entire situation and has the long-term perspective can make the judgment of whether or not the short-term harm of releasing terrorists who may kill Israeli civilians is worth the long-term benefit of a better and superior army that might be better able to defeat the enemy at war. If the "experts" determined that the enhanced power of its fighting force outweighs the damage from the released terrorists, then it would be valid, according to Rabbi Yossi, the *Sheiltot*, and *Ha'amek She'aila*. This seems to have been the rationale in the exchanges.

This new concept also helps explain a very strange ruling of Shmuel in the Talmud.[30] He says that a community may kill up to one-sixth of its own population without punishment. Tosafot explains that this refers to wartime. Based on the discussion above, we might understand what is being stated here. If, in order to survive and be victorious in war, it is necessary that many citizens in the population be sacrificed, it is permissible up to sixteen percent (one-sixth), since only this painful sacrifice will guarantee the future survival of that Jewish community. Shmuel also looked at the long-term benefit versus the terrible short-term loss of life.

---

28. *Responsa Mishpat Kohen*, Israel, 143
29. *Shulchan Aruch, Yoreh De'ah* 252:4

30. *Shavuot* 35b with Tosafot commentary

## A FURTHER IMPLICATION FOR A JEWISH SOCIETY OF TODAY

Based on the entire discussion and the new idea of looking at the long term needs of the community, the following dilemma can also be raised in a society that wants to live by Jewish and Torah principles: It is known that in the State of Israel, as well as in most countries in the world, there are many sick people who have non-functioning kidneys and are kept alive through dialysis or kidney machines. Similarly, many people today replace their non-functioning lungs with machines that allow them to breathe, and there are even artificial hearts (when transplants are not available) that can keep people alive. The number of people who need these machines far exceeds their availability, and many people die each year as a result. If a Torah-observant member of the Knesset (parliament) is involved in the finance committee and votes on the entire budget (before it is presented to the entire Knesset), then which expenses should be spent by overall budget and which should not be used? Each budget is filled with many line items, costing hundreds of millions of shekels to pay for the building of new roads, tens of millions of shekels to pay for public gardens, and millions of shekels to subsidize the Israeli Philharmonic Orchestra. If instead, all of this money was diverted to be used to pay for additional kidney or lung machines, then hundreds of lives would immediately be saved each year. Since saving the lives of people who are dying is the highest and most important value in Judaism, how can this observant Jew ever vote for a budget that does not divert every shekel to fill this crucial need? As a Torah Jew observing Jewish law, is this person ever permitted to vote for

a budget that allocates money for roads, gardens, and orchestras, knowing that if these monies would go instead towards machines that supply artificial kidneys, lungs, and hearts, hundreds or even thousands of more lives will be saved during the upcoming year?

If this member of the Knesset thinks about the needs of the individuals in Israeli society, then indeed, he would be obligated to vote only for these life-saving machines and nothing else in the budget. But as was pointed out above, when it comes to a community or Israeli society, the crucial element is to look at the broad, long-term view. What would happen if no money at all would be allocated for roads, gardens, and the Israeli Philharmonic? In the short term, the harm would be relatively inconsequential, like the city without water for laundry needs. But in the long term, parks and gardens would disappear and affect the quality of life of the Israeli population. Without repaired roads and new roads to match the demand of increased traffic, the inconvenience would greatly frustrate Israeli motorists. The loss of the Philharmonic Orchestra would engender protests from devotees of classical music. People would become angry and eventually people would probably leave the country en masse or simply stop paying taxes. With many fewer citizens, the state budget's income would be greatly reduced, the army's need for enough soldiers would not be satisfied, and very future of the state would be jeopardized.

Therefore, by looking at the long-term needs of the State of Israel, even an observant Knesset member could and should vote for these gardens, roads, and the Israeli Philharmonic as part of the Jewish law obligation to insure the long-term viability of the State.

# PROPPING ONESELF UP - *GENAIVAT DA'AT*

THERE ARE TWO UNETHICAL WAYS that people often make themselves feel superior to others. They get others to look up to them, even though they do not deserve the attention or praise. Or, these people say or do something to make others feel badly about themselves. Essentially these are two sides of the same coin. Therefore, this chapter will gaining favor in the eyes of others without deserving it, called *Genaivat Da'at*. What exactly is the sin of telling somebody something so that he or she should feel better about you? Why is it a sin at all? How can we define this concept? What exactly is forbidden and permitted to do or say in this area? Finally, how severe is this sin on the scale of Jewish transgressions?

## THE DEFINITION AND TORAH PRECEDENTS OF FALSELY PROPPING ONESELF UP

The Hebrew term for falsely propping oneself up, called *Genaivat Da'at*, which technically means "stealing someone else's thoughts." It signifies a conscious effort by an individual to look better than he or she actually deserves to be viewed in the eyes of another person or other people or, similarly, it means making an object for sale appear more desirable and valuable that it really is. There are two places, one in the Torah and other in the Prophets, where this phrase is used. The first relates to the evil Lavan, after his son-in-law Jacob, who lived in Lavan's home for twenty years, snuck away at night because he was afraid that Lavan would never let him leave. Lavan's reaction to Jacob's leaving (when he caught up to him) was to say, "What did you do? Why did you *steal my heart*?" In the next verse he again says, "*you stole me*," because he escaped and ran away.[1] Rashi says these phrases in the verse refer to

*Genaivat Da'at* – i.e., that Lavan accused Jacob of appearing to be friendly, appreciative, and satisfied with his life in Lavan's house, when he obviously was not. Chatam Sofer comments that this feigning by Jacob to Lavan would generally be forbidden for a Jew, even towards a non-Jew like Lavan, but he explains that Jacob legitimately did this only because he was afraid for his life.[2]

Later on, Abasalom, King David's son, wanted to ingratiate himself with the people. He took chariots and horses and placed fifty people in front of him in order to impress the masses. When some individuals had a lawsuit against another person, and there was no one to hear the case, Abasalom would stand by the gates of the city (the place of judgment) and tell people that if he were made a judge (though what he really meant was, "if he were king"), he would hear their case and give them justice. When anyone came to bow to him, Absalom would kiss the person's hand. (He did all of this to make the people feel he was on their side and cared about them, when in truth he was not and did not.) The verse says that Absalom "stole the hearts of the people" through these actions.[3] Absalom made the people feel that he was a better person and more deserving than he really was, and that he cared about them much more than he actually did. This is *Genaivat Da'at* – i.e., propping oneself in the eyes of others when it is undeserved.

These stories and phrases are reflected in Jewish law. The original source in the Mishna forbids taking objects for sale and making them appear better and more worthy than they actually are, in order to be sold at a higher price. This is forbidden as *Genaivat Da'at*. Thus, the Mishna says that a vendor of fruit may not mix up fruit of better value with fruit of lesser

1. Genesis 31:26-27

2. Rashi and Chatam Sofer commentaries to Genesis 31:26-27
3. Samuel II 15:1-6 with Ralbag commentary

value, since it will all appear to be of better quality (and more expensive) than it really is.[4] The Mishna continues with other cases. It is forbidden for the same reason to mix less expensive wine with more expensive wine unless the combination made it superior wine. Similarly, it is forbidden to dilute the wine with water (lowering the quality), without informing the customer that this was done to the wine. In the same vein, the Mishna forbids the mixing of five different qualities of grain, making it appear as though the best quality was present throughout the grain. One may not take the refuse (the non-edible part) of the fruit from the top, put it in the middle, and then sell the entire bin of fruit by weight, making it appear that the entire amount is all edible fruit, thereby deceiving the customer. Finally, it is forbidden to take used items and paint to them in order to make them appear (and sell) as new. This is true with cattle and even with people who are servants. The principle remains: It is forbidden to present something as better than it really is. This is the basic law, but the implications for daily life go far beyond the marketplace and laws of Jewish commerce.

## EXAMPLES OF *GENAIVAT DA'AT* IN THE TALMUD AND IN JEWISH LAW

Deceiving people to make them think you or your objects are better than they actually are, is defined in the Tosefta as a form of stealing, the verb used in the Scripture. In fact, Tosefta says that of the seven types of theft in Judaism, this kind of theft – making people think that you or your items are better than the really are – is the worst type of theft possible.[5] The Talmud gives several example of this.

Many of the examples cited in the Talmud describe situations in which *Genaivat Da'at* is violated today as common practice in twenty-first century society.[6] For example, a person may not invite a friend over for a meal if he

knows in advance that the friend cannot or will not accept the invitation. The reason that the person doing the inviting violates *Genaivat Da'at,* in that he or she receives undeserved good will from the invited guest. The invited person thinks that the seemingly potential host really cares about him or her, when the truth is that the person had no real intention to invite the guest at all. (If the inviter truly wants the person to be his guest, even if he knows the friend cannot, it is *not* a violation.) This can prompt undeserved good will that may cause the invited person to unnecessarily go out of his way to do a favor in the future, and, thus, this is a violation of *Genaivat Da'at*, which is improper and forbidden in Judaism. This concept is further demonstrated by another case on the same page in the Talmud.

It was the custom at that time to store wine in large barrels. Apparently, once a barrel was opened, the wine started to gradually deteriorate. Thus, it was a truly great honor for a guest when a host opened up a new barrel of wine just for him. The Talmud records that Rabbi Judah had on one occasion just sold a number of bottles of wine and would have had to shortly open up a new barrel anyway. When Ulla came over as a guest, Rabbi Judah opened the barrel of wine and served Ulla. The Talmud says this violates the principal of *Genaivat Da'at* because Ulla assumed the barrel was being opened specifically for him due to his importance (and not because of the previous sale). Here we see that even when a person does not even say anything misleading, it can violate the principle of undeserved good will. In order not to violate the prohibition, Rabbi Judah would have had to tell Ulla that he has sold wine and that's why he was opening up the barrel.

Similarly, a Jew may not sell non-kosher meat to a non-Jew at non-kosher meat prices without specifically indicating that the meat is not kosher. The non-Jew will think it *is* kosher meat being sold by the Jew and believe that he is getting a bargain price for this more expensive meat. Therefore, he will naturally think better of this Jew. That is a violation of

4. Mishna *Bava Metzia* 4:11-12
5. Tosefta *Bava Kama* 7:3
6. *Chullin* 94a with Rashi commentary

undeserved good will, unless the Jew informs the non-Jew that the meat is not kosher. In this case, the Jew violates the principle, even though he technically does nothing wrong. As long as the wrong impression is being created and the good will gained is undeserved, it is a violation of Jewish law. In a modern example of this case, a Jew would not be able to give away a delicious cake (full of *Chametz*-leaven) to his non-Jewish neighbor on the day before Pesach without informing the non-Jew that because of the upcoming holiday he *must* get rid of the cake. Otherwise, the non-Jew would feel indebted (undeservedly so) and may feel obligated to do something good for this Jew in the future as a result.

There are many other examples of the violation of this principle in the Talmud and later commentaries. Normative Judaism does codify this concept into Jewish law. Maimonides cites the general concept and many of the specific cases mentioned in the Talmud.[7] But then he adds that even one word that will falsely enhance a person's image or possession in the eyes of someone else violates this Jewish law. *Shulchan Aruch* codifies each case of the Talmud into normative Jewish law.[8] The Sema commentary on *Shulchan Aruch* explains that anytime a person will be favorably judged in a situation that is undeserved, he violates this law.[9] Thus, full disclosure is required any time the buyer or friend may have a false sense of enhancement of the person or product – i.e., it is required to inform a customer when a seller paints used goods, which then may appear as new (but the seller need not inform the customer if he paints new merchandise).

## CONCEPTUAL DERIVATION OF GENAIVAT DA'AT

Why is *Genaivat Da'at* forbidden? What is the underlying concept that forbids the practice of gaining underserved benefit? According to

the Ritva, "stealing" someone's thoughts or attitude is actually a form of theft.[10] Rabbeinu Yonah, however, disagrees. According to him, the underlying reason this sin is forbidden is because it is lying to others, not theft.[11]. The Chatam Sofer compares this sin to idol worship, and says this sin is an act of *Mirma*-fraud.[12] He then goes on to say that as terrible as the people of Shechem were in kidnapping (and raping) his daughter Dina, Yaakov could not agree to the plan of his sons Shimon and Levi to deceive the people into circumcision, because this was an act of *Genaivat Da'at*.

## THE SEVERITY OF THE SIN OF GENAIVAT DA'AT – UNDESERVED GOOD WILL

There are many sins listed in the Torah and by the Rabbis. But this sin is especially grave. Falsely obtaining the good will of others, *Genaivat Da'at*, is such a harsh sin that Rabbeinu Yonah calls it a violation of the foundation of a person's soul.[13] The Tosefta says this kind of stealing is like stealing directly from God.[14] And Rabbi Eliezer of Metz says that of all the types of thieves, he who fools others into thinking that he is better than he actually deserves, is the worst kind of thief of all.[15].

## WHEN THIS PRACTICE IS PERMITTED AND IS NOT CONSIDERED A SIN

If a person uses *Genaivat Da'at* to mislead another person for the purpose of keeping that individual away from a sin or causing the person to perform a commandment, then in this case it is permitted, according to some opinions.[16] Similarly, if the purpose of misleading an individual or getting him or her to

---

7. Maimonides, *Hilchot De'ot* 2:6
8. *Shulchan Aruch, Choshen Mishpat* 228:6-9
9. *Sefer Meirat Einayim* on *Choshen Mishpat* 228:7, 10, 15

10. Ritva commentary on *Chulin* 94a
11. *Sha'arei Teshuva* 3:184
12. Chazon Ish, *Emunah U'bitachon*, chapter 4
13. *Sha'arei Teshuva* 3:184
14. Tosefta *Bava Kama* 3:7
15. *Sefer Yerai'im* 124
16. *Pele Yo'etz* on "*Genaiva*"

think better of you than you deserve involves someone who already hates you, or when this act will bring the parties who hate each other closer together, thereby eliminating this enmity, then it is permitted.[17] This is precisely what Aaron the High Priest did in order for enemies to cease their hatred of each other. He said to each person individually that the other person really wanted to make peace but was embarrassed to take the first step (which was not the case). When the two parties subsequently met, both former enemies usually made peace as a result. This clearly would normally be a violation of *Genaivat Da'at* on Aaron's part, since each person's standing was falsely improved in the other's eyes after Aaron's words. But since it was for a higher purpose – promoting peace between two people – it was permitted. Finally, the *Zohar* states that misleading people in order to get them to learn more Torah is permissible.[18] That is why in the Torah, there us a cantillation stop after the "*Lo*" – "Thou shalt not," and before "*Tignov*" – "steal," indicating that there are times that it is permitted to steal. "Stealing the heart" of a Jew in order to help him or her want to learn more Torah is one of those permitted times.

## EXAMPLES OF *GENAIVAT DA'AT* IN TODAY'S WORLD

There are numerous examples and issues related to this prohibition that have occurred in the twentieth and twenty-first centuries and were addressed by leading Rabbis. One question, relevant to synagogues and fundraising today, was already discussed in the 1600s. Regarding giving *Tzedaka*, charity, publically, it is known that many people give *Tzedaka* in reaction to the amount that others give. Knowing this, is it permitted for one person to announce a larger gift than he actually will give (with the permission of the organization), in order to entice others to give larger amounts to *Tzedaka*?

Rabbi Shmuel Eidels forbids this practice and castigates Jews and Jewish community leaders who gave less than they publicly announced they would give, since this is the classic case of *Genaivat Da'at*, receiving undeserved good will for larger than their actual donations.[19]

In the twentieth century, Rabbi Moshe Feinstein was asked if it is permitted to steal the state-wide New York Regents exams in advance of the test, so that the student will attain good grades (without learning or studying), in order to enable him to spend more time learning Torah and still graduate with a state high school diploma.[20] Rabbi Feinstein forbade this not only because of *Genaivat Da'at* – i.e., that educators would mistakenly believe students learned and mastered the material when they did not, but it also violates the commandment not to steal. Therefore, even if this act will lead to more Torah learning it is strictly forbidden. In a book on telling the truth and lying, Rabbi Yaakov Fisch asked the question of whether or not a person can enter a store and pretend not to be interested in an item (that he really desires), so that the seller will lower the price (in a country where the prices are can be negotiated). Since this would be fooling the seller into thinking in that this person is less interested in the item than he really is, would it be considered *Genaivat Da'at*? Rabbi Fisch answers that this practice is perfectly legitimate and does not violate the prohibition of *Genaivat Da'at*.[21] In fact, Abraham did precisely this in negotiating to buy the Cave of Machpela. He did not disclose why he wanted it (for his Sara's and his own burial, and because Adam and Eve were buried there). Thus, seeming uninterested in a particular product in order to lower its price is considered perfectly legal and a legitimate business practice in Judaism, and it is not the same as receiving undeserved good will.

Rabbi Shmuel Eliezer Stern, a contemporary Rabbi, was asked by a supermarket owner

17. Knesset Gedolah, *Choshen Mishpat* 228:7 (in the name of *Damesek Eliezer*)
18. *Zohar* 2:93b

19. Maharsha commentary on *Sukkah* 29b
20. *Responsa Igrot Moshe, Choshen Mishpat* 2:30
21. *Titen Emet LeYaakov* 5:121

who had a certain canned item that sold for 10 shekels each (about $3.50), but they were not selling well at all. Would it be permitted for him to put the cans in a prominent large bin and write, "Five cans for only 50 Shekels, until supplies are gone" (even though this was the same price as before)? Since most people would assume this is a sale item, is it *Genaivat Da'at* or not? Since he is not technically writing or selling anything that is not true, perhaps it would be permitted? He concludes that since most people assume that such a sign indicates a sale and a reduced price from the normal one, this is a clear case of underserved good will and would be prohibited.[22] It is also forbidden for someone selling a house or apartment to lie and say that there are others interested at the asking price (or at a higher price) when there are none, since this too is falsely propping up the value of the home. Similarly, a storeowner may not write a higher price on an item (higher than the regular price), and then put a line thought it and underneath write the normal, actual price. This too implies to the buyer that the item is on sale and was once selling at the higher price, which is false.

One very pertinent and important area that has been asked and spoken about at length regarding its application to this Jewish law applies to prospective marriage partners: Should the prospective bride or groom disclose a serious illness that may or will surely destroy the *Shidduch*, the potential marriage? As far back as the thirteenth century, this question was posed to Rabbi Yehudah HaChasid, and he rules that if the sickness is serious enough for the sick person to be convinced that disclosure would definitely or most likely break off the relationship, then it is *Genaivat Da'at* to hide this fact, and full disclosure must take place before the marriage is agreed upon.[23] This is because the potential healthy bride or groom assumes his or her partner is "better" than he or she really is, the classic definition of "undeserved good will," since the health of a person

is certainly one important factor in choosing a partner. One of the greatest recognized Jewish law experts of the twenty-first century also dealt with this issue at length.[24] Unlike other cases involving the question of misrepresentation regarding the profit in a store, the case here deals with a very crucial Jewish value – the importance of getting married. Thus, in order to insure that women get married, Rabbi Kanievsky allows a certain amount of "fudging" of the facts, and cites a line in Rashi to support this idea. He brings the case of a desperate orphan girl who had very few marriage prospects in Europe in the 1920s. But when she said that she was a relative of Chofetz Chaim, she was able to receive marriage offers.[25] When they later asked the Chofetz Chaim if she was indeed a relative (she was not) and if this was permitted, he responded that if the entire marriage hung on this condition, then yes, it was all right to say she was his relative even though she was not, because all Jews are technically related (and responsible) for one another. Rabbi Kanievsky then writes that he personally asked about this issue to another great expert in Jewish law, Rabbi Yosef Shalom Elyashiv, and Rabbi Elyashiv ruled that if the "lie" is a very small one, such as saying that she is nineteen years old when she is really twenty years old, then it is permitted in order to get married. But a greater change or lie than this is not permitted. Rabbi Shlomo Zalman Auerbach, however, was adamant and ruled that it is forbidden to change even a small fact or truth or withhold any important information. Rabbi Kanievsky then quotes another famous Rabbi, Aaron Kotler, who said that a groom who says that he is twenty-eight when he is actually thirty has not done something forbidden and would not violate *Genaivat Da'at*. After bringing *Sefer Chasidim* quoted above, it is clear that Rabbi Kanievsky believes that if the withheld or changed information would certainly not affect the agreement to marry, then it is permitted to slightly fudge the truth. But

---

22. *Responsa Shvivai Eish*, section 2, Parshat Behar
23. *Sefer Chasidim* 507

24. *Responsa Kehilat Yaakov*, Yevamot 7:44
25. *Titen Emet LeYaakov*, 5:38

if there is a chance that the information would destroy the relationship had the other party known, then full disclosure must take place.

Rabbi Eliezer Waldenberg deals with a different aspect of possible fraud or misrepresentation.[26] Doctors who are competing for positions in hospitals are asked to submit resumes (biographical information), which include articles published in medical journals. Apparently, the number of articles published and their quality play a significant role in hiring or not hiring doctors for certain positions. Rabbi Waldenberg was asked if a doctor may falsify the number of articles and the contents (when there is no health risk to any patient), in order to be offered the job which that doctor believes that he is most qualified for among all the candidates. This is certainly a case of receiving undeserved good will, the classic definition of *Genaivat Da'at*. It is for this reason that Rabbi Waldenberg absolutely forbids this practice and any falsification of a curriculum vitae (resume). He says that falsifying a resume is both lying and *Genaivat Da'at*, and that the prohibition of *Genaivat Da'at* applies to the written word as well as to the spoken word.

Finally, Rabbi Feinstein discusses another case of many people applying for a particular job. One observant candidate has (premature) gray hair and is convinced that the gray hair makes him appear older, which will disqualify him from the job, even though knows that he is fully qualified, and the color of his hair has no impact whatsoever on the performance of the job. Rabbi Feinstein was asked if this person is allowed to darken his hair artificially for the interview in order to get the job, as this may mislead the interviewer's impression and be considered *Genaivat Da'at*.[27] He ruled that indeed a person may indeed darken his hair for this purpose, and it does not violate the prohibition of imitating the garb of women (who very often change their hair color) and is also not *Genaivat Da'at*, because the color of the hair (unlike the articles in medical journals) is not relevant to the actual work.

There are many more cases in daily life that relate to this issue, and the general rule is that underserved good will is forbidden.

---

26. *Responsa Tzitz Eliezer* 15:12

27. *Responsa Igrot Moshe, Yoreh De'ah* 2:61

# PUTTING OTHERS DOWN - ONA'AT DEVARIM

THERE ARE TWO UNETHICAL WAYS that people often make themselves feel superior to others. They get others to look up to them, even though they do not deserve the attention or praise. Or, these people say or do something to make others feel badly about themselves. Essentially these are two sides of the same coin. This chapter will investigate one of these Jewish concepts and sins, making a person feel pain by intentionally saying or doing something to that person. This is the sin of *Ona'at Devarim*, or "hurting another person through words." What exactly is the sin of saying something that causes someone to feel badly? If the words are true, is it a sin at all? How can we specifically define this concept in Jewish law? What exactly is forbidden and permitted to do or say in this area? Finally, how severe is this sin on the scale of Jewish transgressions?

## HURTING OTHERS WITH WORDS – IN THE TORAH AND THE DEFINITION

Very often, human beings put others down and cause them to feel anguish. Where does the Torah discuss this? What is the actual definition of the sin, and where and when is it permitted or prohibited?

In three verses in the Torah, it says the words "*Lo Tone*" twice, which can be translated as "You shall not defraud," or more accurately, "You shall not cause distress" to your neighbor.[1] Why twice? What is the difference between the two verses? Rashi explains based on the Talmud (and it is clear from the context of the verse) that the first verse refers to defrauding or distressing a customer in a sale, since the verse refers to selling. This signifies that it is forbidden to overcharge a customer for an item, make the sale price significantly greater

than the going rate (usually at least one-sixth above market value). The second verse refers to causing distress to a person with words. When Rashi explains this verse, he brings two different cases that cause distress to a person and represent the sin. First he says it is forbidden to "*Yaknit*," which is most accurately translated as teasing a person – i.e., making the person feel anguish by saying something that will distress him. The second example is asking the advice of a person in an area that he or she has absolutely no knowledge or expertise. Like the teasing, this will expose the person, make him or her feel embarrassed, and cause psychological pain. Therefore, both types of *Ona'ah*, grief, which cause a person needless distress – financial and psychological – are forbidden.[2]

Some specific cases of verbal *Ona'ah* are pointed out in the Mishna, while others are expanded upon in the Talmud. The Mishna states that it is a sin of *Ona'ah* to enter a store and ask the salesman the price of an item - if the customer has absolutely no intention at all to buy the merchandise.[3] According to most opinions, this will unnecessarily cause distress to the salesman, who now has expectations of possibly making a sale, but there is actually no chance of that happening. (This will be discussed in greater detail below.) The second example of the Mishna is more clear-cut: It is forbidden to tell a newly religious person (*Ba'al Teshuva*), "I remember when you were a sinner," as this will cause the person unnecessary distress and psychological pain. Similarly, concludes the Mishna, a person may not remind the son of converts that his parents were sinners before they converted.

The Talmud repeats the examples of the Mishna and adds more cases explaining what

---

1. Leviticus 25:14, 17

2. Rashi commentary on Leviticus 25:17
3. Mishna *Bava Metzia* 4:10

is considered the sin of verbal *Ona'ah*.[4] If someone legitimately converts to Judaism (this would also apply to a newly religious person), it is forbidden to taunt this person and ask, and "The same lips that ate non-kosher food now want to learn the holy Torah?" That Talmud continues and says that if someone is suffering terribly in life, either experiencing a great and debilitating sickness or has buried his children, for instance, it is forbidden to go over to this person (as did the friends of Job) and say, "Do you know why you suffered? It was a punishment for your actions." (It is important to note that just as the friends of Job were mistaken in explaining his suffering, so too, people who try to explain the reason for anyone else's pain are usually wrong, and that is another reason why it is forbidden) Another example cited by the Talmud is the situation in which a person wants to buy wheat, and you send him (as a joke) to a person who you know has never sold wheat in his life. It causes distress to both the person desiring to purchase the wheat, wasting his time, as well as the person to whom he was referred. Rabbi Judah says that if a person has no money to buy an item, he may not go into a store and inquire about the details of the item as if he is trying to buy it (similar to the window shopping case in the Mishna). Finally, the Talmud states that the verse prohibiting intentional verbal distress concludes with the words, "You shall fear God, I am the Lord." Rashi, both on the verse and in the Talmud, explains this idea more deeply.[5] In many of the circumstances described above, it is impossible to detect the actual intention of the person causing the verbal distress. In the case of the wheat, for example, the person may later say, "I really thought he did sell wheat," and no one can know for sure what was in that person's heart. Therefore, in these cases (and in any other cases in which an onlooker cannot detect the true intention of the perpetrator of the sin), the verse always says, "You shall fear

your God, I am the Lord." This indicates that there are only two who truly know the person's intention – that person and God. God will indeed punish the person, even though no human court can ever punish that individual, as it cannot determine intention.

## DEFINING THE EXACT NATURE OF THE SIN OF *ONA'AH* – CAUSING DISTRESS

Although we now know the general prohibition of *Ona'ah* – i.e., causing anguish to another person by a verbal statement, the commentators tried to define precisely the nature of the sin and the emotion behind the words that cause this sin. As we noted above, Rashi defined the act as one of teasing (*Lehaknit*).[6] But in the Talmud, Rashi defines this sin slightly differently. He says that these are words that cause pain to the heart of a person and almost bring a person to tears.[7] Rabbeinu Yonah disagrees and defines *Ona'ah* as words that cause the person (psychological) pain and inner stress.[8] Maimonides defines this sin as anything that hurts a person and makes him or her angry.[9] *Shulchan Aruch* differs radically in his definition of this sin. He says that *Ona'ah* are words that terrify a person and cause him or her to be frightened.[10] Although all of these emotions are somewhat related, each commentary sees the origin and basis of the sin in a slightly different manner.

Chinuch uses the words of Maimonides about not causing pain and anger, but then explains that the goal of this Mitzvah is to promote peace between people.[11] If individuals are careful not to cause any hurt to others, their sensitivity to all human beings will be heightened, and people would certainly live in more peace and harmony. He says that a Jew not only may not cause pain to others, but also

---

4. *Bava Metzia* 58b

5. Rashi commentaries on Leviticus 25:17 and *Bava Metzia* 58b, s.v. "*She'harai*"

6. Rashi commentary on Leviticus 25:17

7. Rashi commentary on *Bava Metzia* 59b, s.v. "*Chutz*"

8. *Sha'arei Teshuva* 3:25

9. Maimonides, *Sefer HaMitzvot*, negative Mitzvah 251

10. *Shulchan Aruch, Choshen Mishpat* 420:34

11. *Sefer HaChinuch*, Mitzvah 338

may not embarrass them through his or her words. And even to hint to someone anything that might cause him or her distress is forbidden, because the Torah was very careful about this particular commandment since it affects people so harshly, much more than the loss of money. Then Chinuch speaks about how to react to someone who is causing pain with words. The victim of *Ona'ah* is not expected to be like an inert rock and not react to the psychological pain that was caused, because that is not normal. While it is forbidden to initiate harsh words, if a fool does hurt a person with words, it is permitted to answer that person back in kind. Just as Judaism does not expect a person to remain dormant and not respond when physically attacked by another person, the Torah similarly does not expect a person to be quiet when verbally attacked either.

Rabbi Avraham Karelitz (1878-1953) follows the general path of Rashi and Rabbeinu Yonah in defining *Ona'ah* to signify words that cause psychological pain,[12] but then also says that he was very careful his entire life not to cause any discomfort to *any* person, even for one minute![13]

When it comes to *Ona'ah* through words in the marketplace, the exact nature of the offense is a bit more difficult to define. Everyone agrees that one may not walk into a store and ask the price of an item without any intention to buy it and that this too is verbal *Ona'ah*. The question is why. *Sefer Chasidim* seems to explain the reason as the fact that the inquiry about price raises the hopes of the merchant or salesperson to make a sale imminently (especially when a person is paid by commission, i.e., according to the number of sales).[14] When the sale is then not made the hopes of the seller are inevitably dashed and this causes him or her distress. This is not forbidden if there was indeed a possibility of a sale, since this is a normal aspect of any business. But to intentionally raise the hopes of the seller without any real

prospect of a sale is the sin of causing unnecessary distress. Rashbam seems to say that while the shopper is wasting the time of the proprietor or salesperson since he or she no intention to buy, it takes their time away from someone else who could have actually bought the item.[15] This causes the business owner or salesperson unnecessary psychological pain.

Meiri gives a different reason for the sin.[16] He says that when a person rejects the item (that he or she never had any intention to buy), other customers in the store will see this and believe that the item is not worth the asking price and that is why the person did not buy it. This may cause the merchant financial loss and will certainly cause him or her distress. Shitta Mekubetzet quotes the Ra'avad and seems to agree with *Sefer Chasidim*, and says that a person's hopes are heightened any time someone takes an interest in a piece of merchandise for sale.[17] By falsely raising the hopes of the salesperson, since the buyer has no intention to buy, he or she causes the seller distress.

## THE IMPORTANCE AND SEVERITY OF THIS SIN

There are numerous statements in the sources that show that causing distress to another human being is not just "another" sin, but indeed one of the most severe sins in the entire Torah. The Talmud states that after the Temple was destroyed, the various "gates" by which a Jew could reach heaven and God were closed – all except for one: the gate of *Ona'ah*, verbal distress. Rashi explains that this signifies that if someone calls out to God about other sins and pain caused by other people, this person may or may not be answered. But he who cries out to God due to the pain of *Ona'ah*, he or she will certainly be answered by God.[18] And *Sefer Chasidim* states that one who calls out to God in pain because of verbal wrongdoing perpetrated upon him or her, that person will

---

12. Chazon Ish, *Kovetz Igrot*, section 1
13. Chazon Ish, *Kovetz Igrot* 1:33
14. *Sefer Chasidim* 311

15. Rashbam commentary on *Bava Metzia* 58b
16. Meiri commentary on *Bava Metzia* 58b
17. *Shitah Mekubetzet* commentary on *Bava Metzia* 58b
18. *Bava Metzia* 59a with Rashi commentary

be answered quickly and the sinner will be hastily punished.[19]

The Talmud also states that the sin of hurting a person financially is not as severe as hurting a person verbally, and it gives three reasons for this statement.[20] In the verse describing the causing of financial pain, the phrase, "You shall fear God," does not appear, but it does appear at the end of the verse describing the sin of causing psychological pain. Second, a person can "undo" the sin of the causing financial loss by compensating the aggrieved individual with cash later on. But almost nothing can remove the pain suffered from words. Finally, the sin of causing financial loss only affects a person's possessions, while causing psychological pain affects the person's body. Maharal strengthens this idea by stating that causing pain to a person's soul is far worse than causing pain to an individual's money, since the soul belongs directly to God.[21] Another Talmudic passage says that the punishment for other sins is carried out by God's messengers, while the punishment for causing a person verbal pain is carried out by God Himself.[22] Rabbi Nachman in the Talmud taught that anyone who embarrasses another person publicly though words is tantamount to a murderer.[23] The Talmud then continues and explains that the phrase used here to signify that he embarrasses is that he "whitens the face of the individual," because the embarrassment causes the blood of a person to actually leave one's face and make the person turn pale. This "loss of blood" is symbolically equivalent to actual loss of blood through murder.

Abaye says that every sinner goes down to *Gehinom*, a place of punishment, but only three types of sinners never rise from there. One of them is he who embarrasses someone else publicly.[24] Tosafot explains that normally a person is not left there eternally, but rises after twelve months. However, he who embarrasses another publicly completely loses his or her share in the World to Come.[25] Rabbi Abahu states that there are three sins that are so heinous that God's eyes never depart from them until the perpetrator is punished: idol worship, stealing, and *Ona'ah* – verbal abuse.[26]

Pele Yo'etz summarizes the entire scope of this sin when he defines this concept in a similar manner as the Rabbis defined the commandment to love your fellow neighbor: Do not cause any pain to someone else that you would not want to be caused to you.[27] Even small talk or a joke that hurts someone are included in this sin. The severity of this sin is codified in Jewish law and not left to mere philosophy. *Shulchan Aruch* rules that hurting someone verbally is far worse than hurting him or her financially, and that the victim of verbal abuse who calls out to God is immediately answered.[28]

## HOW FAR DOES THIS SIN EXTEND?

The sin of causing verbal pain to other people is so antithetical to Judaism that its prohibition extends far beyond the usual action of sins in other areas. Thus, the Talmud wisely stresses that, in particular, a man should be very careful with his wife in not heaping any verbal abuse upon her, and this is codified as part of normative Jewish law.[29] This concept is particularly poignant because many men have the ability to control themselves and act like a perfect gentleman with other people in the course of business or even with strangers, but always manage to say the wrong thing and cause hurt to their wives at home. And the sources allude to the fact that it is far easier to "fall into the trap" and cause pain to one's spouse than it is with other people.

19. *Sefer Chasidim* 658
20. *Bava Metzia* 58b
21. Maharal, *Netivot Olam* 2, Ahavat Re'a 2
22. *Bava Metzia* 59a with Rashi commentary
23. *Bava Metzia* 58b with Rashi commentary
24. *Bava Metzia* 58b

25. Tosafot commentary on *Bava Metzia* 58b, s.v. "Chutz"
26. *Bava Metzia* 59a with Rashi commentary
27. Pele Yo'etz on "Ona'ah"
28. *Shulchan Aruch, Choshen Mishpat* 228:1
29. *Bava Metzia* 59a; *Shulchan Aruch, Choshen Mishpat* 228:3

This sin of causing pain to others is so severe that the Rabbis ascribed the prohibition of causing pain even if no words were actually uttered by the sinner. Thus, Rabbi Judah Ha-Chasid speaks about a person who intentionally lets mucus come out of his nose or does any other disgusting act with the intention of repulsing someone who sees it.[30] This person has sinned as part of Ona'ah, since he or she has intentionally caused distress to another person. Even making a face that will repulse or distress another person, without saying anything, makes a person guilty of this sin according to another Rabbi of the Middle Ages.[31] These rulings may be based on the Talmudic passage that describes the story of Rabbi Rachumi who used to study out of his home city and would only return to his wife each year on the day before Yom Kippur.[32] One year he was so engrossed in his study that he simply forgot to return to his wife, who was anxiously anticipating his arrival, and he thereby caused her great distress. She became so depressed that she began to cry. At that moment, Rabbi Rachumi was sitting on a roof that collapsed and he died. Thus, we see that this Rabbi died because he inadvertently caused great distress to his wife, even though all he did was forget to return home. Therefore, even without words and even in a different city, this non-act is considered the sin of Ona'ah, since it caused such great psychological pain, and Rabbi Rachumi was punished with death by the hand of God.

*Sefer Chasidim* describes another situation in which doing nothing but merely sitting caused someone distress and was therefore a violation of the sin of Ona'ah.[33] If a person is a known genius in Talmud, and he sits in a class where the Talmud teacher is not as bright or as learned as he is, the teacher will feel threatened simply by having the genius sitting there and saying nothing. This is considered a violation of the sin of Ona'ah by the Talmud genius, as it causes distress to another Jew. Rabbeinu

Yonah specifically states that to be guilty of this sin, it makes no difference if the psychological pain is caused through action or words, because we look at the result and not the specific cause.[34] Rabbi Abraham Danzig, a nineteenth century decisor, agrees and rules as such in his book of Jewish law.[35]

There are two caveats to this sin, however. A person must actually intend to cause anguish to someone else in order to be guilty of this sin, and not merely do something unintentional that results in another person feeling distressed (besides Rabbi Rachumi, who was judged more harshly because he was a great Rabbi). Thus, both Chinuch and Nachmanides stress the intentional aspect of the sin in order to be culpable.[36] Unfortunately, as pointed out above, it is often the case with this sin that the only person who knows whether the pain caused was indeed intentional is the perpetrator (and of course God.) According to two opinions, in order to be guilty of this sin in certain circumstances, the pain caused must be so great that it actually causes fear in the victim. Thus, Rabbeinu Yonah writes that if a person causes pain to the community where the people are actually afraid of this person, only then is he or she guilty of the sin of Ona'ah.[37] Similarly, *Shulchan Aruch* says that if a person intentionally causes someone to be afraid, like sneaking up from behind and scaring him or her, the man or woman doing so is guilty of the sin of Ona'ah, but is punished by God and not man.[38]

PRACTICAL AND UNUSUAL
APPLICATIONS OF THIS SIN TODAY

There is no shortage of practical cases that demonstrate this sin, neither in ancient times nor today, as we have demonstrated through the sources. However, the Rabbis in more

---

30. *Sefer Chasidim* 641
31. *Sefer Yerai'im* 180
32. *Ketuvot* 62b
33. *Sefer Chasidim* 972

34. *Igeret HaTeshuva*, 3
35. *Chayei Adam* 2:143
36. *Sefer HaChinuch*, Mitzvah 243; Nachmanides commentary on Leviticus 25:14-15
37. *Sha'arei Teshuva* 3:165
38. *Shulchan Aruch, Choshen Mishpat* 420:34

modern times have faced Jewish law questions based on cases brought before them that show unusual applications of this sin. For example, Rabbi Moses Sofer was asked in the nineteenth century about the town's *Shochet*-ritual slaughterer, whose wife gave birth to a girl. Then, this new father contacted the *Mohel*, who performs *Brit Milah*-circumcision on boys, to circumcise his newborn, either as a joke or only to cause him distress. When the *Mohel* travelled quite a distance and discovered that the newborn was a girl and not a boy (and that he would not be compensated for his time), Rabbi Sofer was asked about this situation.[39] Rabbi Sofer castigates the *Shochet*, says he is guilty of *Ona'ah*, and advises the community to remove this new father from his community position as *Shochet*, slaughterer of kosher meat.

In the twentieth century, Rabbi Moshe Feinstein was asked about a situation in which, in a family with two brothers, the younger brother found a prospective wife before the older brother.[40] Since this situation caused psychological pain and embarrassment to the older brother and to the parents (*Ona'ah,* even though this was not intentional), Rabbi Feinstein was asked whether they can and should delay the marriage of the younger brother until the older brother is married. In addition, in this case, the father of the bride was adamant not to delay the marriage. Rabbi Feinstein rules that since many grooms get married later due to many reasons, including learning Torah, any embarrassment that was felt was misplaced. Therefore, he not only allows the marriage to take place now, but he suggests not delaying at all since it is a Mitzvah to get married and no one should postpone performing a Mitzvah.

Another area that many recent Rabbis have written about is the sin of *Ona'ah* by depriving someone of his or her sleep, causing distress. Although not mentioned in the Talmud or later commentaries, already in the this question was discussed. Rabbi Eliezer Greenwald

(1867-1928) was asked about a situation in which an observant Jew overslept one morning. The question was if this person should be woken up in order to recite the prayers in their proper time (within the first third of the daylight hours).[41] On the one hand, it is known that this person is very careful about praying in the proper time and waking him up will help him. On the other hand, a person who is sleeping is not culpable and considered *Anoos*, meaning that it is not his fault due to his sleeping and not a sin. If it is known that the person would certainly want to be woken up, of course it is permitted to do so. And if the person goes to bed so late at night that there is little chance that he will wake up on time, then he is no longer considered *Anoos*. But the larger question of intentionally depriving someone of sleep is an important one. One of the great Rabbis of the twentieth century, Rabbi Elchanan Wassermann (1874-1941) writes of an incident that took place when he visited the city of Radin and the Yeshiva of the Chafetz Chaim (Rabbi Yisrael Meir Kagan).[42] One Rabbi had dozed off at the end of Shabbat and asked Rabbi Wasserman to wake him for the monthly prayer recited for the moon (on Saturday night). When the Chafetz Chaim saw that he was about to wake up this Rabbi (who had asked him to do so), the Chafetz Chaim stopped him, turned pale, and asked him, "How can you wake him up? It is a clear violation of *Ona'ah*!"

A contemporary Rabbi, Yaakov Bloi, has written extensively about the sin of depriving someone of his or her sleep and considers this act a clear violation of the sin of *Ona'ah*.[43] He discusses the sin of making noise in a neighborhood where it will disturb others who are sleeping. For example, someone in a top floor apartment will surely wake up sleeping people in an apartment below by making loud noise, and making noise during hours (late at night or even during the day) when an individual knows that certain people in the area are

---

39. *Responsa Chatam Sofer, Choshen Mishpat* 176
40. *Responsa Igrot Moshe, Even Ha'ezer* 2:1
41. *Responsa Keren David, Orach Chaim* 18
42. *Kovetz Maamarim Vigeirut*, section 2, p. 1
43. *Pitchei Choshen* 15:3

sleeping, is forbidden. He cites the 11:00 pm hour as the time when in most societies, it is prohibited for Jews to make any further noise, since most people go to sleep by that hour. But he does allow for an occasional *Simcha* (joyous celebration) past that hour, since most people understand this need and are willing to allow this noise on an occasional basis. However, if it is known that someone is sick in one apartment, the Jewish law changes to require more sensitivity for this person regarding sleeping and reducing noise even during the day.

## WHEN *ONA'AH*, CAUSING DISTRESS TO OTHERS, IS PERMITTED

There are numerous circumstances in Judaism when what would normally be a sin is permitted. This is true with this sin as well, as severe as it is. One was briefly mentioned above. When an evil person makes another individual feel psychological pain, it is permitted to "give it back to him or her" and answer these hurtful words with words by the victim (just as in a physical attack one is not expected to remain a punching bag, but can and should return the punches to defend himself or herself). This can be learned from a Talmudic passage in which a eunuch berated Rabbi Yehoshua, who was bald. The eunuch asked him mockingly, "How far it is to Baldtown?" He responded, "It is as far as it is from here to Eunuchtown," thereby making fun of the man who insulted him.[44] Thus, we see that Rabbi Judah answered back and legitimately caused distress to the man who had caused him distress. Similarly, the Talmud brings another story of the High Priest during the time that Shemaya and Avtalyon lived.[45] They were descended from converts, as everyone knew, and were the most popular scholars of their generation, who went out of their way to make peace between people. As the Kohen Gadol- High Priest, left the Temple, an entourage of people followed him. But when they saw Shemaya and Avtalyon, they

left the High Priest and naturally went to them. This angered the Kohen Gadol. When Shemaya and Avtalyon later visited the Kohen Gadol, he said to them (in anger), "May the descendants of non-Jews come in peace," a slur and insult that is specifically forbidden (in the Talmud, as brought above). Rather than remain quiet after being verbally abused, they answered him and said, "May the descendants of non-Jews, who do the work of Aaron (speaking about themselves, who worked towards peace) arrive in peace. But the descendant of Aaron (speaking about that High Priest) who does not do the work of Aaron, does not come in peace." Thus, by answering this jealous High Priest with an insult of their own, they showed that this reaction is permitted in this circumstance.

Another situation that permits speaking harshly to a Jew is when this person is a chronic sinner, and the person is convinced that through these harsh words to the sinning man, he can bring this sinner to righteousness. Rabbi Yechiel Michel Epstein rules this as permitted in Jewish law.[46] But Rabbi Epstein warns that this practice is only for select individuals, and the person's intentions have to be pure. A Jew should not use this Jewish law as an excuse or rationalization to badmouth an evil person whom he detests.

There is another discussion in Judaism about whether or not it is permitted to lie, which is normally a sin, in order to avoid *Ona'ah*, causing a person psychological pain. This is the basis of an argument between the House of Shammai and the House of Hillel.[47] At a wedding, is it permitted to say that the bride is beautiful, even if it is clear that she is physically ugly or deformed? The House of Shammai says no, and one must say, "The bride as she is," regarding all brides. The House of Hillel says that a person should lie and say each bride is beautiful at her wedding in order to make her feel good and not feel pain (as does the phrase "the bride as she is"). It seems that the House of Hillel was able to convince

---

44. *Shabbat* 152a
45. *Yoma* 71b with Rashi commentary
46. *Aruch HaShulchan, Choshen Mishpat* 228:1
47. *Ketuvot* 16b

the House of Shammai when the Talmudic passage continues. The House of Hillel asked the House of Shammai about the case in which a wife brings home a dress from the market (that cannot be returned) that she likes it very much, and then she asks her husband if she looks good in it. The dress is actually ugly, but if the husband says so, it will cause distress (unnecessarily) to the wife. Thus, all parties seem to agree that it is preferable to lie (about the way the wife looks in the dress), rather than cause her psychological pain through harsh words. In addition, to *that* groom on *that* night, the bride is indeed beautiful, so it is not a total lie, just as to that wife, the dress is indeed beautiful (see the chapter "When Is Lying Permitted in Judaism? For an expansion upon this theme). The importance of telling *every* bride that she is beautiful, no matter how she looks, is brought down in Jewish law by *Shulchan Aruch*.[48] Rabbi Judah Chasid writes that a person may lie in order to avoid words that would embarrass someone or make him or her feel pain.[49] But, like *Shulchan Aruch* says, the person should try to lie in a way that there is some truth in it, so that it is not a total absolute lie.

---

48. *Shulchan Aruch, Even Ha'ezer* 85:1
49. *Sefer Chasidim* 642

# REVENGE: IS IT EVER JUSTIFIED?

REVENGE IS DEFINED AS THE INFLIC-
tion of punishment in return for injury
or insult, or the desire to retaliate or
repay an injury or wrong. It is a basic human
emotion or action, which is both intense and
natural. One can explain the very first sin inflicting injury in history as Cain's revenge for
God's favoring Abel over Cain (in their sacrifices to God), which drove Cain to murder his
brother. If this emotion is so natural, can it be
forbidden? What does Judaism specifically say
about the act of revenge? Is it ever permitted
in Judaism? If yes, then what is considered
permitted revenge and what is forbidden revenge? Are there different types of revenge in
Judaism, or is the general definition sufficient
to be called a Jewish sin? The chapter will explore these questions, the feeling of revenge,
the sin, the definition of the act, and when it
is permitted and forbidden from a Jewish perspective – all through traditional sources.

## THE INTENSITY OF THIS EMOTION

Unlike other sentiments, which may vary from
person to person or situation to situation,
Judaism recognizes the intensity of the emotion of revenge. Meiri says that revenge is an
emotion that "attacks the evil inclination" and
forces man to give into it.[1] Chinuch states that
this emotion is so powerful that most people
in the world will not stop searching after the
person who wronged them until they pay back
the evil or injury that was done to them.[2] The
classic book of Jewish ethical behavior, *Mesilat
Yesharim*, describes how difficult the sentiment
of revenge is. A person cannot escape these
feelings, as they cause him or her great pain,
and the feeling of payback or revenge is indeed so sweet. Thus, resisting the urge to act
upon this feeling is indeed difficult, and it is

only easy for angels to ignore this emotion.[3]
In explaining the prohibition against taking
revenge in the Torah, Chizkuni writes that the
feeling of seething rage completely overtakes
a human being.[4] In another section, Chinuch
explains that God does not expect a person to
be wronged and pained by another, and to remain inert like a rock, without feeling the need
to pay back.[5] If this is so, if the desire for revenge is so great, what then is a Jew supposed
to do when confronted by these emotions?

## REVENGE IS GOD'S DOMAIN

In verse after verse, God tells us that revenge is
to be left only to God. Even though normally
Jews are supposed to imitate the ways of God,[6]
the realm of revenge is God's alone. Thus, it
states in Psalms that vengeance and revenge
belong only to God.[7] Isaiah says that God
tells those who are afraid and who have been
wronged that He will take revenge for what has
been done.[8] Sometimes God will take revenge
against His own people, the Jews who have
wronged Him by sinning, by letting the enemies of the Jews vanquish the Jewish people.[9]
But in most of Scripture, God's revenge is on
*behalf* of the Jewish people, as God promises
to put on the "cloak" of revenge and repay
those who wronged the Jews.[10] One prophet
calls God a vengeful God, full of revenge towards those who have wronged God,[11] since
God repeatedly promises revenge upon the

---

1. Meiri commentary to *Avot* 3:4
2. *Sefer HaChinuch*, Mitzvah 241
3. *Mesilat Yesharim*, chapter 11
4. Chizkuni commentary on Leviticus 19:18
5. *Sefer HaChinuch*, Mitzvah 338
6. Deuteronomy 28:9, Nachmanides commentary on
   Deuteronomy 11:1
7. Psalms 94:1
8. Isaiah 35:4
9. Leviticus 26:25
10. Isaiah 59:17-19
11. Nachum 1:2-3

enemies of the Jews who have wronged the Jewish people.[12]

But why is it that in regard to all other traits and actions, Jews should imitate the behavior of God, and only in the case of revenge does God operate alone, not wanting His actions to be emulated? Perhaps it is precisely because revenge is such an intense and volatile feeling that God forbade it completely from the realm of man's actions. Human beings would not know how to use this feeling properly and repay a wrong in the proper proportion. Just as Cain murdered Abel as revenge for a sacrifice favored by God, which was certainly an "overreaction," perhaps no person can properly control rage and feeling the need for revenge, and therefore cannot administer it properly against another human being who is deserving of punishment. That is why it is left only to God to take revenge and avenge a sin properly, in a way that is exact compensation for a wrong committed. Chizkuni implies as much when he says that only God can assuage the feeling of revenge within man.[13]

There is one place in the Torah where God does command the Jews to take revenge, and perhaps this exception proves the rule. When the Midianites confronted the Jewish people in the desert, it is the only time in the Torah when the Jews were attacked spiritually and not physically. God's name was publicly shamed. Therefore, it is possible that this is why only here God asked the Jews to avenge these actions and take revenge upon the Midianites.[14] In a related incident, Pinchas took revenge against the Midianite woman and Jewish man who were publicly fornicating as a religious act before the *Ba'al Pe'or* idol. Pinchas' action caused the plague that had killed "only" 24,000 Jews to cease. God immediately praises this act of revenge by Pinchas, and rewards him with the covenant of peace.[15] But why is Pinchas praised for taking revenge, if revenge is the exclusive domain of God? The Talmud

explains that, indeed, Pinchas was viewed by the Rabbis as wrong and sinful for taking revenge and for doing this act without receiving legal Rabbinic permission.[16] It is for this reason that God had to "step in" and publicly declare Pinchas as a hero in this specific situation, before the Rabbis put him to death for his actions. But why did God praise Pinchas' action if revenge is not generally considered "Jewish" or in the domain of human beings? Once again, this exception proves the rule. Because in this instance God's name was being desecrated by the idol worship and people were dying as a result, Pinchas was correct to "take the law into his own hands" and avenge the sin against God. But in general, revenge is forbidden by Jews or by human beings.

One of the most famous narratives in the Torah in which revenge apparently took place was the story of Dina, Jacob's daughter. Shechem, the son of Chamor and ruler of the town also named Shechem, kidnapped Dina and raped her. Dina's brothers were furious, and arranged a "deal" with the people of Shechem, who wanted their city and Jacob's family to become one. The brothers said that if the males of Shechem circumcised themselves, they would be able to marry into the Jewish family. After they were all circumcised, Simon and Levi walked into the town and killed not only Shechem and Chamor, but also the entire townspeople, who could not fight back because of their recent circumcisions. Jacob became very angry with his two sons for this act, but they defended themselves saying, "Should our sister be turned into a prostitute?"[17] How are we to understand this story? Was the act of Simon and Levi in killing the people of the town an act of revenge or not? Were their actions correct? Without delving too deeply into the story, there is considerable disagreement about whether or not Simon and Levi did the right thing. On the surface, Jacob was still angry at them many years later for their act of revenge, and he cursed Simeon

12. Jeremiah 16:10, Ezekiel 25:17
13. Chizkuni commentary on Leviticus 19:18
14. Numbers 31:1-2
15. Numbers 25:7-12

16. Jerusalem Talmud, *Sanhedrin* 48b
17. Genesis, chapter 34

and Levi on this deathbed.[18] Nachmanides states that the brothers were indeed wrong and sinful in their act of revenge.[19] Even those commentaries that defend the action of these brothers explain their actions differently, never legitimizing revenge. Maimonides writes that the attack of the people of the town was indeed justified, as they deserved the punishment of death under Noahide law for allowing the rape and kidnapping to continue without protest.[20] Maharal justifies Simeon and Levi's action as an act of war between two nations, not one family pitted against another family.[21] But no commentary justifies the act of revenge by Simeon and Levi as legitimate.

## DEFINING THE ACT OF REVENGE JEWISHLY: *NEKIMA* – RETALIATION

The Torah clearly prohibits the act of revenge in one of the most famous verses in the Torah, with the words at the end of the verse following, "You shall love your neighbor as yourself."[22] But the Torah uses two distinct and different verbs for the sin of revenge – "Nekima," retaliation, and "Netira," grudge. The verse says that both are prohibited. In order to understand the Jewish definition and implications of revenge, both of these terms need to be defined and explained in detail, and, as we will see, each of the terms is a different aspect of the sin of revenge.

The simple definition of revenge, *Nekima*, would seem to be as Rabbeinu Yonah explains it: Do not do unto the other person as he did unto you.[23] Tit for tat. Repayment in kind for something that hurt you. (An "eye for an eye" in the Torah never was meant, according to any commentary, to actually remove someone's eye as punishment. Thus, this is *not* a proper example or expression of revenge.) Chizkuni defines the prohibition of revenge

as an action of retribution regarding money or the body.[24] Rashbam defines it as repaying one act of evil with another act of evil.[25] Malbim defines the retribution in greater detail – that it must be a similar action committed to another for an action previously done to him, such as withholding a favor from the person who did not do you a favor in the past.[26] Rabbi Berlin says that it is not only evil to pay back a bad deed for a good deed done for you, but paying back a bad deed for a bad deed done for you is also evil. That is revenge.[27]

These commentaries explain the verse, but do not attempt to explain the term revenge in the legal sense. What precisely is the definition of revenge? Is it revenge if a person damages you and you take him or her to court? Clearly not. Similarly, it is not revenge if you defend yourself while someone is attacking you. The Talmud attempts to define this sin. It explains that *Nekima*, retaliation, is violated if one day a person asks his neighbor to borrow garden implement but is refused. The next day that neighbor asks the original man to borrow *his* garden implement, and the man refuses by saying, "I am not lending the item to you because you did not lend it to me yesterday."[28] This is *Nekima* and is a Torah sin. This seems, on the surface, to be a pretty innocuous offense – refusing to lend an object as "payback." But the underlying principle shows the depth of this transgression. Of course, it is easy to understand that when someone harms a person financially or physically, it is forbidden to take revenge by doing the same (or worse) to him or her in retaliation. But even a case of refusal to lend a simple item that costs the person nothing, a case that was not even an action but mere words, and a situation in which the person did not suffer an actual loss, would still be considered vengeful and a form of revenge. This still demonstrates that same emotion which is forbidden: I am giving you

---

18. Genesis 49:5-7
19. Nachmanides commentary on Genesis 34:13, 49:5
20. Maimonides, *Hilchot Melachim* 9:14
21. Gur Aryeh commentary on Genesis 34:13
22. Leviticus 19:18
23. *Sha'arei Teshuva* 3:219

24. Chizkuni commentary on Leviticus 19:18
25. Rashbam commentary on Leviticus 19:18
26. Malbim commentary on Leviticus 19:18
27. *Ha'amek Davar* commentary on Leviticus 19:19
28. *Yoma* 23a

back just as you gave me yesterday. This is a Torah violation and a sin in Judaism.

Maimonides, in his *Book of Commandments*, defines this sin in more concrete terms: A Jew is forbidden to search out an individual in order to repay an evil act that he suffered by the hand of this man (or a pain that was caused by this person).[29] In his code, Maimonides calls the act of revenge a very evil trait, but understands how difficult it is to resist the urge and action to "get someone back" when the person feels that he or she has been wronged.[30] Yet, Maimonides says that the Jewish way is to be the "bigger person" and to lend the object to the neighbor the next day, even though he did not lend it yesterday. Overcoming one's natural desires of retribution is part of being Jewish and requires great inner strength indeed. But that is what Jewish law demands. This seems to be the consensus in defining this commandment in Jewish law.[31]

Rabbi Judah of Regensburg (1140-1271), known as Rabbi Yehuda Chasid, writes that revenge is a sin even if a relative of the person wronged "gives it back" to the person. Forbidden revenge can take the form of an action, words, or cursing. Revenge can even be an innocuous act that is normally permitted on its own (it is not revenge or even forbidden to initially refuse to lend your neighbor an implement if asked). But if these normally permitted acts or words are undertaken in response to a similar action or words, then they become forbidden as revenge. He advises that Jews who live in an area where retribution is common should move away.[32]

Chinuch comments and adds that if someone feels wronged, he or she is not expected to keep it inside and just suffer. It is not a sin to tell the offending person how one feels.[33] But what is forbidden is to keep the anger inside (see chapter, "Anger") and then wait for an opportunity to reciprocate in order to intentionally cause the other person to feel what that person feels. That is revenge that is forbidden.[34] Thus, there is a fine line here between what is permitted and what is forbidden. Keeping hatred inside completely is not recommended and is prohibited. Expressing that hatred in the extreme is a form of revenge.[35] Thus, a Jew can express his or her displeasure as a reaction to a particular action, but the expression cannot be a means of "getting back" at the person for what happened.

Rabbi Yisrael Meir Kagan highlights a point of contention about this commandment.[36] If a person was caused bodily damage by someone else, is it considered revenge if that person reacts and retaliates for this damage by causing the perpetrator physical harm? Chinuch says yes, and forbids such retaliation, while others permit Jews to "hit back" if attacked physically. All agree, however, that in monetary matters one may not take revenge by committing a specific act in order to deprive someone else of money, to even steal, or to cause him or her property damage as an act of retaliation. Of course, in all of these cases of bodily or property damage, reacting by calling the police and bringing someone to court and justice is certainly *not* an act of revenge, but is perfectly legitimate and even encouraged in Judaism.

## DEFINING THE ACT OF REVENGE JEWISHLY: *NETIRA* – GRUDGE

The second concept of revenge that is forbidden by the Torah is called in Hebrew "*Netira*," which we have translated as "grudge." How is this prohibition of revenge different from *Nekima*, discussed above? The commentaries are fairly unified in explaining that while *Nekima* is revenge either by an action or non-action (not lending the garden tool out of a feeling of revenge, for example), *Netira* is a sin of emotion only, a feeling or a thought.

---

29. Maimonides, *Sefer HaMitzvot*, negative Mitzvah 304
30. Maimonides, *Hilchot De'ot* 7:7
31. *Sefer Mitzvot Gedolot*, negative Mitzvah 60
32. *Sefer Chasidim* 557
33. *Sefer HaChinuch*, Mitzvah 338

34. *Sefer HaChinuch*, Mitzvah 241
35. *Sefer HaChinuch*, Mitzvah 338
36. *Sefer Shemirat HaLashon*, "Peticha," 8-9; Be'er Mayim Chaim

Thus, Chizkuni differentiates between the two by defining *Nekima* as an action and *Netira* as a thought.[37] Malbim defined *Nekima* as something a person does towards another individual, while *Netira* as a sin in one's heart alone.[38] Rashbam says that *Nekima* is payback for one evil with another evil, while *Netira* remains in one's heart.[39]

The Talmud gives a much more concrete example that differentiates these two concepts of revenge. In the case of lending the garden implement, as was pointed out above, when the neighbor does not lend his tool to the man the second day as an act of revenge, this is *Nekima*. However, if the neighbor *does* lend him the garden implement (after he was the denied the garden tool the day before), then he has done an admirable act. But if at the same time the lender says, "You see, I am not like you. I am lending it to you, even though you did not lend it to me yesterday," *that is Netira*. The man technically did nothing wrong. No action of revenge. But his motivation in lending the garden implement was clearly revenge and to show up his neighbor. That is the Talmud's definition of *Netira*.[40] In forming the Jewish law, Maimonides follows the Talmud's definition of *Netira*, and adds that as long as a Jew keeps the feeling or revenge and hatred for not receiving the initial item in his or her heart (or any other act that causes a grudge and engenders feelings of revenge), that revenge will come out in one form or another. God is commanding each Jew to attempt, as much as possible, to erase the emotion from one's heart.[41] *Sefer Mitzvot Gedolot* also rules like Maimonides and the Talmud.[42] *Orchot Tzadikim* reiterates that *Netira* is one of the few commandments in the Torah that a Jew violates by merely having a feeling of a grudge in his or her heart, without any action.[43]

## WHY IS REVENGE FORBIDDEN FOR JEWS?

If the feeling of revenge is such a basic and intense human emotion, then why should the Torah not let Jews act upon this feeling and retaliate when they feel they have been legitimately wronged? Why is revenge forbidden, especially if it is a feeling that people often cannot control? Why should Jews have to go against their nature to overcome their desire for revenge?

Chinuch gives a philosophical answer as to why Jews should not feel the emotion of revenge or act upon it.[44] When something is done to a person, rather than blame the other person who did it, a believing Jew should realize that God desired, for some reason, that this person should experience this particular pain. The other individual who caused the pain was only a vehicle for this "punishment" mandated by God. Thus, since God desired for some reason that the person should feel this emotion, blaming the other person (even though he did what he did out of free will) is pointless. When a Jew realizes this, he or she will look at this action done to him and try to understand what caused God's punishment, rather than blame the "messenger" of the pain and seek revenge.

In defining heroism and true strength, the Mishna says that according to Judaism this is achieved by overcoming one's natural desires (see chapter, "Jewish Heroes").[45] Much of the Torah and the observance of Mitzvot are related to God's desire for the Jew to go against his or her basic nature and act in a moral manner by observing the precepts of the Torah. Fighting one's basic desire to seek revenge is indeed difficult. But the Torah says this is certainly possible, and every Jew is commanded to do so. Rabbi Moshe Chaim Luzzato states that even though it is extremely difficult to overcome, and revenge is such a sweet feeling to any person, the Jew is commanded to

37. Chizkuni commentary on Leviticus 19:18
38. Malbim commentary on Leviticus 19:18
39. Rashbam commentary on Leviticus 19:18
40. *Yoma* 23a
41. Maimonides, *Hilchot De'ot* 7:8
42. Semag, negative Mitzvah 81
43. "Gate of Cruelty," chapter 8 in *Orchot Tzadikim*

44. *Sefer HaChinuch*, Mitzvah 241
45. Mishna *Avot* 4:1

overcome this tendency and nevertheless be strong.[46]

Another commentary states that while revenge is permitted for non-Jews who are not obligated to keep the Torah's precepts, for them not acting upon their emotions and not seeking revenge is an act of special kindness, since they fight and overcome their natural instincts.[47] But for the Jew who is commanded to observe this commandment, there is an additional benefit. It says in the Talmud that for any Jew who is able to succeed and go against his or her natural inclinations (to keep the Mitzvot), all of that person's transgressions are removed from him or her.[48] Rabbi Shlomo Ganzfried (1804-1886) gives a novel reason why a Jew should not take revenge.[49] He writes that the "best" revenge is to do nothing against the person who has wronged him or her. When the wronged individual does not retaliate, the person who originally offended him or her will hear that this person such so special (in acting in this manner), and will begin to think about his or her own transgression that caused that natural feeling to retaliate. But if retaliation against that person *does* take place, it will give the individual actual pleasure knowing that he or she "got under his skin." Thus, by not taking revenge, the second person will come out as the better and more respected person.

It should be noted that there is a fine line between the concept of "justice," which is always advisable and legitimate, and one who seeks "revenge," which always has negative connotations and is forbidden. Almost everyone who seeks revenge will not call it revenge, but "justice" carried out in order to correct how that person has been wronged. And seeking justice is certainly a Mitzvah.[50] Because of this rationalization that will become the mantra of anyone seeking revenge, that may be part of the reason why the Torah prohibited this sin altogether. The Jerusalem Talmud gives

another reason to explain that revenge is philosophically absurd.[51] If all Jews are considered like one body and all are connected, then any one Jew cannot seek revenge against another Jew. It would be analogous to a person who accidentally cut one hand with a knife in his other hand. The damaged hand would never "seek revenge" against that other hand, since it belongs to the same body. Conceptually, it is no different when a Jew seeks revenge against another Jew.

Finally, the key to the reason that the urge for revenge and the urge to retain a grudge should be overcome and forgotten comes from the verse itself that prohibits this sin. It is not an accident that the commandment to love one's neighbor as oneself is placed at the end of the verse prohibiting revenge.[52] Since no one would want anyone else to commit revenge against him or her for something he or she did, so too, no one should not take revenge against any individual who feels wronged and who feels as though he or she deserves the right to take that revenge. Because this is so difficult to do, it is the ultimate test of the verse to love one's neighbor as oneself. Any Jew who can bury this urge and not commit revenge can be said to truly love someone else as much as he loves himself.

## WHEN IS REVENGE PERMITTED IN JUDAISM?

Despite the clear prohibitions to retaliate, there are several instances in which Judaism *does* recognize a form of revenge. Each of them needs to be understood in its own context, and it will be explained why each is permitted, as there is usually a greater principle involved in each case of permitting revenge, more important than overcoming the natural urge to bear a grudge and act upon it.

The Talmud states that any Torah scholar that does not take revenge is not a Torah

46. *Mesilat Yesharim*, 11
47. Semag, negative Mitzvah 12
48. *Rosh Hashana* 17a
49. *Kitzur Shulchan Aruch* 30:8
50. Deuteronomy 16:20

51. Jerusalem Talmud, *Nedarim* 30a
52. Leviticus 19:18

scholar.[53] Maimonides codifies this into Jewish law.[54] When and why is this an exception to the rule? Why is it that a Torah Scholar is permitted to take revenge when other Jews are not? The answer is that the Torah scholar can only take revenge when it is his Torah being challenged and insulted. This act is not only an affront to that particular learned Jew, but to the Torah itself and even to God. When the honor of the Torah is at stake and is affronted, then any act cannot go unanswered, and the Torah scholar must give back to the person who tried to demean the Torah.

In the same vein, when God's name is being desecrated publicly, a Jew is obligated to take revenge, as did Pinchas in the desert, who was praised by God (see chapter, "Jealousy"). Based on that incident and the Talmud, Maimonides allows a Jew to take revenge when God's name is being desecrated, but only if four specific conditions are met: (1) The clear desecration of Judaism or God must be in public, (2) It must be an act that takes place during the actual desecration of God or Judaism and not something planned later on as retaliation, (3) If the person stops to ask permission to retaliate from the law authorities or Rabbis who deal in Jewish law, then it would forbidden, as it must be an act that is spontaneous and in the heat of the moment, and (4) If the person trying to defend the Torah's or God's honor is hurt or even killed during the attack, no legal proceedings may later be taken against the person who hurt or killed this person.[55]

There are two specific scenarios in which the emotion of revenge is most natural, and the Torah allows the emotion to be acted upon, but only in a supervised manner. The first case involves witnesses to a heinous crime who see a murderer kill an innocent person in cold blood. It is very natural for anyone seeing such an act to try to avenge the innocent victim and take revenge upon that murderer. Jewish law does not allow the witness to "take the law into his

own hands" and kill that murderer on the spot as an act of revenge, no matter how justified. Rather, the witness must alert the authorities and bring this evil person to a court proceeding and then testify there.[56] But the feelings of that witness are still inside. It is for this reason that when the murderer is found guilty, the Torah commands that the witnesses actually take their act of revenge by being the first to kill the murderer in the court supervised execution.[57] In describing this execution, Maimonides emphasizes how it is the witnesses who must take the lead in the execution.[58]

There are often others involved in every murder case who feel an even greater desire to take revenge against the murderer – the relatives of the victim. The Torah acknowledges these intense feelings of revenge and says that under certain circumstances, the relative of a murdered person can indeed take revenge and kill the murderer.[59] When there is a case of deliberate and intentional murder, Maimonides rules that the relatives, those who stand to inherit, are like the witnesses and therefore at the forefront of the execution.[60] Thus, their sense of retribution can be satisfied by taking part in the killing of the person who murdered their relative.

But there is another circumstance in which the feelings of revenge may be the greatest of all because the murderer is never executed – the case of accidental murder, when a person has killed someone accidentally and the death might have been prevented if everyone had been more careful. In that situation, Jewish law mandates that the killer go to a city of refuge until the Kohen Gadol-High Priest, dies. In this situation, the pain and desire for revenge of the relatives are never assuaged, since the killer never dies at the hands of the court. How does the Torah and Judaism deal with these intense feelings to avenge the victim in this situation?

53. *Yoma* 22b
54. Maimonides, *Hilchot Talmud Torah* 7:13
55. Maimonides, *Hilchot Issurei Biah* 12:4-5

56. Maimonides, *Hilchot Rotze'ach* 1:5
57. Deuteronomy 17:7
58. Maimonides, *Hilchot Rotze'ach* 15:1
59. Numbers 35:19
60. Maimonides, *Hilchot Rotze'ach* 1:2

The Torah does acknowledge and empathizes with the anger and feelings of revenge by the aggrieved relatives. First, if the accidental killer ever leaves the city of refuge (illegally, before the death of the Kohen Gadol), then the relatives are allowed to kill him with impunity.[61] In addition, after the person has been judged to be an accidental killer and is on his way to the city of refuge, the Talmud understands the great anger of the relatives and is afraid that the relatives may try to kill that accidental killer on his way to the city of refuge. Therefore, the court appoints two Torah scholars to accompany the accidental killer to the city, in case they meet up with the relatives of the victim. As they attempt to calm down the relatives seeking revenge, the Torah scholars attempt to convince them not to act illegally and kill that person then and there.[62] When the Kohen Gadol dies after many years and the entire people mourn his death, it is hoped that this public mourning and the effect of time will overcome the relative's desire for revenge. Maimonides explains all of these laws in detail, which demonstrate Judaism's great sensitivity towards the feelings of one who seeks revenge.[63]

There is one additional area, somewhat controversial, which allows revenge to take place in certain circumstances. Since the sin of revenge is a result of anger and a need to retaliate because of those feelings, when there is absolutely no anger, sometimes what appears to be revenge can take place for educational purposes, and there is no sin. Rabbi Elchanan Wasserman (1874-1941) speaks in general and says that if sins are committed for educational purposes as a demonstration to others, without negative feelings or intentions, they are sometimes permitted.[64] Rabbi Abraham Weinfeld, a contemporary Rabbi, argues that if parents (or others) want to demonstrate how revenge is wrong and hurtful by showing a child or someone else what an act of revenge is and how painful it can be, then it is permitted.[65] He brings as a proof Rashi's comments regarding the need to cut an animal (or human being) for surgery in order to heal the sickness or injury, when the cutting is painful, and yet the person doing the cutting and healing is not deemed guilty of damaging the animal.[66] So too, says Rashi, a parent sometimes must admonish or even hit a child to teach him or her a powerful lesson for life. But this act is permitted only if it is done out of love for the child and never out of anger.

61. Deuteronomy 19:6
62. *Makkot* 10b
63. Maimonides, *Hilchot Rotze'ach* 5:7-11

64. *Kovetz He'arot*, Rav Elchanan Wasserman, *Yevamot* 70
65. *Responsa Lev Avraham* 128
66. Rashi commentary on *Sanhedrin* 84b

# SACRIFICE ONE TO SAVE MANY

THE DILEMMA OF KILLING ONE PERson to save many people seems to be a simple enough concept to understand. But a classic moral dilemma always pits two different values against one another. What are the two values in conflict here? It is the ethical concept to save a life versus the ethical prohibition to kill and end a life. In this case, the only way to save many lives is to do the unthinkable and actually kill someone innocent and end his or her life. Rather than discuss this dilemma in the abstract, actual scenarios based on real-life cases will be presented. However, instead of having to decide what to do in a matter of seconds, as is the situation that occurs quite regularly in reality, this chapter will present what Judaism believes is the right action based on the myriad of ancient sources.

## THE SCENARIOS AND DILEMMAS

David is a soldier in the midst of a war zone. Suddenly, a hand grenade is thrown into the room in which many soldiers are standing and only David sees it. If he does nothing, 15 soldiers will be killed in a few seconds (but not David).

**Situation #1:**

If David diverts the grenade with his hands, 5 out of those 15 soldiers will die, but if he does nothing, all 15 soldiers will die. May David divert the grenade so that 5 and not all 15 soldiers die?

**Situation #2:**

In similar circumstances, if David falls on the grenade, only he will die and no other soldier will even be injured. If David does nothing, he and 14 others will be killed. May David throw himself on the grenade, killing himself, thereby preventing other soldiers from dying? Must he do this?

**Situation #3:**

If he quickly throws the grenade in another direction, only three soldiers will be killed, but different soldiers from the 15 people who would die if he does nothing. May David divert the grenade to kill 3 soldiers and thereby save the lives of 15?

These questions are essentially some of the same dilemmas that relate to situations and events that took place or might have taken place on 9/11. Thus, the same dilemmas above can be posed in a different manner, knowing in hindsight now what actually happened on September 11, 2001:

**Situation #1:**

As the hijacked plane is hurtling towards the World Trade Center, one man on the ground (who understands what is about to happen) has a rocket-propelled grenade (RPG) launcher which is designed to shoot down planes. If he shoots down the plane, he will kill the 350 people inside, but will prevent the plane from reaching the tower, thereby saving thousands of lives. If he does nothing, the 350 people in the plane and thousands in the Tower will all be killed. Should he shoot down the plane?

**Situation #2:**

On September 11, 2001, after terrorists took control of the plane, the passengers of flight United Airlines 93 understood (through cell phone contacts) what had already happened – i.e., they knew that other planes had already hit the Twin Towers and that their plane would be used to hit a large building in order to inflict maximum damage and loss of life. They decided to sacrifice themselves (since they would be killed anyway) in order to prevent the plane from reaching the intended target, the White House, which would then kill hundreds of additional innocent people. Should they have intentionally killed themselves and crashed the plane in order to save the lives of hundreds in the White House?

Other actual events confronted real people with these decisions, like those faced by some

Israelis a few years ago. On December 27, 2002, terrorists entered the settlement of Otniel on a Friday night. The Yeshiva was in the middle of Friday night Shabbat dinner and, as is customary, the students were serving and clearing the food that was prepared in advance. The terrorist, intending to kill as many Yeshiva boys as possible, entered the dining room building through the kitchen where only one Yeshiva student, Noam Apter, happened to be preparing the food to be served. As the terrorist entered the kitchen, Noam quickly realized and understood the situation. He noticed that the key to the dining room from the kitchen was in the door. Noam knew that if he could lock that dining room door, he would probably save the hundreds of students inside, as they would hear the commotion before the terrorist would be able to enter into the dining room. But at the same time, Noam also understood that the terrorist would certainly kill him. Should Noam run and try to get away from the terrorist and possibly save his own life, or should he try to get to that key and lock the door, thereby saving the lives of many more Israelis in the dining room? This is similar to Situation #2. In fact, Noam ran to the door, locked it, and threw the key outside the window. The terrorist instantly killed Noam, but the shots alerted the Yeshiva boys inside, most of whom were also soldiers carrying guns. The terrorist was killed before he could fire any more shots to kill anyone else other than Noam Apter. Did Noam do the right thing? Was it allowed? Was it obligatory?

Four years later, in the summer of 2006, the Israeli army was fighting the Hezbollah forces in Lebanon. In one of the battles, the Hezbollah fighters threw a hand grenade into a shack full of Israeli soldiers, almost identical to the dilemma presented above. One solider, Roee Klein, saw the grenade, analyzed the situation, and immediately fell on the grenade (Situation #2), instantly killing himself, but as a result of his actions no other solider died. Did Roee do the right thing from a Jewish perspective, giving up his own life to save the lives of others?

This chapter will explore the various issues involved in both of these dilemmas: (a) whether or not it is permissible to kill one or more persons in order to save many more people from dying, and (b) whether or not one is allowed to sacrifice oneself in order to save others from dying. Judaism discussed these ideas and values in depth hundreds or even thousands of years ago, which provides a basis in Jewish values to respond to these real-life situations of today.

## THE GENERAL IMPORTANCE OF LIFE IN JUDAISM

Before we can begin to discuss the value of one life versus another life (or lives) in Judaism, we must first examine the value that Judaism places on life in general, even though this is discussed elsewhere in this volume (see chapter "Conceiving to Abort for Stem Cells & Other Stem Cell Issues" and others). Maimonides, based on the Talmudic discussion, rules that human life is so important that one may violate every Mitzvah-commandment in the Torah except for three specific Mitzvot-commandments, in order to preserve it.[1] Thus, Jewish law *requires* a Jew to violate 610 commandments rather than give up his or her life. The only exceptions are killing another person, adultery, and idol worship. Only in these cases a person must be ready to die rather than violate these Mitzvot (under gunpoint).

Thus, if faced with a situation in which a Jew must choose between violating (one of the 610) Mitzvot or remaining alive, Maimonides, the Rambam, does not leave the choice up to that Jew, but rather clearly says that one *must* violate the Mitzvah and stay alive. If a person chooses instead to become a "martyr" and give up his or her life for Judaism, Maimonides says he or she is morally wrong and is culpable. The punishment is equivalent to "death."

The Talmud, based on the verse in Leviticus,[2] explains why Judaism places such a high value on human life. It says that if a person

---

1. Maimonides, *Hilchot Yesodai HaTorah* 5:1-2
2. Leviticus 18:5

can live another day to do more Mitzvot, it is imperative to violate one Mitzvah today. Thus, it can be said that except for three circumstances, there is no value in Judaism more important than the preservation of life.[3] The juxtaposition of "He shall live by them" after stating in the same verse "You shall keep my statutes," shows us that Jews should read the verse, "You shall keep my statutes ... *as long as you live by them.*" Rabbi Judah, based on our first verse, will say that a Jew's purpose in life is to do Mitzvot. If Jews are alive, they can do more Mitzvot. Therefore, one can violate one Mitzvah (of the 610) in order to stay alive and do other Mitzvot.

In order to arrive at the same conclusion, Rabbi Shimon uses a different verse commanding the Jewish people to keep or preserve the Shabbat. By using this new verse of "keeping/preserving," Rabbi Shimon is claiming that only one who will keep Shabbat in the future is allowed to violate the Shabbat now. Thus, it is permitted to violate one Mitzvah or one Shabbat so that a Jew will remain alive to keep and preserve the Shabbat in the future. Given this high priority on preserving human life, we can begin to examine the conflict, first by the pitting of one human life against another life. The *Code of Jewish Law* rules according to this passage and according to Maimonides, thus showing the importance of preserving life in Judaism.[4]

## KILLING ONE LIFE TO SAVE ONE LIFE

Before the specific dilemmas outlined above can be analyzed, we must discuss what happens when one life is threatened by another life. Whose life takes precedence? The Talmud first discusses this situation in reference to an abortion. According to the Mishna, as long as the baby is still inside the womb, if it threatens the life of the mother, the fetus should be

killed in order to save the mother's life.[5] The reason for this is clear. Although the fetus has some Jewish and legal aspects of life (for example, a Jew violates the Shabbat to save a fetus, according to most Rabbis, discussed in chapter "Stem Cell Dilemmas"), it still is not equal to a fully formed and independent life. The fetus has the status of a potential life. Thus, the mother's life, an actual life, takes precedence over the life of the fetus, a potential life. However, the Mishna continues, once the head of the baby shows itself or most of the baby leaves the womb, then the one-minute-old baby is considered a full life, and one may *not* sacrifice the baby to save the mother (or vice versa). The Mishna concludes and states clearly: "*One may not destroy one life in order to save another life.*" Thus, a newborn has the same value as its mother, and we may *never* choose whose life is more valuable and sacrifice the "less valuable" life. It is clear from the Mishna that we cannot choose one life over another when they are both in danger (and the circumstances are equal).

Therefore, the Jewish value learned for our dilemmas is that we can never evaluate whose life is "more valuable" (e.g., whether to save the baby since it has a longer potential for life than the mother, or to save the mother since she can contribute to society now while the baby cannot), and thus man can never choose to save one life over another life based on our determination of the value of that life. This is what the Mishna means when it says, "One may not set aside one person's life for that of another," and this has become part of normative Jewish law and Jewish values.[6] So, for example, we would not save a Talmudic scholar over an ignorant and assimilated Jew just because the former has more Torah knowledge.

Why is this so? Why can't we save one life by sacrificing another life? The Talmud, in a different passage, reaffirms the principle and gives us a clue to the reason. The Talmud describes a case in which a man threatens to kill

---

3. *Yoma* 85b
4. *Shulchan Aruch, Yoreh De'ah* 157:1

5. Mishna *Ohalot* 7:6
6. *Shulchan Aruch, Choshen Mishpat* 425:2

you unless you kill another (innocent) person (and there is no chance to wrestle the gun away from him and kill him, which is permitted and is the best possible resolution of this scenario). One might think that since preservation of (your) life is so important in Judaism, you would be permitted to kill the other person in this case, since an innocent person is going to die anyway (and I have to preserve my life before someone else's). Yet the Talmud says that it is forbidden to kill another person in such a circumstance (similar to the first source, which says that murder is one of the three exceptions to preserving life).[7]

But why is this so? Logically, we might have thought that if it comes down to my life versus someone else's life, my life should always win out, and I may kill someone else to preserve my own life. However, the above passage says you may not do this. Why not? Apparently, there is a great distinction between actually killing someone else and "letting yourself be killed." It is true that your life does take precedence – if you already own that canteen of water in the desert and you have to do nothing to save your own life. In that case, you should not give any water to your friend who will die if you do not give him or her the water, since your life takes precedence (you are already considered saved). But if your friend has the canteen (that would be similar to our case), then it is forbidden to take the canteen away from him and save yourself, thereby killing your friend. Your life comes first as long as you do no action to stay alive. But you may not act and kill your friend in order to stay alive. (The fact that you will inevitably die as a result of not killing and not acting is *not* the same thing as your taking a specific action to kill someone else. Even though you will die, you did nothing to bring about your death. But if you kill the other person, you have done an act that brought about the death of an innocent in order to preserve your life. That is forbidden.)

The same source brings the adage, "Who said that your blood is redder than his blood?"

This signifies "Who said your life is more valuable than his?" Maybe his life is more valuable than yours? We don't know! Man can never know. And since we do not know, we can *never* make a judgment to say whose life is more important and kill one to save another. This Talmudic passage reiterates the value mentioned earlier about the mother and her infant: Human beings can never judge whose life is more valuable and make a determination based on their own evaluation.

Thus, *we* cannot know for sure whose life is truly more valuable. But it is possible from God's perspective that one life is indeed more valuable. Thus, the question is: Why can't we say whose life is more valuable based on age, health, income, potential income, and potential benefit to the society? The Rabbis help us answer this question when they say that when someone destroys a human being, it is as if he has destroyed an entire world.[8] The Mishna makes it clear that in God's eyes *every* human being is considered equal in value, and each person's value is that of the entire world. Since no one can put a price tag on the value of the entire world (as it too large to even consider), we may use the analogy that just as the value of the entire world is infinite, so too, the value of each human being is infinite. Any mathematician will confirm that one calculation of infinity can never be greater or smaller than a different infinity, because infinity is simply infinity, and a one-minute-old baby has the same infinite value as the greatest *Talmid Chacham*-Jewish scholar. Therefore, each person has the same infinite value before God and man. The second part of the Mishna in *Sanhedrin* (referred to above) also alludes to this idea. Only one man, Adam, was created, so that later on no one could say that he or she was greater than anyone else. Since people all came from the same source and origin, all human beings are considered of equal and infinite value.

---

7. *Sanhedrin* 74a

8. *Sanhedrin* 37a

## OUR QUESTION: KILL ONE LIFE TO SAVE MANY LIVES?

Now that we know that Jews may never sacrifice one person in order to save another person, the question is whether one life can be sacrificed to save *many* lives. The Tosefta seems to describe a case that is similar to one of our dilemma situations.[9] A terrorist threatens to kill an entire group of people at gunpoint unless the group gives him a specific person that he asks for (within the group), in which case he will spare the lives of the entire group and only kill that person. May the group hand over the person in order to save the people in the group? The Tosefta says *no*! Even though in the end that specific person will die in either case anyways, it is still forbidden to give over the person to be killed, even though by giving over the one person, you would be saving the lives of many people!

We have read the Tosefta and understand the words. But where is the logic? They can save the lives of many people by giving over one who is doomed in either scenario. And even if they follow the Tosefta and refuse to give over that one individual, he or she will be killed with the group anyways, so what was accomplished by refusing? *Why* is it forbidden? This case is similar to our Situation #1. If they kill one person or a few people, who would be killed anyways with everyone else (with the grenade or people on the plane hurtling toward the tower), they can save many more people from dying. And yet, the Tosefta says they *cannot* give them the one person to be killed, even though that person and everyone else would now be killed as a result of their refusal. What is the logic? Aren't people supposed to save as many lives as possible in Judaism?

If we return to two of the principles learned above, we might find an answer. It was pointed out and explained there that no Jew may take any action to save himself or herself if it comes at the expense of another's life. Thus, no action can be taken that will bring about someone's death (i.e., giving that person over to the murderers), even if it means saving many lives. In addition, since it was shown that each person's life has infinite value, then mathematically, 100 infinities is still the same infinite number and equal to one infinity, and thus Jews cannot kill one person, or one infinity, to save many people, or many infinities, according to the Tosefta. It would be no different mathematically and conceptually from killing one (infinite value) person to save another (infinite value) person.

The Mishna does say that if the specifically requested person was *already* guilty of death, like Sheva Ben Bichri (who was a murderer, as explained below), then that is a different story in Jewish law. Then *we* did not pick this person to die. He was already selected to die through his own actions and his life is already over in a legal sense. Then we are sending a dead man to die, and this is permitted if it will save many other lives.

Who was Sheva ben Bichri? From the book of Samuel we can see that he was truly evil and deserving of death.[10] This man rebelled against the king, King David – an offense punishable by death. Joab, David's general, surrounded the city where Sheva lived and was about to kill the inhabitants of the entire city. When the citizens heard this, they killed Sheva ben Bichri and threw his head over the wall to Joab. When Joab saw this, he spared the city. This is similar to our case in that all of the people's lives were in danger and Joab would have killed them all, including Sheva Bin Bichri. The people killed one person (who was already guilty of death) and "gave" him to Joab, thus saving the rest from death. Therefore, we see that if the murderers specified a person "like Sheva ben Bichri," who was guilty of death, it is permissible to give him to them and thus save everyone else.

Maimonides writes that Jewish law follows this Tosefta. It is clear from Maimonides that we may never kill one innocent person intentionally in order to save the lives of the rest of

---

9. Tosefta *Terumot* 7:23

10. Samuel II 20:20-122

the group, even though that man will be killed in any event.[11] Thus, according to Maimonides, the man with the RPG may *not* shoot down the plane hurtling towards the World Trade Center, and David may *not* divert the grenade to kill some of the soldiers who would be killed anyway (Situation #1).

Based on this analysis, it *certainly* would be forbidden in Situation #3 to divert the grenade to soldiers who would never have been killed to begin with, in order to kill fewer soldiers and save more lives. The overriding principle of Maimonides is "never surrender a Jewish soul." We may take no action to bring about the death of any Jew, even if it will save many lives. He makes the situation much clearer than the Tosefta and answers our question about the case in which the murderers specified the innocent person. Clearly, the act of handing over someone (whom you know will be killed) is forbidden according to Maimonides.

But as we often see in Judaism, there is another side to the question.

There is an almost identical passage to the one brought in the Tosefta in the Jerusalem Talmud.[12] It begins almost word for word like the Tosefta, but then continues beyond the Tosefta. After quoting the "exception" of Sheva ben Bichri (according to Resh Lakish), however, Rabbi Yochanan then disagrees with the entire premise. He says that as long as the terrorists (the murderers) specified one person to be handed over, even if this person was innocent (*not* like Sheva ben Bichri), then the group *may* turn over this person in order to save the lives of the group!

Therefore, we see from this passage the contrary opinion – according to Rabbi Yochanan, one *may* (or should) sacrifice one innocent life in order to save many innocent lives. According to Rabbi Yochanan, then, should the man with the rocket shoot down the plane in order to save thousands in the tower (we can say that the passengers were specified by the terrorists when they were hijacked)? And can

David then divert the grenade to kill five of the fifteen people instead of all of them? (Maybe these five would *not* be considered chosen by Rabbi Yochanan?) More importantly, is there any later support in Jewish law for this seemingly lone opinion?

Even though we saw that Maimonides rules according to the Tosefta, Meiri makes a cogent argument and rules according to Rabbi Yochanan (against the opinion of Maimonides). Meiri says that you *do* sacrifice one life to save many lives, bringing proof for his ruling.[13] He shows that in every argument (save for three exceptional cases), we always rule according to Rabbi Yochanan against his brother-in-law Resh Lakish (and this is *not* one of the exceptions)![14] (This presents a question to Maimonides as to why he rules against Rabbi Yochanan, which is discussed at length and answered by the commentaries of Maimonides.) In fact, the Vilna Gaon, in his commentary on *Shulchan Aruch*, questions how Maimonides can rule against Rabbi Yochanan, and he simply leaves it as a question.[15]

Meiri proves his point even further, saying that Rabbi Yochanan is the author of the entire Jerusalem Talmud, which even Maimonides himself agrees with.[16] Thus, it makes sense to rule like Rabbi Yochanan against Resh Lakish in the Jerusalem Talmud, and give over one innocent person to be killed in order to save many. This argument remains and seems not to be resolved (between Maimonides and the Meiri, the Babylonian Talmud and the Jerusalem Talmud). Resh Lakish and Maimonides (and the original Tosefta) believe that Jews may *not* give over one person to be killed in order to save many, while Rabbi Yochanan and Meiri rule that Jews may (or must) kill the few in order to save the many, if they were specified. According to whom does the *Code of Jewish Law, Shulchan Aruch*, rule? Rabbi Yosef Caro is silent, but his Ashkenazic counterpart,

---

11. Maimonides, *Hilchot Yesodai HaTorah* 5:5
12. Jerusalem Talmud, *Terumot* 47a

13. *Beit Habechira* commentary on *Sanhedrin* 72b
14. *Yevamot* 36a
15. *Biur HaGra, Shulchan Aruch, Yoreh De'ah* 157:16
16. Maimonides, Introduction to his Mishna commentary

Rema, who is part of *Shulchan Aruch*, does comment.

## CURRENT JEWISH LAW

Although Rabbi Yosef Caro is silent, Rabbi Moshe Isserles mentions our case and brings the Meiri's view as the main Jewish law[17] – i.e., if the terrorists single out one of the group for killing, the group *may* give this person over on condition that the person and the group would have been killed as the alternative. But then Rema brings the alternative view (Maimonides) as "there are those who rule . . ." So both views are mentioned in *Shulchan Aruch*. One noted commentary on the *Shulchan Aruch* clearly rules according to the positions of Rabbi Yochanan and Meiri.[18]

Twenty and twenty-first century Rabbis bring actual cases that are similar to those discussed above. Among them are:

1. A man is standing and behind him is another man. Someone shoots an arrow at the first man with the intent to kill him. If he bends down in order to avoid being hit, he knows the other man will be killed. Can he bend down to avoid being killed knowing that the man behind him will die as a result?
2. There is a famous case of a group of people hiding from the Nazis during the Holocaust. They must be silent as the Nazis search the home for Jews (where they are hiding). An infant in the group starts to cry. If the baby is not silenced, the Nazis will hear the cry and consequently find and kill everyone in the group, including the infant. May the mother (or anyone else in the group) silence the baby if this means killing the infant?
3. A patient in a hospital is connected to a very expensive machine that is keeping him alive. If he is disconnected, he will surely die, but then this machine can save the lives of many other patients who need it. Is it permitted to disconnect the machine and let one

person die in order to save the lives of many others?
4. The question of the airplane hurtling towards a tall building is actually discussed after 9/11. Is it permitted or even obligatory to shoot down the plane and kill its passengers (who would die anyway) in order to save all the people in the building from being killed?
5. Twenty people are on a boat that will sink from too much weight. If the captain selects five of them to be thrown off, the other fifteen can be saved. May he throw off the five passengers in order to save the others? And if so, how should he determine who gets thrown off?
6. A large apartment building has collapsed. Some people are still alive inside, but in order to get to these people, the rescuers will have to kill a few other people. Is it permitted to use machines that will kill a few in order to save the many?
7. A bus is driving along on a major street, and the brakes suddenly stop working. If the bus driver continues on the path the bus is travelling, he will kill many people. But if he turns the steering wheel, he will kill a few (different) people. May he turn the steering wheel?

A major twentieth century expert in Jewish law who is respected across the board, comments on a dilemma that seems very similar to the last case and to the case in the Tosefta. Rabbi Karelitz (who lived in Israel and passed away in 1953) wrote about an arrow that is headed towards many people, and questions if it is permitted to alter its path so that that it kills only one person (even if that person is not specified).[19] This seems to be the case of Situation #1, when the soldier diverts the grenade to other soldiers. By diverting the grenade (or arrow), only a few people will be killed rather than many. Someone familiar with the actual incident presented explained that the specific event that Rabbi Karelitz was referring to was the case with the bus. Is the bus driver moving the steering wheel similar to the case described in Situation #1 or Situation #3? Rabbi Karelitz

---

17. Rema, *Shulchan Aruch, Yoreh De'ah* 157:1
18. *Turei Zahav* on *Yoreh De'ah* 157:7

19. Chazon Ish on *Sanhedrin* 25

answers that the bus driver may indeed move the steering wheel, and explains that this is different from the case in the Tosefta, because moving the steering wheel is not an act of killing (since the deaths would have happened if no action is taken), while giving over the person is an act of killing. And yet, almost all more modern Rabbis use this ruling to show that we rule like Rabbi Yochanan and Meiri.

Another giant in Jewish law of the twentieth century, Rabbi Moshe Feinstein, rules (after a long explanation of the argument) that we do follow the view of Rabbi Yochanan.[20] An equally respected commentator, Rabbi Eliezer Waldenberg, disagrees. He says that because both sides of the argument are very strong and we are in doubt as to what the correct opinion is, we do nothing, and thus in effect, rule according to the view of Maimonides.[21]

Rabbi Shimon Efrati (1908-1988) suffered through the Holocaust and wrote about situations of Jewish law that occurred during that terrible period. Regarding the case of the crying infant who would alert the Nazis to the hiding Jews and endanger their lives, he writes that he was there when some of his relatives were actually faced with that situation. They did not quiet the baby and were actually caught and killed by the Nazis. But as a matter of Jewish law, even if someone had smothered the child to save the lives of everyone else involved, they would not have been wrong. Thus, he says that either option in this situation can be followed.[22] Rabbi Lorintz compiled the responsa of Rabbi Chaim Kanievsky (who was born in 1938) and wrote about the 9/11 dilemma of shooting down the plane streaking for the tower, which would otherwise kill everyone in both the tower and the plane, similar to Situation #1. He says that it would be permitted to shoot down the plane, based on Rabbi Karelitz's responsa (about changing the direction of the arrow) and many more lives would be saved.[23] He also writes about

the case in which a building had collapsed and in order to save many, some have to be killed in the process (or else everyone would be killed).[24] Once again, after a long discussion, his principle is the same, and he would allow killing some in order to save many more people who were involved in the accident. Rabbi Yitzchak Silberstein comments on this last case with slightly different circumstances, and comes to the same conclusion.[25]

## IF ONE PERSON VOLUNTEERS TO DIE, DOES THAT MAKE A DIFFERENCE?

In our original dilemma (Situation #1) one person could volunteer to die and all would be saved except for that person. That is exactly what happened with Noam Apter and Roee Klein. Would that action be permitted, or even obligatory? Are there are any precedents in the Bible or in the Talmud for this? Actually there are. There are three cases in the Prophets and Talmud that seem to answer this question in the affirmative.

The first case is the story of Purim and Queen Esther. When Mordechai asked Esther to go to the king to save the Jewish people, Esther knew that it was not her turn to see the king and she would almost certainly be killed for coming to him without an invitation. Thus, she asked (Mordechai and herself) if she was permitted to sacrifice herself in order to try to save the lives of all the Jewish people, and Mordechai ordered her to go in any case.[26] This seems similar to Situation #2 and the people on the United 93 flight, who chose to be killed in order to prevent additional deaths, as they knew they would die anyways. The fact that Esther did go to the king seems to indicate that it was permitted. Rabbi Kook writes that she was *obligated* to do so, to be ready to sacrifice herself in order to save many.[27]

However, the case of Esther and our

20. *Responsa Igrot Moshe, Yoreh De'ah* 2:60
21. *Responsa Tzitz Eliezer* 15:70
22. *Responsa Gei HaHariga* 1
23. *Mishnat Pikuach Nefesh* 50
24. *Mishnat Pikuach Nefesh* 7-8
25. *Assia*, 45-48, Tevet 5749. pp. 62-68
26. Esther 4:8-13
27. *Responsa Mishpat Kohen* 143, "Mai Esther"

Situation #2 may not be the same. Even though Rabbi Kook establishes the principle of volunteering to be killed in order to save many lives, in the case of Esther, it was not *certain* death like it is in the situation of the grenade and United Airlines flight 93. Thus, Esther's risk was not definite death, only possible death. In addition, Esther was trying to save the entire Jewish people. Maybe that is an unusual situation, far different from an "ordinary" case of volunteering to sacrifice oneself to save many.

The case of Jonah, however, seems to be identical to our case of Situation #2. When the storm was threatening to certainly kill everyone on board, Jonah knew that the storm had come about because of his previous actions.[28] He volunteered to sacrifice himself by jumping overboard (not knowing he would be rescued by God and swallowed by a large fish), in order to save the remaining people on board. According to the commentaries, this seemed to be permissible and the right thing to do. If Jonah had not jumped overboard, everyone, including Jonah, would have died. This seems to be identical to the case of the soldier jumping on the grenade and the passengers on the plane who were willing to sacrifice themselves in order to save others from death. If the soldier had not volunteered, everyone, including the soldier, would have been killed. Thus, it seems that volunteering for death is certainly praiseworthy.

There is one more case in the Talmud that seems to support the notion that it is permissible to volunteer to be killed in order to save many lives. Although the specific concept of a blood libel was popularized by the Christians much later in history, an almost identical concept is already found in the Talmud.[29] The Gemara (with the explanation of Rashi) describes the case in Lod, where the daughter of the king was found murdered. Some people immediately (and falsely) accused the Jews of the crime, and the king believed them. He ordered *all* of the Jews in the area to be killed. In order to save the rest of the Jews, two brothers named Pappus and Lulianus, who were innocent, came forward and said that they had committed the crime. The king then killed only them. Rashi says of these two (who certainly did not commit the crime, but offered to die in order to save every other Jew in the area) that there is no one else in the Garden of Eden who could compare to their high level.

Thus, while there is an argument between the Babylonian and Jerusalem Talmuds (and between Maimonides and the Meiri) about Jews actively giving over a person to die in order to save everyone else, it seems clear from this Talmudic passage and according to nearly all of the commentaries that volunteering to die in order to save many people from being killed is indeed praiseworthy.

---

28. Jonah 1:10-12

29. *Ta'anit* 18b with Rashi commentary

# SELF-ESTEEM IN JUDAISM

ELF-ESTEEM IS A TERM THAT RE-
flects a person's overall evaluation or ap-
praisal of his or her own worth. Self-esteem encompasses beliefs (for example, "I am
competent," "I am worthy") and emotions
such as triumph, despair, pride, and shame.
Synonyms of self-esteem include self-worth,
self-regard, self-respect, and self-integrity. It
is a self-concept, a self-evaluation of what we
think about ourselves. It is often not based on
actual facts, but on how each person views
himself or herself. Studies have shown that a
person with a high level of self-esteem, who
may not be as gifted as he thinks he or she is,
generally does better and excels more than
the person who is objectively more gifted and
talented with a low self-esteem. Therefore, in
an age in which more people (particularly
children and adolescents) think less and less
of themselves, achieving proper self-esteem is
important for each person. Feeling good about
oneself helps each person become happier and
achieve success in life (by any self-standard).
But how is self-esteem achieved? How can a
person who has low self-esteem be convinced
of his or her own greatness?

As a people, Jews have always had overall
high self-esteem. In order to survive intact as
a distinct group, a minority culture in diverse
foreign lands, Jews always believed that they
were as good (or better) than others. Thus, for
example, when other immigrant groups came
to the United States en masse, they usually
did not adjust and rise socioeconomically as
quickly as did the millions of Jewish immi-
grants in the twentieth century who immi-
grated to the USA. This largely has to do with
self-esteem and a general sense of well-being
in life. Even today, in all surveys, Jews in the
State of Israel are some of the happiest and
contented people on earth, with high self-esteem, even though the country has been
threatened with utter destruction since its
birth more than sixty years ago. How and why

is this achieved? How can individual Jews who
feel incompetent and unworthy learn to feel
the opposite? What messages within Judaism
can help each person feel good about himself
or herself?

## THE IMPORTANCE OF EACH AND EVERY PERSON IN THE WORLD

Traditional Jews realize that there is a piece
of God, as it were, inside every human being.[1]
That is what makes man special as a species,
and it makes each member of the human race
a special, unique, and important individual as
well. The godliness inside every person gives
him or her enormous value as, according to the
Talmud, each person has incalculable worth,
regardless of his or her identity or level of intelligence and accomplishment, since a single
individual has the value of an entire world.[2]
This general awareness and knowledge should
help every person think better of himself or
herself. King David wrote that each individual
is so special that he or she is just a little lower
than the angels. But just one verse before this,
he wrote that man is "nothing." This seems
to be a contradiction.[3] The Midrash explains
that when people have either a low or proper
level of self-esteem, they should know that
they have achieved a status so high that only
angels are higher. But if a person has excessive
self-esteem and as a result thinks too highly
of himself, God (and King David) tells this
person not to "think you are so great," since
God created the mosquito before you, so you
are not really all that special.[4]

That each person has a bit of God inside of
him or her is itself is a level of greatness, and
should give each person a feeling of self-worth.
But the Mishna states that an even greater

---

1. Genesis 1:26-27
2. *Sanhedrin* 37a
3. Psalms 8:5-6
4. Midrash, *Vayikra Rabbah* 14a

feeling of well-being is achieved in that man can be aware of how special he or she really is. It is one thing to be special. It is quite another to realize and be conscious of that that unique situation and use that specialness to maximize one's potential.[5]

Maimonides adds to this notion by saying that man should realize how lucky he is to be part of a species that is so unique.[6] He is the only creature in the world that can truly distinguish between right and wrong, as animals do not have this gift. And because animals are basically preprogrammed at birth, they have very few choices about what to do with their lives. But man has infinite choices before him, and can use his or her life to accomplish whatever he or she desires, without anyone forcing him or her to choose any particular path. That free choice by man in every sphere is a great gift that people should appreciate and take full advantage of. Thus, Judaism teaches that every person is so special and important that he or she is considered at the center of the world. In fact, it is proper to say to oneself and actually believe that the entire world was created for "me and my needs."[7] Sadly there are many Jews, even observant Jews, who do not appreciate this concept. Thus, they value a Torah scroll much more than they value each person, who is viewed as much more valuable than a Torah,[8] and they, therefore, treat the Torah with more respect than they treat each person. When the Torah passes them, they will stand up, but when a person passes, they often do not stand up. And when the Torah is about to fall, they rush to prevent it from falling. But when an elderly person is about to fall, they do not run quite as quickly to prevent that person from falling. This is utterly wrong from a Jewish perspective, as each person is much more valuable than a Torah scroll.

Jews should feel especially lucky and blessed, and particularly good about themselves. Because of the rich heritage passed down to every Jew, all Jews, says the Mishna, should feel like the son or daughter of a king, part of royalty.[9] For all of these reasons, Jews should realize that they are great. In other words, they should feel extremely good about life and about themselves.

## THE INDIVIDUALITY OF EACH JEW

Along with that infinite value, the same Mishna reveals another secret about each person in the world.[10] It is true that each person should feel special about his or her infinite worth, and it is also true that each person has equal value before God (since everyone came from the same one man, Adam). On the other hand, God made all (normal) people in a similar manner to somewhat resemble each other, with two eyes, ears, lips, arms and legs, and one nose, mouth, head, etc. Yet, God also created each person unique, with a distinct personality and talents, as well as distinctive physical features such as fingerprints, voice prints, iris scan, and footprints. This uniqueness of each person also makes him or her special, knowing that there is no one in the entire world quite like this individual. The Talmud specifically says that each Jew's mind and personality is as unique as his or her face.[11] And because every person is different, King Solomon cautioned that each person should be taught in a manner that is specifically suited for him or her.[12] That includes testing, style of teaching, and how a student's progress is measured. It is incompatible with Jewish thought to compare students to each other, to teach everyone in the same manner, and to hold all children to one standard.

Not only is each human being unique, but each species of animals and plants in the world was also created in a unique manner, with a specific and different purpose.[13] But unlike animals, which are grouped by species (see

5. Mishna *Avot* 3:14
6. Maimonides, *Hilchot Teshuva* 5:1
7. *Sanhedrin* 37a
8. *Makkot* 22b
9. Mishna *Shabbat* 14:4
10. Mishna *Sanhedrin* 4:5
11. *Berachot* 58a
12. *Proverbs* 22:6
13. *Psalms* 104:24

chapter, "The Differences Between Man and Animal"), each human being is a unique distinct individual, as noted above. It is for this reason that each individual has his or her unique mission in life, as is recited in the Rosh Hashana prayers.[14] Finding one's special purpose and goal that combines one's talents, environment, and all other factors, can be difficult. But once a person discovers that mission, he or she should try to maximize efforts and maximize potential in fulfilling that goal in life. The path to discovery of that mission, says Rabbeinu Yonah, is to know oneself very well, to understand one's strengths and weaknesses, and to come close to God by fulfilling that mission. This will give a person great self-esteem as long as the individual does not attempt a task greater than was meant for his or her talents and abilities.[15]

## DO NOT PUMP YOURSELF UP BY PUTTING OTHERS DOWN

Some people may (wrongly) feel that they can feel better about themselves by putting other people down. While this may temporarily make a person feel better, at the end of the day, every person knows his or her true value and worth. Just as you were created in the image of God with some Godliness inside of you, so too was every other person.[16] Based on this verse, the Midrash says that even if you feel that others have put you down and therefore you feel you have the right to also put others down, you may not do so.[17] Since everyone has some Godliness inside, not only is this not the correct manner in which to behave, but by doing so, you are also putting down God Himself in the process. Logically, a person may reason that by hurting the other person, his or her own self-worth will be enhanced. But that is not how it works in Jewish law and in life. Thus, it is forbidden to curse oneself (since each person is a being with Godliness

inside), and a Jew may not curse others if he or she feels they have been wronged.[18] Even if the person being cursed will not find out about it, it is still forbidden to do so (see the chapter, "Putting Others Down" for a deeper analysis of this idea). That is why the Torah forbids you to curse a deaf person, even though the deaf person will never hear those terrible words.[19] First, each person knows what he or she has done, and the verse ends with the phrase, "you shall fear God, I am God" to demonstrate that God also knows. In addition, the person who curses has diminished God, once again, by cursing one of His creations. In summary then, one is not only forbidden to put others down, but it will never enhance that person's self-esteem in the long run.

What then can a person do to feel better about himself or herself and enhance his or her self-esteem?

## HELPING YOURSELF FEEL BETTER ABOUT YOURSELF

One of the most important aspects of helping any person do better, feel better, and realize his or her great potential, is knowing that he or she is not alone. In addition to help from family and friends, there is always another area each person can count on for help – God. The Midrash promises that if a person makes even a small effort to make himself a better person, God will do the "heavy lifting" and help with the rest.[20] The phrase in the Midrash is "you open up a small hole the size of a pin needle, and God will make that opening the size of a hall."

In fact, Judaism stresses in many places that feeling good about oneself and how a person is judged (and should judge oneself) is a function of effort, and not accomplishment. A Jew should not feel diminished in any way if he or she does not accomplish as much as he or she wants to or even by how much is expected, as

14. Musaf service for Rosh Hashana
15. Rabbeinu Yonah, Sha'ar HaAvodah 1
16. Genesis 5:1
17. Midrash, Beraishit Rabbah 24:7

18. Mishna Shavuot 4:13
19. Leviticus 19:14
20. Midrash, Shir HaShirim Rabbah 5:3

long as he or she tried maximumally and gave all possible effort. That is why the Talmud specifically states that achieving more or achieving less in any realm is not the main goal or way to judge a person.[21] (The context there was Torah study, one of the highest values in Judaism.) Rather, a person is judged by how much effort was exerted in the endeavor. Therefore, from a Jewish perspective, to feel better about oneself, a person has to answer one simple question: Did you try your best? If the individual did, then the achievement is secondary and even unimportant. It is interesting that it is specifically at a ceremony of achievement of Torah study that this concept is highlighted by the Rabbis, in the wording of the text that a Jew recites upon completion of a Talmud tractate. In differentiating between non-Jewish values and Jewish values, that text says that non-Jews run to non-Torah related pursuits and Jews run to Torah-related pursuits.[22] Then it says that both non-Jews and Jews put in effort. But non-Jews are not rewarded for the effort alone, but only for how much was accomplished (as this is the standard in the world at large), while Jews are rewarded for effort alone. Therefore, a person should feel great if he gives his or her all, even if very little or nothing was achieved.

The same idea is related to possibly the greatest Jew of all time, Moses. The Torah states that Moses was the humblest of all people in the world.[23] On this verse, one commentary asks how could it be possible that Moses, who was the greatest prophet, the only one who spoke face to face with God,[24] stood up to Pharaoh, and stayed in heaven for forty day and nights without eating in order to write the Torah,[25] could think of himself as worthless, with low self-esteem?[26] One answer he espouses is that indeed Moses recognized his enormous talent and worth and how special he really was.

Realizing that all of his talents and greatness were from God, Moses did not think of himself as great, because he himself did not do anything special, but his accomplishments were due only to God's help. Furthermore, Moses tried to use all of his talents and gifts to help others. If we learn from Moses and attribute anything we are good or great at to God and then use our abilities to help others, we will inevitably feel good about ourselves – but in the proper way, with modesty, like Moses. Therefore, Moses had very high self-esteem, while still remaining the most humble man on earth.

Another way that we can improve our self-esteem is by not committing one of the basic sins in the Torah. Unlike any other commandment, it says that Jews have to run away from a falsehood, and they have a prohibition not to lie.[27] Part of the prohibition about lying is not to lie to oneself! A person should not deceive himself or herself and think that he or she is worse or less talented or gifted than one actually is. A person also cannot lie and think that he or she is better than one actually is. But certainly, it would also be forbidden to put oneself down unnecessarily. Therefore, each person must do an honest reckoning of one's personality, achievements, and actions, and then judge oneself honestly. Most people with low self-esteem judge themselves too harshly. In judging one's actions, it is important that each individual do just that – judge actions, but not thoughts. It is important in judging oneself that each person *not* compare himself or herself with others. Why not? First, as was demonstrated above, each person is different, with unique qualities and potential. Second, just as we fool ourselves by often misjudging our accomplishments, talents, etc., we also misjudge the accomplishments and greatness of others. We often wish to emulate others, when these people are actually not worth emulating. When Rabbi Yosef was approaching death, he briefly entered the world beyond before he returned. He reported that in the world of truth over there, the reality that we

---

21. *Berachot* 5b
22. Text from the ceremony upon completion of a Talmud tractate
23. Numbers 12:3
24. Deuteronomy 34:10
25. Exodus 34:28
26. *Ketav VeKabblah* commentary on Numbers 12:3

27. Exodus 23:7, Leviticus 19:11

seem to believe is truth here in this world, is exactly the opposite of the objective truth and reality of beyond.[28] Thus, there are those who are thought of highly in this world, but in the world of objective truth are not thought of as anything special, and vice versa. Thus, we have to be honest in how we compare or contrast ourselves with others.

In addition, it is natural that everyone has bad or evil thoughts that are never acted upon. People with low self-esteem often punish themselves for these thoughts. Judaism, in general, believes that a Jew is judged by what he or she does, and not by one's thoughts, according to the Talmud.[29] After an evil action, the thoughts are added to the sin. However, thoughts alone almost never indict a Jew and are not considered culpable. Therefore, a person should never put himself or herself down for just bad thoughts. In addition, a person should be honest about his or her own potential as part of the prohibition not to lie to oneself. People with low self-esteem often think that they have limited potential and feel as though they are inadequate in a particular area. But by the very fact that each individual was born as a human being, they automatically have enormous potential, as opposed to the life and nature of animals, which have very little potential to grow after they are born (in a non-physical sense).[30] Each person, knowing that he or she has unlimited potential, should help every individual dream big and try to accomplish that dream. Even if the accomplishment falls short, that should not minimize any person's self-esteem. Yet, every human being should understand the unlimited potential given to him or her by God, and this should help that person think better of himself or herself.

Low self-esteem is even recognized in Jewish law as a legitimate concern. If a woman has low self-esteem because she was born with a large nose, and this really bothers her and causes great psychological pain, then Jewish law permits this woman to violate the Jewish prohibition forbidding a Jew to intentionally cause himself for herself physical harm and a create a wound, and allows this person to have cosmetic surgery – simply in order to feel better about herself and raise her self-esteem.[31]

## IN THE END, THOUGH, IT IS ALL UP TO ME

A person with low self-esteem can study the sources to realize each person's individuality and greatness. This person can understand that God will help those who attempt to help themselves. A person may have very supportive parents and friends telling him or her that he or she is a better person than he or she believes. But in the end, the change has to start with each person. Every individual has to help himself or herself in all areas, especially with regard to self-esteem. This idea can be demonstrated by many different sources within the Jewish tradition.

If a person tries to find something – himself or his self-esteem – and says, "I tried but had absolutely no success," then the Talmud says that we do not believe him – i.e., we assume that this person did not try hard enough. If a person truly attempts to find something – anything important – he or she will get there if he or she puts in enough effort.[32] The Mishna says that the gain is equal to the pain, – the more effort a person puts in, the more reward or result he or she will see (not necessarily tangible reward, as we saw above that in Judaism, people are not judged by accomplishments, but only by effort).[33] As we saw above, each person's actions and each person's mission will be brought before God for judgment.[34] But each person has to try and accomplish only according to his or her unique ability, not by any other standard. God will judge based on one's effort to accomplish.

---

28. *Pesachim* 50a
29. *Kiddushin* 39b
30. Maharal, *Drush on the Torah* 9b, 11b
31. *Responsa Igrot Moshe, Choshen Mishpat* 2:66
32. *Megillah* 6b
33. Mishna *Avot* 5:22
34. Musaf service on Rosh Hashana

This concept was clearly demonstrated by a certain Eliezer, who was a terrible sinner in every aspect of his life, according to the Talmud, and had a very low opinion of himself.[35] Even others had a low opinion of him, as one of the prostitutes he used to visit regularly said, "you, Eliezer, are such a bad person and such a chronic sinner, that there is no chance that you will ever repent and become a good person." This woke up Eliezer and he tried to repent. He tried and he summoned all parts of nature to help him repent, but they refused. In the end, Eliezer realized that repentance and raising his self-esteem were only up to him (as a first step). As he repented he died, and was called by God "Rabbi Eliezer" because his repentance was complete. Among the many lessons this passage teaches us, it demonstrates that if a person wants to better himself or herself, it is possible no matter how low one feels, but the repentance has to begin with that person's own desire and recognition that it can be done.

The opposite story concerned the ten spies sent by Moses to spy the land of Israel. Each of these people was a leader of his tribe and was called a "special" and distinguished person in the Torah.[36] How, then, did these men fall so quickly and bring back a bad report about the land of Israel, which caused the people to believe them and sin? The Torah gives us a clue to the answer. It was due to low self-esteem that they developed, despite their previous high position among the Jewish people. When telling over their exploits to the Jews, these spies describe the inhabitants of the land of Israel as "giants" of men. The verse says, "We were like insects in their eyes, and also in our own eyes."[37] We can understand how these people imagined how the others pictured them, but how did they know for sure how they appeared and were evaluated? Rashi offers one explanation that the spies actually heard the inhabitants speaking about the spies as "ants."[38] But other commentaries simply say that this was all in their imaginations. And later on, when the next generation actually fought and conquered these people in the land of Israel, it does not say anywhere that all of the Canaanites were giants. Since they felt so humbled and imagined themselves to be so low, both physically and psychologically, the Torah ends with the words "and so we were in our own eyes." This experience turned these leaders into ants – in their own minds. They now had such low self-esteem, all imagined, that they could no longer say anything positive about their experience or about the land of Israel as a place that God would help them conquer. So it was low self-esteem that turned these experienced leaders into scared individuals. We can learn from this that only if a person feels himself or herself to be worthy will he or she indeed become that worthy person.

In fact, we have proof that their low self-esteem falsely led them to the wrong conclusion about how the Canaanites felt about them. Thirty-eight years later, when the second group of two spies entered the land of Israel, the person who hid them, Rachav, states the feeling of all the Canaanites: "I know that the Lord has given you the land, and that your terror has fallen upon us, and that all the inhabitants of the land faint because of you."[39] For forty years, after the splitting of the sea defeating the Egyptians and the defeat of Amalek, the Canaanites were living in fear of the Jews. But the Jewish people and the spies thought differently because of their low self-esteem.

The same phenomenon occurred with the first king of the Jewish people, Saul. When he assumed the kingship, he was not only physically tall, but he had strong self-esteem. But when things did not go his way, his self-esteem became smaller and smaller, which was not justified. When Saul allowed the Amalekites to live, against the specific instructions of God, Samuel the prophet asked him why he had done so. Saul answered that he had to listen to the "polls" because this was what the people wanted. Samuel then calls Saul a

---

35. *Avodah Zara* 17b
36. Numbers 13:2-3 with Rashi commentary on verse 3
37. Numbers 13:33
38. Rashi commentary on Numbers 13:33

39. Joshua 2:9-11

"small person," not worthy of being a king of Israel.[40] Saul had lost his self-confidence, had lowered his self-esteem until he could no longer function, and was eventually deposed as king. Self-esteem is dependent, once again, on each person's feeling based on the objective facts, and a person needs to fight a feeling of inadequacy like the one that Saul developed.

Maimonides stresses a similar idea in another context. He says that many foolish people in the world believe that their destiny is already decided for them and that their futures are really not up to them, as many people with low self-esteem believe.[41] Maimonides points out that what each person does with his or her life is totally up to himself or herself. If a person wants to achieve the greatest heights (however that person defines it), it is possible if a person has the proper self-esteem and puts in the maximum effort to achieve. Each person can be as great as Moses or the opposite. But no one should think that it is not up to him or her.

Knowing and doing are two different things. An individual can understand intellectually how to achieve strong self-esteem, but doing it is a much harder task. How does a person go from knowing to acting upon that knowledge? Each person has to find his or her own way. The Rabbis give one suggestion: Help others with their self-esteem, and yours will come. Rabbi Yochanan says that every person should try to make others smile and try to help others to feel important.[42] That will help you achieve a sense of self-importance and a healthy self-esteem. That is also why it is a Jewish law that a very poor person who subsists only on donations is nevertheless obligated to give some of what he or she has received to another poor person, even poorer than he or she is.[43] Why? The knowledge that someone is worse off than you and that you can help them always enhances a person's dignity and self-esteem.

## TOO MUCH SELF-ESTEEM IS NOT A JEWISH VALUE AND NOT HEALTHY

Some people have *too much* self-esteem and think that they are so terrific and even better than everyone else. They do not measure themselves by any objective standards and believe that no one is as good as they are. There is one word for this characteristic of having too much self-esteem: haughtiness. How does Judaism feel about people who have this trait of haughtiness, brought on (very often) by too much self-esteem?

King Solomon says that God despises people who are so haughty, who think of themselves as so high and great, with too much self-esteem.[44] The Mishna tells each Jew do be very humble (not to have low self-esteem, but like Moses, as explained above, to know and accurately measure one's greatness but to attribute it to God and use one's terrific talents to help others). Maimonides rules this not only as a goal to seek in life, but also as a Jewish law.[45]

But how does a person achieve this difficult task once he or she has achieved a healthy self-esteem, to keep too much self-esteem in check? The Mishna says that a Jew should not look at his or her needs first, but should look first to what God wants from each Jew. And if God's will comes in conflict with that person's desires or needs, God's will always come first.[46] Another Mishna also has some sound advice for anyone who has achieved great things in life but thinks that he or she is indeed great, full of too much self-esteem. (The Mishna speaks about Torah learning, but this advice can apply to all spheres of life and success.) If a Jew achieved much, he or she should not feel that it is something so terrific, because this is why each person was created.[47] God gave each person talent – to learn, to excel in music, business or any other field. If people succeed, they are only doing what God expects of them.

40. Samuel I 15:16-19
41. Maimonides, *Hilchot Teshuva* 5:2
42. *Ketuvot* 11b
43. Maimonides, *Hilchot Matnot Aniyim* 7:5

44. Proverbs 16:5
45. Mishna *Avot* 4:4; Maimonides, *Hilchot De'ot* 2:3
46. Mishna *Avot* 2:4
47. Mishna *Avot* 2:8

An individual should use one's talent and success to help others, but not feel too great about oneself.

How does the traditional Jew remind himself or herself (especially in ancient times) that the focus is about God and not about him? In almost every endeavor (in the time of the Torah when most of the economy was connected to farming), the Torah says that before a Jew can enjoy the fruits of his or her labor, before a person pats himself on the back for his achievements, he or she must first give something back to God and acknowledge that it was God that made this all possible.[48] Therefore, in an agrarian society, where possessions were not measured by how much money was in the bank, but by crops and sheep, before a person could eat any food he or she had produced with his or her hands and months of toil, he or she first had to give a small percentage to God. This is Jewish law with regard to grain, domestic animals that are born, and any other physical achievement in that society. We could and should learn to translate that pattern to many activities today, besides the usual 10-20% for set aside for *Tzedaka*-charity, in Jewish law. *Sefer HaChinuch* explains the reasons for these commandments in the manner described above.[49] One lowers one's own self-esteem if one realizes that no achievement could have been accomplished without God's help.

In order to preclude people developing a self-esteem that is too strong, the Rabbis also advise acting like Hillel, who was very modest, and not with the personality of exactitude that was displayed by Shammai.[50] On the other hand, Hillel was no shrinking violet who thought very little of himself. As he entered a Sukkot celebration, Hillel once remarked, "If I am here, all is here."[51] (This statement should not be understood on the simple level, since a modest person would never say something so outlandish. The explanation is beyond the realm of this volume.) But a balance must be struck between a good, healthy self-esteem and too much or too little self-worth, both of which cause the person problems. That is why right after stating that man is "nothing," equal to a mosquito, the next verse states that man is just a little lower than the angels.[52] A person with low self-esteem should concentrate on the second verse, while a person who has too much self-esteem should study the first verse.

The prophet Jeremiah warned about the person who has so much success in areas such as knowledge, strength, and finances. These achievements can easily go to the person's head and raise his or her self-esteem to an unacceptable level. Therefore, he says that a person should not attribute achievements to oneself, but only to God, and only he who concentrates on becoming closer to God can truly be proud.[53] And a little anxiety in this area – lowering one's self-esteem – is good for a person, to help prevent that individual from becoming evil.[54] Finally, although the verse in its simple reading seems to say, "God's Torah is perfect and revives the soul,"[55] the term *"Meshivat Nafesh"* can also be translated as "self-esteem." Thus, when a person realizes that it is God's Torah, not his or her Torah, and that all efforts in life should be God-centered, then that individual's self-esteem will be perfected.

48. Exodus 23:9, Leviticus 23:10, Numbers 15:20, Deuteronomy 18:4
49. *Sefer HaChinuch*, Mitzvah 606
50. *Shabbat* 30b
51. *Sukkah* 53a
52. Psalms 8:5-6 with Midrash, *Vayikra Rabbah* 14:1
53. Jeremiah 9:22-23
54. Proverbs 28:14
55. Psalms 19:8

# SEXUAL ABUSE OF CHILDREN – JUDAISM'S VIEW

IT IS VERY DIFFICULT TO WRITE about sexual abuse, just as it is difficult to acknowledge that sexual abuse of children of all ages happens every day. Because of the shame involved, this difficulty is more pronounced in the Jewish community, and even more so in the observant Jewish community. In the secular community, sexual abuse of children has been the subject of great concern for some time now and has become the focus of many legislative and professional initiatives. But discussing this taboo subject has only recently begun to take place in the general Jewish community, and even more recently in the Haredi (ultra-Orthodox) population. Before this, many claimed and some even believed that this problem did not even exist at all in these communities. But the issue and possible crisis of sexual abuse of children exists on some level in all Jewish communities. Therefore, knowing how to respond to this problem as Jews is extremely important.

It seems like a clear-cut issue, not a subject for a moral or ethical debate. Any perpetrator of sexual abuse against children should be in jail and certainly separated from any further contact with children. Whether it is a parent, teacher, youth leader, camp counselor, Rabbi, or principal, any adult who sexually abuses children should be punished severely for his actions. What possible ethical discussion or issues could exist within the context of such a subject?

And yet, there are many important questions to address. First of all, the track record of the Jewish community in its reaction to problems in this area has not been stellar. In the past, some suspected child abusers in public positions have often been allowed to "slide" without being removed from their positions, with those having more notoriety allowed the greatest leeway. Too often, Rabbis or teachers guilty of such crimes have been permitted to move away from the community without

public exposure of their deeds, and then continue their abhorrent activities all over again with unsuspecting children in another Jewish community.

In addition to this inexcusable behavior by the community (which needs to be addressed and explained), several other moral issues surrounding this subject need to be examined. For example, what is the proper reaction if someone sees such a heinous crime taking place? How should a Jew react when he hears about such a sin? At the stage that a person is merely suspected of harming one child, without any proof, how should this individual be treated from a Jewish perspective? The removal of a suspected person from his position due to suspicion of committing a vile act, or even a mere public accusation, will immediately damage this human being's reputation for the rest of his life. For the small minority of suspected people who are accused but not guilty, how should the community proceed in the absence of concrete proof? How does the sin of *Lashon Harah*, slanderous speech (i.e., speaking badly about an individual even if the accusation is true), play into this issue? Is it right to go straight to the police or should a Rabbi first be consulted? Should publicizing a guilty individual's crime in the Jewish community take place if this will engender a desecration of God's name in the general community, especially if the perpetrator is religious and a person of note? Publicizing an individual's crime(s) will almost certainly destroy that person's family, who are innocent individuals. Should that be taken into account as well? This chapter will discuss these issues, based on the sources.

## DEFINITION OF SEXUAL ABUSE OF CHILDREN

There are many definitions for sexual abuse of a child, but the simplest definition of an offender is any adult who uses a child for sexual stimulation, including asking or pressuring a child to engage in sexual activities or indecent exposure with intent to gratify the offender's sexual desires. In trying to explain this concept to young children in order to warn them, they should be told that "If an adult touches you any place that is covered by a bathing suit," that is wrong, and the child should report it to a responsible adult. The effects of sexual abuse extend far beyond childhood. Sexual abuse robs children of their childhood and creates a loss of trust, feelings of guilt, and self-abusive behavior. It can lead to antisocial behavior, depression, identity confusion, loss of self-esteem, and other serious emotional problems. It can also lead to difficulty with intimate relationships later in life. The sexual victimization of children is clearly ethically and morally wrong, both in the Jewish tradition and in most secular societies.

## REACTING TO SEEING OR KNOWING ABOUT DEFINITE SEXUAL ABUSE

In the United States, there are laws directing a person's reaction to the sexual abuse of a child. Every state has a law mandating "professionals" – including doctors, nurses, therapists, welfare personnel, and teachers – to report such abuse, but only in three states is failure to report considered a felony. In thirty-nine states, not reporting the sexual abuse of children is only a misdemeanor. Eighteen states have a law requiring non-professionals to report such an act, with no specification for those failing to report.

In contradistinction, the attitude and ruling about this in crime in Judaism is very definitive. Not acting and/or not reporting is a clear sin, and reporting the molestation of a child fulfills one of the 613 commandments in the Torah, as Judaism forbids any person, not only professionals, from standing by and doing nothing.[1] Maimonides records this law with specific examples, including any sexual act against a person's will.[2] In addition to

reporting, a Jew's first obligation is to prevent an imminent act from occurring, or stopping an act that he or she witnesses. The Code of Jewish Law goes one step further and even requires a Jews to hire others to stop the act if the witness cannot do it by himself.[3] This applies to any situation in which one person is harming another person, but certainly when the victim is a defenseless child.

Judaism actually stresses the prevention of the act, and one commentary states that reporting to the proper authorities (who these are will be discussed below) should take place *before* the act is committed, if possible, in order to prevent harm to any person and any child.[4] The Talmud says that before any act of sin is committed, the perpetrator should be warned that it is a sin and that one's immoral desires should not be acted upon. If the person does not listen, the warning should be repeated again and again. The Talmud also says that even if a teacher is about to do a sin, a child (or student) is permitted to warn the teacher against it.[5] Another Talmudic passage states that if a person is told about an imminent sin but does nothing to prevent it, that person's inaction renders him or her culpable, as if he/she committed the sin itself.[6] This implies that if Jews know about a situation of sexual abuse and do nothing about it, they are considered part of that sin.

Jewish law even allows a person to do an act that would normally be forbidden in order to stop an act of sin such as child abuse. Rabbi Yisrael Meir Kagan, who was famous for enunciating the laws forbidding speaking evil about other people, writes that while it is not normally permitted to reveal someone's bad behavior to another person, if a man witnesses an adulterous relationship, it is a Mitzvah, a commandment, to tell the husband about the adulterous woman, in order to end the illicit relationship. But he adds a caveat (which will be discussed below as well) that this Jewish

---

1. Leviticus 19:16
2. Maimonides, *Hilchot Rotze'ach* 1:15

3. *Shulchan Aruch, Choshen Mishpat* 426:1
4. *Ha'amek Davar* on Leviticus 10:16
5. *Bava Metzia* 31a
6. *Nidah* 61a

law only applies when the person actually saw the act and did not just hear about it second hand from someone else.[7] In a similar manner, normally it is forbidden to strike another person, but a Jew is permitted to strike the sinner to force him or her to stop the act of sinning.[8] Thus, it is not sufficient to report sexual abuse if one actually witnesses the act. A Jew is obligated to stop the act, even it means striking the perpetrator (in a situation where the onlooker will not endanger himself or herself). Although one Jewish law authority says that permission to hit the molester only applies if the individual does not hate the person (due to previous experiences),[9] others disagree and say that if a Jew must hit this perpetrator to make him desist, it is permitted to do so even if the two adults are enemies.[10] Another Jewish law authority from the last century, after explaining at length the severity of the sin of striking another human being, also says that in this particular case it is permitted if that is the only way to make a sinner stop hurting another person.[11]

Rabbi Moshe Shternbuch of the twenty-first century speaks specifically about this aspect of sexual abuse and how doing nothing is forbidden, especially regarding a person in a position of authority.[12] He says that if a student comes to the principal complaining that a certain teacher is molesting children in the class, the principal is forbidden to ignore the accusation of that child and must put the teacher on constant surveillance while investigating the matter carefully and immediately.

## SUSPICION WITHOUT ADEQUATE PROOF: WHAT IS THE RIGHT THING TO DO?

Very rarely is an abuser of children foolish enough to be seen and get caught in the act. Thus, in practice, preventing the abuse beforehand or during the act is almost impossible. But even after the abuse has taken place, the most we can hope for is that the child will come forth to complain, or sometimes a doctor or another professional will see signs of abuse. However, the evidence of abuse is often circumstantial and can be explained away in different ways. If the accused abuser denies the charge and only one child complains, what are the right steps to take in such a situation? Believing the child regarding a teacher or parent's supposed offense will often result in the teacher losing his job or the immediate removal of the child from the parent's custody. But it is possible that sometimes the child is mistaken in his or her understanding of what happened or is inventing allegations that never happened, and in those situations, a teacher's career may be ruined forever as a result of that mistake. (Later apologies can never undo the damage.) Likewise, a parent may improperly be deprived of custody of his child. What then should be done when it is a situation of "he says, she says" or the proof is only circumstantial? (Once two or more children come forth, there is a much stronger basis to take action.)

A Jewish court can only rule and act upon the valid report of two legitimate witnesses,[13] a situation that is almost impossible in cases of sexual abuse of children. And the testimony of a child is not admitted at all in a Jewish court. What then is the right thing to do according to Judaism at the stage of innuendo, suspicion, and/or accusation without actual proof?

The Rabbis had enough savvy to understand how and when to act even without adequate witnesses and to differentiate between accusations and substantiations, between circumstantial evidence and proof. The Talmud asks how King David could have acted upon the *Lashon Harah* (slanderous speech) of Tziba? It answers that he saw other things besides Tziba's words that convinced him of the facts, and he did not act on the words alone.[14] Thus, we

7. Chofetz Chaim, *Hilchot Issurei Lashon Hara* 4 (side comment)
8. Rosh commentary on *Bava Kama* 3:13
9. *Me'irat Einayim* on *Tur, Choshen Mishpat* 421:28
10. *Turei Zahav* on *Tur, Choshen Mishpat* 421
11. *Kitzur Shulchan Aruch* 184:1
12. *Teshuvot Vehanhagot* 5.398

13. Deuteronomy 19:15
14. *Shabbat* 56a

see that sometimes, besides actual witnesses, evidence can be intuitive and common sense can be employed to act upon it, thereby ameliorating the need to rely solely upon mere accusations. Sometimes even an allegation is enough to justify punishment under certain circumstances (i.e., if other circumstantial evidence helps determine the facts in the case). Therefore, in particular circumstances and in the absence of valid witnesses, the Talmud states that it is permitted to give a person the punishment of flogging based merely on a rumor of evildoing.[15] Rabbi Ashi said that it is permitted to curse an adulterer based only upon what people are saying, even without any evidence at all.[16] One commentator on the Talmud wrote regarding the immorality of a son-in-law living in his in-laws' home: If there is a rumor that he is having an affair with his mother-in-law, he may be flogged if she has a reputation for improper behavior.[17]

Another Talmudic passage discusses the topic of gossip and innuendo and how we should react to it. The first part of the passage says, "where there is smoke there must be fire" – i.e., that every accusation has some truth to it, be it only the intent to commit the sin the person is accused of. The next part of the passage shows that Moses himself was accused of adultery, and then it explains that Moses had enemies.[18] Thus, any time a person has enemies in the community, accusations (without specific proof) can be disregarded as the attempt of enemies trying to destroy a person. Finally, it says that the usual cycle for rumors, gossip, and accusations lasts a day and a half. If the same rumors persist long after that and the person has no known enemies, they can be taken seriously. One Talmudic commentary states this specifically: when a rumor persists in a community regarding sins of a sexual nature, and when these rumors continue for a long period, it is permitted to flog this person

as punishment, providing he has no enemies.[19] Regarding the husband who suspects his wife of adultery in the Torah (the topic of *Sotah*), one commentary explains why the husband is not considered a sinner, even if it turns out that the wife was not an adulteress. He explains that after the husband warned his wife not to be seen with the other man, she simply disregarded the warning, and her suspicious behavior alone made her worthy of the accusation by the husband.[20] Thus, all the circumstances surrounding an accusation must be taken into account before acting or not acting upon it.

*Sefer Yerai'im* states that while we may not believe *Lashon Harah* (evil or slanderous speech) as truth, a person may nevertheless treat the person spoken about with suspicion.[21] And if other factors substantiate the rumor, then one may indeed act upon the "slanderous speech." This is Jewish law according to one authority.[22] Another authority states that a Jewish court has the power to act in a meta-legal manner and punish a person even without witnesses, if it is clear to the judges, even without proof, that this person had acted in an improper or sinful manner.[23] The Rabbi most associated with the avoidance of speaking evil or believing what is spoken, writes that although every Jew is obligated to judge each situation optimistically and for the good of each person,[24] if one cannot find a positive side in a specific situation and the circumstances point to the fact that the person did do what he is accused of, then one can believe the accusations as truth.[25] The author of the *Code of Jewish Law* adds that if this person is a repeat offender in this particular sin, then accusation and rumor is sufficient to believe that he actually did it.[26]

The sum total of all of these opinions is that sometimes allegations are enough to act upon

---

15. *Kiddushin* 81a
16. *Megillah* 25b
17. Meiri on *Kiddushin* 12b
18. *Mo'ed Katan* 18b

19. *Yam Shel Shlomo* on *Yevamot* 10:20
20. Seforno commentary on Numbers 5:31
21. *Sefer Yerai'im* 192
22. *Sefer Mitzvot HaGadol, Lo Ta'ase* 10
23. *Aruch HaShulchan, Choshen Mishpat* 2:1
24. Mishna *Avot* 1:6
25. Chofetz Chaim, *Hilchot Issurei Lashon Hara* 7:10-11
26. *Beit Yosef*, on *Tur, Choshen Mishpat* 388:13

as fact if other factors corroborate the rumor/accusation/charge. Who determines these factors today, will be discussed below. However, two famous Rabbis of the 20th and 21st centuries discussed the specific situation of teachers who sexually abuse their students. They both say that when the evidence dictates it, the person should be put away, even if there are no valid witnesses. However, Rabbi Elyashiv states that we also have to be worried about the student who has a personal vendetta against a particular teacher and is clever enough to turn that anger into an accusation of sexual abuse.[27] Chazon Ish spoke of a situation in which a new group of teachers moved to a city and tried to take the jobs of the existing teachers of Torah by spreading accusations of the veteran teachers' sexual abuse of the students.[28] In cases like these, where there may clearly be an ulterior motive behind the accusations, one must be very careful not to believe them. In these situations, clear proof is required before acting.

## SHOULD THE ABUSER BE GIVEN TO THE SECULAR AUTHORITIES OR NOT?

Throughout Jewish history, wherever Jews lived in the Diaspora, there has almost always been a very strained relationship between the Jewish community and the local government. Usually, local governments found ways to punish Jews simply because they were Jews, regardless of their generally lawful behavior. Even today in certain observant communities, Jews are wary of handing over sinners and criminals to the police, preferring to punish sinners within the community. This is true even in the United States and in some communities in Israel. There is a reluctance to give over any sinner, and specifically a child abuser, to the local authorities in order to be judged in secular courts. On the other hand, these religious communities realize that they do not have the authority or the means to incarcerate

a person who deserves to be in prison. Nevertheless, the reluctance to hand over child molesters to the police persists in some areas. Is there any justification for this? Should individuals who are guilty of committing heinous acts be dealt with by the Jewish *Bet Din* or not? The sources on this issue are quite revealing.

Even though the Rabbis of previous generations legitimately did not trust the secular authorities (before Western countries began treating Jews fairly), nevertheless we see that in certain circumstances the Rabbis understood that criminals must be turned over to the local police. Although the sources do not specifically speak about child abusers, we infer that the same rule applies. Already in the thirteenth century, Maimonides ruled that anyone who is a threat to the Jewish community may be given over and punished by the local non-Jewish authorities.[29] In a similar vein, Rabbi Moshe Isserles wrote that counterfeiters who potentially cause damage to the larger Jewish community can be given over to the non-Jewish court system, much like a sexual abuser.[30] In a different paragraph, Rabbi Isserles wrote that if a Jew commits a type crime that the secular authorities will pursue seriously, then it is a duty to hand this person over to the secular police, because the person poses a threat to the Jewish community as long as he is free.[31] This law also applies to any Jewish adult who molests children.

Modern day Rabbis and community leaders also rule that child abusers may be given over to the secular police and court system. As noted above, Rabbi Elyashiv, the acknowledged leader of the Haredi Jewish community in Israel, ruled that teachers who sexually abused children should be given over to the secular authorities as long as it is clear to all that the person is actually guilty of the crimes with which he is charged.[32] Rabbi Waldenberg was asked by an observant doctor about a child who was brought into the emergency room,

27. *Kovetz Teshuvot* 3:231
28. *Emunah U'Bitachon* 3:1
29. Maimonides, *Hilchot Chovel U'Mazik* 8:11
30. Rema, *Shulchan Aruch, Choshen Mishpat* 368:12
31. Rema, *Shulchan Aruch, Choshen Mishpat* 425:1
32. *Kovetz Teshuvot* 3:231

clearly abused by one or both parents who ostensibly were observant Jews. The observant doctor knew that he must report this situation to the police, but he also knew that since the authorities would most likely not return the child to his or her parents, this child would probably be given over to a secular institution or secular foster parents. He asked Rabbi Waldenberg if he was permitted to report the abuse to the police, given this probable outcome. Rabbi Waldenberg answered that since the child's life would be endangered upon returning home, going to the police is tantamount to saving a life, even if the child were to wind up in a secular environment.[33]

Rabbi Shternbuch was asked about a similar case in which the person is a danger to the community. If an observant man is an irresponsible driver who puts people in danger with his wild driving or driving without a license, should he be given over to the local secular authorities? Rabbi Shternbuch answers in the affirmative, provided that a Rabbi or religious court first warns him of the consequences of his reckless driving. If he disregards the warning, it is appropriate to give him over to the police.[34] In a similar case, Rabbi Ovadiah Yosef was asked about a driver who intentionally hid a disease like epilepsy from the government, in order to obtain a driver's license. If this person has an episode while driving, he could severely hurt or kill other drivers. Rabbi Yosef rules that without a doubt this person's medical information must be given over to the authorities because, like the child molester, he poses a danger to society.[35] Rabbi Moshe Feinstein also rules that a butcher who says he is selling kosher meat but actually sells non-kosher meat should be handed over to the secular authorities, though only after the local Jewish court has tried to persuade him to stop the fraudulent sale. If they are unsuccessful, he should then be brought to the police.[36] Thus, it seems clear that in any situation in which a person

is a threat to the community and cannot be stopped forever by them, there is an obligation to give this person over to the local police and secular courts.

## SHOULD THE SINNER BE WARNED FIRST TO STOP?

Before taking the drastic step of turning over a Jewish, observant (in other areas) abuser to the police, should this person be given a warning to stop his behavior, and only if he persists, should he then be arrested? We saw that both Rabbi Shternbuch and Rabbi Feinstein believe that this person should first be brought to a Jewish court, and if the person continues his behavior after he is warned by the court, only then should he be given over to the secular police. But they were speaking about cases of bad drivers and thieves. Would this apply to adults who sexually abuse children?

Rashi explains that the purpose of the warning is only to distinguish between an intentional act and an accidental act in order to determine the proper punishment.[37] But in the situation of a "pursuer," when we have an obligation to insure that an immoral act is stopped, warning is not necessary. Since we saw that saving a child from a child abuser is an obligation, the idea of giving this person "one more chance," which can be used to harm another victim, is not applicable at all. In addition, since many studies have demonstrated that sex offenders can never truly be cured (and continue to have the urge to commit these crimes throughout their lifetimes), warning in this case (unlike the case of drivers or thieves who may stop if scared enough) will have little or no impact. Therefore, *Kitzur Shulchan Aruch* rules that in money matters, such as the case of a counterfeiter, a warning from the Jewish community may be in order before giving this person over to the police. But regarding sexual abuse, since every additional act may destroy a

---

33. *Responsa Tzitz Eliezer* 19:52
34. *Teshuvot VeHanhagot* 1:803
35. *Responsa Yechave Da'at* 4:60
36. *Responsa Igrot Moshe, Choshen Mishpat* 1:8

---

37. Rashi commentary on *Sanhedrin* 102b

child's life for years, no one should give a molester "one last chance" to reform.[38]

## SHOULD RABBIS BE CONSULTED BEFORE TAKING ANY CONCRETE STEPS?

It seems very clear cut that when individuals know that an adult is sexually abusing children, the person should be immediately arrested and put in jail for a long time. And yet, there are always special sensitivities involved in such cases regarding the victim, his or her family, and the family of the sinner. We saw above that both Rabbis Shternbuch and Feinstein suggest that a Jewish court should be consulted first, before proceeding to the secular authorities. Rabbi Yoel Sirkis ruled even more stringently in the 1600's: In *any* case that involves the non-Jewish authorities, a Rabbi or Jewish court *must* first rule on the particular issue, and only then, if they rule guilty, should the abuser be handed over to the police.[39] A contemporary Rabbi, Tzvi Gertner, writing about the specifics of child abuse by teachers, acknowledges the seriousness of the crime and says that if left unrestricted, a teacher who abuses children can ruin the lives of hundreds of youngsters. Therefore, he admonishes, the right way to deal with such a person is to utilize the advice of Rabbis who have specific knowledge and expertise in this area.[40] Rabbi Karelitz writes that because of the sensitivities involved, especially to the victims, at least the sources or responsa of Rabbis must be consulted before moving forward.[41] It seems clear from these Jewish authorities that it is not only prudent but also obligatory for steps to be taken to stop such offenders, and this should be done in consultation with local Rabbis who have experience in such matters.

## REPENTANCE FOR SUCH SINNERS?

Judaism teaches that the process of repentance and atonement is possible for almost all sins, as we see from the daily blessings in the *Amidah* (blessings 5 and 6) and the entire day of Yom Kippur once a year. Would this dictum and concept also apply to sexual abusers of children? Rabbi Elyashiv writes that first the perpetrator must admit fully to his sins.[42] If it can be shown that he has gone through a process of rehabilitation and is no longer a threat to anyone, only then can he be returned to the classroom (or to his position) after this long process. If it is true that the urge to molest can never be removed, then obviously full repentance can never be achieved and this person should never have any further contact with children. Rabbi Halberstam writes that the offender must sit first for many years in jail and go through extensive therapy with psychologists and psychiatrists.[43] If after this long process the professionals say he is rehabilitated, only then can this person return to normal society. Chofetz Chaim, however, warns us that these kinds of offenders are very astute at saying the right words and proclaiming that they have been rehabilitated while continuing to abuse children.[44] Their actions speak much louder than their words. Therefore, we should not believe them and their claims of repentance and reform until this is verified by experts.

## PUBLICIZE OR NOT? USING COMMON SENSE

As mentioned above, until now the tendency in the Jewish community throughout the ages, especially in the more observant communities, was to hide all cases of sexual abuse of children, specifically when the perpetrators are leaders or well-known figures in the community. Is this the right course of action or not?

On the one hand, keeping each shameful

---

38. *Kitzur Shulchan Aruch* 184:9
39. *Bayit Chadash* on *Shulchan Aruch, Choshen Mishpat* 28:3
40. Rabbi Tzvi Gertner in *Yeshurun* 15, pp. 644-645
41. *Emunah U'Bitachon* 3:2
42. *Responsa Sho'eil U'maishiv* 1:185
43. Rabbi Moshe Halberstam, *Yeshurun* 15, p. 646
44. Chofetz Chaim, *Hilchot Lashon Hara* 4:7

incident "in-house" without publicizing what happened or singling out the person who committed the crime makes sense. Each time incidents like these are publicized to the greater (non-Jewish) community, God's name is profaned. People think less of God and Judaism because of what this person did, especially if the perpetrator is a Rabbi or well-known personality. The sin of desecrating God's name is serious indeed, so much so that anyone who profanes God's name is worthy of being separated from the Jewish community[45] and/or publicly censured.[46] In addition, by publicizing the perpetrator's name, the entire family of this person, who are certainly innocent bystanders (who may have also suffered in different ways) will be publicly shamed as well, and their lives may be forever ruined. On the other hand, Rabbi Yonah Gerondi says that *not* publicizing the offender's name will cause an even greater desecration of God's name because the identity of this sinner may never be known or exposed.[47] Indeed, it has often happened in cases in which the community did not publicize the facts in child abuse cases that the Rabbi or perpetrator simply moved to another community and then victimized other children. The importance of avoiding desecration of God's name in every situation in life is a paramount value in Judaism according to Rabbi Luzzato.[48] Thus, knowing the right thing to do about this issue and how to behave in each case requires great sensitivity, which is another reason that Rabbinic authorities should be consulted.

Indeed, knowing precisely how to proceed in each situation is often very difficult. That is why the element of common sense, as well as consultation with professionals, is needed. This idea of common sense is not independent and separated from Jewish thought, since Judaism embraces the idea of using common sense in each situation, in addition to strict adherence to Jewish law. Thus, the Talmud tells us that the Second Temple was destroyed because Jews strictly obeyed the law without using the element of common sense that goes beyond the strict Jewish law.[49] There is the concept of the pious fool who carefully follows the details of Jewish law but does not see the bigger picture. An example of this is the man who can save a drowning woman, but because she is unclothed he refuses to do so, thereby following the laws of modesty but ignoring the larger picture of saving a life. Things have not changed much in two thousand years. The Rosh Yeshiva of Yeshivat Torah Voda'as wrote about the Yeshiva boy who reasoned it is better to marry a non-Jewish woman than a non-observant Jewish woman who will not observe the laws of family purity.[50] While it is true that fewer actual sins will be perpetrated by marrying the non-Jew, it is foolish piety to think that Judaism desires this. Hundreds of years ago, Rabbi Yehuda Chasid wrote that there are actions in Judaism that we should do even if they are not specifically written in Jewish law, as well as other acts we should refrain from – all due to common sense and logic.[51] Both Maimonides[52] and Nachmanides[53] echo this idea.

Therefore in the case of a child abuser, because many difficult decisions often arise in apprehending and prosecuting the perpetrator, one has to be very careful how to proceed. Jewish thought and Jewish law, along with common sense and the advice of professionals and qualified Rabbis who are well-versed in these issues, are all important components to use in reaching a just decision on how to properly deal with the various facets concerning the problem of sexual abuse of children. Each specific situation must be analyzed and acted upon within the specific details and context of that circumstance.

45. *Shulchan Aruch, Yoreh De'ah* 242:11
46. *Shulchan Aruch, Yoreh De'ah* 343:43
47. Rabbeinu Yonah commentary on Proverbs 24:28
48. *Mesilat Yesharim*, chapter 11

49. *Bava Metzia* 30b
50. *Emet LeYaakov, Vayechi* 137
51. *Sefer Chasidim* 153
52. Maimonides, *Guide for the Perplexed* 3:17
53. Nachmanides commentary on Genesis 6:13

# SHOULD RESPECT BE GIVEN TO A LEADER THAT SINNED?

WITHOUT MENTIONING THE SPE-
cific names of many of the well-
known personalities involved, over
the past few years there have unfortunately
been many Jewish (and non-Jewish) leaders who have sinned and who have been
convicted of crimes in a very public manner,
which has brought shame upon them as well
as upon the entire Jewish community. This
list includes presidents of Israel, Jewish mayors, Israeli Prime Ministers, Chassidic Rebbes,
and heads of Yeshivas in both the Ashkenazic
and Sephardic communities. The purpose
of this chapter is not to analyze why this has
become such a widespread and public trend
lately (for that, see the chapter, "The Jewish
View of Greed and the Madoff Scandal").
Rather, this chapter analyzes how as individuals and as a Jewish community should react
to these leaders after they have served their
time, expressed contrition, and have returned
to society. Should we give them honor for the
positions they once held, or should these people be shunned for the disgrace they brought
upon themselves and the community? If
one of these people walks into a synagogue,
should he or she be greeted like any other
Jew and given an honor such as an *Aliyah* to
the Torah? Does it make a difference if the
person is an observant Jew or not? Should it
make a difference if the person has expressed
remorse or is jail time enough to allow a person to re-enter society and be treated like anyone else? If the person wishes to return to his
or her former status, should the community
now allow this person a "second chance," or
refuse to support him or her? Although the
frequency and circumstances are not an exact
parallel, the Jewish sources have much to say
on this subject and can provide us with much
insight and guidance.

## DEFINING HONOR IN JUDAISM

Normally, when we speak about showing a
person honor, the dictionary defines that
concept as "high respect, as that shown for
special merit." But in Judaism, the word "*Kavod*" – "honor" has two distinct meanings. In
addition to the high esteem we give someone,
in Judaism, *Kavod* also signifies basic human
dignity.[1] Thus, when the Torah commands
children to honor their parents,[2] most people
normally understand this to signify giving parents respect and treating them with reverence
or esteem. But the Talmud defines honoring
one's parents as giving them enough food and
drink to survive, making sure they are dressed,
and helping infirm parents in and out of the
house.[3] This honor is not respect and high esteem, but rather according them basic human
dignity.

Therefore, the honor that is due to every
human being – *Kavod*, basic human dignity –
must also be accorded to a leader who sinned.
Even a sinner or an enemy is due that minimal
honor in Judaism. Thus, it is forbidden to rejoice when one's enemy falls,[4] although a Jew
can be happy that he or she was saved from
tragedy. Similarly, even the worst type of sinner, a murderer, is accorded basic human dignity in Judaism. For that reason, the Torah says
that after a murderer is hanged, one may not
leave the body overnight because that would
demonstrate a lack of dignity for the human
body (even that of a murderer).[5] In a similar
manner, the Talmud says that God berated the
angels who wanted to sing when the Egyptians
died in the sea and the Jews were saved. God

---

1. *Berachot* 19b
2. Exodus 20:12
3. *Kiddushin* 31b
4. Mishna *Avot* 4:19
5. Deuteronomy 21:22-23, codified by Maimonides, *Hilchot Sanhedrin* 15:7

said, "My creations are dying and you want to sing praises?" Even though these Egyptians were murderers of Jewish babies, evil to the core, they were still God's creations and had to be accorded minimal human dignity, and thus, the angles were not permitted to sing at their downfall.[6] This sentiment is reflected in Jewish custom and law as well. We symbolically remove ten drops from their joyous cup of wine at the Seder because of the agony the evil Egyptians suffered during the Ten Plagues. And the prayer service on Pesach is also changed because of this sentiment.[7] On every other holiday, Jews recite the full *Hallel* prayer in praise of God. But because the Egyptians died, Jews symbolically reduce singing their praise of God and eliminate two paragraphs during the last six days of Passover. For the same reason, even a sinner who is a Jewish leader must be accorded the minimum level of human dignity and may not be shunned by the community. Every human being retains a part of God inside of him or her[8] and thus must be accorded basic human dignity and honor.

However, when it comes to Jewish leaders, there is one caveat. The *Code of Jewish Law* states that if a leader or Rabbi retains his evil ways, then this person must be shunned by the Jewish community, even though his talents may be desperately needed by the community.[9] Thus, Judaism does not separate between one's moral values and actions, and the ability to perform one's duties admirably. Until a person has admitted his sin and has returned to the proper path, the community may and should ignore the person. But once this change has occurred, this leader must be accorded the minimum honor and dignity, and as with any sinner, may not be reminded of his checkered past.[10]

## CAN THE COMMUNITY GIVE A SINNER A PUBLIC HONOR OR SHOWING OF RESPECT?

Regarding the leader who has "served his time" and is contrite, the question is: Can this person be given special honor because of his past leadership, or do we afford him only the basic human dignity and nothing more, due to his past sins? Can and should this person be accorded an honor, like an *Aliyah* in the synagogue, because he is now an upstanding individual (and we ignore his past sins)?

The closest source that will help answer this question involves a bit of introduction. In today's modern society, if a person does something "wrong" by accident, without specific intent, that person is usually given a reprieve and is not looked down upon. However, Judaism does not quite view the person in the same manner. If a person commits a sin "by accident," i.e., without intent, but it could have been prevented if he had been paying closer attention, then this person is viewed as a sinner in Judaism. Though not as guilty as an intentional sinner, this person has to bring a sin offering (in Temple times), for example, for his *Shogeg*, accidental sin (and this sin is often ascribed in the Torah to a Jewish leader).[11] If a Jew accidentally kills someone (when a little more sensitivity might have prevented the action), then this person is "punished" by being banished to a city of refuge until the High Priest dies.[12] The Talmud speaks about our case in such a context.

Each city of refuge was populated by Levites. Like the Witness Protection Program today, no one in the city of refuge knew who was a sinner who had accidentally killed someone and who was simply a "regular" resident. Thus, if in the synagogue on Shabbat they would ask such an accidental sinner to come up to the Torah for an honor, the Mishna states that the person must inform the congregation at that point that he was an accidental sinner. If

6. *Megillah* 10b
7. *Shulchan Aruch, Orach Chaim* 490:4
8. Genesis 1:27
9. *Shulchan Aruch, Yoreh De'ah* 246:8
10. *Bava Metzia* 58b

11. Leviticus 4:2-3
12. Numbers 35:11

the congregation still wishes to give him the honor, it may do so.[13] Therefore, we see that if a person is contrite after sinning and the congregation knows he was a sinner who is contrite, they may indeed offer him an honor. However, let us not forget that in this situation, we are speaking about a sinner who sinned accidentally, and there is no parallel source to our question about bestowing an honor upon an intentional sinner who is now contrite. In either event, it seems that the congregation may decide about bestowing an honor or not.

## RESTORING A SINNER TO A FORMER POSITION OF LEADERSHIP

After the leader has "served his time" and is contrite, may he or she resume the mantle of leadership and be accorded this honor by the community once again? In the Jewish community of old (and sometimes today), there were two kinds of leadership positions – one achieved through personal achievement alone and another was a position inherited from one's parents. In both kinds of leadership, there is a Mishnaic argument about this question between Rabbi Meir and Rabbi Judah. Rabbi Meir says that a leader who sinned and is now contrite may indeed be restored to the former position of leadership, whether the position was due to his own merits[14] or due to his father's status.[15] In both cases, Rabbi Judah argues and says that once a leader is tainted with sin and immorality, he may never again be given any leadership position.

Since there is a Talmudic argument about whether a fallen leader can be restored to his former position, we must investigate the position of the later commentaries and Rabbis on this issue. One famous Mishna commentary rules like Rabbi Meir, and believes that a leader who has sinned and repented can indeed be reappointed to his former position.[16] But Ritva

disagrees and says that we rule according to Rabbi Judah – i.e., that a fallen leader is never reappointed, even if he has paid the price for his crime and repented. But Ritva then qualifies his ruling, saying that this may only apply when the crime is severe, such as murder, entering into servitude, or other such egregious crimes or sins. If, however, the sins are less severe, as long as the person repented, he may be reappointed to his former leadership position.[17] Maimonides has no such qualifications in his ruling and says that we rule like Rabbi Judah and never reappoint a leader who has fallen, even if he has repented fully.[18] The three-way argument is never clearly resolved by later authorities, but we often rule like Maimonides in such situations. In fact, one later authority does state that we rule like Maimonides – i.e., a Jewish leader never returns to his former position of honor and power.[19]

However, until now we have been speaking about Jewish leadership in general. We will see that there are major differences between which kind of Jewish leader sins and how we look at each leadership position in Judaism.

## KOHEN GADOL-HIGH PRIEST, WHO SINS

Although the argument exists about all other Jewish leaders, nearly everyone agrees that a sinning Kohen Gadol-High Priest, indeed returns to his leadership after he has repented. The Talmud states that after he is punished, the Kohen Gadol is reinstated to his position.[20] Why is this leader different? This is because the source of his leadership is the holiness derived from birth, which traces back to the original High Priest, Aaron. This holiness cannot be removed, even through sin. Maimonides validates this approach, explaining that since the source of power of other leaders is their actions, they deserve permanent removal if

---

13. Mishna *Makkot* 2:8
14. Mishna *Makkot* 2:8
15. *Makkot* 13a
16. Rebbeinu Ovadia Bartenura commentary on *Makkot* 2:8
17. Ritva commentary on *Makkot* 13a
18. Maimonides, *Hilchot Reotze'ach* 7:13-14 and commentary on Mishna *Makkot* 2:8
19. *Aruch HaShulchan, Choshen Mishpat* 425:29
20. Jerusalem Talmud, *Sanhedrin* 9b

they act immorally. But since the source of the Kohen Gadol's leadership is his holiness due to birth, it cannot be permanently removed.[21]

## THE *NASI* WHO SINS

The Torah speaks of a Nasi-political Jewish leader, a leader who sins "accidentally," but is nevertheless considered a sinner who must bring a sin offering for this action.[22] What of about a *Nasi* who sins intentionally? Can or should he be returned to office after he repents and brings a sin offering? Should he be accorded the honor due to a former leader even if he does not return to his former position?

First, we must define the term *Nasi* that the Torah is speaking about. In Modern Hebrew, a *Nasi* is a president. But even that title can be imprecise or misleading and therefore begs definition, since the role of a president of a country is defined differently even today, varying from nation to nation. In some countries, such as the United Sates, the president is the Commander-in-Chief, elected by the people (indirectly). He is the leader of the executive branch of government, with greater political power than any other elected official. In other countries, such as Israel, the president is only a titular position, that represents the state at formal affairs, but does not have any real political clout. He is elected by the congress (or Knesset), and it is the prime minister whose role is closest to the president of the United States. What then is a *Nasi* in the Torah and Talmud?

The Mishna declares that a *Nasi* is equivalent to a king, which in today's world would mean the position is similar to the presidency of the United States, which accords the president full military and political authority.[23] Maimonides explains that the meaning of the title of *Nasi* changed over time in Judaism. [24] While it referred to power that was equivalent

to the monarchy in the time of Scripture, by Talmudic times, the *Nasi* became the head of the high court of Judaism, the Sanhedrin. It was a Rabbinical position, with much power in Jewish law and some political clout as well in a community where the Sanhedrin was the highest court. As an aside, Maimonides reminds us that the Torah forbids Jews to curse the sitting *Nasi*, or king.[25] Even if the person who holds the title is deplorable and miserable at his job (a moral sinner), this person may still not be cursed due to his current position. Cursing the man is equivalent to cursing the office, and respect for the office must be retained, no matter who has the post. But once this *Nasi* is removed, no such prohibition exists.

In his description of the *Nasi* as a politician who rules the country, Rabbeinu Bechaye, who lived in the 1300s, sounds as though he is describing modern political life. He says that in referring to the sins of other Jewish leaders, the Torah begins the verse with the word "*Im*" – "if." Only in the case of a *Nasi* does the verse begin with the word "*Asher*" – "when." The reason is that (in contrast with the situation in other positions of Jewish leadership) it is almost inevitable that the *Nasi* is going to sin due to his hubris. It is a question of "when" rather than "if" when it came to the *Nasi*. A High Priest is aware of his holiness, and a Rabbi at the head of the Rabbinical court is aware of his religious duty, but a king who derives his power from his actions often thinks too highly of himself, and this will inevitably lead to sin. Unlike the Torah, Rabbeinu Bechaye is speaking about intentional sins as well.[26]

Regarding returning a *Nasi* to his previous position after he has been punished, we have seen the argument above. But there is another Talmudic source that sheds additional light on this person and position. The Jerusalem Talmud states that after the intentional sinning, the *Nasi* is given lashes for his sin, and this *Nasi* is never returned to his former position

---

21. Maimonides, Commentary on Mishna *Horayot* 3:2
22. Leviticus 4:22
23. Mishna *Horayot* 3:3
24. Maimonides, *Sefer HaMitzvot*, negative Mitzvah 316

25. Exodus 22:27 with Nachmanides commentary
26. Rabbeinu Bechaye commentary on Leviticus 4:22

because "he may kill them."[27] What does this signify? Who may kill whom and why?

Radvaz, who lived in the sixteenth century, says that if the *Nasi* returns to his former political position and regains the power he once had, he may decide to arrange matters to murder the Rabbis of the Jewish court that judged the *Nasi* as a sinner. It is for that reason that we do not return him to power. Radvaz continues and states that if the *Nasi* would never be in a position to exact revenge on those Rabbis, then he could indeed be reinstated.[28] But the Radvaz remains a minority opinion. *Kesef Mishne* (Rabbi Yosef Caro) commentary on Maimonides has a totally different understanding of this Talmudic passage. *Kesef Mishne* implies that it is better that this person should have his life shortened rather than be reinstated to a position of power. How could anyone who intentionally sins while he is in a leadership position be brought back to power? *Kesef Mishne* then offers an alternative reading of the Talmud passage: It would be as if the *people* had killed this *Nasi* if he were to return to power, since they would defame and ridicule this person, who is no longer worthy of any position of leadership. Therefore, he can never be returned to his former position. This reaction of the people leads us to another natural consequence when any Jewish leader sins.[29]

THE REACTION OF THE MASSES
AND HOW THEY LOOK AT GOD

In the modern era, each time a Jewish leader acts immorally, Jews all over the world are afraid how non-Jews will now perceive Judaism as a result. If a Jewish leader can act this way, this must be a reflection on the entire religion and the entire people. This reaction to fallen leaders has been felt and noted throughout Jewish history.

Maimonides says that even if a leader is acting in a technically correct manner and is not breaking any laws or Mitzvot-commandments, if the people perceive that he should not be acting in a particular manner, not only is the act forbidden to him, but it also constitutes a "desecration of God's name."[30] Something of this nature occurred in the State of Israel in 1977, when the wife of Prime Minister Yitzchak Rabin had a small foreign bank account in the United States, which at that time was illegal. This small infraction by the wife of the Prime Minister brought down the government and eventually led to the political upheaval in Israel, with a new party elected led by Menachem Begin. The Prime Minister did nothing illegal or immoral, but the perception was that this infraction was not "proper" for a prime minister's wife, and by association, for a prime minister.

What exactly is a "desecration of God's name"? Any action that will make people think less of God desecrates His name, and any act that makes people think better of God makes His name holy. This idea is articulated in the Talmud in describing some Jews whose actions embarrass their fellow Jews, and other Jews whose actions make their coreligionists proud. The Talmud speaks of people who are ostensibly "religious," keep Mitzvot in some areas, and are learned in Torah, but then act immorally and sin. The Talmud states that these are the worst kind of people who desecrate God's name. Thus, a public figure who brings shame to himself by his actions, also brings shame to Judaism and desecrates God's name. And a supposedly religious leader, an observant Jew (in most areas of Jewish life) who acts immorally, certainly desecrates God's name even more.[31] Even after the person is punished and repents, this kind of desecration of God's name does not dissipate so quickly. It is unfortunate that it the past few years, many of the prominent Jews who have sinned and committed crimes have also been supposedly "religious" people, which has caused God's name to be

27. Jerusalem Talmud, *Sanhedrin* 9b
28. Radvaz commentary on Maimonides, *Hilchot Sanhedrin* 17:9
29. *Kesef Mishne* commentary on Maimonides, *Hilchot Sanhedrin* 17:8

30. Maimonides, *Sefer HaMitzvot*, negative Mitzvah 63
31. *Yoma* 86a

desecrated around the world numerous times.

This public humiliation and desecration of God's name complicates how to behave towards the final category of a Jewish leader who sins, the Rabbi and teacher.

## THE RABBI-TEACHER WHO SINS

The Talmud describes a situation in which one of the prominent Rabbis of the Sanhedrin "did something objectionable" – i.e., he sinned. The Rabbis posed the question: What is the proper way to react to this person, who was apparently so important that his teaching was needed by the other Rabbis and by the people? On the one hand, if they publicly excommunicate this Rabbi, then his needed teaching would be lost. On the other hand, if they did not excommunicate him, it would create a public desecration of God's name, by not reacting to the sin of such a person. Rabbi Judah did not hesitate and promptly excommunicated this Rabbi. Later on, on that same Talmudic page, it says that if a (prominent or observant) person feels that the evil inclination is getting the best of him and he is about to sin, it is preferable that he should go to a place where no one recognizes him, dress like a non-Jew, and commit the sin there, rather than desecrate God's name publicly.[32]

Then the Talmud speaks about a case in which the sin by a Rabbi is not done in public, but it is a situation that a very public figure, such as the head of the high court, sins, and it is known only among other Rabbis. How should they react? Rabbi Huna says that in this case the sinner is not publicly excommunicated or shamed, but he is reprimanded by his peers privately (in order to avoid public desecration of God's name), quoting to him the verse, "Be dignified and remain at home" (Kings II 14:10). But if his inappropriate behavior continues despite these admonitions, then this Rabbi must be publicly excommunicated and punished, because not to do so would desecrate God's name (when the public

would eventually find out).[33] Rashi explains the phrase, "Be dignified," in two ways. It could either signify, "Act as a person who feels humiliated and stay home," or it can mean, "Act like the dignity your position demands and stay at home." Either way, the first approach is to quietly reprimand the Rabbi for the one-time sin in order not to publicize the sin and cause God's name to be desecrated. But if the immoral behavior persists, then it is proper to publicize the sin and the person is then removed from his position. What does Jewish law say is the proper reaction to this sensitive situation?

Maimonides echoes the basic thrust of the Talmud. He says that any public figure who sins should not be publicly humiliated unless the sin was egregious, like the sins of Yerovam (see Kings I), whose sins were very severe and caused other Jews to sin. But other sins should be addressed and punished privately. Even a great Torah scholar should be dealt with privately, certainly at first. Rabbis should not rush to publicly excommunicate him.[34] The Code of Jewish Law essentially quotes Maimonides word for word, but then adds that if the sins involved leaving Jewish observance entirely or creating a public desecration of God's name, then the Rabbi should be publicly and immediately excommunicated from the community.[35]

Maimonides adds a caveat in another section of his book of Jewish law: If the perpetrator was the head of the Jewish high court, then he receives lashes and is immediately removed from his position without the possibility to return even as a "regular" judge of the Sanhedrin-Jewish High Court.[36] We can summarize, then, that if the sin is particularly severe or if the person is in a very high public position, then immediate and public action is necessary. And once a Rabbi is removed from his position, one may not learn from this Rabbi as long as he remains a sinner or unrepentant,

---

32. Mo'ed Katan 17a

33. Mo'ed Katan with Rashi commentary
34. Maimonides, Hilchot Talmud Torah 7:1
35. Shulchan Aruch, Yoreh De'ah 344:42
36. Maimonides, Hilchot Sanhedrin 17:9

even if the entire community "needs" his wisdom.[37] As noted above, in Jewish thought, we do not separate between the Torah learned and the personality or character of a person, as students can learn bad traits even if great wisdom is present.

What about all the Torah that was taught by this great Rabbi for the many years *before* he sinned? Should it be thrown out because this person was removed from his position and is no longer respected or accepted? Or is the Torah that he taught still valid and to be studied nevertheless? The Talmud compares this Torah scholar who sinned to a walnut. Even though the outside of the walnut can be dirty and sullied, the inside remains pristine. Thus, the Torah this person taught remains valid and can be learned even after the teacher has been removed.[38]

The most famous Rabbi in the Talmud who went off the path and rejected Judaism was Rabbi Elisha ben Avuyah, who was called "*Acher*-the other one," after he left Judaism. The Torah that he taught before he rejected Judaism is still quoted in the Talmud as valid.[39] But Rabbi Meir, Elisha's most famous student, never gave up on his teacher and continued to learn from him, even after Elisha abandoned Jewish observance (though this was against the wishes of some of Rabbi Meir's colleagues). The Talmud records an incident when "Acher" was riding on a horse on Shabbat (against Jewish law) and Rabbi Meir was walking alongside him to learn Torah from him. At one point, "Acher" informed Rabbi Meir that he had to stop and return, for if he continued, Rabbi Meir would be violating the Sabbath by walking more than 2,000 cubits out of the city. Rabbi Meir returned but never abandoned his teacher and his belief that in the end, Rabbi Elisha would return to Judaism and Jewish practice.[40] According to the Midrash, Rabbi Meir fought both with and for his teacher during his entire lifetime, even after Elisha ben Avuyah died. In the end, Rabbi Meir received a signal from God that his Rebbe had indeed returned and died a righteous man.[41]

---

37. Maimonides, *Hilchot Talmud Torah* 4:1
38. *Chagiga* 15b
39. *Mo'ed Katan* 20a
40. *Chagiga* 15a
41. Midrash, *Kohelet Rabbah* 7:16

As we were growing up, most of us heard a variation of the following "rules" from our parents: "Do the right thing. I do not care what your friends are doing. You have to behave properly. (If all the other kids jumped off a bridge, would you do it too?) It makes no difference what other people think, as long as you do the right thing." The first two statements seem to be ideas everyone can agree on – act morally and resist peer pressure. But is the last statement really the ideal? Should people not care what others think of them or their actions? If each individual acts ethically in a given situation, but it looks unethical to others, should people still take that action? Is it really ethical and moral to not be concerned about how others react to the way people conduct themselves? Judaism has much to say about these questions and this moral issue.

## JUDAISM VERY MUCH CARES WHAT OTHERS THINK ABOUT OUR ACTIONS

In Judaism, how people react to a Jew's action is indeed very important. The very essence of being Jewish is how one impacts not only upon oneself but also upon others. Therefore, to consider the reaction of others as unimportant is to contradict a fundamental precept in Judaism, because it does not allow a Jew to fulfill his or her overall mission. The very first Jew, Abraham, is promised by God that he will be a blessing to all people of the world, not just to Jews. This indicates that others would aspire to be like Abraham.[1] Every action that Abraham took was scrutinized by others, and rightly so. Had Abraham acted in a way that would have affected people negatively, he would not have been able to succeed in his goal to inspire others to believe in one God.

This is not just Abraham's mission, but it is also the mission of every Jew. Therefore, the Talmud explains how a person fulfills one of the main guiding principles of Judaism:[2] "You shall love God with all your heart . . ."[3] A Jew is obligated to act in a manner that will cause people to say how great this person is and how special God must be to inspire such behavior. By learning and keeping the Torah's teachings, a Jew creates a *Kiddush Hashem*-Sanctification of God's Name. Therefore, what other people think of our actions is certainly important in Judaism. The Midrash tells us that had the personalities in the Bible such as Reuven and Boaz (and others) known that their actions would be recorded in the Torah and scrutinized by millions throughout the ages, they would have acted in a much more careful manner, especially when they did not behave in a totally righteous manner.[4] How people reacted to their actions was important to them, as it should be to all Jews.

When considering the proper path in life, says the Mishna, it is not enough that we choose deeds that will bring honor only to God. They also must bring honor to other human beings.[5] Therefore, every time a person decides upon any behavior, he or she must be very conscious that not only it is the right thing to do in that individual's eyes and even in God's eyes, but it must likewise be behavior that others will interpret as ethical as well. This concept – acting ethically in both God's eyes and in the eyes of others – is derived from the Torah story of the two and a half tribes who wished to remain on the east side of the Jordan River. Even though they displayed the right motives, they had to demonstrate that their actions were ethical to God and also to their fellow Jews. (For this reason, the men left

---

1. Genesis 12:3 with Rashi commentary

2. *Yoma* 86a
3. Deuteronomy 6:5
4. Midrash, *Vayikra Rabbah* 34:8
5. Mishna *Avot* 2:1

their homes and families to fight alongside the other tribes for fourteen years.)[6] It is a Torah imperative that Jews take into account how their actions are perceived by others – i.e., Jews must always behave in a way that is not only moral, but that also *appears* moral to others. King Solomon echoes the same imperative when he writes that Jews need to be right and seek favor both in God's eyes and in men's eyes.[7] Traditional Jews ask God to help them achieve this goal each day when they recite the Grace After Meals.[8]

This concept of taking an action specifically to assure that one does not appear guilty in the eyes of others is such an important one that it saved the Jewish people twice in the desert. If not for this idea, the entire Jewish people, as we know it, would simply not exist today. After the first great sin that the people committed in the desert by worshipping the Golden Calf, God wanted to destroy the entire nation and begin again with Moses. What was Moses' argument that saved the Jewish people from destruction? Moses tells God that if He were to destroy the Jewish people, the Egyptians would (completely erroneously) think that God was simply too weak to fulfill His promise to bring them into the holy land (see Ibn Ezra commentary) and *that* is the reason the Jewish people were destroyed, rather than because of their sins.[9] Though the Egyptians would have been totally mistaken to think this way, and God's punishment of death would have been deserved (an omnipotent God could certainly have brought them to the land of Israel), God relents and does not destroy the people in order to avoid a *Chilul Hashem*-desecration of His name. Moses uses the same argument less than two years later one more time. The Jews sin, once again, in believing the ten spies' negative report and not having faith that God would make them victorious in their conquest of the land of Israel. Once again God wishes to

destroy the people. This time, Moses spells out what people would say if this were to occur: The Egyptians would say that God had some powers, but not enough strength to lead them successfully into the land of Israel and triumph over the seven nations living there, and that is why God had to destroy the Jews in the desert.[10] As foolish and incorrect as this argument was, God says to Moses that he forgives the Jewish people "because of your words." Thus, how something *appears* is as important as doing the right thing. Even God changed His plans and the Jewish people were saved because of how the situation would appear to the nations the world, even though, had He acted as He had wanted to, of course God would have been right and the nations mistaken.

Rabbi Moses Sofer (1762-1839), one of the most outstanding and pious Rabbis in Europe, writes that one of the most difficult precepts he encountered in trying to fulfill all of Judaism's commandments is this one. It was far easier for him to remain "clean" and righteous in the eyes of God than to "remain clean in the eyes of his fellow man."[11] People are always filled with all kinds of suspicions and thoughts, even about Rabbis, so a Jew must work very diligently not only to *be* guiltless but also to *appear* guiltless in the eyes of others.

HOW FAR SOME PEOPLE WENT SO THAT OTHER PEOPLE WOULD NOT THINK THEM SINFUL

There are numerous incidents related in the Talmud describing how people and families went "the extra mile" in their actions in order to insure that they would be above suspicion, even when they had done absolutely nothing wrong. For example, the family of Garmu was responsible for baking the dough, of the finest quality, for the *Lechem Hapanim*, the Bread of Display for the Temple. The Rabbis praised them because this family consciously would not allow any clean flour to enter their own

---

6. Numbers 32:22
7. Proverbs 3:4
8. End of the last blessing of *Birkat HaMazon* (Grace after Meals)
9. Exodus 32:11-12, 14

10. Numbers 14:11-20
11. *Responsa Chatam Sofer* 6:59

homes so that no one would suspect them of using the dough designated for the Temple for their own needs.[12] Abba Hoshiya was a launderer who made sure to always wear clothing made of a special type of cotton (not commonly found) so that people could not say that when he washed their clothes, he took little pieces of material from them and made a garment for himself.[13] The family of Avtinas was responsible for mixing the spices that created the incense in the Temple.[14] The Rabbis praised them because whenever a woman in their family got married, she would not wear any perfume at all at the wedding, and when the men in the family got married, they made sure that their brides would not wear perfume as well. They did all of this so that they would be above suspicion that they may have used the spices meant for the Temple incense for their personal use. Moses was responsible for both building the *Mishkan*-Tabernacle, and keeping the accounts for all of the gifts and how they were used. Even though no accounting of each donation was required, Moses insisted on giving a detailed public accounting so that even he, the great and respected leader, would be above suspicion that he took some of the donations for his personal use.[15]

The obligation to act in a manner that eliminates suspicion, even when a person does nothing wrong, is so important that Jewish law required that anyone who entered the Temple area where the money was stored had to wear clothing without pockets or any other places that might be used to stash coins. Thus, the person had to go in barefoot, since coins could be stored in shoes. Similarly, one could not wear a coat, an amulet, or any other type of clothing that might allow a person to store a coin. In this way, if the person later became wealthy, no one could attribute this wealth to money stolen from the Temple.[16] Tiferet Yisrael commentary points out that in all of these cases, the people went beyond the original Torah requirement of this principle that was delineated in the desert when the tribes of Reuven, Gad, and half of the tribe of Menashe wanted the land on the eastern side of the Jordan River and asked to stay behind while the other tribes fought for the rest of the land. In that case, these tribes wanted something special and tangible for themselves, but they had to make sure that their actions did not appear to be selfish, subversive, or insensitive to others (and that is why Moses told them to fight alongside the other tribes before returning to their land and cattle). However, in the cases delineated above, the people did absolutely nothing wrong or suspicious in any way and gained nothing. Yet they still took steps to ensure that no one could suspect them of any improper activity.[17] This shows to what degree Jews have to care what people think of them and their actions. Even when they do nothing remotely wrong or suspicious, they should anticipate what people might think and should avoid any activity that could arouse suspicion and compromise their integrity.

*Sefer HaChinuch* adds another layer to this sensitivity. If the person in question is very prominent, in addition to violating "keeping clean in the eyes of the people," any action that (wrongly) looks suspicious also automatically involves desecration of God's name. Thus, a Torah scholar has to avoid any situation that might even remotely look wrong, even if he is completely in the right. So if the Torah scholar is doing something that he knows to be moral and right, if it may look to others like a sin, he may not do it for both of these reasons.[18]

## HOW THIS CONCEPT RELATES SPECIFICALLY TO JEWISH LAW

As a result of this concept, there are many instances in daily Jewish living when a person acts in complete accordance with Jewish law (Halacha), but to someone else, a particular

---

12. *Yoma* 38a
13. Jerusalem Talmud, *Bava Kama* 44b
14. *Yoma* 38a
15. *Midrash Tanchuma, Pikudei* 5
16. Mishna *Shekalim* 3:2

17. Tiferet Yisrael commentary on Mishna *Shekalim* 3:2
18. *Sefer HaChinuch*, Mitzvah 295

action might look like a sin that violates Jewish law. If that situation arises, the person is forbidden from doing that action, even though it would normally be permitted by Halacha. When a normally permitted act is prohibited because someone else may think it is a sin, it is considered either *Marit Ayin* (how it looks) or *Cheshad* (we are afraid because . . .) in Jewish law. There are numerous examples of this in the Talmud and in the codes of Jewish law, and as usual, there is some disagreement about the finer points of the laws, even though all agree on the basic principle. Only a few examples will be brought here.

One classic case is the person who gets caught in the rain on Shabbat and his clothing is soaking wet. It is perfectly permissible to put these clothing out in the sun to dry without violating any Shabbat laws. But if people see these clothes drying, they may suspect that the person washed them on Shabbat, which is forbidden. Thus, the Mishna states that any individual may not dry these clothes in the sun on Shabbat in a place where people can see them (because they might suspect that individual washed them on Shabbat). But in the privacy of one's backyard, the clothing may be laid out to dry. Another classic case in the Talmud is the person who lives in a corner house, with windows facing two different streets. If that homeowner lights Chanukah candles in the windows facing one street, he has completely fulfilled the Mitzvah-commandment of lighting Chanukah candles. But people who pass by only on the other street will see no candles in those windows and possibly think that this man has not lit Chanukah candles and has sinned by neglecting a Rabbinical Mitzvah. Therefore our concept – caring what others think even when doing the right thing – *obligates* him to light candles in *both* windows, so that no one should think he has sinned by forgetting to light the *Menorah*.[19] Other examples abound. For instance, the eating or drinking of both human and animal blood is forbidden in Jewish law, but drinking the blood of fish is

permitted. If a person wanted, for some reason, to drink the blood of a fish (in some places this is considered a delicacy), it would be forbidden to do so even though there is nothing forbidden about this act. Since people might assume it is blood that came from an animal, it is forbidden. However, if there is some sign that it is from fish, i.e., some fish bones or other parts of the fish were lying next to it, then it would be permitted.[20]

Similarly, if the coins in a person's pocket happened to fall on the ground in front of a statue that was an idol, which some people consider a god, it would be forbidden to bend down and pick them up. Even though that Jew has no intention to do so, others looking at this scene might think that he or she is bowing down to an idol and thus it is forbidden[21]. Likewise is the case of a water fountain located near the statue of an idol. If bending down is required to reach the water, some may think the drinker is bending down to worship, and therefore, it would be forbidden to drink from that fountain.[22] That is how far this concept extends and how seriously Judaism takes this idea. Another situation that is very common today is the use of a liquid that looks like milk but comes from non-dairy sources. In earlier times, it was milk that comes from nuts or coconuts that looked like cow's milk. Even though perfectly permitted in Jewish law, a Jew may not use this milk with meat because it looks like one is doing the forbidden act of mixing meat and (dairy) milk together.[23] However, mixing this non-dairy "milk" with chicken would be permitted, since chicken itself is not Biblically considered meat (and therefore could be used with even dairy milk according to Biblical law), but the Rabbis forbade it in order to avoid confusion. A prohibition due to a Rabbinic confusion on top of another possible Rabbinic confusion (i.e., suspicion it is dairy milk) would indeed be

---

19. *Shabbat* 23a

20. *Shulchan Aruch, Yoreh De'ah* 66:9
21. *Mishna Shabbat* 22:4
22. *Avodah Zara* 12a
23. Rema, *Shulchan Aruch, Yoreh De'ah* 87 with *Turei Zahav* commentary

permitted. This law had very practical implications when Coffee Rich non-dairy creamer came on the market more than 50 years ago. It was forbidden then to serve it with coffee in a kosher restaurant after a meat meal unless the container was left on the table, because people might think it was actual milk. (Jewish law therefore required visible proof that no sin was being committed.) Now, when almost everyone is familiar with non-dairy creamers, people are not so quick to assume it is milk and therefore it is permissible to serve a non-dairy creamer with a meat meal even without the carton on the table. (More about this particular case is discussed below.)

Though not common today, since kosher meat that has already been slaughtered is readily available, in the time of the Talmud (before refrigeration), most Jews had to know how to slaughter meat in order to eat it. Jewish law requires that the blood of a slaughtered animal be covered up properly. Heretics and Sadducees who did not believe in the Oral Torah used to slaughter into an open pit, which is technically permitted. But since this was the standard way that heretics and Sadducees operated, the Mishna forbids slaughtering in this manner, lest people think that this upstanding Jew is a heretic or Sadducee. However, the Mishna continues and says that if one does this in the privacy of his own home, where no one can (supposedly) see, then it would be permitted.[24] We will see below whether or not this idea and the laws of *Marit Ayin* and *Cheshad* apply in a private situation.

THE DIFFERENCES BETWEEN THE CONCEPTS OF *MARIT AYIN* AND *CHESHAD*

On the surface, it appears that the concepts of *Marit Ayin* ("how it looks") and *Cheshad* ("we are afraid because . . .") are identical, and they seem to be used interchangeably in the Talmud. However, later authorities present three distinctions between these two concepts.

Rabbi Abraham Teumim (1800-1868) writes that *Marit Ayin* is something that appears like a sin regarding a Jewish law that everyone already knows is forbidden, like coconut milk mixed with meat, for example (because everyone is aware that combining meat and milk is prohibited).[25] Since all know the "apparent" sin is forbidden, this kind of act (which is actually perfectly legal and moral but appears wrong) would be forbidden even in the privacy of one's home, since if people happen to see it, they would immediately question how this can be done. A *Cheshad*, however, is an act that appears to be forbidden, but not everyone knows that it is a definite sin. Thus, this type of act is permitted in private, like the example brought above of slaughtering into a pit. A clearer distinction between the two concepts, based on the above notion, is a psychological difference in how the person seeing the action will react. If a person who is watching you do an action that appears to be sinful (but is not, in actuality) thinks that if you are doing it, this act must be permitted, since you are such an upstanding Jew who is careful about Halacha-Jewish law, then this is a *Cheshad*. So if, for example, the person sees you eating fish blood and thinks that Jewish law must now permit drinking animal blood, then it is a *Cheshad*. But if the person who sees you doing the act is sure it is a sin (even if it is not) and will then think that *you* are a sinner, then it is a case of *Marit Ayin*. Thus, since everyone knows that eating meat and milk together is forbidden, by putting coconut milk into meat, the person will think that you have become a sinner – and that is *Marit Ayin*. Both explanations are mentioned by Rashi,[26] but Rabbi Moshe Feinstein makes this distinction. Finally, *Marit Ayin* involves an "apparent" sin that is Rabbinically forbidden, while the *Cheshad* can even involve what appears to be a Biblical sin.[27] The *Encyclopedia Talmudit* summarizes all three opinions and distinctions.[28]

---

24. Mishna *Chulin* 2:9

25. *Chesed LeAvraham, Orach Chaim* 21
26. Rashi commentary on *Shabbat* 64b
27. *Responsa Igrot Moshe, Orach Chaim* 4:82
28. *Encyclopedia Talmudit*, vol. 17 "*Cheshad – Marit*

## DO THESE LAWS APPLY EVEN IN THE PRIVACY OF ONE'S HOME?

In the Talmud, Rav made a statement that seems counterintuitive. He states that in a case of *Marit Ayin*, all Jewish laws that are forbidden because they look like a sin, even though technically permitted, are also forbidden within one's home, even in a "room within a room."[29] Why should something that is only forbidden because we are afraid of what an onlooker will think, continue to be prohibited when there are no onlookers? Numerous reasons have been given. One is that if the Rabbis permit it privately, a person might forget and do it publicly. Others say that even in the privacy of one's home, it is possible that "nosy neighbor" might see the action, even though a person thinks the situation is private. In the twenty-first century, this idea has proven to be a reality. There are many times when "private" actions in one's home, when a person was "sure" no one was looking, have been captured on camera, either with telephoto lenses, hidden cameras, a cell phone camera, or even a very small, remote-controlled plane. But is Rav's premise indeed Jewish law?

Rashi, in citing the Mishna discussed above, which says that a person may indeed dry his clothing on Shabbat in the privacy of his own home, points out that this opinion disagrees with Rav's principle that this concept is valid even in the privacy of one's home.[30] The Jerusalem Talmud also cites many instances in which others disagree with Rav about this principle.[31] Tosafot commentary, in citing that there is indeed a fundamental argument between those who agree and those who disagree that this concept is also valid in private, adds that even Rav would agree that the only time an action is forbidden in the privacy of one's home is if it looks like a sin for which one would be Biblically culpable, but for a sin

that appears to be a Rabbinic transgression, even Rav agrees that it would be permitted privately.[32]

This argument continues in the post-Talmudic period as well, with the Rif and Rabbeinu Nissim disagreeing with Rav that *Marit Ayin* applies in private,[33] while Tosafot, Rosh, and others agree with Rav. Finally, Rabbi Joseph Caro in his *Code of Jewish Law*, rules according to Rav. Thus, when people might suspect a Jew is doing something wrong even if he or she is not, it is forbidden both in public and in private to act in this manner, but only when the suspected sin would be Biblically forbidden.[34] This is good advice, especially in the age of the super telephoto lens.

## OTHER JEWISH LAW PRACTICAL ISSUES THAT RELATE TO THIS CONCEPT

There are two specific interesting areas in which these concepts of *Marit Ayin* and *Cheshad* have led to discussions involving practical implications for observant Jews of today.

### Make a Blessing?

We saw above that in certain circumstances, the Rabbis obligated a Jew to do something even though the act itself would normally not be required, but it was only performed because of what people might think. In those cases, would the Jew have to recite a blessing? After all, the only reason to perform these acts is to quell people's possible suspicions. *Shulchan Aruch* brings the case of the person living in the corner house with windows facing two different streets. While he obligates this Jew to light two Menorahs, he writes that a second blessing is not said on the second Menorah.[35] Rashba disagrees and says that a second blessing should be recited. He cites the case of a cow that was slaughtered while almost about

---

*Ayin"*

29. *Shabbat* 64b

30. Rashi commentary on *Shabbat* 64b, s.v. *"Aval Lo Keneged Ha'am"*

31. Jerusalem Talmud, *Klayim* 40b

32. Tosafot on *Chulin* 41a, s.v. *"U'veshuk"*

33. Rabbeinu Nisim on Rif, *Beitza* 4b

34. *Shulchan Aruch, Orach Chaim* 301:45 with *Mishna Berura* commentary (165)

35. *Shulchan Aruch, Orach Chaim* 671:8

to give birth. If the calf emerges alive and healthy, there is a Jewish law that this animal does not need to be slaughtered before eating it, since it is considered already slaughtered, having been inside the slaughtered cow (called a *Ben Pakua*). Nevertheless, so that people will not think that a Jew is eating a cow that was not slaughtered (or that it is no longer required to ritually slaughter cows), the Rabbis ruled that a Jew is required to slaughter even this cow. Rashba says that the slaughterer recites the standard blessing on slaughtering this cow that you recite for every cow that requires slaughtering.[36] Why? Just as the Rabbis require a blessing and establish so many other Jewish laws Rabbincally, the idea of not appearing to do sin (even if doing nothing wrong) is also a Rabbinic law. Thus, like any other Rabbinic act requiring a blessing, a blessing would also be mandated in this case.

## A NON-JEW DOING A JOB FOR A JEW ON SHABBAT

While it is forbidden on Shabbat for a Jew to ask a non-Jew to do a certain prohibited Shabbat activity for him or her, it is permitted to contract with a non-Jew on Thursday or Friday to do such a job, without specifying that it be done on Shabbat. If the non-Jew wishes to do it on Shabbat, it is completely permissible. But what if the work given to the non-Jew on Thursday involves working in the Jew's backyard? Won't some people think that the Jew asked the non-Jew to do work on Shabbat itself and thus forbidden as *Marit Ayin*? The Talmud asks this question and says that if the work (such as laundering or repairing a car) is done on the premises of the non-Jew, it is perfectly permissible, since no one knows or sees that he is doing the work specifically for this Jew. But if the work is done in the Jew's backyard or an area of town where many Jews pass by on Shabbat and they know the work is for a particular Jew, then it would be forbidden. However,

in an area where Jews do not live or walk, it would be permitted.[37] This is precisely how the *Code of Jewish Law* rules and it coincides with the parameters of our overriding idea – that only when someone would think that the person is doing a forbidden action (even if this is not the actual case) would that action be prohibited. However, three sentences later *Shulchan Aruch* discusses another case and brings a ruling that seems to contradict this basic idea.[38]

Some Jews used to collect the taxes for the local governor, from Jews and non-Jews alike, and this job entailed a seven-day work week. Since this activity was obviously forbidden on Shabbat, a Jew in this profession was forced to hire a non-Jew to collect the taxes for him on that day. But in this situation, everyone would see and know that the non-Jew was working for the Jewish tax collector on Shabbat. Logically then, it should have been forbidden. However, *Shulchan Aruch* and the Rema both say this is permitted, and they give a new reason for this: Failure to hire the non-Jew for this purpose would result in a great financial loss and possibly even the loss of the Jewish tax collector's job. Therefore, in this case it would be permitted, even though, to other Jews, the non-Jew seems to working for the Jew on Shabbat.[39] (This situation is technically permitted since the deal was not made on Shabbat or for Shabbat specifically.) The idea that financial loss plays a role in the concepts of *Marit Ayin* and *Cheshad* is already mentioned in the Talmud.[40] But regarding this ruling in *Shulchan Aruch*, the twentieth century Rabbi Israel Meir Kagan writes at length and says that it applies *only* to the specific case of tax collection, and should not be extrapolated to other situations that seem similar. He specifically mentions observant Jews who own taverns and bars, where Friday night is the busiest night of the week. When the Jewish owners pay non-Jews to run

---

36. *Responsa Rashba* 1:525

37. *Mo'ed Katan* 12a with Rashi commentary
38. *Shulchan Aruch, Orach Chaim* 244:1
39. *Shulchan Aruch, Orach Chaim* 244:4
40. *Ketuvot* 60a

the bar for them so that the owners could reap all the profits, they are engaging in a forbidden act.[41] Rabbi Kagan explains that unlike the tax collection case, the work in taverns and the like is designated only for Shabbat. Moreover, in the case of tax collections, the non-Jew kept all the profits accrued on Shabbat, which would not be the case in the tavern. Therefore, it is not advisable for Jews to hire non-Jews to work for them on Shabbat.

## APPLYING THESE IDEAS TO JEWISH LIVING IN THE TWENTY-FIRST CENTURY

The ideas of *Marit Ayin* and *Cheshad* raise many practical questions for Jews of the twenty-first century. With modern inventions, many new situations arise in which the actions themselves are not forbidden, but may appear to be to others. (For example, in the early 1900s, the idea of a Shabbat clock turning out the lights on Friday night might have been a problem of *Marit Ayin*, but now it is known that this is done in most observant Jews' homes. Therefore, seeing lights go out in such homes on Shabbat would not be *Marit Ayin* today.) Concerning the subject of food alone, many questions abound: Would it be permissible to bake rolls for Pesach that look like bread, using Matzah meal that is completely kosher for Pesach? People might think that it is bread which is now permitted on Passover, or that the person eating such a roll is committing a sin. Similarly, food producers have created "Bac-Os," which look and taste somewhat like bacon but are fully kosher. Is it permitted to buy and eat these? Clocks and other electronic devices can automatically do many actions that are forbidden on Shabbat. While it is technically permitted for a Jew to use these on Shabbat, people might think that a Jew performed these actions himself rather than thinking that he relied on the machines. Are they permitted or not? The

Rabbis of today have discussed these and other issues, enumerated below.

Already in the 1600s, an Italian Rabbi came up against these questions, and Rabbi Da Silva (1656-1695) ruled that only those specific *Marit Ayin* cases mentioned in the Talmud and in the previous books of Jewish law should be respected and observed. But regarding new cases, such as the baking of kosher for Passover items that look like *Chametz* (leavened products), one need not worry.[42] The *Encyclopedia Talmudit* seems to agree with this overall analysis.[43] Of course, many twentieth and twenty-first century Rabbis were asked specific questions and wrote responsa that are very instructive, not only for Jewish law, but for the ethics and morality of this overall concept. Only a few examples are brought below.

Rabbi Moses Feinstein, the "dean" of Jewish law in the United States in the twentieth century, writes about a number of situations that presented themselves and relate to the concepts discussed. Since a married Jewish woman is supposed to cover her hair according to Jewish law, many women today cover their hair with wigs made of human hair, which is permitted by almost all Halachik-Jewish law authorities. But what if the wig is so professional looking that it appears as if it is the woman's own hair? People might think that she is violating this law by not covering her hair, even though she is actually keeping the law. May she still wear the wig in this situation? Rabbi Feinstein says that women may indeed wear such wigs today for several reasons. First, it is already well known that many religious women wear wigs in order to fulfill the requirement to cover their own hair, so most people who see this woman and know she is an observant Jewess in all other areas will not suspect her in this area. Then he says that if one looks carefully, it is possible to see that this is a wig. Finally, he reiterates the words of

41. *Mishna Berurah* 35 on *Shulchan Aruch, Orach Chaim* 244

42. Pri Chadash on *Shulchan Aruch, Orach Chaim* 461:2
43. *Encyclopedia Talmudit*, vol. 17 "*Cheshad  Marit Ayin*"

Rabbi Da Silva and says that today we do not forbid what was not forbidden by the Rabbis of the Talmudic or Gaonic periods.[44]

Another question asked of Rabbi Feinstein involved travelling in a car to the synagogue on Friday night after the time of candle lighting but before sunset, as candle lighting usually takes place eighteen or twenty minutes before sunset. A woman usually accepts Shabbat early when lighting candles, but she can make a stipulation not to accept Shabbat until right before sunset if she wishes. Then, even after lighting candles, she can legitimately travel in a car, along with a man, who accepts Shabbat later, immediately following the *Mincha*-afternoon prayer in the synagogue. The person seeing a woman in the car after candle lighting but before sunset might think that she is violating the Shabbat. Is travelling in the car at that time then permitted? Rabbi Feinstein says yes, and establishes several important principles about *Marit Ayin*. First, he generally says that a situation is considered *Marit Ayin* only when more than 50% of the time it involves an action that is actually forbidden, though the person is doing it now in a permitted manner. That, as we have discussed, constitutes *Marit Ayin*. In this case, however, most observant people who drive their cars to synagogue after candle lighting time do so legitimately. Thus, this is not a case of *Marit Ayin*. Furthermore, he says that only a very small percentage of people will mistakenly believe that this observant person is actually violating the Shabbat, so that the case would not qualify as *Marit Ayin* for this reason as well.[45] In general, when the percentage of people thinking this is a sin is small (probably less than 50%), there is no problem of *Marit Ayin*.

There is also a question about the permissibility of going to the bathroom or buying a can of soda in a non-kosher restaurant. Jews who see an observant Jew going into the restaurant for these purposes may mistakenly think he

is buying non-kosher food or (in Israel) that this restaurant is now kosher. May a person buy kosher food that is sold in a non-kosher restaurant, or even just go inside to use the bathroom there? Rabbi Feinstein writes that this would indeed be a violation of *Marit Ayin* and *Cheshad*. But if this person is very thirsty, there are no other places nearby to purchase the soda, and there are no Jews in the vicinity (or no one he recognizes that will see him go in), then it is permitted. If he sees Jews that he recognizes, he should first explain to them why he is going in, so that they will not get the wrong idea.[46]

Another contemporary expert in Jewish law of the twentieth and twenty-first century who lived in Jerusalem is Rabbi Ovadia Yosef. He was asked about a kosher hotel that serves non-dairy creamer in coffee following the meat meal. As noted above, this is perfectly legitimate today. But in this particular hotel, many of the guests are non-observant tourists who, upon witnessing this, would probably think it is now permitted to drink milk after a meat meal. Rabbi Yosef answers that ideally there should be some indication that this is non-dairy creamer and not milk, either that it be served in a separate kind of dish or the packaging be brought onto the table. But even if not, since waiting six hours between meat and milk is only a custom (the real Torah prohibition is not eating them together at the same time), and waiting a few minutes in between is sufficient from the perspective of Torah law, it would not be considered *Marit Ayin* and could be served even without the container.[47]

With all of these technical issues, one may lose sight of the overall concept that is crucial in Judaism: Jews should care what other people think and how other people view them, and Jews may not do anything which appears wrong, even if it is completely moral and correct. Chatam Sofer reiterates how hard it is to fulfill this precept, but how important it is at

---

44. *Responsa Igrot Moshe, Even Ha'ezer* 2:12
45. *Responsa Igrot Moshe, Orach Chaim* 1:96

46. *Responsa Igrot Moshe, Orach Chaim* 2:40
47. *Responsa Yabia Omer*, section 6, *Yoreh De'ah* 8

the same time.[48] As we saw, even though the two-and-a-half tribes seemed to do everything right according to the directions of Moses, there still lingered some doubt and suspicion of their motives by the other tribes, and this was so even though they fought fourteen years alongside their brethren before returning home. And it was for this reason, this skepticism of other Jews, that in the end these two and a half tribes were the first of the Jewish people to be destroyed by the enemy many hundreds of years later.

---

48. *Responsa Chatam Sofer* 6:59

# SPORTS AND JUDAISM

I N A FAMOUS 1980S SATIRICAL COM-
edy film, one scene depicts a flight attendant asking a passenger if he would
like something to read on the trip. He asks
for something with a very short text, and she
hands him a magazine called *Greatest Jewish
Athletes* described in the film as "the world's
shortest book." This exemplifies a commonly
accepted notion that Jews generally do not
participate in sports, and if they do, they certainly do not excel in them. This chapter will
examine this perception, and show why it was
a misconception in the past and still is today.
It will also attempt to show how the attitude
of traditional Judaism towards sports is both
complex and multilayered. Is there a difference, from the Jewish perspective, between
participating in sports and watching them as
entertainment? Are any sports more forbidden
or permitted from a Jewish viewpoint? Let us
examine these and other questions through
the sources.

## SPORTS IN THE JEWISH BIBLE

References to and the participation of Jews
in sports are already found in Prophets and
Psalms. The practice of shooting arrows at a
target is mentioned in the books of Samuel,
Job, and Lamentations.[1] The idea of attaining
proficiency in using a sling with a stone in order to hit a target can be seen not only in the
famous story of David and Goliath, but also
in other contexts in Samuel and Zachariah.[2]
Long jumping[3] and running[4] are used as met-
aphors by King David, indicating that these
activities were already prevalent at that time,
and that is the reason that they could be used
as imagery in poetry and music. All of these
sports and skills mentioned, like those in all

other societies in ancient times, relate to the
aptitude that was needed in these activities as
a preparation to wage war, and only later did
these activities become entertainment sports.

There are also numerous references to feats
of strength in the Torah, as this aptitude of
brute strength, often needed and used in
numerous sports, seems to be admired in Judaism. Jacob used his considerable physical
strength to remove the large stone covering
the town well, an act that normally required
several shepherds to accomplish.[5] Moses
performed a similar feat of strength for the
daughters of Jethro.[6] Samson's great strength
is well known, and it was this unique quality
that allowed him to kill one thousand Philistines with the jawbone of a donkey.[7] One of
the physical characteristics that made King
Saul worthy of the monarchy was his unusual
great height and strength.[8]

But the most dramatic sports reference in
the Jewish Bible is the story of the confrontation between Avner and Yoav.[9] These two
opposing camps during King David's rule
met, and each side selected twelve athletes to
compete against each other in various sports.
This athletic confrontation and competition
did not end well, as immediately afterwards
both sides engaged in war in which the forces
of Avner defeated the army of Yoav. This first
negative association between sports and Judaism foreshadowed some of the later opinions
about sports in Jewish thought.

## SPORTS IN THE TIME OF THE TALMUD

Although no direct description of sports
activities is mentioned in the Talmud, there

---

1. Samuel I 20:20, Job 16:12, Lamentations 3:12
2. Judges 20:16, Samuel I 17:40, Zachariah 9:15
3. Psalms 19:6
4. Psalms 18:30

5. Genesis 29:6-10
6. Exodus 2:15-19
7. Judges 15:15-16
8. Samuel I 9:2 with Malbim commentary
9. Samuel II 2:12-17

is ample evidence in many of the Talmud's legal discussions to infer that sports were an integral part of Jewish life in Talmudic times. For example, in describing the Temple service performed by the Kohanim-Priests, the very first and prestigious daily service was to remove the ashes from the Altar. Since many Kohanim desired this privilege, a footrace was held, and the fastest Kohen would be granted this honor.[10] If the result of the race was a tie, then a lottery was held to determine the winner. Later on, after one Kohen-Priest was injured in a race, they abandoned this practice and only conducted lots to determine which Kohen would perform this service. This shows that not only was sports encouraged, but it was even a part of the daily activities in the Temple.

In determining which objects become ritually impure and which do not, the Mishna discusses the status of a ball, and which type of balls are ritually pure and which are ritually impure.[11] The inside of those ancient balls were made of cloth or grass. This demonstrates that balls used for playing sports were prevalent in Mishnaic times.

In describing the final day of the Sukkot holiday, now called Hoshana Rabbah, a day in which the *Arava* (willow) is beaten as part of the service, the Mishna declares that after the service, the children would play some kind of sport or game with the *Lulavim*-palm branches and eat the *Etrogim*-citrons.[12] The Talmud explains this practice[13] and Rashi gives the details, writing that the adults would try, as a sport or game, to take the *Lulavim* from the children as a way of adding to the joy of the holiday.[14] After citing Rashi's explanation, Tosafot disagrees and says that this was a sport played exclusively by the children.[15]

In a different context, the Talmud deliberates the culpability of accidently killing an individual with a ball that ricochets off a wall.[16] The Talmud elaborates and says that if the ball strikes a person beyond a rebound of four cubits, the thrower of the ball should not normally be guilty, but because in this game a greater rebound off the wall is the desired outcome, then perhaps even beyond four cubits the person throwing the ball would be guilty. Once again, Rashi describes in greater detail this game played in Talmudic times, which is remarkably like the sport of handball played today.[17] In discussing the activities forbidden on Shabbat but permitted during the rest of the week, the Mishna declares that one of these activities is wrestling on the ground or (as described by some commentaries) mud-wrestling![18] Apparently, this was a commonly practiced sport in Mishnaic times.

## SPORTS IN JEWISH COMMUNITIES AFTER TALMUDIC TIMES

In the thirteenth century, a question of Jewish law was presented to Tzadok ben Aryeh the doctor.[19] He was asked about carrying a leather ball, a ball filled with hair, or a ball made of wood on Shabbat, and whether these could be used to play sport on Shabbat, which he forbade. Thus, we see Jews were also actively playing ball sports in the Middle Ages. Tosafot commentary, which was previously cited in discussing the sports played on the last day of Sukkot, also mentions that in his time (in France and Germany in the Middle Ages) it was the custom at Jewish weddings for the friends of the groom to engage in jousting contests while riding on horses! This was done in order to fulfill the obligation to make the groom and bride happy at their wedding.[20] In comparison, some of the outrageous activities and wild performances seen at some religious Jewish weddings today (for the same purpose) actually seem very mild. An authority in Jewish law around the same period actually rules

10. Mishna *Yoma* 2:1-2
11. Mishna *Kelim* 29:1, 10:4, 23:1
12. Mishna *Sukkah* 4:7-8
13. *Sukkah* 46b
14. Rashi commentary on *Sukkah* 46b
15. Tosafot commentary on *Sukkah* 46b, s.v. "*Miyad*"

16. *Sanhedrin* 77b
17. Rashi commentary on *Sanhedrin* 77b
18. Mishna *Shabbat* 22:6
19. *Shibolei HaLeket, Shabbat* 121
20. Tosafot commentary on *Sukkah* 46b, s.v. "*Miyad*"

that when jousting at weddings, if one of the Jewish jousters gets hurt, his clothing is ruined, or the horse is damaged, the injured party cannot sue for damages, since the purpose was to gladden the groom and any damage is understood as accidental.[21]

Rabbi Eliezer ben Yoel HaLevi (known as the Raviyah) lived in Germany a century earlier and writes of a question in Jewish law presented to him involving a suit of armor.[22] A Jew borrowed a suit of armor from his friend in order to participate in a tournament, and he left a certain amount of money as a surety. The armor was lost and only much later did the friend demand more compensation than originally given as surety. Dr. Aptowitzer, the editor of this volume who cites this text, asserts that this is first written proof that Jews participated in sport tournaments as early as the 1100s. Tosafot also mentions ball playing in that time.[23]

In 1386, there were also tournaments in Wiesenfeld, Germany involving Jews. In the 1400s, sports competitions in Germany, in which Jews actively took part, also involved running, jumping, throwing, and bowling. At a popular festival in fifteenth century in Rome, Jews participated in its sports competitions, in which each day of the week was designated for a different category according to age and ethnicity. Tuesday was reserved for Jews. Jews excelled in these games in the years 1487, 1502, and 1513. In the sixteenth century, a famous Jew named Ott was so outstanding at the Augsburg, Germany games, that he was invited by the Austrian prince to train his courtiers.[24]

The problem of playing or not playing ball games on Shabbat has been an issue in the Jewish community for centuries. In every society that this is discussed, there necessarily must have been Jews who clearly desired to play sports on Shabbat and who were playing at other leisure times already. In the sixteenth

century, *Shulchan Aruch* ruled that playing sports on Shabbat and the festivals was forbidden for Jews of Sephardic descent, but Rabbi Isserles permitted these sports activities for the Ashkenazi world.[25] Rabbi Isserles, in a different section, again emphasizes the permissibility of sports activity on Shabbat.[26] But all agree that playing sports was permitted and apparently took place extensively in the Jewish community on non-Shabbat days. In the early twentieth century, the issue of playing sports on Shabbat was still a raging debate, and the preeminent authority on Jewish law, Rabbi Yisrael Meir Kagan, writes that though certainly sports add to the joy of the festival, they should be restricted to children and not be played by adults.[27]

In contemporary times, in fact, there are ample records of Jews both participating in and excelling in professional sports, contradicting the stereotype that Jews are not athletes. In the United States, for example, Jews have participated in all the major sports of baseball, basketball, and American football. Adolph "Dolph" Schayes, for example, was designated and honored as one of the fifty greatest NBA (National Basketball Association) players ever. In swimming, until Michael Phelps broke his records, the greatest swimmer was Mark Spitz who achieved seven gold medals at the 1972 Olympics. Nancy Lieberman, one of the greatest women's basketball players ever, played and coached in the WNBA, and is a member of the Basketball Hall of Fame. Aly Raisman captained the gold-medal-winning American Gymnastic team and also received and individual gold medal in gymnastics at the 2012 Olympic Games. But in order to demonstrate how extensively Jews were involved in sports, we will select just one country and one specific sport as an example – baseball, America's pastime.

21. *Or Zarua*, section 2, *Hilchot Sukkah and Lulav*, 315
22. *Responsa Raviya*, 1027, brought in *Sefer Mavo Raviyah*
23. Tosafot Commentary on *Beitzah* 12a, s.v. "*Chag*"
24. *Encyclopedia Judaica*, 15:292-293

25. *Shulchan Aruch, Orach Chaim* 308:45
26. Rema on *Shulchan Aruch, Orach Chaim* 518:1
27. *Mishna Berurah* commentary on *Shulchan Aruch, Orach Chaim* 518, no. 9

## JEWISH BASEBALL PLAYERS IN THE UNITED STATES

The very first professional baseball player ever in 1866 was a Jew named Lipman E. "Lip" Pike. In the early days of baseball, William Nash, a third baseman, was a member of the pennant winning Boston teams of 1890-1893. James Roseman, an outfielder, was a player on the New York team that won the pennant in 1884. Erskine Mayer won twenty-one games in each of the 1914 and 1915 seasons with Philadelphia, and in those same seasons, Benjamin Kauf was the batting champion of the Federal League. Buddy Meyer won the American League batting title in 1935 with a .349 average, with a .303 lifetime batting average and two World Series. Hank Greenberg, the superstar of his era, was looked up to by all Americans, and hit fifty-eight home runs in 1938 (second only to Babe Ruth for 23 years), won two Most Valuable Player awards and is in the Baseball Hall of Fame. Al Rosen was the MVP in 1953, and Larry Sherry won the MVP of the 1959 World Series. Sandy Koufax was arguably the best pitcher ever in baseball and the youngest man ever elected to the Baseball Hall of Fame. Both he and Hank Greenberg refused to play in the World Series on Yom Kippur, an act of principle to their Jewish faith that was very difficult due to its unpopularity at the time. (Most Jewish baseball players have never had to face this conflict.) Koufax later won two games in that World Series, including the finale that won the championship for his 1965 Dodgers team.

In a later era, Rod Carew, who never officially converted but married a Jewish woman and raised his children as Jewish, had 3053 hits, a .328 lifetime batting average. Steve Stone won twenty-five games in 1980 and received the Cy Young Award as the best pitcher. Ian Kinsler (born in 1982) is a three-time all-star, who went six for six in one game (and hit for the cycle) and is one of less than fifteen players ever to hit thirty home runs and steal thirty bases in the same season. Ryan Braun won the MVP award in 2011 and is one of the premier players in the game (despite his 2013

suspension). In the spring of 2015, the Detroit Tigers had three noted Jews on their team.

Clearly, Jews have been active in baseball (and all professional sports), and have often risen to the top ranks. Thus, anyone who claims that Jews do not play sports and do not excel in sports is clearly mistaken.

## JEWISH ATTITUDE TOWARDS SPORTS

There is no clear statement in the Torah, Mishna, or Talmud concerning how Judaism regards sports. The fact that sports were never condemned at all in any of these volumes seems to indicate that they were tolerated and maybe even approved of (as was seen in the act of foot racing in the Temple). And yet, an analysis of the verb in Hebrew for sports seems to indicate a negative attitude of Judaism towards participation in these kinds of activities.

Part of the Jewish attitude towards sports can be gleaned from the Hebrew verb for engaging in sports, used both in Prophets as well as today in Modern Hebrew: "*Lisachek*." This is the identical verb used in other contexts in the Jewish Bible, giving it its meaning in the context of sports as well. This verb *Lisachek* is used by King David to indicate derision and by Jeremiah to indicate mocking.[28] On the other hand, this verb is used elsewhere by King Solomon and his father King David to indicate happiness and laughter.[29] In Judges, when Samson is brought into the arena after his hair is cut, the verb is indeed utilized to indicate a sporting activity,[30] but in Proverbs it is again used to indicate foolishness.[31] Therefore, sports seem to be associated with mocking and derision, but also with laughter and foolishness. This is borne out by a similar word in Hebrew (the Hebrew letters *Tzadi* and *Sin* are sometimes interchangeable), the verb "*Litzachek*," which alternately signifies mocking, playing, and joking (according to most commentaries).[32] The

---

28. Psalms 104:26, Jeremiah 48:26
29. Ecclesiastes 10:19, Psalms 126:1-2
30. Judges 27:16
31. Proverbs 10:23
32. Genesis 21:9, Exodus 32:6, Genesis 19:14

idea of sports offering a diversion from "real life" in order to engender happiness but also foolishness was continued later in the use of the English word for this activity: "sport." The origin of the verb in English is actually "disport" which signifies "to divert one's thoughts." Thus, the Jewish concept of sports to be used as a diversion from the real goals in life can be viewed as both a foolishness to be mocked, and yet as something which brought smiles to the faces of participants.

And yet, with all of the derivations of the word mentioned above, we can find no place in the Torah, Prophets, Talmud, or the writings of later Rabbis that specifically prohibits Jewish participation in sports, or even an outcry to desist from such activities. The great Resh Lakish, whose thoughts and opinions are found on hundreds of pages in the Talmud usually arguing with his brother-in-law, Rabbi Yochanan, used to be an accomplished athlete before he became observant. Then, when Resh Lakish sold himself to the Lydians, which he knew would lead to his eventual death, the Talmud records that he took with him stone in a bag (as a means of some kind of sport to possibly escape) to later use before his death, but there is no condemnation of this activity in the Talmud.[33] It is known that one of the reasons that the Second Temple was destroyed was because of Sabbath desecration.[34] Thus, when Tur Shimon declared that the Temple was destroyed because people played ball on Shabbat, a source found both in the Midrash[35] as well as the Jerusalem Talmud,[36] it is clear that the violation and sin was that of desecrating the Shabbat, and not because of engaging in sport. Thus, engaging in sports, if not encouraged, was certainly accepted in Judaism and never condemned. The fact that the High Priest allowed a sports competition to determine the "winner" who would receive the first honor of the daily service in the Temple, mentioned above, demonstrates that sports

were not only permitted, but accepted as part of daily religious life.[37]

This attitude continued into the twentieth century (and presumably today). When Rabbi Moses Feinstein was asked if it is legitimate for an observant Jew to become a professional athlete, he dismissed any notion that it might be forbidden to engage in activity that might result in injury or even death, and clearly permitted playing sports in order to earn a livelihood. (This cannot be said to be the Jewish view concerning all occupations.)[38] An earlier Torah giant of the nineteenth century, Rabbi Epstein, explained the fascination of Jews (and all people) with sports as an activity that was pleasant and desired by the masses.[39]

ENGAGING IN SPORTS AS A MEANS OF EXERCISE

A Jew need not take part in a sports competition for the purpose of winning (see chapter, "Competition") in order to be active in sports. Sports can also be used as a means to exercise the body. Improving the health of the body is actually a religious act, one of the 613 Torah commandments, to protect one's body from harm.[40] One commentary quotes Maharsha, who asks why at the end of the verse about protecting the safety of the body it also mentions that Jews should not have any idols or physical representations of God. What is the connection between these two diverse ideas in the same verse? He answers that just as converting a totally spiritual God into a physical being violates a religious Torah principle, so too, by ignoring and not protecting the physical representation that God gave them, Jews also violate a religious principle of the Torah.[41] Thus, exercise of the body as a means to keep it healthy seems to be a religious act. Isaiah also taught that just as God guides souls to make them better and maximize them, so too God

33. *Gittin* 47a
34. *Shabbat* 119b
35. Midrash, *Eicha Rabbah* 2:4
36. Jerusalem Talmud, *Ta'anit* 24b
37. Mishna *Yoma* 2:1
38. *Responsa Igrot Moshe, Choshen Mishpat* 1:104
39. *Aruch HaShulchan, Orach Chaim* 518:8
40. Deuteronomy 4:9, 4:15
41. *Orot HaChumash*, Parshat Va'etchanan 4:15

guides bodies to maximize them as well.[42]

Maimonides, the preeminent Jewish thinker of the Middle Ages who was also a physician (and wrote medical books), stressed the importance of keeping the body healthy. He states that a healthy body is what God demands of human beings, and Jews cannot fulfill the precepts of the Creator or come to fully know Him unless their bodies are healthy.[43] Maimonides further writes that as long as a person exercises and is not too bloated from overeating, that person will not fall ill and the body will remain strong. If a person remains sedentary, even if he or she eats properly, that individual will experience pain regularly throughout life.[44] In another context, Maimonides states that all physical activities, including exercise (as well as eating, sleeping, etc.) should be done for the purpose of creating a healthy body, which then can help a person acquire the correct ideas and proper values as a Jew.[45] In his *Guide for the Perplexed*, Maimonides even enumerates examples of physical exercises to be practiced, including playing ball, wrestling, repeatedly raising one's arms, and breath control. He goes on to say that some view these sports as foolishness, but Torah scholars see them as means to achieve the true goals of a Jewish life.[46]

One contemporary Rabbi echoes the general attitude of Maimonides, but warns the Jew not to reverse his or her priorities by making exercise a priority and the spiritual commandments less significant. As long as an individual realizes that the exercises are for the ultimate purpose of the spirit and that the body's health is only a means to an end, then physical exercise is to be encouraged.[47] In 1903, Chafetz Chaim (Rabbi Yisrael Meir Kagan) gave a talk to his students in which he also stressed maintaining the balance between spiritual and physical aspects of Judaism, but in the reverse. He said that students in his Yeshiva in Radin, Poland should not spend too much time learning Torah while totally ignoring their bodies. It is important to make sure that the health of the body remains strong and a person does not become ill. He advised walking at night and swimming in the river. He also warned the students not to be tempted to learn so much Torah that they ignore entirely the needs of their bodies, because in the end, they could become ill and be unable to learn Torah properly, thus losing even more time from learning Torah.[48]

Various personal stories about leading Rabbis of the twentieth century concerning their actions or attitudes regarding physical exercise also show the importance of this activity in Jewish thought. Rabbi Yaakov Kaminetzky, founder and head of the Torah VeDa'as Yeshiva in New York, always stressed the importance of physical exercise. When he was a student in the Lomza Yeshiva in Europe, he was known as the best swimmer in the Yeshiva.[49] Since it is a Torah obligation to teach one's child to swim,[50] he reasoned that every parent must first know how to swim well. When he was asked if it is proper for Yeshiva students to ride a bicycle, Rabbi Kaminetzky answered that if he only had a bicycle to ride in his youth, he would not have had to walk so much in his later years in order to maintain his health. Rabbi Abraham Kook (1865-1935) writes about the importance of maintaining a healthy body and that the body is no less holy than the spirit God has given each human being.[51] His son, Rabbi Tzvi Yehudah Kook, spoke about his father when the elder Rabbi Kook was a student in Riga and lived with two "roommates," who would later become great European Rabbis. These Rabbis used to wrestle each other in order to maintain their health. The Chief Rabbi of

---

42. Isaiah 58:11
43. Maimonides, *Hilchot De'ot* 4:1
44. Maimonides, *Hilchot De'ot* 4:14-15
45. Maimonides, Introduction to *Shmoneh Perakim*
46. Maimonides, *Guide for the Perplexed* 3:25
47. Rabbi Moshe Shternbuch, *Ta'am VaDa'at*, *Va'etchanan* 4:9

48. Mussar talk of Rabbi Kagan in the Radin Yeshiva, 1903
49. "The Development of the Body and Jewish Law", Dr. Aaron Arend, *Development of the Jewish Body*, Israeli Ministry of Education, 2007, p. 47
50. *Kiddushin* 30h
51. Rabbi Abraham Isaac HaKohen Kook, *Orot*, section 80

Israel, Rabbi Shlomo Goren (1918-1994), former Chief Rabbi of the Israeli Army, used to do fifty pushups daily. And the sainted Chafetz Chaim once remarked that he should do physical exercise, but refrains only due to laziness.[52]

Rabbi Raphael Halperin (1924-2011) was great Torah scholar who learned in the Chevron Yeshiva (Jerusalem) and Lomza Yeshiva (Petach Tikva). At the age of eighteen, he became a professional bodybuilder and then a champion wrestler in 1950. When Rabbi Halperin met Rabbi Aaron Kotler, founder of the Lakewood Yeshiva, in the 1950s, Rabbi Kotler told him admiringly, "We have many Rabbis, but you are the only religious champion athlete." Other Rabbis told him that his victories in the wrestling ring sanctify God's name.[53] Another contemporary Chief Rabbi of Israel wrote that the commandment to preserve one's body is a positive Torah commandment, and that almost the entire Torah can be violated in order to preserve one's physical body and life.[54] He goes on to say that keeping one's body healthy is a spiritual act and then debates whether this obligation is actually a Torah commandment or only demanded by the Rabbis. In any event, it seems that the majority of Rabbis in contemporary Judaism view sports or any other exercise to be a valid Jewish activity that should be encouraged.

## SPORTS AS ENTERTAINMENT

Although we have demonstrated above that sports participation is permitted in Judaism and that sports, as exercise, is to be encouraged, it is equally clear that the normative Jewish view of sports for entertainment purposes seems to be discouraged or even forbidden. The first Jewish reference to sports as entertainment for the masses can be seen

in the story of Samson. When the Philistines thought that Samson no longer had any strength left after cutting his hair, they took him from jail into the arena to have sport with him ("*Viyisachek Lanu*" – "Let him make sport for us").[55] They used Samson in the stadium as a grand spectacle, the sport of entertainment, until God helped Samson demolish the entire structure and destroy those Philistines (as well as himself). But this Biblical story involving non-Jewish Philistines does not demonstrate the antipathy of the Rabbis towards Jews going to arenas to watch sports as a spectacle.

In the time of the Greeks, the *Book of the Maccabees* describes the Jewish Hellenists who wanted to completely adapt the ways of the Greeks as part of their culture. The very first thing they did was to build a house of sport or a gymnasium in Jerusalem, and then they ceased circumcising their sons, leaving traditional Judaism completely.[56] Thus, we see that building houses of sport used for entertainment is tantamount to adapting the ways of non-Jews and abandoning Judaism.

The very first verse in Psalms praises Jews who do not follow the "counsel of the wicked." What is the "counsel of the wicked"? The Talmud explains that these are people who visit (Roman) stadiums to witness, view, and be entertained by performances of sport, magic, etc.[57] But the Talmudic passage continues with another opinion: Rabbi Nathan that says that Jews *should* go to (Roman) stadiums, because the custom then was that the shouting of the crowd helped decide if a victim was to be killed or not be killed, and if the Jews go, they might save potential victims from death. In addition, in order to allow the Jewish widows of the victims of these "sports" to remarry after their deaths, it was necessary that Jews actually witness the death in person. Finally, the passage concludes that Jews should not go to (Roman) theaters or circuses, since these prominently display the Roman idols. Therefore, we

---

52. "The Development of the Body and Jewish Law", Dr. Aaron Arend, *Development of the Jewish Body*, Israeli Ministry of Education, 2007, p. 47
53. "The Development of the Body and Jewish Law", Dr. Aaron Arend, *Development of the Jewish Body*, Israeli Ministry of Education, 2007, p. 46
54. Rabbi Bakshi-Doron, *Responsa Binyan Av* 73:1

55. Judges 16:25-31
56. *Book of the Maccabees* 1:14-17
57. Psalms 1:1, *Avodah Zara* 18b

see that the entire atmosphere of such sports spectacles is antithetical to Judaism, especially if the purpose of attending such events is only to revel and be entertained.

The controversy about Jews at sporting events for entertainment purposes continued to be discussed even after Talmudic times. A question was asked of Rabbi Yisrael MeBruna (1400-1480) if Jews are permitted to watch non-Jews "at the track" – i.e., horse races by non-Jews. The Rabbi answered that if the purpose of watching these events is to buy horses or learn the sport in order to participate, then it is permitted. But if it is purely for fun, then it is forbidden.[58] In the contemporary period, this question has again been asked of leading Rabbis. Rabbi Menashe Klein was asked about the permissibility of Jews attending sporting events that involve gambling, such as horse racing. He says if the primary purpose is to watch the event and not to win money, then it is not forbidden as gambling. But then he also discusses the question of attending sporting events even without wagering, just for pleasure. He first says that there is no formal prohibition about watching sports. But then he writes that every minute watching sporting events takes away from Torah learning and encourages even more time-wasting activities. For this reason, as well as that it is not the right "atmosphere" for observant Jews (based on the Talmud's point that this is a place of "bad counsel"), he forbids attending such sporting events. He then even prohibits watching or listening to these events on television and radio for the same reason mentioned above – taking time away for Torah learning.[59] Rabbi Moses Feinstein was asked a similar question – i.e., if observant Jews can attend stadiums with sporting events in our days.[60] Although attending these events does not violate the general prohibition of "imitating the ways of the non-Jews," Rabbi Feinstein nevertheless decries the frivolousness of the activity itself

as well as the people who attend such events, which make such an activity forbidden. It also takes away time from Torah learning, as mentioned above.

The majority opinion, then, is that experiencing sports as entertainment is a violation of the prohibition of participating in frivolous activities with frivolous people, as well as diverting time that could be used more productively and in a more Jewish manner.

## ARE WRESTLING AND BOXING PERMITTED IN JUDAISM?

In November 2008, a boxer named Yuri Foreman won the World Boxing Association super welterweight boxing championship in Las Vegas, Nevada. Normally, this would not create big news, even in the Jewish world. But Yuri Forman is not only Jewish but also an Orthodox Jew, who was studying to be a Rabbi. How could an observant Jew possibly legitimately box? Isn't it forbidden according to Jewish law? On the surface, it seems that the sports of boxing and wrestling should be permitted just like any other sports. Wrestling is already found in the Torah, when Jacob wrestled with a "man," an angel of Esau, say the commentaries.[61] We even saw above that the roommates of Rabbi Kook wrestled with each other. What could be the problem or issue of Jews wrestling or Jews boxing?

Unlike other sports, in wrestling and especially in boxing, the chances of inflicting damage and bodily harm on the opponent are very high, since essentially that is the goal of the activity in defeating an opponent. The same verse used above to encourage exercise and keep the body healthy is also the same verse that may prohibit boxing and wrestling, because these activities almost always result in some bodily damage, which may violate the commandment of keeping the body healthy.[62] The Talmud clearly states that causing someone else bodily harm is forbidden, just as

58. *Responsa Mohari MiBruna* 71
59. *Responsa Mishna Halacha* 6:270
60. *Responsa Igrot Moshe, Yoreh De'ah* 4:11

61. Genesis 32:25-26 with Rashi commentary
62. Deuteronomy 4:9, 4:15

causing bodily harm to oneself, is forbidden.[63] If harming another human being intentionally is forbidden, then all wrestling and certainly all boxing should be forbidden for a Jew. And yet we see that these sports are permitted in certain circumstances. How can this be?

Maimonides helps to provide an answer to this question. Although he rules it is forbidden to harm one's own body and certainly someone else's body, the prohibition is only if it is done between two people so angry at each other that they come to blows.[64] The wording of Maimonides, "Derech Nitzayon" – "in the manner of arguing," is based on the Torah word in the verse describing two people arguing that and then coming to blows (and accidentally striking a pregnant woman).[65] Therefore, only if people were arguing with each other and intending to cause bodily harm out of anger would a person be forbidden from striking another person. But a blow to the body in the course of a sporting match apparently would be permitted. On the other hand, Maimonides also rules that while it is permitted to intentionally destroy someone's property if the owner allows you to do so, it is forbidden to damage someone intentionally even if the person allows you to hurt him or her (since people's bodies belong to God and not to us).[66] Nevertheless, if the purpose of the sport is not merely to cause bodily harm and damage such as in boxing and wrestling, but to defeat the opponent, perhaps this type of blow is indeed permitted.

This very question was asked of Rabbeinu Asher in the fourteenth century.[67] If two people were wrestling and one person struck a blow to the opponent's eye which prevented him from seeing, is the opponent who inflicted the damage liable in the same manner as someone who intentionally inflicts damage on someone else or not? Rabbeinu Asher answers that normally a person is liable even

if the blow was not intentional. In this case, however, because both opponents entered the ring willingly and knowing that damage might occur in the course of the bout, and because the blow was not intended to inflict permanent damage, then both opponents accept the risk when they enter the ring, and a participant in the sport is not liable. This would seem to permit such an activity from a Jewish perspective. This view of wrestling and boxing and the liability for damage it may cause was codified by the son of Rabbeinu Asher in his book, the Tur.[68] Based on these rulings, Shulchan Aruch, the Code of Jewish Law, also rules that wrestling and boxing are indeed permitted and that any damage as a result of the match does not make an individual liable for damages.[69]

In the twentieth and twenty-first centuries, this ruling has been upheld. It was reported that in the Yeshiva of Brisk (Brest-Litovsk) at the beginning of the twentieth century, Rabbi Chaim Soloveitchik used to box with his students and was not worried about possible damage, since it took place in the context of a sporting event and not due to hatred.[70] In the 1950s, the Chief Rabbi of Israel was asked about having organized boxing matches in a Jewish school in England for observant boys. Rabbi Unterman reiterated that, according to the wording of Maimonides, only if the damage comes with the intention of anger between two people arguing can a person be held liable for inflicting a harming blow.[71] Just as the inflictor of lashes in a Jewish court is not liable for causing damage, and just as a Mohel is not liable for any minor damage as a result of a normal circumcision, so too, damage inflicted unintentionally in the course of a boxing match cannot be deemed as libelous. Hence, boxing is a legitimate Jewish sport and Yuri Foreman can continue his career in boxing, even as an Orthodox Jew.

63. Bava Kama 91b
64. Maimonides, Hilchot Chovel U'Mazik 5:1
65. Exodus 21:22 with Rashi commentary
66. Maimonides, Hilchot Chovel U'Mazik 5:11
67. Responsa Rosh 201:6

68. Tur, Choshen Mishpat 421:5
69. Shulchan Aruch, Choshen Mishpat 421:5
70. David Holzer, "The Rav Thinking Aloud: Transcripts of personal Conversations with Rabbi Joseph B. Soloveitchik," p. 13
71. Responsa Shevet Yaakov, section 1, p. 230

# THE TORAH REACTION TO THE MADOFF SCANDAL, OTHER SCANDALS, AND GREED

THE SPATE OF PUBLIC ARRESTS IN the past few years by Jews who have swindled the government and many other people points to a serious breakdown in Jewish values. The most famous of these cases involves Bernie Madoff, who cheated people out of more than 50 billion dollars. Although he is not Orthodox, almost of all of Bernie Madoff's victims were Jewish. This is compounded by the arrests of several Orthodox Rabbis for their alleged roles in scandals on the western and eastern coasts of the United States, which include Rabbis in the Chassidic, Lithuanian, and Sephardic communities, as well as other Jews who have also been in the news for similar reasons. A very influential lobbyist was sent to jail for stealing from the government and Native American tribes, while purporting to live an Orthodox and moral life aside from these crimes. The same phenomenon has been witnessed in Israel, as one president of the country was forced to resign for accepting bribes, and a sitting prime minister stepped down after being indicted and later convicted for bribe taking and many other financial irregularities. A past mayor of Jerusalem was convicted for similar crimes, and more recently, several mayors of smaller towns were forced to leave their posts for illegal financial dealings. It seems that this pandemic of unethical behavior in this particular area has affected the entire Jewish community, while it affects many in the non-Jewish world as well. It is clear that the values of the entire Western world "allowed" for these crimes to take place. And for every public official caught, there are many more who are guilty but not yet found out.

This atmosphere of greed that led to these behaviors, not only by leaders, but also by entire societies, needs to be addressed. It is clear that the voracious desire for money and wealth is not only a Jewish problem, but a value affecting everyone in Western society.

What is Judaism's take on this rampant avarice affecting both leaders and others in the Jewish community, even those who profess to live by Jewish values? Can and should the Jewish community do anything about this phenomenon? This chapter will examine the specific Jewish attitude towards greed through sources and through examples from the past.

## REFERENCES TO GREED IN SCRIPTURE

Before defining greed in Jewish terms and in the Jewish Bible, the term needs to be defined in general. Greed has many definitions. Some dictionaries say it is an "excessive consumption of or desire for wealth and power." Others believe that greed is defined as "the excessive, extreme desire for something, often more than one's proper share." Some people (allegedly attributed to Malcolm Forbes) have cynically defined the attitude of the greedy towards life as "the person who dies with the most 'toys' wins". Whatever the definition, greed consists of people's constant drive to obtain material goods and wealth, often at the expense of others and at the expense of staying within the boundaries of the law.

There are very few references to the actual Hebrew word for greed – "*Betza*" – in the Torah or Prophets. The only specific Torah reference to this word refers to one quality needed for Jewish leadership, specifically the judges that Yitro-Jethro, the father-in-law of Moses, advised him to appoint. One of their necessary qualities must be that they "despise greed."[1] Nachmanides explains that for people to be proper judges, they must despise even the idea of money in general, the obtainment of physical possessions, and they should not even care about their own wealth at all. There-

---

1. Exodus 18:21

333

fore, such a person can never be tempted to accept bribes when they are offered to him.[2] Riva explains that since his own possessions are meaningless to him, if this judge is threatened by a litigant that he will burn down the judge's field if the judge rules against him, the threat will not faze or cause fear in this judge. Rabbeinu Bechaye brings this explanation, but then adds that hating greed signifies that a judge despises people who intentionally steal from others in order to gain wealth.[3] Tur also explains that such a judge has no desire to be rich, which inoculates him from ever accepting a bribe.[4]

The greedy person is also referred to by Prophets, and the psychology behind such an individual is amplified by the commentaries. King Solomon wrote that a greedy person will find trouble in his own house, but whoever hates gifts will live (a longer and better life).[5] Rabbi Elijah Kramer, known as Vilna Gaon, explains that a greedy person is only interested in accumulating more and more wealth. But in the end, he or she will lose everything, even his home. Rabbi Meir Wisser, known as the Malbim, says that a person who illegally gains wealth at the expense of other people believes that each additional acquisition enhances the honor of is home. However, the reality is that the person who makes his fortune at the expense of others actually destroys his home, since he destroys his reputation. On the other hand, the person who refuses all financial help from any human being and is even unwilling to accept gifts, but rather lives with only the money he legitimately accumulates by himself, understands that all comes from God, and in the end he will gain the most.[6] Unfortunately, we know that the greed that pervades all of Western society, i.e., the great desire to accumulate more and more, has indeed destroyed homes both figuratively and

literally. Friendships and families have been ruined by the insatiable need for one family member to accumulate wealth at the expense of spending time in the home with family. In addition, today many families have lost the homes in which they have lived for years due to foreclosures that result from greedy behavior. Their avarice allowed them to buy homes that they could not truly afford but were able to purchase with almost no down payment. However, they were too blinded by their desires to understand that they would never be able to maintain the rate of payments.

Proverbs also says that a prince who lacks understanding (of the power of his greed) will feel oppressed, but he who has no covetous or greedy desires will prolong his days.[7] Rashi explains that this greedy individual is unaware of how much he is destroying his life by unscrupulously cheating others for his own gain.[8] Even in the eleventh century, Rashi understood how a person's avarice could destroy him or her. Rabbi Levi ben Gershon (known as Ralbag or Gersonides), who lived two hundred years later, explains that a greedy person is a smooth talker, like a lion who controls others through fear of its roar. Underneath the talk and that roar, however, there is no real substance, and the greedy person will eventually be exposed for what he truly is, while the person who despises greed will live long and gain the respect of others in his life. Malbim, who lived in the nineteenth century, describes the greedy schemer like Bernie Madoff. He says that if this greedy person is clever, he will use the greed to get others to give him their funds. But if this greedy person is foolish, he will simply rob people. Either way, when the mastermind (or robber) is found out, his days are numbered and his life is shortened. On the other hand, the individual who earns money honestly will never live in fear of being caught, and his life will be lengthened.[9] How insightful this comment is. While Bernie Madoff

2. Nachmanides commentary on Exodus 18:21
3. Riva and Rabbeinu Bechaye commentaries on Exodus 18:21
4. Tur HaAroch commentary on Exodus 18:21
5. Proverbs 15:27
6. Gra and Malbim commentaries on Proverbs 15:27

7. Proverbs 28:16
8. Rashi commentary on Proverbs 28:16
9. Rabbeinu Gershom and Malbim commentaries on Proverbs 28:16

was paying dividends for years to many clients that defied all market logic, his investors never bothered to question him or the inflated amounts they received because of their own greed. As long as he was making them large profits, their greed and desire for more money did not allow them to inquire too deeply (or at all) about how it was being accomplished, even though (in retrospect) the signs were all there for anyone to objectively see what was happening. These ideas are also echoed in a third Proverbs text, which also uses this word, "*Betza*-greed," and says that the attribute of greediness takes away one's life.[10]

There are many other verses that discuss or imply concepts related to avarice, without using the actual word "*Betza*," especially as they are interpreted by the commentaries. For example, in one of the most famous paragraph in the entire Torah, the *Shema*, it says that a Jew should love God with "all his heart, with all his soul, and with all his *Me'od* (might)."[11] Rashi explains that the third phrase actually signifies that a Jew should love God with all his money, i.e., God should be more important to him or her than money is. Rashi then answers an unasked question: Why is "money" in "third place" in the verse, after loving God with all of one's heart and soul? Certainly, if a Jew loves God with all of his or her heart and soul, loving God with money is obvious or redundant? Rashi answers that there are certain people who are so greedy that to them, money and possessions are more important than even their lives. For them, it is harder to love God with all of their money than to love Him with all of their soul. Maharal expands on Rashi's words and says that we already encountered Jews in the Torah who are very greedy – the two-and-a-half tribes that wanted to stay out of Israel proper in order to have grazing land for their multitude of cattle. (More about them will be explained below.) Why does this verse, then, have to remind us of this lesson again – that God is more important than worldly goods? He answers that for some greedy people, the idea of acquiring more money actually gives them a sense of life and a reason to live. These people are so greedy that their entire existence is about accumulation of more wealth. Thus, God commands that even these Jews must put God before their money.[12] Rabbi Chaim ibn Attar (1696-1743) gives a similar explanation, but he says the verse is not speaking about actual money, but rather about the desire for money. For greedy people whose entire life hinges on their great and insatiable desire for money, they should learn to love God with that same insatiable desire.[13]

Jeremiah described his era and his society, which seems very similar to ours today. He says that *everyone* in his time, from the least to the greatest in that society, had a greedy desire.[14] Rabbi Dovid Altshuler explains that the High Priest and prophet referred to by Jeremiah in that verse were also filled with greed, and these refer to a corrupt High Priest and a false prophet, who worshipped idols.[15] Jeremiah also warns the Jew not to boast about his or her accomplishments of wisdom, strength/heroism, or accumulated wealth. They should only "boast" about God, who is just and is the basis and source of all of these three accomplishments, which God allows people to achieve and which can be removed from them at any time. If people have attained any of these three achievements without full belief in God, the success is worthless and will not protect any individual.[16] Thus, the greedy, wealthy person who ignores God is disdained by Jeremiah, who says he is leading a misguided life. Job agrees with this attitude and states that a person who has insatiable greed will ultimately not save anything that he or she has accumulated.[17] King Solomon also said that a "lover of money" will never be satisfied, since, like any

---

10. Proverbs 1:19
11. Deuteronomy 6:5

12. Rashi and *Gur Aryeh* (Maharal) commentaries on Deuteronomy 6:5
13. *Ohr HaChaim* commentary on Deuteronomy 6:5
14. Jeremiah 8:10
15. *Metzudat David* commentary on Jeremiah 8:10
16. Jeremiah 9:22 23
17. Job 20:20

addiction, what is enough for today is never enough for tomorrow.[18] Long before psychologists classified greed as an actual addiction, as many have recently done, King Solomon alluded to this concept thousands of years ago. Ibn Ezra explains this "lover of money" literally. This is a special kind of greedy person who does not like to accumulate possessions, but only desires to build up his or her bank account, i.e., to become the wealthiest person in the world, simply to have the money and not even use it.[19]

All greedy people are, by definition, truly ignorant of the fundamental concept that everything in the world belongs to God, even those goods that are in a person's home or his or her money in the bank.[20] God can arrange for these people to be wiped out very quickly with a super-storm that destroys people's worldly goods or with bank failures that wipe out entire fortunes. Many people unfortunately learned this lesson when Bernie Madoff destroyed their hard-earned life fortunes overnight. Only when people understand what Chagai taught – that all money and gold belongs to God and He decides who keeps it and who does not[21] – will they begin to have a proper perspective on life and towards worldly goods. Some have interpreted the verse about not making idols out of gold and silver[22] in a literal sense – do not make money into an idol, something other than God that a person believes has ultimate power. In fact, some commentaries have shown that the Hebrew word for money or silver, "Kesef," actually means an insatiable desire. Thus, Ecclesiastes is really teaching that when a Jew's desire for Torah is the same as a greedy person's desire for money, then he has achieved God's true will.[23] The word "Kesef" "desire," is even used by King

David to describe his desire and longing to be close to God.[24]

Because it is so easy for powerful people to become greedy, God tried to ensure that the most powerful person in Jewish society, the king, would not succumb to this natural inclination. Therefore, He forbade the king from taking too many wives (physical desire) or having too many horses (material desire). God also commanded the Jewish king to write an "extra" Torah scroll (in addition to the one that each Jew is commanded to write), to bring it with him wherever he went, and also to study it carefully. In this way, the king will be reminded that he must obey the Torah and not grow haughty, which will lead to greediness.[25] Unfortunately, as is the case with today's most powerful people, i.e., the CEOs of major companies who earn hundreds of millions of dollars yearly while, at the same time reducing the wages or benefits of their workers, all these Torah safeguards did not prevent most Jewish kings in the past from succumbing to their greedy desires.

When God promises the Jewish people wealth, but also peace, as a reward for keeping the commandments, Rabbi Avraham Shmuel Binyamin Sofer (1815-1872) comments that when most societies become wealthy, like most countries in the twenty-first century who have achieved great wealth in comparison to previous generations, nevertheless, there will always be some people who have more wealth than others. This will naturally lead to jealousy and greed to accumulate more, even from people who have "enough" to live a very good and comfortable life. Thus, God's promise to the Jewish people is that if they keep all of the commandments, God will create a wealthy society that will have peace as well, i.e., a life without jealousy and greed.[26] King Solomon, who was vastly wealthy, understood that a good name is a far more important achievement in life than "good oil," or great wealth.[27]

---

18. Ecclesiastes 5:9
19. Ibn Ezra commentary on Ecclesiastes 5:9
20. Psalms 24:1
21. Chagai 2:8 with Rashi commentary
22. Exodus 20:20
23. Ecclesiastes 10:19 with *Chomat Anach* (Chida) commentary

24. Psalms 84:3 with Rashi and Ibn Ezra commentaries
25. Deuteronomy 17:15-20
26. Leviticus 26:3-6 with Ktav Sofer commentary
27. Ecclesiastes 7:1

This has been shown to be true for those in the Jewish and non-Jewish communities, like Bernie Madoff and others who have been caught swindling other people or the government, and have permanently lost their good names, their most valuable asset.

While the Talmudic and accepted understanding of the sins that led to the destruction of the First Temple were that the Jewish people worshipped idols, and committed murder and adultery,[28] Isaiah describes a different reason why the Temple was destroyed, as he portrays a society at that time that seems very similar to the money-hungry culture we live in today.[29] Unlike Jeremiah's similar expression, Isaiah's "*Eicha*-how?" shows a city of Jerusalem bereft of honesty and justice, full of bribes often leading to murder.[30] Isaiah asks how it is that Jerusalem, which used to be a city of faith, turned into a city of lies like a harlot who lies to her husband?[31] The people demonstrated greed as they fooled their customers much in the same way that Madoff did with his customers. They took coins of copper and painted them with silver, so that they would appear much more expensive than they really were. The customers thought they were receiving valuable silver coins instead of relatively worthless copper coins.[32] And just as it is with some in the twenty-first century, it was the leaders of the Jewish community who conspired with the thieves and made deals with each other, saying, "I will lie and cover for you today, if you do the same for me tomorrow."[33] It was these sins, according to Isaiah, that led to the Temple's destruction.

## NARRATIVES IN THE TORAH RELATING TO GREED

There are numerous stories and recorded incidents in the Torah that involve avarice, as understood by the classic commentaries. By examining these accounts in the verses, we will shed even more light on the Jewish attitude towards greed and why this quality is so heinous.

According to Rabbeinu Bechaye, the second sin in the Torah, that of Cain, was based on his greed. He worked the land and brought a sacrifice to God from that land, only because he desired to take the entire planet from his brother Abel. He was cursed and forced to till the land in great labor as a punishment for his greediness.[34] Ten generations later, the society in Noah's generation was acting both on its rampant lust and its great desire for goods, which eventually doomed it.[35] Because that society was lawless, there was no need to hide their greed or stealing the way it is done today. Rather, they openly took anything they wanted.[36] According to Rabbi Shlomo Ephraim Luntschitz (1550-1619), it was their constant greed for more and more to satiate their endless desires that made this generation evil.[37] In the end, despite the myriad other sins that this generation committed, God decided to destroy the entire world only because of the sin of greed.[38]

Even after the world had been destroyed due to the sin of greed, ten generations later, the generation of the Tower of Babel had not changed their essential values. Using a newly invented building material called brick, they built a massive tower to create a name for themselves and challenge God.[39] The Midrash says that the chief value of that civilization was worldly goods, and the most important among these goods was their precious bricks. Thus, when a person fell off the tower and died

---

28. *Yoma* 9b
29. Isaiah 1:21-23
30. Radak commentary on Isaiah 1:21
31. *Metzudat David* commentary on Isaiah 1:21
32. Rashi and Radak commentaries on Isaiah 1:22
33. Radak and Metzudat David commentaries on Isaiah 1:23

34. Rabbeinu Bechaye commentary on Genesis 4:7
35. Genesis 6:11-13
36. Rashi commentary on Genesis 6:11
37. *Kli Yakar* commentary on Genesis 5:5
38. *Sanhedrin* 108a, Rashi commentary on Genesis 6:13
39. Genesis 11:1-5

while building this seven-mile skyscraper, no one paid attention or cared. But if one brick fell and was lost, they stopped building, sat down, and wept.[40] It sounds preposterous to care more about money or goods than human life. Yet, we live in a society today that is not essentially different in its values. Three examples from the operations of large companies are enough to prove how this idea exists in our own times. In the 1970s the Ford Company was in a rush to release their new Pinto car, despite the fact that it was well aware that its gas tank was prone to fire in the event of an accident and would cause many unnecessary deaths. It would have cost an additional $11 per car to install a part that would have fixed this problem. An internal memorandum revealed that Ford did a cost-benefit analysis and concluded that it would cost them about $200,000 per death for each potential lawsuit. With an estimated 900 deaths, they figured, it would be cheaper to pay the bereaved families that money than install the part. Therefore, they consciously released the car without this part, which resulted in hundreds of deaths. Is this any different than the Tower of Babel generation who placed their precious bricks above people's lives?

More recently, it was reported (New York Times, May 11, 2013) that a Johns Hopkins University study found that a company had injected small amounts of arsenic into their chickens because this chemical roxarsone kills intestinal parasites, promotes growth, and makes meat look pinker. Although this was not an illegal action, this company knowingly increased people's chances of contracting cancer and other diseases as a result. Similarly, a poultry plant in upstate New York was treating its fowl with potentially toxic chemicals in order to remove contaminants that escape notice as processing line speeds accelerated, in part to meet growing consumer demand for chicken and turkey. When a thirty-seven-year-old federal poultry inspector, Jose Nevarro, died when his lungs bled out, only then did

an investigation begin that eventually halted this practice (as reported in the Washington Post on April 25, 2013). Today, it is the greed of companies – i.e., their desire for profit above all other considerations – that endangers lives and sometimes kills people, which is no different from the Tower of Babel generation's practices.

In contrast, the Torah tells us that Abraham was extremely wealthy with cattle, gold, and silver, and showed the world that it is possible to have wealth and power and not necessarily become greedy.[41] In the same vein, when it says that Abraham died an old man and was satisfied with life,[42] Nachmanides points out that this informs us that because Abraham was not greedy at all, he was always satisfied with what he had and was never desirous of obtaining more and more. Therefore, he did not waste his life on the continual pursuit of material possessions.[43]

Part of the insidious nature of greed is the need not only to have it, but also to show off one's wealth and accomplishments to others. Jacob was well aware of this and that how appearances matter. Therefore, even though he and his family were not particularly in need of food, when there was a famine in the land of Israel and almost all of the surrounding families required food from Egypt, Jacob nevertheless instructed his sons to go to Egypt to obtain food. Why? The Talmud explains that Jacob was careful that his family should not appear to be showing off its wealth by not requiring Egyptian food to survive.[44] Unfortunately, it appears that this message did not carry over to the next few generations. Two generations later, it says that the new Egyptian king did not know Joseph, i.e., he ignored all that Joseph had done to save Egyptian society, and he began to enslave the Jews. What caused this sudden change of attitude towards Joseph and the Jewish people? The verse immediately prior to this one about the new king says that

---

40. Midrash, Pirkei DeRabbi Eliezer 24

41. Genesis 13:2 with Ktav Sofer commentary
42. Genesis 25:8
43. Nachmanides commentary on Genesis 25:8
44. Genesis 41:57-58, 42:1-2, Ta'anit 10b

as the Jewish people multiplied greatly, they became exceedingly eminent "*Bime'od, Meo'd*," which is usually translated as "mighty." But we know from the Talmud and the explanation of the *Shema* cited above that this word also signifies "wealth." Thus, some interpret this verse to signify that the Jewish people showed off their wealth to the Egyptians (rather than keep it private), which is one of the symptoms of greed. It was for this reason that the Egyptian king and Egyptian people turned against the Jews, despite everything that Joseph had done to save and lead the country.[45]

Later, some Jews from the generation in the desert showed that they had not learned their lesson about the Jewish antipathy towards greed. Barely a year after escaping Egyptian slavery with their lives, a group of Jews were not satisfied with the daily manna, which provided for all of their nourishment needs and was delicious. In addition, though they possessed many cattle, in their greed they refused to "sacrifice" their own wealth for the taste of meat, which they desired even though they had never enjoyed meat in Egypt. God knew that if He did not deliver on their request, it would possibly appear to some that God was incapable of giving them meat in the middle of the desert. Therefore, He gave them quail. It was the way that these Jews reacted to the quail that God had sent that truly demonstrates their greed. If they really just wanted to taste meat, then the first thing they should have done was grab a quail, slaughter it the kosher way, roast it, and then savor its taste. However, the Torah records that when the quail came, the birds were stationery in the air, their formation measuring about twelve miles by twelve miles and three to four feet thick. Rather than immediately prepare to eat them, the people gathered the quail, and each Jew put them into his or her individual pile, with this process continuing for more than twenty-four consecutive hours. Only afterwards did they begin to eat the quail. This demonstrates their enormous greed and desire to put the meat "in the bank," into those piles, rather than enjoy its taste, thereby indicating their true intent. In this way, they believed, they would not have to rely on God to send their daily portion of manna. It was for this reason that these Jews were killed by God one month later.[46]

Forty years later, another group of Jewish men showed greed by demonstrating that their possessions were more important than their children, wives, and spiritual connection to their people and their land. The two-and-a-half tribes of Reuben, Gad, and half of the tribe of Menashe, were blessed with extremely large herds of cattle. They feared that entry into the land of Israel would deprive them of the large grazing area needed for their cattle, and hence make them lose some of their wealth. Therefore, they asked Moses to let them remain and live on the east side of the Jordan, which has vast grazing areas, rather than live in the land of Israel. In their request to Moses they indicated their priority by mentioning their cattle before they mentioned their wives and children, and they also left out God's name completely in the conversation with Moses. Only later, after the men committed to fight with their brethren for fourteen years in order to conquer the promised land, and only after they included God in their words and got their priorities straight (at the urging of Moses), did Moses agree to their request. Nevertheless, the sages tell us that it was these particular tribes that were destroyed first (before any other tribes) many years later, because of their initial sin of greed, putting their cattle (which constituted their wealth) above settling in the land of Israel.[47]

## THE ONE SOCIETY THAT MOST RESEMBLES TODAY'S WESTERN WORLD – SODOM

Although there are some similarities between the societies in the narratives above and twenty-first century life, the one place in the ancient

---

45. Exodus 1:7-8, *Berachot* 54a

46. Numbers 11:4, 7-9, 18-10, 31-34
47. Numbers 32:1, 5-7, 16-17, 25-26 with *Da'at Zekainim* commentary

world that most resembles today's world seems to be that of Sodom. This sounds like a harsh evaluation, but if we compare the atmosphere and values of that society, according to traditional Jewish texts, we will see many parallels.

The first reference to Sodom in the Mishna, at first blush, does not seem to render this city as such an evil place. It says that a person who believes that "what is yours is mine and what is mine is mine" is truly evil, while a person who believes that "what is yours is yours and what is mine is mine" is a an average person. But some believe this latter attitude was a characteristic of Sodom.[48] What is wrong with caring about only your possessions and letting others care about their possessions? Apparently, this indicates a feeling and general value that "I only have to worry about me, and no one else." In a purely capitalistic society, this is the core value – everybody only worries about his or her own welfare and does not help anyone out unless it is in his or her interest to do so. That is Sodom. In the extreme, this leads to the law that was passed in Sodom that anyone who helped out any poor person would be burned to death. The Midrash then records that the daughter of Lot, who had been brought up to be kind by her great-uncle Abraham, secretly helped out a needy person. When she was caught doing this, the Sodom government actually killed her. This is what caused God to decree destruction upon the entire city.[49] Another similar Midrash speaks about two young girls meeting at the well. One looked sickly because she did not have food at home. Her friend helped her by giving her wheat and when she was found out, the Sodom authorities killed her.[50] A third Midrash speaks of a Sodom practice in which any guest who came to visit Sodom was raped and all of his or her money was taken.[51] The reason the Sodom citizens took the money of strangers or did not give anything to the poor was *not* because the people of Sodom were poor and needed the

money. It was the choicest and richest area, the most luscious region in the country, and the people were all very wealthy. Rather, their core value of greed, never to part with their money, did not allow them to ever help anyone, and they felt they had to "punish" all guests and make even more money through them. While helping others is not considered evil in Western countries today, and most people believe that it is indeed their government's obligation to help the poor, nevertheless, many people retain the "each-person-for-himself" attitude, and in practice, most people today do not go out of their way to help others.

Another source describes the lewdness and sexual immorality that took place in Sodom, where adultery was very common. There is a famous story about the residents in Sodom who constructed special beds – all one size – in order to house the guests who came there. If people were shorter than the beds, the "hosts" physically stretched their bodies until they fit the bed exactly. If they were too tall for the beds, they cut off their limbs until they fit into the bed. Finally, the same source records that when poor people came to Sodom to beg for help (since it was so wealthy), every person was given special coins, ostensibly to help them. But when these poor people tried to use these coins to buy food and pay for anything in the city, no one would accept them. The poor eventually died from starvation, and the people then retrieved their coins from the corpses. The Sodom citizens then fought over the clothing of these poor people.[52] The last example shows the true values of Sodom. On the surface, they seemingly cared about others, building beds for guests and giving the poor money. But, in truth, it was only a large show. Why would wealthy people fight over the tattered clothes of the dead poor people? This demonstrates the extent of their insatiable desire to own yet another item, even one that they would never use. Although today people are not as cruel and callous as the Sodomites,

48. Mishna *Avot* 5:10
49. Midrash, *Beraishit Rabbah* 49
50. Midrash, *Beraishit Rabbah* 49:6
51. Midrash, *Beraishit Rabbah* 50:7

52. *Sefer HaYashar (Sefer Toldot Ha'adam)*, *Parshat Vayera*, pp. 58-62

there are many people who will fight others to obtain even a small amount of additional wealth, and many others who on the outside seem like giving people, but in reality never part with the wealth they have accumulated. This is particularly true of large corporations that ostensibly try to help people or the environment, but often are only concerned only with enhancing their image in order to increase sales even further. In Sodom, the prime motivator was greed, and as Pirkei DeRabbi Eliezer says, it was all about accumulating more and more wealth.[53]

## THE ATTITUDE OF THE RABBIS TOWARDS GREED

The issue of greed or its avoidance is not simply "another" value in Judaism. How a Jew behaves with regard to money matters is front and center on the scale of Jewish values. The Talmud says that the very first question a person will be asked when he or she gets to heaven will be, "How ethically did you behave in business and money matters?"[54] Only then will a Jew be asked about his or her Torah learning. The questions about keeping Shabbat and kosher are far down on the list. The Midrash says that a person who is not greedy, but ethical and caring in business dealings, will earn the respect of everyone he or she knows, and it will be considered as if this Jew kept the entire Torah.[55]

When Alexander the Great visited Jerusalem and heard about the wonders of the Jewish people, he received an eyeball from the "Garden of Eden." He put the eyeball on a scale, but no matter how much gold and silver were put on the other side of the scale to balance it, the eyeball outweighed it. Alexander wanted to know why this was so, and the Rabbis explained that this eyeball represented the greed of the human being, which can never be satisfied.[56] Why? The Rabbis clarified that it is in the nature of human beings that regardless of whatever goods they have accumulated until the present, their desire for more goods constantly increases. Therefore, if a person believes that when he or she will have a certain amount it will be enough, human nature is such that when that amount is reached, that person's desire for more goods will automatically be increased. This is such a truism that the Midrash states that a person always dies with less than half of his or her desires for material goods fulfilled.[57] This is true whether the person dies poor or was the richest person in the world. A person's desire for wealth increases in direct proportion to that individual's affluence. That is why it is also true that if a person's main value is the accumulation of wealth, he or she can never be satisfied in life. This is the very definition of greed and also the definition of an addiction – the need constantly outpaces the consumption. Only when a person learns that there are higher values in life than money and accumulated wealth, will that individual also realize that all prosperity comes from God and that a person should be satisfied with whatever goods and money he or she has. Thus, the Jewish definition of the concept of wealth is subjective. If a person is appreciative of what he or she has, not matter how much or how little it may be, he or she is considered wealthy. If the person is unsatisfied and remains greedy, then that person is never considered wealthy.[58]

Generally, say the Rabbis, the more wealth a person has, the more worried he or she will be (in order to increase that wealth and/or not lose it).[59] Thus, the greedy person is more worried and tense than other people, since his or her focus is always on getting or making more. Rabbi Mazuz adds that a greedy person who constantly runs after increasing wealth will take up almost all of his or her time in this pursuit, and will not have time for significant Torah learning or any other spiritual pursuits.

53. Midrash, *Pirkei DeRabbi Eliezer* 25
54. *Shabbat* 31a
55. Midrash, *Mechilta*, "*Vayasa*" 1
56. *Tamid* 32b

57. Midrash, *Kohelet Rabbah* 3:13
58. Mishna *Avot* 4:1
59. Mishna *Avot* 2:7

As a result, this person will almost always lose his or her share in the World to Come.[60]

There are two types of greedy people. There are those who are openly greedy and proud of their accumulation of wealth, even at the expense of others, and who need to show off their possessions. Then there are greedy people, like Bernie Madoff, who are secretly greedy and feign concern for others while surreptitiously stealing from them. Which is worse? The Torah seems to believe that the second category is a worse type of greed because a robber who openly steals pays back only what he or she stole, but a thief who steals without people knowing it pays back double. Why? The thief who steals from people in secret shows more fear of human beings than fear of God. For that reason, his punishment is more severe.[61] And people who pretend to help society through their wealth, but their true values are only greed and accumulating more wealth, are disdained by God. This is proven by a discussion between the Roman leaders who occupied the Land of Israel and God. God asked them what they did in life. Fearful of God, they replied that we built roads, bridges, and accumulated wealth, but did all of this only so that the Jewish people could sit and learn Torah. God then castigated them and said that what they did and built was only for their own physical pleasure and greediness. They did not realize that everything belongs to God in any event.[62] Thus, greedy people and greedy corporations pretending to benefit society, but secretly using this benefit to gain even more wealth are worse than openly greedy individuals.

A person who does not realize that all prosperity comes from above can indeed turn especially greedy. The classic Talmudic definition of a greedy person is "the individual who has food in his basket, but still asks 'what will I eat tomorrow?'" Even when this person has enough to survive and thrive, it is not sufficient for him or her, and the Talmud calls this person lacking any faith in God.[63] In fact, one can tell the true values of a person, says the Talmud, by how an individual acts in three situations: when the person is drunk, how he spends his or her money, and how he or she behaves when angry.[64]

Rabbi Eliezer Papo (1786-1827) perhaps best summed up the Jewish attitude on greed. He states that just like the verse says that life and death are in the hands of the tongue,[65] so too, life and death are in the hands of money. Wealth can give or take away life. He also says that there are many other sins that a Jew often does in order to accumulate excessive wealth (see next section). And a person whose focus is on greed, i.e., accumulating more and more wealth, will necessary forgo many important commandments not at all related to money. A greedy Jew who uses his money and wealth improperly will lose his share in the World to Come. But if a Jew uses his or her wealth properly, that will increase his or her share in the World to Come.[66]

## OTHER SINS NECESSARILY VIOLATED BY THE GREEDY PERSON

In addition to the intrinsic sin and violation of ethical behavior by the greedy individual, the greedy Jew also necessarily violates a host of other sins in the process of displaying greed (many of which are discussed in other chapters in this volume). For example, by immorally taking money from others due to greed, a Jew is guilty of stealing, a Torah violation.[67] Even taking a very minor amount is still considered stealing.[68] And if the person is not aware that he or she is being swindled, this is the classic definition of stealing.[69]

Another sin that a greedy person is guilty of (by swindling victims without their

---

60. *Avot Al Banim*
61. *Bava Kama 79b*
62. *Avodah Zara 2b*
63. *Sotah 48b*
64. *Eiruvin 65b*
65. Proverbs 19:21
66. *Pele Yo'etz* on "*Kesef*"
67. Leviticus 19:11
68. Maimonides, *Hilchot Genaiva* 1:2
69. Maimonides, *Hilchot Genaiva* 1:3

knowledge) is that of being a hypocrite. It is a Torah violation not to be "whole with God," i.e., act the same on the inside and the outside.[70] In fact, Rabban Gamliel would throw out any student from the *Beit Midrash*-House of Jewish Learning, if he showed any hypocrisy.[71] All those arrested for swindling others or cheating the government, at one time, seemed to act legitimately – until they were caught. They all acted hypocritically, especially those who supposedly were Torah-observant Jews. Maimonides states that it is absolutely forbidden to speak one way and think another way (or act differently in secret).[72] According to the commentaries, this action is a Torah violation, much like a land that appears fruitful on the surface, but beneath the ground everything is rotten.[73] When King David specified the formula for a long and meaningful life, he stated that a Jew should not speak with guile. Rabbi David Kimchi understands this to be acting hypocritically, i.e., speaking one way but acting in a different manner.[74] Thus, an individual can achieve a great life by refraining from being a hypocrite. This is especially true in business, regarding which one's word should be one's bond, and a violation of one's word violates a Torah law.[75] Of the three types of individuals whom God hates most in this world, the number one category is a person who acts hypocritically.[76] Thus, if one's greed leads to speaking to people nicely as he or she cheats them, this is the ultimate sin.

Another sin that most greedy people are guilty of in swindling others is *Genaivat Da'at*, receiving undeserved benefit. If someone believes that another individual is helping him or her when the person is not helping at all, then that person is guilty of *Genaivat Da'at*. (See chapter, "Falsely Propping Oneself Up and Putting Others Down"). This is particularly

true in the business realm. This sin is violated if an item or commodity such as an investment opportunity, a car, or even a fruit, is portrayed as truly great when in reality it is not.[77] Of the seven types of thieves described in Judaism, the Jew who swindles in this manner is called the worst.[78] A Jew may not gain favor undeservedly, even from non-Jews. For example, if a greedy person seems to be offering "the deal of a lifetime" and "lets the person in on the ground floor," the investor is especially grateful. In addition to stealing from that individual, this greedy person is guilty of *Genaivat Da'at*.[79] Even pronouncing one word that makes others think that he looks better than he truly deserves is considered *Genaivat Da'at* and is forbidden.[80] The *Code of Jewish Law* spells out all of the circumstances of *Genaivat Da'at*, and most greedy people violate one or more of these laws when they deal with other human beings in business.[81] Rabbeinu Yonah calls this sin a "fundamental sin of the soul."[82]

Finally, when greedy Jewish people are finally exposed for what they truly are, then they are often guilty of probably the greatest sin in the Torah – desecrating God's name.[83] If the greedy person is identified as an observant Jew, the desecration of God's name is even greater, because when someone thinks less of God because of this Jew's actions, this sin has been perpetrated.[84] The entire purpose of Judaism and one's life as a Jew is to sanctify God's name in the world.[85] The greedy person who gets caught doing illegal activities does just the opposite. The Torah commands each Jew to love God.[86] Part of that love is to make God beloved to others through one's actions and one's words.[87] Thus, a greedy Jew who causes

---

70. Deuteronomy 18:13
71. *Berachot* 28a
72. Maimonides, *Hilchot De'ot* 2:6
73. Numbers 33:35 with Ibn Ezra and Malbim commentaries
74. Psalms 34:13-14 with Radak commentary
75. Leviticus 19:36, *Bava Metzia* 49a
76. *Pesachim* 113b
77. Mishna *Bava Metzia* 4:11-12
78. Tosefta *Bava Kama* 7:3
79. *Chulin* 94a
80. Maimonides, *Hilchot De'ot* 2:6
81. *Shulchan Aruch, Choshen Mishpat* 228:6-9
82. *Sha'arei Teshuva* 3:184
83. Leviticus 22:32
84. *Yoma* 86a
85. Midrash, *Tana Debei Eliyahu* 26:2
86. Deuteronomy 6:5
87. *Yoma* 86a

others to despise God has also violated this commandment. Pele Yo'etz calls this the worst sin in the Torah and the most difficult one from which to repent. He says that sanctifying or desecrating God's name very often occurs in the realm of business and how people act around money. In our days, when every observant Jew is considered God's "representative" in the sense that he affects how God is perceived by most others, it is especially crucial that all actions by a Jew who supposedly keeps the commandments should uphold God's image. Therefore, for an observant Jew today, there are additional reasons not to engage in any activity even slightly resembling greed. [88]

---

88. *Pele Yo'etz* on *"Chilul Hashem"*

# TOLERANCE AND INTOLERANCE IN JUDAISM

**W**HEN PEOPLE ARE ASKED whether they are generally tolerant or intolerant, almost everyone will say that they are most definitely tolerant of others, and they truly believe it. However, when examining how most of these people actually live, a different reality emerges. This dichotomy arises because although most people truly believe that they tolerate others whose views and lifestyles are different from their own, the fact is that when they actually encounter someone who is different from them, it is very difficult for them to be fair, objective, and permissive towards those who do not share their attitudes, behaviors, and opinions. Why is this so? The human being's natural tendency is to be uncomfortable with anyone who is different. For example, if a person suddenly comes into a crowded room with purple hair, it is interesting how the atmosphere in the room quickly changes and how that person is treated, even if he or she never even says one word or does anything. Thus, tolerant individuals have to fight their basic nature in order to treat those who disagree with them in lifestyle, opinion, and attitude, as equals. Most religions are usually intolerant of those who disagree with its values and tenets. How tolerant, then, is Judaism, with those who disagree with normative Jewish practice, ideas, and underlying values? This chapter will not examine how some Jews behave (which often is not the measure of Jewish values), but rather, how the sources tell Jews to behave and how significant traditional Jewish personalities in the past have behaved and spoken of others who are different. It also will examine when and why Judaism is intolerant.

## TOLERANCE OF THE DIFFERING OPINION OF OTHERS

Most people are naturally convinced that their view and opinion is the correct one, and they have little tolerance of others who do not share that opinion. Judaism teaches us just the opposite: Respect the opinion of others and learn from it, even when it differs from your own. Therefore, Ben Zoma teaches in the Mishna that a true scholar is someone who can learn from everyone, even those whose opinions differ radically from his or hers.[1] In another Mishna, Jews are taught that a wise person is he who lets the other person finish his or her thought while speaking, without interrupting, even though that individual's viewpoint may not make sense, may be diametrically opposed to the wise person's outlook, or may even be against basic Jewish values.[2] Judaism tolerates anyone's view, and thus, that opinion should not be cut off. In fact, the structure of the entire Talmud also teaches this idea. On points of Jewish law, on nearly every page of the Mishna and Gemara, diametrically opposing opinions are recorded. When written down, the editors could have easily omitted those views not included in normative Jewish practice. But instead, they recorded every view in order to emphasize that all opinions are valid, even those not enacted into Jewish law. This is most dramatically demonstrated in the very first words of the entire Talmud, the very first Mishna in *Berachot*. The Rabbis argue with Rabban Gamliel about the latest time that the *Shema* prayer may be recited at night. The Rabbis say that it can be prayed until midnight, while Rabban Gamliel says it can be recited all night. But then the Mishna then records that Rabban Gamliel's own sons followed the view of the Rabbis (since Jewish law follows the majority opinion) and not the view of their father. One night, when they came home after midnight and did not know what to do, Rabban Gamliel explained how they could still recite the *Shema* at that time, since the Rab-

---

1. Mishna *Avot* 4:1
2. Mishna *Avot* 5:7

bis essentially agreed with their father's view (of all night), but only declared midnight as the deadline in order to prevent people from staying up very late and then accidentally falling asleep.[3] Therefore, we see that the sons of Rabban Gamliel respected the Rabbis enough to tolerate and actually follow their view, even when it disagreed with that of their own father.

In the Talmud, there are vehement arguments between The House of Shammai and the House of Hillel on points of Jewish law. Which view is followed in Halacha, in Jewish law? The Talmud tells us that Jewish law almost always follows the view of Beit Hillel. But if both views are valid, why does Beit Hillel emerge victorious almost every time? The Talmud explains the reason is because they were so tolerant of Beit Shammai's view that disagreed with their own, and it was due to their kindness and modesty, as they always mentioned Beit Shammai's opinion before their own.[4]

The idea of tolerating and respecting the opinion of those who disagree with you is not limited to theoretical debates in Judaism. In the *Code of Jewish Law*, Rabbi Caro must decide and rule finally according to the one opinion that is to be followed by all Jews. But then, after stating the "final opinion," he often says that if there is a mitigating reason, Jews should follow the opposite view. For example, *Shulchan Aruch*-Code of Jewish Law rules that in a specific situation, we follow the opinion that the wine could not be ritually used if it was previously drunk by someone. That is his final ruling. But then, a few sentences later, he also rules that if it was difficult to obtain that wine, then we follow the opposite view and *can* use wine that was already previously drunk.[5] Thus, even though Jewish law Halacha is supposed to be "cut and dried," even the final Jewish law tolerates minority opinions. In another example of this process, *Shulchan Aruch* reverses himself and even allowed a Matzah

on Passover that had a bit of *Chametz* (leaven) that was removed from it to be eaten on Pesach, in a case that the monetary loss would have been substantial.[6] This pattern can be found throughout the four sections of *Shulchan Aruch*, demonstrating the tolerance and power of opinions that are different and usually not followed, but still respected enough to be used when needed.

The Talmud itself states that the intellectual battles of Rabbis who disagree with each other are a very positive phenomenon, like two pieces of iron that sharpen each other when rubbed together.[7] When Resh Lakish passed away, Rabbi Yochanan's students tried to comfort him by praising his Torah lectures in order to appease Rabbi Yochanan on the terrible loss of Resh Lakish, who was his study partner (and brother-in-law). They sent the brightest student, Rabbi Eleazar, who gave Rabbi Yochanan great compliments following a discourse. But Rabbi Yochanan wept, explaining that this was no substitute for Resh Lakish. He missed his study partner *because* Resh Lakish would always argue with him and try to dispute the main points of Rabbi Yochanan's talks.[8] To Rav Yochanan, this is true Jewish learning: presenting, arguing, being questioned, and, through this process, arriving at the truth. This process represents a true tolerance of conflicting ideas.

## THE NAMES OF THE JEWISH PEOPLE IN THE TORAH ALSO REPRESENT THIS IDEA

The very names of the Jews as a Jewish people in the Torah all refer to disagreements and arguments. The first name describing the Jewish people, named for its founding father, is Abraham "the Hebrew." His descendants were often called Hebrews. Among the various explanations of this word is the Midrash that states that Abraham was called this because

---

3. Mishna *Berachot* 1:1
4. *Eiruvin* 13b
5. *Shulchan Aruch, Orach Chaim* 182:3, 7
6. *Shulchan Aruch, Orach Chaim* 467:11, *Yoreh De'ah* 23:2
7. *Ta'anit* 7a
8. *Bava Metzia* 84a

of his lone opinion and philosophy of life that different from everyone else's and not tolerated by the non-Jewish world.[9] He fought for his beliefs and was able to survive even threats to his life. The second reference to the Jewish people, still used today, is "Israel," the name given to Jacob after he fought with the angel. The verse itself describes the meaning of this name – "You fought with God."[10] Thus, this name, too, signifies fighting and disagreement. Finally, the name Jew is "*Yehudi*," originally signifying anyone from the tribe of Judah. But Mordechai, from the tribe of Benjamin, was also called *Yehudi*. The Midrash explains "*Yehudi*" as describing his being different, by refusing to bow down to Haman.[11] Therefore, all of the names of the Jewish people describe a nation that disagrees, fights for its values, and is different.

## MINORITY OPINIONS IN JUDAISM ARE NOT ONLY TOLERATED, BUT RESPECTED

The very first reference to the concept of following a majority opinion in deciding a Jewish law comes from the Torah.[12] This refers to a majority of judges who decide the guilt or innocence of an accused criminal. But the very fact that a minority can speak up and try to convince the majority that it has the correct view, shows that Judaism tolerates minority opinions, even in cases that they do not rule that way. This was further demonstrated by how the highest Jewish court, the *Sanhedrin*, deliberated capital crimes and other issues that affected the entire Jewish nation. The physical set up of the *Sanhedrin* was that of a semicircle, which is imitated today by the Knesset, the Israeli parliament. The Talmud states that the younger and less experienced members of the deliberative body would sit on the sides, while the more prominent members sat towards the middle. But when they began deliberations, the first members who spoke were those that sat on the sides, the newest members, who gave their opinions first. This was the intentional order, so that the less experienced judges would not be influenced or intimidated by the opinion of the veterans.[13] Thus, we see that Judaism not only tolerated different views, but actually encouraged and wanted different viewpoints on each subject that was judged.

The lone opinion of great Rabbis was respected, even if not followed in practice. There was one exception, however. Rabbi Eliezer was so admired by his own townspeople that they followed his lone view when it came to circumcision on Shabbat. He allowed the *Mohel* (the person who performs the circumcision) to carry his equipment to the *Brit Milah* on Shabbat, whereas the Rabbis forbade this (but only allowed the circumcision itself on Shabbat). Rabbi Yitzchak taught that not only were the people of Rabbi Eliezer's town not castigated for following their Rabbi (against the majority, the usual practice in Jewish law), but they were also vindicated in their practice by an event that took place later. When the enemy forbade circumcision for Jews all over the land of Israel, they did not decree this ban against one particular town, which happened to be that place where Rabbi Eliezer had lived. The Rabbis took this as a sign showing that the townspeople in Rabbi Eliezer's city were correct in following Rabbi Eliezer against all of the other Rabbis and normative Jewish law.[14]

## LEGITIMATE AND ILLEGITIMATE ARGUMENTS IN JUDAISM

The Mishna defines what is considered a valid argument in Judaism and when another person's opposing view should not be tolerated.[15] The arguments in the Talmud between the Houses of Shammai and Hillel, as noted above, are legitimate in Judaism, while the argument

---

9. Genesis 14:13; Midrash, *Beraishit Rabbah* 42:13
10. Genesis 32:29
11. Esther 2:5; Midrash, *Esther Rabbah* 6:2
12. Exodus 23:2

---

13. *Sanhedrin* 32b, 36a
14. *Shabbat* 130a
15. Mishna *Avot* 5:17

by Korach in the Torah against Moses is illegitimate. What is the difference? From a Jewish perspective, there can certainly be legitimate differences of opinion about any issue, and those differences should not only be tolerated, but also respected – as long as the goals of both sides is to seek the truth, as did the arguments of Hillel and Shammai. But when there are ulterior or personal motives as the basis for the disagreements, such as the argument of Korach with Moses (who argued for the purpose of attaining more political power), then that argument is not legitimate. The Houses of Shammai and Hillel demonstrated this principle not only in how they argued, but also with regard to how they later behaved. Even though their disputes over aspects of Jewish law had serious consequences, the people of both the House of Shammai and the House of Hillel left their vehement disagreements in the halls of the *Beit Midrash*-Jewish House of Learning and readily married each other's families. They somehow found ways within Jewish law to marry, even though their serious disagreements sometimes centered specially around the laws of permitted and forbidden Jewish marriages! The Talmud concludes that they accomplished this only because of their great friendship, and that they put the concept of peace into practice.[16] Thus, people who have these values and put them into practice are able to disagree vehemently, still remain friends, and even stay as close as relatives.

## ACKNOWLEDGING THAT DIFFERENCES BETWEEN PEOPLE EXIST SHOWS TOLERANCE

If Judaism acknowledges that there are legitimate differences between people and that not everyone is the same, then this is the beginning point of tolerance of others who are different. The blessing a Jew says upon seeing a multitude of Jews reflects this "secret" that Jews are not monolithic, and just as each person's face is somewhat different from everyone

else's, so too, each person's values and attitudes differ from others.[17] Thus, just as each person was created with unique facial features, voice patterns, and fingerprints, so too does each person have a unique way of thinking and conceptualizing the world. Understanding this will help people become tolerant of those who differ from their way of thinking (which most see as the "right" way). Likewise, there is not only one "right" way to understand and live as a Jew. The Midrash says that there are seventy different paths to understanding the Torah.[18] This signifies that there are many legitimate avenues to find authentic Judaism. In the same way that each person's face is a little different from everyone else's, so may Judaism's "face" appear in (seventy) different forms. Therefore, people with a legitimate Torah perspective should be tolerant of others with different legitimate perspectives.

These differences also explain an anomaly in the Torah when the Ten Commandments were given. When God spoke to the Jewish people, each person heard the same message from God, but in a distinctive manner. That is why the first commandment of the Ten Commandments is stated in the singular, says the Midrash.[19] Every person learns in an individual way and hears the Torah messages in a manner appropriate for him or her. And because every human being is distinguishable from others, each prophet, charged with delivering essentially the same message from God to the people, delivered it in his or her inimitable way.[20] Everyone has his or her "style," and people must be tolerant of those whose "style" differs from theirs. Moses, the leader of the Jewish people, learned this truth through forty years of leading the Jewish people. This is the reason that when Moses was about to die, he asked God to appoint a leader to succeed him who had the capacity to understand that each Jew requires a different type of leadership, depending on his or her temperament. When

---

16. *Yevamot* 14b

17. *Berachot* 68a
18. Midrash, *Bamidbar Rabbah* 13:15
19. Midrash, *Pesikta Derav Kehana* 12:27
20. *Sanhedrin* 89a

God chose Joshua, he made sure to inform Moses that the new leader indeed had this quality of understanding each person according to his or her specific needs.[21]

In keeping with this perceptive on the nature of human beings, the Mishna states that one of the most amazing aspects of man's creation is that there are many characteristics of the human being which are common to every person, while at the same time, there are features that make each individual unlike any other person created before or to be thereafter.[22] Thus, some aspects of humankind unite all people, while there exists to be other components of the human makeup that allow each person to remain different and special. The Rabbis understood this, so that even when they enacted laws, they understood that some people would not be able to keep these edicts. As long as most, but not all, of the Jewish people would keep them, an edict was enacted.[23]

## TOLERANCE OF SINNERS IN JUDAISM

Judaism has special sensitivity towards sinners and recognizes that they, too, are an integral part of the overall Jewish community. Thus, the most sacred day of the Jewish year, Yom Kippur, cannot commence until the community receives "permission" from the transgressors to pray with them in seeking forgiveness on this Day of Atonement.[24] A similar thought is represented by the content of the spices brought in the Temple. All eleven spices are required in the daily incense offering on the Altar. If even one spice is missing, the penalty is death if the deficient offering is brought as a sacrifice. Yet one spice, the *Chelbonah*, is a foul-smelling plant.[25] Thus, Jews acknowledge in symbolic terms that the species representing

the entire community cannot be offered to God until *all* parts of the community are present, even the "foul-smelling" transgressors.

On Sukkot, the holiday of Tabernacles, Jews are commanded to bring together the Four Species. The Midrash compares each species to a different type of Jew: one with Torah learning and observance (*Etrog*), one who has Torah learning but is non-observant (*Hadas*), one with observance but lacking in Torah learning (*Lulav*), and one with neither Torah learning nor observance (*Arava*). The commandment is not fulfilled until all four species (which represent the different types of Jews) are brought together as one.[26] Moreover, the seventh day of the holiday of Sukkot is called Hoshana Rabbah, and there is a tradition that this is the final day of forgiveness and atonement of the High Holiday season (reminiscent of Yom Kippur). Yet almost the entire focus of the prayer service is the *Arava*, which represents the sinning Jew or the Jew who has neither Torah learning or observance (see previous source). In fact, at one point in the service, the three other species (types of Jews) are set aside, and only the *Arava* is handled from that point onward. Thus, to achieve atonement, every Jew must focus on the needs of the sinning Jew, or the Jew who has no Torah learning and no observance.[27] This sensitivity to sinners was also taught by Beruriah, the wife of Rabbi Meir. She castigated her husband for praying that sinners should die, convincing him that he was in error and that Judaism only advocates the disappearance of sin and/or the habitual sinners. Beruriah then urged her husband to pray that these men would repent.[28] It is important to note that when rebuking the sinner for his or her evil ways, a Jew must possess sensitivity. There is a general commandment in the Torah to admonish Jewish sinners in order to induce them to repent.[29] Why is it

---

21. Midrash, *Bamidbar Rabbah* 21:2; Rashi commentary on Numbers 27:18

22. Mishna *Sanhedrin* 4:5

23. *Bava Batra* 60b; Maimonides, *Hilchot Mamrim* 2:5

24. Yom Kippur Machzor, right before the *Kol Nidre* prayer

25. *Kritot* 6a, 6b

26. Midrash, *Vayikra Rabbah* 30:12

27. Rema on *Shulchan Aruch, Orach Chaim* 664:7; Shelah commentary on Sukkah, *Perek Ner*, Mitzvah 7

28. *Berachot* 10a

29. Leviticus 19:17

that the commandment not to hate someone and the commandment to rebuke are placed in the very same verse? This teaches that even when one rebukes a person who is sinning, the rebuke may never be with even the smallest portion of hate. In addition, because one may not rebuke with any feeling of hatred, Rabbi Elazar believed that in his generation there did not exist any person who could perform the act of proper rebuke – i.e., there was no one who could rebuke someone else without at least a twinge of hatred. Rabbi Tarfon believed that there was no one who could accept rebuke in the proper spirit. Therefore, since rebuke can only be given when the erring person can accept rebuke in the proper spirit and the person giving the rebuke does so in the proper spirit, it is almost impossible to fulfill this Torah commandment today.[30]

It seems that God looks for some redeeming value even in sinners in order to help them. The generation of the Tower of Babel committed the sin of rebellion against God, while the generation of the flood committed the relatively minor sin of stealing. Yet, those who built the tower were saved from death and were only punished by being dispersed throughout the world, speaking different languages. Even though they were intolerant, not permitting any dissenting opinion,[31] they nevertheless had one redeeming value – unity (despite the fact that their unity was directed toward their rebellion against God).[32] This power to unite, even for the wrong reasons, was enough "justification" for God not to destroy them. Thus, even in the case of a sinner, God seeks to find at least one redeeming quality. The great sensitivity that Jews should show even to an evil person who has sinned can be demonstrated in a statement by Shammai in the Mishna. He says that Jews are obligated to greet every person with a warm countenance, graciously.[33] The Mishna does not say to greet only nice people in this manner. The obligation is to greet everyone, even evil people, even non-believers, graciously. Even non-Jews or people of other faiths must be greeted in this way. And the specific wording of Shammai's statement is also strange. The words actually say, "Greet the entire person (*Kol Ha'adam*) graciously." Why is this idea expressed in this manner? Very often it is difficult to find something nice about a person to be gracious about. But if an individual searches hard enough, then he or she can find something good about any person. Thus, if someone looks at the entire person, he or she should be able to discover some aspect of the individual that is positive, and will then be able to greet him or her graciously. This is true even for sinners.

## TOLERANCE AND RESPECT EVEN FOR ONE'S ENEMIES

One would think that Judaism would draw the line about tolerance when it comes to those who seek to destroy Judaism and Jews. And yet, that the sources tell us that even non-Jews who torture and kill Jews must be tolerated and respected to some degree. In the Torah, the Egyptians represent the most reprehensible human beings who killed Jewish babies and Jewish adults, as they demanded backbreaking slave work from the Jews. When the Egyptians were finally defeated, it is logical that the angels (and later the Jewish people) rejoiced and sang in joy. Yet, God castigated the angels for their singing, saying that these human beings, no matter how despicable, are creations of God, and singing at their downfall is immoral and should cease.[34] The Jewish people also symbolically limit their joy in the defeat of the Egyptians, because they are still human beings. That is why at the Seder, Jews remove a drop from their wine cup for each of the Ten Plagues suffered by the Egyptians.[35] Even though the entire Seder celebrates freedom from Egyptian oppression, rejoicing upon the

---

30. *Arachin* 16b
31. Genesis 11:1 with Seforno commentary
32. Rashi commentary on Genesis 11:9
33. Mishna *Avot* 1:15

34. *Sanhedrin* 39b
35. Rema on *Shulchan Aruch, Orach Chaim* 483:7

actual suffering of one's enemy is not a Jewish concept.

This idea is not limited to the Egyptian enemy. Referring to when King Ahab was defeated, the Talmud also states that it is improper to rejoice when an enemy falls.[36] This is true whenever Jews defeat their enemies. Rejoice, yes, but for the victory and the survival of Jews and Judaism and not for the suffering and death of other people.[37] This concept was not limited to statements in the Talmud or Midrash, but was codified as part of Jewish law, making it not only immoral but also illegal for a Jews to rejoice at the downfall of their enemies.[38]

## TOLERANCE ALSO SIGNIFIES NOT EMBARRASSING SINNERS

Respect and sensitivity to sinners also requires not embarrassing them needlessly. When God designed the Tabernacle (and later the Temple), He commanded Aaron to set up the place of the sin offering in the very same place as the burnt offering.[39] Why? The Talmud explains that if there was one particular place that the sin offering were to be offered, then all of the sinners would gather there and all would know that these are transgressors, causing a very embarrassing situation. In order to avoid this, God demonstrated great sensitivity, and commanded the sin offering and burnt offering to be brought from the same spot so that no one would be able to distinguish between these two groups of Jews.[40]

This was not the first time that God went out of His way not to embarrass Jewish sinners. In Egypt, too, there were Jewish sinners and non-believers (the majority of Jews, according to some opinions) who either did not want to leave Egypt or did not deserve to do so. In order not to publicly punish these people, God made sure that they died in Egypt during the plague of darkness, so that no one would see them die or recognize why these people did not leave Egypt with the rest of the Jewish people.[41] Similarly, the original seventy Elders of the Jewish people in Egypt, appointed by Pharaoh, were not worthy individuals. They were afraid to confront Pharaoh with Moses and they inappropriately partied at Mount Sinai after God gave the Ten Commandments. But rather than punish them publicly and embarrass them, God waited almost a year and killed them along with other sinners who died by fire in a rebellion against God.[42]

This concept has been carried out in practical Jewish law today as well. If a Jew's father becomes a known apostate, then this Jew should not be called to the Torah in the same manner as other Jews with his name as the son of his father, but rather, his grandfather's name should be used instead. In certain situations, the father of one's mother is used, and sometimes simply "Abraham" is used instead of the father's name, since Abraham is the ultimate father of all Jewish people. All of this is done not to embarrass the sinner or the child of a sinner.[43]

## TOLERANCE AND RESPECT FOR ALL PEOPLE, ESPECIALLY JEWS

Judaism espouses tolerance and respect for every person, regardless of that person's standing or beliefs. The Mishna states that only if a Jew has tolerance and respect for others will God have tolerance and respect for that individual.[44] In a similar manner, another passage says that a Jew should be tolerant and respectful of every other person because at some point, every person will have his or her moment of importance (his fifteen minutes, perhaps?) in this world.[45] For the same reason, a Jew should judge everyone favorably – i.e., if a person can

---

36. *Sanhedrin* 39b
37. Chronicles II 20:20-21, *Megillah* 10b
38. Mishna *Avot* 4:19
39. Leviticus 6:18
40. *Sotah* 32b

41. Rashi commentary on Exodus 13:8
42. Numbers 11:14, 17; Rashi commentary on Numbers 11:14:17 and Exodus 5:1
43. Rema on *Shulchan Aruch, Orach Chaim* 139:3
44. Mishna *Avot* 3:10
45. Mishna *Avot* 4:3

view another's actions in one of two ways, that person should always assume the good and moral interpretation of events.[46] (See the chapter, "Judging Favorably," for an expansion on this theme).

What is the reason that a Jew should demonstrate such an attitude of tolerance and respect? *Avot DeRabbi Natan* explains Shammai's dictum, cited above, about greeting every person with a smile no matter his or her moral standing.[47] This attitude, which tolerates all people and does not prejudge them before encountering and engaging them, says the Mishna, is the equivalent of giving each person precious gifts, because it shows an inherent respect and likability for every human being – something that every person craves when meeting others. The reason, says the Talmud, is clear. Since only one human being was created in the original creation, it demonstrates to all subsequent human beings that no one person is better or of a higher standing than anyone else, and no one can say that "I am better than you because my father was greater," since every human being shares the same ultimate father, Adam.[48] When asked by a non-Jew who wished to convert to describe the essence of Judaism in one line, Hillel responded that a Jew should treat all people the way he or she would want to be treated.[49] A fundamental principle of Judaism, then, is tolerance and respect for all other people.

This is specifically put into practice within the Jewish community, as the Torah stresses the equality of all Jews, no matter their standing or background. Maimonides stresses that a Jew must not only be tolerant and respectful of other Jews, but he must also actually love them. And this love is extended to each and every Jew, even the most different (e.g., the convert to Judaism with a very different background and the weakest member of a Jewish society). In fact, it is forbidden to hate any Jew.[50] The Torah was given at a time when no society in the world had rules of equality for every member of the population, and the weakest members were legally treated as inferiors, while royalty had a different set of rules and laws that applied to them. Yet, the Torah stresses repeatedly that the laws of the Judaism apply equally to the weakest members of the society, such as the convert (the obligation to love the convert and treat him or her fairly is mentioned thirty-six times in the Torah), the widow, and the orphan. Similarly, the king and other Jewish leaders are obligated to keep the Torah in the same way as everyone else.[51]

It was due to the intolerance and disrespect of Talmud scholars for each other that the 24,000 students of Rabbi Akiva died, and the Jewish people today commemorate this great loss with a thirty-three day period of mourning between Passover and Shavuot.[52] Judaism does not just believe in platitudes and declarations of its values. Rather, it puts these ideas of tolerance and respect for others into practice on an everyday level. This is the reason that it is forbidden to ignore the plight of a Jew in trouble or ignore even the lost object of someone else by passing by and not picking it up. The Jew is commanded to show respect and tolerance of others by helping and retuning lost objects, no matter who are the owners.[53]

## TOLERANCE THAT LEADS TO JEWISH UNITY

Tolerance of all Jews, no matter their backgrounds, beliefs, or lifestyles, leads to the ultimate goal – Jewish unity. It was only that one and only time when the Jewish people united as one, expressed through the singular use of the verb in the verse (of camping), that they were worthy to hear God's voice directly when they received the Torah.[54] In fact, every

---

46. Mishna *Avot* 6:1
47. *Avot DeRabbi Natan* 13:5
48. *Sanhedrin* 37a
49. *Shabbat* 31a

50. Maimonides, *Hilchot De'ot* 6:3-5
51. Exodus 12:49, 22:20, 23:9; Leviticus 19:10, 19:33-34; Numbers 9:14, 15:125-16; Deuteronomy 10:18-19
52. *Yevamot* 62b
53. Leviticus 19:16, Deuteronomy 22:1-3
54. Exodus 19:2 with Rashi commentary

Jew is commanded to be responsible for *every* other Jew, not only the Jews who agree with a particular viewpoint, lifestyle, or behavior pattern.[55] When there is cohesive feeling and action, Jewish unity results. The Midrash states that the Jews are compared to one large sheep, because just as when one limb suffers pain, the entire animal feels the hurt, so too when one Jew suffers, the entire Jewish people should also feel the pain. Rabbi Shimon compares the situation to a person who bores a hole in a ship, and as the others get upset that the entire ship will go down causing everyone to drown, the man says, "I only put a hole in the area that belongs to me." So it is with the Jewish people. Every action by every Jew affects the entire Jewish people.[56]

## TOLERANCE AND RESPECT FOR NON-JEWS

Most religions teach respect for members of that religion, but are intolerant of those that do not practice or believe in that faith. Judaism teaches tolerance for non-Jews as well as Jews. The sources referenced above as well as a verse said by the prophet Malachi stress that God is a father to all human beings, not only Jews, and all human beings are created in God's image as equals.[57] The Torah does not say that only Jews were created as special with God's image, but this is so for every human being.[58] Although the Jews have a special mission in this world, the non-Jew is respected by the Jew. Why is this so? How can Judaism respect the non-Jew who does not accept God in the same way that Jews do?

One answer to this question can be gleaned by the placement of two consecutive verses in the Torah. Most people who have studied the Torah or Judaism are aware of the key verse (mentioned above as possibly the very essence of Judaism) commanding Jews love their fellow as they love themselves – i.e., to treat others

as they would want to be treated. But what is the verse that immediately follows these well-known and important words? God commands the Jew not to mate animals of different species, not to plant together seeds of different species, and not to wear a garment that contains wool (the symbol of the animal world) and flax (the symbol of the plant world).[59] Why? What is the connection between these two verses? The second verse stresses that species and creations of God that are created as separate and different should remain separate and different. Thus, although God wants Jews to love others, He does not want everyone to become the same and homogenized as a result. A Jew should love others, even though they remain different or, perhaps, because they are different. Therefore, Judaism does not wish or attempt to change non-Jews and make them just like Jews. While conversion to Judaism is tolerated, it is not encouraged. Remaining different and still loving those who are different is at the heart of Judaism.

Perhaps this concept was most demonstrated in the Bible by Abraham. Abraham's essential characteristic was *Chesed*-kindness. There was one group of people whose essential characteristic was the opposite of Abraham's, as they were mean-spirited, insensitive, and actually nasty. Yet, when God wants to kill these Sodomites for their abominable behavior, it is the kind-hearted Abraham who fights his natural tendencies to root out such evil people, lacking any kindness, from the world. Rather, Abraham asks God to let the city's inhabitants live.[60] Why? Although these people represented everything that Abraham abhorred, they were still human beings and deserved "tolerance," even though they were so different and abhorrent to Abraham. This is the ultimate Jewish tolerance of non-Jews.

Although Jews do not believe in active proselytizing of non-Jews, Jews are supposed to be role models of behavior to everyone else. In this way, the non-Jews will eventually see by

---

55. *Shavuot* 39a
56. Midrash, *Vayikra Rabbah* 4:6
57. Malachi 2:10
58. Genesis 1:27

59. Leviticus 19:18-19
60. Genesis 18:20-33

themselves that the moral path of Judaism is superior to all other modes of living.[61] This idea is encapsulated in the very first words of God to Abraham, a microcosm of Jewish history.[62] God first promises Abraham to create a separate nation from his progeny, then all the other nations will praise and imitate Abraham's people and be blessed, which is the ultimate goal of Judaism and Creation. Therefore, even though Jews do not believe in proselytizing, they are obligated to be cognizant about whether their actions sanctify God's name or desecrate God's name before others. Because of this particular obligation to behave especially morally before the non-Jew, the Jew must be sensitive not to defame God, and it is far worse than even erasing a letter from the Torah.[63] It is also for this reason that stealing from a non-Jew is worse than stealing from a Jew,[64] since stealing from a Jew violates only the prohibition against theft, while stealing from a non-Jew also violates the prohibition against desecrating God's name.

In his book of Jewish law, Maimonides shows that Judaism not only tolerates non-Jews, but even offers the ultimate reward to non-Jews. While no other religions promise reward for those who do not follow that faith, Judaism declares that non-Jews who keep the seven basic Noahide laws (basic ideas and laws for all societies) attain the World to Come, without doing anything specifically "Jewish."[65] Moreover, the sacrifices brought to the Temple during one major Jewish holiday are not for the benefit of Jews, but are for the non-Jewish nations of the world. Thus, the seventy sacrifices on the seven days of Sukkot are brought to help all of the non-Jews in the world.[66] The Midrash says that if the non-Jews had been aware of this fact, they would never have destroyed the Holy Temple.[67]

Judaism and Jews appreciate non-Jews who have achieved greatness. Thus, a non-Jew who masters Torah is compared to a Jewish Kohen Gadol-High Priest.[68] A non-Jew who has achieved wisdom is looked up to as well and called a *Chacham*, a wise person, the same term used for a Jewish scholar.[69] The Talmud says that a Jew who sees a wise non-Jew or a non-Jewish king should recite a blessing,[70] and this idea is codified as part of Jewish law.[71] A Jew must go out of his or her way to greet a non-Jew and be polite to him or her,[72] and non-Jewish poor must be provided for, just as Jewish poor are taken care of by the Jewish community.[73]

## WHERE AND WHEN JUDAISM IS INTOLERANT

There is one area in which Judaism is absolutely intolerant. When ideas and actions that are completely antithetical to Jewish values are found within the Jewish community, the Torah in the book of Deuteronomy warns repeatedly to get rid of this in any form, using the words, to "remove the evil from your midst."[74] For the same reason, Judaism does not wish that non-Jews who live a lifestyle and belief system antithetical to Judaism should be living among Jews, as they will certainly influence their Jewish neighbors negatively. Therefore, when the Torah commands Jews not to bring an abomination into their homes, the commentaries suggest that this signifies the law not to rent or sell homes to idol worshippers who want to live within the Jewish community.[75] One of the 613 commandments for Jews is not to imitate the ways of non-Jews, especially the ways of the Egyptians and Canaanites, whose

61. Isaiah 42:6, 49:6
62. Genesis 12:1-3
63. Yevamot 79a
64. Tosefta *Bava Kama* 10:8
65. Maimonides, *Hilchot Melachim* 8:11
66. Numbers 29:12-24, *Sukkah* 55b
67. Midrash, *Bamidbar Rabbah* 1:3

68. *Bava Kama* 38a
69. *Megillah* 16a
70. *Berachot* 58a
71. *Shulchan Aruch, Orach Chaim* 224:7
72. Mishna *Shevi'it* 5:9
73. *Gittin* 61a
74. Deuteronomy 13:6, 17:7, 17:12, 19:19, 21:21, 22:21, 22:22, 22:24, 24:7
75. Deuteronomy 7:26 with Rabbeinu Bechaye commentary

lifestyles are so antithetical to Judaism.[76] Intolerance of idol worship and non-Jewish values is so strong that if Jews build a community of idol worshippers, it is a Torah Mitzvah, a Biblical commandment, to completely destroy that community, its inhabitants, and even its contents.[77]

Specifically in the Land of Israel, the place that should exemplify Jewish values most, it is forbidden to give non-Jews a foothold in the land if they worship idols and live an anti-Jewish lifestyle.[78] The Mishna magnifies this law and gives details.[79] Idol worshippers can live in areas of the city (or out of the city) where the Jewish population does not reside. These laws are enacted in an effort to prevent Jews from having regular contact and interaction with people whose lifestyle is hostile to Judaism and its values. Judaism cannot tolerate such a situation. It is for this reason that Maimonides rules that Jews are obligated to destroy all forms of idol worship and not permit idol worshippers to live among Jews, even on a temporary basis. However, he qualifies this

ruling, limiting it only in the Land of Israel and only when the Jews control the land. The reason behind this commandment, says a commentary on Maimonides, is not to permit even a foothold of values alien to Judaism to take root, whenever possible.[80] That commentary, *Kesef Mishne*, wrote his own book of Jewish law, *Shulchan Aruch*, and includes these laws as well in his Code of Jewish law.

This idea has recently become an emotional issue in the State of Israel today, where some Rabbis forbid selling land in the Jewish communities to Arabs, and the politics of the issue have been more at the forefront than actual Jewish law. Most Jewish law authorities hold that the Arabs of today are not in the same category as the idol worshippers referred to by the Mishna, Maimonides, and *Shulchan Aruch*. Nevertheless, for any group of people who will actively undermine Jewish values in a given community, Judaism expresses intolerance if they will negatively influence the Jews already living there.

---

76. Leviticus 18:3
77. Deuteronomy 13:13-19
78. Deuteronomy 7:1-3 with Rashi commentary
79. Mishna *Avodah Zara* 1:4, 8, 9

80. Maimonides, *Hilchot Avodah Zara* 7:1, 10:6 with *Kesef Mishne* commentary

תִּקְבֹּץ אֶל־תּוֹךְ רְחֹבָהּ וְשָׂרַפְתָּ בָאֵשׁ אֶת־הָעִיר וְאֶת־כָּל־
שְׁלָלָהּ כָּלִיל לַד' אֱלֹקֶיךָ וְהָיְתָה תֵּל עוֹלָם לֹא תִבָּנֶה
עוֹד: וְלֹא־יִדְבַּק בְּיָדְךָ מְאוּמָה מִן־הַחֵרֶם לְמַעַן יָשׁוּב
ד' מֵחֲרוֹן אַפּוֹ וְנָתַן־לְךָ רַחֲמִים וְרִחַמְךָ וְהִרְבֶּךָ כַּאֲשֶׁר
נִשְׁבַּע לַאֲבֹתֶיךָ: כִּי תִשְׁמַע בְּקוֹל ד' אֱלֹקֶיךָ לִשְׁמֹר אֶת־
כָּל־מִצְוֹתָיו אֲשֶׁר אָנֹכִי מְצַוְּךָ הַיּוֹם לַעֲשׂוֹת הַיָּשָׁר בְּעֵינֵי
ד' אֱלֹקֶיךָ:

### 78) דברים ז:ב-ג ופירוש רש"י
וּנְתָנָם ד' אֱלֹקֶיךָ לְפָנֶיךָ וְהִכִּיתָם הַחֲרֵם תַּחֲרִים אֹתָם
לֹא תִכְרֹת לָהֶם בְּרִית וְלֹא תְחָנֵּם: וְלֹא תִתְחַתֵּן בָּם בִּתְּךָ
לֹא תִתֵּן לִבְנוֹ וּבִתּוֹ לֹא תִקַּח לִבְנֶךָ:

ולא תחנם – ... ד"א לא תתן להם חנייה בארץ:

### 79) משנה עבודה זרה א:ד, ח, ט
עיר שיש בה עבודה זרה. חוצה לה מותר. היה חוצה
לה עבודה זרה. תוכה מותר. מהו לילך לשם. בזמן
שהדרך מיוחדת לאותו מקום. אסור. ואם היה יכול
להלך בה למקום אחר. מותר. עיר שיש בה עבודה
זרה היו בה חנויות מעוטרות ושאינן מעוטרות. זה
היה מעשה בבית שאן. ואמרו חכמים. המעוטרות
אסורות ושאינן מעוטרות מותרות:

... אין משכירין להם בתים בארץ ישראל. ואין צריך
לומר שדות. ובסוריא משכירין להם בתים. אבל לא
שדות. ובחוץ לארץ מוכרין להם בתים ומשכירין
שדות. דברי רבי מאיר. רבי יוסי אומר בארץ ישראל
משכירין להם בתים. אבל לא שדות. ובסוריא מוכרין
בתים ומשכירין שדות. ובחוצה לארץ מוכרין אלו
ואלו:
אף במקום שאמרו להשכיר. לא לבית דירה אמרו.
מפני שהוא מכניס לתוכו עבודה זרה. שנאמר (דברים

---

ז) ולא תביא תועבה אל ביתך. ובכל מקום לא ישכיר
לו את המרחץ. מפני שהיא נקראת על שמו:

### 80) רמב"ם, הלכות עבודה זרה ז:א, י':ו ופירוש כסף משנה

מצות עשה היא לאבד עבודת כוכבים ומשמשיה
וכל הנעשה בשבילה שנאמר אבד תאבדון את כל
המקומות ונאמר כי כה תעשו להם וגו', ובארץ
ישראל מצוה לרדוף אחריה עד שנאבד אותה מכל
ארצנו, אבל בחוץ לארץ אין אנו מצווין לרדוף
אחריה אלא כל מקום שנכבוש אותו נאבד כל עבודת
כוכבים שבו, שנאמר ואבדתם את שמם מן המקום
ההוא, בארץ ישראל אתה מצווה לרדוף אחריהן ואי
אתה מצווה לרדוף אחריהן בחוץ לארץ.
אין כל הדברים האלו אמורים אלא בזמן שגלו
ישראל לבין העובדי כוכבים או שיד עכו"ם תקיפה
על ישראל אבל בזמן שיד ישראל תקיפה עליהם
אסור לנו להניח עובדי כוכבים בינינו, ואפילו יושב
ישיבת עראי או עובר ממקום למקום בסחורה לא
יעבור בארצנו אלא עד שיקבל עליו שבע מצות
שנצטוו בני נח שנאמר לא ישבו בארצך אפילו לפי
שעה, ואם קבל עליו שבע מצות הרי זה גר תושב,
ואין מקבלין גר תושב אלא בזמן שהיובל נוהג אבל
שלא בזמן היובל אין מקבלין אלא גר צדק בלבד.
כסף משנה – ... ורבינו משמע ליה דכיון דטעמא
משום פן יחטיאו אותך לי אפילו בישיבת עראי או
בעובר ממקום למקום איכא למיחש להכי הילכך
על כרחך לומר דישיבה דכתיבא בהו אפילו כל דהו
קאסר ומשבע אומות ילפינן לשאר עובדי כוכבים
דהא בהו נמי שייך פן יחטיאו:

### 67) מדרש, במדבר רבה א:ג

א"ר יהושע בן לוי אלו היה אר"ה אומות העולם יודעים מה היה המקדש יפה להם קסטריות היו מקיפים אותו כדי לשומרו שהיה יפה להם יותר משל ישראל שכן שלמה סדר תפלה (מלכים א ח) וגם אל הנכרי אשר לא מעמך ישראל הוא וכתיב (שם מלכים א' ח) ועשית ככל אשר יקרא אליך הנכרי אבל כשהוא בא אצל ישראל מה כתיב (דה"ב דברי הימים ב' ו) ונתת לאיש ככל דרכיו אשר תדע את לבבו אם היה ראוי לו היה נותן לו ואם לאו לא היה נותן לוד

### 68) בבא קמא לח.

ר' אומר: מנין שאפילו נכרי ועוסק בתורה שהוא ככהן גדול? ת"ל: (ויקרא י"ח) אשר יעשה אותם האדם וחי בהם, כהנים ולוים וישראלים לא נאמר אלא אדם, הא למדת, שאפילו נכרי ועוסק בתורה הרי הוא ככהן גדול

### 69) מגילה טז

אמר רבי יוחנן: כל האומר דבר חכמה, אפילו באומות העולם נקרא חכם

### 70) ברכות נח

תנו רבנן: הרואה חכמי ישראל אומר ברוך שחלק מחכמתו ליראיו, חכמי אומות העולם אומר ברוך שנתן מחכמתו לבשר ודם. הרואה מלכי ישראל אומר ברוך שחלק מכבודו ליראיו, מלכי אומות העולם אומר ברוך שנתן מכבודו לבשר ודם. אמר רבי יוחנן: לעולם ישתדל אדם לרוץ לקראת מלכי ישראל, ולא לקראת מלכי ישראל בלבד אלא אפילו לקראת מלכי אומות העולם

### 71) שולחן ערוך, אורח חיים רכד:ז, ט

הרואה חכמי אומות העולם עובדי כוכבים שחכמים בחכמות העולם בא"י אמ"ה שנתן מחכמתו לב"ו:
מצוה להשתדל לראות מלכים [אפ' מלכי עובדי כוכבים

### 72) משנה שביעית ה:ט

ומחזיקין ידי נכרי בשביעית. אבל לא ידי ישראל. ושואלין בשלומן. מפני דרכי שלום:

### 73) גיטין סא.

אין ממחין ביד עניי נכרים בלקט בשכחה ובפאה, מפני דרכי שלום.

### 74) דברים יג:ו, יז:ז, יז:יב, יט:יט, כא:כא, כב:כב, כב:כד, כד:ז

והנביא ההוא או חלם החלום ההוא יומת כי דבר סרה על ד' אלקיכם המוציא אתכם מארץ מצרים והפדך מבית עבדים להדיחך מן הדרך אשר צוך ד'

אלקיך ללכת בה ובערת הרע מקרבך:
יד העדים תהיה בו בראשנה להמיתו ויד כל העם באחרנה ובערת הרע מקרבך:
והאיש אשר יעשה בזדון לבלתי שמע אל הכהן העמד לשרת שם את ד' אלקיך או אל השפט ומת האיש ההוא ובערת הרע מישראל:
ועשיתם לו כאשר זמם לעשות לאחיו ובערת הרע מקרבך:
ועשיתם לו כאשר זמם לעשות לאחיו ובערת הרע מקרבך:
והוציאו את הנער אל פתח בית אביה וסקלוה אנשי עירה באבנים ומתה כי עשתה נבלה בישראל לזנות בית אביה ובערת הרע מקרבך:
כי ימצא איש שכב עם אשה בעלת בעל ומתו גם שניהם האיש השכב עם האשה והאשה ובערת הרע מישראל:
והוצאתם את שניהם אל שער העיר ההוא וסקלתם אתם באבנים ומתו את הנער על דבר אשר לא צעקה בעיר ואת האיש על דבר אשר ענה את אשת רעהו ובערת הרע מקרבך:
כי ימצא איש גנב נפש מאחיו מבני ישראל והתעמר בו ומכרו ומת הגנב ההוא ובערת הרע מקרבך:

### 75) דברים ז:כו ופירוש רבינו בחיי

ולא תביא תועבה אל ביתך והיית חרם כמהו שקץ תשקצנו ותעב תתעבנו כי חרם הוא:
ולא תביא תועבה אל ביתך – מכאן למדו חז"ל (עבודה זרה טו.) בדרך אסמכתא שאסור להשכיר ביתו לגוי לבית דירה מפני שהגוי מכניס לתוכו עבודה זרה וישראל זה המשכיר עובר, שהרי שכירות אינו קונה הקרקע לשוכר, וקרקע לאו של עובד גלולים הוא אלא של ישראל הוא לפיכך הוא עובר עליו. אבל מצינו קצת מן הגאונים ז"ל שכתבו שאין זה אלא בארץ ישראל לפי ששם עיקר עבודה זרה, וכן נראה בירושלמי (עבודה זרה פ"א ה"י), וכן דעת רבינו חננאל ז"ל, וכן אנו נוהגין בזה היתר עכשיו, אבל הרמב"ן ז"ל כתב, בעל נפש צריך לפרוש מלהשכיר אפילו בארץ ישמעאלים:

### 76) ויקרא יח:ג

כמעשה ארץ מצרים אשר ישבתם בה לא תעשו וכמעשה ארץ כנען אשר אני מביא אתכם שמה לא תעשו ובחקתיהם לא תלכו:

### 77) דברים יג:יג-יט

כי תשמע באחת עריך אשר ד' אלקיך נתן לך לשבת שם לאמר: יצאו אנשים בני בליעל מקרבך וידיחו את ישבי עירם לאמר נלכה ונעבדה אלהים אחרים אשר לא ידעתם: ודרשת וחקרת ושאלת היטב והנה אמת נכון הדבר נעשתה התועבה הזאת בקרבך: הכה תכה את ישבי העיר ההוא לפי חרב החרם אתה ואת כל אשר בה ואת בהמתה לפי חרב: ואת כל שללה

### 55) שבועות לט.

...מלמד שכל ישראל ערבים זה בזה

### 56) מדרש, ויקרא רבה ד:ו

תני חזקיה (ירמיה נ) שה פזורה ישראל נמשלו ישראל לשה מה שה הזה לוקה על ראשו או בא' מאבריו וכל אבריו מרגישין כך הן ישראל, אחד מהן חוטא וכולן מרגישין, (במדבר טז) האיש אחד יחטא תני רשב"י משל לבני אדם שהיו יושבין בספינה נטל אחד מהן מקדח והתחיל קודח תחתיו אמרו לו חבריו מה אתה יושב ועושה אמר להם מה אכפת לכם לא תחתי אני קודח אמרו לו שהמים עולין ומציפין עלינו את הספינה כך אמר איוב (איוב יט) ואף אמנם שגיתי אתי תלין משוגתי, אמרו לו חבריו (שם איוב לד) כי יוסף על חטאתו פשע בינינו יספוק, אתה מספיק בינינו את עונותיך.

### 57) מלאכי ב:י'

הלוא אב אחד לכלנו הלוא אל אחד בראנו מדוע נבגד איש באחיו לחלל ברית אבתינו:

### 58) בראשית א:כז

ויברא אלקים את־האדם בצלמו בצלם אלקים ברא אתו זכר ונקבה ברא אתם:

### 59) ויקרא יט:יח-יט

לא־תקם ולא־תטר את־בני עמך ואהבת לרעך כמוך אני ד': את־חקתי תשמרו בהמתך לא־תרביע כלאים שדך לא־תזרע כלאים ובגד כלאים שעטנז לא יעלה עליך:

### 60) בראשית יח:כ-לג

ויאמר ד' זעקת סדם ועמרה כי־רבה וחטאתם כי כבדה מאד: כא ארדה־נא ואראה הכצעקתה הבאה אלי עשו כלה ואם־לא אדעה: כב ויפנו משם האנשים וילכו סדמה ואברהם עודנו עמד לפני ד': כג ויגש אברהם ויאמר האף תספה צדיק עם־רשע: כד אולי יש חמשים צדיקם בתוך העיר האף תספה ולא־תשא למקום למען חמשים הצדיקם אשר בקרבה: כה חללה לך מעשת |כדבר הזה להמית צדיק עם־רשע והיה כצדיק כרשע חללה לך השפט כל־הארץ לא יעשה משפט: כו ויאמר ד' אם־אמצא בסדם חמשים צדיקם בתוך העיר ונשאתי לכל־המקום בעבורם: כז ויען אברהם ויאמר הנה־נא הואלתי לדבר אל־אדני ואנכי עפר ואפר: כח אולי יחסרון חמשים הצדיקם חמשה התשחית בחמשה את־כל־העיר ויאמר לא אשחית אם־אמצא שם ארבעים וחמשה: כט ויסף עוד לדבר אליו ויאמר אולי ימצאון שם ארבעים ויאמר לא אעשה בעבור הארבעים: ל ויאמר אל־נא יחר לאדני ואדברה אולי ימצאון שם שלשים ויאמר לא אעשה אם־אמצא שם שלשים: לא ויאמר הנה־נא הואלתי לדבר אל־אדני אולי ימצאון שם עשרים

ויאמר לא אשחית בעבור העשרים: לב ויאמר אל־נא יחר לאדני ואדברה אך־הפעם אולי ימצאון שם עשרה ויאמר לא אשחית בעבור העשרה: לג וילך ד' כאשר כלה לדבר אל־אברהם ואברהם שב למקמו:

### 61) ישעיה מב:ו, מט:ו

אני ד' קראתיך בצדק ואחזק בידך ואצרך ואתנך לברית עם לאור גוים:
...ונתתיך לאור גוים להיות ישועתי עד־קצה הארץ:

### 62) בראשית יב:א-ג

ויאמר ד' אל־אברם לך־לך מארצך וממולדתך ומבית אביך אל־הארץ אשר אראך: ואעשך לגוי גדול ואברכך ואגדלה שמך והיה ברכה: ואברכה מברכיך ומקללך אאר ונברכו בך כל משפחת האדמה:

### 63) יבמות עט.

מוטב שתעקר אות אחת מן התורה ואל יתחלל שם שמים בפרהסיא.

### 64) תוספתא בבא קמא י:ח

חמור גזל הנכרי מגזל ישראל מפני חילול השם.

### 65) רמב"ם הלכות מלכים ח:יא

כל המקבל שבע מצות ונזהר לעשותן הרי זה מחסידי אומות העולם, ויש לו חלק לעולם הבא

### 66) במדבר כט:יב-כד, סוכה נה:

יב ובחמשה עשר יום לחדש השביעי מקרא־קדש יהיה לכם כל־מלאכת עבדה לא תעשו וחגתם חג לד' שבעת ימים: יג והקרבתם עלה אשה ריח ניחח לד' פרים בני־בקר שלשה עשר אילם שנים כבשים בני־ שנה ארבעה עשר תמימם יהיו: ... יז וביום השני פרים בני־בקר שנים עשר אילם שנים כבשים בני־ שנה ארבעה עשר תמימם: כ וביום השלישי פרים עשתי־עשר אילם שנים כבשים בני שנה ארבעה עשר תמימם: כא ומנחתם ונסכיהם לפרים לאילם ולכבשים במספרם כמשפט: ... כג וביום הרביעי פרים עשרה אילם שנים כבשים בני־שנה ארבעה עשר תמימם: ... כו וביום החמישי פרים תשעה אילם שנים כבשים בני־שנה ארבעה עשר תמימם: ... כט וביום הששי פרים שמנה אילם שנים כבשים בני־ שנה ארבעה עשר תמיממ: ... לב וביום השביעי פרים שרעה אילם שנים כבשים בני־ שנה ארבעה עשר תמימם: ... לה ביום השמיני עצרת תהיה לכם כל־מלאכת עבדה לא תעשו: לו והקרבתם עלה אשה ריח ניחח לד' פר אחד איל אחד כבשים בני־ שנה שבעה תמימם: לז מנחתם ונסכיהם לפר לאיל ולכבשים במספרם כמשפט:
אמר רבי (אליעזר): הני שבעים פרים כנגד מי כנגד שבעים אומות. פר יחידי למה כנגד אומה יחידה.

במצרים ישב עמהם, שנאמר לך ואספת את זקני
ישראל (שמות ג, טז.), אלא באש תבערה מתו,
וראוים היו מסיני לכך, דכתיב ויחזו את האלהים
(שמות כד, יא.), שנהגו קלות ראש, כנושך פתו
ומדבר בפני המלך, וזהו ויאכלו וישתו, ולא רצה
הקב"ה ליתן אבלות במתן תורה ופרע להם כאן:

### 43) רמ"א על שולחן ערוך, אורח חיים קלט:ג

ומי שאביו מומר לעבודת כוכבים קורין אותו בשם
אבי אביו אבל לא בשמו לבד שלא לביישו ברבים
(תרומת הדשן סי' נ"א וס' חסידים) ודוקא שלא עלה
מימיו בשם אביו אבל אם הוא גדול והורגל באותה
העיר לעלות בשם אביו והמיר אביו לעבודת כוכבים
קוראים אותו בשם אביו כמו שהורגל שלא לביישו
ברבים וכן אם איכא למיחש לאיבת המומר (מהר"ם
פאדוואה סי' פ"ז) ואסופי ושתוקי קורין אותו בשם
אבי אמו ואם אינו ידוע קורין אותו בשם אברהם
כמו לגר

### 44) אבות ג:י'

הוא היה אומר כל שרוח הבריות נוחה הימנו. רוח
המקום נוחה הימנו. וכל שאין רוח הבריות נוחה
הימנו. אין רוח המקום נוחה הימנו:

### 45) אבות ד:ג

הוא היה אומר אל תהי בז לכל אדם. ואל תהי מפליג
לכל דבר. שאין לך אדם שאין לו שעה ואין לך דבר
שאין לו מקום

### 46) אבות א:ו

והוי דן את כל האדם לכף זכות:

### 47) אבות דרבי נתן ט:ג:ה

והוי מקבל את כל האדם בסבר פנים יפות כיצד ...
המקבל את חבירו בסבר פנים יפות אפי' לא נתן לו
כלום מעלה עליו הכתוב כאילו נתן לו כל מתנות
טובות שבעולם:.

### 48) סנהדרין לז.

לפיכך נברא אדם יחידי ... ומפני שלום הבריות,
שלא יאמר אדם לחבירו אבא גדול מאביך

### 49) שבת לא.

מעשה בנכרי אחד שבא לפני שמאי, אמר לו: גיירני
על מנת שתלמדני כל התורה כולה כשאני עומד על
רגל אחת. דחפו באמת הבנין שבידו. בא לפני הלל,
גייריה. אמר לו: דעלך סני לחברך לא תעביד זו היא
כל התורה כולה, ואידך פירושה הוא, זיל גמור

### 50) רמב"ם הלכות דעות ו:ג-ה

ג מצוה על כל אדם לאהוב את כל אחד ואחד
מישראל כגופו שנאמר ואהבת לרעך כמוך, לפיכך

---

צריך לספר בשבחו ולחוס על ממונו כאשר הוא חס
על ממון עצמו ורוצה בכבוד עצמו, והמתכבד בקלון
חבירו אין לו חלק לעולם הבא.
ד אהבת הגר שבא ונכנס תחת כנפי השכינה שתי
מצות עשה, אחת מפני שהוא גר והתורה אמרה
מפני שהוא בכלל ריעים ואחת ואהבתם את הגר, צוה
על אהבת הגר כמו שצוה על אהבת עצמו שנאמר
ואהבת את ה' אלקיך, הקב"ה עצמו אוהב גרים
שנאמר ואוהב גר.
ה כל השונא אחד מישראל עובר בלבו עובר בלא תעשה
שנאמר לא תשנא את אחיך בלבבך ...

### 51) שמות יב:מט, כב:כ, כג:ט, ויקרא יט:י', יט:לג-לד, במדבר ט:יד, טו:טו-טז, דברים י':יח-יט

תּוֹרָה אַחַת יִהְיֶה לָאֶזְרָח וְלַגֵּר הַגָּר בְּתוֹכְכֶם:
וְגֵר לֹא־תוֹנֶה וְלֹא תִלְחָצֶנּוּ כִּי־גֵרִים הֱיִיתֶם בְּאֶרֶץ
מִצְרָיִם:
וְגֵר לֹא תִלְחָץ וְאַתֶּם יְדַעְתֶּם אֶת־נֶפֶשׁ הַגֵּר כִּי־גֵרִים
הֱיִיתֶם בְּאֶרֶץ מִצְרָיִם:
וְכַרְמְךָ לֹא תְעוֹלֵל וּפֶרֶט כַּרְמְךָ לֹא תְלַקֵּט לֶעָנִי וְלַגֵּר
תַּעֲזֹב אֹתָם אֲנִי ד' אֱלֹקֵיכֶם:
וְכִי־יָגוּר אִתְּךָ גֵּר בְּאַרְצְכֶם לֹא תוֹנוּ אֹתוֹ: כְּאֶזְרָח מִכֶּם
יִהְיֶה לָכֶם הַגֵּר הַגָּר אִתְּכֶם וְאָהַבְתָּ לוֹ כָּמוֹךָ כִּי־גֵרִים
הֱיִיתֶם בְּאֶרֶץ מִצְרָיִם אֲנִי ד' אֱלֹקֵיכֶם:
... חֻקָּה אַחַת יִהְיֶה לָכֶם וְלַגֵּר וּלְאֶזְרָח הָאָרֶץ:
הַקָּהָל חֻקָּה אַחַת לָכֶם וְלַגֵּר הַגָּר חֻקַּת עוֹלָם לְדֹרֹתֵיכֶם
כָּכֶם כַּגֵּר יִהְיֶה לִפְנֵי ד': תּוֹרָה אַחַת וּמִשְׁפָּט אֶחָד יִהְיֶה
לָכֶם וְלַגֵּר הַגָּר אִתְּכֶם:
עֹשֶׂה מִשְׁפַּט יָתוֹם וְאַלְמָנָה וְאֹהֵב גֵּר לָתֶת לוֹ לֶחֶם
וְשִׂמְלָה: וַאֲהַבְתֶּם אֶת־הַגֵּר כִּי־גֵרִים הֱיִיתֶם בְּאֶרֶץ
מִצְרָיִם:

### 52) יבמות סב

אמרו: שנים עשר אלף זוגים תלמידים היו לו לרבי
עקיבא, מגבת עד אנטיפרס, וכולן מתו בפרק אחד
מפני שלא נהגו כבוד זה לזה, והיה העולם שמם

### 53) ויקרא יט:טז, דברים כב:א-ג

לֹא תַעֲמֹד עַל־דַּם רֵעֶךָ אֲנִי ד':
לֹא־תִרְאֶה אֶת־שׁוֹר אָחִיךָ אוֹ אֶת־שֵׂיוֹ נִדָּחִים וְהִתְעַלַּמְתָּ
מֵהֶם הָשֵׁב תְּשִׁיבֵם לְאָחִיךָ: וְאִם־לֹא קָרוֹב אָחִיךָ אֵלֶיךָ
וְלֹא יְדַעְתּוֹ וַאֲסַפְתּוֹ אֶל־תּוֹךְ בֵּיתֶךָ וְהָיָה עִמְּךָ עַד דְּרֹשׁ
אָחִיךָ אֹתוֹ וַהֲשֵׁבֹתוֹ לוֹ: וְכֵן תַּעֲשֶׂה לַחֲמֹרוֹ וְכֵן תַּעֲשֶׂה
לְשִׂמְלָתוֹ וְכֵן תַּעֲשֶׂה לְכָל־אֲבֵדַת אָחִיךָ אֲשֶׁר־תֹּאבַד
מִמֶּנּוּ וּמְצָאתָהּ לֹא תוּכַל לְהִתְעַלֵּם:

### 54) שמות יט:ב ורש"י שם

וַיִּסְעוּ מֵרְפִידִים וַיָּבֹאוּ מִדְבַּר סִינַי וַיַּחֲנוּ בַּמִּדְבָּר וַיִּחַן־
שָׁם יִשְׂרָאֵל נֶגֶד הָהָר:
ויחן שם ישראל – כאיש אחד בלב אחד, אבל שאר
כל החניות בתרעומות ובמחלוקת

## (28) ברכות י'.

הנהו בריוני דהוו בשבבותיה דרבי מאיר והוו קא מצערו ליה טובא, הוה קא בעי רבי מאיר רחמי עליהו כי היכי דלימותו. אמרה ליה ברוריא דביתהו: מאי דעתך? משום דכתיב: (תהלים ק"ד) יתמו חטאים, מי כתיב חוטאים? חטאים כתיב ועוד, שפיל לסיפיה דקרא: ורשעים עוד אינם, כיון דיתמו חטאים ורשעים עוד אינם? אלא, בעי רחמי עליהו דלהדרו בתשובה ורשעים עוד אינם

## (29) בראשית יא:א, ו ופירוש ספורנו על פסוק ו

וַיְהִי כָל הָאָרֶץ שָׂפָה אֶחָת וּדְבָרִים אֲחָדִים:
וַיֹּאמֶר ד' הֵן עַם אֶחָד וְשָׂפָה אַחַת לְכֻלָּם וְזֶה הַחִלָּם לַעֲשׂוֹת וְעַתָּה לֹא יִבָּצֵר מֵהֶם כֹּל אֲשֶׁר יָזְמוּ לַעֲשׂוֹת:
הן עם אחד – כי אמנם הבטול המפר עצות ומניא מחשבות הוא המחלוקת הקורה אם לסבת הדתות ואם לסבת הלשונות. והנה אלה היו עם אחד בענין הדת כי היו כלם מסכימים בדעת אנשי הצא"בה ועם זה היה כלם מסכימים בלשון:

## (30) פירוש רשי על בראשית יא:ט

ומשם הפיצם – ... וכי אי זו קשה של דור המבול או של דור הפלגה, אלו לא פשטו יד בעיקר, ואלו פשטו יד בעיקר להלחם בו, ואלו נשטפו ואלו לא נאבדו מן העולם, אלא שדור המבול היו גזלנים והיתה מריבה ביניהם, לכך נאבדו, ואלו היו נוהגים אהבה ורעות ביניהם, שנאמר שפה אחת ודברים אחדים, למדת ששנאוי המחלוקת וגדול השלום:

## (31) ויקרא יט:יז

לֹא תִשְׂנָא אֶת אָחִיךָ בִּלְבָבֶךָ הוֹכֵחַ תּוֹכִיחַ אֶת עֲמִיתֶךָ וְלֹא תִשָּׂא עָלָיו חֵטְא:

## (32) ערכין טז

א"ר טרפון: תמה אני אם יש בדור הזה שמקבל תוכחה, אם אמר לו טול קיסם מבין עיניך, אמר לו טול קורה מבין עיניך. אמר רבי אלעזר בן עזריה: תמיהני אם יש בדור הזה שיודע להוכיח.

## (33) משנה אבות א:טו

שמאי אומר ... והוי מקבל את כל האדם בסבר פנים יפות:

## (34) סנהדרין לט:

דאמר רבי שמואל בר נחמן אמר רבי יונתן: מאי דכתיב (שמות י"ד) ולא קרב זה אל זה כל הלילה, באותה שעה בקשו מלאכי השרת לומר שירה לפני הקדוש ברוך הוא, אמר להן הקדוש ברוך הוא: מעשה ידי טובעין בים ואתם אומרים שירה לפני?

## (35) רמ"א של שולחן ערוך, אורח חיים תעג:ז

ונוהגין לזרוק מעט מן הכוס באצבע (ד"ע) כשמגיע

---

לדם ואש ותמרות עשן וכן כשמזכיר המכות דצ"ך עד"ש באח"ב בכלל ובפרט הכל ט"ז פעמים (מהרי"ל) ויהיה הפת מגולה בשעה שאומר ההגדה עד לפיכך שאוחז הכוס בידו ואז יכסה הפת (אגור וב"י):

## (36) סנהדרין לט:

(מלכים א' כ"ב) ויעבר הרנה במחנה אמר רבי אחא בר חנינא: (משלי י"א) באבד רשעים רנה באבוד אחאב בן עמרי רנה. ומי חדי קודשא בריך הוא במפלתן של רשעים? הכתיב (דברי הימים ב' כ') בצאת לפני החלוץ ואמרים הודו לה' כי לעולם חסדו, ואמר רבי יונתן: מפני מה לא נאמר בהודאה זו כי טוב לפי שאין הקדוש ברוך הוא שמח במפלתן של רשעים:

## (37) דברי הימים ב' כ:כ-כא ומגילה י:

וַיַּשְׁכִּימוּ בַבֹּקֶר וַיֵּצְאוּ לְמִדְבַּר תְּקוֹעַ וּבְצֵאתָם עָמַד יְהוֹשָׁפָט וַיֹּאמֶר שְׁמָעוּנִי יְהוּדָה וְיֹשְׁבֵי יְרוּשָׁלַ‍ִם הַאֲמִינוּ בַּד' אֱלֹקֵיכֶם וְתֵאָמֵנוּ הַאֲמִינוּ בִנְבִיאָיו וְהַצְלִיחוּ: וַיִּוָּעַץ אֶל הָעָם וַיַּעֲמֵד מְשֹׁרְרִים לַד' וּמְהַלְלִים לְהַדְרַת קֹדֶשׁ בְּצֵאת לִפְנֵי הֶחָלוּץ וְאֹמְרִים הוֹדוּ לַד' כִּי לְעוֹלָם חַסְדּוֹ:
והא כתיב (דברי הימים ב' כ') בצאת לפני החלוץ ואמרים הודו לה' כי לעולם חסדו, ואמר רבי יוחנן: מפני מה לא נאמר כי טוב בהודאה זו לפי שאין הקדוש ברוך הוא שמח במפלתן של רשעים.

## (38) משנה אבות ד:יט

שמואל הקטן אומר (משלי כד) בנפל אויבך אל תשמח ובכשלו אל יגל לבך. פן יראה יי ורע בעיניו והשיב מעליו אפו:

## (39) ויקרא ו:יח

דַּבֵּר אֶל אַהֲרֹן וְאֶל בָּנָיו לֵאמֹר זֹאת תּוֹרַת הַחַטָּאת בִּמְקוֹם אֲשֶׁר תִּשָּׁחֵט הָעֹלָה תִּשָּׁחֵט הַחַטָּאת לִפְנֵי ד' קֹדֶשׁ קָדָשִׁים הִוא:

## (40) סוטה לב

... כדי שלא לבייש את עוברי עבירה, שהרי לא חלק הכתוב מקום בין חטאת לעולה

## (41) פירוש רש"י על שמות יג:ח

וחמשים – ... דבר אחר חמושים מחומשים, אחד מחמשה יצאו, וארבעה חלקים מתו בשלשת ימי אפילה:

## (42) במדבר יא:יד,טז, ופירוש רש"י שם

לֹא אוּכַל אָנֹכִי לְבַדִּי לָשֵׂאת אֶת כָּל הָעָם הַזֶּה כִּי כָבֵד מִמֶּנִּי ... וַיֹּאמֶר ד' אֶל מֹשֶׁה אֶסְפָה לִּי שִׁבְעִים אִישׁ מִזִּקְנֵי יִשְׂרָאֵל אֲשֶׁר יָדַעְתָּ כִּי הֵם זִקְנֵי הָעָם וְשֹׁטְרָיו וְלָקַחְתָּ אֹתָם אֶל אֹהֶל מוֹעֵד וְהִתְיַצְּבוּ שָׁם עִמָּךְ:
אספה לי – הרי תשובה לתלונתך שאמרת לא אוכל אנכי לבדי, והזקנים הראשונים היכן היו, והלא אף

אחת גזרה מלכות הרשעה גזרה על ישראל על
המילה, ועל אותה העיר לא גזרה.

### 15) משנה אבות, ה:יז
כל מחלוקת שהיא לשם שמים. סופה להתקים.
ושאינה לשם שמים. אין סופה להתקים. איזו היא
מחלוקת שהיא לשם שמים. זו מחלוקת הלל ושמאי.
ושאינה לשם שמים. זו מחלוקת קורח וכל עדתו:

### 16) יבמות יד:
ת"ש: אע"פ שנחלקו ב"ש וב"ה בצרות, ובאחיות, ובגט
ישן, ובספק אשת איש, ובמגרש את אשתו ולנה עמו
בפונדק, בכסף ובשוה כסף, בפרוטה ובשוה פרוטה,
לא נמנעו ב"ש מלישא נשים מבית הלל, ולא ב"ה
מבית שמאי, ללמדך, שחיבה וריעות נוהגים זה בזה

### 17) ברכות נח.
תנו רבנן: הרואה אוכלוסי ישראל אומר: ברוך חכם
הרזים. שאין דעתם דומה זה לזה, ואין פרצופיהן
דומים זה לזה

### 18) מדרש במדבר רבה יג:טו
יש שבעים פנים בתורה

### 19) מדרש, פסיקתא דרב כהנא יב:כז
... כך הקב"ה כשהיה מדבר כל אחד ואחד מישר'
היה אומ' עמי הדבר מדבר, אנכי ד' אלקיכם אין כת'
כאן, אלא אנכי י"י אלקיך (שם שמות כ). א"ר יוסי
בר' חנינא ולפי כוחן של כל אחד ואחד היה הדיבר
מדבר עמו. ואל תתמה על הדבר הזה, שהיה המן
יורד לישראל כל אחד ואחד היה טועמו לפי כוחו,
התינוקות לפי כוחן, והבחורים לפי כוחן, הזקנים לפי
כוחן

### 20) סנהדרין פט.
ואין שני נביאים מתנבאין בסיגנון אחד

### 21) מדרש במדבר רבה כא:ב, פירוש רש"י על
במדבר כז:יח
... שכן משה מבקש מן הקב"ה בשעת מיתה אמר
לפניו רבש"ע גלוי וידוע לפניך דעתן של כל אחד
ואחד ואין דעתן של בניך דומין זה לזה וכשאני
מסתלק מהן בבקשה ממך מנה עליהם מנהיג שיהא
סובלם לאחד ואחד לפי דעתו
**אשר רוח בו** – כאשר שאלת, שיוכל להלוך כנגד א
רוחו של כל אחד ואחד:

### 22) משנה סנהדרין ד:ה
לפיכך נברא אדם יחידי ... ולהגיד גדולתו של
הקדוש ברוך הוא, שאדם טובע כמה מטבעות בחותם
אחד כולן דומין זה לזה, ומלך מלכי המלכים הקדוש
ברוך הוא טבע כל אדם בחותמו של אדם הראשון

---

ואין אחד מהן דומה לחבירו.

### 23) בבא בתרא ס:, רמב"ם הלכות ממרים ב:ה
אין גוזרין גזירה על הצבור אלא אם כן רוב הצבור
יכולין לעמוד בה

### 24) מחזור יום כיפור, לפני "כל נדרי"
עַל דַּעַת הַמָּקוֹם וְעַל דַּעַת הַקָּהָל בִּישִׁיבָה שֶׁל
מַעְלָה וּבִישִׁיבָה שֶׁל מַטָּה אָנוּ מַתִּירִין לְהִתְפַּלֵּל עִם
הָעֲבַרְיָנִין:

### 25) כריתות ו,.:
ת"ר: פיטום הקטרת, הצרי והציפורן והחלבנה
והלבונה ... חיסר אחת מכל סממניה חייב מיתה.
א"ר חנא בר בזנא א"ר שמעון חסידא: כל תענית
שאין בה מפושעי ישראל אינה תענית, שהרי חלבנה
ריחה רע, ומנאה הכתוב עם סממני קטרת.

### 26) מדרש ויקרא רבה ל:יב
ד"א פרי עץ הדר אלו ישראל מה אתרוג זה יש בו
טעם ויש בו ריח כך ישראל יש בהם בני אדם שיש
בהם תורה ויש בהם מעשים טובים כפות תמרים אלו
ישראל מה התמרה הזו יש בו טעם ואין בו ריח כך
הם ישראל יש בהם שיש בהם תורה ואין בהם מעשים
טובים וענף עץ עבות אלו ישראל מה ההדס יש בו ריח
ואין בו טעם כך ישראל יש בהם שיש בהם מעשים
טובים ואין בהם תורה וערבי נחל אלו ישראל מה
ערבה זו אין בה טעם ואין בה ריח כך הם ישראל
יש בהם בני אדם שאין בהם לא תורה ולא מעשים
טובים ומה הקב"ה עושה להם לאבדן אי אפשר אלא
אמר הקב"ה יוקשרו כולם אגודה אחת והן מכפרין
אלו על אלו ואם עשיתם כך אותה שעה אני מתעלה
הה"ד (עמוס ט) הבונה בשמים מעלותיו ואימתי הוא
מתעלה כשהן עשויין אגודה אחת

### 27) רמ"א על שולחן ערוך, אורח חיים תרסד:ז של"ה,
מסכת סוכה, פרק נר מצוה ז
והמנהג פשוט ליטול הערבה עם הלולב בשחרית
בשעת הנענוע ובשעת הקפה עד שעת החבטה
ונוטלים הערבה לבדה ויותר טוב שלא ליטלה עם
הלולב כלל ואף הנוטלה עם הלולב נ"ל דלאחר
שהקיף יסיר הלולב מידו ויאחוז הערבה שהם
ההושענות שעושין לבד כל זמן שאומרים תחנונים
על המים ומנענעים ההושענות בשעה שאומרים
ההושענות ואח"כ חובטים אותם:
ליל הושענא רבה – נוהגין בארץ ישראל כמו ליל
שבועות ועוסקים כל הלילה בתורה גם בתפלות,
ומקצת קהילות מהמלכות הזה נוהגים שאומרים
איזה הושענות ובקשות המסודרות להם, ואומרים
כמה פעמים אל מלך ויעבור, ותוקעים תשר"ת
כשאומרים י"ג מדות, והכל לעורר הלבבות לתשובה.

# SOURCES ON TOLERANCE AND INTOLERANCE IN JUDAISM

**1) אבות ד:א**

בן זומא אומר איזהו חכם. הלומד מכל אדם

**2) אבות ה:ז**

חכם ... אינו נכנס לתוך דברי חברו

**3) משנה ברכות א:א**

מאימתי קורין את שמע בערבית. משעה שהכהנים
נכנסים לאכל בתרומתן. עד סוף האשמורה
הראשונה. דברי רבי אליעזר. וחכמים אומרים עד
חצות. רבן גמליאל אומר עד שיעלה עמוד השחר.
מעשה שבאו בניו מבית המשתה. אמרו לו. לא קרינו
את שמע. אמר להם. אם לא עלה עמוד השחר. חייבין
אתם לקרות. ולא זו בלבד. אלא כל מה שאמרו
חכמים עד חצות. מצותן עד שיעלה עמוד השחר....
אם כן. למה אמרו חכמים עד חצות. כדי להרחיק את
האדם מן העבירה:

**4) עירובין יג:**

שלש שנים נחלקו בית שמאי ובית הלל, הללו
אומרים הלכה כמותנו והללו אומרים הלכה כמותנו.
יצאה בת קול ואמרה: אלו ואלו דברי אלוקים חיים
הן, והלכה כבית הלל. וכי מאחר שאלו ואלו דברי
אלקים חיים מפני מה זכו בית הלל לקבוע הלכה
כמותן מפני שנוחין ועלובין היו, ושונין דבריהן
ודבריה בית שמאי

**5) שולחן ערוך, אורח חיים קפב:ג,ז**

ג צריך שלא יהא פגום ...
ז בשעת הדחק מברכין על כוס פגום:

**6) שולחן ערוך, אורח חיים תסז:יא, יורה דעה כג:ב**

אם נמצאת חטה בקועה בעיסה או במצה אפויה יסיר
ממנה כדי נטילת מקום והשאר מותר ויש מי שאוסר
כל העיסה או אותה מצה וראוי לחוש לדבריו אם לא
במקום הפסד מרובה או בשעת הדחק:
... יש להחמיר כסברא זו אלא א"כ הוא שעת הדחק
או הפסד מרובה שאז יש לסמוך על סברא ראשונה:

**7) תענית ז.**

מאי דכתיב (משלי כ"ז) ברזל בברזל יחד, לומר לך:
מה ברזל זה, אחד מחדד את חבירו אף שני תלמידי
חכמים מחדדין זה את זה בהלכה

**8) בבא מציעא פד.**

נח נפשיה דרבי שמעון בן לקיש, והוה קא מצטער

רבי יוחנן בתריה טובא. אמרו רבנן: מאן ליזיל
ליתביה לדעתיה ניזיל רבי אלעזר בן פדת, דמחדדין
שמעתתיה. אזל יתיב קמיה. כל מילתא דהוה אמר
רבי יוחנן אמר ליה: תניא דמסייעא לך. אמר: את
כבר לקישא? בר לקישא, כי הוה אמינא מילתא
הוה מקשי לי עשרין וארבע קושייתא, ומפריקנא
ליה עשרין וארבעה פרוקי, וממילא רווחא שמעתא.
ואת אמרת תניא דמסייע לך, אטו לא ידענא דשפיר
קאמינא? הוה קא אזיל וקרע מאניה, וקא בכי ואמר:
היכא את בר לקישא, היכא את בר לקישא

**9) בראשית יד:יג ומדרש, בראשית רבה מב:יג**

וַיָּבֹא הַפָּלִיט וַיַּגֵּד לְאַבְרָם הָעִבְרִי וְהוּא שֹׁכֵן בְּאֵלֹנֵי
מַמְרֵא הָאֱמֹרִי אֲחִי אֶשְׁכֹּל וַאֲחִי עָנֵר וְהֵם בַּעֲלֵי בְרִית־
אַבְרָם:
ויגד לאברם העברי, רבי יהודה ורבי נחמיה ורבנן,
רבי יהודה אומר כל העולם כולו מעבר אחד והוא
מעבר אחד

**10) בראשית לב:כט**

וַיֹּאמֶר לֹא יַעֲקֹב יֵאָמֵר עוֹד שִׁמְךָ כִּי אִם־יִשְׂרָאֵל כִּי־
שָׂרִיתָ עִם־אֱלֹהִים וְעִם־אֲנָשִׁים וַתּוּכָל:

**11) אסתר ב:ה ומדרש, אסתר רבה ו:ב**

אִישׁ יְהוּדִי הָיָה בְּשׁוּשַׁן הַבִּירָה וּשְׁמוֹ מָרְדֳּכַי בֶּן יָאִיר
בֶּן־שִׁמְעִי בֶּן־קִישׁ אִישׁ יְמִינִי:
למה נקרא שמו יהודי והלא ימיני הוא לפי שייחד
שמו של הקב"ה כנגד כל באי עולם, הה"ד לא יכרע
ולא ישתחוה

**12) שמות כג:ב**

לֹא־תִהְיֶה אַחֲרֵי־רַבִּים לְרָעֹת וְלֹא־תַעֲנֶה עַל־רִב לִנְטֹת
אַחֲרֵי רַבִּים לְהַטֹּת:

**13) סנהדרין לו:, לב.**

משנה. סנהדרין היתה כחצי גורן עגולה, כדי שיהיו
רואין זה את זה. ושני סופרי הדיינין עומדים לפניהם,
אחד מימין ואחד משמאל, וכותבין דברי מחייבין
ודברי מזכין
דיני נפשות מתחילין מן הצד

**14) שבת קל.**

תנו רבנן: במקומו של רבי אליעזר היו כורתין עצים
לעשות פחמין לעשות ברזל בשבת ... אמר רבי
יצחק: עיר אחת היתה בארץ ישראל שהיו עושין
כרבי אליעזר, והיו מתים בזמנם. ולא עוד אלא שפעם

88) פלא יועץ- ערך "חילול ד'"

ידוע שהוא חמור מכל עבירות שבתורה עד שאמרו
רז"ל שאינו מתכפר אלא עם תשובה ויסורין ויום
הכיפורים ויום המות. אי לזאת יחרד האיש וילפת
ויזהר וישמר מכל שהוא חילול ה' והדבר הקשה
שחילול ה' הוא הכל לפי מה שהוא אדם ולפי מה
שמחזיקין אותו העולם אם גורם שידברו עליו
תועה הוי חילול ה' ... אבל כל אדם אינו חייב אלא
כשיעורו ואשר בכחו לעשות יעשה ויזהר
עד מקום שידו מגעת וישתדל בכל עוז להשמר מן
הכיעור ומן הדומה לו ושלא ימצאו מקום לדבר
עליו ובפרט בענין הממון צריכה רבה שלא יהא הכסף
נחשב בעיניו למאומה במקום דאיכא למיחש אחת מני
אלף לחילול ה' או לחשש גזל או שהם נדנוד איסור
יתגבר וישליך כספו וזהבו שמוטב שימות ברעב ולא
יהא רשע לפני המקום שעה א' וכל שכן שדורשי ה'
לא יחסרו כל טוב ובפרט בדורות הללו צריך זהירות

גדולה ושמירה יתירה כי הן בעון רבו המתפרצים
שנפשם שוקקה לדבר תועה על הת"ח ועל יראי ה'
וחושבי שמו ואפי' אם יהיו כל דרכיו משפט כמלאך
ה' צבאות לא יבא ולא יהיה שיכשל בדבר קטון בין
באונס בין בשוגג או שיחשדוהו במה שאין בו או
שישמעו עליו שום שמועה רעה לא יחתרו לדעת
אמתותן של דברים היכי הוה עובדא ותכף פוערין
פיהם לבלי חק ויהיו מלעיגים במלאכי אלקי"ם
ואפילו על הקטנים המתחילין ללמוד אם פיהם ואומרים
ראו בן שלומד גמרא או חזו גברא שהוא ת"ח או
חזו גברא שמחזיקין אותו לחסיד או לירא שמים כך
וכך מעשיו ואין מכריע לכף זכות רק פותחים כולם
לחובה אוי להם ולנפשם כי גמלו רעה והם יטלו חלק
בראש בעון חילול ה' וכמה רעות עושים שמדברים
לשון הרע והגורמים ...

**78) תוספתא בבא קמא פרק ז:ג**

שבעה גנבין הן הראשון שבכולן גונב דעת הבריות ... שכל הגונב דעת הבריות נקרא גנב שנא' (ש"ב טו) "ויגנב אבשלום את לב אנשי ישראל" ...

**79) חולין צד. ורש"י שם**

דאמר שמואל: אסור לגנוב דעת הבריות, ואפילו דעתו של עובד כוכבים ... אמר אביי: תרנגולת טרפה הואי, ויהבה ניהליה במר דשחוטה ... תניא, היה ר' מאיר אומר: אל ירהב אדם לחבירו לסעוד אצלו ויודע בו שאינו סועד, ולא ירבה לו בתקרובת ויודע בו שאינו מקבל, ולא יפתח לו חביות המכורות לחנוני אא"כ הודיעו, ולא יאמר לו סוך שמן מפך ריקן, ואם בשביל כבודו מותר. איני, והא עולא איקלע לבי רב יהודה, פתח לו חביות המכורות לחנוני אודועי אודעיה, ואיבעית אימא: שאני עולא דחביב ליה לרב יהודה, דבלאו הכי נמי פתוחי מפתח ליה.

**80) רמב"ם, הלכות דעות ב:ו**

ואסור לגנוב דעת הבריות ואפילו דעת הנכרי, כיצד לא ימכור לנכרי בשר נבילה במקום בשר שחוטה, ולא מנעל של מתה במקום מנעל של שחוטה, ולא יסרהב בחבירו שיאכל אצלו והוא יודע שאינו אוכל, ולא ירבה לו בתקרובת והוא יודע שאינו מקבל, ולא יפתח לו חביות שהוא צריך לפותחן למוכרן כדי לפתותו שבשביל כבודו פתח וכן כל כיוצא בו, **ואפילו מלה אחת של פיתוטי ושל גניבת דעת אסור**, אלא שפת אמת ורוח נכון ולב טהור מכל עמל והוות.

**81) שולחן ערוך, חושן משפט רכח:ו-ט**

ו אסור לרמות בני אדם במקח וממכר או לגנוב דעתם ... ואין לגנוב דעת הבריות בדברים שמראה שעושה בשבילו ואינו עושה אסור. כיצד: לא יסרהב (בחבירו) שיסעוד עמו והוא יודע שאינו סועד, ולא ירבה לו בתקרובת והוא יודע שאינו מקבל, ולא יפתח חבית הפתוחות לחנוני וזה סובר שפתחם בשבילו, אלא צריך להודיעו שלא פתחם בשבילו, ואם הוא דבר דאיבעי ליה לאסוקי אדעתיה שאינו עושה בשבילו, ומטעה עצמו שסובר שעושה בשבילו לכבודו, כגון: שפגע בחבירו בדרך וסובר זה שיצא לקראתו לכבדו, אין צריך להודיעו.

ז לא יאמר לו סוך שמן מפך זה והוא ריקן, ולילך לבית האבל ובידו כלי ריקן וסובר האבל שהוא מלא יין, ואם הוא עושה כדי לכבדו מותר.

ח לא ימכור לו עור של בהמה מתה בחזקת שהיא שחוטה, ולא ישלח לו חבית של יין ושמן צף על פיו. ט אין מפרכסין לא אדם ולא בהמה ולא כלים. כגון: לצבוע זקן עבד העומד למכור כדי שיראה כבחור, ולהשקות הבהמה מי סובין שמנפחין וזוקפין שערותיה כדי שתראה שמינה, וכן אין מקרדין פירוש קרוד: במגרדת או מסרקת ששניו דקים, ולא

---

מקרצפין פירוש קרצוף: מגרדת או מסרק ששניו עבים אותה כדי לזקוף שערותיה, ולצבוע כלים ישנים כדי שיראו כחדשים, ואין נופחין בקרבים כדי שיראו שמנים ורחבים, ואין שורין הבשר במים כדי שיראה לבן ושמן.

**82) שערי תשובה ג:קפד**

... אמרו רבותינו זכרונם לברכה (חולין צד, א): אסור לגנוב דעת הבריות ואפילו דעת נכרי. והנה החטא הזה חמור אצל חכמי ישראל יותר מגזל הנכרי, יען וביען כי שפת שקר אשמה רבה, ונתחייבנו על גדרי האמת, כי הוא מיסודי הנפש:

**83) ויקרא כב:לב**

וְלֹא תְחַלְּלוּ אֶת־שֵׁם קָדְשִׁי וְנִקְדַּשְׁתִּי בְּתוֹךְ בְּנֵי יִשְׂרָאֵל אֲנִי ד' מְקַדִּשְׁכֶם:

**84) יומא פו.**

יצחק דבי רבי ינאי אמר: כל שחביריו מתביישין מחמת שמועתו (היינו חילול השם) ... שיהא קורא ושונה ומשמש תלמידי חכמים, ויהא משאו ומתנו בנחת עם הבריות, מה הבריות אומרות עליו אשרי אביו שלמדו תורה, אשרי רבו שלמדו תורה. אוי להם לבריות שלא למדו תורה, פלוני שלמדו תורה ראו כמה נאים דרכיו, כמה מתוקנים מעשיו, עליו הכתוב אומר (ישעיהו מט) ויאמר לי עבדי אתה ישראל אשר בך אתפאר. אבל מי שקורא ושונה ומשמש תלמידי חכמים ואין משאו ומתנו באמונה, ואין דבורו בנחת עם הבריות, מה הבריות אומרות עליו אוי לו לפלוני שלמד תורה, אוי לו לאביו שלמדו תורה, אוי לו לרבו שלמדו תורה, פלוני שלמד תורה ראו כמה מקולקלין מעשיו וכמה מכוערין דרכיו.

**85) מדרש, תנא דבי אליהו כו:ב**

לא נתנה תורה על מנת כן אלא לקדש שמו הגדול שנאמר ויאמר עבדי אתה ישראל וגו' (ישעיה מ"ט ג') מיכן אמרו ירחיק אדם עצמו מן הגזל מישראל ומן הגוי ואפילו מכל אדם שבשוק שהגונב לגוי לסוף שהוא גונב לישראל והגוזל לגוי לסוף שהוא גוזל לישראל נשבע לגוי לסוף שהוא נשבע מכחש לגוי לסוף מכחש על ישראל שופך דמים לגוי לסוף שהוא שופך דמים לישראל ולא נתנה תורה על מנת כן אלא לקדש שמו הגדול

**86) דברים ו:ה**

וְאָהַבְתָּ אֵת ד' אֱלֹקֶיךָ בְּכָל־לְבָבְךָ וּבְכָל־נַפְשְׁךָ וּבְכָל־מְאֹדֶךָ:

**87) יומא פו.**

"ואהבת את ה' אלקיך" שיהא שם שמים מתאהב על ידך

אסורות חילול שבת וי"ט ורוב העבירות שאדם עושה
הוא על בצע כסף ועון חילול ה' על גביהן וכן מי
שממונו חביב עליו מבטל רוב מצות ותפלות וברכות
ות"ת כנגד כולם וכשמקיים אותם הם פסולות מחמת
המהירות והכיליות ולבו בל עמו כי לבצעו פונה בכל
פינות שהוא פונה ומעלים עין מן הצדקה וכדמבעי
ליה למעבד לא עביד וכהנה רעות רבות באופן שיש
עושר שמור לבעליו לרעתו שעל ידו יורש באופן שיש
ויורד לבאר שחת ובאמת אמרו אדם ניכר בכיסו
כי הן אמת כי גבר אויב יצר הממון ובפרט בדור הזה
הוא דור ממון שאדם להוף אחר הממון יותר מכל
העבירות ומכל התענוגים וממונו של אדם חביב
עליו יש יותר מגופו ... ובכן יש קונה עולמו בממונו
שמרבה צדקה מרבה מצות ומע"ט וקונה שם טוב
לעצמו קונה לו דברי תורה קונה לו חיי העוה"ב
וכבר איתנא סימנא דבר תורה מעות קונות שלכל
דברי תורה וכל דבר טוב צריך מעות והכסף יענה
את הכל מי חכם וישמור אלה ולא יהא נרדם סוף
דבר הכל נשמע את האלקים ירא ואת מצותיו שמור
כי זה כל האדם:

## 67) ויקרא יט:יא
לֹא תִּגְנֹבוּ וְלֹא־תְכַחֲשׁוּ וְלֹא־תְשַׁקְּרוּ אִישׁ בַּעֲמִיתוֹ:

## 68) רמב"ם, הלכות גניבה א:ב
אסור לגנוב כל שהוא דין תורה.

## 69) רמב"ם, הלכות גניבה א:ג
איזה הוא גנב, זה הלוקח ממון אדם בסתר ואין
הבעלים יודעין,

## 70) דברים יח:יג
תָּמִים תִּהְיֶה עִם ד' אֱלֹקֶיךָ:

## 71) ברכות כח.
שהיה רבן גמליאל מכריז ואומר כל תלמיד שאין
תוכו כברו לא יכנס לבית המדרש ...

## 72) רמב"ם, הלכות דעות ב:ו
אסור לאדם להנהיג עצמו בדברי חלקות ופיתוי ולא
יהיה אחד בפה ואחד בלב אלא תוכו כברו והענין
שבלב הוא הדבר שבפה ואסור לגנוב דעת הבריות
ואפילו דעת הנכרי כיצד לא ימכור לנכרי בשר נבילה
במקום בשר שחוטה ולא מנעל של מתה במקום
מנעל של שחוטה ולא יסרהב בחבירו שיאכל אצלו
והוא יודע שאינו אוכל ולא ירבה לו בתקרובת והוא
יודע שאינו מקבל ולא יפתח לו חביות שהוא צריך
לפותחן למוכרן כדי לפתותו שבשביל כבודו פתח
וכן כל כיוצא בו ואפילו מלה אחת של פיתוי ושל
גניבת דעת אסור אלא שפת אמת ורוח נכון ולב טהור
מכל עמל והוות:

## 73) במדבר לה:לג ופירושי אבן עזרא מלבי"ם
וְלֹא־תַחֲנִיפוּ אֶת־הָאָרֶץ אֲשֶׁר אַתֶּם בָּהּ כִּי הַדָּם הוּא
יַחֲנִיף אֶת־הָאָרֶץ וְלָאָרֶץ לֹא־יְכֻפַּר לַדָּם אֲשֶׁר שֻׁפַּךְ־בָּהּ
כִּי־אִם בְּדַם שֹׁפְכוֹ:
יחניף – עשות רע בסתר:
ולא תחניפו את הארץ – החנף הוא מי שאין תוכו
כברו, נגלהו כצדיק והוא רשע באמת, והונח על
הארץ, כשאין תוכה כברה. נראית ארץ טובה
ופירותיה זרים ורעים, וזה בא ע"י חנופה מדה כנגד
מדה, ועז"א והארץ חנפה תחת יושביה (ישעיה כ"ד),
וגם בא לעונש על ש"ד כמ"ש ותחנף הארץ בדמים,
וז"ש אל תגרמו אל הארץ שתהיה מחנפת לכם, ולפ"ז
הוא שלילה וגם ר"ל שע"י שתהיו חנפים תחניפו את
הארץ, וא"כ הוא אזהרה על החנופה, ור' יאשיה
דריש ששרש חנף חן אף חנה אף, ובארתי דבר זה
בארך בפי' התו"ה ויקרא (סי' קנ"ב) עיי"ש:

## 74) תהילים לד:יג-יד ופירוש רד"ק
מִי־הָאִישׁ הֶחָפֵץ חַיִּים אֹהֵב יָמִים לִרְאוֹת טוֹב: נְצֹר
לְשׁוֹנְךָ מֵרָע וּשְׂפָתֶיךָ מִדַּבֵּר מִרְמָה:
ושפתיך מדבר מרמה – שלא תדבר אחד בפה ואחד
בלב. ואלו הן שפתי מרמה, שמרמֶה את חבירו,
שמדבר לו טובות וחושב בלבו רעתו, כמו שאמר
הכתוב (ירמיה ט, ז), בפיו שלום את רעהו ידבר
ובקרבו ישים ארבו. וזהו מצות לא תעשה שבלב, כמו
(ויקרא יט, יז), לא תשנא את אחיך בלבבך. ואמר
(משלי ג, כט), אל תחרש על רעך רעה והוא יושב
לבטח אתך:

## 75) ויקרא יט:לו, בבא מציעא מט.
מֹאזְנֵי צֶדֶק אַבְנֵי־צֶדֶק אֵיפַת צֶדֶק וְהִין צֶדֶק יִהְיֶה לָכֶם
אֲנִי ד' אֱלֹקֵיכֶם אֲשֶׁר־הוֹצֵאתִי אֶתְכֶם מֵאֶרֶץ מִצְרָיִם:
מיתיבי רבי יוסי ברבי יהודה אומר מה תלמוד לומר
הין צדק והלא הין בכלל איפה היה אלא לומר לך
שיהא הן שלך צדק ולאו שלך צדק אמר אביי ההוא
שלא ידבר אחד בפה ואחד בלב מי

## 76) פסחים קיג:
שלשה הקדוש ברוך הוא שונאן המדבר אחד בפה
ואחד בלב ...

## 77) משנה, בבא מציעא ד:יא-יב
(יא) אין מערבין פרות בפרות. אפילו חדשים
בחדשים. ואין צריך לומר חדשים בישנים. באמת
ביין התירו לערב קשה ברך. מפני שהוא משביחו.
אין מערבין שמרי יין ביין. אבל נותן לו את שמריו.
מי שנתערב מים ביינו. לא ימכרנו בחנות אלא אם כן
הודיעו. ולא לתגר אף על פי שהודיעו. שאינו אלא
לרמות בו. מקום שנהגו להטיל מים ביין. יטילו:
(יב) ... ומודים שלא יבור מעל פי מגורה. אין
אלא כגונב את העין. אין מפרכסין לא את האדם ולא
את הבהמה ולא את הכלים:

וראה כל איש את אשתו ואת בתו ביד רעהו ואין
אומר דבר. ויעשו להם ככה מהבקר עד הערב, ושבו
אחרי כן איש לביתו ואישה לאוהלה בערב. ככה יעשו
להם כל הימים ארבעה ימים בשנה... ויעשו להם כל
אנשי סדום ועמורה, על פי ארבעת שופטיהם, מיטות
בנויות ברחוב הערים. והיה כל איש אשר יבא והלך
אל הערים האלה, ועמדו עליו והחזיקו בו, והביאו
אותו אל אחת מהמיטות ההן... והיה אם האיש ההוא
קצר מהמיטה ההיא, ומשכוהו ששת האנשים ההם
אלה מזה ואלה מזה, ויצעק אליהם ולא יענוהו. ואם
יהיה האיש ההוא ארך בקומה מהמיטה אלה ואלה מזה, עד
משכו צלעות המטה מצדיה
הגיע האיש ההוא לשערי מות. והיה בצעקו אליהם,
וענו אותו ואמרו לו: ככה יעשה לאיש אשר יבוא
בארצנו... היה בבוא אביון אל ארצם, ונתנו לו כסף
וזהב, והעבירו קול בכל העיר לבלתי תת לו פת לחם
לאכול. והיה אם ישב האביון בארץ ימים ומת ברעב,
כי לא ימצא פת לחם לאכול. ובמותו יבואו כל אנשי
העיר ולקחו את כספם וזהבם אשר נתנו לו. והיה
כל איש אשר ידע את כספו ואת זהבו אשר נתן לו,
ייקח והלך לו. וגם כל בגדי העני וכל לבושו יפשיטו
מעליו במותם ונלחמו כולם עליהם, והיה אשר יחזק
על רעהו ייקח אותם. ואחרי כן יישאוהו ויקברוהו
ערם תחת אחד השיחים אשר במדברות. ככה יעשו
כל הימים, לכל הבא אליהם אשר ימות יומת בארצם.

### 53) מדרש, פרקי דרבי אליעזר כה

(אנשי סדום) ... ולא בטחו בצל יוצרם אלא על רוב
עשרם

### 54) שבת לא.

אמר רבא בשעה שמכניסין אדם לדין אומרים לו
נשאת ונתת באמונה קבעת עתים לתורה...

### 55) מדרש, מכילתא בשלח, ויסע א

והישר בעיניו תעשה זה משה ומתן מלמד שכל מי
שנושא ונותן באמונה רוח הבריות נוחה הימינו
ומעלין עליו כאילו קיים את כל התורה כולה.

### 56) תמיד לב:

אמר להון אנא נמי מלכא אנא מיחשב חשיבנא הבו לי
מידי יהבו ליה גולגלתא חדא אתייה תקליה לכוליה
דהבא וכספא דידיה בהדיה לא הוה מתקליה אמר
להון לרבנן מאי האי אמרי גולגלתא דעינא דבישרא
ודמא דלא קא שבע אמר להו ממאי דהכי הוא שקלי
קלילי עפרא וכסייה לאלתר תקלא

### 57) מדרש קהלת רבה ג:יג

דאמר ר' יודן בש"ר איבו אין אדם יוצא מן העולם
וחצי תאותו בידו אלא אם אית ליה מאה בעי דיעבדון
תרתי מאה ומאן דאית ליה תרתי מאה בעי דיעבדון
ארבעה

### 58) משנה אבות ד:א

איזהו עשיר השמח בחלקו.

### 59) משנה אבות ב:ז

מרבה נכסים. מרבה דאגה.

### 60) אבות על בנים (הרב מזאוז)

... כי מי שרדף הרבה אחר תאות הממון הוא מקדיש
כל זמנו רק במשא ומתן ואינו יכול לקבוע עתים
לתורה ולעבודת השי"ת והוא מאבד חלקו בעוה"ב
וזהו והאומר התנא נגד שמא מי שנמשך אחרי
פירסום שמו של עוה"ז זהו אינו שם שלועיקרי
ויסודי ורוצה להיות לו שם כאחד העשירים הגדולים
בזה היא אבד שמיה שהוא מאבד שמו העיקרי שיהיה
לו בעוה"ב והוא מטעם האמור.

### 61) בבא קמא עט:

שאלו תלמידיו את רבן יוחנן בן זכאי: מפני מה
החמירה תורה בגנב יותר מגזלן? אמר להן: זה השוה
כבוד עבד לכבוד קונו, וזה לא השוה כבוד עבד
לכבוד קונו,

### 62) עבודה זרה ב:

אמר להם הקב"ה: במאי עסקתם? אומרים לפניו:
רבש"ע, הרבה שווקים תקנינו, הרבה מרחצאות
עשינו, הרבה כסף וזהב הרבינו, וכולם לא עשינו
אלא בשביל ישראל כדי שיתעסקו בתורה. אמר להם
הקב"ה: שוטים שבעולם, כל מה שעשיתם לצורך
עצמכם עשיתם, תקנתם שווקים להושיב בהן זונות,
מרחצאות - לעדן בהן עצמכם, כסף וזהב שלי הוא,
שנאמר: (חגי ב) לי הכסף ולי הזהב נאם ה' צבאות

### 63) סוטה מח:

רבי אליעזר הגדול אומר: כל מי שיש לו פת בסלו
ואומר מה אוכל למחר אינו אלא מקטני אמנה.

### 64) עירובין סה:

בשלשה דברים אדם ניכר בכוסו ובכיסו ובכעסו...

### 65) משלי יח:כא

מָוֶת וְחַיִּים בְּיַד־לָשׁוֹן וְאֹהֲבֶיהָ יֹאכַל פִּרְיָהּ:

### 66) פלא יועץ- ערך "כסף"

כחיב כסף נבחר לשון צו" וכתיב בצל החכמה בצל
הכסף והביטה וראה שהוקש הכסף ללשון והוקש
לחכמה שם רמז שכמו מות חיים ביד לשון
מאן דבעי חיי בלישניה מאן דבעי מיית בלישניה ...
אף אנו נאמר לענין הכסף מאן דבעי חיי בכסף מאן
דבעי מיית אחר הכסף כי רוב העבירות הן נגררות מחמת
היות אדם להוט אחר הכסף כגון גזל גניבה אונאה
ועושק שבועת שוא שבועת שקר שמעו על ובמדות
השגת גבול מחלוקת קנאה שנאה תחרות מאכלות

### 46) במדבר יא:ד, ז-ט, יח-כ, לא-לד

וְהָאסַפְסֻף אֲשֶׁר בְּקִרְבּוֹ הִתְאַוּוּ תַּאֲוָה וַיָּשֻׁבוּ וַיִּבְכּוּ גַּם בְּנֵי יִשְׂרָאֵל וַיֹּאמְרוּ מִי יַאֲכִלֵנוּ בָּשָׂר:

וְהַמָּן כִּזְרַע גַּד הוּא וְעֵינוֹ כְּעֵין הַבְּדֹלַח: שָׁטוּ הָעָם וְלָקְטוּ וְטָחֲנוּ בָרֵחַיִם אוֹ דָכוּ בַּמְּדֹכָה וּבִשְּׁלוּ בַּפָּרוּר וְעָשׂוּ אֹתוֹ עֻגוֹת וְהָיָה טַעְמוֹ כְּטַעַם לְשַׁד הַשָּׁמֶן:

וּבְרֶדֶת הַטַּל עַל הַמַּחֲנֶה לָיְלָה יֵרֵד הַמָּן עָלָיו:

וְאֶל הָעָם תֹּאמַר הִתְקַדְּשׁוּ לְמָחָר וַאֲכַלְתֶּם בָּשָׂר כִּי בְּכִיתֶם בְּאָזְנֵי ד' לֵאמֹר מִי יַאֲכִלֵנוּ בָּשָׂר כִּי טוֹב לָנוּ בְּמִצְרָיִם וְנָתַן ד' לָכֶם בָּשָׂר וַאֲכַלְתֶּם: לֹא יוֹם אֶחָד תֹּאכְלוּן וְלֹא יוֹמָיִם וְלֹא חֲמִשָּׁה יָמִים וְלֹא עֲשָׂרָה יָמִים וְלֹא עֶשְׂרִים יוֹם: עַד חֹדֶשׁ יָמִים עַד אֲשֶׁר יֵצֵא מֵאַפְּכֶם וְהָיָה לָכֶם לְזָרָא יַעַן כִּי מְאַסְתֶּם אֶת ד' אֲשֶׁר בְּקִרְבְּכֶם וַתִּבְכּוּ לְפָנָיו לֵאמֹר לָמָּה זֶּה יָצָאנוּ מִמִּצְרָיִם:

וְרוּחַ נָסַע מֵאֵת ד' וַיָּגָז שַׂלְוִים מִן הַיָּם וַיִּטֹּשׁ עַל הַמַּחֲנֶה כְּדֶרֶךְ יוֹם כֹּה וּכְדֶרֶךְ יוֹם כֹּה סְבִיבוֹת הַמַּחֲנֶה וּכְאַמָּתַיִם עַל פְּנֵי הָאָרֶץ: וַיָּקָם הָעָם כָּל הַיּוֹם הַהוּא וְכָל הַלַּיְלָה וְכֹל יוֹם הַמָּחֳרָת וַיַּאַסְפוּ אֶת הַשְּׂלָו הַמַּמְעִיט אָסַף עֲשָׂרָה חֳמָרִים וַיִּשְׁטְחוּ לָהֶם שָׁטוֹחַ סְבִיבוֹת הַמַּחֲנֶה: הַבָּשָׂר עוֹדֶנּוּ בֵּין שִׁנֵּיהֶם טֶרֶם יִכָּרֵת וְאַף ד' חָרָה בָעָם וַיַּךְ ד' בָּעָם מַכָּה רַבָּה מְאֹד: וַיִּקְרָא אֶת שֵׁם הַמָּקוֹם הַהוּא קִבְרוֹת הַתַּאֲוָה כִּי שָׁם קָבְרוּ אֶת הָעָם הַמִּתְאַוִּים:

### 47) במדבר לב:א, ה-ו, טז-יז, כה-כו, ופירוש דעת זקנים מבעלי תוספות

וּמִקְנֶה רַב הָיָה לִבְנֵי רְאוּבֵן וְלִבְנֵי גָד עָצוּם מְאֹד וַיִּרְאוּ אֶת אֶרֶץ יַעְזֵר וְאֶת אֶרֶץ גִּלְעָד וְהִנֵּה הַמָּקוֹם מְקוֹם מִקְנֶה:... וַיֹּאמְרוּ אִם מָצָאנוּ חֵן בְּעֵינֶיךָ יֻתַּן אֶת הָאָרֶץ הַזֹּאת לַעֲבָדֶיךָ לַאֲחֻזָּה אַל תַּעֲבִרֵנוּ אֶת הַיַּרְדֵּן: וַיֹּאמֶר מֹשֶׁה לִבְנֵי גָד וְלִבְנֵי רְאוּבֵן הַאַחֵיכֶם יָבֹאוּ לַמִּלְחָמָה וְאַתֶּם תֵּשְׁבוּ פֹה:... וַיִּגְּשׁוּ אֵלָיו וַיֹּאמְרוּ גִּדְרֹת צֹאן נִבְנֶה לְמִקְנֵנוּ פֹּה וְעָרִים לְטַפֵּנוּ: וַאֲנַחְנוּ נֵחָלֵץ חֻשִׁים לִפְנֵי בְּנֵי יִשְׂרָאֵל עַד אֲשֶׁר אִם הֲבִיאֹנֻם אֶל מְקוֹמָם וְיָשַׁב טַפֵּנוּ בְּעָרֵי הַמִּבְצָר מִפְּנֵי יֹשְׁבֵי הָאָרֶץ:... וַיֹּאמֶר בְּנֵי גָד וּבְנֵי רְאוּבֵן אֶל מֹשֶׁה לֵאמֹר עֲבָדֶיךָ יַעֲשׂוּ כַּאֲשֶׁר אֲדֹנִי מְצַוֶּה: טַפֵּנוּ נָשֵׁינוּ מִקְנֵנוּ וְכָל בְּהֶמְתֵּנוּ יִהְיוּ שָׁם בְּעָרֵי הַגִּלְעָד: וַעֲבָדֶיךָ יַעַבְרוּ כָּל חֲלוּץ צָבָא לִפְנֵי ד' לַמִּלְחָמָה כַּאֲשֶׁר אֲדֹנִי דֹּבֵר:

וּמִקְנֶה רַב הָיָה – לְפִי שֶׁהָיוּ עֲשִׁירִים בְּיוֹתֵר חִבְּבוּ מָמוֹנָם וּבִשְׁבִיל חֲבוֹב מָמוֹנָם פֵּירְשׁוּ מֵאֲחֵיהֶם וְיֵשְׁבוּ לָהֶם חוּץ לְאֶרֶץ יִשְׂרָאֵל וּלְפִיכָךְ גָּלוּ תְּחִלָּה לְכָל הַשְּׁבָטִים שֶׁנֶּאֱמַר וַיַּגְלֵם לָראוּבֵנִי וְלַגָּדִי וְלַחֲצִי שֵׁבֶט הַמְנַשֶּׁה וְזֶ"שׁ כִּי לֹא מִמּוֹצָא וּמִמַּעֲרָב וְלֹא מִמִּדְבַּר הָרִים כִּי אֱלֹקִים שֹׁפֵט זֶה יַשְׁפִּיל וְזֶה יָרִים כְּלוֹמַר כָּל מַה שֶּׁאָדָם עָמֵל וְיוֹצֵא בִּסְחוֹרָה וְהוֹלֵךְ מִמִּזְרָח לַמַּעֲרָב וְדוֹחֵק אֶת הַשָּׁעָה לְהִתְעַשֵּׁר אֵינוֹ נַעֲשֶׂה עָשִׁיר בִּשְׁבִיל זֶה וְאַפִ' יֵלֵךְ בַּמִּדְבָּרִיּוֹת וְאֶל הֶהָרִים מֵהוּ וְלֹא מִמִּדְבַּר הָרִים אָמַר ר' אַבָּא כָּל הֶהָרִים שֶׁבַּמִּקְרָא הָרִים מַמָּשׁ חוּץ מִזֶּה שֶׁהוּא לְשׁוֹן הֲרָמָה כְּלוֹמַר שֶׁאֵין הָאָדָם מִתְרוֹמֵם בָּזֶה כִּי אֱלֹקִים שֹׁפֵט זֶה יַשְׁפִּיל וְזֶה יָרִים נוֹטֵל נְכָסִים מִזֶּה וְנוֹתְנָם לָזֶה שֶׁמָּם נְכָסִים נִקְרָא וְלָמָּה נִקְרָא שְׁמָם נְכָסִים שֶׁהֵם נִכְסִין מִזֶּה וְנִגְלִין לָזֶה.... וְהַשְּׁלֹשָׁה הַלָּלוּ בִּזְמַן שֶׁאֵינָן מֵאֵת

הַקָּבָּ"ה סוֹפָן לִיפָּסֵק מִמֶּנּוּ וְכֵן שָׁנוּ רַזַ"ל שְׁנֵי חֲכָמִים הָיוּ וַהֲיוּ עֲשִׁירִים עָמְדוּ בָּעוֹלָם. אֶחָד מִיִּשְׂרָאֵל וְאֶחָד מֵאוּמּוֹת הָעוֹלָם קֹרַח וְהָמָן וּשְׁנֵיהֶם נֶאֶבְדוּ מִן הָעוֹלָם. וְכֵן אָז"ל עֹשֶׁר שָׁמוּר לִבְעָלָיו לְרָעָתוֹ זֶה עָשְׁרוֹ שֶׁל קֹרַח וְשֶׁל הָמָן וְכָל כָּךְ לָמָּה לְפִי שֶׁלֹּא הָיְתָה מַתְּנָתָן מֵאֵת הַקָּבָּ"ה אֶלָּא חָטְפוּ אוֹתָן לָהֶם:

### 48) משנה אבות ה:י'

אַרְבַּע מִדּוֹת בָּאָדָם. הָאוֹמֵר שֶׁלִּי שֶׁלִּי וְשֶׁלְּךָ שֶׁלָּךְ. זוֹ מִדָּה בֵּינוֹנִית. וְיֵשׁ אוֹמְרִים זוֹ מִדַּת סְדוֹם. שֶׁלִּי שֶׁלְּךָ וְשֶׁלְּךָ שֶׁלִּי. עַם הָאָרֶץ. שֶׁלִּי שֶׁלְּךָ וְשֶׁלְּךָ שֶׁלָּךְ. חָסִיד. שֶׁלִּי שֶׁלִּי וְשֶׁלְּךָ שֶׁלִּי. רָשָׁע:

### 49) מדרש בראשית רבה מט

רַבִּי יְהוּדָה אוֹמֵר הִכְרִיזוּ בִּסְדוֹם כָּל מִי שֶׁהוּא מַחֲזִיק בְּפַת לֶחֶם לֶעָנִי וְאֶבְיוֹן יִשָּׂרֵף בָּאֵשׁ פְּלוֹטִית בִּתּוֹ שֶׁל לוֹט הָיְתָה נְשׂוּאָה לְאֶחָד מִגְּדוֹלֵי סְדוֹם רָאֲתָה עָנִי אֶחָד מְדֻקָּר בִּרְחוֹב הָעִיר וְעָגְמָה עָלֶיהָ נַפְשָׁהּ מַה הָיְתָה עוֹשָׂה בְּכָל יוֹם כְּשֶׁהָיְתָה יוֹצְאָה לִשְׁאוֹב מַיִם הָיְתָה נוֹתֶנֶת בְּכַד שֶׁלָּהּ מִכָּל מַה שֶּׁבְּבֵיתָהּ וּמַאֲכֶלֶת לְאוֹתוֹ עָנִי אָמְרוּ מֵאַיִן חַי הָעָנִי הַזֶּה וּכְשֶׁיָּדְעוּ בַּדָּבָר הוֹצִיאוּהָ לִישָׂרֵף אָמְרָה רִבּוֹן הָעוֹלָמִים עֲשֵׂה מִשְׁפָּטִי וְדִינִי וְעָלְתָה צַעֲקָתָהּ לִפְנֵי כִסֵּא הַכָּבוֹד בְּאוֹתָהּ שָׁעָה אָמַר הַקָּבָּ"ה אֵרְדָה נָּא [וְאֶרְאֶה] אִם צַעֲקַת הַנַּעֲרָה הַזֹּאת עָשׂוּ אַנְשֵׁי סְדוֹם אֶהְפֹּךְ יְסוֹדוֹתֶיהָ לְמַעְלָה הַכְּצַעֲקָתָם אֵינוֹ אוֹמֵר אֶלָּא הַכְּצַעֲקָתָהּ:

### 50) מדרש בראשית רבה מט:ו

מַעֲשֶׂה בִשְׁתֵּי נְעָרוֹת שֶׁיָּרְדוּ לִשְׁתּוֹת וְלִמְלֹאת מַיִם אָמְרָה אַחַת לַחֲבֶרְתָּהּ לָמָּה פָנַיִךְ חוֹלָנִיּוֹת אָמְרָה לָהּ כָּלוּ מְזוֹנוֹתֶיהָ וּכְבָר הִיא נְטוּיָה לָמוּת מֶה עָשְׂתָה מִלְּאָה אֶת הַכַּד קֶמַח וְהֶחֱלִיפוּ זוֹ מַה שֶּׁבְּיַד זוֹ וְכֵיוָן שֶׁהִרְגִּישׁוּ בָהּ נְטָלוּהָ וּשְׂרָפוּהָ אָמַר הַקָּבָּ"ה אֲפִ' אֲנִי מְבַקֵּשׁ לִשְׁתּוֹק דִּינָהּ שֶׁל נַעֲרָה אֵינוֹ מַנִּיחַ אוֹתִי לִשְׁתּוֹק הה"ד

### 51) מדרש בראשית רבה נז:ז

וַיֹּאמְרוּ גַּשׁ הָלְאָה קְרַב לְהַלָּן וַיֹּאמְרוּ הָאֶחָד בָּא לָגוּר וַיִּשְׁפֹּט שָׁפוֹט דִּין שֶׁדָּנוּ רִאשׁוֹנִים אַתָּה בָּא לַהֲרוֹס רַבִּי מְנַחֲמָא מִשֵּׁם רַבִּי בִּיבִי כָּךְ הִתְנוּ אַנְשֵׁי סְדוֹם בֵּינֵיהֶם אָמְרוּ כָּל אַכְסְנַאי שֶׁהוּא בָּא לְכָאן יְהוּ בוֹעֲלִים אוֹתוֹ וְנוֹטְלִים אֶת מָמוֹנוֹ אֲפִילוּ אוֹתוֹ שֶׁכָּתוּב בּוֹ וְשָׁמְרוּ דֶּרֶךְ ד' אָנוּ בּוֹעֲלִים אוֹתוֹ וְנוֹטְלִים אֶת מָמוֹנוֹ:

### 52) ספר הישר (ספר תולדות האדם), פרשת וירא, עמודים נח-סב

... וַתְּהִי לָהֶם בִּקְעָה בְּאַרְצָם רְחָבָה מְאֹד ... וּבָהּ מַעְיָנוֹת מַיִם וּדְשָׁאִים. וְהָלְכוּ שָׁמָּה כָּל אַנְשֵׁי סְדוֹם וַעֲמוֹרָה אַרְבָּעָה יָמִים בַּשָּׁנָה, הֵם וּנְשֵׁיהֶם וּבְנֵיהֶם וְכָל אֲשֶׁר לָהֶם, וְשָׂמְחוּ שָׁמָּה בְּתֻפִּים וּבִמְחוֹלוֹת. וַיְהִי בְעֵת שִׂמְחָתָם, וְעָמְדוּ יַחַד וְהֶחֱזִיקוּ אִישׁ בְּאֵשֶׁת רֵעֵהוּ וְאִישׁ בְּבַת רֵעֵהוּ הַבְּתוּלָה, וְהִתְעַלְּלוּ בָּהֶן וְשָׁכְבוּ אֶתְהֶן,

בָּשָׂר בָּא לְפָנַי כִּי מָלְאָה הָאָרֶץ חָמָס מִפְּנֵיהֶם וְהִנְנִי מַשְׁחִיתָם אֶת הָאָרֶץ:

**36) פירוש רש"י על בראשית ו:יא**
ותמלא הארץ חמס - גזל (ס"א שנאמר (יונה ג) ומן החמס אשר בכפיהם)

**37) פירוש כלי יקר על בראשית ה:ה**
וירא ה' כי רבה רעת האדם - לפי שחטאו בזנות ואותה תאוה רבה והולכת תמיד ולא ישבע לעולם כארז"ל (סוכה נב ע"ב) אבר קטן באדם משביעו רעב וכן חטאו בגזל ואוהב חמס וכסף לא ישבע כסף אלא תאותו רבה והולכת תמיד וכל יצר מחשבות לבו רק רע כל היום ר"ל כל היום לא ישבע מתאותו אין שעה ביום שיהיה שבע בה אלא כל שעה הוא מוסיף על תאותו

**38) סנהדרין קח., פירוש רש"י על בראשית ו:יג**
אמר רבי יוחנן בא וראה כמה גדול כחה של חמס שהרי דור המבול עברו על הכל ולא נחתם עליהם גזר דינם עד שפשטו ידיהם בגזל שנאמר כי מלאה הארץ חמס מפניהם והנני משחיתם את הארץ כי מלאה הארץ חמס - לא נחתם גזר דינם אלא על הגזל (סנהדרין קח)

**39) בראשית יא:א-ה**
וַיְהִי כָל הָאָרֶץ שָׂפָה אֶחָת וּדְבָרִים אֲחָדִים: וַיְהִי בְּנָסְעָם מִקֶּדֶם וַיִּמְצְאוּ בִקְעָה בְּאֶרֶץ שִׁנְעָר וַיֵּשְׁבוּ שָׁם: וַיֹּאמְרוּ אִישׁ אֶל רֵעֵהוּ הָבָה נִלְבְּנָה לְבֵנִים וְנִשְׂרְפָה לִשְׂרֵפָה וַתְּהִי לָהֶם הַלְּבֵנָה לְאָבֶן וְהַחֵמָר הָיָה לָהֶם לַחֹמֶר: וַיֹּאמְרוּ הָבָה | נִבְנֶה לָּנוּ עִיר וּמִגְדָּל וְרֹאשׁוֹ בַשָּׁמַיִם וְנַעֲשֶׂה לָּנוּ שֵׁם פֶּן נָפוּץ עַל פְּנֵי כָל הָאָרֶץ: וַיֵּרֶד ד' לִרְאֹת אֶת הָעִיר וְאֶת הַמִּגְדָּל אֲשֶׁר בָּנוּ בְּנֵי הָאָדָם:

**40) מדרש, פרקי דרבי אליעזר כד**
... שבנו אותו גבוה כשבעה מילין מקנה מעלת היו לו במזרחו ובמערבו ואלו שהיו מעלו מעלין לבנים היו עולין ממזרחו ואלו שהיו יורדין היו יורדין ממערבו ואם נפל אדם ומת לא היו שמים לבם עליו ואם נפלה לבנה היו יושבין ובוכין ואומרין מתי תעלה אחרת תחתי

**41) בראשית יג:ב ופירוש כתב סופר**
וְאַבְרָם כָּבֵד מְאֹד בַּמִּקְנֶה בַּכֶּסֶף וּבַזָּהָב:
ואברם כבד מאד במקנה בכסף ובזהב - ... ועוד יש לפרש, הנה אוהב כסף השמח ושש בעושרו ולא יכבד משא שמירת עושרו עליו, הוא יגע וטורח ועל כל הטרחות תכסה אהבתו למצוא מבוקשו בכסף ובזהב ובאהבתו ישגה תמיד. אבל ירא ה' אשר מכיר הבל קניני עולם הזה יכבד עליו עושר רב, ושלמה המע"ה אמר [משלי ל, ח] ריש ועושר אל תתן לי. וחובת הלבבות [בפתיחה לשער הבטחון] מביא חסיד אחד

שאמר ה' יצילני מפזור נפש, ונ"ל לכן כתיב ואברם כבד מאד במקנה בכסף, צריך להבין לשון כבד מאוד, הול"ל היה לו כסף וכו', ונ"ל שכונת הקרא שהיה לו למשא, ובכבד עליו מקנה והון רב, ולא חפץ באלה, אבל ראה והבין כי חפץ ורצון ה' הוא שסיבב כל הסיבות האלו, לכן לקח כל העושר מאת פרעה. וכן היה ביוצאי מצרים שאמרו ז"ל [ברכות ט:] שלא רצו ליטול כסף וזהב של מצרים ואמרו הלוואי שנצא בעצמינו, והיה עליהם לטורח לשאת משא כבד, ולא היתה תשוקתם לכסף וזהב. אבל ה' ציוה דבר נא וישאלו וכו', ודומה ליציאת אברהם ממצרים. וזהו כונת המדרש ואברהם כבד, הה"ד ויוציאם בעל כרחם בכסף וזהב וק"ל:

**42) בראשית כה:ח**
וַיִּגְוַע וַיָּמָת אַבְרָהָם בְּשֵׂיבָה טוֹבָה זָקֵן וְשָׂבֵעַ וַיֵּאָסֶף אֶל עַמָּיו:

**43) פירוש רמב"ן על בראשית כה:ח**
זקן ושבע - שראה כל משאלות לבו ושבע כל טובה, וכן ושבע ימים (להלן לה כט), ששבעה נפשו בימים, ולא יתאוה שיחדשו בו הימים דבר, וכענין שנאמר בדוד וימת בשיבה טובה שבע ימים ועושר וכבוד (דהי"א כט כח). והוא ספור חסדי השם בצדיקים, ומדה טובה בהם שלא יתאוו במותרות, כענין שנאמר בהם תאות לבו נתת לו (תהלים כא ג), ולא כמו שנאמר באשר אוהב כסף לא ישבע כסף (קהלת ה ט), ואמרו בו (קהלת רבה א יג) אין אדם יוצא מן העולם וחצי תאוותיו בידו, יש בידו מנה מתאוה מאתים, השיגה ידו למאתים מתאוה לעשות ארבע מאות, שנאמר אוהב כסף לא ישבע כסף:
ובבראשית רבה (סב ב) אמרו הקב"ה מראה להם לצדיקים מתן שכרן שהוא עתיד ליתן להם לעולם הבא, ונפשם שבעה והם ישנים. נתעוררו החכמים בזה ופירשו הכתוב שאומר "ושבע" במראה הזו:

**44) בראשית מא:נז-מב:א-ב, תענית י'**
וְכָל הָאָרֶץ בָּאוּ מִצְרַיְמָה לִשְׁבֹּר אֶל יוֹסֵף כִּי חָזַק הָרָעָב בְּכָל הָאָרֶץ: וַיַּרְא יַעֲקֹב כִּי יֶשׁ שֶׁבֶר בְּמִצְרָיִם וַיֹּאמֶר יַעֲקֹב לְבָנָיו לָמָּה תִּתְרָאוּ: וַיֹּאמֶר הִנֵּה שָׁמַעְתִּי כִּי יֶשׁ שֶׁבֶר בְּמִצְרָיִם רְדוּ שָׁמָּה וְשִׁבְרוּ לָנוּ מִשָּׁם וְנִחְיֶה וְלֹא נָמוּת:
... שנאמר (בראשית מ"ב) ויאמר יעקב לבניו למה תתראו אמר להם יעקב לבניו: אל תראו עצמכם כשאתם שבעין לא בפני עשו ולא בפני ישמעאל, כדי שלא יתקנאו בכם.

**45) שמות א:ז-ח, ברכות נד.**
וּבְנֵי יִשְׂרָאֵל פָּרוּ וַיִּשְׁרְצוּ וַיִּרְבּוּ וַיַּעַצְמוּ בִּמְאֹד מְאֹד וַתִּמָּלֵא הָאָרֶץ אֹתָם: וַיָּקָם מֶלֶךְ חָדָשׁ עַל מִצְרָיִם אֲשֶׁר לֹא יָדַע אֶת יוֹסֵף:
ובכל מאדך - בכל ממונך

הַמִּצְוָה יָמִין וּשְׂמֹאול לְמַעַן יַאֲרִיךְ יָמִים עַל־מַמְלַכְתּוֹ
הוּא וּבָנָיו בְּקֶרֶב יִשְׂרָאֵל:

### 26) ויקרא כו:ג-ו ופירוש כתב סופר

אִם־בְּחֻקֹּתַי תֵּלֵכוּ וְאֶת־מִצְוֹתַי תִּשְׁמְרוּ וַעֲשִׂיתֶם אֹתָם:
וְנָתַתִּי גִשְׁמֵיכֶם בְּעִתָּם וְנָתְנָה הָאָרֶץ יְבוּלָהּ וְעֵץ הַשָּׂדֶה
יִתֵּן פִּרְיוֹ: וְהִשִּׂיג לָכֶם דַּיִשׁ אֶת־בָּצִיר וּבָצִיר יַשִּׂיג אֶת־
זֶרַע וַאֲכַלְתֶּם לַחְמְכֶם לָשֹׂבַע וִישַׁבְתֶּם לָבֶטַח בְּאַרְצְכֶם:
וְנָתַתִּי שָׁלוֹם בָּאָרֶץ וּשְׁכַבְתֶּם וְאֵין מַחֲרִיד וְהִשְׁבַּתִּי חַיָּה
רָעָה מִן־הָאָרֶץ וְחֶרֶב לֹא־תַעֲבֹר בְּאַרְצְכֶם:

וְנָתַתִּי שָׁלוֹם בָּאָרֶץ וּשְׁכַבְתֶּם וְאֵין מַחֲרִיד. אחז"ל
[שלהי עוקצין] אין כלי מחזיק ברכה לישראל אלא
השלום. נ"ל עניינו, שבאמת אוהב כסף לא ישבע
ולעולם משתוקק ליותר, ועפ"י הרוב אם לעצמו יש
די לו במה שיש לו אבל ע"י שרואה שלחבירו יש
יותר מתקנא בו, וכואב ונאנח על שלחבירו יש יותר
ממנו. ושמעתי לפרש מה שנאמר [ה, יא] מתוקה
שנת העובד אם מעט ואם הרבה יאכל והשבע לעשיר
איננו מניח לו לישן, כי היה די לעובד במעט שיש לו,
רק שרואה השבע של העשיר ע"י זה אינו מסתפק
בשלו וחפץ עוד עד שאינו מניח לו לישן, ונכון הוא.
וכל זה כשיש קנאה ושנאה בין איש לרעהו, אבל
בשכולם אוהבים זה לזה, ואוהב את רעהו כעצמו לא
יתקנא בו, ולא יקשה בעיניו כשראה בחבירו שיש
לו יותר ממנו וזהו שלום האמתי. וזה כונת התנא
אין כלי מחזיק ברכה לישראל, היינו שאין הברכה
בשלימותה רק ע"י השלום, אז יש ברכה שלמה. וזהו
שאמר רש"י ז"ל שאמרו אם אין שלום אין כלום,
שכל זמן שאין שלום אמיתי אין לאדם אין די בשיש לו,
ואינו עשיר עשיר השמח בחלקו. וזהו שאמר ושכבתם ואין
מחריד, ע"ד אין מניח לו לישן, והבטיח שלא תחרדו
ע"י אחרים משינתכם, כי יהיה לך שלום בארץ,
וק"ל:

### 27) קהלת ז:א

טוֹב שֵׁם מִשֶּׁמֶן טוֹב וְיוֹם הַמָּוֶת מִיּוֹם הִוָּלְדוֹ:

### 28) יומא ט:

מקדש ראשון מפני מה חרב? מפני שלשה דברים
שהיו בו: עבודה זרה, וגלוי עריות, ושפיכות דמים.

### 29) ישעיה א:כא-כג

אֵיכָה הָיְתָה לְזוֹנָה קִרְיָה נֶאֱמָנָה מְלֵאֲתִי מִשְׁפָּט צֶדֶק
יָלִין בָּהּ וְעַתָּה מְרַצְּחִים: כַּסְפֵּךְ הָיָה לְסִיגִים סָבְאֵךְ
מָהוּל בַּמָּיִם: שָׂרַיִךְ סוֹרְרִים וְחַבְרֵי גַּנָּבִים כֻּלּוֹ אֹהֵב
שֹׁחַד וְרֹדֵף שַׁלְמֹנִים יָתוֹם לֹא יִשְׁפֹּטוּ וְרִיב אַלְמָנָה לֹא
יָבוֹא אֲלֵיהֶם:

### 30) פירוש רד"ק על ישעיה א:כא

מלאתי משפט ... וגם בירושלם העמיד למשפט ה'
ולריב וגו', ועתה אין בה משפט כמו שאמר בסמוך
כלו אוהב שחד ורודף שלמונים:

---

צדק ילין בה – ... וירושלם היה הצדק תמידי בה
ועתה מרצחים:

### 31) פירוש מצודת דוד על ישעיה א:כא

איכה – מתאונן לומר איך ירושלים עיר אמונה
נהפכה להיות משקרת בה' כזונה המשקרת בבעלה.

### 32) פירושי רש"י ורד"ק על ישעיהו א:כב

כספך היה לסיגים – שהיו עושין מעות נחשת ומצפין
אותן בכסף להונות בהם.

כספך – עושים בה מטבע שקר וחושבים בני אדם
כי כלו כסף ויש בו סיגים נחשת ובדיל והדומים
להם ומחופף בכסף ומטעין בו בני אדם וכן מוכרי
יין חושבים הקונים שהם קונים יין חי והוא מעורב
במים, סבאך הוא היין הנמכר בחנות ...

### 33) פירושי רד"ק ומצודת דוד על ישעיהו א:כג

שריך – השרים שהיה להם לתקן המעוות הם
סוררים ומעוותים היושר והם חברי גנבים כי הגנבים
חולקים עמהם לפיכך לא ייסרו אותם, ולא ימנעום
מלגונגום:

כלו – דרך כלל על השרים כי כלם בדרך אחד לפיכך
אמר כלו בלשון יחיד והם אוהבים לקבל שחד ומטים
המשפט:

סוררים – סרים מדרך הטוב ומתחברים עם הגנבים.
כלו – כל העם.

שלמונים – האחד אומר לחבירו הצדיקני היום בדיני
ולמחר אצדיקך בדינך:

### 34) רבינו בחיי על בראשית ד:ז

... ועל דרך השכל קין והבל יש בשמם התעוררות
ורמז לענין הויה והפסד כי הם אחים סמוכים זה לזה.
וקין רמז לקנין לעולם הזה, והבל רמז למי שדעתו
שפלה ומכביל אותו הקנין. וכן היתה מנחתו הצאן
שהיא שפלה מכל בעלי חיים ועל כן דבק בו רצון
ה' יתברך, הוא שכתוב וישע ה' אל הבל ואל מנחתו.
והיתה מנחתו של קין מפרי האדמה כי היה אוהב
קניני העולם הזה ועבודת הגוף שאין בו קיימא
ונמשך אחר התאוות הגופניות ועל כן לא חל עליו
רצון ה' יתברך, הוא שכתוב ואל קין ואל מנחתו
לא שעה. המכביל הזה נהרג כי איננו חושש לעסקי
העולם ואינו עושה מן העולם הזה עיקר, והאוהב
קניני העולם הזה נתקלל ואמר לו נע ונד תהיה
בארץ כי כן אוהב כסף לא ישבע כסף והולך ומטלטל
ממקום למקום בימים ובמדברות במקום גדודי חיות
ולסטים ואין לו מנוחה אפילו שעה אחת אבל כל ימיו
מכאובים:

### 35) בראשית ו:יא-יג

וַתִּשָּׁחֵת הָאָרֶץ לִפְנֵי הָאֱלֹהִים וַתִּמָּלֵא הָאָרֶץ חָמָס:
וַיַּרְא אֱלֹהִים אֶת־הָאָרֶץ וְהִנֵּה נִשְׁחָתָה כִּי־הִשְׁחִית כָּל־
בָּשָׂר אֶת־דַּרְכּוֹ עַל־הָאָרֶץ: וַיֹּאמֶר אֱלֹהִים לְנֹחַ קֵץ כָּל־

### 12) פירוש רש"י, מהר"ל (גור אריה) על דברים ו:ה

**ובכל מאודך** – בכל ממונך יש לך אדם שממונו חביב עליו מגופו לכך נאמר בכל מאודך.

**שממונו חביב עליו מגופו** – תימה, אם כן דיבר הכתוב נגד הסכלים, שהרי בני גד ובני ראובן – שחסו על ממונם יותר ממה שחסו על בניהם ונשותיהם – נאמר (קהלת י', ב) "לב כסיל לשמאלו", ולמה צריך לכתוב לדבר מאלו אנשים. ויראה לומר, דמי שהוא אוהב את ממונו יותר מגופו, משום שהממון מחיה את האדם, שהוא סבה לחיותו, ודבר שהוא סבה לחיות שלו – הוא קודם לו במעלה בדבר מה, ולפיכך הוא אוהב אותו יותר מגופו.... בשביל שיש לממון האדם מעלה שהוא מחיה את הנפש ...

### 13) פירוש אור החיים על דברים ו:ה

והנה שני הדרגות אלו ישנם בגדר המצטער והמתגדר, שהמאכל אחרי אוכלו ואחרי שתו יחדל ממנו החפץ בו, וכמו כן תאות לבו אחר גמר מעשה דרך גבר בעלמה (משלי ל יט) ישתנה הדבר אצלו עד אחר זמן, לזה בא דבר ה' בהדרגה ג' בגדר השיעור, ואמר ובכל מאודך פירוש בכל ממון שאתה חפץ בו, וכשם שהממון אמר הכתוב (קהלת ה ט) אוהב כסף לא ישבע כסף, כי כשאדם מגיע לקנות קנין עצום אז יתעצם חפצו לחפוץ בהוני הונות והולכת תאותו וגדלה, וכמו כן יצו ה' באהבתו שלא תשתער ותוגבל, וכשיגיע גדר אחד תגדל בו האהבה לגדר עליון מזה, ולדרך זה השיעור אומרו מאודך, לא מה שקנה, אלא שחפץ לקנות:

ובזה יתייישב גם כן מה שהיה קשה בו אם אתה אומר מה שקנית אם כן אין מצוה זו שוה בכל, שהרי עני אין בו מצוה זו, גם באנשים לא תהיה להם המצוה בהשואה, מה שאין כן במצות שבכל ונפשך שהכל שוים בו, ולפי דרכנו יבא על נכון:

### 14) ירמיהו ח:י

לָכֵן אֶתֵּן אֶת־נְשֵׁיהֶם לַאֲחֵרִים שְׂדוֹתֵיהֶם לְיוֹרְשִׁים כִּי מִקָּטֹן וְעַד־גָּדוֹל כֻּלֹּה בֹּצֵעַ בָּצַע מִנָּבִיא וְעַד־כֹּהֵן כֻּלֹּה עֹשֶׂה שָּׁקֶר:

### 15) פירוש מצודת דוד על ירמיהו ח:י

**לאחרים** – לעם אחר. **ליורשים** – כל מי שירצו לרשת. **כולם בוצע בצע** – כולם גוזלים הון. **מנביא** – נביא השקר. **כהן** – כהן הבעל:

### 16) ירמיהו ט:כב-כג

כֹּה אָמַר ד' אַל־יִתְהַלֵּל חָכָם בְּחָכְמָתוֹ וְאַל־יִתְהַלֵּל הַגִּבּוֹר בִּגְבוּרָתוֹ אַל־יִתְהַלֵּל עָשִׁיר בְּעָשְׁרוֹ: כִּי אִם־בְּזֹאת יִתְהַלֵּל הַמִּתְהַלֵּל הַשְׂכֵּל וְיָדֹעַ אוֹתִי כִּי אֲנִי ד' עֹשֶׂה חֶסֶד מִשְׁפָּט וּצְדָקָה בָּאָרֶץ כִּי־בְאֵלֶּה חָפַצְתִּי נְאֻם־ד':

### 17) איוב כ:כ

כִּי לֹא יָדַע שָׁלֵו בְּבִטְנוֹ בַּחֲמוּדוֹ לֹא יְמַלֵּט:

---

### 18) קהלת ה:ט

אֹהֵב כֶּסֶף לֹא־יִשְׂבַּע כֶּסֶף וּמִי־אֹהֵב בֶּהָמוֹן לֹא תְבוּאָה גַּם־זֶה הָבֶל:

### 19) פירוש אבן עזרא על קהלת ה:ט

**אוהב כסף** – נפשו לא תשבע:

ומי אוהב **בהמון לא תבואה** – יש מי שאוהב לקבץ ממון בבגדים ומיני סחורות ולא יאהב תבואה גם זה הבל, וגם ישוב על אוהב כסף והוא המקבץ כסף וזהב בלבד וי"א מי שאוהב בהמון לא תבואה לו ופירוש המון קנות עבדי' ושפחו' ושמשי' רבים והענין שיאהב להיות המון לפניו:

### 20) תהילים כד:א

לְדָוִד מִזְמוֹר לַד' הָאָרֶץ וּמְלוֹאָהּ תֵּבֵל וְיֹשְׁבֵי בָהּ:

### 21) חגי ב:ח ופירוש רש"י

לִי הַכֶּסֶף וְלִי הַזָּהָב נְאֻם ד' צְבָאוֹת:

**לי הכסף ולי הזהב** – ובידי להביא לאשר חפצתי בו:

### 22) שמות כ:כ

לֹא תַעֲשׂוּן אִתִּי אֱלֹהֵי כֶסֶף וֵאלֹהֵי זָהָב לֹא תַעֲשׂוּ לָכֶם:

### 23) קהלת י':יט ופירוש חומת אנך (חיד"א)

לִשְׂחוֹק עֹשִׂים לֶחֶם וְיַיִן יְשַׂמַּח חַיִּים וְהַכֶּסֶף יַעֲנֶה אֶת־הַכֹּל:

וכי תימא במקום שמחה אנו רואים שצריכה התורה יגיעה רבה. לז"א

**והכסף יענה** את הכל והכסף לשון תאוה כמו "נכספה גם כלתה" ר"ל אם יהיה חשקך בתורה יגיע לתכלית מבוקשו זש"ם "והכסף יענה את הכל" בין חכם בין טפש על ידי התשוקה ישיג התורה:

### 24) תהילים פד:ג ופירושי רש"י ואבן עזרא

נִכְסְפָה וְגַם־כָּלְתָה נַפְשִׁי לְחַצְרוֹת ד' לִבִּי וּבְשָׂרִי יְרַנְּנוּ אֶל־קֵל חָי:

**נכספה. כלתה. נחמדה** – נתאותה

**נכספה** – התאותה וכמעט כלתה מרוב התאוה והטעם שעברה חק התאוה על כן מלת גם:

### 25) דברים יז:טו-כ

שׂוֹם תָּשִׂים עָלֶיךָ מֶלֶךְ אֲשֶׁר יִבְחַר ד' אֱלֹהֶיךָ בּוֹ מִקֶּרֶב אַחֶיךָ תָּשִׂים עָלֶיךָ מֶלֶךְ לֹא תוּכַל לָתֵת עָלֶיךָ אִישׁ נָכְרִי אֲשֶׁר לֹא־אָחִיךָ הוּא: רַק לֹא־יַרְבֶּה־לּוֹ סוּסִים וְלֹא־יָשִׁיב אֶת־הָעָם מִצְרַיְמָה לְמַעַן הַרְבּוֹת סוּס וַד' אָמַר לָכֶם לֹא תֹסִפוּן לָשׁוּב בַּדֶּרֶךְ הַזֶּה עוֹד: וְלֹא יַרְבֶּה־לּוֹ נָשִׁים וְלֹא יָסוּר לְבָבוֹ וְכֶסֶף וְזָהָב לֹא יַרְבֶּה־לּוֹ מְאֹד: וְהָיָה כְשִׁבְתּוֹ עַל כִּסֵּא מַמְלַכְתּוֹ וְכָתַב לוֹ אֶת־מִשְׁנֵה הַתּוֹרָה הַזֹּאת עַל־סֵפֶר מִלִּפְנֵי הַכֹּהֲנִים הַלְוִיִּם: וְהָיְתָה עִמּוֹ וְקָרָא בוֹ כָּל־יְמֵי חַיָּיו לְמַעַן יִלְמַד לְיִרְאָה אֶת־ד' אֱלֹהָיו לִשְׁמֹר אֶת־כָּל־דִּבְרֵי הַתּוֹרָה הַזֹּאת וְאֶת־הַחֻקִּים הָאֵלֶּה לַעֲשֹׂתָם: לְבִלְתִּי רוּם־לְבָבוֹ מֵאֶחָיו וּלְבִלְתִּי סוּר מִן

# SOURCES ON THE TORAH REACTION TO THE MADOFF SCANDAL, OTHER SCANDALS, AND GREED

## 1) שמות יח:כא

וְאַתָּה תֶחֱזֶה מִכָּל־הָעָם אַנְשֵׁי־חַיִל יִרְאֵי אֱלֹקִים אַנְשֵׁי אֱמֶת שֹׂנְאֵי בָצַע וְשַׂמְתָּ עֲלֵהֶם שָׂרֵי אֲלָפִים שָׂרֵי מֵאוֹת שָׂרֵי חֲמִשִּׁים וְשָׂרֵי עֲשָׂרֹת:

## 2) פירוש רמב"ן על שמות יח:כא

**שונאי בצע** – ... אבל הלשון במכילתא אינו כן, אלא כך שנויה שם שונאי בצע, שהן שונאין לקבל ממון בדין, דברי רבי יהושע רבי אלעזר המודעי אומר, שונאי בצע, אלו שהן שונאין ממון עצמם, אם ממון עצמם שונאין קל וחומר ממון חבריהם פירש רבי יהושע שונאי בצע, שונאי שוחד, כמו כולו בוצע בצע (ירמיה ו יג), איש לבצעו מקצהו (ישעיה נו יא) רבי אלעזר המודעי דרש כי הם השונאים הממון הרב, ואין להם חפץ ברבוי כסף וזהב, כענין אם אשמח כי רב חילי וכי כביר מצאה ידי (איוב לא כה) כי הממון יקרא בצע, מה בצע כי נהרוג את אחינו (בראשית לז כו), ואם בצע כי תתם דרכיך (איוב כב ג), והחרמתי לה' בצעם וחילם לאדון כל הארץ (מיכה ד יג):

## 3) פירוש ריב"א על שמות יח:כא

**שנאי בצע** – ששונאין את ממונם בדין כההיא דאמרינן כל דיינא דמפקין ממונא מיניה בדינא לאו דיינא הוא (ב"ב כה):

## 4) פירוש טור הארוך על שמות יח:כא

**שונאי בצע.** לפי הפשט על השוחד דבר הפסוק. ויש מפרשים, שונאי ריבוי ממון, שאינו יגע להעשיר. ופירש"י שונא ממון עצמן בדין, כההוא דאמרינן (ב"ב נח, ב) כל דיינא דמפקין מיניה ממונא בדינא לאו דיינא הוא, לומר, כל ממון שידעו בו שאדם יכול להוציאו מידם בדין, ישנאוהו ויחזירוהו מעצמם ולא ירד עמו לדין, ואפילו הוא שלהם באמת, כגון שקנה מהם עבד בלא עדים והאחר מוציאו ממנו בדין. ויש מפרשים (כ"ה בתנחומא יתרו ב) שונא ממונו, כגון אם הבעל דין אלם ומגזם לו להפסיד ממונו אם לא יטה הדין, אל ישמע לו ולא יחוש להפסד ממונו:

## 5) משלי טו:כז

עֹכֵר בֵּיתוֹ בּוֹצֵעַ בָּצַע וְשׂוֹנֵא מַתָּנֹת יִחְיֶה:

## 6) פירושי גר"א ומלבי"ם על משלי טו:כז

**עוכר ביתו וגו'** – פי' הבוצע בצע שמאסף תמיד ממון שאינו שלו סופו שגם ביתו יוטל ממנו ונעכר ...
**עוכר ביתו בוצע בצע** – מי שהוא בוצע בצע שמרויח

---

ממון שלא ביושר, בל תחשוב כי ירבה בבצע הלז כבוד ביתו, בהפך בזה עוכר ביתו, כמ"ש הוי בוצע בצע רע לביתו וכו' כי אבן מקיר תזעק וכו', ובהפך מי ששונא – אף מתנות – ולא יהנה משל אחרים רק מה שמרויח ע"י יגיע כפו, בל תאמר שימות ברעב או יחלה מרוב עבודה, בהפך עי"ז יחיה כי הכל תלוי בהשגחת ה':

## 7) משלי כח:טז

נָגִיד חֲסַר תְּבוּנוֹת וְרַב מַעֲשַׁקּוֹת שֹׂנֵא [שֹׂנֵא] בֶצַע יַאֲרִיךְ יָמִים:

## 8) פירוש רש"י על משלי כח:טז

**נגיד חסר תבונות** – מתוך שהוא חסר תבונה הוא רב מעשקות כי אינו נותן לב על חייו ומרבה לעשוק שהרי השונא בצע יאריך ימים:

## 9) פירושי רלב"ג ומלבי"ם על משלי כח:טז

**נגיד** – וזה דרך הנגיד שהוא חסר תבונות ורב מעשקות אך הנגיד שהוא שונא בצע יאריך ימים המונהגים ממנו בהנהגתו הישרה ובשמירתו אותם מהרע ובהפך הענין ברשע שיכסף לטרפם או ירצה בזה הנה בדמיון הארי הנוהם ברשע שישמעו קולו החיות ויברחו כן הענין ברשע המושל על עם דל כי לא יוכלו שאתו וימרדו בו וכן הענין בנגיד חסר תבונות ורוב מעשקות אך מי שהוא שונא בצע יאריך ימים על ממלכתו:

**נגיד חסר תבונות ורב מעשקות** – הנה הנגיד הרשע אם אינו רב מעשקות ימצאון תחת ממשלתו אנשים שמרויחים ממון ומתקיימים, וכן גם הוא רב מעשקות – אם י"ל תבונה, יניח ג"כ את הסוחרים הבוצעים בצע, שיקח מהם מס ומתנות והם ירבו עושר למענו, אבל אם הוא גם חסר תבונות – אז תיכף כשיראה איש שי"ל בצע וממון הורג אותו כדי לקחת ממונו, כי אינו חושב מחשבת שימצאו עשירים וסוחרים בממשלתו כי אין תבונה בו לדאוג על ימים הבאים, ואז רק שונאי בצע יאריך ימים – רק מי שאינו בוצע ומרויח והוא נראה בעיניו אינו מסוכן למות, אבל הבוצע ומרויח לא יאריך ימים, ומפרש כי.

## 10) משלי א:יט

כֵּן אָרְחוֹת כָּל־בֹּצֵעַ בָּצַע אֶת־נֶפֶשׁ בְּעָלָיו יִקָּח:

## 11) דברים ו:ה

וְאָהַבְתָּ אֵת ד' אֱלֹקֶיךָ בְּכָל לְבָבְךָ וּבְכָל נַפְשְׁךָ וּבְכָל מְאֹדֶךָ:

אין ע"ז איסור חבלה ויש לי ראיה לכך ממה שהעירירו המפרשים על זה דאיהא בגמרא כי איסור חובל הותר מכללו אצל בי"ד כי הם מלקין מי שמחויב ללקות ולמה לא אומרים כי הותר מכללו לענין מצות מילה שעושים חבלה בגוף הילד אולם לפי"ז

אתי שפיר כי החבלה שעושים בגוף הילד אינה באה כדי לצערו ולהכאיבו ואינה דרך נציון ולכן לא מצינו הותר מכללו אלא לענין מלקות בי"ד שהכונה היא לעונשו ולצערו כמ"ש בתורה ונקלה אחיך לעיניך והדברים מאירים

וכי ינצו אנשים – זה עם ח זה, ונתכוון להכות את חבירו, והכה את האשה (מכילתא פ״ח):

## 66) רמב״ם הלכות חובל ומזיק ה:י״א

ועוד יש הפרש בין נזקי גופו לנזקי ממונו, שהאומר לחבירו סמא עיני קטע את ידי על מנת שאתה פטור הרי זה חייב בחמשה דברים שהדבר ידוע שאין אדם רוצה בכך. אבל האומר לחבירו קרע את כסותי שבר את כדי על מנת שאתה פטור הרי זה פטור, ואם לא אמר לו על מנת שאתה פטור הרי זה חייב לשלם אף על פי שהרשהו להשחית.

## 67) שו״ת רא״ש כא:ו

שאלה: ב׳ =שנים= שנתאבקו יחד, והפיל האחד את חבירו לארץ ונפל עליו, ובנפלו עליו סימא עינו של התחתון, נ״ל דפטור מה׳ דברים; ואף על גב דקיי״ל: אדם מועד לעולם, בין שוגג בין מזיד בין באונס בין ברצון בין ישן בין ער, היכא דהוה אנס גמור, פטור. כדאיתא בריש פרק המניח (כ״ז): המניח את הכד ברשות הרבים, ובא אחר ונתקל בה ושברה, פטור; ופריך עלה בגמ׳ (שם): ואמאי, איבעי ליה לעיוני ומיזל; ומשני: אמרי דבי רב משמיה דרב: בממלא ר״ה =רשות הרבים= כולה; ושמואל אמר באפלה; ורבי אלעא אמר: לפי שאין דרכן של בני אדם להתבונן בדרכים; אלמא, דבאונס כי האי, אדם פטור. ואמרינן בירושלמי: היה ישן במטה ובא חברו וישן אצלו, הראשון פטור בנזקי שני. ואמרינן בפרק הגוזל בתרא (קי״ב), ובפרק אלו נערות (ל״ד): הניח להם אביהם פרה שאולה וטבחוה ואכלוה, משלמין דמי בשר בזול, היינו לפי הנאתם, אבל דמי כל הבשר לא, משום דאנוסין היו, שלא היה להם לידע שאינה של אביהם. ואמרינן בפרק המניח (ל״ב): היה בעל חבית ראשון ובעל קורה אחרון, ונשברה חבית בקורה, ואם עמד בעל החבית, פטור. ואמרינן בפרק שור שנגח את הפרה (מ״ז): אם נכנס לחצר בעל הבית שלא ברשות והזיקו בעל הבית, פטור, היכא דלא הוה ידע ליה. ותניא נמי בפרק המניח (לב א): איסי בן יהודה אומר: רץ חייב, מפני שהוא משנה, ומודה איסי בן יהודה ברץ בע״ש =בערב שבת= בין השמשות, שהוא פטור, משום שרץ ברשות; ואם היו שניהם רצים, והזיקו זה את זה שלא בכוונה, פטורין. וכן בנדון זה, נתאבקו זה עם זה מדעת שניהם, והזיקו זה את זה שלא בכוונה, כי הדבר ידוע כשהשניהם נתאבקו עיקר כונתם שיפיל האחד את חברו, וכשהאחד נותן על חברו, א״א =אי אפשר= לו לצמצם ולכוין שיפילהו בנחת כדי שלא יזיקו, כי בכל כחן מתאבקין, וכל אחד מכוין להפיל חברו, אם יזיקנו, ואדעתא דהכי נתאבקו יחד. נאם הכותב, אשר בן הרב ר׳ יחיאל זצ״ל.

## 68) טור, חושן משפט תכא:ה

שאלה לא״א הרא״ש ז״ל שנים שהתאבקו יחד והאחד

הפיל חבירו לארץ ונפל עליו וסימא עינו של התחתון [בהפלתו] מה דינו. תשובה נראה דפטור מה׳ דברים אע״ג דקיי״ל אדם מועד לעולם היכא דהוי אונס פטור כדאיתא בירושלמי היה ישן ובא חבירו ושכב אצלו הראשון פטור בנזקי שני ותניא גבי ב׳ שרצו בר״ה והזיקו זה בזה שלא בכוונה פטורין ובנדון זה שהתאבקו זה עם זה מדעת שניהם והזיקו זה את זה שלא בכוונה כי הדבר ידוע בב׳ מתאבקין יחד עיקר כוונתם שיפיל אחד לחבירו ואי אפשר לאדם לצמצם ולכוין שיפילהו בנחת שלא יוזק כי בכל כוחם הם מתאבקים וכל אחד מהם מכוין להפיל חבירו ומחלו זה על זה ואדעתא דהכי התאבקו יחד:

## 69) שולחן ערוך, חושן משפט תכא:ה

שנים שנתאבקו יחד, ואחד הפיל חבירו לארץ ונפל וסימא את עינו פטור.

## 70) "The Rav Thinking Aloud: Transcripts of personal Conversations with Rabbi Joseph B. Soloveitchik," David Holzer, page 13

"Moshe mentioned that he saw Rabbi Willig outside playing with this students, to which the Rav replied that Rav Chaim (Soloveitchik, his grandfather, Head of the Yeshiva in Brisk) used to box with his students. When asked if this was a problem of *Chavalah* [wounding], the Rav answered that it is only a problem if done with *Sinah* [hatred], but not if done with *Ahava* (love). Moshe then asked about the *Inyan* (issue) of not being *Misachek* (playing sports) with *Talmidim* (students), to which the Rav responded he doesn't know about that; this is just what he saw."

## 71) שו״ת שבט מיהודה (הרב איסר יהודה אונטרמאן), חלק א, דף רל

דוגמא שלישית קצרה נמצאה באותו פרק עצמו הל׳ חובל ה א וז״ל כל המכה אדם כשר מישראל בין קטן בין גדול בין איש בין אשה דרך נציון עובר בלא תעשה שנאמ׳ לא יוסיף ומפרשים עמלו להבין למה צריך הרמב״ם להוסיף מלה זו דרך נציון היינו מלשון כי ינצו אנשים לאמר לצערו ולהכאיבו שאינה נזכרת בגמרא בשום מקום ואמרתי ע״ז דרבנו בא לפרש לנו דין חדש שהוא אקטואלי בימינו כי נשאלתי בהיותי באנגליא מיהודים חרדים אם מותר לצעירים להתאגרף כמו שנוהגים בבתי ספר שלהם כשאחד עושה חבלה בחברו ואם אין בזה לאו מה״ת שלא לחבול בחברו עניתי ע״ז בקונטרס שלם שאין איסור וזה מבוסס על דברי רבנו כי רק חבלה דרך נציון וקטטה שכוונתו לגרום להברו כאב וצער אבל כשרצונו רק להראות גבורתו ותוקף שריריו בלבד

הנה מבואר מדברי מוהר"י ברונא הנ"ל דלא התיר לילך ולראות אלא משום שהולך ללמוד אומנות שיכול לקנות סוסים לרוץ בהם שכך ה' מנהגם בזמנם אבל אם לא הולך ללמוד אומנות אלא לראות השחוק ולשמוח בשמחתם אסור.

ומינה נראה שאסור לצאת ולהמרות גם במשחקים בכדור (באל פליי בלע"ז) לבד ממה שיש בו משום ביטול זמן יש בו משום איסור הנ"ל ובגמ' ע"ז י"ח ע"ב ת"ר ההולך לאיצטדינין ולכרקום ... הרי זה מושב לצים ועליהם הכתוב אומר אשרי האיש אשר לא הלך בעצת רשעים וגו' כי אם בתורת ה' חפצו הא למדת שדברים אלו מביאים את האדם לידי ביטול תורה ופרש" כולם מיני שחוק וליצנות הרי מבואר שבכל אלו יש בהם איסור משום אשר לא הלך ובביטול תורה ועוד וא"כ זה אסור אפילו לראות על הראדיא או טעלעוויזיא דג"כ יש בו משום ביטול תורה כמובן ופשוט הוא אפילו נימא דאין בו משום מושב לצים שהרי בביתו הוא אבל אסור משום בטול תורה ומשום אל תשמח אל גיל כעמים ולכן כל מי שיראת ה' נוגע בלבבו ירחק מהם.

## 60) שו"ת אגרות משה יורה דעה חלק ד סימן יא

א. אם אסור מצד בחוקותיהם לא תלכו, ללכת לתיאטרון ואיצטדיון ספורט בימינו באלו שנקראו תיאטרון שעושין שם עניני שחוק, וכן איצטדיון, שהם המקומות שמשמחקין ספארט, לא שייכים בהו ענין "ובחוקותיהם לא תלכו" (ויקרא קדושים יח:יג), דהוא דווקא כשהוא חוק להעכו"ם לעשות איזה דבר בעלמא, אף כשאין זה מחוקי הע"ז שלהם, אבל עכ"פ הם עניני חוקים שהנהיגו ביניהם – לא רק דברים של פריצות אלא אף דברים בעלמא – שלא ידוע טעם, כדאיתא ברמ"א יו"ד סימן קע"ח סעיף א'. ואין כוונת הרמ"א במש"כ או בדבר שנהגו למנהג ולחוק ואין טעם בדבר דאיכא למיחש ביה משום דרכי האמורי ושיש בו שמץ ע"ז מאבותיהם, שהוא ספק, אלא שהוא בדין ודאי. דמאחר דאין טעם נגלה ומובן, יש לנו לתלות שהוא עניין מחוקי עבודה זרה. אבל כשאיכא טעם למה שעושין, כהא דאיצטדינין וכרקום שאיתא בע"ז דף י"ח ע"ב שהוא לליצנות, ליכא בזה משום ע"ז, אף שהוא דבר אסור מצד אסור ליצנות וכל ההולך שם עובר באיסור מושב לצים ובביטול תורה – לא רק על זמן זה – אלא שגורם לו להיות בטל לגמרי מתורה כמפורש שם. וכ"ש בתיאזרון הנמצא כעת במדינתנו, וכן האיצטדיון של משחקי ספארט, ואף במדינות אחרות, דעושין זה סתם אינשי מהנכרים שבעיר שלא שייך כלל לעניני ע"ז ...

## 61) בראשית לב:כה-כו

וַיִּוָּתֵר יַעֲקֹב לְבַדּוֹ וַיֵּאָבֵק אִישׁ עִמּוֹ עַד עֲלוֹת הַשָּׁחַר: וַיַּרְא כִּי לֹא יָכֹל לוֹ וַיִּגַּע בְּכַף־יְרֵכוֹ וַתֵּקַע כַּף־יֶרֶךְ יַעֲקֹב

בְּהֵאָבְקוֹ עִמּוֹ: וַיֹּאמֶר שַׁלְּחֵנִי כִּי עָלָה הַשָּׁחַר וַיֹּאמֶר לֹא אֲשַׁלֵּחֲךָ כִּי אִם־בֵּרַכְתָּנִי:

## 62) בבא קמא צא:

דאין אדם רשאי לחבל בעצמו, אחרים שחבלו בו חייבין. ואין אדם רשאי לחבל בעצמו? והתניא: יכול נשבע להרע בעצמו ולא הרע יהא פטור? ת"ל: (ויקרא ה') להרע או להיטיב, מה הטבה רשות, אף הרעה רשות, אביא נשבע להרע בעצמו ולא הרע אמר שמואל: באשב בתענית. כוותה גבי הרעת אחרים להשיבם בתענית, אחרים מי מיטיב להו בתעניתא? אין דמהדק להו באנדרונא. והתניא: איזהו הרעת אחרים? אכה פלוני ואפצע את מוחן אלא תנאי היא, דאיכא למ"ד: אין אדם רשאי לחבל בעצמו, ואיכא מ"ד: אדם רשאי לחבל בעצמו. מאן תנא דשמעת ליה דאמר: אין אדם רשאי לחבל בעצמו? אילימא האי תנא הוא, דתניא: (בראשית ט') ואך את דמכם לנפשותיכם אדרש ר' אלעזר אומר: מיד נפשותיכם אדרש את דמכם ודלמא קטלא שאני אלא האי תנא הוא, דתניא: מקרעין על המת האמורי, אמר רבי אלעזר: שמעתי, שהמקרע על המת יותר מדאי לוקה משום בל תשחית, וכ"ש גופו ודלמא בגדים שאני כי הא דרבי יוחנן קרי למאני מכבדותא, ורב חסדא כד הוה מסגי ביני היזמי והגא, מדלי להו למאניה, אמר: זה מעלה ארוכה, וזה אינו מעלה ארוכה אלא האי תנא הוא, דתניא: אמר ר"א הקפר ברבי, מה ת"ל: (במדבר ו') וכפר עליו מאשר חטא על הנפש? וכי באיזה נפש חטא זה? אלא שציער עצמו מן היין, והלא דברים ק"ו: ומה זה שלא ציער עצמו אלא מן היין נקרא חוטא, המצער עצמו מכל דבר על אחת כמה וכמה.

## 63) רמב"ם הלכות חובל ומזיק ה:א

אסור לאדם לחבול בין בעצמו בין בחבירו, ולא החובל בלבד אלא כל המכה אדם כשר מישראל בין קטן בין גדול בין איש בין אשה דרך נציון הרי זה עובר בלא תעשה, שנ' דברים כ"ה ג' לא יוסיף להכותו, אם הזהירה תורה שלא להוסיף בהכאת החוטא קל וחומר למכה את הצדיק.

## 64) רמב"ם הלכות חובל ומזיק ה:א

אסור לאדם לחבול בין בעצמו בין בחבירו, ולא החובל בלבד אלא כל המכה אדם כשר מישראל בין קטן בין גדול בין איש בין אשה דרך נציון הרי זה עובר בלא תעשה, שנ' (דברים כה:ג) "לא יוסיף להכותו" ...

## 65) שמות כא:כב ופירוש רש"י

וְכִי־יִנָּצוּ אֲנָשִׁים וְנָגְפוּ אִשָּׁה הָרָה וְיָצְאוּ יְלָדֶיהָ וְלֹא יִהְיֶה אָסוֹן עָנוֹשׁ יֵעָנֵשׁ כַּאֲשֶׁר יָשִׁית עָלָיו בַּעַל הָאִשָּׁה וְנָתַן בִּפְלִלִים:

חַטָּאִים לֹא עָמָד וּבְמוֹשַׁב לֵצִים לֹא יָשָׁב:
תנו רבנן: ההולך לאיצטדינין ולכרקום, וראה שם את
הנחשים ואת החברין, בוקיון ומוקיון ומוליון ולוליון,
בלורין סלגורין הרי זה מושב לצים, ועליהם הכתוב
אומר: (תהלים א) אשרי האיש אשר לא הלך וגו' כי
אם בתורת ה' חפצו, הא למדת, שדברים הללו מביאין
את האדם לידי ביטול תורה. ורמינהו: [הולכין]
לאיצטדינין מותר מפני שצווח ומציל, ולכרקום מותר
מפני ישוב מדינה, ובלבד שלא יתחשב עמהם, ואם
נתחשב עמהם אסור קשיא איצטדינין אאיצטדינין,
קשיא כרקום אכרקום בשלמא כרקום אכרקום ל"ק:
כאן במתחשב עמהן, כאן בשאין מתחשב עמהן, אלא
איצטדינין אאיצטדינין קשיא תנאי היא [דתניא:] אין
הולכין לאיצטדינין מפני מושב לצים, ור' נתן מתיר
מפני שני דברים, אחד מפני שצווח ומציל, ואחד
מפני שמעיד עדות אשה להשיאה.

### 58) שו"ת מוהר"י מברונא עא

נשאלתי אם מותר לצאת ולראות שמחת הערלים
כשממרים ומריצים סוסיהם כל הקודם סוסו ירויח
זהב וכה"ג, אם יש לדמותו לצידת חיות ועופות
שאוסר בפרק קמא בעבודה זרה (יח:)
והתרתי דלא דמי כי אין זה לשמחה אך ללמוד
אומנות ולקנות סוסים לרוץ בהם להנצל מאויבים
וכן ראיתי מבעלי מעשים:
אך בהא מספקנא אם מותר לילך ולראות
כשמשמחים יחד לרכוב זה כנגד זה במוטות וכדים
שקורין לטעד"ן.

### 59) שו"ת משנה הלכה (הרב מנשה קליין) ו:רע

אי מותר לראות במשחק הימורים שעושים גוים
ובדין משחק בקוביא מע"כ ידידי וכו' הי"ו.
בדבר השאלה אי מותר לישראל לצאת ולראות
שחוק העמים כשממרים ומריצים את הסוסים (רעיס
טראק בלע"ז) וכל הקודם סוסו ירויח וזוכה בפרס
וקורין לו (הארס רעיס בלע"ז) אי יש בזה איסור
משום משחק בקוביא או שדומה לצידת חיות ועופות
שאוסר בפ"ק דע"ז י"ח ב'. הנה כנראה דשאלה זו הוא
רק לראות משחקים העמים ולא להרויח במשחק אבל
באמת בתרווייהו השאלה ולענין להרויח יהי' הדבר
תלוי אי זה הוא אומנתו או שיש לו אומנות אחרת
בכדי שיפסל לעדות ועיין משנה סנהדרין פ"ג מ"ג
ואלו הן הפסולין (לעדות) המשחק בקוביא והמלוה
ברבית ומפריחי יונים ...
אמנם לצאת ולראות השחוק למי שנהנה מזה לפום
ריהטא ליכא איסור ברם ראיתי בשו"ת מוהר"י ברונא
סי' ע"א שנשאל בשחוק שעושים כזה וכתב ז"ל דלא
דמי לצידת חיות ועופות כי אין זה לשמחה אך ללמוד
אומנות ולקנות סוסים לרוץ בהם להנצל מאויבים
וכתב וכן ראיתי לבעלי מעשים, אך בהא מספקנא אם
מותר לילך ולראות כשמשמחים יחד לרכוב זה כנגד
זה במוטות וכדים שקורין לטעדין ע"כ.

ללמוד ממעשה זה ובפרט שהגוי הוא קרא הפסוק
המנחת חינוך מצוה תקמ"ו הביא מקור להלכה
מדברי הגמ' בשבועות לו דאסור לאדם לקלל עצמו
על יסוד הפסוק השמר לך ושמור נפשך מאד אולם
נראה שאין זה אלא אסמכתא שהרי פשט הכתוב
הוא לשמור שמירה רוחנית והנה בסה"מ להרמב"ם
לא מצאנו שמנה מצות שמירת הנפש כמצות עשה
או מצות ל"ת להשמר מסכנה ויש שהסמיכו החיוב
למצות מעקה או לכתוב לא תעמוד על דם רעך
וראיתי בזוהר הרקיע מל"ת אות קי"ח שפירש הפסוק
דהשמר לך ושמור נפשך לא רק לענין שכחת הר
סיני כמבואר בכתוב אלא לענין שמירת הנפש והביא
מהגמ' בשבועות שהמקלל עצמו לוקה מפסוק זה
וכן דברי הרמב"ם שכתב פסוק זה על מקלל וכתב
שאזהרה זו של שמירת הנפש מן התורה נכפלה בו
ונשמרתם מאד לנפשותיכם ומזה יצא איסור גילוי
והחמירו בו יותר מבשאר איסורים ועיין בציוני זיו
הזוהר שם שהביא בהרחבה דברי האחרונים בזה

### 55) שופטים טז:כה:לא

וַיְהִי כִּי טוֹב [כְּטוֹב] לִבָּם וַיֹּאמְרוּ קִרְאוּ לְשִׁמְשׁוֹן
וִישַׂחֶק־לָנוּ וַיִּקְרְאוּ לְשִׁמְשׁוֹן מִבֵּית הָאֲסִירִים
[הָאֲסוּרִים] וַיְצַחֵק לִפְנֵיהֶם וַיַּעֲמִידוּ אוֹתוֹ בֵּין
הָעַמּוּדִים: וַיֹּאמֶר שִׁמְשׁוֹן אֶל־הַנַּעַר הַמַּחֲזִיק בְּיָדוֹ
הַנִּיחָה אוֹתִי וַהֲמִשֵׁנִי [וַהֲמִישֵׁנִי] אֶת־הָעַמֻּדִים אֲשֶׁר
הַבַּיִת נָכוֹן עֲלֵיהֶם וְאֶשָּׁעֵן עֲלֵיהֶם: וְהַבַּיִת מָלֵא הָאֲנָשִׁים
וְהַנָּשִׁים וְשָׁמָּה כֹּל סַרְנֵי פְלִשְׁתִּים וְעַל־הַגָּג כִּשְׁלֹשֶׁת
אֲלָפִים אִישׁ וְאִשָּׁה הָרֹאִים בִּשְׂחוֹק שִׁמְשׁוֹן: וַיִּקְרָא
שִׁמְשׁוֹן אֶל־יְדֹוָד וַיֹּאמַר אֲדֹנָי יֱדֹוִד זָכְרֵנִי נָא וְחַזְּקֵנִי נָא אַךְ
הַפַּעַם הַזֶּה הָאֱלֹקִים וְאִנָּקְמָה נְקַם־אַחַת מִשְּׁתֵי עֵינַי
מִפְּלִשְׁתִּים: וַיִּלְפֹּת שִׁמְשׁוֹן אֶת־שְׁנֵי | עַמּוּדֵי הַתָּוֶךְ אֲשֶׁר
הַבַּיִת נָכוֹן עֲלֵיהֶם וַיִּסָּמֵךְ עֲלֵיהֶם אֶחָד בִּימִינוֹ וְאֶחָד
בִּשְׂמֹאלוֹ: וַיֹּאמֶר שִׁמְשׁוֹן תָּמוֹת נַפְשִׁי עִם־פְּלִשְׁתִּים
וַיֵּט בְּכֹחַ וַיִּפֹּל הַבַּיִת עַל־הַסְּרָנִים וְעַל־כָּל־הָעָם אֲשֶׁר
בּוֹ וַיִּהְיוּ הַמֵּתִים אֲשֶׁר הֵמִית בְּמוֹתוֹ רַבִּים מֵאֲשֶׁר הֵמִית
בְּחַיָּיו: וַיֵּרְדוּ אֶחָיו וְכָל־בֵּית אָבִיהוּ וַיִּשְׂאוּ אֹתוֹ וַיַּעֲלוּ |
וַיִּקְבְּרוּ אוֹתוֹ בֵּין צָרְעָה וּבֵין אֶשְׁתָּאֹל בְּקֶבֶר מָנוֹחַ אָבִיו
וְהוּא שָׁפַט אֶת־יִשְׂרָאֵל עֶשְׂרִים שָׁנָה:

### 56) ספר מכבים א:א:יד-יז

ויהי בעת ההיא ויצאו אנשים בני-בלייעל מקרב
ישראל, וידיחו את עם הארץ לאמור. הבה נכרתה
ברית את הגויים אשר סביבותינו, כי מאז אשר סרנו
מאחריהם מצאונו צרות רבו ורעות. וייטב הדבר
בעיני העם, וישלחו מלאכים אל המלך, ויצווה המלך
בידם ללכת בדרכי הגויים ובחוקותיהם. ויקימו בית
משחק בירושלים במשפט הגויים, ולא מלו עוד את
בניהם, ויעזבו את ברית הקודש ללכת בחוקותם,
ויתמכרו לעשות הרע בעיני ה'.

### 57) תהילים א:א, עבודה זרה יח:

אַשְׁרֵי־הָאִישׁ אֲשֶׁר לֹא הָלַךְ בַּעֲצַת רְשָׁעִים וּבְדֶרֶךְ

לקנות החכמות ולקנות מעלות המדות ומעלות
השכליות, עד שיגיע לתכלית ההיא ...

## 46) רמב"ם, מורה נבוכים ג:כו

כי אשר יעשה פעולות ההתעמלות להתמיד בו
הבריאות, כשחוק בכדור, או התאבקות, או משיכת
הידים, או עצירת הנשימה; או פעולות יכון בהם
הכתיבה, כעשיית הקולמוס ועשית הניר – יהיה אצל
אנשים סכלים פעולת שחוק, ואצל החכמים אינו
פעולת שחוק. והפעולה הטובה היא הפעולה אשר
עשאה הפועל לכונת תכלית נכבדת – רצוני לומר,
הכרחית או מועילה – ותגיע התכלית ההיא:

## 47) טעם ודעת, הרב משה שטרנבוך, ואתחנן ד:ט

ומכאן יש להזהיר לאותם השוקדים ביותר על
בריאות וחוסן גופם שלא יעשו העיקר טפל והטפל
יהיה להם לעיקר ולא ישכחו חובתם בשמירת מצות
הנפש בהתעסקם בשמירת גופם כי עיקר שמירת
הנפש בריבוי תורה ומצות היא והוא מזונו הרוחני
של האדם אשר בה תתקיים נפשו ואין הגוף אלא
אמצעי לקיום הנשמה בעולם החמרי ...

## 48) שיחת מוסר של הרב ישראל מאיר הכהן, בישיבת ראדין, תרס"ג

אל תרבו ללמוד הרבה יותר מדאי, צריך האדם
לשמור את הגוף שלא ייחלש, שלא יחלה, כי על כן
צריך לנוח ולהנפש לשאוף רוח צח.. צריך לטייל
לפנות ערב, או לשבת בבית ולנוח. וכשאפשר יש
לרחוץ בנהר כדי לחזק את הגוף, כי ההתמדה היתרה
הרי היא עצת היצר, לעמול יותר מדאי (בתורה)
למען ייחלש הגוף, ויהיה מוכרח אח"כ ליבטל
מתלמוד תורה כלל, אז יצא שכרו בהפסדו.

## 49) "תרבות הגוף עם בעימות עם הלכה", ד"ר אהרון ארנד,משרד החינוך, תרבות הגוף היהדות (תשס"ז) דף 47

הרב יעקב קמנצקי הקפיד על פעילות גופנית
סדירה.בצעירותו נודע כשחיין הטוב ביותר בישיבת
לומז'ה. השקפתו היתה: אם חייב האב ללמד את בנו
שחייה (קידושין כט ע"א) הרי חייב האדם בעצמו
לדעת לשחות, ואם כך – עליו להיטיב לשחות.
פעם הוא נשאל אם מתאים לבחור ישיבה לרכב על
אופניים. תשובתו: הלוואי והיה ברשותי זוג אופניים
בצעירותי, אזי לא הייתי חייב להרבות בהליכה כיוח
למען בריאותי ...

## 50) קידושין ל:

כשם שחייב להשיאו אשה, כך חייב ללמדו אומנות,
אם תורה היא כשם שחייב ללמדו תורה, כך חייב
ללמדו אומנות. ויש אומרים: אף להשיטו בנהר. מאי
טעמא? חיותיה הוא.

---

## 51) הרב קוק, קבצים "אורות" פיסקה פ

גדולה היא תביעתנו הגופנית גוף בריא אנו צריכים
התעסקנו הרבה בנפשיות שכחנו את קדושת הגוף
שכחנו שיש לנו בשר קודש לא פחות ממה שיש לנו
רוח הקודש עזבנו את החיים המעשיים

## 52) "תרבות הגוף עם בעימות עם הלכה", ד"ר אהרון ארנד,משרד החינוך, תרבות הגוף היהדות (תשס"ז) דף 47

הרב צבי יהודה קוק נהג לספר כי כשהיה אביו,
הראי"ה, בריגה וגר בדירה עם ר' יוסף יוזל הורוביץ
הסבא מנוברהרדוק, (בעל 'מדרגת האדם') ועם ר'
אהרון וולקין (בעל שו"ת 'זקן אהרון') היו שני
האחרונים מתאבקים לשם בריאות. רב שהעיד על
עיסוקו שלו בפעילות גופנית היה הרב שלמה גורן,
שהיה הרב הראשי לישראל (נפטר ב1994) שסיפר
באחד הראיונות שנתן לעיתון 'הצופה' כי הוא עושה
50 'שכיבות סמיכה' מדי יום. ו'החפץ חיים' שכבר
ראינו שייחס חשיבות לפעילות גופנית, שמעתי כי
העיד על עצמו שאינו עוסק בפעילות גופנית רק
מחמת עצלנותו.

## 53) "תרבות הגוף עם בעימות עם הלכה", ד"ר אהרון ארנד,משרד החינוך, תרבות הגוף היהדות (תשס"ז) דף 46

... אולם הרב רפאל הלפרין, מחבר 'אטלס עץ
חיים' ולשעבר אלוף העולם בהיאבקות ראווה,
מעיד באוטוביוגרפיה שלו כי בשנות ה־50, כשהגיע
לארצות הברית במסגרת קרבות היאבקות חופשית
שהיה משתתף בהם, בעת שביקר בליקווד אצל הרב
אהרון קוטלר, מגדולי התורה בארצות הברית, אמר
לו הרב: 'רבנים יש לנו הרבה, אבל גיבורים ובפרט
גיבור בן תורה אין לנו'. אדמו"רים אחרים אמרו לו
שבניצחונותיו בהיאבקות על הגויים הוא מקדש שם
שמים.

## 54) שו"ת בנין אב, הרב בקשי-דורון עג:א

מצות שמירת הגוף כמצות עשה שמירת הנפש
וזהירות מסכנה היא מהמחויבים החשובים ביותר
וכידוע שפיקוח נפש דוחה כל התורה והנה למרות
החומרא שבחיוב זה מקורו לא ברור רגילים
לקרוא את הפסוק (דברים ד:טו) "ונשמרתם מאוד
לנפשותיכם" כמצוה של שמירת הנפש או מהכתוב
"רק השמר לך ושמור נפשך" (שם ד:ט) אולם
כשנתבונן בפסוקים נראה שמורים הם על שמירה
רוחנית כפי שנאמר שם "רק השמר לך ושמור נפשך
מאוד פן תשכח את הדברים אשר ראו עיניך" ולא
על שמירת הגוף מסכנה אמנם מצאנו מקור מהגמ'
בברכות לב שהביאה מעשה בחסיד אחד שהיה
מתפלל בדרך וסיכן עצמו ואמר לו אותו קיסר כתוב
בתורתכם רק השמר לך וגו' ומבואר שמהפסוק זה יש
חיוב להישמר מסכנה אולם כתבו המפרשים שאין

**(37) משנה יומא ב:א-ב**

בראשונה, כל מי שרוצה לתרום את המזבח, תורם. ובזמן שהן מרובין, רצין ועולין בכבש, וכל הקודם את חברו בארבע אמות זכה. ואם היו שניהם שוין, הממונה אומר להם הצביעו. ומה הן מוציאין, אחת או שתים, ואין מוציאין אגודל במקדש: מעשה שהיו שניהם שוין ורצין ועולין בכבש, ודחף אחד מהן את חברו, ונפל ונשברה רגלו. וכיון שראו בית דין שבאין לידי סכנה, התקינו שלא יהו תורמין את המזבח אלא בפיס. ארבעה פיסות היו שם, וזה הפיס הראשון:

**(38) שו"ת אגרות משה, חושן משפט א:קד**

נשאלתי מאחד אם מותר להתפרנס ממשחק זריקת הכדורים שנקרא באל בלע"ז שיש לחוש לסכנה כדאירע לאחד מכמה אלפים שנסתכן. והשבתי שלע"ד יש להתיר דהא מפורש בב"מ דף קי"ב על קרא דואליו נושא נפשו מפני מה נתלה באילן ומסר את עצמו למיתה לא על שכרו אלמא דמותר להתפרנס אף כשאיכא חשש סכנה לאופן רחוק. וממילא אף כשיש חשש שיהרוג אחרים באופן רחוק כזה מותר דמאי שנא מחשש דליהרג בעצמו דגם להרוג את עצמו יש איסור לא תרצח ומ"מ מותר בחשש רחוק כזה לצורך פרנסה א"כ גם בחשש סכנת אחרים נמי יש להתיר בחשש רחוק כזה וגם אם לא נימא כן לא היה רשאי בעל האילן לשכור אותו. אבל ודאי מסתבר שהוא דוקא כשהאחר ג"כ נכנס לזה ברצונו דודאי אין לו רשות להכניס אף בספק הרחוק כזה את אלו שלא ידעו או לא רצו להכנס אף בספק רחוק כזה.

**(39) ערוך השולחן, אורח חיים תקיח:ח**

וכתב רבינו הרמ"א דמותר לשחוק בכדור אפילו ברשות הרבים אף על גב שאינו אלא טיול בעלמא עכ"ל ויש מתרעמים על זה שאין זה שמחה וטיול רק לקטנים ולא לגדולים [שם ומג"א סק"ד בשם יש"ש] ובאמת אין זה תרעומות דכיון דחביב עליו לפי דעתו השפלה איך נמנע ממנו עוד כתב דאם הניח עירוב מותר לטלטל ולהוציא כל שיש לו תורת כלי אף על פי שאינן לצורך היום כלל עכ"ל דלא עדיף יום טוב משבת אבל בלא עירוב אפילו מחצר לחצר אסור שלא לצורך כלל [מג"א סק"ד] ...

**(40) דברים ד:ט, טו**

רַק הִשָּׁמֶר לְךָ וּשְׁמֹר נַפְשְׁךָ מְאֹד פֶּן תִּשְׁכַּח אֶת הַדְּבָרִים אֲשֶׁר רָאוּ עֵינֶיךָ וּפֶן יָסוּרוּ מִלְּבָבְךָ כֹּל יְמֵי חַיֶּיךָ וְהוֹדַעְתָּם לְבָנֶיךָ וְלִבְנֵי בָנֶיךָ: וְנִשְׁמַרְתֶּם מְאֹד לְנַפְשֹׁתֵיכֶם כִּי לֹא רְאִיתֶם כָּל תְּמוּנָה בְּיוֹם דִּבֶּר ד' אֲלֵיכֶם בְּחֹרֵב מִתּוֹךְ הָאֵשׁ:

**(41) אורות החומש, פרשת ואתחנן, ד:טו**

ומה קשור שמירה זאת לזכור שלא לעשות פסל

---

תמונת כל סמל לשמירת הנפש והגוף מסכנות והמהרש"א ז"ל הקשה כן ונראה לומר שאותו שר אציל רמז בזה שהנה הפסוק קורא לזה שמירת הנפש שלא לשכח מה שראינו במעמד סיני ואכן כן הוא שמירת הנפש והרוח היא אותו דבר כשמירת הגוף מסכנות לשכח את מעמד ההוד וההדר של מעמד הר סיני של בכל דרכיך דעהו והוא יישר אורחותיך זהו שמירת הנפש והיא שמירת הגוף וכן להישמר מתמונת סמל שאין ע"ז שאין אידיאלים אחרים היא שמירת הגוף והנפש גם יחד וע"כ נלמדים הם אחד משני כוונתו זוהי כוונתו של אותו שר ומכאן למד הרמב"ם שדברים המסוכנים לגוף אסורים ונלמדים מפסוק זה זכירת מעמד הר סיני וזכירה שלא להוסיף אידיאלים אחרים הם השמירה מאד לגוף ולנפש הם הכוחות הפנימיים השמורים וכמוסים עמנו בדרך עץ החיים וע"ז השיב לו אותו חסיד שמרתי באותו רגע את הנפש ממש שהרי דברתי עם הקב"ה וממילא נשמר גם הגוף כפי שראינו מהמעשה ממש וע"כ נתפייס אותו שר

**(42) ישעיהו נח:יא**

וְנָחֲךָ ד' תָּמִיד וְהִשְׂבִּיעַ בְּצַחְצָחוֹת נַפְשֶׁךָ וְעַצְמֹתֶיךָ יַחֲלִיץ וְהָיִיתָ כְּגַן רָוֶה וּכְמוֹצָא מַיִם אֲשֶׁר לֹא יְכַזְּבוּ מֵימָיו:

**(43) רמב"ם, הלכות דעות ד:א**

הואיל והיות הגוף בריא ושלם מדרכי השם הוא, שהרי אי אפשר שיבין או ידע דבר מידיעת הבורא והוא חולה, לפיכך צריך להרחיק אדם עצמו מדברים המאבדין את הגוף, ולהנהיג עצמו בדברים המבריאין והמחלימים ...

**(44) רמב"ם, הלכות דעות ד:יד-טו**

ועוד כלל אחר אמרו בבריאות הגוף, כל זמן שאדם מתעמל ויגע הרבה ואינו שבע ומעיו רפין אין חולי בא עליו וכחו מתחזק, ואפילו אוכל מאכלות הרעים. וכל מי שהוא יושב לבטח ואינו מתעמל, או מי שמשהא נקביו, או מי שמעיו קשין, אפילו אכל מאכלות טובים ושמר עצמו על פי הרפואה, כל ימיו יהיו מכאובים וכחו תשש, ואכילה גסה לכל גוף כל אדם כמו סם המות, והוא עיקר לכל החלאים, ורוב החלאים שבאים על האדם אינם אלא או מפני מאכלים רעים, או מפני שהוא ממלא בטנו ואוכל אכילה גסה אפילו ממאכלים טובים, הוא ששלמה אמר בחכמתו שומר פיו ולשונו שומר מצרות נפשו, כלומר שומר פיו מלאכול מאכל רע או משבוע ולשונו מלדבר אלא בצרכיו.

**(45) רמב"ם, הקדמה לשמונה פרקים**

... שישים הכונה באכילתו, בשתיתו, במשגלו, שנתו, יקיצתו, תנועתו ומנוחתו בבריאות גופו לבד, והכונה בבריאות גופו, שתמצא הנפש כליה בריאים ושלמים

---

להתאפק עוד ומכרתים אז י"ב חדשים בי"ג ישנים ...

Kolnische Schillinge .1 (קולוניא דינרי)

Turnier, turnay .2 (מלחמה בשלום שנלחמו הפרשים [Ritter] זה בזה).

שיהודי אשכנז השתתפו בטורני רוח לא נודע עד עתה רק ממאה החמש עשרה למספרם ... ועתה אנו רואים שהיה כן כבר במאה ה שתים עשרה למספרם.

### 23) תוספות, ביצה יב. ד"ה "חג"

... דשרי גם טיול דהא אשכחן נמי דמשחקין בכדור שקורין פלוט"א בלע"ז ביו"ט ברה"ר אע"ג דליכא אלא טיול

### Encyclopedia Judaica 15:292–293 (24

"In 1386 there were Jewish tourneys in Wiesenfeld, Germany. In the 15th century, competitions were held in Augsburg, Germany, in running, jumping, throwing and bowling in which Jews also participated ... in the same century, at the popular festival initiated in Rome, sports competitions were also included: Monday was for youth, Tuesday was for Jews (under 20 years of age), Wednesday for older boys, etc.... It is known that Jews distinguished themselves in these games in 1487, 1502 and 1595. There is even a song about Jewish runners, composed in 1513 ... In the 16th century, there was a famous Austrian Jew by the name of Ott who was outstanding at the Augsburg games and was even invited by the court of the Austrian prince in order to train the courtiers."

### 25) שולחן ערוך, אורח חיים שח:מה

אסור לשחוק בשבת ויו"ט בכדור: הגה ויש מתירין ונהגו להקל (תוס' פ"ק דביצה) :

### 26) שולחן ערוך, אורח חיים תקיח:א

הגה (ביום טוב).. מותר לשחוק בכדור אפי' בר"ה אע"ג שאינו אלא טיול בעלמא (תוס' ור' ירוחם) ואם הניח עירוב מותר לטלטל ולהוציא כי כל שיש לו תורת כלי אע"פ שאינו לצורך היום כלל (ר"ן פ"ב דביצה)

### 27) משנה ברורה על שולחן ערוך, אורח חיים תקיח, ס"ק ט

בכדור אפילו בר"ה – ר"ל אע"ג דעי"ז רגיל להעביר ד"א ממקום למקום אפ"ה מותר דהוא בכלל טיול ושמחת יו"ט ורש"ל כתב דדבר תימה הוא להתיר זה דאין בו צורך היום כלל אלא שחוק של ילדים והנח להם אבל לגדולים שנוהגין כן מנהג רע הוא דאין זה שמחה וטיול אלא שיחת ילדים וקלות ראש ובלא"ה אין דין זה מוסכם לכו"ע דדעת המחבר לאסור

---

כמבואר לעיל בסימן ש"ח סעיף מ"ה.

### 28) תהילים קד:כו, ירמיהו מח:כו

שם אניות יהלכון לויתן זה צרת לשחק בו:
השקיתו כי על־ד' הגדיל וספק מואב בקיאו והיה לשחק גם־הוא:
פתיתני ד' ואפת חזקתני ותוכל הייתי לשחק כל־היום כלה לעג לי:

### 29) קהלת י':ט, תהילים קכו:א-ב

לשחוק עשים לחם ויין ישמח חיים והכסף יענה את־הכל
שיר המעלות בשוב ד' את־שיבת ציון היינו כחלמים:
אז ימלא שחוק פינו ולשוננו רנה אז יאמרו בגוים הגדיל ד' לעשות עם־אלה:

### 30) שופטים כז:טז-טז

והבית מלא האנשים והנשים ושמה כל סרני פלשתים ועל־הגג כשלשת אלפים איש ואשה הראים בשחוק שמשון:

### 31) משלי י':כג

כשחוק לכסיל עשות זמה וחכמה לאיש תבונה:

### 32) בראשית כא:ט, שמות לב:ו, בראשית יט:יד

ותרא שרה את־בן־הגר המצרית אשר־ילדה לאברהם מצחק:
וישכימו ממחרת ויעלו עלת ויגשו שלמים וישב העם לאכל ושתו ויקמו לצחק:
ויצא לוט וידבר | אל־חתניו | לקחי בנתיו ויאמר קומו צאו מן־המקום הזה כי־משחית ד' את־העיר ויהי כמצחק בעיני חתניו:

### 33) גיטין מז.

ריש לקיש זבין נפשיה ללודאי, שקל בהדיה חייתא וגלגלתא, אמר: גמירי, דיומא בתרא כל דבעי מינייהו עבדי ליה, כי היכי דליחול אדמיה.

### 34) שבת קיט:

אמר אביי: לא חרבה ירושלים אלא בשביל שחללו בה את השבת ...

### 35) מדרש, איכה רבה ב:ד

טור שמעון הוה מפיק תלת מאה גרבין ולמה חרבו אי תימא מן הזנונות והלא לא היתה אלא ריבה אחת והוציאוה משם א"ר הונא משום שהיו משחקין בכדור בשבת

### 36) ירושלמי, תענית כד:

טור שמעון הוה מפיק תלת מאון דגרבין דמרקיע לקייטא כל ערובות שובא. ולמה חרב יש אומר מפני הזנונות וי"א שהיו משחקין בכדור

מיד התינוקות שומטין את לוליבהן ואוכלין אתרוגיהן:

### 13) סוכה מו:

איתיביה ריש לקיש לרבי יוחנן: מיד תינוקות שומטין את לוליבהן ואוכלין אתרוגיהן. מאי לאו הדין לגדולים לא, תינוקות דוקא. איכא דאמרי, איתיביה רבי יוחנן לריש לקיש: מיד התינוקות שומטין את לוליבהן ואוכלין אתרוגיהן. תינוקות אין, גדולים לא הוא הדין דאפילו גדולים, והאי דקתני תינוקות אורחא דמלתא קתני.

### 14) רש"י על סוכה מה,, מו:

מיד תינוקות שומטין את לוליבהן – הגדולים שומטין את לוליבי הקטנים מידם בשביעי.
ואוכלין אתרוגיהן – של תינוקות, ואין בדבר לא משום גזל, ולא משום דרכי שלום, שכך נהגו מחמת שמחה.
מיד תינוקות שומטין כו' – בשביעי קאי במתניתין, ויש מפרשים: מיד תינוקות, כלומר: מיד, אחר סיום מצות לולב התינוקות שומטין את לוליבהן ...

### 15) תוספות על סוכה מה. ד"ה "מיד"

מיד תינוקות שומטין לוליבהן – לולבי התינוקות שומטין הגדולים מידן ואוכלין אתרוגיהן של תינוקות ואין בדבר גזל ולא משום דרכי שלום אלא שכך נהגו בו מחמת שמחה כך פי' בקונט' ... ועוד יש לומר דמתני' לא איירי כלל שיחטפו הגדולים מידן של תינוקות אלא מיד כלומר לאלתר התינוקות שומטין לוליבי עצמן מתוך הערבה לפי שהלולב ארוך ושוחקין בו ואתרוגיהן היו אוכלין ...

### 16) סנהדרין עז:

ותנא תונא: כגון אלו המשחקין בכדור שהרגו, במזיד נהרגין, בשוגג גולין.... תני רב תחליפא בר מערבא קמיה דרבי אבהו: כגון אלו המשחקין בכדור שהרגו, תוך ארבע אמות פטור, חוץ לארבע אמות חייב. אמר ליה רבינא לרב אשי: היכי דמי? אי דקא ניחא ליה אפילו פורתא נמי. אי דלא ניחא ליה אפילו טובא נמי לא אמר ליה: סתם משחקין בכדור, כמה (דעייל טפי) (מסורת הש"ס: דאזלי מיניה) מינה ניחא ליה.

### 17) פירוש רש"י על סנהדרין עז:

כגון אלו המשחקין בכדור שהרגו – רגילין תינוקות להכות הכדור בכותל בכח כדי שתתחזור לאחוריה הרבה, ולאחר שזורק הוא רץ וחבירו אוחז את הכדור ומכה אותו בה אם היה יכול לכוון ההוא דזרק בכותל, אשמעינן תנא נתכוין שתתהרוג את חבירו בחזרתה לאחוריה ויש בו כדי להמית חייב. **כגון אלו המשחקין בכדור שהרגו תוך ארבע אמות פטורין** – אם היה המוכה עומד בתוך ארבע אמות של

---

כותל ולא הספיקה לחזור ארבע אמות עד שמצאתו והרגתו פטור הזורק מגלות.

### 18) משנה שבת כב:ו

סכין וממשמשין בבני מעים. אבל לא מתעמלין ולא מתגרדין. אין יורדין לקורדימא.

### 19) ספר שבולי הלקט ענין שבת סימן קכא

צדקיהו בן אברהם הרופא 1210-1280
שאלו את ר' אליעזר הכדור והאמום ומשקולת קטנה ופירש רבינו שלמה זצ"ל כדור פילוטא מחופה עור ומליאה מתוכה שיער של איל בדוחק והאמום של עור הוא כעין מנעל וממלא אותו שיער ובו היו עושין מנעלים כעין שעושין רצענין בדפוס של עץ ונחלקו בהן ר' אליעזר וחכמים בסדר טהרות בשני דברים חכמים אומרים אינם מקבלין טומאה ... אבל אלו הכדורים שלנו אפי' כלי לא חשיבי ומחשבת השחוק שחישב לשחק בו לא משוי ליה כלי מ"מ בין שיש תורת כלי עליו בין שאין תורת כלי עליו נראה שאסור לשחק בו ולטלטלו בשבת ויום טוב שהרי אין צריך בטילטולו ואפי' לכסות בו על צליחותו אינו ראוי דהא ממאיס על ידי ששוחקים בו ומטניף בטיט ועפר וכן כדור של עץ אסור לטלטלה ולשחק בה וכן מצינו במדרש איכה טור שמעון הוי מפיק תלת מאה גרבין דמרקוע בכל ערובת שבא לאילין קייטיא ולמה חרב אין תימר משום זנות והלא ריבה אחת היתה שם והוציאוה משם ולמה חרב ולמה אמר רב הונא על ידי שהיו משחקים בכדור בשבת:

### 20) תוספות על סוכה מה. ד"ה "מיד"

מיד תינוקות שומטין לוליבהן – ... ויש ללמוד מכאן לאותן בחורים שרוכבים בסוסים לקראת חתן ונלחמים זה עם זה וקורעין בגדו של חבירו או מקלקל לו סוסו שהן פטורין כך נהגו מחמת שמחת חתן ...

### 21) אור זרוע, חלק ב, הלכות סוכה ולולב שטו

... כתב רבי' שמשון יש ללמוד מיכן לאותן הבחורים הרוכבים בסוסים לקראת חתן ונלחמים זה עם זה וקורע בגדו של חבירו או מקלקל [לו סוסו] שהן פטורין הואיל וכבר נהגו מחמת שמחת חתן

### 22) שו"ת ראבי"ה תתרכ, בספר מבוא האבי"ה

ראובן תבע שמעון לדין ואמר באחי אליך להשאיל שריונך להחזיר לך לסוף שבועיים או כ"ו דינר קולניש 1) ישנים והנחתי לך משכון עליהם, וכשהחזרתי מן הטורניי 2) אמרתי לך שאבד השיריון והוצרכתי לאותו משכון למקצחו ונתתי לך י"ד דינר קולניש מטבע חדש בחשבון. והנה אני תובע לפרות משכוני י"ז דינרים חדשים והעודף ואתן לך כ"ז דינר קולניש. השיב שמעון: הלא מזה החילוף יש כבר יותר מחצי שנה. ואז היה מוטל עליך לפרוע לי חובי לאלתר והיית דוחה אותי מיום ליום עד כי לא יכולתי

# SOURCES ON SPORTS AND JUDAISM

### 1) שמואל א' כ:כ, איוב טז:יב, איכה ג:יב

וַאֲנִי שְׁלֹשֶׁת הַחִצִּים צִדָּה אוֹרֶה לְשַׁלַּח־לִי לְמַטָּרָה:
שָׁלֵו הָיִיתִי וַיְפַרְפְּרֵנִי וְאָחַז בְּעָרְפִּי וַיְפַצְפְּצֵנִי וַיְקִימֵנִי
לוֹ לְמַטָּרָה:
דָּרַךְ קַשְׁתּוֹ וַיַּצִּיבֵנִי כַּמַּטָּרָא לַחֵץ:

### 2) שופטים כ:טז, שמואל א' יז:מ, זכריה ט:טו

מִכֹּל הָעָם הַזֶּה שְׁבַע מֵאוֹת אִישׁ בָּחוּר אִטֵּר יַד־יְמִינוֹ
כָּל־זֶה קֹלֵעַ בָּאֶבֶן אֶל־הַשַּׂעֲרָה וְלֹא יַחֲטִא:
וַיִּקַּח מַקְלוֹ בְּיָדוֹ וַיִּבְחַר־לוֹ חֲמִשָּׁה חַלֻּקֵי אֲבָנִים |
מִן־הַנַּחַל וַיָּשֶׂם אֹתָם בִּכְלִי הָרֹעִים אֲשֶׁר־לוֹ וּבַיַּלְקוּט
וְקַלְעוֹ בְיָדוֹ וַיִּגַּשׁ אֶל־הַפְּלִשְׁתִּי:
ד' צְבָאוֹת יָגֵן עֲלֵיהֶם וְאָכְלוּ וְכָבְשׁוּ אַבְנֵי־קֶלַע וְשָׁתוּ
הָמוּ כְּמוֹ־יָיִן וּמָלְאוּ כַּמִּזְרָק כְּזָוִיּוֹת מִזְבֵּחַ:

### 3) תהילים יט:ו

וְהוּא כְּחָתָן יֹצֵא מֵחֻפָּתוֹ יָשִׂישׂ כְּגִבּוֹר לָרוּץ אֹרַח:

### 4) תהילים יח:ל

כִּי־בְךָ אָרֻץ גְּדוּד וּבֵאלֹקַי אֲדַלֶּג־שׁוּר:

### 5) בראשית כט:ו-י'

וַיֹּאמֶר לָהֶם הֲשָׁלוֹם לוֹ וַיֹּאמְרוּ שָׁלוֹם וְהִנֵּה רָחֵל בִּתּוֹ
בָּאָה עִם־הַצֹּאן: וַיֹּאמֶר הֵן עוֹד הַיּוֹם גָּדוֹל לֹא־עֵת
הֵאָסֵף הַמִּקְנֶה הַשְׁקוּ הַצֹּאן וּלְכוּ רְעוּ: וַיֹּאמְרוּ לֹא נוּכַל
עַד אֲשֶׁר יֵאָסְפוּ כָּל־הָעֲדָרִים וְגָלְלוּ אֶת־הָאֶבֶן מֵעַל פִּי
הַבְּאֵר וְהִשְׁקִינוּ הַצֹּאן: עוֹדֶנּוּ מְדַבֵּר עִמָּם וְרָחֵל |
בָּאָה עִם־הַצֹּאן אֲשֶׁר לְאָבִיהָ כִּי רֹעָה הִוא: וַיְהִי כַּאֲשֶׁר רָאָה
יַעֲקֹב אֶת־רָחֵל בַּת־לָבָן אֲחִי אִמּוֹ וְאֶת־צֹאן לָבָן אֲחִי
אִמּוֹ וַיִּגַּשׁ יַעֲקֹב וַיָּגֶל אֶת־הָאֶבֶן מֵעַל פִּי הַבְּאֵר וַיַּשְׁקְ
אֶת־צֹאן לָבָן אֲחִי אִמּוֹ:

### 6) שמות ב:טז-יט

וּלְכֹהֵן מִדְיָן שֶׁבַע בָּנוֹת וַתָּבֹאנָה וַתִּדְלֶנָה וַתְּמַלֶּאנָה
אֶת־הָרְהָטִים לְהַשְׁקוֹת צֹאן אֲבִיהֶן: וַיָּבֹאוּ הָרֹעִים
וַיְגָרְשׁוּם וַיָּקָם מֹשֶׁה וַיּוֹשִׁעָן וַיַּשְׁקְ אֶת־צֹאנָם: וַתָּבֹאנָה
אֶל־רְעוּאֵל אֲבִיהֶן וַיֹּאמֶר מַדּוּעַ מִהַרְתֶּן בֹּא הַיּוֹם:
וַתֹּאמַרְןָ אִישׁ מִצְרִי הִצִּילָנוּ מִיַּד הָרֹעִים וְגַם־דָּלֹה דָלָה
לָנוּ וַיַּשְׁקְ אֶת־הַצֹּאן:

### 7) שופטים טו:טו-טז

וַיִּמְצָא לְחִי־חֲמוֹר טְרִיָּה וַיִּשְׁלַח יָדוֹ וַיִּקָּחֶהָ וַיַּךְ־בָּהּ
אֶלֶף אִישׁ: וַיֹּאמֶר שִׁמְשׁוֹן בִּלְחִי הַחֲמוֹר חֲמוֹר חֲמֹרָתָיִם
בִּלְחִי הַחֲמוֹר הִכֵּיתִי אֶלֶף אִישׁ:

### 8) שמואל א' ט:ב ופירוש מלבי"ם

וְלוֹ־הָיָה בֵן וּשְׁמוֹ שָׁאוּל בָּחוּר וָטוֹב וְאֵין אִישׁ מִבְּנֵי

---

יִשְׂרָאֵל טוֹב מִמֶּנּוּ מִשִּׁכְמוֹ וָמַעְלָה גָּבֹהַּ מִכָּל־הָעָם:
... וְכֵן הָיָה שָׁלֵם בְּתָארוֹ וְיָפְיוֹ כִּי הָיָה מִשִּׁכְמוֹ וּמַעְלָה
גָּבֹהַּ מִכָּל הָעָם – עַד שֶׁהָיָה מְיֻחָד בִּגְבוּרָה (מִצַּד
אָבִיו) וּבְטוֹב הַמִּדּוֹת וּבְתוֹאַר הַקּוֹמָה וְיִצְלַח לַמְּלוּכָה:

### 9) שמואל ב' ב:יב-יז

וַיֵּצֵא אַבְנֵר בֶּן־נֵר וְעַבְדֵי אִישׁ־בֹּשֶׁת בֶּן־שָׁאוּל מִמַּחֲנַיִם
גִּבְעוֹנָה: וְיוֹאָב בֶּן־צְרוּיָה וְעַבְדֵי דָוִד יָצְאוּ וַיִּפְגְּשׁוּם
עַל־בְּרֵכַת גִּבְעוֹן יַחְדָּו וַיֵּשְׁבוּ אֵלֶּה עַל־הַבְּרֵכָה מִזֶּה
וְאֵלֶּה עַל־הַבְּרֵכָה מִזֶּה: וַיֹּאמֶר אַבְנֵר אֶל־יוֹאָב יָקוּמוּ
נָא הַנְּעָרִים וִישַׂחֲקוּ לְפָנֵינוּ וַיֹּאמֶר יוֹאָב יָקֻמוּ: וַיָּקֻמוּ
וַיַּעַבְרוּ בְמִסְפָּר שְׁנֵים עָשָׂר לְבִנְיָמִן וּלְאִישׁ בֹּשֶׁת בֶּן־
שָׁאוּל וּשְׁנֵים עָשָׂר מֵעַבְדֵי דָוִד: וַיַּחֲזִקוּ אִישׁ | בְּרֹאשׁ
רֵעֵהוּ וְחַרְבּוֹ בְּצַד רֵעֵהוּ וַיִּפְּלוּ יַחְדָּו וַיִּקְרָא לַמָּקוֹם
הַהוּא חֶלְקַת הַצֻּרִים אֲשֶׁר בְּגִבְעוֹן: וַתְּהִי הַמִּלְחָמָה
קָשָׁה עַד־מְאֹד בַּיּוֹם הַהוּא וַיִּנָּגֶף אַבְנֵר וְאַנְשֵׁי יִשְׂרָאֵל
לִפְנֵי עַבְדֵי דָוִד:

### 10) משנה יומא ב:א-ב

בָּרִאשׁוֹנָה, כָּל מִי שֶׁרוֹצֶה לִתְרוֹם אֶת הַמִּזְבֵּחַ, תּוֹרֵם.
וּבִזְמַן שֶׁהֵן מְרֻבִּין, רָצִין וְעוֹלִין בַּכֶּבֶשׁ, וְכָל הַקּוֹדֵם
אֶת חֲבֵרוֹ בְּאַרְבַּע אַמּוֹת זָכָה. וְאִם הָיוּ שְׁנֵיהֶם שָׁוִין,
הַמְמֻנֶּה אוֹמֵר לָהֶם הַצְבִּיעוּ. וּמָה הֵן מוֹצִיאִין, אַחַת
אוֹ שְׁתַּיִם, וְאֵין מוֹצִיאִין אֲגוּדָל בַּמִּקְדָּשׁ:
מַעֲשֶׂה שֶׁהָיוּ שְׁנֵיהֶם שָׁוִין וְרָצִין וְעוֹלִין בַּכֶּבֶשׁ, וְדָחַף
אֶחָד מֵהֶן אֶת חֲבֵרוֹ, וְנָפַל וְנִשְׁבְּרָה רַגְלוֹ. וְכֵיוָן שֶׁרָאוּ
בֵית דִּין שֶׁבָּאִין לִידֵי סַכָּנָה, הִתְקִינוּ שֶׁלֹּא יְהוּ תוֹרְמִין
אֶת הַמִּזְבֵּחַ אֶלָּא בְּפַיִס. אַרְבָּעָה פְיָסוֹת הָיוּ שָׁם, וְזֶה
הַפַּיִס הָרִאשׁוֹן:

### 11) משנה כלים כח:א, י"ד כג:א

שָׁלֹשׁ עַל שָׁלֹשׁ שֶׁנִּתְּנָה בְכַדּוּר. אוֹ שֶׁעֲשָׂאָהּ כַּדּוּר בִּפְנֵי
עַצְמָהּ. טְהוֹרָה. אֲבָל שְׁלֹשָׁה עַל שְׁלֹשָׁה שֶׁנִּתְּנוּ בְכַדּוּר.
טָמֵא. עֲשָׂאוֹ כַּדּוּר בִּפְנֵי עַצְמוֹ. טָהוֹר. מִפְּנֵי שֶׁהִתְפַּר
מֵעַמְטוֹ:
הַכַּדּוּר וְהַפְקַעַת שֶׁל גֶּמִי שֶׁנִּתְּנָן עַל פִּי הֶחָבִית. אִם
מֵרַח מִן הַצְּדָדִין. לֹא הַצִּיל. עַד שֶׁיְּמָרַח מִלְמַעְלָן
וּמִלְמַטָּן. וְכֵן בַּמְּטַלִּית שֶׁל בֶּגֶד. הָיְתָה שֶׁל נִיר אוֹ שֶׁל
עוֹר וְקֹשַׁר...ה בַּמְּשִׁיחָה. אִם מֵרַח מִן הַצְּדָדִין. הִצִּיל.
הַכַּדּוּר וְהָאֵמוּם וְהַקְּמֵיעַ וְהַתְּפִלִּין שֶׁנִּקְרְעוּ. הַנּוֹגֵעַ
בָּהֶן. טָמֵא. וּבַמֶּה שֶׁבְּתוֹכוֹ. טָהוֹר. הָאֻכָּף שֶׁנִּקְרַע.
הַנּוֹגֵעַ בַּמֶּה שֶׁבְּתוֹכוֹ. טָמֵא. מִפְּנֵי שֶׁהִתְפַּר מֵחַבְּרוֹ:

### 12) משנה סוכה ד:ז-ח

... רַבִּי יוֹחָנָן בֶּן בְּרוֹקָה אוֹמֵר, חֲרִיּוֹת שֶׁל דֶּקֶל הָיוּ
מְבִיאִין וְחוֹבְטִין אוֹתָן בַּקַּרְקַע בְּצִדֵּי הַמִּזְבֵּחַ, וְאוֹתוֹ
הַיּוֹם נִקְרָא יוֹם חִבּוּט חֲרִיּוֹת:

אסור אף לאנשים לא שייך לאסור בזה משום מראית
העין, דלא איכפת לן שיודעו האמת שלאנשים מותר
כיון שעדיין לא קבלו שבת.

### 46) שו"ת אגרות משה, אורח חיים ב:מ

ובדבר אם מותר לאכול ברעסטאראנס שמכינים שם
רק מאכלי חלב אבל הם של אנשים מחללי שבת, הנה
אף שם אפשר להיות כמה מאכלות אסורות כדגים
טמאים, וגם השומן שממטגנים בהם אפשר שהם
מבהמות אסורות ונבלות, וגם גבינות אסורות, ויש
גם דברים שאסורים משום בשולי עכו"ם, ולכן אף
ליכנס לשם לאכול דברים הידועים שאין בהם שום
חשש איסור יש לאסור מפני מראית עין וחשד. אך
אם הוא רעב ביותר שמצטער טובא ואין שם מקום
אחר לאכול יכול ליכנס לשם לאכול דברים הידועים
למותרין, אבל צריך שיהיה בצנעא דבמקום צערא
ופסידא לא גזרו רבנן כדאיתא בכתובות דף ס'. והיינו
שלא יהיו מבחוץ מכיריו, דלפני אלו הנמצאים בפנים
הרי יראו שלוקח רק דברים הידועים למותרים. ואם
יש שם מבחוץ מכיריו צריך לומר להם שמצטער
טובא ולכן נכנס לשם ליקח דבר הידוע למותר. אבל
בלא מצטער טובא אין ליכנס לשם כלל.

### 47) שו"ת יביע אומרת חלק ו, יורה דעה ח

אודות מה שנהגו כעת בכמה בתי מלון להגיש
לאורחים אחר ארוחה בשרית, כוס חלב סינטטי
שאין בו כל תערובת של חלב אמיתי, אלא הוא חלב
צמחוני בלבד, האם אין לחוש בזה משום מראית

---

העין של התיירים המתגוררים במלון שיחשבו
שהותרה הרצועה לשתות חלב אחר מאכלי בשר
בסעודה אחת.

... שכל שאין האיסור ניכר בעת אכילתו או שתייתו
לא חיישינן משום מראית העין ... שאם יש היכר
מצד הקערות והצלוחות שמגישים בהם חלב שקדים,
אחר מאכלי הבשר, ומעלין אותם עם מגדנות ופירות,
מותר, והויל והדבר ניכר מצד מקומו ושעתו שהוא
חלב שקדים, יותר מהנחת שקדים עמו ... מסקנא
דדינא שהמנהג הזה בדין יסודו, ואין להחמיר עליהם
להצריכם שיתנו שקדים עם החלב הצמחוני הזה.

### 48) חתם סופר, ליקוטי שו"ת ו:נט

... ואני הרהרתי כמה פעמים אם אפשר שקיים אדם
בעולם מקרא זה על מתכונתו ואולי על זה כייל
שהע"ה קהלת ז' כ' אדם אין צדיק בארץ אשר יעשה
טוב ולא יחטא רצתו לומר שאפי' בעשייתו כל טוב
א"א שלא יחטא עכ"פ באופן השני הנ"ל ביציאת ידי
הבריות ואינני כדי להזכיר אבותינו הקדושים מ"מ
תורה היא וחוכך אני בבני גד וראובן אשר עליהם
נאמר מקרא זה והייתם נקיים מה' ומ"מ לא
יצאו ידי חובת המקרא הזה בשלימות כי על לא חנם
גלו ראשונה לפני כל השבטים וקראו חז"ל עליהם
מקרא הזה משלי כ' כ"א נחלה מבוהלת בראשונה
ואחריתה לא תבורך עיין ברבה פ' מטות (כב:ט)

בהכאת המטבע (הגהות מיימוני פ"ו וע"ל סימן
רנ"ב) ויזהר שלא ישב הישראל אצל הא"י בשבת
כשעושק ' (ו') במלאכתו במטבע או בקבלת המכס
(מרדכי פ"ק דשבת) :

### 40) כתובות ס.

תניא, נחום איש גליא אומר: צינור שעלו בו קשקשין,
ממעכן ברגלו בצנעא בשבת ואינו חושש. מאי
טעמא? מתקן כלאחר יד הוא, ובמקום פסידא לא
גזרו בה רבנן. אמר רב יוסף: הלכה כנחום איש גליא.

### 41) משנה ברורה לה על שולחן ערוך,
אורח חיים רמד

**לא חששו-** דע דמשמע מכל הפוסקים דלא התירו
אפי' במקום הפסד גדול אלא באופן זה שצייר השו"ע
דהיינו או בקיבולת או שמשכיר לו את גוף הריוח
דבכל זה העובד גלולים דנפשיה קעביד אבל
בשכיר יום ממש אסור בכל גווני ומזה תדע שאותן
האנשים המחזיקים בית משקה שלוקחין מע"ש איזה
א"י בביתן על יום השבת לעסוק במכירת המשקה
(לה) שלא כדין הם עושין דאף אם נחשוב מניעת
ריוח יום השבת להפסד גדול מ"מ הלא לא התירו
בשכיר יום ממש וגם דאולי הוא רק בכלל מניעת
הריוח כמו שכתבו האחרונים לענין תנור ומרחץ
וע"כ אין להתיר אלא באופן שציירו השו"ע והרמ"א
או (לו) שיקנה לו מע"ש כל הדברים שנותן לו למכור
(לז) ואף דעכ"פ עדיין העסק נקרא על שם ישראל זה
מותר משום פסידא ולפי מה שכתבנו לקמיה בשם
הט"ז יהיה מותר בזה לישראל לישב מרחוק ולשמור
שלא יגנוב האי"י מהעסק אך שיזהר שלא יתערב
בהעסק ושלא ידבר עמו כלום מעניינים ההם והוא
דבר שקשה ליזהר להתיר כשיושב שם אך
העולם נוהגים להתיר והנח להם מוטב שיהיו שוגגין
ואל יהיו מזידין [תו"ש] והבוטח בה' ואינו מחפש
צדדי קולות על שבת אשריו:

### 42) פרי חדש על שולחן ערוך אורח חיים תסא:ב
(1656-1695)

עוד כתב בתשובה הנזכר שמותר לעשות סופגנין
ממצה אפוי' וכת' בס' כנה"ג שלעשות פאשטוליש
הנהוגות בכל שבת זכר למן ... ואף במצה אפויה
משום מעשה שהיה שאשת חבר עשתה כן ושכינתה'
חשבה שהיה קמח ממש ולמחר טגנה דגים בקמח
ממש ולפיכך יש' לאסור מפני מראית חיין ואני אומ'
שהכל מותר מן הדין ואין לנו לגזור גזירות מדעתנו
ומה בכך אם אשה אחת טעתה ... והרי בש"ס לא
חששו למראית העין מהא דגרסינן בפרק כ"ש לא למחי
אינש קדרה בקמחא דאבשונא דילמא לא בשיל שפיר
ואתי לידי חימוץ הא לאו הכי שרי ... ובין לפירוש
רש"י שפירש קמחא דאבשונא ובין לפי' הערוך
דחסיסי הוי קמח של עדשים וכמה שכת' התוספות
נמצינו למדים מכל הני דכל שמותר מעיקר הדין

עבדינן בפסחא ולא חיישינן למראית העין והכי
נקטינן:

### 43) אנציקלופדיה תלמודית, כרך יז, "חשד:
מראית עין"

במקום שלא הוזכר בתלמוד בפירוש שאסרו חכמים
מפני מראית העין, יש מהאחרונים שכתבו שאין
אוסרים דבר מותר הנראה כדבר אסור משום מראית
העין, ולכן בשר חיה, שחלבה מותר, מותר לאכלו
בלא ניקור החלב, אף על פי שבשרה נראה כבשר
בהמה שחלבה אסור, וכן [טור תקפד] מצינו שמותר
לאפות פת בפסח במקום של עדשים215, ולא אסרוהו
מפני מראית העין, שנראה כקמח חטים

### 44) שו"ת אגרות משה, אבן העזר ב:יב

... ויש עוד טעם גדול במה שלא אסרו בפאה נכרית,
דכיון דידוע לכל שיש ללבוש פאה נכרית שתהיה
נדמית כשערות האשה עצמה אין לאסור דמה"ת
יחשדוה הרואים מרחוק ואלו שאין מסתכלין כ"כ
בנשים שהשער הנראה הוא משערות האשה עצמה
כיון שהיא מוחזקת לאשה כשרה ויודעין שמקרוב
ודאי מכירין שאין שערותיה והרואים אותה בקרוב
ומסתכלין הרי ברוב הפעמים יכירו שהיא פאה
נכרית. ואין לומר שבמדינתנו זו בזה"ז שנתפרצה
שרוב נשים בעוה"ר אין מכסות ראשן שלכן יאמרו
גם עליה שהיא מהפרוצות בזה, שלכן אף שלא אסרי
רבנן אנן יש לאסור, חדא דאנו אין מחדשין איסור מה
שלא אסרו מתחלה בגמ' והגאונים ...

### 45) שו"ת אגרות משה, אורח חיים א:צו

בדבר נסיעה לאנשים בקאר /במכונית/ אחר הדלקת
הנרות לביהמ"ד סמוך ערך שני מינוטין /דקות/ לכל
היותר אם יש איזה חשש איסור

איסור מראית העין הוא רק בדבר שנעשה זה ברוב
הפעמים באופן האסור והוא עושה זה באופן המותר
אסרו מפני מראית העין, כגון לעשות ע"י עכו"ם
בקבלנות מלאכה כזו שהרבה עושים בשכירי יום
שהוא אופן האסור, לכן אסרו גם בקבלנות משום
מראית העין ... אבל לעשות דבר היתר מפורסם
בשביל איזה אנשים שיטעו לחשוב שהוא דבר איסור
לא אסרו. ועובדא זו שידוע לכל שנשים מקבלות
שבת בהדלקת הנרות ואנשים מקבלים שבת בתוספת
קטן כי זמן הדלקת הנרות קבוע בעשרים מינוטין
קודם השקיעה כאן וברוב המקומות וא"כ הוא דבר
מפורסם לכל אף לנשים שהאנשים עדיין מותרין
במלאכה קרוב לי"ח מינוט אף לכתחלה אם לא
יקבלו שבת, ... והיו עוד אחד עשר מינוטין מהרגע
שישבתי בקאר. ... עוד אחד עשר מינוטין למלאכה
לכתחלה שאפשר בזה הזמן ליסע בקאר אף דרך
רחוקה חמשה פעמים מהשיעור שעד הישיבה, ועוד
ישארו איזה מינוטין לתוספת שבת. ורק אפשר יש
איזה נשים טועות שחושבות שמזמן הדלקת הנרות

בחדרי חדרים אסור. מתניתא פליגא על רב ...
מתניתא פליגא על רב ... מתניתא פליגא על רב

### 32) תוספות על חולין מא. ד"ה ובשוק"

ובשוק לא יעשה כן – אע"ג דאמר רב (שבת דף סד:)
כל מקום שאסרו חכמים מפני מראית העין אפילו
בחדרי חדרים אסור היינו כמו שוטחן בחמה אבל לא
כנגד העם שאם היו רואים אותו כן בצינעא
היה שם חשד כמו בשוק אבל כאן הרואה שעושה
בביתו אומר לנקר חצרו הוא עושה ומיהא בירושלמי
יש דהך משנה פליג אדרב מההיא ונראה שאין
הש"ס שלנו סובר כן מדלא הקשה ממתניתין לרב
כמו שהקשה מזוג שבצואר ומשני תנאי היא בפרק
במה אשה (שם דף סד:) וכל הנהו דפריך לרב בפ"ק
דמסכת ע"ז (דף יב.) מי שנתפזרו לו מעותיו לפני
עבודת כוכבים ויש לו קוץ ברגלו ומשני להו קאמר
בירושלמי דפליגי אדרב והא דאמר בפרק אע"פ
(כתובות דף ס.) צינור שעלו בו קשקשים בשבת
ממעכו ברגלו בצינעא בשבת ואינו חושש בההוא נמי
מודה רב דלא שייך שם חשד דהא מדאורייתא שרי
למעכו לכתחלה בשבת:

### 33) רבינו ניסים על הרי"ף ביצה ד:

... מחלוקת ברה"י דב"ש אית להו ורב יהודה א"ר
דאמר כל מקום שאסרו חכמים משום מראית העין
אפי' בחדרי חדרים אסור וב"ה לית להו אבל בר"ה
דברי הכל אסור והרב אלפסי ז"ל לא הביא מכל זה
כלום לפי שהוא פסק בפ' חבית [סי' תקנ"ב] כהא
דאמר ר"י אמר רב הלכך על כרחיך אמר ב"ה אפילו
ברה"ר שרי דאי הוו אסרי ברה"י נמי הוו
אסרי אלא ודאי בכל ענין שרו:

אבל רבינו נסים גאון ז"ל כ' דליתא לדרב משום
דאשכחן כמה מתני' דפליגי עליה ...

### 34) שולחן ערוך, אורח חיים שא:מה ומשנה ברורה שם קסה

מי שנשרו כליו במים הולך בהם ואינו חושש שמא
יבא לידי סחיטה ולא ישטחם לנגבם מפני מראית
העין שלא יחשדוהו שכבסן בשבת ואפילו בחדרי
חדרים שאין שם רואים אסור.

בחדרי חדרים – הטעם דלא חלקו חכמים בתקנתן.
כתבו התוספות והרא"ש דוקא במקום שיש חשש
שיחשדוהו הרואים שעשה איסור דאורייתא כגון כאן
בכיבוס בזה אסור אפילו בחדרי חדרים משא"כ בדבר
שהוא איסור דרבנן אפילו למה שיסברו הרואים לא
החמירו לאסור בזה כ"א בפרהסיא והובא דבר זה
במ"א וט"ז ושארי אחרונים:

### 35) שולחן ערוך, אורח חיים תרע"א:ח

חצר שיש לו ב' פתחים מב' רוחות צריך להדליק
בשתיהן ) מפני החשד ואם ב' הפתחים ברוח א' (והם
בבית אחד) (כל בו) די לו באחד מהם. הגה ואם

---

מדליק בב' פתחים אינו מברך רק באחד מהם ובשני
מדליק בלא ברכה (ר"ן)

### 36) שו"ת רשב"א א:תקכה

שאלת עוד הא דאמר רבא (פסחים פ"ק דף ו')
עיסת ארנונא חייבת בחלה משום דלית לה קלא אם
חייב לברך על הפרשתה? דנראה שאינו חייב כיון
שאינו אלא משום הרואין ולא מן הדין דהא כתוב
עריסותיכם. וכן הדומין לזה כבן פקועה שהפריס על
גבי קרקע.
תשובה כל שהצריכו חכמים להפריש או לשחוט
מאיזה טעם שאמרו מצוה מדבריהם היא. ועל
מצוה של דבריהם מברכין.

### 37) מועד קטן יב. ופירוש רש"י שם

והאמר שמואל: מקבלי קיבולת, בתוך התחום אסור,
חוץ לתחום מותר אדם חשוב שאני. ואיכא דאמרי:
סייועי סייע בתיבנא בהדייהו, רב חמא שרא להו
לאבונגרי דבי ריש גלותא למיעבד להו עבידתא
בחולא דמועדא. אמר: כיון דאגר לא קא שקלי
שרשויי הוא דקא משרשו ליה. ולית לן בה. תנו רבנן:
מקבלין קיבולת במועד לעשותה לאחר המועד,
ובמועד אסור.
מקבלי קיבולת בתוך התחום אסור – ליתן מלאכה
לנכרי בקיבולת כי עבדי ליה בשבתא, דידעי כולי
עלמא ואמרי: היום בשבת יהב ליה, והא דשרי בית
הלל בפרק קמא דשבת (יז, ב) ליתן כלים לכובס
בערב שבת עם חשיכה, ואפילו בתוך התחום, משום
דכביסה בנכרי מידי דלא מינכר הוא, ולֵיכא חשדא, אבל
מידי דמינכר בתוך התחום אסור, משום חשדא.

### 38) שולחן ערוך, אורח חיים רמד:א

פוסק עם הא"י על המלאכה וקוצץ דמים והא"י עושה
לעצמו ואע"פ שהוא עושה בשבת מותר בד"א בצנעה
שאין מכירים הכל שזו המלאכה הנעשית בשבת של
ישראל היא אבל אם היתה ידועה ומפורסמת אסור
שהרואה את הא"י עוסק אינו יודע שקצץ ואומר
שפלוני שכר האינו יהודי לעשות מלאכה בשבת
לפיכך הפוסק עם הא"י לבנות לו חצירו או כותלו או
לקצור לו שדהו אם היתה המלאכה במדינה או בתוך
התחום אסור לו להניחה לעשות לו מלאכה בשבת
מפני הרואים שאינם יודעים שפסק

### 39) שולחן ערוך, אורח חיים רמד:ו

יהודי הקונה מכס ומשכיר לו א"י לקבל מכס בשבת
מותר אם הוא בקבלות דהיינו שאומר לו לכשתגבה
מאה דינרים אתן לך כך וכך. הגה וכן יוכל להשכיר
המכס לכל השבתות לא"י והא"י יקח הריות של
שבתות לעצמו ולא חיישינן שיאמרו לצורך ישראל
הוא עושה דבמקום פסידא כה"ג לא חששו (ב"י)
וישראל הממונה על מטבע של מלך דינו כדין
הממונה על המכס ואע"פ שמשמיעים קול בשבת

### 23) רמ"א, שולחן ערוך, יורה דעה פז ופירוש טורי זהב ד

הגה ונהגו לעשות חלב משקדים ומניחים בה בשר עוף הואיל ואינו רק מדרבנן אבל בשר בהמה יש להניח אצל החלב שקדים משום מראית העין כמו שנתבאר לעיל..

**כמו שנתבאר לעיל** – למד מדם דגים לאסור לאכול בשר עוף בחלב של שקדים אא"כ הניחו משקדים אצלו משום מראית עין ודחה דבריו שאין ראיה מדם שמצינו בו איסור כרת משא"כ בבשר עוף בחלב שהוא דרבנן

### 24) משנה חולין ב:ט

אין שוחטין לגומא כל עיקר, אבל עושה גומא בתוך ביתו בשביל שיכנס הדם לתוכה ובשוק לא יעשה כן, שלא יחקה את הצדוקים

### 25) חסד לאברהם (תאומים), אורח חיים כא

... כי חשדא ומראית עין שני ענינים נפרדים הם ורחוקים זמ"ז דהרי יש דבר שאסרו משום מראית עין אף' בחדרי חדרים אסור ובדבר שגזרו משום חשדא בצינעה שרי וע"כ דמראית העין היינו בדבר שנראה בעיני העולם לאיסור ברור ולכן גזרו אף בחדרי חדרים דכל שיודע לשום אדם יהי' מי שיהי' והואיל והוא רואה שעושה איסור ברור ואיכא מראית עין ולכן גם ברבים שייך חשדא דמה מועיל מה שהם רבים ולא חשידי אם האיסור נראה ברור בעיני משא"כ חשדא ל"ש בדבר שהוא ספק השקול אם עושה בהיתר או באיסור ואם עושה כן בפרהסיא ימצאו אנשים שיחשידו בכשרים שעושה איסור ולכן בצינעה מותר ...

### 26) פירוש רש"י על שבת סד:

כל שאסרו חכמים משום מראית העין – שלא יחשדוהו באיסור, כגון שריון וקסדא ומגפיים, או לא יקשור גמלים זה בזה דמיחזי כאזיל לחינגא.

**ולא בזוג אף על פי שהוא פקוק** – ואינו מוליד קול לא תצא בהמה בו, וטעמא פרישנא בפרק במה בהמה (שבת נד, ב) משום דמיחזי כאזיל לחינגא. ותניא בברייתא דבחצר דליכא מראית העין מותר.

### 27) שו"ת אגרות משה, אורח חיים ד:פב

לע"ד שאיסור חשדא שילפינן בשקלים פ"ג מ"ב מקרא ד'והייתם נקיים מה' ומישראל" הוא איסור מדאורייתא מצד עצמו שמחוייב שלא לעשות דבר שיחשדוהו וגם מהטעמים שצריך להניח פאה בסוף משום שדהו חשדא בשבת דף כ"ג ע"א וא"כ א"צ לחקור איזה גדר איסור שייך להיות בזה דזה עצמו הוא האיסור. ויש עניני מראית עין דהיכא דלא שייך חשד שהוא עושה דבר היתר והכל רואים מה שעושה רק שיבואו לדמות לדבר שזה מותר כ"כ מותר גם דבר שמדמין לזה הוא ודאי רק

---

מדרבנן וצריך לאיזה גדר שיוכלו לאסור. וכן יש מראית עין כהא דעכו"ם בקבלנות י"ז ע"ב תוד"ה אין שמצד חשדא דאורייתא אין לאסור דכיון דאיכא גם אופן היתר אף שהוא באופן שאינו טוב להבעלים כשכיר יום מ"מ אין לחשוד דכמה מצות ואיסורין הוא בקושי להאדם ולא יחשדו כל שהוא עובר עליהן ואם אחד חושד הוא עושה איסור דחושד בכשרים, אך מ"מ אסרו שלא יהיה מקום לבעלי לשון הרע לדבר עליו או שהרוצים להקל יאמרו בכוונה שגם הוא עושה בשכיר יום כמו שטוב להבעלים, הוא רק איסור דרבנן מטעם מ"ע =מראית עין= ולא משום איסור חשד וצריך גדר לאסור. ובטעם זה הוא דין מי שנשרו כליו בדרך שוטחן בחמה וכדומה ולא הוזכר שם חשד בגמ' אלא רש"י כתב שיחשדוהו שכבסן בדף קמ"ו ע"ב לטעם על המ"ע אבל לא שהחשד הוא האיסור, הוא נמי רק מדרבנן אבל היכא שאמר בגמ' מפני החשד הוא מדאורייתא מאיסור והייתם נקיים מישראל ומהא דפאה ולכן א"צ גדר אחר להאיסור דזה עצמו הוא האיסור ולפ"ז אין שייך תירוצך. ולכן הנכון לפרש כדבארתי שהשנים יהיו בכל הדרך ותרי לא חשידי.

### 28) אנציקלופדיה תלמודית, כרך יז, "חשד:מראית עין"

יש שכתבו שמראית העין הוא דבר שבעיני הרואים נראה בבירור שעושה איסור, ולכן אף בחדרי חדרים אסור, שמא יזדמן שם אדם שרואהו, וחשד הוא כשהדבר שקול אם זה עושה איסור או [טור תקסט] היתר, ודוקא בפרהסיא אסרו שמא ימצאו בני אדם שיחשדוהו שעובר עבירה, אבל בצינעא לא גזרו, לפי שאפילו יראהו אדם שמא יתלה בהיתר. ויש שכתבו שמראית העין הוא באופן שהרואה יהא סבור שמותר לעשות דבר זה וילמד ממנו לעשותו, וחשד הוא באופן שהדבר ברור לכל שאסור לעשות כן, אלא שיאמרו פלוני זה עושה איסור

### 29) שבת סד:

אמר רב יהודה אמר רב: כל מקום שאסרו חכמים מפני מראית העין אפילו בחדרי חדרים אסור. תנן: ולא בזוג אף על פי שפקוק, ותניא אידך: פוקק לה זוג בצוארה ומטייל עמה בחצר תנאי היא, דתניא: שוטחן בחמה, אבל לא כנגד העם, רבי אליעזר ורבי שמעון אוסרין.

### 30) פירוש רש"י על שבת סד:

**אבל לא כנגד העם** – שלא יאמרו כבסן בשבת האי תנא סבר דמידי דמראית העין מותר בחדרים. אוסרין - כרב.

### 31) ירושלמי, כלאים מ:

רב אמר כל שהוא אסור מפני מראית העין אפילו

ועונשו יותר קשה מאד מאד עד לאין מספר ממי שאינו יוצא ידי שמים ח"ו והוא מש"ס ס"פ יה"כ פ"ו ע"א בענין חלול ה' ראין לו כפרה כלל ר"ל ושיעור חלול ה' כגון

רב דשקיל בשרא ולא יהיב דמי לאלתר שם ובעו"ה שכיח בדברי הבריות למדן כזה יעשה דבר זה והוא שגור בפיהם ואפילו על חסד סברא בעלמא ...

### 12) יומא לח.

בית גרמו היו בקיאין במעשה לחם הפנים ... ועל דבר זה מזכירין אותן לשבח: מעולם לא נמצאת פת נקיה ביד בניהם, שלא יאמרו ממעשה לחם הפנים זה ניזונין, לקיים מה שנאמר (במדבר לב) "והייתם נקים מה' ומישראל".

### 13) ירושלמי, בבא קמא מד:

אבא הושעיה איש טרייא הוה קצר והוה עבד ליה חדא איסדרין מן הד עמר. דלא יהוון אמרין מדידן לבש:

### 14) יומא לח.

בית אבטינס היו בקיאין במעשה ... ועל דבר זה מזכירין אותן לשבח: מעולם לא יצאת כלה מבושמת מבתיהן, וכשנושאין אשה ממקום אחר מתנין עמה שלא תתבסם, לקיים מה שנאמר והייתם נקים מה' ומישראל.

### 15) מדרש, תנחומא פקודי ה

זה"כ "ולא יחשבו את האנשים אשר יתנו את הכסף על ידם לתת לעושי המלאכה כי באמונה הם עושים" (מ"ב מלכים ב' יב) ... ומשה היה גזבר על מלאכת המשכן לעצמו ... כיון שבא ליתן חשבון אמר להם כך וכך יצא למשכן וביותר עשיתי למשכן העדות ... דבר אחר איש אמונות רב ברכות זה משה שנתמנה גזבר על המשכן, שנו רבותינו אין עושין שררה על הצבור פחות משנים ומשה היאך נעשה יחידי גזבר אלא אע"פ שהיה משה הצדיק נאמן על פי הגבורה דכתיב (במדבר יב) בכל ביתי נאמן הוא קורא לאחרים ומחשב על ידיהם שנאמר ביד איתמר בן אהרן הכהן, זה"כ "ולא יחשבו את האנשים אשר יתנו את הכסף על ידם לתת לעושי המלאכה כי באמונה הם עושים

### 16) משנה שקלים ג:ב

אין התורם נכנס לא בפרגוד חפות, ולא במנעל, ולא בסנדל, ולא בתפלין, ולא בקמיע, שמא יעני, ויאמרו מעוין מתרומת הלשכה העני, או שמא יעשיר, ויאמרו מתרומת הלשכה העשיר. לפי שאדם צריך לצאת ידי הבריות כדרך שצריך לצאת ידי המקום, שנאמר (במדבר לב) "והייתם נקים מי"י ומישראל", ואומר (משלי ג)

"ומצא חן ושכל טוב בעיני אלקים ואדם":

### 17) פירוש תפארת ישראל על משנה שקלים ג:ב

ואדם – נ"ל דלהכי נקט קרא בתרא, דאי מקרא קמא, הו"א דוקא בגורם שיחשדוהו אסור, כבני גד שמאנו לעבור לא"י, וע"ז גרמו שיחשדום כאילו מתפחדין מכנענים, להכי היו צריכים להכריע דעת הרואה כשיראו הם עוברים לפני החלוץ, אבל הכא לא עשה התורם דבר שיגרום שיחשדוהו, דהרי כל אדם נמי לובש פרגוד חפות, קמ"ל ומצא חן, דמשמע דלא לבד להנקות מחשד, אלא צריך שישתדל שימצא חן

### 18) ספר החינוך רצה

והחלק אשר על הפרט, שיעשה איש מעשה מגמילות חסדים ומעשים טובים מעשה אחד שיראה לרבים שהוא עבירה, וכגון המעשה ההוא אינו ראוי לכמו האיש החסיד ההוא שיעשהו אף על פי שהוא מעשה היתר, חילל את השם

### 19) שבת כג.

אמר רב הונא: חצר שיש לה שני פתחים צריכה שתי נרות. (ואמר) (מסורת הש"ס: [אמר]) רבא: לא אמרן אלא משתי רוחות, אבל מרוח אחת לא צריך. מאי טעמא? אילימא משום חשדא, חשדא דמאן? אילימא חשדא דעלמא אפילו משתי רוחות נמי ליבעי אי חשדא דבני מתא אפילו מרוח אחת נמי לא ליבעי לעולם משום חשדא דבני מתא, וזימנין דמחלפא בהאי ולא חלפי בהאי, ואמרי: כי היכי דבהאי פיתחא לא אדליק, בהך פיתחא נמי לא אדליק. ומנא תימרא דחיישינן לחש דתניא, אמר רבי שמעון: בשביל ארבעה דברים אמרה תורה להניח פיאה בסוף שדהו: מפני גזל עניים, ומפני ביטול עניים, ומפני החשד, ומשום (ויקרא יט) בל תכלה.

### 20) שולחן ערוך, יורה דעה סו:ט

דם דגים אף על פי שהוא מותר בכלי אסור משום מראית עין לפיכך אם ניכר שהוא מדגים כגון שיש בו קשקשים מותר:

### 21) משנה שבת כב:ד

... מי שנשרו כליו בדרך במים. מהלך בהן ואינו חושש. הגיע לחצר החיצונה. שוטחן בחמה. אבל לא כנגד העם:

### 22) עבודה זרה יב.

נתפזרו לו מעותיו בפני עבודת כוכבים לא ישחה ויטלם, מפני שנראה כמשתחוה לעבודת כוכבים, ואם אינו נראה מותר. מעיין המושך לפני עבודת כוכבים לא ישחה וישתה, מפני שנראה כמשתחוה לעבודת כוכבים, ואם אינו נראה מותר.

# SOURCES FOR SHOULD WE CARE
# WHAT OTHERS THINK?

**1) בראשית יב:ג ופירוש רש"י על יב:ג**

וַיֹּאמֶר ד' אֶל־אַבְרָם לֶךְ־לְךָ מֵאַרְצְךָ וּמִמּוֹלַדְתְּךָ וּמִבֵּית אָבִיךָ אֶל־הָאָרֶץ אֲשֶׁר אַרְאֶךָּ: וְאֶעֶשְׂךָ לְגוֹי גָּדוֹל וַאֲבָרֶכְךָ וַאֲגַדְּלָה שְׁמֶךָ וֶהְיֵה בְּרָכָה: וַאֲבָרֲכָה מְבָרֲכֶיךָ וּמְקַלֶּלְךָ אָאֹר וְנִבְרְכוּ בְךָ כֹּל מִשְׁפְּחֹת הָאֲדָמָה:

**ונברכו בך** – יש אגדות רבות וזהו פשוטו אדם אומר לבנו תהא כאברהם

**2) יומא פו.**

אביי אמר: כדתניא, (דברים ו) ואהבת את ה' אלקיך שיהא שם שמים מתאהב על ידך, שיהא קורא ושונה ומשמש תלמידי חכמים, ויהא משאו ומתנו בנחת עם הבריות, מה הבריות אומרות עליו אשרי אביו שלמדו תורה, אשרי רבו שלמדו תורה. אוי להם לבריות שלא למדו תורה, פלוני שלמדו תורה ראו כמה נאים דרכיו, כמה מתוקנים מעשיו, עליו הכתוב אומר (ישעיהו מט) ויאמר לי עבדי אתה ישראל אשר בך אתפאר. אבל מי שקורא ושונה ומשמש תלמידי חכמים ואין משאו ומתנו באמונה, ואין דבורו בנחת עם הבריות, מה הבריות אומרות עליו אוי לו לפלוני שלמד תורה, אוי לו לאביו שלמדו תורה, אוי לו לרבו שלמדו תורה, פלוני שלמד תורה ראו כמה מקולקלין מעשיו וכמה מכוערין דרכיו, עליו הכתוב אומר (יחזקאל לו) באמר להם עם ה' אלה ומארצו יצאו.

**3) דברים ו:ה**

וְאָהַבְתָּ אֵת ד' אֱלֹקֶיךָ בְּכָל־לְבָבְךָ וּבְכָל־נַפְשְׁךָ וּבְכָל־מְאֹדֶךָ:

**4) מדרש ויקרא רבה לד:ח**

אמר ר' יצחק למדתך תורה דרך ארץ שכשיהא אדם עושה מצוה יהא עושה אותה בלב שמח שאלו היה ראובן יודע שהקב"ה מכתיב עליו (בראשית לז) וישמע ראובן ויצילהו מידם היה טוענו ומוליכו אצל אביו ואלו היה יודע בועז שהקב"ה מכתיב עליו ויצבט לה קלי עגלים פטומים היה מאכילה ר' כהן ורבי יהושע ברבי סימון בשם ר' לוי אמרו לשעבר היה אדם עושה מצוה והנביא כותבה ועכשיו אדם עושה מצוה מי כותבה אליהו והמשיח והקב"ה חותם על ידיהם

**5) משנה אבות ב:א**

רבי אומר איזוהי דרך ישרה שיבור לו האדם. כל שהיא תפארת לעושיה ותפארת לו מן האדם.

**6) במדבר לב:כב**

וְנִכְבְּשָׁה הָאָרֶץ לִפְנֵי ד' וְאַחַר תָּשֻׁבוּ וִהְיִיתֶם נְקִיִּם מֵד' וּמִיִּשְׂרָאֵל וְהָיְתָה הָאָרֶץ הַזֹּאת לָכֶם לַאֲחֻזָּה לִפְנֵי ד':

**7) משלי ג:ד**

וּמְצָא־חֵן וְשֵׂכֶל־טוֹב בְּעֵינֵי אֱלֹקִים וְאָדָם:

**8) ברכת המזון, קטע "במרום"**

וְנִשָּׂא בְרָכָה מֵאֵת ד'. וּצְדָקָה מֵאֱלֹקֵי יִשְׁעֵנוּ. וְנִמְצָא חֵן וְשֵׂכֶל טוֹב בְּעֵינֵי אֱלֹקִים וְאָדָם:

**9) שמות לב:יא-יב, יד**

וַיְחַל מֹשֶׁה אֶת־פְּנֵי ד' אֱלֹקָיו וַיֹּאמֶר לָמָה ד' יֶחֱרֶה אַפְּךָ בְּעַמֶּךָ אֲשֶׁר הוֹצֵאתָ מֵאֶרֶץ מִצְרַיִם בְּכֹחַ גָּדוֹל וּבְיָד חֲזָקָה: לָמָּה יֹאמְרוּ מִצְרַיִם לֵאמֹר בְּרָעָה הוֹצִיאָם לַהֲרֹג אֹתָם בֶּהָרִים וּלְכַלֹּתָם מֵעַל פְּנֵי הָאֲדָמָה שׁוּב מֵחֲרוֹן אַפֶּךָ וְהִנָּחֵם עַל־הָרָעָה לְעַמֶּךָ: ... וַיִּנָּחֶם ד' עַל־הָרָעָה אֲשֶׁר דִּבֶּר לַעֲשׂוֹת לְעַמּוֹ:

**10) במדבר יד:יא-כ**

וַיֹּאמֶר ד' אֶל־מֹשֶׁה עַד־אָנָה יְנַאֲצֻנִי הָעָם הַזֶּה וְעַד־אָנָה לֹא־יַאֲמִינוּ בִי בְּכֹל הָאֹתוֹת אֲשֶׁר עָשִׂיתִי בְּקִרְבּוֹ: אַכֶּנּוּ בַדֶּבֶר וְאוֹרִשֶׁנּוּ וְאֶעֱשֶׂה אֹתְךָ לְגוֹי־גָּדוֹל וְעָצוּם מִמֶּנּוּ: וַיֹּאמֶר מֹשֶׁה אֶל־ד' וְשָׁמְעוּ מִצְרַיִם כִּי־הֶעֱלִיתָ בְכֹחֲךָ אֶת־הָעָם הַזֶּה מִקִּרְבּוֹ: וְאָמְרוּ אֶל־יוֹשֵׁב הָאָרֶץ הַזֹּאת שָׁמְעוּ כִּי־אַתָּה ד' בְּקֶרֶב הָעָם הַזֶּה אֲשֶׁר־עַיִן בְּעַיִן נִרְאָה אַתָּה ד' וַעֲנָנְךָ עֹמֵד עֲלֵהֶם וּבְעַמֻּד עָנָן אַתָּה הֹלֵךְ לִפְנֵיהֶם יוֹמָם וּבְעַמּוּד אֵשׁ לָיְלָה: וְהֵמַתָּה אֶת־הָעָם הַזֶּה כְּאִישׁ אֶחָד וְאָמְרוּ הַגּוֹיִם אֲשֶׁר־שָׁמְעוּ אֶת־שִׁמְעֲךָ לֵאמֹר: מִבִּלְתִּי יְכֹלֶת ד' לְהָבִיא אֶת־הָעָם הַזֶּה אֶל־הָאָרֶץ אֲשֶׁר־נִשְׁבַּע לָהֶם וַיִּשְׁחָטֵם בַּמִּדְבָּר: וְעַתָּה יִגְדַּל־נָא כֹּחַ אֲדֹנָי כַּאֲשֶׁר דִּבַּרְתָּ לֵאמֹר: ד' אֶרֶךְ אַפַּיִם וְרַב־חֶסֶד נֹשֵׂא עָוֹן וָפָשַׁע וְנַקֵּה לֹא יְנַקֶּה פֹּקֵד עֲוֹן אָבוֹת עַל־בָּנִים עַל־שִׁלֵּשִׁים וְעַל־רִבֵּעִים: סְלַח־נָא לַעֲוֹן הָעָם הַזֶּה כְּגֹדֶל חַסְדֶּךָ וְכַאֲשֶׁר נָשָׂאתָה לָעָם הַזֶּה מִמִּצְרַיִם וְעַד־הֵנָּה: וַיֹּאמֶר ד' סָלַחְתִּי כִּדְבָרֶךָ:

**11) חתם סופר, ליקוטי שו"ת ו:נט**

העתרתי בדבריך ובגלגולי סבותיך אשר לא היה לי לנחת ודע בני ותלמידי ש... כי כל ימי הייתי מצטער על המקרא הזה והייתם נקיים מה' ומישראל (במדבר לב:כב) וב' חובות אלו נקיות מה' יתב' והנקיות מישראל עמו שהם שני רוכבים צמדים על גבנו ויותר **אפשרי לצאת ידי החוב הראשון היינו ידי שמים יותר הרבה ויותר מלצאת ידי הבריות כי הם חושבים מחשבות זרות ונושאים ונותנים מנורות בלבנה**

מעשים רעים בנערותו ובזקנותו עושה מעשים טובים
ד"א טוב אחרית דבר מראשיתו יש לך אדם שהוא
למד תורה בנערותו ומשכחה ובזקנותו הוא חוזר
עליה הוי טוב אחרית דבר מראשיתו א"ל ר' עקיבא
רבך לא כך אמר אלא טוב אחרית דבר כשהוא טוב
מראשיתו וכן היה מעשה אבויה אבי מגדולי הדור
וכשבא למולני קרא לכל גדולי ירושלים וקרא לכל
גדולי הדור וקרא לר' אליעזר ולר' יהושע עמהם
וכשאכלו ושתו שרון אילין אמרין מזמורין ואילין
אמרין אלפכטרין א"ר אליעזר לר' יהושע אילין
עסקין בדידהון ואנן לית אנן עסקין בדידן והתחילו
בתורה ומן התורה לנביאים ומן הנביאים לכתובים
והיו הדברים שמחין כנתינתן מסיני והאש מלהטת
סביבותיהן עיקר נתינתן לא מסיני נתנו באש שנאמר
(דברים ד') וההר בוער באש עד לב השמים אמר
הואיל וכך הוא גדול כחה של תורה הבן הזה אם
מתקיים לי הריני נותנו לתורה וע"י שלא היתה כוונת
מחשבתו לש"ש לא נתקיימה בי תורתי ומה את אמר
תובן (איוב כ"ח) לא יערכנה זהב וזכוכית אמר ליה
ומה אמרת ביה א"ל אלו דברי תורה שקשין לקנות
ככלי זהב וזכוכית א"ל עקיבא רבך לא אמר כן אלא
מה כלי זהב וזכוכית אם נשברו יש להם תקנה אף
תלמיד חכם שאיבד משנתו יכול הוא לחזור עליה
אמר ליה חזור עול לך א"ל למה עד כאן תחום שבת
אמר ליה מנן את ידע א"ל מטלפי סוסי שכבר הלך
אלפים אמה א"ל וכל הדא חכמתא אית בך ולית
את חוזר בך א"ל לית בחילי א"ל למה אמר ליה
רוכב הייתי על הסוס ומטייל אחורי בית המקדש
ביום הכפורים שחל להיות בשבת ושמעתי בת קול
מצפצפת ואומרת (ירמיה ג') שובו בנים שובבים

(מלאכי ג') שובו אלי ואשובה אליכם חוץ מאלישע
בן אבויה שהיה יודע כחי ומרד בי ומהיכן היה לו
ראה אדם אחד עלה לראש הדקל בשבת ונטל האם
על הבנים וירד בשלום ובמוצאי שבת ראה אדם
אחד עלה לראש הדקל ונטל הבנים ושלח את האם
וירד והכישו נחש ומת אמר כתיב (דברים כ"ב) שלח
תשלח את האם ואת הבנים תקח לך למען ייטב לך
והארכת ימים היכן טובו של זה והיכן אריכת ימיו
של זה ולא ידע שדרשה ר' עקיבא למען ייטב לך
בעולם שכלו טוב והארכתי ימים לעולם שכלו ארוך
ויש אומרים ע"י שראה לשונו של ר' יהודה הנחתום
נתון בפי הכלב אמר מה הלשון שיגע בתורה כל ימיו
כך לשון שאינו יודע ויגע בתורה עאכ"ו אמר א"כ לא
מתן שכר לצדיקים ולא תחיית המתים ויש אומרים
על ידי שכשהיתה אמו מעוברת בו עברה על בתי
עבודת כוכבים והריחה ונתנו לה מאותו המין ואכלה
והיה מפעפע בכריסה כאריסה של חכינה חולה
חלה אלישע בן אבויה אתון אמרין לר"מ אלישע חולה
אזל לגביה א"ל חזור בך אמר ליה ועד כדון מקבלין
א"ל ולא כתיב (תהלים צ') תשב אנוש עד דכא עד
דדוכדכה של נפש באותה שעה בכה אלישע בן אבויה
ומת והיה ר' מאיר שמח ואמר דומה שמתוך תשובה
נסתלק ר' וכיון שקברוהו באתה האור לשרוף את
קברו אתון אמרין ליה לר' מאיר קבר רבך נשרף יצא
ופרש טליתו עליה אמר ליה (רות ג') ליני הלילה
בעולם הזה שכלו לילה והיה בבקר אם יגאלך טוב
יגאל מהו והיה בבקר בעולם שכלו טוב אם יגאלך
טוב זה הקב"ה שנאמר (תהלים קמ"ה) טוב ה' לכל
ואם לא יחפוץ לגאלך וגאלתיך אנכי חי ה' שכבי עד
הבקר ודמכת ליה

## 30) רמב"ם, ספר המצוות, לא תעשה סג

והחלק המיוחד הוא שיעשה אדם ידוע במעלה ובטוב פעולה אחת תראה בעיני ההמון שהיא עבירה ושאין דמיון הפועל ההוא ראוי לנכבד כמוהו לעשות אע"פ שהפועל מותר הנה הוא חלל את השם ... וכבר נכפל לאו זה ואמר "לא תחלל את שם אלקיך אני ה'" ...

## 31) יומא פו.

יצחק דבי רבי ינאי אמר: כל שחביריו מתביישין מחמת שמועתו (היינו חילול השם) ... שיהא קורא ושונה ומשמש תלמידי חכמים, ויהא משאו ומתנו בנחת עם הבריות, מה הבריות אומרות עליו אשרי אביו שלמדו תורה, אשרי רבו שלמדו תורה. אוי להם לבריות שלא למדו תורה, פלוני שלמדו תורה - ראו כמה נאים דרכיו, כמה מתוקנים מעשיו, עליו הכתוב אומר (ישעיהו מט) ויאמר לי עבדי אתה ישראל אשר בך אתפאר. אבל מי שקורא ושונה ומשמש תלמידי חכמים ואין משאו ומתנו באמונה, ואין דבורו בנחת עם הבריות, מה הבריות אומרות עליו אוי לו לפלוני שלמד תורה, אוי לו לאביו שלמדו תורה, אוי לו לרבו שלמדו תורה, פלוני שלמד תורה ראו כמה מקולקלין מעשיו וכמה מכוערין דרכיו

## 32) מועד קטן יז.

ההוא צורבא מרבנן דהוו סני שומעניה. אמר רב יהודה: היכי ליעביד? לשמתיה צריכי ליה רבנן, לא לשמתיה קא מיתחיל שמא דשמיא ... שמתיה רב יהודה ...

רבי אילעאי אומר: אם רואה אדם שיצרו מתגבר עליו ילך למקום שאין מכירין אותו, וילבש שחורים ויתעטף שחורים, ויעשה מה שלבו חפץ, ואל יחלל שם שמים בפרהסיא ....

## 33) מועד קטן יז. ופירוש רש"י שם

אמר רב הונא: באושא התקינו: אב בית דין שסרח אין מנדין אותו, אלא אומר לו: (מלכים ב' י"ד) "הכבד ושב בביתך". חזר וסרח מנדין אותו, מפני חילול השם. ופליגא דריש לקיש. דאמר ריש לקיש: תלמיד חכם שסרח אין מנדין אותו בפרהסיא, שנאמר (הושע ד') וכשלת היום וכשל גם נביא עמך לילה כסהו כלילה.

**הכבד** – בלשון הזה: אומרים לו עשה עצמך כאדם שכבד עליו ראשו, ושב בביתך, בלשון כבוד אומר לו, לישנא אחרינא: הכבד   התכבד, כבוד שתשב בביתך.

## 34) רמב"ם, הלכות תלמוד תורה ז:א

חכם זקן בחכמה וכן נשיא או אב בית דין שסרח אין מנדין אותו בפרהסיא לעולם, אלא אם כן עשה כירבעם בן נבט וחביריו, אבל כשחטא שאר חטאות מלקין אותו בצנעה, שנאמר וכשלת היום וכשל גם נביא עמך לילה אע"פ שכשל כסהו כלילה, ואומרים

---

לו הכבד ושב בביתך, וכן כל תלמיד חכם שנתחייב נידוי אסור לבית דין לקפוץ ולנדותו במהרה אלא בורחין מדבר זה ונשמטין ממנו, וחסידי החכמים היו משתבחים שלא נמנו מעולם לנדות תלמיד חכם אף על פי שנמנין להלקותו אם נתחייב מלקות, ואפילו מכת מרדות נמנין עליו להכותו.

## 35) שולחן ערוך, יורה דעה של"ד:מב

חכם זקן בחכמה או אב בית דין שסרח אין מנדין אותו בפרהסיא לעולם אלא אם כן עשה כירבעם בן נבט וחביריו אבל כשחטא שאר חטאות מלקין אותו בצינעא וכן כל ת"ח שנתחייב נידוי אסור לב"ד לקפוץ ולנדותו במהרה אלא בורחין ונשמטים ממנו וחסידי החכמים היו משתבחים שלא נמנו מעולם לנדות תלמיד חכם ואע"פ שנמנים להלקותו אם נתחייב מלקות או מכת מרדות ואי סני שומעניה כגון שמתעסק בספרי אפיקורוס ושותה במיני זמר או שחביריו מתביישין ממנו ושם שמים מתחלל על ידו משמתינן ליה:

## 36) רמב"ם, הלכות סנהדרין יז:ט

אבל ראש הישיבה שחטא מלקין אותו ואינו חוזר לשררותו גם אינו חוזר להיות כאחד משאר הסנהדרין שמעלין בקודש ולא מורידין.

## 37) רמב"ם, הלכות תלמוד תורה ד:א

... וכן הרב שאינו הולך בדרך טובה אע"פ שחכם גדול הוא וכל העם צריכין לו אין מתלמדין ממנו עד שובו למוטב, שנאמר "כי שפתי כהן ישמרו דעת ותורה יבקשו מפיהו כי מלאך ה' צבאות הוא", אמרו חכמים אם הרב דומה למלאך ה' צבאות תורה יבקשו מפיהו אם לאו אל יבקשו תורה מפיהו.

## 38) חגיגה טו:

למה נמשלו תלמידי חכמים לאגוז? לומר לך: מה אגוז זה, אף על פי שמלוכלך בטיט ובצואה - אין מה שבתוכו נמאס, אף תלמיד חכם, אף על פי שסרח - אין תורתו נמאסת.

## 39) מועד קטן כ.

מעשה ומת אביו של רבי צדוק בגינזק, והודיעוהו לאחר שלש שנים, ובא ושאל את אלישע בן אבויה וזקנים שעמו, ואמרו: נהוג שבעה ושלשים.

## 40) חגיגה טו:

תנו רבנן: מעשה באחר שהיה רוכב על הסוס בשבת, והיה רבי מאיר מהלך אחריו ללמוד תורה מפיו. אמר לו: מאיר, חזור לאחריך, שכבר שיערתי בעקבי סוסי עד כאן תחום שבת. אמר ליה: אף אתה חזור בך.

## 41) מדרש קהלת רבה ז:טז

טוב אחרית דבר מראשיתו יש לך אדם שעושה

שלימה אפילו לכתחלה ממנין אותו לכל הראוי לו ...

### 18) רמב"ם, הלכות רוצח ז:יג-יד, פירוש המשניות למכות ב:ח

רוצח ששב לעירו אחר מות הכהן הגדול הרי הוא כשאר כל אדם ואם הרגו גואל הדם נהרג עליו שכבר נתכפר לו בגלותו. ואף על פי שנתכפר לו אינו חוזר לשררה שהיה בה לעולם אלא הרי הוא מורד מגדולתו כל ימיו הואיל ובאה תקלה זו הגדולה על ידו.

... והלכה כר' יהודה בשני המאמרים, ושררה, מעלה וגדולה

### 19) ערוך השולחן, חושן משפט תכה:כט

ומ"מ אינו חוזר לשררה שהיה בה קודם שהוגלה עד עולם דהואיל שבא על ידו תקלה גדולה משפיכת דמים אינו ראוי לשום התמנות

### 20) תלמוד ירושלמי, סנהדרין ט:

א"ר לעזר כהן גדול שחטא מלקין אותו ואין מעבירין אותו מגדולתו. א"ר מנא כתיב "כי נזר שמן משחת אלקיו אני ה'" (ויקרא כא:יב) כביכול מה אני בקדושתי אף אהרן בקדושתו.

### 21) רמב"ם, פירוש המשניות, הוריות ג:ב

כהן גדול אם עבר במום או זקן וכיוצא בהם הוא עומד בקדושתו לפי ששמן המשחה שנמשח בו אינו מבטל מעשיהו ... אבל הנשיא אין לו גדולה אלא כשמצותו נעשית ושבטל ענין זה הרי הוא כהדיוט:

### 22) ויקרא ד:כב

אֲשֶׁר נָשִׂיא יֶחֱטָא וְעָשָׂה אַחַת מִכָּל-מִצְוֹת ד' אֱלֹקָיו אֲשֶׁר לֹא-תֵעָשֶׂינָה בִּשְׁגָגָה וְאָשֵׁם:

### 23) משנה הוריות ג:ג ורמב"ם, ספר המצוות, לא תעשה שטז

ואיזהו הנשיא זה המלך

... שהזהירנו מלקלל הנשיא והוא אמרו "ונשיא בעמך לא תאר" וזה השם רוצה לומר נשיא ישימהו הכתוב על המלך אשר לו הממשלה אמר "אשר נשיא יחטא". והחכמים ישימוהו במוחלט על ראש הישיבה של שבעים זקנים לבד ובכל התלמוד והמשנה יאמרו נשיאים ואבות בית דין ... ודע שזה הלאו כולל גם כן הנשיא עם המלך כי ענין לאו זה הוא שמזהיר שלא לקלל כל מי שיש לו ממשלה לצוות והוא במעלה העליונה בין שהיתה מעלת שלטונית או מעלת תורית והיא הישיבה ...

### 24) רמב"ם, ספר המצוות, לא תעשה שטז

... שהזהירנו מלקלל הנשיא והוא אמרו "ונשיא בעמך לא תאר" וזה השם רוצה לומר נשיא ישימהו הכתוב על המלך אשר לו הממשלה אמר "אשר נשיא

---

יחטא". והחכמים ישימוהו במוחלט על ראש הישיבה של שבעים זקנים לבד ובכל התלמוד והמשנה יאמרו נשיאים ואבות בית דין ... ודע שזה הלאו כולל גם כן הנשיא עם המלך כי ענין לאו זה הוא שמזהיר שלא לקלל כל מי שיש לו ממשלה לצוות והוא במעלה העליונה בין שהיתה מעלת שלטונית או מעלת תורית והיא הישיבה ...

### 25) שמות כב:כז ופירוש רמב"ן

אֱלֹהִים לֹא תְקַלֵּל וְנָשִׂיא בְעַמְּךָ לֹא תָאֹר:
ונשיא בעמך לא תאור – הנשיא על העם, והוא המלך, והזהיר שלא יאור שלא יחייב אותו כאשר יחייב אותו במשפט:

### 26) פירוש רבינו בחיי על ויקרא ד:כב

אשר נשיא יחטא. לשון אשר כלשון אם, ושיעורו אם נשיא יחטא, וכמוהו "את הברכה אשר תשמעו" (דברים יא, כז), שיעורו אם תשמע. או אפשר לאמר שהוא לשון ודאי, ולזה לא נכתב אם נשיא יחטא כמו שאמר אם הכהן המשיח יחטא, ואמר אם כן אם כל עדת ישראל ישגו, כי הכהן הגדול נזהר מן החטא לפי שעיני כל ישראל תלויות עליו בין לעניני צרכי גופם ומזונותם בין לעניני כפרת נפשותם, וכן הסנהדרין גם כן נזהרים הם מן החטא לפי שרוח הקודש נוספת עליהם, ולפיכך הזכיר בהם בחטאם לשון ספק, אבל בנשיא הזכיר החטא בלשון ודאי לפי שהנשיא לבו גס מאד בו, ומדת הגאוה שהיא סיבת החטא מצויה עמו לגודל ממשלתו, ולזה הזהירה התורה את המלך ותוכיחנו במדה הזאת, הוא שכתוב (שם יז:כ) "לבלתי רום לבבו מאחיו" ...

### 27) תלמוד ירושלמי, סנהדרין ט:ב

וריש לקיש אמר נשיא שחטא מלקין אותו בב"ד של שלשה. מה מחזרון ליה א"ר חגיי משה אין מחזרין ליה די קטל לון

### 28) פירוש רדב"ז על הרמב"ם, הלכות סנהדרין יז:ט

... כלומר אם יחזירו אותו לנשיאותו, קטיל להו לבית דין. היינו הוא עלול להתנקם בדיינים שדנו אותו. לפי נימוק זה, הדין שנשיא שחטא אינו חוזר לתפקידו מוגבל רק למי שעלולים להתנקם במי שדנו אותם, כגון נשיא ושכמותו. לעומת זאת, אם ממלא התפקיד שחטא אינו עלול להתנקם במי שדנו אותו, אין מניעה שיחזור לתפקידו.

### 29) כסף משנה על רמב"ם, הלכות סנהדרין יז:ח

כהן גדול שחטא וכו'. ירושלמי ... אמר רבי חגי מוטב דינון מחזרין ליה דו קטלין ליה ונראה דמשמע ליה ז"ל דה"ק מוטב שאותן המחזירים אותו יהרגוהו שלא יאריך ימים כיון שהיה מעולה וחטא במזיד בענין שנתחייב מלקות אי נמי מה שאמר שהוא כאילו הורגים אותו הוא מפני שבני אדם יזלזלו אותו הילכך לא יחזירוהו ...

# SOURCES ON SHOULD RESPECT BE GIVEN TO A LEADER THAT SINNED?

**1) ברכות יט:**
תא שמע: גדול כבוד הבריות שדוחה [את] לא תעשה שבתורה.

**2) שמות כ:יב**
כַּבֵּד אֶת־אָבִיךָ וְאֶת־אִמֶּךָ לְמַעַן יַאֲרִכוּן יָמֶיךָ עַל הָאֲדָמָה אֲשֶׁר־ד' אֱלֹקֶיךָ נֹתֵן לָךְ

**3) קידושין לא:**
איזהו מורא, ואיזהו כיבוד ... כיבוד מאכיל ומשקה, מלביש ומכסה, מכניס ומוציא.

**4) משנה אבות ד:יט**
שמואל הקטן אומר (משלי כד) בנפול אויביך אל תשמח ובכשלו אל יגל לבך.

**5) דברים כא:כב-כג, רמב"ם, הלכות סנהדרין טו:ז**
וְכִי־יִהְיֶה בְאִישׁ חֵטְא מִשְׁפַּט־מָוֶת וְהוּמָת וְתָלִיתָ אֹתוֹ עַל־עֵץ: לֹא־תָלִין נִבְלָתוֹ עַל־הָעֵץ כִּי־קָבוֹר תִּקְבְּרֶנּוּ בַּיּוֹם הַהוּא כִּי־קִלְלַת אֱלֹקִים תָּלוּי וְלֹא תְטַמֵּא אֶת־אַדְמָתְךָ אֲשֶׁר ד' אֱלֹקֶיךָ נֹתֵן לְךָ נַחֲלָה:
כיצד מצות הנתלין אחר שסוקלין אותן משקעין את הקורה בארץ ועץ יוצא ממנה ומקיפין שתי ידיו זו לזו ותולהו סמוך לשקיעת החמה ומתירין אותו מיד, ואם לן עוברין עליו בלא תעשה שנאמר "לא תלין נבלתו על העץ".

**6) מגילה י':**
בקשו מלאכי השרת לומר שירה, אמר הקדוש ברוך הוא: מעשה ידי טובעין בים ואתם אומרים שירה?

**7) שולחן ערוך, אורח חיים תצב:ד**
כל הימים של חוש"מ ושני ימים אחרונים של יו"ט קורין ההלל בדילוג כמו בראש חודש:

**8) בראשית א:כז**
וַיִּבְרָא אֱלֹקִים אֶת־הָאָדָם בְּצַלְמוֹ בְּצֶלֶם אֱלֹקִים בָּרָא אֹתוֹ זָכָר וּנְקֵבָה בָּרָא אֹתָם:

**9) שולחן ערוך, יורה דעה רמו:ח**
הרב שאינו הולך בדרך טובה אע"פ שחכם גדול הוא וכל העם צריכים לו אין למדין ממנו עד שיחזור למוטב.

**10) בבא מציעא נח:**
"לא תונו איש את עמיתו" באונאת דברים. הא כיצד?

---

אם היה בעל תשובה אל יאמר לו זכור מעשיך הראשונים

**11) ויקרא ד:ב-ג**
דַּבֵּר אֶל־בְּנֵי יִשְׂרָאֵל לֵאמֹר נֶפֶשׁ כִּי־תֶחֱטָא בִשְׁגָגָה מִכֹּל מִצְוֹת ד' אֲשֶׁר לֹא תֵעָשֶׂינָה וְעָשָׂה מֵאַחַת מֵהֵנָּה: אִם הַכֹּהֵן הַמָּשִׁיחַ יֶחֱטָא לְאַשְׁמַת הָעָם וְהִקְרִיב עַל חַטָּאתוֹ אֲשֶׁר חָטָא פַּר בֶּן־בָּקָר תָּמִים לַד' לְחַטָּאת:

**12) במדבר לה:יא**
וְהִקְרִיתֶם לָכֶם עָרִים עָרֵי מִקְלָט תִּהְיֶינָה לָכֶם וְנָס שָׁמָּה רֹצֵחַ מַכֵּה־נֶפֶשׁ בִּשְׁגָגָה:

**13) משנה מכות ב:ח**
כיוצא בו רוצח שגלה לעיר מקלטו ורצו אנשי העיר לכבדו. יאמר להם רוצח אני. אמרו לו אף על פי כן. יקבל מהן. שנאמר (דברים יט) "וזה דבר הרוצח" ... וחוזר לשררה שהיה בה. דברי רבי מאיר. רבי יהודה אומר לא היה חוזר לשררה שהיה בה:

**14) משנה מכות ב:ח**
... וחוזר לשררה שהיה בה. דברי רבי מאיר. רבי יהודה אומר לא היה חוזר לשררה שהיה בה:

**15) מכות יג.**
חוזר לשררה שהיה בה כו'. תנו רבנן: (ויקרא כ"ה) "ושב אל משפחתו ואל אחזת אבותיו ישוב" למשפחתו הוא שב, ואינו שב למה שהחזיקו אבותיו, דברי ר"י ר"מ אומר: אף הוא שב למה שהחזיקו אבותיו,

**16) רבינו עובדיה מברטנורה על משנה מכות ב:ח**
לא היה חוזר לשררה שהיה בה - דכתיב (ויקרא כה) ושב אל משפחתו ואל אחזת אבותיו ישוב למשפחתו הוא חוזר ואינו חוזר למה שהוחזקו אבותיו. ואין הלכה כר' יהודה:

**17) חידוש ריטב"א על מכות יג**
וניחא ליה למנקט כחו דר' יהודה דהלכתא כוותיה ואלו בברייתא בעי לאשמועינן לר' מאיר שהוא חוזר אפילו למה שהוחזקה אבותיו אע"פ שלא הוחזק הוא עצמו ... ואע"פ שהרג בשוגג וכ"ש שאין ממנין בשום מינוי למי שהרג במזיד. ואפשר שאף ר' יהודה לא נחלק כאן אלא בשפיכות דמים או בשנמכר ונעשה עבד לאחרים שהם דברים חמורים ומאוסים מאוד אבל בשאר עבירות דעלמא כל שחזר בתשובה

הַחוֹב, צָרִיךְ לְשָׁפְטוֹ לְצַד הַחוֹב, אַחֲרֵי שֶׁנִּתְחַזֵּק לְרָשָׁע גָּמוּר בִּשְׁאָר עִנְיָנָיו, וְכֵן אָמְרוּ רַבּוֹתֵינוּ "לֹא תוֹנוּ אִישׁ אֶת עֲמִיתוֹ", עִם שֶׁאִתְּךָ בַּתּוֹרָה וּבְמִצְווֹת, אַל תּוֹנֵהוּ בִּדְבָרִים, וַאֲשֶׁר לֹא שָׁת לִבּוֹ לִדְבַר ה', מֻתָּר לְהַכְלִימוֹ בְּמַעֲלָלָיו וּלְהוֹדִיעַ תּוֹעֲבוֹתָיו וְלִשְׁפֹּךְ בּוּז עָלָיו, וְעוֹד אָמְרוּ, מְפַרְסְמִין אֶת הַחֲנֵפִים מִפְּנֵי חִלּוּל ה', וְכָל שֶׁכֵּן (לֹא) אִם הוֹכִיחַ אוֹתוֹ בָּזֶה וְלֹא חָזַר, דְּמֻתָּר לְפַרְסְמוֹ וּלְגַלּוֹת עַל חֲטָאָיו בְּשַׁעַר בַּת רַבִּים וְלִשְׁפֹּךְ בּוּז עָלָיו, עַד שֶׁיַּחֲזֹר לְמוּטָב, וּכְמוֹ שֶׁכָּתַב הָרַמְבַּ"ם בְּסוֹף פֶּרֶק ו' מֵהִלְכוֹת דֵּעוֹת (הֲלָכָה ח'), אַךְ יֵשׁ לִזָּהֵר שֶׁלֹּא לְשַׁכֵּחַ (לֵב) פְּרָטִים אֲחָדִים הַמִּצְטָרְכִים לָזֶה, וּכְתַבְתִּים בְּבְאֵר מַיִם חַיִּים:

### (45) שולחן ערוך, יורה דעה רמב:יא
לאפרושי מאיסורא כגון שרואה אדם עובר עבירה מפני שאינו יודע שהוא אסור או מפני רשעתו מותר להפרישו ולומר לו שהוא אסור בפני רבו רבו מקום שיש חילול השם אין חולקין כבוד לרב:

### (46) שולחן ערוך, יורה דעה שלד:מג
... על כ"ד דברים מנדין את האדם ואלו הן ... ט"ו המביא רבים לידי חילול השם.

### (47) פירוש רבינו יונה על משלי כד:כח
... ואם הוא רשע ואין בני אדם מכירין בו והוא מחזיק כאיש צדיק ביניהם אין לוחשין על מעשיו (אלא) באזני הצנועים בלבד. אבל [מצוה] לפרסמו עד אשר רוע פעולותיו יודעו לרבים, כי יש נזקים גדולים בכבוד הרשעים, כי ידיחו רבים מדרך טובה וישפילו כבוד הצדיקים ויקריבו החטאים, אף כי יש חילול השם בכבודם, כי מקצת בני אדם מכירים במעשיהם, ואומרים כי אין שפלות לאיש בעבירות, ולא נגרע מערכו במעשיו הרעים, ואין כח בחטאים להשפיל בני אדם והוא ששנינו (יומא פו, ע"ב) מפרסמין את החנפים מפני חלול השם ...

### (48) מסילת ישרים, פרק יא
ענפי חילול השם גם כן הם רבים וגדולים כי הרבה צריך האדם להיות חס על כבוד קונו, ובכל מה שיעשה צריך שיסתכל ויתבונן מאד שלא יצא משם מה שיוכל להיות חילול לכבוד שמים חס וחלילה, וכבר שנינו, אחד שוגג ואחד מזיד בחילול השם... והענין, שכל אדם לפי מדריגתו ולפי מה שהוא נחשב בעיני הדור, צריך שיתבונן לבלתי עשות דבר בלתי הגון לאיש כמותו, כי כפי רבות חשיבותו וחכמתו כן ראוי שירבה זהירותו בדברי העבודה ודקדוקו בה, ואם איננו עושה כן, הרי שם שמים מתחלל בו חס וחלילה, כי כבוד התורה הוא, שמי שמרבה הלימוד בה ירבה כמו כן ביושר ובתיקון המדות, וכל מה שיחסר מזה למי שמרבה בלימוד, גורם ביזיון ללימודו עצמו, וזה חס וחלילה חילול לשמו יתברך, שנתן לנו את תורתו הקדושה וצונו לעסוק בה להשיג על ידה שלימותנו.

### (49) בבא מציעא ל:
לא חרבה ירושלים אלא על שדנו בה דין תורה. אלא דיני דמגיזתא לדיינו? אלא אימא: שהעמידו דיניהם על דין תורה, ולא עבדו לפנים משורת הדין.

### (50) אמת ליעקב, ויחי, עמוד קלז
דוגמא מעשית שלא לפי הדין ניתן להביא מהשאלה הבאה אדם שיש לו ברירה בין לישא בת ישראל שלא תשמור על טהרת המשפחה ובין לישא גויה מה עדיף? התלמיד שלא שימש כל צרכו בודאי יאמר: הלא איסורי נדה הם בכרת ואילו בעילת עכו"ם אינו אלא לאו בעלמא שאינו ענוש כרת בודאי אם יכל עליו לבחור בגויה האמת היא לא כן הרמב"ם אף שדעתו היא שביאת שפחה אינה אלא מדרבנן פוסק (הלכות איסורי ביאה יב:ז-ח) בזה"ל: עזן זה אע"פ שאין בו מיתת בית דין אל יהי קל בעיניך אלא יש בו הפסד שאין בכל העריות כמותו שהבן מן הערוה בנו הוא לכל דבר ובכלל ישראל יחשב ואע"פ שהוא ממזר והבן מן הגויה אינו בנו שנאמר כי יסיר את בנך מאחרי מסיר אותו מלהיות אחרי ה' ודבר זה גורם להדבק בגוים שהבדילנו הקב"ה מהם ולשוב מאחר ה' ולמעול בו עכ"ל ברור לפ"ז שעליו לבחור בבת ישראל אע"פ שהיא אינה שומרת טהרת המשפחה ...

### (51) ספר החסידים קנג
... ומצינו בתורה שכל מי שיכול להבין אע"פ שלא נצטווה, נענש עלי' על שלא שם על לבו ... אלא שהי' לו לחשוב שמא שלא ברצון הקב"ה הוא ...

### (52) רמב"ם, מורה נבוכים ג:יז
ואמרו, "במדה שאדם מודד – בה מודדין לו", וזה – לשון ה'משנה'. ובארו בכל מקום שהמשפט מחויב בהכרח בחוקו ית', והוא, שיגמול העובד על כל מה שיעשה ממעשי הבור והישר – ואף על פי שלא צווה בו על ידי נביא – ושיענוש על כל מעשה רע שיעשהו האיש – ואף על פי שלא הוזהר ממנו על ידי נביא – אחר שהוא דבר שהשכל מזהיר ממנו – רצוני לומר, ההזהרה מן העול והחמס. אמרו, "אין הקדוש ברוך הוא מקפח זכות כל בריה", ואמרו, "כל האומר קודשא בריך הוא ותרן הוא יתותרן מעוהי"; אלא, מאריך אפיה וגבי דיליה"; ואמרו, "אינו דומה מצווה ועושה למי שאינו מצווה ועושה" – ובארו שהוא – אף על פי שלא צווה – 'נותנים לו שכרו';

### (53) פירוש רמב"ן על בראשית ו:יג
חמס – הוא הגזל והעושק. ונתן לנח הטעם בחמס ולא הזכיר השחתת הדרך, כי החמס הוא החטא הידוע והמפורסם. ורבותינו אמרו (סנהדרין קח.) שעליו נתחתם גזר דינם. והטעם מפני שהוא מצוה מושכלת אין להם בה צורך לנביא מזהיר, ועוד שהוא רע לשמים ולבריות.

**40) הרב צבי גרטנר, ישורון טו, דף תרלד-תרלה**

בדבר השאלה העומדת על הפרק כעת בארה"ב שהנה כידוע התגלו בשנים האחרונות אצל אומות העולם מקרים רבים של מורים ואנשי חינוך המתעללים התעללות מינית וואו פיזית בתלמידיהם\חניכיהם והענין קיבל פרסום רב אצלם ומחמת גודל הנזק גופני ועאכו"כ נפשי הנגרם לילדים הנופלים קרבן להתעללות כזו שברבים מן המקרים חייהם וחיי משפחתם נהרסים התחילה הממשלה להחמיר ביותר בענינים אלו הן על העבריינים עצמם והן על אנשי חינוך וכל מי שבא במגע מקצועי עם ילדים שמטילים עליהם חובת דיווח לרשויות בכל מקרה של חשש וחשד והמשתרשל או הנמנע מלדווח תוך זמן קצר מאד חשוף לעונשי קנס ומאסר ואף לתביעות אזרחיות מצד הורי הילדים שנפגעו כתוצאה מאי הדיווח

ולדאבונינו ובעוה"ר אף על מחננו לא פסע הנגע והיו מקרים שונים כנ"ל גם אצלנו ר"ל ונשאלת השאלה מה יעשה מורה ומחנך וכו' אם מעשה כזה בא לידי שיש אומרים הרי כל אדם בחזקת כשרות הוא עומד ולכן אסור למוסרו לרשויות ובפרט אם לא תבעוהו תחילה בבית דין ונפסק על ידם שדברים כהוויתם והוא דבר שכמעט ואי אפשר ובפרט בזמן הזה שאין כח בית דין יפה לכופו לעמוד בדין ועוד שגם אם יבוא לבית דין הרי בדרך כלל תשתית הראיות בדברים כאלו מבוססת על עדות קטנים ופסולים ואומדנות או על הודאת בעל דין ולהוציא אדם מחזקתו צריך עדות כשרה ולא של קטנים ופסולים או אומדנות וכל שכן לא הודאתו שאין אדם משים עצמו רשע ואחרים

אומרים הרי בהצלת נפשות ולאפרושי מאיסורא קעסקינן שכפי הנשמע מרבנים ואנשי מקצוע העוסקים בשטח זה הלקוי בדבר זה עלול לפגוע בעשרות ולפעמים מאות ילדים וקרוב לודאי שאין לו תקנה בתשובה גרידא עד שילווה בטיפול מקצועי לתקופה ממושכת ומה גם שהרשויות מטילות חובת דיווח וכאמור ובפרט כי ברוב המקרים אין לרשויות ענין להעניש העבריין אלא מאלצים אותו לעבור תהליך שיקום שלכן אין ספק שרשאים וחייבים לדווח ובתנאי שהענין נבדק כראוי על ידי רבנים מובהקים ואנשי מקצוע ונמצא שדברים בגוו ולדוגמא בכמה ערים בארה"ב הקימה הקהילה בית דין מיוחד המטפל בענינים אלון ולאחר בדיקת ואימות הענין לפי ראות עיניהם ולעת הצורך הם מתירים את הפניה לרשויות באלול תשס"ד פורסם הנחיות מטעם ועד ראשי הישיבות של "תורה ומסורה" על דרכי הפעולה בבית הספר שבמקרה ומתעורר חשש ומחד אצל אחד המורים על מאן דהו שמתעולל בתלמיד מודיע המורה על כך למנהל בית הספר והמנהל יברר הענין תוך התייעצות עם מורה הוראה או רב מוסמך בעל נסיון בענינים אלו וכן עם איש מקצוע ובמידה ויתאמת שיש רגלים לדבר על המנהל לדווח הלאה לרשויות וכנדרש בחוק

**41) אמונה ובטחון (חזון איש) ג:ב**

ב. מחובות המוסריות שישתדל האדם לטעת בלבבו את העיקר הגדול הזה, שבכל מקרה אשר הוא נפגש עם רעהו צריך לשקול בפלס ההלכה לדעת מי הוא הרודף ומי הוא הנרדף, והלא לימוד המוסר מנחיל אהבה וחמלה להנרדף, וחמת מרורות להרודף, ומה נוראה היא המכשלה ורבת הפוקה להיות מן המחליפים את הרודף לנרדף ואת הנרדף לרודף, ואשר לדעת אמתתו לנו מצוקי תבל רבותנו ז"ל, זולת אין מקום מסרום לנו מצוקי תבל רבותנו ז"ל:

**42) שו"ת שואל ומשיב (רב אלישיב) א:קפה**

בשנת תרי"ג אירע בעיר אחד שנשמע קול על מלמד אחד שמתגורר שם זה שמנה שנים והילדים אשר למדו אצלו בקטנותם וכעת הם בני י"ג שנה ויותר הם מעידים שבקטנותם כאשר למדו אצלו טימא אותם במשכב זכר ר"ל...וע"כ על כשתי שהמראוי להסיר כתר המלמדות מעל ראשו וחושו לנפשם עד אשר ישוב בתשובה שלמה ובסגופים כראוי ואז ישוב לקבל דברי חבירות ויהיה לו לכפרה על חטאיו וכל זמן שאינו מתודה על חטאיו לא שייך תשובה כמ"ש התב"ש בסמ"ב

**43) הרב משה הלברשטם, ישורון טו, דף תרמו**

אם נבוא לדון בדבר השאלה הבאה בזה באיש רע מעללים שיצרו אונסו לחטוא ולהרשיע וניתן למוסרו לשלטונות כדי שיעצרוהו בתפיסה לכמה שנים עדי ירגיע עצמו וישוב אל ה' בכל ליבו הנה ע"פ המורם מכל הנ"ל אין כל חטא ופשע במסירה זו ואדרבה מצוה היא זו שבכך גורמים שימנע מלעשות מעשיו המגונים בשנית דהרי אין לחוש שהשלטונות יענישוהו במיתה וכל עיקר העונש שיושת עליו הוא שיושיבוהו לכמה שנים בבית הסוהר ויוכל להרוויח בכך שיצמידו לו פסיכולוג או פסיכיאטער שישגיח עליו ועל תהלוכותיו בעינא פקיחא ואולי יוכל למצוא מזור לנפשו הנאבקת והנאנקת ע"י הטיפול הפסיכולוגי הנה בכה"ג פשוט שיפה שעה אחת קודם להצלתו ולהצלת משפחתו

**44) חפץ חיים, הלכות לשון הרע ד:ז**

וְכָל אֵלּוּ הַדִּינִין שֶׁכָּתַבְנוּ הוּא דַּוְקָא בְּאִישׁ, אֲשֶׁר מִנְהֲגוֹ וְדַרְכּוֹ לְהִתְחָרֵט עַל חֲטָאָיו, (כט) אֲבָל אִם בָּחַנְתָּ אֶת דַּרְכּוֹ, כִּי אֵין פַּחַד אֱלֹהִים לְנֶגֶד עֵינָיו וְתָמִיד יִתְיַצֵּב עַל דֶּרֶךְ לֹא טוֹב, כְּמוֹ הַפּוֹרֵק מֵעָלָיו עֹל מַלְכוּת שָׁמַיִם אוֹ שֶׁאֵינוֹ נִזְהָר מֵעֲבֵרָה אַחַת, אֲשֶׁר עַל שַׁעַר עַמּוֹ יוֹדְעִים שֶׁהִיא עֲבֵרָה, דְּהַיְנוּ בֵּין שֶׁאוֹתָהּ הָעֲבֵרָה, שֶׁהוּא רוֹצֶה לְגַלּוֹת, עָשָׂה הַחוֹטֵא כַּמָּה פְּעָמִים בְּמֵזִיד אוֹ שֶׁעָבַר בְּמֵזִיד כַּמָּה פְּעָמִים עֲבֵרָה אַחַת הַמְפֻרְסֶמֶת לַכֹּל שֶׁהִיא עֲבֵרָה, אִם כֵּן מוּכָח מִזֶּה מֵחֲמַת שֶׁבָּהּ מֵחֲמַת שֶׁבָּר יִצְרוֹ עָלָיו עָבַר עַל דִּבְרֵי ה' כִּי אִם בִּשְׁרִירוּת לִבּוֹ הוּא הוֹלֵךְ, וְאֵין פַּחַד אֱלֹהִים לְנֶגֶד עֵינָיו, לָכֵן מֻתָּר לְהַכְלִימוֹ (ל) וּלְסַפֵּר בִּגְנוּתוֹ בֵּין בְּפָנָיו וּבֵין שֶׁלֹּא בְּפָנָיו. וְאִם הוּא עָשָׂה מַעֲשֶׂה אוֹ יְדַבֵּר דָּבָר, וְיֵשׁ לְשָׁפְטוֹ לְצַד הַזְּכוּת וּלְצַד

**34) תשובות והנהגות א:תתג**

נהג יהודי הרגיל לנסוע במהירות מופרזת או בלי רשיון אם מותר למוסרו למשטרה פורש בשולחן ערוך חושן משפט שפ"ג ס"ק י"ב שאם עוסק בזיופים ומסוכן מזהירים אותו ואם אינו משגיח לאזהרה יכולים למוסרו עי"ש בביאור הגר"א שיש לו דין רודף אף שאינו מתכוין ואף שאינו רק גרמא ואע"פ שאינו אלא חשששא עי"ש ואין לך מסוכן כמו הנוסע תכופות במהירות מופרזת או בלי ידיעת מלאכת הנהיגה כראוי שלכן לא השיג רשיון שאלו עלולים להרוג ח"ו ודינם כרודף לכן התקנה של נהיגה כראוי וברשיון היא בצדק וביושר ולטובת הציבור וחייבין לשמור תקנות אלו ואם הוא מזלזל בהם ויש חשש שיבוא לאבד נפשות ראוי הוא לעונש מרתיע אף מאסר ועיין תשב"ץ ח"ג סימן קס"ח לאוסרו על ידי נכרים ובמהרשד"ם ח"מ נ"ח סעיף ו'

אמנם כדאי לא למוסרו מיד אלא להתרותו תחילה ע"י רב העיר או הבית דין שאם ימשיך בדרכו ימסרו אותו למשטרה ויענש כראוי לו שבהתראה סתם אינו מאמין שבאמת ימסרוהו ואם בכל זאת מתעקש בדרכו ומזלזל בציבור ימסרוהו ומרן הגאון רבי יעקב קנייבסקי זצ"ל רגז מאד על אלו העוברים חוקי תנועה שנוסדו לפיקוח נפש דציבור ושמעתי על אחד שבא לפניו שחושש מאד שיקבל עונש חמור על שעבר על חוקי התנועה ורוצה לבקש ברכתו שיפטרו אותו והגיב במחאה חריפה מאד שהאמת שראוי לעונש אף שלא היה לו במשפטיהם וע"כ נראה שאם הוא בגדר מועד ואי אפשר לנו להענישו בעצמנו ועלול להזיק ראוי ברשותבית דין או רב העיר למוסרי ומצוה קעביד להציל את הציבור ממזיק שעלול אפילו לסכן את חייהם

**35) שו"ת יחווה דעת ד:ס**

**שאלה:** המשתדל להשיג רשיון נהיגה, והוא חולה במחלה סמויה מתגלית על ידי בדיקת רופא רגילה. האם מותר לרופאו האישי או למי שיודע בבירור על מחלתו, להודיע על כך למשרד הרישוי, למנוע בעדו השגת הרשיון בכדי שלא יגרום לתאונות ואסונות בנהיגתו, או שמא יש בזה איסור משום רכילות ולשון הרע?

**תשובה:** נאמר בתורה לא תלך רכיל בעמך ... ומכל מקום נראה שכל זה הוא באופן שמתכוין רק להשמיץ את חבירו ולבזותו, אבל אם מתכוין לתועלת מסויימת או להרחיק נזק מותר. וראיה לזה ממה שכתב הרמב"ם (בפרק א' מהלכות רוצח הלכה יד) וזו לשונו: כל היכול להציל את חבירו ואינו מצילו, עובר על לא תעמוד על דם רעך, לפיכך הרואה את חבירו טובע בים או שלסטים באים עליו, ויכול להצילו, או ששמע שאנשים חושבים עליו רעה וטומנים לו פח, ולא גילה אוזן חבירו להודיעו, הרי זה עובר על מה שנאמר בתורה לא תעמוד על דם רעך. ע"כ. וכן פסקו הטור והשלחן ערוך בחושן

---

משפט (סימן תכ"ו סעיף א'). ולכן בנידון שלנו שהחולה במחלה סמויה, כמו מחלת הנפילה וכיוצא בה, מעלים ממשרד הרישוי את דבר מחלתו, כדי להשיג רשיון נהיגה, ויכול להיות שיקבל התקפת – המחלה בשעה שהוא נוהג, בודאי שהחובה ומצוה להודיע למשרד הרישוי על מחלתו של זה, כדי שלא יגרום נזק או סכנה לציבור ...

**36) שו"ת אגרות משה, חושן משפט א:ח**

קבלתי מכתבכם בדבר הרשע אשר זייף חותמות ותלה אותם על נבלות וטרפות ומכר ליהודים בתור כשרות, שהנידון הוא אם למסרו לערכאות המדינה שידונו קשה בכסף ובמאסר, או שידונו אותו הרבנים בדיני ישראל. לע"ד אף שפשעו גדול מאד וכנראה אינו בעל תשובה כלל, מ"מ כל זמן שלא ראינו שדייני ישראל אינם יכולים להפסיקו אין לדונו בערכאות משני טעמים. חדא דאפילו לא ידונו בערכאות אלא כדיני התורה אסור לדון בערכאות כדאיתא בחו"מ ר"ס כ"ו. ועוד הא ודאי הם ידונו במאסר ובממון שלא כדיני ישראל שיש לחוש לאיסור מסור, שאסור למסור ישראל ביד עכו"ם בין בגופו בין בממונו ואפילו היה רשע ובעל עבירות כדאיתא בחו"מ סימן שפ"ח סעיף ט'. ורק כשיראו שאין דייני ישראל יכולים להפסיקו אז יש היתר, אחר שיתרו בו שיתבעו אותו ... וכ"ש שהוא שלא להכשיל כמה בנ"א באיסורים, ... אבל כשיכולים להפסיקו בדייני ישראל יש לאסור גם בשביל שיגרמו שישבע שבועת שוא ... ולכן נראה לע"ד שמתחלה ידונו אותו בועד הרבנים בכל מה שבידם והעיקר לפוסלו מלמכור דברים כשרים ואם לא יציית אז יביאוהו לדון בערכאות.

**37) פירוש רש"י על סנהדרין עב**

קסבר – רב הונא רודף אין צריך התראה לענין להצילו בנפשו, דלא ניתנה התראה אלא לענין בית דין דלא מצי למקטליה אם הרג בלא התראה.

**38) קיצור שולחן ערוך קפד:ט**

מִי שֶׁעוֹסֵק בְּזִיּוּפִים וְיֵשׁ לָחוּשׁ שֶׁיְּסַכֵּן בָּזֶה רַבִּים, דִּינוֹ כְּמוֹ רוֹדֵף וּמֻתָּרִין בּוֹ לַעֲשׂוֹת שֶׁלֹּא יַעֲשֶׂה. וְאִם אֵינוֹ מַשְׁגִּיחַ, מֻתָּר לְמָסְרוֹ לְמַלְכוּת וְלוֹמַר שֶׁאֵין אַחֵר מִתְעַסֵּק בָּזֶה אֶלָּא פְּלוֹנִי לְבַדּוֹ, וְכֵן יָחִיד שֶׁמַּעֲלִילִים עָלָיו בִּגְלָלוֹ, יָכוֹל לוֹמַר לָהֶם, אֲנִי אֵינֶנִּי עוֹשֶׂה אֶלָּא פְּלוֹנִי לְבַדּוֹ:

**39) ב"ח על שולחן ערוך, חושן משפט כח:ג**

ומה שכתב הרא"ש כל שכן בזמן הזה וכו'. .... ומכל מקום נהגו ברוב הקהלות שאין לשום בר ישראל להעיד לגוי על ישראל חבירו אלא אם כן ישאל תחילה לבית הדין ועל פיהם יעשה לא יטה ימין ושמאל ואם מעיד בלא שאלת בית דין עונשים אותו אף על פי שלא עבר על דין תורה..

**28) אמונה ובטחון (חזון איש) ג:א**

חובות המוסריות המה לפעמים גוף אחד עם פסקי
ההלכה, וההלכה היא המכרעת את האסור ואת
המותר של בורת המוסר. כיצד, אמרו ב"ב כ"א ב'
בדמלמדי תינוקות אין טענה של פסקנ לחיות, הרי
שיש בעיר מלמדים מתפרנסים מעמלם ולפתאום
באו מלמדים אחרים מעיר אחרת, וכטבע בני אדם
אינם שבעים רצון מהישנשנת, קפצו כלם על האורחים
החדשים ומלמדי העיר נזוקו.:

המקופחים פשטו שנאתם בלבב על הרודפים
החדשים, ומשנאת הלב יצאו לבקש עליהם תואנות
מומים ועלילות, ולמדו לשונם דבר רע עליהם,
ומרעה אל רעה יצאו להוציא דבת שוא ולעורר
רחמי בני העיר נגד האכזריות של הבאים החדשים,
עד שהוסיפו בקטטות ומריבות ולעתים נוקמים בהם
נקמות כאשר תמצא ידם.:

הנה כל מעשיהם היו מנוקים מכל חטא ואון לוא
היתה ההלכה כמותם שיכולים לעכב על החדשים,
והחדשים היו החוטאים בנפשותם למרות נגד
ההלכה שנאמרה למשה רבנו ע"ה בסיני, אין כאן
איסור מחלוקת ולא איסור לשון הרע ושנאת חנם,
ויש כאן נלחמת מצוה לעמיד הדת על תלה.:

אבל עכשו שהההלכה הכריעה דקנאת סופרים תרבה
חכמה, ויסוד הזה נעלה מחיותא דאנשים פרטיים,
הנה האורחים הבאים עשו כהלכה וקמים כנגדם
שופכים דם נקיים, וכששונאים אותם בלב עוברים
על לא תשנא אחיך, כשמדברים עליהם רע עוברים
על איסור לה"ר, כשמקהילים קהלות לקטטות
עוברים על לא תהי' כקרח, כשנוקמים בהם בהעדר
הטבה עוברים משום לא תקום.:

וכשאמרו בגמ' ב"ב שם ומודה ר"ה במקרי דרדקי
דלא מצי מעכב נכללה בהלכה זו הרבה הלכות
מוסריות אשר תפגשנה מתוצאות ההלכה.:

**29) רמב"ם, הלכות חובל ומזיק ח:יא**

וכן כל המיצר לציבור ומצער אותן מותר למסרו ביד
גוים להכותו ולאסרו ולקנסו, אבל מפני צער יחיד
אסור למסרו, ואסור לאבד ממונו של מסור ואע"פ
שמותר לאבד גופו שהרי ממונו ראוי ליורשיו.

**30) רמ"א על שולחן ערוך, חושן משפט שפח:יב**

הגה: (וע"ל סי' תכה ס"א) מי שעוסק בזיופים וכדומה
ויש לחוש שיזיק שיזיק רבים, מתרין בו שלא יעשה, ואם
אינו משגיח יכולין למסרו לומר שאין אחר מתעסק
בו אלא זה לבד. מי שרוצה לברוח ולא לשלם לעכו"ם
מה שחייב, ואחר גילה הדבר אין לו דין מוסר שהרי
לא הפסידו רק שהוצרך לשלם מה שחייב, מכל מקום
ברעה עשה דהוי כמשיב אבידה לעכו"ם, ואם גרם לו
היזק חייב לשלם לו מה שגרם לו (מהר"ם מרוזבורק).

**31) רמ"א על שולחן ערוך, חושן משפט תכה:א**

הגה: ... מי שממסכן רבים כגון שעוסק בזיופים

במקום שהמלכיות מקפידות, דינו כרודף ומותר
למסרו למלכות (נימוקי מהר"ם מריזבורג כמו
שנתבאר לעיל סימן שפח סי"ב).

**32) קובץ תשובות (רב אלישיב) ג:רלא**

... אכן כל זה להתיר להודיע לממשלה הוא באופן
שהדבר ברור שאין ידו במעל, ובזה יש משום תיקון
העולם אך באופן שאין אפילו רגלים לדבר, אלא איזה
דמיון אם נתיר את הדבר לא רק שאין בזה משום תיקון
עולם אלא הרס העולם שי ויתכן שבגלל איזה
מרירות של תלמיד כלפי המורה מעליל על המורה
או בגלל איזה דמיון שוא מכניסים אדם למצב שטוב
מותו מחייו. – על לא עול הכפר, ואין אני רואה שום
היתר בדבר.

**33) שו"ת ציץ אליעזר, יט:נב**

שאלה. ילד המוכה. לדאבוני אין הדבר נדיר שמביאים
תינוק או ילד לביה"ח כשהוא כולו פצוע קשה
עם שברים בגולגולת ובגפיים, דימומים ובאברים
פנימיים, ממכות או כוויות קשות (ממים רותחים
או מסגריות וכדומה) עד מצב של ממש פקוח נפש,
כשכל החבלות האלו נעשו במזיד ע"י אחד או שני
הורי, וכפי שכתבתי כבר בחחו"מ של ספרי (סימן
תכ"ד סק"ב עמוד רי"ט) כשמתלוננים במשטרה, אז
אחרי שהתינוק טופל ומשתחרר מביה"ח מעבירים
אותו ע"י צו בית המשפט למשפחה אומנת או למוסד
כדי להציל אותו מהוריו, כי כבר היו מקרים לא
מעטים שכשהחזירו את התינוק לביתו, מוכה אח"כ
למות, שאלתי היא מה יהיה הדין כשהרופא יודע
שהסיכויים הם טובים שיעבירו את התינוק לבית או
למוסד לא דתי, או אפילו בחו"ל לבית או מוסד של
עכו"ם, האם עדיין עליו להתלונן למשטרה, או לא.

**תשובה** ... בקשר לשאלתו הראשונה, לענ"ד נראה
בכזאת. אם קים ממש חשש מבוסס שהורי הילד
ישובו קרוב לודאי להכותו שוב במכות אכזריות
כאלה, ועוד יותר מזה עד למות, במקרה כזה, מכיון
שהרופא רק מוסר על המצב למשטרה עם בקשת
לראות להציל את הילד מידי הורי, אזי חייב הרופא
לעשות זאת כדי להציל נפש אחת מישראל מרדת
שחת, ומה שיעשה לאחר מיכן המשרד הממשלתי
כדי להצילו הרי הרופא בזה רק בבחינה של גורם
בלבד, ואין לפני עור ממש כי הרי גם בטוח במאה
אחוז שיעבירו אותו דוקא למוסד של עכו"ם, או לא
ו(תד", יעיון בע"ז ד' ט"ו, ובתבואות שור סי' ט"ז ס"ק
כ"ד שכתובת לדייק מדברי הגמ' הנ"ז דמשמע מזה
דאין אזהרה דלפ"ע כי אם היכא דאיכא מכשול ודאי
ע"ש, וכ"כ עוד פוסקים.

נוסף על זה הרי הילד עד שיגדל איננו עובר עי"כ
שום עבירה, וכשיגדל הרי יתכן גם שיחזירוהו למקום
שיוכל לשמור על יהדותו. (יעיון שו"ת חתם סופר
חאו"ח סימן פ"ג, וכף החיים סימן או"ח סימן שמ"ג ס"ק
כ"ב ע"ש).

אדם נחשד בדבר אלא אם כן עשאו, ואם לא עשה
כולו עשה מקצתו, ואם לא עשה מקצתו הרהר בלבו
לעשותו, ואם לא הרהר בלבו לעשותו ראה אחרים
שעשו, ושמח. מתיב רבי יעקב: (מלכים ב' י"ז)
ויחפאו בני ישראל דברים אשר לא כן על ה' אלהיהם
התם להכעיס הוא דעבוד. תא שמע: (תהלים ק"ו)
ויקנאו למשה במחנה לאהרן קדוש ה', רב שמואל
בר יצחק אמר: מלמד שכל אחד קינא לאשתו ממשה
התם משום קינאה הוא דעבוד. תא שמע, אמר רבי
יוסי: יהא חלקי עם מי שחושדין אותו בדבר ואין בו.
ואמר רב פפא: לדידי חשדון ולא הוה בי לא קשיא
הא בקלא דפסיק, הא בקלא דלא פסיק. וקלא דלא
פסיק עד כמה? אמר לי אביי: אמרה לי אם: דומי דמתא
יומא ופלגא. והני מילי דלא פסק בינתי בינתי, אבל פסק
בינתי בינתי לית לן בה. וכי פסק בינתי בינתי לא אמרן אלא
דלא פסק מחמת יראה, אבל פסק מחמת יראה לא.
ולא אמרן אלא דלא הדר נבט, אבל הדר נבט לא. ולא
אמרן אלא דלית ליה אויבים, אבל אית ליה אויבים
אויבים הוא דאפקוה לקלא.

### 19) פירוש ים של שלמה על יבמות י':כ

... וכן יש להן להלקות אדם ששמעתו רעה, (והם)
[והעם] מרננין אחריו, שהוא עובר על העריות,
והוא שיהא קול שאינו פוסק, ולא יהי' לו אויבי'
שמוציאים עליו דבה רעה,

### 20) פירוש ספורנו על במדבר ה:לא

ונקה האיש מעון – אף על פי שחשד בכשרה, כי היא
גרמה לו שעברה על התראתו וגרמה רגלים לדבר,
כאמרם ז"ל: לא קיבל דוד לשון הרע, דברים הנכרים
חזא ביה (שבת נו,א) במפיבשת ...

### 21) ספר יראים קצב

לא תשא שמע שוא – הזהיר היוצר בפ' ואלה
המשפטים שלא יקבל אדם לשה"ר דכתיב "לא תשא
שמע שוא" ואומר האי לישנא אף על גב דלקבולי לא
מקבלינן מיחש חיישינן לה. ואם אדם רואה בחבירו
דברים ועניינים שנראה שהדבר אמת רשאי להאמין
ולא לקבל כדאמרינן בשבת פ' במה אשה יוצאה [נ"ו
א'] לא קבל דוד לשה"ר אלא דברים ניכרים חזא ביה
במפיבשת.

### 22) ספר מצוות הגדול, לא תעשה י'

ואם אדם רואה בחבירו צדדים ועניינים שנראה דבר
אמת רשאי להאמין ולקבל כדאמ' בשבת פרק במה
בהמה (נו, א) לא קיבל דוד לשון הרע מ"ט דברים
נכרים חזא ביה במפיבשת (יראים סי' קצב):

### 23) ערוך השולחן, חושן משפט ב:א

אף על פי שאין דנין בחו"ל דיני נפשות ומלקות
וקנסות מ"מ אם אם רואים ב"ד שהשעה צריכה לכך
שהעם פרוצים בעבירות דנים הכל כפי צורך השעה

---

ואפילו כשרואים ליחיד שהוא פרוץ בעבירות יכולים
לקנסו כפי ראות עיניהם ובלבד שתהיה כוונתם
לשמים ואפילו אין בדבר עדות גמורה אלא שיש
רגלים לדבר וקלא דלא פסיק וליכא אויבים דמפקי
לקלא ...

### 24) חפץ חיים, הלכות איסורי לשון הרע, כלל ז:י-יא

וְאִם יֵשׁ עָלָיו דְּבָרִים הַנִּכָּרִים, שֶׁנִּרְאָה עַל יְדֵי זֶה, שֶׁמַּה
שֶּׁמְּסַפְּרִין עָלָיו הוּא אֱמֶת, דִּינָא הָכֵי (הַדִּין כָּךְ), אִם
יֵשׁ בָּעִנְיָן הַזֶּה, אֲפִלּוּ אִם הַדָּבָר אֱמֶת, לְשָׁפְטוֹ לְצַד
זְכוּת, אוֹ בְּעִנְיְנֵי שְׁלִילַת הַמַּעֲלוֹת, אוֹ בְּכָל שְׁאָר
הַפְּרָטִים, הַמְבֹאָרִים לְעֵיל בְּסָעִיף ז', לֹא שַׁיָּךְ בָּזֶה
דְּבָרִים הַנִּכָּרִים, דְּוַדַּאי אָנוּ מְחֻיָּבִין לְדוּנוֹ לְכַף זְכוּת
כֵּיוָן שֶׁהוּא אִישׁ בֵּינוֹנִי כְּדֵי שֶׁלֹּא יִתְבַּזֶּה עַל יְדֵי זֶה
בְּעֵינֵינוּ וְכַנַּ"ל, אֲבָל אִם הוּא דָּבָר אֲשֶׁר אֵין לִמְצֹא צַד
זְכוּת עַל הָעוֹשְׂקוֹ, מֻתָּר לְהַאֲמִין וּלְקַבֵּל:
[הַגָּהָ"ה – וּבְכָל זֹאת צְרִיכִין לְהִזָּהֵר מְאֹד וְלַחְקֹר
בְּשֶׁבַע חֲקִירוֹת, אִם הֵם בֶּאֱמֶת דְּבָרִים הַנִּכָּרִים, וְלִזָּהֵר
בְּכָל הַתְּנָאִים שֶׁצָּרִיךְ לָזֶה וּכְדִלְקַמָּן, כִּי הַיֵּצֶר מַטְעֶה
אֶת הָאָדָם בָּזֶה מְאֹד וְיַמְרְאֶה לוֹ כַּמָּה דְּבָרִים הַנִּכָּרִים
שֶׁהֵם אֱמֶת, כְּדֵי שֶׁיַּאֲמִין בָּזֶה וְיִלְכְּדֶנּוּ עַל יְדֵי זֶה
בְּרֶשֶׁת שֶׁל עֲוֹן קַבָּלַת לָשׁוֹן הָרָע, וְעַל כֵּן אַל יְמַהֵר
לְהָקֵל בָּזֶה]:
יא. וְדַוְקָא אִם הֵם נִכָּרִים מַמָּשׁ, דְּהַיְנוּ (כו) שֶׁהֵם
מַגִּיעוֹת לְעִנְיַן הַסִּפּוּר, וְגַם רָאָה אֶת הַדְּבָרִים הַנִּכָּרִים
בְּעַצְמוֹ. אֲבָל אִם הֵם רְחוֹקִין מִזֶּה רַק הוּא כְּעֵין
דָּבָר הַנִּכָּר קְצָת, אוֹ שֶׁלֹּא רָאָה אֶת הַדְּבָרִים הַנִּכָּרִים
בְּעַצְמוֹ (כז) רַק שְׁמָעָן מִפִּי אֲחֵרִים, אֵין לוֹ בָּזֶה שׁוּם
יִתְרוֹן כְּלָל:

### 25) משנה אבות, א:ו

והוי דן את כל האדם לכף זכות:

### 26) בית יוסף על טור חושן משפט שפח:יג

ומ"ש בשם בעל העיטור. כתוב בתשובות הרשב"א
סימן קפ"א אם רגיל לעשות כן כל שאומר לעשות
כאילו עשה והרי הוא בכלל הבא להרגך [השכם
להרגו] כההיא דרבי שילא המתין לראות
היעמדו דבריו ואפילו מי שאינו רגיל בכך אם הכרנו
בו שהוא רוצה לעשות כההיא דרב כהנא הרי הוא
כאילו ידענו בבירור שיעשה:

### 27) קובץ תשובות (רב אלישיב) ג:רלא

... אכן כל זה להתיר למשמשלה ההודיע הוא באופן
שהדבר ברור שאכן ידו במעל, ובזה יש משום תיקון
העולם אך באופן שאין אפילו רגלים לדבר, אלא איזה
דמיון אם נתיר הדבר לא רק שאין בזה משום תיקון
עולם אלא הרס העולם שי ויתכן שבגלל איזה
מרירות של תלמיד שילא המורה מעליל על המורה
או בגלל איזה דמיון שוא מכניסים אדם למצב שטוב
מותו מחייו. – על לא עול הכפר, ואין אני רואה שום
היתר בדבר.

אחרי' הרי לא יפה עשה באותן הפעמים אמנם בהאי
מעשה שפיר קעביד ומצוה קעביד ומ"מ נ"ל לחלק
ביניהם דמכה למכה א' מישראל אין פוטרין אותו אם
לא שיש בירור גמור שלא יוכל להציל בענין אחר
משא"כ במציל את קרובו אין מדמדקי' כ"כ ואפי'
במקום שאין בירור שלא היה יכול להציל בענין אחר
דקרובו כגופו דמי ואע"ג דאי' בס' ד' דאין פטור
על ההכאה אם ההכאה יוכל להציל ממנו בלא"ה היינו במכה
כדי להציל ממון אבל כאן שזה מכה קרובו והוה
במכהו בעצמו ואפי' בספק הצלה יכול להכות במכה
וזה נ"ל מדודקק בלשון הרא"ש והטור בקרובו כתבו
כדי להציל קרובו ובא' מישראל כתבו אם אינו יכול
להציל בע"א מורה על החילוק שכתבו והוא נכון:

### 11) קיצור שולחן ערוך, קפד:א

אָסוּר לְאָדָם לְהַכּוֹת אֶת חֲבֵרוֹ, וְאִם הִכָּהוּ עוֹבֵר בְּלֹא
תַעֲשֶׂה, שֶׁנֶּאֱמַר, אִם בֶּן הַכּוֹת הָרָשָׁע וְגוֹמֵר, אַרְבָּעִים
יַכֶּנּוּ לֹא יוֹסִיף פֶּן יוֹסִיף וְגוֹמֵר, אִם הִקְפִּידָה תּוֹרָה
בְּהַכָּאַת הָרָשָׁע שֶׁלֹּא לְהַכּוֹתוֹ יוֹתֵר עַל רִשְׁעוֹ, קַל
וָחֹמֶר בְּהַכָּאַת צַדִּיק. וְכָל הַמֵּרִים יָד עַל חֲבֵרוֹ לְהַכּוֹתוֹ
אַף עַל פִּי שֶׁלֹּא הִכָּהוּ נִקְרָא רָשָׁע, שֶׁנֶּאֱמַר, וַיֹּאמֶר
לָרָשָׁע לָמָּה תַכֶּה רֵעֶךָ, "לָמָּה הִכִּיתָ" לֹא נֶאֱמַר, אֶלָּא
"לָמָּה תַכֶּה", אַף עַל פִּי שֶׁעֲדַיִן לֹא הִכָּהוּ נִקְרָא רָשָׁע.
וְכָל מִי שֶׁהִכָּה אֶת חֲבֵרוֹ הָיָה מְחֻרָם בְּחֵרֶם הַקַּדְמוֹנִים
וְלֹא צֵרְפוּהוּ לְמִנְיַן עֲשָׂרָה לְכָל דָּבָר שֶׁבִּקְדֻשָׁה, עַד
שֶׁהִתִּירוּ לוֹ בֵּית דִּין אֶת הַחֵרֶם כְּשֶׁיְּקַבֵּל עָלָיו לִשְׁמֹעַ
אֶת דִּינָם. וְאִם הִכָּה אֶחָד הִכָּה אוֹתוֹ אוֹ לְיִשְׂרָאֵל אַחֵר וְאִי
אֶפְשָׁר לְהַצִּיל אֶת עַצְמוֹ אוֹ אֶת חֲבֵרוֹ מִיַּד מַכֵּהוּ אֶלָּא
עַד שֶׁיַּכֶּה אוֹתוֹ, מֻתָּר לְהַכּוֹתוֹ:

### 12) שו"ת תשובות והנהגות (רב שטרנבוך) ה:שצח

וּדְבָרָיו של המנהל הם הבל הבלים ופותח פתח
לשחיתות ר"ל וחובת ראש ישיבה ומנהל לשמוע
כל רינון וחשד על המתרחש בתחומו שכן עיקר
חובתו לשמור על נפשותיהם של התלמידים ולכן
צריך לחשוש לכל דבר אפילו אינו מצוי כלל ואף
שמקמינן אדם על חזקת כשרותו מכל מקום
מה שנוגע לשמירת התלמידים אם נראה אפילו
נדנוד ספק שהזקן ילדים או בחורים חייבין לסלק
את החשוד בינתיים או להעמיד שמירה מיוחדת
ותמידית עליו ועיקר איסור סיפור וקבלת לשון הרע
הוא אם נובע מכך ששנאו או מקנא בו ואין כוונתו
לש"ש אבל כשכוונתו להורות חייב
לחשוש לכל טענה או רינון על מנת למנוע נזקים
והחשש המ___ך מאיסור לשון הרע עלול לגרום
לקלקול רבים

ופעם אחת כשהייתי אצל כ"ק האדמו"ר רבי ישראל
אלתר האדמו"ר מגור שאל אותי אודות בחור אחד
וכיון שחשש שאני מפקפק אם להגיד מפני לשון הרע
אמר "דע לך דבבית הזה אין איסור לשון הרע
לתועלת וכל מה שאני שומע אני פועל ועושה והכל
יהא תמיד בזה תועלת"

---

והנה שמעתי על אסיפת רבנים בה עמד הקדוש
ה"חפץ חיים" זצ"ל ודרש על ענין לשון הרע ובקש
מהרבנים הנוכחים שיחתמו על התחייבות להזהר
מלשון הרע והגאון רבי חיים עוזר זצ"ל היסס לחתום
ויש בזה סיפורים שונים וכפי ששמעתי השיב שרב
בעירו צריך לידע ולשמוע הכל אפילו בחשש רחוק
מאד ולעשות בירור יסודי אם יש בדברים ממש
ובמידה שיחתום עלול להחמיר מדאי וזה יגרום
קלקול לרבים ולכן טוב יותר לתקן ללמוד הלכות
לשון הרע

סוף דבר מצוה גדולה לספר כל חשש וחשש והמנהל
צריך לשמוע ולחשוש ולשמור על התלמידים שמירה
מעולה ואם מתרשל הרי הוא בכלל ארור עושה
מלאכת ה' רמייה והיום יש הרבה כלי משחית לקלקל
הנוער וחובה לשמור שמירה מעולה על קודש
הקדשים התלמידים העוסקים בתורת ה' כמבואר
בלשון הרמב"ם סוף הלכות שמיטה ויובל ע"ש ריקני
באתי לעודדו שלא ינוח ולא ישקוט ושכרו רב מאד
ויסכר פי דובר שקר הסותם פיות ומזלזל בדברים
הנוגעים לדיני נפשות

### 13) דברים יט:טו-טז

... אעפ"כ אמרי' הואיל וסני שומעני מוטה דלא
ילפי מיני' ושמוהו עאכו"כ במלמד שחשדוהו כנ"ל
ורשע בזה, שרבע את הנערים ר"ל דחייב למתו כדי
שלא יהי' מלמד, אול יהיו שכיח בביתו להחטיאם
ר"ל ושאין להשחית

לֹא-יָקוּם עֵד אֶחָד בְּאִישׁ לְכָל-עָוֹן וּלְכָל-חַטָּאת בְּכָל-
חֵטְא אֲשֶׁר יֶחֱטָא עַל-פִּי | שְׁנֵי עֵדִים אוֹ עַל-פִּי שְׁלֹשָׁה-
עֵדִים יָקוּם דָּבָר:

### 14) שבת נו.

ושמואל אמר: לא קיבל דוד לשון הרע, דברים
הניכרים חזא ביה'

### 15) קידושין פא.

אמר רב: מלקין על לא טובה השמועה

### 16) מגילה כה:

אמר רב אשי: האי מאן דסנאי שומעניה שרי ליה
לבזוייה בגימ"ל ושי"ן. האי מאן דשפיר שומעניה
שרי לשבוחיה, ומאן דשבחיה ינוחו לו ברכות על
ראשו.

### 17) פירוש מאירי על קידושין יב:

חתן הדר בבית חמיו אם היא חשודה ממנו מלקין
אותו על לא טובה השמועה הוא כל שאינה חשודה
אף על פי שהדבר מכוער אינו בר מלקות:

### 18) מועד קטן יח:

ואמר רב משום רבי ראובן בן איצטרובילי, ואמרי לה
במתניתא תנא, אמר רבי ראובן בן איצטרובילי: אין

# SOURCES ON SEXUAL ABUSE OF CHILDREN – JUDAISM'S VIEW

**1) ויקרא יט:טז**

לֹא־תֵלֵךְ רָכִיל בְּעַמֶּיךָ לֹא תַעֲמֹד עַל־דַּם רֵעֶךָ אֲנִי ד':

**2) רמב"ם, הלכות רוצח א:טו**

הרואה רודף אחר חבירו להרגו או אחר ערוה לבועלה ויכול להציל ולא הציל, הרי זה ביטל מצות עשה שהיא וקצותה את כפה ועבר על שני לאוין על לא תחוס עינך ועל לא תעמוד על דם רעך.

**3) שולחן ערוך, חושן משפט תכו:א**

הרואה את חבירו טובע בים או ליסטים באין עליו או חיה רעה באה עליו, ויכול להצילו הוא בעצמו או שישכור אחרים להציל ולא הציל, או ששמע עכו"ם או מוסרים מחשבים עליו רעה או טומנים לו פח ולא גילה אוזן חבירו והודיעו, או שידע בעכו"ם או באנס שהוא בא על חבירו ויכול לפייסו בגלל חבירו ולהסיר מה שבלבו ולא פייסו וכיוצא בדברים אלו, עובר על לא תעמוד על דם רעך

**4) פירוש נציב על ויקרא יט:טז**

... שאף ע"ג שאזהרה לא תלך רכיל מכ"מ לא תעמוד על דם רעך היינו אם יודע שאיש א' רוצה לירד לחייו של אדם אחר ה"ז מחויב להודיע ואסור לעמוד ע"ד רעך:

**5) בבא מציעא לא.**

ואימא (ויקרא י"ט) הוכח חדא זימנא, תוכיח תרי זמני? אמר ליה: הוכח אפילו מאה פעמים משמע, תוכיח אין לי אלא הרב לתלמיד, תלמיד לרב מנין תלמוד לומר הוכח תוכיח, מכל מקום.

**6) נדה סא.**

תנא: הוא הבור שמילא ישמעאל בן נתניה חללים, דכתיב (ירמיהו מ"א) והבור אשר השליך שם ישמעאל את כל פגרי אנשים אשר הכה ביד גדליה. וכי גדליה הרגן? והלא ישמעאל הרגן אלא מתוך שהיה לו לחוש לעצת יוחנן בן קרח ולא חש מעלה עליו הכתוב כאילו הרגן. אמר רבא: האי לישנא בישא, אע"פ דלקבולי לא מבעי מיחש ליה מבעי. הנהו בני גלילא דנפק עלייהו קלא דקטול נפשא, אתו לקמיה דרבי טרפון, אמרו ליה: לטמרינן מר אמר להו: היכי נעביד? אי לא אטמרינכו חזו יתייכו, אטמרינכו הא אמור רבנן האי לישנא בישא, אע"ג דלקבולי לא מבעי מיחש ליה מבעי.

**7) חפץ חיים, הלכות איסורי לשון הרע, כלל ד הגה"ה**

[הגה"ה – וְכָל זֶה שֶׁכָּתַבְנוּ בְּאֵלוּ הַסְּעִיפִים הוּא בְּשֶׁאֵין

---

הַדָּבָר הַזֶּה מוֹעִיל לְאַפְרוּשֵׁי מֵאִסּוּרָא, אֲבָל אִם הוּא (יט) מוֹעִיל לְאַפְרוּשֵׁי מֵאִסּוּרָא, כְּגוֹן, שֶׁרָאָה לְאֵשֶׁת אִישׁ שֶׁזִּנְּתָה, דְּמִן הַדִּין נֶאֶסְרָה עֲבוּר זֶה לְהַבַּעַל, אֲפִלּוּ רָאָה דָבָר בִּיחִידִי, צָרִיךְ (כ) לְגַלּוֹת (כא) לְהַבַּעַל כְּדֵי לְהַפְרִישׁוֹ מֵאִסּוּר, וְדַוְקָא אִם רָאָה בְּעַצְמוֹ שֶׁזִּנְּתָה, דְּמִן הַדִּין נֶאֶסְרָה עַל יְדֵי זְנוּת לְהַבַּעַל, אֲבָל אִם שָׁמַע זֶה מֵאֲנָשִׁים אֲחֵרִים, דְּמִן הַדִּין לֹא נֶאֶסְרָה עַל יְדֵי זֶה לְהַבַּעַל, אוֹ שְׁאָר אָפְנִים כַּיּוֹצֵא בָזֶה – אָסוּר לְגַלּוֹת. וַאֲפִלּוּ אִם רָאָה בְּעַצְמוֹ שֶׁזִּנְּתָה, לֹא יְגַלֶּה, רַק אִם הוּא מְשׁוֹעָר, (כב) שֶׁאֶפְשָׁר שֶׁהַבַּעַל יַאֲמִין לוֹ כִּבֵי תְּרֵי (כִּשְׁנֵי עֵדִים) וְיִפְרֹשׁ עַל יְדֵי זֶה מִמֶּנָּה, אֲבָל בְּלָאו הָכִי אָסוּר לוֹ לְגַלּוֹת דָּבָר זֶה לְהַבַּעַל וְכָל שֶׁכֵּן לְזוּלָתוֹ]:

**8) רא"ש, בבא קמא ג:יג**

וכן אם רואה אדם שישראל מכה את חבירו ואין יכול להציל אם לא שיכה את המכה מכת נפש מותר להכות המכה לאפרושי מאיסורא. כדאמרינן לעיל (דף כח.) בנרצע שנשא שפחה כנענית וכלו ימיו שרבו מותר לחבול בו לאפרושי מאיסורא:

**9) סמ"ע על טור, חושן משפט תכא:כח**

כדי לאפרושי מאיסורא. בטור כתב עוד בבא א' לפני בבא זו וכן הדין באדם הרואה את חבירו שמכה לאביו או בנו או אחיו והרואה הכה המכה כדי להציל את קרובו שפטור עכ"ל ודקדקתי בפרישה מדלא כייל אחיו ובנו עם סיפא דרואה מכה לא' מישראל גם כתב בכל א' טעם בפני עצמו דבמציעתא כתב כדי להציל את קרובו ובסיפא כ' כדי לאפרושי מאיסורא וכתבתי דאיכא בינייהו נ"מ לדינא והוא דאם זה הבא להציל ולהכות המכה אינו בר הכי דרגיל לאפרושי מאיסורא דכמה פעמים רואה שמכה א' לחבירו ואינו חושש לאפרושי המכה מאיסורא אז אמרינן דאסור להכות לזה המכה דודאי מכח שנאה בא להכותו ולא בא להפרישו מהאיסור מה שא"כ ברואה מכה אביו ובנו ואחיו דמותר להציל קרובו בהכאה אף שאין מדרכו להפריש אחרים והמחבר דלא חילק בינייהו אפשר משום דלא הרגיש בזה דבאמת טעם הגון הוא לחלק בינייהו ודוק:

**10) ט"ז על טור, חושן משפט תכא**

הסמ"ע מחלק בין אם רגיל בכך או לא ואני יודע טעם לזה החילוק דכיון דדינא הוא שיכול להציל ע"י הכאה את המוכה מ"ל בזה יש לו שנאה על המוכה מ"מ הוא עושה מצוה להציל את המוכה וכי בכוונת הלב תליא מלתא ואף שאין דרכו כן לפעמים

---

ראוי לו לעורר לבבו בדברי פיהו ולחשוב כי הכל
הגיע אליו מאת אדון העולם ...

**50) שבת ל:**

תנו רבנן: לעולם יהא אדם ענוותן כהלל ואל יהא
קפדן כשמאי.

**51) סוכה נג.**

תניא, אמרו עליו על הלל הזקן כשהיה שמח בשמחת
בית השואבה אמר כן: אם אני כאן הכל כאן, ואם איני
כאן מי כאן

**52) תהילים ח:ה-ו, מדרש, ויקרא רבה יד:א**

מָה־אֱנוֹשׁ כִּי־תִזְכְּרֶנּוּ וּבֶן־אָדָם כִּי תִפְקְדֶנּוּ: וַתְּחַסְּרֵהוּ
מְעַט מֵאֱלֹקִים וְכָבוֹד וְהָדָר תְּעַטְּרֵהוּ:
אם זכה אדם אומרים לו אתה קדמת למלאכי השרת

ואם לאו אומרים לו זבוב קדמך, יתוש קדמך ...

**53) ירמיהו ט:כב-כג**

כֹּה אָמַר ד' אַל־יִתְהַלֵּל חָכָם בְּחָכְמָתוֹ וְאַל־יִתְהַלֵּל
הַגִּבּוֹר בִּגְבוּרָתוֹ אַל־יִתְהַלֵּל עָשִׁיר בְּעָשְׁרוֹ: כִּי אִם־
בְּזֹאת יִתְהַלֵּל הַמִּתְהַלֵּל הַשְׂכֵּל וְיָדֹעַ אוֹתִי כִּי אֲנִי ד'
עֹשֶׂה חֶסֶד מִשְׁפָּט וּצְדָקָה בָּאָרֶץ כִּי־בְאֵלֶּה חָפַצְתִּי
נְאֻם־ד':

**54) משלי כח:יד**

אַשְׁרֵי אָדָם מְפַחֵד תָּמִיד וּמַקְשֶׁה לִבּוֹ יִפּוֹל בְּרָעָה:

**55) תהילים יט:ח**

תּוֹרַת ד' תְּמִימָה מְשִׁיבַת נָפֶשׁ עֵדוּת ד' נֶאֱמָנָה
מַחְכִּימַת פֶּתִי:

וגבעות, אמר: הרים וגבעות בקשו עלי רחמים,
אמרו לו: עד שאנו מבקשים עליך נבקש על עצמנו,
שנאמר: (ישעיהו נד) כי ההרים ימושו והגבעות
תמוטינה. אמר: שמים וארץ בקשו עלי רחמים,
אמרו: עד שאנו מבקשים עליך נבקש על עצמנו,
שנאמר: (ישעיהו נא) כי שמים כעשן נמלחו והארץ
כבגד תבלה. אמר: חמה ולבנה בקשו עלי רחמים,
אמרו לו: עד שאנו מבקשים עליך נבקש על עצמנו,
שנאמר: (ישעיהו כד) וחפרה הלבנה ובושה החמה.
אמר: כוכבים ומזלות בקשו עלי רחמים, אמרו לו:
עד שאנו מבקשים עליך נבקש על עצמנו, שנאמר:
(ישעיהו לד) ונמקו כל צבא השמים. אמר: אין הדבר
תלוי אלא בי, הניח ראשו בין ברכיו וגעה בבכיה
עד שיצתה נשמתו. יצתה בת קול ואמרה: ר"א בן
דורדיא מזומן לחיי העולם הבא.

### 36) במדבר יג:ב-ג, ורש"י על יג:ג
שְׁלַח־לְךָ אֲנָשִׁים וְיָתֻרוּ אֶת־אֶרֶץ כְּנַעַן אֲשֶׁר־אֲנִי
נֹתֵן לִבְנֵי יִשְׂרָאֵל אִישׁ אֶחָד אִישׁ אֶחָד לְמַטֵּה אֲבֹתָיו
תִּשְׁלָחוּ כֹּל נָשִׂיא בָהֶם:
**כולם אנשים** – כל אנשים שבמקרא לשון חשיבות,
ואותה שעה כשרים היו.

### 37) במדבר יג:לג
וְשָׁם רָאִינוּ אֶת־הַנְּפִילִים בְּנֵי עֲנָק מִן־הַנְּפִלִים וַנְּהִי
בְעֵינֵינוּ כַּחֲגָבִים וְכֵן הָיִינוּ בְּעֵינֵיהֶם:

### 38) פירוש רש"י על במדבר יג:לג
וכן היינו בעיניהם – שמענו אומרים זה לזה נמלים
(רא"ם ובס"א חגבים) יש בכרמים כאנשים (סוטה לה):

### 39) יהושע ב:ט-יא
וַתֹּאמֶר אֶל־הָאֲנָשִׁים יָדַעְתִּי כִּי־נָתַן ד' לָכֶם אֶת־הָאָרֶץ
וְכִי־נָפְלָה אֵימַתְכֶם עָלֵינוּ וְכִי נָמֹגוּ כָּל־יֹשְׁבֵי הָאָרֶץ
מִפְּנֵיכֶם: כִּי שָׁמַעְנוּ אֵת אֲשֶׁר־הוֹבִישׁ ד' אֶת־מֵי יַם־
סוּף מִפְּנֵיכֶם בְּצֵאתְכֶם מִמִּצְרָיִם וַאֲשֶׁר עֲשִׂיתֶם לִשְׁנֵי
מַלְכֵי הָאֱמֹרִי אֲשֶׁר בְּעֵבֶר הַיַּרְדֵּן לְסִיחֹן וּלְעוֹג אֲשֶׁר
הֶחֱרַמְתֶּם אוֹתָם: וַנִּשְׁמַע וַיִּמַּס לְבָבֵנוּ וְלֹא־קָמָה עוֹד
רוּחַ בְּאִישׁ מִפְּנֵיכֶם כִּי ד' אֱלֹקֵיכֶם הוּא אֱלֹקִים בַּשָּׁמַיִם
מִמַּעַל וְעַל־הָאָרֶץ מִתָּחַת:

### 40) שמואל א' ט"ו:ט-יט
וַיֹּאמֶר שְׁמוּאֵל אֶל־שָׁאוּל הֶרֶף וְאַגִּידָה לְּךָ אֵת אֲשֶׁר
דִּבֶּר ד' אֵלַי הַלָּיְלָה וַיֹּאמְרוּ [וַיֹּאמֶר] לוֹ דַּבֵּר: וַיֹּאמֶר
שְׁמוּאֵל הֲלוֹא אִם־קָטֹן אַתָּה בְּעֵינֶיךָ רֹאשׁ שִׁבְטֵי
יִשְׂרָאֵל אָתָּה וַיִּמְשָׁחֲךָ ד' לְמֶלֶךְ עַל־יִשְׂרָאֵל: וַיִּשְׁלָחֲךָ
ד' בְּדָרֶךְ וַיֹּאמֶר לֵךְ וְהַחֲרַמְתָּה אֶת־הַחַטָּאִים אֶת־עֲמָלֵק
וְנִלְחַמְתָּ בוֹ עַד כַּלּוֹתָם אֹתָם: וְלָמָּה לֹא־שָׁמַעְתָּ בְּקוֹל
ד' וַתַּעַט אֶל־הַשָּׁלָל וַתַּעַשׂ הָרַע בְּעֵינֵי ד':

### 41) רמב"ם, הלכות תשובה ה:ב
אל יעבור במחשבתך דבר זה שאומרים טפשי

---

אומה"ע ורוב גולמי בני ישראל שהקב"ה גוזר על
האדם מתחלת בריתו להיות צדיק או רשע, אין
הדבר כן אלא כל אדם ראוי לו להיות צדיק כמשה
רבינו או רשע כירבעם או חכם או סכל או רחמן או
אכזרי או כילי או שוע וכן שאר כל הדעות, ואין לו מי
שיכפהו ולא גוזר עליו ולא מי שמושכו לאחד משני
הדרכים אלא הוא מעצמו ומדעתו נוטה לאי זו דרך
שירצה ...

### 42) כתובות קיא:
דאמר ר' יוחנן: טוב המלבין שינים לחבירו יותר
ממשקהו חלב

### 43) רמב"ם, הלכות מתנת עניים ז:ה
ואפילו עני המתפרנס מן הצדקה חייב ליתן צדקה
לאחר.

### 44) משלי טז:ה
תּוֹעֲבַת ד' כָּל־גְּבַהּ־לֵב ...

### 45) משנה אבות ד:ד, רמב"ם, הלכות דעות ב:ג
רבי לויטס איש יבנה אומר מאד מאד הוי שפל רוח.
... ולפיכך נאמר במשה רבינו ענו מאד ולא נאמר
ענו בלבד, ולפיכך צוו חכמים מאד מאד הוי שפל
רוח, ועוד אמרו שכל המגביה לבו כפר בעיקר
שנאמר ורם לבבך ושכחת את ה' אלקיך

### 46) משנה אבות ב:ד
... בטל רצונך מפני רצונו

### 47) משנה אבות ב:ח
רבן יוחנן בן זכאי קבל מהלל ומשמאי. הוא היה אומר
אם למדת תורה הרבה. אל תחזיק טובה לעצמך כי
לכך נוצרת.

### 48) שמות כג:יט, ויקרא כג:י', במדבר טו:כ, דברים
יח:ד, ספר החינוך, מצוה תרו
רֵאשִׁית בִּכּוּרֵי אַדְמָתְךָ תָּבִיא בֵּית ד' אֱלֹקֶיךָ לֹא־תְבַשֵּׁל
גְּדִי בַּחֲלֵב אִמּוֹ:
דַּבֵּר אֶל־בְּנֵי יִשְׂרָאֵל וְאָמַרְתָּ אֲלֵהֶם כִּי־תָבֹאוּ אֶל־הָאָרֶץ
אֲשֶׁר אֲנִי נֹתֵן לָכֶם וּקְצַרְתֶּם אֶת־קְצִירָהּ וַהֲבֵאתֶם אֶת־
עֹמֶר רֵאשִׁית קְצִירְכֶם אֶל־הַכֹּהֵן:
רֵאשִׁית עֲרִסֹתֵכֶם חַלָּה תָּרִימוּ תְרוּמָה כִּתְרוּמַת גֹּרֶן כֵּן
תָּרִימוּ אֹתָהּ:
רֵאשִׁית דְּגָנְךָ תִּירֹשְׁךָ וְיִצְהָרֶךָ וְרֵאשִׁית גֵּז צֹאנְךָ
תִּתֶּן־לוֹ:

### 49) ספר החינוך, מצוה תרו
מצות קריאה על הבכורים ... לפי שהאדם מעורר
מחשבותיו ומצייר בלבבו האמת בכח דברי פיו, על
כן בהטיבו אליו השם ברוך הוא ובברכו אותו ואת
אדמתו לעשות פירות, וזכה להביאם לבית אלקינו,

### 19) ויקרא יט:יד
לֹא-תְקַלֵּל חֵרֵשׁ וְלִפְנֵי עִוֵּר לֹא תִתֵּן מִכְשֹׁל וְיָרֵאתָ מֵאֱלֹקֶיךָ אֲנִי ד':

### 20) מדרש רבה, שיר השירים ה:ג
אמר הקב"ה לישראל בני פתחו לי פתח אחד של תשובה כחודה של מחט ואני פותח לכם פתחים שיהיו עגלות וקרוניות נכנסות בו.

### 21) ברכות ה:
אחד המרבה ואחד הממעיט ובלבד שיכוין לבו לשמים

### 22) מתוך נוסח של סיום מסכתא
... שאנו משכימים והם משכימים, אנו משכימים לדברי תורה, והם משכימים לדברים בטלים. אנו עמלים והם עמלים, אנו עמלים ומקבלים שכר, והם עמלים ואינם מקבלים שכר. אנו רצים והם רצים, אנו רצים לחיי העולם הבא, והם רצים לבאר שחת ...

### 23) במדבר יב:ג
וְהָאִישׁ מֹשֶׁה עָנָו מְאֹד מִכֹּל הָאָדָם אֲשֶׁר עַל פְּנֵי הָאֲדָמָה:

### 24) פירוש כתב וקבלה על במדבר יב:ג
... ואף שלא היה ונעלם ממנו סגולותיו היקרות, ידע שהוא אב לחכמים ולנביאים, בכל זה היו כל זולתו הפחותים ממנו נחשבים מאד בעיניו, העביר זכרון סגולותיו ומעלותיו הנפלאות מנגד עיני לבו והטה עיניו לטובת כל זולתו, ונפש כל אחד מישראל היה יקר בעיניו יותר מנפש עצמו, עד שבחר להמחות מספר החיים למען הציל נפשות ישראל ...

### 25) דברים לד:י
וְלֹא-קָם נָבִיא עוֹד בְּיִשְׂרָאֵל כְּמֹשֶׁה אֲשֶׁר יְדָעוֹ ד' פָּנִים אֶל-פָּנִים:

### 26) שמות לד:כח
וַיְהִי-שָׁם עִם-ד' אַרְבָּעִים יוֹם וְאַרְבָּעִים לַיְלָה לֶחֶם לֹא אָכַל וּמַיִם לֹא שָׁתָה וַיִּכְתֹּב עַל-הַלֻּחֹת אֵת דִּבְרֵי הַבְּרִית עֲשֶׂרֶת הַדְּבָרִים:

### 27) שמות כג:ז, ויקרא יט:יא
מִדְּבַר-שֶׁקֶר תִּרְחָק וְנָקִי וְצַדִּיק אַל-תַּהֲרֹג כִּי לֹא-אַצְדִּיק רָשָׁע:
לֹא תִּגְנֹבוּ וְלֹא-תְכַחֲשׁוּ וְלֹא-תְשַׁקְּרוּ אִישׁ בַּעֲמִיתוֹ:

### 28) פסחים נ
כי הא דרב יוסף בריה דרבי יהושע בן לוי חלש ואתנגיד. כי הדר, אמר ליה אבוה: מאי חזית? אמר ליה: עולם הפוך ראיתי, עליונים למטה ותחתונים למעלה.

---

### 29) קידושין לט:
מחשבה רעה אין הקב"ה מצרפה למעשה.

### 30) מהר"ל, דרוש על התורה ט:, יא:
... כי כל מה שראוי שיהיה בהם נמצא בם מיד כשנבראו. ולכך נקראת היותר עצמות שבהם בהמה, כלומר בה כי מה שראוי שימצא בה הרי הוא מתחלה בה. שאם נברא השור לחרוש והחמור לישא משא הרי נמצא בהם בהבראם, ואין דבר בו בכח שיצא בה אחר כך אל הפעל. אבל האדם לא נקרא רק שיהיה הוא מוציא שלימותו אל הפעל, בבחינת האדמה הזאת אשר ממנה נוצר וכל זמן שלא הוציא שלימותו אל הפעל נחשב אדמה בכח בלבד. ... שהב"ח נקראים בהמה על שם שיש בה מה, דהיינו מה שנבראת הבהמה עליו נמצא עמה בבריאותה, ואילו האדם נקרא אדם מפני שהוא אדמה שהיא בכח בלבד ...

### 31) שו"ת אגרות משה חושן משפט חלק ב סימן סו
נשאלתי בנערה שרוצה ליפות עצמה כדי שיקפצו עליה לקדשה ע"י מה שהמציאו עתה הרופאים ע"י נתוח שהוא חבלה בגופה אם מותרת מצד האיסור לחבול בעצמו.... וא"כ בנערה ליפות עצמה שהוא לטובתה וברצונה יש להתיר בפשיטות אף אם לא נסבור כהרמב"ם בחדושו דבעינן שיהיה דרך נציון ובזיון ... אלא צריך לומר דכיון שהוא לנוי שלכן הוא לטובתו שרוצה בזה ליכא איסור דחבול והוי מזה ראיה ממש לעובדא דידן שכ"ש בנערה שהשיפוי יותר צורך וטובה לה מלאיש דהא איתא בכתובות דף נ"ט ע"ב תני ר"ח אין אשה אלא ליופי שודאי יש להחשיב שהוא לטובתה ומותרת לחבול בשביל להתיפות.

### 32) מגילה ו:
ואמר רבי יצחק, אם יאמר לך אדם: יגעתי ולא מצאתי אל תאמן, לא יגעתי ומצאתי אל תאמן, יגעתי ומצאתי תאמן.

### 33) משנה אבות, ה:כב
בן הא הא אומר לפום צערא אגרא:

### 34) מתוך תפילת מוסף של ראש השנה
כי זכר כל היצור לפניך בא. מעשה איש ופקדתו ...

### 35) עבודה זרה יז:
אמרו עליו על ר"א בן דורדיא, שלא הניח זונה אחת בעולם שלא בא עליה. פעם אחת שמע שיש זונה אחת בכרכי הים והיתה נוטלת כיס דינרין בשכרה, נטל כיס דינרין והלך ועבר עליה שבעה נהרות. בשעת הרגל דבר הפיחה, אמרה: כשם שהפיחה זו אינה חוזרת למקומה, כך אלעזר בן דורדיא אין מקבלין אותו בתשובה. הלך וישב בין שני הרים

# SOURCES ON SELF-ESTEEM IN JUDAISM

**1) בראשית א:כו-כז**

וַיֹּאמֶר אֱלֹקִים נַעֲשֶׂה אָדָם בְּצַלְמֵנוּ כִּדְמוּתֵנוּ וְיִרְדּוּ בִדְגַת הַיָּם וּבְעוֹף הַשָּׁמַיִם וּבַבְּהֵמָה וּבְכָל־הָאָרֶץ וּבְכָל־הָרֶמֶשׂ הָרֹמֵשׂ עַל־הָאָרֶץ: וַיִּבְרָא אֱלֹקִים אֶת־הָאָדָם בְּצַלְמוֹ בְּצֶלֶם אֱלֹקִים בָּרָא אֹתוֹ זָכָר וּנְקֵבָה בָּרָא אֹתָם:

**2) סנהדרין לז.**

לפיכך נברא אדם יחידי, ללמדך שכל המאבד נפש אחת (מישראל) מעלה עליו הכתוב כאילו איבד עולם מלא, וכל המקיים נפש אחת (מישראל) מעלה עליו הכתוב כאילו קיים עולם מלא.

**3) תהילים ח:ה-ו**

מָה־אֱנוֹשׁ כִּי־תִזְכְּרֶנּוּ וּבֶן־אָדָם כִּי תִפְקְדֶנּוּ: וַתְּחַסְּרֵהוּ מְעַט מֵאֱלֹקִים וְכָבוֹד וְהָדָר תְּעַטְּרֵהוּ:

**4) מדרש, ויקרא רבה יד:א**

אם זכה אדם אומרים לו אתה קדמת למלאכי השרת ואם לאו אומרים לו זבוב קדמך, יתוש קדמך ...

**5) משנה אבות ג:יד**

הוא היה אומר חביב אדם שנברא בצלם. חבה יתרה נודעת לו שנברא בצלם. שנאמר (בראשית ט). כי בצלם אלהים עשה את האדם. חביבין ישראל שנקראו בנים למקום. חבה יתרה נודעת להם שנקראו בנים למקום. שנאמר (דברים יד). בנים אתם לה' אלהיכם. חביבין ישראל. שנתן להם כלי חמדה. חבה יתרה נודעת להם שנתן להם כלי חמדה שבו נברא העולם. שנאמר (משלי ד). כי לקח טוב נתתי לכם. תורתי אל תעזבו:

**6) רמב"ם, הלכות תשובה ה:א**

... הוא שכתוב בתורה "הן האדם היה כאחד ממנו לדעת טוב ורע", כלומר הן מין זה של אדם היה יחיד בעולם ואין מין כמו שני דומה לו בזה הענין שיהא הוא מעצמו בדעתו ובמחשבתו יודע הטוב והרע ועושה כל מה שהוא חפץ ואין מי שיעכב בידו מלעשות הטוב או הרע וכיון שכן הוא פן ישלח ידו.

**7) סנהדרין לז.**

לפיכך כל אחד ואחד חייב לומר: בשבילי נברא העולם.

**8) מכות כב**

אמר רבא: כמה טפשאי שאר אינשי דקיימי מקמי ספר תורה ולא קיימי מקמי גברא רבה, דאילו בס"ת כתיב ארבעים, ואתו רבנן בצרו חדא.

**9) משנה שבת יד:ד**

רַבִּי שִׁמְעוֹן אוֹמֵר, כָּל יִשְׂרָאֵל בְּנֵי מְלָכִים הֵם:

**10) משנה סנהדרין ד:ה**

לפיכך נברא אדם יחידי, ללמדך שכל המאבד נפש אחת מישראל מעלה עליו הכתוב כאילו איבד עולם מלא, וכל המקיים נפש אחת מישראל מעלה עליו הכתוב כאילו קיים עולם מלא. ומפני שלום הבריות, שלא יאמר אדם לחבירו אבא גדול מאביך ... ולהגיד גדולתו של הקדוש ברוך הוא, שאדם טובע כמה מטבעות בחותם אחד - כולן דומין זה לזה, ומלך מלכי המלכים הקדוש ברוך הוא טבע כל אדם בחותמו של אדם הראשון - ואין אחד מהן דומה לחבירו.

**11) ברכות נח.**

שאין דעתם דומה זה לזה, ואין פרצופיהן דומים זה לזה.

**12) משלי כב:ו**

חֲנֹךְ לַנַּעַר עַל־פִּי דַרְכּוֹ גַּם כִּי־יַזְקִין לֹא־יָסוּר מִמֶּנָּה:

**13) תהילים קד:כד**

מָה־רַבּוּ מַעֲשֶׂיךָ ד' כֻּלָּם בְּחָכְמָה עָשִׂיתָ מָלְאָה הָאָרֶץ קִנְיָנֶךָ:

**14) מתוך תפילת מוסף של ראש השנה**

כִּי זֵכֶר כָּל הַיְצוּר לְפָנֶיךָ בָּא. מַעֲשֵׂה אִישׁ וּפְקֻדָּתוֹ ...

**15) רבינו יונה, שער העבודה א**

הפתח הראשון הוא שידע האיש העובד ערך עצמו ויכיר מעלתו ... יוסיף אומץ לקנות מעלות ומדות אשר יתקרב בהם לבוראו וידבק אליו ... כפי כחו והשגת ידו ...

**16) בראשית ה:א**

זֶה סֵפֶר תּוֹלְדֹת אָדָם בְּיוֹם בְּרֹא אֱלֹקִים אָדָם בִּדְמוּת אֱלֹקִים עָשָׂה אֹתוֹ:

**17) מדרש בראשית רבה כד:ז**

זה כלל גדול בתורה, שלא תאמר הואיל ונתבזיתי יתבזה חבירי עמי הואיל ונתקללתי יתקלל חבירי עמי, א"ר תנחומא אם עשית כן דע למי אתה מבזה, בדמות אלקים עשה אותו.

**18) משנה שבועות ד:יג**

המקלל עצמו וחבירו בכולן. עובר בלא תעשה.

וַיָּבוֹא הֲתָךְ וַיַּגֵּד לְאֶסְתֵּר אֵת דִּבְרֵי מָרְדֳּכָי: וַתֹּאמֶר אֶסְתֵּר לַהֲתָךְ וַתְּצַוֵּהוּ אֶל־מָרְדֳּכָי: כָּל־עַבְדֵי הַמֶּלֶךְ וְעַם־מְדִינוֹת הַמֶּלֶךְ יֹדְעִים אֲשֶׁר כָּל־אִישׁ וְאִשָּׁה אֲשֶׁר יָבוֹא־אֶל־הַמֶּלֶךְ אֶל־הֶחָצֵר הַפְּנִימִית אֲשֶׁר לֹא־יִקָּרֵא אַחַת דָּתוֹ לְהָמִית לְבַד מֵאֲשֶׁר יוֹשִׁיט־לוֹ הַמֶּלֶךְ אֶת־שַׁרְבִיט הַזָּהָב וְחָיָה וַאֲנִי לֹא נִקְרֵאתִי לָבוֹא אֶל־הַמֶּלֶךְ זֶה שְׁלוֹשִׁים יוֹם: וַיַּגִּידוּ לְמָרְדֳּכַי אֵת דִּבְרֵי אֶסְתֵּר: וַיֹּאמֶר מָרְדֳּכַי לְהָשִׁיב אֶל־אֶסְתֵּר אַל־תְּדַמִּי בְנַפְשֵׁךְ לְהִמָּלֵט בֵּית־הַמֶּלֶךְ מִכָּל־הַיְּהוּדִים:

## 27) רב קוק, שו"ת משפט כהן קמג, "מאי אסתר"

... וא"כ אפילו בלא הצלת הרבים ג"כ היתה יכולה, בשביל הצלת עצמה, להכניס את עצמה לספק זה, וא"כ בשביל הצלת הרבים מצוה וחובה איכא ... שוב הכירה (אסתר) את ההיתר, וממילא את החובה

## 28) יונה א:י'-י"ב

וַיִּירְאוּ הָאֲנָשִׁים יִרְאָה גְדוֹלָה וַיֹּאמְרוּ אֵלָיו מַה־זֹּאת עָשִׂיתָ כִּי־יָדְעוּ הָאֲנָשִׁים כִּי־מִלִּפְנֵי ד' הוּא בֹרֵחַ כִּי הִגִּיד לָהֶם: וַיֹּאמְרוּ אֵלָיו מַה־נַּעֲשֶׂה לָּךְ וְיִשְׁתֹּק הַיָּם מֵעָלֵינוּ כִּי הַיָּם הוֹלֵךְ וְסֹעֵר: וַיֹּאמֶר אֲלֵיהֶם שָׂאוּנִי וַהֲטִילֻנִי אֶל־הַיָּם וְיִשְׁתֹּק הַיָּם מֵעֲלֵיכֶם כִּי יוֹדֵעַ אָנִי כִּי בְשֶׁלִּי הַסַּעַר הַגָּדוֹל הַזֶּה עֲלֵיכֶם:

## 29) תענית יח: ופירוש רש"י שם

כשבקש טוריינוס להרוג את לולינוס ופפוס אחיו בלודקיא

בלודקיא – הרוגי לוד אין כל בריה יכולה לעמוד במחיצתן בגן עדן, ויש אומרין: שנהרגו על בתו של מלך שנמצאת הרוגה, ואמרו: היהודים הרגוה, וגזרו גזרה על שונאיהן של ישראל, ועמדו אלו ופדו את ישראל, ואמרו: אנו הרגנוה, והרג המלך לאלו בלבד.

מפני נפש אבל לא באופן דילן שממילא לא ינצל
... אלא שנראה שאין הדברים אמורים אלא ברודף
לרצונו משא"כ בנ"ד שהרוצה רודף לאונסו אין כאן
מצוה בדוקא להורגו אלא רשות ונהרד בכה"ג שלא
רצה להרוג את הרודף ונהרג על ידו "קדוש יאמר לו"
וקיים "ונקדשתי בתוך בני ישראל" ולכן אלו. (והיו
מקרים כאלו במשפחתי הי"ד) שלא רצו להציל נפש
ע"י החנקת ילד מישראל קדשו שם שמים. אבל זה
שכן עשה א"צ להיות לבו נוקפו מכיוון שכדין עשה
בכדי להציל נפשות מישראל ...

## 23) משנת פיקוח נפש נ

האם מותר להפיל מטוס כשחוטפין רוצים לפוצץ
אותו על בנין גבוה

יש לעיין אם נחטף מטוס ורוצים החוטפים לפוצצו
על בנין רב קומות כדי להרבות ההרוגים (וכמעשה
דארע בבנין התאומים בארה"ב) האם מותר לפוצץ
המטוס באויר קודם שיגיע למטרתו ובפשטותו דומה
הדבר לדינא דעכו"ם שאומרים לישראלתנו לנו אחד
מכם ואם לאו נהרוג את כולכם דאסור למסור להם
נפש מישראל ויהרגו כולם ... וא"כ גם בנידון דידן
הגם דבלא"ה כל נוסעי המטוס ייהרגו בעוד זמן מה
מ"מ א"א לילד ולהרוג ליחידים אפילו לחיי שעה כדי
להציל הרבים אמנם למאי דכתב החזו"א ביו"ד סימן
ס"ט דמותר להטות החץ כדי להציל הרבים הגם
דעי"ז יהרג היחיד דחשיבא מעשה הצלה עיי"ש יש
להסתפק בנידון דידן מהו.... ושאלתי לדבר לרבנו
הגר"ח קניבסקי שליט"א והשיב רבנו "נסתפקנו בזה"
(והנה באמת שהיה מקום לדון בזה מפנים אחרות
דמסתברא סהדי דכאו"א מיושבי המטוס אם היה
יודע הדברים כהוויתן רוצה שיפילו המטוס ולהציל
לנפשות הרבות שזוממים להורגן ובזה י"ל דבודאי
שרי וכמעשה דלוליינוס ופפוס (בתענית יח:) שמסרו
נפשם להציל הרבים ואין כל בריה לעמוד במחיצתן
והכא עדיפא דהתם הם עצמם לא היו בגזירה ... ואם
הוא באופן שבמטוס ישנם רק לחוטפים אלא דאם
המטוס קודם שיגיע לבנין הגבוה יפול שבריו במקום
ישוב כמה יחידים בזה ודאי הדבר דומה להטיית
החץ שדן החזו"א דעלינו להשתדל בהצלת הרבים

## 24) משנת פיקוח נפש מט:ז-ח

ומעשה שנפל בית רב קומות על כל יושביו ואנשים
הרבה שכולם ימותו ברעב ובצמא וכדי לפנות
להריסות אנו גורמים

להריגתם של חלק מהאנשים אולם רק באופן זה
נוכל להציל להרבה מן הלכודים ויש לדון אם מותר
לעשות כן דלכאורה הרי אסור להרוג אדם כדי
להציל לאחרים וא"כ אין לנו רשות לפנות להריסות
הבנין ... אמנם לדברי החזו"א דמותר להטות החץ
להציל הרבים הגם בנידון דמפולת הרי אנו עוסקים
במעשה הצלה דרבים ואין כאן פעולת הריגה, איברא
דיש לחלק דבהטית חץ אנו באים למנוע לדבר

ההורג ובזה התיר החזו"א הגם שע"ז יהרוג החץ
ליחיד אולם

בנידון דמפולת אנו באים להציל ללכודים שלא
ימותו ברעב ובצמא או בחניקה אולם אין כאן סילוק
מעשה ההריגה כי אם פעולת הצלה לחודא ואפשר
דבכגון דא לא התיר החזו"א הצלה דברים כשע"ז
אנו עושים מעשה הריגה דיחיד ...

## 25) אסיא, מה-מו, טבת תשמ"ט, עמודים 62-68, הרב יצחק זילברשטיין
### שאלה

א שבעה אנשים נוסעים בים והספינה על נוסעיה
עומדת להיטבע מכובד האנשים כדי להקל מעומס
הספינה חייב רב החובל להשליך לים שלושה
מהנוסעים ובזה יינצלו הנותרים האם הדבר מותר
ב בית שקרס תחתיו ורבים נלכדו מתחת לעיי
המפולת המצילים חייבים לעלות עליו עם טרקטור
ומנוף וקרוב לודאי שבפעולות ההצלה ייהרגו בידים
חלק מהלכודים האם הדבר מותר

... לאור כל זאת אם נראה אם שבעה אנשים נוסעים בים
וכולם עומדים להיטבע יש מקום למסור לרב החובל
שלושה מהנוסעים להטילם לים כדי על מנת להציל
את הנותרים כשם שנטה הפנים מאירות להתיר
הריגת העובר כדי להציל את האם וכשם שמביא
מהר"מ חלואה שיטה המתירה לראובן להרוג את
שמעון באופן שאם לא יהרגנו יהרוג המושל את
ראובן וגם את שמעון ומסתבר שבאופן זה מותר
להטיל גורלות מי יהיה השלושה שיוטלו לים ומה
שתמה החזון איש אם כן למה יהרגו כולם יטילו
גורלות הרי כתבו היד רמ"ה ומהר"ם חלואה והלחם
משנה וחסדי דוד במשניות אהלות שלא בטוח
שהאחד שימסרו ודאי ייהרג כי שמא יצליח להימלט
אבל כאשר ברור הדבר שייהרג מותר למוסרו אך
מדברי החזון איש הנ"ל נראה דגם כשברור שכולם
ייהרגו אסור. ונראה שהוא הדין במפולת אם בלי
פעולות הצלה ימותו כולם מותר לעלות עם טרקטור
ומנוף להציל ואעפ"י שקרוב לודאי שייהרג בידים
אנשים הרי בלי הצלה כולם ימותו ודומה לפנים
מאירות ולמהר"ם חלואה הנ"ל ומדבריהם יוצא שאין
להתחשב בחיי שעה כשנתין להציל לחיי עולם ...
וטעם ההיתר דאם לא נעשה פעולות הצלה ימותו
כולם ועכ"פ כשאין ודאות ממש שייהרג מסתבר
שמותר ובפרט שיש לצרף לכך את שיטת החזון איש
הסובר שאם חץ נופל לעבר קבוצת אנשים מותר
להם להטות את החץ לעבר השני שיש בו פחות
אנשים משום שהטיית החץ נחשבת לפעולת הצלה
שבמקרה כרוכה בהריגה

## 26) אסתר ד:ח-יג

וְאֶת־פַּתְשֶׁגֶן כְּתָב־הַדָּת אֲשֶׁר־נִתַּן בְּשׁוּשָׁן לְהַשְׁמִידָם
נָתַן לוֹ לְהַרְאוֹת אֶת־אֶסְתֵּר וּלְהַגִּיד לָהּ וּלְצַוּוֹת עָלֶיהָ
לָבוֹא אֶל־הַמֶּלֶךְ לְהִתְחַנֶּן־לוֹ וּלְבַקֵּשׁ מִלְּפָנָיו עַל־עַמָּהּ:

**13) פירוש בית הבחירה על סנהדרין עב:**

מכל מקום אמרו שם, שאם ייחדוהו להם כשבע בן בכרי, כלומר "תנו לנו את פלוני ונהרגהו, ואם לאו נהרוג את כולכם ימסרו להם כל כיש בו הצלת שנים בשביל אחד ... הא כל להצלת רבים אפילו לא נתחייב מיתה או שנתחייב ולא בדיננו, הואיל וייחדוהו, מותר

ויראה כרב יוחנן שהרי זה שנחלקו שניהם הלכה כמותו, וכל שכן בתלמוד שלו

**14) יבמות לו.**

אמר רבא: הלכתא כוותיה דריש לקיש בהני תלת ...

**15) גר"א על שולחן ערוך, יורה דעה קנז:טז**

...והרמב"ם פסק כר"ל משום ההוא עובדא דריב"ל שם וצ"ע

**16) רמב"ם, הקדמה לפירוש המשניות**

... כתבו התלמוד הירושלמי, והמחברו הוא רבי יוחנן

**17) רמ"א, שולחן ערוך, יורה דעה קנז:א**

... עובדי כוכבים שאמרו לישראל תנו לנו אחד מכם ונהרגנו לא יתנו להם אחד מהם אלא א"כ יחדוהו ואמרו תנו לנו פלוני (משנה פ' ח' דתרומות והרמב"ם פ"ה מהלכות יסודי התורה) ויש אומרים דאפילו בכה"ג אין למסרו אא"כ חייב מיתה כשבע בן בכרי (ב"י בשם רש"י ור"ן)

**18) טורי זהב על יורה דעה קנז:ז**

נ"ל נכון בפי' הירושלמי וברמב"ם ולענין הלכה יש לנו לפסוק כן כר"ל ולא ימסרוהו אא"כ חייב מיתה כשבע בן בכרי כדעה השניה שהביא רמ"א כאן וכן פסק מו"ח ז"ל:

**19) חזון איש על סנהדרין, 25#**

ויש לעיין באחד רואה חץ הולך להרוג אנשים רבים, ויכול להטותו לצד אחר ויהרוג רק אחד שבצד אחר, ואלו שבצד זה יצולו, ואם לא יעשה כלום, יהרגו הרבים והאחד ישאר בחים. ואפשר דלא דמי למוסרים אחד להריגה, דהתם המסירה היא פעולה האכזרית של הר ית נגת נפש, ובפעולה זה ליכא הצלת אחרים בטבע של הפעולה, אלא המקרה גרם עכשיו הצלה לאחרים. גם הצלת האחרים קשור במה שמוסרים להריגה נפש מישראל. אבל ... טיית החץ מצ ד זה לצד אחר היא בעיקרה פעולת הצלה. דיש לנו להשתדל למעט אבידת ישראל בכל מאי דאפשר.

**20) אגרות משה, יורה דעה, ב:ס**

... וזה מוכרח לומר להרמב"ם שפוסק כר"ל וכתב טעם רודף בעובר וא"כ א"א לומר ... ומחוייב

מיתה כשבע בן בכרי שכתב הרמב"ם מוכרח לומר שכוונתו רק מחוייב מיתה להליסטים ... נמצא לפי מה שביארתי בדברי ר' יוחנן ומוכרח כן שכל ההיתר בייחדוהו הוא רק מחמת שהוא נחשב כרודף אף שהוא שלא בכוונה ... ולפי זה יש לפרש בטעם ר"ל שפליג על ר' יוחנן ... שסובר דהוא עכ"פ מעשה מסירה ואסור גם מצד עצם החיים, שלכן יהיה אסור לדידיה גם בייחדו לטומאה ... וגם לפ"מ שביארתי לכו"ע כדסובר התפארת ישראל, ולכן מסתבר שיש לסמוך על המתירין לדינא.

**21) שו"ת ציץ אליעזר טו:ע:**

... אם רשאים לעשות פעולת הצלה למען הצלת רבים ממיתה כאשר על ידי זאת הפעולה ייהרג יחיד ...

ובהקדם דברי הגאון החזו"א ז"ל לסנהדרין סי' כ"ה שכותב לחתור חקירה חמורה למעשה, דמה יהא הדין באחד שרואה חץ הולך להרוג אנשים רבים ויכול להטותו לצד אחר ויהרג רק אחד שבצד אחר, ואלו שבצד זה יצולו, ואם לא יעשה כלום יהרגו הרבים והאחד ישאר בחים. ומתחילה נוטה החזו"א לומר שצריך להטותו לצד האחר ולא דמי למוסרים אחד להריגה וכו' מפני שהטיית החץ מצד זה לצד אחר היא בעיקרה פעולת הצלה ואינה קשורה כלל בהריגת היחיד שבצד האחר ורק עכשיו במקרה נמצא בצד האחר נפש מישראל, ולכן, אחרי שבצד זה יהרגו נפשות רבות, ובצד האחר רק אחד, אפשר דיש לנו להשתדל למעט אבידת ישראל בכל מאי דאפשר....ולכן נלענ"ד דבכל כגון דא של חקירת החזו"א ז"ל קובע יותר השב ואל תעשה עדיף כי הרי ישנה טענה של מאי חזית דדמא דזה סומק מדמא של חבירו, ובהריגה ודאית אין חילוק בין יחיד לרבים, ולא אמרינן דרבים עדיפא, ולולינוס ופפוס שנהרגו בשביל להציל את ישראל כמ"ש רש"י בתענית ד' י"ח ע"ב (שמביא החזו"א שם מזה) הוא מפני שאחרת גם המה היו בהסכנה ליהרג ...

**22) שו"ת מנחת ההריגה א**

הצלה ממעט ע"י גרימת מותו של ילד

שאלה: בדבר השאלה אשר שמעה תסמר שערות ראש והיא בבונקר - במחבוא ישבה עדה שלמה של יהודים שהסתתרו מהמת המציק הצורר ימ"ש ... ובעת שהרשעים הללו ערכו חיפושים למצוא את האומללים האלו פרץ תינוק שחיה בין הנחבאים בבכי ... השאלה חמותר לשים כר בפי התינוק כדי להשתיקו. במעשה זה הי' חשש לסכנה שמא יחנק הילד ... בנדון דידן יש לצרף עוד שבתינוק הבוכה הזה שעי"ז גורם להמתתם של כל הנחבאים יש עליו דין של רודף ...... וא"כ בההיא דידן כיון שכולם יהרגו אין כאן ספק שיכולו להטיל עליו כי יש עליו דין רודף באונס ובזה אין להורגו רק אם הוא ינצל, ומדין אין דוחים נפש

# SOURCES ON SACRIFICE ONE TO SAVE MANY

## 1) רמב"ם, הלכות יסודי התורה ה:א-ב

... כיצד כשיעמוד עובד כוכבים ויאנוס את ישראל לעבור על אחת מכל מצות האמורות בתורה או יהרגנו יעבור ואל יהרג שנאמר "במצות אשר יעשה אותם האדם וחי בהם", וחי בהם ולא שימות בהם, ואם מת ולא עבר הרי זה מתחייב בנפשו. במה דברים אמורים בשאר מצות חוץ מעבודת כוכבים וגלוי עריות ושפיכת דמים, אבל שלש עבירות אלו אם יאמר לו עבור על אחת מהן או תהרג, יהרג ואל יעבור ...

## 2) ויקרא יח:ה

וּשְׁמַרְתֶּם אֶת־חֻקֹּתַי וְאֶת־מִשְׁפָּטַי אֲשֶׁר יַעֲשֶׂה אֹתָם הָאָדָם וָחַי בָּהֶם אֲנִי ד':

## 3) יומא פה:

רבי שמעון בן מנסיא אומר: (שמות לא) "ושמרו בני ישראל את השבת", אמרה תורה: חלל עליו שבת אחת, כדי שישמור שבתות הרבה. אמר רבי יהודה אמר שמואל: אי הואי התם הוה אמינא: דידי עדיפא מדידהו, (ויקרא יח) "וחי בהם" ולא שימות בהם.

## 4) שולחן ערוך, יורה דעה קנז:א

כל העבירות שבתורה חוץ מעבודת כוכבים וגלוי עריות ושפיכת דמים אם אומרים לו לאדם שיעבור עליהם או יהרג אם הוא בצינעה יעבור ואל יהרג ואם ירצה להחמיר על עצמו וליהרג רשאי אם העובד כוכבי' מכוין להעבירו על הדת. הגה ואם יוכל להציל עצמו בכל אשר לו צריך ליתן הכל ולא יעבור לא תעשה

## 5) משנה אוהלות ז:ו

האשה שהיא מקשה לילד.מחתכין את הולד במעיה ומוציאין אותו אברים אברים מפני שחייה קודמין לחייו. יצא רובו אין נוגעין בו שאין דוחין נפש מפני נפש:

## 6) שולחן ערוך, חושן משפט תכה:ב

לפיכך: העוברת שהיא מקשה לילד, מותר לחתוך העובר במעיה בין בסם בין ביד מפני שהוא כרודף אחריה להרגה, ואם הוציא ראשו אין נוגעין בו שאין דוחין נפש מפני נפש, וזהו טבעו של עולם.

## 7) סנהדרין עד.

ההוא דאתא לקמיה דרבה, ואמר ליה:אמר לי מרי דורא זיל קטליה לפלניא, ואי לא – קטלינא לך. – אמר ליה: לקטלוך ולא תיקטול. מי יימר דדמא דידך סומק טפי דילמא דמא דהוא גברא סומק טפי.

## 8) סנהדרין לז.

לפיכך נברא אדם יחידי, ללמדך שכל המאבד נפש אחת (מישראל) מעלה עליו הכתוב כאילו איבד עולם מלא, וכל המקיים נפש אחת (מישראל) מעלה עליו הכתוב כאילו קיים עולם מלא. ומפני שלום הבריות, שלא יאמר אדם לחבירו אבא גדול מאביך ...

## 9) תוספתא, תרומות ז:כג

סיעה של בני אדם שאמרו להם נכרים תנו לנו א' מכם ונהרגהו ואם לאו הרי אנו הורגין את כולן יהרגו כולן ואל ימסרו להם נפש אחת מישראל אבל אם ייחדוהו להם כגון שיחדו לשבע בן בכרי יתנוהו להם ואל יהרגו

## 10) שמואל ב', כ:כ-כב

וְשָׁם נִקְרָא אִישׁ בְּלִיַּעַל וּשְׁמוֹ שֶׁבַע בֶּן־בִּכְרִי אִישׁ יְמִינִי וַיִּתְקַע בַּשֹּׁפָר וַיֹּאמֶר אֵין־לָנוּ חֵלֶק בְּדָוִד וְלֹא נַחֲלָה־לָנוּ בְּבֶן־יִשַׁי אִישׁ לְאֹהָלָיו יִשְׂרָאֵל: וַיַּעַל כָּל־אִישׁ יִשְׂרָאֵל מֵאַחֲרֵי דָוִד אַחֲרֵי שֶׁבַע בֶּן־בִּכְרִי וְאִישׁ יְהוּדָה דָּבְקוּ בְמַלְכָּם מִן־הַיַּרְדֵּן וְעַד־יְרוּשָׁלָ͏ִם: ... וַיַּעַן יוֹאָב וַיֹּאמֶר חָלִילָה חָלִילָה לִי אִם־אֲבַלַּע וְאִם־אַשְׁחִית: לֹא־כֵן הַדָּבָר כִּי אִישׁ מֵהַר אֶפְרַיִם שֶׁבַע בֶּן־בִּכְרִי שְׁמוֹ נָשָׂא יָדוֹ בַּמֶּלֶךְ בְּדָוִד תְּנוּ־אֹתוֹ לְבַדּוֹ וְאֵלְכָה מֵעַל הָעִיר וַתֹּאמֶר הָאִשָּׁה אֶל־יוֹאָב הִנֵּה רֹאשׁוֹ מֻשְׁלָךְ אֵלֶיךָ בְּעַד הַחוֹמָה: וַתָּבוֹא הָאִשָּׁה אֶל־כָּל־הָעָם בְּחָכְמָתָהּ וַיִּכְרְתוּ אֶת־רֹאשׁ שֶׁבַע בֶּן־בִּכְרִי וַיַּשְׁלִכוּ אֶל־יוֹאָב וַיִּתְקַע בַּשֹּׁפָר וַיָּפֻצוּ מֵעַל־הָעִיר אִישׁ לְאֹהָלָיו וְיוֹאָב שָׁב יְרוּשָׁלַ͏ִם אֶל־הַמֶּלֶךְ:

## 11) רמב"ם, הלכות יסודי התורה ה:ה

אם אמרו להם עובדי כוכבים תנו לנו אחד מכם ונהרגנו ואם לאו נהרוג כולכם, יהרגו כולם ואל ימסרו להם נפש אחת מישראל, ואם יחדוהו להם ואמרו תנו לנו פלוני או נהרוג כולכם, אם היה מחוייב מיתה כשבע בן בכרי יתנו אותו להם, ואין מורין להם כן לכתחלה, ואם אינו חייב מיתה יהרגו כולם ואל ימסרו להם נפש אחת מישראל.

## 12) תלמוד ירושלמי, תרומות מז

תני סיעות בני אדם שהיו מהלכין בדרך פגעו להן גוים ואמרו תנו לנו אחד מכם ונהרוג אותו ואם לאו הרי אנו הורגים את כולכם אפי' כולן נהרגים לא ימסרו נפש אחת מישראל ייחדו להן אחד כגון שבע בן בכרי ימסרו אותו ואל ייהרגו א"ר שמעון בן לקיש והוא שיהא חייב מיתה כשבע בן בכרי ורבי יוחנן אמר אע"פ שאינו חייב מיתה כשבע בן בכרי

**62) מכות י':**

בגואל הדם הכתוב מדבר. תנן: מוסרין לו שני ת"ח, שמא יהרגנו בדרך וידברו אליו ...

**63) רמב"ם, הלכות רוצח ה:ז-י"א**

בתחילה אחד שוגג ואחד מזיד מקדימין לערי מקלט ובית דין של אותה העיר שהרג בה מביאין אותם משם ודנין אותן שנ' ושלחו זקני עירו ולקחו אותו משם מי שנתחייב מיתה ממיתין אותו שנ' ונתנו אותו ביד גואל הדם מי שנפטר פוטרים אותו שנ' והצילו העדה את הרוצח מיד גואל הדם מי שנתחייב גלות מחזירין אותו למקומו שנ' והשיבו אותו העדה אל עיר מקלטו: כשמשיבין אותו מוסרין לו שני תלמידי חכמים שמא יהרגנו גואל הדם בדרך ואומרין להם אל תנהגו בו מנהג שופכי דמים בשוגג בא מעשה לידו: רוצח בשגגה שהרגו גואל הדם חוץ לתחום עיר מקלטו פטור שנ' (דברים י"ט ו') ולו אין משפט מות: אחד ההורגו בדרך קודם שיכנס לעיר מקלטו או שהרגו בחזירתו עם השנים ששומרים אותו נכנס לעיר מקלטו ויצא לתחומה בזדון הרי זה התיר עצמו למיתה ורשות לגואל הדם להרגו ואם הרגו כל אדם אין חייבין עליו שנ' (במדבר ל"ה כ"ז) אין לו דם: יצא חוץ לתחום עיר מקלטו בשגגה כל ההורגו בין גואל הדם בין שאר אדם גולה על ידו הרגו בתוך תחום עיר מקלטו אפילו גואל הדם הרי זה נהרג עליו:

**64) קובץ הערות לרב אלחנן ואסרמן, יבמות סימן ע**

... נראה דכל האיסורין שבין אדם לחבירו אינן איסורין אלא על דרך קילקול והשחתה שלא לצורך וכמו בלאו דלא תשנא אח אחיך דין האיסור אינו בשנאת חנם היינו שלא ראה בו דבר ערוה אבל אם ראה עליו דבר ערוה מותר לשנאותו ואין דשם הטעם משום דאינו בכלל קי"ג ע"ב ז"ה שנאה דאם ישנאהו בשביל טעם אחר עובר עליו בלאו ולא הותר אלא לשנאתו בשביל דבר ערוה שראה בו וכן דחובל כתב הרמב"ם פ"ה ה"א דהאיסור הוא דוקא אם חובל

דרך נציון והיינו מדחזינן דמותר לרב להכות תלמידו והא דאיתא בסוגיא דפ' הנחנקין הנ"ל אחר שגגת לאו על כרחך צ"ל דאינו אלא חומרא מדרבנן. וכן בלאו דאלמנה ויתום לא תענון כתב הרמב"ם בהל' דעות פ"ו ה ה אם עינה אותן בלאו דלא תלך רכיל מותר לספר לה"ר על בעלי מחלוקת כדי להשקיט המריבה וכן בלאו דאונאת דברים מותר להקניטו בדברים דרך תוכחה וכן מותר להלבין פנים דרך תוכחה אם לא חזר בו אחר שהוכיחו בסתר ומותר גם לקללו בשביל זה כמו שעשו כל הנביאים בישראל והוא לשון הרמב"ם בהל' דעות פ"ו ומוכח מכ"ז דכל האיסורין האלו הותרו לצורך תועלת

**65) שו"ת לב אברהם קכ"ח (ביאור דעת חינוך)**

שעיקר לאו דלא תקום ולא תטור אינו עובר אלא אם אדם נקיט השנאה בלבו, וע"ז בלבד עובר על לא תטור, ואם מחמת הרגש זה נוקם נקמתו עובר על לא תקום. אבל העושה מעשה נקמה בלא כל הרגש של שנאה שבלב, אלא בדרך חינוך ללמדו דעת ולהראות לו איך מרגישים אנשים הצריכים לשאול טובה מאחר והאחר מסרב, ואז כאשר כוונתו לטובתו אין כאן לאו דלא תקום ולאו דלא תטור כלל, וזהו דין באמת לכל אדם כמו שאהב המכה את בנו ורב המכה את תלמידו אינו עובר על לאו דלא יוסף להכותו, כן משום חינוך בלא הרגשת נקמה אין עוברין בלאוין אלו. אלא שזהו אחת מהעבודות הקשות שבמקדש שידע אינש בנפשי' שרק טובת חבירו והדרכתו הניעתו לעשות מעשה נקמה.

**66) פירוש רש"י על סנהדרין פד'**

מה מכה בהמה ישלמנה לרפואה - כגון מקיז דם פטור מן התשלומין, שהרי לא הזיקה. אף מכה אדם - דהיינו אביו. לרפואה פטור - ממיתה, ואף על גב דחבורה היא. ואהבת לרעך כמוך - לא הוזהרו ישראל מלעשות לחבריהם אלא דבר שאינו חפץ לעשות לעצמו.

בעלבונותיו ומצטער צער גדול, והנקמה לו מתוקה
מדבש, כי היא מנוחתו לבדה. על כן לשיהיה בכחו
לעזוב מה שטבעו מכריח אותו ... חזק ואמיץ הוא.
והוא קל רק למלאכי השרת ... :

### 47) סמ"ג לא תעשה יב

... ושאר כל אדם שמתקוטטים עם חביריהם אף על פי
שאין לאו בזה אם ינקום מחבירו [מ"מ] מדת חסידות
היא להעביר על מדותיו כדאמרי' (שם ביומא) כל
המעביר על מדותיו מעבירין לו על כל פשעיו, וכן
דוד היה משתבח במדותיו הטובות ואמר (תהלים ז,
ה) אם גמלתי שולמי רע וגו', וההוא חסידא (מגילה
כח, א) דכל אימת דסליק לפוריא הוה אמר שרי
ומחיל כל מאן דמצערן לי:

### 48) ראש השנה יז.

כל המעביר על מדותיו מעבירין לו על כל פשעיו,
שנאמר "נשא עון ועבר על פשע"

### 49) קיצור שולחן ערוך ל:ח

אִם תִּרְצֶה לְהִנָּקֵם מֵאוֹיְבֶיךָ, תּוֹסִיף מַעֲלוֹת טוֹבוֹת
וְתֵלֵךְ בְּדַרְכֵי יְשָׁרִים, וּבָזֶה מִמֵּילָא תִּנָּקֵם מִשּׂוֹנְאֶיךָ, כִּי
הוּא יִצְטַעֵר עַל מִדּוֹתֶיךָ וְיִתְאַבֵּל, בְּשָׁמְעוֹ שִׁמְךָ הַטּוֹב.
אֲבָל אִם תַּעֲשֶׂה מַעֲשִׂים מְכֹעָרִים, אָז יִשְׂמַח שׂוֹנַאֲךָ עַל
קְלוֹנְךָ וְחֶרְפָּתֶךָ, וְהִנֵּה הוּא מִתְנַקֵּם בָּךְ:

### 50) דברים טז:כ

צֶדֶק צֶדֶק תִּרְדֹּף לְמַעַן תִּחְיֶה וְיָרַשְׁתָּ אֶת הָאָרֶץ
אֲשֶׁר ד' אֱלֹקֶיךָ נֹתֵן לָךְ:

### 51) תלמוד ירושלמי, נדרים ל.

כתיב לא תקום ולא תטור את בני עמך. היך עבידא
הוה מקטע קופד ומחת סכינא לידוי תחזור ותמחי
לידיה.

### 52) ויקרא יט:יח

לֹא תִקֹּם וְלֹא תִטֹּר אֶת בְּנֵי עַמֶּךָ וְאָהַבְתָּ לְרֵעֲךָ כָּמוֹךָ
אֲנִי ד':

### 53) יומא כב:

אמר רב: מפני מה נענש שאול מפני שמחל על כבודו
... ואמר רבי יוחנן משום רבי שמעון בן יהוצדק:
כל תלמיד חכם שאינו נוקם ונוטר כנחש אינו
תלמיד חכם

### 54) רמב"ם, הלכות תלמוד תורה ז:יג

... במה דברים אמורים כשבזהו או חרפהו בסתר
אבל תלמיד חכם שבזהו או חרפו אדם בפרהסיא
אסור לו למחול על כבודו ואם מחל נענש שזה בזיון
תורה אלא נוקם ונוטר הדבר כנחש עד שיבקש ממנו
מחילה ויסלח לו.

---

### 55) רמב"ם, הלכות איסורי ביאה יב:ד-ה

כל הבועל כותית בין דרך חתנות בין דרך זנות אם
בעלה בפרהסיא והוא שיבעול לעיני עשרה מישראל
או יתר אם פגעו בו קנאין והרגוהו הרי אלו משובחין
וזריזין, ודבר זה הל"מ הוא ראיה לדבר זה מעשה
פנחס בזמרי.

ואין הקנאי רשאי לפגוע בהן אלא בשעת מעשה
כזמרי שנאמר ואת האשה אל קבתה אבל אם פירש
אין הורגין אותו, ואם הרגו נהרג עליו, ובא הקנאי
ליטול רשות מב"ד אין מורין לו ואע"פ שהוא
בשעת מעשה, ולא עוד אלא אם בא הקנאי להרוג את
הבועל ונשמט הבועל והרג הקנאי כדי להציל עצמו
מידו אין הבועל נהרג עליו, והבא על בת גר תושב
אין הקנאין פוגעים בו אבל מכין אותו מכת מרדות.

### 56) רמב"ם, הלכות רוצח א:ה

רוצח שהרג בזדון אין ממיתין אותו העדים ולא
הרואים אותו עד שיבא לבית דין וידינוהו למיתה,
שנ' במדבר ל"ה י"ב ולא ימות הרוצח עד עמדו לפני
העדה למשפט, והוא הדין לכל מחוייבי מיתת בית
דין שעברו ועשו שאין ממיתין אותן עד שיגמר דינם
בבית דין.

### 57) דברים יז:ז

יַד הָעֵדִים תִּהְיֶה בּוֹ בָרִאשֹׁנָה לַהֲמִיתוֹ וְיַד כָּל הָעָם
בָּאַחֲרֹנָה וּבִעַרְתָּ הָרָע מִקִּרְבֶּךָ:

### 58) רמב"ם, הלכות רציחה טו:א

כיצד מצות הנסקלין ... ואחד מן העדים דוחפו על
מתניו מאחוריו והוא נהפך ונופל על לבו לארץ, אם
מת בה יצא שהרי נאמר סקול יסקל או ירה יירה
הנה השוה הנסקל שנפל עליו האבן עם הנדחף
שנפל הוא בעצמו על הארץ, ואם לא מת מדחיפה
זו מגביהין העדים אבן שהיתה מונחת שם משא שני
בני אדם והעד השני מרפה את ידו ומשליך האבן על
לבו, אם מת בו יצא ואם לאו רגימתו בכל ישראל
שנאמר יד העדים תהיה בו בראשונה להמיתו ויד כל
העם באחרונה.

### 59) במדבר לה:יט

גֹּאֵל הַדָּם הוּא יָמִית אֶת הָרֹצֵחַ בְּפִגְעוֹ בוֹ הוּא יְמִיתֶנּוּ:

### 60) רמב"ם, הלכות רוצח, א:ב

מצוה ביד גואל הדם שנ' (במדבר ל"ה י"ט) גואל הדם
הוא ימית את הרוצח וכל הראוי לירושה הוא גואל
הדם לא רצה גואל הדם או שלא היה יכול להמיתו או
שאין לו גואל דם בית דין ממיתין את הרוצח בסייף:

### 61) דברים יט:ו

פֶּן יִרְדֹּף גֹּאֵל הַדָּם אַחֲרֵי הָרֹצֵחַ כִּי יֵחַם לְבָבוֹ וְהִשִּׂיגוֹ
כִּי יִרְבֶּה הַדֶּרֶךְ וְהִכָּהוּ נָפֶשׁ וְלוֹ אֵין מִשְׁפַּט מָוֶת כִּי לֹא
שֹׂנֵא הוּא לוֹ מִתְּמוֹל שִׁלְשׁוֹם:

## 35) ספר החינוך, רלה

... שנאמר [ויקרא י"ט, י"ז] "לא תשנא את אחיך
בלבבך". ולשון ספרא, לא אמרתי אלא שנאה שהיא
בלב. וכמו כן בערכין [ט"ז ע"ב] בשנאה שבלב
הכתוב מדבר. אבל כשיראה לו שנאה וידוע שהוא
שונאו אינו עובר על זה הלאו, אמנם הוא עובר על
"לא תקום ולא תטור" ...

## 36) ספר שמירת הלשון, פתיחה, לאוין ח-ט, באר מים חיים

אבל מדברי ספר החינוך במצוה רמ"א משמע דמה"ת
נאמרו הלאוין דלא תקום ולא תטור אפילו אם ציערו
צער הגוף דז"ל במצוה הנ"ל שלא לנקום כלומר
שנמנענו לקחת נקמה מישראל העניך הוא כגון
ישראל שהרע או ציער לחבירו בא' מכל הדברים
ונוהג רוב בני העולם הוא שלא יסורו מלחפש אחר
מי שהרע להם עד שיגמלוהו כמעשהו הרע או
יכאיבוהו כמו שהכאיבם ומזה העניך ימנענו הש"י
באומרו לא תקום, ולשון ספרא עד היכן כוחה של
נקימה וכו'. א"ל השאילני מגלך וכו'. משרשי המצוה
שידע האדם ויתן אל לבו כי כל אשר יקרהו מטוב
ועד רע הוא סיבה שתבוא אליו מאת הש"י, ומיד
האדם מיד איש אחיו לא יהיה דבר בלתי רצונו ב"ה,
על כן כשיצערהו או יכאיבהו אדם ידע בנפשו כי
עונותיו גרמו לו והש"י גזר עליו בכך ולא ישית
מחשבותיו לנקום ממנו כי הוא אינו סיבת רעתו כי
העון הוא המסבב וכמו שאמר דוד ע"ה הניחו לו
ויקלל כי אמר לו ה', תלה הענין בחטאו ולא בשמעי
בן גרא וכו' עכ"ל....

היוצא מדברינו אם ציערו צערא דגופא מחלוקת בין
הראשונים אם מותר מן התורה לנקום ממנו וספיקא
דאוריתא לחומרא. אבל אם העולה שיש לו עליו הוא
עבור עניני ממון לכולי עלמא אסור לנקום ממנו בכל
גוונא כמ"ש בפנים:

## 37) פירוש חזקוני על ויקרא יט:יח

לא תקם – במעשה.
ולא תטר – במחשבה.

## 38) פירוש מלבי"ם על ויקרא יט:יח

לא תקם ולא תטר – הנקמה הוא בפועל. שנקם
מחברו על אשר הרע לו. ויהי' או במעשה כשעשה לו
רע במעשה, או במניעת הטובה אם מנע טוב מאתו.
והנטירה היא בלב.

## 39) פירוש רשב"ם על ויקרא יט:יח

לא תקם – לגמול לו רעה תחת רעה:
ולא תטר – אפי' בלבבך אלא עבור על מדתך

## 40) יומא כג.

איזו היא נקימה ואיזו היא נטירה ... ואיזו היא
נטירה אמר לו השאילני קרדומך אמר ליה לא למחר

---

אמר לו השאילני חלוקך אמר לו הילך איני כמותך
שלא השאלתני זו היא נטירה

## 41) רמב"ם, הלכות דעות ז:ח

וכן כל הנוטר לאחד מישראל עובר בלא תעשה
שנאמר ולא תטור את בני עמך, כיצד היא הנטירה,
ראובן שאמר לשמעון השכיר לי ביתי או השאילני
שור זה ולא רצה שמעון, לימים בא שמעון לראובן
לשאול ממנו או לשכור ממנו ואמר לו ראובן הא לך
הריני משאילך ואיני כמותך לא אשלם לך כמעשיך,
העושה כזה עובר בלא תטור, אלא ימחה הדבר מלבו
ולא יטרנו, שכל זמן שהוא נוטר את הדבר וזוכרו
שמא יבא לנקום, לפיכך הקפידה תורה על הנטירה
עד שימחה העון מלבו ולא יזכרנו כלל, וזו היא
הדעה הנכונה שאפשר שיתקיים בה יישוב הארץ
ומשאם ומתנם של בני אדם זה עם זה.

## 42) סמ"ג לא תעשה פא

פא. מצות לא תעשה שלא לנטור שנאה בלב על
חבירו. שנאמר (ויקרא יט, יח): "ולא תטור". נטירה
היא, שנוטר השנאה בלבו, כגון שיאמר לו: הריני
משאילך, ואין אני משלם לך כפעלך שלא השאלתני,
זוהי נטירה, שנוטר השנאה בלב. אלא צריך להשאיל
לו בלב שלם, ולא יהא לו שום שנאה בלב, אלא ימחה
הדבר מלבו, ולא יטרנו ולא יזכרנו כלל. ושתי מדות
הללו המה רעות למאד, שכל דברי העולם הזה הבל
והבאי, ואינן כדאי לנקום ולנטור עליהן. ונוהג בכל
מקום ובכל זמן, בזכרים ובנקבות:

## 43) אורחות צדיקים, שער שמיני "אכזריות"

ועוד המידה הזאת בנפשו של אדם להשיג נקמה
באויביו, כדכתיב (משלי ו לד): "ולא יחמול ביום
נקם", פירוש, כשיש נקמה – אין חמלה אלא
אכזריות, והכתוב אומר (ויקרא יט יח): "לא תקום
ולא תטור", אפילו ליטור בלב הזהרנו, כל שכן שלא
לעשות מעשה בידים להכות את חבירו.

## 44) ספר החינוך רמא

שלא לנקום:
משרשי המצוה, ... ומיד האדם מיד איש אחיו
לא יהיה דבר בלתי רצון השם ברוך הוא, על כן
כשיצערהו או יכאיבהו אדם ידע בנפשו כי עוונותיו
גרמו והשם יתברך גזר עליו בכך, ולא ישית
מחשבותיי לנקום ממנו כי הוא אינו סיבת רעתו, כי
העוון הוא המסבב ...

## 45) משנה אבות ד:א

איזהו גבור. הכובש את יצרו.

## 46) מסילת ישרים יא

גם השנאה והנקימה קשה מאד להימלט ממנה
לב התול אשר לבני האדם, כי האדם מרגיש מאד

דבר, כגון זה שפרצו בהם לעשות להם נבלה, אף
על גב דלא עשה רק אחד מהם – כיון דמכלל העם
הוא, כיון שפרצו להם תחלה – מותרים ליקח נקמתם
מהם. והכי נמי כל המלחמות שהם נמצאים כגון
"צרור את המדיינים וגו'" (במדבר כה, יז), אף על
גב דהיו הרבה שלא עשו – אין זה חילוק, כיון שהיו
באותה אומה שעשה רע להם – מותרין לבא עליהם
למלחמה, וכן הם כל המלחמות:

### 22) ויקרא יט:יח
לֹא תִקֹּם וְלֹא תִטֹּר אֶת בְּנֵי עַמֶּךָ וְאָהַבְתָּ לְרֵעֲךָ כָּמוֹךָ
אֲנִי ד':

### 23) שערי תשובה, ג:ריט
אַל תֹּאמַר כַּאֲשֶׁר עָשָׂה – לִי כֵּן אֶעֱשֶׂה – לּוֹ, כִּי אִם
גֻּלָּה עַל חֶטְאֶךָ, לֹא תִקֹּם וְלֹא תִטֹּר לַעֲשׂוֹת לוֹ כַּאֲשֶׁר
עָשָׂה לָךְ.

### 24) פירוש חזקוני על ויקרא יט:יח
ולא תטר – בממון דבר הכתוב, אבל בשל גוף, אינו
זקוק למחול לו עד שיפיסנו.
לא תקם – במעשה.

### 25) פירוש רשב"ם על ויקרא יט:יח
לא תקם – לגמול לו רעה תחת רעה:

### 26) פירוש מלבי"ם על ויקרא יט:יח
לא תקם ולא תטר – הנקמה הוא בפועל. שנוקם
מחברו על אשר הרע לו. ויהי' או במעשה כשעשה לו
רע במעשה, או במניעת הטובה אם מנע טוב מאתו.
והנטירה היא בלב.

### 27) פירוש העמק דבר על ויקרא יט:יח
לא תקם וגו' – אם אפילו חטא ודאי נגדך מכ"מ
נקמה אינה מדת הקדושה בישראל (וכתיב משיב
רעה תחת טובה לא תמוש רעה מביתו. ופירשו חז"ל
בב"ר ס"פ נח לא רק משיב רעה תחת טובה אלא אפי'
משיב רעה תחת רעה. והיינו משום שדייקו חז"ל
לשון משיב. דלא שייך לשון השבה אלא מה שחייב
והאיך שייך לשון השבת רעה על טובה.

### 28) יומא כג. ורש"י שם
דתניא: איזו היא נקמה ואיזו היא נטירה, נקמה,
אמר לו: השאילני מגלך, אמר לו: לאו. למחר אמר לו
הוא: השאילני קרדומך אמר לו: איני משאילך, כדרך
שלא השאלתני זו היא נקמה ...

### 29) רמב"ם, ספר המצוות לא תעשה שד
שהזהירנו שלא לנקום מקום קצתנו מקצתנו והוא שעשה
לו מעשה אחד ולא יסור מלחפש אחריו עד שיגמלהו
כמעשהו הרע או יכאיבהו כמו שהכאיבו הזהיר האל
מזה ואמר לא תקם ובספרא עד היכן כחה של נקמה

---

אמר לו השאילני מגלך ולא השאילו למחר אמר לו
השאילני קרדומך אמר לו אינו משאילך כשם שלא
השאלתני מגלך לכך נאמר לא תקם ועל זה הדמיון
היקש בכל העניינים:

### 30) רמב"ם, הלכות דעות ז:ז
הנוקם מחבירו עובר בלא תעשה שנאמר לא תקם,
ואע"פ שאינו לוקה עליו דעה רעה היא עד מאד, אלא
ראוי לו לאדם להיות מעביר על מדותיו על כל דברי
העולם שהכל אצל המבינים דברי הבל והבאי ואינן
כדי לנקום עליהם, כיצד היא הנקימה אמר לו חבירו
השאילני קרדומך אמר לו איני משאילך, למחר צריך
לשאול ממנו אמר לו חבירו השאילני קרדומך אמר
לו איני משאילך כדרך שלא השאלתני כששאלתי
ממך הרי זה נוקם, אלא כשיבוא לו לשאול יתן בלב
שלם ולא יגמול לו כאשר גמלו וכן כל כיוצא באלו,
וכן אמר דוד בדעותיו הטובות אם גמלתי שולמי רע
ואחלצה וגו'.

### 31) סמ"ג לא תעשה פ
פ. מצות לא תעשה שלא לנקום מחבירו. שנאמר
(ויקרא יט, יח): "לא תקם". נקימה היא, שהוא גומל
למריע לו כמעשהו, כגון שאמר לחבירו: השאילני
קרדומך ולא השאיל לו, למחר צריך לחבירו לשאול
ממנו, ואמר לו: אין אני משאילך, כדרך שלא
השאלתני כששארתי לשאול ממך, הרי זה נקימה,
שנוקם ממנו וגומל לו כמעשהו הרע. ונוהג בכל
מקום ובכל זמן, בזכרים ובנקבות:

### 32) ספר חסידים תרנז
כל המבקש נקמה מאותם שעשו לו רעה, ונענשו
על ידו, כשיעשה דבר כיוצא בו או הוא או זרעו,
יענשו, אע"פ שלא היו מענישים אותו עבור זה אם
לא היה מבקש נקמה, אחר שביקש נקמה יענישוהו
מדה כנגד מדה. אל ידור אדם במקום שאנשים או
נשים מקללים ומענישים, ויתפלל על זה להרחיקו
מהם וממונשן:

### 33) ספר החינוך, מצוה שלח
... ואולם לפי הדומה אין במשמע שאם בא בישראל
אחד והתחיל והרשיע לצער חבירו בדברים הרעים
שלא יענהו השומע ואי שפשר להיות אדם כאבן
שאין לה הופכים ועוד שיהיה בשתיקתו כמודה על
החירופין ובאמת לא תצוה התורה להיות האדם כאבן
שותק למחרפיו כמו למברכים אבל תצוה אותנו
שנתרחק מן המדה הזאת ושלא נתחיל להתקוטט
ולחרף בני אדם ...

### 34) ספר החינוך רמא
... ועובר עליה וקבע בלבו לשנוא חבירו על שהרע
לו עד שיגמלהו כרעתו עבר על לאו זה ...

הָאָרֶץ וַיִּקַּח אֹתָהּ וַיִּשְׁכַּב אֹתָהּ וַיְעַנֶּהָ: ג וַתִּדְבַּק נַפְשׁוֹ
בְּדִינָה בַּת־יַעֲקֹב וַיֶּאֱהַב אֶת־הַנַּעֲרָ וַיְדַבֵּר עַל־לֵב הַנַּעֲרָ:
ד וַיֹּאמֶר שְׁכֶם אֶל־חֲמוֹר אָבִיו לֵאמֹר קַח־לִי אֶת־
הַיַּלְדָּה הַזֹּאת לְאִשָּׁה: ה וְיַעֲקֹב שָׁמַע כִּי טִמֵּא אֶת־דִּינָה
בִתּוֹ וּבָנָיו הָיוּ אֶת־מִקְנֵהוּ בַּשָּׂדֶה וְהֶחֱרִשׁ יַעֲקֹב עַד־
בֹּאָם: ו וַיֵּצֵא חֲמוֹר אֲבִי־שְׁכֶם אֶל־יַעֲקֹב לְדַבֵּר אִתּוֹ:
וּבְנֵי יַעֲקֹב בָּאוּ מִן־הַשָּׂדֶה כְּשָׁמְעָם וַיִּתְעַצְּבוּ הָאֲנָשִׁים
וַיִּחַר לָהֶם מְאֹד כִּי־נְבָלָה עָשָׂה בְיִשְׂרָאֵל לִשְׁכַּב אֶת־
בַּת־יַעֲקֹב וְכֵן לֹא יֵעָשֶׂה: ח וַיְדַבֵּר חֲמוֹר אִתָּם לֵאמֹר
שְׁכֶם בְּנִי חָשְׁקָה נַפְשׁוֹ בְּבִתְּכֶם תְּנוּ נָא אֹתָהּ לוֹ לְאִשָּׁה:
ט וְהִתְחַתְּנוּ אֹתָנוּ בְּנֹתֵיכֶם תִּתְּנוּ־לָנוּ וְאֶת־בְּנֹתֵינוּ
תִּקְחוּ לָכֶם: י וְאִתָּנוּ תֵּשֵׁבוּ וְהָאָרֶץ תִּהְיֶה לִפְנֵיכֶם שְׁבוּ
וּסְחָרוּהָ וְהֵאָחֲזוּ בָּהּ: יא וַיֹּאמֶר שְׁכֶם אֶל־אָבִיהָ וְאֶל־
אַחֶיהָ אֶמְצָא־חֵן בְּעֵינֵיכֶם וַאֲשֶׁר תֹּאמְרוּ אֵלַי אֶתֵּן:
יב הַרְבּוּ עָלַי מְאֹד מֹהַר וּמַתָּן וְאֶתְּנָה כַּאֲשֶׁר תֹּאמְרוּ אֵלָי
וּתְנוּ־לִי אֶת־הַנַּעֲרָ לְאִשָּׁה: יג וַיַּעֲנוּ בְנֵי־יַעֲקֹב אֶת־שְׁכֶם
וְאֶת־חֲמוֹר אָבִיו בְּמִרְמָה וַיְדַבֵּרוּ אֲשֶׁר טִמֵּא אֵת דִּינָה
אֲחֹתָם: יד וַיֹּאמְרוּ אֲלֵיהֶם לֹא נוּכַל לַעֲשׂוֹת הַדָּבָר הַזֶּה
לָתֵת אֶת־אֲחֹתֵנוּ לְאִישׁ אֲשֶׁר־לוֹ עָרְלָה כִּי־חֶרְפָּה הִוא
לָנוּ: טו אַךְ־בְּזֹאת נֵאוֹת לָכֶם אִם תִּהְיוּ כָמֹנוּ לְהִמֹּל
לָכֶם כָּל־זָכָר: טז וְנָתַנּוּ אֶת־בְּנֹתֵינוּ לָכֶם וְאֶת־בְּנֹתֵיכֶם
נִקַּח־לָנוּ וְיָשַׁבְנוּ אִתְּכֶם וְהָיִינוּ לְעַם אֶחָד: יז וְאִם־לֹא
תִשְׁמְעוּ אֵלֵינוּ לְהִמּוֹל וְלָקַחְנוּ אֶת־בִּתֵּנוּ וְהָלָכְנוּ:
יח וַיִּיטְבוּ דִבְרֵיהֶם בְּעֵינֵי חֲמוֹר וּבְעֵינֵי שְׁכֶם בֶּן־חֲמוֹר:
יט וְלֹא־אֵחַר הַנַּעַר לַעֲשׂוֹת הַדָּבָר כִּי חָפֵץ בְּבַת־יַעֲקֹב
וְהוּא נִכְבָּד מִכֹּל בֵּית אָבִיו: כ וַיָּבֹא חֲמוֹר וּשְׁכֶם בְּנוֹ
אֶל־שַׁעַר עִירָם וַיְדַבְּרוּ אֶל־אַנְשֵׁי עִירָם לֵאמֹר: כא
הָאֲנָשִׁים הָאֵלֶּה שְׁלֵמִים הֵם אִתָּנוּ וְיֵשְׁבוּ בָאָרֶץ וְיִסְחֲרוּ
אֹתָהּ וְהָאָרֶץ הִנֵּה רַחֲבַת־יָדַיִם לִפְנֵיהֶם אֶת־בְּנֹתָם נִקַּח־
לָנוּ לְנָשִׁים וְאֶת־בְּנֹתֵינוּ נִתֵּן לָהֶם: כב אַךְ־בְּזֹאת יֵאֹתוּ
לָנוּ הָאֲנָשִׁים לָשֶׁבֶת אִתָּנוּ לִהְיוֹת לְעַם אֶחָד בְּהִמּוֹל
לָנוּ כָּל־זָכָר כַּאֲשֶׁר הֵם נִמֹּלִים: כג מִקְנֵהֶם וְקִנְיָנָם וְכָל־
בְּהֶמְתָּם הֲלוֹא לָנוּ הֵם אַךְ נֵאוֹתָה לָהֶם וְיֵשְׁבוּ אִתָּנוּ:
כד וַיִּשְׁמְעוּ אֶל־חֲמוֹר וְאֶל־שְׁכֶם בְּנוֹ כָּל־יֹצְאֵי שַׁעַר
עִירוֹ וַיִּמֹּלוּ כָּל־זָכָר כָּל־יֹצְאֵי שַׁעַר עִירוֹ: כה וַיְהִי בַיּוֹם
הַשְּׁלִישִׁי בִּהְיוֹתָם כֹּאֲבִים וַיִּקְחוּ שְׁנֵי־בְנֵי־יַעֲקֹב שִׁמְעוֹן
וְלֵוִי אֲחֵי דִינָה אִישׁ חַרְבּוֹ וַיָּבֹאוּ עַל־הָעִיר בֶּטַח וַיַּהַרְגוּ
כָּל־זָכָר: כו וְאֶת־חֲמוֹר וְאֶת־שְׁכֶם בְּנוֹ הָרְגוּ לְפִי־חָרֶב
וַיִּקְחוּ אֶת־דִּינָה מִבֵּית שְׁכֶם וַיֵּצֵאוּ: כז בְּנֵי יַעֲקֹב בָּאוּ
עַל־הַחֲלָלִים וַיָּבֹזּוּ הָעִיר אֲשֶׁר טִמְּאוּ אֲחוֹתָם: כח אֶת־
צֹאנָם וְאֶת־בְּקָרָם וְאֶת־חֲמֹרֵיהֶם וְאֵת אֲשֶׁר־בָּעִיר וְאֶת־
אֲשֶׁר בַּשָּׂדֶה לָקָחוּ: כט וְאֶת־כָּל־חֵילָם וְאֶת־כָּל־טַפָּם
וְאֶת־נְשֵׁיהֶם שָׁבוּ וַיָּבֹזּוּ וְאֵת כָּל־אֲשֶׁר בַּבָּיִת: ל וַיֹּאמֶר
יַעֲקֹב אֶל־שִׁמְעוֹן וְאֶל־לֵוִי עֲכַרְתֶּם אֹתִי לְהַבְאִישֵׁנִי
בְּיֹשֵׁב הָאָרֶץ בַּכְּנַעֲנִי וּבַפְּרִזִּי וַאֲנִי מְתֵי מִסְפָּר וְנֶאֶסְפוּ
עָלַי וְהִכּוּנִי וְנִשְׁמַדְתִּי אֲנִי וּבֵיתִי: לא וַיֹּאמְרוּ הַכְזוֹנָה
יַעֲשֶׂה אֶת־אֲחוֹתֵנוּ:

### 18) בראשית מט:ה-ז

שִׁמְעוֹן וְלֵוִי אַחִים כְּלֵי חָמָס מְכֵרֹתֵיהֶם: בְּסֹדָם אַל־
תָּבֹא נַפְשִׁי בִּקְהָלָם אַל־תֵּחַד כְּבֹדִי כִּי בְאַפָּם הָרְגוּ
אִישׁ וּבִרְצֹנָם עִקְּרוּ־שׁוֹר: אָרוּר אַפָּם כִּי עָז וְעֶבְרָתָם כִּי

---

קָשָׁתָה אֲחַלְּקֵם בְּיַעֲקֹב וַאֲפִיצֵם בְּיִשְׂרָאֵל:

### 19) פירוש רמב"ן על בראשית לד:יג, מט:ה

... וְיִתָּכֵן שֶׁהָיָה הַכַּעַס לְיַעֲקֹב שֶׁאֵרַר אַפָּם עַל
אַנְשֵׁי הָעִיר אֲשֶׁר לֹא חָטְאוּ לוֹ, וְהָרָאוּי לָהֶם שֶׁיַּהַרְגוּ
שְׁכֶם לְבַדּוֹ. וְזֶהוּ מַה שֶּׁאָמַר הַכָּתוּב וַיַּעֲנוּ בְנֵי יַעֲקֹב
אֶת שְׁכֶם וְאֶת חֲמוֹר אָבִיו בְּמִרְמָה ... וְרַבִּים יִשְׁאֲלוּ,
וְאֵיךְ עָשׂוּ בְנֵי יַעֲקֹב הַצַּדִּיקִים הַמַּעֲשֶׂה הַזֶּה לִשְׁפֹּךְ
דָּם נָקִי. וְהָרַב הֵשִׁיב בְּסֵפֶר שׁוֹפְטִים (רמב"ם הלכות
מלכים פי"ד ה"ט) וְאָמַר שֶׁבְּנֵי נֹחַ מְצֻוִּין עַל הַדִּינִין,
וְהוּא לְהוֹשִׁיב דַּיָּנִין בְּכָל פֶּלֶךְ וּפֶלֶךְ לָדוּן בְּשֵׁשׁ מִצְוֹת
שֶׁלָּהֶן, וּבֶן נֹחַ שֶׁעָבַר עַל אַחַת מֵהֶן הוּא נֶהֱרָג בְּסַיִף,
רָאָה אֶחָד שֶׁעָבַר עַל אַחַת מֵהֶן וְלֹא דָנוּהוּ לְהָרְגוֹ הֲרֵי
זֶה הָרוֹאֶה יֵהָרֵג בְּסַיִף. וּמִפְּנֵי זֶה נִתְחַיְּבוּ כָּל בַּעֲלֵי
שְׁכֶם הֲרִיגָה שֶׁהֲרֵי שְׁכֶם גָּזַל, וְהֵם רָאוּ וְיָדְעוּ וְלֹא
דָנוּהוּ: וְאֵין דְּבָרִים הַלָּלוּ נְכוֹנִים בְּעֵינַי, שֶׁאִם כֵּן הָיָה
יַעֲקֹב אָבִינוּ חַיָּב לִהְיוֹת קוֹדֵם וְזוֹכֶה בְּמִיתָתָם, וְאִם
פָּחַד מֵהֶם לָמָּה כָעַס עַל בָּנָיו וְאָרַר אַפָּם אַחַר כַּמָּה
זְמַנִּים, וְעָנַשׁ אוֹתָם וְחִלְּקָם וַהֲפִיצָם, וַהֲלֹא הֵם זָכוּ
עָשׂוּ מִצְוָה וּבָטְחוּ בֵאלֹהִים וְהִצִּילָם: ... וּמַה יְּבַקֵּשׁ
בָּהֶן הָרַב חִיּוּב, וְכִי אַנְשֵׁי שְׁכֶם, אוֹיֵב, וְכָל שִׁבְעָה עֲמָמִין לֹא
עוֹבְדֵי עֲבוֹדָה זָרָה וּמְגַלֶּה עֲרָיוֹת וְעוֹשִׂים כָּל תּוֹעֲבוֹת
הַשֵּׁם הָיוּ ...

... וּכְבָר פֵּרַשְׁתִּי (לְעֵיל לד יג) כִּי יַעֲקֹב קָצַף עַל
שִׁמְעוֹן וְלֵוִי בְּהָרְגָם אַנְשֵׁי הָעִיר בַּעֲבוּר שֶׁעָשׂוּ חָמָס,
כִּי הֵם לֹא חָטְאוּ לָהֶם כְּלָל וּבָאוּ בַּבְּרִית וְנִמֹּלוּ ...

### 20) רמב"ם, הלכות מלכים ט:יד

וְכֵיצַד מְצֻוִּין הֵן עַל הַדִּינִין חַיָּבִין לְהוֹשִׁיב דַּיָּנִין
וְשׁוֹפְטִים בְּכָל פֶּלֶךְ וּפֶלֶךְ לָדוּן בְּשֵׁשׁ מִצְוֹת אֵלּוּ
וּלְהַזְהִיר אֶת הָעָם וּבֶן נֹחַ שֶׁעָבַר עַל אַחַת מִשֶּׁבַע מִצְוֹת
אֵלּוּ יֵהָרֵג בְּסַיִף וּמִפְּנֵי זֶה נִתְחַיְּבוּ כָּל בַּעֲלֵי שְׁכֶם
הֲרִיגָה שֶׁהֲרֵי שְׁכֶם גָּזַל וְהֵם רָאוּ וְיָדְעוּ וְלֹא דָנוּהוּ ...

### 21) פירוש גור אריה על בראשית לד:יג

... אַךְ קָשֶׁה אִם שְׁכֶם חָטָא כָּל הָעִיר מֶה חָטְאוּ לֵהָרֵג,
וְתֵירֵץ הָרַמְב"ם (הלכות מלכים פ"ט הי"ד) דִּבְנֵי נֹחַ
מְצֻוִּים עַל הַדִּינִין, וַעֲבֵירָה אַחַת שֶׁעוֹבֵר – נֶהֱרָג עַל
יָדוֹ, וְכָאן רָאוּ הַמַּעֲשֶׂה הָרַע הַזֶּה וְלֹא דָנוּהוּ, לְכָךְ הָיוּ
חַיָּבִין מִיתָה שֶׁלֹּא הָיוּ דָנִין אוֹתָם. וּבֶאֱמֶת דָּבָר תְּמִיהָה
הֵם אֵלּוּ הַדְּבָרִים, כִּי אֵיךְ אֶפְשָׁר לָהֶם לָדוּן אֶת בֶּן
נְשִׂיא הָאָרֶץ (פָּסוּק ב), כִּי הָיוּ יְרֵאִים מֵהֶם, וְאַף עַל גַּב
שֶׁנְּטָטוּ עַל הַדַּיָּנִין – הַיְנוּ כְּשֶׁיּוּכְלוּ לָדוּן, אֲבָל אוֹנֶס
רַחֲמָנָא פַּטְרֵהּ (ב"ק כח ע"ב), וְאֵיךְ אֶפְשָׁר לָהֶם לָדוּן
אוֹתָם: וְנִרְאֶה דְּלָא קַשְׁיָא מִידֵי, מִשּׁוּם דְּלָא דְּמֵי שְׁנֵי
אֻמּוֹת, כְּגוֹן בְּנֵי יִשְׂרָאֵל וּכְנַעֲנִים, שֶׁהֵם שְׁנֵי אֻמּוֹת,
כְּדִכְתִיב (פסוק טז) "וְהָיִינוּ לְעַם אֶחָד" – וּמִתְּחִלָּה
לֹא נֶחְשְׁבוּ לְעַם אֶחָד, וּלְפִיכָךְ הֻתַּר לָהֶם לִלְחוֹם כְּדִין
אֻמָּה שֶׁבָּא לִלְחוֹם עַל אֻמָּה אַחֶרֶת, שֶׁהִתִּירָה הַתּוֹרָה.
וְאַף עַל גַּב דְּאָמְרָה הַתּוֹרָה (דברים כ, י) "כִּי תִקְרַב אֶל
עִיר לְהִלָּחֵם עָלֶיהָ וְקָרָאתָ אֵלֶיהָ לְשָׁלוֹם", הַיְנוּ הֵיכָא
דְּלָא עָשׂוּ לְיִשְׂרָאֵל דָּבָר, אֲבָל הֵיכָא דְּעָשׂוּ לְיִשְׂרָאֵל

# SOURCES ON REVENGE: IS IT EVER JUSTIFIED?

## 1) פירוש מאירי על אבות ג:ד

הנטירות והנקימות הם מהדברים שתוקף יצר הרע מכריח בהעברתם

## 2) ספר החינוך רמא

.. ונוהג רוב בני אדם שבעולם הוא שלא יסורו מלחפש אחרי מי שהרע להן עד שיגמלוהו כמעשהו הרע או יכאיבוהו כמו שהכאיבם ...

## 3) מסילת ישרים יא

גם השנאה והנקימה קשה מאד להימלט ממנה לב הותל אשר לבני האדם, כי האדם מרגיש מאד בעלבונותיו ומצטער צער גדול, והנקמה לו מתוקה מדבש, כי היא מנוחתו לבדה. על כן לשיהיה בכחו לעזוב מה שטבעו מכריח אותו ... חזק ואמיץ הוא. והוא קל רק למלאכי השרת ...:

## 4) פירוש חזקוני על ויקרא יט:יח

**לא תקם** – לפי שהחימה מכבשתך ...

## 5) ספר החינוך, מצוה שלח

... ואולם לפי הדומה אין במשמע שאם בא בישראל אחד והתחיל והרשיע לצער חבירו בדברים הרעים שלא יעננו השומע שאי שפשר להיות אדם כאבן שאין לה הופכים ועוד שיהיה בשתיקתו כמודה על החירופין ובאמת לא תצוה התורה להיות האדם כאבן שותק למחרפיו כמו למברכים אבל תצוה אותנו שנתרחק מן המדה הזאת ושלא נתחיל להתקוטט ולחרף בני אדם ...

## 6) דברים כח:ט ופירוש רמב"ן על דברים יא:א

יְקִימְךָ ד' לוֹ לְעַם קָדוֹשׁ כַּאֲשֶׁר נִשְׁבַּע לָךְ כִּי תִשְׁמֹר אֶת מִצְוֹת ד' אֱלֹקֶיךָ וְהָלַכְתָּ בִּדְרָכָיו: ... שנאמר במקום אחר (מ"א ב ג ) לשמור את משמרת ה' אלקיך ללכת בדרכיו, ואמרו (שבת קלג:) מה הוא חנון ורחום אף אתה היה חנון ורחום ...

## 7) תהילים צד:א

אֵ־ל־נְקָמוֹת ד' אֵ־ל נְקָמוֹת הוֹפִיעַ:

## 8) ישעיהו לה:ד

אִמְרוּ לְנִמְהֲרֵי־לֵב חִזְקוּ אַל־תִּירָאוּ הִנֵּה אֱלֹקֵיכֶם נָקָם יָבוֹא גְּמוּל אֱלֹקִים הוּא יָבוֹא וְיֹשַׁעֲכֶם:

## 9) ויקרא כו:כה

וְהֵבֵאתִי עֲלֵיכֶם חֶרֶב נֹקֶמֶת נְקַם־בְּרִית וְנֶאֱסַפְתֶּם אֶל־עָרֵיכֶם וְשִׁלַּחְתִּי דֶבֶר בְּתוֹכְכֶם וְנִתַּתֶּם בְּיַד־אוֹיֵב:

## 10) ישעיהו נט:יז-יט

וַיִּלְבַּשׁ צְדָקָה כַּשִּׁרְיָן וְכוֹבַע יְשׁוּעָה בְּרֹאשׁוֹ וַיִּלְבַּשׁ בִּגְדֵי נָקָם תִּלְבֹּשֶׁת וַיַּעַט כַּמְעִיל קִנְאָה: כְּעַל גְּמֻלוֹת כְּעַל יְשַׁלֵּם חֵמָה לְצָרָיו גְּמוּל לְאֹיְבָיו לָאִיִּים גְּמוּל יְשַׁלֵּם: וְיִירְאוּ מִמַּעֲרָב אֶת־שֵׁם ד' וּמִמִּזְרַח־שֶׁמֶשׁ אֶת־כְּבוֹדוֹ כִּי־יָבוֹא כַנָּהָר צָר רוּחַ ד' נֹסְסָה בוֹ:

## 11) נחום א:ב-ג

אֵ־ל קַנּוֹא וְנֹקֵם ד' נֹקֵם ד' וּבַעַל חֵמָה נֹקֵם ד' לְצָרָיו וְנוֹטֵר הוּא לְאֹיְבָיו: ד' אֶרֶךְ אַפַּיִם וּגְדָל [וּגְדָל] ־כֹּחַ וְנַקֵּה לֹא יְנַקֶּה ד' בְּסוּפָה וּבִשְׂעָרָה דַּרְכּוֹ וְעָנָן אֲבַק רַגְלָיו:

## 12) ירמיהו מו:י', יחזקאל כה:יז

וְהַיּוֹם הַהוּא לַאדֹ־נָי ד' צְבָאוֹת יוֹם נְקָמָה לְהִנָּקֵם מִצָּרָיו וְאָכְלָה חֶרֶב וְשָׂבְעָה וְרָוְתָה מִדָּמָם כִּי זֶבַח לַאדֹ־נָי ד' צְבָאוֹת בְּאֶרֶץ צָפוֹן אֶל־נְהַר־פְּרָת: וְעָשִׂיתִי בָם נְקָמוֹת גְּדֹלוֹת בְּתוֹכְחוֹת חֵמָה וְיָדְעוּ כִּי אֲנִי ד' בְּתִתִּי אֶת־נִקְמָתִי בָּם:

## 13) פירוש חזקוני על ויקרא יט:יח

**לא תקם** – ... אבל הקב"ה שהוא כובש את החימה כתיב נוקם ה' ובעל חימה.

## 14) במדבר לא:א-ב

וַיְדַבֵּר ד' אֶל־מֹשֶׁה לֵּאמֹר: נְקֹם נִקְמַת בְּנֵי יִשְׂרָאֵל מֵאֵת הַמִּדְיָנִים אַחַר תֵּאָסֵף אֶל־עַמֶּיךָ:

## 15) במדבר כה:ז-יב

וַיַּרְא פִּינְחָס בֶּן־אֶלְעָזָר בֶּן־אַהֲרֹן הַכֹּהֵן וַיָּקָם מִתּוֹךְ הָעֵדָה וַיִּקַּח רֹמַח בְּיָדוֹ: וַיָּבֹא אַחַר אִישׁ־יִשְׂרָאֵל אֶל־הַקֻּבָּה וַיִּדְקֹר אֶת־שְׁנֵיהֶם אֵת אִישׁ יִשְׂרָאֵל וְאֶת־הָאִשָּׁה אֶל־קֳבָתָהּ וַתֵּעָצַר הַמַּגֵּפָה מֵעַל בְּנֵי יִשְׂרָאֵל: וַיִּהְיוּ הַמֵּתִים בַּמַּגֵּפָה אַרְבָּעָה וְעֶשְׂרִים אָלֶף: וַיְדַבֵּר ד' אֶל־מֹשֶׁה לֵּאמֹר: פִּינְחָס בֶּן־אֶלְעָזָר בֶּן־אַהֲרֹן הַכֹּהֵן הֵשִׁיב אֶת־חֲמָתִי מֵעַל בְּנֵי־יִשְׂרָאֵל בְּקַנְאוֹ אֶת־קִנְאָתִי בְּתוֹכָם וְלֹא־כִלִּיתִי אֶת־בְּנֵי־יִשְׂרָאֵל בְּקִנְאָתִי: לָכֵן אֱמֹר הִנְנִי נֹתֵן לוֹ אֶת־בְּרִיתִי שָׁלוֹם:

## 16) תלמוד ירושלמי סנהדרין מח:

ופינחס שלא ברצון חכמים א"ר יודה בר פזי ביקשו לנדותו אילולי שקפצה עליו רוח הקודש ואמרה והיתה לו ולזרעו אחריו ברית כהונת עולם וגומר.

## 17) בראשית לד

א וַתֵּצֵא דִינָה בַּת־לֵאָה אֲשֶׁר יָלְדָה לְיַעֲקֹב לִרְאוֹת בִּבְנוֹת הָאָרֶץ: ב וַיַּרְא אֹתָהּ שְׁכֶם בֶּן־חֲמוֹר הַחִוִּי נְשִׂיא

ייתון בני עממין לשלם לשון גנאי הוא, לפי שבאו מבני בניו של סנחריב, כדאמרינן במסכת גיטין (נז, ב).

דעבדי עובדא דאהרן רודפי שלום.

דלא עבד עובדא דאהרן שהוניתנו אונאת דברים, ואמר מר (בבא מציעא נח, ב) לא תונו איש את עמיתו (ויקרא כה) באונאת דברים הכתוב מדבר, אם היה בן גרים לא יאמר לו זכור מעשה אבותיך.

**46) ערוך השולחן, חושן משפט רכח:א**

וי"א דאין מצווין על אונאת דברים שלא לאנותו רק למי שאינו בעל עבירות אבל לרשע מותר לאנות בדברים דשמעא ע"י זה ישוב בתשובה ולכן אם כוונתו לשמים לאנותו לרשע בדברים כדי שישוב בתשובה יכול לעשות כן וכן מי שמאנה את עצמו שהולך בדרך לא טוב וסובר שהולך בדרך הישר מותר לאנותו שאדם כזה אינו מכלל הישוב ודרך ארץ ...

**47) כתובות טז:**

תנו רבנן: כיצד מרקדין לפני הכלה? בית שמאי

אומרים: כלה כמות שהיא, ובית הלל אומרים: כלה נאה וחסודה. אמרו להן ב"ש לב"ה: הרי שהיתה חיגרת או סומא, אומרי' לה, כלה נאה וחסודה? והתורה אמרה: (שמות כ"ג) מדבר שקר תרחק אמרו להם ב"ה לב"ש: לדבריכם, מי שלקח מקח רע מן השוק, ישבחנו בעיניו או יגננו בעיניו? הוי אומר: ישבחנו בעיניו, מכאן אמרו חכמים: לעולם תהא דעתו של אדם מעורבת עם הבריות.

**48) שולחן ערוך, אבן העזר סה:א**

מצוה לשמח חתן וכלה ולרקד לפניהם ולומר שהיא נאה וחסודה (פי' מן ותשא חסד לפניו) אפילו אינה נאה

**49) ספר חסידים תרמב**

יכול אדם לשקר כדי שלא יתבייש חבירו, וכשישקר יעסוק לשנות כדי שלא יהא נראה כל כך שקר לגמרי

ופשוט שבדברים הכרחיים וכן בדברים שגרתיים מסתבר שאין בזה איסור משום שעל דעת כן דר אדם בקומה שיש שכן מעליו וכי אי אפשר להזהר בכגון אלה וסבר וקיבל אבל יש דברים שאפשר למנוע כגון כשיש צורך להוציא ולהזיז מטות אפשר לעשות בשעה מוקדמת יותר ואע"פ שזה גורם לפעמים אי נעימות וכי מפני אי נעימות שלו מותר לגרום צער לחבירו ולהפריע למנוחתו בשעה מאוחרת וכן רצוי שבשעות הערב לילך בבית בנעלי בית רכים ולא להפעיל מקדחות או מכונת כביסה וכדומה ועוד נראה שאע"פ שלכתחלה אין לחשוש רק בשעה שדרך בני אדם שוכבים אם יודע שהשכן ישן מוקדם מהרגיל בגלל סיבה או אפילו שינת צהרים או אפילו סתם מנוחה יש להזהר בכל אלו אע"פ שאפשר שמדינא אין השכן יכול למנוע ממנו שימוש בביתו בדרך הרגילה ובכלל יש להמנע מרעש מיותר שלפעמים מצטער השכן בכך ומתבייש מלהגיד לו וע" עוד בדיני נזיקין בהלכות נזקי שכנים בספר הנ"ל דן בכמה צדדים של גזל שינה שעפ"י מנהג המדינה אין להקים רעש לאחר השעה ה-11 בלילה מה הדין במסיבה או בשמחה אם צריך להפסיק והביא שם תשובת גדול אחר מבלי לפרש שמו שמכיון שזה נעשה נוהג מקובל יש לנהוג כן ולענ"ד נראה שהעושה שמחה בביתו אפשר שאינו קשור לשעה זו שכן דרך שכנים לוותר במקרים מיוחדים וגם זה בכלל סבור וקיבל וכמובן שגם לזה יש גבול וגם יש בזה משום לפנים משורת הדין וע" להלן עוד דן שם בדין בית מדרש וישיבה הסמוכים למקום מגורים אם מותר ללמוד בקול רם ותשובת אותו גדול שיתכן שיכולים השכנים להתנגד מראש שלא יקבעו שם ישיבה אבל אם לא התנגדו או שהישיבה קדמה הרי ירע וסבור וקיבל וצ"ע שלא ציין לדברי השו"ע בסימן קנו סעיף ג שכתב וכן יש לו לאחד מבני החצר ללמוד תינוקות ישראל תורה בתוך ביתו ואין השכנים יכולים למחות בידו ולומר אין אנו יכולים לישן מקול התינוקות וה"הלכל מילי דמצוה שאינם יכולים למחות בידו ע"כ ומשמע שבכל אופן מותר ואפשר שיש לחלק דשאני התם שהוא אחד מבני החצר אבל כשיבא אחר שלא מבני החצר לקבוע שם ללמוד תשב"ר אפשר שיכולים לעכב וכבר הערתי בזה בספר צדקה ומשפט פרק יב ואי"ה בדיני נזקי שכנים אנסה לברר הלכה זו וה"ה גם במה שדן שם בדין בית מדרש שאומרים סליחות באשמורת או בחצות אם יכולים השכנים למחות עוד דל שם במקרה שיש שכן חולה וכתב גדול שבודאי חייבים להתחשב בחולה ומשמע שם שגם בביהמד"ר כתב כן והנה בשו"ע שם בסעיף ב כתב המחבר שיכולים השכנים לעכב על אחד מהם הרוצה לעשות בביתו דבר המקים רעש. ודעת הרמ"א שכל שעושה בביתו ובחנותו אין יכולים לעכב עליו וסיים הרמ"א דהיינו דוקא בבריאים אבל כשיש חולה יכולים לעכב וכתב הנתיה"מ שם שאפילו חלה אח"כ משום דלא שייך חזקה בזה עיי"ש ומשמע שבמקום

חולי לא שייך הסברא דסבור וקיבל ולפי זה יש לדון בכל האמור לעיל שההיתר הוא משום דסבור וקיבל שבמקום חולי יכול מדינא לעכב עליו ויש להסתפק אם דין חולה נאמר גם בתך דסעיף ג והיינו במילי דמצוה ששם ההיתר הוא לאו משום דסבור וקיבל ויש לדון דא"כ במקום שיש חולה יבטלו הלימוד והתפלה מביהכנ"ס והביהמד"ר ולא מצאתי דבר זה וצ"ע וראיתי בחזו"א בב"ב סימן יג ס"ק יא שדן בדין חולה שיכול לעכב ויתבאר בע"ה בדיני נזיקין ואעתיק כאן הנוגע לענינינו וז"ל נראה שאין דברי הריב"ש שבחולה יכול לעכב אלא בעושה דבר שאינו עיקר דירה כמו בעושה אריגה וכי' שאין זה מצוי בכל אדם ולא ברוב בני אדם אבל אם עושה דברים שרוב ב"א עושין ולפעמים תשמישן ודיבורים משמיע קול שמפריע את החולה אינו יכול למחות אף אם החולה קדם ורשאי אדם לבנות בית אצל אבירו ולהכניס את העוללים והיונקים שצועקים בלילה ואין החולה יכול לעכב עליו שהרי אינו יכול לצאת מדירתו ע"כ ומדבריו נראה שכל דבר הרגיל לעשות במקום מסים בכלל זה ולפי"ז נראה שגם בביהמד"ר וביהכנ"ס אין החולה יכול לעכב ואפשר שכשעושים לפעמים שמחה גם זה בכלל תשמיש דירה באופן המקובל ולפי"ז דברי הריב"ש לא קאי גם במלמדי תינוקות וצ"ע בזה ועפ"ז האמור נראה דלאו דוקא בביהמד"ר דה"ה ליחיד הלומד בביתו אשיב כמילי דמצוה ואין השכן יכול לעכב עליו מללמוד בקול ומ"מ נראה שכל שאפשר לעשות באופן שלא יפריע מנוחת השכן חייב להשתדל בכך ועכ"פ לפנים משורת הדין וכן יש להזהר בערבסכות בשעת הקמת הסוכה שיש רעש שאע"פ שמצד הדין נראה שאינו יכול לעכב עליו אפילו בשעות הלילה נראה כי מסברא נראה שגם לזה יש גבול דלא מסתכר שיכול לעשות רעש בחצות הלילה מן הראוי להתחשב במנוחת השכנים ובסבלם

## 44) שבת קנב. ורש"י שם

אמר ליה ההוא גוזאה לרבי יהושע בן קרחה: מהכא לקרחינא כמה הוי? אמר ליה: כמהכא לגוזניא. מהכא לקרחינא כמה הוי – כמה מהלך יש מכאן עד הקרח, ולהקניטו על קרחתו נתכוון.

## 45) יומא עא: ורש"י שם

תנו רבנן: מעשה בכהן גדול אחד שיצא מבית המקדש, והוו אזלי כולי עלמא בתריה. כיון דחזיונהו לשמעיה ואבטליון שבקוהו לדידיה ואזלי בתר שמעיה ואבטליון. לסוף אתו שמעיה ואבטליון לאיפטורי מיניה דכהן גדול אמר להן: ייתון בני עממין לשלם אמרו ליה: ייתון בני עממין לשלם דעבדין עובדא דאהרן, ולא ייתי בר אהרן לשלם דלא עביד עובדא דאהרן.
לסוף אתו שמעיה ואבטליון לאיפטורי מיניה ליטול רשות ממנו, ולפרוש לצד ביתן.

**38) שולחן ערוך, חושן משפט תכ:לד**

המבעית את חבירו, אע"פ שחלה מהפחד, פטור מדיני אדם וחייב בדיני שמים; והוא שלא נגע בו, כגון שצעק לו מאחוריו, או שנראה לו באפילה וכיוצא בו

**39) שו"ת חתם סופר, חושן משפט קעו**

גי"ה קבלתי ע"ד השוחט מיכאל ראב שוחט בכפר א' פגע באיש א' נכבד כה' מיכאל פשקיז מקהלתו דמעלתו והתל בו נכבד א' על מצוה זו וביום א' העבר נסע ר' מיכאל מהלך ארבעה שעות מקהלתו לכפר ההוא והנה שיקר בו ונקבה ילדה והי' לשחוק בעיני כל ונפשו בשאלתו וכן הגאון אבדק"ק ס"ה שואל אם יש להעביר השוחט מאומנתו על מעשה הנ"ל או מה לעשות לו ... ומכ"ש דאיכא עלי' רשעת לאו דלא תונו שכשכנגדו שיכולים להעבירו מאומנתו עד שיפייס את שכנגדו בכל מה שראוי' לפי הנ"ל ולקבל תשובתו על חוצפתו ולאו של אונאה ועד אז אני מסכים להעבירו ב"ד קבלו ב"ד טענת הצדדי' ואמתלאותם וימצא את השוחט חייב.

**40) שו"ת אגרות משה אבן העזר ב:א**

נשאלתי מהגאב"ד דשארמאש שליט"א באח צעיר שנזדמן לו שידוך הגון ואבי הכלה רוצה דוקא שישאנה תיכף ולא יחכה עד שיזדמן לאחיו הגדול שידוך וישא תחלה משום שרוצה שישה קודם שימלאו לו עשרים שנה והאח הגדול מצטער מזה אם ראשי הצעיר לישא תחלה ואם האב רשאי לעזור להצעיר כדרך האב לבנו.

והנה פשוט לע"ד דף"ר לכתחלה יכול אח צעיר לישא אשה אף שאחיו הגדול לא נזדמן לו עדיין אשה לישאנה כי הרי הוא מחוייב לישא אשה ואיך שייך שלא יקיים חיובו בשביל שאחיו הגדול לא מקיים ... אינו רוצה אבי האשה להכות משום שרוצה שהחתונה תהיה קודם שנמלאו לו עשרים שנה ואם לא יתבטל העניין משום שאינו רוצה בחתן שיהיה יותר מבן כ' שנה והוא שידוך הגון שודאי אין עליו להפסיד ענין חשוב בשביל זה... ומה שרצה כתר' לומר דאולי יש להצעיר להמנע משום שהוא בושת עבור הגדול והוא כעין הלבנת פנים שהוא איסור חמור, הנה גם לענין הבושה הוא רק שבעצמו מתביש מזה דהא הרבה יש שמתאחרין מלישא בשביל הרבה טעמים אם בשביל שיש שרוצים ללמוד שחושבין שאחר הנישואין שיהיה רחים בצוארו לא יוכל ללמוד.. וגם מסתבר שלא שייך לאסור לאדם מלעשות עסקיו וכל צורכי גופו בטענה שאחר יתביש ע"י זה במה שהוא לא הצליח כמותו.

ולכן איני רואה שום איסור ואף לא שום דבר שלא כהוגן בזה שישא הצעיר אשה תחלה ואדרבה זכה במצוה רבא דנישואין ופו"ר שחייב בן עשרים ולא יצטרך לבקש זכותים להנצל מהעונש דאמר רבא ותנא דב"ר ישמעאל והוא דבר ברור לדינא.

**41) שו"ת קרן לדוד של הרב אליעזר גרינוואלד, אורח חיים יח**

שאלת חכם הגיעני ואשר עלה ונסתכ"ק במי שהוא ישן בזמן תפלה אם חבירו להקיצו כדי שלא יעבור זמן תפלה או כדי שיתפלל בצבור

... סיומא דהאי דינא דבמצוה חיובית לא מבעי' במצוה של תורה ודאי צריך להעירו אפי' אי חשבינן לי' לאונס מ"מ כיון דאונסא כמאן דעביד ל"א ובר חיובא מקרי אף בשעת שינה מחוייבין לזכותו במצוה, אלא אפי' במצוה דרבנן אם הוא

מקפיד על כך שלא לעבור זמן תפלה ומצטער על כך כשתבטל מהמצוה הוי בכלל גמ"ח ומצוה וחיובא להקיצו לזכותו במצוה כמ"ש המג"א סי' נ"ה אבל אם אינו מקפיד ע"ז אין חיוב להקיצו דאין כאן חיוב תוכחה כיון דלא נחשב בזה כעובר אדרבנן דהא אונס הוא כנ"ל אמנם היינו דוקא כשנרדם בשינה באונס דכיון דאונס הוא לא חל עליו חיוב מצוה דרבנן כלל אבל כשהלך לישן במכוין אף שהיה עדיין שהות, מ"מ כיון דהי"ל להזהר שלא תחטפנו שינה ויעבור זמן תפלה' אף דהשתא אונס הוא הו"ל תחילתו בפשיעה וסופו באונס דקיימ"ל דלאו אונס הוא כמבואר בב"מ צ"ג וכ"פ כרמב"ם פ"ג מה שומרים ובש"ע חו"מ סי' רצ"א כנלע"ד בס"ד

**42) קובץ מאמרים של הרב גר"א ווסרמן, חלק ב, עמוד ו**

פעם אחת בהיותי בראדין ביקש ממני רבי משה לנדינסקי ראש הישיבה לקראו מחדרו בעת שיצאו הקהל לקידוש לבנה כשהתחילו לצאת הלכתי אליו לקראו אך מצאתיו שנרדם על גבי הספר ונסוגתי לאחור ניגשתי אל החפץ חיים ושאלתי ר' משה ביקש ממני לקראו לקידוש לבנה ועכשיו שנרדם מה לעשות לעורר אותו או לאו והשיבני בקורטוב התרגשות קא סלקא דעתך? לעורר אדם משינתו??ונתחוור לי אז עוד א' מע' פנים למקרא כתוב (ויקרא כה:י') "לא תונו איש את עמיתו"

**43) פתחי חושן, פרק טו, ס"ק ג**

בספר "הזהרו בממון חבריכם" (עמוד קנו ואילך) האריך בענין גזל שינה ונראה פשוט שמכיון שצער גדול הוא הרי זה בכלל "לא תונו" ולשון גזל אינו מדויק כ"כ בזה אבל איסור צער ודאי יש בזה וכ"כ בשו"ת קרן לדוד או"ח סימן יח שאסור מן התורה להקיץ חבירו בשנתו משום צער והאריך שם לדון אם מותר ואם חייב להקיצו כדי שיקיים מצוה דאורייתא או דרבנן או לאפרושי מאיסורא ומה שדן בדין צער בע"ח באדם יתבאר בע"ה בדיני נזיקין ועוד האריך לדון אם ישן מיקרי בר דעת וגם עובר משום "ואהבת לרעך כמוך" והזכיר שם במי שעושה רעש בביתו או ברחוב בשעה שהשכנים ישנים ונראה פשוט שה"ה הגר בקומה עליונה ועושה רעש באופן שמפריע לשכן שלמטה במנוחתו ת"ז בכלל מצער

### 23) בבא מציעא נח: ורש"י שם

תני תנא קמיה דרב נחמן בר יצחק: כל המלבין פני
חבירו ברבים כאילו שופך דמים. אמר ליה: שפיר קא
אמרת, דחזינא ליה דאזיל סומקא ואתי חוורא
דדש ביה – כבר הורגל בכך שמכנים אותו כן, ואין
פניו מתלבנות, ומכל מקום זה להכלימו מתכוין.

### 24) בבא מציעא נח:

אמר ליה אביי לרב דימי: במערבא במאי זהירי?
אמר ליה: באחוורי אפי. דאמר רבי חנינא: הכל
יורדין לגיהנם, חוץ משלשה. הכל סלקא דעתך?
אלא אימא: כל היורדין לגיהנם עולים, חוץ משלשה
שיורדין ואין עולין. ואלו הן: הבא על אשת איש,
והמלבין פני חבירו ברבים, והמכנה שם רע לחבירו.
מכנה היינו מלבין אף על גב דדש ביה בשמיה.

### 25) תוספות על בבא מציעא נח: ד"ה "חוץ"

חוץ מג' שיורדין ואין עולין – אין לפרש דאין עולין
לעולם ... אלא ה"פ כל היורדין עולין מיד ואין אור
של גיהנם שולט בהן ... אבל יש מהם נדונין לעולם
המלבין פני חבירו ברבים דאמר בסמוך אין לו חלק
לעולם הבא ויש שעולין לאחר י"ב חדש ...

### 26) בבא מציעא נט. ופירוש רש"י שם

אמר רבי אבהו: שלשה אין הפרגוד ננעל בפניהם:
אונאה, וגזל, ועבודה זרה.
**פרגוד** מחיצה שבין שכינה לצבא מרום.
**אינו ננעל** להפסיד ראייתן מן המקום, אלא תמיד
רואה אותם עד שיפרע.

### 27) פלא יועץ, ערך "אונאה"

... והכלל הוא שכל שמצער חבירו בדבריו הוי
אונאת דברים וכדי לידע באיזה דברים מצטער
חבירו יקיים תמיד מארז"ל שאמרו דעלך סני לחברך
לא תעביד ורבים מעמי הארץ זה דרכם כסל למו
שמצטערים את חבריהם דרך שחוק וקלות ראש
כדי להרבות שמחה של ... אפילו על שיחה קלה
שמדברין לו והוא אינו מרגיש בצער חבירו וחושב
בדא מאי אם אני מצער אותו בשביל שעשה עמי
שלא כהוגן הדין עמי לצערו ואם הוא דרך שחוק
אין כאן צער כי כן דרכם של בני אדם ולשחוק
אמרתי מהולל ומתוך כך אין איש נחם על רעתו כי
לא יחשוב לו עון אשר חטא אבל ראוי לדעת כי לא
הותר לצער בדברים אפילו למי שציער אותו אם לא
דרך תוכחת מגולה מאהבה ...

### 28) שולחן ערוך, חושן משפט רכח:א

כשם שאונאה במקח וממכר כך אונאה בדברים,
וגדולה אונאת דברים מאונאת ממון שזה ניתן
להשבון וזה לא ניתן להשבון זה בגופו וזה בממונו,
והצועק על אונאת דברים נענה מיד.

---

### 29) בבא מציעא נט. ושולחן ערוך, חושן משפט רכח:ג

אמר רב: לעולם יהא אדם זהיר באונאת אשתו,
שמתוך שדמעתה מצויה אונאתה קרובה,
צריך ליזהר באונאת אשתו לפי שדמעתה מצויה.

### 30) ספר חסידים תרמא

אדם שהוציא ניעו מחוטמו, והוא הולך לו, ובא אחר
ונמאס בו, אותו שהוציא הניע יבא לדין, לפי שגרום
מיאוס לחבירו. וגם אם הביא את בניו או בנותיו עמו
בית חבירו ...

### 31) ספר יראים, סימן קפ

... וכשם שאונאה בדברים כך בעין רע שמראה לו
פנים רעים

### 32) כתובות סב:

כי הא דרב רחומי הוה שכיח קמיה דרבא במחוזא,
הוה רגיל דהוה אתי לביתיה כל מעלי יומא דכיפורי.
יומא חד משכתיה שמעתא, הוה מסכיא דביתהו
השתא אתי השתא אתי, לא אתא, חלש דעתה אחית
דמעתא מעינה, הוה יתיב באיגרא, אפחית איגרא
מתותיה ונח נפשיה.

### 33) ספר חסידים תתקעב

מי שהוא חריף ומפולפל, ובעבור ענוונותו ילך
במקום שהרב אומר לתלמידיו ההלכה, ואותו הרב
אינו חריף ומפולפל, ויתבייש שזה יושב שם, אותו
חריף חוטא אע"פ שאינו מקשה לו:

### 34) אגרת התשובה של רבינו יונה, יום שלישי

אסור לצער איש מישראל בין בדברים בין במעשה
שנא' 'לא תונו איש את עמיתו' וארז"ל באונאת
דברים הכתוב מדבר ולשון אונאה לשון צער

### 35) חיי אדם ב:קמג

מצער אחד מישראל בין בדברים בין במעשה,
שנאמר "לא תונו" וגו'

### 36) ספר החינוך, מצוה רמג, פירוש רמב"ן על ויקרא כה:יד-טו

... וכל שכן אם הזיק אותו בממון או צערו בשום
דבר לדעת, ביטל עשה זו ...
ואני חושב עוד סברא, שודאי המאנה את חבירו
לדעת עובר בלאו ...

### 37) שערי תשובה ג:קסה

והשלשה פנים שהם מצד העם: האחד – כי הוא
מצער את הצבור בהטלת אימתו, ונאמר (ויקרא כה,
יז): "ולא תונו איש את עמיתו", והוא על ענין הצער
בדברים כאשר בארנו כבר:

בדבר עד שאמרו [שם] שלא יתלה עיניו על המקח
בשעה שאין לו דמים. וראוי להזהר שאפילו ברמז
דבריו לא יהי נשמע חירוף לבני אדם, כי התורה
הקפידה הרבה באונאת הדברים, לפי שהוא דבר
קשה מאד ללב הבריות, והרבה מבני אדם יקפידו
עליהן יותר מן הממון, וכמו שאמרו זכרונם לברכה
[שם] גדולה אונאת דברים מאונאת ממון, שבאונאת
דברים הוא אומר [שם, שם] ויראת מאלקיך וגו'. ולא
יהיה באפשר לכתוב פרט כל הדברים שיש בהן צער
לבריות, אבל כל אחד צריך להזהר כפי מה שיראה,
כי השם ברוך הוא יודע את כל פסיעותיו וכל
רמיזותיו, כי האדם יראה לעינים והוא יראה ללבב
... ואולם לפי הדומה, אין במשמע שאם בא ישראל
אחד והתחיל והרשיע לצער חבירו בדברים הרעים
שלא יענהו השומע, שאי אפשר להיות האדם כאבן
שאין לה הופכים, ועוד שיהיה בשתיקתו כמודה על
החירופים, ובאמת לא תצוה התורה להיות האדם
כאבן שותק למחרפיו כמו למברכיו, אבל תצוה אותנו
שנתרחק מן המדה הזאת, ושלא נתחיל להתקוטט
ולחרף בני אדם ... ויש לנו ללמוד דבר זה, שמותר
לנו לענות כסיל, לפי הדומה, מאשר התירה התורה
הבא במחתרת להקדים ולהורגו, שאין ספק שלא
נתחייב האדם לסבול הנזקין מיד חבירו, כי יש לו
רשות להנצל מידה, וכמו כן מדבריו אשר מלא
מרמות ותוך, בכל דבר שהוא יכול להנצל ממנו ...

### 12) קובץ אגרות חזון איש, חלק א
... והרי צריך ליזהר שלא לגרום צער לחברו בדיבור
קל, אל לרגע, ויש בזה לא תעשה דאורייתא כדאמרו
סוף פרק הזהב.

### 13) חזון איש, קובץ אגרות א:לג
... מאד חובתי להזהר לגרום אי נעימות לבני אדם
אף לרגע אחת

### 14) ספר חסידים שיא
אל יפתה את בני אדם כך וכך רצו ליתן לו בסחורה,
או שיאמר אני קניתי בכך וכך, ועל זה נאמר (צפני'
ג יג) שארית ישראל לא יעשו עולה ולא ידברו כזב
ולא ימצא בפיהם לשון תרמית, ואל יתעה החפצים
לקנות, שיראה להם פנים כאומר למכור אותם
חפצים שבידו, ואין בלבו, והם אינם קונים במקום
אחר, כי סבורים שזה ימכור להם, וכתיב (ויקרא כה
יז) לא תונו שהונונהו בדברים, כי סבורים שזה ימכור
להם, וכתיב (ויקרא כה יז) לא תונו שהונונהו בדברים,
וכתיב (זכרי' ח טז) דברו אמת איש אל רעהו:

### 15) רשב"ם על פסחים קיב
אל תעמוד על המקח – לסחור והמוכר ישראל הוא
ואין לך דמים לקנות המקח ונמצא מפסידו חנם שלא
יקחנו אחר מאחר שאתה מהפך בו:

---

### 16) פירוש מאירי על בבא מציעא נח:
אמר המאירי כשם שיש אונאה במקח וממכר כך יש
אונאה בדברים ר"ל (1) שאסור להונות את חברו
ולגרום לו פסידא בדבריו והוא שאמר לא יאמר לו
בכמה חפץ זה והוא אינו רוצה ליקח שהרי מתוך
שהוא בוש לומר שאינו רוצה ליקח משפיל לו מקחו
לומר שאינו שוה כל כך ואחרים שומעים ונמצא
גורם לו פסידא (2) ואפילו לא היה שם אדם מ"מ
הוא מטריחו ומצערו שחשב למכור ולא מכר

### 17) שיטה מקובצת על בבא מציעא נח:
לא יתלה עיניו על המקח וכו' פירוש מפני שמשביח
דעתו של מוכר. הראב"ד.

### 18) בבא מציעא נט. ופירוש רש"י שם
אמר רבי אלעזר: מיום שנחרב בית המקדש ננעלו
שערי תפילה ... אמר רב חסדא: כל השערים ננעלים
חוץ משערי אונאה
חוץ משערי אונאה הצועק על אונאת דברים אין
השער ננעל בפניו.

### 19) ספר חסידים תרנח
ממהרים להפרע מן האדם כשצועקים עליו, מאשר
לא יצעקו עליו, שנאמר (דברים טו ט) וקרא עליך
אל ה', וכתיב (שמות כב כב) כי אם צעק יצעק אלי
שמע אשמע צעקתו ...

### 20) בבא מציעא נח:
אמר רבי יוחנן משום רבי שמעון בן יוחאי: גדול
אונאת דברים מאונאת ממון, שזה נאמר בו (ויקרא
כה) "ויראת מאלקיך" וזה לא נאמר בו "ויראת
מאלקיך". ורבי אלעזר אומר: זה בגופו וזה בממונו.
רבי שמואל בר נחמני אמר: זה ניתן להישבון, וזה לא
ניתן להישבון.

### 21) מהר"ל, נתיבות עולם ב, אהבת רע ב
יש לך לדעת כי הפרש יש בין אונאה ובין כאשר הוא
מכה את חבירו ומצערו, כי האונאה בפרט הוא לנפש
האדם אשר מקבל האונאה ואין האונאה לגוף, כי מה
אונאה יעשה אל הגוף. וכן הכתוב אומר (שמות כ"ב)
וגר לא תונו ולא תלחצנו כי אתם ידעתם את נפש
הגר וגו', הרי כי תלה אונאה בנפש שהיא מקבלת
אונאה. וכל בושה היא לנפש כמו שהתבאר למעלה,
ומפני כי האונאה היא לנפש והנפש היא בידו של
הקב"ה

### 22) בבא מציעא נט. ופירוש רש"י שם
אמר רבי אלעזר: הכל נפרע בידי שליח חוץ מאונאה,
שנאמר ובידך אנך.
על ידי שליח נפרעים על כל עבירות על ידי שליח.
ובידו לא מסרה לשליח.

# SOURCES ON PUTTING OTHERS DOWN – ONA'AT DEVARIM

**1) ויקרא כה:יד, יז**

וְכִי־תִמְכְּרוּ מִמְכָּר לַעֲמִיתֶךָ אוֹ קָנֹה מִיַּד עֲמִיתֶךָ אַל־תּוֹנוּ אִישׁ אֶת־אָחִיו:

וְלֹא תוֹנוּ אִישׁ אֶת־עֲמִיתוֹ וְיָרֵאתָ מֵאֱלֹקֶיךָ כִּי אֲנִי ד' אֱלֹקֵיכֶם:

**2) פירוש רש"י על ויקרא כה:יז**

ולא תונו איש את עמיתו – כאן הזהיר על אונאת דברים (ת"כ פרק ד, א.), שלא יקניט איש את חבירו, ולא ישיאנו עצה שאינה הוגנת לו, לפי דרכו והנאתו של יועץ ...

**3) משנה בבא מציעא ד:י'**

כשם שאונאה במקח וממכר. כך אונאה בדברים. לא יאמר לו בכמה חפץ זה. והוא אינו רוצה לקח. אם היה בעל תשובה. לא יאמר לו זכור מעשיך הראשונים. אם הוא בן גרים. לא יאמר לו זכור מעשה אבותיך. שנאמר (שמות כב) "וגר לא תונה ולא תלחצנו":

**4) בבא מציעא נח:**

תנו רבנן: (ויקרא כ"ה) "לא תונו איש את עמיתו" באונאת דברים הכתוב מדבר. אתה אומר באונאת דברים, או אינו אלא באונאת ממון? כשהוא אומר (ויקרא כ"ה) "וכי תמכרו ממכר לעמיתך או קנה מיד עמיתך" הרי אונאת ממון אמור, הא מה אני מקיים (ויקרא כ"ה) "לא תונו איש את עמיתו" באונאת דברים. הא כיצד? אם היה בעל תשובה אל יאמר לו זכור מעשיך הראשונים, אם היה בן גרים אל יאמר לו זכור מעשה אבותיך, אם היה גר ובא ללמוד תורה אל יאמר לו פה שאכל נבילות וטריפות, שקצים ורמשים בא ללמוד תורה שנאמרה מפי הגבורה. אם היו יסורין באין עליו, אם היו חלאים באין עליו, או שהיה מקבר את בניו, אל יאמר לו כדרך שאמרו לו חביריו לאיוב (איוב ד') "הלא יראתך כסלתך תקותך ותם דרכיך זכר נא מי הוא נקי אבד". אם היו חמרים מבקשין תבואה ממנו, לא יאמר להם לכו אצל פלוני שהוא מוכר תבואה ויודע בו שלא מכר מעולם. רבי יהודה אומר: אף לא יתלה עיניו על המקח בשעה שאין לו דמים, שהרי הדבר מסור ללב, וכל דבר המסור ללב נאמר בו ויראת מאלקיך.

**5) פירוש רש"י על בבא מציעא נח:, ויקרא כה:יז**

שהרי דבר המסור ללב – ולפיכך נאמר בו ויראת מאלקיך, האי שהרי ליתן טעם למה נאמר בו יראה נקט ליה, והכי קאמר: שהרי כל הדברים הללו אין טובתן ורעתן מסורה להכיר אלא ללבו של עושה,

הוא יודע אם לעקל אם לעקלקלות, ויכול הוא לומר לא עשיתי כי אם לטובה, הייתי סבור שיש לך תבואה למכור או היית חפץ לקנות מקח זה. וכל דבר המסור ללב של אדם, נאמר בו הוי ירא מן היודע מחשבות, אם לטובה אם לאונאה.

ולא תונו איש את עמיתו – ... ואם תאמר מי יודע אם נתכוונתי לרעה, לכך נאמר ויראת מאלקיך, היודע מחשבות הוא יודע. כל דבר המסור ללב, שאין מכיר אלא מי שהמחשבה בלבו, נאמר בו ויראת מאלקיך:

**6) ויקרא כה:יז ורש"י שם**

וְלֹא תוֹנוּ אִישׁ אֶת־עֲמִיתוֹ וְיָרֵאתָ מֵאֱלֹקֶיךָ כִּי אֲנִי ד' אֱלֹקֵיכֶם:

ולא תונו איש את עמיתו – כאן הזהיר על אונאת דברים (ת"כ פרק ד, א.), שלא יקניט איש את חבירו, ולא ישיאנו עצה שאינה הוגנת לו, לפי דרכו והנאתו של יועץ, ואם תאמר מי יודע אם נתכוונתי לרעה, לכך נאמר ויראת מאלקיך, היודע מחשבות הוא יודע. כל דבר המסור ללב, שאין מכיר אלא מי שהמחשבה בלבו, נאמר בו ויראת מאלקיך:

**7) פירוש רש"י על בבא מציעא נט: ד"ה "חוץ משערי אונאה"**

חוץ משערי אונאה – לפי שצער הלב היא, וקרוב להוריד דמעות.

**8) שערי תשובה של רבינו יונה ג:כד**

... באונאת דברים הכתוב מדבר, והוא מענין הצער והמצוק ...

**9) רמב"ם, ספר המצוות לא תעשה רנא**

שהזהירנו מהונות קצתנו את קצתנו בדברים והוא שנאמר לו מאמרים יכאיבוהו ויכעיסוהו

**10) שולחן ערוך, חושן משפט תכ:לד**

המבעית את חבירו, אע"פ שחלה מהפחד, פטור מדיני אדם וחייב בדיני שמים; והוא שלא נגע בו, כגון שצעק לו מאחריו, או שנראה לו באפילה וכיוצא בו

**11) ספר החינוך, מצוה שלח**

שלא להונות אחד מישראל בדברים, כלומר שלא נאמר לישראל דברים שיכאיבוהו ויצערוהו ואין בו כח לתת להעזר מהם ... שורש מצוה זו ידוע, כי הוא לתת שלום בין הבריות, וגדול השלום שבו הברכה מצויה בעולם וקשה המחלוקת ... מדיני המצוה ... שלא להכאיב הבריות בשום דבר ולא לביישם, והפליגו

בפירסומים שמפרסמים), והאם משתנה הפסק
כתוצאה מכך שרוב האנשים שקוראים בחוברות
האלה הם עכו"ם, ע"פ. וכפי שכבו' הוסיף להסביר
לי בע"פ, לא יוכל לצאת עי"ז איזה תקלה בטיפול
מסולף וקביעת דיאגנוזה לא נכונה, דאחרת, כפי
שהסברתי לו, פשוט הדבר כביעתא בכותחא שיש
בזה איסור גמור מכמה בחינות. וזאת תשובתי בע"ה.
... כי בעצם עוברים על איסור זה של מדבר שקר
תרחק גם אם משקרים בכתב, ולא רק בעל פה, יעוין
ביד רמה על בבא בתרא ד' קע"ב ד' קע"א ד"ה אמר להו
רב לספריה (אות ק"ח) דכות כן בפשיטות דלכתוב
שקר ודאי אסור משום מדבר שקר תרחק ע"ש ...
וכעת אשיב לו בראשונה על שאלתו, אם ישנו בכה"ג
איסור משום גונב דעת הבריות ואגיד לו, שכן ישנו,
ולא משנה גם בזה שרוב הקוראים הם עכו"ם ...
ופשוט הדבר שהאיסור בזה הוא אפילו בכתב ...
ולפי האמור פשוט גם זאת, דגם בהעלמת מקצת
פרטים אשר משתנה עי"כ הענין משתנה עי"כ ישנו בזה משום
גניבת דעת הבריות ... לאור האמור והמתבאר נראה

להלכה בנידון שאלת כבו', כי אסור לשנות בפרטים
שמפרסמים, וגם לא להעלים פרטים אם הענין
משתנה על ידי כן, והגם שאין העונש בזה כעונש
המשקר ללא תועלת, ומכל שכן לא כמי שמזיק עי"כ
לחבירו, אבל הוא בכלל למדו לשונם דבר שקר,
והאמת צריך להיות נר לרגלנו.

### 27) אגרות משה יורה דעה, חלק ב:סא

... ובאם כוונת צביעתו הוא לא ליפוי אלא כדי
שיקבלוהו למשרה באופן שאין איסור אונאה
כגון שיודע שיעשה המלאכה כצעיר מסתבר שיש
להתיר כמו בלובש מפני החמה והצנה שהתיר
הב"ח כדהביאו הט"ז סק"ד והש"ך /סי' קפ"ב/ סק"ז
והסכימו לזה כיון שהוא רק דבר אחד ולא מתדמה
בזה לאשה. אחרי כתבי זה נזדמן לי לראות ספר
המאור להגרא"מ פריל שמדבר בזה וכן תשובה
מהגאון ר' משה מרדכי עפשטיין הר"מ דסלאבאדקא
והעלו ג"כ להתיר לצבוע בשביל השגת משרה
כשליכא איסור אונאה עיי"ש.

בהסכמתם ובסתמא הכוונה היא על דעת בפועל אלא
שאין הם עומדים בזה ועיין היטב בתשובות והנהגות
ח"ד סי' רט"ו בזה ו בא י בס"ד בוה דבר נפלא בשו"ת
יוסף אומץ לרבינו החיד"א סי' נ"ז שהאריך בענין
ת"ח אחד שהיה רגיל להעלות את דמי העליה בבית
הכנסת בכדי להעלות דמיהם ולהוסיף להכנסת בית
הכנסת וסיכם הגבאים שאם העליה תישאר בידו או
יפרע חצי דמיהם והחיד"א בזרוע שם כתב להוכיחו
בתוקף דאין ראוי לעשות כדבר הזה מכמה טעמי
עויין שם היטב:

### 23) ספר חסידים תקז

לא יכסה אדם מום בני ביתו, אם צריכים בניו או
קרוביו להזדווג, אם יש להם חולי שאלו היו יודעים
אותם המזדווגים עמהם אותו חולי, לא היו מזדווגים,
יגלה להם, פן יאמרו קדושי טעות היו, אלא יפרידם
ולא יהיו ברע יחדיו. או אם יש מעשים רעים להם
שאלו היו יודעים, לא היו מתחתנים בהם, לכך
יפרסם. וכן לענין צדקה שאם היו יודעים לא היו
נותנים להם הרבה, יגיד לנותנים:

### 24) קהלת יעקב, יבמות סימן מד

... ושאל אם מחוייב עכ"פ להגיד ענינו (שהוא חולה)
להמשודכת א' שמא אם לא יגיד יהא חשש קדושי
טעות והב' את"ל שאין כאן חשש קדושי טעות שמא
עכ"פ מחוייב להגיד שלא תהא אונאה וגונב דעת
אחרים להינשא בחזקת כשר גמור בלא שום פקפוק
... וא"כ לפ"ז ה"נ נד"ד אי אפשר דהוי בו צד מקח טעות
וחוזר, אכן נראה לענ"ד דאין כאן בית מיחוש למקח
טעות ... ולשאלה הב' ... דמ"מ גניבת דעת איכא
ע"ש בסמ"ע, וא"כ לכאורה ה"נ נד"ד צריך להודיע
... ומ"מ התירו לו להינשא במקום שאין מכירין
אותו מבלי להגיד ענינו דהא אי יגעי לא יהבי לישא
אישה, אלמא דכה"ג שהוא כשר עפ"י ד"ת אינו מחוייב
להגיד פגמו. וטעמא דלא אסרינן כה"ג משום גניבת
דעת י"ל כעין הנ"ל דגבי כל מרח אפילו מום שאינו
מבטל המקח ... מ"מ אומדנא הוא שלא היה רוצה
בזה אחרי שכבר נתקשרו בחבה, וקשין גירושין, ומי
יודע מה יזדמן לו עוד, ומשו"ה כל כה"ג שבדיעבד
לא ירצה לוותר על הקנין אע"פ שיש בו מום זה ...

### 25) תתן אמת ליעקב, פרק ה, סימן לח

האם מותר לשנות בענין שידוכין
עיין ב"ב ט"ז דכתיב באויב "ולב אלמנה ארנן" דכל
היכא דהוה אלמנה דלא הוו נסבי לה זה הוה אזיל שדי
שמי' עילוי' והוו אתי נסבי לה ופרש"י שדי שמי'
עלווה אומר שהיא קרובתו או מדבר בה להשיאנה
ע"כ ונראה לדייק מדברי רש"י דמותר לשקר בכי
האי גוונא עבור שידוכין ... וסיפר הצדיק רבי שלמה
בלוך זצ"ל תלמידו של החפץ חיים זצ"ל שפעם קרה
שידוכו יתומה עם בחור בן תורה והשדכן אמר
להבחור שהיתומה היא קרובה של החפץ חיים

ובא הבחור אליו ושאל אם זה אמת, והשיבו שכן
וכאשר שאלו אותו בני הבית אח"כ היתכן הרי אין
היא קרובה שלנו השיב ואמר שבאופן זה כדי לשדך
יתומה והכל תלוי אם היא קרובה שלנו או לא יכולים
לסמוך על זה שכל ישראל קרובים זה לזה (הצדיק
ר' שלמה דף י"ט).... ונסתפקתי אם אפשר ללמוד
מכאן היתר לשנות לכל א' בכה"ג ... ולמעשה פסק
רבינו הגאון ר' ישראל יעקב פישר זצ"ל דיש להתיר
ולשנות בכה"ג לכל מי שהולך בשידוכין וקשה להתיר
ולבו נשבר בקרבו ... ושאלתי את הגאון רבי יוסף
שלום אלישיב שליט"א ואמר דמתיר רק שינוי קטן
דהיינו אם היא בת עשרים יכול לומר שהיא בת
תשע עשרה אבל לא יותר מזה ושאלתי הגאון רבי
שלמה זלמן אויערבך זצ"ל ואסר בזה לשנות אף
שינוי קטן. אבל שמעתי מעשה שהי' שהתיר הגרש"ז
אויערבאך זצ"ל לשנות לבחור מבוגר בכמה שנים
בשעת הדחק הכל לפי הענין (מפי אחד מבני ביתו
הרוצה בעילום שמו) והג"רב זילבר שליט"א כתב לי
וז"ל אודות לשנות בענין שידוך בנוגע להגיל פשוט
הוא דאסור לשנות מה שדרך להקפיד ע"ז ועובדא שמענא
משני ת"ח ההתיר הגר"א קוטלר זצ"ל לבחור שהיה
בגיל שלושים לשנות ולומר שהוא בן עשרים ושמונה
... אבל זה נלע"ד ברור לכל הדעות דאם הבחורה
באמת יותר מבת ארבעים שנה דאסור לומר עליה
שהיא פחותה מבת ארבעים לפי גמ' ב"ב קיט: דאי
לא נישאת קודם ארבעים שוב אינה יולדת ... ועוד
יש לציין מ"ש ספר חסידים תק"ז לא יכסה אדם מום
בני ביתו אם צריכים בניו או קרוביו להזדווג אם יש
להם חולי שאלו הוי יודעים אותם המזדווגים עמהם
אותו חולי לא הוי מזדווגים יגלה להם פן יאמרו
קדושי טעות הוי אלא יפרידם ולא יהיו ברע יחיו או
אם יש מעשים רעים להם שאלו היו יודעים לא היו
מתחתנים בהם לכך יפרסם ע"כ ... אמנם יש להוסיף
דמצינו גם דהותר גניבת דעת עבור שידוכין כמבואר
בערכין כ"ג: דערב דכתובה דברי הכל לא משתעבד
ופרש"י דמצוה קא עביד לזוווגם ולא מידי מחסר לה
דהא לא יהיבא זווי ע"כ ...

### 26) ציץ אליעזר, חלק טו:יב

... שאלתו היא. היות ולאחרונה רבו פרסומי
מחקרים ותוצאותיהם בעתונים רפואיים בכל שטחי
הרפואה, ובחלקו הדבר נובע מהעובדא שהההחלטה
להתקבלות רופא חדש לעבודה בבית חולים
מבוססת במדה רבה על מספר המאמרים שפירסם,
הנ"ל מביא להתחרות בין הרופאים, וכדי להגדיל את
מספר הפרסומים נאלצים הרופאים לפעמים לשנות
פרטים במקרים שמפרסמים, ע"י שינוי גיל, סידור
סיפור מהלך המחלה, העלמה או הוספת פרטים וכו',
כדי שהפירסום יהיה מעניין יותר, ויגביר את סיכוייו
להתקבל לעבודה, לכן נפשו בשאלתו! האם ע"י
שינוי הפרטים האלה עוברים על איסור גניבת דעת
הבריות (כי למיטב ידיעתו קורה כן לעתים תכופות

של עובדי כוכבים אסור שלא מצינו שהתהירה תורה בעובדי כוכבים.

### 16) פלא יועץ, ערך "גניבה"

ויש מין גניבה אחרת שדשו בה רבים הלא היא גניבת דעת הבריות ויש מיני ממינים הכלל הוא שכל שמשתדל לידע מה שבלב חבירו ברוב דברים הדברים גניבת דעת אקרי ואסור אם לא שעושה לש"ש להציל עשוק מיד עושקו או לאפרושי מאיסורא וכן המראה חיבה יתירה לחבירו ואין פיו ולבו שוים גניבת דעת מיקרי והולך בתום ילך בטח:

### 17) כנסת הגדולה, חושן משפט רכח:ז (בשם דמשק אליעזר)

ואסור לגנוב דעת הבריות וכו' – נ"ב אם הוא שונא לו מתמול מותר לגנוב דעתו אפילו במה פעמים כדי שעל ידי כך יעשו אהובים. דמשק אליעזר דף רמ"ב

### 18) זוהר, ב:צג:

לא תגנב. אי לאו דפסקא טעמא הוה אסיר אפילו למגנב דעתא דרביה באורייתא או דעתא דחכם לאסתכלא ביה או דיינא דדאין דינא לפום טענה דאצטריך ליה למגנב דעתא דרמאה ולמגנב דעתא דתרוויהו לאפקא דינא לנהורא. ובמה דפסקא טעמא אסיר ושרי.

### 19) מהרש"א על סוכה כט:

ופוסקי צדקה ברבים. היינו שבעלי בתים מנהיגי הקהילה פוסקין צדקה מרובה ואינן נותנין כולה שאומרים שלא היה דעתן לכך אלא בשביל אחרים שיתנו נדבות כראוי ודו"ק:

### 20) אגרות משה, חושן משפט, חלק ב:ל

הנה בדבר שאלתו על מה ששמע שבישיבות מתירין להתלמידים לגנוב את התשובות להשאלות במבחני הסיום שעושה המדינה (Regents – רידזענס) כדי להנות ולקבל את התעודות שנגמרו בטוב, הנה דבר זה אסור לא רק מדינא דמלכותא אלא מדין התורה, ואין זה רק גניבת דעת שג"כ אסור כדאמר שמואל בחולין דף צ"ד ע"א שאסור לגנוב דעת הבריות ואפילו דעתו של עכו"ם וכ"ש הכא שהוא גניבת דעת לכולי עלמא אף לישראל, אלא דהוא גם גניבת דבר ממש דהא בשיריצה לפרונחמו כמשך הזמן להשריר עצמו אצל אחד לעבוד בעסקיו ורוצים ברוב הפעמים במי שגמר היטב למודיו דחול והוא יראה לו התעודה איך שגמר בטוב ועל סמך זה קבלוהו שזהו גניבת ממון ממש ... שגם בשביל למוד התורה אסור לגנוב ...

### 21) תתן אמת ליעקב, פרק ה, סימן קכא

מי שמאד רוצה לקנות איזה דבר, האם יש בזה משום גניבת דעת אם עושה את עצמו כאילו אינו חפץ כ"כ

---

לקנות כדי שהלה ויזיל המחיר. לענ"ד יש ללמוד מדברי הזוה"ק פ' חיי שרה דף קכ"ז לענין זה שאין זה איסור בדבר ויש ללמוד מאברהם אבינו דרך ארץ לעשות כן דזה לשון הזוהר שם ע"פ הסולם. ר' יהודה אמר אברהם היה יודע בזה סימן באותה המערה היינו מערת המכפלה ולבו וצונו היה שם וכו', בא וראה בחכמה עשה אברהם, בשעה שבקש קבר לשרה כי כשבקש לא בקש מיד באותה שעה המערה ולא אמר שרוצה להפרד מהם אלא שאמר "תנו לי אחוזת קבר עמכם ואקברה מתי מלפני". ולא הזכיר לא את עפרון ולא את המערה ואם תאמר שעפרון לא היה שם, אינו כן, אלא הי' שם, וכי יעלה על דעתך שאברהם רצה להקבר ביניהם בין הטמאים או שרצונו היה להתחבר עמהם, עד שאמר להם תנו לי אחוזת קבר עמכם, אלא בחכמה עשה ואנו למדים דרך ארץ ממה שעשה אברהם, כי משום שתשוקתו ורצונו היה באותה המערה אע"פ שעפרון היה שם לא רצה לבקש ממנו מיד ולגלות לו את הרצון שהיה לו במערה ושאל תחילה מה שלא צריך לו, ולאחרים ולא לעפרון עכ"ל.

### 22) שביבי אש, חלק ב, פרשת בהר

הנה נשאלתי האם מותר לו לבעל סופרמקט לעשות צדקי למכור סחורתו והוא לוקח קופסאות שימורים שמחירם עשרה שקלים ליחידה והם עומדים במקומם במנוחה ואף אחד אינו רוכשם ועלתה בדעתו של המוכר להכניסם לתוך עגלה ולכתוב שלט "חמשה בחמשים ש"ח עד לגמר המלאי" וע"י ז מיהרו הלקוחות וקנו ביום אחד את כל המלאי או ונשאלת השאלה האם שפיר דמי למיעבד הכי או יש בזה משום גניבת דעת ואיסורי אחריני דהרי בכך הוא מאחז את עיניו ומטעה אותו ... ומעתה בנידון דילן אף שבאמת אין הוא מסתיר או מעלים מאומה מטיב הסחורה מכל מקום איכא למימר רזה נמי הוי בכלל הערמה ואונאה דכיון דהוא מציג את הסחורה באופן שע"י ז יוכל הקונה לטעות בדמיונו ולחשוב שיש לפניו הזדמנות מיוחדת ולולי זאת לא היה קונה דהיינו שאין לו מוכן לשלם את מחירה הרגיל ורק אם הוא בגדר מציאה והזדמנות ובמה שהוא מציג את הסחורה בצורה מיוחדת כאילו היא הזדמנות אין לך אונאה גדולה מזו ולכאורה הוא הדין במי שרוצה למכור דירה או חפצים ואומר לקונה שלפניו שיש לו קונים נוספים שחפצים במכר זה או שאומר לו שיש לו קונים אחרים שרוציה ורוציצ'ה למשלח יותר במחיר זה יחרן דהוי נמי בכלל אונאה דמטעה אותו לידי החלטה לקנות שאינו נכון וע"י ז הוא מביא אותו לידי החלטה לקנות ויש הרבה הטעיות כעין אילו שמצויות בשוק כותבים מחיר גבוה ועושים על זה סימן מחיקה ולצידו כותבים את המחיר הנמוך ואם אין המחיר המחוק נכון גם זה נחשב להטעיה ... ובאמת מצינו בדברי המהרש"א בסוכה דף כט. דמבואר מדבריו דמטעם זה נענשים בעלי הבתים שמכריזין בשמם ואינם נותנים עיי"ש ומיהו למימר דאיהו איירי כשמכריזים

בשבילו, אלא צריך להודיעו שלא פתחם בשבילו,
ואם הוא דבר דאיבעי ליה לאסוקי אדעתיה שאינו
עושה בשבילו, ומטעי עצמו שסובר שעושה בשבילו
לכבודו, כגון: שפגע בחבירו בדרך וסבור זה שיצא
לקראתו לכבדו, אין צריך להודיעו.

ז לא יאמר לו סוך שמן מפך זה והוא ריקן, ולילך
לבית האבל ובידו כלי ריקן וסובר האבל שהוא מלא
יין, ואם הוא עושה כדי לכבדו מותר.

ח לא ימכור לו עור של בהמה מתה בחזקת שהיא
שחוטה, ולא ישלח לו חבית של יין ושמן צף על פיה.
ט אין מפרכסין לא אדם ולא בהמה ולא כלים. כגון:
לצבוע זקן עבד העומד למכור כדי שיראה כבחור,
ולהשקות הבהמה מי סובין שמנפחין וזוקפין
שערותיה כדי שתראה שמינה, וכן אין מקרדין
פירוש קרוד: במגרדת או מסרקת ששיני דקים, ולא
מקרצפין פירוש קרצוף: מגרדת או מסרק ששיני
עבים אותה כדי לזקוף שערותיה, ולצבוע כלים
ישנים כדי שיראו כחדשים, ואין נופחין בקרבים כדי
שיראו שמנים ורחבים, ואין שורין הבשר במים כדי
שיראה לבן ושמן.

### 9) ספר מאירת עינים על שולחן ערוך, חושן משפט רכח ס"ק ז', י', טו

אם יש מום במקחו כו' - פי' אע"פ שאין בו אונאת
ממון מ"מ ה"ל להודיע והוא דומה לגניבת דעת
דאסור אע"פ שאין בו חסרון

והוא ריקן - פירוש והוא יודע בו שלא יסוך ומ"ה
דוקא אסור מפני גניבת דעת דחבירו יחזיק לו טובה
חנם אבל אם הי' בו שמן אף שיודע בו שלא יסוך
מותר לו לדבר בא וסוך ממנו מפני הכבוד וכמ"ש
לפני זה:

ולצבוע כלים ישנים - ז"ל ואין השבח שמשביחין
בצבע כמו העילוי שמעלה אותם בדמים אבל חדשים
מותר לצובעם כדי ליפות' שבלא"ה הן חדשים
וטובים עכ"ל:

### 10) חידושי ריטב"א על חולין צד.

ואיסור גניבת דעתו של נכרי כתבו קצת רבותינו
בשם בעלי התוספות ז"ל שהוא איסור תורה דנפקא
לן מדכתיב "לא תגנובו ולא תכחשו וגו'".... והיינו
נמי דיהביה אנחתא בלא תגנבו. ואע"ג דלא אשכחן
גניבה סתם על גניבת דעת אלא לשון גניבת לב
בכאן נכתב לא תגנבו סתם לכלול גניבת ממון
ובתוספתא דב"ק איתא שלשה גנבים הם גדול
שבכולם גונב דעת הבריות:

### 11) שערי תשובה, שער ג, קעח, קפד

וזה דבר כת שקרים. ענין הכת הזו נחלק לתשעה
חלקים. החלק האחד - איש כזב, אשר תורה עזב,
ירע וישחית במענה פיו, כמו המכחש בעמיתו
בפקדון או בתשומת יד או בשכר שכיר, שנאמר
(ויקרא יט, יא): "ולא תכחשו ולא תשקרו איש

בעמיתו", וכן העונה ברעהו עד שקר, שנאמר (שמות
כ, יג): "לא תענה ברעך עד שקר ...

החלק השביעי - מי שמתעה את חברו בדיבורו כי
עשה עמו טובה או דיבר טוב עליו ולא עשה. אמרו
רבותינו זכרונם לברכה (חולין צד, א): אסור לגנוב
דעת הבריות ואפילו דעת נכרי. והנה החטא הזה
חמור אצל חכמי ישראל יותר מזגל הנכרי, יען וביען
כי שפת שקר אשמה רבה, ונתחייבנו על גדרי האמת,
כי הוא מיסודי הנפש:

### 12) חזון איש, אמונה ובטחון, פרק ד

... ואמרו שם צ"ב א' כל המחליף בדיבורו כאילו
עובר עכו"ם כתיב הכא והייתי בעיניו כמתעתע
וכתיב התם הבל המה מעשה תעתועים ... ואם שנאוי
הוא השקר הקל שאינו פוגע בחבירו בשקרו, משנה
תועבה היא המרמה שחץ שחטו לשום לשום דבר מרמה
שכוון כזביו כדי להוליך את רעהו שולל, וקראו
חז"ל לחלי הזאת גנבת דעת, ואמרו בגמ' חולין צ"ד
א' אסור לגנוב דעת הבריות אפילו דעתו של עובד
כו"מ והאריכו שם בגמ' בפרטים הרבה: וכ' הרמב"ן
בפי' התורה בראשית ל"ד ד' דאנשי שכם היו נדונים
למיתה מן הדין שלא היו שומרים ז' מצוות ולא קבעו
דינים והרי תפשו את דינה ועינו אותה, ומכל מקום
לא הסכים יעקב אבינו עמהם מפני ששימשו בגנבת
דעת אחרי שלב אנשי שכם היה בטוח באמונתם
ובישרתם לבם שלא יעשו עמהם רע:

### 13) שערי תשובה ג:קפד

... אמרו רבותינו זכרונם לברכה (חולין צד, א): אסור
לגנוב דעת הבריות ואפילו דעת נכרי. והנה החטא
הזה חמור אצל חכמי ישראל יותר מזגל הנכרי, יען
וביען כי שפת שקר אשמה רבה, ונתחייבנו על גדרי
האמת, **כי הוא מיסודי הנפש:**

### 14) תוספתא, בבא קמא ז:ג

ולא עוד אלא שמעלין עליו כאילו היה יכול לגנוב
דעת העליונה היה גונב

### 15) ספר יראים סימן קכד

ג' גנבים הן הראשון שבכולם גונב דעת הבריות
והמרבה לו בתקרובת ויודע בו שאינו מקבל מסרב
בו לאכול ויודע בו שאינו אוכל. ואין לומר שאיסור
גניבת דעת במידי דממון שהרי מצינו שנענש
אבשלום עליו בסוטה פ"א [ט' ב'] תנן לפי שגנב ג'
גניבות לב אביו ולב ב"ד ולב כל ישראל נתקעו בו ג'
שבטים שנאמר ויקח ג' שבטים בכפו ויתקעם בלב
אבשלום לב אנשי ישראל ממון ונפשות גונב נפש
וחמור גונב דעת מגונב ממון ונפשות גונב נפש
מאחיו מבני ישראל ולא מבני עובדי כוכבים. ממון,
אמרי' בב"ק בשור שנגח את הפרה ראה ויתר גוים
התיר ממונם של כנענים לישראל וגונב דעת אפי'

**1)** בראשית לא:כו-כז ופירוש רש"י וחתם סופר שם

וַיֹּאמֶר לָבָן לְיַעֲקֹב מֶה עָשִׂיתָ וַתִּגְנֹב אֶת-לְבָבִי וַתְּנַהֵג אֶת-בְּנֹתַי כִּשְׁבֻיוֹת חָרֶב: לָמָּה נַחְבֵּאתָ לִבְרֹחַ וַתִּגְנֹב אֹתִי וְלֹא-הִגַּדְתָּ לִי וָאֲשַׁלֵּחֲךָ בְּשִׂמְחָה וּבְשִׁרִים בְּתֹף וּבְכִנּוֹר:

**ותגנב אתי – גנבת את דעתי:**

... למה גנבת את אלהי – י"ל כך כי גנבת דעת הבריות אסור אפי' דעתו של עכו"ם [חולין צ"ד], וצ"ל כי ירא יעקב שיעכבנו מחזור לבית אביו ...

**2)** ופירושי רש"י וחתם סופר על בראשית לא:כו-כז

**ותגנב אתי – גנבת את דעתי:**

... למה גנבת את אלהי – י"ל כך כי גנבת דעת הבריות אסור אפי' דעתו של עכו"ם [חולין צ"ד], וצ"ל כי ירא יעקב שיעכבנו מחזור לבית אביו ...

**3)** שמואל ב' טו:א-ו ופירוש רלב"ג שם

וַיְהִי מֵאַחֲרֵי כֵן וַיַּעַשׂ לוֹ אַבְשָׁלוֹם מֶרְכָּבָה וְסֻסִים וַחֲמִשִּׁים אִישׁ רָצִים לְפָנָיו: וְהִשְׁכִּים אַבְשָׁלוֹם וְעָמַד עַל-יַד דֶּרֶךְ הַשָּׁעַר וַיְהִי כָּל-הָאִישׁ אֲשֶׁר-יִהְיֶה-לּוֹ-רִיב לָבוֹא אֶל-הַמֶּלֶךְ לַמִּשְׁפָּט וַיִּקְרָא אַבְשָׁלוֹם אֵלָיו וַיֹּאמֶר אֵי-מִזֶּה עִיר אַתָּה וַיֹּאמֶר מֵאַחַד שִׁבְטֵי-יִשְׂרָאֵל עַבְדֶּךָ: וַיֹּאמֶר אֵלָיו אַבְשָׁלוֹם רְאֵה דְבָרֶיךָ טוֹבִים וּנְכֹחִים וְשֹׁמֵעַ אֵין-לְךָ מֵאֵת הַמֶּלֶךְ: וַיֹּאמֶר אַבְשָׁלוֹם מִי-יְשִׂמֵנִי שֹׁפֵט בָּאָרֶץ וְעָלַי יָבוֹא כָּל-אִישׁ אֲשֶׁר-יִהְיֶה-לּוֹ-רִיב וּמִשְׁפָּט וְהִצְדַּקְתִּיו: וְהָיָה בִּקְרָב-אִישׁ לְהִשְׁתַּחֲוֹת לוֹ וְשָׁלַח אֶת-יָדוֹ וְהֶחֱזִיק לוֹ וְנָשַׁק-לוֹ: וַיַּעַשׂ אַבְשָׁלוֹם כַּדָּבָר הַזֶּה לְכָל-יִשְׂרָאֵל אֲשֶׁר-יָבֹאוּ לַמִּשְׁפָּט אֶל-הַמֶּלֶךְ וַיְגַנֵּב אַבְשָׁלוֹם אֶת-לֵב אַנְשֵׁי יִשְׂרָאֵל:

ויגנב אבשלום את לב אנשי ישראל – ר"ל באלו הכזבי' כאלו גנב לבם מאת המלך דוד ולקחו לו כי בזה משך לב העם אליו:

**4)** משנה, בבא מציעא ד:יא-יב

(יא) אין מערבין פרות בפרות. אפילו חדשים בחדשים. ואין צריך לומר חדשים בישנים. באמת בין התירו לערב קשה ברך. מפני שהוא משביחו. אין מערבין שמרי יין ביין. אבל נותן לו את שמריו. מי שנתערב מים ביינו. לא ימכרנו בחנות אלא אם כן הודיעו. ולא לתגר אף על פי שהודיעו שאינו אלא לרמות בו. מקום שנהגו להטיל מים ביין. יטילו:

(יב) ... ומודים שלא יבור מעל על פי מגורה. שאינו אלא כגונב את העין. אין מפרכסין לא את האדם ולא את הבהמה ולא את הכלים:

**5)** תוספתא בבא קמא פרק ז:ג

שבעה גנבין הן הראשון שבכולן גונב דעת הבריות ...

שכל הגונב דעת הבריות נקרא גנב שנא' (ש"ב

---

טו) "ויגנב אבשלום את לב אנשי ישראל" ...

**6)** חולין צד. ורש"י שם

דאמר שמואל: אסור לגנוב דעת הבריות, ואפילו דעתו של עובד כוכבים ... אמר אביי: תרנגולת טרפה הואי, ויהבה ניהליה במר דשחוטה. תניא, היה ר' מאיר אומר: אל יסרהב אדם לחבירו לסעוד אצלו ויודע בו שאינו סועד, ולא ירבה לו בתקרובת ויודע בו שאינו מקבל, ולא יפתח לו חביות המכורות לחנוני אא"כ הודיעו, ולא יאמר לו סוך שמן מפך ריקן, ואם בשביל כבודו מותר. איני, והא עולא איקלע לבי רב יהודה, פתח לו חביות המכורות לחנוני אודועי אודעיה, ואיבעית אימא: שאני עולא דחביב ליה לרב יהודה, ודבלאו הכי נמי פתוחי מפתח ליה.

לא יסרהב – לא יפציר בו הואיל ויודע שלא יעשה משום דגונב דעתו להחזיק לו טובה בחנם כסבור שמן הלב מסרהב לו כן.

ולא יפתח לו כו' – כל חביותיהם מגופות היו וכשבא אדם חשוב אצלו פותח לו חבית להשקותו יין חזק ואם מכר חבית לחנוני שלמה ועדיין היא אצלו לא יפתחנה לאורח הבא לו מפני שגונב לבו להחזיק לו טובה חנם כסבור זה הפסד גדול ע"י שהרי תשאר חבית זו חסרה ותתקלקל יינה וזה ימסרנה מיד לחנוני שימכרנה לו.

ואם בשביל כבודו – של אורח להודיע לבריות שחביב עליו מותר.

שמתעהו – גונב דעתו.

**7)** רמב"ם, הלכות דעות ב:ו

ואסור לגנוב דעת הבריות ואפילו דעת הנכרי, כיצד לא ימכור לנכרי בשר נבילה במקום בשר שחוטה, ולא מנעל של מתה במקום מנעל של שחוטה, ולא יסרהב בחבירו שיאכל אצלו והוא יודע שאינו אוכל, ולא ירבה לו בתקרובת והוא יודע שאינו מקבל, ולא יפתח לו חביות שהוא צריך לפותחן למוכרן כדי לפתותו שבשביל כבודו פתח וכן כל כיוצא בו, ואפילו מילה אחת של פיתוי ושל גניבת דעת אסור, אלא שפת אמת ורוח נכון ולב טהור מכל עמל והות.

**8)** שולחן ערוך, חושן משפט רכח:ו-ט

ו אסור לרמות בני אדם במקח וממכר או לגנוב דעתם ... ואין לגנוב דעת הבריות בדברים שמראה שעושה בשבילו ואינו עושה אסור. כיצד: לא יסרהב (בחבירו) שיסעוד עמו והוא יודע שאינו סועד, ולא ירבה לו בתקרובת והוא יודע שאינו מקבל, ולא יפתח חביות הפתוחות לחנוני וזה סובר שפתחם

ההלכה נמצא שלא כן הדבר, ובמלחמה ההלכה בזה
אחרת ...

### 28) שו"ת משפט כהן (עניני א"י) סימן קמג ד"ה ולענין הצלת

עניני הכלל דמלחמות יוצאים הם מכלל זה דוחי
בהם, שהרי גם מלחמת רשות מותרת היא, +ע'
העמק דבר בראשית ט' ה' ואפי' מלך ישראל מותר
לעשות מלחמת הרשות אע"ג שכמה מישראל יהרגו
ע"י ואיך מצינו היתר להכניס נפשות רבות בסכנה
בשביל הרווחה, אלא דמלחמה והלכות צבור שאני.

### 29) שולחן ערוך, יורה דעה רנב:ד

אין פודין השבויים יותר מכדי דמיהם מפני תיקון
העולם שלא יהיו האויבים מוסרים עצמם עליהם
לשבותם אבל אדם יכול לפדות את עצמו בכל מה
שירצה וכן לת"ח או אפי' אינו ת"ח אלא שהוא תלמיד
חריף ואפשר שיהיה אדם גדול פודים אותו בדמים
מרובים

### 30) שבועות לה: ותוספות שם

דאמר שמואל: מלכותא דקטלא חד משיתא בעלמא
לא מיענשא
דקטלא חד משיתא בעלמא כו'. בהוצאת למלחמת
הרשות קאמר:

### 25) שולחן ערוך, יורה דעה רנב:ד

אין פודין השבויים יותר מכדי דמיהם מפני תיקון
העולם שלא יהיו האויבים מוסרים עצמם עליהם
לשבותם אבל אדם יכול לפדות את עצמו בכל מה
שירצה

### 26) שולחן ערוך, יורה דעה רנב:יב

האב חייב לפדות את הבן אי אית ליה לאב ולית ליה
לבן: הגה וה"ה קרוב אחר קרוב קודם דלא כל
הימנו שיעשירו עצמם ויטילו קרוביהם על הצבור

### 27) שו"ת ציץ אליעזר חלק יג סימן ק

א. במלחמה אם מחוייבים, או עכ"פ מותרים,
להכניס את עצמם בספק סכנה כדי להציל את
חברם החייל המוטל פצוע בשטח מסוכן וחשוף
לאויב. ב. ספק עבירה בג' העבירות אם יהרג ואל
יעבור.

(ו) וא"כ לכאורה יש להחיל את כל האמור במסקנת
ההלכה על נידון שאלתנו, ולומר שלא מיבעיא
שאינם מחוייבים להכניס א"ע בספק סכנה משום
ספק סכנה של חבירו החייל, ויתכן גם שאפי' אינם
רשאים בכך, אלא אפילו להכניס א"ע בספק סכנה
משום ודאי סכנה של חבירו החייל ג"כ אינם מחוייבי',
ולפי הרדב"ז, העושה כן הר"ז חסיד שוטה.

(ז) אולם בהתבוננות ובחדירה יותר מעמיקה בנבכי

נערה כדקתני ... (כתובות נב.) רשב"ג אומק אין פודין את השבויין יותר על כדי דמיהם וכו' ...

### 13) שולחן ערוך, יורה דעה רנב:ד
... אבל אדם יכול לפדות את עצמו בכל מה שירצה. ...

### 14) משנה גיטין ד:ו
מתני'. אין פודין את השבויין יתר על כדי דמיהן, מפני תיקון העולם ואין מבריחין את השבויין, מפני תיקון העולם רשב"ג אומר: מפני תקנת השבויין.

### 15) גיטין מה.
איבעיא להו: האי מפני תיקון העולם משום דוחקא דצבורא הוא, או דילמא משום דלא לגרבו ולייתו טפי? ת"ש: דלוי בר דרגא פרק לברתיה בתליסר אלפי דינרי זהב. אמר אביי: ומאן לימא לן דברצון חכמים עבד? דילמא שלא ברצון חכמים עבד? ואין מבריחין את השבויין, מפני תיקון העולם רשב"ג אומר: מפני תקנת שבויין. מאי ביניהו? איכא ביניהו, דליכא אלא חד.

### 16) כתובות נב.
תנו רבנן: נשבית, והיו מבקשין ממנו עד עשרה בדמיה פעם ראשונה פודה, מכאן ואילך, רצה פודה, רצה אינו פודה

### 17) ברכות כד., שולחן ערוך, אבן העזר עה:ב, משנה ברורה על שלחן ערוך, אורח חיים שסו:א
... אשתו כגופו

### 18) בבא מציעא סב.
... עד שבא רבי עקיבא ולימד: וחי אחיך עמך ‏ חייך קודמים לחיי חבירך.

### 19) טור, יורה דעה רנא
כתב ה"ר סעדיה חייב אדם להקדים פרנסתו לכל אדם ואינו חייב לתת צדקה עד שיהיה לו פרנסתו שנא' וחי אחיך עמך חייך קודמין לחיי אחיך וכן אמרה הצרפית לאליהו ועשיתי לי ולבני כו' תחילה ואח"כ לבני והודה לה אליהו ואמר לה לך ולבנך תעשה באחרונה:

### 20) פרי מגדים על שולחן ערוך, אורח חיים עב, חכמת אדם קמה
... ומיהו שם כתב דבכלל ואהבת לרעיך כמוך הוא. וע' במהרש"א שבת פרק ב' דמה "דסני" לך הא הטבה אין בכלל זה יע"ש דחייך קודמים, וכן משמע בשורש הא' וע' מה שכתבתי בפתיחה כוללת מזה וצ"ע עי' תי"ט פרק ג' דברכות משנה פרנסת עצמו קודם לכל אדם ואינו חייב ליתן צדקה עד שיהיה לו פרנסתו דכתיב וחי אחיך עמך משמע

חייך קודמין לחיי אחיך ואחר כך יקדים פרנסת אביו ואמו אם הם עניים ואם ידו משגת לפרנסם ממעותיו ומפרנסם ממעות מעשר אמרו חכמים תבא לו מארה לביתו שמבזה אביו ואמו לפרנסם ממעות צדקה.

### 21) נדרים פ:
מעיין של בני העיר, חייהן וחיי אחרים חייהן קודמין לחיי אחרים ... כביסתן וכביסת אחרים כביסתן קודמת לכביסת אחרים, חיי אחרים וכביסתן חיי אחרים קודמין לכביסתן, רבי יוסי אומר: כביסתן קודמת לחיי אחרים

### 22) שאילתות דרב אחאי גאון פרשת ראה שאילתא קמז ד"ה ברם צריך
... מאי כביסה קודם לחיי אחריתי או חיי אחרים קודם לכביסתן במקום כביסה חיי אחרים קודם או דילמא כיון דלא מחוורי מניהון אתו לידי צערא והילכתא כביסה שלהן קודם לחיי אחרים ...

### 23) פירוש העמק שאלה על שאילתות קמז
... דאותה תקנה לא היה אלא לתועלת רבים והיינו דדייק לשון התקנה "בני העיר" וכו' ... דסכנת צמא ברור שימותו בצמא משאין כן (בהמתן) אפשר יבואו לידי סכנה ... אבל כמה בני אדם אינם באים לידי שעמום בהעדר הכביסה ... וכביסתן ממילא הלכה כרבי יוסי שאין להכנס בספק סכנת נפשות בשביל ודאי פדיון נפש של חברו ... דעיקר פלוגתא דתנא קמא ורב יוסי היא פלוגתא דבן פטורי ורבי עקיבא (בבא מציעא סב:) שנים היו מהלכין במדבר ואין ביד אחד אלא קיתון של מים אם שותהו אחד מגיע לישוב ואם שותים אותו שנים שניהם מתים. דרש בן פטורי ישתו שניהם וימותו שנאמר "וחי אחיך עמך". אמר ליה רבי עקיבא "וחי אחיך עמך" חייך קודמין לחיי חברך ... ולכאורה דעת בן פטורי תמוה, וכי בשביל שאי אפשר לקיים "וחי אחיך" מחויב הוא להמית את עצמו חס ושלום? ואיזו תועלת תהיה מה שיתן גם לחברו? אלא הענין שאם ישתושניהם על כל פנים יחיו יום או יומיים גם שניהם, שלא יגיעו לישוב, ואולי עד כה יזדמן להם מים, משאין כן אם לא יתן לחברו הרי ימות בודאי בצמא. ובא רבי עקיבא ודרש "וחי אחיך עמך"

### 24) בבא מציעא סב:
שנים שהיו מהלכין בדרך, וביד אחד מהן קיתון של מים, אם שותין שניהם מתים, ואם שותה אחד מהן מגיע לישוב. דרש בן פטורא: מוטב שישתו שניהם וימותו, ואל יראה אחד מהם במיתתו של חבירו. עד שבא רבי עקיבא ולימד: וחי אחיך עמך חייך קודמים לחיי חבירך.

**1) ויקרא יט:טז**

לֹא-תֵלֵךְ רָכִיל בְּעַמֶּיךָ לֹא תַעֲמֹד עַל-דַּם רֵעֶךָ אֲנִי ד':

**2) שולחן ערוך, חושן משפט תכו:א**

הרואה את חבירו טובע בים או ליסטים באין עליו או חיה רעה באה עליו, ויכול להצילו הוא בעצמו או שישכור אחרים להציל ולא הציל, או ששמע עכו"ם או מוסרים מחשבים עליו רעה או טומנים לו פח ולא גילה אוזן חבירו והודיעו, או שידע בעכו"ם או באנס שהוא בא על חבירו ויכול לפייסו בגלל חבירו ולהסיר מה שבלבו ולא פייסו וכיוצא בדברים אלו, עובר על לא תעמוד על דם רעך.

**3) שולחן ערוך,אורח חיים שכט:ג**

מי שנפלה עליו מפולת ספק חי ספק מת ספק הוא שם ספק אינו שם מפקחין עליו אע"פ שיש בו כמה ספיקות:

**4) סנהדרין לז.**

וכל המקיים נפש אחת מישראל מעלה עליו הכתוב כאילו קיים עולם מלא

**5) כתובות יב:**

ברי ושמא ברי עדיף

**6) רמב"ם הלכות מתנת עניים ח:י'**

פדיון שבויים קודם לפרנסת עניים ולכסותן, ואין לך מצוה גדולה כפדיון שבויים שהשבוי הרי הוא בכלל הרעבים והצמאים והערומים ועומד בסכנת נפשות, והמעלים עיניו מפדיונו הרי זה עובר על לא תאמץ את לבבך ולא תקפוץ את ידך ועל לא תעמוד על דם רעך ועל לא ירדנו בפרך לעיניך, ובטל מצות פתח תפתח את ידך לו, ומצות וחי אחיך עמך, ואהבת לרעך כמוך, והצל לקוחים למות והרבה דברים כאלו, ואין לך מצוה רבה כפדיון שבויים.

**7) שולחן ערוך, יורה דעה רנב: ב**

המעלים עיניו מפדיון שבויים עובר על לא תאמץ את לבבך ועל לא תקפוץ את ידך ועל לא תעמוד על דם רעך ועל לא ירדנו בפרך לעיניך ובטל מצות פתוח תפתח ידך לו ומצות וחי אחיך עמך ואהבת לרעך כמוך והצל לקוחים למות והרבה דברים כאלו:

**8) שולחן ערוך, יורה דעה רנב:א**

פדיון שבויים קודם לפרנסת עניים ולכסותן ואין מצוה גדולה כפדיון שבויים הילכך לכל דבר מצוה שגבו מעות בשבילו יכולים לשנותן לפדיון שבויים ואפי' אם גבו לצורך בנין ב"ה ואפי' אם קנו העצים והאבנים והקצום לצורך הבנין שאסור למכרם בשביל מצוה אחרת מותר למכרם לצורך פדיון שבויים אבל אם בנאוהו כבר לא ימכרו אותו

**9) שולחן ערוך, יורה דעה רנב:ג**

כל רגע שמאחר לפדות השבויים היכא דאפשר להקדים הוי כאילו שופך דמים:

**10) שולחן ערוך, יורה דעה רנב:ד**

אין פודין השבויים יותר מכדי דמיהם מפני תיקון העולם שלא יהיו האויבים מוסרים עצמם עליהם ...

**11) שו"ת רדב"ז א:מ**

שאלת ממני אודיעך דעתי על הא דתנן אין פודין את השבויים יותר על כדי דמיהן אי הוי דמיהן כעבד הנמכר בשוק או הוי דמיהן כמו שנמכרים השבויים עכו"ם:

תשובה כבר נהגו כל ישראל לפדות את השבויים יותר מכדי דמיהן הנמכרי' בשוק שהרי זקן או קטן אין שוה בשוק יותר מעשר' דינרין ופודין אותו בק' או יותר וטעמא דמנהגא הוא משום דקי"ל דטעמא הוא דילמא ליגרו ליתו וימסרו עצמן לשבות מהם הרי אנו רואי' בזמן הזה שהשבאים אין יוצאים לכתחלה בשביל ישראל אלא לכל מי שימצאו הילכך אפי' שפודין אותם יותר ממה ששוה בשוק כיון שאין פודין אותם יותר ממה שנפדין שאר עכו"ם מותר והנח להם לישראל שהם גומלי חסד בני גומלי חסד והכי איכא למידק ממתני' דלא קתני אין פודין את השבויים יותר מכדי שיווין אלא יותר מכדי דמיהן משמע דמיהן של שבויים הרגיל בכל השבויים. אבל לפדותם אותם יותר מכדי שאר השבוי' של שאר לשונות עכו"ם אין ראוי ...

**12) שו"ת מהר"ם מלובלין טו**

... אמנם נ"ל פשוט דאין דאין מחוייבין לפדותן יותר מכדי דמיו ולא ידעתי מהיכי תיתי שיעלה על הדעת שיהיו מחוייבים לפדותו יותר מכדי דמיו דמ"ש משאר שבויים חוץ מת"ח כמבואר בכבפסוקי' דהא הכא שייכי טעמים לתרי שינויים דגמר' טעמא דדוחקא דצבורא ... כי אם יפדו אותס בסך גדול בכל יום יעלילו על כל בר ישראל שיכנס לבתיהם ... ופירושו של כדי דמיו היינו כפי שבשוק כעבד מהא שכתב הרמב"ם פרק ל' מהלכות ... וטעמו משום דהוא פוסק כרשב"ג דפליג התם בפרק

**81) שולחן ערוך, אורח חיים תקעא:א**
היושב בתענית אם יכול לסבול התענית נקרא קדוש
וא"ל כגון שאינו בריא וחזק נקרא חוטא:

**82) תוספתא, בבא מציעא ח:ב**
אין הפועל רשאי ... מרעיב ומסגיף את עצמו ...

**83) שולחן ערוך, אורח חיים תקעא:א**
ת"ח אינו רשאי לישב בתענית מפני שממעט
במלאכת שמים אא"כ כשהצבור מתענים שלא יפרוש
עצמו מהם ומלמדי תינוקות דינם כת"ח:

יאכל הכזית מעט מעט בכדי שיעור אכילת פרס דמעיקר הדין יוצא בזה כדלקמן סימן תע"ה ס"ו ואם ג"ז א"א לו מפני בריאותו עכ"פ יאכל מעט או ילעוס בפיו לזכר טעם מרירות אך לא יברך ע"ז:

### 70) מנחת אשר, בראשית לט

... ועיין שו"ת אבני נזר (יו"ד ח"ב ס' שכ"א) וכן בחלקת יואב בקונטרס בדיני אונס שכתבו דאין האדם חייב ליפול למשכב כדי לקיים מצות עשה משום דלא גרע מחומש בנכסיו עי"ש ... דאין צריך לחלות וליפול למשכב על מצוות עשה ... ונראה כנ"ל כיון דיש בזה חבלה וצער גדול הוי כחולה ... ונראה עיקר דלהלכה דלגבי סכנת אבר או כל נזק רפואי שאין לו מזור ועלול להיות בלתי הפיך ודאי אינו חייב לחלות לקיים מצ"ע ואפשר דאף חטא יש בזה דאין האדם רשאי לחבל בעצמו כמבואר בב"ק (צא:) ולא מצינו שהתירו לצורך מצוה ...

### 71) הלכה ורפואה (הרב משה הרשלר), תרופות ורפואות בשבת ח:ד

... אבל אם יש לו צער גדול מחמת הכאב ובשביל זה נחלש בשאר הגוף שרי לעשות כל הרפואות והיינו דהוה סכ"נ
ובפמ"ג שם כתב דהוה כחולה שא"ב סכנה ...

### 72) שולחן ערוך, אורח חיים רנ:ב, רפח:ב

ירבה בבשר ויין ומגדנות כפי יכלתו:
י"א שאדם שמזיק לו האכילה דאז עונג הוא לו שלא לאכול לא יאכל: הגה וכן מי שיש לו עונג אם יבכה כדי שילך הצער מלבו מותר לבכות בשבת (אגור בשם שבולי לקט) :

### 73) תענית יא.

אמר שמואל: כל היושב בתענית נקרא חוטא. סבר כי האי תנא, דתניא: רבי אלעזר הקפר ברבי אומר: מה תלמוד לומר (במדבר ו') וכפר עליו מאשר חטא על הנפש, וכי באיזה נפש חטא זה? אלא שציער עצמו מן היין, והלא דברים קל וחומר: ומה זה שלא ציער עצמו אלא מן היין נקרא חוטא, המצער עצמו מכל דבר ודבר על אחת כמה וכמה.

### 74) תענית כב:

רבי יוסי אומר: אין היחיד רשאי לסגף את עצמו בתענית, שמא יצטרך לבריות ואין הבריות מרחמות עליו.

### 75) תענית יא:

רבי אלעזר אומר: נקרא קדוש, שנאמר (במדבר ו') "קדוש יהיה גדל פרע שער ראשו". ומה זה שלא ציער עצמו אלא מדבר אחד נקרא קדוש, המצער עצמו מכל דבר ודבר על אחת כמה וכמה.

### 76) רמב"ם, הלכות דעות ג:א

שמא יאמר אדם הואיל והקנאה והתאוה והכבוד וכיוצא בהם דרך רעה הן ומוציאין את האדם מן העולם, אפרוש מהן ביותר ואתרחק לצד האחרון, עד שלא יאכל בשר ולא ישתה יין ולא ישא אשה ולא ישב בדירה נאה ולא ילבוש מלבוש נאה אלא השק והצמר הקשה וכיוצא בהן כגון כהני העובדי כוכבים, גם זה דרך רעה היא ואסור לילך בה, המהלך בדרך זו נקרא חוטא, שהרי הוא אומר בנזיר וכפר עליו מאשר חטא על הנפש, אמרו חכמים ומה אם נזיר שלא פירש אלא מן היין צריך כפרה המונע עצמו מכל דבר ודבר על אחת כמה וכמה, לפיכך צוו חכמים שלא ימנע אדם עצמו אלא מדברים שמנעתו התורה בלבד, ולא יהא אוסר עצמו בנדרים ובשבועות על דברים המותרים, כך אמרו חכמים לא דייך מה שאסרה תורה אלא שאתה אוסר עליך דברים אחרים, ובכלל הזה אלו שמתענין תמיד אינן בדרך טובה, ואסרו חכמים שיהא אדם מסגף עצמו בתענית, ועל כל הדברים האלו וכיוצא בהן צוה שלמה ואמר אל תהי צדיק הרבה ואל תתחכם יותר למה תשומם.

### 77) רמב"ם, הלכות נזיר י:יד

האומר הריני נזיר ... אבל הנודר לה' דרך קדושה הרי זה נאה ומשובח ועל זה נאמר נזר אלקיו על ראשו קדש הוא לה', ושקלו הכתוב כנביא ...

### 78) משנה אבות ו:א ופירוש רמב"ם, ורמב"ם, הקדמה לשמונה פרק ד

רבי מאיר אומר כל העוסק בתורה לשמה. זוכה לדברים הרבה ... ומכשרתו להיות צדיק חסיד ישר ונאמן.
חסיד – עושה לפנים משורת הדין
... ולזה הענין לא היו החסידים מניחים תכונות נפשותיהם תכונה הממוצעת בשוה, אך היו נוטים מעט לצד היתר או החסר על דרך הסייג והשמירה, רצוני לומר על דרך משל, שהיו נוטים מן הזהירות לצד העדר הרגש ההנאה מעט, מן הגבורה – לצד מסירות נפשו בסכנות מעט, מטוב הלב – לצד יתרון טוב הלב מעט, מן הענוה – לצד שפלות הרוח מעט, וכן בשאר הענינים. ואל זה הענין רמזו באמרם, לפנים משורת הדין ...

### 79) תהילים קמה:יז

צַדִּיק ד' בְּכָל דְּרָכָיו וְחָסִיד בְּכָל מַעֲשָׂיו:

### 80) רמב"ם, ספר המצוות, מצוה ח

היא שצונו להדמות בו ית' לפי יכלתנו והוא אמרו והלכת בדרכיו וכבר כפל צווי זה ואמר ללכת בכל דרכיו ובא בפירוש זה מה הקדוש ברוך הוא נקרא רחום אף אתה היה רחום מה הקב"ה נקרא חנון אף אתה היה חנון מה הקב"ה רחום אף אתה היה צדיק מה הקב"ה נקרא חסיד אף אתה היה

ההכאה בין ברגעי בין במימי רגלים אין מכין אותו
יותר שנאמר ונקלה אחיך לעיניך כיון שנקלה
פטור ...

### 64) ויקרא כג:כט, תהילים לה:יג
כִּי כָל הַנֶּפֶשׁ אֲשֶׁר לֹא תְעֻנֶּה בְּעֶצֶם הַיּוֹם הַזֶּה וְנִכְרְתָה
מֵעַמֶּיהָ:
וַאֲנִי בַּחֲלוֹתָם לְבוּשִׁי שָׂק עִנֵּיתִי בַצּוֹם נַפְשִׁי וּתְפִלָּתִי
עַל חֵיקִי תָשׁוּב:

### 65) סוכה כו., רמב"ם, הלכות סוכה ו:ב
תנו רבנן: חולה שאמרו לא חולה שיש בו סכנה,
אלא אפילו חולה שאין בו סכנה, אפילו חש בעיניו,
ואפילו חש בראשו ... דאמר רבא: מצטער פטור
מן הסוכה. והא אנן תנן: חולין ומשמשיהם פטורים
מן הסוכה. חולה אין, מצטער לא אמרי: חולה הוא
ומשמשיו פטורים, מצטער הוא פטור, משמשיו לא.
חולים ומשמשיהן פטורים מן הסוכה, ולא חולה שיש
בו סכנה אלא אפילו חש בראשו ואפילו חש בעיניו,
מצטער פטור מן הסוכה הוא ולא משמשיו, ואיזה
הוא מצטער זה שאינו יכול לישן בסוכה מפני הרוח
או מפני הזבובים והפרעושים וכיוצא בהן או מפני
הריח.

### 66) רמב"ם, הלכות תפילין ד:יג
... מצטער ומי שאין דעתו מיושבת ונכונה עליו
פטור מן התפילין שהמניח תפילין אסור לו להסיח
דעתו מהן ...

### 67) שו"ת רדב"ז ג:תכה, ב:תרפ"ז
... דאמר ר' יהושע לעולם ישלים אדם פרשיותיו
עם הצבור עדיף מכל הני דאמרן לעיל ... ולענין
החולה רואה אני שהוא פטור לגמרי ולא יהא אלא
מצטער שהוא פטור מן הסוכה שהיא מצות עשה של
תורה.
שאלת ממני על מה שנהגו להסתפר בראש חדש אייר
אם הוא מנהג הגון או לא.
תשובה ... תו איכא טעמא דאיכא צער בגידול
השיער למי שרגיל להסתפר ולא עדיף האי מנהגא
ממצות עשה של סוכה דקי"ל מצטער פטור

### 68) שולחן ערוך, אורח חיים תעב:י, משנה ברורה ס"ק לה
מי שאינו שותה יין מפני שמזיקו או שונאו צריך
לדחוק עצמו ולשתות לקיים מצות ארבע כוסות:
מפני שמזיקו. ר"ל שמצטער בשתייתו וכואב בראשו
מזה ואין זה בכלל זה כשיפול למשכב מזה:

### 69) משנה ברורה על שולחן ערוך, אורח חיים תעג, ס"ק מג
יחזור אחר ראשון ראשון. ומי שהוא חולה או איסטניס
מותר לו ליקח לו מאיזה מין שערב עליו ביותר וגם

לבנות שיהיו (ב"י) שחורות אפילו שערה אחת וכן
אסור לאיש להסתכל במראה (וע"ל סימן קנ"ו) :

### 57) נשמת אברהם, חלק ה, דף סט הערה 1
וכן אסור לאיש לצבוע – שאל מו"ר הגרי"י נויבירט
שליט"א למורנו ורבנו הגרש"ז אויערבאך זצ"ל
הלכה למעשה בחור בן 20 שנה שששערות ראשו
וזקנו לבנות (ולא מחמת מחלה) ומתבייש לצאת בין
האנשים, האם מותר לו לצבוע אותן שיהיו שחורות?
ואמר הגאון זצ"ל שמותר לבחור לצבוע את השערות
שלו (בתנאי שלא יהיה אונאה לגבי שידוך וכו') כדי
שלא יתבייש כי שערות לבנות בבחור צעיר נקרא
מום ואין איסור בהסרת מום.

### 58) שולחן ערוך, חושן משפט יז:יא
צריך הדיין לפסוק הדין מיד אחר שיתברר לו שאם
מענה את הדין ומאריך בדברים הברורים כדי לצער
אחד מבעלי הדינים הרי זה בכלל לא תעשו עול

### 59) בבא מציעא נח:, רמב"ם הלכות מכירה יד:יג
אם היו יסורין באין עליו, אם היו חלאים באין עליו,
או שהיה מקבר את בניו, אל יאמר לו כדרך שאמרו
לו חביריו לאיוב (איוב ד') הלא יראתך כסלתך
תקותך ותם דרכיך זכר נא מי הוא נקי אבד
כיצד היה בעל תשובה לא יאמר לו זכור מעשיך
הראשונים, ואם היה בן גרים לא יאמר לו זכור מעשה
אבותיך, היה גר ובא ללמוד תורה לא יאמר לו פה
שאכל נבילות וטריפות יבא וילמוד תורה שניתנה
מפי הגבורה, היו חלאים ויסורים באין עליו או שהיה
מקבר את בניו, לא יאמר לו כדרך שאמרו חביריו
לאיוב הלא יראתך כסלתך זכור נא מי הוא נקי אבד.

### 60) בראשית לח:כד-כו
וַיְהִי | כְּמִשְׁלֹשׁ חֳדָשִׁים וַיֻּגַּד לִיהוּדָה לֵאמֹר זָנְתָה תָּמָר
כַּלָּתֶךָ וְגַם הִנֵּה הָרָה לִזְנוּנִים וַיֹּאמֶר יְהוּדָה הוֹצִיאוּהָ
וְתִשָּׂרֵף: הִוא מוּצֵאת וְהִיא שָׁלְחָה אֶל חָמִיהָ לֵאמֹר
לְאִישׁ אֲשֶׁר אֵלֶּה לּוֹ אָנֹכִי הָרָה וַתֹּאמֶר הַכֶּר נָא לְמִי
הַחֹתֶמֶת וְהַפְּתִילִים וְהַמַּטֶּה הָאֵלֶּה: וַיַּכֵּר יְהוּדָה וַיֹּאמֶר
צָדְקָה מִמֶּנִּי כִּי עַל כֵּן לֹא נְתַתִּיהָ לְשֵׁלָה בְנִי וְלֹא יָסַף
עוֹד לְדַעְתָּהּ:

### 61) סוטה י':
אמר רבי יוחנן משום ר' שמעון בן יוחי: נוח לו לאדם
שיפיל עצמו לתוך כבשן האש ואל ילבין פני חבירו
ברבים. מנלן? מתמר.

### 62) ספר החינוך, מצוה רמ
... לפי שהבושת צער גדול לבריות, אין גדול ממנו.

### 63) רמב"ם, הלכות סנהדרין טז:ט, יז:ה
האיש המכה צריך להיות יתר בדעה וחסר בכח
מי שאמדוהו וכשהתחיל ללקות נתקלקל מכח

**45) ברכות סא:**

בשעה שהוציאו את רבי עקיבא להריגה זמן קריאת
שמע היה, והיו סורקים את בשרו במסרקות של
ברזל, והיה מקבל עליו עול מלכות שמים. אמרו לו
תלמידיו: רבינו, עד כאן? אמר להם: כל ימי הייתי
מצטער על פסוק זה בכל נפשך אפילו נוטל את
נשמתך, אמרתי: מתי יבא לידי ואקיימנו, ועכשיו
שבא לידי לא אקיימנו? היה מאריך באחד עד
שיצתה נשמתו באחד

**46) ברכות ה:**

אמר רבי יוחנן: נגעים ובנים אינן יסורין של אהבה
... אמר ליה: חביבין עליך יסורין? אמר ליה: לא הן
ולא שכרן.

**47) ערכין טז:**

דתניא דבי רבי ישמעאל: כל שעברו עליו ארבעים
יום בלא יסורין קיבל עולמו. במערבא אמרי:
פורענות מזדמנת לו.

**48) תענית כג.**

אמר ליה: שמע מינה דניימי שבעין שנין. חזא
לחמריה דאתיילידא ליה רמכי רמכי. אזל לביתיה,
אמר להו: בריה דחוני המעגל מי קיים? אמרו ליה:
בריה ליתא, בר בריה איתא. אמר להו: אנא חוני
המעגל. לא הימנוהו. אזל לבית המדרש, שמעינהו
לרבנן דקאמרי: נהירן שמעתתין כבשני חוני המעגל,
דכי הוי עייל לבית מדרשא, כל קושיא דהוו להו
לרבנן הוה מפרק להו. אמר להו: אנא ניהו, ולא
הימנוהו, ולא עבדי ליה יקרא כדמבעי ליה, חלש
דעתיה, בעי רחמי ומית. אמר רבא, היינו דאמרי
אינשי: או חברותא או מיתותא.

**49) שולחן ערוך, אורח חיים שלא:א**

יולדת היא כחולה שיש בו סכנה ומחללין עליה
השבת לכל מה שצריכה קוראין לה חכמה ממקום
למקום ומילדין (אותה) _ומדליקין לה נר אפילו היא
סומא ...

**50) מלכים א׳ יז:כא-כד**

וַיִּתְמֹדֵד עַל הַיֶּלֶד שָׁלֹשׁ פְּעָמִים וַיִּקְרָא אֶל־ד׳ וַיֹּאמַר
ד׳ אֱלֹקַי תָּשָׁב נָא נֶפֶשׁ־הַיֶּלֶד הַזֶּה עַל־קִרְבּוֹ: וַיִּשְׁמַע
ד׳ בְּקוֹל אֵלִיָּהוּ וַתָּשָׁב נֶפֶשׁ־הַיֶּלֶד עַל־קִרְבּוֹ וַיֶּחִי: וַיִּקַּח
אֵלִיָּהוּ אֶת־הַיֶּלֶד וַיֹּרִדֵהוּ מִן־הָעֲלִיָּה הַבַּיְתָה וַיִּתְּנֵהוּ
לְאִמּוֹ וַיֹּאמֶר אֵלִיָּהוּ רְאִי חַי בְּנֵךְ: וַתֹּאמֶר הָאִשָּׁה אֶל־
אֵלִיָּהוּ עַתָּה זֶה יָדַעְתִּי כִּי אִישׁ אֱלֹקִים אָתָּה וּדְבַר־ד׳
בְּפִיךָ אֱמֶת:

**51) תוספות בבא מציעא קיד: ד"ה "אמר"**

אמר ליה לאו כהן (אתה). תימה לר"י היאך החיה
בנה של האלמנה כיושן כהן היה דכתיב (מלכים א
יז) ויתמודד על הילד וגו' ויש לומר שהיה ברור לו

<hr>

שיחייהו לכך היה מותר משום פיקוח נפש:

**52) שו"ת אגרות משה יורה דעה ב:קעד**

ומש"כ התוס' בב"מ דף קי"ד דאליהו שהיה כהן
דהקשה הר"י דאיך החיה את בן הצרפית שהוצרך
להיות עמו באהל באחד ואם נשאו ונגע בו דהוא
משום שהיה ברור לו שיחיה והיה מותר לו משום
פקוח נפש, צריך לומר דאין כוונתם משום פקוח נפש
דהמת אלא משום פקוח נפש דהאם שהיתה מצטערת
מאד על שבשביל מצותה הגדולה והאמונה בהשי"ת
ובנביאיו לפרנס את אליהו מת בנה כמפורש בקרא
שטענה זה ...

**53) נשמת אברהם, חלק ה, דף לט, הערה 1**

... ושמעתי ממו"ר הגרי"י נויבירט שליט"א ששאל
לכאורה יוצא מכאן שאדם שרואה את כל רכושו
עולים באש בשבת ועקב זה יש תשש שמרוב צער
יחלה ויסתכן שיהיה מותר לכבות את האש בשבת
כדי למנוע סכנת נפשות של וזה לא כפי שפסק הגאון
האדר"ת ז"ל בקונטרס עובר אורח סי' שלדג יראה
מה שכתב הגרש"ז אויערבאך זצ"ל בספרו מנחת
שלמה וכן בשמירת שבת כהלכתה שצ"ע מה טעם לא
חוששין לזה וכן ואפילו אם יש ממש סכנת אבר בלי
סכנת נפשות אין מחללין שבת ואין חוששין שיצטער
הרבה עד שיחלה וכן לא מצינו דמתחשבן בחייבי
מיתת בית דין עם הצער וספק סכנה של הקרובים:

**54) שמירת שבת כהלכתה, פרק לב, הערה קעד**

ואף להסוברים ששבת רק דחויה, ולא הותרה אצל
פקו"נ, מ"מ אין חיוב להצטער אלא בשביל הצלת
נפש ולא כדי למנוע מלאכה הנעשית בהיתר לצורך
פקו"נ, וכמו שמותר לכל אדם להרוג בשבת את הבא
במחתרת לגנוב ממון חברו ואין עליו שום חיוב
לפייסו בממון כדי למנוע רציחה וחילול שבת

**55) שבת נ: ורש"י שם**

אמימר ומר זוטרא ורב אשי הוו יתבי, אייתו לקמייהו
ברדא. אמימר ורב אשי משו, מר זוטרא לא משא.
אמרו ליה: לא סבר לה מר להא דאמר רב ששת
ברדא שרי? אמר להו רב מרדכי: בר מינה דמר,
דאפילו בחול נמי לא סבירא ליה. סבר לה כי הא
דתניא: מגרר אדם גלדי צואה וגלדי מכה שעל בשרו
בשביל צערו, אם בשביל ליפות אסור. ואינהו כמאן
סברוה כי הא דתניא: רוחץ אדם פניו ידיו ורגליו בכל
יום בשביל קונו, משום שנאמר (משלי טז) כל פעל
ה' למענהו.

משום ליפות את עצמו אסור – משום לא ילבש גבר
שמלת אשה (דברים כב).

**56) שולחן ערוך, יורה דעה קפב:ו**

אסור ללקט אפילו שער אחד לבן מתוך השחורות
משום לא ילבש גבר וכן אסור לאיש לצבוע (שערות

עליו השלום (משלי טז, ו): "בחסד ואמת יכופר עון",
כי קנין התורה נקרא קנין האמת, כמו שאמר (משלי
כג, כג): "אמת קנה ואל תמכור", ונאמר (תהלים
קיט, קמב): "ותורתך אמת". ואמרו רבותינו זכרונם
לברכה (ויקרא רבה קדושים כה, א): "עץ חיים היא
למחזיקים בה" (משלי ג, יח) – עבר אדם על כריתות
או מיתות בית דין, אם היה רגיל לקרוא פרק אחד ביום
יקרא שני פרקים, אם היה רגיל לקרוא פרשה אחת
יקרא שתי פרשיות. ומשני פנים תגן עליו התורה מן
היסורים: האחת – כי אמרו רבותינו זכרונם לברכה
(קדושין לא, ב): תלמוד תורה

## 35) רמב"ם, הלכות ברכות י:ג, טור, אורח חיים רכב:ב-ג

שמע שמועה טובה מברך ברוך אתה יי' אלקינו מלך
העולם הטוב והמטיב, שמע שמועה רעה מברך ברוך
דיין האמת, וחייב אדם לברך על הרעה בטוב נפש
כדרך שמברך על הטובה בשמחה שנאמר ואהבת
את יי' אלקיך וגו' ובכל מאדך, ובכלל אהבה היתירה
שנצטוינו בה שאפילו בעת שייצר לו יודה וישבח
בשמחה.

## 36) חפץ חיים, שם עולם, פרק ג

וכן כל ענייני צער שמזדמן לאדם, שאחד מחרפו
ומגדפו, הוא הכל מן השמים על עונותיו, אלא
שמגלגלין חוב על ידי חייב, וכמו שאמרו חז"ל על
הפסוק והשבות אל לבבך, שעונותיך הם המחרפין
אותך. וכן אם אחד הכה אותו אפילו במזיד, הוא גם
כן השגחה מלמעלה, אלא שמגלגלין וכנ"ל, וראיה
ממה שאמר הכתוב וכי יריבון אנשים והכה איש את
רעהו וגו' שבתו יתן ורפא ירפא מכאן אמרו חז"ל
שניתנה רשות לרופא לרפאות דלא לימא רחמנא
מחי ואיהו מסי, והרי הכתוב מדבר שאחד הכה את
רעהו במזיד על ידי מריבה אלא על כרחך דגם זה
בידי שמים.

## 37) ספר החינוך, מצוה רמא

... שידע האדם ויתן אל לבו כי כל אשר יקרהו מטוב
עד רע, הוא סיבה שתבוא עליו מאת השם ברוך
הוא, ומיד האדם מיד איש אחיו לא יהיה דבר בלתי
רצון השם ברוך הוא, על כן כשיצערהו או יכאיבהו
אדם ידע בנפשו כי עוונותיו גרמו והשם יתברך גזר
עליו בכך,

## 38) שמואל ב' טז:י-יב ופירוש רלב"ג

וַיֹּאמֶר הַמֶּלֶךְ מַה לִּי וְלָכֶם בְּנֵי צְרֻיָה כִּי {כֹּה} יְקַלֵּל
כִּי ד' אָמַר לוֹ קַלֵּל אֶת דָּוִד וּמִי יֹאמַר מַדּוּעַ עָשִׂיתָה
כֵּן: וַיֹּאמֶר דָּוִד אֶל אֲבִישַׁי וְאֶל כָּל עֲבָדָיו הִנֵּה בְנִי אֲשֶׁר
יָצָא מִמֵּעַי מְבַקֵּשׁ אֶת נַפְשִׁי וְאַף כִּי עַתָּה בֶּן הַיְמִינִי
הַנִּחוּ לוֹ וִיקַלֵּל כִּי אָמַר לוֹ ד':
(אוּלַי יִרְאֶה ד' בְּעֵונִי {בְּעֵינִי} וְהֵשִׁיב ד' לִי טוֹבָה תַּחַת
קִלְלָתוֹ הַיּוֹם הַזֶּה:

---

אוּלַי יִרְאֶה ד' בעיני – ר"ל אולי ישגיח השם בעבור
עיני והרצון בזה בעבור מה שעיני רואה מהבזויים
האלו ואני סובלם לכבוד הש"י ואע"פ שיש לאל ידי
להנקם משמעוי הנה מפני זאת התכונה הטובה אני
בה מסבול אלי החרפות אולי ישיב לי השם ית' טובה
תחת קללתו אשר קלל אותי היום הזה:

## 39) מדרש תהילים כו:ב

... ארבעה הן שלקו, אחד לקה והיה מבעט, אחד
לקה והיה מצחק, ואחד לקה ומבקש אוהבו, ואחד
אמר למה הרצועה תלויה הכוני בה. אחד לקה והיה
מבעט, זה איוב שלקה ובעט ... והשני שהיה לקה
והיה מצחק, זה אברהם, ... השלישי היה לוקה
ומבקש מאוהבו, זה חזקיהו, ... והרביעי אמר למה
הרצועה תלויה הכוני בה, זה דוד, ... וכן דוד אמר
אשרי הגבר אשר תיסרנו יה (תהלים צד יב).

## 40) ברכות יז.

רבא בתר צלותיה אמר הכי ... יהי רצון מלפניך ה'
אלקי שלא אחטא עוד, ומה שחטאתי לפניך מרק
ברחמיך הרבים אבל לא על ידי יסורין וחלאים רעים.

## 41) ספר חסידים, תשנא

אם חלה שום אדם, אל יתלה חולי זו ושמחמת שום
מאכל או שום משקה בא חליו, ולא ה' פעל כל זאת,
ואפי' חבלוהו בני אדם רעים, אלא יאמר עונותיו
גרמו לו, שהרי כתיב (זכר' ח י) ואשלח את כל
האדם איש ברעהו, וכתיב (עמוס ג:ו) אם תהיה רעה
בעיר וה' לא עשה, אלא ודאי עשה. ואומר (בראשית
מב:כח) מה זאת עשה אלקים לנו, לכן יתפלל אדם
על מיני פגעים מנגעי אדם ונגעי שמים:

## 42) כתובות קד.

סליקא אמתיה דרבי לאיגרא אמרה עליוני' מבקשין
את רבי והתחתוני' מבקשין את רבי יהי רצון שיכופו
תחתונים את העליונים כיון דחזai כמה זימני דעייל
לבית הכסא וחלץ תפילין ומנח להו וקמצטער
אמרה יהי רצון שיכופו עליונים את התחתונים ולא
הוו שתקי רבנן מלמיבעי רחמי שקלה כוזא שדייא
מאיגרא (לארעא) אישתיקו מרחמי ונח נפשיה דרבי

## 43) פירוש ר"ן על נדרים מ.

נראה בעיני דה"ק פעמים שצריך לבקש רחמים על
החולה שימות כגון שמצטער החולה בחליו הרבה
ואי אפשר לו שיחיה כדאמרינן בפרק הנושא דכיון
דחזאי אמתיה דרבי דעל כמה זימנין לבית הכסא
ואנח חפילין וקא מצטער אמרה יהי רצון שיכופו
העליונים את התחתונים כלומר דלימות רבי ומש"ה
קאמר דהמבקר חולה מועילו בתפלתו אפילו לחיות

## 44) קהלת י':יח

בַּעֲצַלְתַּיִם יִמַּךְ הַמְּקָרֶה וּבְשִׁפְלוּת יָדַיִם יִדְלֹף הַבָּיִת:

(ישעי' מ ב) כי נרצה עונה, וכתיב (שם) כי מלאה צבאה:

### 24) רמב"ם, הלכות חובל ומזיק א:א, ז

החובל בחבירו חייב לשלם לו חמשה דברים נזק וצער ורפוי ושבת ובושת ...
ומנין שמזיק חבירו בצער בפני עצמו שהרי נאמר באונס (דברים כב:כט) "תחת אשר ענה" והוא הדין לכל המצער את חבירו בגופו שהוא חייב לשלם דמי הצער.

### 25) רמב"ם, הלכות חובל ומזיק ב:ט-י'

כמה הוא הצער, הכל לפי הניזק, יש אדם שהוא רך וענוג ביותר ובעל ממון ואילו נתנו לו ממון הרבה לא היה מצטער מעט ויש אדם שהוא עמל וחזק ועני ומפני זוז אחד מצטער צער הרבה, ועל פי הדברים האלה אומדין ופוסקין הצער. כיצד משערין הצער במקום שחסרו אבר, הרי שקטע ידו או אצבעו אומדין ואומרים כמה כזה רוצה ליתן בין לקטוע לו אבר זה בסייף או לקטוע אותו בסם אם גזר המלך עליו לקטוע ידו או רגלו ואומדין כמה יש בין זה לזה ומשלם המזיק

### 26) שולחן ערוך, חושן משפט תכ:טו

צער כיצד: הרי שקטע אצבעו, אומדים כמה אדם רוצה ליתן בין לקטוע לו אבר זה בסייף או לקטוע אותו בסם אם גזר המלך לקטוע אבר בסייף, ומה שיש בין זה לזה משלם לו.
הגה: ובמקום דאיכא צער לחוד, משערין אם היה גזר המלך לכוות אותו בשפוד על צפרנו וכדומה כמה היה נותן להנצל מצער זה (טור בשם הרא"ש).

### 27) רמב"ם, הלכות רוצח א:ד

ומוזהרין בית דין שלא ליקח כופר מן הרוצח ואפילו נתן כל ממון שבעולם ואפילו רצה גואל הדם לפטרו שאין נפשו של זה הנהרג קנין גואל הדם אלא קנין הקב"ה שנאמר (במדבר ל"ה ל"א ל"ג) ולא תקחו כופר לנפש רוצח

### 28) סוטה כ.

אינה מספקת לשתות עד שפניה מוריקות ועיניה בולטות והיא מתמלאת גידין, והם אומרים: הוציאוה, שלא תטמא העזרה. אם יש לה זכות היתה תולה לה, יש זכות תולה שנה אחת, יש זכות תולה לה ב' שנים, יש זכות תולה ג' שנים. מכאן אומר בן עזאי: חייב אדם ללמד את בתו תורה, שאם תשתה תדע שהזכות תולה לה.

### 29) רמב"ם, הלכות סוטה ג:כ

סוטה שהיה לה זכות תלמוד תורה אע"פ שאינה מצווה על תלמוד תורה הרי זו תולה לה ואינה מתה לשעתה אלא נימוקת והולכת וחלאים כבדים באין

---

עליה עד שתמות אחר שנה או שתים או שלש לפי זכותה והיא מתה בצביית בטן ובנפילת איברין.

### 30) שולחן ערוך, אורח חיים שכח:א-ב

מי שיש לו מיחוש בעלמא והוא מתחזק והולך כבריא אסור לעשות לו שום רפואה ואפי' ע"י א"י גזירה משום שחיקת סממנים:
מי שיש לו חולי של סכנה מצוה לחלל עליו את השבת והזהריז ה"ז משובח והשואל ה"ז שופך דמים:

### 31) שולחן ערוך, אורח חיים שכח:יז

חולה שנפל מחמת חליו למשכב ואין בו סכנה: הגה או שיש לו מיחוש שמצטער וחלה ממנו כל גופו שאע"פ שהולך כנפל למשכב דמי (המגיד פ"ב) אומרים לא"י לעשות לו רפואה אבל אין מחללין עליו את השבת באיסור דאורייתא אפי' יש בו סכנת אבר. ולחלל עליו ישראל באיסור דרבנן בידים יש מתירים אפילו אין בו סכנת אבר

### 32) ברכות ה.

אמר רבי שמעון בן לקיש: כל העוסק בתורה יסורין בדילין הימנו ...

### 33) ברכות ה.

אמר רבא ואיתימא רב חסדא: אם רואה אדם שיסורין באין עליו יפשפש במעשיו, שנאמר (איכה ג') נחפשה דרכינו ונחקורה ונשובה עד ה' פשפש ולא מצא יתלה בבטול תורה ...

### 34) שערי תשובה, שער רביעי יא

אם עבר אדם על כריתות ועל מיתות בית דין ועשה תשובה אחרי כן לא נרצה העון בלי יסורים, כי התשובה תולה ויסורים ממרקים, יכין לבו לעשות מצות המגינות מן היסורים כמו מצות הצדקה, כי היא מצלת גם מן המות, שנאמר (משלי י, ב): "וצדקה תציל ממות", ומי שאין לו ממון לעשות צדקה – ידבר טוב על העני, ויהיה לו לפה לבקש אחרים להטיב עמו. ואמרו רבותינו זכרונם לברכה (בבא בתרא ט, א): גדול המעשה יותר מן העושה. וכן יעסוק במצות גמילות חסדים לעזור את חבירו בעצמו והשתדלותו, כמו שאמרו רבותינו זכרונם לברכה (סוכה מט, ב): גדולה גמילות חסדים מן הצדקה, שהצדקה בממונו וגמילות חסדים בין בגופו ובין בממונו, והצדקה לעניים בלבד וגמילות חסדים בין לעניים ובין לעשירים. וכן ידבר על לב העני ויכבדהו וינחמהו מצרתו, כענין שנאמר (ישעיה נח, י): "ותפק לרעב נפשך", ואמרו רבותינו זכרונם לברכה (בבא בתרא ט, ב): כי המפייסו בדברים גדול מן הנותן צדקה. וכן יעסוק במצות בקור חולים וקבורת מתים ותנחומי אבלים ולשמח חתן וכלה, כי כל אלה מדרכי החסד. וכנגד כולן מצות תלמוד תורה לשם שמים. וכל המועצות שזכרנום הן בכלל מה שאמר שלמה המלך

עיניו באשה אחת, והעלה לבו טינא. ובאו ושאלו
לרופאים, ואמרו: אין לו תקנה עד שתבעל. אמרו
חכמים: ימות, ואל תבעל לו.

### 16) רמב"ם, הלכות יסודי התורה ה:ו

כענין שאמרו באונסין כך אמרו בחלאים, כיצד מי
שחלה ונטה למות ואמרו הרופאים שרפואתו בדבר
פלוני מאיסורין שבתורה עושין, ומתרפאין בכל
איסורין שבתורה במקום סכנה חוץ מעבודת כוכבים
וגילוי עריות ושפיכת דמים שאפילו במקום סכנה
אין מתרפאין בהן, ואם עבר ונתרפא עונשין אותו
בית דין עונש הראוי לו

### 17) שולחן ערוך, חושן משפט תכ:א

אסור לאדם להכות חבירו; ואם הכהו עובר בלאו,
שנאמר: פן יוסיף (דברים כה, ג). ואם הקפידה תורה
בהכאת רשע שלא להכותו יותר על רשע, קל וחומר
בהכאת צדיק. והמרים יד על חבירו להכותו, אף על
פי שלא הכהו, נקרא רשע:

### 18) דברים כה:ג, רמב"ם, הלכות סנהדרין טז:יב

אַרְבָּעִים יַכֶּנּוּ לֹא יֹסִיף פֶּן־יֹסִיף לְהַכֹּתוֹ עַל־אֵלֶּה מַכָּה
רַבָּה וְנִקְלָה אָחִיךָ לְעֵינֶיךָ:
... ואם הוסיף רצועה אחת על האומד ומת הרי החזן
גולה, ואם לא מת הרי החזן עבר על מצות לא תעשה
שנאמר "לא יוסיף"

### 19) שו"ת ציץ אליעזר יד:לה

אודות מה שבבתי חולים נותנים למתלמדים לבצע
זריקות לתוך הורידים וגורמים לחבלות ... והנה
עיני ראו, ועל גופי חשתי, איך שבביצוע הזריקות
שמבצעים המתלמדים הם גורמים, עקב אי בקיאותם
והתמחותם המוחלטת עדנה בזה, לחבלות לאברים
שעושים בהם את הזריקה, המקום מתנפח ונעשה
כחול וצהוב וכל האבר מתחיל לכאוב עד שמן
הצורך להניח על המקום הנפוח והכאוב תחבושת עם
ספירט. וזה נמשך כמה ימים ויותר עד שמתרפאים
מזה. ונשאלת איפוא השאלה, דאיך מותר לעשות
זאת למסור ביצוע הזריקות כנ"ז למתלמדים? הא
אסור לחבול בחבירו, והגם דזה לא יכול להגיע
לידי מצב של סיכון, אבל יש בזה מכל מקום מיתה
משום עבירה על לאו של איסור חבלה.... מה שיותר
חמור שלא שואלים בזה אפילו רשות מהחולה על
כך? להודיע לו ולבקש שיסכים שמתלמד יבצע
זאת וימחול אם יגרום לו ע"י חבלה אלא המתלמד
נגש עם הזריקה ישר למטה החולה ובא[ין] אומר
ובאין דברים מבצע את פעולתו וגורם לו לחבלות
ולכאבים כנ"ל.

### 20) שו"ת רדב"ז תשכח

שאלת ממני אודיעך דעתי אם האדם הוא בכלל
עשה דטעינה ופריקה. תשובה הרשב"א ז"ל העלה
בתשובת שאלה שהוא בכלל ולמד אותה מק"ו דשור
וחמור דאי משום צערא דבעלי חיים כ"ש צערא
דישראל גופיה ... ומ"מ מודה אני שהוא בכלל ג"ח
=גמילות חסדים= בכלל ואהבת לרעך כמוך אבל
שיהיה בכלל עשה דטעונה /דטעינה/ ופריקה לא
מסתברא לי. ומה שכתב הרשב"א ז"ל ועוד דאפי'
במשאוי הראוי מה נעשה לנתקל ורובץ תחת משאו
ע"כ. גם בעל הדין מודה דחייב להציל אותו מערתו
ולהשיב לו אבידת גופו א' משום לא תעמוד על דם
רעך וכל כי האי גוונא אבל אינו בכלל עשה דטעינה
ופריקה.

### 21) ספר חסידים תרסו

כל מעשה גרמות שאדם גורם צער לחבירו, נענש,
ואף אם יעשה צער על חנם לבהמה, כגון שמשים
עליה משאוי יותר מאשר יכולה לשאת, ואינה יכולה
ללכת ומכה אותה, עתיד ליתן את הדין, שהרי צער
בע"ח דאורייתא. כתיב בענין בלעם (במדבר כב) על
מה הכית [את] אתונך, וכנגד שאמר לו יש חרב
בידי כי עתה הרגתיך (שם שם כט), לכן נהרג בחרב
... כתיב [דכתיב] (דברים יג יח) ונתן לך רחמים
ורחמך, ר' יהודה אומר משום רבן גמליאל הרי הוא
אומר ונתן לך רחמים ורחמך הרי סימן זה מסור
בידך, כל זמן שאתה רחמן רחמו עליך:

### 22) שבת נה.

ואין יסורין בלא עון.

### 23) ספר חסידים קסד

אדם שהיה הולך בספינה או במדבר שאר העם
נוצלו והוא לא נוצל, או שלהם ניצול ושלו נאבד,
הוא לוקה והם אינם לוקים, ראוי לגרוע מעונותיו.
ואם הצער שאדם מקבל שקול כנגד עונותיו, הרי
נתכפרו עונותיו, והזכיות במקומם עומדות. ואין
מחליפין עון בזכות, שאין עבירה מכבה מצוה. ובלבד
שהצער שקיבל לא יהיה לדבר עבירה, כגון שרואה
אשה ומצטער עלי' שאינה שלו, ועיניו גרמו לו, ועוד
בושת יש לו לתובעה אולי לא תחפוץ היא, או ירא
שהיא תודיע בושתו לבני אדם. וכן צער של גניבה
שיבוש מבני אדם, ואינו מצער בשביל העבירות
שנשמע בשביל בושת בני אדם ואינו יכול לעשות מה
שלבו חפץ, כי אז עונשו גדול ביותר:
אבל אם קבל עליו צערו בשביל הקב"ה כגון שמונע
מעשעשוע בניו וכנותיו, שישמע שבוכין ואשתו
מגדלתן והוא מצטער שבוכין, ואינו עומד בשביל
שעוסק בתורה, ואינו הולך לטייל עם בני וילדיו,
על זה יקבל שכר על זה הצער, וצער של גיהנם
ממעטים לו:
וכן צער אשה רעה ואינו חוטא, ודקדוקי עניות ואינו
עושה עולה, וצער יסורים בגופו או במיתת אוהביו,
או שמצטער על צער אוהביו ועל צער אחרים, הכל
מחשבים לו כנגד צער גיהנם, כנגד עונותיו, שנאמר

**1) ויקרא כו:יח, כח**
וְאִם־עַד־אֵלֶּה לֹא תִשְׁמְעוּ לִי וְיָסַפְתִּי לְיַסְּרָה אֶתְכֶם שֶׁבַע עַל־חַטֹּאתֵיכֶם:
וְהָלַכְתִּי עִמָּכֶם בַּחֲמַת־קֶרִי וְיִסַּרְתִּי אֶתְכֶם אַף־אָנִי שֶׁבַע עַל־חַטֹּאתֵיכֶם:

**2) בראשית לד:כה**
וַיְהִי בַיּוֹם הַשְּׁלִישִׁי בִּהְיוֹתָם כֹּאֲבִים וַיִּקְחוּ שְׁנֵי־בְנֵי־יַעֲקֹב שִׁמְעוֹן וְלֵוִי אֲחֵי דִינָה אִישׁ חַרְבּוֹ וַיָּבֹאוּ עַל־הָעִיר בֶּטַח וַיַּהַרְגוּ כָּל־זָכָר:

**3) בראשית מט:טו**
וַיַּרְא מְנֻחָה כִּי טוֹב וְאֶת־הָאָרֶץ כִּי נָעֵמָה וַיֵּט שִׁכְמוֹ לִסְבֹּל וַיְהִי לְמַס־עֹבֵד:

**4) ישעיה מו:ז, נג:ד**
יִשָּׂאֻהוּ עַל־כָּתֵף יִסְבְּלֻהוּ וְיַנִּיחֻהוּ תַחְתָּיו וְיַעֲמֹד מִמְּקוֹמוֹ לֹא יָמִישׁ אַף־יִצְעַק אֵלָיו וְלֹא יַעֲנֶה מִצָּרָתוֹ לֹא יוֹשִׁיעֶנּוּ:
אָכֵן חֳלָיֵנוּ הוּא נָשָׂא וּמַכְאֹבֵינוּ סְבָלָם וַאֲנַחְנוּ חֲשַׁבְנֻהוּ נָגוּעַ מֻכֵּה אֱלֹקִים וּמְעֻנֶּה:

**5) פירוש רש"י על בבא מציעט צג: ד"ה "סיגפה"**
סיגפה – עינה ברעב, או העמידה בקיץ בחמה ובחורף בצינה, לענות נפש (במדבר ל') מתרגם לסגפא נפש.

**6) בראשית טז:ט, שמות א:יב**
וַיֹּאמֶר לָהּ מַלְאַךְ ד' שׁוּבִי אֶל־גְּבִרְתֵּךְ וְהִתְעַנִּי תַּחַת יָדֶיהָ:
וְכַאֲשֶׁר יְעַנּוּ אֹתוֹ כֵּן יִרְבֶּה וְכֵן יִפְרֹץ וַיָּקֻצוּ מִפְּנֵי בְּנֵי יִשְׂרָאֵל:

**7) ויקרא כג:כט, תהילים לה:יג**
כִּי כָל־הַנֶּפֶשׁ אֲשֶׁר לֹא־תְעֻנֶּה בְּעֶצֶם הַיּוֹם הַזֶּה וְנִכְרְתָה מֵעַמֶּיהָ:
וַאֲנִי בַּחֲלוֹתָם לְבוּשִׁי שָׂק עִנֵּיתִי בַצּוֹם נַפְשִׁי וּתְפִלָּתִי עַל־חֵיקִי תָשׁוּב:

**8) שבת יא. ורש"י שם**
ואמר רבא בר מחסיא אמר רב חמא בר גוריא אמר רב: כל חולי ולא חולי מעים, כל כאב ולא כאב לב, כל מיחוש ולא מיחוש ראש.
כאב – הוא ההולך ובא, כגון כאב שן, כאב מכה.
מיחוש – חששא בעלמא לפי שעה, וקל.

**9) עבודה זרה כח: ורש"י שם**
דמר שמואל היא. ההיא אמתא דהואי בי מר שמואל

דקדחא לה עינא בשבתא, צווחא וליכא דאשגח בה, פקעא עינא. למחר נפק מר שמואל ודרש: עין שמרדה מותר לכוחלה בשבת מאי טעמא? דשוריייני דעינא באובנתא דליבא תלו. כגון מאי? אמר רב יהודה: כגון רירא, **דיצא**, דמא, דימעתא, וקידחא ותחלת אוכלא, לאפוקי סוף אוכלא ופצוחי עינא דלא.
**דיצא** – אישפונד"ט לשון נעיצה ותחיבה. קדחא – חמימות.

**10) הושע ה:יג, סנהדרין צב:**
וַיַּרְא אֶפְרַיִם אֶת־חָלְיוֹ וִיהוּדָה אֶת־מְזֹרוֹ וַיֵּלֶךְ אֶפְרַיִם אֶל־אַשּׁוּר וַיִּשְׁלַח אֶל־מֶלֶךְ יָרֵב וְהוּא לֹא יוּכַל לִרְפֹּא לָכֶם וְלֹא־יִגְהֶה מִכֶּם מָזוֹר:
ואין מזור אלא יסורין, שנאמר (הושע ה') וירא אפרים את חליו ויהודה את מזורו.

**11) ביצה לב:**
תנו רבנן: שלשה חייהן אינם חיים, ואלו הן: המצפה לשלחן חברו, ומי שאשתו מושלת עליו, ומי שיסורין מושלין בגופו.

**12) ברכה יב בעמידה לחול**
הָשִׁיבָה שׁוֹפְטֵינוּ כְּבָרִאשׁוֹנָה וְיוֹעֲצֵינוּ כְּבַתְּחִלָּה. וְהָסֵר מִמֶּנּוּ יָגוֹן וַאֲנָחָה. וּמְלֹךְ עָלֵינוּ אַתָּה ד' לְבַדְּךָ בְּחֶסֶד וּבְרַחֲמִים. וְצַדְּקֵנוּ בַּמִּשְׁפָּט. בָּרוּךְ אַתָּה ד'. מֶלֶךְ אוֹהֵב צְדָקָה וּמִשְׁפָּט:

**13) ברכת "השכיבנו" בתפילת ערבית**
הַשְׁכִּיבֵנוּ ד' אֱלֹקֵינוּ לְשָׁלוֹם. וְהַעֲמִידֵנוּ מַלְכֵּנוּ לְחַיִּים וּפְרוֹשׂ עָלֵינוּ סֻכַּת שְׁלוֹמֶךָ. וְתַקְּנֵנוּ בְּעֵצָה טוֹבָה מִלְּפָנֶיךָ. וְהוֹשִׁיעֵנוּ לְמַעַן שְׁמֶךָ. וְהָגֵן בַּעֲדֵנוּ. וְהָסֵר מֵעָלֵינוּ אוֹיֵב דֶּבֶר וְחֶרֶב וְרָעָב וְיָגוֹן. וְהָסֵר שָׂטָן מִלְּפָנֵינוּ וּמֵאַחֲרֵינוּ. וּבְצֵל כְּנָפֶיךָ תַּסְתִּירֵנוּ. כִּי אֵל שׁוֹמְרֵנוּ וּמַצִּילֵנוּ אָתָּה. כִּי אֵל מֶלֶךְ חַנּוּן וְרַחוּם אָתָּה. וּשְׁמוֹר צֵאתֵנוּ וּבוֹאֵנוּ לְחַיִּים וּלְשָׁלוֹם מֵעַתָּה וְעַד עוֹלָם:

**14) שולחן ערוך, אורח חיים שכח:יז**
חולה שנפל מחמת חליו למשכב ואין בו סכנה: הגה או שיש לו מיחוש שמצטער וחלה ממנו כל גופו שאז אע"פ שהולך כנפל למשכב דמי (המגיד פ"ב) אומרים לא"י לעשות לו רפואה אבל אין מחללין עליו את השבת באיסור דאורייתא אפי' יש בו סכנת אבר. ולחלל עליו ישראל באיסור דרבנן בידים מתירים אפילו אין בו סכנת אבר

**15) סנהדרין עה.**
אמר רב יהודה אמר רב: מעשה באדם אחד שנתן

שתוקנה אז (כפי שנזכר בספר שמלת /שלמת /חיים
ח"א סי' ע"ז), ואין להוסיף על הגזירה, ובדומה לזה
ראיתי שכותב בספר שו"ת חלקת יעקב ח"א סי'
ס"ב על כלי הרדיו בנוגע לאיסור זימרה בכלי שלא
במקום מצוה עיי"ש, ושם היתה הגזירה בזמן חז"ל,
ומכש"כ שיש להתיר השמעת הקלטות מנגינות
בע"פ [ואפילו בפטיפון] בחתונות, שאין כל הוכחה
ואסמכתא ברורה שגם על זה התקינו בירושלים
גאוני הדור שבדור הקודם [והטייפ עוד לא היה],
ואשר בכלל רובא דעלמא נוהגים בזה היתר.

### 79) עשה לך רב, חלק ג:ד

... איני רואה שום איסור בשמיעת תקליטי מוסיקה
לכל סוגיה קלאסית או מודרנית וכן שירים שהם סתם
גיבובי מילים בעלמא וכל המטרה היא המוסיקה אך
אם תכנו אינו טוב אף שהוא בשפה זרה כיון שאפילו
יחידים מבינים ודאי שאסור ...

### 80) שו"ת הליכות שלמה, הלכות ספירת העומר יד, וס"ק כב

איש להמנע בימים אלה (ספירת העומֶר) מכל שירה
המעוררת לריקוד ומחול, אבל שירה המרוממת את
האדם אך אינו מביאתו לריקוד וממחול, מותרת.
(כב) וכן שמיעת פרקי חזנות ונגינות "קלאסיות:
וכדומה, יש להתיר.

All this information is culled from the (81
Journal of Halacha and Contemporary Society, vol. 14, pages 22–24, footnote 13

שיתחדש אע"פ שלא הי' בשעת הגזירה דודאי אסור
משום דהגזירה היתה על מיני כלי זמר, והסברא
נותנת דאף כ"ז שיתחדש בכלל, אבל הרדיו שאין
רואים כלל המנגן ובא ממרחק רב עפ"י חדשות
הטבע מיקרי פנים חדשות ואינו בכלל הגזירה, ואף
שהיא רק סברא בעלמא ומי שירצה יכול לדחותה
מ"מ סניף יש.

### 78) שו"ת ציץ אליעזר, חלק טו,:לג (חלק ג)

ומה שמוסיף כבו' לשאול, דאם נאמר שדין
טייפרקורד כזמר בכלי, האם הוא ממש כדין זמר
בכלי שיר כמו כינור והדומה או דרגה בין זה לשיר
בפה, ונפק"מ להנוהגים איסור בכלי זמר בירושלים
בחתונות כידוע, דאם הוא ממש ככלי זמר אזי אסור,
ואם הוא פחות מזה אזי יהיה מותר, ע"כ. הנה כבר
חויתי דעתי לעיל שזה תלוי מאין מקור השירים
והניגונים שהוקלטו בטייף, אם משירה וזימרה בפה
מותר, ואם זה נובע ממה שהקליטו מכלי – שיר אזי
דינו כהשמעה מכלי – זמר. אמנם ראיתי בספר שלמת
חיים ח"ד סי' כ"א אות ג' שמחבר הספר שאל את
הגרי"ח זאננפעלד ז"ל אם מנהג ירושלים חל גם על
כלי הגראמיפון, /דפטיפון/ והשיב בקצרה ובזה"ל:
ודאי גם זה בכלל, אבל השאלה שם נחלקה לשנים
הן על שירה בפה שקלטה והן על מה שקלטה ניגונים
של כלי שירה כדיעו"ש, ולא ברור איפוא אם מה
שענה דגם זה בכלל המכוון על כל גוונא, או דילמא
רק כשמשמיעה ניגונים שקלטה מכלי שיר, וגם אם
נאמר שגם הכלי – גראמפאן בכלל יש עדיין לומר
שחלות התקנה לא חלה גם על הטייף, מכיון שזה לא
היה עדיין בזמנם של הגאונים מקאליש ומבריסק ז"ל

בתשובת שאלה דאפי' בפה אסור אף בלא משתה
ואין חילוק בין לשון עברי ולשון ערבי כ"ש אם הן
דברי ניבול לשומעו שאסור אף בלא מליצה וניגון
וה"מ שירת אהבים כגון לשבח יפה ביופיו וכיוצא
בו אבל מותר לומר שירות ותשבחות על היין בבית
המשתה ואסור לאדם שימלא שחוק פיו בזמן הזה
שנאמר אז ימלא שחוק פינו:

### 72) רמב"ם, הלכות תענית ה:יד

וכן גזרו שלא לנגן בכלי שיר וכל מיני זמר וכל
משמיעי קול של שיר אסור לשמוח בהן ואסור
לשמען מפני החורבן, ואפילו שירה בפה על היין
אסורה שנאמר ישעיהו כ"ד בשיר לא ישתו יין, וכבר
נהגו כל ישראל לומר דברי תושבחות או שיר של
הודאות לאל וכיוצא בהן על היין.

### 73) שולחן ערוך, אורח חיים תקס:ג

וכן גזרו שלא לנגן בכלי שיר וכל מיני זמר וכל
משמיעי קול של שיר לשמוח בהם: הגה וי"א דוקא
מי שרגיל בהם כגון המלכים שעומדים ושוכבים
בכלי שיר או בבית המשתה (טור): ואסור לשומעם
מפני החורבן ואפי' שיר בפה על היין אסורה שנאמר
בשיר לא ישתו יין וכבר נהגו כל ישראל לומר דברי
תשבחות או שיר של הודאות וזכרון חסדי הקב"ה על
היין: הגה וכן לצורך מצוה כגון בבית חתן וכלה הכל
שרי (תוספות וסמ"ג והגהות מיימוני):
הגה וי"א דוקא מי שרגיל בהם כגון המלכים שעומדים
ושוכבים בכלי שיר או בבית המשתה (טור):
הגה וכן לצורך מצוה כגון בבית חתן וכלה הכל שרי
(תוספות וסמ"ג והגהות מיימוני):

### 74) ערוך השולחן, אורח חיים תקס:ז

וכן גזרו שלא לנגן בכלי שיר וכל מיני זמר וכל
משמיעי קול של שיר לשמוח בהם ואסור לשומען
מפני החורבן שנאמר אל תשמח ישראל אל גיל
כעמים וי"א דוקא מי שרגיל בזה אסור כמו השרים
שעומדים ושוכבים בכלי שיר וכן בבית המשתה
אסור אם אינה שמחה של מצוה ואפילו מי שאינו
רגיל בזה אסור אבל לצורך מצוה כגון בבית חתן
וכלה הכל מותר וגם שם אין לשמוח ביותר ובסעודת
הסיום מותר ומצוה לשמוח בשמחת התורה וכתב
רבינו הב"י בסעיף ג' דכבר נהגו כל ישראל לומר
דברי תשבחות או שיר של הודאות וזכרון חסדיו של
הקב"ה על היין עכ"ל כלומר דבכה"ג אפילו בסעודת
רשות מותר

### 75) חיי אדם קלז:ג ומשנה ברורה תקס:יג

וכן גזרו שלא לשמוע שום כלי שיר, ואפילו שיר בפה
וכל מיני שמחה, אסור ואסור למלאות פיו שחוק
בעולם הזה והמזמרין בשעת מלאכתן, אסור ואם
ידוע שלא ישמע, מוטב שיהיו כו' אבל לשמחת חתן
וכלה, הכל שרי:

---

**ואפילו שיר בפה** על היין אסור. וב"ח פסק דאפילו
בלא יין ג"כ אסור דאמרינן בגמרא דוקא זמרא של
מושכי הספינות או מושכי הבקרים שרי שאינו אלא
לזרוזי במלאכתם אבל דגרדאי אסור שהוא לשחוק
בעלמא וע"כ נשים המזמרות בפה בעת מלאכתן יש
למחות להן ואם אינן שומעות מוטב שיהיו שוגגין ...

### 76) שו"ת אגרות משה, אורח חיים א:קסו

היוצא מזה דבפומא רגיל לאסור שלא בבית משתה
ולמי שאינו רגיל משום דכמעט כל הראשונים מתירין
רק הרמב"ם בתשובתו נגד עצמו בהלכותיו....
אבל ודאי דמהראוי לבעל נפש להחמיר כהרמב"ם
בתשובתו והב"ח פסק כותיה אף שראייתו אינה
כלום מ"מ ראוי להחמיר ... ואם הוא לדבר מצוה
משמע מתוס' ומרמ"א שמותר אף שאינו לשמחת
חתן וכלה דהא נקטו כגון בבית חתן וכלה הכל שרי
משמע דחתן וכלה שנקטו הוא רק לציור וה"ה לכל
דבר מצוה. אבל הבענקעטס שעושין לצורך צדקה
מסופקני אם הוא בכלל היתר דבר מצוה מאחר
שהסעודה והשמחה אינה מצוה בעצם רק שהוא
לאסוף עי"ז הרבה אנשים שיתנדבו אבל אפשר
יש להחשיב שהוא לדבר מצוה כיון שהוא לכבוד
מקיימי מצות צדקה ולכן טוב להחמיר ואם אפשר
ואין למחות באלו המקילין. וע"י הרדיו /הרדיו/ אם
נשמע זמרא דפומא מותר ואם בכלי זמר אסור. ובימי
ספירה יש לאסור בזמרא דמנא אף להמתירין..

### 77) שו"ת חלקת יעקב, חלק א:סב (חלק ב)

מי יתן והי' אשר יתכשר דרא להיזהר מבלתי שמוע
זמרת הרדיו, אבל לדאבונינו העולם אינם נזהרים
כלל ורק חסידים ואנשי מעשה, וראיתי בני
עלי' והם מועטים, וצריכין למשכוני אנפשי' להתיר
וללמד זכות, ... וזמרת הרדיו עכ"פ יש לסמוך
על שיטת רש"י ותוס' בגיטין דרך בית המשתה
על יין או שרגיל בכך כלשון הרמ"א כגון המלכים
שעומדים ושוכבים בכלי שיר, וכלשון התוס' גיטין
ז' א' ד"ה זמרא, "שמתענג ביותר" ובהגהות מרדכי
ריש גיטין דדוקא במשתה בלא אכילה הוא דאסור,
שכן דרך עכו"ם אבל במשתה של אכילה מותר,
ומובא גם במשנ"ב להלכה, ומה שהביא משו"ע נ"ג
משירי נכרים דאסור אינו ענין לכאן, דהא מבואר
שם במג"א ס"ק ל"א דזה דוקא בניגון שמנגנים כן
לע"ז, ובבאה"ט שם בשם ב"ח בתשובה ניגון שמיוחד
בבית ע"ז וזה נוגע לאבק ואביזרהו דע"ז, אבל ברדיו
ידוע שאינו זמרא ע"ז רק זמר סתם ויש רק חשש
אבלות דאחר החורבן ועל זה אנו סומכין על שיטות
הנ"ל להתיר, ואם לפעמים נשמע קול אשה או שירי
חשק ועגבות ודאי היא דאסור וצריכין להיזהר.
ויש עוד סברא גדולה להתיר כיון דבשעת הגזירה
לאסור הזמרא מטעם אבלות לא היה עדיין הרדיו
לא חל הגזירה על הרדיו ... לא נגזור ונתחדש גזירה
חדשה ונשאר בהיתרו, ואין זה דומה למין כלי זמר

## 64) שו"ת ציץ אליעזר חלק יג סימן יב

אם מותר לנגן קטעי תפלה ובקשות בניגוני – עגבים

... וניתן לומר שהדברים עוד ק"ו שאסור להתפלל לפני הקב"ה בניגונים מתועבים כאלה, באשר משחיתים המה כל חלקה טובה ... בתי הכנסיות, בניגוני – עגבים הרי זה כמכניסים אל הקודש אש – זרה אשר לא צוה ה', אשר השורף ומכלה את כל בשריפה – נשמה ... ולא עוד אלא שהמנגנים והמאזינים עוד יתבעו לדין שמים על השתמשם בשרביטו של מלך מלכי – של עולם לישא את שמו לשוא להשמיע ע"כ ניגוני תועבה כאלה. ולכן שומר נפשו ירחק מזה, ולהשומעים ולבער צרעת זה תבוא עליהם ברכת טוב.

## 65) שו"ת יחווה דעת, חלק ב:ה

... ונראה שהמכוון הוא שאומר שירי הגויים עם המילים שלהם שהם שירי עגבים, וכמו שכתב בשו"ת הרי"ף (סימן רפא) בזו הלשון: שליח צבור שמרנן בפיו שירי ישמעאלים ומוציא מפיו דברי נבלה מסלקין אותו ממשרתו, ועליו כיוצא בו נאמר נתנה עלי בקולה על כן שנאתיה, והובא להלכה בספר אורחות חיים הלכות תפלה (אות עח). וכן בספר כל בו. וכן פסקו הרמ"א בהגה אורח חיים (סימן נג סעיף כה), והרדב"ז בתשובה (חלק ב סימן תתט). אבל לומר שירי קודש ופזמונים במנגינה שחוברה בלחן של שירי עגבים, נראה שאין בזה איסור כלל ... אולם מרן החיד"א בספר ברכי יוסף (סימן תקס) כתב, שמה שאוסר המעשה רוקח לשורר פיוטים וקדיש וקדושה בלחן של שירי עגבים ונוכרים ... בזו הלשון: ולפי שהשיר והשבח להשם יתברך ראוי שיהיה בתכלית השלמות, שכך נאמר "בנבל עשור זמרו לו", כלומר, בכל מאמצי הכח, זאת היתה לי לחבר רוב השירים שלי על פי ניגוני הערבים, לפי שהם מגביהים קולם ומנעימים את שירתם יותר מזולתם. ואמנם ראיתי קצת חכמים שמתאוננים רע על המחברים שירות ותשבחות לה' יתברך על פי ניגונים אשר לא מבני ישראל המה, אולם אין הדין עמם, כי אין בכך כלום. עד כאן. וכן הסכים להלכה רבי אברהם אלקלעי בספר זכור לאברהם (מערכת קדיש). ובאמת שמעשה רב בכמה גאוני ישראל שחיברו שירות ותשבחות על פי הלחן של מנגינות שירי עגבים, ומהם שירי הבקשות הנאמרים כיום בכל ליל שבת ברוב קהל ועדה בבתי הכנסת של הספרדים ועדות המזרח בארץ ובתפוצות הגולה אשר יסודתם בהררי קודש ...

## 66) משנה סוטה ט:יא וסנהדרין מא.

משבטלה סנהדרין, בטלה השיר מבית המשתאות, שנאמר (ישעיה כד) בשיר לא ישתו יין וגו':

## 67) ירושלמי סוטה מה. ופירוש מאירי על סוטה (בבלי) מז., ח.

אמר רב חסדא בראשונה היתה אימת סנהדרין עליהן

ולא היו אומרים דברי נבלה בשיר. אבל עכשיו שאין אימת סנהדרין עליהן הן אומרים דברי נבלה בשיר. אמר המאירי משבטלו סנהדרין בטל השיר מבית המשתאות ר"ל בית חופת חתנים ורמז לדבר זקנים משער שבתו בחורים מנגינתם ופרשו בתלמוד המערב שבזמן הסנהדרין היתה אימת סנהדרין עליהם ולא היו אומרים דבר נבלה בשיר:

כל השירים שאין בהם שבח להב"ה אסור לזמר בהם והם התחלת הפקר ושעמום וסבתם דרך הערה אמרו זימרא בביתא חורבא בסיפא שנאמר קול ישורר בחלון חרב בסף ומ"מ כל שנעשה להזדרז במלאכה שלא יתנמנמו ולא יתרשלו במלאכתם מותר ועל זה אמרו זימרא מנגדי ר"ל מושכי ספינות בחבל וכן דבקרי ר"ל שמזמרין לפניהם בשעת חרישם לכוין השוורים לתלמיהם שהולכין לקול השיר שהוא ערב עליהם מאד אבל כל שאינו אלא לשחוק אף בבעלי מלאכה אסור והוא שאמרו דגירדאי אסור ולא עוד אלא שאותם זמירות שבבית המשתאות הם גרמת הפסד וסבת הוצאה יתירה דרך סיפור העידו על רב הונא שגזר על בני דורו שלא לזמר בבית המשתאות ונכנס זול ביניהם עד שבאו עופות ותבואות לשער מזולזל ביותר ואעפ"כ לא היו רוצים לקנותם ורב חסדא זלזל בכך וחזרו לזמירותיהם ונתיקר הכל עד שכמעט לא היו מוצאים למכור

## 68) הושע ט:א

אַל־תִּשְׂמַ֨ח יִשְׂרָאֵ֤ל ׀ אֶל־גִּיל֙ כָּֽעַמִּ֔ים כִּ֥י זָנִ֖יתָ מֵעַ֣ל אֱלֹהֶ֑יךָ אָהַ֣בְתָּ אֶתְנָ֔ן עַ֖ל כָּל־גָּרְנ֥וֹת דָּגָֽן׃

## 69) סוטה מח.

אמר רב הונא: זמרא דנגדי ודבקרי שרי, דגרדאי אסיר. רב הונא בטיל זמרא,

## 70) פירוש רש"י על סוטה מח.

זמרי דנגדי – מושכי ספינות בחבל שרי שאינו אלא לזרזם במלאכתם.

ודבקרי – שמזמרין בשעה שחורשין ואינו אלא לכוין את השוורים לתלמיהם שהולכין לקול השיר דערב עליהם.

דגרדאי – אינו אלא לשחוק.

בטל זמרא – גזר על דורו שלא יזמרו ביתם ובבית משתאות.

## 71) טור, אורח חיים תקס

משום בחורבן הבית תקנו שבכל דבר שמחה שיהיה בה זכר לחורבן הבית ... ואסרו כל מיני שיר בין בכלי בין בפה ופירש"י כגון לשורר בבית המשתה והתוס' מפרשים דאפי' בלא משתה נמי ודוקא למי שרגיל בכך כההיא דאיתא בירוש' ריש גלותא הוה קאים ודמיך בזמרא פירוש בשכבו ובקומו היו מזמרין לפניו ומלשון הרמב"ם ז"ל משמע דבכלי אסור לשמוע בכל ענין ובפה על היין דוקא אבל הוא ביאר

## 52) סוכה נ:

אמר רב יוסף: מחלוקת בשיר של קרבן, רבי יוסי
סבר: עיקר שירה בכלי, ועבודה היא, ודוחה את
השבת. ורבנן סברי: עיקר שירה בפה, ולאו עבודה
היא, ואינה דוחה את השבת. אבל שיר של שואבה -
דברי הכל שמחה היא ואינה דוחה את השבת.

## 53) רמב"ם, הלכות כלי המקדש ג:ו

... וחליל זה דוחה שבת מפני שהוא חליל של קרבן
וחליל של קרבן עבודה היא ודוחה את השבת.

## 54) מדרש, במדבר רבה טו:יא

קח את הלוים הלכה כמה בכנור היו שהיו
הלוים מנגנים בו א"ר יהודה ז' נימין היו בכנור שנא'
(תהלים טז) שובע שמחות את פניך נעימות אל תהי
קורא שובע אלא שבע שמחות וכן דוד אומר (שם
קיט) שבע ביום הללתיך על משפטי צדקך ולימות
המשיח נעשית שמונה שכן דוד אומר בניגון (שם ו)
למנצח בנגינות על השמינית ולעתיד לבא נעשית
עשר שנא' (שם קמד) אלהים שיר חדש אשירה לך
בנבל עשור ומי התקין להם שמואל ודוד שנא' (ד"ה
א ט) המה יסד דוד ושמואל הרואה באמונתם והם
העמידו חלוקי השיר והיו הלוים עומדים על הדוכן
ומזמרים לפני מי שאמר והיה העולם ראה חיבה
שחיבב הקב"ה את הלוים כך אמר הקב"ה למשה
הרבה הלוים חביבין לפני קח אותם לשמי לשררה
מנין ממה שקרינו בענין קח את הלוים:

## 55) ברכות כו:

רבי יוסי ברבי חנינא אמר: תפלות אבות תקנום רבי
יהושע בן לוי אמר: תפלות כנגד תמידין תקנום.

## 56) מדרש, במדבר רבה טו:יא

קח את הלוים הלכה כמה בכנור היו שהיו
הלוים מנגנים בו א"ר יהודה ז' נימין היו בכנור שנא'
(תהלים טז) שובע שמחות את פניך נעימות אל תהי
קורא שובע אלא שבע שמחות וכן דוד אומר (שם
קיט) שבע ביום הללתיך על משפטי צדקך ולימות
המשיח נעשית שמונה שכן דוד אומר בניגון (שם ו)
למנצח בנגינות על השמינית ולעתיד לבא נעשית
עשר שנא' (שם קמד) אלהים שיר חדש אשירה לך
בנבל עשור ומי התקין להם שמואל ודוד שנא' (ד"ה
א ט) המה יסד דוד ושמואל הרואה באמונתם והם
העמידו חלוקי השיר והיו הלוים עומדים על הדוכן
ומזמרים לפני מי שאמר והיה העולם ראה חיבה
שחיבב הקב"ה את הלוים כך אמר הקב"ה למשה
הרבה הלוים חביבין לפני קח אותם לשמי לשררה
מנין ממה שקרינו בענין קח את הלוים:

## 57) ספר חסידים תשסח

מי שקולו נעים ואין הקב"ה נהנה מקולו, ראוי לו שלא
בא לעולם. ואם הקב"ה נהנה, עליו נאמר (שה"ש ב

---

יד) השמיעני את קולך כי קולך ערב ומראך נאוה,
וכתיב (ש"ב כג א) ונעים זמירות ישראל, וכתיב
(תהלים ג ה) קולי אל ה' אקרא.

## 59) שולחן ערוך, אורח חיים נג:ד-ה

ש"ץ צריך שיהיה הגון ואיזהו הגון שיהא ריקן
מעבירות ושלא יצא עליו שם רע אפילו בילדותו
ושיהיה עניו ומרוצה לעם ויש לו נעימה וקולו ערב
ורגיל לקרות תורה נביאים וכתובים:
אם אין מוצאין מי שיהיה בו כל המדות האלו יבחרו
הטוב שבצבור בחכמה ובמעשים טובים: הגה ואם
היה כאן עם הארץ זקן וקולו נעים והעם חפצים בו
ובן י"ג שנה המבין מה שאומר ואין קולו נעים הקטן
הוא קודם (מרדכי ספ"ק דחולין) מי שעבר עבירה
בשוגג כגון שהרג הנפש בשגגה וחזר בתשובה

## 60) כף החיים פלאגי, כח:ה

דרב גדול ומובהק נענש בעולם הבא על שהיה גוער
שמאריכין בזמירות בנגונים, ומאן דהוא דקל
הביאוהו לגן עדן בכבוד, על שהיה אומר הזמירות
בניגון ובקול נעים

## 61) ספר חסידים תשסט

... ויזהר מי שיש לו קול נעים שלא יזמר נגונים
נכרים, כי עבירה היא, ולכך נברא קולו נעים, לשבח
בוראו, ולא לעבירה. ואדם יפה ישמור עצמו מניאוף,
כי לא לכך נברא יפה:

## 62) שו"ת הרי"ף רפא

... ש"ץ שמוציא מפיו דברים שאינם הגונים כגון
שהוציא מפיו דבר נבלה ומרנן בשירי ישמעאל
מסלקין אותו על כיוצא בו נאמר נתנה עלי בקולה
על כן שנאתיה ...

## 63) שו"ת אגרות משה יורה דעה חלק ב סימן נו, קיא

הנה הניגונים שמזמרים הנוצרים בבית תיפלתם ודאי
אסור לשמעם אף ע"י הראדיא ואף ע"י פאנאגראף,
ולא רק הניגונים שמזמרים עתה אלא אפילו מה
שהיו מזמרים מכבר אע"פ שהפסיקו עתה לזמר
באותן הניגונים אסור. וגם הניגון שחיבר איזה נוצרי
ניגון על פסוק מתהלים על הלשון שהעתיקו, אסור
כי סתם הניגונים שמחברים הנוצרים לפסוקי תהלים
הוא לזמר לתפלותיהן שזה אסור. ואם הוא מכיר
שלא היתה כוונת מחבר הניגון לזמר לעבודתם אלא
לזמר בעלמא להנאת זמרה אף שמחבר הזמר הוא
נוצרי ועכו"ם אין בזה איסור, אבל סתמא יש להחזיק
שהוא לעבודתם ואסור ...
ובדבר לשמוע הניגונים שמנגנין לע"ז ודאי אסור
דהא המנגן לע"ז אף לאלו שאין דרכו בכך עובר
בלאו שהוא דרך כבוד כמו מנשק וכדומה ... וא"כ
ודאי אסור להתכוין לשמוע ... ואף אם אין בקול
איסור דאורייתא דאין בו ממש מ"מ אסור מדרבנן ...

**39) שמואל א' ב:א**

וַתִּתְפַּלֵּל חַנָּה וַתֹּאמַר עָלַץ לִבִּי בַּד' רָמָה קַרְנִי בַּד' רָחַב פִּי עַל־אוֹיְבַי כִּי שָׂמַחְתִּי בִּישׁוּעָתֶךָ:

**40) ישעיה ל:כט**

הַשִּׁיר יִהְיֶה לָכֶם כְּלֵיל הִתְקַדֶּשׁ־חָג וְשִׂמְחַת לֵבָב כַּהוֹלֵךְ בֶּחָלִיל לָבוֹא בְהַר־ד' אֶל־צוּר יִשְׂרָאֵל:

**41) בראשית ד:כא**

וְשֵׁם אָחִיו יוּבָל הוּא הָיָה אֲבִי כָּל־תֹּפֵשׂ כִּנּוֹר וְעוּגָב:

**42) תהילים סח:כו**

קִדְּמוּ שָׁרִים אַחַר נֹגְנִים בְּתוֹךְ עֲלָמוֹת תּוֹפֵפוֹת:

**43) פירוש מלבים על תהילים סח:כו**

שרים, נגנים – השיר בפה והניגון בכלי, והשרים הולכים אחר נוגנים קודם הליכות ה':

**44) ברכות ג:**

כנור היה תלוי למעלה ממטתו של דוד, וכיון שהגיע חצות לילה בא רוח צפונית ונושבת בו ומנגן מאליו, מיד היה עומד ועוסק בתורה עד שעלה עמוד השחר.

**45) פירוש בניהו בן יהוידע על ברכות ג:**

שם כינור היה תלוי למעלה ממטתו. נראה לי הרמז בזה על רוח קדוש אלהי, ורמזו אותו חכמינו ז"ל בכינור שהוא אותיות כ"ו נ"ר, שם שם הוי"ה שמספרו כ"ו מאיר לו כמו נר, באותו הרוח הקדוש הנברא מעסק תורתו שעסק קודם שכבו על מטתו, והוא כעניין המגיד של מרן בית יוסף ז"ל, שהיה נברא מן עסק המשנה שהיה לומד, וזה הרוח הקדוש הוא מקשר דוד של מטה עם דוד שלמעלה, ואמר כיון שהגיע חצות לילה רוח צפונית מנשבת בו, רמזו ברוח צפונית על לאה אשר עת תיקון שלה הוא בחצות לילה, וקראה צפונית כי היא בסוד עלמא דאתכסייא, וכמו שכתוב בתיקונים, הטעם דלאה נקברה באתכסייא תוך מערת המכפלה ורחל באתגליא על אם הדרך, ודוק היטב:

**46) משנה תמיד ג:ח**

... מיריחו היו שומעין קול המגרפה. מיריחו היו שומעין קול העץ שעשה בן קטין מוכני לכיור. מיריחו היו שומעין קול גביני כרוז. מיריחו היו שומעין קול החליל. מיריחו היו שומעין קול הצלצל. מיריחו היו שומעין קול השיר. מיריחו היו שומעין קול השופר.

**47) רמב"ם, הלכות כלי המקדש ג:ג-ד**

ג לוי האונן מותר לעבוד ולשורר, ואין פוחתין משנים עשר לוים עומדים על הדוכן בכל יום לומר שירה על הקרבן ומוסיפין עד לעולם ואין אומרין שירה אלא בפה בלא כלי שעיקר השירה שהיא עבודתה

---

בפה, ואחרים היו עומדים שם מנגנין בכלי שיר, מהן לוים ומהן ישראלים מיוחסין המשיאין לכהונה, שאין עולה על הדוכן אלא מיוחס, ואין אלו המשוררים על פי הכלים עולין למנין השנים עשר.

ד ובמה הם מנגנין, בנבלים וחלילים וכנורות וחצוצרות והצלצל, ואין פוחתין משני נבלים ולא מוסיפין על ששה, ואין פוחתין משני חלילים ולא מוסיפין על שנים עשר, ואין פוחתין משתי חצוצרות ולא מוסיפין על עשרים ומאה, ואין פוחתין מתשעה כנורות ומוסיפין עד לעולם, והצלצל אחד בלבד.

**48) רמב"ם, הלכות כלי המקדש ג:ה**

... והחלילין שהיו מנגנין בהן היה אבוב שלהן של קנה, מפני שקולו ערב ולא היה מחלק אלא אבוב יחידי מפני שהוא מחלק יפה

**49) שקלים ה:א**

אלו הן הממונין שהיו במקדש ... בן ארזה על הצלצל, הוגרס בן לוי על השיר

**50) משנה סוכה ה:ה**

אין פוחתין מעשרים ואחת תקיעות במקדש, ואין מוסיפין על ארבעים ושמונה. בכל יום היו שם עשרים ואחת תקיעות (במקדש), שלש לפתיחת שערים, ותשע לתמיד של שחר, ותשע לתמיד של בין הערבים. ובמוספין היו מוסיפין עוד תשע. ובערב שבת היו מוסיפין עוד שש, שלש להבטיל העם ממלאכה, ושלש להבדיל בין קודש לחול. וערב שבת שבתוך החג היו שם ארבעים ושמונה, שלש לפתיחת שערים, שלש לשער העליון, ושלש לשער התחתון, ושלש למלוי המים, ושלש על גבי מזבח, תשע לתמיד של שחר, ותשע לתמיד של בין הערבים, ותשע למוספין, שלש להבטיל את העם מן המלאכה, ושלש להבדיל בין קודש לחול:

**51) משנה סוכה ה:א, ד**

(א) החליל חמשה וששה. זהו החליל של בית השואבה, שאינו דוחה לא את השבת ולא את יום טוב. אמרו, כל מי שלא ראה שמחת בית השואבה, לא ראה שמחה מימיו:

(ד) חסידים ואנשי מעשה היו מרקדים לפניהם באבוקות של אור שבידיהן, ואומרים לפניהן דברי שירות ותשבחות. והלויים בכנורות ובנבלים ובמצלתים ובחצוצרות ובכלי שיר בלא מספר, על חמש עשרה מעלות היורדות מעזרת ישראל לעזרת נשים, כנגד חמשה עשר שיר המעלות שבתהלים, שעליהן לויים עומדין בכלי שיר ואומרים שירה. ועמדו שני כהנים בשער העליון שיורד מעזרת ישראל לעזרת נשים, ושתי חצוצרות בידיהן. קרא הגבר, תקעו והריעו ותקעו. הגיעו למעלה עשירית, תקעו והריעו ותקעו ...

כל התורה שאין הספור שבה מבואר יפה ...

**28) בראשית ד:כא**

וְשֵׁם אָחִיו יוּבָל הוּא הָיָה אֲבִי כָּל־תֹּפֵשׂ כִּנּוֹר וְעוּגָב:

**29) במדבר כא:יז**

אָז יָשִׁיר יִשְׂרָאֵל אֶת־הַשִּׁירָה הַזֹּאת עֲלִי בְאֵר עֱנוּ־לָהּ:

**30) שופטים ה:א**

וַתָּשַׁר דְּבוֹרָה וּבָרָק בֶּן־אֲבִינֹעַם בַּיּוֹם הַהוּא לֵאמֹר:

**31) מלכים א' ג:יג-טו**

וַיֹּאמֶר אֱלִישָׁע אֶל־מֶלֶךְ יִשְׂרָאֵל מַה־לִּי וָלָךְ לֵךְ אֶל־נְבִיאֵי אָבִיךָ וְאֶל־נְבִיאֵי אִמֶּךָ וַיֹּאמֶר לוֹ מֶלֶךְ יִשְׂרָאֵל אַל כִּי־קָרָא ד' לִשְׁלֹשֶׁת הַמְּלָכִים הָאֵלֶּה לָתֵת אוֹתָם בְּיַד־מוֹאָב: וַיֹּאמֶר אֱלִישָׁע חַי־ד' צְבָאוֹת אֲשֶׁר עָמַדְתִּי לְפָנָיו כִּי לוּלֵי פְּנֵי יְהוֹשָׁפָט מֶלֶךְ־יְהוּדָה אֲנִי נֹשֵׂא אִם־אַבִּיט אֵלֶיךָ וְאִם־אֶרְאֶךָּ: וְעַתָּה קְחוּ־לִי מְנַגֵּן וְהָיָה כְּנַגֵּן הַמְנַגֵּן וַתְּהִי עָלָיו יַד־ד':

**32) שמואל א' י':ה-ו**

אַחַר כֵּן תָּבוֹא גִּבְעַת הָאֱלֹקִים אֲשֶׁר־שָׁם נְצִבֵי פְלִשְׁתִּים וִיהִי כְבֹאֲךָ שָׁם הָעִיר וּפָגַעְתָּ חֶבֶל נְבִאִים יֹרְדִים מֵהַבָּמָה וְלִפְנֵיהֶם נֵבֶל וְתֹף וְחָלִיל וְכִנּוֹר וְהֵמָּה מִתְנַבְּאִים: וְצָלְחָה עָלֶיךָ רוּחַ ד' וְהִתְנַבִּיתָ עִמָּם וְנֶהְפַּכְתָּ לְאִישׁ אַחֵר:

**33) דברי הימים א' כה:א**

וַיַּבְדֵּל דָּוִיד וְשָׂרֵי הַצָּבָא לַעֲבֹדָה לִבְנֵי אָסָף וְהֵימָן וִידוּתוּן הַנִּבְּאִים בְּכִנֹּרוֹת בִּנְבָלִים וּבִמְצִלְתָּיִם וַיְהִי מִסְפָּרָם אַנְשֵׁי מְלָאכָה לַעֲבֹדָתָם:

**34) שמואל א' טז:יד-כג**

וְרוּחַ ד' סָרָה מֵעִם שָׁאוּל וּבִעֲתַתּוּ רוּחַ־רָעָה מֵאֵת ד': וַיֹּאמְרוּ עַבְדֵי־שָׁאוּל אֵלָיו הִנֵּה־נָא רוּחַ־אֱלֹקִים רָעָה מְבַעִתֶּךָ: יֹאמַר־נָא אֲדֹנֵנוּ עֲבָדֶיךָ לְפָנֶיךָ יְבַקְשׁוּ אִישׁ יֹדֵעַ מְנַגֵּן בַּכִּנּוֹר וְהָיָה בִּהְיוֹת עָלֶיךָ רוּחַ־אֱלֹהִים רָעָה וְנִגֵּן בְּיָדוֹ וְטוֹב לָךְ: וַיֹּאמֶר שָׁאוּל אֶל־עֲבָדָיו רְאוּ־נָא לִי אִישׁ מֵיטִיב לְנַגֵּן וַהֲבִיאוֹתֶם אֵלָי: וַיַּעַן אֶחָד מֵהַנְּעָרִים וַיֹּאמֶר הִנֵּה רָאִיתִי בֵּן לְיִשַׁי בֵּית הַלַּחְמִי יֹדֵעַ נַגֵּן וְגִבּוֹר חַיִל וְאִישׁ מִלְחָמָה וּנְבוֹן דָּבָר וְאִישׁ תֹּאַר וַד' עִמּוֹ: וַיִּשְׁלַח שָׁאוּל מַלְאָכִים אֶל־יִשָׁי וַיֹּאמֶר שִׁלְחָה אֵלַי אֶת־דָּוִד בִּנְךָ אֲשֶׁר בַּצֹּאן: וַיִּקַּח יִשַׁי חֲמוֹר לֶחֶם וְנֹאד יַיִן וּגְדִי עִזִּים אֶחָד וַיִּשְׁלַח בְּיַד־דָּוִד בְּנוֹ אֶל־שָׁאוּל: וַיָּבֹא דָוִד אֶל־שָׁאוּל וַיַּעֲמֹד לְפָנָיו וַיֶּאֱהָבֵהוּ מְאֹד וַיְהִי־לוֹ נֹשֵׂא כֵלִים: וַיִּשְׁלַח שָׁאוּל אֶל־יִשַׁי לֵאמֹר יַעֲמָד־נָא דָוִד לְפָנַי כִּי־מָצָא חֵן בְּעֵינָי: וְהָיָה בִּהְיוֹת רוּחַ־אֱלֹקִים אֶל־שָׁאוּל וְלָקַח דָּוִד אֶת־הַכִּנּוֹר וְנִגֵּן בְּיָדוֹ וְרָוַח לְשָׁאוּל וְטוֹב לוֹ וְסָרָה מֵעָלָיו רוּחַ הָרָעָה:

**35) שמואל ב' כג:א**

וְאֵלֶּה דִּבְרֵי דָוִד הָאַחֲרֹנִים נְאֻם דָּוִד בֶּן־יִשַׁי וּנְאֻם הַגֶּבֶר

---

הָקֵם עַל מְשִׁיחַ אֱלֹהֵי יַעֲקֹב וּנְעִים זְמִרוֹת יִשְׂרָאֵל:

**36) מדרש שיר השירים רבה ד:ה**

משל למה"ד לחבורה של אנשים שמבקשים לומר הימנון למלך אמר להם המלך כלכם נעימים כלכם חסידים כלכם משובחין לומר הימנון לפני אלא איש פלוני יאמר על ידי כלכם למה שקולו ערב כך בשעה שבקשו עשרה צדיקים לומר ספר התהלים אמר להם הקדוש ב"ה כלכם נעימים וחסידים ומשובחים לומר הימנון לפני אלא דוד יאמר על ידי כלכם למה שקולו ערב הה"ד (ש"ב כ"ג) ונעים זמירות ישראל רבי הונא בשם רבי אחא אמר מי מנעים זמירותיהם של ישראל דוד

**37) תרגום יונתן, הקדמה לשיר השירים (מהדורת מכון הרב מצליח, בני בקר תשס"ד)**

שירים ותשבחות שאמר שלמה הנביא ברוח נבואה לפני רבון כל העולם ה' עשר שירות נאמרו בעולם הזה שירה זו משובחת מכולן שירה ראשונה אמר אדם הראשון בשעה שנתכפר לו עוונו ובא יום השבת והגן עליו פתח פיו ואמר מזמור שיר ליום השבת (תהלים נב:א). שירה שניה אמר משה עם בני ישראל בשעה שקרע להם אדון העולם את ים סוף. פתחו כולם ואמרו כאחד שירה שכן כתוב "אז ישיר משה ובני ישראל" _(שמות טו:א). שירה שלישית אמרו בני ישראל בשעה שניתנה להם באר המים שכן כתוב "אז ישיר ישראל נמטר" (במדבר כא:יז). שירה רביעית אמר משה הנביא כשהגיעה שעתו ליפטר מן העולם והוכיח בשירה זו את עם בית ישראל שכן כתוב "האזינו השמים ואדברה" (דברים לג:א). שירה חמישית אמר יהושע בן נון כשערך מלחמה בגבעון ועמדו לו השמש והירח שלושים ושש שעות ופסקו מלומר שירה, פתח פיו הוא ואמר שירה שכן כתוב "אז ידבר יהושע לה'" (יהושע יד:יג). שירה ששית אמרו ברק ודבורה ביום שמסר ה' את סיסרא ומחנהו ביד בני ישראל שכן כתוב "ותשר דבורה וברק בן אבינועם" (שופטים ה:א). שירה שביעית אמרה חנה כשניתן לה בן מאת ה', שכן כתוב "ותתפלל חנה ותאמר" (שמואל א' ב:א). שירה שמינית אמר דוד מלך ישראל על כל הנסים שעשה לו הקב"ה פתח פיו ואמר שירה שכן כתוב "וידבר דוד לה'" (שמואל ב' כג:א). שירה תשיעית אמר שלמה מלך ישראל ברוח הקדש לפני רבון כל העולם ה' והשירית העשירית עתידים בני הגלויות בזמן שיצאו מהגולה שכן כתוב ומפורש ע"י הנביא ישעיה כאמור (ישעיה ל:כט) "השיר יהיה לכם כליל התקדש חג"

**38) יהושע י':יב**

אָז יְדַבֵּר יְהוֹשֻׁעַ לַד' בְּיוֹם תֵּת ד' אֶת־הָאֱמֹרִי לִפְנֵי בְּנֵי יִשְׂרָאֵל וַיֹּאמֶר | לְעֵינֵי יִשְׂרָאֵל שֶׁמֶשׁ בְּגִבְעוֹן דּוֹם וְיָרֵחַ בְּעֵמֶק אַיָּלוֹן:

בשם שמואל מנין לעיקר שירה מן התורה שנאמר
(דברים יח) ושרת בשם ה' איזהו שירות שבשם ה'
הוי אומר זו שירה רבי יצחק אמר מהכא (תהלים
פא) שאו זמרה ותנו תוף כנור נעים עם נבל רב נחמן
בר יצחק אמר מהכא (ישעיה כד) המה ישאו קולם
ירונו בגאון ה' וגו' תני תנא ולבני קהת לא נתן כי עבודת
הקודש עליהם בכתף ישאו ממשמע שנאמר בכתף
איני יודע שישאו מה תלמוד לומר ישאו אין ישאו
אלא לשון שירה וכן הוא אומר שאו זמרה ותנו תוף
וגו' ואומר ישאו קולם ירונו רבי יהושע בן חנניא אחי ר' יהושע
אמר מהכא (שמות טו) משה ידבר והאלהים יעננו
בקול על עסקי קול רבי אסא אמר מהכא (ד"ה ב
ה) ויהי כאחד למחצצרים ולמשוררים להשמיע
קול אחד רבי יונתן אומר מהכא (במדבר יח) ולא
ימותו גם הם גם אתם מה אתם בעבודת מזבח אף הם
בעבודת מזבח רבי יוחנן אמר מהכא לעבוד עבודת
עבודה איזו היא עבודה שצריכה עבודה הוי אומר
זו שירה:

### 23) ערכין יא.

איזו היא עבודה שבשמחה ובטוב לבב? הוי אומר:
זה שירה..

### 24) זהר, חלק ב יט.

אמר רבי יהודה. למה נקראו השרים של מטה לוים.
על שנלוים ונחברים למעלה כאחד. והשומע נלוה
ונדבק נפשו למעלה.

### 25) ספר בן יהוידע, סנהדרין צא:

שם כך האומר שירה בעולם הזה זוכה ואומרה
לעולם הבא שנאמר אשרי יושבי ביתך

### 26) דברים לא:יט

וְעַתָּה כִּתְבוּ לָכֶם אֶת הַשִּׁירָה הַזֹּאת וְלַמְּדָהּ אֶת בְּנֵי
יִשְׂרָאֵל שִׂימָהּ בְּפִיהֶם לְמַעַן תִּהְיֶה לִּי הַשִּׁירָה הַזֹּאת
לְעֵד בִּבְנֵי יִשְׂרָאֵל:

### 27) פירוש העמק דבר בהקדמה לספר בראשית

וְעַתָּה כִּתְבוּ לָכֶם אֶת הַשִּׁירָה הַזֹּאת וְלַמְּדָהּ אֶת בְּנֵי
יִשְׂרָאֵל שִׂימָהּ בְּפִיהֶם לְמַעַן תִּהְיֶה לִּי הַשִּׁירָה הַזֹּאת
לְעֵד בִּבְנֵי יִשְׂרָאֵל:
והנה בנדרים דף ל"ח העלו המקרא "כתבו את
השירה" שהוא כל התורה והביאו ראיה מסיפי' דקרא
"למען תהיה לי חשירה לעד" הא מיהא יש
להבין היאך נקרא כה"ת שירה והרי לא נכתבה בלשון
של שירה אלא ע"כ יש בה טבע וסגולת השירה שהוא
דבור בלשון מליצה דידוע לכל מבין מבי& עם תלמוד
דמשונה המל^ה מספור פרזי בשני ענינים בטבע
ובסגולה א) דבשיר אין הענין מבואר יפה כמו ^יור
פרזי וצריך לעשות הערות מן הצד דזה החרוז כיוון
לזה הספור וזה החרוז כגון לזה ולא מיקרי דרוש
אלא כך הוא טבע השיר אפילו של ... כך הוא טבע

### 17) פירוש רש"י על שמות טו:א

אז ישיר משה – אז כשראה הנס, עלה בלבו שישיר
שירה. וכן אז ידבר יהושע (יהושע י, יב.). וכן ובית
יעשה לבת פרעה (מלכים־א ז, ח.), חשב בלבו שיעשה
לה. אף כאן ישיר, אמר לו לבו שישיר, וכן עשה,

### 18) מדרש שמות רבה כג:ד

ד"א אז ישיר משה הה"ד (משלי לא) פיה פתחה
בחכמה ותורת חסד על לשונה מיום שברא הקב"ה
את העולם ועד שעמדו ישראל על הים לא מצינו אדם
שאמר שירה להקב"ה אלא ישראל ברא אדה"ר ולא
אמר שירה הציל אברהם מכבשן האש ולא אמר שירה
ולא אמר שירה וכן יצחק מן המאכלת ולא אמר שירה
וכן יעקב מן המלאך ומן עשו ומן אנשי שכם ולא
אמר שירה כיון שבאו ישראל לים ונקרע להם מיד
אמרו שירה לפני הקב"ה שנא' אז ישיר משה ובני
ישראל הוי פיה פתחה בחכמה אמר הקב"ה לאלו
הייתי מצפה ואין אז אלא שמחה שנאמר (תהלים
קכז) אז ימלא שחוק פינו א"ר יהודה בן פזי מה ראו
ישראל לומר שירה באז אלא אמרו מתחלה היה הים
הזה יבשה ועמדו דורו של אנוש והכעיסו לפניו באז
שנאמר (בראשית ד) אז הוחל לקרא בשם ה' ועשאו
הקב"ה ים ופרע מהם שנאמר (עמוס ה) הקורא למי
הים וישפכם על פני הארץ ועכשיו ים היה ונעשה לנו
יבשה שנאמר ובני ישראל הלכו ביבשה בתוך הים
נקלסנו באז שהפך לנו ים ליבשה הוי אז ישיר משה
ובני ישראל ואין אז אלא לשון בטחון שנאמר (משלי
ג) אז תלך לבטח דרכך:

### 19) אוצר מדרשים, רבי עקיבא ו

שאלמלא שירה וזמרה שישראל אומרים לפני בכל
יום לא בראתי עולמי. אפילו ישראל שכל העולם כלו
נברא בשבילן לא בראתים אלא בשביל שירה שנאמר
עם זו יצרתי לי תהלתי יספרו (ישעיה מ"ד).

### 20) מדרש אותיות דרבי עקיבא א

אמר הקדוש ברוך הוא אפתח לשון פה של כל בני
בשר ודם כדי שיהיו מקלסין לפני בכל יום וממליכין
אותי בארבע רוחות העולם שאלמלא שירה וזמרה
שהם אומרים לפני בכל יום לא בראתי את עולמי:
ומנין שלא ברא הקדוש ברוך הוא את העולם אלא
בשביל שירה וזמרה

### 21) ערכין יא.

מה כפרה מעכבת, אף שירה מעכבת

### 22) מדרש, במדבר רבה ו:י'

תני השיר מעכב את הקרבן דברי רבי מאיר וחכ"א
אינו מעכב אר"א טעמיה דר"מ מהאי קרא (במדבר
ח) ואתנה את הלוים נתונים וגו' לכפר על ב"י וגו' מה
כפרה מעכבת אף שירה מעכבת ורבנן מוקמין מהאי
קרא מה כפרה ביום אף שירה ביום אמר רבי יהודה

(1 **Dr. Alexandra Lamont, University of Leicester, 2001**

**2) סוטה ל:**
מנין שאפי׳ עוברים שבמעי אמן אמרו שירה? שנאמר: (תהלים סח) "במקהלות ברכו אלקים ה׳ ממקור ישראל."

**3) טור אורח חיים נא**
ברוך שאמר וכו׳ צריך לאומרו בניגון ובנעימה כי שוא שיר נאה ...

**4) כף החיים פלאגי, כח:כד**
בתפילות שבת לא יעשה שינוי בניגון, כמו שעושה בחול, דבאמצעיות דהן בקשות ושאלת צרכיו, צריך לאומרם בהכנעה בקול נמוך, וכשחוזר לברכת רצה, צריך להגביה קולו בניגון, אלא בשבת מתחילה ועד סוף יהיה בניגון אחד, ובהרמת קול בשוה, ואפילו בלחש, ירים קולו מעט מבחול, כמנהג רבינו האר"י, שהיה משים הפרש בתפילותיו משבת לחול, מתחילת התפילה עד לבסוף:

**5) ליקוטי מוהר"ן, מהדורא קמא מט**
וְזֶה לְשׁוֹן תִּשְׁרֵי, לְשׁוֹן שִׁירָה. וּלְשׁוֹן פֶּסַח, פֶּה סָח (שַׁעַר הַכַּוָּנוֹת דַּף פ"ב). כְּמוֹ שֶׁכָּתוּב (יְשַׁעְיָה ל׳): "הַשִּׁיר יִהְיֶה לָכֶם כְּלֵיל הִתְקַדֶּשׁ חָג". כִּי יִתְעַר שִׁיר וְנִגּוּנָא בְּעָלְמָא, בִּבְחִינַת פֶּ"ה סָ"ח. בִּבְחִינַת (תְּהִלִּים ל'):

**6) אליהו רבה, אורח חיים רפד**
כתב שיירי כנסת הגדולה אומרים מי שעשה ניסים קודם ראש חודש אב בניגון נשבר ונדכה, עד כאן, ועיין סימן תכ"א

**7) תוספות שם "והשונה" על מגילה לב.**
השונה בלא זמרה. שהיו רגילין לשנות המשניות בזמרה לפי שהיו שונין אותן על פה וע"י כך היו נזכרים יותר:

**8) משנה ברורה ובאר היטב על שולחן ערוך, אורח חיים נ**
וכתב של"ה כשאומר איזהו מקומן או במה מדליקין או פיטום הקטורת יעשה קול ניגון דמשניות ע"ש

**9) מגילה לב.**
אמר רבי יוחנן: כל הקורא בלא נעימה ושונה בלא זמרה עליו הכתוב אומר (יחזקאל כ׳) וגם אני נתתי להם חקים לא טובים וגו'.

**10) משנה ברורה על שולחן ערוך, אורח חיים קמב:ד**
... דה"ה בנגינת הטעמים כשהענין משתנה עי"ז כגון שקרא משרת במקום מפסיק מחזירין אותו

**11) שערי תשובה, הלכות מגילה תרצו**
יש לנהוג לזמר זמירות ותשבחות שאז בודאי הוא סעודת מצוה ולרמוז לזה מסיים וטוב לב משתה תמיד והוא עפ"י מה דאמרינן בערכין דף י"א מנין לעיקר שירה מה"ת כו׳ איזה עבודה שהיא בשמחה ובטוב לבב הוי אומר זה שירה

**12) תהילים יט:ב**
הַשָּׁמַיִם מְסַפְּרִים כְּבוֹד־קֵל וּמַעֲשֵׂה יָדָיו מַגִּיד הָרָקִיעַ:

**13) אוצר מדרשים, רבי עקיבא ד**
שאלמלא שירה וזמרה שהם אומרים לפני בכל יום ויום לא בראתי את עולמי. ומנין שלא ברא הקב"ה את העולם אלא בשביל שירה וזמרה שנאמר (תהלים צ"ו) הוד והדר לפניו עוז ותפארת במקדשו (תהלים צ"ו) הוד והדר לפני בשמים ועוז ותפארת במקדשו בארץ.

**14) ליקוטי מוהר"ן, מהדורא בתרא סג**
כִּי כָל רוֹעֶה וְרוֹעֶה יֵשׁ לוֹ נִגּוּן מְיֻחָד לְפִי הָעֲשָׂבִים וּלְפִי הַמָּקוֹם שֶׁהוּא רוֹעֶה שָׁם, כִּי כָל בְּהֵמָה וּבְהֵמָה יֵשׁ לָהּ עֵשֶׂב מְיֻחָד, שֶׁהִיא צְרִיכָה לְאָכְלוֹ. גַּם אֵינוֹ רוֹעֶה תָּמִיד בְּמָקוֹם אֶחָד. וּלְפִי הָעֲשָׂבִים וְהַמָּקוֹם שֶׁרוֹעֶה שָׁם, כֵּן יֵשׁ לוֹ נִגּוּן. כִּי כָל עֵשֶׂב וָעֵשֶׂב יֵשׁ לוֹ שִׁירָה שֶׁאוֹמֵר, שֶׁזֶּה בְּחִינַת פֶּרֶק שִׁירָה, וּמִשִּׁירַת הָעֲשָׂבִים נַעֲשֶׂה נִגּוּן שֶׁל הָרוֹעֶה. וְזֶה סוֹד מַה שֶּׁכָּתוּב (שָׁם ד):

**15) אוצר מדרשים, קדושה ז**
אמר רב שלש כתות של מלאכי השרת אומרות שירה בכל יום, אחת אומרת קדוש ואחת אומרת קדוש ואחת אומרת קדוש ה' צבאות מלא כל כל הארץ כבודו. מיתבי ישראל חביבין לפני המקום יותר ממלאכי השרת, שישראל אומרים שירה בכל שעה שירצו ואילו מה"ש מלאכי השרת אין אומרים שירה אלא פעם אחת ביום ואמרי לה פעם אחת בחדש ואמרי לה פעם אחת בשנה ואמרי לה פעם אחת בשבוע (שמיטה) ואמרי לה פעם אחת ביובל ואמרי לה פעם אחת לעולם

**16) שמות יד:לא-טו:א**
וַיַּרְא יִשְׂרָאֵל אֶת־הַיָּד הַגְּדֹלָה אֲשֶׁר עָשָׂה ד׳ בְּמִצְרַיִם וַיִּירְאוּ הָעָם אֶת־ד׳ וַיַּאֲמִינוּ בַּד׳ וּבְמֹשֶׁה עַבְדּוֹ: אָז יָשִׁיר־מֹשֶׁה וּבְנֵי יִשְׂרָאֵל אֶת־הַשִּׁירָה הַזֹּאת לַד׳ וַיֹּאמְרוּ לֵאמֹר אָשִׁירָה לַד׳ כִּי־גָאֹה גָּאָה סוּס וְרֹכְבוֹ רָמָה בַיָּם:

לברך אמרו לי: בריך, כל היכא דמברכת לרחמנא מברכת. מוטב דאמינא להו אנשאי יונה דדהבא. אמר להו: אנטרו לי, דאנשאי יונה דדהבא. אזיל ובריך, ואשכח יונה דדהבא

### 65) מדרש ילקוט שמעוני לא.

מעשה היה ר' מאיר בר' מאיר שהיה יושב במנחה בשבת ודורש ומתו שני בניו, מה עשתה אמן הניחה שניהם על המטה ופירשה סדין עליהם, במוצאי שבת בא רבי מאיר מבית המדרש אמר לה היכן שני בני, אמרה לו לבית המדרש הלכו, אמרה לו צפיתי בבית המדרש, ולא ראיתים, נתנה לו הכוס של הבדלה והבדיל וחזר, ואמר לה היכן שני בני אמרה לו פעמים שהלכו למקום פלוני ועכשו הם באים, הקריבה לפניו לאכול, לאחר שאכל אמרה לו רבי שאלה יש לי לשאול, א"ל אמרי רי שאלתך, אמר לה רבי קודם היום בא אחד ונתן לי פקדון ועכשו בא ליטול אחזיר לו או לאו, אמר לה בתי מי שיש לו פקדון אינו צריך להזיר לרבו, אמרה לו חוץ מדעתך לא הייתי מחזרת אותו, מה עשתה תפשה אותו בידו והעלהו לחדר והקריבה אותו למטה, נטלה הסדין מעליהם וראה שניהם מתים מונחים על המטה, התחיל בוכה ...

### 66) נדרים נ.

ר' עקיבא איתקדשת ליה ברתיה (דבר) דכלבא שבוע, שמע (בר) כלבא שבוע אדרה הנאה מכל נכסיה, אזלא ואיתנסיבה ליה. בסיתוא הוה גנו בי תיבנא, הוה קא מנקיט ליה תיבנא מן מזייה, אמר לה: אי הוי לי, רמינא ליך ירושלים דדהבא. אתא אליהו אידמי להון כאנשא וקא קרי אבבא, אמר להו: הבו לי פורתא דתיבנא, דילדת אתתי ולית לי מידעם לאגונה. אמר לה ר' עקיבא לאנתתיה: חזי גברא דאפילו תיבנא לא אית ליה.

### 67) שולחן ערוך, אורח חיים תקסה:ו ומגן אברהם ומשנה ברורה שם

המתענה ומפרסם עצמו לאחרים להשתבח שהוא מתענה, הוא נענש על כך:

מגן אברהם – ... ומ"מ מדת חסידות הוא שיאמר שאינו מתענה כדאיתא בב"מ דף כ"ג שאם ישאלוהו אם למד מסכתא יאמר שלא למד פירש"י שמדת ענוה הוא זו ...

משנה ברורה – ומפרסם עצמו וכו' – משמע שאם שואלין אותו אם התענה מותר לומר האמת כיון שאינו עושה להשתבח ולהתפאר ומ"מ נכון הוא שבכל גווני יאמר שאינו מתענה כדי שלא להחזיק טיבותא לנפשיה ...

### 68) מלכים א' א:מ, חולין צ:, שולחן ערוך יורה דעה שדמ:א

וַיַּעֲלוּ כָל-הָעָם אַחֲרָיו וְהָעָם מְחַלְלִים בַּחֲלִלִים

וּשְׂמֵחִים שִׂמְחָה גְדוֹלָה וַתִּבָּקַע הָאָרֶץ בְּקוֹלָם:

אמר רבי אמי: דברה תורה לשון הואי, דברו נביאים לשון הואי, דברו חכמים לשון הואי... מעשה היה ונמנו עליה שלש מאות כהנים לפנותה. פרכת דתנן: רבן שמעון בן גמליאל אומר משום רבי שמעון הסגן, פרוכת עוביה טפח, ועל שבעים ושנים נירים נארגת, ועל כל נימא ונימה עשרים וארבעה חוטין ארכה ארבעים באמה ורחבה עשרים באמה, ומשמונים ושתי רבוא נעשת, ושתים עושים בשנה, ושלש מאות כהנים מטבילין אותה.

### 69) שולחן ערוך יורה דעה שדמ:א

מצוה גדולה להספיד על המת כראוי ומצותו להרים קולו לומר עליו דברים המשברים את הלב כדי להרבות בכיה ולהזכיר שבחו ואסור להפליג בשבחו יותר מדאי אלא מזכירין מדות טובות שבו ומוסיפין בהם קצת רק שלא יפליג ואם לא היו בו מדות טובות כלל לא יזכיר עליו וחכם וחסיד מזכירין להם חכמתם וחסידותם וכל המזכיר על מי שלא היה בו כלל או שמוסיף להפליג יותר מדאי על מה שהיה בו גורם רעה לעצמו ולמת:

### 70) יבמות סג.

רב הוה קא מצערא ליה דביתהו כי אמר לה עבידי לי טלופחי עבדא ליה חימצי חימצי עבדא ליה טלופחי כי גדל חייא בריה אפיך לה אמר ליה איעליא לך אמך אמר לה אנא הוא דקא אפיכנא לה אמר ליה היינו דקא אמרי אינשי דנפיק מינך טעמא מלפך את לא תעביד הכי שנאמר "למדו לשונם דבר שקר העוה" וגו'

### 71) סוכה מו: ופירוש ערוך לנר

אמר רבי זירא: לא ליקני איניש הושענא לינוקא ביומא טבא קמא. מאי טעמא? דינוקא מקנא קני, אקנויי לא מקני, ואשתכח דקא נפיק בלולב שאינו שלו.
ואמר רבי זירא: לא לימא איניש לינוקא דיהיבנא לך מידי ולא יהיב ליה, משום דאתי לאגמוריה שיקרא, שנאמר (ירמיהו ט') למדו לשונם דבר שקר.
...וכשישאל לו הקטן הרי הרי נתן לו שכך אמר לו אבל במחשבתו לא הי' לשם מתנה או התחכמות אחר שהי' עושה באופן שהי' חושב הקטן שקבל במתנה ולא קבל וע"ז מלמדו לדבר שקר במרמה וזה אסור משום דכתיב למדו לשונם דבר שקר

### 72) סוכה מו:

ואמר רבי זירא: לא לימא איניש לינוקא דיהיבנא לך מידי ולא יהיב ליה, משום דאתי לאגמוריה שיקרא, שנאמר (ירמיהו ט') למדו לשונם דבר שקר.

### 52) עירובין נג:

אמר רבי יהושע בן חנניה...פעם אחת נתארחתי אצל אכסניא אחת, עשתה לי פולין. ביום ראשון אכלתים ולא שיירתי מהן כלום, שנייה ולא שיירתי מהן כלום. ביום שלישי הקדיחתן במלח. כיון שטעמתי משכתי ידי מהן. אמרה לי: רבי, מפני מה אינך סועד? אמרתי לה: כבר סעדתי מבעוד יום.

### 53) עזרא י:א-ב ופירוש מלבי"ם

וּכְהִתְפַּלֵּל עֶזְרָא וּכְהִתְוַדֹּתוֹ בֹּכֶה וּמִתְנַפֵּל לִפְנֵי בֵּית הָאֱלֹקִים נִקְבְּצוּ אֵלָיו מִיִּשְׂרָאֵל קָהָל רַב מְאֹד אֲנָשִׁים וְנָשִׁים וִילָדִים כִּי בָכוּ הָעָם הַרְבֵּה בֶכֶה:וַיַּעַן שְׁכַנְיָה בֶן יְחִיאֵל מִבְּנֵי עֵילָם. וַיֹּאמֶר לְעֶזְרָא אֲנַחְנוּ מָעַלְנוּ בֵּאלֹקֵינוּ וַנֹּשֶׁב נָשִׁים נָכְרִיּוֹת מֵעַמֵּי הָאָרֶץ וְעַתָּה יֵשׁ מִקְוֶה לְיִשְׂרָאֵל עַל זֹאת:

... וע"כ נחשב החטא הזה כאלו יצא מכלל העם, מטעם ערבות, ע"ז אמר אנחנו מעלנו, וכלל גם עצמו ואת הכלל שכולם מעלו בזה,

### 54) שו"ת שבט הלוי (ברה ווזנר) חלק ב' יורה דעה סימן קיט

... בגבאי צדקה שאוסף מעות עבור ת"ח גדול שהוא במצוקה גדולה ושאל אם מותר לו לומר שאוסף עבור הכנסת כלה כדי שיקבל יותר וכבר אמר להגבאי שדבר פשוט שאין לשנות מצדקה לצדקה כמבואר בשו"ע יו"ד והביא מדברי הש"ך סי' רנ"ז ס"ק ז' שבני העיר יכולים לשנות מצדקה לצדקה אבל דוקא דבר שהוא קבוע... ולדידי יראה לענ"ד דמותר לשנות, רק הדבר ספק בידו אם מותר להטעות את חבירו לומר שגובה להכנסת כלה אבל אם כבר גבה להכנסת כלה יראה דמותר לשנות כאשר אבאר בעזה"י.

### 55) פירוש מאירי על יבמות סה:

.... ויש אומרים מצוה שהרי נצטוה שמואל עגלת בקר תקח בידיך ואמרת לזבוח לה' ואף על פי שכך עשה מכל מקום עיקר הליכתו למשוח לדוד היתה והוא אמר שעיקר ביאתו לזבוח לה'

### 56) פירוש ערוך לנר על יבמות סה:

... ועוד י"ל דשם שרה לא שינתה כלל רק רק אמרה מילתא דמשתמע לתרי אפי ...

... ולכן י"ל הם אמרו לישנא דמשתמע לתרי אפי דבאמת לא שלחו רק אביך צוה לפני מותו לאמר יהיה כונתם בזה שצוה מה שצוה כדכתיב ויכל יעקב לצות את בניו ... והם שנו ואמרו לשון שיש לטעות בו מזה הוכיח שמותר לשנות מפני השלום

### 57) בראשית יא:כט ופירוש רש"י

ויקח אברם ונחור להם נשים שם אשת אברם שרי ושם אשת נחור מלכה בת הרן אבי מלכה ואבי יסכה:
רש"י: יסכה – זו שרה על שם שסוכה ברוח הקודש

---

וְהַכֹּל סוכין ביפיה (ס"א כמו שנאמר ויראו אותה שרי פרעה) ועוד יסכה לשון נסיכות (וכן הוא סנהדרין לט להדיא) כמו שרה לשון שררה:

### 58) כתובות טז:

תנו רבנן כיצד מרקדין לפני הכלה בית שמאי אומרים כלה כמות שהיא ובית הלל אומרים כלה נאה וחסודה אמרו להן בית שמאי לבית הלל הרי שהיתה חיגרת או סומא אומרי' לה כלה נאה וחסודה והתורה אמרה מדבר שקר תרחק אמרו להם בית הלל לבית שמאי אומרים לדבריכם מי שלקח מקח רע מן השוק ישבחנו בעיניו או יגננו בעיניו הוי אומר ישבחנו בעיניו מכאן אמרו חכמים לעולם תהא דעתו של אדם מעורבת עם הבריות

### 59) עבודה זרה טז:

ת"ר: כשנתפס ר"א למינות, העלוהו לגרדום לידון. אמר לו אותו הגמון: זקן שכמותך יעסוק בדברים בטלים הללו? אמר לו: נאמן עלי הדיין. כסבור אותו הגמון: עליו הוא אומר, והוא לא אמר אלא כנגד אביו שבשמים. אמר לו: הואיל והאמנתי עליך, דימוס, פטור אתה.

### 60) נדרים סב: ודברים ד:כד

ואמר רבא: שרי ליה לצורבא מרבנן למימר עבדא דנורא אנא לא יהיבנא אכרגא, מ"ט? לאברוחי אריא מיניה קאמר.
כִּי ד' אֱלֹקֶיךָ אֵשׁ אֹכְלָה הוּא אֵל קַנָּא:

### 61) ניב שפתים, הלכות איסורי שקר ב:ט-י-י'

ואפילו אם אינו יכול להשכין שלום אלא א"כ ישקר, מ"מ אם יכול לומר בלישנא דמשמע דתרי אנפי לא יוציא מפיו שקר גמור. עוד נראה פשוט דאף כשאין לו ברירה והוא מוכרח לשקר, יראה למעט בדברי שקר ולא יאמר רק מה שמוכרח לצורך שלום.

### 62) ספר ניב שפתים, הלכות איסורי שקר, כלל ג

כשם שהתירו לשנות מפני השלום, כך התירו לשנות כדי לקיים מצוות ואפילו מצוה מדרבנן ואפילו מידה טובה, כגון אם נוהג עצמו איזה מנהג טוב שאינו חייב מצד הדין, כגון שמתענה, ושאלוהו אם מתענה, נכון שיאמר שאינו מתענה כדי שלא להחזיר טיבותא לנפשיה ... וה"ה נמי דמותר לשנות כדי שלא יעבור על איסור

### 63) רמב"ם, הלכות ברכות ד:א

כל המברך ברכת המזון או ברכה אחת מעין שלש צריך לברך אותה במקום שאכל,

### 64) ברכות נג:

רבה בר בר חנה הוה קאזיל בשיירתא, אכל ואשתלי ולא בריך אמר: היכי אעביד? אי אמינא להו אנשאי

תועלת מזה, או שמשקר מתוך אהבת השקר, זה לא הותר ...

ומתבאר בתוך דברי האחרונים דטעמא דמלתא הוא משום דכל שקר שהוא בדבר ההוה או העתיד, האדם מתרגל עי"ז יותר לשקר, וכל היכא שאדם מתרגל לשקר, לא הותר אפילו מפני שלום משום שנאמר "למדו לשונם דבר שקר" כדאמרינן יבמות סג. עוד יש לומר עפ"י המבואר בתרגום אונקלוס פרשת בלק (כג:יט) דשקר הדבר העבר הוי שקר בדיבור, אבל שקר בדבר העתיד הוי שקר במעשה עי"ש.

### 41) רי"ף על בבא מציעא כג: ומהרש"א על יבמות סה:

... אבל הך דשלום מצוה לשנות ומ"ש ר"נ אומר מצוה כו'. הוסיף לומר שהרי הקב"ה צוה לו לשנות ...

### 42) סוטה מא:

מותר להחניף לרשעים בעולם הזה, שנאמר: (ישעיהו לב) לא יקרא עוד לנבל נדיב ולכילי לא יאמר שוע, מכלל דבעולם הזה שרי.

### 43) משנה נדרים ג:ד

נודרין להרגין ולחרמין ולמוכסין ... שהן של בית המלך אף על פי שאינן של בית המלך.

### 44) נדרים סב:

וא"ר יהודה: מנדה זו מנת המלך, בלו זו כסף גולגלתא, והלך זו ארנונא. ואמר רבא שרי ליה לצורבא מרבנן למימר עבדא דנורא אנא לא יהיבנא אכרגא, מ"ט? לאברוחי אריא מיניה קאמר.

### 45) יומא פג:

... למחר אמרו לו: הב לן כיסן אמר להו: לא היו דברים מעולם ... אמרו ליה: אמאי לא אמרת לן מר? אמר להו: אימר דאמרי אנא חששא, אחזוקי מי אמרי? משכוהו ועיילוהו לחנותא, חזו טלפחי אשפמיה, אזלו ויהבו סימנא לדביתהו, ושקלוהו לכיסייהו ואייתו

### 46) שולחן ערוך, חושן משפט שלג:ה

במה דברים אמורים: בדבר שאינו אבוד, אבל בדבר האבוד כגון פשתן להעלות מהמשרה, או שכר חמור להביא חלילין למת או לכלה וכיוצא בהם, אחד פועל ואחד קבלן אינו יכול לחזור בו ... כיצד מטען, אומר להם סלע קצצתי לכם בואו וטלו שתים עד שיגמרו מלאכתם ולא יתן להם אלא מה שפסק תחילה, ואפילו נתן להם השתים מחזיר מהם התוספת.

### 47) בבא מציעא כג: ותוספות שם

דאמר רב יהודה אמר שמואל בהני תלת מילי עבידי

---

רבנן דמשנו במליוהו במסכת ובפוריא ובאושפיזא באושפיזא – ... והא דלא חשיב הכא מותר לשנות מפני דרכי שלום כדאמרינן פרק הבא על יבמתו (יבמות דף סה:) משום דהני נמי משום דרכי שלום הן ורגילין יותר מאחרים להכי נקט הני:

### 48) רמב"ם, הלכות גזילה ואבידה יד:יג

במה דברים אמורים בתלמיד ותיק שאינו משנה בדבורו כלל אלא בדברי שלום או במסכתא או במטה או בית שהוא מתארח בו כיצד היה עוסק במסכת נדה ואמר במקומות אני שונה כדי שלא ישאלו אותו שאלות בענין נדה או שישן במטה זו ואמר בזה אני ישן שמא ימצא שם קרי או שנתארח אצל שמעון ואמר אצל ראובן אני מתארח כדי שלא יטריחו על זה שנתארח אצלו או שהביא שלום בין אדם לחבירו והוסיף וגרע כדי לחבבן זה לזה הרי זה מותר אבל אם באו עדים שששנה בדבורו חוץ מדברים אלו אין מחזירין לו את האבידה בטביעות עין

### 49) שולחן ערוך, חושן משפט רסב:כא

במה דברים אמורים: בתלמיד ותיק שאינו משנה בדיבורו כלל אלא בדברי שלום, או במסכתא הגה: פירוש: אם ישאלוהו על מסכתא אחת אם היא סדורה בידו יענה לאו דרך ענוה, או בפוריא הגה: פירוש: אם שאלוהו חבירו על מטה זו אם לא יאמר לא פן יראו בה קרי ויתגנה (תוס' וכן כתב הרמב"ם), או באושפיזא הגה: (פירוש: כדאמרינן בערכין מברך רעהו בקול גדול וגו', קללה תחשב לו שלא יספר בשבחו שקבלוהו בסבר פנים יפות בין בני אדם שאינם מהוגנים, שלא יקפצו עליו ויכלו ממונו

### 50) מלכים ב' ח:ז-י'

וַיָּבֹא אֱלִישָׁע דַּמֶּשֶׂק וּבֶן־הֲדַד מֶלֶךְ־אֲרָם חֹלֶה וַיֻּגַּד־לוֹ לֵאמֹר בָּא אִישׁ הָאֱלֹקִים עַד־הֵנָּה: וַיֹּאמֶר הַמֶּלֶךְ אֶל־חֲזָאֵל קַח בְּיָדְךָ מִנְחָה וְלֵךְ לִקְרַאת אִישׁ הָאֱלֹקִים וְדָרַשְׁתָּ אֶת־ד' מֵאוֹתוֹ לֵאמֹר הַאֶחְיֶה מֵחֳלִי זֶה: וַיֵּלֶךְ חֲזָאֵל לִקְרָאתוֹ וַיִּקַּח מִנְחָה בְיָדוֹ וְכָל־טוּב דַּמֶּשֶׂק מַשָּׂא אַרְבָּעִים גָּמָל וַיָּבֹא וַיַּעֲמֹד לְפָנָיו וַיֹּאמֶר בִּנְךָ בֶן־הֲדַד מֶלֶךְ־אֲרָם שְׁלָחַנִי אֵלֶיךָ לֵאמֹר הַאֶחְיֶה מֵחֳלִי זֶה: וַיֹּאמֶר אֵלָיו אֱלִישָׁע לֵךְ אֱמָר־לֹא [לוֹ] חָיֹה תִחְיֶה וְהִרְאַנִי ד' כִּי־מוֹת יָמוּת:

### 51) סנהדרין יא.

מעשה ברבן גמליאל שאמר: השכימו לי שבעה לעלייה. אמר: מי הוא שעלה שלא ברשות? ירד שמואל הקטן ואמר: אני הוא שעליתי שלא ברשות, ולא לעבר השנה עליתי, אלא ללמוד הלכה למעשה הוצרכתי. אמר לו: שב בני, שב. ראויות כל השנים כולן להתעבר על ידך, אלא אמרו חכמים: אין מעברין את השנה אלא במזומנין לה. ולא שמואל הקטן הוה, אלא איניש אחרינא, ומחמת כיסופא הוא דעבד.

נאה וחסודה אפילו אינה נאה

### 31) פירוש הרש"ש על כתובות יז

... משא"כ כשלוקח מן השוק שאינו מכירו להשיבנו לו אם נתאנה מה לו לחברו לגלות לגלות לו מומין להדאינו באין תועלת

### 32) אורחות צדיקים, שער כב

הרביעי המשקר בסיפור דברים ששמע, ומחליף מקצתם ומתכוין להחליף, ואין לו שום ריוח באותו שקר, וגם לא יזיק אותו שקר לחבירו. ופעמים שהוא מספר דברים שהוא בודה כולם מלבו, ויש לו עונש שאוהב שקר בלא תועלת. ועל זה אמר שלמה המלך, עליו השלום (משלי ו יט): "יפיח כזבים עד שקר" – יש לך לידע, שזאת המידה תביאהו להעיד שקר באחיו מחמת שהוא אוהב שקר. ויש אנשים שמחליפים מקצת דברים ששמעו בלי דעת, כי אינם שמים על לב שהם שומעים הדברים לחקור על אמיתתם – גם זו מידה רעה, ועל זה אמר שלמה המלך, עליו השלום (משלי כא כח): "ואיש שומע לנצח ידבר", פירוש: מי שנותן לב לשמוע להבין תוכן הענין והדברים אשר יספרו עבור שסיפרו אותם על דרך האמת, שלא יימצא בפיו לשון שקר, אותו האיש לנצח ידבר, כי יתאוו בני אדם לשמוע דבריו ולא יגערו בו על דבריו:

התשיעי המספר בסיפור דברים ששמע, ומחליף בדברים על אודות חפצו, ואין הפסד לשום אדם בזה, אך יש לו מעט הנאה בשקרו, אף על פי שאינו מרויח ממון בכך. כגון (יבמות סג א): רב שאמר לאשתו: עשי לי טלופחי! ועשתה לו חימצי, וכשאמר חימצי עשתה לו טלופחי: הלך חייא בנו והפך הדברים: כשהיה חפץ [רב] חימצי, אמר לאמו תעשי טלופחי – והיא עשתה חימצי. וזה הבן עשה לכבוד האב, כדי שיהא לו מזומן המאכל שחפץ, ואף על פי כן מיחה [רב] בידו שלא לעשות עוד, משום (ירמיה ט ד): "למדו לשונם דבר שקר". אך אין עונש בזה השקר כעונש המשקרים על לא דבר, כאשר הזכרנו בחלק רביעי. עד כאן תשעה חלקי שקר:

### 33) שערי תשובה, שער שלישי קפא

החלק הרביעי – המשקר בספור הדברים אשר שמע ומחליף קצתם במתכוין, ואין לו תועלת בשקריו ולא הפסד לזולתו, ... וזה החלק התירוהו לקיים מצות ודרישת טובה ושלום. ואמרו (כתובות יז, א): כי מותר לשבח הכלה לפני החתן ולאמר שהיא נאה וחסודה אף על פי שאינה כן. ואמרו (יבמות סה, ב): מותר לשנות בדברי שלום, שנאמר (בראשית נ, טז-יז): "אביך צוה לפני מותו לאמר כה תאמרו ליוסף אנא שא נא וגו'

### 34) ספר חסידים תכו

דע אע"פ שאמרו מותר לשנות בדברי שלום, אם יבא

נכרי או יהודי ויאמר לאדם תלוה לי מעות, ואינו מלוה לו ברצון, כי ירא פן לא יפרע לו, אינו יכול לומר אין לי, כי מה שאמרו שמותר לשנות בדברי שלום, זהו בשכבר עבר הדבר:

### 35) ספר טעמי המנהגים, עמוד תקס

ובספר חסידים תכו כתב דמותר לשנות מפני דרכי שלום הוא דוקא בדבר שכבר עבר ולא בדבר דלהבא. ובספר דברי שאול חלק א' על מסכת יבמות כתב כי בדבר שלעבר לא שייך שירגיל עצמו בדבר שקר, דכבר עבר הדבר. אבל בדבר דלהבא אם נתיר לו לשנות, אז מהנקל לו לאמר על כל דבר שהוא מפני דרכי שלום וירגיל עצמו בשקר עד אין קץ.

### 36) אבות דרבי נתן יב

אוהב שלום כיצד מלמד שיהא אדם אוהב שלום בישראל בין כל אחד ואחד כדרך שהיה אהרן אוהב שלום בין כל אחד ואחד ... כשהיה אהרן מהלך בדרך פגע בו באדם רשע ונתן לו שלום למחר בקש אותו האיש לעבור עבירה אמר אוי לי היאך אשא עיני אחר כך ואראה את אהרן בושתי הימנו שנתן לי שלום נמצא אותו האיש מונע עצמו מן העבירה. וכן שני בני אדם שעשו מריבה זה עם זה הלך אהרן וישב אצל אחד מהם אמר לו בני ראה חברך מהו אומר מטרף את לבו וקורע את בגדיו אומר אוי לי היאך אשא את עיני ואראה את חברי בושתי הימנו שאני הוא שסרחתי עליו הוא יושב עד שמסיר קנאה מלבו. והלך אהרן ויושב אצל האחר וא"ל בני ראה חברך מהו אומר מטרף את לבו וקורע את בגדיו ואומר אוי לי היאך אשא את עיני ואראה את חברי בושתי הימנו שאני הוא שסרחתי עליו הוא יושב אצלו עד שמסיר קנאה מלבו.

### 37) פירוש בן יהוידא על יבמות סה:

... לכך מספר שקר עולה מספר דרך שלום, ללמד אם הוא דרך שלום מותר לומר שקר

### 38) מגן אברהם על שולחן ערוך, אורח חיים קנו

הא דמותר לשנות מפני השלום היינו בדבר שכבר עבר ולא בלהבא [ס"ח סי' תכ"ו].

### 39) משנה ברורה על שולחן ערוך, אורח חיים קנו

וכן ירחק משקר בתכלית הריחוק [עי' שבועות ל"א] אך מפני השלום מותר לשנות

### 40) ניב שפתים, הלכות איסורי שקר, ב:טו

ודע עוד דרבינו יונה חילק את כת שקרנים לט' חלקים, והעולה מדבריו, דלא הותר לשנות מפני השלום אלא שקר שאין לו תועלת בו, ולא הפסד לזולתו, וגם אין משקר מאהבת השקר, ואדרבה מואס את השקר בלבו, ורק מפני ההכרח לעשות שלום הוא משקר, אבל שקר שיש בו הפסד לזולתו, או שיש בו

**19)** יבמות סה:
וא"ר אילעא משום רבי אלעזר בר' שמעון: מותר לו
לאדם לשנות בדבר השלום, שנאמר: (בראשית נ')
אביך צוה וגו' כה תאמרו ליוסף אנא שא נא וגו'. ר'
נתן אומר: מצוה, שנאמר: (שמואל א' ט"ז) ויאמר
שמואל איך אלך ושמע שאול והרגני וגו'. דבי רבי
ישמעאל תנא: גדול השלום, שאף הקדוש ברוך הוא
שינה בו, דמעיקרא כתיב: (בראשית י"ח) ואדני זקן,
ולבסוף כתיב: ואני זקנתי.

**20)** בראשית נ:טו
ויראו אחי־יוסף כי־מת אביהם ויאמרו לו ישטמנו
יוסף והשב ישיב לנו את כל־הרעה אשר גמלנו אתו:

**21)** בראשית נ:טז-יז
ויצוו אל־יוסף לאמר אביך צוה לפני מותו לאמר:
כה־תאמרו ליוסף אנא שא נא פשע אחיך וחטאתם
כי־רעה גמלוך ועתה שא נא לפשע עבדי אלקי אביך
ויבך יוסף בדברם אליו:

**22)** שמואל א' טז:ב-ה
ויאמר שמואל איך אלך ושמע שאול והרגני ויאמר ד'
עגלת בקר תקח בידך ואמרת לזבח לד' באתי: וקראת
לישי בזבח ואנכי אודיעך את אשר־תעשה ומשחת
לי את אשר־אמר אליך: ויעש שמואל את אשר דבר
ד' ויבא בית לחם ויחרדו זקני העיר לקראתו ויאמר
שלם בואך ויאמר | שלום לזבח לד' באתי התקדשו
ובאתם אתי בזבח ויקדש את־ישי ואת־בניו ויקרא
להם לזבח:

**23)** בראשית יח:יב
ותצחק שרה בקרבה לאמר אחרי בלתי היתה־לי
עדנה ואדני זקן:

**24)** בראשית יח:יג
ויאמר ד' אל־אברהם למה זה צחקה שרה לאמר האף
אמנם אלד ואני זקנתי:

**25)** סוטה מא.
למה הדבר דומה? לאדם שזימן את חבירו והכיר
בו שמבקש להורגו, אמר לו: טעם תבשיל זה שאני
טועם כתבשיל שטעמתי בבית המלך, אמר: ידע ליה
מלכא, מיחתפי ולא קטיל ליה,

**26)** עבודה זרה יז:
אתיוהו לרבי אלעזר בן פרטא, אמרו: מ"ט תנית,
ומ"ט גנבת? אמר להו: אי סייפא לא ספרא, ואי
ספרא לא סייפא, ומדהא ליתא הא נמי ליתא. ומ"ט
קרו לך רבי? רבן של תרסיים אני. אייתו ליה תרי
קיבורי, אמרו ליה: הי דשתיא והי דערבא. איתרחיש
ליה ניסא, אתיא זיבוריתא אותיבא על דשתיא ואתאי
זיבורא ויתיב על דערבא, אמר להו: האי דשתיא והאי

דערבא. א"ל: ומ"ט לא אתית לבי אבידן? אמר להו:
זקן הייתי ומתיירא אני שמא תרמסוני ברגליכם.
[אמרו:] ועד האידנא כמה סבי איתרמוס? אתרחיש
ניסא, ההוא יומא אירמס חד סבא.

**27)** ספר יראים, עמוד ח:דרלה ופירוש תועפות רעם
ורבינו חידש כאן דשקר שאינו בא לידי רעה לא
הזהירה תורה עליו ... ונראה לדברי רבינו דרעה
לבריות אינו דוקא רעה רעה בממון ... ואף ה"ה דפליגי
על ב"ש אינו אלא דס"ל לב"ה דאין זה נקרא גונב
דעת הבעל ... אבל אם באמת מספר אדם לחבירו
דבר שקר וגונב דעתו שהאמת אתו, אף ב"ה מודו
דהתורה הזהירה על זה "מדבר שקר תרחק" ...

**28)** כתובות טז: ורש"י ותוספות שם
תנו רבנן כיצד מרקדין לפני הכלה בית שמאי
אומרים כלה כמות שהיא ובית הלל אומרים כלה
נאה וחסודה אמרו להן בית שמאי לבית הלל
הרי שהיתה חיגרת או סומא אומרי' לה כלה נאה
וחסודה והתורה אמרה מדבר שקר תרחק אמרו להם
בית הלל לבית שמאי אומרים לדבריכם מי שלקח
מקח רע מן השוק ישבחנו בעיניו או יגננו בעיניו הוי
אומר ישבחנו בעיניו מכאן אמרו חכמים לעולם תהא
דעתו של אדם מעורבת עם הבריות
כיצד מרקדים – מה אומרים לפניה.
מכאן אמרו – מדברי ב"ה שאמרו ישבחנה.
תהא דעתו של אדם מעורבת עם הבריות – לעשות
**לאיש ואיש כרצונו.**
ישבחנו בעינו או יגננו בעיניו. וב"ש סברי אע"ג
דישבחנו בעיניו אין להם לחכמים לתקן להזיק
לומר שקר דהתורה אמרה מדבר שקר תרחק:

**29)** מסכת כלה, פרק י'
(ברייתא) כיצד מרקדין לפני הכלה ב"ש אומרים
כלה כמות שהיא וב"ה אומרים כלה נאה וחסודה
אמר להם ב"ש אפילו היא חגרת או סומא אומרם
מדבר שקר תרחק א"ל ב"ה מקח רע ישבחנו בעיניו
או יגננו בעיניו ישבחנו בעיניו לפיכך ב"ה אומר תהא
דעתו של אדם מעורבת עם הבריות. גמ' וב"ה נמי
ליכא הכא נמי דלמא נאה במעשיה נאה מבית אבות
וחסידה בדנפשיה דאחזקיה בבישתא לא מחזיקנן
וב"ש אומר מי כתיב משקר הרחק מדבר אפילו סתם
וב"ה אומר כי אמר רחמנא מדבר שקר משום ונקי
וצדיק הא לקיומי שפיר דמי וב"ה נמי דמיתביה
ממקח וליתביה מדאורייתא דתניא גדול השלום
שאפילו הקב"ה שינה בו דמעיקרא כתיב ואדני זקן
ולבסוף כתיב ויאמר ה' אל אברהם וגו' ואני זקנתי
הכי קאמרי לא מיביעא מדאורייתא דשפיר דמי אלא
אף לבריתא דמדאורייתא שפיר דמי כלפליא איפוך

**30)** שולחן ערוך, אבן העזר סה:א
מצוה לשמח חתן וכלה ולרקד לפניה, ולומר שהיא

## 14) רמב"ם, הלכות יסודי התורה ה:א-ב

.. כיצד כשיעמוד עובד כוכבים ויאנוס את ישראל
לעבור על אחת מכל מצות האמורות בתורה או
יהרגנו יעבור ואל יהרג שנאמר במצות אשר יעשה
אותם האדם וחי בהם, וחי ולא ולא שימות בהם,
ואם מת ולא עבר הרי זה מתחייב בנפשו. במה
דברים אמורים בשאר מצות חוץ מעבודת כוכבים
וגלוי עריות ושפיכת דמים, אבל שלש עבירות אלו
אם יאמר לו עבור על אחת מהן או תהרג, יהרג ואל
יעבור ...

## 15) בראשית יב:י-יג

וַיְהִי רָעָב בָּאָרֶץ וַיֵּרֶד אַבְרָם מִצְרַיְמָה לָגוּר שָׁם כִּי־
כָבֵד הָרָעָב בָּאָרֶץ: וַיְהִי כַּאֲשֶׁר הִקְרִיב לָבוֹא מִצְרָיְמָה
וַיֹּאמֶר אֶל־שָׂרַי אִשְׁתּוֹ הִנֵּה־נָא יָדַעְתִּי כִּי אִשָּׁה יְפַת־
מַרְאֶה אָתְּ: וְהָיָה כִּי־יִרְאוּ אֹתָךְ הַמִּצְרִים וְאָמְרוּ אִשְׁתּוֹ
זֹאת וְהָרְגוּ אֹתִי וְאֹתָךְ יְחַיּוּ: אִמְרִי־נָא אֲחֹתִי אָתְּ לְמַעַן
יִיטַב־לִי בַעֲבוּרֵךְ וְחָיְתָה נַפְשִׁי בִּגְלָלֵךְ:

## 16) שמואל א' כא:יא-טו

וַיָּקָם דָּוִד וַיִּבְרַח בַּיּוֹם־הַהוּא מִפְּנֵי שָׁאוּל וַיָּבֹא אֶל־
אָכִישׁ מֶלֶךְ גַּת: וַיֹּאמְרוּ עַבְדֵי אָכִישׁ אֵלָיו הֲלוֹא־זֶה
דָוִד מֶלֶךְ הָאָרֶץ הֲלוֹא לָזֶה יַעֲנוּ בַמְּחֹלוֹת לֵאמֹר הִכָּה
שָׁאוּל בַּאֲלָפָיו [בַּאֲלָפָו] וְדָוִד בְּרִבְבֹתָיו [בְּרִבְבֹתָיו]:
וַיָּשֶׂם דָּוִד אֶת־הַדְּבָרִים הָאֵלֶּה בִּלְבָבוֹ וַיִּרָא מְאֹד מִפְּנֵי
אָכִישׁ מֶלֶךְ־גַּת: וַיְשַׁנּוֹ אֶת־טַעְמוֹ בְּעֵינֵיהֶם וַיִּתְהֹלֵל
בְּיָדָם וַיְתָו עַל־דַּלְתוֹת הַשַּׁעַר וַיּוֹרֶד רִירוֹ אֶל־זְקָנוֹ:
וַיֹּאמֶר אָכִישׁ אֶל־עֲבָדָיו הִנֵּה תִרְאוּ אִישׁ מִשְׁתַּגֵּעַ לָמָּה
תָּבִיאוּ אֹתוֹ אֵלָי:

## 17) שמות א:טו-יט

וַיֹּאמֶר בְּיַלֶּדְכֶן אֶת־הָעִבְרִיּוֹת וּרְאִיתֶן עַל־הָאָבְנָיִם
אִם־בֵּן הוּא וַהֲמִתֶּן אֹתוֹ וְאִם־בַּת הִוא וָחָיָה: וַתִּירֶאןָ
הַמְיַלְּדֹת אֶת־הָאֱלֹהִים וְלֹא עָשׂוּ כַּאֲשֶׁר דִּבֶּר אֲלֵיהֶן
מֶלֶךְ מִצְרָיִם וַתְּחַיֶּיןָ אֶת־הַיְלָדִים: וַיִּקְרָא מֶלֶךְ־מִצְרַיִם
לַמְיַלְּדֹת וַיֹּאמֶר לָהֶן מַדּוּעַ עֲשִׂיתֶן הַדָּבָר הַזֶּה וַתְּחַיֶּיןָ
אֶת־הַיְלָדִים: וַתֹּאמַרְןָ הַמְיַלְּדֹת אֶל־פַּרְעֹה כִּי לֹא
כַנָּשִׁים הַמִּצְרִיֹּת הָעִבְרִיֹּת כִּי־חָיוֹת הֵנָּה בְּטֶרֶם תָּבוֹא
אֲלֵהֶן הַמְיַלֶּדֶת וְיָלָדוּ:

## 18) שופטים ד:יז-כא

וְסִיסְרָא נָס בְּרַגְלָיו אֶל־אֹהֶל יָעֵל אֵשֶׁת חֶבֶר הַקֵּינִי כִּי
שָׁלוֹם בֵּין יָבִין מֶלֶךְ־חָצוֹר וּבֵין בֵּית חֶבֶר הַקֵּינִי: וַתֵּצֵא
יָעֵל לִקְרַאת סִיסְרָא וַתֹּאמֶר אֵלָיו סוּרָה אֲדֹנִי סוּרָה
אֵלַי אַל־תִּירָא וַיָּסַר אֵלֶיהָ הָאֹהֱלָה וַתְּכַסֵּהוּ בַּשְּׂמִיכָה:
וַיֹּאמֶר אֵלֶיהָ הַשְׁקִינִי־נָא מְעַט־מַיִם כִּי צָמֵאתִי וַתִּפְתַּח
אֶת־נֹאוד הֶחָלָב וַתַּשְׁקֵהוּ וַתְּכַסֵּהוּ: וַיֹּאמֶר אֵלֶיהָ עֲמֹד
פֶּתַח הָאֹהֶל וְהָיָה אִם־אִישׁ יָבוֹא וּשְׁאֵלֵךְ וְאָמַר הֲיֵשׁ־
פֹּה אִישׁ וְאָמַרְתְּ אָיִן: וַתִּקַּח יָעֵל אֵשֶׁת־חֶבֶר אֶת־יְתַד
הָאֹהֶל וַתָּשֶׂם אֶת־הַמַּקֶּבֶת בְּיָדָהּ וַתָּבוֹא אֵלָיו בַּלָּאט
וַתִּתְקַע אֶת־הַיָּתֵד בְּרַקָּתוֹ וַתִּצְנַח בָּאָרֶץ וְהוּא־נִרְדָּם
וַיָּעַף וַיָּמֹת:

---

וְיֵשׁ עוֹד אֲחֵרִים שֶׁחַלָּיִם קַל מֵחוֹלֵי הָרִאשׁוֹנִים, וְהֵם
אוֹתָם שֶׁאֵינָם קְבוּעִים כָּל כָּךְ בְּשֶׁקֶר, אֶלָּא שֶׁלֹּא יָחוֹשׁוּ
לְהִתְרַחֵק מִמֶּנּוּ, וְאִם יִזְדַּמֵּן לָהֶם יֹאמְרוּהוּ, וּפְעָמִים
רַבּוֹת יֹאמְרוּהוּ דֶּרֶךְ שְׂחוֹק אוֹ כַּיּוֹצֵא בָּזֶה בְּלֹא כַוָּנָה
רָעָה. וְאָמְנָם הֶחָכָם הוֹדִיעָנוּ, שֶׁכָּל זֶה הוּא הֵפֶךְ רְצוֹן
הַבּוֹרֵא בָּרוּךְ הוּא וּמִדַּת חֲסִידָיו, הוּא מַה שֶּׁכָּתוּב
(משלי יג): "דְּבַר שֶׁקֶר יִשְׂנָא צַדִּיק", וְהוּא מַה שֶּׁבָּאָה
עָלָיו הָאַזְהָרָה (שמות כג): "מִדְּבַר שֶׁקֶר תִּרְחָק".
וְתִרְאֶה שֶׁלֹּא אָמַר מִשֶּׁקֶר תִּשָּׁמֵר, אֶלָּא מִדְּבַר שֶׁקֶר
תִּרְחָק, לְהָעִיר אוֹתָנוּ עַל הַהַרְחָק הַגָּדוֹל וְהַבְּרִיחָה
הַרְבֵּה שֶׁצָּרִיךְ לִבְרוֹחַ מִזֶּה. וּכְבָר נֶאֱמַר (צפניה ג):
"שְׁאֵרִית יִשְׂרָאֵל לֹא יַעֲשׂוּ עַוְלָה וְלֹא יְדַבְּרוּ כָזָב וְלֹא
יִמָּצֵא בְּפִיהֶם לְשׁוֹן תַּרְמִית":

וַחֲכָמִים זִכְרוֹנָם לִבְרָכָה אָמְרוּ (שבת נה): חוֹתָמוֹ שֶׁל
הַקָּדוֹשׁ בָּרוּךְ הוּא אֱמֶת. וּבְוַדַּאי שֶׁאִם הָאֱמֶת הוּא מַה
שֶּׁבָּחַר בּוֹ הַקָּדוֹשׁ בָּרוּךְ הוּא לְקָחְתּוֹ לַחְתּוֹם לוֹ, כַּמָּה
יִהְיֶה הֶפְכּוֹ מְתוֹעָב לְפָנָיו. וְהִזְהִיר הַקָּדוֹשׁ בָּרוּךְ הוּא
עַל הָאֱמֶת אַזְהָרָה רַבָּה וְאָמַר (זכריה ח): "דַּבְּרוּ אֱמֶת
אִישׁ אֶת רֵעֵהוּ". וְאָמַר (ישעיה טז): "וְהוּכַן בַּחֶסֶד כִּסֵּא
וְיָשַׁב עָלָיו בֶּאֱמֶת", וְאָמַר (שם סג):
וַיֹּאמֶר אַךְ עַמִּי הֵמָּה בָּנִים לֹא יְשַׁקֵּרוּ. הָא לָמַדְתָּ, שֶׁזֶּה
תָּלוּי בָּזֶה. וְאָמַר (זכריה ח):
וְנִקְרְאָה יְרוּשָׁלַיִם עִיר הָאֱמֶת, לְהַגְדִּיל חֲשִׁיבוּתָהּ.
וּכְבָר אָמְרוּ ז"ל (מכות כד): וְדוֹבֵר אֱמֶת בִּלְבָבוֹ,
כְּגוֹן רַב סַפְרָא וְכוּ', לְהוֹדִיעֲךָ עַד הֵיכָן חוֹבַת הָאֱמֶת
מַגַּעַת. וּכְבָר אָסְרוּ לַתַּלְמִיד חָכָם לְשַׁנּוֹת בְּדִבּוּרוֹ
חוּץ מִשְּׁלֹשָׁה דְבָרִים. וְאֶחָד מִן הָעַמּוּדִים שֶׁהָעוֹלָם
עוֹמֵד עָלָיו הוּא הָאֱמֶת, אִם כֵּן מִי שֶׁדּוֹבֵר שֶׁקֶר כְּאִלּוּ
נוֹטֵל יְסוֹדוֹ שֶׁל עוֹלָם, וְהַהֵפֶךְ מִזֶּה, מִי שֶׁמַּזְהִיר בָּאֱמֶת
כְּאִלּוּ מְקַיֵּם יְסוֹדוֹ שֶׁל עוֹלָם. וּכְבָר סִפְּרוּ חֲכָמִים ז"ל
(סנהדרין צז): מֵאוֹתוֹ הַמָּקוֹם שֶׁהָיוּ זְהִירִים בָּאֱמֶת
שֶׁלֹּא הָיָה מַלְאַךְ הַמָּוֶת שׁוֹלֵט שָׁם, וּלְפִי שֶׁאִשְׁתּוֹ שֶׁל
רַבִּי פְּלוֹנִי שִׁנְּתָה בִּדְבָרֶיהָ אַף עַל פִּי שֶׁהָיָה לְכַוָּנָה
טוֹבָה, גֵּירְתָה בָּהֶם מַלְאַךְ הַמָּוֶת עַד שֶׁגֵּירְשׁוּהוּ מִשָּׁם
בַּעֲבוּר זֶה, וְחָזְרוּ לִשְׁלוֹמָם. וְאֵין צָרִיךְ לְהַאֲרִיךְ בַּדָּבָר
הַזֶּה שֶׁהַשֵּׂכֶל מְחַיְּבוֹ וְהַדַּעַת מַכְרִיחוֹ:

## 13) סנהדרין צז.

אָמַר רָבָא: מֵרִישׁ הֲוָה אֲמִינָא לֵיכָּא קוּשְׁטָא בְּעָלְמָא,
אֲמַר לִי הַהוּא מֵרַבָּנָן וְרַב טָבוּת שְׁמֵיהּ, וְאָמְרִי לַהּ רַב
טָבִיוֹמֵי שְׁמֵיהּ, דְּאִי הֲווֹ יָהֲבִי לֵיהּ כָּל חַלְלֵי דְעָלְמָא
לָא הֲוָה מְשַׁנֵּי בְּדִבּוּרֵיהּ: זִמְנָא חֲדָא אִיקְלַע לְהַהוּא
אַתְרָא, וְקוּשְׁטָא שְׁמֵיהּ, וְלָא הֲווֹ מְשַׁנּוּ בְּדִבּוּרַיְיהוּ,
וְלָא הֲוָה מָיֵית אִינִישׁ מֵהֶתֶם בְּלָא זִמְנֵיהּ. נְסִיבִי
אִיתְּתָא מִינְהוֹן, וְהָווּ לִי תַּרְתֵּין בְּנִין מִינָהּ. יוֹמָא חַד
הֲוָה יָתְבָא דְּבֵיתְהוּ וְקָא חָיְיפָא רֵישָׁא, אֲתָאי שִׁיבַבְתָּא
טְרַפָא אַדַּשָׁא. סָבַר: לָאו אֹרַח אַרְעָא, אֲמַר לַהּ: לֵיתָא
הָכָא. שְׁכִיבוּ לֵיהּ תַּרְתֵּין בְּנִין, אֲתוֹ אִינְשֵׁי דְאָתְרָא
לְקַמֵּיהּ, אָמְרוּ לֵיהּ: מַאי הַאי? אֲמַר לְהוּ: הָכִי הֲוָה
מַעֲשֶׂה. אֲמַרוּ לֵיהּ: בְּמָטּוּתָא מִינָּךְ, פּוּק מֵאַתְרִין, וְלָא
תְגָרֵי בְּהוּ מוֹתָנָא בְּהָנָךְ אִינְשֵׁי.

החלק הרביעי – המשקר בספור הדברים אשר שמע ומחליף קצתם במתכוין, ואין לו תועלת בשקריו ולא הפסד לזולתו, אבל כה כה משפטו מאהבתו שקר מדבר צדק סלה, ופעמים שהוא בודה מלבו ספור הדברים כולו. והאיש הזה יקל ענשו מצד אחד, על כי אין הפסד לאיש בשקריו ופחזותו, אבל גדול מאד ענשו בעז פניו ואהבת השקר, ויכבד עונו, כי יאהבהו לבלי תועלת. ואמר שלמה עליו השלום (משלי ו, יט): "יפיח כזבים עד שקר"

החלק הששי – המבטיח את חברו להטיב עמו וישקר וישים דבריו לאל מלתו, כי אחרי אשר אמר להיטיב עמו בלשון הבטחה ובטח בו לב חברו, אין לו לחלל הבטחתו, כי זה דרך שקר, והוא כאדם עבר ברית

החלק השביעי – מי שמתעה את חברו לאמר כי עשה עמו טובה או דבר טוב עליו ולא עשה. אמרו רבותינו זכרונם לברכה (חולין צד, א): אסור לגנוב דעת הבריות ואפילו דעת נכרי. והנה החטא הזה חמור אצל חכמי ישראל יותר מגזל הנכרי, יען ובעין כי שפת שקר אשמה רבה, ונתחייבנו על גדרי האמת, כי הוא מיסודי הנפש:

החלק השמיני – מי שמשתבח במעלות שאינן נמצאות בו. אמר שלמה עליו השלום (משלי יז, ז): "לא נאוה לנבל שפת יתר אף כי לנדיב שפת שקר", פירוש: אין לנבל להתגאות ולהתנשא במעלת אבותיו, כי אמרו במקרא שלמעלה מזה (שם פסוק ו): "ותפארת בנים אבותם", אף כי אין לנדיב להתכבד בשקר ולאמר: כה עשיתי ופזרתי ונתתי! ולא כן עשה. וזה גנאי לכל אדם וכל שכן לנדיב, וגנה נדבותיו אשר עשה, כי הלל נפשו על מה שלא עשה, כי זאת תהיה לעדה, כי לבו בכל צדקותיו אשר עשה אך לשם ולתהלה. ואמרו רבותינו זכרונם לברכה (ירושלמי סוף שביעית): כי מי שמכבדים אותו במדרגות הכבוד הראויות לתת למי שהוא יודע שתי מסכתות, והוא אינו יודע זולתי אחת, עליו שיאמר להם: אחת לבדה אני יודע! כל שכן כי אסור לכזב ולהתפאר לאמר: שמענו כאלה רבות!

החלק התשיעי – בנים לא ישקרו בספור דברים אשר ישמעו והגדת מאורעות, אבל יחליפו דברים על אודות חפציהם מאין הפסד לאדם בדבר, אך ימצאו כמעט הנאה בשקרותם אף על פי שאינם מרויחים ממון בכך. ואמרו רבותינו (יבמות סג, א): כי גם זה אסור, והוא שנאמר (ירמיה ט, ד): "למדו לשונם דבר שקר"

## (11) פלא יועץ, ערך אמת

שפת אמת תכון לעד ומצלת ... ויש רבים מעמי הארץ אשר למדו לשונם דבר שקר ונעשה להם כהיתר גמור עד שיש שמשקרים בסיפורים של הבל בלי שום תועלת. עליהם אמר הכתוב "הוי מושכי העון בחבלי השוא" ... ואם היצה"ר החליק אליו בעיניו ומראה לו שמרויח הרבה על ידי השקר סוף סוף בלי ספק שחסר יבואנו ככתוב בדברי

קבלה עושה עושר ולא במשפט בחצי ימיו יעזבנו ובאחריתו יהיה נבל או יהיה עושר שמור לבעליו לרעתו בעוה"ז ובעוה"ב וה' לא ימנע טוב להולכים בתמים. ורעת השקר היא רעה בעיני אלקים ואדם כי מי שהוא שקרן הוא נבזה ונמאס וגנאי הדבר לעין כל ... והמדברים שקר כמו"מ שעושים עם גוים גורמים חילול ה' שאומרים הגוים ידוע הדבר שיהודי שקרן כזבן עולן וכהנה רעות מדברים עליהם ונותנים מום בקדשים וידוע חומר איסור חילול ה' וכמה איסורים נגררים מן השקר לפי הענין ... ראוי לאדם להתחזק לחנך את בניו במדת האמת וממנו יראו שמקפיד על דבר אמת וכן יעשו ויעמוד על המשמר עליהם שלא ימצא בפיהם לשון תרמית ואם יעשו דבר שלא כהוגן יעשה שידוד על האמת ובכן ימחול להם באותו פעם ולא יכם רק יזרזם שלא יוסיפו ... כי מלבד האיסור שבו גנאי הדבר לחזור מדבורו ואמרו ממי שפרע מדור המבול ומדור הפלגה הוא עתיד ליפרע ממי שאינו עומד בדבורו לכן יחשוב מאד קודם שיוציא דבור מפיו אם יוכל לקיימו ואם הוציא דבר מפיו מוצא שפתיו ישמור כאלו השבע שבועה. ומאחר שתורתנו הקדושה היא תורת אמת מה מאד צריך ליזהר להגות בה באמת ולהיות מודה על האמת ולקבל האמת ממי שאמרו אפילו קטן שבקטנים ...

אמרו רז"ל במדרש משלי כשנכנס נח לתיבה בא גם כן שקרא ליכנס אמר לו צא ובקש לך בת זוג שכל הבאים אל התיבה זכר ונקבה באו הלך ומצא את פחתא (היזק) אמר לה רצונך שתנשאי עמי אמרה לו מה תתן לי השיב לה כל מה שארויח אתן לך ומשם ואילך כל דמרויח שקרא פחתא נקיט ליה.

## (12) מסילת ישרים יא, מדת הנקיות

והנה דבר השקר גם הוא חולי רע נתפשט מאד בבני האדם, ואולם מדריגות מדריגות יש בו: יש בני אדם שאמונתם ממש הוא השקרנות, הם ההולכים ובודים מלבם כזבים גמורים למען הרבות שיחה בין הבריות או להחשב מן החכמים ויודעי דברים הרבה, ועליהם נאמר (משלי יב): "תועבת ה' שפתי שקר". ואומר (ישעיה נט):"שפתותיכם דברו שקר", לשונכם עולה תהגה. וכבר גזרו חכמים ז"ל (סוטה מב): ארבע כתות אינם מקבלות פני השכינה, ואחת מהם כת שקרנים: ויש אחרים קרובים להם במדריגה, אף על פי שאינם כמוהם ממש, והם המכזבים בספוריהם ודבריהם, והיינו, שאין אמונתם בכך ללכת ולבדות ספורים ומעשים אשר לא נבראו ולא יהיו, אבל בבואם לספר דבר מה, יערבו בהם מן השקרים כמו שיעלה על רוחם, ויתרגלו בזה עד ששב להם כמו טבע, והם הבדאים אשר אי אפשר להאמין לדבריהם, וכמאמרם ז"ל (סנהדרין פט): כך הוא עונשו של בדאי, שאפילו אומר אמת, אין שומעין לו, שכבר הטביעו בהם הרעה הזאת שלא יוכלו לצאת דבריהם נקיים מן הכזב מתוך פיהם. הוא מה שהנביא מצטער ואומר (ירמיה ט): "למדו לשונם דבר שקר העוה נלאו":

# SOURCES ON LYING – WHEN IS IT PERMITTED IN JUDAISM?

**1) ויקרא יט:לו, בבא מציעא מט.**

מֹאזְנֵי צֶדֶק אַבְנֵי־צֶדֶק אֵיפַת צֶדֶק וְהִין צֶדֶק יִהְיֶה לָכֶם אֲנִי ד' אֱלֹקֵיכֶם אֲשֶׁר־הוֹצֵאתִי אֶתְכֶם מֵאֶרֶץ מִצְרָיִם:
רבי יוסי ברבי יהודה אומר: מה תלמוד לומר (ויקרא י"ט) הין צדק? והלא הין בכלל איפה היה? אלא לומר לך: שיהא הן שלך צדק, ולאו שלך צדק

**2) ספר חרדים, מצוות עשה בפה, מצוה כו**

מצות עשה לדבר אמת אפילו במילדי דעלמא דליכא בהו דררא דממונא שנאמר "מדבר שקר תרחק" משמע אפילו ליכא רק דיבור בעלמא

**3) סוטה מב.**

א"ר ירמיה בר אבא, ארבע כיתות אין מקבלות פני שכינה: כת ליצים, וכת חניפים, וכת שקרים, וכת מספרי לשון הרע.... כת שקרים, דכתיב (תהלים קא) "דובר שקרים לא יכון לנגד עיני"

**4) ויקרא יד:לה, ופירושי רש"י וגור אריה**

וּבָא אֲשֶׁר־לוֹ הַבַּיִת וְהִגִּיד לַכֹּהֵן לֵאמֹר כְּנֶגַע נִרְאָה לִי בַּבָּיִת:
כנגע נראה לי בבית – אפי' תלמיד חכם שיודע שהוא נגע ודאי, לא יפסוק דבר ברור לומר חנגע נראה לי, אלא כנגע נראה לי (ת"כ פרשתא ה:י. נגעים פי"ב ה:ה):
שאפילו חכם גמור וכו' – אין הטעם שאם יאמר "נגע נראה לי בבית" יהיה כל שבבית טמא, דודאי אין טומאה של בית רק על פי כהן, אבל טעם הדבר "דובר שקרים לא יכון" (תהלים קא:ז), דהא כל זמן שלא נזקק לו הכהן לאו נגע הוא (רש"י פסוק לו), ואיך יאמר 'נגע נראה לי בבית:

**5) רמב"ם, הלכות דעות ה:ז, יג**

תלמיד חכם לא יהא צועק וצווח בשעת ... ולא ישנה בדבורו, ולא יוסיף ולא יגרע אלא בדברי שלום וכיוצא בהן ...
משאו ומתנו של תלמיד חכם באמת ובאמונה, אומר על לאו לאו ועל הן הן ...

**6) שפת תמים (חפץ חיים) פרק ב**

ויש כח ביד העון הזה להורידו מנכסיו, ולהענישו בכמה אופנים שונים בזה ובבא. מטעם כי העון הזה של המרמה הוא כלול על פי רוב מכמה וכמה עונות, וביותר מגזל ואונאה ושקר, שכל אחד בפני עצמו הוא עון חמור

**7) סנהדרין פט.**

כך עונשו של בדאי, שאפילו אמר אמת אין שומעין לו.

**8) ישעיהו ו:ה**

וָאֹמַר אוֹי לִי כִּי נִדְמֵיתִי כִּי אִישׁ טְמֵא שְׂפָתַיִם אָנֹכִי וּבְתוֹךְ עַם טְמֵא שְׂפָתַיִם אָנֹכִי יֹשֵׁב כִּי אֶת הַמֶּלֶךְ ד' צְבָאוֹת רָאוּ עֵינָי:

**9) כבוד שמים (חפץ חיים) חלק ב:ו**

ע"י דיבורים אסורים נמשכת רוח הטומאה על השפתים וכמו שכתוב בישעיה ו:ה "כי איש טמא שפתים אנכי" וביותר מזה שנמשכת הטומאה גם על ראשו והאות לזה שבעת טהרתו של מצורע כתיב "והנותר בשמן אשר על כף הכהן יתן על ראש המטהר וגו'" שלא מצינו כן בכל הטמאים שיצטרך לטהר ראשו.

**10) שערי תשובה, שער שלישי קעח-קפו**

וזה דבר כת שקרים. ענין הכת הזו נחלק לתשעה חלקים. החלק האחד – איש כזב, אשר תורה עזב, וירע וישחית במענה פיו, כמו המכחש בעמיתו בפקדון או בתשומת יד או בשכר שכיר, שנאמר (ויקרא יט, יא): "ולא תכחשו ולא תשקרו איש בעמיתו", וכן העונה ברעהו עד שקר, שנאמר (שמות כ, יג): "לא תענה ברעך עד שקר". ומן החלק הזה כלל התרמית והאונאות במסחרים ובשותפות, שנאמר (ויקרא כה, יד): "אל תונו איש את אחיו", ונאמר (תהלים נה, יב): "ולא ימיש מרחובה תוך ומרמה", ונקרא איש און ונקרא בליעל, והוא כבד עון בכתות הרשעים, כאשר הקדמנו בשערי יראת חטא. ומדות זה איש האון שהוא קורץ בעיניו ומולל באצבעותיו, כמו שנאמר (משלי ו, יב-יג): "אדם בליעל איש און וגו', קורץ בעיניו מולל ברגליו מורה באצבעותיו":
החלק השני – המשקר ואין בעצם השקר נזק והפסד לחברו, אך יתכוין בו לעשותו סבה אל הנזק ואל הרע, כמו המתעה את חברו, שיאמין בו כי הוא אוהב וריע נאמן עמו, ומתכוין בזה כדי שיבטח בו ולא ישמר ממנו, ויוכל להדיח עליו רעה, כענין שנאמר (ירמיה ט, ז): "בפיו שלום את רעהו ידבר ובקרבו ישים ארבו", ונאמר אחריו (שם פסוק ח): "העל אלה לא אפקד בם נאם ה' אם בגוי אשר כזה לא תתנקם נפשי". ואלה שני החלקים נענש על שני דברים: על השקר ועל הנזק הצרור בכנפיו, כי השקר מלבד צד הנזק הוא תועבת ה', שנאמר (משלי יב, כב): "תועבת ה' שפתי שקר"

של השחוק גם כי יזקין לא יסור ממנו אם לא שבכח
יגבר איש

## 53) סיני, ירחון לתורה למדע ולספרות, כרך מח,
## יעקב בזק, דף קטז

על מקרה מחריד שאירע בדורנו שומעים אנו מתוך
שאלה שנשאל הרב עובדיה הראייה חבר בית
הדין הגדול בירושלים על יהודי בסינגפור שלאחר
שהפסיד את כל ממונו במשחק קלפים עם אחד
הגויים החליט להמשיך ולשחק על אשתו לאחר
שהפסיד גם במשחק זה עברה האישה לרשותו של
הגוי שזכה בה ולקחה לביתו והולידה ממנו בנים
ובנות הרב נשאל אם הבנים והבנות כשרים לבוא
בקהל ואין בהם חשש ממזרות. אין ספק שהקרבן
העיקרי למללת הקלפנות הוו השחקן עצמו, המאבד
את כל זמנו וממונו במשחקי הקוביא וכן בני משפחתו
הנשארים מוזנחים ללא השגחת האב וללא פת לחם
בודאי שדבר זה כשלעצמו דיו כדי להצדיק את
האיסור שהטיל מטיל על משחקים אלה. אולם נוסף
לתוצאות השליליות הישירות של המשחק בקלפים
היינו: איבוד ממון ביטול זמן והזנחת עצמו ובני ביתו
קיימות גם תוצאות לווי נוספות הפוגעות בציבור
בכללו כגון מעילה גניבה פשיטות רגל מעשי אלימות
ומקרי איבוד עצמו לדעת. בדו"ח משנת 1933 של
ועדה מלכותית בריטית שנתמנתה לדון בבעית
ההימורים והקלפנות נמסר כי במשך תקופה של 12
שנים (1895-1907) אירעו באנגליה 156 מקרים של
איבוד לדעת ונסיון איבוד לדעת על רקע של משחקי
קוביא וכמו כן 719 מעשי גניבות; ומעילות 1442
מקרים של פשיטות רגל על אותו רקע.

**54) שו"ת יביע אומר חלק ז – חושן משפט סימן ו**
נשאלתי האם מותר מן הדין להשתתף בקניית
כרטיסי הגרלה של מפעל הפיס?
... מסקנא דדינא שהספרדים ועדות המזרח אסור
להם להשתתף בקניית כרטיסי מפעל הפיס, וכל שכן
כרטיסי ספורט למיניהם שמשחקים בשבת ומחללים
שבת בפרהסיא, ונמצא שהוא מסייע ידי עוברי
עבירה. ואף לאשכנזים יש לאסור בזה. (וע' בשו"ת
ישכיל עבדי חלק ח' עמוד פט ס"ס ה).

### 55) שו"ת תשובות והנהגות ד:שיא
עכ"פ נראה שבקניית כרטיס לא שייך אסמכתא,
והיינו בין לאשכנזים ובין לספרדים.
ומיהו בארץ ישראל חברת ההגרלות "מפעל הפיס"
היא ביד הממשלה, וחלק ניכר מהכסף המתקבל
אצלם הוא עבור החפשיים ומוסדותיהם, ואולי יש
כאן ענין של מסייע ידי עוברי עבירה. אבל האמת
היא שבלאו הכי כל מה שקונין בכל הארץ חלק
מהתשלום הוא מס ערך מוסף, והם אח"כ משתמשים
בו גם לעבירות חמורות רח"ל, רק ע"כ אנן בדידן ולא
חוששין לזה מכיון שאין בידינו לשנות ולהכריע בזה
כלום, ולכן מדינא אין עלינו אחריות מה שהם עושים
בכסף זה.

ודע שרוב ההגרלות של מוסדות שהכסף הולך
לצדקה, יש לצרף עוד שלהרבה פוסקים אין דין
אסמכתא בהקדש, והוא הדין בזמנינו ישיבות
וכוללים הם בכלל צדקה, ואם יפסיד הלא מנחם את
עצמו שהכסף הלך לכולל או שאר צדקה, ולכן יש
להקל טפי.

שקר להפסיד ממון חבירו לפיכך אם יש לו אומנות אחרת כשר:

ומפריחי יונים והוא והוא שאומר לחבירו אם תקדום יונתי לשלך למקום פלוני תתן לי כך וכך ואם שלך תקדום אתן לך כך וכך והוא הדין העושין כן בכל מיני בהמה וחיה ועוף גם אלו אינו פסולין אלא כשאין להם אומנות אחרת. כתב הרמב"ם מפריחי יונים בישוב פסולין שחזקתם שגוזלין יונים של אחרים וכן מפרש טעמא לפי שאינו עוסק בישובו של עולם גבי קוביא וחזקתו שהוא אוכל מן הקוביא שהוא אבק גזל ולפי זה אם יש לו ממון אחר שאוכל ממנו אינו פסול אבל לפי הטעם שפירשתי פסול לעולם:

**47)** רמ"א, שולחן ערוך, חושן משפט רז:יג, שע:ג

... יש אומר הא דמשחק בקוביא לא הוי אסמכתא הוא מטעם דמאחר ששניהן מתנין זה כנגד זה ולא אחד יוכל להפסיד אגב דבעי למקני גמר ומקני, ולכן כל שנים שהמרו זה עם זה קנו אם קנו מידן, ודוקא שאין בידן גם כן אבל מה שבידן לא כמו שנתבאר גבי ערבון בסמוך סעיף יא (טור ומרדכי פרק איזהו נשך בשם ר"ת), ואפילו בזה יש חולקין, ולכן הוצרכו לתת טעמים אחרים גבי משחק בקוביא.

(טור הביאו בס"ו) יש מי שאומר שהמשחק בקוביא עם העכו"ם אין בו משום גזל, אבל יש בו איסור עוסק בדברים בטלים, שאין ראוי לאדם שיעסוק כל ימיו אלא בדברי חכמה ויישובו של עולם, וחלקו עליו לומר שאינו פסול אלא אם כן אין לו אומנות אחרת. הגה: אבל אם יש לו אומנות אחרת אפילו משחק עם ישראל אינו פסול (טור) וע"ל סימן רז סי' יג, וכבר פשט המנהג הכשרא כסברא האחרונה לשחוק בקוביא ואין פסול אלא מי שאין לו אומנות אלא הוא, ואם שחק עמו באמנה אם חייב לשלם ע"ל סימן רז ושם.

**48)** משנה ברורה ס"ק כב על שולחן ערוך, אורח חיים שכב

ולהטיל גורל וכו' – היינו דמי שיזכה בגורל יטול הגדולה ומי שיתחייב יטול הקטנה הוא בכלל שחיקת קוביא ממש. [קוביא (יט) הוא מה שמשחקין בעצים] וקוביא הוא (כ) אבק גזל מדבריהם שאין דעתו להקנותו בקנין גמור ולהכי אסור אף בחול ואף דבעה"ב עם ב"ב לא שייך גזל כלל שהרי הכל שלו מ"מ אסור דלמא אתי לסרוכי בקוביא עם אחרים (כא) ובאחרים בודאי אסור בחול וכ"ש בשבת דקוביא דמי למקח וממכר:

**49)** ספר חסידים תתרכו

אל ירחם אדם על אכזרים. ואל ירחם על מי שאינו מרחם על עצמו. ואל ירחם על מי שהוא כפוי טובה. כגון מי שמרמה את חבירו, וגונב וגוזל ומסית ומדיח ורכיל. ואל ירחם על מי שאינו מרחם על עצמו, כגון מפזר מעות שלא לצורך, ואינו נשמע כשיועצים אותו אל תוציא המעות בהבלים. ואל ירחם על מי

---

שהוא משחק בקוביא ואומר תרחם עלי שלא יביישני ולא יכלימני פלוני שהרויח עלי זהוב, טוב שיתבייש המשחק, ועוד שלא יהא מסייע לעוברי עבירה.

**50)** פירוש שלטי גבורים למרדכי על שבועות כט. מצאתי בתוספות פ' השולח וז"ל אמנם נהג מורי הרי"ף להתיר באנשים קלים פן יכשלו לעבור על שבועתם כי יצר של קוביא גדול מאד לרגילים בו, וכן היה אומר רבינו טוביה דכל נדר של קוביא עתה יש להתיר בו כל השוגים כי אין יכול להתאפק ולמשול ברוחם עכ"ל:

"Gambling in the Synagogue", Leo **(51** Landman, Tradition (10:1), 1968 page **77**

The popular yen for gambling led the communities to enact communal restrictions to suppress it. Most communities lifted these restrictions for special days or auspicious occasions. In fact, the numerous exceptions to the restrictions in themselves show how popular gaming was and how difficult it was for the communities to enforce their edicts. These bans were lifted on days when Tachanun was not recited, i.e., days such as Chanukah, Purim, the intermediary days of Passover or Sukkot, on days of the New Moon, etc. However, on major festivals gaming was prohibited except for women and children.14 The fasts also were days when the communities relaxed their restrictions against gambling. The Takkanot of Bologna 1416–18 specifically stated: "… on fast days, too, one may play cards in order to forget the pain, provided one wagers no more than one quattrino at a game per person." The same reason permitted women in childbirth and those who were sick to engage in gambling activities so that they might distract their minds from pain they might otherwise experience.

**52)** פלא יועץ, ערך "שחוק"

וגם בזה רבו המתפרצים אשר זה דרכם כסל למו ואומנותם בכך לאבד כמה לילות וכמה ימים בשחוק בבתים ובגנות ובקרנות ומשקיעים כמה ממון וכמה נפשות עד שיש שמכלים את ממונם אף אם כביר מצאה ידם לכל יש מוצא וסוף שגוזלים וחומסים ובני ביתם מוטלים ברעב עוללים שאלו לחם פורש אין להם שאין מתעסקים בישובו של עולם להביא לביתם טרף לביתה ועבירה גוררת עבירה שמבטלים תפלות ומצות בעדנא שיצה"ר תוקפם ועומדים בשחוק קשה להם לפרוש הימנו יותר מפרישת הצפורן מן הבשר ועל חייהם אינם חסים ואין מכינים עצמם מן השחוק אפילו לאכול בשעת אכילה ולישן בשעת שינה ומי שהורגל במנהג הרע

מבריסק "עתה הנני מבין גם את הרישא של הפסוק
שעלה בגורל".

באותה תקופה נקלע גם הגאון ר' אהרן קוטלר
לוילנא והגיע אליו הזמנתו של הגאון ר' משה
פיינשטיין שסידר לו רשיון כניסה לארה"ב, אך ר'
אהרן לא יכול היה להכריע בין אר"י וארה"ב, החליט
איפוא להטיל את גורל הגר"א ועלה הפסוק "ויאמר
ד' אל אהרן לך לקראת משה המדברה" וכך פירש
את הפסוק שילד ר' אהרן קטלר לקראת ר' משה
פיינשטיין הנמצא במדבר הרוחני שהיה שם באותה
תקופה, ואמנם עלתה בידי ר' אהרן ואתו שאר גדולי
ישראל להקים עולה של תורה בארה"ב.

### 40) אוצר ידיעות השלם, דף תקופה

בשנת התשי"א כאשר אספו את גוויות הלוחמים
שנשלחו לגוש עציון שנטמנו בקבר ארעי בתנאים
מוגבלים תחת אימת המלחמה ולא התאפשר
להקפיד על עריכת רישום מדויק שיאפשר את
זיהויים מתוך כל הנופלים הצליחו לזהות במדויק
רק עשרים ושלוש גוויות ולגבי היתר אף שידעו
שהם גופותיהם של שנים עשר הלוחמים האחרים לא
יכלו לקבוע בוודאות מי היא גופת פלוני או אלמוני
ההורים השכולים פנו לרב צבי פסח פראנק רבה
הראשי של ירושלים הרב פראנק שיגר שליח לר'
אריה לוין ובקש ממנו שיערוך גורל והנה שמימית
ומדהימה כשאמרו את שמו של אחד החללים הגיעו
לפסוק לשמו

לשם בנימין בוגולובסקי יצא הפסוק "וממטה
בנימין" בגורל

לעודד בן ימיני יצא הפסוק "הלא בן ימיני"
ליעקב בן עתר יצא הפסוק "כל הנפש הבא ליעקב"
ליוסף ברוך יצא הפסוק "ויאתר יוסף הבו מקניכם"
לאיתן גאון יצא הפסוק "וענה גאון ישראל"
לאליהו הרשקוביץ יצא הפסוק "ויקח אליהו את
הילד"

ליצחק זבולוני יצא הפסוק "ולזבולון אמר"
לאלכסנדר כהן יצא הפסוק "כהניך ילבשו צדק"
ליעקב כהן יצא הפסוק "נשבע ה' ולא ינחם אתה כהן"
לישראל מרזל יצא הפסוק "גם בבל לנפול חללי
ישראל"

לשאול מנואלי יצא "אתת שאלתי"

### 41) שופטים יד:יב-יג

וַיֹּאמֶר לָהֶם שִׁמְשׁוֹן אָחוּדָה־נָּא לָכֶם חִידָה אִם־הַגֵּד
תַּגִּידוּ אוֹתָהּ לִי שִׁבְעַת יְמֵי הַמִּשְׁתֶּה וּמְצָאתֶם וְנָתַתִּי
לָכֶם שְׁלֹשִׁים סְדִינִים וּשְׁלֹשִׁים חֲלִפֹת בְּגָדִים: וְאִם־
לֹא תוּכְלוּ לְהַגִּיד לִי וּנְתַתֶּם אַתֶּם לִי שְׁלֹשִׁים סְדִינִים
וּשְׁלֹשִׁים חֲלִיפוֹת בְּגָדִים וַיֹּאמְרוּ לוֹ חוּדָה חִידָתְךָ
וְנִשְׁמָעֶנָּה:

### 42) משנה סנהדרין ג:ג

ואלו הן הפסולין, המשחק בקוביא.. אמר רבי יהודה:

---

אימתי בזמן שאין להן אומנות אלא הוא, אבל יש להן
אומנות שלא הוא כשרין.

### 43) סנהדרין כד:

משחק בקוביא מאי קא עביד? אמר רמי בר חמא:
משום דהוה אסמכתא, ואסמכתא לא קניא. רב ששת
אמר: כל כי האי גוונא לאו אסמכתא היא. אלא: לפי
שאין עסוקין ביישובו של עולם. מאי בינייהו? איכא
בינייהו דגמר אומנותא אחריתי. (ותנן) (מסורת
הש"ס: דתנן) אמר רבי יהודה: אימתי בזמן שאין
להן אומנות אלא הוא, אבל יש להן אומנות שלא
הוא (הרי זה) כשרים. אלמא טעמא דמתניתין משום
יישובו של עולם הוא, קשיא לרמי בר חמא וכי תימא
פליגי רבנן עליה דרבי יהודה והא אמר רבי יהושע
בן לוי: כל מקום שאמר רבי יהודה אימתי ובמה אינו
אלא לפרש דברי חכמים.

### 44) פירוש רש"י על סנהדרין כד:

אסמכתא – היינו דבר דאינו נותן לו מדעתו אלא
סומך על דבר שאינו, דסבור שהוא יכול לנצח,
ופעמים שמנצחין אותו.

לא קניא – והוה ליה כעין גזילה בידו.

כל כי האי גוונא לאו אסמכתא הוא – והיכי דמי
אסמכתא כגון דאם אובר ולא אעביד אשלם
במיטבא (בבא מציעא עו, א) וכגון משליש את שטרו
דגט פשוט (בבא בתרא קסח, א) דסומך על לא דבר,
דסבור כל זה בידי לעשות, ומרישא כי מתני אדעתא
דלא יהיב ליה לאסמכתא קא מתני, דטועה וסבור לא
יבא לידי כך, אבל הכא לא סמיך אמידי, דהא לא
ידע אי נצח אי לא נצח, ואפילו הכי אתני שמע מינה
מספיקא אתני גמר ואקני, ולא גזילה היא.

### 45) רמב"ם, הלכות עדות י:ד

ועוד יש שם רשעים שהן פסולין לעדות אע"פ שהן
בני תשלומין ואינן בני מלקות, הואיל ולוקחים ממון
שאינו שלהם בחמס פסולין ... וכן משחק בקוביא
והוא שלא תהיה לו אומנות אלא הוא, הואיל ואינו
עוסק ביישובו של עולם הרי זה בחזקת שאוכל מן
הקוביא שהוא אבק גזל, ולא בקוביא בלבד אלא
אפילו משחקים בקליפי אגוזים וקליפי רומנים, וכן
לא יונים בלבד אמרו אלא אפילו המשחקים בבהמה
חיה ועוף ואומר כל הקודם את חבירו או כל הנוצח
את חבירו יטול כל שעליו את שניהם וכן כל כיוצא
בשחוק זה, והוא שלא תהיה לו אומנות אלא שחוק
זה הרי הוא פסול, וכל אלו פסולין מדבריהם.

### 46) טור, חושן משפט לד

משחקים בקוביא פסולים ולאו דוקא בקוביא אלא
אפי' בכל מיני שחוק אפי' בקליפי רימונים ואגוזים
ודוקא כשאין לו אומנות אחרת אלא הוא והטעם
מפני שאז אינו מתעסק בישובו של עולם ולא ידע
כמה טורח האדם אחר הממון ונקל בעיניו להעיד

שנאמר "תמים תהיה עם ה"א" וזה שייך רק בגורלות
אדלהבא ולא בגורלות שבא להכריע למי לתת הזכות
בה וב"כ הגרש"ק בשו"ת אלף לך שלמה (סי' ס"ב)
להשואל ששאל אותו איך נוהגין להטיל גורל בקדיש
הא נפסק להלכה דאין שואלין בגורלות והשיב ע"ז
דכוונת השו"ע הוא רק על שאלות בגורלות עד
להבא כגון אם יהיה חולה או אם ימצא האבידה
וכיו"ב אבל להפיס בין ב' ענינים איזה מהם שייך לזה
או לזה ודאי שרי ואין שייך לומר בזה "תמים תהיה"
שהרי בביהמ"ק היו מפייסין מי שוחט וכו' ...

גורל שאינו לדעת ע"י זה עתידות אם זה אסור
ב ועתה נעמוד נא על המחקר בסוג גורל ששם ב'
פתקים בקלפי ובאחד כתוב לעשות או לילך בדבר
שעומד עתה על הפרק וכד'. ובהשני כתב לא
לעשות או שלא לילך אם גם זה בכלל אסור לשאול
בגורלות האי' בשו"ע יו"ד ושם הנה מצד הסברא
נראה דהא דאסור לשאול בגורלות הוא דוקא
כשרוצה לדעת ע"י זה היצלח דרכו או לא וזה אסור
משום דכתיב תמים תהיה עם ה"א ... משא"כ באדם
שעומד לו עתה ב' אפשרויות ואינו יודע להחליט
ומה להעדיף ומה לדחות שפיר רשאי לעשות גורל
וכפי אשר יצא מהגורל כן יעשה דכפי הנראה כן הוא
רצון הבוב"ה ...

### 33) גיטין סח.

כי קא נפיק, כרו ליה בירא ושדו ליה ציפתא עילויה,
ואמרי ליה: ליתי מר לינח, נחר ליה רב חסדא
מאחוריה, אמר ליה לינוקא: פסוק לי פסוקיך, אמר
ליה: (שמואל ב' ב') נטה לך על ימינך או על שמאלך.
אמר ליה לשמעיה: מאי קא חזית? אמר ליה: ציפיתא
דשידיא, אמר ליה: הדר מינה. לבתר דנפק, אמר ליה
רב חסדא: מנא הוה ידע מר? אמר ליה: חדא, דנחר
לי מר ועוד, דפסק לי ינוקא פסוקא ועוד, דחשידי
עבדי דלא מעלו.

### 34) חולין צה:

רב בדיק במברא, ושמואל בדיק בספרא, רבי יוחנן
בדיק בינוקא.

### 35) מדרש אסתר רבה ז:יג

ובשעה שנחתמו אותן האגרות ונתנו ביד המן ויבא
שמח הוא וכל בני חבורתו ופגעו במרדכי שהוא
הולך לפניהם וראה מרדכי שלשה תינוקות שהיו
באים מבית הספר ורץ מרדכי אחריהם וכשראה
המן וכל חבורתו שהיה רץ מרדכי אחרי התינוקות
הלכו אחרי מרדכי לדעת מה ישאל מרדכי מהם כיון
שהגיע מרדכי אצל התינוקות שאל לאחד מהם פסוק
לי פסוקיך א"ל (משלי ג') אל תירא מפחד פתאום
ומשואת רשעים כי תבא פתח השני ואמר אני קריתי
היום ובזה הפסוק עמדתי מבית הספר (ישעיה ח')
עוצו עצה ותופר דברו דבר ולא יקום כי עמנו אל
פתח השלישי ואמר (שם מ"ו) ועד זקנה אני הוא ועד

---

שיבה אני אסבול אני עשיתי ואני אשא ואני אסבול
ואמלט כיון ששמע מרדכי כך שחק והיה שמח שמחה
גדולה

### 36) פירוש ט"ז על שולחן ערוך, יורה דעה קעט:ב
... ופסוק לי פסוקיך הוי כעין נבואה קטנה

### 37) פירוש ש"ך על שולחן ערוך, יורה דעה קעט:ה
וכן מותר כו' – משמע דעת הרב והפוסקים דאפי'
לעשות מעשה ולסמוך עליו לעתיד על הפסוק מותר
דחשיב קצת נבואה

### 38) קובץ תל תלפיות, פסח תשס"ז
גורל על ידי פתיחת ספר
ג אך מה דאיכא לעיונא דהנה בברכי יוסף שם ס"ק
י' איתא כתב מהריק"ש נ"ל דלכו"ע מותר לפתוח
בתורה לראות הפסוק העולה כי היא חיינו וכמו
ששמעינו ביאשיה מעשה על שמצא ס"ת גלול
באותו פסוק וכן עמא דבר עכ"ל וע"כ הברכ"י שם
וז"ל והנה אמרו בילקוט משלי (סדי"ט) אם בקשת
ליטול עצה מן התורה הוי נוטל וכן בדוד הוא
אומר בפיקודיך אשיחה עכ"ל ומשמע דליטול עצה
מן התורה אפשר דבכלל זה הוא לפתוח בתורה
ולראות פסוק המזדמן ומצאתי בקונטרס כ"י להרב
מהר"ר אליהו הכהן ז"ל בעל שבט מוסר שכתב וז"ל
קבלתי מרבותי כשהיו רוצים לעשות איזה דבר והיו
מסופקים אם לעשותו אם לאו היו נוטלים חומש או
נ"ך והיו פותחים אותו ורואים בראש הדף מה פסוק
היה מוצא וכפי מה שמראה אותו פסוק היו עושים
... מה שמראה אותו פסוק כן היו עושים ונמצא
שהיו מתיעצים עם התורה כדת מה לעשות בכל
עניניהם וזה עצמם רומז מאמרם ז"ל ליטול עצה מן
התורה אפשר ...

### 39) גדולי הדורות, הרב יחיאל מיכל שטרן, דף 253
כך מספר הרמ"מ ישר שהחפץ חיים השתמש לפרקים
בגורל זה והיה מתענה אותו היום, היה זה כאשר
לטובת ישיבתו בראדין היה על החפץ חיים לנסוע
למרכזים הרוסיים המרוחקים לצורך אסיפת כספים
ונרתע מפני נסיעה וו ומן רב היסס ולבסוף השתמש
בגורל הגר"א ועלה בגורל הפסוק "אנכי ארד עמך
מצרימה ואנכי אעלך גם עלה" והיו נחשבים בעיניו
תשובות אלו כדברי נבואה _תולדות החפץ חיים).
כך השתמש בזה גם הגרי"ז סאלווייציק מבריסק
כשנקלע לוילנא עם פרוץ מלחמת העולם השניה
ונסתפק אם לנסוע לארץ ישראל או לארה"ב, החליט
להטיל גורל הגר"א ועלה בגורל הפסוק "יעלו הרים
ירדו בקעות אל מקום זה יסדת להם" סוף הפסוק –
מקום זה יסדת להם וכ"י דרך היבשה
דרך סוריה ולבנון לא"י בנסיעתו זו נסע בדרך
שעלתה למרומי הרים וירדה בקעות, ואז אמר הרב

---

ראינו מן התורה ומן נביאים וכתבים שסמכו על
הגורל באשר נעשה בלי מחשבות אדם ופעולת אנוש
מצד התחכמות "אך בגורל תחלק הארץ" וכן סמכו
על הגורל במיתת עכן ויונתן לולא שפדאוהו העם לא
מצד הוראתו ונאמר בחוק יוטל הגורל ומהשם כל
משפטו, ואף באומות העולם היה מקובל זה כמו גבי
יונה והמן הרשע לפשטיה דקרא מפני שקרוב הדבר
שאם הגורל כהוגן ידבק בו השגחה עליונה מה שאין
כן אם הגורל מקולקל אין מבוא לומר שמי שזכה
מאת ה' היתה זאת הן שהקליקול על ידי תחבולת
אנוש או בשגגה על כל פנים הגורל ...

### (25) שולחן ערוך, יורה דעה קעט:א

אין שואלין בחוזים בכוכבים ולא בגורלות (הגה
משום שנאמר תמים תהיה עם ה' אלקיך (ב"י בשם
תוספות דע"פ ובשם ספרי) ...

### (26) פירוש בית יוסף על טור יו"ד סימן קעט

דאיתא בספרי מנין שאין שואלין בגורלות שנאמר
(דברים יח יג) תמים תהיה

### (27) דברים יח:יג ופירוש רש"י שם

תָּמִים תִּהְיֶה עִם ד' אֱלֹקֶיךָ:
תמים תהיה עם ה' אלקיך- התהלך עמו בתמימות
ותצפה לו, ולא תחקור אחר העתידות, אלא כל מה
שיבוא עליך קבל בתמימות, ואז תהיה עמו ולחלקו:

### (28) שו"ת יביע אומר חלק ו, חושן משפט ד

... ותמיהני שאיך יתכן לסמוך על הגורל בדיני
נפשות, שהרי אפי' בממון אמרינן דהוי אסמכתא
דלא קניא, כ"ש בעניין נפשות. והראיות שהביא
אינם ראיות כלל ... ואעיקרא אין להביא ראיה מן
המלחים שהיו עכו"ם שעשו מה כפי ההלכה שלנו ...
עכ"פ הרי שלחן ערוך לפנינו וגמרא ערוכה דלא
מהני גורל לשום עניין אפי' בדיני ממונות, ויש לו דין
אסמכתא ... וממחוורתא שר' יהודה החסיד חזר בו
ממ"ש (בסי' תרעד), והסכים (בסי' תש"א) שבזה"ז
אין לעשות מעשה כזה ... כלל העולה מכל הנ"ל
שאין לסמוך בנ"ד על הגורל שנעשה על דעת חברי
הגוף הבוחר למנות התח שזכה בגורל לרב העיר,
ועליהם להתאסף שנית לבחור ברוב דעות את
המועמד שיראה בעיניהם כמתאים למשרה רמה זו.
וקרוב אני לומר שאפי' אם הגורל נעשה גם בהסכמת
שני המועמדים, לא מהני הגורל

### (29) פתחי תשובה על שולחן ערוך, יורה דעה סימן קנז ס"ק יג

תנו לנו א' מכם - בתשובת נו"ב תניינא חי"ד סימן
ע"ד נשאל בן המחבר שר שצריך יהודים לעבודתו
ומבקש מהיהודים שימסרו לו איזה נערים אם מותר
למסור לו והשיב דפשוט שאסור ואף אם יש איזה
נערים קלים ופרוצים ביותר אין אנו יכולים לדון

דיני נפשות והרבה הילדות עושה וניתן להענישם
בתפיסה אבל חלילה למסור אותם להדיחם לגמרי
מקהל ישראל ובפרט שלא נתברר בעדות ברורה אם
עברו עבירה חמורה לכן שארית ישראל לא יעשו
עולה כזו אך את זה יכולים לעשות להשתדל על פירוש
כשר שלא יקחו אותו כי כ"ז שלא אמרו בפירוש שאותו
הם מבקשים אבל אם כבר בא על הפקודה על אחד
קשה להורות להשתדל עבורו ובד"ז קשה להורות
וע"ז אמרו חז"ל כשם שמצוה לומר דבר הנשמע
כו' והמשכיל בעת ההיא ידום אבל עכ"פ מחוייבים
למחות ביד מי שרוצה למסור בידים ע"ש ועיין
בתשובת יד אליהו ס"ס מ"ג ועיין בס' תפארת למשה
שכתב דעל פי גורל שרי כעובדא דיונה וגבעונים
וסרח בת אשר ע"ש:

### (30) חזון איש, הלכות עבודה זרה סח

בפתחי תשובה הביא בשם התפל"מ דע"פ הגורל
אפשר למסור את היחיד כמו שמצינו אצל יונה.
תמוה דא"כ למה תני בתוספתא ובירושלמי יהרגו
כולם ואל ימסרו הו"ל למתמני יפילו גורל ...

### (31) מנחת אשר, חלק ד, חומש במדבר סימן עב

... ברם במקום אחר (אות תש"א) כתב (ר, יהודה
החסיד) דיורדי הים שנקלעו לסערת ים שמותר להם
להטיל גורל לפי שדורות הראשונים מסור היה בידם
סוד הגורל וידעו ותכונתו ומשפטו ואולם בדורות
האחרונים שנסתתמו מעיינות החכמה חלילה לנו
מעשות כדבר הזה וכ"כ בכנסת הגדולה חו"מ ס'
קע"ג'גולוקאורה סתר הספר חסדים את משנתו בהלכה
זו. ונראה בזה דהא דכתב למנוע הגורל (אות תש"א)
הוא במקום שנקלעו על פי דרך הטבע לסערה בלב
ים ובמקום סכנה הטבעית נאסרו בהטלת גורל
... אמנם ביו"ד סימן קע"ט ס"א שנינו אין שואלין
בחוזים בכוכבים ולא
בגורלות הרי דאסור לשאול בגורל ופשוט דאין
איסור אלא לשאול עתידות וכד' דומיא דחוזים
בכוכבים וזה אסור
משום תמים תהיה כמ"ש שם הרמ"א וכ"כ בספר
חסד לאלפים לבעל הפלא יועץ אות ד' וז"ל למעבד
בלי צורך למען לדעת עתידות לא אריך למעבד
הכי הולך בתום ילך בטח" (משלי י:ט) ואין זה עניין
לחלוקת ממון ע"י גורל ומ"מ פשוט להלכה ולמעשה
ראין תוקף בגורל אלא בחלוקת ממון עפ"י הסכמה
ולא בשום עניין אחר.

### (32) קובץ תל תלפיות, פסח תשס"ז

בדין אם מותר להשתמש בגורל שיהיה
הכרעה בהספק שעומד לו על הפרק
א הנה נפסק להלכה ביו"ד ס' קע"ט ס"א דאין
שואלין בגורלות והנה פשוט הדבר בכלל יד יי-
שעושים גורל למי לתת הזכות בחפץ וכדומ...
כל האיסור לשאול בגורלות הוא משום שזה נגד למה

שוות כגון ת' והאחרים יש להם מנין הפחות מזה
אז בטל גורל וצריכים כולם להטיל גורל מחדש ...
ב' או ג' שהפילו גורל ולמחרת בא עוד אחד בטלה
החלוקה וצריכין להטיל גורל מחדש כמ"ש בח"מ סי'
קע"ה ס"ג. ב' אחין שחלקו ובא להן אח ממדינת הים
בטלה החלוקה ואם היה בעיר ולא בא איבד זכותו
(") דמדלא בא ודאי מחל להן שיהיה אחרון כמ"ש
בח"מ סי' קע"ו סכ"ה ...

### 18) משלי טז:לג
בַּחֵיק יוּטַל אֶת־הַגּוֹרָל וּמֵד' כָּל־מִשְׁפָּטוֹ:

### 19) פירוש רש"י על במדבר כו:נד
לרב תרבה נחלתו – ... והגורל היה על פי רוח
הקודש ...

### 20) שו"ת יביע אומר חלק ו – חושן משפט ד
... וחזות קשה הוגד לי בשו"ת גאוני קדמאי (סי'
ס) וז"ל: יורשים שרצו למכור ירושתם מדעת כולם
ולא רצה אחד מהם למכור חלקו, מה הדין? תשובה,
הרשות בידו ויהיה לו חלקו, ואין יכולים אחיו למכור
חלקו. ואם אין חלקו מבורר מפילין גורלות, ובכל
מקום שיפול הגורל יטלנו, ואין רשות לאדם מישראל
לעבור על הגורל, **שאין הגורל אלא מפי שמים, שנא'**
**על פי הגורל תחלק הארץ, והעובר על הגורל כעובר**
**על עשרת הדברות. עכ"ל.**

### 21) ספר חסידים תרעט
בני אדם שעוברים בים, ועמדה עליהם רוח סערה
לשבר הספינה, או להטביעה בים, ושאר הספינות
עוברות בשלום, בידוע שיש בספינה מי שחייב,
ורשאים להפיל גורלות, על מי שיפול הגורל ג'
פעמים זה אחר זה, רשאים להפילו בים, ומתפללים
שלא יפול על הזכאי אלא על החייב, שנאמר (ש"א
יד מא) ה' אלקי ישראל הבה תמים, וכתיב (יונה א
ז) ויפול הגורל על יונה, וכתיב (שם שם יב) שאוני
והטילוני אל הים, ולמה לא אמרו לו ליונה תשליך
עצמך אל הים, אלא לא רצה להשליך עצמו. ועוד
גוים היו בספינה, ומוטב שישליכוהו הם. ואם יש שם
כלי או עריבה קטנה, אל ישליכוהו בים אלא יתנוהו
שם באותה כלי ואם ינצל ינצל. קודם שנכנסים בים
אם יבא רוח סערה, מי שחטא בדבר שיש בו סקילה
אפי' בשוגג, שיפילו גורלות, ועל שיפול להטילו בים
לא יפרוש בים:

### 22) ספר חסידים תשא
בני אדם שבספינה והיה רוח סערה, אין רשאים
להפיל גורלות, שאם יפול על אחד מהם צריך
להטילו בים, אין זה לעשות כאשר עשו ליונה בן
אמיתי, השתא אסמכתא לא קניא לענין ממון, וכ"ש
לענין נפשות שלא יסמכו ע"פ הגורל, ואשר כתיב
(ש"א יד מב) ויאמר שאול הפילו בינו ובין יהונתן

בנו וילכד יהונתן, שם היה ארון ומה' כל משפט,
והם ידעו באיזה ענין להטיל, אבל עתה אין לסמוך
על הגורל, שנאמר (יהושע יח ו) ויריתי לכם גורל
פה לפני ה' אלקינו. ואפי' בממון אין מפילים גורל
אלא כשחולקים בשוה, אבל אין משמין שתי חתיכות
כנגד חתיכה אחת אא"כ שום שתיהן כאחת, ולא
חתיכה גדולה כנגד חתיכה קטנה אלא בשוה באומד
הדעת. ולפי שהיו צריכים שני שעירי יום הכפורים
גורל, לכך היו שוים במראה ובקומה:

### 23) שו"ת חוות יאיר, סא
... מ"מ גורל שאני דבלה"ן מסוגל להשגחה ע' שו"ת
גאוני קדמאי (סי' ס) שאין הגורל אלא מפי שמים
שנא' "עפ"י הגורל תחלק הארץ" והעובר על הגורל
כעובר על עשרת הדברות. כי ראינו מן התורה ומן
הנביאים ומן הכתובים שסמכו על הגורל באשר נעשה
בלי מחשבות אדם ופעולות אנוש מצד התחכמות אך
בגורל תחלק הארץ וכן סמכו על הגורל במיתת עכן
ויונתן לולי שפדאוהו העם אם לא מצד הודאתו ונאמר
בחיק יוטל הגורל ומה' כל משפטו ואפילו בא"ה היה
מקובל זה כמו גבי יונה והמן הרשע לפשטי' דקרא
+ע' תשו' בעל יד דוד בתשו' מגד שמים סימן י"ד
שדחה דברי המחבר משום שעכן הודה מעצמו, ועוד
דהתם עפ"י הדיבור הוי. מפני שקרוב הדבר שאם
הגורל כהוגן ידבק בו השגחה עליונה כמ"ש הבה
תמים ...

### 24) שו"ת שדי חמד ח:יד
ואם אפשר לסמוך על הגורל בנפשות היינו בני אדם
שהיו בספינה ועמד נחשול על הים או רוח סערה
לטבעה וכמעשה דיונה הנה הרב מדרש תלפיות
בענף גורל עמד בסתירת דברי ספר החסידים דבס'
תש"א כתב השתא אסמכתא לא קניא לענין ממון כל
שכן לענין נפשות שלא יסמכו על הגורל, ומה שאמר
שאול להפיל גורלות בינו ובין יונתן בנו וילכד יונתן
שם היה ארון ומה' כל משפטו והם ידעו באיזה ענין
להפיל אבל עתה אין לסמוך על הגורל וכו' והקש
על זה דבס' תר"ף (תרעט) כתב להיפך וז"ל בני
אדם שעוברים בים ועמד עליהם רוח סערה לשבר
הספינה או להטביע בים ושאר הספינות עוברות
בשלום בידוע שיש בספינה מי שחייב ורשאים להפיל
גורל על פי שיפול הגורל שלשה פעמים זה אחר זה
להטילו לים ומתפללים שלא יפול הגורל על הזכאי
וכו' ותירץ דהתם מדבר שהרוח סערה בכל האניות
שבים בשוה ולכך אין להפיל גורל שמא אין חייב
ביניהם אבל כאן מדבר שכל האניות עוברות בשלום
ודוקא עליהם רוח סערה ענין כזה מורה באצבע שיש
ביניהם גורם הצער כענין יונה ולכך מפילים גורלות
עכ"ל ... וגם הספר חסידים עצמו בסי' תש"א כתב
דאין להפיל גורל על נפש אדם וכו' אמנם התות
יאיר סי' ס"א כתב נגד האמור בענין עכן ויונתן ויונה
ולמד מנייהו לענין ממון והוא פלא עכ"ל ... כי ראינו

חסרים, אברור ששה משבט זה וחמשה משבט זה הריני מטיל קנאה בין השבטים, מה עשה? בירר ששה והביא שבעים ושנים פיתקין, על שבעים כתב זקן ושנים הניח חלק, בללן ונתנן בקלפי, אמר להם: בואו וטלו פיתקיכם כל מי שעלה בידו זקן אמר: כבר קידשך שמים, מי שעלה בידו חלק אמר: המקום לא חפץ בך, אני מה אעשה לך? כיוצא בדבר אתה אומר: (במדבר ג') ולקחת חמשת שקלים לגולגלת, אמר משה: כיצד אעשה להן לישראל? אם אומר לו תן לי פדיונך וצא יאמר לי: כבר פדאני בן לוי. מה עשה? הביא עשרים ושנים אלפים פיתקין, וכתב עליהן בן לוי, ועל שלושה ושבעים ומאתים כתב עליהן חמשה שקלים, בללן ונתנן בקלפי. אמר להן: טלו פיתקיכם. מי שעלה בידו בן לוי אמר לו: כבר פדאך בן לוי. מי שעלה בידו חמשת שקלים, אמר לו: תן פדיונך וצא.

### 10) משנה יומא ב:ב-ג

בראשונה, כל מי שרוצה לתרום את המזבח תורם. ובזמן שהן מרובין רצין ועולין בכבש, כל הקודם את חבירו בארבע אמות זכה. ואם היו שניהן שוין הממונה אומר להן: הצביעו. ומה הן מוציאין ־ אחת או שתים. ואין מוציאין אגודל במקדש. מעשה שהיו שניהם שוין ורצין ועולין בכבש, ודחף אחד מהן את חבירו, ונפל ונשברה רגלו. וכיון שראו בית דין שבאין לידי סכנה, התקינו שלא יהו תורמין את המזבח אלא בפיס: ארבעה פיסות היו שם, וזה הפיס הראשון: הפיס השני, מי שוחט, מי זורק, ומי מדשן מזבח הפנימי, ומי מדשן את המנורה, ומי מעלה אברים לכבש, הראש והרגל, ושתי הידים, העוקץ והרגל, החזה והגרה, ושתי הדפנות, והקרבים, והסולת, והחבתין, והיין. שלושה עשר כהנים זכו בו. אמר בן עזאי לפני רבי עקיבא משום רבי יהושע, דרך הלוכו היה קרב:

### 11) יומא כג.

תנו רבנן: מעשה בשני כהנים שהיו שניהן שוין ורצין ועולין בכבש, קדם אחד מהן לתוך ארבע אמות של חבירו נטל סכין ותקע לו בלבו.

### 12) בבא בתרא קו:

תניא, ר' יוסי אומר: האחין שחלקו, כיון שעלה גורל לאחד מהן קנו כולם.

### 13) רמב"ם, הלכות שכנים יב:א-ב

האחין או השותפין שבאו לחלוק את השדה וליטול כל אחד חלקו אם היתה כולה שוה ואין שם מקום טוב ומקום רע אלא הכל אחד חולקין לפי המדה בלבד, ואם אמר אחד מהם תנו לי חלקי מצד זה כדי שיהא סמוך לשדה אחר שלי ויהיה הכל שדה אחת שומעין לו וכופה אותו על זה שעיכוב בדבר זה מדת סדום היא, אבל אם היה חלק אחד ממנה

---

טוב או קרוב לנהר יותר או קרוב לדרך ושמו אותה היפה כנגד הרע ואמר תנו לי בשומא שלי מצד זה אין שומעין לו אלא נוטל בגורל ...
הבכור שחלק נוטל שני חלקים שלו כאחד אבל היבם שחלק עם אחיו נכסי האב נוטל חלקו וחלק אחיו בגורל, אם עלו במקום אחד עלו ואם עלו בשתי מקומות עלו.

### 14) פירוש לחם משנה על רמב"ם, הלכות שכנים ב:יא

האחין שחלקו ועשו ביניהם גורל כו' – נראה מדברי רשב"ם שהגורל עושה קנין אפילו דלא החזיק וכן נראה מדברי רבינו ז"ל שכתב הטור בסימן קע"ג נראה דלא מהני גורל בלא חזקה וא"ת אם החזיק אפילו בלא גורל נמי כדקאמר רב אשי דאם החזיק קנה ואפילו אחד מהם לבדו וכדכתב הטור בשם אביו וא"כ מאי אהני גורל. וי"ל דכי מהני חזקה היינו כשחלקו קודם ואח"כ החזיק אע"פ שלא קנו ולהכי אהני גורל דאע"ג דלא חלקו אלא שעלה הגורל והלך והחזיק בלא מחאת חבירו קודם החזיקה מהני כאלו חלקו ואח"כ החזיק, זו נ"ל דעת הרא"ש ז"ל ואולי שזו היא כוונת הר"א ז"ל בהשגות שכתב על רבינו ז"ל שלא נתחוורו דבריו אפשר דמשום שהבין כן בדברי רבינו ז"ל שהגורל עושה קנין השיג עליו שאינו כן אלא דצריך חזקה וכסברת הרא"ש ז"ל:

### 15) משנה שבת כג:ב ופירוש תפארת ישראל

מפיס (בשבת) אדם עם בניו ועם בני ביתו על השולחן, ובלבד שלא יתכוין לעשות מנה גדולה כנגד מנה קטנה.
על השלחן – כי כך היה מנהגם לבלי להטיל קנאה בין הבנים, (כשבת דף י' ע"ב), ודוקא בב' לטיבותא, שהחלקים כולן שלו דכוותנו רק שלא להטיל קנאה בין הבנים אבל חדא לטיבותא, שרוצה להגריל בינו לחבירו, אף שהחלקים שוין, עכ"פ מדמקפידין להגריל, דמי למקח וממכר, ולהכי אפילו במגריל בין בניו, וכמ"כ אין החלקים שוין, י"א דאף בחול אסור, משום קוביא, וי"א דבכה"ג אף בשבת שרי.

### 16) שולחן ערוך, אורח חיים שכב:ו

המחלק לבני ביתו מנות בשבת יכול להטיל גורל לומר למי שיצא גורל פלוני יהיה חלק פלוני שלו והוא שיהיו החלקים שוים ואינו עושה אלא כדי להשוותם שלא להטיל קנאה ביניהם ...

### 17) מגן אברהם על שולחן ערוך, אורח חיים תקלב:ב

הגאון בלבוש כתב כאן דיני קדיש והנני מוסיף דבר שנתחדש אצלי כמ"ש רמ"מ סי' פ' בתשובה שהאיר ציצ"ט שלו כל הקדישים של אותו יום אפי' קדיש של פרקים ושל שיר השירים ושל רות עכ"ל ...
כשמטילין גורל ד' או ה' ויש בהן ב' שיש להן אותיות

# SOURCES ON LOTTERIES, GAMBLING, AND BUYING LOTTERY TICKETS – THE JEWISH VIEW

### 1) ויקרא טז:ח

וְנָתַן אַהֲרֹן עַל־שְׁנֵי הַשְּׂעִירִם גֹּרָלוֹת גּוֹרָל אֶחָד לַד' וְגוֹרָל אֶחָד לַעֲזָאזֵל:

### 2) במדבר כה:נד-נה

אַךְ־בְּגוֹרָל יֵחָלֵק אֶת־הָאָרֶץ לִשְׁמוֹת מַטּוֹת־אֲבֹתָם יִנְחָלוּ: עַל־פִּי הַגּוֹרָל תֵּחָלֵק נַחֲלָתוֹ בֵּין רַב לִמְעָט:

### 3) דברי הימים א' כה:ח ופירוש מצודת דוד

וַיַּפִּילוּ גוֹרָלוֹת מִשְׁמֶרֶת לְעֻמַּת כַּקָּטֹן כַּגָּדוֹל מֵבִין עִם־תַּלְמִיד:

**גורלות** – מי ישמש ראשון ועבודתם היה ללנן בכלים. **משמרת לעומת** – כמו משמרת לעומת משמר' וקצר בדבר המובן. **מבין** – היותר נבון בדבר השיר עם מי שצריך להתלמד עוד ולא הועיל לו רוח בינתו להקדימו ראשון:

### 4) יהושע ז:יד-כ

וְנִקְרַבְתֶּם בַּבֹּקֶר לְשִׁבְטֵיכֶם וְהָיָה הַשֵּׁבֶט אֲשֶׁר־יִלְכְּדֶנּוּ ד' יִקְרַב לַמִּשְׁפָּחוֹת וְהַמִּשְׁפָּחָה אֲשֶׁר־יִלְכְּדֶנָּה ד' תִּקְרַב לַבָּתִּים וְהַבַּיִת אֲשֶׁר יִלְכְּדֶנּוּ ד' יִקְרַב לַגְּבָרִים: וְהָיָה הַנִּלְכָּד בַּחֵרֶם יִשָּׂרֵף בָּאֵשׁ אֹתוֹ וְאֶת־כָּל־אֲשֶׁר־לוֹ כִּי עָבַר אֶת־בְּרִית ד' וְכִי־עָשָׂה נְבָלָה בְּיִשְׂרָאֵל: וַיַּשְׁכֵּם יְהוֹשֻׁעַ בַּבֹּקֶר וַיַּקְרֵב אֶת־יִשְׂרָאֵל לִשְׁבָטָיו וַיִּלָּכֵד שֵׁבֶט יְהוּדָה: וַיַּקְרֵב אֶת־מִשְׁפַּחַת יְהוּדָה וַיִּלְכֹּד אֵת מִשְׁפַּחַת הַזַּרְחִי וַיַּקְרֵב אֶת־מִשְׁפַּחַת הַזַּרְחִי לַגְּבָרִים וַיִּלָּכֵד זַבְדִּי: וַיַּקְרֵב אֶת־בֵּיתוֹ לַגְּבָרִים וַיִּלָּכֵד עָכָן בֶּן־כַּרְמִי בֶן־זַבְדִּי בֶּן־זֶרַח לְמַטֵּה יְהוּדָה: וַיֹּאמֶר יְהוֹשֻׁעַ אֶל־עָכָן בְּנִי שִׂים־נָא כָבוֹד לַד' אֱלֹקֵי יִשְׂרָאֵל וְתֶן־לוֹ תוֹדָה וְהַגֶּד־נָא לִי מֶה עָשִׂיתָ אַל־תְּכַחֵד מִמֶּנִּי: וַיַּעַן עָכָן אֶת־יְהוֹשֻׁעַ וַיֹּאמַר אָמְנָה אָנֹכִי חָטָאתִי לַד' אֱלֹקֵי יִשְׂרָאֵל וְכָזֹאת וְכָזֹאת עָשִׂיתִי:

### 5) שופטים כ:ה-יג

וַיָּקֻמוּ עָלַי בַּעֲלֵי הַגִּבְעָה וַיָּסֹבּוּ עָלַי אֶת־הַבַּיִת לָיְלָה אוֹתִי דִּמּוּ לַהֲרֹג וְאֶת־פִּילַגְשִׁי עִנּוּ וַתָּמֹת: וָאֹחֵז בְּפִילַגְשִׁי וָאֲנַתְּחֶהָ וָאֲשַׁלְּחֶהָ בְּכָל־שְׂדֵה נַחֲלַת יִשְׂרָאֵל כִּי עָשׂוּ זִמָּה וּנְבָלָה בְּיִשְׂרָאֵל: הִנֵּה כֻלְּכֶם בְּנֵי יִשְׂרָאֵל הָבוּ לָכֶם דָּבָר וְעֵצָה הֲלֹם: וַיָּקָם כָּל־הָעָם כְּאִישׁ אֶחָד לֵאמֹר לֹא נֵלֵךְ אִישׁ לְאָהֳלוֹ וְלֹא נָסוּר אִישׁ לְבֵיתוֹ: וְעַתָּה זֶה הַדָּבָר אֲשֶׁר נַעֲשֶׂה לַגִּבְעָה עָלֶיהָ בְּגוֹרָל: וְלָקַחְנוּ עֲשָׂרָה אֲנָשִׁים לַמֵּאָה לְכֹל שִׁבְטֵי יִשְׂרָאֵל וּמֵאָה לָאֶלֶף וְאֶלֶף לָרְבָבָה לָקַחַת צֵדָה לָעָם לַעֲשׂוֹת לְבוֹאָם לְגֶבַע בִּנְיָמִן כְּכָל־הַנְּבָלָה אֲשֶׁר עָשָׂה בְּיִשְׂרָאֵל: וַיֵּאָסֵף כָּל־אִישׁ יִשְׂרָאֵל אֶל־הָעִיר כְּאִישׁ אֶחָד חֲבֵרִים: וַיִּשְׁלְחוּ שִׁבְטֵי יִשְׂרָאֵל אֲנָשִׁים בְּכָל־שִׁבְטֵי בִנְיָמִן לֵאמֹר

---

מָה הָרָעָה הַזֹּאת אֲשֶׁר נִהְיְתָה בָּכֶם: וְעַתָּה תְּנוּ אֶת־הָאֲנָשִׁים בְּנֵי־בְלִיַּעַל אֲשֶׁר בַּגִּבְעָה וּנְמִיתֵם וּנְבַעֲרָה רָעָה מִיִּשְׂרָאֵל וְלֹא אָבוּ [בְּנֵי] בִּנְיָמִן לִשְׁמֹעַ בְּקוֹל אֲחֵיהֶם בְּנֵי־יִשְׂרָאֵל:

### 6) שמואל א' יד:מא-מו

וַיֹּאמֶר שָׁאוּל אֶל־ד' אֱלֹקֵי יִשְׂרָאֵל הָבָה תָמִים וַיִּלָּכֵד יוֹנָתָן וְשָׁאוּל וְהָעָם יָצָאוּ: וַיֹּאמֶר שָׁאוּל הַפִּילוּ בֵּינִי וּבֵין יוֹנָתָן בְּנִי וַיִּלָּכֵד יוֹנָתָן: וַיֹּאמֶר שָׁאוּל אֶל־יוֹנָתָן הַגִּידָה לִּי מֶה עָשִׂיתָה וַיַּגֶּד־לוֹ יוֹנָתָן וַיֹּאמֶר טָעֹם טָעַמְתִּי בְּקָצֵה הַמַּטֶּה אֲשֶׁר־בְּיָדִי מְעַט דְּבַשׁ הִנְנִי אָמוּת: וַיֹּאמֶר שָׁאוּל כֹּה־יַעֲשֶׂה אֱלֹקִים וְכֹה יוֹסִף כִּי־מוֹת תָּמוּת יוֹנָתָן: וַיֹּאמֶר הָעָם אֶל־שָׁאוּל הֲיוֹנָתָן יָמוּת אֲשֶׁר עָשָׂה הַיְשׁוּעָה הַגְּדוֹלָה הַזֹּאת בְּיִשְׂרָאֵל חָלִילָה חַי־ד' אִם־יִפֹּל מִשַּׂעֲרַת רֹאשׁוֹ אַרְצָה כִּי־עִם־אֱלֹקִים עָשָׂה הַיּוֹם הַזֶּה וַיִּפְדּוּ הָעָם אֶת־יוֹנָתָן וְלֹא־מֵת: וַיַּעַל שָׁאוּל מֵאַחֲרֵי פְּלִשְׁתִּים וּפְלִשְׁתִּים הָלְכוּ לִמְקוֹמָם:

### 7) יונה א:ד-ז

וַד' הֵטִיל רוּחַ־גְּדוֹלָה אֶל־הַיָּם וַיְהִי סַעַר־גָּדוֹל בַּיָּם וְהָאֳנִיָּה חִשְּׁבָה לְהִשָּׁבֵר: וַיִּירְאוּ הַמַּלָּחִים וַיִּזְעֲקוּ אִישׁ אֶל־אֱלֹהָיו וַיָּטִלוּ אֶת־הַכֵּלִים אֲשֶׁר בָּאֳנִיָּה אֶל־הַיָּם לְהָקֵל מֵעֲלֵיהֶם וְיוֹנָה יָרַד אֶל־יַרְכְּתֵי הַסְּפִינָה וַיִּשְׁכַּב וַיֵּרָדַם: וַיִּקְרַב אֵלָיו רַב הַחֹבֵל וַיֹּאמֶר לוֹ מַה־לְּךָ נִרְדָּם קוּם קְרָא אֶל־אֱלֹקֶיךָ אוּלַי יִתְעַשֵּׁת הָאֱלֹהִים לָנוּ וְלֹא נֹאבֵד: וַיֹּאמְרוּ אִישׁ אֶל־רֵעֵהוּ לְכוּ וְנַפִּילָה גוֹרָלוֹת וְנֵדְעָה בְּשֶׁלְּמִי הָרָעָה הַזֹּאת לָנוּ וַיַּפִּלוּ גּוֹרָלוֹת וַיִּפֹּל הַגּוֹרָל עַל־יוֹנָה:

### 8) אסתר ג:ז, ט:כד-כו

בַּחֹדֶשׁ הָרִאשׁוֹן הוּא־חֹדֶשׁ נִיסָן בִּשְׁנַת שְׁתֵּים עֶשְׂרֵה לַמֶּלֶךְ אֲחַשְׁוֵרוֹשׁ הִפִּיל פּוּר הוּא הַגּוֹרָל לִפְנֵי הָמָן מִיּוֹם לְיוֹם וּמֵחֹדֶשׁ לְחֹדֶשׁ שְׁנֵים־עָשָׂר הוּא־חֹדֶשׁ אֲדָר:

כִּי הָמָן בֶּן־הַמְּדָתָא הָאֲגָגִי צֹרֵר כָּל־הַיְּהוּדִים חָשַׁב עַל־הַיְּהוּדִים לְאַבְּדָם וְהִפִּיל פּוּר הוּא הַגּוֹרָל לְהֻמָּם וּלְאַבְּדָם: וּבְבֹאָהּ לִפְנֵי הַמֶּלֶךְ אָמַר עִם־הַסֵּפֶר יָשׁוּב מַחֲשַׁבְתּוֹ הָרָעָה אֲשֶׁר־חָשַׁב עַל־הַיְּהוּדִים עַל־רֹאשׁוֹ וְתָלוּ אֹתוֹ וְאֶת־בָּנָיו עַל־הָעֵץ: עַל־כֵּן קָרְאוּ לַיָּמִים הָאֵלֶּה פוּרִים עַל־שֵׁם הַפּוּר עַל־כֵּן עַל־כָּל־דִּבְרֵי הָאִגֶּרֶת הַזֹּאת וּמָה־רָאוּ עַל־כָּכָה וּמָה הִגִּיעַ אֲלֵיהֶם:

### 9) סנהדרין יז.

שבעה שאמר לו הקדוש ברוך הוא למשה אספה לי שבעים איש מזקני ישראל אמר משה: כיצד אעשה? אברור ששה מכל שבט ושבט נמצאו שנים יתרים, אברור חמשה מכל שבט ושבט נמצאו מכל שבט ושבט נמצאו עשרה

---

במעלה הזאת וכן למעשים ולמצוות התלויים בארץ שהם מעין עבודת הכרם לכרם אולם שלא ככרם העושה ענבים גם במקום אחר אין עם הסגולה יכול להדבק בענין האלוהי כי אם בארץ הזאת:

**16) דברים יא:יג-יז**

וְהָיָה אִם־שָׁמֹעַ תִּשְׁמְעוּ אֶל־מִצְוֹתַי אֲשֶׁר אָנֹכִי מְצַוֶּה אֶתְכֶם הַיּוֹם לְאַהֲבָה אֶת־ד' אֱלֹקֵיכֶם וּלְעָבְדוֹ בְּכָל־לְבַבְכֶם וּבְכָל־נַפְשְׁכֶם: וְנָתַתִּי מְטַר־אַרְצְכֶם בְּעִתּוֹ יוֹרֶה וּמַלְקוֹשׁ וְאָסַפְתָּ דְגָנֶךָ וְתִירֹשְׁךָ וְיִצְהָרֶךָ: וְנָתַתִּי עֵשֶׂב בְּשָׂדְךָ לִבְהֶמְתֶּךָ וְאָכַלְתָּ וְשָׂבָעְתָּ: הִשָּׁמְרוּ לָכֶם פֶּן־יִפְתֶּה לְבַבְכֶם וְסַרְתֶּם וַעֲבַדְתֶּם אֱלֹהִים אֲחֵרִים וְהִשְׁתַּחֲוִיתֶם לָהֶם: וְחָרָה אַף־ד' בָּכֶם וְעָצַר אֶת־הַשָּׁמַיִם וְלֹא־יִהְיֶה מָטָר וְהָאֲדָמָה לֹא תִתֵּן אֶת־יְבוּלָהּ וַאֲבַדְתֶּם מְהֵרָה מֵעַל הָאָרֶץ הַטֹּבָה אֲשֶׁר ד' נֹתֵן לָכֶם:

**17) ויקרא כו:ג-ה**

אִם־בְּחֻקֹּתַי תֵּלֵכוּ וְאֶת־מִצְוֹתַי תִּשְׁמְרוּ וַעֲשִׂיתֶם אֹתָם: וְנָתַתִּי גִשְׁמֵיכֶם בְּעִתָּם וְנָתְנָה הָאָרֶץ יְבוּלָהּ וְעֵץ הַשָּׂדֶה יִתֵּן פִּרְיוֹ: וְהִשִּׂיג לָכֶם דַּיִשׁ אֶת־בָּצִיר וּבָצִיר יַשִּׂיג אֶת־זָרַע וַאֲכַלְתֶּם לַחְמְכֶם לָשֹׂבַע וִישַׁבְתֶּם לָבֶטַח בְּאַרְצְכֶם:

**18) ויקרא יח:כה**

וַתִּטְמָא הָאָרֶץ וָאֶפְקֹד עֲוֹנָהּ עָלֶיהָ וַתָּקִא הָאָרֶץ אֶת־יֹשְׁבֶיהָ:

**19) דברים יא:יב**

אֶרֶץ אֲשֶׁר־ד' אֱלֹקֶיךָ דֹּרֵשׁ אֹתָהּ תָּמִיד עֵינֵי ד' אֱלֹקֶיךָ בָּהּ מֵרֵשִׁית הַשָּׁנָה וְעַד אַחֲרִית שָׁנָה:

**20) בראשית יב:א**

וַיֹּאמֶר ד' אֶל־אַבְרָם לֶךְ־לְךָ מֵאַרְצְךָ וּמִמּוֹלַדְתְּךָ וּמִבֵּית אָבִיךָ אֶל־הָאָרֶץ אֲשֶׁר אַרְאֶךָּ:

**21) בראשית יג:טו-יז**

כִּי אֶת־כָּל־הָאָרֶץ אֲשֶׁר־אַתָּה רֹאֶה לְךָ אֶתְּנֶנָּה וּלְזַרְעֲךָ עַד־עוֹלָם: וְשַׂמְתִּי אֶת־זַרְעֲךָ כַּעֲפַר הָאָרֶץ אֲשֶׁר אִם־יוּכַל אִישׁ לִמְנוֹת אֶת־עֲפַר הָאָרֶץ גַּם־זַרְעֲךָ יִמָּנֶה: קוּם הִתְהַלֵּךְ בָּאָרֶץ לְאָרְכָּהּ וּלְרָחְבָּהּ כִּי לְךָ אֶתְּנֶנָּה:

**22) בראשית כו:ג-ד**

גּוּר בָּאָרֶץ הַזֹּאת וְאֶהְיֶה עִמְּךָ וַאֲבָרְכֶךָּ כִּי־לְךָ וּלְזַרְעֲךָ אֶתֵּן אֶת־כָּל־הָאֲרָצֹת הָאֵל וַהֲקִמֹתִי אֶת־הַשְּׁבֻעָה אֲשֶׁר נִשְׁבַּעְתִּי לְאַבְרָהָם אָבִיךָ: וְהִרְבֵּיתִי אֶת־זַרְעֲךָ כְּכוֹכְבֵי הַשָּׁמַיִם וְנָתַתִּי לְזַרְעֲךָ אֵת כָּל־הָאֲרָצֹת הָאֵל וְהִתְבָּרֲכוּ בְזַרְעֲךָ כֹּל גּוֹיֵי הָאָרֶץ:

**23) בראשית כח:יג-יד**

וְהִנֵּה ד' נִצָּב עָלָיו וַיֹּאמַר אֲנִי ד' אֱלֹקֵי אַבְרָהָם אָבִיךָ

---

וֵאלֹקֵי יִצְחָק הָאָרֶץ אֲשֶׁר אַתָּה שֹׁכֵב עָלֶיהָ לְךָ אֶתְּנֶנָּה וּלְזַרְעֶךָ: וְהָיָה זַרְעֲךָ כַּעֲפַר הָאָרֶץ וּפָרַצְתָּ יָמָּה וָקֵדְמָה וְצָפֹנָה וָנֶגְבָּה וְנִבְרְכוּ בְךָ כָּל־מִשְׁפְּחֹת הָאֲדָמָה וּבְזַרְעֶךָ:

**24) פירוש רש"י על בראשית א:א**

בראשית – אמר רבי יצחק לא היה צריך להתחיל את התורה אלא מהחודש הזה לכם שהיא מצוה ראשונה שנצטוו בה ישראל ומה טעם פתח בבראשית משום (תהלים קי"א) כח מעשיו הגיד לעמו לתת להם נחלת גוים שאם יאמרו אומות העולם לישראל ליסטים אתם שכבשתם ארצות שבעה גוים הם אומרים להם כל הארץ של הקב"ה היא הוא בראה ונתנה לאשר ישר בעיניו ברצונו נתנה להם וברצונו נטלה מהם ונתנה לנו:

**25) בבא בתרא ס:**

אמר להן בני בואו ואומר לכם שלא להתאבל כל עיקר אי אפשר שכבר נגזרה גזרה ולהתאבל יותר מדאי אי אפשר שאין גוזרין גזירה על הצבור אא"כ רוב צבור יכולין לעמוד בה דכתיב במארה אתם נארים ואותי אתם קובעים הגוי כולו אלא כך אמרו חכמים סד אדם את ביתו בסיד ומשייר בו דבר מועט וכמה אמר רב יוסף אמה על אמה אמר רב חסדא כנגד הפתח עושה אדם כל צרכי סעודתו ומשייר דבר מועט מאי היא אמר רב פפא כסא דהרסנא עושה אשה כל תכשיטיה ומשיירת דבר מועט מאי היא אמר רב בת צדעא שנאמר אם אשכחך ירושלם תשכח ימיני זכור על ראש שמחתי אמר רב יצחק זה אפר מקלה שבראש חתנים א"ל רב פפא לאביי היכא מנח לה במקום תפילין שנאמר לשום לאבלי ציון לתת להם פאר תחת אפר וכל המתאבל על ירושלים זוכה ורואה בשמחתה

**26) רות א:טז**

אֹמֶר רוּת אַל־תִּפְגְּעִי־בִי לְעָזְבֵךְ לָשׁוּב מֵאַחֲרָיִךְ כִּי אֶל־אֲשֶׁר תֵּלְכִי אֵלֵךְ וּבַאֲשֶׁר תָּלִינִי אָלִין עַמֵּךְ עַמִּי וֵאלֹקַיִךְ אֱלֹקָי:

**27) מדרש מכילתא בשלח י'**

ארבעה נקראו נחלה בית המקדש נקרא נחלה שנאמר בהר נחלתך. ארץ ישראל נקראת נחלה שנאמר (דברים ט"ו) בארץ אשר ה' אלקיך נותן לך נחלה. וכן התורה נקראת נחלה שנאמר (במדבר כ"א) וממתנה נחליאל. וכן ישראל קרויין נחלה שנאמר (יואל ד') עמי ונחלתי ישראל. אמר הקדוש ברוך הוא יבא ישראל שנקראו נחלה ויבנו בית המקדש שנקרא נחלה בזכות התורה שנקראת נחלה

# SOURCES ON LAND OF ISRAEL
## AND THE JEWISH PEOPLE

**1) מדרש, ויקרא רבה יג:ה**
מלמד שאין תורה כתורת ארץ ישראל ואין חכמה כחכמת א"י

**2) תלמוד ירושלמי, ברכות יא:**
ר' יהושע בן לוי אמר לא הזכיר תורה בארץ מחזירין אותו מה טעם ויתן להם ארצות גוים מפני מה בעבור ישמרו חוקיו ותורותיו ינצורו.

**3) חגיגה ה:**
כיון שגלו ישראל ממקומן אין לך ביטול תורה גדול מזה

**4) מדרש, שמות רבה ב:ב**
וראה מה כורש אומר (עזרא א) אל האלקים אשר בירושלים אמר להן אע"פ שהוא חרב האלהים אינו זז משם א"ר אחא לעולם אין השכינה זזה מכותל מערבי שנאמר (שיר ב) הנה זה עומד אחר כתלנו

**5) מדרש, ויקרא רבה (מרגליות) יג:ב**
מדד הקב"ה בכל ההרים ולא מצא הר שתתשרה שכינה עליו אלא הר המורייה מדד הקב"ה בכל עיירות ולא מצא עיר שיבנה בה בית המקדש אלא ירושלם

**6) משנה כלים א:ו**
עשר קדושות הן. ארץ ישראל מקודשת מכל הארצות.

**7) רמב"ם, הלכות בית הבחירה ב:ב**
ומסורת ביד הכל שהמקום שבנה בו דוד ושלמה המזבח בגורן ארונה הוא המקום שבנה בו אברהם המזבח ועקד עליו יצחק והוא המקום שבנה בו נח כשיצא מן התיבה והוא המזבח שהקריב עליו קין והבל ובו הקריב אדם הראשון קרבן כשנברא ומשם נברא אמרו חכמים אדם ממקום כפרתו נברא:

**8) פירוש רש"י על בראשית כח:יא**
ויפגע במקום – לא הזכיר הכתוב באיזה מקום אלא במקום הנזכר במקום אחר הוא הר המוריה שנ' בו וירא את המקום מרחוק:
ויפגע – כמו (יהושע טז) ופגע ביריחו ופגע בדבשתה (ברכות כז) ורבותינו פירשו לשון תפלה

**9) פסחים ח:**
דאמר רבי אמי כל אדם שיש לו קרקע עולה לרגל ושאין לו קרקע אין עולה לרגל

**10) דברים טז:ז**
וּבִשַּׁלְתָּ וְאָכַלְתָּ בַּמָּקוֹם אֲשֶׁר יִבְחַר ד' אֱלֹקֶיךָ בּוֹ וּפָנִיתָ בַבֹּקֶר וְהָלַכְתָּ לְאֹהָלֶיךָ:

**11) מדרש ספרי, עקב ז, פירוש רש"י על דברים יא:יח**
ד"א ואבדתם מהרה: אע"פ שאני מגלה אתכם מן הארץ לח"ל היו מצויינים במצות שכשאתם חוזרים לא יהיו לכם חדשים. משל למלך שכעס על אשתו וחזר' בבית אביה אמר לה הוי מקושט' בתכשיטיך וכשתחזרי לא יהו עליך חדשים כך אמר להם הקב"ה לישראל בני היו מצויינים במצות שכשאת' חוזרים לא יהיו עליכם חדשים שירמיהו אמר (ירמיה לא) הציבי לך ציונים אלו המצות שישראל מצויינים בהם. ושמתם את דברי – אף לאחר שתגלו היו מצויינים במצות הניחו תפילין עשו מזוזות כדי שלא יהיו לכם חדשים כשתחזרו וכן הוא אומר הציבי לך ציונים:

**12) דברים ד:א**
וְעַתָּה יִשְׂרָאֵל שְׁמַע אֶל הַחֻקִּים וְאֶל הַמִּשְׁפָּטִים אֲשֶׁר אָנֹכִי מְלַמֵּד אֶתְכֶם לַעֲשׂוֹת לְמַעַן תִּחְיוּ וּבָאתֶם וִירִשְׁתֶּם אֶת הָאָרֶץ אֲשֶׁר ד' אֱלֹקֵי אֲבֹתֵיכֶם נֹתֵן לָכֶם:

**13) סוטה יד.**
דרש רבי שמלאי מפני מה נתאוה משה רבינו ליכנס לא"י וכי לאכול מפריה הוא צריך או לשבוע מטובה הוא צריך אלא כך אמר משה הרבה מצות נצטוו ישראל ואין מתקיימין אלא בא"י אכנס אני לארץ כדי שיתקיימו כולן

**14) כתובות קי':**
לעולם ידור אדם בא"י אפי' בעיר שרובה עובדי כוכבים ואל ידור בחוץ לארץ ואפילו בעיר שרובה ישראל שכל הדר בארץ ישראל דומה כמי שיש לו אלוה וכל הדר בחוצה לארץ דומה כמי שאין לו אלוה

**15) ספר כוזרי ב:יא-יב**
(יא) אמר הכוזרי: אולם אני לא שמעתי כי יש לאנשי ארץ ישראל יתרון על שאר בני אדם:
(יב) אמר החבר: כך גם הכרם זה שאתם אומרים כי הכרם מצליח בו לולא היו נוטעים בו את הגפנים ועושים את כל מלאכת עבודת הכרם הדרושה לגדולים לא היה עושה ענבים והנה המעלה המיוחדת באה ראשונה לעם אשר הוא הסגלה והגרעין (כמו שהזכרתי למעלה) ואחרי זה גם יש לארץ חלק

**45) דברים א:כז**
וַתֵּרָגְנוּ בְאָהֳלֵיכֶם וַתֹּאמְרוּ בְּשִׂנְאַת ד' אֹתָנוּ הוֹצִיאָנוּ מֵאֶרֶץ מִצְרָיִם לָתֵת אֹתָנוּ בְּיַד הָאֱמֹרִי לְהַשְׁמִידֵנוּ:

**46) ברכות ס:**
אמר רב הונא ... לעולם יהא אדם רגיל לומר כל דעביד רחמנא לטב עביד. כי הא, דרבי עקיבא דהוה קאזיל באורחא, מטא להההיא מתא, בעא אושפיזא לא יהבי ליה. אמר: כל דעביד רחמנא לטב. אזל ובת בדברא, והוה בהדיה תרנגולא וחמרא ושרגא. אתא זיקא כבייה לשרגא, אתא שונרא אכליה לתרנגולא, אתא אריה אכלא לחמרא. אמר: כל דעביד רחמנא לטב. ביה בליליא אתא גייסא, שבייה למתא. אמר להו: לאו אמרי לכו כל מה שעושה הקדוש ברוך הוא הכל לטובה.

**47) תענית כא.**
ואמאי קרו ליה נחום איש גם זו דכל מילתא דהוה סלקא ליה אמר גם זו לטובה.

**48) שולחן ערוך, אורח חיים רלו:ה**
לעולם יהא אדם רגיל לומר כל מה דעביד רחמנא לטב עביד:

**49) משנה אבות ב:יג**
ואל תהי רשע בפני עצמך:

**50) פירוש רמב"ם על משנה אבות ב:יג**
ואל תהי רשע בפני עצמך – כשיחשוב אדם עצמו חסר ופחות לא יגדל בעיניו חסרון שיעשהו

**51) פירוש רבינו יונה, שערי עבודה, פתיחה**
פתח הראשון הוא שידע האיש העובד ערך עצמו ויכיר מעלתו ומעלת אבותיו וגדולתם וחשיבותם וחבתם אצל הבורא יתברך. וישתדל ויתחזק תמיד להעמיד עצמו במעלה ההיא ולהתנהג בה תמיד בכל יום ויום יוסיף אומץ לקנות מעלות ומדות אשר יתקרב בהם לבוראו וידבק אליו.

וירץ לקראתו- כסבור ממון הוא פ' טעון, שהרי עבד
הבית בא לכאן בעשרה גמלים טעונים (ב"ר שם):

ויחבק- כשלא ראה עמו כלום, אמר, שמא זהובים
הביא והנם בחיקו (ב"ר שם):

וינשק לו - אמר, שמא מרגליות הביא והם בפיו
(ב"ר שם):

### 36) משנה יומא א:ה

מסרוהו זקני בית דין לזקני כהונה, והעלוהו לעלית
בית אבטינס, והשביעוהו ונפטרו והלכו להם. ואמרו
לו, אישי כהן גדול, אנו שלוחי בית דין, ואתה שלוחנו
ושליח בית דין, משביעין אנו עליך במי ששכן שמו
בבית הזה, שלא תשנה דבר מכל מה שאמרנו לך. הוא
פורש ובוכה, והן פורשין ובוכין:

### 37) יומא יט

הוא פורש ובוכה - שחשדוהו צדוקי, והם פורשין
ובוכין דאמר רבי יהושע בן לוי: כל החושד בכשרים
לוקה בגופו.

### 38) פירוש רש"י על

שחשדוהו צדוקי - לתקן הקטורת ולתת אותה על
מחתת האש בהיכל, ולהכניסה אחרי כן לבית קדשי
הקדשים, שכן אומרים הצדוקים, כדלקמן:
**החושד בכשרים לוקה בגופו** - דכתיב (שמות פרק ד)
הן לא יאמינו לי וגו' וכתיב והנה ידו מצורעת כשלג:

### 39) פירוש רבינו יונה משנה אבות א:ו

והוי דן את כל האדם לכף זכות - ... אבל אין הדברים
... ברשע גמור ... גם מן הרשע הגמור לא אמר, כי
אם אפילו מעשיו כלו טוב, ואין נראה עליו
משום צד וענין, יש לאדם לדונו לכף חובה ולומר,
לפנים עשה ואין תוכו כברו, וכמו שנאמר (משלי
כו, כה), "כי יחנן קולו אל תאמן בו כי שבע תועבות
בלבו". וכן כתב הרב רבינו משה בן מימון זצ"ל. ועל
ענין זה אמר שלמה בחכמתו (משלי כא, יב), "משכיל
צדיק לבית רשע, מסלף רשעים לרע", ר"ל בני אדם
חושבים כי הצדיקים מפני שאינם יודעים לעשות
רע אינם מכירים דרכי רשע, כי לא יבינו העושים
אותו, ואין הדבר כן, כי הצדיק, "משכיל לבית רשע"
יודע ומכיר ומשגיח רוע מעלליו יותר משאר בני
אדם שאינם קפדים בדבר כל כך ולא יתנו אותו אל
לבם, "מסלף רשעים לרע", הצדיק כשרואה מעשה
רשעים הנראים בדרך טוב, מסלף אותו ומטהו לרע,
לאמר, פעל און, כי לא נתכוון למצוה, אך לשום
עצמו בחזקת הטובים:

### 40) ספר חפץ חיים, איסורי לשון הרע ג:ח

ח. וַאֲפִילוּ בְּמָקוֹם שֶׁהַכַּף חוֹב מַכְרִיעַ יוֹתֵר, דְּמִצַּד
הַדִּין לֵיכָּא אִסּוּרָא כָּל כָּךְ, אִם יַכְרִיעֵהוּ לְכַף חוֹבָה,
הַיְנוּ לְעִנְיָן (יב) שֶׁיֵּשֵׁב בְּעֵינֵי עַצְמוֹ עָלָיו, שֶׁעָשָׂה
שֶׁלֹּא כַּדִּין, אֲבָל אֵין לְמַהֵר לֵילֵךְ וּלְבַזּוֹתוֹ עֲבוּר זֶה

---

אֵצֶל אֲחֵרִים, אִם לֹא שֶׁיַּשְׁלִימוּ כָּל הַפְּרָטִים הַמְבֹאָרִים
לְקַמָּן בִּכְלַל ד' וְה' וּבִכְלַל י', כִּי יֵשׁ הַרְבֵּה דְבָרִים,
שֶׁאֲפִלּוּ אִם אֵין הַדִּין עִמּוֹ, גַּם כֵּן אָסוּר לְבַזּוֹתוֹ עֲבוּר
זֶה, כַּמְבֹאָר הַמְעַיֵּן בִּכְלָלִים אֵלּוּ:

### 41) טור חושן משפט יז

ואם באו לפניו אחד כשר ואחד רשע לא יאמר הואיל
וזה רשע וחזקתו משקר וזה בחזקת שאינו משנה
בדיבורו אטה הדין על הרשע אלא ישוה יהיו שני
בעלי הדינין בעיניו כרשעים ובחזקת שכל אחד
מהם טוען שקר וידון לפי מה שיראה לו מן הדברים
וכשיפטרו מלפניו אז יהיו בעיניו ככשרים כשקבלו
עליהם את הדין וידון כל אחד לכף זכות:

### 42) שערי תשובה ג:ריח

... ונאמר (משלי כט, כו): "תועבת צדיקים איש
עול", ונאמר (שם ח, יג): "יראת ה' שנאת רע". ואמרו
(סנהדרין נב, א): רשע בן צדיק - מותר לקרותו
רשע בן רשע, צדיק בן רשע - מותר לקרותו צדיק
בן צדיק... ואם האיש ההוא רוב מעשיו לרוע או
בחנותו כי אין יראת אלקים בלבבו, תכריע מעשיו
ודבריו לכף חובה, שנאמר (משלי כא, יב): "משכיל
צדיק לבית רשע מסלף רשעים לרע", וכבר הקדמנו
לך פירושו:

### 43) רמב"ם, הלכות חובל ומזיק ה:ד

קנס קנסו חכמים לאלו השוטים בעלי זרוע שהיה
הנחבל נאמן ונשבע בנקיטת חפץ שזה חבל בו חבל
זה ונוטל מה שראוי לו, והוא שיהיו שם עדים. כיצד,
היו שני עדים מעידים אותו שנכנס לתוך ידו שלם
ויצא חבול ולא ראוהו בעת שחבל בו והוא אומר
לא חבלתי והלה אומר אתה חבלת בי הרי זה נשבע
ונוטל.

הנחבל כיצד ראוהו עדים שנכנס תחת ידו של חבירו
שלם ויצא חבול ולא ראוהו בשעה שחבל בו וזה
אומר חבל בי וזה אומר לא חבלתי בו הרי זה נשבע
ונוטל ז) ואם יש הוכחה שזה חבל בו כגון שהיתה
החבלה במקום שאי אפשר לו לחבול בעצמו כגון
שהיתה בין כתיפיו וכיוצא בזה ולא היה אחר עמהם
הרי זה נוטל בלא שבועה ואפילו יש אחר עמהם
אי ברור לעדים שאותו אחר לא חבל בו כאילו אין
עמהם אחר דמי ונוטל בלא שבועה.

### 44) שולחן ערוך, חושן משפט צ:ו

העידו עדים שהיו לבעל הבית זה כך וכך כלים
וראו אחד שנכנס לביתו ויצא ולא נכנס שם אדם
אחר וקודם שיכנס שם אדם אחר מנו אותם כלים
ונמצאו חסרים ולא היה שם מקום שיפלו בו אותם
כלים יש מי שאומר שיטול בעל הבית בלא שבועה
אותם כלים שחסרו מאותו אדם שהעידו עליו
שנכנס שם.

מאזנים ואין לו הכרע לכאן ולכאן כגון כגון שאין
אנו יודעים ממעשיו אם צדיק הוא אם רשע ועשה מעשה
שאפשר לדונו לזכות ואפשר לדונו לחובה. מדת
חסידות הוא לדונו לכף זכות.

### 25) פירוש רבינו יונה משנה אבות א:ו
והוי דן את כל האדם לכף זכות – זה מדבר על אדם
שאין יודעין בו אם הוא צדיק אם רשע, או מכירין
אותו והוא איש בינוני, פעמים עושה רע ופעמים
עושה טוב, ואם יעשה דבר שיש לדונו לחובה ויש
לדונו לזכות בשקול הדעת, או אפילו לפי הנראה
נוטה לכף חובה יותר, אם משום צד וענין יכול לדונו
לזכות, יש לו לומר, לטובה נתכוון.

### 26) פירוש רמב"ם משנה אבות א:ו
והוי דן את כל האדם לכף זכות – ענינו כשיהיה אדם
שלא תדע בו אם צדיק הוא או רשע כשתראהו שיעשה
מעשה או יאמר דבר שאם תפרשהו על דרך אחת
יהיה טוב ואם תפרשהו על דרך אחרת יהיה רע, קח
אותו על הטוב ולא תחשוב בו רע ...

### 27) פחד יצחק, אגרות וכתבים, איגרת לח
ועוד יסוד אחד עלינו לבאר כאן הנה נתחייבנו
במצות "בצדק תשפוט את עמיתך" פירושה של
מצוה זו הוא לדון לכף זכות והשיעור בזה של דיון
לכף זכות מבואר בראשונים שזה תלוי בטיבו של
האדם הנידון למשל מי שהמדרגה שלו הוא מדרגה
של מחצה זכיות ומחצה עוונות אז חובת הדיון לכף
זכות נוהגת בו במעשה שיש בו חמשים אחוז לצד
זכות וחמשים אחוז לצד חוב וכדומה הכל לפי ערך
(כמבואר ברבנו יונה י) שהאחוזים של צד הזכות
נמצאים הם בערך מצב הזכויות של האדם הנידון
אמנם כל זה הוא רק בנוגע למעשה שנעשה ע"י אדם
שיש בו צדדים לחובה וצדדים לזכות אז המצוה של
"בצדק תשפוט את עמיתך" מחייבת אותנו להכריע
לצדדי הזכות לפי ערכו של אותו אדם ...

### 28) ספר חפץ חיים, הלכות לשון הרע, פתיחה
ולפעמים עובר נמי (ג) בְּמִצְוַת עֲשֵׂה ד"בְּצֶדֶק תִּשְׁפֹּט
עֲמִיתֶךָ". כְּגוֹן שֶׁרָאָה אֶת חֲבֵרוֹ שֶׁדִּבֶּר אוֹ עָשָׂה מַעֲשֶׂה,
וְיֵשׁ בַּדָּבָר הַזֶּה לְשָׁפְטוֹ לְצַד הַטּוֹב וּלְצַד הַזְּכוּת אוֹ
לְהָפְכוֹ, אֲפִלּוּ אִם הוּא אִישׁ בֵּינוֹנִי, נִתְחַיַּבְנוּ מִן הַתּוֹרָה
בְּמִצְוַת עֲשֵׂה לָדוּן אוֹתוֹ לְכַף זְכוּת. (וְאִם הָאִישׁ
הַהוּא יְרֵא אֱלֹקִים, נִתְחַיַּבְנוּ לָדוּן אוֹתוֹ לְכַף זְכוּת, גַּם
כִּי הַדָּבָר נוֹטֶה יוֹתֵר הַדָּבָר לְכַף חוֹבָה מִלְּכַף זְכוּת)
וּמִי שֶׁהוֹלֵךְ וּמְסַפֵּר בִּגְנוּתוֹ עָבַר הַדִּבּוּר הַזֶּה שֶׁדִּבֵּר
אוֹ הַמַּעֲשֶׂה הַזֶּה שֶׁעָשָׂה, אוֹ הַמְקַבֵּל, שֶׁנִּתְחַזֵּק אֶצְלוֹ
לִגְנוּת, עֲבוּר זֶה שֶׁשָּׁמַע עָלָיו, וְלֹא דָן אוֹתוֹ לְכַף זְכוּת
עוֹבֵר בְּמִצְוַת עֲשֵׂה זוֹ:

### 29) ספר חפץ חיים, באר מים חיים, פתיחה
... דהרמב"ם איירי שם באדם שאין אני מכירו אם

הוא צדיק אם רשע לזה בודאי אין אני מחויב מן
התורה לדונו לכף זכות רק מדה טובה בעלמא ...
אבל אנן איירינן באיש שאני מכירו שאינו רשע רק
מן הבינונים, שם הוא חיובא דאורייתא ...

### 30) ספר חפץ חיים, איסורי לשון הרע ג:ז
ז. וְדַע עוֹד כְּלָל גָּדוֹל וְעִקָּר בְּעִנְיָנִים אֵלּוּ, (ח) אִם
הוּא רוֹאֶה אָדָם, שֶׁדִּבֶּר דָּבָר אוֹ עָשָׂה מַעֲשֶׂה, בֵּין מִמַּה
שֶׁבֵּין אָדָם לַמָּקוֹם אוֹ מִמַּה שֶׁבֵּין אָדָם לַחֲבֵרוֹ, וְיֵשׁ
לִשְׁפֹּט דְּבָרוֹ וּמַעֲשֵׂהוּ לְצַד הַטּוֹב וּלְצַד הַזְּכוּת, אִם
הָאִישׁ הַהוּא יְרֵא אֱלֹקִים, נִתְחַיֵּב לָדוּן אוֹתוֹ לְכַף
זְכוּת, אֲפִלּוּ אִם הַדָּבָר קָרוֹב וְנוֹטֶה אֵצֶל הַדַּעַת יוֹתֵר לְכַף
חוֹבָה. וְאִם הוּא מִן הַבֵּינוֹנִים, אֲשֶׁר יִזָּהֲרוּ מִן הַחֵטְא
וּפְעָמִים יִכָּשְׁלוּ בּוֹ, אִם הַסָּפֵק שָׁקוּל, צָרִיךְ לְהַטּוֹת
הַסָּפֵק וּלְהַכְרִיעוֹ לְכַף זְכוּת, כְּמוֹ שֶׁאָמְרוּ רַזַ"ל, הַדָּן
אֶת חֲבֵרוֹ לְכַף זְכוּת, (ט) הַמָּקוֹם יְדִינֵהוּ לְכַף זְכוּת,
וְהוּא נִכְנָס בִּכְלָל מַאֲמָרוֹ יִתְבָּרַךְ, "בְּצֶדֶק תִּשְׁפֹּט
עֲמִיתֶךָ". (י) וַאֲפִלּוּ אִם הַדָּבָר נוֹטֶה יוֹתֵר לְכַף חוֹבָה,
נָכוֹן מְאֹד שֶׁיִּהְיֶה הַדָּבָר אֶצְלוֹ כְּמוֹ סָפֵק וְאַל יַכְרִיעֵהוּ
לְכַף חוֹבָה. וּבְמָקוֹם שֶׁהַדָּבָר נוֹטֶה לְכַף זְכוּת, דִּבְדַּאי
אָסוּר עַל פִּי הַדִּין לְדוּנוֹ לְכַף חוֹבָה, וְהוּא דָן אוֹתוֹ
לְכַף חוֹבָה, וּבִשְׁבִיל זֶה הָלַךְ וְגִנָּהוּ, לְבַד שֶׁעָבַר בָּזֶה עַל
"בְּצֶדֶק תִּשְׁפֹּט עֲמִיתֶךָ", (יא) עוֹד עָבַר בָּזֶה עַל
אִסּוּר סִפּוּר לָשׁוֹן הָרָע:

### 31) סנהדרין קב:
רב אשי אוקי אשלשה מלכים. אמר: למחר נפתח
בחברין. אמר: אתא מנשה איתחזי ליה בחלמיה. אמר:
חברך וחבירי דאבוך קרית לן? מהיכא בעית
למישרא המוציא? אמר ליה: לא ידענא. אמר ליה:
מהיכא דבעית למישרא המוציא לא גמירת, וחברך
קרית לן? אמר ליה: אגמריה לי, ולמחר דרישנא ליה
משמך בפירקא. אמר ליה: מהיכא דקרים בישולא.
אמר ליה: מאחר דחכימתו כולי האי, מאי טעמא קא
פלחיתו לעבודה זרה?

### 32) רבי עובדיה מברטנורה על משנה אבות א:ו
והוי דן את כל האדם לכף זכות – ... אבל אדם
שהוחזק ברשע מותר לדונו לחובה שלא אמרו (שבת
צז) אלא החושד בכשרים לוקה בגופו מכלל שהחושד
ברשעים אינו לוקה:

### 33) משלי כו:כה
כִּי־יְחַנֵּן קוֹלוֹ אַל־תַּאֲמֶן־בּוֹ כִּי שֶׁבַע תּוֹעֵבוֹת בְּלִבּוֹ:

### 34) משלי כא:יב
מַשְׂכִּיל צַדִּיק לְבֵית רָשָׁע מְסַלֵּף רְשָׁעִים לָרָע:

### 35) בראשית כט:יג ופירוש רש"י שם
וַיְהִי כִשְׁמֹעַ לָבָן אֶת־שֵׁמַע יַעֲקֹב בֶּן־אֲחֹתוֹ וַיָּרָץ
לִקְרָאתוֹ וַיְחַבֶּק־לוֹ וַיְנַשֶּׁק־לוֹ וַיְבִיאֵהוּ אֶל־בֵּיתוֹ וַיְסַפֵּר
לְלָבָן אֵת כָּל־הַדְּבָרִים הָאֵלֶּה:

שכל אדם חייב לדון חבירו לכף זכות, שהוא בכלל המצוה, יהיה סיבה להיות בין אנשים שלום ורעות. ונמצא שעיקר כל כוונות המצוה להועיל ביישוב בני אדם עם יושר הדין, ולתת ביניהם שלום עם סילוק החשד איש באיש:

### 14) פירוש רש"י על שבת קכז.

... היינו תלמוד תורה, דן את חבירו לכף זכות בכלל הבאת שלום, דמתוך שהוא מכריעו לזכות, ואמר: לא חטא לי בזאת, אנוס היה, או לטובה נתכוון יש שלום ביניהן, ור' יוחנן לפרש לך אתא, דבכלל שלשה דמתניתין איתנהו להנך ששה, ואיכא נמי לכבוד אב ואם, ור' יוחנן לא פליג עליה.

### 15) ספר מצוות קטן, רכג

... ובכלל זה לדון חבירו לכף זכות שמתוך שידונו לכף זכות שוב אינו חוטא וישוב לבוראו פן יכריע כל העולם לחובה וכן מעשה במסכת שבת (דף קכ"ז)

### 16) יומא יט:

דאמר רבי יהושע בן לוי: כל החושד בכשרים לוקה בגופו.

### 17) פלא יועץ "סנגוריא"

... וכזאת יבקש לדון לכף זכות וכל הדן לכף זכות המקום ידין אותו לכף זכות צא ולמד איך מה זכות יצחק אבינו על ישראל באמור כמה שנותיו של אדם וכו' דל וכו' דל והבן דוק ותראה חסדיו יתברך כי חפץ חסד הוא ומקבל כל מין טענה מהמלמד זכות ...

### 18) ספר יסוד שורש והעבודה, א:ח

... שרואה בחבירו שעשה איזה מעשה או יצא מפיו איזה דבור שלכאורה הוא נגד רצון הבורא ית' יש לדון אותו תיכף לכף זכות ויחשוב במחשבתו בזה"ל הריני מוכן ומזומן לקיים מ"ע של בצדק תשפוט עמיתך ויתאמץ בהתאמצות גדול במחשבתו למצוא לו איזה זכות במעשהו או בדבור ההוא ואז כשהוא צדיק בעיניו בודאי יתאמץ לו ג"כ לעשות רצונו באיזה ענינים שיהי' ביכלתו ולקיים בזה מ"ע של ואהבת

### 19) מדרש תהילים קכה

תני, רבי ישמעאל אומר, אם ראית תלמיד חכם עובר עבירה בלילה אל תהרהר אחריו ביום, שמא עשה תשובה.

### 20) סנהדרין קי.

אמר רבי אבהו: כל המהרהר אחר רבו כאילו מהרהר אחר שכינה.

### 21) פירוש רמב"ם משנה אבות א:ו

והוי דן את כל האדם לכף זכות – ... אבל אם יהיה

---

האדם נודע שהוא צדיק מפורסם ובפעולות הטובות ונראה לו פועל של שכל ענייניו מורים שהוא פועל רע ואין אדם יכול להכריעו לטוב אלא בדוחק גדול ואפשר רחוק הוא ראוי שתקח אותו שהוא טוב אחר שיש שום צד אפשרות להיותו טוב ואין מותר לך לחשדו, ועל זה אמרו [שבת צז] כל החושד בכשרים לוקה בגופו.

### 22) פירוש רבינו יונה משנה אבות א:ו

והוי דן את כל האדם לכף זכות – ... אבל אין הדברים כן בצדיק גמור ... כי הצדיק אפילו במעשה שכולו רע ונוטה לכף חובה מכל עבר, ידינהו לזכות, לאמר, כי בשגגה היתה היוצאת מלפני השליט, וראה והביט ובקש מחילה, וכמו שאמרו רז"ל (ברכות יט, א), אם ראית תלמיד חכם שעבר עבירה בלילה אל תהרהר אחריו ביום, שמא עשה תשובה, שמא ס"ד, אלא אימא ודאי אימא עשה תשובה. פי', "שמא ס"ד", שאם הדבר אליו כשמא, על כל פנים מהרהר אחריו, או פירושו, "שמא ס"ד" כיון שהוא ת"ח ועד עתה לא אירע דבר קלקלה בידו על כל פנים מיד עשה תשובה. הנה לך, כי אין לדון לכף חובה צדיק גמור לעולם, וממנו לא הוצרך לומר, והוי דן את כל האדם לכף זכות.

### 23) שבת קכז:

תנו רבנן: הדן חבירו לכף זכות דנין אותו לזכות. ומעשה באדם אחד שירד מגליל העליון ונשכר אצל בעל הבית אחד בדרום שלש שנים. ערב יום הכפורים אמר לו: תן לי שכרי, ואלך ואזון את אשתי ובני. אמר לו: אין לי מעות. אמר לו: תן לי פירות. אמר לי: אין לי. תן לי קרקע. אין לי. תן לי בהמה. אין לי. תן לי כרים וכסתות. אין לי. הפשיל כליו לאחוריו, והלך לביתו בפחי נפש. לאחר הרגל נטל בעל הבית שכרו בידו, ועמו משוי שלשה חמורים, אחד של מאכל ואחד של משתה ואחד של מיני מגדים, והלך לו לביתו. אחר שאכלו ושתו נתן לו שכרו. אמר לו: בשעה שאמרת לי תן לי שכרי ואמרתי אין לי מעות במה חשדתני? אמרתי: שמא פרקמטיא בזול נזדמנה לך, ולקחת בהן. ובשעה שאמרת לי תן לי בהמה ואמרתי אין לי בהמה במה חשדתני? אמרתי: שמא מושכרת ביד אחרים. בשעה שאמרת לי תן לי קרקע ואמרתי אין לי קרקע במה חשדתני? אמרתי: שמא מוחכרת ביד אחרים היא. ובשעה שאמרתי לך אין לי פירות במה חשדתני? אמרתי שמא אינן מעושרות. ובשעה שאמרתי לך אין לי כרים וכסתות במה חשדתני? אמרתי: שמא הקדיש כל נכסיו לשמים. אמר ליה: העבודה, כך היה הדרתי כל נכסי בשביל הורקנוס בני שלא עסק בתורה, וכשבאתי אצל חבירי בדרום התירו לי כל נדרי. ואתה, כשם שדנתני לזכות המקום ידין אותך לזכות.

### 24) רבי עובדיה מברטנורה על משנה אבות א:ו

והוי דן את כל האדם לכף זכות – כשהדבר בכף

## 1) ויקרא יט:טו

לֹא־תַעֲשׂוּ עָוֶל בַּמִּשְׁפָּט לֹא־תִשָּׂא פְנֵי־דָל וְלֹא תֶהְדַּר פְּנֵי גָדוֹל בְּצֶדֶק תִּשְׁפֹּט עֲמִיתֶךָ:

## 2) משנה אבות א:ו

יהושע בן פרחיה ונתאי הארבלי קבלו מהם. יהושע בן פרחיה אומר ... והוי דן את כל האדם לכף זכות:

## 3) שבועות ל.

ד"א: "בצדק תשפוט עמיתך" הוי דן את חבירך לכף זכות. תני רב יוסף: "בצדק תשפוט עמיתך" עם שאתך בתורה ובמצות השתדל לדונו יפה.

## 4) מדרש, ספרא קדושים ד:ד

"בצדק תשפוט עמיתך" הוי דן את כל האדם לכף זכות:

## 5) משנה אבות ב:ד

הלל אומר ... ואל תדין את חברך עד שתגיע למקומו.

## 6) ספר חסידים לא

... ואהוב את הבריות והוי דן את כל האדם לכף זכות, וזהו שאמרה תורה (ויקרא יט טו) בצדק תשפוט עמיתך, ותהי שפל בפני כל.

## 7) סמ"ג, מצות עשה קו

... דבר אחר בצדק תשפוט עמיתך הוי דן את חבירך לכף זכות תני רב יוסף בצדק תשפוט עמיתך עם שאתך בתורה ובמצות השתדל לדונו יפה יפה

## 8) רמב"ם, ספר המצוות, מצות עשה קעז

היא שנצטוו הדיינין להשוות בין בעלי דיניו ושיהיה נשמע כל אחד מהם עם אורך דבריו או קצורם והוא אמרו ית' בצדק תשפוט עמיתך ובא הפירוש בספרא שלא יהא אחד מדבר כל צרכו ואחד את אומר לו קצר דבריך וזו אחת מהכוונות שכולל עליהם הצווי הזה ובו גם כן שכל איש מצווה לדון דין תורה כשהיה יודע בו ושישבית הריב שבין בעלי דינים ובבאור אמרו אחד דן את חבירו דבר תורה שנאמר "בצדק תשפוט עמיתך" ויש בו עוד שראוי לדון את חבירו לכף זכות ולא יפרש מעשיו ודבריו אלא לטוב וחסד וכבר נתבארו משפטי מצוה זו במקומות מפוזרים מן התלמוד:

## 9) רמב"ם, הלכות דעות ה:ז

תלמיד חכם לא יהא צועק וצווח בשעת דבורו

---

כבהמות וחיות, ולא יגביה קולו ביותר אלא דבורו בנחת עם כל הבריות, וכשידבר בנחת יזהר שלא יתרחק עד שיראה כדברי גסי הרוח, ומקדים שלום לכל האדם כדי שתהא רוחו נוחה הימנו, ודן את כל האדם לכף זכות, מספר בשבח חבירו ולא בגנותו כלל, אוהב שלום ורודף שלום

## 10) ספר חפץ חיים, באר מים חיים, פתיחה

... וגם הרבינו יונה בספרו שערי תשובה כתב שהיא מצות עשה דאורייתא. וממנו העתקתי כמעט כל דברי שבסעיף זה שבפנים ... ואל יתפוס עלי הקורא לאמר שבודאי הרמב"ם חולק על רבינו יונה והסמ"ג והסמ"ק, וסובר שהוא רק מדה בעלמא ולא מצות עשה, והראיה שהרמב"ם כתב שם בסוף מאמרו במשנה הנ"ל שהוא מדרכי החסידות, דזה אינו דהרמב"ם איירי שם באדם שאין אני מכירו אם הוא צדיק אם רשע לזה בודאי אין אני מחויב מן התורה לדונו לכף זכות רק מדה טובה בעלמא, וכן ברמב"ם בפרק ה' מהלכות דעות בהלכה ז' שמונה זה בין מדותיו של תלמיד חכם ומשמע דהוא רק מדה בעלמא, התם איירי גם כן בכהאי גוונא. ותדע דהא העתיק שם לשון המשנה דאבות הוי דן את כל אדם לכף זכות, אבל אנן איירינן באיש שאני מכירו שאינו רשע רק מן הבינונים, שם הוא חיובא דאורייתא. והראיה מהרמב"ם גופה בספר המצוות במצות קע"ז הנ"ל כתב בהדיא ובכללה גם כן שיתחייב שידין את חבירו לכף זכות מלשון שיתחייב משמע בהדיא דאיירי בכל אדם דהתרי"ג מצות נאמרו לכל ישראל. וראה כי דברינו אמת, דבמשנה דאבות הנ"ל דאיירי במדות נאמר והוי דן את כל אדם לכף זכות ובגמרא ובמימרא דשבועות הנ"ל דאיירי בבאור המצות עשה דבצדק וכו' נאמר והוי דן את חבירך לכף זכות, חבירך, משמע שאתה מכירו שאיננו רשע:

## 11) מדרש ילקוט שמעוני, ויקרא יט תרי"א

תנו רבנן הדן את חברו לכף זכות [דנין אותו לכ"ז].

## 12) שבת קכז.

ששה דברים אדם אוכל פירותיהן בעולם הזה, והקרן קיימת לו לעולם הבא. ואלו הן: הכנסת אורחין, ובקור חולים, ועיון תפלה, והשכמת בית המדרש, והמגדל בניו לתלמוד תורה, והדן את חברו לכף זכות.

## 13) ספר החינוך, מצוה רל"ה

שראוי לכל אדם לדון את חבירו לכף זכות, ולא יפרש מעשיו ודבריו אלא לטוב ... במה שאמרנו

---

**(35 ברא‍שית מט:ח-י'**

יְהוּדָה אַתָּה יוֹדוּךָ אַחֶיךָ יָדְךָ בְּעֹרֶף אֹיְבֶיךָ יִשְׁתַּחֲווּ לְךָ בְּנֵי אָבִיךָ: גּוּר אַרְיֵה יְהוּדָה מִטֶּרֶף בְּנִי עָלִיתָ כָּרַע רָבַץ כְּאַרְיֵה וּכְלָבִיא מִי יְקִימֶנּוּ: לֹא-יָסוּר שֵׁבֶט מִיהוּדָה וּמְחֹקֵק מִבֵּין רַגְלָיו עַד כִּי-יָבֹא שִׁילֹה וְלוֹ יִקְּהַת עַמִּים:

**(36 סנהדרין קב.**

מר רבי אבא: אחר שתפשו הקדוש ברוך הוא לירבעם בבגדו, ואמר לו: חזור בך, ואני ואתה ובן ישי נטייל בגן עדן, אמר לו, מי בראש: בן ישי בראש אי הכי לא בעינא.

**(37 רמב"ם, הלכות מלכים יא:ד, א**

ואם יעמוד מלך מבית דוד הוגה בתורה ועוסק במצות כדוד אביו, כפי תורה שבכתב ושבעל פה, ויכוף כל ישראל לילך בה ולחזק בדקה, וילחם מלחמות ה', הרי זה בחזקת שהוא משיח, אם עשה והצליח ובנה מקדש במקומו וקבץ נדחי ישראל הרי זה משיח בודאי

המלך המשיח עתיד לעמוד ולהחזיר מלכות דוד

ליושנה לממשלה הראשונה, ובונה המקדש ומקבץ נדחי ישראל, וחוזרין כל המשפטים בימיו כשהיו מקודם, מקריבין קרבנות, ועושין שמטין ויובלות ככל מצותה האמורה בתורה, וכל מי שאינו מאמין בו, או מי שאינו מחכה לביאתו, לא בשאר נביאים בלבד הוא כופר, אלא בתורה ובמשה רבינו,

**(38 עמידה של חול, ברכות יד, טו, יז**

וְלִירוּשָׁלַיִם עִירְךָ בְּרַחֲמִים תָּשׁוּב. וְתִשְׁכֹּן בְּתוֹכָהּ כַּאֲשֶׁר דִּבַּרְתָּ. וּבְנֵה אוֹתָהּ בְּקָרוֹב בְּיָמֵינוּ בִּנְיַן עוֹלָם. וְכִסֵּא דָוִד מְהֵרָה לְתוֹכָהּ תָּכִין: בָּרוּךְ אַתָּה ד'. בּוֹנֵה יְרוּשָׁלָיִם:

אֶת צֶמַח דָּוִד עַבְדְּךָ מְהֵרָה תַצְמִיחַ. וְקַרְנוֹ תָּרוּם בִּישׁוּעָתֶךָ. כִּי לִישׁוּעָתְךָ קִוִּינוּ כָּל הַיּוֹם. בָּרוּךְ אַתָּה ד'. מַצְמִיחַ קֶרֶן יְשׁוּעָה:

רְצֵה ד' אֱלֹקֵינוּ בְּעַמְּךָ יִשְׂרָאֵל וּבִתְפִלָּתָם וְהָשֵׁב אֶת הָעֲבוֹדָה לִדְבִיר בֵּיתֶךָ. וְאִשֵּׁי יִשְׂרָאֵל וּתְפִלָּתָם. בְּאַהֲבָה תְקַבֵּל בְּרָצוֹן. וּתְהִי לְרָצוֹן תָּמִיד עֲבוֹדַת יִשְׂרָאֵל עַמֶּךָ: וְתֶחֱזֶינָה עֵינֵינוּ בְּשׁוּבְךָ לְצִיּוֹן בְּרַחֲמִים: בָּרוּךְ אַתָּה ד'. הַמַּחֲזִיר שְׁכִינָתוֹ לְצִיּוֹן:

[ושמואל] אמר: עבדים היינו.

**18) פסחים קח.**

בין הכוסות הללו, אם רצה לשתות ישתה, בין שלישי
לרביעי לא ישתה.

**19) שולחן ערוך, אורח חיים תעט:א**

אחר כך מוזגין לו כוס שלישי ומברך עליו ברכת
המזון ובורא פרי הגפן ושותהו בהסיבה ולא יברך
אחריו ולא ישתה יין בינו לכוס רביעי:

**20) מדרש בראשית רבה סח:ה**

מכאן קבעו חכמים ד' כוסות של לילי פסח ...
כנגד ד' גאולות שנאמרו במצרים והוצאתי והצלתי
וגאלתי ולקחתי

**21) שמות ו:ו-ח**

(1) ... וְהוֹצֵאתִי אֶתְכֶם מִתַּחַת סִבְלֹת מִצְרַיִם (2)
וְהִצַּלְתִּי אֶתְכֶם מֵעֲבֹדָתָם (3) וְגָאַלְתִּי אֶתְכֶם בִּזְרוֹעַ
נְטוּיָה וּבִשְׁפָטִים גְּדֹלִים: (4) וְלָקַחְתִּי אֶתְכֶם לִי לְעָם
וְהָיִיתִי לָכֶם לֵאל, קים וִידַעְתֶּם כִּי אֲנִי ד' אֱלֹקֵיכֶם
הַמּוֹצִיא אֶתְכֶם מִתַּחַת סִבְלוֹת מִצְרָיִם: וְהֵבֵאתִי אֶתְכֶם
אֶל הָאָרֶץ ...

**22) תלמוד ירושלמי, מגילה כה:**

רבי לוי בשם ר"ח בר חנינה אין מפסיקין בין פרה
להחודש אמר רבי לוי סימניהון דאילין פרשתא בין
הכוסות הללו אם רצה לשתות ישתה בין השלישי
לרביעי לא ישתה רבי לוי בשם רבי חמא בר חנינה
בדין הוא שתקדים החודש לפרה שבאחד בניסן
הוקם המשכן ובשני נשרפה הפרה ולמה פרה קודמת
שהיא טהרתן של כל ישראל

**23) במדבר יט:א-יב**

וַיְדַבֵּר ד' אֶל מֹשֶׁה וְאֶל אַהֲרֹן לֵאמֹר: זֹאת חֻקַּת הַתּוֹרָה
אֲשֶׁר צִוָּה ד' לֵאמֹר דַּבֵּר | אֶל בְּנֵי יִשְׂרָאֵל וְיִקְחוּ אֵלֶיךָ
פָרָה אֲדֻמָּה תְּמִימָה אֲשֶׁר אֵין בָּהּ מוּם אֲשֶׁר לֹא עָלָה
עָלֶיהָ עֹל: וּנְתַתֶּם אֹתָהּ אֶל אֶלְעָזָר הַכֹּהֵן וְהוֹצִיא אֹתָהּ
אֶל מִחוּץ לַמַּחֲנֶה וְשָׁחַט אֹתָהּ לְפָנָיו: וְלָקַח אֶלְעָזָר
הַכֹּהֵן מִדָּמָהּ בְּאֶצְבָּעוֹ וְהִזָּה אֶל נֹכַח פְּנֵי אֹהֶל מוֹעֵד
מִדָּמָהּ שֶׁבַע פְּעָמִים: וְשָׂרַף אֶת הַפָּרָה לְעֵינָיו אֶת עֹרָהּ
וְאֶת בְּשָׂרָהּ וְאֶת דָּמָהּ עַל פִּרְשָׁהּ יִשְׂרֹף: וְלָקַח הַכֹּהֵן
עֵץ אֶרֶז וְאֵזוֹב וּשְׁנִי תוֹלָעַת וְהִשְׁלִיךְ אֶל תּוֹךְ שְׂרֵפַת
הַפָּרָה: וְכִבֶּס בְּגָדָיו הַכֹּהֵן וְרָחַץ בְּשָׂרוֹ בַּמַּיִם וְאַחַר
יָבֹא אֶל הַמַּחֲנֶה וְטָמֵא הַכֹּהֵן עַד הָעָרֶב: וְהַשֹּׂרֵף אֹתָהּ
יְכַבֵּס בְּגָדָיו בַּמַּיִם וְרָחַץ בְּשָׂרוֹ בַּמָּיִם וְטָמֵא עַד הָעָרֶב:
וְאָסַף | אִישׁ טָהוֹר אֵת אֵפֶר הַפָּרָה וְהִנִּיחַ מִחוּץ לַמַּחֲנֶה
בְּמָקוֹם טָהוֹר וְהָיְתָה לַעֲדַת בְּנֵי יִשְׂרָאֵל לְמִשְׁמֶרֶת לְמֵי
נִדָּה חַטָּאת הִוא: וְכִבֶּס הָאֹסֵף אֶת אֵפֶר הַפָּרָה אֶת
בְּגָדָיו וְטָמֵא עַד הָעָרֶב וְהָיְתָה לִבְנֵי יִשְׂרָאֵל וְלַגֵּר הַגָּר
בְּתוֹכָם לְחֻקַּת עוֹלָם: הַנֹּגֵעַ בְּמֵת לְכָל נֶפֶשׁ אָדָם וְטָמֵא

---

שִׁבְעַת יָמִים: הוּא יִתְחַטָּא בוֹ בַּיּוֹם הַשְּׁלִישִׁי וּבַיּוֹם
הַשְּׁבִיעִי יִטְהָר וְאִם לֹא יִתְחַטָּא בַּיּוֹם הַשְּׁלִישִׁי וּבַיּוֹם
הַשְּׁבִיעִי לֹא יִטְהָר:

**24) שמות יב:א-ב**

וַיֹּאמֶר ד' אֶל מֹשֶׁה וְאֶל אַהֲרֹן בְּאֶרֶץ מִצְרַיִם לֵאמֹר:
הַחֹדֶשׁ הַזֶּה לָכֶם רֹאשׁ חֳדָשִׁים רִאשׁוֹן הוּא לָכֶם לְחָדְשֵׁי
הַשָּׁנָה:

**25) שולחן ערוך, אורח חיים תפט:ח**

אם שכח לברך באחד מהימים בין יום ראשון בין
משאר ימים סופר בשאר ימים בלא ברכה אבל אם
הוא מסופק אם דילג יום אחד ולא ספר יספור בשאר
ימים בברכה:

**26) שולחן ערוך, אורח חיים כה:ט**

אסור להפסיק בדיבור בין תפלה של יד לתפלה
של ראש

**27) שמות ז:טז, ז:כו, ט:א, ט:יג**

... שַׁלַּח אֶת עַמִּי וְיַעַבְדֻנִי

**28) שמות יט:ו**

וְאַתֶּם תִּהְיוּ לִי מַמְלֶכֶת כֹּהֲנִים וְגוֹי קָדוֹשׁ אֵלֶּה הַדְּבָרִים
אֲשֶׁר תְּדַבֵּר אֶל בְּנֵי יִשְׂרָאֵל:

**29) רות א:טז**

עַמֵּךְ עַמִּי וֵאלֹקַיִךְ אֱלֹקָי:

**30) בראשית מז:יב**

וַיְכַלְכֵּל יוֹסֵף אֶת אָבִיו וְאֶת אֶחָיו וְאֵת כָּל בֵּית אָבִיו
לֶחֶם לְפִי הַטָּף:

**31) בראשית מו:כח ופירוש רש"י**

וְאֶת יְהוּדָה שָׁלַח לְפָנָיו אֶל יוֹסֵף לְהוֹרֹת לְפָנָיו גֹּשְׁנָה
וַיָּבֹאוּ אַרְצָה גֹּשֶׁן:
לפניו – קודם שיגיע לשם. ומדרש אגדה להורות
לפניו, לתקן לו בית תלמוד שמשם תצא הוראה:

**32) בראשית מח:כב**

וַאֲנִי נָתַתִּי לְךָ שְׁכֶם אַחַד עַל אַחֶיךָ אֲשֶׁר לָקַחְתִּי מִיַּד
הָאֱמֹרִי בְּחַרְבִּי וּבְקַשְׁתִּי:

**33) מלכים א' יב:כה**

וַיִּבֶן יָרָבְעָם אֶת שְׁכֶם בְּהַר אֶפְ_ַ__ יט__ וַיֵּשֶׁב בָּהּ וַיֵּצֵא מִשָּׁם
וַיִּבֶן אֶת פְּנוּאֵל:

**34) סוכה נב,:**

.... עַל משיח בן יוסף שנהרג ...
אמר רב חנא בר ביזנא אמר רבי שמעון חסידא
משיח בן דויד ומשיח בן יוסף ...

# SOURCES ON JUDAISM – A RELIGION OR A NATION?

**1) דברים יז:יח-יט**

וְהָיָה כְשִׁבְתּוֹ עַל כִּסֵּא מַמְלַכְתּוֹ וְכָתַב לוֹ אֶת־מִשְׁנֵה הַתּוֹרָה הַזֹּאת עַל־סֵפֶר מִלִּפְנֵי הַכֹּהֲנִים הַלְוִיִּם: וְהָיְתָה עִמּוֹ וְקָרָא בוֹ כָּל־יְמֵי חַיָּיו לְמַעַן יִלְמַד לְיִרְאָה אֶת־ד' אֱלֹקָיו לִשְׁמֹר אֶת־כָּל־דִּבְרֵי הַתּוֹרָה הַזֹּאת וְאֶת־הַחֻקִּים הָאֵלֶּה לַעֲשֹׂתָם:

**2) בראשית מב:ג-ה**

וַיֵּרְדוּ אֲחֵי־יוֹסֵף עֲשָׂרָה לִשְׁבֹּר בָּר מִמִּצְרָיִם: וְאֶת־בִּנְיָמִין אֲחִי יוֹסֵף לֹא־שָׁלַח יַעֲקֹב אֶת־אֶחָיו כִּי אָמַר פֶּן־יִקְרָאֶנּוּ אָסוֹן: וַיָּבֹאוּ בְּנֵי יִשְׂרָאֵל לִשְׁבֹּר בְּתוֹךְ הַבָּאִים כִּי־הָיָה הָרָעָב בְּאֶרֶץ כְּנָעַן:

**3) פירוש רש"י על בראשית מב:ג**

וירדו אחי יוסף. ולא כתב בני יעקב, מלמד שהיו מתחרטים במכירתו, ונתנו לבם להתנהג עמו באחוה, ולפדותו בכל ממון שיפסקו עליהם:

**4) שמות א:א**

וְאֵלֶּה שְׁמוֹת בְּנֵי יִשְׂרָאֵל הַבָּאִים מִצְרָיְמָה אֵת יַעֲקֹב אִישׁ וּבֵיתוֹ בָּאוּ:

**5) שמות ב:א ופירוש רש"י**

וַיֵּלֶךְ אִישׁ מִבֵּית לֵוִי וַיִּקַּח אֶת־בַּת־לֵוִי:
**ויקח את בת לוי** – פרוש היה ממנה מפני גזירת פרעה, (וחזר ולקחה, וזהו וילך, שהלך בעצת בתו שאמרה לו גזרתך קשה משל פרעה, אם פרעה גזר על הזכרים ואתה גם כן על הנקבות. ברש"י ישן) והחזירה ועשה בה לקוחין שניים,

**6) שמות י':י-יא**

וַיּוּשַׁב אֶת־מֹשֶׁה וְאֶת־אַהֲרֹן אֶל־פַּרְעֹה וַיֹּאמֶר אֲלֵהֶם לְכוּ עִבְדוּ אֶת־ד' אֱלֹקֵיכֶם מִי וָמִי הַהֹלְכִים: וַיֹּאמֶר מֹשֶׁה בִּנְעָרֵינוּ וּבִזְקֵנֵינוּ נֵלֵךְ בְּבָנֵינוּ וּבִבְנוֹתֵנוּ בְּצֹאנֵנוּ וּבִבְקָרֵנוּ נֵלֵךְ כִּי חַג־ד' לָנוּ: וַיֹּאמֶר אֲלֵהֶם יְהִי כֵן ד' עִמָּכֶם כַּאֲשֶׁר אֲשַׁלַּח אֶתְכֶם וְאֶת־טַפְּכֶם רְאוּ כִּי רָעָה נֶגֶד פְּנֵיכֶם: לֹא כֵן לְכוּ־נָא הַגְּבָרִים וְעִבְדוּ אֶת־ד' כִּי אֹתָהּ אַתֶּם מְבַקְשִׁים וַיְגָרֶשׁ אֹתָם מֵאֵת פְּנֵי פַרְעֹה:

**7) שמות: יב:ג-ד**

דַּבְּרוּ אֶל־כָּל־עֲדַת יִשְׂרָאֵל לֵאמֹר בֶּעָשֹׂר לַחֹדֶשׁ הַזֶּה וְיִקְחוּ לָהֶם אִישׁ שֶׂה לְבֵית־אָבֹת שֶׂה לַבָּיִת: וְאִם־יִמְעַט הַבַּיִת מִהְיוֹת מִשֶּׂה וְלָקַח הוּא וּשְׁכֵנוֹ הַקָּרֹב אֶל־בֵּיתוֹ בְּמִכְסַת נְפָשֹׁת אִישׁ לְפִי אָכְלוֹ תָּכֹסּוּ עַל־הַשֶּׂה:

**8) שמות: יב:ז**

וְלָקְחוּ מִן־הַדָּם וְנָתְנוּ עַל־שְׁתֵּי הַמְּזוּזֹת וְעַל־הַמַּשְׁקוֹף

---

עַל הַבָּתִּים אֲשֶׁר־יֹאכְלוּ אֹתוֹ בָּהֶם:

**9) במדבר א:ב**

שְׂאוּ אֶת־רֹאשׁ כָּל־עֲדַת בְּנֵי־יִשְׂרָאֵל לְמִשְׁפְּחֹתָם לְבֵית אֲבֹתָם בְּמִסְפַּר שֵׁמוֹת כָּל־זָכָר לְגֻלְגְּלֹתָם:

**10) שבועות לט. ושולחן עריך, חושן משפט פז:כב**

שכל ישראל ערבים זה לזה

**11) מדרש, ויקרא רבה ד:ו**

תני חזקיה (ירמיה נ) שה פזורה ישראל נמשלו ישראל לשה מה שה הזה לוקה על ראשו או א' מאבריו וכל אבריו מרגישין כך הן ישראל אחד מהן חוטא וכולן מרגישין (במדבר טז) האיש אחד יחטא תני רשב"י משל לבני אדם שהיו יושבין בספינה נטל אחד מהן מקדח והתחיל קודח תחתיו אמרו לו חבריו מה אתה יושב ועושה אמר להם מה אכפת לכם לא תחתי אני קודח אמרו לו שהמים עולין ומציפין עלינו את הספינה

**12) תלמוד ירושלמי, נדרים ל.**

כתיב לא תקום ולא תטור את בני עמך. היך עבידא הוה מקטע קופד ומחת סכינא לידוי תחזור ותמחי לידיה.

**13) שמות ג:יב**

וַיֹּאמֶר כִּי־אֶהְיֶה עִמָּךְ וְזֶה־לְּךָ הָאוֹת כִּי אָנֹכִי שְׁלַחְתִּיךָ בְּהוֹצִיאֲךָ אֶת־הָעָם מִמִּצְרַיִם תַּעַבְדוּן אֶת־הָאֱלֹקִים עַל הָהָר הַזֶּה:

**14) שמות יט:ה**

וְעַתָּה אִם־שָׁמוֹעַ תִּשְׁמְעוּ בְּקֹלִי וּשְׁמַרְתֶּם אֶת־בְּרִיתִי וִהְיִיתֶם לִי סְגֻלָּה מִכָּל־הָעַמִּים כִּי־לִי כָּל־הָאָרֶץ:

**15) יחזקאל מה:כא ורש"י שם**

בָּרִאשׁוֹן בְּאַרְבָּעָה עָשָׂר יוֹם לַחֹדֶשׁ יִהְיֶה לָכֶם הַפָּסַח חָג שְׁבֻעוֹת יָמִים מַצּוֹת יֵאָכֵל:
**שבועות** – על שם שמתחילין ממנו לספור שבעה שבועות

**16) הגדת פסח, לכני כוס שני**

בְּכָל דּוֹר וָדוֹר חַיָּב אָדָם לִרְאוֹת אֶת עַצְמוֹ כְּאִלּוּ הוּא יָצָא מִמִּצְרָיִם.

**17) פסחים קטז.**

מתחיל בגנות ומסיים בשבח מאי בגנות? רב אמר: מתחלה עובדי עבודה גלולים היו אבותינו.

קדושה ולומד ממנו ד"ת ולפ"ז גם אגרת שלום
הכתובה בלה"ק שרי לקרות דיש ללמוד מתוכו
הלשון ...

### 73) רמ"א, שולחן ערוך, יורה דעה רלז:ו
(מי שנשבע בשמים ובארץ ושמש וכיוצא בהם אע"פ
שאין כוונתו אלא למי שבראם אינה שבועה ...) הגה
וכל זה שלא נטל בידו אבל אם נטל בידו כתב אשורית
אפילו אינו רק חכמה חיצונית או אל"ף בי"ת שאין בו
רק אותיות אם נשבע בהן והן בידו הוי שבועה

### 74) מדרש ויקרא רבה לב:ה
רב הונא אמר בשם בר קפרא בשביל ד' דברים נגאלו
ישראל ממצרים שלא שנו את שמם ואת לשונם ולא
אמרו לשון הרע ולא נמצא ביניהן אחד מהן פרוץ
בערוה ...

### 75) ספר מצוות גדולות, לא תעשה נ
שלא ללכת בחוקות הגוים לא במלבושיהן ולא
במנהגיהן שנאמר (ויקרא כ, כג) ולא תלכו בחוקות
הגוי וגומ' ונא' (ויקרא יח, ג) ובחוקותיהן לא תלכו
ונאמר (דברים יב, ל) השמר לך פן תנקש אחריהם
וגומר הכל בעניין אחד הוא מזהיר שיהא ישראל
מובדלין מן הגוים במלבוש ובמנהג **בדבור** ...

### 76) ירושלמי שבת ט:
דתני רשב"י בו ביום גזרו על פיתן ועל גבינתן ועל
יינן ... ועל לשונן ...

### 77) שו"ת אגרות משה, אבן העזר ג:לה
... ומצד עצם הדבר שמשנים את שמותיהם לשמות
נכרים ודאי הוא דבר מגונה מאד מאחר שחז"ל

שיבחו זה וחשבו זה מהדברים שבשבילם נגאלו
ממצרים, אבל איסור ממש לא מצינו בזה.
והוא כמו לא שינו את לשונם דג"כ הוא מהארבעה
דברים שחשיב התם, שחזינן שאף שהוא מצוה לדבר
בלה"ק כדאיתא בספרי ס"פ עקב והובא ברש"י בפ'
החומש שם על הפסוק לדבר בם, מ"מ אינו איסור
דהא כל ישראל מדברים בלשון חול של האומות
מזמן שגלינו בחטאינו בין האומות ...

### 78) שו"ת דברי יציב, יורה דעה נב-נג
... נזכה שימין ה' רוממה ימין ה' עושה חיל ונזכה
למלאה הארץ דעה את ה' ויקבץ אותנו מארבע
כנפות הארץ ויקויים כי אז אהפוך אל עמים שפה
ברורה (צפניה ג' ט') שפירשו האבן עזרא בשם רבינו
משה והמצודות דהיינו לשון הקודש ובמהר"י קרא
שידברו מלות לשון הקודש שהוא לשון מובחר וזה
פלא ונראה שהגויים גם אז לא ידברו בלשון הקודש
שבו נברא העולם רק ידברו בלשון שיש בו כמה
מלים לשון הקודש וכמו שהנהיגו אבותינו לנו לאחר
שגלו ורק זרע אברהם יצחק ויעקב ידברו כולם ממש
בלשון הקודש שבו ניתנה תורה ובו נברא העולם
אכיה"ר.

... ועיין בראשית רבה פרשה י"ח "לזאת יקרא
אשה כי מאיש לוקחה זאת "מכאן שניתחנה התורה
בלשון הקודש וכו' כשם שניתחנה חורה בלה"ק כך
נברא העולם בלה"ק עיי"ש. והא גופא שניתנה תורה
בלשון זה מורה על ערך קדושתה אלא משום שהיה
מקום לומר דבשביל שישראל קדושים בדור ההוא
השתמשו בלשון זה לכן קמ"ל יתר על כן שגם בריאת
העולם בלשון הקודש שהקב"ה משתמש בלשון זה
והבן.

**60) אוצרות המוסר, שער דיבור ושתיקה נב**

... וכתב מהר"י אייבשיץ (יערות דבש ז' אדר תקח"ל) "הביטו נא וראו כמה גדלה מעלת לשון הקודש והיא המקרבת ישועה וגאולה. עיין ראשית חכמה (שער הקדושה פרק ז' דף קכ"ה בנדפס) על מעלת מי שמדבר בלשון הקודש וכתב של"ה ואשרי מי שמרגיל את עצמו לדבר בלשון הקודש אף בימי החול (מסכת שבת גר מצוה ח"ב דף קט"ז) ...

**61) ספר חסידים תתקצד**

אמרו לזקן במה הארכת ימים, אמר כי היו אורחים בביתי, ולא היו מבינים בלשוני, והיו מדברים עמי בלשון עברית (בבית המרחץ), ואני לא דברתי מעולם בבית המרחץ ובבית הכסא ואפי' דברים של חול, אע"פ שמותר, והואיל ועשיתי גדר ותוספת, הוסיפו לי אף שנותי:

**62) זוהר, שמות קלב:**

והא אוקימנא כל קדושה דאיהו בלשון הקודש יחיד אסיר ליה למימר.

**63) שיטה מקובצת, ברכות יג ד"ה "לימא קסבר רבי"**

... אבל הראב"ד ז"ל כתב וזה לשונו ... ואין אדם יוצא ידי והגית בו אלא בלשון הקדש:

**64) אגרות הגר"א ע"פ פתיחת הגר"א, דף מט**

והש"ה (מסכת שבת סה) כתב אף בדברים ההכרחיים לדבר נוהגים אנשי מעשה שלא לדבר בשבת כי אם בלשון הקודש ולא בלשון חול כי קדוש היום לאדונינו ושבת אות הוא בינו יתברך לבינינו על כן אין לדבר אלא בלשון

**65) פירוש בניהו בן יהודיא על סוטה מב.**

שם משוח מלחמה בשעה שהוא מדבר אל העם בלשון הקודש. היינו משום דכתיב ודבר אל העם, כלומר דבור המיוחד לעם הזה, שהוא לשון הקודש שניתן לישראל דוקא. ונ"ל הטעם שצריך לדבר בלשון הקודש ...

הקודש אף מה שמוכרח לדבר ... כדי לקיים זכור את יום השבת

**66) רמב"ם, הלכות תפילה יב:יא**

אין הקורא רשאי להגביה קולו יותר מן המתרגם, והמתרגם לא יגביה קולו יותר מן הקורא, ואין המתרגם רשאי לתרגם עד שיכלה הפסוק מפי הקורא, ואין הקורא רשאי לקרות פסוק אחר עד שיכלה התרגום מפי התורגמן, ואין התורגמן נשען לא לעמוד ולא לקורה אלא עומד באימה וביראה, ולא יתרגם מתוך הכתב אלא על פה, ואין הקורא רשאי לסייע לתורגמן שלא יאמרו תרגום כתוב בתורה, והקטן מתרגם על ידי גדול ואין כבוד לגדול

שיתרגם על ידי קטן, ולא יהיו המתרגמין שנים כאחד אלא אחד אחד קורא ואחד מתרגם.

**67) שולחן ערוך, אורח חיים קא:ד**

יכול להתפלל בכל לשון שירצה וה"מ בצבור אבל ביחיד לא יתפלל אלא בלשון הקודש וי"א דה"מ כשישאל צרכיו כגון שהתפלל על חולה או על שום צער שיש לו בביתו אבל תפלה הקבועה לצבור אפילו יחיד יכול לאומרה בכל לשון

**68) משנה ברורה על שולחן ערוך, אורח חיים קא:ד**

בכל לשון - ומצוה מן המובחר הוא דוקא בלשון הקודש .. דמה שהתירו להתפלל בכל לשון היינו דוקא באקראי אבל לקבוע בקביעה תמידית ולהעמיד ש"ץ ולהשכיח לה"ק לגמרי זה א"א בשום אופן עי"ש ועוד מחמת כמה וכמה טעמים נכוחים האריכו כל גאוני הזמן בספר דברי הברית והסכימו שאיסור גמור הוא לעשות כן ולאפוקי מכתות חדשות שנתפרצו למדינה מחוץ בזה והעתיקו את כל נוסח התפלה ללשון ... וכשם שרוצים להשכיח זכרון ירושלים כן רוצים להשכיח לשה"ק מישראל ...

**69) ביאור הלכה על שולחן ערוך, אורח חיים קא:ד**

יכול להתפלל בכל וכו'. ... ורצונו בזה הוא רק כדי שיתפלל בכונה אבל אם אינו בכי האי גוונא יתפלל בלה"ק והטעם כי לה"ק יש לו סגולות רבות מכל לשונות והוא הלשון שהקב"ה מדבר בו עם נביאיו כמו שכתב הרמב"ן בפ' תשא וחז"ל אמרו בלה"ק נברא העולם כדכתיב לזאת יקרא אשה כי מאיש לוקחה זאת וגם כשתקנו כנה"ג את נוסח התפלה היו ק"ך זקנים ומהם כמה נביאים והמה נימנו על כל ברכה בתיבותיה ובצירופי אותיותיה בכמה סודות נעלמות ונשגבת וכשאנו אומרין דברים אלו כלשונם של כנה"ג אף שאין אנו יודעין מ"מ עלתה לנו תפלתינו כהוגן כי התיבות בעצמן פועלין קדושתן למעלה משא"כ כשמתפללין בלע"ז:

**70) פלא יועץ, ערך "לעז"**

... שסגולת לשון הקודש רבה היא עד שאמרו שמי שיכול לדבר לעולם אפילו מילי דעלמא בלה"ק קונה קדושה והדברים עתיקים ובכל אות ואות יש רזין עלאין ובונה בשמים עליותיו אף אם לא ידע מאי קאמר קמי שמיא גליא ומעשה ידינו כוננה עלינו ...

**71) רמ"א, שולחן ערוך, אורח חיים שז:טז**

הגה ונראה לדקדק הא דאסור לקרות (בשבת) בשיחת חולין וסיפורי מלחמות היינו דוקא אם כתובים בלשון לעז אבל בלשון הקודש שרי

**72) משנה ברורה סג על שולחן ערוך, אורח חיים שז:טז**

אבל בלשון הקודש וכו' - דהלשון בעצמו יש בו

לדבר בם – משעה שהבן יודע לדבר למדהו תורה
צוה לנו משה, שיהא זה למוד דבורו, מכאן אמרו,
כשהתינוק מתחיל לדבר, אביו מסיח עמו בלשון
הקודש ומלמדו תורה (ספרי מו.), ואם לא עשה כן,
הרי הוא כאלו קוברו, שנאמר ולמדתם אותם את
בניכם מ לדבר בם וגו':

### 48) תוספתא חגיגה א:ג

יודע לדבר אביו מלמדו שמע ותורה ולשון קודש
ואם לאו ראוי לו שלא בא לעולם..

### 49) שמות ל:יב-יג

כִּי תִשָּׂא אֶת־רֹאשׁ בְּנֵי־יִשְׂרָאֵל לִפְקֻדֵיהֶם וְנָתְנוּ אִישׁ
כֹּפֶר נַפְשׁוֹ לַד' בִּפְקֹד אֹתָם וְלֹא־יִהְיֶה בָהֶם נֶגֶף בִּפְקֹד
אֹתָם זֶה יִתְּנוּ כָּל־הָעֹבֵר עַל־הַפְּקֻדִים מַחֲצִית הַשֶּׁקֶל
בְּשֶׁקֶל הַקֹּדֶשׁ עֶשְׂרִים גֵּרָה הַשֶּׁקֶל מַחֲצִית הַשֶּׁקֶל
תְּרוּמָה לַד':

### 50) פירוש רמב"ן על שמות ל:יב

... וכן כל כסף קצוב האמור בתורה, יקרא לו הכתוב
שקל הקודש. וכן טעם אצלי במה שרבותינו קוראין
לשון התורה "לשון הקודש", שהוא מפני שדברי
התורה והנבואות וכל דברי קדושה כולם בלשון
ההוא נאמרו. והנה הוא הלשון שהקב"ה יתעלה שמו
מדבר בו עם נביאיו ועם עדתו, אנכי ולא יהיה לך
ושאר דברות התורה והנבואה, ובו נקרא בשמותיו
הקדושים אל, אלהים, צבאות, ושדי, ויו"ד ה"א,
והשם הגדול המיוחד, ובו ברא עולמו, וקרא שמות
שמים וארץ וכל אשר בם, ומלאכיו וכל צבאיו לכולם
בשם יקרא מיכאל וגבריאל בלשון ההוא, ובו קרא
שמות לקדושים אשר בארץ אברהם יצחק ויעקב
ושלמה וזולתם: ...

### 51) משנה אבות ה:א ופירוש רב עובדיה מברטנורה

בַּעֲשָׂרָה מַאֲמָרוֹת נִבְרָא הָעוֹלָם.
בעשרה מאמרות – תשעה ויאמר. ובראשית נמי
מאמר הוא דכתיב (תהלים לג) בדבר ה' שמים נעשו:

### 52) מדרש ילקוט שמעוני, בראשית ב:רמז

... לזאת יקרא אשה כי מאיש מכאן שניתנה תורה
בלשון הקדש כשם שניתנה בלשון הקדש כך נברא
העולם בלשון הקדש שמעת מימיך אומר גיני גיניא
אנתרופי אנתרופא גברא גברתא אלא איש ואשה למה
שהלשון הזה נופל על הלשון הזה ...

### 53) בראשית יא:א ופירוש רש"י

וַיְהִי כָל־הָאָרֶץ שָׂפָה אֶחָת וּדְבָרִים אֲחָדִים:
שפה אחת – לשון הקודש:

### 54) פירוש רבינו בחיי על שמות ל:יג

... וקראו קודש מפני שכל המצוות הם עיקר
הקדושה, ויש בקצת המצוות צורך למטבע ההוא

---

כמצות פדיון הבן שהמצוה חמשת שקלים, גם מצות
הערכין שהם נקראים קודש שקלים צריכה לשקלים. ומן
הטעם הזה אנחנו קורין לשון תורתנו לשון הקודש,
מפני שהוא לשון של קדושה כולל כמה מיני קדושות
וכל עניני קדושה ישתמשו בו כי הוא הלשון שבו
הקב"ה דיבר עם בני ישראל עשרת הדברות, ובו
מדבר עם הנביאים ועם המלאכים, ושבעים שמות
יש לו כולם הם לשון הקודש, גם שמות המלאכים
נקראים בלשון הקודש, שהרי גבריאל נקרא על שם
הגבורה ורפאל מלשון רפואה ... והוא הלשון שבו
נברא העולם וכמו שדרשו חז"ל (בראשית רבה יח,
ד) העולם נברא בלשון הקודש שנאמר (בראשית ב,
כג) לזאת יקרא אשה כי מאיש לוקחה זאת ...

### 55) רמב"ם, מורה נבוכים ג:ח

אלה הם הדברים כולם לא הונח להם שם ראשון כלל
בלשון העברי, אלא ידובר בהם בשמות מושאלים
וברמיזות. והיתה הכוונה בזה – שאלה הדברים אין
ראוי לזכרה שיושם להם שמות, אבל הם ענינים
שצריך לשתוק מהם, וכשיביא הצורך לזכרם – יעשה
לו תחבולה בכנויים ממילות אחרות, כאשר נסתר,
בעשותם בעת הצורך, בכל יכולתנו ...

### 56) ספר כוזרי, מאמר רביעי

... אך הלשון האלוהית לשון אשר האלוה בראה
ולמדה לאדם ושמה על לשונו ובלבו היא בלא ספק
השלמה בלשונות שכנוייה מתאימים ביותר לכל
הדברים אשר עליה יורו כמו שאמר הכתוב וכל
אשר יקרא לו האדם נפש חיה הוא שמו ראוי לומר
ראוי הוא שם זה המתאים למכנה בו ומודיע טיבו
ובזה היתרון ללשון הקדש ואף המלאכים מרגישים
בה יותר מבכל לשון..

### 57) משנה אבות ב:א ופירוש הרמב"ם

הוי זהיר במצוה קלה כבחמורה. שאין אתה יודע מתן
שכרן של מצות.
אח"כ אמר שצריך ליזהר במצוה שיחשב בה שהיא
קלה כשמחת הרגל ולמידת לשון הקדש כמצוה
שהתבאר לך חומרתה שהיא גדולה כמילה וציצית
ושחיטת הפסח, ושם סיבת זה שאין אתה יודע מתן
שכרן של מצוות

### 58) תלמוד ירושלמי, שבת ט.

תני בשם ר"מ כל מי שהוא קבוע בארץ ישראל. ואוכל
חוליו בטהרה. ומדבר בלשון הקודש וקורא את שמע
בבוקר ובערב מובטח לו שהוא מחיי העולם הבא:

### 59) ירושלמי, שקלים יד:

תנא בשם ר"מ }אומר{ כל מי שקבוע בארץ ישראל
ומדבר בלשון הקודש ואוכל פירותיו בטהרה וקורא
ק"ש בבוקר ובערב יהא מבושר שכן עולם הבא

### 33) מדרש תנחומא, האזינו ז

... לעולם יבדוק אדם בשמות לקרוא לבנו הראוי להיות צדיק כי לפעמים השם גורם טוב או גורם רע

### 34) מדרש ויקרא רבה לב:ה

בשביל ד' דברים נגאלו ישראל ממצרים שלא שנו את שמם ואת לשונם ...

### 35) מדרש, במדבר רבה יג:יט

... כנגד ג' מדות טובות שהיו בידן של ישראל במצרים ובזכותן נגאלו שלא שינו את שמם ולא שינו את לשונם ושגדרו עצמם מן העולם

### 36) מהר"ל, גבורות השם מג

בזכות שלא שנו את שמם ראובן ושמעון נחתי ראובן ושמעון סלקי ולא היו קורין לראובן רופינוס ולשמעון לא היו קורין לוליני ... פירוש המאמר הזה, כי גאולה של מצרים היה בשביל שלא היו מתאחדים עם מצרים והיה לישראל התחברות עם המצרים לא היו יוצאים משם, שהרי יש להם התחברות עם מצרים ואיך יצאו מתוכם. ולפיכך אילו שינו שמם בשם מצרים או היו מדברים בלשון מצרים היה לישראל חבור עמהם ולא היו יוצאים ...

### 37) שמות א:א ופירוש הטור

וְאֵלֶּה שְׁמוֹת בְּנֵי יִשְׂרָאֵל הַבָּאִים מִצְרָיְמָה אֵת יַעֲקֹב אִישׁ וּבֵיתוֹ בָּאוּ.

... ואלה שמות בני ישראל הבאים. ר"ת שביה שאפילו כשהיו בשביה "שמות בני ישראל", שלא שינו שמותם. וזהו שאחז"ל שבשביל ג' דברים נגאלו ממצרים, בשביל שלא שינו שמותם ...

### 38) בראשית מא:מה

וַיִּקְרָא פַרְעֹה שֵׁם יוֹסֵף צָפְנַת פַּעְנֵחַ וַיִּתֶּן לוֹ אֶת אָסְנַת בַּת פּוֹטִי פֶרַע כֹּהֵן אֹן לְאִשָּׁה וַיֵּצֵא יוֹסֵף עַל אֶרֶץ מִצְרָיִם:

### 39) שו"ת מהר"ם שיק, יורה דעה קסט

... מ"מ ראיתי שראוי להשיב על הדבר אשר שאל שיש בני אדם שמכנים עצמם בשם הגוים ומעלתו נ"י הוכיח אותם דהרי אמרו במדרש שבזכות זה שלא שינו את שמם זכינו לצאת ממצרים והם משיבים שלזה די כמה שיש להם שם יהודי לקרותם בו לעלות לתורה וזה דבר הבל וטפשות כי בודאי יש בזה איסור דאורייתא כמ"ש הרמב"ם בפ' י"א מהלכי' ע"ז דמקרא מלא נאמר בסוף פרשת קדושים "ואבדיל אתכם מן העמים להיות לי לעם" ומשם ילפינן בספרי דאין רשאין לדמות להם בשום אופן וכל שהוא עושה לדמות להם עובר על מה שנאמר בתור' דאסור לנו לדמות להם וכשם שאסור לנו להדמות להם במלבושים ובהילוכים ובשאר מנהגיהם ה"ה וכ"ש דאסור לדמות להם בשמם ועלינו לעשות

---

כמו שעשו אבותינו שנאמר בהם "ויהי שם לגוי גדול" דרשו חז"ל מלמד שהיו ישראל מצויינים שם.

### 40) שו"ת אגרות משה, אורח חיים ד:סו

אם לשנות שם לעז לשם בלה"ק [=בלשון הקודש= שקרוא לבתו ע"ש אמו בע"ה י"ג כסלו תש"מ לאברך אחד.

הנה בדבר שמות של לעז שכתבתי שאף שהוא דבר מגונה אינו איסור שלכן חזינן שכמה שמות של לעז מכל מדינה ומדינה נעשו במשך הזמן דגלות הארוך שנתחלפו המדיניות, שאף שמסתמא צווחו מתחלה נשתקעו השמות בין ישראל עד שנקראו כבר לשמות ישראל ובשמות נשים הם ביותר אצלינו שאנו מבני אשכנז הם משמות אשכנז ומגולי ספרד הרבה שמות משל ספרד ... ובאם ליכא שום טעם לשום שם יש ודאי לבחור בשם אחד מהנביאים והצדיקים שבקראי או למי שהכרנוהו בדור זה לצדיק וגאון ואף כשהוא חי.

### 41) ראש השנה טז:

ארבעה דברים מקרעין גזר דינו של אדם, אלו הן: צדקה, צעקה, שינוי השם, ושינוי מעשה.

### 42) קהלת ז:א

טוֹב שֵׁם מִשֶּׁמֶן טוֹב וְיוֹם הַמָּוֶת מִיּוֹם הִוָּלְדוֹ:

### 43) פירושי רש"י על קהלת ז:א

טוב שם משמן טוב – ... שמן טוב לשעה ושם טוב לעולם שנאמר (תהלים עב) יהי שמו לעולם, שמן טוב הולך מקיתון לטרקלין ולא יותר ושם טוב לסוף העולם ...

### 44) יומא לח:

נאמר "ושם רשעים ירקב". מאי ושם רשעים ירקב? אמר רבי אלעזר: רקיבות תעלה בשמותן, דלא מסקינן בשמייהו

### 45) דברים יא:יט

וְלִמַּדְתֶּם אֹתָם אֶת בְּנֵיכֶם לְדַבֵּר בָּם בְּשִׁבְתְּךָ בְּבֵיתֶךָ וּבְלֶכְתְּךָ בַדֶּרֶךְ וּבְשָׁכְבְּךָ וּבְקוּמֶךָ:

### 46) מדרש ספרי עקב י

ולמדתם אותם את בניכם לדבר בם – ... מכאן אמרו כשהתינוק מתחיל לדב' אביו מדבר עמו לשון הקודש ומלמדו תורה ואם אין מדבר עמו לשון הקודש ואינו מלמדו תורה ראוי לו כאלו קוברו שנ' ולמדתם אותם את בניכם לדבר בם אם למדתם אותם את בניכם ירבו ימיכם וימי בניכם ואם לאו יקצרו ימיכם

### 47) דברים יא:יט ופירוש רש"י על דברים יא:יט

וְלִמַּדְתֶּם אֹתָם אֶת בְּנֵיכֶם לְדַבֵּר בָּם בְּשִׁבְתְּךָ בְּבֵיתֶךָ וּבְלֶכְתְּךָ בַדֶּרֶךְ וּבְשָׁכְבְּךָ וּבְקוּמֶךָ:

לקרותו סוס ולזה נאה לקרותו חמור ולזה נאה לקרותו שור וכן לכלם שנאמר ויקרא האדם שמות

### 25) פירוש רבינו בחיי על בראשית ב:יט

וכל אשר יקרא לו האדם נפש חיה הוא שמו. אמרו במדרש (במדבר רבה יט, ג) העביר הקב"ה לפניו כל הבהמות והחיות וקרא להן שמות, ואמר לזה נאה לקרותו אריה ולזה נאה לקרותו חמור ולזה סוס וכן על כל דבר ודבר, והנה בזה נתפרסמה חכמתו הגדולה כמו שהיה בצלם אלקים ומעשה ידי ה' יתברך:ונראה לי ביאור המדרש הזה כי האדם הבין בחכמתו ושכלו טבע כל בהמה וחיה וקרא לכל אחת ואחת שם מעין הטבע והמדה שהכיר בה והאותיות שיצרף בשמותיהן הכל לפי טבעיהן ומדותיהן, והנה היו שמות מושכלות, כאמרך הכיר בחכמתו טבע האריה שהוא גבור גדול שבחיות עד שהנביאים המשילו בו את ה' יתברך כאומרו (הושע יא, י) אחרי ה' ילכו כאריה ישאג, והעלה שמו אריה מפני שאותיות אריה רוחניות, כי האל"ף וההי"א והיו"ד הן אותיות ה' יתברך והרי"ש פירושו רוח, ואם כן עצם השם של אריה מבאר ענינו:

### 26) שמואל א' כ:כה

אַל־נָ֣א יָשִׂ֣ים אֲדֹנִ֣י ׀ אֶת־לִבּ֡וֹ אֶל־אִישׁ֩ הַבְּלִיַּ֨עַל הַזֶּ֜ה עַל־נָבָ֗ל כִּ֤י כִשְׁמוֹ֙ כֶּן־ה֔וּא נָבָ֣ל שְׁמ֔וֹ וּנְבָלָ֖ה עִמּ֑וֹ וַאֲנִי֙ אֲמָ֣תְךָ֔ לֹ֤א רָאִ֙יתִי֙ אֶת־נַעֲרֵ֣י אֲדֹנִ֔י אֲשֶׁ֖ר שָׁלָֽחְתָּ׃

### 27) בראשית ה:כט ופירושי רש"י וספורנו

וַיִּקְרָ֧א אֶת־שְׁמ֛וֹ נֹ֖חַ לֵאמֹ֑ר זֶ֞ה יְנַחֲמֵ֤נוּ מִֽמַּעֲשֵׂ֙נוּ֙ וּמֵעִצְּב֣וֹן יָדֵ֔ינוּ מִן־הָ֣אֲדָמָ֔ה אֲשֶׁ֥ר אֵֽרֲרָ֖הּ ד':

זה ינחמנו – יניח ממנו את עצבון ידינו עד שלא בא נח לא היה להם כלי מחרישה והוא הכין להם והיתה הארץ מוציאה קוצים ודרדרים כשזורעים חטים מקללתו של אדה"ר ובימי נח נחה וזהו ינחמנו. ואם לא תפרשהו כך אין טעם הלשון נופל על השם ואתה צריך לקרות שמו מנחם:

זה ינחמנו – התפלל שזה ינחמנו בהמציאו מנוחה ממעשיהם כי מלת נח תורה מנוחה כמו ונוח מאויביהם:

### 28) פירוש האלשי"ך (תורת משה) על שמות לה:ל-לג

על כן הקדים ואמר ראו כאילו בחוש הראות אתם רואים כי קרא אותו יתברך ולא אני. ובמה תראו, הלא הוא בשם כי כשמו כן הוא בצלאל, וכן כמה דברים כיוונה דעתו אל רצון הבורא יתברך יותר ממנו כאילו בצל אל היה,

### 29) שמות ג:יג ופירושי רמב"ן

וַיֹּ֨אמֶר מֹשֶׁ֜ה אֶל־הָֽאֱלֹהִ֗ים הִנֵּ֨ה אָנֹכִ֣י בָא֮ אֶל־בְּנֵ֣י יִשְׂרָאֵל֒ וְאָמַרְתִּ֣י לָהֶ֔ם אֱלֹהֵ֥י אֲבוֹתֵיכֶ֖ם שְׁלָחַ֣נִי אֲלֵיכֶ֑ם וְאָֽמְרוּ־לִ֣י מַה־שְּׁמ֔וֹ מָ֥ה אֹמַ֖ר אֲלֵהֶֽם:

... ולפי דעתי היה משה גם בעת ההיא אב בחכמה

---

גדול במעלת הנבואה, ודרך שאלה בקש שיודיעהו מי השולח אותו, כלומר באי זו מדה הוא שלוח אליהם, כענין שנאמר ישעיה (ישעיה מח טז) ועתה ה' אלהים שלחני ורוחו, והנה אמר ישאלוני על שליחותי אם היא במדת אל שדי שעמדה בה לאבות, או במדת רחמים מחודשים ביצירה וזה בעבור שאמר לו אנכי אלהי אביך אלהי אברהם (לעיל פסוק ו) ולא פירש שם משמותיו הקדושים כלל, ושמע משה שהבטיחו על מעמד הר סיני ומתן תורה, והוא היודע כי התורה לא תנתן בשם אל שדי הנזכר באבות רק השם הגדול שבו היה העולם, ועל כן שאל מה אמר אליהם:

### 30) ברכות ז:

מנא לן דשמא גרים? אמר רבי אליעזר דאמר קרא: (תהלים מו) לכו חזו מפעלות ה' אשר שם שמות בארץ, אל תקרי שמות אלא שמות.

### 31) יומא פג.

רבי מאיר הוה דייק בשמא רבי יהודה ורבי יוסי לא הוו דייקי בשמא. כי מטו להההוא דוכתא בעו אושפיזא, יהבו להו. אמרו לו: מה שמך? אמר להו: כידור. אמר: שמע מינה אדם רשע הוא, שנאמר (דברים לב) כי דור תהפכת המה. רבי יהודה ורבי יוסי אשלימו ליה כיסייהו רבי מאיר לא אשלים ליה כיסיה. אזל אותביה בי קיבריה דאבוה אתחזי ליה בחלמיה: תא שקיל כיסא דמנח ארישא דההוא גברא. למחר אמר להו: הכי אתחזי לי בחלמא אמרי ליה: חלמא דבי שמשי לית בהו ממשא. אזל רבי מאיר, ונטריה כולי יומא ואייתיה. למחר אמרו לו: הב לן כיסן אמר להו: לא היו דברים מעולם. אמר להו רבי מאיר: אמאי לא דייקיתו בשמא?

### 32) שער הגלגולים, פרק לה, לקוטים גלגולים, סוג חיבוט הקבר

וכל נשמה יש לה שם כפי בחי' האבר שממנו חוצבה וכאשר נולד האדם ואביו ואמו קוראים לו שם אינו במקרה ובהזדמן כי אם השי"ת מזמין בפיו השם המוכרח אל הנשמה הזאת כפי המקום שהיא תלויה באבר האדם העליון כמש"ה אשר שם שמ"ת בארץ והשם הזה נרשם למעלה בכסא הכבוד וגם למעלה נקרא בשם הזה וכמו שיש שם קבוע אל הנשמה הקדושה כך יש שם קבוע אל הקליפה שהוא היצה"ר הנכנס באדם מיום הולדו ...

... ונמצא כי כל אדם מישראל מלבד השם שיש לו שקרוא לו אביו ואמו בעת שנימול והוא השם הנקרא אל נשמת אדם כי השם שקורין לו אביו ואמו הוא נחשב למעלה בכסא כבוד וכן הוא ג"כ נק' למעלה כי הדברים אינם במקרה כי הקב"ה מזמין אותו בפי אביו ואמו שיקראו לו זה השם ...

כגון לסיים בלשון לספה"נ, או יותר טוב שיסיים
בלשון למה"נ, ור"ל למנהג הנהוג ...

### 15) שו"ת באר משה (שטרן) חלק ח:יח-יט

..ודע שבודאי במחאה טשעק שכל אדם כותב צריכין
להיות מאוד נזהר לכתב למשל חודש נאוועמבער
יום ג' או ד' וכיוצ"ב אבל לא לכתב תחת בחודש
נאוועמבער חודש "הי"א כי החודש הי"א הוא שבט
ולא נאוועמבער וכן לכתוב בחודש דעצעמבער ולא חודש
י"ב דחודש י"ב הוא אדר ולא דעצעמבער ...

### 16) מדרש מכילתא, פרשת החודש ז

רבי יצחק אומר לא תהא מונה כדרך שאחרים מונין
אלא תהא מונה לשם שבת:

### 17) שמות כ:ח ופירוש רמב"ן

זָכוֹר אֶת־יוֹם הַשַּׁבָּת לְקַדְּשׁוֹ:
וטעם לקדשו. שיהא זכרוננו בו להיות קדוש
בעינינו, כמו שאמר וקראת לשבת עונג לקדוש ה'
מכובד (ישעיה נח יג) .... ולכך אמרו ז"ל (חולין
ה.) שהשבת שקולה כנגד כל מצות שבתורה, כמו
שאמרו בע"ז, מפני שבה נעיד על כל עיקרי האמונה
בחדוש ובהשגחה ובנבואה. ובמכילתא (כאן) רבי
יצחק אומר, לא תהא מונה כדרך שהאחרים מונים,
אלא תהא מונה לשם שבת. ופירושה, שהגוים מונין
ימי השבוע לשם הימים עצמם, יקראו לכל יום שם
בפני עצמו, או על שמות המשרתים, כנוצרים, או
שמות אחרים שיקראו להם, וישראל מונים כל הימים
לשם שבת, אחד בשבת, שני בשבת, כי זו מן המצוה
שנצטוינו בו לזכרונו תמיד בכל יום. וזה פשוטו של
מקרא, וכך פירש ר"א ...

### 18) דרשות הרמב"ן לראש השנה

שהרי ימי השבוע אין להם שם בישראל, ובשאר
האומות כל אחד שמו עליו, כגון הנוצרים שקורין
אותם על שם שבעה כוכבי לכת כצנ"ש חל"ם שהם
ראשי הימים, ואומרים וכו', אבל בישראל אין להם
שם אלא שקורין אותם לשם מצות שבת ואומרים
אחד בשבת שני בשבת וכו' כדי שנזכור השבת בכל
יום, וזהו פשוטו של מקרא שאמר זכור את יום
השבת שנזכור אותו תמיד בכל הימים, וכך אמרו
רז"ל במכילתא ר' יצחק אומר לא תהא מונה כדרך
שאחרים מונין אלא תהא מונה לשם שבת, כלומר כל
הימים תהא מונה אליו וממנו, ועל כן לא קראו להם
לא שם עצם ולא שם תאר אלא לשם שבת הם
נקראים ...

### 19) תורת משה על פרשת בא

החדש הזה לכם ראש חדשים ראשון הוא וכו' – כ'
הרמב"ן אין שם פרט לחדשים בתורה רק ימי שבת
ושני כדי להיות זכרון ליציאת מצרים וכן ימי שבת
מונים כך יום ראשון בשבת יום שני וכן כולם והוא

בכלל זכור את יום השבת וזה תוכחת מוסר שנכתב
מהמכתבים וכדומה יום ראשון בשבת וחודש ראשון
להעיד על בריאת שמים וארץ בששת ימים וינח ביום
השביעי ועל יציאת מצרים לא ח"ו כמספרם של
אומות העולם ...

### 20) שו"ת באר משה (שטרן) חלק ח:יח-יט

... ובאמת חידוש גדול בעיני למה יש שום מחבר
שיש לעורר על מה שאנו קורין יום ראשון א' בשבת
זונטיג ב' בשבת מאנטיג וכו' שלא כדין ושלא כהלכה
ואח"כ מצאתי בתשו' כ"ק מרן אדמו"ר מסאטמאר
זצוקלה"ה דברי יואל שע"י מה שאנו קורין יום ראשון
של כל יום ואומרים היום יום ראשון בשבת וכו' זה
נקרא שפיר זכירה תמידית דפח"ח ש"י אבל עדיין
צע"ג דמדברי הרמב"ן משמע שצריך להיות מנין
השבוע יום א' יום ב' שגור בכל עניניו ומי התיר
לנו לקרות זונטיג מאנטיג וגו' תחת יום א' יום ב'
ואיך אנו פטורים להחליף דבר המפורש לפי פי'
הרמב"ן עפ"י המכילתא בשם ר' יצחק באיזה אחר
כדרך האומות העולם ואיך אנו דורסים ברגלינו על
הלכה זו מדהזכרנו פעם א' בבקר כן והדבר צ"ת
ועיון רב ...

### 21) הליכות שלמה (רב שלמה זלמן אוירבך), הלכות תפילה יא:יד

קודם שיר של יום אמר רבנו "זכור את יום השבת
לקדשו" היום יום פלוני וכו'
ס"ק יז – והיינו משום דעת הרמב"ן (שמות כ:ח)
דמצוה לזכור את יום השבת בכל יום. ומיהו עיקר
ההלכה אינה כהרמב"ן אלא המצוה היא רק יום
השבת גופא לקדשו בדברים ועל הכוס וכו' ומשום
כך אין לחוש למה שאין מזכירין את היום בשבוע
בימים שאומרים בהם מזמורים אתוים (ע"פ מנהג
הגר"א ז"ל)

### 22) חיי אדם, חלק שני, א:א

... וכן כשמונין מנין הימים, יהיו מונים על שם
השבת, דהיינו יום ראשון בשבת, ויום שני בשבת, וכן
כולם, כי קדושת השבת היא נמשכת לכל יום, כי הוא
המרכז האמצעי שכל ימי השבוע יונקים ממנו. יום
א' ב' ג' נקראין אחר השבת, שהם מקבלים קדושה
משבת העבר. וימים ד' ה' ו' נקראים קודם שבת, כי הם
מושפעים ומקבלים קדושה משבת הבא ...

### 23) בראשית ב:כ

וַיִּקְרָא הָאָדָם שֵׁמוֹת לְכָל־הַבְּהֵמָה וּלְעוֹף הַשָּׁמַיִם וּלְכֹל
חַיַּת הַשָּׂדֶה וּלְאָדָם לֹא־מָצָא עֵזֶר כְּנֶגְדּוֹ:

### 24) מדרש ילקוט שמעוני, מלכים א' רמז

ויחכם מכל האדם. מאדם הראשון. מה היה חכמתו
אתה מוצא כשבראו הקב"ה העביר כל בהמה
חיה ועוף, א"ל מה שמותן של אלו, א"ל לזה נאה

אין לדעתי כל חשש של לא ישמע על פיך, וגם לא משום גרמא להזכרה. ועוד זאת כידוע אין המנין האזרחי שמונים בו מכוון בכלל למנין אותו האיש, וכבר האריך את ההוכחות הברורות לכך ידידי הגר"ע יוסף שליט"א בספרו שו"ת יביע אומר ח"ג יו"ד סי' ט, קחנו משם... ואם כי בודאי באין כל צורך ורק לשם חיקוי, אין לכתוב התאריך למנינם, ויש להדר ולהנהיג לכתוב לפי התאריך העברי... אבל כשיש הכרח מסחרי או משרדי ומכ"ש לכתוב למנינם, על כגון דא לא אמורים תוקף דברי הח"ס... ונראה לומר עוד גם זאת, דאולי כל תוקף דברי הח"ס בזה אמורים בהיכא שמזכיר במפורש שגם זה לספה"נ,... ועוד זאת נראה לי לומר דאם בסמוך לתאריך האזרחי ידקדק בעצמו לכתוב במפורש גם התאריך העברי בשניו ובחדשיו, אזי באופן כזה לא יהא בדבר גם משום גנאי בהיות דמראה במפורש שאינו מזיח מלמנות למנין ב"י... הן אמנם אילו זכינו היו אלו שהכח בידם לכך מנהיגים שעכ"פ בכל הנוגע לעניננו הפנימיים בכאן יכתבו רק התאריך העברי, אבל עכשיו שלא זכינו ומשרד אחד גורר את משנהו להכרח להזכיר תאריך מנינם, על כן נלפענ"ד שבאופנים הנ"ל שיכתבו למנ"ן או למספרם...

## 11) שו"ת באר משה (שטרן) חלק ח:יח-יט

...וכשכותבים השנה בטשיק בודאי יהי' נזהר לכתוב למשל בשנת אלף ותשע מאות ושמונים רק לכתוב 980 או 80, ומעיד אני על עצמי שתמיד כתבתי רק 80 או 980 ושום טשעק לא חזר אם הי' מעות בהבאנק ותהלה לא-ל לכל מי שאמרתי לעשות כן קבלו בסבר פנים יפות והבטיחו אותי לכתוב כן ופעם לתמהתי הגדולה קבלתי מישיבה אחת בארצינו הקדושה קבלה על המעות ששלחתי והי' כתוב תאריך הנוצרי וגם החודש תחת אקטאבער החודש העשירי והחזרתי המכתב וכתבתי להם להראות להגאון הראש הישיבה שליט"א ומאז כותבים הכל לפי השנה והחודש שלנו ולא ח"ו שלהם...

יט- הנה ראיתי בב' ספרי אחרונים דברים תמוהים שאין להם שום יסוד בהלכה והעלו להקל להזכיר מספר הנוצרים כי טעות הוא שמספרם הוא לידת "אותו איש" כי הוא נולד ד' שנים לפני מספר הנוצרים עיי"ש ופליאה נשגבה בעיני דבריהם דמה בכך שנולד ד' שנים לפני מספר שני הנוצרים הלא כל הגוים מאמינים וגם להבדיל אנן כן יודעים שמספר שני הנוצרים מספרים ללידת "אותו איש" והם תקנו לכתוב לכבודו ולתפארתו וכן מפורסם ביניהם ואם אנו (ז) ג"כ נכתב המספר הנוצרים נותנים יקר ותפארת וכבוד "למשיחם" היינו לאותו איש...

...והיותר מחמיר בהזכרת מספר הנוצרים הוא רבינו הק' מהר"מ שיק (חיו"ד סי' קע"א) שחושש שהמזכיר מספרם עובר בזה איסור דהוריתא ושם אלקים אחרים לא תזכירו עיי"ש...

## 12) שו"ת תשובות והנהגות (רב משה שטרנבוך) חושן משפט א:תתל

שאלה אם מותר לכתוב על שטר את התאריך הלועזי השנה והחודש כפי חשבון הגויים – אין אני רואה בזה נדנוד של איסור לכתוב תאריך לועזי ומצינו גם בזמן חז"ל שכתבו שטרות לפי מנין היוונים אבל ראיתי בפירוש לחם הפנים מהרב מבולגריי זצ"ל שמעורר שאסור לכתוב לשמיני כיון שלדידן החודש הראשון הוא ניסן וכאן מונה הוא החדשים לפי מנינם ע"ש ולא הבנתי דבריו כלל דכל מה דחיבין למנות את ניסן כחודש ראשון הוא רק לפי חשבון שלנו שמונין לפי הלבנה אבל לחשבונם שמונין לפי החמה אזי לא שייך למנות בזה מנין כראשון וכודאי מותר והחתם סופר זצ"ל העלה שמקיימין מצוה בזה שמונים לפי ניסן שנאמר החודש הזה לכם ראש חדשים אבל מדינא נראה שאין שום איסור מנין החמה מותר לציין במכתב לכותב צ'קים ושטרות לתשלום משכורות או שכירות חודש כפי חדשיהם וכן סיפר לי מרן הגריז"ס זצ"ל שאביו הגר"ח מבריסק זצ"ל שילם ליהודי שכירות כפי חדשיהם כמו שנצטוטה ולא חשש כלל אמנם נאה הדבר ויאה שכל כותב לחבירו יכתוב כפי הלוח העברי שלנו שעלינו להתגאות בחישוב תקופות ושנים כפי מנין שלנו דוקא ולשבח בכך את הקב"ה שלא שם חלקנו כהם וגורלנו ככל המונם ולדעת הח"ס הנ"ל לכאורה היה כדאי לכתוב תמיד מנין החודש ניסן הוא החודש הראשון וכו' כגון בחודש תמוז "חודש הרביעי חודש תמוז" ונקיים בכך מ"ע אבל לא נהגו כן בדרשת הרמב"ן לר"ה שמבאר הענין

## 13) שו"ת ילקוט יוסף (רב עובדיה יוסף), שובע שמחות א:א, לו

יש לכתוב בהזמנות את התאריך של החתונה בתאריך עברי כגון אור ל' לחודש וכו', והרוצים לכתוב בהזמנות גם תאריך לועזי לא יכתבו מספר החודש דהיינו החודש הראשון או השני וכו' אלא יכתבו ינואר פברואר וכדומה וכזה עדיף יותר ויכתבו אחר התאריך הלועזי "למספרם"

## 14) שו"ת ציץ אליעזר, חלק ח:ח

... והנה היביע אומר שם מציע כשכותבים לפי מנינים להזכיר במפורש שמות החדשים שלהם ולא לכתוב בספירה של החדש הראשון או השני וכו', ואני כתבתי לו דלפי דעתי להזכיר במפורש שמות החדשים שלהם הוא יותר גרוע כי כפי שטמעתי /ששמעתי/ בבירור שמות החדשים שלהם מכוונים לשמות אלילים, ויצא איפוא שדוקא כשמזכיר במפורש שמות החדשים שלהם אז הו"ל כמזכיר שם עכו"ם [והערה זאת ממשמשת ובאה גם על ספר גנזי יוסף סי' ק"ו שמביא ג"כ לכתוב בכזאת עיי"ש]. ולכן עדיפא יותר שיכתוב בסתם במספרים השנה והחדש שלהם, ויזהר שלא להזכיר שהוא לספירת הנוצרים

מאשור זכר לגאולה השנית כי הבינו שצווי מנין
החדשים מניסן היה זמניי ולא צווי נצחי אע"פ שלא
נזכר בו זמן:

### 6) בני יששכר, מאמרי חודש ניסן א

שמות החדשים עלו עמהם מבבל כן אמרו רז"ל ויצא
להם זה מדלי נמצא שום שם חודש בדברי נבואה
רק בכתובים במגילת אסתר בעזרא ונחמיה ונראה לי
דודאי שמות החדשים נתקבלו גם מסיני רק שהיה
בבחינת תורה שבעל פה דהרי נזכרו השמות של
חדשים בתרגום והתרגום נתקבל בסיני כידוע אבל
התרגום הוא תורה שבעל פה אבל לא נתנו לכתוב
בכתב עד שעלו מבבל ...

### 7) חתם סופר, דרוש לז' אב, שנת תק"ע

.. וה"נ במנין שאנו מונין לבריאת עולם זוכרים אנחנו
כי העולם מחודש וארץ ישראל ראוי לנו ואפ"ה
גלינו מארצינו ולא כאותם חדשים מקרוב המונים
שכותבים בריש מגילתא מנין לידת משיח הנוצרים
וכותב וחותם עצמו אין לו חלק באלקי ישראל אוי
להם כי גמלו לנפשם רעה בתורת ה' מאסו וחכמת
מה להם

### 8) שו"ת מהר"ם שיק, יורה דעה קע"א, שמות כג:יג

... אבל מה שעשו עוד (על המצבה) שכתבו מספר
השנים כרך החדשים ג"כ בלשון לע"ז זה עבירה
ומכופלת דמספר החדשים שלהם אינם מכוונים
למספר ב"י ומה שסיימו למספר השנים למספר
הנוצרי לדעתי זה איסור דאורייתא שהרי בפ'
משפטים נאמר "ושם אלקים אחרים לא תזכירו"
וּבְכֹל אֲשֶׁר אָמַרְתִּי אֲלֵיכֶם תִּשָּׁמֵרוּ וְשֵׁם אֱלֹהִים אֲחֵרִים
לֹא תַזְכִּירוּ לֹא יִשָּׁמַע עַל פִּיךָ:

### 9) שו"ת יביע אומר, יורה דעה, חלק ג:ט

נשאלתי אודות הכותבים אגרות ומכתבים לחבריהם,
וכותבים התאריך למנין הנוצרים, אם יש למחות
בידיהם משום ובחקותיהם לא תלכו. או אין בזה
איסור גמור מן הדין.

(1) בטרם תחיל הארץ /הארש/ אבא העיר והיתה
לבאר כי אין הדבר ברור כלל שמנין הנוצרים הוא
ללידת ישוע הנוצרי יש"ו. שהרי לפי מ"ש רז"ל
בסוטה (מז) ובסנהדרין (קז:), יש"ו היה חי בזמנו של
יהושע בן פרחיה, אשר דחאו בשתי ידים ... נמצא
שהרבה שנים לפני תחלת מספרם כבר מת יש"ו. וכ"כ
הראב"ד בס' הקבלה ... ומסורת אמת יש בידינו מן
הש"ס שלא החליפו שום דבר ... והנוצרים אומרים
שמת מ"ב שנה קודם החורבן כדי לתלות החרבן בעון
הריגתו ... ומחלוקת היא בין חכמי ישראל לחכמי
אוה"ע. ..... שמנין הנוצרים הוא למלכות הרומיים
ולא ללידת יש"ו. ע"ש.

(2) ומעתה הבא נבא לנ"ד, כי נראה שאם כותבי
התאריך הלועזי אינם חושבים בכוונה מכוונת שמנין

---

זה ללידת אותו האיש, רק לפי שכן נוהגים העולם
הבקיאים יותר בתאריך האזרחי, (ובפרט במקומות
שגם משרדי הממשלה מונים למספר הנוצרים.)
אין בזה איסור משום ובחקותיהם לא תלכו. הואיל
ובאמת דעת רז"ל היא שאין מספרם מתאים ללידת
ישו הנוצרי, וטעות הוא ביד החושבים כן. ואף את"ל
שהואיל ונראה שכוונת הנוצרים במספרם זה היא
ללידת אותו האיש, כל מי שכותב התאריך הלועזי
בתר דידהו אזיל. מ"מ הואיל ואין כוונתו אלא
לכתוב התאריך המפורסם יותר אין בזה איסור משום
ובחקותיהם לא תלכו

... הוית להגאון מהר"ם שיק (חיו"ד סי' קעא......
אולם לפמש"כ לעיל שאין זה חשבון זה מכוון ללידתו
של אותו האיש, לפ"ד רז"ל, נראה שאין בזה גם
משום ושם אלהים אחרים לא תזכירו. ובלא"ה יש
להעיר לפמ"ש הר"א ממיץ בס' יראים (סי' עה) וז"ל,
ונ"ל שאינו אסור להזכיר אלא שם הניתן לאליל
לשם אלהות ... ולפ"ז הדבר ברור שאין כל איסור
בספירת התאריך הלועזי, ... אבל במצבות וכיו"ב
ודאי שאין ראוי לכתוב תאריך לועזי....אבל איסור
ממש לא שמענו. ולכן אין צורך למחות בהנוהגים
כן מתוך שיגרא בעלמא. ובפרט בחו"ל. שכל משרדי
הממשלה ואילי המסחר והתעשיה מונים למספר.
אך יש להעיר להם שלא יקראו את החודש ינואר
החודש הראשון, או פברואר השני. וכו'. וכן בכתיבה.
**אלא יש לבחור הרע במיעוטו שיקראום בשמותם
המפורסמים.** וכמ"ש הרמב"ן (פר' בא) וז"ל, וטעם
החדש הזה לכם ראש חדשים, שימנוהו ישראל חודש
הראשון ...

### 10) שו"ת ציץ אליעזר, חלק ח:ח

על אודות מה ששאלתני אם אין איסור בהזכרת
תאריך העמים במכתבים משום לא ישמע על פיך,
וממילא אם יש לו שותפות צריך לדקדק מראש
שגם שותפו יזהר בזה בדומה לנפסק באו"ח סי'
קנ"ו דיזהר מלהשתתף עם הכותי שמא יתחייב
לו שבועה ועובר משום לא ישמע על פיך, והוסיף
ששמע מרב אחד שאמר שבשבח"ס כותב לאסור זה.

.... הרי דמיאסר קאסר המהר"ם שיק הזכרת תאריך
העמים על מצבה משום לא תזכירו, וא"כ ה"ה יש
לאסור מה"ט גם הזכרת התאריך ע"ג מכתבי"
ומסמכים. אבל לאחר העיון נראה די"ל דעד כאן
אסר בזה המהר"ם שיק משום לא תזכירו כי אם היכא
שמזכיר במפורש שזהו למספר הנוצרי כגון שעם
סיום כתיבת התאריך מסיים בלשון לספה"נ. אבל
אם לא מסיים בכזאת ובכל כה"ג משום לא תזכירו
שמונים העמים אין בכל כה"ג משום לא תזכירו ...
אבל זאת מידה שפיר יש לומר דמה דמה שחשש ברישא
דדבריו לפסול את הגט משום הזכרת שם עבודת
כוכבים, כוונתו בדווקא בהיכא שסיים שם גם וכתב
"לספירת הנוצרים" ... עכ"פ בהיכא שאינו מזכיר גם
המלים לספה"נ וכותב רק חשבון התאריך של חשבון העמים

# SOURCES ON JEWISH AND SECULAR DATES, NAMES, AND LANGUAGE

### 1) שמות יב:א-ב

וַיֹּאמֶר ד' אֶל-מֹשֶׁה וְאֶל-אַהֲרֹן בְּאֶרֶץ מִצְרַיִם לֵאמֹר: הַחֹדֶשׁ הַזֶּה לָכֶם רֹאשׁ חֳדָשִׁים רִאשׁוֹן הוּא לָכֶם לְחָדְשֵׁי הַשָּׁנָה:

### 2) פירוש רמב"ן על שמות יב:ב

... וטעם החדש הזה לכם ראש חדשים, שימנו אותו ישראל חדש הראשון, וממנו ימנו כל החדשים שני ושלישי עד תשלום השנה בשנים עשר חדש, כדי שיהיה זה זכרון בנס הגדול, כי בכל עת שנזכיר החדשים יהיה הנס נזכר, ועל כן אין לחדשים שם בתורה, אלא יאמר בחדש השלישי (להלן יט א), ואומר ויהי בשנה השנית בחדש השני נעלה הענן (במדבר י יא), ובחדש השביעי באחד לחודש וגו' (שם כט א), וכן כלם: ...

... וכבר הזכירו רבותינו זה הענין, ואמרו שמות חדשים עלו עמנו מבבל (ירושלמי ר"ה א ב, ב"ר מח ט), כי מתחלה לא היו להם שמות אצלנו, והסבה בזה, כי מתחלה היה מניננו זכר ליציאת מצרים, אבל כאשר עלינו מבבל ונתקיים מה שאמר הכתוב (ירמיה טז יד) ולא יאמר עוד חי ה' אשר העלה את בני ישראל מארץ מצרים כי אם חי ה' אשר העלה ואשר הביא את בני ישראל מארץ צפון, חזרנו לקרא החדשים בשם שנקראים בארץ בבל, להזכיר כי שם עמדנו ומשם העלנו העל"ו הש"י. כי אלה השמות ניסן אייר וזולתם שמות פרסיים, ולא ימצא רק בספרי נביאי בבל (זכריה א ז, עזרא ו טו, נחמיה א א) ובמגילת אסתר (ג ז). ולכן אמר הכתוב בחדש הראשון הוא חדש ניסן, כמו הפיל פור הוא הגורל (שם). ועוד היום הגוים בארצות פרס ומדי כך הם קוראים אותם ניסן ותשרי וכלם כמונו. והנה נזכיר בחדשים הגאולה השנית כאשר עשינו עד הנה בראשונה:

### 3) דרשות הרמב"ן לראש השנה

... וכן החדשים לא היה להם שם בתורה ולא בישראל אבל היו ישראל אומרים כמו שהתורה אומרת בחדש ש[הראשו]ן, וכן ויהי בשנה השנית רחדש השני נעלה הענן, ובחודש השביעי באחד לחודש וכן כולם, ופירושו בחודש הראשון לגאולתינו ממצרים ובחדש השביעי ליציאת מצרים, וזהו פירוש ראשון הוא לכם שאינו ראשון בשנה אבל הוא ראשון לנו שנקרא אותו ראשון לגאולה שלנו ואלו השמות שאנו קורין אותן ניסן אייר סיון, שמות פרסיים הם ולא תמצא אותם לא בתורה ולא בנביאים אלא בכתבי הקדש הנעשים בבבל ... אמרו בבראשית רבה (פמ"ח ט) וכן בירושלמי (ר"ה פ"א ה"ב) שמות החדשים עלו

---

עמהם מבבל כלומר שמתחילה לא היו להם שמות בישראל עד שיצאנו מבבל והעלינו השמות משם, והסבה בזה לפי שמתחילה נצטוינו למנותם בזכרון גאולת מצרים, וכשיצאנו מבבל ונצטוינו לא אמר עוד חי ה' אשר העלה את בני ישראל מארץ מצרים כי אם חי ה' אשר העלה ואשר הביא את בני ישראל מארץ צפון וגו', חזרנו לקרות חדשינו לגאולת צפון, ולא שנשנה השמות הראשונים ונשכח גאולת מצרים אלא שנצרף שם שמות בבל להודיע ולזכור ששם עמדנו ומשם הוציאנו הוציאנו ה', וכל זה נתחדש ביציאתנו ממצרים, אבל קודם לכן החדשים הנזכרים בתורה כגון במבול בראשון באחד לחדש ובחדש השביעי והעשירי הנמנים שם ...

### 4) ספר העיקרים ג:טז

... וכאשר עלו מבבל ראו לעשות זכר לגאולה השנית ועשו זה בשני דברים ... וכן עשו דבר אחר זכר לגאולה השנית והוא שהניחו מלמנות מנין החדשים מניסן כמו שהיו רגילים למנות זכר ליציאת מצרים וחזרו למנות מנין אחר לחדשים וזהו שאמרו רבותינו ז"ל שמות החדשים עלו עמהם מאשור כלומר שהיו מונין החדשים בשמותם תשרי מרחשון כסליו כמו שהיו מונין אותם באשור זכר לגאולה השנית ולא שני שלישי רביעי כאשר בתחלה וכן כתב הרמב"ן ז"ל בפרשת בא אל פרעה:

### 5) פירוש אברבנאל על שמות יב

... ואמנם שמות החדשים אשר אתנו העולים מבבל העלום משם כי שמות פרסיים הם וקראום כן לזכרון גאולתם מבבל להודיע כי משם עמדו ומשנם העלום השם יתברך ונראה לי שלא עברו בזה על מצות החדש לפי שהם גם לא נמנעו מלקרוא את החדשים ראשון ושני במספרם כמו שצותה תורה אבל מלבד זה כנו את החודש באותו כנוי שהיו מכנים אותו בבבל וכן נאמר במגלת אסתר בחדש הראשון הוא חדש ניסן שהוא ביאור החודש על דרך הפיל פור הוא הגורל הנה התבאר שענין מצות החדש היא התחלת הנחיית ושאינה סותרות להתחלה הטבעיית ...

ונראה מזה כי הם הבינו שצווי מנין החדשים היה זמני ר"ל כל עוד שתתמיד הגאולה ההיא אבל אחר שגלו שנית משם ונצטוו ע"י ירמיהו ולא יאמר עוד חי ה' אשר העלה את בני ישראל מארץ מצרים כי אם חי ה' אשר העלה את זרע בני ישראל מארץ צפון וגו' (ירמיהו כ"ג) ראו להניח המנין הראשון שהיה זכר ליציאת מצרים וחזרו למנות מנין אחר מתשרי לשנות העולם והשאירו שמות החדשים שעלו עמהם

לֶחֶם לְפִי הַטָּף:
וְכָל־הָאָרֶץ בָּאוּ מִצְרַיְמָה לִשְׁבֹּר אֶל־יוֹסֵף כִּי־חָזַק
הָרָעָב בְּכָל־הָאָרֶץ:

### 84) דברים לג:יב

לְבִנְיָמִן אָמַר יְדִיד ד' יִשְׁכֹּן לָבֶטַח עָלָיו חֹפֵף עָלָיו כָּל־
הַיּוֹם וּבֵין כְּתֵפָיו שָׁכֵן:

### 85) מדרש תהילים קכב:ד

ירושלים הבנויה – א"ר יוחנן אמר הקב"ה לא אבא
בירושלים של מעלה, עד שאבוא לירושלים של מטה
(שנאמר בקרבך קדוש ולא אבוא בעיר (הושע יא:ט)

### 86) שמות יט:ו

וְאַתֶּם תִּהְיוּ־לִי מַמְלֶכֶת כֹּהֲנִים וְגוֹי קָדוֹשׁ אֵלֶּה הַדְּבָרִים
אֲשֶׁר תְּדַבֵּר אֶל־בְּנֵי יִשְׂרָאֵל:

### 87) סנהדרים קב.

אמר רבי אבא: אחר שתפשו הקדוש ברוך הוא
לירבעם בבגדו, ואמר לו: חזור בך, ואני ואתה ובן
ישי נטייל בגן עדן, אמר לו, מי בראש: בן ישי בראש
אי הכי לא בעינא.

### 88) מלכים א' יב:כה

וַיִּבֶן יָרָבְעָם אֶת־שְׁכֶם בְּהַר אֶפְרַיִם וַיֵּשֶׁב בָּהּ וַיֵּצֵא מִשָּׁם
וַיִּבֶן אֶת־פְּנוּאֵל:

### 89) בראשית מח:כב

וַאֲנִי נָתַתִּי לְךָ שְׁכֶם אַחַד עַל־אַחֶיךָ אֲשֶׁר לָקַחְתִּי מִיַּד
הָאֱמֹרִי בְּחַרְבִּי וּבְקַשְׁתִּי:

### 90) תהילים קלז:ה-ו

אִם־אֶשְׁכָּחֵךְ יְרוּשָׁלִָם תִּשְׁכַּח יְמִינִי: תִּדְבַּק־לְשׁוֹנִי |
לְחִכִּי אִם־לֹא אֶזְכְּרֵכִי אִם־לֹא אַעֲלֶה אֶת־יְרוּשָׁלִַם עַל
רֹאשׁ שִׂמְחָתִי:

**69) קידושין מט:**
עשרה קבים יופי ירדו לעולם, תשעה נטלה ירושלים, ואחד כל העולם כולו.

**70) סוכה נא:**
מי שלא ראה ירושלים בתפארתה לא ראה כרך נחמד מעולם

**71) ברכות ט:, ביצה יד:, תמיד כז:**
קהלא קדישא דבירושלים:

**72) אבות דרבי נתן לה:א, יומא כא.**
עשרה נסים נעשו לאבותינו בבהמ"ק [מעולם לא הסריח בשר הקדש] ולא הפילה אשה מריח בשר הקודש ((עשרה נסים נעשו לאבותינו בירושלים)) לא ניזוק אדם בירושלים מעולם] ולא נפגע אדם בירושלים ולא נכשל אדם בירושלים מעולם ולא נפלה דליקה בירושלים מעולם לא היתה מפולת בירושלים מעולם לא אמר אדם לחבירו לא מצאתי תנור לצלות פסחים בירושלים. מעולם לא אמר אדם לחבירו לא מצאתי מיטה שאישן עליה בירושלים. מעולם לא אמר אדם לחבירו צר לי המקום שאלין בירושלים.

עשרה נסים נעשו בבית המקדש: לא הפילה אשה מריח בשר הקדש, ולא הסריח בשר הקדש מעולם, ולא נראה זבוב בבית המטבחים, ולא אירע קרי לכהן גדול ביום הכפורים, ולא נמצא פסול בעומר, ובשתי הלחם, ובלחם הפנים, עומדים צפופים ומשתחוים רווחים, ולא הזיק נחש ועקרב בירושלים מעולם, ולא אמר אדם לחברו צר לי המקום שאלין בירושלים.

**73) יומא לט:**
כלה שבירושלים אינה צריכה להתקשט מריח קטורת.

**74) מדרש, קהלת רבה א:כ**
ד"א כל הנחלים הולכים אל הים כל ישראל אינם מתכנסין אלא לירושלים ועולים בפעמי רגלים בכל שנה ושנה, והים איננו מלא, וירושלים אינה מתמלאת לעולם דתנינן עומדין צפופים ומשתחוים רווחים, ר' שמואל בר חובה בשם ר' אחא אמר ארבע אמות ריווח בין כל אחד ואחד ואמה מכל צד כדי שלא יהא שומע תפלתו של חבירו ויטעה, אל מקום שהנחלים הולכים,

**75) מדרש תהילים קכב:ד**
ירושלים הבנויה – א"ר יוחנן אמר הקב"ה לא אבוא בירושלים של מעלה, עד שאבוא לירושלים של מטה (שנאמר בקרבך קדוש ולא אבוא בעיר (הושע יא:ט)

**76) ישעיה נד:יא-יג**
עֲנִיָּה סֹעֲרָה לֹא נֻחָמָה הִנֵּה אָנֹכִי מַרְבִּיץ בַּפּוּךְ אֲבָנַיִךְ

וִיסַדְתִּיךְ בַּסַּפִּירִים: וְשַׂמְתִּי כַּדְכֹד שִׁמְשֹׁתַיִךְ וּשְׁעָרַיִךְ לְאַבְנֵי אֶקְדָּח וְכָל גְּבוּלֵךְ לְאַבְנֵי חֵפֶץ: וְכָל בָּנַיִךְ לִמּוּדֵי ד' וְרַב שְׁלוֹם בָּנָיִךְ:

**77) מדרש תהילים צג:ב**
אמר ר' יהודה אמר הקב"ה לאומות העולם בניתם בתי עבודה זרה שלכם, וכיון שאני אומר לכם בנו את ירושלים, אתם אומרים עניה סוערה לא נוחמה (ישעיה נד יא), הוי עצת עני תבישו, וכאן הוא אומר הבישותה כי (ה') (אלקים) מאסם (תהלים צג:ו), כסבורים אתם שה' מאסם, והלא כבר נאמר לא מאסתים (ויקרא כו:מד), מי יתן מציון ישועות ישראל בשוב (ה') (אלקים) שבות עמו יגל יעקב ישמח ישראל, ועשו וישמעאל מתאנחים.

**78) ברכות סד.**
שנאמר (ישעיהו נ"ד) "וכל בניך למודי ה' ורב שלום בניך", אל תקרי בניך אלא בוניך

**79) בבא בתרא עה.**
(ישעיהו נח) ושמתי כדכד שמשותיך א"ר שמואל בר נחמני: פליגי תרי מלאכי ברקיעא, גבריאל ומיכאל, ואמרי לה: תרי אמוראי במערבא, ומאן אינון? יהודה וחזקיה בני רבי חייא, חד אמר: שוהם, וחד אמר: ישפה, אמר להו הקב"ה: להוי כדין וכדין.

**80) שמות כח:יז-כ**
וּמִלֵּאתָ בוֹ מִלֻּאַת אֶבֶן אַרְבָּעָה טוּרִים אָבֶן טוּר אֹדֶם פִּטְדָה וּבָרֶקֶת הַטּוּר הָאֶחָד: וְהַטּוּר הַשֵּׁנִי נֹפֶךְ סַפִּיר וְיָהֲלֹם: וְהַטּוּר הַשְּׁלִישִׁי לֶשֶׁם שְׁבוֹ וְאַחְלָמָה: וְהַטּוּר הָרְבִיעִי תַּרְשִׁישׁ וְשֹׁהַם וְיָשְׁפֵה מְשֻׁבָּצִים זָהָב יִהְיוּ בְּמִלּוּאֹתָם:

**81) פירוש רשב"ם על בבא בתרא עה.**
שמשותיך – חומותיך פליגי בה – באבנים של חומות ירושלים ממה יהיו אלו אבנים שעתידים להיות. כדין וכדין – כדברי זה וכדברי זה והיינו כדכוד משהם וישפה תבנה ואע"פ שמקרא זה קדם לבני ר' חייא טובא יש לומר שכך נתנבא ישעיה שכדברי כל המפרשים עתידה להבנות.

**82) פירוש מהרש"א על בבא בתרא עה.**
שוהם או ישפה שהם ב' אבנים אחרונים שהם בחושן בטור הרביעי ע"ש אור בגאולה הרביעית של עתיד שהיא גאולה הרביעית ובשוהם היה מפותח שם יוסף ובישפה בנימין ע"פ כונה זו ובגאולה הרביעית יהיה תחלה אור ישראל ע"י משיח בן יוסף ואורו של ירושלים שהוא בחלקו של בנימין וז"ש להוי כדין וכדין ע"פ שתי הכוונות שאמרנו וק"ל:

**83) בראשית מז:יב, מא:מז**
וַיְכַלְכֵּל יוֹסֵף אֶת אָבִיו וְאֶת אֶחָיו וְאֵת כָּל בֵּית אָבִיו

כהן גדול קול הברה, ולא תהא שינה חוטפתו.
מיקירי ירושלים – מחשובי ירושלים עושין כך ...

### 55) יומא א:ז
בקש להתנמנם, פרחי כהונה מכין לפניו באצבע
צרדה, ואומרים לו, אישי כהן גדול, עמוד והפג אחת
על הרצפה. ומעסיקין אותו עד שיגיע זמן השחיטה:

### 56) סוכה לז
אמר רבי מאיר: מעשה בביקירי ירושלים שהיו אוגדין
את לוליביהן בגימוניות של זהב

### 57) סוכה מא:
כך היה מנהגן של אנשי ירושלים, אדם יוצא מביתו
ולולבו בידו, הולך לבית הכנסת לולבו בידו, קורא
קריאת שמע ומתפלל ולולבו בידו, קורא בתורה
ונושא את כפיו מניחו על גבי קרקע. הולך לבקר
חולים ולנחם אבלים לולבו בידו, נכנס לבית
המדרש משגר לולבו ביד בנו וביד עבדו וביד
שלוחו, מאי קא משמע לן? להודיעך כמה היו זריזין
במצות.

### 58) סופרים יב:יד
כך היו נקיי הדעת שבירושלים עושין כשהיו מוציאין
את התורה ומחזירין היו הולכין אחריה מפני כבודה.

### 59) תענית כו:
אמר רבן שמעון בן גמליאל: לא היו ימים טובים
לישראל כחמשה עשר באב וכיום הכפורים, שבהן
בנות ירושלים יוצאות בכלי לבן שאולין, שלא לבייש
את מי שאין לו, כל הכלים טעונין טבילה. ובנות
ירושלים יוצאות וחולות בכרמים. ומה היו אומרות:
בחור שא נא עיניך וראה מה אתה בורר לך, אל תתן
עיניך בנוי, תן עיניך במשפחה, (משלי ל"א) שקר
החן והבל היפי אשה יראת ה' היא תתהלל, ואומר:
(משלי ל"א) תנו לה מפרי ידיה ויהללוה בשערים
מעשיה.

### 60) סופרים יח:ה
וכן היה מנהג טוב בירושלים להתענות בניהם
ובנותיהם הקטנים ביום צום בן [י"א] שנה עד עצם
היום בן שתים עשר להשלים, ואח"כ סבלו ומקרבו
לפני כל זקן וזקן כדי לברכו לחזן ולהתפלל עליו
שיזכה בתורה ובמעשים טובים וכל מי שהיה לו
גדול ממנו בעיר היה עומד ממקומו והולך לפניו
והיה משתחוה לו להתפלל בעדו ללמד שהן נאין
ומעשיהם נאים ולבן לשמים ולא היו מניחים בניה
קטנים אחריהם אלא היו מוליכן אותן לבתי כנסיות
כדי לזרזם במצות.

### 61) בבא בתרא צג:
עוד מנהג גדול היה בירושלים, מפה פרוסה על גבי

---

הפתח כל זמן שמפה פרוסה אורחין נכנסין, נסתלקה
המפה אין האורחין נכנסין.

### 62) בבא מציעא כח:
תנו רבנן: אבן טוען היתה בירושלים, כל מי שאבדה
לו אבידה נפנה לשם, וכל מי שמוצא אבידה נפנה
לשם. זה עומד ומכריז, וזה עומד ונותן סימנין
ונוטלה. וזו היא ששנינו: צאו וראו אם נמחת אבן
הטוען.

### 63) דברים טו:י
נָתוֹן תִּתֵּן לוֹ וְלֹא־יֵרַע לְבָבְךָ בְּתִתְּךָ לוֹ כִּי בִּגְלַל | הַדָּבָר
הַזֶּה יְבָרֶכְךָ ד' אֱלֹקֶיךָ בְּכָל־מַעֲשֶׂךָ וּבְכֹל מִשְׁלַח יָדֶךָ:

### 64) מדרש ספרי ראה סד
לו – בינך לבינו מכאן אמרו (שקלים פ"ה) לשכת
חשאים היתה בירושלם:

### 65) משנה שקלים ה:ו
שתי לשכות היו במקדש, אחת לשכת חשאים, ואחת
לשכת הכלים, לשכת חשאים יראי חטא נותנים
לתוכה בחשאי, ועניים בני טובים מתפרנסים מתוכה
בחשאי. לשכת הכלים, כל מי שהוא מתנדב כלי,
זורקו לתוכה. ואחת לשלשים יום, גזברין פותחין
אותה. וכל כלי שמוצאין בו צורך לבדק הבית,
מניחין אותו. והשאר נמכרין בדמיהן ונופלין ללשכת
בדק הבית:

### 66) סופרים יט:יב
כר"א בן הורקנוס דאמר ראה שלמה כח של גומלי
חסדים ובנה להם לישראל שני שערים אחד לחתנים
ואחר לאבלים ולמונדים בשבת היו מתקבצין
יושבי ירושלים ועולין להר הבית ויושבין בין שני
שערים הללו כדי לגמול חסדים לזה ולזה משחרב
בית המקדש התקינו שיהו החתנים והאבלים באים
לכנסת כדי לגמול להם חסד חתנים לקלסן ולהלוותם
לבתיהן אבלים לאחר שיגמרו החזן תפלה של מוסף
הולך לו אחורי דלתי של בית הכנסת או בפני הכנסת
ומוצא שם האבלים וכל קרוביו ואומר עליהם ברכה
ואחר כך אומר קדיש ...

### 67) ירושלמי חגיגה כו:
א"ר יהושע בן לוי (תהלים קכז) "ירושלם הבנויה
כעיר שחוברה לה יחדיו" עיר שהיא עושה כל ישראל
לחברים

### 68) מדרש תהילים צא:ז
שנאמר "ויירא ויאמר מה נורא המקום הזה, אין זה
כי אם בית אלקים" (בראשית כח:יז), מכאן אמרו, כי
כל מי שהוא מתפלל בירושלים, כאילו מתפלל לפני
כסא הכבוד, ששער השמים הוא שם, ופתח פתוח
לשמוע תפלה, שנאמר "וזה שער השמים"

מחנות ומחנה לויה שנאמר בה וסביב למשכן יחנו, ומחנה שכינה והוא מפתח חצר אהל מועד ולפנים, וכנגדן לדורות, מפתח ירושלים עד הר הבית כמחנה ישראל, ומפתח הר הבית עד פתח העזרה שהוא שער ניקנור כמחנה לויה, ומפתח העזרה ולפנים מחנה שכינה, והחיל ועזרת הנשים מעלה יתירה בבית עולמים.

### 43) רמב"ם, הלכות בית הבחירה ז:יד
ירושלים מקודשת משאר העיירות המוקפות חומה, שאוכלין קדשים קלים ומעשר שני לפנים מחומתה, ואלו דברים שנאמרו בירושלים: אין מלינין בה את המת, ואין מעבירין בתוכה עצמות אדם ואין משכירין בתוכה בתים, ואין נותנין בתוכה מקום לגר תושב, ואין מקיימין בה קברות חוץ מקברי בית דוד וקבר חולדה שהיו בה מימות נביאים הראשונים, ואין נוטעין בה גנות ופרדסים, ואינה נזרעת ואינה נחרשת שמא תסרח, ואין מקיימין בה אילנות חוץ מגינת ורדים שהיתה שם מימות נביאים הראשונים, ואין מקיימין בה אשפה מפני השרצים, ואין מוציאין הימנה זיזין וגזוזטראות לר"ה מפני אהל הטומאה, ואין עושין בה כבשונות מפני העשן, ואין מגדלין בה תרנגולות מפני הקדשים, וכן לא יגדלו הכהנים תרנגולים בכל א"י מפני הטהרות, ואין הבית נחלט בה, ואינה מטמא בנגעים, ואינה נעשית עיר הנדחת, ואינה מביאה עגלה ערופה לפי שלא נתחלקה לשבטים.

### 44) כתובות קי:
משנה. הכל מעלין לארץ ישראל ואין הכל מוציאין, הכל מעלין לירושלים ואין הכל מוציאין, אחד האנשים ואחד הנשים ... הכל מעלין לירושלים לאתויי מאי? לאתויי מנה היפה לנוה הרעה... ת"ר: הוא אומר לעלות, והיא אומרת שלא לעלות כופין אותה לעלות, ואם לאו תצא בלא כתובה, היא אומרת לעלות, והוא אומר שלא לעלות כופין אותו לעלות, ואם לאו יוציא ויתן כתובה. היא אומרת לצאת, והוא אומר שלא לצאת כופין אותה שלא לצאת, ואם לאו תצא בלא כתובה הוא אומר לצאת, והיא אומרת שלא לצאת כופין אותו שלא לצאת, ואם לאו יוציא ויתן כתובה

### 45) ירושלמי, כתובות כב.
הוא רוצה לעלות לירושלם והיא אינה רוצה כופין אותה לעלות היא רוצה לעלות והוא אינו רוצה אין כופין אותו לעלות הוא רוצה לצאת לח"ל והיא אינה רוצה אין כופין אותה היא רוצה לצאת והוא אינו רוצה כופין אותה שלא לצאת:

### 46) רמב"ם, הלכות אישות יג:כ
אמר האיש לעלות לארץ ישראל והיא אינה רוצה תצא בלא כתובה, אמרה היא לעלות והוא אינו רוצה

יוציא ויתן כתובה, והוא הדין לכל מקום מארץ ישראל עם ירושלים, שהכל מעלין לארץ ישראל ואין הכל מוציאין משם והכל מעלין לירושלם ואין הכל מוציאין משם.

### 47) טור, אבן העזר עה
אבל מח"ל לא"י כופין לעלות אפילו מנוה היפה לנוה הרע ואפילו ממקום שרובו ישראל למקום שרובן עכו"ם ואין מוציאין מא"י לח"ל אפילו מנוה הרע שרובו עכו"ם למקום היפה שרובן ישראל אמר האיש לעלות לא"י והיא אינה רוצה או שהיא שם ומבקשת לצאת תצא בלא כתובה האשה שאומרת לעלות והוא אינו רוצה או שרוצה לצאת משם יוציא ויתן כתובה וה"ה נמי לכ"מ מא"י לירושלים שהכל מעלין מא"י לירושלים ואין מוציאין משם ...

### 48) ירושלמי, כתובות סז:
אמר ר' פינחס בשם ר' הושעיה ארבע מאות ושישים בתי כנסיות היו בירושלם וכל אחת ואחת היה לה בית ספר ובית תלמוד בית ספר למקרא ובית תלמוד למשנה

### 49) בבא מציעא כו. ופירושי רש"י ותוספות שם
מעות שנמצאו ... בירושלים, בשאר ימות השנה חולין, בשעת הרגל הכל מעשר, ואמר רבי שמעיה בר זעירא: מאי טעמא הואיל ושוקי ירושלים עשויין להתכבד בכל יום.

### 50) פירוש רש"י על בבא מציעא כו.
ושוקי ירושלים עשויין להתכבד בכל יום – ואם נפלו שם לפני הרגל כבר מצאום מכבדי השוק, אבל הר הבית אין צריך להתכבד בכל יום, שאין טיט ועפר קולט שם מתוך שהוא משופע, ועוד שאין אדם נכנס שם במנעל ובאבק שעל רגליו.

### 51) פירוש תוספות על בבא מציעא כו.
עשויין להתכבד בכל יום – וא"ת והלא אין מתכבדות אלא בשביל שרצים שלא יטמאו הטהרות ולא בשביל המעות ...

### 52) מועד קטן יא.
עד ימיו היה פטיש מכה בירושלים כו'. עד ימיו אין, מכאן ואילך לא? לא קשיא ... רב פפא אמר: כאן קודם גזירה, כאן לאחר גזירה.

### 53) מדרש, שמות רבה נב:ה
א"ר יוחנן כיפה של חשבונות היתה חוץ לירושלים וכל מי שמבקש לחשב הולך לשם למה שלא יחשב בירושלים ויצר לפי שנקראת "משוש כל הארץ"

### 54) יומא יט: ורש"י שם
מיקירי ירושלים לא היו ישנין כל הלילה, כדי שישמע

והיא החזקה שבהם – **שלא יבקש כל 'שבט' היותו** '**בנחלתו' ולמשול בו**, והיה נופל עליו מן המחלוקת והקטטה, כמו שנפל בבקשת 'הכהונה' – ולזה באה המצוה שלא יבנה 'בית הבחירה' אלא אחר 'הקמת מלך', עד שתהיה המצוה לאחד, ותסתלק המחלוקת – כמו שבארנו ב"ספר שופטים":

**25) בראשית יד:יח**
וּמַלְכִּי־צֶדֶק מֶלֶךְ שָׁלֵם הוֹצִיא לֶחֶם וָיַיִן וְהוּא כֹהֵן לְאֵל עֶלְיוֹן:

**26) תרגום אונקלוס על בראשית יד:יח**
וּמַלְכִּי צֶדֶק מַלְכָּא דִירוּשְׁלֵם אַפֵּיק לְחֵם וַחֲמָר וְהוּא מְשַׁמֵּשׁ קֳדָם אֵל עִלָּאָה:

**27) בראשית כב:יד**
וַיִּקְרָא אַבְרָהָם שֵׁם הַמָּקוֹם הַהוּא ד' יִרְאֶה אֲשֶׁר יֵאָמֵר הַיּוֹם בְּהַר ד' יֵרָאֶה:

**28) פירוש רש"י על בראשית כב:יד**
ד' יִרְאֶה – .... ה' יבחר ויראה לו את המקום הזה, להשרות בו שכינתו ולהקריב כאן קרבנות:

**29) מדרש, בראשית רבה נו:י'**
אברהם קרא אותו יראה שנאמר ויקרא אברהם שם המקום ההוא ה' יראה שם קרא אותו שלם שנאמר (בראשית יז) ומלכי צדק מלך שלם אמר הקב"ה אם קורא אני אותו יראה כשם שקרא אותו אברהם שם אדם צדיק מתרעם ואם קורא אני אותו שלם אברהם אדם צדיק מתרעם אלא הריני קורא אותו ירושלים כמו שקראו שניהם יראה שלם ירושלים

**30) ישעיהו מח:ב, נחמיה יא:א**
כִּי־מֵעִיר הַקֹּדֶשׁ נִקְרָאוּ וְעַל־אֱלֹקֵי יִשְׂרָאֵל נִסְמָכוּ ד' צְבָאוֹת שְׁמוֹ:
וַיֵּשְׁבוּ שָׂרֵי־הָעָם בִּירוּשָׁלָם וּשְׁאָר הָעָם הִפִּילוּ גוֹרָלוֹת לְהָבִיא | אֶחָד מִן־הָעֲשָׂרָה לָשֶׁבֶת בִּירוּשָׁלַם עִיר הַקֹּדֶשׁ וְתֵשַׁע הַיָּדוֹת בֶּעָרִים:

**31) ישעיהו כז:יג, דניאל ט:טז**
וְהָיָה בַּיּוֹם הַהוּא יִתָּקַע בְּשׁוֹפָר גָּדוֹל וּבָאוּ הָאֹבְדִים בְּאֶרֶץ אַשּׁוּר וְהַנִּדָּחִים בְּאֶרֶץ מִצְרָיִם וְהִשְׁתַּחֲווּ לַד' בְּהַר הַקֹּדֶשׁ בִּירוּשָׁלָם:
אֲדֹנָי כְּכָל־צִדְקֹתֶךָ יָשָׁב־נָא אַפְּךָ וַחֲמָתְךָ מֵעִירְךָ יְרוּשָׁלַם הַר־קָדְשֶׁךָ כִּי בַחֲטָאֵינוּ וּבַעֲוֹנוֹת אֲבֹתֵינוּ יְרוּשָׁלַם וְעַמְּךָ לְחֶרְפָּה לְכָל־סְבִיבֹתֵינוּ:

**32) זכריה ח:ג**
כֹּה אָמַר ד' שַׁבְתִּי אֶל־צִיּוֹן וְשָׁכַנְתִּי בְּתוֹךְ יְרוּשָׁלָם וְנִקְרְאָה יְרוּשָׁלַם עִיר הָאֱמֶת וְהַר־ד' צְבָאוֹת הַר הַקֹּדֶשׁ:

**33) תהילים מו:ה**
נָהָר פְּלָגָיו יְשַׂמְּחוּ עִיר־אֱלֹקִים קְדֹשׁ מִשְׁכְּנֵי עֶלְיוֹן:

**34) תהילים מח:ג**
יְפֵה נוֹף מְשׂוֹשׂ כָּל־הָאָרֶץ הַר־צִיּוֹן יַרְכְּתֵי צָפוֹן קִרְיַת מֶלֶךְ רָב:

**35) דברים יב:ט**
כִּי לֹא־בָאתֶם עַד־עָתָּה אֶל־הַמְּנוּחָה וְאֶל־הַנַּחֲלָה אֲשֶׁר־ד' אֱלֹקֶיךָ נֹתֵן לָךְ:
ת"ר: "כי לא באתם עד עתה אל המנוחה ואל הנחלה", מנוחה זו שילה, נחלה זו ירושלים ... דברי רבי יהודה ר"ש אומר: מנוחה זו ירושלים, נחלה זו שילה ... רבי שמעון בן יוחי אומר: זו וזו ירושלים.

**36) זבחים קיט.**
כִּי לֹא־בָאתֶם עַד־עָתָּה אֶל־הַמְּנוּחָה וְאֶל־הַנַּחֲלָה אֲשֶׁר־ד' אֱלֹקֶיךָ נֹתֵן לָךְ:
ת"ר: "כי לא באתם עד עתה אל המנוחה ואל הנחלה", מנוחה זו שילה, נחלה זו ירושלים ... דברי רבי יהודה ר"ש אומר: מנוחה זו ירושלים, נחלה זו שילה ... רבי שמעון בן יוחי אומר: זו וזו ירושלים.

**37) סנהדרין ב. ורש"י שם**
אין מוסיפין על העיר ועל העזרות אלא על פי בית דין של שבעים ואחד.
**על העיר** – ירושלים:

**38) משנה כלים א:ח**
לפנים מן החומה מקודש מהם. שאוכלים שם קדשים קלים ומעשר שני.

**39) מגילה טו.**
[נביא] שמו ושם עירו מפורש בידוע שהוא מאותה העיר, שמו ולא שם עירו בידוע שהוא מירושלים.

**40) מגילה כו.**
במאי קמיפלגי? תנא קמא סבר: לא נתחלקה ירושלים לשבטים, ורבי יהודה סבר: נתחלקה ירושלים לשבטים ובפלוגתא דהני תנאי, דתניא: מה היה בחלקו של יהודה ... והאי תנא סבר: לא נתחלקה ירושלים לשבטים. דתניא: אין משכירים בתים בירושלים, מפני שאינן שלהן.

**41) משנה שקלים ד:ב**
פרה ושעיר המשתלח ולשון של זהורית, באין מתרומת הלשכה. כבש פרה, וכבש שעיר המשתלח ולשון שבין קרניו, ואמת המים, וחומת העיר ומגדלותיה, **וכל צרכי העיר, באין משירי הלשכה.**

**42) רמב"ם, הלכות בית הבחירה ז:יא**
שלש מחנות היו במדבר, מחנה ישראל והוא ארבע

וַיִּקְרָא אַבְרָהָם שֵׁם־הַמָּקוֹם הַהוּא ד' יִרְאֶה אֲשֶׁר יֵאָמֵר הַיּוֹם בְּהַר ד' יֵרָאֶה: וַיִּקְרָא מַלְאַךְ ד' אֶל־אַבְרָהָם שֵׁנִית מִן־הַשָּׁמָיִם: וַיֹּאמֶר בִּי נִשְׁבַּעְתִּי נְאֻם־ד' כִּי יַעַן אֲשֶׁר עָשִׂיתָ אֶת־הַדָּבָר הַזֶּה וְלֹא חָשַׂכְתָּ אֶת־בִּנְךָ אֶת־יְחִידֶךָ: כִּי־בָרֵךְ אֲבָרֶכְךָ וְהַרְבָּה אַרְבֶּה אֶת־זַרְעֲךָ כְּכוֹכְבֵי הַשָּׁמַיִם וְכַחוֹל אֲשֶׁר עַל־שְׂפַת הַיָּם וְיִרַשׁ זַרְעֲךָ אֵת שַׁעַר אֹיְבָיו: וְהִתְבָּרֲכוּ בְזַרְעֲךָ כֹּל גּוֹיֵי הָאָרֶץ עֵקֶב אֲשֶׁר שָׁמַעְתָּ בְּקֹלִי:

### 20) דברי הימים ב' ג:א

וַיָּחֶל שְׁלֹמֹה לִבְנוֹת אֶת־בֵּית־ד' בִּירוּשָׁלַם בְּהַר הַמּוֹרִיָּה אֲשֶׁר נִרְאָה לְדָוִיד אָבִיהוּ אֲשֶׁר הֵכִין בִּמְקוֹם דָּוִיד בְּגֹרֶן אָרְנָן הַיְבוּסִי:

### 21) תהילים קכב:ג ופירוש רש"י

יְרוּשָׁלַם הַבְּנוּיָה כְּעִיר שֶׁחֻבְּרָה־לָּהּ יַחְדָּו:
כעיר שחוברה לה – כשעלה שכתוב זו לזו שנאמר (דברים י"ב) אל המנוחה ואל הנחלה זו שילה נחלה זו ירושלים, ורבותינו אמרו יש ירושלים הבנויה בשמים ועתידה ירושלים של מטה להיות כמותה:

### 22) רמב"ם, הלכות בית הבחירה א:ג-ד

כיון שנבנה המקדש בירושלים נאסרו כל המקומות כולן לבנות בהן בית לד' ולהקריב בהן קרבן, ואין שם בית לדורי הדורות אלא בירושלים בלבד ובהר המוריה שבה נאמר ויאמר דויד זה הוא בית ד' האלקים וזה מזבח לעולה לישראל ואומר זאת מנוחתי עדי עד. בנין שבנה שלמה כבר מפורש במלכים, וכן בנין העתיד להבנות אע"פ שהוא כתוב ביחזקאל אינו מפורש ומבואר ואנשי בית שני כשבנוהו בימי עזרא בנוהו כבנין שלמה ומעין דברים המפורשים ביחזקאל.

### 23) רמב"ם, הלכות בית הבחירה ז:יד

ירושלים מקודשת משאר העיירות המוקפות חומה, שאוכלין קדשים קלים ומעשר שני לפנים מחומתה ...

### 24) רמב"ם, מורה נבוכים ג:נ

ואין ספק אצלי גם כן שהמקום אשר ייחדו אברהם בנבואה היה אצל 'משה רבינו' ואצל רבים, שאברהם בנבואה היה ידוע אצל 'משה רבינו' ואצל רבים, שאברהם צוה אותם שישאר תמיד בית עבודה – כמו שבאר המתרגם ואמר, 'ופלח וצלי אברהם תמן, באתרא ההוא, ואמר קדם יי, הכא יהון פלחין דריא וגו'". ואשר לא התבאר ב'תורה' ולא נזכר בפרט, אבל רמז אליו ואמר, "אשר יבחר יי וגו'" יש בו אצלו שלש חכמות. האחת מהן – שלא יחזיקו בו האומות וילחמו עליו מלחמה חזקה, כשידעו שזה המקום מן הארץ הוא תכלית התורה; והשנית – שלא יפסידוהו מי שהוא בידם עתה וישחיתוהו בכל יכלתם; והשלישית,

<br>

אמרו חכמים: סד אדם את ביתו בסיד, ומשייר בו דבר מועט. וכמה? אמר רב יוסף: אמה על אמה. אמר רב חסדא: כנגד הפתח. עושה אדם כל צרכי סעודה, ומשייר דבר מועט. מאי היא? אמר רב פפא: כסא דהרסנא. עושה אשה כל תכשיטיה, ומשיירת דבר מועט.

### 14) מדרש תנחומא קדושים י'

ארץ ישראל יושבת באמצעיתו של עולם וירושלים באמצעיתה של א"י, ובית המקדש באמצע ירושלים וההיכל באמצע בית המקדש והארון באמצע ההיכל ואבן שתיה לפני הארון שממנה נשתת העולם, למה נקרא אבן שתיה שממנה הושתת העולם

### 15) מדרש במדבר רבה יב:ד, מדרש תנחומא, פקודי ג

ולמה נקרא שמה אבן שתיה, מפני שממנה התחיל הקב"ה לבראות את עולמו, וברא ב"ה את בית המקדש למעלה שנאמר (שמות טו) מכון לשבתך פעלת ה', אל תקרא מכון אלא מכוון לשבתך

### 16) רמב"ם, הלכות בית הבחירה ב:ב

ומסורת ביד הכל שהמקום שבנה בו דוד ושלמה המזבח בגורן ארונה הוא המקום שבנה בו אברהם המזבח ועקד עליו יצחק, והוא המקום שבנה בו נח כשיצא מן התיבה, והוא המזבח שהקריב עליו קין והבל, ובו הקריב אדם הראשון קרבן כשנברא ומשם נברא, אמרו חכמים אדם ממקום כפרתו נברא.

### 17) בראשית ד:ג-ה, ח

וַיְהִי מִקֵּץ יָמִים וַיָּבֵא קַיִן מִפְּרִי הָאֲדָמָה מִנְחָה לַד': וְהֶבֶל הֵבִיא גַם־הוּא מִבְּכֹרוֹת צֹאנוֹ וּמֵחֶלְבֵהֶן וַיִּשַׁע ד' אֶל־הֶבֶל וְאֶל־מִנְחָתוֹ: וְאֶל־קַיִן וְאֶל־מִנְחָתוֹ לֹא שָׁעָה וַיִּחַר לְקַיִן מְאֹד וַיִּפְּלוּ פָּנָיו ... וַיֹּאמֶר קַיִן אֶל־הֶבֶל אָחִיו וַיְהִי בִּהְיוֹתָם בַּשָּׂדֶה וַיָּקָם קַיִן אֶל־הֶבֶל אָחִיו וַיַּהַרְגֵהוּ:

### 18) בראשית ח:כ

וַיִּבֶן נֹחַ מִזְבֵּחַ לַד' וַיִּקַּח מִכֹּל הַבְּהֵמָה הַטְּהֹרָה וּמִכֹּל הָעוֹף הַטָּהוֹר וַיַּעַל עֹלֹת בַּמִּזְבֵּחַ:

### 19) בראשית כב:א-ה, יד-יח

וַיְהִי אַחַר הַדְּבָרִים הָאֵלֶּה וְהָאֱלֹקִים נִסָּה אֶת־אַבְרָהָם וַיֹּאמֶר אֵלָיו אַבְרָהָם וַיֹּאמֶר הִנֵּנִי: וַיֹּאמֶר קַח־נָא אֶת־בִּנְךָ אֶת־יְחִידְךָ אֲשֶׁר־אָהַבְתָּ אֶת־יִצְחָק וְלֶךְ־לְךָ אֶל־אֶרֶץ הַמֹּרִיָּה וְהַעֲלֵהוּ שָׁם לְעֹלָה עַל אַחַד הֶהָרִים אֲשֶׁר אֹמַר אֵלֶיךָ: וַיַּשְׁכֵּם אַבְרָהָם בַּבֹּקֶר וַיַּחֲבֹשׁ אֶת־חֲמֹרוֹ וַיִּקַּח אֶת־שְׁנֵי נְעָרָיו אִתּוֹ וְאֵת יִצְחָק בְּנוֹ וַיְבַקַּע עֲצֵי עֹלָה וַיָּקָם וַיֵּלֶךְ אֶל־הַמָּקוֹם אֲשֶׁר־אָמַר־לוֹ הָאֱלֹקִים: בַּיּוֹם הַשְּׁלִישִׁי וַיִּשָּׂא אַבְרָהָם אֶת־עֵינָיו וַיַּרְא אֶת־הַמָּקוֹם מֵרָחֹק: וַיֹּאמֶר אַבְרָהָם אֶל־נְעָרָיו שְׁבוּ־לָכֶם פֹּה עִם־הַחֲמוֹר וַאֲנִי וְהַנַּעַר נֵלְכָה עַד־כֹּה וְנִשְׁתַּחֲוֶה וְנָשׁוּבָה אֲלֵיכֶם:

# SOURCES ON JERUSALEM – ITS MEANING
## FOR THE JEWISH PEOPLE

**1) שולחן ערוך, אורח חיים צד:א**

בקומו להתפלל אם היה עומד בח"ל יחזיר פניו כנגד ארץ ישראל ויכוין גם לירושלים ולמקדש ולבית קדשי הקדשים היה עומד בא"י יחזיר פניו כנגד ירושלים ויכוין גם למקדש ולבית קה"ק ...

**2) ברכה י"ד של בעמידה של חול**

וְלִירוּשָׁלַיִם עִירְךָ בְּרַחֲמִים תָּשׁוּב. וְתִשְׁכֹּן בְּתוֹכָהּ כַּאֲשֶׁר דִּבַּרְתָּ. וּבְנֵה אוֹתָהּ בְּקָרוֹב בְּיָמֵינוּ בִּנְיַן עוֹלָם. וְכִסֵּא דָוִד מְהֵרָה לְתוֹכָהּ תָּכִין: בָּרוּךְ אַתָּה ד'. בּוֹנֵה יְרוּשָׁלָיִם:

**3) ברכה שלישית של ברכת המזון**

רַחֵם נָא ד' אֱלֹקֵינוּ עַל יִשְׂרָאֵל עַמֶּךָ. וְעַל יְרוּשָׁלַיִם עִירְךָ. וְעַל צִיּוֹן מִשְׁכַּן כְּבוֹדֶךָ ... וּבְנֵה יְרוּשָׁלַיִם עִיר הַקֹּדֶשׁ בִּמְהֵרָה בְיָמֵינוּ. בָּרוּךְ אַתָּה ד'. בּוֹנֵה בְרַחֲמָיו יְרוּשָׁלָיִם:

**4) ברכה אחרונה "על המחיה"**

בָּרוּךְ אַתָּה ד' אֱלֹקֵינוּ מֶלֶךְ הָעוֹלָם עַל: (עַל הַיַּיִן – עַל הַגֶּפֶן וְעַל פְּרִי הַגֶּפֶן) (עַל מְזוֹנוֹת – עַל הַמִּחְיָה וְעַל הַכַּלְכָּלָה) ...
רַחֵם (נָא) ד' אֱלֹקֵינוּ עַל יִשְׂרָאֵל עַמֶּךָ וְעַל יְרוּשָׁלַיִם עִירְךָ וְעַל צִיּוֹן מִשְׁכַּן כְּבוֹדֶךָ וְעַל מִזְבְּחֶךָ וְעַל הֵיכָלֶךָ, וּבְנֵה יְרוּשָׁלַיִם עִיר הַקֹּדֶשׁ בִּמְהֵרָה בְיָמֵינוּ וְהַעֲלֵנוּ לְתוֹכָהּ וְשַׂמְּחֵנוּ בְּבִנְיָנָהּ ...

**5) סוטה מא.**

ת"ר: [מברכין] עַל התורה כדרך שמברכין בבהכ"נ, ועל העבודה ועל ההודאה ועל מחילת עון כתיקנן, על המקדש בפני עצמו, ועל הכהנים בפני עצמן, על ישראל בפני עצמן, ועל ירושלים בפני עצמה. והשאר תפלה

**6) ברכות אחרי ההפטרה**

רַחֵם עַל צִיּוֹן כִּי הִיא בֵּית חַיֵּינוּ. וְלַעֲלוּבַת נֶפֶשׁ תּוֹשִׁיעַ בִּמְהֵרָה בְיָמֵינוּ: בָּרוּךְ אַתָּה ד'. מְשַׂמֵּחַ צִיּוֹן בְּבָנֶיהָ:

**7) ברכה רביעית מתוך "שבע ברכות" בחתונה**

שׂוֹשׂ תָּשִׂישׂ וְתָגֵל הָעֲקָרָה. בְּקִבּוּץ בָּנֶיהָ לְתוֹכָהּ בְּשִׂמְחָה. בָּרוּךְ אַתָּה ד' מְשַׂמֵּחַ צִיּוֹן בְּבָנֶיהָ:

**8) שולחן ערוך, אבן העזר סה:ג**

צריך לתת אפר בראש החתן במקום הנחת תפילין זכר לאבילות ירושלים דכתיב לשום לאבילי ציון פאר תחת אפר: הגה ויש מקומות שנהגו לשבר כוס

---

אחר שבע ברכות וזהו מנהג נוהג במדינות אלו ...

**9) שולחן ערוך, אורח חיים תקס:א**

משחרב בית המקדש תקנו חכמים שהיו באותו הדור שאין בונים לעולם בנין מסוייד ומכוייר כבנין המלכים אלא טח ביתו בטיט וסד בסיד ומשייר מקום אמה על אמה כנגד הפתח בלא סיד והלוקח חצר מסוייודת ומכויירת (פי' מצויירת) הרי זו בחזקתה ואין מחייבים אותו לקלוף בכותלים:

**10) שו"ת אגרות משה, אורח חיים ה:כ**

ומה שנוהגין לומר המקום ינחם אותך בתוך שאר אבלי ציון וירושלים ...

**11) ר' משה שטרנבוך, חכמה ודעת על בראשית מב:כח**

ונראה שזהו הכוונה בניחום אבלים שאומרים "המקום ינחם אתכם בתוך שאר אבלי ציון וירושלים" והכוונה כמו שאי אפשר לנו להבין מדוע במשך אלפיים שנה דור אחר דור אנחנו בגלות עם הריגות ורציחות לצדיקים ואפילו לקטנים וטף שאי אפשר לבשר ודם להשיג את מחשבת הקב"ה ורצונו וזאת אומרים לאבלים תתנחמו גם אתם כמו אבלי ציון וירושלים שבודאי כך רצונו ית' מה שאירע לכם ואי אפשר לבשר ודם להבין את דרכיו

**12) תוספתא נדרים א:ט**

איזו הוא איסור [הכתוב] בתורה האומר הרי עלי שלא לאכול בשר שלא [לשתות יין כיום שראיתי את ירושלים חריבה וכיום שנהרג בו פלוני] אסור:

**13) בבא בתרא ס:**

ת"ר: כשחרב הבית בשניה, רבו פרושין בישראל שלא לאכול בשר ושלא לשתות יין. נטפל להן ר' יהושע, אמר להן: בני, מפני מה אי אתם אוכלין בשר ואין אתם שותין יין? אמרו לו: נאכל בשר שממנו מקריבין על גבי מזבח, ועכשיו בטל? נשתה יין שמנסכין על גבי המזבח, ועכשיו בטל? אמר להם: א"כ, לחם לא נאכל, שכבר בטלו מנחות אפשר בפירות. פירות לא נאכל, שכבר בטלו בכורים אפשר בפירות אחרים. מים לא נשתה, שכבר בטל ניסוך המים שתקו. אמר להן: בני, בואו ואומר לכם: שלא להתאבל כלל אי אפשר שכבר נגזרה גזרה, ולהתאבל יותר מדאי אי אפשר שאין גוזרין גזירה על הצבור אא"כ רוב צבור יכולין לעמוד בה, דכתיב: (מלאכי י') במארה אתם נארים ואותי אתם קובעים הגוי כולו, אלא כך

**76) סוטה ט. ופירושי רש"י ומאירי**

תנו רבנן: סוטה נתנה עיניה במי שאינו ראוי לה, מה שביקשה לא ניתן לה, ומה שבידה נטלוהו ממנה שכל הנותן עיניו במה שאינו שלו, מה שמבקש אין נותנין לו, ומה שבידו נוטלין הימנו ... וכן מצינו בקין, וקרח,

רש"י – קרח – על הכהונה ונבלע.

מאיר"י – ... לפי הדרש קרח בנשיאות בלעם.

**77) שו"ת שבט קהתי ג:שכט**

... בענין לאו דלא תתמוד דאינו נוהג בחפץ העומד למכירה ונראה דחפץ שאינו עומד למכירה אלא אם יתנו לו סכום גדול ימכרנו אבל באין רוצה למכור אם אין נותנים לו סכום פחות נראה דאסור להפציר ימכור בפחות כיון דאין החפץ עומד למכירה ודו"ק

**78) ספר חרדים, כא:ב-ה**

... וכשישתדל ליקח הקרקע או המטלטלין מחבירו שלא היה בדעתו למוכרן אלא שהפציר עליו או הרבה עליו רעים או הרבה לו דמים עד שלקחו אז עבר על לא תתמוד דאין חימוד אלא על ידי מעשה אבל על לאו דלא תתאוה משגמר והסכים בלבו להשתדל בכל עוז לקנותו ממנו מיד עבר דאין תאוה אלא בלבד ...

**79) שערי תשובה ג:מג**

לא תתמוד בית רעך (שמות כ, יד), לא תתאוה בית רעך (דברים ה, יח). הוזהרנו בזה שלא להתעולל עלילות ברשע לקחת שדה וכרם וכל אשר לרענו, גם כי נתן מכרם. והוזהרנו על מחשבת הדבר הרע הזה שלא נסכים במחשבתנו לעשותו, שנאמר: לא תתמוד. ואם יכסוף אדם שימכור לו חברו שדה או כרם או אחד מחפציו ולא יש את נפשו למכרו, ואם יפצר בו ברוב דברי תחנונים יבוש להשיב פניו, אסור לפצור בו, כי זה לו כמו הכרח ואונס. והתומד לקחת כל חפץ והוא איש נכבד, שאם ישאל שאלה אור פניו לא יפילון אסור לשאול לשאול מעם רעהו מקח או מתת, בלתי אם ידע כי נתן יתן לו בנפש חפצה ולא ירע לבבו בתתו לו:

ומה שכתבתי בענין לא תחמוד דדעת רבינו יונה ז"ל בס' שע"ת דהמפציר ליתן לו מתנה עובר בלא תחמוד וכ"ק שליט"א כ' אולי דעת יחיד הוא איני כדאי לדון

---

דה"ק דלענ"ד הקלושה והרטושה הדברים מוכיחים מעצמם ואפי' לא אמרן ר"י הי' ראוי לדון כן מהיקש שכליי לפי פסק הרמב"ם והשו"ע סימן שנ"ט סעי' יוד כל התומד עבדו או אמתו או כליו הז או כ"ד שאפשר שיקנהו ממנו והכביד עליו רעים והפציר בו עד שלקחו ממנו הר"ז עובר בלא תתמוד הנה דאע"ג דבסוף מכר מדעתו מ"מ כיון בסיבת הפצרתו עד שהוציאו מרצונו עובר בלא תתמוד במכר שנתן לו מעות כן כש"כ **במתנה שאם מפציר לו מתנה עובר**

**80) ספר החינוך תטז**

ונוהגת בכל מקום ובכל זמן, בזכרים ונקבות. גם כל בני העולם מחוייבין בה, לפי שהיא ענף למצות גזל שהיא אחת מן השבע מצוות שנצטוו עליהם כל בני העולם.

**81) ספר חסידים צט**

לא תתמוד אשת (שמות כ יז) כתיב בלא וא"ו לא תתמוד, אזהרה שלא ליפות עצמו כדי שישר בעיני אשת רעהו, ויכניס אהבתו ויפיו בלבה, לא תהי' חומד לאשת רעך. ועוד קרי לא תתמוד שלא ישבח אשה יפה בפני חבירו, שמא יגרור אחריה והי' כך חטא, כלומר לא תתמוד אשת רעך לאחרים ...

**82) סוטה ט.**

שכל הנותן עיניו במה שאינו שלו, מה שמבקש אין נותנין לו, ומה שבידו נוטלין הימנו.

**83) ספר מצוות הקטן יט**

... מצינו בנחש הקדמוני, שהיה סבור (ליהנות) [להיות] מלך על כל החיות והבהמות, ועכשיו ארור מכל הבהמה. היה סבור ללכת בקומה זקופ', ועכשיו על גחונך תלך. היה סבור לאכול מעדנים כאדם, ועכשיו ועפר תאכל כל ימי חייך. היה סבור להרוג אדם וליקח חוה אשתו, ועכשיו איבה אשית. וכן בקין וקרח ובלעם ודואג האדומי ואחיתופל ואבשלום וגחזי ואדוניה ועוזיה והמן שנתנו עיניהם במה שאינו שלהם. ולא מבעיא שמה שבקשו לא נתנו להם. אלא אף מה שבידם נטלו ... וגם אוי לו לחומד שכל ימיו מכאובים ולא ישמח. והשמח בחלקו שמח הוא לעולם.

הבעלים למכור אע"פ שהרבה להם בדמים והפציר
רעים יבא לידי גזל ...

### 64) שולחן ערוך, חושן משפט שנט:י'-י"א

כל החומד עבדו או אמתו או ביתו או כליו של חבירו
או כל דבר שאיפשר שיקנהו ממנו, והכביד עליו
רעים והפציר בו עד שלקחו ממנו, הרי זה עובר בלא
תחמוד. וכל המתאוה ביתו או אשתו וכליו של חבירו
וכל כיוצא בזה, כיון שחשב בלבו איך יקנה דבר זה
ונפתה בלבו בדבר, עבר בלא תעשה של לא תתאוה,
ואין תאוה אלא בלב בלבד.

התאוה מביא לידי חמוד והחמוד מביא לידי גזל ...
על שאמר בכאן עין הרע בלשון זכר שזהו
העויין רע.

### 65) מדרש מכילתא, פרשת החודש ח

לא תחמוד בית רעך. כלל. ועבדו ואמתו ושורו
וחמורו. פרט. כלל ופרט אין בכלל אלא מה שבפרט.
וכשהוא אומר וכל אשר לרעך חזר וכלל. אי כלל כלל
הראשון הרי אמרת אלא כלל וכלל ופרט אין
בכלל אלא מה שבפרט אי אתה דן אלא כעין הפרט
מה הפרט מפורש בדבר שהוא קונה ומקנה אף כלל
מפורש בדבר שהוא קונה ומקנה ... אי מה הפרט
מפורש בדבר שאינו בא ברשותך אלא ברצון בעלים
אף אין לי אלא דבר שאי איפשר לבא ברשותך אלא
ברצון בעלים יצא שאתה חומד בתו לבנך או בנו
לבתך או אפי' חומד בדבור ת"ל (שם ה') "לא תחמוד
כסף וזהב עליהם" מה להלן עד שעושה מעשה אף כאן
עד שעושה מעשה:

### 66) טור, חושן משפט ש"ע"א

עוד לשון א"א הרא"ש ז"ל בתשובות ג' עבירות הן
בענין גזילת קרקע הראשונה במחשבה שחמד (ס"א
שהתאוה) ממון חבירו בלבו והשנית בדיבור שדבר
אילו היה אותו ממון של זה שלו והשלישית זה
שמוציא מחשבתו לפועל והולך וגוזל ממון חבירו:

### 67) שולחן ערוך, חושן משפט שנ"ט:י'

כל החומד עבדו או אמתו או ביתו או כליו של חבירו
או כל דבר שאיפשר שיקנהו ממנו, והכביד עליו
רעים והפציר בו עד שלקחו ממנו, הרי זה עובר בלא
תחמוד. כל המתאוה ביתו או אשתו וכליו של חבירו
וכל כיוצא בזה, כיון שחשב בלבו איך יקנה דבר זה
ונפתה בלבו בדבר, עבר בלא תעשה של לא תתאוה,
ואין תאוה אלא בלב בלבד.

### 68) פלא יועץ ערך חמדה

... וכל המשתדל ליטול חפץ של חבירו בחנם או
ברצי כסף עובר על לא תחמוד ואפי' אם לא השתדל
רק חשב בלבו שהיה חפץ שיבא זו לידו הרי עבר על
לאו דלא תתאוה

### 69) זוהר יתרו ב:צ"ג

לא תחמד לא פסיק טעמא כלל. ואי תימא אפי'
חמודא דאורייתא אסיר כיון דלא פסקא. תא חזי
בכלהו עבדא אורייתא כלל ובהאי עבדת פרט.
בית רעך שדהו ועבדו וגו' בכל מילי דעלמא. אבל
אורייתא איהי חמודתא תדיר שעשועים גנזי דחיי
ארכא דיומין בעלמא דין ובעלמא דאתי.

### 70) שו"ת בצל חכמה ג:נ"ג

... מבואר דדוקא לימוד התורה ממעטינן לי שצריך
ללמדה בחינם ואינו בקונה ומקנה, אבל ס"ת תפילין
ומזוזות אף שאינו רוצה בהם רק לצורך מצוה דומיא
דלימוד התורה הרי הם בכלל לא תחמוד כל אשר
לרעך, כיון שהם בקונה ומקנה שא"צ ליתנם לחברו
בחנם, וכמ"כ שופר, לולב, מצה וכה"ג שאפשר
להשתמש בהם לצורכי חול דשייך בהו ולאו דלא
תחמוד ודלא תתאוה אף שהוא חומד ומתאוה
להם רק לצורך מצוה בלבד ... לפי"ז בודאי בקונה
שופר, לולב, מצה וכל כה"ג שבעצם מילי דעלמא
נינהו שייך בהו דלא לאו תחמוד גם כשהוא רוצה
בהם לצורך מצוה בלבד, שהרי הם דומיא דפרטי
דכתיבי, לא תחמוד בית רעך וגו' ושורו וחמורו,
והרי אסור לחמוד בית חבירו כדי לקיים בו מצות
מזוזה

### 71) פירוש רבינו בחיי על שמות כ:י"ד

... ואמנם מצינו חמדת שהיא מותרת והיא חמדת
התורה והמצוות, וכמו שאמרו חז"ל (בבא בתרא
כא.) קנאת סופרים תרבה חכמה, והחמדה והקנאה
הזאת היא מותרת ויש לאדם שכר עליה.

### 72) ספר שמירת הלשון, חלק ב', חתימת הספר ד

לְכְאוֹרָה יֵשׁ בָּזֶה הַלָּאו דְּ"לֹא תַחְמֹד". וְכֵן כָּל כְּהַאי
גַּוְנָא מַתָּנוֹת שֶׁל רְשׁוּת [לַאֲפוּקֵי שֶׁל צְדָקָה], שֶׁאֵין
בְּלִבּוֹ שֶׁל הַנּוֹתֵן לְתֵּן, כִּי אִם לְאַחַר הַפְצָרַת רֵעִים, יֵשׁ
בָּזֶה מִשּׁוּם "לֹא תַחְמֹד"

### 73) מנחת חינוך, מצוה ל"ח

והנה לכאורה טעמא בעי כיון שבפחות משוה פרוטה
משום שישראל מוחל וכאן לענין הלאו דלא החמוד
לא מהני לדעת הר"מ אף מתרצה בסוף מ"מ עבר
ונראה דעיקר הטעם הוא מכלל השיעורין שאצל דיני
ממון הכל בפרוטה ופחות משוה פרוטה לא נקרא
ממון ...

### 74) כלה רבתי ו

ת"ש ושמעינהו לכלהו דלא תחמוד אפילו ממון
פלוני לי

### 75) שו"ת ארץ צבי (אריה צבי פראמער) סימן ד

... דחימוד הוא רק בחפץ שאינו מצוי וכו' ...

ובשביל כי טבע המעשה שעשה פינחס להרוג נפש
בידו. היה נותן להשאיר בלב הרגש עז גם אח"כ. אבל
באשר היה לש"ש מש"ה באה הברכה שיהא תמיד
בנחת ובמדת השלום. ולא יהא זה הענין לפוקת לב.
וע' כ"ב ז בס' דברים י"ג:י"ח ברוצחי עיר הנדחת:

**48) דברים י"ג:י"ג-י"ז**
כִּי תִשְׁמַע בְּאַחַת עָרֶיךָ אֲשֶׁר ד' אֱלֹקֶיךָ נֹתֵן לְךָ לָשֶׁבֶת
שָׁם לֵאמֹר: יָצְאוּ אֲנָשִׁים בְּנֵי בְלִיַּעַל מִקִּרְבֶּךָ וַיַּדִּיחוּ
אֶת יֹשְׁבֵי עִירָם לֵאמֹר נֵלְכָה וְנַעַבְדָה אֱלֹהִים אֲחֵרִים
אֲשֶׁר לֹא יְדַעְתֶּם: וְדָרַשְׁתָּ וְחָקַרְתָּ וְשָׁאַלְתָּ הֵיטֵב וְהִנֵּה
אֱמֶת נָכוֹן הַדָּבָר נֶעֶשְׂתָה הַתּוֹעֵבָה הַזֹּאת בְּקִרְבֶּךָ: הַכֵּה
תַכֶּה אֶת יֹשְׁבֵי הָעִיר הַהִוא לְפִי חָרֶב הַחֲרֵם אֹתָהּ וְאֶת
כָּל אֲשֶׁר בָּהּ וְאֶת בְּהֶמְתָּהּ לְפִי חָרֶב: וְאֶת כָּל שְׁלָלָהּ
תִּקְבֹּץ אֶל תּוֹךְ רְחֹבָהּ וְשָׂרַפְתָּ בָאֵשׁ אֶת הָעִיר וְאֶת כָּל
שְׁלָלָהּ כָּלִיל לַד' אֱלֹקֶיךָ וְהָיְתָה תֵּל עוֹלָם לֹא תִבָּנֶה
עוֹד:

**49) דברים י"ג:י"ח**
וְלֹא יִדְבַּק בְּיָדְךָ מְאוּמָה מִן הַחֵרֶם לְמַעַן יָשׁוּב ד'
מֵחֲרוֹן אַפּוֹ וְנָתַן לְךָ רַחֲמִים וְרִחַמְךָ וְהִרְבֶּךָ כַּאֲשֶׁר
נִשְׁבַּע לַאֲבֹתֶיךָ:

**50) גר"א, אבן שלמה, פרק ג**
כל העבירות והחטאים באים מחדה כמו שאמרו "לא
תחמוד" כולל כל הדברות וכל התורה. והסתפקות,
שהוא ההפוך, הוא יסוד כל התורה, והוא אמונה
שלמה שלא לדאוג דאגת מחר
תני ר' חייא פרשה זו נאמרה בהקהל מפני שרוב גופי
תורה תלויין בה ר' לוי אמר מפני מעשרת הדברות
כלולין בתוכה

**51) מדרש ויקרא רבה כד:ה**
תני ר' חייא פרשה זו נאמרה בהקהל מפני שרוב גופי
תורה תלויין בה ר' לוי אמר מפני מעשרת הדברות
כלולין בתוכה/ לא תחמוד וכתיב הכא ואהבת לרעך
כמוך

**52) מדרש בראשית רבה כד:ז**
ר"ע אומר (ויקרא יט) ואהבת לרעך כמוך זה כלל
גדול בתורה

**53) פלא יועץ ערך חמדה**
יודעים רעת החמדה כי רבה וכתרו המפ' שהיא
העשירית ממעשרת הדברות והיא גדולה מכולם שע"י
החמדה יכול לעבור על כל התורה

**54) משנה אבות ה:י"ט**
כָּל מִי שֶׁיֵּשׁ בְּיָדוֹ שְׁלֹשָׁה דְבָרִים הַלָּלוּ, מִתַּלְמִידָיו שֶׁל
אַבְרָהָם אָבִינוּ. וּשְׁלֹשָׁה דְבָרִים אֲחֵרִים, מִתַּלְמִידָיו שֶׁל
בִּלְעָם הָרָשָׁע. עַיִן טוֹבָה, וְרוּחַ נְמוּכָה, וְנֶפֶשׁ שְׁפָלָה,
מִתַּלְמִידָיו שֶׁל אַבְרָהָם אָבִינוּ.

**55) פירוש ברטנורה על משנה אבות ה:י"ט**
עין טובה – מסתפק במה שיש לו ואינו חומד ממון
אחרים. שכן מצינו באברהם שאמר למלך סדום
(בראשית יד) אם מחוט ועד שרוך נעל ואם אקח
מכל אשר לך:

**56) פירוש רבינו יונה על משנה אבות ב:י"ב**
ר' אליעזר אומר, עין טובה. מי ששמח בחלקו.

**57) פירוש הרמב"ן על שמות כ"ג:י"ג**
... ומי יחמוד לא יזיק לעולם לחברו.

**58) שמות כ:י"ד**
לֹא תַחְמֹד בֵּית רֵעֶךָ לֹא-תַחְמֹד אֵשֶׁת רֵעֶךָ וְעַבְדּוֹ
וַאֲמָתוֹ וְשׁוֹרוֹ וַחֲמֹרוֹ וְכֹל אֲשֶׁר לְרֵעֶךָ:

**59) דברים ה:י"ח**
וְלֹא תַחְמֹד אֵשֶׁת רֵעֶךָ וְלֹא תִתְאַוֶּה בֵּית רֵעֶךָ שָׂדֵהוּ
וְעַבְדּוֹ וַאֲמָתוֹ שׁוֹרוֹ וַחֲמֹרוֹ וְכֹל אֲשֶׁר לְרֵעֶךָ:

**60) ספר מצוות הגדול (סמ"ג) קנה**
כתוב בעשרת הדברות לא תחמוד וכתוב שם עוד
לא תתאוה והכל אחד ותני' במכילתיה לא תחמוד
יכול אפילו בדברים תלמוד לומר (דברים ז, כה)
לא תחמוד כסף וזהב עליהם ולקחת לך עד שיעשה
מעשה ... כתוב בדברים לא תחמוד אשת רעך ולא
תתאוה בית רעך ולפי דבריו החמיר בבית מבאשת
איש אלא החמדה והתתאוה הכל אחד וכן פירשו
אונקלוס לא תירוג וכן (בראשית ב, ט) ונחמד למראה
מתרגמינין דמרגג למיחזי וכן פירש רבינו שלמה
(ואתחנן) כי הכל אחד:

**61) פירוש רש"י על דברים ה:י"ז**
לא תתאוה – לא תירוג, אף הוא לשון חמדה, כמו
נחמד למראה (בראשית ב, ט.), דמתרגמינין דמרגג
למיחזי:

**62) זוהר, חלק ג:רסא.**
אמר רבי יוסי מאי ולא תתאוה כיון דכתיב ולא
תחמוד דהא בהאי סגי. א"ל זכאין אינון מארי קשוט
חמידה חד דרגא. תאוה דרגא אחרא. חמידה דאי
אזיל למיסב דיליה ההיא חמידה דנקיט אזיל
למעבד עובדא. תאוה לאו הכי דהא אפילו דלא
יניקט אורחא למהך אבתריה והא אוקמוה חברייא.

**63) רמב"ם, הלכות גזילה א:י'-י"א**
כל המתאוה ביתו או אשתו וכליו של חבירו וכל
כיוצא בהן משאר דברים שאפשר לו לקנותן
ממנו כיון שחשב בלבו היאך יקנה דבר זה ונפתה
לבו בדבר עבר בלא תעשה שנ' דברים ה' י"ח לא
תתאוה ואין תאוה אלא בלב בלבד. התאוה מביאה
לידי חימוד והחימוד מביא לידי גזל, שאם לא רצו

אָמְרָה אִילּוּלֵי שֶׁהִיא צַדֶּקֶת לֹא הָיְתָה יוֹלֶדֶת, וַתֹּאמֶר אֶל יַעֲקֹב הָבָה לִי בָּנִים וְאִם אַיִן מֵתָה אָנֹכִי.

### (34) מגילה יג
אָמַר: אֵין אִשָּׁה מִתְקַנְּאָה אֶלָּא בְּיֶרֶךְ חֲבֶרְתָּהּ.

### (35) שמות כה:ה
לֹא תִשְׁתַּחֲוֶה לָהֶם וְלֹא תָעָבְדֵם כִּי אָנֹכִי ד' אֱלֹקֶיךָ אֵל קַנָּא פֹּקֵד עֲוֹן אָבֹת עַל בָּנִים עַל שִׁלֵּשִׁים וְעַל רִבֵּעִים לְשֹׂנְאָי:

### (36) שמות לד:יד, דברים ה:ט, ו:יד-טו
לֹא תִשְׁתַּחֲוֶה לָהֶם וְלֹא תָעָבְדֵם כִּי אָנֹכִי ד' אֱלֹקֶיךָ אֵל קַנָּא פֹּקֵד עֲוֹן אָבֹת עַל בָּנִים וְעַל שִׁלֵּשִׁים וְעַל רִבֵּעִים לְשֹׂנְאָי:
לֹא תֵלְכוּן אַחֲרֵי אֱלֹהִים אֲחֵרִים מֵאֱלֹהֵי הָעַמִּים אֲשֶׁר סְבִיבוֹתֵיכֶם: כִּי אֵל קַנָּא ד' אֱלֹקֶיךָ בְּקִרְבֶּךָ פֶּן יֶחֱרֶה אַף ד' אֱלֹקֶיךָ בָּךְ וְהִשְׁמִידְךָ מֵעַל פְּנֵי הָאֲדָמָה:

### (37) מדרש מכילתא ו
כִּי אָנֹכִיה' אֱלֹקֶיךָ בְּקִנְאָה אֵל קַנָּא. אֲנִי שַׁלִּיט בַּקִּנְאָה וְאֵין קִנְאָה שׁוֹלֶטֶת בִּי שֶׁנֶּאֱמַר (תהלים קכ"א) הִנֵּה לֹא יָנוּם וְלֹא יִישָׁן שׁוֹמֵר יִשְׂרָאֵל. דָּבָר אַחֵר אֲנִי ה' אֱלֹקֶיךָ אֵל קַנָּא אֲנִי שַׁלִּיט בַּקִּנְאָה וְאֵין קִנְאָה שׁוֹלֶטֶת בִּי אֲנִי שַׁלִּיט בַּנוּמָה וְאֵין נוּמָה שׁוֹלֶטֶת בִּי שֶׁנֶּאֱמַר' הִנֵּה לֹא יָנוּם וְלֹא יִישָׁן שׁוֹמֵר יִשְׂרָאֵל. דָּבָר אַחֵר אֲנִי ה' אֱלֹקֶיךָ אֵל קַנָּא בַּקִּנְאָה אֲנִי נִפְרָע מִן עֲבוֹדָה זָרָה אֲבָל רַחוּם וְחַנּוּן אֲנִי בִּדְבָרִים אֲחֵרִים. שָׁאַל פִילוֹסוֹפוֹס אֶחָד אֶת רַבָּן גַּמְלִיאֵל כְּתִיב בַּתּוֹרַתְכֶם כִּי ה' אֱלֹקֶיךָ אֵל קַנָּא וְכִי יֵשׁ כֹּחַ בַּעֲבוֹדָה זָרָה לְהִתְקַנּוֹת בָּהּ גִּבּוֹר מִתְקַנֶּה בְּגִבּוֹר חָכָם מִתְקַנֶּה בְּחָכָם עָשִׁיר מִתְקַנֶּה בֶּעָשִׁיר אֶלָּא יֵשׁ כֹּחַ בַּעֲבוֹדָה זָרָה לְהִתְקַנּוֹת בָּהּ אָמַר לוֹ אִלּוּ אָדָם קוֹרֵא לְכַלְבּוֹ בְּשֵׁם אָבִיו וּכְשֶׁהוּא נוֹדֵר בְּחַיֵּי כֶּלֶב זֶה בְּמִי הָאָב מִתְקַנֵּא בַּבֵּן אוֹ בַּכֶּלֶב

### (38) מדרש דברים רבה ב:יח
וּכְתִיב (דברים ד) כִּי ה' אֱלֹקֶיךָ אֵשׁ אוֹכְלָה הוּא אֵל קַנָּא רַבָּנָן אָמְרֵי הוֹאִיל וְאֵין בַּעֲבוֹדַת כּוֹכָבִים מַמָּשׁ לָמָּה קוֹרֵא אוֹתָן אֱלֹהוּת אָמַר ר' פִּנְחָס בַּר חָמָא כְּדֵי לִיתֵּן שָׂכָר לְכֹל מִי שֶׁפּוֹרֵשׁ מִמֶּנָּה אָמַר הקב"ה אע"פ שֶׁאֵין בָּהּ מַמָּשׁ כֵּיוָן שֶׁפּוֹרֵשׁ אָדָם מִמֶּנָּה מַעֲלֶה אֲנִי עָלָיו כְּאִלּוּ הוּא עוֹבֵד לְמִי שֶׁיֵּשׁ בּוֹ מַמָּשׁ

### (39) ברכות לא:
דִּבְּרָה תוֹרָה כִּלְשׁוֹן בְּנֵי אָדָם.

### (40) מדרש תנחומא צד:ו
כִּי ה' אֱלֹקֶיךָ אֵשׁ אוֹכְלָה הוּא אֵל קַנָּא, כֵּיצַד הוּא קַנָּא שֶׁנֶּאֱמַר (הושע ב) וְאֵרַשְׂתִּיךְ לִי בֶּאֱמוּנָה כְּמוֹ שֶׁמְּקַנֵּא הַבַּעַל לְאִשָּׁה כָּךְ הַקב"ה מְקַנֵּא

### (41) במדבר ה:יד
וְעָבַר עָלָיו רוּחַ קִנְאָה וְקִנֵּא אֶת אִשְׁתּוֹ וְהִוא נִטְמָאָה

---

אוֹ עָבַר עָלָיו רוּחַ קִנְאָה וְקִנֵּא אֶת אִשְׁתּוֹ וְהִיא לֹא נִטְמָאָה:

### (42) פירוש רבינו בחיי על שמות כה:ה
וְדַע כִּי לֹא תִמְצָא בְּכָל הַתּוֹרָה קַנָּאָה בְּהקב"ה כִּי אִם בַּעֲוֹן עֲבוֹדַת גִּלּוּלִים, וְהַטַּעַם כִּי כֵּיוָן שֶׁקִּבְּלוּ יִשְׂרָאֵל עֲלֵיהֶם אֱלֹהוּתוֹ שֶׁל הקב"ה בְּקַבָּלַת הַתּוֹרָה הִנֵּה הֵם לְקוּחִים לְחֶלְקוֹ בְּיִחוּד וְהֵם עִם מְיֻחָד לְאָדוֹן יָחִיד וְכַאֲשֶׁר הֵם נִשְׁמָטִים מִמֶּנּוּ פּוֹנִים אֶל אֱלֹהִים אֲחֵרִים רָאוּי שֶׁיְּקַנֵּא בָּהֶם כְּאִישׁ אֲשֶׁר יְקַנֵּא בְּאִשְׁתּוֹ בְּלֶכְתָּהּ לַאֲחֵרִים, וּמִזֶּה לֹא תִמְצָא בְּכָל סִפְרֵי הַנְּבִיאִים שֶׁיִּתְפּוֹשׂ שׁוּם נָבִיא לְשׁוּם אֻמָּה בְּעִנְיַן עֲבוֹדַת גִּלּוּלִים כִּי אִם לְיִשְׂרָאֵל, וְהוּא שֶׁכָּתוּב (דברים ד, יט) אֲשֶׁר חָלַק ה' אֱלֹקֶיךָ אוֹתָם לְכֹל הָעַמִּים תַּחַת כָּל הַשָּׁמַיִם וְאֶתְכֶם לָקַח ה':

### (43) פלא יועץ – קנאה
וְיֵשׁ עוֹד מִין קִנְאָה אַחֶרֶת שֶׁהִיא טוֹבָה עַד מְאֹד לְקַנְאוּת קִנְאַת ה' צְבָאוֹת לְשַׁבֵּר מַלְתָּעוֹת רֶשַׁע וּלְהָקִים דֶּגֶל הַתּוֹרָה וְיָדוּעַ מַעֲלַת פִּינְחָס קַנַּאי בֶּן קַנַּאי בְּקַנְאוֹ קִנְאַת ה' צְבָאוֹת וַיִּקָּרֵא'לוֹ ה' שָׁלוֹם וּבָזֶה נִשְׁתַּבַּח שֵׁבֶט לֵוִי הָאוֹמֵר לְאָבִיו וּלְאִמּוֹ לֹא רְאִיתִיו

### (44) במדבר כה:יא-יג
פִּינְחָס בֶּן אֶלְעָזָר בֶּן אַהֲרֹן הַכֹּהֵן הֵשִׁיב אֶת חֲמָתִי מֵעַל בְּנֵי יִשְׂרָאֵל בְּקַנְאוֹ אֶת קִנְאָתִי בְּתוֹכָם וְלֹא כִלִּיתִי אֶת בְּנֵי יִשְׂרָאֵל בְּקִנְאָתִי: לָכֵן אֱמֹר הִנְנִי נֹתֵן לוֹ אֶת בְּרִיתִי שָׁלוֹם: וְהָיְתָה לּוֹ וּלְזַרְעוֹ אַחֲרָיו בְּרִית כְּהֻנַּת עוֹלָם תַּחַת אֲשֶׁר קִנֵּא לֵאלֹקָיו וַיְכַפֵּר עַל בְּנֵי יִשְׂרָאֵל

### (45) מלכים א' יט:י-יד
וַיֹּאמֶר קַנֹּא קִנֵּאתִי לַד' אֱלֹקֵי צְבָאוֹת כִּי עָזְבוּ בְרִיתְךָ בְּנֵי יִשְׂרָאֵל אֶת מִזְבְּחֹתֶיךָ הָרָסוּ וְאֶת נְבִיאֶיךָ הָרְגוּ בֶחָרֶב וָאִוָּתֵר אֲנִי לְבַדִּי וַיְבַקְשׁוּ אֶת נַפְשִׁי לְקַחְתָּהּ: וַיֹּאמֶר צֵא וְעָמַדְתָּ בָהָר לִפְנֵי ד' וְהִנֵּה ד' עֹבֵר וְרוּחַ גְּדוֹלָה וְחָזָק מְפָרֵק הָרִים וּמְשַׁבֵּר סְלָעִים לִפְנֵי ד' לֹא בָרוּחַ ד' וְאַחַר הָרוּחַ רַעַשׁ לֹא בָרַעַשׁ ד': וְאַחַר הָרַעַשׁ אֵשׁ לֹא בָאֵשׁ ד' וְאַחַר הָאֵשׁ קוֹל דְּמָמָה דַקָּה: וַיְהִי כִּשְׁמֹעַ אֵלִיָּהוּ וַיָּלֶט פָּנָיו בְּאַדַּרְתּוֹ וַיֵּצֵא וַיַּעֲמֹד פֶּתַח הַמְּעָרָה וְהִנֵּה אֵלָיו קוֹל וַיֹּאמֶר מַה לְּךָ פֹה אֵלִיָּהוּ: וַיֹּאמֶר קַנֹּא קִנֵּאתִי לַד' אֱלֹקֵי צְבָאוֹת כִּי עָזְבוּ בְרִיתְךָ בְּנֵי יִשְׂרָאֵל אֶת מִזְבְּחֹתֶיךָ הָרָסוּ וְאֶת נְבִיאֶיךָ הָרְגוּ בֶחָרֶב וָאִוָּתֵר אֲנִי לְבַדִּי וַיְבַקְשׁוּ אֶת נַפְשִׁי לְקַחְתָּהּ:

### (46) מדרש, פסיקתא רבתי ד:ג
מֹשֶׁה קַנַּאי "מִי לַה' אֵלָי" (שמות שם לב:כו) וְאֵלִיָּהוּ קַנַּאי "וַיֹּאמֶר אֵלִיָּהוּ לְכֹל הָעָם גְּשׁוּ נָא אֵלַי" (מלכים א' יח:ל)

### (47) פירוש העמק דבר על במדבר כה:יב
אֶת בְּרִיתִי שָׁלוֹם – בְּשָׂכָר שֶׁהֵנִיחַ כַּעַס וַחֲמַת הקב"ה בֵּרְכוֹ בְּמִדַּת הַשָּׁלוֹם. שֶׁלֹּא יַקְפִּיד וְלֹא יִרְגַּז.

## 20) תענית ח.

רבא אמר: שני תלמידי חכמים שיושבין בעיר אחת
ואין נוחין זה לזה בהלכה מתקנאין באף, ומעלין אותו

## 21) סנהדרין יז.

... שבשעה שאמר לו הקדוש ברוך הוא למשה
אספה לי שבעים איש מזקני ישראל אמר משה: כיצד
אעשה? אברור ששה מכל שבט ושבט נמצאו שנים
יתרים, אברור חמשה מכל שבט ושבט נמצאו
עשרה חסרים, אברור ששה משבט זה וחמשה משבט
זה הריני מטיל קנאה בין השבטים, מה עשה? בירר
ששה ששה, והביא שבעים ושנים פיתקין, על שבעים
כתב זקן ושנים הניח חלק, בללן ונתנן בקלפי, אמר
להם: בואו וטלו פיתקיכם כל מי שעלה בידו זקן
אמר: כבר קידשך שמים, מי שעלה בידו חלק אמר:
המקום לא חפץ בך, אני מה אעשה לך?

## 22) שבת י:

לעולם אל ישנה אדם בנו בין הבנים, שבשביל משקל
שני סלעים מילת שנתן יעקב ליוסף יותר משאר
בניו נתקנאו בו אחיו, ונתגלגל הדבר וירדו אבותינו
למצרים.

## 23) מגילה יב.

תניא, רבי יהודה אומר: הראוי לכסף לכסף, הראוי
לזהב לזהב. אמר לו רבי נחמיה: אם כן אתה מטיל
קנאה בסעודה, אלא: הם של כסף ורגליהן של זהב.

## 24) אבות דרבי נתן ד:ו

בשלשה דברים שינה הקב"ה את בני אדם זה מזה
אלו הן בקול בנעימה ובמראה.... שאלמלא שינה
הקב"ה נעימות בני אדם זה מזה היו מתקנאין זה בזה
לפיכך שינה הקב"ה נעימות בני אדם של זה מזה
נעימה של זה אינו דומה לזה ושל זה אינו דומה לזה.

## 25) פלא יועץ – קנאה

וכל ישראל הם גוף א' כאיש א' וראוי לשמוח על
טובת חברו ולהצטער על צרתו כמו על עצמו בפרט
בשום לב שאפילו בזמן שהרשעים בצער – שכינה
מצטערת, מה הלשון אומרת וכו' כל קבל דנא
כשישראל בנחת ישמח ה' במעשיו ועד שבזמן שאדם
בדוחק ובצער לא יוכל לעבוד את בוראו והדוחק
מעבירו על דעתו ועל דעת קונו וזה צער השמים
משא"כ כשהוא בנחת ובריוח מרבה להטיב ועושה
נחת רוח ליוצרו ובזמן שהרשעים בעולם חרון אף
בעולם, ובהדי הוצא לקי כרבא. ובזמן שהצדיקים
בעולם יתרבה השפע וברכה רבה וברבות הטיבה
רבו אוכליה.

## 26) שבת קלט.

ואמר רבי מלאי: בשכר (שמות ד) וראך ושמח בלבו
זכה לחשן המשפט על לבו.

## 27) סנהדרין קה:

בכל אדם מתקנא, חוץ מבנו ותלמידו

## 28) פלא יועץ – קנאה

אבל יש קנאה טובה כמאמר רבותינו זכרונם לברכה "
קנאת סופרים תרבה חכמה. ויתאוה וישתדל לעלות
במעלות החכמה ובעבודת ה' יתברך שמו כקדושים
אשר בארץ. וחייב אדם לומר מתי יגיע מעשי למעשי
אברהם יצחק ויעקב. ואם רואה שחבירו מוצלח
במעשי, זאת תהיה קנאתו באומרו בודאי שהכל לפי
מעשיו של אדם מעלליו יאכל. ויקנא לבו ביראת
ה' על דרך דכתיב "ותקנא רחל באחותה". ופירשו
רבותינו זכרונם לברכה שקנאה במעשיה הטובות
שאמרה אילו לא היתה טובה ממני לא זכתה להבנות.
ומתוך כך ייטיב מעשיו לעשות נחת רוח ליוצרו כי
זה כל האדם.

## 29) בבא בתרא כא.

קנאת סופרים תרבה חכמה.

## 30) מדרש תהילים לז:א

"לדוד אל תתחר במרעים אל תקנא בעושי עולה",
זהו שאמר הכתוב "אל יקנא לבך בחטאים" (משלי כג
יז), ובמה תקנא, "כי אם ביראת ה' כל היום" (שם שם
משלי כ"ג), אל תקנא בנרן של רשעים, שאינו כלום,
כמה שמן יש בו, שמינית או רביעית, אין לו אחרית,
השמן משתלם, והנר מתכבה מיד, וכן הוא אומר כי
לא תהיה אחרית לרע נר רשעים ידעך (שם משלי כד
כ), הלכה האורה שלו, לכך אמר (דוד) אל יקנא לבך
בחטאים, קנא לנר שאינו נדעך לעולם, ואין האור
שלו פוסקת, ואיזה הוא, זה כי נר מצוה ותורה אור
(שם משלי ו כג), לכך אל יקנא לבך בחטאים, אמר
הקב"ה קנא לי, שאילולי הקנאה אין העולם עומד,
ואין אדם נושא אשה, ואינו בונה בית, שאילולי שקנא
אברהם, לא היה קונה שמים וארץ, ואימתי קנא
שאמר למלכי צדק

## 31) משלי כג:יז

אַל יְקַנֵּא לִבְּךָ בַּחַטָּאִים כִּי אִם בְּיִרְאַת ד' כָּל הַיּוֹם:
רש"י – אל יקנא לבך בחטאים – בהצלחתם להיות
רשע כמותם:
אבן עזרא – כי אם – באיש יראת ה' תקנא:

## 32) בראשית ל:א

וַתֵּרֶא רָחֵל כִּי לֹא יָלְדָה לְיַעֲקֹב וַתְּקַנֵּא רָחֵל בַּאֲחֹתָהּ
וַתֹּאמֶר אֶל יַעֲקֹב הָבָה לִּי בָנִים וְאִם אַיִן מֵתָה אָנֹכִי:

## 33) מדרש, בראשית רבה עא:ו

ותרא רחל כי לא ילדה וגו', ותקנא רחל באחותה,
א"ר יצחק כתיב (משלי כג) אל יקנא לבך בחטאים
כי אם ביראת ה' כל היום, ואת אמרת ותקנא רחל
באחותה אלא מלמד שקנאתה במעשיה הטובים

**1) פלא יועץ – קנאה**

קנאה היא מדה רעה מאד כמאמר התנא 'הקנאה והתאוה והכבוד מוציאין את האדם מן העולם' והנה יצר לב האדם רע וחושק להיות יחיד בחכמה ומעשים בעושר וכבוד ומתוך כך מצטער כשיש אחר כמוהו או גדול וטוב ממנו ומקנא לו ומבקש רעתו ומספר בגנותו. וגדולה שנאה שהיא מחמת קנאה אש אוכלה היא לאין מרפה ומי שיש בו מדה רעה זו כל ימיו מכאובים ואוכל לחם העצבים ואין לו רעים אהובים ומרבה ריבות והוא שמח לאיד ורוצה בתקלת חבירו ...

**2) משלי ו:לד**

כִּי־קִנְאָה חֲמַת־גָּבֶר וְלֹא יַחְמוֹל בְּיוֹם נָקָם:

**3) משלי כז:ד**

אַכְזְרִיּוּת חֵמָה וְשֶׁטֶף אָף וּמִי יַעֲמֹד לִפְנֵי קִנְאָה:

**4) שיר השירים ח:ו**

שִׂימֵנִי כַחוֹתָם עַל־לִבֶּךָ כַּחוֹתָם עַל־זְרוֹעֶךָ כִּי־עַזָּה כַמָּוֶת אַהֲבָה קָשָׁה כִשְׁאוֹל קִנְאָה רְשָׁפֶיהָ רִשְׁפֵּי אֵשׁ שַׁלְהֶבֶתְיָה:

**5) משלי יד:ל**

חַיֵּי בְשָׂרִים לֵב מַרְפֵּא וּרְקַב עֲצָמוֹת קִנְאָה:

**6) איוב ה:ב**

כִּי־לֶאֱוִיל יַהֲרָג־כָּעַשׂ וּפֹתֶה תָּמִית קִנְאָה:

**7) קהלת ט:ו**

גַּם אַהֲבָתָם גַּם־שִׂנְאָתָם גַּם קִנְאָתָם כְּבָר אָבָדָה וְחֵלֶק אֵין־לָהֶם עוֹד לְעוֹלָם בְּכֹל אֲשֶׁר־נַעֲשָׂה תַּחַת הַשָּׁמֶשׁ:

**8) סנהדרין נט:**

הָיָה רבי יהודה בן תימא אומר: אדם הראשון מיסב בגן עדן היה, והיו מלאכי השרת צולין לו בשר, ומסננין לו יין. הציץ בו נחש וראה בכבודו, ונתקנא בן

**9) בראשית ד:ד-ה**

וְהֶבֶל הֵבִיא גַם־הוּא מִבְּכֹרוֹת צֹאנוֹ וּמֵחֶלְבֵהֶן וַיִּשַׁע ד' אֶל־הֶבֶל וְאֶל־מִנְחָתוֹ: וְאֶל־קַיִן וְאֶל־מִנְחָתוֹ לֹא שָׁעָה וַיִּחַר לְקַיִן מְאֹד וַיִּפְּלוּ פָּנָיו:

**10) בראשית לז:יא**

וַיְקַנְאוּ־בוֹ אֶחָיו וְאָבִיו שָׁמַר אֶת־הַדָּבָר:

**11) מדרש משלי א:יט**

אמר ר' יהושע בן לוי לא נמשכו עשרה הרוגי מלכות אלא בחטא מכירתו של יוסף]

**13) מדרש, שיר השירים רבה ח:ז**

קשה כשאול קנאה שקנא עשו ליעקב ... קשה כשאול קנאה שקנאו בו (יוסף) אחיו ... קשה כשאול קנאה קנא שקנא שאול לדוד ... קשה כשאול קנאה קנא שמקנא לה (לאשתו) ואומר לה אל תדברי עם איש פלוני והלכה ודברה עמו מיד ... קשה כשאול קנאה שעתיד הקב"ה לקנא לציון קנאה גדולה ...

כִּי לֹא תִשְׁתַּחֲוֶה לְאֵל אַחֵר כִּי ד' קַנָּא שְׁמוֹ אֵל קַנָּא הוּא:

**14) במדבר יא:כח-כט**

וַיַּעַן יְהוֹשֻׁעַ בִּן־נוּן מְשָׁרֵת מֹשֶׁה מִבְּחֻרָיו וַיֹּאמַר אֲדֹנִי מֹשֶׁה כְּלָאֵם: וַיֹּאמֶר לוֹ מֹשֶׁה הַמְקַנֵּא אַתָּה לִי וּמִי יִתֵּן כָּל־עַם ד' נְבִיאִים כִּי־יִתֵּן ד' אֶת־רוּחוֹ עֲלֵיהֶם:

**15) מדרש דברים רבה ט:ט**

... אותה שעה צעק משה ואמר מאה מיתות ולא קנאה אחת כמא"ד ושלמה מפרשה (שיר ח) כי עזה כמות אהבה קשה כשאול קנאה אהבה שאהב משה ליהושע ומה שקינא משה ביהושע כיון שקיבל עליו למות התחיל הקדוש ברוך הוא מפייסו אמר ליה חייך בעולם הזה הנהגת את בני אף לעתיד לבא על ידך אני מנהיג אותן מנין שנאמר (ישעיה סג) ויזכר ימי עולם משה עמו:

**16) במדבר ה:יד-טו, כט**

וְעָבַר עָלָיו רוּחַ־קִנְאָה וְקִנֵּא אֶת־אִשְׁתּוֹ וְהִוא נִטְמָאָה אוֹ־עָבַר עָלָיו רוּחַ־קִנְאָה וְקִנֵּא אֶת־אִשְׁתּוֹ וְהִיא לֹא נִטְמָאָה: וְהֵבִיא הָאִישׁ אֶת־אִשְׁתּוֹ אֶל־הַכֹּהֵן וְהֵבִיא אֶת־קָרְבָּנָהּ עָלֶיהָ עֲשִׂירִת הָאֵיפָה קֶמַח שְׂעֹרִים לֹא־יִצֹק עָלָיו שֶׁמֶן וְלֹא־יִתֵּן עָלָיו לְבֹנָה כִּי־מִנְחַת קְנָאֹת הוּא מִנְחַת זִכָּרוֹן מַזְכֶּרֶת עָוֹן:

זֹאת תּוֹרַת הַקְּנָאֹת אֲשֶׁר תִּשְׂטֶה אִשָּׁה תַּחַת אִישָׁהּ וְנִטְמָאָה:

**17) אבות ד:כא**

רבי אלעזר הקפר אומר הקנאה והתאוה והכבוד מוציאין את האדם מן העולם:

**19) סוטה מט.**

שני ת"ח הדרין בעיר אחת ואין נוחין זה לזה בהלכה אחד מת ואחד גולה

בְּמָמוֹנוֹ, צְדָקָה לַעֲנִיִּים, גְּמִילוּת חֲסָדִים בֵּין לַעֲנִיִּים בֵּין לַעֲשִׁירִים וְכוּ'. וְהִיא אֶחָד מֵהַדְּבָרִים שֶׁהָאָדָם אוֹכֵל פֵּרוֹתֵיהֶן בָּעוֹלָם הַזֶּה, וְהַקֶּרֶן קַיֶּמֶת לוֹ לָעוֹלָם הַבָּא, כִּדְאִיתָא בְּפֵאָה פֶּרֶק א'

... וּמִי שֶׁמַּעֲלִים עֵינָיו מִמִּצְוָה זוֹ, גָּדוֹל עֲוֹנוֹ, כְּמוֹ שֶׁכָּתַב הָרַבֵּנוּ יוֹנָה בְּשַׁעֲרֵי תְשׁוּבָה בְּמַאֲמָר ס"ז עַל הַפָּסוּק (דְּבָרִים ט"ו ט'), "הִשָּׁמֶר לְךָ פֶּן יִהְיֶה דָבָר עִם לְבָבְךָ בְלִיַּעַל לֵאמֹר קָרְבָה שְׁנַת הַשֶּׁבַע וְכוּ', וְרָעָה עֵינְךָ" וְכוּ'. וְזֶה לְשׁוֹנוֹ הַטָּהוֹר, לְמַדְנוּ מִזֶּה, כִּי הַנִּמְנָע מִלְּהַלְווֹת לְעָנִי, עוֹבֵר בִּשְׁנֵי לָאוִין, שֶׁהֵם, הִשָּׁמֶר, וּפֶן. וְאִם לְעֵת אֲשֶׁר קָרְבָה שְׁנַת הַשֶּׁבַע הִזְהִירָנוּ שֶׁלֹּא נֶחְדַּל

מִלְּהַלְווֹת מִיִּרְאַת דְּבַר הַשְּׁמִטָּה, אַף כִּי בִּזְמַן שֶׁלֹּא יַפְסִיד חוֹבוֹ, כִּי יִגְדַּל חֶטְא הַקּוֹפֵץ יָדוֹ מִלְּהַלְווֹת. וְעַל גֹּדֶל הֶעָוֹן קָרָא הַכָּתוּב מַחְשֶׁבֶת צַר הָעַיִן מִלְּהַלְווֹת דָּבָר בְּלִיַּעַל. עַד כָּאן לְשׁוֹנוֹ.

### (75) אור זרוע, הלכות אבילות תכב:ד

... וְאוֹמֵר לִי לִבִּי אֲנִי יִצְחָק הַמְחַבֵּר כְּשֵׁם שֶׁאֵין קוֹבְרִין רָשָׁע קַל אֵצֶל רָשָׁע חָמוּר כָּךְ אֵין קוֹבְרִין צַדִּיק אֵצֶל חָסִיד דְּצַדִּיק הַיְינוּ שֶׁמְּקַיְּמִים אֶת הַתּוֹרָה כְּדִין שֶׁנּוֹהֵג הֶיתֵּר בַּהֶיתֵּר וְאִיסּוּר בְּאִיסּוּר וְחָסִיד הַיְינוּ שֶׁמְּקַדֵּשׁ עַצְמוֹ בַּמּוּתָּר לוֹ ...

### 69) מדרש תהילים קמו

לפיכך, אם מבקש אדם להיות לוי או להיות כהן
אינו יכול, מפני שלא היה אביו לא לוי ולא כהן. אבל
מבקש להיות צדיק, אפילו היה גוי יכול להיות צדיק,
שאין הצדיקים באים מבית אב אלא מעצמו

### 70) משנה אבות ה:י', יא, יג

ארבע מדות באדם... שלי שלך ושלך שלך. חסיד.
ארבע מדות בדעות... קשה לכעוס ונוח לרצות
חסיד.
ארבע מדות בנותני צדקה.... יתן ויתנו אחרים.
חסיד.
ארבע מדות בהולכי לבית המדרש. הולך ואינו
עושה. שכר הליכה בידו. עושה ואינו הולך. שכר
מעשה בידו. הולך ועושה. חסיד...

### 71) שבת קכ

משנה. מצילין סל מלא ככרות אף על פי שיש בו
מאה סעודות, ועיגול של דבילה, וחבית של יין.
ואומר לאחרים: בואו והצילו לכם. ואם היו פיקחין
עושין עמו חשבון אחר השבת.
גמרא: ... ועיגול של דבילה כו'. חשבון מאי
עבידתיה? מהפקירא קזכו אמר רב חסדא: מדת
חסידות שנו כאן.

### 72) ירושלמי, תרומות מז

עולא בר קושב תבעתיה מלכותא ערק ואזיל ליה
ללוד גבי ריב"ל אתון ואקפון מדינתא אמרו להן אין
לית אתון יהבון ליה לן אנן מחרבין מדינתא סלק
גביה ריב"ל ופייסיה ויהביה לון והוה אליהו זכור
לטוב יליף מתגלי עלוי ולא אתגלי וצם כמה צומין
ואיתגלי עלוי אמר ליה ולמסורות אני נגלה א"ל ולא
משנה עשיתי א"ל וזו משנת החסידים

### 73) רמב"ם, פירוש המשניות אבות ה:ז, ו:א

וחסיד – הוא האיש החכם כשיוסיף במעלה ר"ל
במעלות המדות עד שיטה אל הקצה האחד מעט כמו
שביארנו בפרק הד' ויהיו מעשיו מרובין מחכמתו,
ומפני זה נקרא חסיד. לתוספתו, כי ההפלגה בדבר
יקרא חסיד תהיה ההפלגה ההיא בטוב או ברע ...
הסתכל איך לא קרא הנבון הזכרן חסיד מפני שהיא
מעלה שכלית ומפני שהיא
חסיד עושה לפנים משורת הדין

### 74) שמירת הלשון א:ז

... וְהִיא גְדוֹלָה יוֹתֵר מִמִּצְוַת הַצְּדָקָה, כְּמוֹ שֶׁאָמְרוּ
חֲזַ"ל (סֻכָּה מ"ט ע"ב) אָמַר ר' אֶלְעָזָר, גְּדוֹלָה גְמִילוּת
חֲסָדִים יוֹתֵר מִן הַצְּדָקָה, שֶׁנֶּאֱמַר (הוֹשֵׁעַ י' י"ב), "זִרְעוּ
לָכֶם לִצְדָקָה קִצְרוּ לְפִי חֶסֶד". אִם אָדָם זוֹרֵעַ, סָפֵק
אוֹכֵל סָפֵק אֵינוֹ אוֹכֵל, אָדָם קוֹצֵר וַדַּאי אוֹכֵל. תָּנוּ
רַבָּנָן, בִּשְׁלשָׁה דְּבָרִים גְּדוֹלָה גְמִילוּת חֲסָדִים יוֹתֵר מִן
הַצְּדָקָה, צְדָקָה בְּמָמוֹנוֹ, גְּמִילוּת חֲסָדִים בֵּין בְּגוּפוֹ בֵּין

---

י"ח ... דהאיש הישראלי מחוייב לעשות גם מצוות
שכליות לא מפני השכל אלא מפני צווי הקדוש ברוך
הוא כמ"ש "כי עקב תשמעון את המשפטים וג'
כלומר אפילו המשפטים תשמע מה שצותה התורה
ולא תעשה מפני שכלך אלא כשאר מצוות השמעיות
מ"מ קדושת ישראל אינו ניכר כל כך בהשכליות כמו
בהשמעיות כמ"ש חז"ל ביומא [ס"ז ב] ולכן לא תקנו
ברכות על מצוות שכליות ודרך ארץ שיש מהם בכל
אום ולשון ולא תקנו לברך אשר קדשנו במצוותיו אם
כי אינם עושים רק מפני השכל

### 66) תהילים קמה:יז, ירמיהו ג:יב

צַדִּיק ד' בְּכָל דְּרָכָיו וְחָסִיד בְּכָל מַעֲשָׂיו:
הָלֹךְ וְקָרָאתָ אֶת הַדְּבָרִים הָאֵלֶּה צָפוֹנָה וְאָמַרְתָּ שׁוּבָה
מְשֻׁבָה יִשְׂרָאֵל נְאֻם ד' לוֹא אַפִּיל פָּנַי בָּכֶם כִּי חָסִיד אֲנִי
נְאֻם ד' לֹא אֶטּוֹר לְעוֹלָם:

### 67) מדרש, ספרי עקב מט

מה הקב"ה נקרא צדיק שנ' (תהלים קמה) צדיק ה'
בכל דרכיו וחסיד בכל מעשיו אף אתה הוי צדיק.
הקב"ה נקרא חסיד שנאמ' וחסיד בכל מעשיו אף
אתה הוי חסיד

### 68) רמב"ם, מורה נבוכים א:נג

ש'חסד' ענינו – הפלגה באי זה דבר שמפליגים
בו. ושמשתמש בו בהפלגת גמילות הטוב יותר. וידוע
שגמילות הטוב כולל שני ענינים, האחד מהם –
לגמול טוב למי שאין חוק עליך כלל, והשני – להיטיב
למי שראוי לטובה יותר ממה שהוא ראוי. ורוב
שמוש ספרי הנבואה במלת 'חסד' הוא בהטבה למי
שאין לו חוק עליך כלל. ומפני זה כל טובה שתגיע
מאתו ית' תקרא 'חסד' – אמר, "חסדי יי אזכיר".
ובעבור זה זה המציאות כולו – רצוני לומר, המצאת
האלוה ית' אותו – הוא 'חסד' – אמר, "עולם חסד
יבנה" – ענינו, 'בנין העולם חסד הוא'. ואמר ית'
בסיפור 'מדותיו', 'ורב חסד':
ומלת 'צדקה' היא נגזרת מ'צדק', והוא היושר,
והיושר הוא – להגיע כל בעל חוק לחוקו ולתת
לכל נמצא מן הנמצאות כפי הראוי לו. ולפי הענין
הראשון לא יקראו בספרי הנבואה החוקים שאתה
חייב בהם לזולתך, כשתשלמם, 'צדקה' – כי
כשתפרע לשכיר שכרו או תפרע חובך – לא יקרא
זה 'צדקה'. אבל החוקים הראויים עליך לזולתך מפני
מעלת המדות, כרפואת מחץ כל מחוץ, יקרא 'צדקה'
– ומפני זה זה אמר בהשבת המשכון, "ולך תהיה צדקה"
– כי כשתתנהג בדרך מעלות המדות כבר עשית צדק
לנפשך המשכלת, כי שילמת לה חוקה. ומפני הקרא
כל מעלת מדות 'צדקה' – אמר,,והאמין ביי, ויחשבה
לו צדקה" – רצוני לומר, מעלת האמונה; וכן אמרו
ע"ה, "וצדקה תהיה לנו – כי נשמור לעשות וג'":
אבל מלת 'משפט' היא לשון לשון במה שראוי על הנדון
– יהיה זה חסד או נקמה:

**52) תהילים לד:יג, טו**
מִי־הָאִישׁ הֶחָפֵץ חַיִּים אֹהֵב יָמִים לִרְאוֹת טוֹב: ... סוּר
מֵרָע וַעֲשֵׂה־טוֹב בַּקֵּשׁ שָׁלוֹם וְרָדְפֵהוּ:

**53) אבות ה:י**
ארבע מדות באדם. האומר שלי שלי ושלך שלך. זו
מדה בינונית. ויש אומרים זו מדת סדום.

**54) ויקרא יט:טז, שולחן ערוך, חושן משפט תכו:א**
לֹא־תֵלֵךְ רָכִיל בְּעַמֶּיךָ לֹא תַעֲמֹד עַל־דַּם רֵעֶךָ אֲנִי ד':
הרואה את חבירו טובע בים או ליסטים באין עליו
או חיה רעה באה עליו, ויכול להצילו הוא בעצמו או
שישכור אחרים להציל ולא הציל, או ששמע עכו"ם
או מוסרים מחשבים עליו רעה או טומנים לו פח
ולא גילה אוזן חבירו והודיעו, או שידע בעכו"ם או
באנס שהוא בא על חבירו ויכול לפייסו בגלל חבירו
ולהסיר מה שבלבו ולא פייסו ויכו"צא בדברים אלו,
עובר על לא תעמוד על דם רעך.

**55) מיכה ו:ח ופירוש אבן עזרא**
הִגִּיד לְךָ אָדָם מַה־טּוֹב וּמָה־ד' דּוֹרֵשׁ מִמְּךָ כִּי אִם־
עֲשׂוֹת מִשְׁפָּט וְאַהֲבַת חֶסֶד וְהַצְנֵעַ לֶכֶת עִם־אֱלֹקֶיךָ:
הגיד – זאת היא תשובת הנביא ככה הגיד לך
אתה האדם האומר במה אקדם ד' מה טוב בעיניו
שתעשה והוא איננו מבקש אילים ולא בנך רק עשות
משפט שלא תעשה עול בעמיתך ולא תוננו בדיבור
או בהון רק תעשה חסד עמו בכל יכולתך והצנע
לכתך עם השם לבדו שתלך בדרכיו בתם לבב הפך
קשי עורף:

**56) ביצה לב**
כל המרחם על הבריות בידוע שהוא מזרעו של
אברהם אבינו, וכל מי שאינו מרחם על הבריות
בידוע שאינו מזרעו של אברהם אבינו

**57) דרך ה', ב:ד**
... ואז השגיח ית"ש על כל בני האדם, וראה כל
המדריגות שהיה ראוי שיקבעו בם האנשים ההם
כפי מעשיהם, וקבעם בם בבחינתם השרשיית כמ"ש.
והנה כפי מה שהונחו הם, כן נגזר עליהם שיהיו
מוציאים התולדות, כפי מה שכבר שוער שהיה ראוי
לשרש ההוא.

**58) רמב"ם, הלכות מתנים י':א, בראשית יח:יט**
חייבין אנו להזהר במצות צדקה יותר מכל מצות
עשה, שהצדקה סימן לצדיק זרע אברהם אבינו
שנאמר כי ידעתיו למען אשר יצוה את בניו לעשות
צדקה ...
כִּי יְדַעְתִּיו לְמַעַן אֲשֶׁר יְצַוֶּה אֶת־בָּנָיו וְאֶת־בֵּיתוֹ אַחֲרָיו
וְשָׁמְרוּ דֶּרֶךְ ד' לַעֲשׂוֹת צְדָקָה וּמִשְׁפָּט לְמַעַן הָבִיא ד'
עַל־אַבְרָהָם אֵת אֲשֶׁר־דִּבֶּר עָלָיו:

**59) פירוש שפת אמת על פרשת לך לך, תרל"ה,**
ופי' מו"ז ז"ל מ"ש מגן אברהם שהקב"ה הבטיח לו
שיה' ממנו נקודה בכל איש ישראל אשר הוא ית'
מגין עלי' שלא יוכל לקלקל אותה כו'. ונקודה זו
מסייע לכל איש ישראל כפי מדריגתו וז"ש מנח לא
העמדתי מגינים כו'. והבן

**60) דברים ד:כ ופירוש רש"י שם**
וְאֶתְכֶם לָקַח ד' וַיּוֹצִא אֶתְכֶם מִכּוּר הַבַּרְזֶל מִמִּצְרָיִם
לִהְיוֹת לוֹ לְעַם נַחֲלָה כַּיּוֹם הַזֶּה:
כור – הוא כלי שמזקקים בו את הזהב.

**61) ישעיהו מח:י**
הִנֵּה צְרַפְתִּיךָ וְלֹא בְכָסֶף בְּחַרְתִּיךָ בְּכוּר עֹנִי:

**62) נדרים כ.**
תניא: (שמות כ) בעבור תהיה יראתו על פניכם זו
בושה, לבלתי תחטאו מלמד שהבושה מביאה לידי
יראת חטא מיכן אמרו: סימן יפה באדם שהוא ביישן.
אחרים אומרים: כל אדם המתבייש לא במהרה הוא
חוטא, ומי שאין לו בושת פנים בידוע שלא עמדו
אבותיו על הר סיני.

**63) יבמות עט.**
אמר, שלשה סימנים יש באומה זו: הרחמנים,
והביישנין, וגומלי חסדים רחמנים, דכתיב: (דברים
י"ג) ונתן לך רחמים ורחמך והרבך ביישנין, דכתיב:
(שמות כ) בעבור תהיה יראתו על פניכם גומלי
חסדים, דכתיב: (בראשית י"ח) למען אשר יצוה את
בניו ואת ביתו וגו', כל שיש בו שלשה סימנים הללו
ראוי להדבק באומה זו.

**64) ירמיהו ט:כב-כג**
כֹּה אָמַר ד' אַל־יִתְהַלֵּל חָכָם בְּחָכְמָתוֹ וְאַל־יִתְהַלֵּל
הַגִּבּוֹר בִּגְבוּרָתוֹ אַל־יִתְהַלֵּל עָשִׁיר בְּעָשְׁרוֹ: כִּי אִם־בְּזֹאת
יִתְהַלֵּל הַמִּתְהַלֵּל הַשְׂכֵּל וְיָדֹעַ אוֹתִי כִּי אֲנִי ד' עֹשֶׂה חֶסֶד
מִשְׁפָּט וּצְדָקָה בָּאָרֶץ כִּי־בְאֵלֶּה חָפַצְתִּי נְאֻם־ד':

**65) ערוך השולחן, חושן משפט תכז:י**
ושאלתי מאת הרב החסיד למסור מפתח על המצוות
מפני מה מברכין במקצתן ומקצתן אין מברכין עליהן
כגון מי שעומד מפני רבו או חכם והנותן צדקה לעני
והלואת מעות והשבת העבוט ושלוח הקן ומעקה
ובקור חולים ונחום אבלים ומכניסי חתן וכלה לחופה
ועל לקט שכחה ופאה ופרט ועוללות ופטר חמור
עריפתו ונתינתו ונתינת בכור לכהן וראשית הגז
ומתנות ונתן זרוע לחיים וקיבה ומגיש וסומך והבאת
שלום ומורא וכבוד ומוכיח חבירו והשמטת כספים
ושלוח עבדים ומשמח גר יתום ואלמנה והשבת
אבדה וטעינה ופריקה ומצות חליצה ויבום עכ"ל
ותירץ דכל מצוה שאינה בינו לבין עצמו אבל תלויה
באחרים א"צ לברך עכ"ל וכ"כ בתשו' הרשב"א סי'

### 39) בראשית יח:ג ורש"י שם
וַיֹּאמַר אֲדֹנָי אִם־נָא מָצָאתִי חֵן בְּעֵינֶיךָ אַל־נָא תַעֲבֹר מֵעַל עַבְדֶּךָ:
ויאמר אדני אם נא וגו' – והיה אומר להקב"ה להמתין לו עד שירוץ ויכניס את האורחים.

### 40) מדרש ילקוט שמעוני יח:פב
אמר רב יהודה אמר רב גדולה הכנסת אורחים מהקבלת פני שכינה דכתיב ויאמר אם נא מצאתי חן בעיניך אל נא תעבור מעל עבדך. אמר ר' אלעזר בא וראה שלא כמדת הקב"ה מדת בשר ודם מדת בשר ודם אין קטן יכול לומר לגדול המתן עד שאבוא אצלך אבל בהקב"ה כתיב אל נא תעבור מעל עבדך. אמר ר' יוחנן ששה דברים שאדם עושה אותם אוכל מפירותיהם בעולם הזה והקרן קיימת לו לעולם הבא ואלו הן הכנסת אורחים ובקור חולים והשכמת בית המדרש ועיון תפלה והמגדל בניו לתלמוד תורה והדן את חבירו לכף זכות. ובהני שייכי נמי כבוד אב ואם וגמילות חסדים והבאת שלום בין אדם לחבירו ותלמוד תורה כנגד כולן:

### 41) כף החיים פלאגי ה:ו
גדולה הכנסת אורחים כהשכמת בית המדרש, ורב דימי אמר יותר מהשכמת בית המדרש, אמר רב יהודה אמר רב, גדולה הכנסת אורחים יותר מהקבלת פני שכינה, ומהדברים שאדם אוכל מפירותיהם בעולם הזה והקרן קיימת לו לעולם הבא, אחד מהם הוא הכנסת אורחים, ובספר החסידים סימן כו כתב, בא וראה כמה גדול פת לעוברי דרכים, שהרי מיכה שעשה הפסל והעמידו אצל המשכן, עד שהיו מתערבים עשן הפסל ועשן המערכה, ואמר הקדוש ברוך הוא הניחו לו, לפי שהיתה פיתו מצויה לעוברי דרכים, ובמדרש רבה פרשת נשא אמרו דנכתב שמו של מיכה כשם הצדיקים, לפי שהיה מקבל אורחים:

### 42) רמ"א, שולחן ערוך, אורח חיים שלג:א, ) ופירוש משנה ברורה ח
וכל שבות שהתירו משום צורך מצוה מותר גם כן (ח) לצורך אורחים
לצורך אורחים – שבעה"ב המזמנם עושה מצוה וכמו שאחז"ל דגדולה הכנסת אורחים יותר מהקבלת פני השכינה

### 43) רש"י על בראשית יא:ט
ומשם הפיצם- למד שאין להם חלק לעולם הבא, וכי אי זו קשה של דור המבול או של דור הפלגה, אלו לא פשטו יד בעיקר, ואלו פשטו יד בעיקר להלחם בו, ואלו נשטפו ואלו לא נאבדו מן העולם, אלא שדור המבול היו גזלנים והיתה מריבה ביניהם, לכך נאבדו, ואלו היו נוהגים אהבה וריעות ביניהם, שנאמר שפה אחת ודברים אחדים, למדת ששנאוי המחלוקת וגדול השלום:

### 44) ברכות יט:, רמב"ם, הלכות שבת כו:כג, שולחן ערוך, יורה דעה, שעב:א
תא שמע: גדול כבוד הבריות שדוחה [את] לא תעשה שבתורה.

גדול כבוד הבריות שדוחה את לא תעשה שבתורה הגה כהן שהכה שוכב ערום והוא באהל עם המת ולא ידע אין להגיד לו אלא יקראו לו סתם שיצא כדי שילביש עצמו תחלה אבל אם כבר הגידו לו אסור להמתין עד שילביש עצמו ... אבל אם ... טומאה דרבנן תחלה דגדול כבוד הבריות

### 45) ישעיהו נח:ה-ז
הֲכָזֶה יִהְיֶה צוֹם אֶבְחָרֵהוּ יוֹם עַנּוֹת אָדָם נַפְשׁוֹ הֲלָכֹף כְּאַגְמֹן רֹאשׁוֹ וְשַׂק וָאֵפֶר יַצִּיעַ הֲלָזֶה תִּקְרָא־צוֹם וְיוֹם רָצוֹן לַד': הֲלוֹא זֶה צוֹם אֶבְחָרֵהוּ פַּתֵּחַ חַרְצֻבּוֹת רֶשַׁע הַתֵּר אֲגֻדּוֹת מוֹטָה וְשַׁלַּח רְצוּצִים חָפְשִׁים וְכָל־מוֹטָה תְּנַתֵּקוּ: הֲלוֹא פָרֹס לָרָעֵב לַחְמֶךָ וַעֲנִיִּים מְרוּדִים תָּבִיא בָיִת כִּי־תִרְאֶה עָרֹם וְכִסִּיתוֹ וּמִבְּשָׂרְךָ לֹא תִתְעַלָּם:

### 46) ישעיה א:טו
וּבְפָרִשְׂכֶם כַּפֵּיכֶם אַעְלִים עֵינַי מִכֶּם גַּם כִּי־תַרְבּוּ תְפִלָּה אֵינֶנִּי שֹׁמֵעַ יְדֵיכֶם דָּמִים מָלֵאוּ:

### 47) הושע ו:ו ומדרש ילקוט שמעוני תקכב
כִּי חֶסֶד חָפַצְתִּי וְלֹא־זָבַח וְדַעַת אֱלֹקִים מֵעֹלוֹת:
"כי חסד חפצתי ולא זבח" אמר הקב"ה חביב עלי חסד שאתם גומלים זה לזה יותר מכל הזבח שזבח שלמה לפני

### 48) ישעיה ג:י' וקידושין מ.
אִמְרוּ צַדִּיק כִּי־טוֹב כִּי־פְרִי מַעַלְלֵיהֶם יֹאכֵלוּ:
"אמרו צדיק כי טוב כי פרי מעלליהם יאכלו" וכי יש צדיק טוב, ויש צדיק שאינו טוב? אלא, טוב לשמים ולבריות זהו צדיק טוב, טוב לשמים ורע לבריות זהו צדיק שאינו טוב.

### 49) בראשית ו:ה, ח:כא
וַיַּרְא ד' כִּי רַבָּה רָעַת הָאָדָם בָּאָרֶץ וְכָל־יֵצֶר מַחְשְׁבֹת לִבּוֹ רַק רַע כָּל־הַיּוֹם:
וַיָּרַח ד' אֶת־רֵיחַ הַנִּיחֹחַ וַיֹּאמֶר ד' אֶל־לִבּוֹ לֹא אֹסִף לְקַלֵּל עוֹד אֶת־הָאֲדָמָה בַּעֲבוּר הָאָדָם כִּי יֵצֶר לֵב הָאָדָם רַע מִנְּעֻרָיו וְלֹא־אֹסִף עוֹד לְהַכּוֹת אֶת־כָּל־חַי כַּאֲשֶׁר עָשִׂיתִי:

### 50) סוכה נב.
תנא ליה: כל הגדול מחבירו יצרו גדול הימנו אמר רבי יצחק: יצרו של אדם מתגבר עליו בכל יום, שנאמר (בראשית ו) רק רע כל היום

### 51) מדרש תנחומא, ויקרא ו
אמר הקב"ה בעולם הזה על ידי יצר הרע ששולט בכם הייתם חוטאים אבל לעולם הבא אני עוקרו מכם ...

**25) מלאכי ב:י'**

הֲלוֹא אָב אֶחָד לְכֻלָּנוּ הֲלוֹא אֵ־ל אֶחָד בְּרָאָנוּ מַדּוּעַ נִבְגַּד אִישׁ בְּאָחִיו לְחַלֵּל בְּרִית אֲבֹתֵינוּ:

**26) משלי כא:ג, סוכה מט**

עֲשֹׂה צְדָקָה וּמִשְׁפָּט נִבְחָר לַד' מִזָּבַח:
גדול העושה צדקה יותר מכל הקרבנות, שנאמר (משלי כא:ג) "עשה צדקה ומשפט נבחר לד' מזבח".

**27) צפניה ג:יג**

שְׁאֵרִית יִשְׂרָאֵל לֹא־יַעֲשׂוּ עַוְלָה וְלֹא־יְדַבְּרוּ כָזָב וְלֹא־יִמָּצֵא בְּפִיהֶם לְשׁוֹן תַּרְמִית כִּי־הֵמָּה יִרְעוּ וְרָבְצוּ וְאֵין מַחֲרִיד:

**28) אבות ד:יז**

הוא היה אומר יפה שעה אחת בתשובה ומעשים טובים בעולם הזה. מכל חיי העולם הבא. ויפה שעה אחת של קורת רוח בעולם הבא. מכל חיי העולם הזה:

**29) משנה אבות ו:ט**

... לפי שבשעת פטירתו של אדם. אין מלוין לו לאדם לא כסף ולא זהב ולא אבנים טובות ומרגליות. אלא תורה ומעשים טובים בלבד:

**30) סוטה ג:**

א"ר שמואל בר נחמני א"ר יונתן: כל העושה מצוה אחת בעוה"ז מקדמתה והולכת לפניו לעוה"ב

**31) מדרש תהילים קיח:יז**

פתחו לי שערי צדק - לעולם הבא אמרו לו לאדם מה היה מלאכתך, והוא אומר מאכיל רעבים הייתי, והם יאמרו לו זה השער לה' מאכיל רעבים הכנס בו, משקה צמאים הייתי, והם אומרים לו זה השער לה', משקה צמאים הכנס בו, מלביש ערומים הייתי, והם אומרים לו זה השער לה', מלביש ערומים הכנס בו, וכן מגדל יתומים, וכן עושי צדקה, וכן גומלי חסדים, ודוד אמר אני עשיתי את כולם, יפתחו לי את כולם, לכך נאמר פתחו לי שערי צדק אבא בם אודה י"ה.

**32) מדרש תנא דבי אליהו רבה יח**

וכן אמרו חכמים מעשיך יקרבוך ומעשיך ירחקוך הא כיצד עשה אדם דברים מכוערים ודברים שאינם ראוים מעשיו מרחיקים אותו מן השכינה שנאמר (ישעיהו נט:ב) "כי אם עונותיכם היו מבדילי"ם ביניכם לבין אלקיכם וחטאתיכם הסתירו פנים מכם משמוע" אבל אם עשה אדם מעשים טובים מקרבין אותו אצל השכינה שנאמר (שם נז) "כי כה אמר רם ונשא וגו' (ישעיה נז:טו)

**33) שמות כ:יב, דברים כב:ו-ז, דברים כה:טו, מורה נבוכים ג:מח**

כַּבֵּד אֶת־אָבִיךָ וְאֶת־אִמֶּךָ לְמַעַן יַאֲרִכוּן יָמֶיךָ עַל

הָאֲדָמָה אֲשֶׁר ד' אֱלֹקֶיךָ נֹתֵן לָךְ:
כִּי יִקָּרֵא קַן־צִפּוֹר | לְפָנֶיךָ בַּדֶּרֶךְ בְּכָל־עֵץ אוֹ עַל־הָאָרֶץ אֶפְרֹחִים אוֹ בֵיצִים וְהָאֵם רֹבֶצֶת עַל־הָאֶפְרֹחִים אוֹ עַל־הַבֵּיצִים לֹא־תִקַּח הָאֵם עַל־הַבָּנִים: שַׁלֵּחַ תְּשַׁלַּח אֶת־הָאֵם וְאֶת־הַבָּנִים תִּקַּח־לָךְ לְמַעַן יִיטַב לָךְ וְהַאֲרַכְתָּ יָמִים:
אֶבֶן שְׁלֵמָה וָצֶדֶק יִהְיֶה־לָּךְ אֵיפָה שְׁלֵמָה וָצֶדֶק יִהְיֶה־לָּךְ לְמַעַן יַאֲרִיכוּ יָמֶיךָ עַל הָאֲדָמָה אֲשֶׁר ד' אֱלֹקֶיךָ נֹתֵן לָךְ:
וזה הטעם גם כן ב'שילוח הקן', כי הביצים אשר שכבה האם עליהם והאפרוחים הצריכים לאמם על הרוב אינם ראוים לאכילה, וכשישלח האם ותלך לה, לא תצטער בראות לקיחת הבנים. ועל הרוב יהיה סיבה להניח הכל, כי מה שהיה לוקח ברוב הפעמים אינו ראוי לאכילה: ואם אלו הצערים הנפשיים חסר התורה עליהם בבהמות ובעופות, כל שכן בבני האדם כולם.

**34) פירוש רש"י על בראשית יא:לב**

וימת תרח בחרן - ... ולמה הקדים הכתוב מיתתו של תרח ליציאתו של אברם ... לפיכך קראו הכתוב מת, (ס"א ועוד) שהרשעים אף בחייהם קרוים מתים והצדיקים אף במיתתן קרוים חיים ...

**35) שמירת הלשון א:ז**

... וּבָזֶה מְעוֹרֵר מִדַּת הַחֶסֶד לְמַעְלָה, כְּמוֹ שֶׁאָמְרוּ חַזַ"ל, שֶׁאוֹמֵר הַקָּדוֹשׁ בָּרוּךְ הוּא, וּמָה אֵלּוּ, שֶׁהֵן בְּעַצְמָן צְרִיכִין חֶסֶד, עוֹשִׂין חֶסֶד זֶה עִם זֶה, אֲנִי, שֶׁאֲנִי מָלֵא חֶסֶד וְרַחֲמִים, עַל אַחַת כַּמָּה וְכַמָּה ... עוֹד אָמְרוּ חַזַ"ל (בְּיַלְקוּט תְּהִלִּים), הַחֶסֶד עוֹמֵד לוֹ לָאָדָם עַד סוֹף כָּל הַדּוֹרוֹת, שֶׁנֶּאֱמַר (תְּהִלִּים ק"ג ז'), "וְחֶסֶד ה' מֵעוֹלָם וְעַד עוֹלָם עַל יְרֵאָיו" וְכוּ', וּמִדָּה זוֹ הִיא אַחַת מִשְּׁלֹשָׁה מִדּוֹת טוֹבוֹת שֶׁהֻטְבְּעוּ בְּיִשְׂרָאֵל, בַּיְשָׁנִים, רַחֲמָנִים וְגוֹמְלֵי חֲסָדִים, כְּמוֹ שֶׁאָמְרוּ חַזַ"ל (יְבָמוֹת ע"ט):

**36) פירוש רש"י על בראשית ו:ט**

אלה תולדת נח נח איש צדיק - ... דבר אחר, ללמדך שעיקר תולדותיהם של צדיקים מעשים טובים

**37) מדרש ילקוט שמעוני תתקלז**

אמר רבי אלעזר בן עזריה מנין למאבד סלע ומצאו עני ונתפרנס בה מעלה עליו הכתוב כאלו זכה, תלמוד לומר לגר ליתום ולאלמוה יהיה, והרי דברים קל וחומר ומה מי שלא נתכוון לזכות וזכה מעלה עליו הכתוב כאלו זכה, מי שמתכוון לזכות וזכה על אחת כמה וכמה.

**38) ישעיה נו:א**

כֹּה אָמַר ד' שִׁמְרוּ מִשְׁפָּט וַעֲשׂוּ צְדָקָה כִּי־קְרוֹבָה יְשׁוּעָתִי לָבוֹא וְצִדְקָתִי לְהִגָּלוֹת:

### 13) בראשית יח:יט

כִּי יְדַעְתִּיו לְמַעַן אֲשֶׁר יְצַוֶּה אֶת־בָּנָיו וְאֶת־בֵּיתוֹ אַחֲרָיו וְשָׁמְרוּ דֶּרֶךְ ד' לַעֲשׂוֹת צְדָקָה וּמִשְׁפָּט לְמַעַן הָבִיא ד' עַל־אַבְרָהָם אֵת אֲשֶׁר־דִּבֶּר עָלָיו:

### 14) אהבת חסד, הקדמה ב

... מדכתב סתם את הדרך בה"א הידיעה, ולא באר איזה דרך, מסתמא היא הדרך הכבושה אשר דרך בה אבינו הראשון, הוא אברהם, שהיה דבור כל ימיו במדת חסד ...

### 15) בבא קמא ק.

כדתני רב יוסף: (שמות י"ח) "והודעת להם" זה בית חייהם, "את הדרך" זו גמילות חסדים, "ילכו" זו ביקור חולים, "בה" זו קבורה,

### 16) דברים יג:ה, כח:ט וסוטה יד.

אַחֲרֵי ד' אֱלֹקֵיכֶם תֵּלֵכוּ וְאֹתוֹ תִירָאוּ וְאֶת־מִצְוֹתָיו תִּשְׁמֹרוּ וּבְקֹלוֹ תִשְׁמָעוּ וְאֹתוֹ תַעֲבֹדוּ וּבוֹ תִדְבָּקוּן: יְקִימְךָ ד' לוֹ לְעַם קָדוֹשׁ כַּאֲשֶׁר נִשְׁבַּע־לָךְ כִּי תִשְׁמֹר אֶת־מִצְוֹת ד' אֱלֹקֶיךָ וְהָלַכְתָּ בִּדְרָכָיו: מאי דכתיב: (דברים יג) אחרי ה' אלקיכם תלכו? וכי אפשר לו לאדם להלך אחר שכינה? והלא כבר נאמר: (דברים ד) "כי ה' אלקיך אש אוכלה הוא" אלא להלך אחר מדותיו של הקב"ה, מה הוא מלביש ערומים, דכתיב: (בראשית ג) ויעש ה' אלהים לאדם ולאשתו כתנות עור וילבישם, אף אתה הלבש ערומים הקב"ה ביקר חולים, דכתיב: (בראשית יח) וירא אליו ה' באלוני ממרא, אף אתה בקר חולים הקב"ה נחם אבלים, דכתיב: (בראשית כה) ויהי אחרי מות אברהם ויברך אלקים את יצחק בנו, אף אתה נחם אבלים הקב"ה קבר מתים, דכתיב: (דברים לד) ויקבר אותו בגיא, אף אתה קבור מתים.

### 17) סוטה יד.

תורה תחלתה גמילות חסדים וסופה גמילות חסדים תחילתה גמילות חסדים, דכתיב: "ויעש ה' אלהים לאדם ולאשתו כתנות עור וילבישם" וסופה גמילות חסדים, דכתיב: "ויקבר אותו בגיא."

### 18) שמונה עשרה, ברכות #1 #2

... גּוֹמֵל חֲסָדִים טוֹבִים ... מְכַלְכֵּל חַיִּים בְּחֶסֶד. מְחַיֶּה מֵתִים בְּרַחֲמִים רַבִּים. סוֹמֵךְ נוֹפְלִים. וְרוֹפֵא חוֹלִים וּמַתִּיר אֲסוּרִים ...

### 19) שמירת הלשון א:ז

וּבֶאֱמֶת מַה מְּאֹד גְּדוֹלָה מִצְוָה זוֹ בְּעֵינֵי ה' יִתְבָּרֵךְ, שֶׁעָלֶיהָ נֶאֱמַר (מִיכָה ו' ח), "הִגִּיד לְךָ אָדָם מַה טּוֹב, וּמָה ה' דּוֹרֵשׁ מִמְּךָ, כִּי אִם עֲשׂוֹת מִשְׁפָּט וְאַהֲבַת חֶסֶד" וְגוֹ'. וְאָמְרוּ חַזַ"ל (סֻכָּה מ"ט ע"ב), עֲשׂוֹת מִשְׁפָּט – זֶה הַדִּין, וְאַהֲבַת חֶסֶד – זוֹ גְּמִילוּת חֲסָדִים, וְגַם הוּא מְקַיֵּם בָּזֶה הַמִּצְוָה ד'"וְהָלַכְתָּ בִּדְרָכָיו", כִּדְאִיתָא בְּסִפְרֵי

---

על הַפָּסוּק (דְּבָרִים כ"ח ט'), "לָלֶכֶת בְּכָל דְּרָכָיו" – אֵלּוּ דַרְכֵי הַקָּדוֹשׁ בָּרוּךְ הוּא, שֶׁנֶּאֱמַר (שְׁמוֹת ל"ד ו'), "ה' ה', קֵל רַחוּם וְחַנּוּן, אֶרֶךְ אַפַּיִם, וְרַב חֶסֶד" וְכוּ'. וְאָמְרִינַן (בָּבָא מְצִיעָא ל' ע"ב), תָּנֵי רַב יוֹסֵף (שְׁמוֹת י"ח כ'), "וְהוֹדַעְתָּ לָהֶם אֶת הַדֶּרֶךְ" – זוֹ גְּמִילוּת חֲסָדִים:

### 20) עמוס ב:ז, ה:ז, מיכה ו:י-יא, ירמיהו ט:ד, ז:ט, ה:ב, כב:יג, מיכה ב:ב

הַשֹּׁאֲפִים עַל־עֲפַר־אֶרֶץ בְּרֹאשׁ דַּלִּים וְדֶרֶךְ עֲנָוִים יַטּוּ וְאִישׁ וְאָבִיו יֵלְכוּ אֶל־הַנַּעֲרָה לְמַעַן חַלֵּל אֶת־שֵׁם קָדְשִׁי: הַהֹפְכִים לְלַעֲנָה מִשְׁפָּט וּצְדָקָה לָאָרֶץ הִנִּיחוּ: הוֹי בֹּנֶה בֵיתוֹ בְּלֹא־צֶדֶק וַעֲלִיּוֹתָיו בְּלֹא מִשְׁפָּט בְּרֵעֵהוּ יַעֲבֹד חִנָּם וּפֹעֲלוֹ לֹא יִתֶּן־לוֹ: עוֹד הַאִשׁ בֵּית רָשָׁע אֹצְרוֹת רֶשַׁע וְאֵיפַת רָזוֹן זְעוּמָה: הַאֶזְכֶּה בְּמֹאזְנֵי רֶשַׁע וּבְכִיס אַבְנֵי מִרְמָה: וְאִישׁ בְּרֵעֵהוּ יְהָתֵלּוּ וֶאֱמֶת לֹא יְדַבֵּרוּ לִמְּדוּ לְשׁוֹנָם דַּבֶּר־שֶׁקֶר הַעֲוֵה נִלְאוּ: הֲגָנֹב רָצֹחַ וְנָאֹף וְהִשָּׁבֵעַ לַשֶּׁקֶר וְקַטֵּר לַבָּעַל וְהָלֹךְ אַחֲרֵי אֱלֹהִים אֲחֵרִים אֲשֶׁר לֹא־יְדַעְתֶּם: וְאִם־חַי־ד' יֹאמֵרוּ לָכֵן לַשֶּׁקֶר יִשָּׁבֵעוּ:

### 21) תהילים טו

מִזְמוֹר לְדָוִד ד' מִי־יָגוּר בְּאָהֳלֶךְ מִי־יִשְׁכֹּן בְּהַר קָדְשֶׁךָ: הוֹלֵךְ תָּמִים וּפֹעֵל צֶדֶק וְדֹבֵר אֱמֶת בִּלְבָבוֹ: לֹא־רָגַל עַל־לְשֹׁנוֹ לֹא־עָשָׂה לְרֵעֵהוּ רָעָה וְחֶרְפָּה לֹא־נָשָׂא עַל־קְרֹבוֹ: נִבְזֶה בְּעֵינָיו נִמְאָס וְאֶת־יִרְאֵי ד' יְכַבֵּד נִשְׁבַּע לְהָרַע וְלֹא יָמִר: כַּסְפּוֹ לֹא־נָתַן בְּנֶשֶׁךְ וְשֹׁחַד עַל־נָקִי לֹא־לָקָח עֹשֵׂה אֵלֶּה לֹא יִמּוֹט לְעוֹלָם:

### 22) סידור, ברכות השחר

אֵלּוּ דְבָרִים שֶׁאֵין לָהֶם שִׁעוּר הַפֵּאָה וְהַבִּכּוּרִים וְהָרְאָיוֹן וּגְמִילוּת חֲסָדִים וְתַלְמוּד תּוֹרָה: אֵלּוּ דְבָרִים שֶׁאָדָם אוֹכֵל פֵּרוֹתֵיהֶם בָּעוֹלָם הַזֶּה וְהַקֶּרֶן קַיֶּמֶת לוֹ לָעוֹלָם הַבָּא. וְאֵלּוּ הֵן. כִּבּוּד אָב וָאֵם. וּגְמִילוּת חֲסָדִים. וּבִקּוּר חוֹלִים. וְהַכְנָסַת אוֹרְחִים. וְהַשְׁכָּמַת בֵּית הַכְּנֶסֶת. וַהֲבָאַת שָׁלוֹם בֵּין אָדָם לַחֲבֵרוֹ. וּבֵין אִישׁ לְאִשְׁתּוֹ. וְתַלְמוּד תּוֹרָה כְּנֶגֶד כֻּלָּם:

### 23) פירוש העמק דבר על דברים ו:יח

ועשית הישר והטוב – עוד יש לעשות גמ"ח בין אדם לחבירו באותה שעה כמו שעשה יהושע ב"נ שתיקן אז עשר תקנות בין אדם לחבירו כדאי' שלהי פ' מרובה: למען ייטב לך ובאת וגו' – שדברים אלו של גמ"ח מביאים טובה וברכה לעולם וה"ה לשכל מצות אלו לעולם אלא באותה שעה מוזהרים ביותר כמש"כ לעיל וע' להלן י"ב כ"ח:

### 24) ויקרא יט:יח

לֹא־תִקֹּם וְלֹא־תִטֹּר אֶת־בְּנֵי עַמֶּךָ וְאָהַבְתָּ לְרֵעֲךָ כָּמוֹךָ אֲנִי ד':

# SOURCES ON IS BEING GOOD THE MOST IMPORTANT THING IN JUDAISM?

## 1) ירושלמי נדרים ל:

ואהבת לרעך כמוך. רבי עקיבה אומר זהו כלל גדול בתורה. בן עזאי אומר (בראשית ה) זה ספר תולדות אדם זה כלל גדול מזה.

## 2) שבת לא.

מעשה בנכרי אחד שבא לפני שמאי, אמר לו: גיירני על מנת שתלמדני כל התורה כולה כשאני עומד על רגל אחת. דחפו באמת הבנין שבידו. בא לפני הלל, גייריה. אמר לו: דעלך סני לחברך לא תעביד זו היא כל התורה כולה, ואידך פירושה הוא, זיל גמור.

## 3) דברים טז:כ

צֶדֶק צֶדֶק תִּרְדֹּף לְמַעַן תִּחְיֶה וְיָרַשְׁתָּ אֶת הָאָרֶץ אֲשֶׁר ד' אֱלֹקֶיךָ נֹתֵן לָךְ:

## 4) מיכה ו:ח ופירוש אבן עזרא

הִגִּיד לְךָ אָדָם מַה טּוֹב וּמָה ד' דּוֹרֵשׁ מִמְּךָ כִּי אִם עֲשׂוֹת מִשְׁפָּט וְאַהֲבַת חֶסֶד וְהַצְנֵעַ לֶכֶת עִם אֱלֹקֶיךָ: הגיד – זאת היא תשובת הנביא במה אקדם ד' מה טוב בעיניו שתעשה והוא איננו מבקש אילים ולא בנך רק עשות משפט שלא תעשה עול בעמיתך ולא תונני בדיבור או בהון רק תעשה חסד עמו בכל יכולתך והצנע לכת עם השם לבדו שתלך בדרכיו בתם לבב הפך קשי עורף:

## 5) דברים ו:יח ופירוש הרמב"ן

וְעָשִׂיתָ הַיָּשָׁר וְהַטּוֹב בְּעֵינֵי ד' לְמַעַן יִיטַב לָךְ וּבָאתָ וְיָרַשְׁתָּ אֶת הָאָרֶץ הַטֹּבָה אֲשֶׁר נִשְׁבַּע ד' לַאֲבֹתֶיךָ: וזה ענין גדול, לפי שאי אפשר להזכיר בתורה כל הנהגות האדם עם שכניו ורעיו וכל משאו ומתנו ותקוני הישוב והמדינות כלם, אבל אחרי שהזכיר מהם הרבה, כגון לא תלך רכיל (ויקרא יט טז), לא תקום ולא תטור (שם פסוק יח), ולא תעמוד על דם רעך (שם פסוק טז), לא תקלל חרש (שם פסוק יד), מפני שיבה תקום (שם פסוק לב), וכיוצא בהן, חזר לומר בדרך כלל שיעשה הטוב והישר בכל דבר, עד שיכנס בזה הפשרה ולפנים משורת הדין, ...

## 6) שמות טו:כו ומכילתא בשלח "ויסע" א שמות טו:כו

וַיֹּאמֶר אִם שָׁמוֹעַ תִּשְׁמַע לְקוֹל ד' אֱלֹקֶיךָ וְהַיָּשָׁר בְּעֵינָיו תַּעֲשֶׂה וְהַאֲזַנְתָּ לְמִצְוֹתָיו וְשָׁמַרְתָּ כָּל חֻקָּיו כָּל הַמַּחֲלָה אֲשֶׁר שַׂמְתִּי בְמִצְרַיִם לֹא אָשִׂים עָלֶיךָ כִּי אֲנִי ד' רֹפְאֶךָ: והישר בעיניו תעשה זה משא ומתן ומלמד שכל מי שנושא ונותן באמונה רוח הבריות נוחה הימינו ומעלין עליו כאלו קיים את כל התורה כולה

## 7) מכילתא בשלח על שמות טו:כו

והישר בעיניו תעשה זה משא ומתן מלמד שכל מי שנושא ונותן באמונה רוח הבריות נוחה הימינו ומעלין עליו כאלו קיים את כל התורה כולה.

## 8) סנהדרין קח.

אמר רבי יוחנן: בא וראה כמה גדול כחה של חמס, שהרי דור המבול עברו על הכל ולא נחתם עליהם גזר דינם עד שפשטו ידיהם בגזל, שנאמר (בראשית ו') כי מלאה הארץ חמס מפניהם והנני משחיתם את הארץ.

## 9) אבן שלמה א:ב

עיקר חיות האדם הוא להתחזק תמיד בשבירת המידות, ואם לאו למה לו חיים?

## 10) שבת לא.

אמר רבא: בשעה שמכניסין אדם לדין אומרים לו: נשאת ונתת באמונה, קבעת עתים לתורה, עסקת בפריה ורביה, צפית לישועה, פלפלת בחכמה, הבנת דבר מתוך דבר?

## 11) מכות כד.

דרש רבי שמלאי: שש מאות ושלש עשרה מצות נאמרו לו למשה ... בא דוד והעמידן על אחת עשרה ... בא ישעיהו והעמידן על שש, דכתיב: (ישעיהו ל"ג) "הולך צדקות ודובר מישרים מואס בבצע מעשקות נוער כפיו מתמוך בשחד אוטם אזנו משמוע דמים ועוצם עיניו מראות ברע". 1. "הולך צדקות" זה אברהם אבינו, דכתיב: (בראשית י"ח) "כי ידעתיו למען אשר יצוה וגו'". 2. "ודובר מישרים" זה שאינו מקניט פני חבירו ברבים. 3. "מואס בבצע מעשקות" כגון ר' ישמעאל בן אלישע. 4. "נוער כפיו מתמוך בשחד" כגון ר' ישמעאל בר' יוסי. 5. "אוטם אזנו משמוע דמים" דלא שמע בזילותא דצורבא מרבנן ושתיק, כגון ר"א ברבי שמעון. 6. "ועוצם עיניו מראות ברע" כדרבי חייא בר אבא, דאמר ר' חייא בר אבא: זה שאינו מסתכל בנשים בשעה שעומדות על הכביסה. וכתיב: (ישעיהו ל"ג) "הוא מרומים ישכון [וגו']".

## 12) מדרש ילקוט שמעוני, שמואל א' כה:קלד, מדרש שמואל כג:ח

... ללמדך שכל הכופר בגמילות חסדים ככופר בעיקר.

**60)** פירוש ריטב"א על מגילה (בבלי) ז.

ואין מדקדקים בדבר פירשו בירוש' שכל הפושט ידו
ליטול יתנו לו לומר שנותנין לכל אדם ואין מדקדקין
אם הוא עני וראוי ליתן לו שאין נתינה זו מדין צדקה
גרידתא אלא מדין שמחה שהרי אף לעשירים יש
לשלוח מנות ולפי' נהגו ליתן מעות פורים לגוים
ואפילו עשירים ...

**61)** שולחן ערוך, אורח חיים תרצד:ג

אין מדקדקים במעות פורים אלא כל מי שפושט
ידו ליטול נותנים לו ומקום שנהגו ליתן אף לעכו"ם
נותנים:

**62)** ב"ח על טור, אורח חיים תרצ"ד:א

חייב **כל אדם וכו'** – כלומר כל אדם אפילו עני המקבל
צדקה חייב לתת ממה שנתנו לו לשאר אביונים

בפורים דאין דין מתנות לאביונים בפורים כדין שאר
צדקה דהכשר מצות פורים כן הוא לתת מתנות ...
ואפילו משלוח מנות חייבים בו העניים אף על פי
שלא יספיק להם בסעודתם לאכול לעצמם ולשלוח
גם לאחרים וכדמשמע מרב חנינא בר אבין ואביי בר
אבין לפי פירוש רבינו לקמן בסימן תרצ"ה אם כן
הוא הדין למתנות לאביונים בפורים אבל שאר **צדקה**
דכל השנה **אין** עני המקבל **הצדקה חייב** בה אלא פעם
אחת בשנה יתן דבר מועט לצדקה כדי לקיים מצות
צדקה וכמו שכתוב ביורה דעה סימן רמ"ח ורמ"ט:

**63)** ט"ז על שולחן ערוך, אורח חיים תרצ"ד:א

**חייב כל אדם** – כתב מו"ח ז"ל אפילו עני המתפרנס
מהצדקה כמו בד' כוסות של פסח מה שאין כן בשאר
צדקה שאינו חייב רק פעם אחד בשנה כדי לקיים
מצות צדקה כמ"ש בי"ד סימן רמ"ח ורמ"ט:

**50) דברים טו:ז**

... וְלֹא תִקְפֹּץ אֶת־יָדְךָ מֵאָחִיךָ הָאֶבְיוֹן:

**51) שו"ת אגרות משה יורה דעה א:קמד**

בדבר אם יכול להפריש צדקה שלו לצורך אחיו כדי שיוכל לישב בשלוה אחר נישואין וללמוד תורה איזה שנים ... והנה כשיש עני שצריך היום לאכילה באופן שאינו פקוח נפש וקרוב שלא חסר לו להיום כלום אבל צריך הוא למחר הוא גם היום בדין עני שרשאי ליטול צדקה שאין לו מאתים זוז, אף שאין הדין מפורש משמע שצריך ליתן להקרוב, שלא מצינו שצריך לדקדק בדין הקדמות של הקרובים לומר שהוא רק כשהן שוין בהצורך בין לההנחיות אלא סתם משמע דאם אף שצורך ליטול צדקה צריך להקדים לקרובו אף שצורך האחר קודם לזמן וליותר דבר נחוץ כיון שעכ"פ הנתינה לתרוייהו הוא מצוה אחת מצות צדקה. ואף בעניים שוין ששניהם קרובים או שניהם רחוקים נמי משמע שיכול ליתן למי שירצה.

**52) מנחת אשר, פרשת ראה כא**

בדבר שאלתו בדיני קדימה בצדקה מה סדר המוקדם והמאוחר בתורת החסד הנני להשיב בקצרה משום רוב טרדה

בפתח הדברים נדגיש דלא סדר קדימה אחד יש בצדקה אלא ד' סדרים שונים ונבאר א' סדר קדימה בין גדרי הצדקה השונים כגון פקו"נ ת"ת צדקה לעניים וכדו' ב' קדימה בין האישים כגון ת"ח קרובי משפחה עניי עירך וכדו' ג' קדימה בין הצרכים השונים מאכל כסות וכדו' ד' קדימה בין האופנים השונים במצות הצדקה וכמ"ש השו"ע ביו"ד סי' רמ"ט ס"ו שמונה מעלות בצדקה וכ"ז ברור ונבאר בקצור את עיקרי ההלכות ...

הנה המעלה העליונה במעלות הצדקה הוא החזקת התורה כמבואר בשו"ע יו"ד סי' רמ"ט סעיף ט"ז ...

.... ואחרי שנתבאר דת"ת קודם לחולים עניים וחולים עניים קודמין לבנין ביהכ"נ ובנין ביהכ"נ קודם לעניים דעלמא נדון קצת בדיני קדימה במצות צדקה

... וא"כ פשוט דעל כל אדם לקיים גם מצות צדקה כפשוטה דהיינו ליתן צדקה לעניים ולגמילות חסדים ואינו יוצא יד"ח בחיזוק מוסדות התורה בלבד אלא אחרון בזה וגם מזה ...

ומתוך כל הנ"ל נתבאר סדר הקדימה כלהלן:

א כל דבר שיש בו פקו"נ כגון חושיב"ס או שאר פקו"נ כמבואר בסי' רנ"א סעיף י"ד וכן פדיון שבויים שדינו כפקו"נ

כמבואר בסי' רנ"ב וזה קודם לכל דבר ומותר אפילו לשנות מצדקה אחרת לצורך פקו"נ ופדיון שבוים והן קודמין אפילו

לת"ת כמבואר שם בט"ז ס"ק ו

ב החזקת ת"ת וזה כולל כל הנצרך לת"ת כגון ביהמ"ד

וספרים וכדו' כמבואר בפשטות המהרי"ק והשו"ע וכך כתב החכמ"א שם

ג חולים עניים ולכאורה משמע דלא רק לצורך ריפוי אלא אף לצורך סיעוד וכדו' כנ"ל

ד בנין ביהכ"נ אך הגר"א ועוד אחרונים פקפקו בקדימה זו כנ"ל

ה נישואין יתום ויתומה ואפשר דבזמנינו שהוצאות הנישואין עצומות ואין ביד האדם בהם הוי כל הכנסת כלה בכלל זה

ן שאר עניי ישראל לפי סדר הקדימה בסי' רמ"ט וסי' רנ"א

**53) אסתר ט:כב**

כַּיָּמִים אֲשֶׁר־נָחוּ בָהֶם הַיְּהוּדִים מֵאֹיְבֵיהֶם וְהַחֹדֶשׁ אֲשֶׁר נֶהְפַּךְ לָהֶם מִיָּגוֹן לְשִׂמְחָה וּמֵאֵבֶל לְיוֹם טוֹב לַעֲשׂוֹת אוֹתָם יְמֵי מִשְׁתֶּה וְשִׂמְחָה וּמִשְׁלוֹחַ מָנוֹת אִישׁ לְרֵעֵהוּ וּמַתָּנוֹת לָאֶבְיוֹנִים:

**54) מגילה ז.**

ומתנות לאביונים. תני רב יוסף: ומשלוח מנות איש לרעהו שתי מנות לאיש אחד. ומתנות לאביונים שתי מתנות לשני בני אדם.

**55) שולחן ערוך, אורח חיים תרצד:א**

חייב כל אדם ליתן לפחות שתי מתנות לשני עניים:

**56) שולחן ערוך, יורה דעה רמח:א**

כל אדם חייב ליתן צדקה אפילו עני המתפרנס מן הצדקה חייב ליתן ממה שיתנו לו

**57) רמב"ם, הלכות מגילה ב:טז-יז**

וחייב לחלק לעניים ביום הפורים, אין פחות משני עניים נותן לכל אחד מתנה אחת או מעות או מיני תבשיל או מיני אוכלין שנאמר ומתנות לאביונים שתי מתנות לשני עניים, ואין מדקדקין במעות פורים אלא כל הפושט ידו ליטול נותנין לו, ואין משנין מעות פורים לצדקה אחרת. יז מוטב לאדם להרבות במתנות אביונים מלהרבות בסעודתו ובשלוח מנות לרעיו, שאין שם שמחה גדולה ומפוארה אלא לשמח לב עניים ויתומים ואלמנות וגרים, שהמשמח לב האמללים האלו דומה לשכינה שנאמר ישעיהו נ"ז להחיות רוח שפלים ולהחיות לב נדכאים.

**58) שבלי הלקט רב**

במעות פורים אין קצבה כל מה שירצה האיש ליתן יתן מפני שהוא צדקה וצדקה כל אחד ואחד לפי עינו הטובה יתן ...

**59) ירושלמי מגילה ה.**

אין מדקדקין במצות פורים אלא כל מי שהוא פושט את ידו ליטול נותנין לו ...

אֲשֶׁר־ד' אֱלֹקֶיךָ נֹתֵן לָךְ לֹא תְאַמֵּץ אֶת־לְבָבְךָ וְלֹא
תִקְפֹּץ אֶת־יָדְךָ מֵאָחִיךָ הָאֶבְיוֹן:

### 36) רמ"א על שולחן ערוך, יורה דעה רנא:ג

הגה פרנסת עצמו קודמת לכל אדם ואינו חייב לתת
צדקה עד שיהיה לו פרנסתו

### 37) משנה ברורה על שולחן ערוך, אורח חיים קנו:ב

עיקר – אלא יעשה רק כדי פרנסתו אך בזה גופא
צריך להזהר מפיתויי היצר שממתהו שכל היום צריך
השתדלות על הרוחה זו. והעיקר שיתבונן בעצמו
מה הוא הכרח האמיתי שאי אפשר בלעדו ואז יכול
להתקיים בידו שתהיה מלאכתו עראי ותורתו עיקר:

### 38) טור יורה דעה רנא

כל הפושט ידו ליטול נותנין לו אפי' נכרי שממפרנסים
עניי נכרים עם עניי ישראל משום דרכי שלום ...

### 39) רמ"א על שולחן ערוך, יורה דעה רמט:ד

הגה ואסור להחזיר העני השואל ריקם אפילו אין לו
רק גרוגרת אחת שנאמר אל ישוב דך נכלם

### 40) שולחן ערוך, יורה דעה רנא:ג

הנותן לבניו ובנותיו הגדולים שאינו חייב במזונותיהם
כדי ללמד את הבנים תורה ולהנהיג הבנות בדרך
ישרה וכן הנותן מתנות לאביו והם צריכים להם
הרי זה בכלל צדקה ולא עוד אלא שצריך להקדימו
לאחרים ואפילו אינו בנו ולא אביו אלא קרובו צריך
להקדימו לכל אדם ...

### 41) כתובות נ.

רבי יוסי בר חנינא תנא מינה ארבעין זימנין, ודמי
ליה כמאן דמנחא ליה בכיסתיה. (תהלים ק"ו) אשרי
שומרי משפט עושה צדקה בכל עת וכי אפשר
לעשות צדקה בכל עת? דרשו רבותינו שבזה,
ואמרו לה רבי אליעזר: זה הזן בניו ובנותיו כשהן
קטנים. רבי שמואל בר נחמני אמר: זה המגדל יתום
ויתומה בתוך ביתו ומשיאן.

### 42) פירוש רש"י על כתובות נ.

זה הזן בניו ובנותיו קטנים – שתמיד יום ולילה הן
עליו והיא צדקה שאינו חייב עליו בהם.

### 43) שולחן ערוך, יורה דעה רנא:ג

... ועניי ביתו קודמין לעניי עירו עירו עניי קודמין
לעניי עיר אחרת ... ויושבי ארץ ישראל קודמין
ליושבי חוצה לארץ:

### 44) משנה הוריות ג:ז

האיש קודם לאשה להחיות ולהשב אבדה, והאשה
קודמת לאיש לכסות ולהוציא מבית השבי.

### 45) כתובות סז.

ת"ר: יתום ויתומה שבאו להתפרנס, מפרנסין את
היתומה ואחר כך מפרנסין את היתום, מפני שהאיש
דרכו לחזור על הפתחים, ואין אשה דרכה לחזור.

### 46) ספר באר שבע על הוריות יג.

ומשמע דפרנסה היינו בין מזון בין כסות, דטעמא
דמפני שהאיש דרכו לחזור וכו' שייך בין במזון בין
בכסות.... וצריך לומר דהאי להחיות אין פירושו
אכילה, אלא דינה של אכילה כדין הכסות. והמשנה
קתני והאשה קודמת לאיש לכסות והוא הדין לאכילה
דחד טעמא הוא כדאמרן ...

### 47) חכמת אדם, קמה:ח

כל דבר שהוא סכנת נפשות כגון לפרוע המס להמלך
ולהשר ואף יש כמה עניים שאין להם ליתן ויכום
ויפשיטום ערומים וכיוצא בזה (סימן רנ"א סעיף י"ד)
וכן שכן פדיון שבוים קודם אפילו מתלמוד תורה
וכל שכן מפרנסת עניים ומלבשותן ואין מצוה גדולה
כפדיון שבויים (סימן רנ"ב סעיף א'):

### 48) בית יוסף על טור יורה דעה קמט

מצות בית הכנסת עדיפא ממצות צדקה דגרסינן
שם [ב] אחזי לרב תרעא דבי כנישתא וכו' וכי לית
תמן בר נש למילף אורייתא או חולים המוטלים
באשפה וקרא עליו (הושע ח יד) וישכח ישראל [את]
עושהו ויבן היכלות מכאן אומר הר' שמואל שטוב
ליתן צדקה לנערים ללמוד תורה או לחולים עניים
מליתן לבית הכנסת עכ"ל מדקאמר בירושלמי חולים
המוטלים באשפה וכן הר' שמואל אומר חולים עניים
ולא קאמר עניים סתם משמע דאם לא היו חולים כי
אם עניים דטוב יותר ליתן לבית הכנסת:

### 49) תשובות והנהגות, חלק א:תקסז

שאלה במצות צדקה מה יש האם הכנסת כלה או
עדיף לתת צדקה לישיבה נוסח השאלה תמוה
שאין מצות הכנסת כלה בארץ ישראל זה לזה
לפעמים צריך לחתן וכלה דברים הכרחיים ממש
ולפעמים מחפשים לקנות דירה עם ג' חדרים ויותר
וכן בישיבות יש ישיבות שיש להם רכוש והשקעות
ויש כאלו שדחוקים לפרנסת יום יום ... וכן פירש
רבינו הגר"א זצ"ל "לא תקפוץ ידך" הכוונה שאם
קופץ אצבעותיו כולם שוין והזהירה תורה לא
לקפוץ אלא לפשוט אצבעותיו בצדקה שכל אצבע
בגודל שונה ואז יחליט במי יש מצוה יותר ולהרבות
בזה ולפי זה השאלה רק כשנשניהם דחוקים ובאותו
מדה של צורך ואז בודאי תלמוד תורה דרבים עדיף
ואתי עשה דרבים ודחי עשה דיחיד אבל יש לבדוק
היטב אם באמת המצב כ"כ נורא ואם כל הכסף יגיע
לישיבה שבלאו הכי יש להעדיף מצות הכנסת כלה
או חתן שהם בצער בצער גדול מאד ...

ענים קטנים שאין נעורין בבקר ולא יגיעו לשדה עד חצי היום, ויש שם זקנים שאינם מגיעין עד המנחה

### 28) רמב"ם, הלכות מתנות עניים ו:ז, ט, י, יב

בעל השדה שעברו עליו עניים והיה לו שם מעשר עני, נותן לכל עני שיעבור עליו מן המעשר כדי שבעו ...

היה לו דבר מועט והעניים מרובין ואין בו כדי ליתן לכל אחד ואחד כשיעור נותן לפניהם והן מחלקין ביניהם אבל המתחלק בבית יש לו טובת הנאה לבעלים ונותנו לכל עני שירצה

אבל אם היה המעשר מחלקו בבית לכל העניים אפילו כזית כזית

### 29) שולחן ערוך, יורה דעה רמט:א

שיעור נתינתה אם ידו משגת יתן כפי צורך העניים ואם אין ידו משגת כל כך יתן עד חומש נכסיו מצוה מן המובחר ואחד מעשרה מדה בינונית פחות מכאן עין רעה וחומש זה שאמרו שנה ראשונה מהקרן מכאן ואילך חומש שהרויח בכל שנה:

### 30) רמב"ם, הלכות מתנות עניים ח:י', שולחן ערוך, יורה דעה רנב:א

פדיון שבויים קודם לפרנסת עניים ולכסותן, ואין לך מצוה גדולה כפדיון שבויים שהשבוי הרי הוא בכלל הרעבים והצמאים והערומים ועומד בסכנת נפשות פדיון שבויים קודם לפרנסת עניים ולכסותן ואין מצוה גדולה כפדיון שבויים הילכך לכל דבר מצוה שגבו מעות בשבילו יכולים לשנותן לפדיון שבויים ואפי' אם גבו לצורך בנין ב"ה ואפי' אם קנו העצים והאבנים והקצום לצורך הבנין שאסור למכרם בשביל מצוה אחרת מותר למכרם לצורך פדיון שבויים אבל אם בנאוהו כבר לא ימכרו אותו

### 31) שולחן ערוך, יורה דעה רמט:טו

גבאי צדקה שיש בידם מעות צדקה ישיאו בהם בתולות עניות שאין צדקה גדולה מזו:

### 32) שולחן ערוך, יורה דעה רמט:טז

יש מי שאומר שמצות בית הכנסת עדיפא ממצות צדקה ...

### 33) שולחן ערוך, יורה דעה רמט:טז

יש מי שאומר שמצות ... צדקה לנערים ללמוד תורה או לחולים עניים עדיף ממצות בית הכנסת:

### 34) שולחן ערוך, יורה דעה רמט:טז

יש מי שאומר שמצות ... צדקה ... לחולים עניים עדיף ממצות בית הכנסת:

### 35) דברים טו:ז

כִּי־יִהְיֶה בְךָ אֶבְיוֹן מֵאַחַד אַחֶיךָ בְּאַחַד שְׁעָרֶיךָ בְּאַרְצְךָ

---

ע"ב], האומר סלע זו לצדקה בשביל שיחיה בני הרי זה צדיק גמור, תירצוה חכמים המפרשים כשגומר הנותן בלבו לתת אותה בין שיחיה או לא יהיה שאין זה מנסה את ה':

### 22) שולחן ערוך, יורה דעה רמז:ד

הצדקה דוחה את הגזירות הקשות וברעב תציל ממות כמו שאירע לצרפית: הגה והיא מעשרת ואסור לנסות הקב"ה כי אם בדבר זה שנאמר ובחנוני נא בזאת וגו' (טור מגמרא פ"ק דתענית) וי"א דוקא בנתינת מעשר מותר לנסות הקב"ה אבל לא בשאר צדקה

### 23) פירוש רב עובדיה מברטנורה על דמאי ו:ג

כשם שחולקין בחולין כך חולקין בתרומה – כשנוטל בעל השדה מחצה ושליש ורביע ממה שהוציאה השדה, נוטל גם כן מחצה ושליש ורביע מן התרומה והמעשרות המוטלות עליה, ונותנן הוא לכל כהן ולוי שירצה

### 24) פירוש רב עובדיה מברטנורה על חלה א:ט

וחומשן – האוכל שוגג משלם קרן לבעלים וחומש לכל כהן שירצה

### 25) תוספתא פאה ב:יג, שולחן ערוך, יורה דעה סא:כח

ארבע מתנות בכרם פרט שכחה ופאה ועוללת שלש בתבואה לקט שכחה ופאה שתים באילן שכחה ופאה כל אלו אין בהן משום טובה ואפילו עני שבישראל מוציאין את שלו מידו ושאר מתנות כהונה כגון הזרוע והלחיים והקיבה יש בהן משום טובה וניתנין לכל כהן שירצה

השוחט בהמת ישראל חבירו, חובה על השוחט ליתן מתנותיה לכהן; ואם שחט בהמת כהן או עובד כוכבים, פטור: הגה – מיהו טובת הנאה לבעלים והוא יכול ליתנם לכל כהן שירצה

### 26) ויקרא כג:כב, דברים כד:יט

וּבְקֻצְרְכֶם אֶת־קְצִיר אַרְצְכֶם לֹא־תְכַלֶּה פְּאַת שָׂדְךָ בְּקֻצְרֶךָ וְלֶקֶט קְצִירְךָ לֹא תְלַקֵּט לֶעָנִי וְלַגֵּר תַּעֲזֹב אֹתָם אֲנִי ד' אֱלֹקֵיכֶם:

כִּי תִקְצֹר קְצִירְךָ בְשָׂדֶךָ וְשָׁכַחְתָּ עֹמֶר בַּשָּׂדֶה לֹא תָשׁוּב לְקַחְתּוֹ לַגֵּר לַיָּתוֹם וְלָאַלְמָנָה יִהְיֶה לְמַעַן יְבָרֶכְךָ ד' אֱלֹקֶיךָ בְּכֹל מַעֲשֵׂה יָדֶיךָ:

### 27) רמב"ם, הלכות מתנות עניים ב:יז

בשלש עתות ביום מחלקין את הפאה לעניים בשדה או מניחים אותם לבוז, בשחר, ובחצי היום, ובמנחה, ועני שבא שלא בזמן זה אין מניחין אותו ליטול, כדי שיהיה עת קבוע לעניים שיתקבצו בו כולן ליטול, ולמה לא קבעו לה עת אחת ביום מפני שיש שם עניות מניקות שצריכות לאכול בתחלת היום, ויש שם

---

## 16) רש"י על ראש השנה ד.

כאן בישראל – שלבו לשמים, ואם מריעין לו בחייו אינו קורא לו תגר (merchant), אלא תולה היסורין בעון, אבל נכרי אם אין מטיבין לו כגמולו קורא תגר:

## 17) בבא בתרא י':

מהו שאמר הכתוב (משלי י"ד) צדקה תרומם גוי וחסד לאומים חטאת? נענה רבי אליעזר ואמר: צדקה תרומם גוי אלו ישראל, דכתיב: (שמואל ב' ז') ומי כעמך ישראל גוי אחד בארץ, וחסד לאומים חטאת כל צדקה וחסד שאומות עובדי כוכבים עושין חטא הוא להן, שאינם עושין אלא להתגדל בו, כמו שנאמר: (עזרא ו') די להוון מהקרבין ניחוחין לאלהה שמיא ומצליין לחיי מלכא ובנוהי. ודעביד הכי לאו צדקה גמורה היא? והתניא: האומר סלע זו לצדקה בשביל שיחיה בני, ובשביל שאזכה לעולם הבא הרי זה צדיק גמור לא קשיא: כאן בישראל, כאן בעובד כוכבים. נענה רבי יהושע ואמר: צדקה תרומם גוי אלו ישראל, דכתיב: ומי כעמך ישראל גוי אחד, וחסד לאומים חטאת כל צדקה וחסד שאומות עובדי כוכבים עושין חטא הוא להן, שאין עושין אלא כדי שתמשך מלכותן,

## 18) מאירי על ראש השנה ד.

האומר סלע זו לצדקה כדי שיחיה בני או כדי שאזכה לחיי העולם הבא אינו מפקיע שכר צדקתו בלשון זה אף על פי שהדבר דומה כעובד על מנת לקבל פרס שאין זה אלא כמתעורר לעמוס על עצמו עול מצות מחמת יראת העונש ואם מגיעהו עונש אח"כ אינו קורא תגר ואינו מהרהר אחר מדותיו של הקב"ה בכך אלא שמצדיק את דינו ומברך על הרעה כעל הטובה ואם עשה על מנת כן ר"ל שאם יגיעהו אח"כ שיקרא תגר ויהרהר אחר מדותיו ית' הרי זה רשע וסכל גמור וזהו שאמרו כאן בישראל כאן באומות העולם ופירשו עליה בתלמוד המערב מפני שהגוי קורא תגר אבל ישראל אינו קורא תגר אלא מברך על הרעה כעל הטובה:

## 19) פני יהושע על ראש השנה ד.

בתוספות ד"ה בשביל שיחיה בני והא דתנן פ"ק דמסכת אבות עכ"ל. ועיין במהרש"א אבל הר"ן ז"ל בדרשותיו כתב בענין אחר דידוע הוא שיש הפרש והבדל בין צדיק גמור ובין חסיד. וראיה לדבריו דלקמן בפירקין [דף י"ז ע"ב] רמי קראי אהדדי כתיב צדיק ה' בכל דרכיו וכתיב וחסיד בכל מעשיו, נמצא דלפי"ז לא קשיא דהכא בישראל נמי לא קאמר אלא דהוי צדיק גמור כשאומר בשביל שיחיה בני אבל חסיד לא הוי משא"כ ההיא דאבות משנת חסידים היא כדאמרינן בעלמא מאן דבעי למיהוי חסידא לקיים מילי דאבות. ולענ"ד הדבר ברור דההיא דבשביל שיחיה בני לא גרע מעובד מיראה ואפ"ה איתא בסוטה [דף ל"א ע"א] דאקריינהו בחלמא

---

דתרוייהו צדיקי גמורי אתון מר מאהבה ומר מיראה, וא"כ על כרחך ההיא דאבות עצה טובה היא שלא לעבוד אלא מאהבה גמורה:

## 20) דרושי הצל"ח, אהבת ציון, דרוש עשירי

... ואמרינן במדרש (תנחומא פ' תשא סי' י"ד) על קרא דהשקיפה ממעון קדשך, גדולה צדקה שמהפכת מדת הדין למדת הרחמים, וא"כ כוונתם היו לעמוד ברשעם ולהנצל מעונש שיהיה מצות הצדקה מחפה עליהם, וכיון שראה ירמיה הנביא שכל כוונתם לא היה בשביל מצות צדקה אלא כדי להנצל מעונש ולעמוד במרדם, א"כ הוי עשיית מצות זו לרשעים האלה מעשה בלי מחשבה, אמנם בעשיית צדקה מועיל המעשה אף בלי מחשבת מצוה כמו דאמרינן (פסחים ח' ע"א) האומר סלע זו לצדקה על מנת שיחיה בני הרי זה צדיק גמור, ואאמ"ו הגאון זצ"ל נתן טעם לזה למה בכל המצות צריך לעשות המצוה לשם שמים ולא על מנת לקבל פרס ובמצות צדקה הוא צדיק גמור אם נותן על מנת שיחיה בני, ואמר אאמ"ו הגאון זצ"ל שכל מצות ה', אם אינו עושה לשם מצוה אין בו ממש ואינו עושה כלום דהא אם נטל לולב או מניח תפילין וציצית ולולא שיש בו מצות הבורא ב"ה אשר צוה לעשות דבר זה אין במעשה הזה שום תועלת מצד עצמו רק המצוה במה שמקיים מצות הבורא ב"ה אשר צוונו לעשות כן אותו קיום המצוה גורם חשיבות ויקר תפארת המעשה ולכך אם אינו עושה לשם מצוה אין בו ממש, אבל בנתינת צדקה אף שאין בו מחשבת מצוה אפ"ה יש תועלת ופעולה בעשייתו דהא העני נהנה ממנו ואין חילוק להעני אם מקבל אותה צדקה לשמה או לא, ולכך ביקש ירמיה שהקב"ה יכשילם בבני אדם שאינם מהוגנין, כדי שא"פי' שכר מעשה לא יהיה בידם:

## 21) ספר החינוך, מצוה תקכד

וכמו כן בכלל האזהרה שלא לעשות מצוות ה' ברוך הוא על דרך הנסיון, כלומר שיעשה אדם מצוה לנסות אם יגמלהו ה' כצדקו, לא לאהבת האל ויראתו אותו. ואל יקשה עליך מה שאמרו לברכה בפרק קמא דמסכת תענית [ט' ע"א], עשר תעשר [דברים י"ד, כ"ב], עשר בשביל שתתעשר, שכבר תירצו שם ואמרו שבכל המצוות נאמר לא תנסו, חוץ מזו דמעשר, שנאמר [מלאכי ג', י'], הביאו את כל המעשר אל בית האוצר וגו' ובחנוני נא בזאת וגו'. והטעם בזו כענין שכתבו [משלי י"ט, י"ז], מלוה ה' חונן דל, כלומר, שהודיענו האל ברוך הוא כי בפרנסנו משרתי ביתו במעשר נמצא התועלת והברכה בממוננו על כל פנים, ולא יעכב זה שום דבר חטא ועון. וטעם איסור הנסיון במצוות, מפני ששכר מצוות אינו בעולם הזה, וכמו שדרשו זכרונם לברכה בריש מסכת עבודה זרה [ג' ע"א], היום לעשותם [דברים ז', י"א], ולמחר, כלומר לעולם הבא, ליטול שכרם, וזה שאמרו זכרונם לברכה [בבא בתרא י'

# SOURCES ON HOW TZEDAKA-CHARITY IS DIFFERENT FROM ALL COMMANDMENTS

**1) דברים יד:כב**

עַשֵּׂר תְּעַשֵּׂר אֵת כָּל־תְּבוּאַת זַרְעֶךָ הַיֹּצֵא הַשָּׂדֶה שָׁנָה שָׁנָה:

**3) משנה אבות א:ג**

אנטיגנוס איש סוכו קבל משמעון הצדיק. הוא היה אומר אל תהיו כעבדים המשמשין את הרב על מנת לקבל פרס. אלא הוו כעבדים המשמשין את הרב שלא על מנת לקבל פרס. ויהי מורא שמים עליכם:

**2) תענית ט.**

אמר ליה: עשר תעשר. אמר ליה: ומאי עשר תעשר? אמר ליה: עשר בשביל שתתעשר. אמר ליה: מנא לך? אמר ליה: זיל נסי. אמר ליה: ומי שרי לנסוייה להקדוש ברוך הוא? והכתיב (דברים ו') לא תנסו את ה'. אמר ליה: הכי אמר רבי הושעיא: חוץ מזו, שנאמר (מלאכי ג') הביאו את כל המעשר אל בית האוצר ויהי טרף בביתי ובחנוני נא בזאת אמר ה' צבאות אם לא אפתח לכם את ארבות השמים והריקתי לכם ברכה עד בלי די, מאי עד בלי די?

**4) מלאכי ג:י**

הָבִיאוּ אֶת־כָּל־הַמַּעֲשֵׂר אֶל־בֵּית הָאוֹצָר וִיהִי טֶרֶף בְּבֵיתִי וּבְחָנוּנִי נָא בָּזֹאת אָמַר ד' צְבָאוֹת אִם־לֹא אֶפְתַּח לָכֶם אֵת אֲרֻבּוֹת הַשָּׁמַיִם וַהֲרִיקֹתִי לָכֶם בְּרָכָה עַד־בְּלִי־דָי:

**5) ראש השנה ד., בבא בתרא י', פסחים ח.**

האומר סלע זו לצדקה בשביל שיחיו בני, ובשביל שאזכה בה לחיי העולם הבא הרי זה צדיק גמור

**6) בבא בתרא י'**

תניא, א"ר אלעזר בר' יוסי: כל צדקה וחסד שישראל עושין בעולם הזה, שלום גדול ופרקליטין גדולין בין ישראל לאביהן שבשמים, שנאמר (ירמיהו ט"ז) "כה אמר ה' אל תבא בית מרזח ואל תלך לספוד ואל תנוד להם כי אספתי את שלומי מאת העם הזה [וגו' את] חחסד ואת הרחמים", חסד זו גמילות חסדים, רחמים זו צדקה. תניא, ר"י אומר: גדולה צדקה שמקרבת את הגאולה, שנאמר: (ישעיהו נ"ו) "כה אמר ה' שמרו משפט ועשו צדקה כי קרובה ישועתי לבא וצדקתי להגלות". הוא היה אומר, עשרה דברים קשים נבראו בעולם: הר קשה ברזל מחתכו, ברזל קשה אור מפעפעו, אור קשה מים מכבין אותו, מים קשים עבים סובלים אותן, עבים קשים רוח מפזרתן, רוח קשה גוף סובלו, גוף קשה פחד שוברו, פחד

קשה יין מפיגו, יין קשה שינה מפכחתו, ומיתה קשה מכולם [וצדקה מצלת מן המיתה], דכתיב: (משלי י') "וצדקה תציל ממות".

**7) משלי י':ב, יא:ד**

לֹא־יוֹעִילוּ אוֹצְרוֹת רֶשַׁע וּצְדָקָה תַּצִּיל מִמָּוֶת:
לֹא־יוֹעִיל הוֹן בְּיוֹם עֶבְרָה וּצְדָקָה תַּצִּיל מִמָּוֶת:

**9) דברים כג:כה**

כִּי תָבֹא בְּכֶרֶם רֵעֶךָ וְאָכַלְתָּ עֲנָבִים כְּנַפְשְׁךָ שָׂבְעֶךָ וְאֶל־כֶּלְיְךָ לֹא תִתֵּן:

**10) רמב"ם, הלכות שכירות יב:א**

הפועלים שהן עושין בדבר שגדולו מן הארץ ועדיין לא נגמרה מלאכתו בין בתלוש בין במחובר ויהיו מעשיהן גמירת המלאכה הרי על בעה"ב מצוה שיניח אותן לאכול ממה שהן עושין בו

**11) שמות כב:כא-כב, דברים כד:יט, דברים טו:יא**

כָּל־אַלְמָנָה וְיָתוֹם לֹא תְעַנּוּן: אִם־עַנֵּה תְעַנֶּה אֹתוֹ כִּי אִם־צָעֹק יִצְעַק אֵלַי שָׁמֹעַ אֶשְׁמַע צַעֲקָתוֹ:
כִּי תִקְצֹר קְצִירְךָ בְשָׂדֶךָ וְשָׁכַחְתָּ עֹמֶר בַּשָּׂדֶה לֹא תָשׁוּב לְקַחְתּוֹ לַגֵּר לַיָּתוֹם וְלָאַלְמָנָה יִהְיֶה לְמַעַן יְבָרֶכְךָ ד' אֱלֹקֶיךָ בְּכֹל מַעֲשֵׂה יָדֶיךָ:
כִּי לֹא־יֶחְדַּל אֶבְיוֹן מִקֶּרֶב הָאָרֶץ עַל־כֵּן אָנֹכִי מְצַוְּךָ לֵאמֹר פָּתֹחַ תִּפְתַּח אֶת־יָדְךָ לְאָחִיךָ לַעֲנִיֶּךָ וּלְאֶבְיֹנְךָ בְּאַרְצֶךָ:

**12) משלי ג:יז**

דְּרָכֶיהָ דַרְכֵי־נֹעַם וְכָל־נְתִיבוֹתֶיהָ שָׁלוֹם:

**13) פסחים קיח.**

בא וראה כמה קשים מזונותיו של אדם, שנשתנו עליו סדרי בראשית.
קשין מזונותיו של אדם כפליים כיולדה ... קשין מזונותיו של אדם יותר מן הגאולה ... קשין מזונותיו של אדם כקריעת ים סוף

**14) כסף משנה על רמב"ם, הלכות תפילין, מזוזה וספר תורה י**

פיקוח נפש דוחה כל מצות שבתורה ...

**15) יבמות עט.**

שלשה סימנים יש באומה זו: הרחמנים, והביישנין, וגומלי חסדים רחמנים

### 34) מדרש, ילקוט שמעוני, ויקרא כ
לא יאמר אדם אי אפשי לאכול בשר חזיר אי אפשי ללבוש כלאים אי אפשי לבוא על הערוה אלא אפשי אבל מה אעשה ואבי שבשמים גזר עלי

### 35) תניא, פרק לב
... אבל מי שאינו חבירו ואינו מקורב אצלו הנה ע"ז אמר הלל הזקן הוי מתלמידיו של אהרן אוהב שלום וכו' אוהב את הבריות ומקרבן לתורה. לומר שאף הרחוקים מתורת ה' ועבודתו ... שמצוה לשנאותם מצוה לאהבם ג"כ ושתיהן הן אמת שנאה מצד הרע שבהם ואהבה מצד בחי' הטוב הגנוז שבהם שהוא ניצוץ אלקות שבתוכם ...

### 36) קהלת ז:כ
כִּי אָדָם אֵין צַדִּיק בָּאָרֶץ אֲשֶׁר יַעֲשֶׂה־טּוֹב וְלֹא יֶחֱטָא:

### 37) רמב"ם, הלכות דעות ז:ג
אמרו חכמים שלש עבירות נפרעין מן האדם בעולם הזה ואין לו חלק לעולם הבא עבודת כוכבים וגילוי עריות ושפיכות דמים ולשון הרע כנגד כולם

### 38) סנהדרין מד.
אמר רבי אבא בר זבדא: אף על פי שחטא ישראל הוא.

### 39) טור, יורה דעה שם
והר"מ מרוטנבורג כתב שעל הכל חייבין לקרוע חוץ מעל מומר ועובד אליל או עובר על כל אחת מכל מצות שבתורה להכעיס שאותו חשוב כמומר אבל אם אדם עושה לפעמים עבירה לתיאבון או שמניח מלעשות המצוה בשביל טורח כגון זה חייב לקרוע עליו כיון שאינו כופר בתורה ואינו עושה להכעיס

### 40) כתבי הגרמ"מ משקלוב, ביאור משנת חסידים, דף רנג
... כי שם הצבור מתפללין, צדיקים בינונים ורשעים

### 41) מדרש ויקרא רבה לב:יב
ד"א פרי עץ הדר אלו ישראל מה אתרוג זה יש בו טעם ויש בו ריח כך ישראל יש בהם בני אדם שיש בהם תורה ויש בהם מעשים טובים כפות תמרים אלו ישראל מה התמרה הזו יש בו טעם ואין בו ריח כך הם ישראל יש בהם שיש בהם תורה ואין בהם מעשים טובים וענף עץ עבות אלו ישראל מה הדס יש בו ריח ואין בו טעם כך ישראל יש בהם שיש בהם מעשים טובים ואין בהם תורה וערבי נחל אלו ישראל מה ערבה זו אין בה טעם ואין בה ריח כך הם ישראל יש בהם בני אדם שאין בהם לא תורה ולא מעשים טובים ומה הקב"ה עושה להם לאבדן אי אפשר אלא אמר הקב"ה יוקשרו כולם אגודה אחת והן מכפרין אלו על אלו
עַל דַּעַת הַמָּקוֹם וְעַל דַּעַת הַקָּהָל בִּישִׁיבָה שֶׁל מַעְלָה וּבִישִׁיבָה שֶׁל מַטָּה מַתִּירִין אָנוּ לְהִתְפַּלֵּל עִם הָעֲבַרְיָנִים:

### 42) מחזור יום כיפור, לפני "כל נדרי"
עַל דַּעַת הַמָּקוֹם וְעַל דַּעַת הַקָּהָל בִּישִׁיבָה שֶׁל מַעְלָה וּבִישִׁיבָה שֶׁל מַטָּה מַתִּירִין אָנוּ לְהִתְפַּלֵּל עִם הָעֲבַרְיָנִים:

### 43) משנה אבות, ב:ד
הלל אומר אל תפרוש מן הצבור.

44) Rabbi Shmuley Boteach "My Jewish Perspective on Homosexuality," Wall Street Journal, October 15, 2010

45) Rabbi Aharon Feldman, "A Letter to a Homosexual Baal Teshuva," Jerusalem Letter, 1, no. 5 (March 24, 1998)

46) Dennis Prager, "Judaism's Sexual Revolution:, Why Judaism (and then Christianity) Rejected Homosexuality" "Crisis Magazine" 11, no. 8 (September 1993)

הָאֵלֶּה וְנִכְרְתוּ הַנְּפָשׁוֹת הָעֹשֹׂת מִקֶּרֶב עַמָּם: וּשְׁמַרְתֶּם אֶת־מִשְׁמַרְתִּי לְבִלְתִּי עֲשׂוֹת מֵחֻקּוֹת הַתּוֹעֵבֹת אֲשֶׁר נַעֲשׂוּ לִפְנֵיכֶם וְלֹא תִטַּמְּאוּ בָּהֶם אֲנִי ד' אֱלֹקֵיכֶם:

**17) ויקרא יח:ג:**
כְּמַעֲשֵׂה אֶרֶץ־מִצְרַיִם אֲשֶׁר יְשַׁבְתֶּם־בָּהּ לֹא תַעֲשׂוּ וּכְמַעֲשֵׂה אֶרֶץ־כְּנַעַן אֲשֶׁר אֲנִי מֵבִיא אֶתְכֶם שָׁמָּה לֹא תַעֲשׂוּ וּבְחֻקֹּתֵיהֶם לֹא תֵלֵכוּ:

**18) סוטה יג:**
"ויקנהו פוטיפר סריס פרעה" אמר רב: שקנאו לעצמו. (בא גבריאל וסירסו) בא גבריאל ופירעו,

**19) בראשית לט:א:**
וְיוֹסֵף הוּרַד מִצְרָיְמָה וַיִּקְנֵהוּ פּוֹטִיפַר סְרִיס פַּרְעֹה שַׂר הַטַּבָּחִים אִישׁ מִצְרִי מִיַּד הַיִּשְׁמְעֵאלִים אֲשֶׁר הוֹרִדֻהוּ שָׁמָּה:

**20) בראשית ו:יב-יג ופירושי רש"י, חזקוני ומזרחי**
וַיַּרְא אֱלֹקִים אֶת־הָאָרֶץ וְהִנֵּה נִשְׁחָתָה כִּי־הִשְׁחִית כָּל־בָּשָׂר אֶת־דַּרְכּוֹ עַל־הָאָרֶץ: וַיֹּאמֶר אֱלֹקִים לְנֹחַ קֵץ כָּל־בָּשָׂר בָּא לְפָנַי כִּי־מָלְאָה הָאָרֶץ חָמָס מִפְּנֵיהֶם וְהִנְנִי מַשְׁחִיתָם אֶת־הָאָרֶץ:

**21) פירושי רש"י, חזקוני ומזרחי על בראשית ו:יב**
רש"י - כי השחית כל בשר – אפילו בהמה חיה ועוף נזקקין לשאינן מינן:
חזקוני - כי השחית כל בשר את דרכו – תשמישו כמו דרך גבר בעלמה וכבר נצטוו תוצא הארץ נפש חיה למינה בהמה ורמש וחיתו ארץ למינהו אבל לא לשאינו מינו לפיכך הנני משחיתם את הארץ מדה כנגד מדה.
מזרחי - כי השחית כל בשר אפילו בהמה חיה ועוף נזקקין לשאינן מינן. דהשחתת דרכו בגלוי עריות קמיירי ...

**22) בראשית ט:כב-כד**
וַיַּרְא חָם אֲבִי כְנַעַן אֵת עֶרְוַת אָבִיו וַיַּגֵּד לִשְׁנֵי־אֶחָיו בַּחוּץ: וַיִּקַּח שֵׁם וָיֶפֶת אֶת־הַשִּׂמְלָה וַיָּשִׂימוּ עַל־שְׁכֶם שְׁנֵיהֶם וַיֵּלְכוּ אֲחֹרַנִּית וַיְכַסּוּ אֵת עֶרְוַת אֲבִיהֶם וּפְנֵיהֶם אֲחֹרַנִּית וְעֶרְוַת אֲבִיהֶם לֹא רָאוּ: וַיִּיקֶץ נֹחַ מִיֵּינוֹ וַיֵּדַע אֵת אֲשֶׁר־עָשָׂה לוֹ בְּנוֹ הַקָּטָן:

**23) סנהדרין ע.**
"ויִיקֶץ נֹחַ מיינו וידע את אשר עשה לו בנו הקטן".
רב ושמואל, חד אמר: סרסו, וחד אמר: רבעו.

**24) בראשית יט:ה**
וַיִּקְרְאוּ אֶל־לוֹט וַיֹּאמְרוּ לוֹ אַיֵּה הָאֲנָשִׁים אֲשֶׁר־בָּאוּ אֵלֶיךָ הַלָּיְלָה הוֹצִיאֵם אֵלֵינוּ וְנֵדְעָה אֹתָם:

---

**25) פירוש רש"י על בראשית יט:ה**
ונדעה אתם - במשכב זכר כמו אשר לא ידעו איש (ב"ר):

**26) בראשית ד:א**
וְהָאָדָם יָדַע אֶת־חַוָּה אִשְׁתּוֹ וַתַּהַר וַתֵּלֶד אֶת־קַיִן וַתֹּאמֶר קָנִיתִי אִישׁ אֶת־ד':

**27) משנה קידושין ד:יט**
מתני'. ...ר' יהודה אומר: לא ירעה רווק בהמה, ולא יישנו שני רווקין בטלית אחת, וחכמים מתירים.
גמ'. מאי טעמא? ... אמרו לו לר' יהודה: לא נחשדו ישראל על משכב זכור ולא על הבהמה ...

**28) רמב"ם, הלכות איסורי ביאה כב:א**
אסור להתיחד עם ערוה מן העריות בין זקנה בין ילדה שדבר זה גורם לגלות ערוה, חוץ מהאם עם בנה והאב עם בתו והבעל עם אשתו נדה, וחתן שפירסה אשתו נדה קודם שיבעול אסור להתיחד עמה אלא אלא היא ישנה בין הנשים והוא ישן בין האנשים, ואם בא עליה ביאה ראשונה ואח"כ נטמאת מותר להתיחד עמה.

**29) רמב"ם, הלכות איסורי ביאה כב:ב**
לא נחשדו ישראל על משכב זכור ועל הבהמה, לפיכך אין אסור להתיחד עמהן, ואם נתרחק אפילו מייחוד זכור ובהמה הרי זה משובח ...

**30) שולחן ערוך, אבן העזר, כד:א**
לא נחשדו ישראל על משכב זכר ועל הבהמה לפיכך אין איסור להתייחד עמהן ואם נתרחק אפי' מיחוד זכר ובהמה הרי זה משובח וגדולי החכמים היו מרחיקין הבהמה כדי שלא יתייחדו עמהם ובדורות הללו שרבו הפריצים יש להתרחק מלהתייחד עם הזכר.

**31) פירוש בית חדש (ב"ח) על טור, אבן העזר כד**
כתב ב"י בש"ע ובדורות הללו שרבו הפריצים יש להתרחק מלהתייחד עם הזכר עכ"ל וכתב כן לפי מדינתו ודורותיו ומשמע דיש להתרחק מדינא קאמר אבל במדינתינו דלא נשמע שפרצו בעבירה זו א"צ להתרחק אלא דמ"מ מי שנתרחק ה"ז משובח:

**32) בראשית ח:כא**
וַיָּרַח ד' אֶת־רֵיחַ הַנִּיחֹחַ וַיֹּאמֶר ד' אֶל־לִבּוֹ לֹא אֹסִף לְקַלֵּל עוֹד אֶת־הָאֲדָמָה בַּעֲבוּר הָאָדָם כִּי יֵצֶר לֵב הָאָדָם רַע מִנְּעֻרָיו וְלֹא־אֹסִף עוֹד לְהַכּוֹת אֶת־כָּל־חַי כַּאֲשֶׁר עָשִׂיתִי:

**33) במדבר טו:לט**
...וְלֹא תָתוּרוּ אַחֲרֵי לְבַבְכֶם וְאַחֲרֵי עֵינֵיכֶם אֲשֶׁר־אַתֶּם זֹנִים אַחֲרֵיהֶם:

# SOURCES ON HOMOSEXUALITY AND HOMOSEXUALS
## IN TRADITIONAL JUDAISM

**1) ויקרא יח:כב**

וְאֶת־זָכָר לֹא תִשְׁכַּב מִשְׁכְּבֵי אִשָּׁה תּוֹעֵבָה הוא:

**2) ויקרא כ:יג**

וְאִישׁ אֲשֶׁר יִשְׁכַּב אֶת־זָכָר מִשְׁכְּבֵי אִשָּׁה תּוֹעֵבָה עָשׂוּ שְׁנֵיהֶם מוֹת יוּמָתוּ דְּמֵיהֶם בָּם:

**3) ויקרא יח:כא-כג**

וּמִזַּרְעֲךָ לֹא־תִתֵּן לְהַעֲבִיר לַמֹּלֶךְ וְלֹא תְחַלֵּל אֶת־שֵׁם אֱלֹהֶיךָ אֲנִי ד': וְאֶת־זָכָר לֹא תִשְׁכַּב מִשְׁכְּבֵי אִשָּׁה תּוֹעֵבָה הוא: וּבְכָל־בְּהֵמָה לֹא־תִתֵּן שְׁכָבְתְּךָ לְטָמְאָה־בָה וְאִשָּׁה לֹא־תַעֲמֹד לִפְנֵי בְהֵמָה לְרִבְעָהּ תֶּבֶל הוא:

**4) מדרש ספרי, אחרי מות ח:ח**

אי כמעשה ארץ מצרים וכמעשה ארץ כנען לא תעשו יכול לא יבנו בניינים ולא יטעו נטיעות כמותם תלמוד לומר ובחוקותיהם לא תלכו לא אמרתי אלא בחוקים החקוקים להם ולאבותיהם ולאבות אבותיהם. ומה היו עושים האיש נושא לאיש והאשה לאשה האיש נושא אשה ובתה והאשה ניסת לשנים לכך אמר ובחוקותיהם לא תלכו:.

**5) רמב"ם, הלכות איסורי ביאה כא:ח**

נשים המסוללות זו בזו אסור וממעשה מצרים הוא שהוזהרנו עליו שנאמר "כמעשה ארץ מצרים לא תעשו", אמרו חכמים מה היו עושים האיש נושא איש ואשה נושא אשה, ואשה נשאת לשני אנשים, אע"פ שמעשה זה אסור אין מלקין עליו, שאין לו לאו מיוחד והרי אין שם ביאה כלל ... וראוי להכותן מכת מרדות הואיל ועשו איסור ...

**6) שולחן ערוך, אבן העזר כ:ב**

נשים המסוללות (פי' המשחקות ומתחככות זו בזו) אסור וממעשה ארץ מצרים שהוזהרנו עליו זה וראוי להכותן מכת מרדות הואיל ועשו דבר איסור ויש לאיש להקפיד על אשתו מדבר זה ומונע הנשים הידועות בכך מליכנס לה וממליצאת היא אליהן:

**7) נדרים נא.**

הכי אמר רחמנא: תועבה – תועה אתה בה.

**8) בראשית א:כח**

וַיְבָרֶךְ אֹתָם אֱלֹהִים וַיֹּאמֶר לָהֶם אֱלֹהִים פְּרוּ וּרְבוּ וּמִלְאוּ אֶת־הָאָרֶץ וְכִבְשֻׁהָ וּרְדוּ בִּדְגַת הַיָּם וּבְעוֹף הַשָּׁמַיִם וּבְכָל־חַיָּה הָרֹמֶשֶׂת עַל־הָאָרֶץ:

---

**9) ספר החינוך, מצוה רט**

משרשי המצוה, לפי שהשם ברוך הוא חפץ ביישוב עולמו אשר ברא, ולכן ציוה לבל ישחיתו זרעם במשכבי הזכרים, כי הוא באמת השחתה שאין בדבר תועלת פרי ולא מצות עונה ...

**10) ישעיהו מה:יח**

כִּי כֹה אָמַר־ד' בּוֹרֵא הַשָּׁמַיִם הוּא הָאֱלֹקִים יֹצֵר הָאָרֶץ וְעֹשָׂהּ הוּא כוֹנְנָהּ לֹא־תֹהוּ בְרָאָהּ לָשֶׁבֶת יְצָרָהּ אֲנִי ד' וְאֵין עוֹד:

**11) דברים ז:כה-כו, יד:ג, דברים יח:ט-יב, יח:כא-כט**

פְּסִילֵי אֱלֹהֵיהֶם תִּשְׂרְפוּן בָּאֵשׁ לֹא־תַחְמֹד כֶּסֶף וְזָהָב עֲלֵיהֶם וְלָקַחְתָּ לָךְ פֶּן תִּוָּקֵשׁ בּוֹ כִּי תוֹעֲבַת ד' אֱלֹהֶיךָ הוּא: וְלֹא־תָבִיא תוֹעֵבָה אֶל־בֵּיתֶךָ וְהָיִיתָ חֵרֶם כָּמֹהוּ שַׁקֵּץ תְּשַׁקְּצֶנּוּ וְתַעֵב תְּתַעֲבֶנּוּ כִּי־חֵרֶם הוּא:

**12) דברים, יד:ג**

לֹא תֹאכַל כָּל־תּוֹעֵבָה:

**13) דברים יח:ט**

כִּי אַתָּה בָּא אֶל־הָאָרֶץ אֲשֶׁר־ד' אֱלֹהֶיךָ נֹתֵן לָךְ לֹא־תִלְמַד לַעֲשׂוֹת כְּתוֹעֲבֹת הַגּוֹיִם הָהֵם:

**14) דברים יח:י-יא**

לֹא־יִמָּצֵא בְךָ מַעֲבִיר בְּנוֹ־וּבִתּוֹ בָּאֵשׁ קֹסֵם קְסָמִים מְעוֹנֵן וּמְנַחֵשׁ וּמְכַשֵּׁף: וְחֹבֵר חָבֶר וְשֹׁאֵל אוֹב וְיִדְּעֹנִי וְדֹרֵשׁ אֶל־הַמֵּתִים:

**15) דברים יח:יב**

כִּי־תוֹעֲבַת ד' כָּל־עֹשֵׂה אֵלֶּה וּבִגְלַל הַתּוֹעֵבֹת הָאֵלֶּה ד' אֱלֹהֶיךָ מוֹרִישׁ אוֹתָם מִפָּנֶיךָ:

**16) דברים יח:כא-כט**

וּמִזַּרְעֲךָ לֹא־תִתֵּן לְהַעֲבִיר לַמֹּלֶךְ וְלֹא תְחַלֵּל אֶת־שֵׁם אֱלֹהֶיךָ אֲנִי ד': וְאֶת־זָכָר לֹא תִשְׁכַּב מִשְׁכְּבֵי אִשָּׁה תּוֹעֵבָה הוא: וּבְכָל־בְּהֵמָה לֹא־תִתֵּן שְׁכָבְתְּךָ לְטָמְאָה־בָהּ וְאִשָּׁה לֹא־תַעֲמֹד לִפְנֵי בְהֵמָה לְרִבְעָהּ תֶּבֶל הוא: אַל־תִּטַּמְּאוּ בְּכָל־אֵלֶּה כִּי בְכָל־אֵלֶּה נִטְמְאוּ הַגּוֹיִם אֲשֶׁר־אֲנִי מְשַׁלֵּחַ מִפְּנֵיכֶם: וַתִּטְמָא הָאָרֶץ וָאֶפְקֹד עֲוֹנָהּ עָלֶיהָ וַתָּקִא הָאָרֶץ אֶת־יֹשְׁבֶיהָ: וּשְׁמַרְתֶּם אַתֶּם אֶת־חֻקֹּתַי וְאֶת־מִשְׁפָּטַי וְלֹא תַעֲשׂוּ מִכֹּל הַתּוֹעֵבֹת הָאֵלֶּה הָאֶזְרָח וְהַגֵּר הַגָּר בְּתוֹכְכֶם: כִּי אֶת־כָּל־הַתּוֹעֵבֹת הָאֵל עָשׂוּ אַנְשֵׁי־הָאָרֶץ אֲשֶׁר לִפְנֵיכֶם וַתִּטְמָא הָאָרֶץ: וְלֹא־תָקִיא הָאָרֶץ אֶתְכֶם בְּטַמַּאֲכֶם אֹתָהּ כַּאֲשֶׁר קָאָה אֶת־הַגּוֹי אֲשֶׁר לִפְנֵיכֶם: כִּי כָּל־אֲשֶׁר יַעֲשֶׂה מִכֹּל הַתּוֹעֵבֹת

יוֹמָא דִּשְׁדִי לֵיהּ אַרְבָּעָה זוּזֵי בְּצִינּוֹרָא דְּדַשָּׁא. יוֹם
אֶחָד אָמַר: אֵיזִיל אֵיחֲזֵי מַאן קָעָבֵיד בֵּי הַהוּא טֵיבוּתָא.
הַהוּא יוֹמָא נְגַהָא לֵיהּ לְמָר עוּקְבָא לְבֵי מִדְרְשָׁא,
אָתְיָא דְּבִיתְהוּ בַּהֲדֵיהּ, כֵּיוָן דַּחֲזִיוֹהוּ דְּקָא מַצְלֵי לֵיהּ
לְדַשָּׁא נְפַק בַּתְרַיְיהוּ, רְהוּט מִקַּמֵּיהּ עָיְילֵי לְהַהוּא
אַתּוּנָא דַּהֲוָה גְּרוּפָה נוּרָא, הֲוָה קָא מִיקַלְיָין כַּרְעֵיהּ
דְּמָר עוּקְבָא אָמְרָה לֵיהּ דְּבִיתְהוּ: שְׁקוֹל כַּרְעֵיךְ אוֹתֵיב
אַכַּרְעַאי. חֲלַשׁ דַּעְתֵּיהּ, אָמְרָה לֵיהּ: אֲנָא שְׁכִיחְנָא
בְּגַוֵּיהּ דְּבֵיתָא וּמְקָרְבָא אַהֲנָיָיתִי. וּמַאי כּוּלֵי הַאי?
דְּאָמַר מָר זוּטְרָא בַּר טוּבִיָּה אָמַר רַב, וְאָמְרֵי לָהּ אָמַר
רַב הוּנָא בַּר בִּיזְנָא אָמַר רְ"שׁ חֲסִידָא, וְאָמְרֵי לָהּ א"ר
יוֹחָנָן מִשּׁוּם רַבִּי שִׁמְעוֹן בֶּן יוֹחַי: נוֹחַ לוֹ לְאָדָם שֶׁיִּמְסוֹר
עַצְמוֹ לְתוֹךְ כִּבְשַׁן הָאֵשׁ וְאַל יַלְבִּין פְּנֵי חֲבֵרוֹ בָּרַבִּים

**18)** מִתּוֹךְ קִינָה לְתִשְׁעָה בְּאָב "אַרְזֵי לְבָנוֹן"
גִּבּוֹרֵי כֹחַ עֲמָלֵיהָ בְּטָהֳרָה ...

**19)** עֲרָכִין יז.
זֶה דּוֹר דּוֹרְשָׁיו מְבַקְשֵׁי פָּנֶיךָ יַעֲקֹב סֶלָה פְּלִיגִי בָּהּ רַבִּי
יְהוּדָה נְשִׂיאָה וְרַבָּנָן, חַד אָמַר: דּוֹר לְפִי פַרְנָס, וְחַד
אָמַר: פַּרְנָס לְפִי דוֹרוֹ.

**20)** שְׁמוֹנֶה עֶשְׂרֵה שֶׁל חוֹל, בְּרָכָה יג
עַל הַצַּדִּיקִים וְעַל הַחֲסִידִים. וְעַל זִקְנֵי עַמְּךָ בֵּית
יִשְׂרָאֵל. וְעַל פְּלֵיטַת סוֹפְרֵיהֶם. וְעַל גֵּרֵי הַצֶּדֶק.
וְעָלֵינוּ. יֶהֱמוּ רַחֲמֶיךָ ד' אֱלֹקֵינוּ. וְתֵן שָׂכָר טוֹב לְכָל
הַבּוֹטְחִים בְּשִׁמְךָ בֶּאֱמֶת. וְשִׂים חֶלְקֵנוּ עִמָּהֶם לְעוֹלָם
וְלֹא נֵבוֹשׁ כִּי בְךָ בָּטָחְנוּ.

**21)** וַיִּקְרָא יט:לו, דְּבָרִים טז:כ
מֹאזְנֵי צֶדֶק אַבְנֵי־צֶדֶק אֵיפַת צֶדֶק וְהִין צֶדֶק יִהְיֶה לָכֶם
אֲנִי ד' אֱלֹקֵיכֶם אֲשֶׁר־הוֹצֵאתִי אֶתְכֶם מֵאֶרֶץ מִצְרָיִם:
צֶדֶק צֶדֶק תִּרְדֹּף לְמַעַן תִּחְיֶה וְיָרַשְׁתָּ אֶת־הָאָרֶץ
אֲשֶׁר־ד' אֱלֹקֶיךָ נֹתֵן לָךְ:

**22)** קִידּוּשִׁין לב:
רַבִּי יוֹסֵי הַגְּלִילִי אוֹמֵר: אֵין זָקֵן אֶלָּא מִי שֶׁקָּנָה חָכְמָה

**23)** פְּסָחִים מט:
תָּנוּ רַבָּנָן: לְעוֹלָם יִמְכּוֹר אָדָם כָּל מַה שֶׁיֵּשׁ לוֹ וְיִשָּׂא בַת
תַּלְמִיד חָכָם. לֹא מָצָא בַת תַּלְמִיד חָכָם יִשָּׂא בַת גְּדוֹלֵי
הַדּוֹר. לֹא מָצָא בַת גְּדוֹלֵי הַדּוֹר יִשָּׂא בַת רָאשֵׁי כְנֵסִיּוֹת,
לֹא מָצָא בַת רָאשֵׁי כְנֵסִיּוֹת יִשָּׂא בַת גַּבָּאֵי צְדָקָה. לֹא
מָצָא בַת גַּבָּאֵי צְדָקָה יִשָּׂא בַת מְלַמְּדֵי תִּינוֹקוֹת

### 1) בראשית י':ח-ט
וְכוּשׁ יָלַד אֶת־נִמְרֹד הוּא הֵחֵל לִהְיוֹת גִּבֹּר בָּאָרֶץ: הוּא־הָיָה גִבֹּר־צַיִד לִפְנֵי ד' עַל־כֵּן יֵאָמַר כְּנִמְרֹד גִּבּוֹר צַיִד לִפְנֵי ד':

### 2) פירוש אבן עזרא על בראשית י':ח-ט
והוא החל - להראות גבורות בני אדם על החיות כי הי' גבור ציד:

### 3) פירוש רש"י על בראשית י':ח-ט
להיות גבור - להמריד כל העולם על הקב"ה בעצת דור הפלגה.
גבור ציד - צד דעתן של בריות בפיו והטען למרוד במקום:

### 4) שופטים ו':יא-יב
וַיָּבֹא מַלְאַךְ ד' וַיֵּשֶׁב תַּחַת הָאֵלָה אֲשֶׁר בְּעָפְרָה אֲשֶׁר לְיוֹאָשׁ אֲבִי הָעֶזְרִי וְגִדְעוֹן בְּנוֹ חֹבֵט חִטִּים בַּגַּת לְהָנִיס מִפְּנֵי מִדְיָן: וַיֵּרָא אֵלָיו מַלְאַךְ ד' וַיֹּאמֶר אֵלָיו ד' עִמְּךָ גִּבּוֹר הֶחָיִל:

### 5) שופטים יא:א
וְיִפְתָּח הַגִּלְעָדִי הָיָה גִּבּוֹר חַיִל וְהוּא בֶּן־אִשָּׁה זוֹנָה וַיּוֹלֶד גִּלְעָד אֶת־יִפְתָּח:

### 6) שמואל א' יד:נב
וַתְּהִי הַמִּלְחָמָה חֲזָקָה עַל־פְּלִשְׁתִּים כֹּל יְמֵי שָׁאוּל וְרָאָה שָׁאוּל כָּל־אִישׁ גִּבּוֹר וְכָל־בֶּן־חַיִל וַיַּאַסְפֵהוּ אֵלָיו:

### 7) שמואל א' טז:יח
וַיַּעַן אֶחָד מֵהַנְּעָרִים וַיֹּאמֶר הִנֵּה רָאִיתִי בֵּן לְיִשַׁי בֵּית הַלַּחְמִי יֹדֵעַ נַגֵּן וְגִבּוֹר חַיִל וְאִישׁ מִלְחָמָה וּנְבוֹן דָּבָר וְאִישׁ תֹּאַר וַד' עִמּוֹ:

### 8) פירושי רד"ק ורלב"ג כלשמואל א' טז:יח
וגבור חיל - שיש לו גבורת הלב לכל דבר כמו שנודעה גבורתו בדבר הארי והדוב:
גבור חיל ואיש מלחמה - הנה קרא גבור חיל מי שהוא בעל אומץ ותוקף ואיש מלחמה מי שהוא יודע להמציא תחבולות עם אויביו וינצחם ...

### 9) מלכים א' יא:כח
וְהָאִישׁ יָרָבְעָם גִּבּוֹר חָיִל וַיַּרְא שְׁלֹמֹה אֶת־הַנַּעַר כִּי־עֹשֵׂה מְלָאכָה הוּא וַיַּפְקֵד אֹתוֹ לְכָל־סֵבֶל בֵּית יוֹסֵף:

### 10) ירמיהו ט:כב
כֹּה אָמַר ד' אַל־יִתְהַלֵּל חָכָם בְּחָכְמָתוֹ וְאַל־יִתְהַלֵּל הַגִּבּוֹר בִּגְבוּרָתוֹ אַל־יִתְהַלֵּל עָשִׁיר בְּעָשְׁרוֹ: כִּי אִם־בְּזֹאת יִתְהַלֵּל הַמִּתְהַלֵּל הַשְׂכֵּל וְיָדֹעַ אוֹתִי כִּי אֲנִי ד' עֹשֶׂה חֶסֶד מִשְׁפָּט וּצְדָקָה בָּאָרֶץ כִּי־בְאֵלֶּה חָפַצְתִּי נְאֻם־ד':

### 11) דברים י':יז
כִּי ד' אֱלֹקֵיכֶם הוּא אֱלֹקֵי הָאֱלֹקִים וַאֲדֹנֵי הָאֲדֹנִים הָאֵל הַגָּדֹל הַגִּבֹּר וְהַנּוֹרָא אֲשֶׁר לֹא־יִשָּׂא פָנִים וְלֹא יִקַּח שֹׁחַד:

### 12) ירמיהו כ':יא, לב:יח
וַד' אוֹתִי כְּגִבּוֹר עָרִיץ עַל־כֵּן רֹדְפַי יִכָּשְׁלוּ וְלֹא יֻכָלוּ בֹּשׁוּ מְאֹד כִּי־לֹא הִשְׂכִּילוּ כְּלִמַּת עוֹלָם לֹא תִשָּׁכֵחַ
עֹשֶׂה חֶסֶד לַאֲלָפִים וּמְשַׁלֵּם עֲוֹן אָבוֹת אֶל־חֵיק בְּנֵיהֶם אַחֲרֵיהֶם הָאֵל הַגָּדוֹל הַגִּבּוֹר ד' צְבָאוֹת שְׁמוֹ:

### 13) תהילים כד:ח, עח:סה
מִי זֶה מֶלֶךְ הַכָּבוֹד ד' עִזּוּז וְגִבּוֹר ד' גִּבּוֹר מִלְחָמָה:
וַיִּקַץ כְּיָשֵׁן אֲדֹנָי כְּגִבּוֹר מִתְרוֹנֵן מִיָּיִן:

### 14) יומא סט:
למה נקרא שמן אנשי כנסת הגדולה שהחזירו עטרה ליושנה. אתא משה אמר (דברים י) האל הגדל הגבר והנורא, אתא ירמיה ואמר: נכרים מקרקרין בהיכלו, איה נוראותיו? לא אמר נורא. אתא דניאל, אמר: נכרים משתעבדים בבניו, איה גבורותיו? לא אמר גבור. אתו אינהו ואמרו: אדרבה, זו היא גבורת גבורתו שכובש את יצרו, שנותן ארך אפים לרשעים. ואלו הן נוראותיו שאלמלא מוראו של הקדוש ברוך הוא היאך אומה אחת יכולה להתקיים בין האומות?

### 15) סוטה יד.
ואמר רבי חמא ברבי חנינא, מאי דכתיב: (דברים יג) אחרי ה' אלקיכם תלכו? וכי אפשר לו לאדם להלך אחר שכינה? והלא כבר נאמר: (דברים ד) כי ה' אלקיך אש אוכלה הוא אלא להלך אחר מדותיו של הקב"ה, מה הוא מלביש ערומים, דכתיב: (בראשית ג) ויעש ה' אלהים לאדם ולאשתו כתנות עור וילבישם, אף אתה הלבש ערומים הקב"ה ביקר חולים, דכתיב: (בראשית יח) וירא אליו ה' באלוני ממרא, אף אתה בקר חולים

### 16) אבות ד:א
... איזהו גבור הכובש את יצרו.

### 17) כתובות סז:
מר עוקבא הוה עניא בשיבבותיה, דהוה רגיל כל

לאידו באשר הוא סוף כל האדם שבוודאי צריך לנחם אבלים כשמת שונאו כי לאחר שמת ודאי אין לחשוש משום שמחה לאיד ומכל מקום יתכן שכאשר בא לנחם אבלים כשמת שונאו מקיים רק את ענין טובת האבלים החיים ולא את ענין טובת המת כי יתכן שאם המנחם הוא שונאו של המת אין למת הנחת הדעת מאותו ואינו דומה לענין לוויית המת שהוא לצורך כבוד ואינו ענין של הנחת הדעת ...

... ונראה שהסברות שכתבו השבט יהודה והמטה משה מדוע שונא צריך לקיים מצות ביקור חולים שייכות גם לענין קיום מצות נחום אבלים על ידי שונא הל לענין החלק של "טובת החיים" ולכאורה גם לענין "טובת המת", שכן מובא בשו"ע (או"ח סימן תרו סע' א-ב) שענין בקשת מחילה שייך לא רק לגבי אנשים חיים אלא אף במתים עבירות שבין אדם לחבירו אין יום הכפורים מכפר עד שיפייסנו ... ... ולכאורה גם סברת המטה משה שאדרבה לשונא יש יותר מצוה לבקר חולה כדי לכוף את יצרו שייכת גם בנחום אבלים שאם היתה שנאה בין המת ובינו או בין האבלים ובינו ודאי שעליו ללכת לנחם ולכוף את יצרו.

---

**66) רץ כצבי (הרב צבי רייזמן), ירח האיתנים יא:ב-ג**

ונראה לדון בענין ניחום אבלים על ידי שונא בהקדם דברי האגרות משה (או"ח ח"ד סימן מ אות יא) שבניחום אבלים יש שני עניינים (א) טובת אבלים החיים שהם טרודים מאד בצערם מחוייבין לדבר על לבו ולנחמו שבשביל זה הרי ג"כ מחוייבין לילך לביתו למקום שהוא נמצא (ב) לטובת המת כדאיתא (בשבת דף קנב ... הרי ממילא ידעינן דכשיש מנחמין איכא בזה גם טובת המת דברי האגרות משה נסבו אודות השאלה אם יכול לקיים מצות ניחום אבלים בטלפון והנה פשוט וברור שמחלוקת המהרי" והרמ"א ופשרת הש"ך שאם יש שנאה בין המנחם והמנוחמים האם צריך השונא ללכת לנחם נאמרה ביחס לענין הראשון של מצות הניחום טובת האבלים החיים ובזה נחלקו האם מצד טובת האבלים מחוייב ללכת לנחמם או לא אולם ביחס לענין השני של מצות הניחום טובת המת לכאורה מה זה משנה שיש שנאה בין האבלים והמנחם החיים לענין טובת המת שעדיין מחוייב בה כשמת שונאו אבלים כשמת שונאו אבלים כשמת שונאו יש ללמוד מדברי הש"ך הנ"ל בשם הב"ח שבליווי המת אין לחשוש משום שמחה

תוספות הדמים אפ"ה יכולין הקהל לומר אין יכולת
כ"כ בידינו להוסיף בדמים: (נג) שפלוני יהיה חזן –
ה"ה בכל המינונים יכול למחות אפילו בחכם מרביץ
תורה [תופס ישיבה] ודוקא כשרוצה לקבל אחר אבל
אם מוחה שאינו רוצה שיהיה מרביץ תורה בקהל
פשיטא שאין במחאתו כלום ואפילו המיעוט יכולין
לכוף לרוב ואפילו ברוצה למנות אחר אם אותו שרוב
הקהל מסכימים עליו הוא עדיף מזה ג"כ אינו יכול
למחות ואפשר דאפילו מיעוט יכולין לכוף לרוב
לשכור מעולה [כנה"ג] כתבו האחרונים שזה הדין
דש"ע הוא דוקא בימיהם אבל היום שידוע שבעו"ה
הרבה מחזיקין במחלוקת בלי טעם וריח וכונתם שלא
לש"ש אם הם היו צריכין לשאול לכל יחיד ויחיד בענין
המינונים בין לענין מינוי הש"ץ או מרביץ תורה
ואב"ד בעיר וכל כה"ג לא היו מסכימים לעולם ע"כ
הולכין אחר רוב פורעי המס ואפילו פסולי קורבי
בינהם [מ"א] ועכשיו המנהג שהולכין אחר ז' טובי
העיר או אחר הנבררים מן הקהל ע"ז כל מקום ומקום
לפי מנהגו [פמ"ג] והכל שלא ירבו המחלוקת ואין
משגיחין על יחיד והמ"א כתב עוד טעם דלא שייך
היום דין דעיכוב יחיד לענין ש"ץ דדוקא בזמניהם
שהיה הש"ץ מוציא רבים י"ח בתפילתו אז היה יחיד
יכול לעכב דאין נעשה שלוחו בע"כ משא"כ עתה
שכולם בקיאים רק הש"ץ הוא לפיוטים אע"פ שאומר
קדיש וברכו אין כל כך קפידא:

**64) שולחן ערוך, יורה דעה שלח:ב ופירוש שפתי כהן**
אפי' הגדול ילך לבקר הקטן ואפילו כמה פעמים
ביום ואפילו בן גילו וכל המוסיף ה"ז משובח ובלבד
שלא יטריח לו: הגה י"א דשונא יכול לילך לבקר
חולה (מהרי"ל קצ"ז) ולא נראה לי אלא לא יבקר
חולה ולא ינחם אבל שהוא שונאו שלא יחשב ששמח
לאידו ואינו לו אלא צער. כן נראה לי (ש"ס פ' כ"ג) :
**אלא לא יבקר כו'** – וכתב הב"ח דלווית את השונא
ליכא למיחש לשמח לאידו באשר הוא סוף כל האדם
אבל לנחם אבל או לבקר חולה שהוא שונאו יש
לחוש לכך ומיהו הכל לפי מה שהוא השנאה ולפי
מה שהם השונאים:

**65) שו"ת אגרות משה אורח חיים חלק ד סימן מ:יא**
ינחום אבלים ע"י הטעלעפאן /הטלפון/ ובדבר אם
מקיים מצות נחום אבלים ע"י הטעלעפאן, הנה בנחום
אבלים איכא תרתי ענינים חדא לטובת אבלים החיים
שהם טרודים מאד בצערם מחוייבין לדבר על לבו
ולנחמו שבשביל זה הרי ג"כ מחוייבין לילך לביתו
למקום שהוא נמצא, ושנית לטובת המת כדאיתא
בשבת דף קנ"ב א"ר יהודה מת שאין לו מנחמין
הולכין עשרה בנ"א =בני אדם= ויושבין במקומו
ומסיק עובדא דמת שאין לו מנחמין שבכל יומא הוה
דביר ר' יהודה בי עשרה ותיתבי בדוכתיה ואיתחזי
ליה בחלמו דר' יהודה ואמר ליה תנוח דעתך שהנחת
את דעתי, הרי ממילא ידעינן דכשיש מנחמין איכא

---

בזה גם טובת המת, ומטעם זה כתב הרמב"ם בפי"ד
מאבל ה"ז יראה לי שנחמת אבלים קודם לבק"ח
=לבקור חולים= שנחום אבלים גמ"ח עם החיים ועם
המתים, ופשוט שאיירי הרמב"ם כשידוע לו שיש שם
מי שיעשה צרכי החולה דאל"כ אף שיש שם בנחמות
אבלים תרתי ואפילו היה יותר מזה היה צריך לילך
אל החולה דפק"נ =דפקוח נפש= דוחה כל המצות,
ואף ת"ת =תלמוד תורה= שא"י יוסף במגילה דף ט"ז
שגדול מהצלת נפשות נפשות מ"מ דוחין ת"ת ואפילו של
רבים להציל אף נפש מישראל, אבל כוונת הרמב"ם הוא
דמצד חשיבות המצות מצד עצמן הרי נחום אבלים
קודם מבק"ח שאית בה תרתי שלכן כשליכא ענין
פק"נ שידוע שיש שם מתעסקין שעכ"פ חייב כל אחד
לבקר החולה צריך לילך לנחם האבלים ול"ק כלום
מה שהקשה הרדב"ז מהא דבק"ח יש בו ענין פק"נ,
ואולי סובר הרדב"ז דמאחר דאיכא פעמים דבבק"ח
ענין פק"נ יש להאדם להקדים תמיד בק"ח קודם נחום
אבלים כדי שלא יבא לטעות איזה פעם וגם אולי בלא
זה אלא כדי שיתרגל לידע דחולה שהוא חי קודם ולא
יצטרך לאמוד בכל פעם שיזדמן בזה. אבל משמע לי
שהרדב"ז סובר שאף בידוע שיש שם מתעסקין בצרכי
החולה מ"מ מצד מצות בק"ח לבד שמתפלל עליו שם
מתקבל יותר התפלה משום ששכינה שרויה למעלה
ממטתו של חולה, דהא אינו מביא הרדב"ז הא דר"ע
אלא הא דרב דימי בנדרים דף מ' דאמר כל המבקר
את החולה גורם לו שיחיה ומפרש בגמ' הגרמא
שיחיה הוא בזה שמבקש עליו רחמים שיחיה הרי
דזה שמתפלל עליו נחשב גורם שיחיה, אבל הרמב"ם
אינו סובר שזה יכריע העדיפות דאיכא תרתי בנחום
אבלים, ל"מ כשהוא רק קדימת זמן בעלמא אלא
אפילו כשא"א לו לקיים אלא אחת מהן שנמצא כשילך
לנחם האבלים לא יוכל לילך לבק"ח מ"מ הא אפשר
להתפלל בביתו ועדיפות התפלה אצל החולה פשיטא
לו שאין בזה להכריע התרתי דאיכא בנחום אבלים.
ומשמע לי שמצד האבל החי שייך לקיים גם ע"י
הטעלעפאן, אבל המצוה שמצד טובת המת לא שייך
אלא דוקא כשיבא לשם במקום שמתנחמין או במקום
שמת, ואף מצד האבל החי נמי ודאי עדיף כשבא לשם
שהוא גם מכבדו שזה עצמו הוא ג"כ ענין תנחומין
כלשון ר"ע במו"ק דף כ"ד כשמתו בניו והספידום
כל ישראל עמד ר"ע ואמר אחב"נ שמעו אפילו שני
בנים חתנים מנוחם הוא בשביל כבוד שעשיתם, וענין
הכבוד לא שייך ע"י הטעלעפאן, דלכן למעשה אם
אפשר לו לילך לבית האבלים שהוא קיום מצוה
שלמה לא שייך שיפטר בטעלעפאן, אך קצת מצוה
יש גם ע"י הטעלעפאן שלכן אם א"א לו ללכת לבית
האבלים כגון מחמת חולי או שהוא טרוד בטירדא
דמצוה יש עליו חיוב לקיים מה שאפשר לו יש לו
לנחם ע"י הטעלעפאן דג"כ איכא בזה מצוה ולא
יאמר כי מאחר שאינו יכול לילך לבית האבלים אין
עליו שוב שום חיוב כלל. וכה"ג כתבתי בתשובה
ביו"ד ח"א סימן רכ"ג לענין בקור חולים עיין שם.

## 55) ספר החינוך, מצוה שלח

...ועובר עליה וקבע שנאה בלבו לאחד מכל ישראל הכשרים, עבר על לאו זה, ואין לוקין עליו לפי שאין בו מעשה. **אבל בשנאת הרשעים אין בו איסור, אלא מצוה לשנאותם אחר שנוכיח אותם על חטאם הרבה פעמים ולא רצו לחזור בהן**, שנאמר [תהילים קל"ט, כ"א] "הלא משנאיך ד' אשנא ובתקוממיך אתקוטט":

## 56) חזון איש, הלכות שחיטה, סימן ב:טז

ונראה דאין דין מורידין אלא בזמן שהשגחתו ית' גלוי כמו בזמן שהיו נסים מצוין ומשמש בת קול ... אבל בזמן ההעלם שנכרתה האמונה מן דלת העם אין במעשה הורדה גדר הפרצה. וכיון שכל עצמנו לתקן איו הדין נוהג בשעה שאין בו תיקון ועלינו להחזירם בעבותות אהבה ולהעמידם בקרן אורה במה שידינו מגעת.

## 57) פסחים קיג: ורש"י שם

שלשה הקדוש ברוך הוא שונאן המדבר אחד בפה ואחד בלב, והיודע עדות בחבירו ואינו מעיד לו והרואה דבר ערוה בחבירו ומעיד בו יחידי כי **מותר לשנוא אותו** – הרואה דבר ערוה בחבירו, אף על פי שאינו רשאי להעיד, מותר לשנאתו:

## 58) דברים יג:ז-ט ופירוש רש"י

כִּי יְסִיתְךָ אָחִיךָ בֶן אִמֶּךָ אוֹ בִנְךָ אוֹ בִתְּךָ אוֹ אֵשֶׁת חֵיקֶךָ אוֹ רֵעֲךָ אֲשֶׁר כְּנַפְשְׁךָ בַּסֵּתֶר לֵאמֹר נֵלְכָה וְנַעַבְדָה אֱלֹהִים אֲחֵרִים אֲשֶׁר לֹא יָדַעְתָּ אַתָּה וַאֲבֹתֶיךָ: מֵאֱלֹהֵי הָעַמִּים אֲשֶׁר סְבִיבֹתֵיכֶם הַקְּרֹבִים אֵלֶיךָ אוֹ הָרְחֹקִים מִמְּךָ מִקְצֵה הָאָרֶץ וְעַד קְצֵה הָאָרֶץ: לֹא תֹאבֶה לוֹ וְלֹא תִשְׁמַע אֵלָיו וְלֹא תָחוֹס עֵינְךָ עָלָיו וְלֹא תַחְמֹל וְלֹא תְכַסֶּה עָלָיו:
**לא תאבה לו** – לא תהא תאב לו לא תאהבנו לפי שנאמר ואהבת לרעך כמוך את זה לא תאהב:

## 59) רמב"ם, ספר המצוות, לא תעשה יז-יח

שהזהיר המוסת מאהוב המסית או להאזין לדבריו והוא אמרו ית' לא תאבה לו ולשון ספרי מכלל שנאמר ואהבת לרעך כמוך יכול אתה אוהב לזה תלמוד לומר לא תאבה לו:
שהזהיר המוסת מעזוב לשנא המסית אבל חייב לשנא אותו בהכרח וכשלא ישנאהו עובר על מצות לא תעשה והוא אמרו ית' ולא תשמע אליו ובא הפירוש מכלל שנאמר עזב תעזוב עמו יכול אתה עוזב לזה תלמוד לומר ולא תשמע אליו:

## 60) ספר החינוך תנז-תנח

שנמנענו כמו כן שלא להטות אוזן לדברי מסית ולא להב אותו בשום דבר. וענין מסית הוא מי שמסית אחד מבני ישראל ללכת לעבוד עבודה זרה, כגון שישבח לו פעולת עבודה זרה וישבחנה לו כדי שילך אחריה ויעבדה ויצא מתחת כנפי השכינה, ועל זה

---

נאמר [דברים י"ג, ט'], לא תאבה לו: שלא לעזוב השנאה מן המסית: שתהיה שנאת המסית קבועה בלבבנו, כלומר שלא נקל בנטירת הנקמה ממנו על כל הרעה אשר חשב לעשות, ועל זה נאמר [דברים י"ג, ט'], ולא תשמע אליו, כלומר אל תהי נשמע אליו להעביר מלבך נטירת נקמתך ממנו, וכן אמרו זכרונם לברכה [ספרי כאן] בפירוש זה הכתוב, מכלל שנאמר בישראל עזוב תעזוב עמו, ותרגם אונקלוס משבק תשבוק מה די בלבך עלוהי, יכול אתה עוזב לזה המסית גם כן, תלמוד לומר ולא תשמע אליו:

## 61) חפץ חיים, באר מים חיים, ס"ק ט

שונאים – וראיה מגמרא הנ"ל במו"ל, והרי בודאי היו שונאים זה לזה, דדתן ואבירם בודאי היו שונאים למשה רבנו ע"ה מכבר כמ"ש כי מתו כל האנשים המבקשים את נפשך משמע דהם עדיין מבקשים, וגם עתה היו שונאים לו כדמוכח קראי בפ' קרח בכל הסיפור, ומשה רבנו ע"ה בודאי היה ג"כ שונאם כמ"ש הלא משנאיך ה' אשנא וכו' והם בודאי בכלל שונאי ה' הם שרצו להדיח את כל ישראל מתורת ה' שהכחישו את נבואתו הקדושה ויציאת מצרים שהיה על ידי ה' והפכו את הקערה על פיה שאמרו מדוע תתנשאו וגו':

## 62) שולחן ערוך, אורח חיים נג:יט

יש מונעים גר מלהיות ש"ץ ונדחו דבריהם אפילו יחיד יכול לעכב ולומר איני רוצה שפלוני יהיה חזן אם לא שכבר הסכים עליו מתחלה: הגה: ודוקא שיהא לאותו יחיד טעם הגון על פי טובי העיר אבל בלאו הכי אין היחיד יכול למחות בש"ץ (מהרי"ק סי' ס') ואם הוא שונאו יכול למחות בו קודם שהסכים עליו (מהר"ם פדואה סימן ק"ד ומהרי"ק שורש מ"ד) ומי שהוא שונא לש"ץ לא יעלה לספר תורה כשקורא התוכחה (אור זרוע):

## 63) פירוש משנה ברורה על שולחן ערוך, אורח חיים נג:יט

(נא) יכול לעכב – בעת ההתמנות והטעם (מב) שהרי התפלות במקום התמידים תקנום וכל ישראל יש להם חלק בתמידים ומי יוכל להקריב קרבנו שלא מדעתו אם לא שכבר הסכים עליו ואז אין יחיד וגם חצי הקהל יכולין להעבירו אפי' רוצים ליתן לו שכר משלם כיון שלא עשה כהוגן אבל רוב הקהל יכולין להעבירו אם נותנין לו שכר משלם [א"ז] ועכשיו הרשות להעבירו רק ביד ז' טובי העיר או הנברים כל מקום ומקום לפי התקנה [פמ"ג]:

(נב) איני רוצה – (מג) ודוקא שיש ש"ץ אחר שיוכלו הקהל להשכירו בדמיו אבל אם אינו בנמצא או שהוא בנמצא אלא שבא להוסיף בדמים יכולין הקהל לומר לו אין בידינו להוסיף אלא הוא יוסיף משלו ואף אם יברר טענתו שזה השני הוא מעולה מן הראשון כנגד

## (47) סנהדרין מו:

תנו רבנן אילו נאמר חטא ותלית היית אומר תולין אותו ואחר כך ממיתין אותו כדרך שהמלכות עושה תלמוד לומר והומת ותלית ממיתין אותו ואחר כך תולין אותו הא כיצד משהין אותו עד סמוך לשקיעת החמה

## (48) דברים כא:כב-כג

וכי יהיה באיש חטא משפט מות והומת ותלית אתו על עץ: לא תלין נבלתו על העץ כי קבור תקברנו ביום ההוא כי קללת אלקים תלוי ולא תטמא את אדמתך אשר ד' אלקיך נתן לך נחלה:

## (49) קהלת ג:ח

עֵת לֶאֱהֹב וְעֵת לִשְׂנֹא עֵת מִלְחָמָה וְעֵת שָׁלוֹם:

## (50) מדרש, קהלת רבה ג:י'

ועת לשנוא בשעת מלחמה

## (51) מגילה טז.

כתיב לכו בנפל אויבך אל תשמח אמר ליה הני מילי בישראל אבל בדידכו כתיב ואתה על במותימו תדרוך

## (52) יומא כב:

בשעה שאמר לו הקדוש ברוך הוא לשאול לך והכית את עמלק אמר ומה נפש אחת אמרה תורה הבא עגלה ערופה כל הנפשות הללו על אחת כמה וכמה ואם אדם חטא בהמה מה חטאה ואם גדולים חטאו קטנים מה חטאו יצאה בת קול ואמרה לו אל תהי צדיק הרבה

## (53) פסחים קיג:

כי האי גוונא דחזיא ביה איהו ערוה דבר עבירה רב נחמן בר יצחק אמר מצוה לשנאתו שנאמר יראת ה' (שנאי) (שנאת) רע

## (54) רמב"ם, הלכות רוצח יג:יד

השונא שנאמר בתורה הוא מישראל לא מאומות העולם והיאך יהיה לישראל שונא מישראל והכתוב אומר (ויקרא י"ט י"ז) לא תשנא את אחיך בלבבך אמרו חכמים כגון שראהו לבדו שעבר עבירה והתרה בו ולא חזר הרי זה מצוה לשנאתו עד שיעשה תשובה ויחזור מרשעו תשובה ואם מצאו נבהל במשאו מצוה לפרוק ולטעון עמו ולא יניחנו נוטה למות שמא תשובה אם מצאו נבהל במשאו מצוה לפרוק ולטעון עמו ולא יניחנו נוטה למות שמא ישתהה בשביל ממונו ויבא לידי סכנה והתורה הקפידה על נפשות ישראל בין רשעים בין צדיקים מאחר שהם נלוים אל ה' ומאמינים בעיקר הדת שנאמר (יחזקאל ל"ג י"א) אמר אליהם חי אני נאם ה' אם אחפוץ במות הרשע כי אם בשוב רשע מדרכו וחיה

## (38) פלא יועץ, ערך "שנאה"

... ויש שונא מחמת שרואה את חברו שאינו הולך בדרך טובה ואי לזאת החי יתן אל לבו כי גם הוא חסר חסרונות

## (39) בראשית יג:ה-יב

וְגַם־לְלוֹט הַהֹלֵךְ אֶת־אַבְרָם הָיָה צֹאן־וּבָקָר וְאֹהָלִים: וְלֹא־נָשָׂא אֹתָם הָאָרֶץ לָשֶׁבֶת יַחְדָּו כִּי־הָיָה רְכוּשָׁם רָב וְלֹא יָכְלוּ לָשֶׁבֶת יַחְדָּו: וַיְהִי־רִיב בֵּין רֹעֵי מִקְנֵה־אַבְרָם וּבֵין רֹעֵי מִקְנֵה־לוֹט וְהַכְּנַעֲנִי וְהַפְּרִזִּי אָז יֹשֵׁב בָּאָרֶץ: וַיֹּאמֶר אַבְרָם אֶל־לוֹט אַל־נָא תְהִי מְרִיבָה בֵּינִי וּבֵינֶךָ וּבֵין רֹעַי וּבֵין רֹעֶיךָ כִּי־אֲנָשִׁים אַחִים אֲנָחְנוּ: הֲלֹא כָל־הָאָרֶץ לְפָנֶיךָ הִפָּרֶד נָא מֵעָלָי אִם־הַשְּׂמֹאל וְאֵימִנָה וְאִם־הַיָּמִין וְאַשְׂמְאִילָה: וַיִּשָּׂא־לוֹט אֶת־עֵינָיו וַיַּרְא אֶת־כָּל־כִּכַּר הַיַּרְדֵּן כִּי כֻלָּהּ מַשְׁקֶה לִפְנֵי | שַׁחֵת ד' אֶת־סְדֹם וְאֶת־עֲמֹרָה כְּגַן־ד' כְּאֶרֶץ מִצְרַיִם בֹּאֲכָה צֹעַר: וַיִּבְחַר־לוֹ לוֹט אֵת כָּל־כִּכַּר הַיַּרְדֵּן וַיִּסַּע לוֹט מִקֶּדֶם וַיִּפָּרְדוּ אִישׁ מֵעַל אָחִיו: אַבְרָם יָשַׁב בְּאֶרֶץ־כְּנָעַן וְלוֹט יָשַׁב בְּעָרֵי הַכִּכָּר וַיֶּאֱהַל עַד־סְדֹם:

## (40) משלי יא:י'

בְּטוּב צַדִּיקִים תַּעֲלֹץ קִרְיָה וּבַאֲבֹד רְשָׁעִים רִנָּה:

## (41) קהלת ג:ח

עֵת לֶאֱהֹב וְעֵת לִשְׂנֹא עֵת מִלְחָמָה וְעֵת שָׁלוֹם:

## (42) תענית ז:

אמר רבה בר בר רב הונא כל אדם שיש לו עזות פנים מותר לקרותו רשע שנאמר רשע איש העז בפניו רב נחמן בר יצחק אמר מותר לשנאותו

## (43) קהלת ח:א

מִי כְּהֶחָכָם וּמִי יוֹדֵעַ פֵּשֶׁר דָּבָר חָכְמַת אָדָם תָּאִיר פָּנָיו וְעֹז פָּנָיו יְשֻׁנֶּא:

## (44) תהילים קלט:כא-כב

הֲלוֹא־מְשַׂנְאֶיךָ ד' אֶשְׂנָא וּבִתְקוֹמְמֶיךָ אֶתְקוֹטָט: תַּכְלִית שִׂנְאָה שְׂנֵאתִים לְאוֹיְבִים הָיוּ לִי:

## (45) פסחים קיג:

אמר רבי שמואל בר רב יצחק אמר רב מותר לשנאתו שנאמר כי תראה חמור שנאך רבץ תחת משאו מאי שונא אילימא שונא נכרי והא תניא שונא שאמרו שונא ישראל ולא שונא נכרי אלא פשיטא שונא ישראל

## (46) ברכות נה:

כי הא דרבא כי הוה חליש יומא קמא לא מגלי מכאן ואילך אמר ליה לשמעיה פוק אכריז רבא חלש מאן דרחים לי לבעי עלי רחמי ומאן דסני לי לחדי לי וכתיב בנפל אויבך אל תשמח ובכשלו אל יגל לבך פן יראה ה' ורע בעיניו והשיב מעליו אפו

אחרים, ועל אחת כמה וכמה אם בפירוש מצוה להם, שלא ילכו ויודיעוהו, דבודאי עובר על לאו זה:

ולפעמים עובר המספר וכו' – ואף שאמרו בגמרא דערכין (ט"ז ע"ב) דבשנאה שבלב הכתוב מדבר והובא דבר זה ברמב"ם במדע פ"ו הלכה ה' וז"ל והמכה חבירו והמחרף אע"פ שאינו רשאי אינו עובר בלא תשא. כוונתו דוקא מחרפו, אף שגברה שנאתו עד שפלטה לחוץ עכ"פ ידע חבריו איך להשמר ממנו, אבל בשנאה שבלב אף דלא ידע איך להשמר ממנו, ולכן אסרה התורה את זה בפרטיות וא"כ בעניננו הנ"ל הוא תרתי לגריעותא. א) שגברה שנאתו כ"כ עד שפלטה לחוץ. ב) שלא ידע חבירו איך להשמר ממנו כיון שבפניו הוא מדבר עמו בדרך שלום ואהבה ואף שלא בפניו הוא מכהו בלשון פיו ...ולשון ספרא לא אמרתי אלא בשנאה שבלב. אמנם כשהראה לו השנאה והודיעו שהוא שונא אותו אינו עובר על לאו זה ועובר על "לא תקום ולא תטור" "ואהבת" עכ"ל. הרי שביאר הרמב"ם בפרוש והראה לו וכו' והודיעו וכו' וכן החינוך כתב ג"כ כלשון הזה של הרמב"ם:

### 30 משפטי השלום, ב:ז, ה

ולפי"ז דוקא כשישנאו בלבו עובר על הלא תעשה אבל כשהראה לו השנאה והודיעו שהוא עובר על לאו זה וכו' מ"מ לכאורה למעשה אין נ"מ בזה שעדיין יעבור על לא תקום ולא תטור ועל ואהבת לרעך כמוך שם "ח אלא ששנאת הלב היא חזקה יותר מן הכל והמג"א והחפץ חיים נקאו בדעה זו
וי"א שאפילו את הבעל עבירה שמותר לשנאותו (יתבאר לקמן) אסור לשנאותו בלבו ולהראות לו פנים יפות אלא יראה ויגלה לו את שנאתו, וכ"ש שאסור לשנוא סתם יהודי מדין "ואהבת לרעך כמוך".

### 31 העמק שאלה על שאילתות כז

... אבל בלא סהדי דעביד איסורא אסור לשנאותו כלל, אלא ודאי כל מותר להכותו ולקללו מותר לשנאותו וכ"כ רבינו להלן ...

### 32 תורת האדם לאדם, קובץ ג (הרב אשר וייס) דף 71

ובשאילתות דר' אחאי סי' כ"ז נראה דעובר בלא תשנא "רק" בשנאה שבלב אלא "אף" בשנאה שבלב וק"ו כשהכהו או צערו וז"ל יכול לא ירננו ולא יקללנו כו' ת"ל בלבבך בשנאה שבלב הכתוב מדבר ועיין בכל דבריו דמשמע דרבותא קמ"ל דעובר אף על שנאת הלב ...

### 33 פירוש המאירי על יומא עה.

לעולם לא תהא שנאת אדם מונעתו מלהטיב לחבירו בכל מה שאפשר לו להיטיב והוא שנאמר "לא תשנא את אחיך בלבבך"

### 34 תורת האדם לאדם, קובץ ג (הרב אשר וייס) דף 71

המאירי ביומא ע"ה ע"א כתב לעולם לא תהא שנאת אדם מונעתו מלהטיב בכל מה שאפשר לו להיטיב והוא שנאמר "לא תשנא את אחיך בלבבך" ומתבאר מדבריו עובר בלאו על עצם השנאה שבלבו ומשמע דאין הלאו על המחשבה והרגשת הלב אלא על הנהגה של שנאה ורק כאשר הביאתו לזולתו למנוע ממנו טובה שהיה עושה לו לולי שנאה שבלבו עובר בלאו וזו שיטה מחודשת

### 35 אורחות צדיקים, שער השישי "שנאה"

יש כמה מיני שנאה: יש שונא את חבירו עבור שהזיק לו בממונו, או שהכהו, או עבור שביישהו, או שהוציא עליו שם רע. על כל אלו וכיוצא בהן לא ישנא את חבירו וישתוק, ... יש רעה, והיא שנאת חנם, והיא החריבה בית שני. ושנאה מחמת קנאה היא רעה ממנה. וראוי לאדם לייסר את נפשו להתרחק מהן. ויש שונא את חבירו עבור שאינו גומל לו חסד, או שאינו נותן לו מתנה כפי חפצו, או שאינו מלוהו לו בשעת דחקו. ראוי לאדם להתרחק מכל זה ומכיוצא בו. אך יקבל מאהבה כל מה שיגזור לו הבורא, ברוך הוא, ולא יבטח באדם, ויחשוב: אילו הייתי זוכה מאת המקום, ברוך הוא, היה נותן לידי זולתו מתנת בשר ודם והלואתם ... וגם אומן שונא בני אומנותו – הכל הבל ורעה רבה, כי יחשוב ששום אדם לא יוכל להרויח יותר ממה שגזר לו הבורא. ... ויש שנאה רעה ממנה – כגון בני אדם השונאים עושי טובה ורודפי צדק, כענין שנאמר (תהלים לח כא): "ישטנוני תחת רדפי טוב" ... אמר החכם: אם תרצה שישנאך חברך – בקרהו תמיד, ואם תרצה שיאהבך – בקרהו לעתים רחוקות ...

### 36 משפטי השלום, ב:ח, י'-י"ב

וכ"ש שלא מצינו שום היתר שנאה מחמת קנאה בהצלחת הזולת (כגון בחיי החברה) או בתחרות עמו (כגון בפרנסה) וידוע שמצוי שהאומן שונא בן אומנתו ולפיכך יש להזהר מזה ביותר אולם כאשר קיימות דעות והשקפות שונות בתפיסת החיים (כגון בין חוגים ועדות מפלגות ומשפחות) או כאשר מומים או מחלות הנהוגות או מעשה הזולת דוחים אותו ונמאסים בעיניו (אפילו מחמת קפידא או איסניס בעלמא) מותר למעט בחברתו כל שאינו עושה מחמת שנאה (ולפעמים מומלץ לעשותו כן כאשר עי"ז יוכלו לכבד זא"ז יותר) אולם יש להזהר בכל אלו מביטול מצוות "ואהבת לרעך כמוך".

### 37 פלא יועץ, ערך "אהבת רעים"

ויש סבות שעליהם תתעורר השנאה בין איש ובין אחיו והכל הבל ורעות רוח יש שונא מחמת שכנגדו חטא כנגדו בגופו או בממונו או בכבודו ... ויש שונא מחמת קנאה ...

י״א שאסור לו לשמעון לשמוע את לשנא את ראובן אבל יכול להתרחק ממנו, ואדרבה יש בזה כפיית היצר וכאשר שמעון יוסיף לו אהבה בעה״י עי״ז ישלים עמו ...

## 18) ויקרא יט:יז

לֹא־תִשְׂנָא אֶת־אָחִיךָ בִּלְבָבֶךָ הוֹכֵחַ תּוֹכִיחַ אֶת־עֲמִיתֶךָ וְלֹא־תִשָּׂא עָלָיו חֵטְא:

## 19) ערכין טז

תנו רבנן: (ויקרא י״ט) לא תשנא את אחיך בלבבך יכול לא יכנו, לא יסטרנו, ולא יקללנו? ת״ל: בלבבך, שנאה שבלב הכתוב מדבר.

## 20) בראשית לד:ד

וַיִּרְאוּ אֶחָיו כִּי־אֹתוֹ אָהַב אֲבִיהֶם מִכָּל־אֶחָיו וַיִּשְׂנְאוּ אֹתוֹ וְלֹא יָכְלוּ דַּבְּרוֹ לְשָׁלֹם:

## 21) פירוש רש״י על בראשית לד:ד

ולא יכלו דברו לשלום – מתוך גנותם למדנו שבחם, שלא דברו אחת בפה ואחת בלב:

## 22) מדרש, ילקוט שמעוני, ויקרא יט תריג

"לא תשנא את אחיך" יכול לא תכנו ולא תסרטנו ולא תקללנו, תלמוד לומר בלבבך שבנאה שבלב הכתוב מדבר

## 23) רמב״ם, ספר המצות, לא תעשה שב

... ולשון הספרי לא אמרתי אלא שנאה שבלב אלא אמנם כשהראה לו השנאה והודיעו שהוא שונא אותו אינו עובר על זה הלאו אבל על לא תקום ולא תטור

## 24) רמב״ם, הלכות דעות ו:ה-ו

כל השונא אחד מישראל עובר בלא תעשה שנאמר "לא תשנא את אחיך בלבבך", ואין לוקין על לאו זה לפי שאין בו מעשה, ולא הזהירה תורה אלא על שנאה שבלב, אבל המכה את חבירו והמחרפו אע״פ שאינו רשאי אינו עובר משום לא תשנא. כשיחטא איש לאיש לא ישטמנו וישתוק ... אלא מצוה עליו להודיעו ולומר לו למה עשית לי כך וכך ולמה חטאת לי בדבר פלוני, שנאמר הוכח תוכיח את עמיתך ...

## 25) ספר החינוך, מצוה שלח

שלא לשנוא שנאת הלב אחד מישראל, שנאמר [ויקרא י״ט, י״ז] "לא תשנא את אחיך בלבבך". ולשון ספרא, לא אמרתי אלא שנאה שהיא בלב. וכמו כן בערכין [ט״ז ע״ב] בשנאה שבלב הכתוב מדבר. אבל כשיראה לו שנאה וידוע שהוא שונא אינו עובר על זה הלאו, אמנם הוא עובר על לא תקום ולא תטור, ועובר כמו כן על עשה, שנאמר [שם, שם י״ח] ואהבת לרעך כמוך. ומכל מקום שנאת הלב היא קשה מכל השנאה הגלויה, ועליה תזהיר התורה ביותר:

## 26) בראשית כא:כה

וְהוֹכִחַ אַבְרָהָם אֶת־אֲבִימֶלֶךְ עַל־אֹדוֹת בְּאֵר הַמַּיִם אֲשֶׁר גָּזְלוּ עַבְדֵי אֲבִימֶלֶךְ:

## 27) פירש רמב״ן על ויקרא יט:יז-יח

לא תשנא את אחיך בלבבך – בעבור שדרך השונאים לכסות את שנאתם בלבם כמו שאמר (משלי כו כד) בשפתיו ינכר שונא, הזכיר הכתוב בהווה.
ואמר הוכח תוכיח את עמיתך. מצוה אחרת, ללמדו תוכחת מוסר, "ולא תשא עליו חטא" שיהיה עליך אשם כאשר יחטא ולא הוכחת אותו. ולזה יטה לשון אונקלוס שאמר, ולא תקבל על דיליה חובא, שלא תקבל אתה עונש בחטא שלו. ואחרי כן צוה שתאהוב אותו. והנה השונא את רעהו עובר בלאו, והאוהב לו מקיים עשה:
והנכון בעיני, כי "הוכח תוכיח", כמו והוכיח אברהם את אבימלך (בראשית כא כה). ויאמר הכתוב, אל תשנא את אחיך בלבבך בעשותו לך שלא כרצונך, אבל תוכיחנו מדוע ככה עשית עמדי, ולא תשא עליו חטא לכסות שנאתו בלב ולא תגיד לו, כי בהוכיחך אותו יתנצל לך, או ישוב ויתודה על חטאו ותכפר לו. ואחרי כן יזהיר שלא תנקום ממנו ולא תטור בלבבך מה שעשה לך, כי יתכן שלא ישנא אותו אבל יזכור החטא בלבו, ולפיכך יזהירנו שימחה פשע אחיו וחטאתו מלבו. ואחרי כן יצוה שיאהב לו כמוהו:

## 28) קהלות יעקב, ערכין ד

הרמב״ן ז״ל בפירושו על התורה פ׳ קדושים על הכתוב לא תשנא את אחיך בלבבך הוכח תוכיח את עמיתך מבאר שלפי פשוטו הכל דין זה שלא תשא את השנאה בלב אלא תתווכח עמו על אודות הדבר שמחמתו אתה שונא אותו שמא יתנצל או יברר שאינו כמו שאתה חושב ושמא יבקש מחילתך וכ׳ היראים במצוה ל״ט ע״ש, ולפי׳ ב׳ במה שמודיעו שנאתו לחבירו אכתי עובר בל״ת זו עד שיודיענו עבור מה הוא שונא לו וישמע מה שמשיב לו על זה ... ומשמע לענ״ד דלדעת הרמב״ן ז״ל ויראים היכא ששונאו מחמת קנאה וכיו״ב או שנאת חנם אז עובר לעולם אע״פ שהודיעו שנאתו והתווכח עמו עבור זה ...
ולפי פירש״י ז״ל אין לנו שום מקור דכשמודיע שנאתו ליכא לאו זה, דמה שכתוב "בלבבך" לא לאפוקי מודיע השנאה אלא ללמד שהשנאה שבלב אסרה תורה בין מודיעו בין אינו מודיעו, אלא שהכ׳ מדבר במי שצריך להכותו לשם תוכחה דע״כ שנאה שבלב אסור שאף על פי שעושה מעשה המורה על שנאה כגון מכהו מ״מ לא יהא שונאו באמת ...

## 29) ספר חפץ חיים, הלכות לשון הרע, פתיחה ופירוש באר מים חיים

ד׳"לֹא תִשְׂנָא אֶת אָחִיךָ בִּלְבָבֶךָ", כְּגוֹן אִם הִפְנָיו שָׁלוֹם יְדַבֵּר אֶת רֵעֵהוּ, וְשֶׁלֹּא בְּפָנָיו מַבְאִישׁ אֶת רֵיחוֹ בִּפְנֵי

**1) ויקרא יט:יז**

לֹא־תִשְׂנָא אֶת־אָחִיךָ בִּלְבָבֶךָ הוֹכֵחַ תּוֹכִיחַ אֶת־עֲמִיתֶךָ וְלֹא־תִשָּׂא עָלָיו חֵטְא:

**2) עובדיה א:יב**

וְאַל־תֵּרֶא בְיוֹם־אָחִיךָ בְּיוֹם נָכְרוֹ וְאַל־תִּשְׂמַח לִבְנֵי־יְהוּדָה בְּיוֹם אָבְדָם וְאַל־תַּגְדֵּל פִּיךָ בְּיוֹם צָרָה:

**3) משלי כד:יז-יח**

בִּנְפֹל אוֹיִבְךָ [אוֹיִבְךָ] אַל־תִּשְׂמָח וּבִכָּשְׁלוֹ אַל־יָגֵל לִבֶּךָ: פֶּן־יִרְאֶה ד' וְרַע בְּעֵינָיו וְהֵשִׁיב מֵעָלָיו אַפּוֹ:

**4) אבות ד:יט**

שמואל הקטן אומר, (משלי כד) בנפול אויבך אל תשמח ובכשלו אל יגל לבך, פן יראה יי ורע בעיניו והשיב מעליו אפו:

**5) יומא ט:**

אבל מקדש שני שהיו עוסקין בתורה ובמצות וגמילות חסדים מפני מה חרב מפני שהיתה בו שנאת חנם ללמדך ששקולה שנאת חנם כנגד שלש עבירות עבודה זרה גלוי עריות ושפיכות דמים

**6) שבת לא.**

שוב מעשה בנכרי אחד שבא לפני שמאי אמר לו גיירני על מנת שתלמדני כל התורה כולה כשאני עומד על רגל אחת דחפו באמת הבנין שבידו בא לפני הלל גייריה אמר לו דעלך סני לחברך לא תעביד זו היא כל התורה כולה ואידך פירושה הוא זיל גמור

**7) ספר החינוך, מצוה רלח**

... כי שנאת הלב גורמת רעות גדולות בין בני אדם להיות תמיד חרב איש באחיו ואיש ברעהו והיא סבה לכל המסורות הנעשים בין האנשים והיא המדה הפחותה והנמאסת..

**8) אבות ב:יא**

רבי יהושע אומר, עין הרע, ויצר הרע, ושנאת הבריות, מוציאין את האדם מן העולם:

**9) ברכות כח:**

אמר להם רבן גמליאל לחכמים כלום יש אדם שיודע לתקן ברכת הצדוקים עמד שמואל הקטן ותקנה

**10) מגילה טז:**

אמר רבא לא מפני שאוהבין את מרדכי אלא מפני ששונאים את המן הכין לו

---

אמר רב חמא בר גוריא אמר רב בשביל משקל שני סלעים מילת שהוסיף יעקב ליוסף משאר אחיו נתגלגל הדבר וירדו אבותינו למצרים

**11) אבות דרבי נתן כג**

איזו גבור שבגבורים זהו שכובש את יצרו ... ויש אומרים מי שעושה שונא אוהבו.

**12) רמב"ם, הלכות רוצח יג:יג**

הפוגע בשנים אחד רובץ תחת משאו ואחד פרק מעליו ולא מצא מי שיטעון עמו מצוה לפרוק בתחילה משום צער בעלי חיים ואחר כך טוען במה דברים אמורים בשהיו שניהם שונאים או אוהבים אבל אם היה אחד שונא ואחד אוהב מצוה לטעון עם השונא תחילה כדי לכוף את יצרו הרע:

**13) שמות כג:ה**

כִּי־תִרְאֶה חֲמוֹר שֹׂנַאֲךָ רֹבֵץ תַּחַת מַשָּׂאוֹ וְחָדַלְתָּ מֵעֲזֹב לוֹ עָזֹב תַּעֲזֹב עִמּוֹ:

**14) סנהדרין לט:**

באותה שעה בקשו מלאכי השרת לומר שירה לפני הקדוש ברוך הוא אמר להן הקדוש ברוך הוא מעשה ידי טובעין בים ואתם אומרים שירה לפני

**15) משנה סנהדרין ג:ה**

האוהב והשונא. אוהב, זה שושבינו. שונא, כל שלא דבר עמו שלשה ימים באיבה.

**16) אורחות צדיקים, שער השישי "שנאה"**

השנאה המידה הזאת יש בה לאו, דכתיב (ויקרא יט יז): "לא תשנא את אחיך בלבבך", ובזה הוזהרנו להסיר מנפשנו מידת השנאה. והיא מידה הגורמת עוונות הרבה, כמו לשון הרע, כי השונא את חבירו מספר לעולם בשנאתו, וקובל עליו, ותמיד דורש רעה עליו, ושמח לאידו, וגורמת נזקו שיזיק לו כשיוכל להזיק לו, ונוקם ונוטר לו, ולא ירחם עליו אפילו הוא דחוק מאד. ומחמת השנאה יגנה את מעשיו הטובים, וישניאם בעיניו ובעיני אחרים, ומונע טוב מבעליו, ולא יודה לו על האמת, ואם חייב לו – הוא נוגשו:

**17) משפטי השלום, ב:ח, י'-יב**

מהות השנאה – מי שמתוך הרגשת כעס או שנאה אינו שואל בשלום חבירו הרי זה עובר על "לא תשנא", ואם לא דיבר עם חבירו שלשה ימים מחמת איבה הרי זה בכלל שונא ופסול לדון אותו בב"ד אע"פ שראובן שונא את שמעון או בני ביתו

**60) שולחן ערוך, אורח חיים שטז:ב**

הצד צבי ישן או סומא או חולה או זקן
פטור: הגה המשסה כלב אחר חיה בשבת הוי צידה
(כלבו) וי"א אף בחול אסור לצוד בכלבים משום
מושב לצים (א"ז) :

**61) (רמ"א) דרכי תשובה, יורה דעה קיז:מד**

חיה ועוף – עיין בשו"ת שמש צדקה חו"ד סי'
כז שהסכים לדברי הרב השואל דאותן האנשים
ההולכים לצוד חיה או עוף בכלי זיין בין שעושים
להרויח ולמכור ובין אותן העושים כן לשחוק ולטייל
בעלמא כולן עבדי איסורא דלא מבעיא אותן העושין
למכור הניצוד עושין איסור דאסור לעשות סחורה
בדבר איסור שתתפסו אומנות של עשו הרשע וקניית
מידת אכזריות להמית בריותיו של הקב"ה על לא
דבר וחובה כפולה ומכופלת על אדם שהתעסק
בישובו של עולם ולא בהשחתת הנבראים דרך שחוק
והיתו עי"ש באורך:

**62) בראשית כה:כז**

הוא היה גבר ציד לפני ד' על כן יאמר כנמרד גבור
ציד לפני ד':

**63) ספר החינוך, מצוה תקנ**

כי מטעמי מצוה זו צער בעלי חיים שאסור מן
התורה ...

**64) גיטין נט:**

כל התורה כולה נמי מפני דרכי שלום היא, דכתי':
(משלי ג') "דרכיה דרכי נועם וכל נתיבותיה שלום".

**65) שו"ת נודע ביהודה מהדורא תניינא – יורה דעה י**

... ואמנם מאד אני תמה על גוף הדבר ולא מצינו
איש ציד רק בנמרוד ובעשו ואין זה דרכי בני אברהם

יצחק ויעקב ופוק חזי לומר תבלה ותחדש כתב
מהרי"ו בפסקיו הביאו רמ"א בא"ח סוף סימן רכ"ג
שאין לומר כן על הנעשה בבהמה משום
ורחמיו על כל מעשיו, ואף שרמ"א כתב עליו שהוא
טעם חלוש היינו מצד שאינו חיוב שבשבילו ימיתו
בהמה וכמה עורות יש שכבר מוכן וכמה מתים
מאליהם ויכולים להשתמש בעורותיהם ועם כל זה
סיים רמ"א שרבים מקפידים על זה, ואיך ימית איש
ישראלי בידים בעלי חיים בלי שום צורך רק לגמור
חמדת זמנו להתעסק בצידה ... אבל מי שאין זה
לצורך פרנסתו ואין עיקר כוונתו כלל בשביל פרנסתו
הוא אכזריות. ועד כאן דברתי מצד יושר ההנהגה
שראוי לאדם להרחיק מזה ועכשיו אני אומר אפילו
איסורא איכא שהרי כל העוסקים בזה צריכין להכנס
ביערות ולהכניס עצמם בסכנות גדולות במקום גדודי
חיות ורחמנא אמר ונשמרתם מאד לנפשותיכם, ומי
לנו גדול ואומן בקי בצידה יותר מעשו שהכתוב העיד
עליו ויהי עשו איש יודע ציד וכו' ופוק חזי מה אמר
הוא על עצמו הנה אנכי הולך למות וגו' ואין מקרא
יוצא מידי פשוטו שהיינו שהוא מסתכן בכל יום בין
גדודי חיות וכן פירשו הרמב"ן, ומעתה איך יכניס עצמו
איש יהודי למקום גדודי חיות רעות ... ומעתה אני
אומר שיש בדבר זה איסור וגם סכנה ... ולדרכנו
יובן דזה המהלך במקום סכנה הוא עובר על דברי
תורה דכתיב ונשמרתם מאד לנפשותיכם ... ולכן
יש בדבר זה מדה מגונה דהיינו אכזריות וגם איסורא
וסכנתא וגם הזכרת עונותיו ולכן השומע לי ישכון
בטח השקט ושאנן בביתו ולא יאבד זמנו בדברים
כאלה. ולולא אהבתי להגביר המפורסם במדות
טובות לא הייתי מזדקק להשיב על שאלה כזו. אבל
להיותי יודע שהגביר בכל כחי כחי את כל בני ביתו שלא יתנו
מקום ללשונאי הגביר שנאה מחמת קנאה שימצאו
מקום להתלונן. והיה זה שלום. מנאי הטרוד.

תשובה: תנן במסכת בבא קמא (עט ע"ב) לא יגדל אדם את הכלב אלא אם כן היה קשור בשלשלת, ופרש"י: מפני שנושך ומנבח ומפלת אשה מיראתו. ע"ש. ובגמרא שם (פג ע"א) אמרינן, תנו רבנן לא יגדל אדם את הכלב אלא א"כ קשור בשלשלת, אבל מגדל הוא בעיר הסמוכה לספר [השוכנת סמוך לעובדי כוכבים וצריכה שימור – רש"י], וקושרו ביום ומתירו בלילה, תניא רבי אליעזר הגדול אומר המגדל כלבים כמגדל חזירים למאי נפקא מינא למיקם עליה באורור, והמשיכה הגמ' לבאר שדנביחת הכלב גורם לאשה להפיל את עוברה וממילא נגרם סילוק השכינה כיון שאין השכינה שורה בישראל על פחות משני אלפים ושני רבבות וכו' ... [ועדיין יש להתבונן מאי הוי דינא שיהיה הכלב נמצא בחצר והוא מוסתר שם, וישימו שלט מבחוץ המודיע שיש כאן כלב, דלכאורה סגי בהכי ומהני, שהרי ממילא ירעו ויזהרו ממנו, ... ומכיון שהכלב נמצא בתוך החצר ואין פחד ממנו כ"כ כיון שהוא כלוא שם ואין חשש שיוכל לנשוך, ובהלה מנביחתו נמי ליכא שהרי יש שלט המודיע זאת יש להתיר. וק"ל ... אלא עתה שאנו אומרים דאיכא הכא פלוגתא דהרמב"ם והטור, דהרמב"ם ס"ל לפרש בין כלב רע לכלב סתם, דכלב רע צריך הריגה והיינו הגמ' דדף טו ע"ב גבי ברייתא דר"נ, והמשנה שכתבה דסגי בשלשלת היינו כלב סתם, ולכן הרמב"ם נקט דינא דבשלשלת שרי לגדל הכלב רק בכלב סתם, אבל לעולם כלב רע כאמור י"ל דצריך להורגו ....

ב) באופן שמגדל את הכלב לשם שמירה, יש להתיר בתנאים כדלקמן:

כל שכלב זה נובח על כל מי שהוא אינו מכיר אפילו אינו נושך דינו כדין "כלב רע", וראוי היכא דאפשר להקפיד שיהיה הכלב נמצא בחצר הבית במשך כל היום וגם יהיה קשור שם בשלשלת או ברצועה חזקה שמא יבוא מישהו לבקר את בני הבית ויכנס לחצר והכלב יזיקו ... ובלילה יכול להתיר לו את הרצועה כדי שיוכל הכלב להסתובב בחצר ולשמור משעה שאין לחוש שמא יבואו בני אדם לבקרו, ואולם יש להקפיד שהשער שבחצר יהיה סגור כדי שלא יוכל הכלב לצאת לבחוץ ולהזיק העוברים והשבים, ורק לאדם שיכנס לתוך החצר ללא רשות יוכל הכלב לתופסו ...

### 53) משנה עבודה זרה א:ז
אין מוכרין להם דובין ואריות וכל דבר שיש בו נזק לרבים.

### 54) עבודה זרה טו:
אין מוכרין להם לא זיין ולא כלי זיין, ואין משחיזין להן את הזיין, ואין מוכרין להן לא סדן ולא קולרין, ולא כבלים ולא שלשלאות של ברזל, אחד עובד כוכבים ואחד כותי ... והאמר רב נחמן אמר רבה בר אבוה: כדרך שאמרו אסור למכור לעובד כוכבים, כך אסור למכור לישראל החשוד למכור לעובד כוכבים ... א"ר דימי בר אבא: כדרך שאסור למכור לעובד כוכבים, אסור למכור ללסטים ישראל.

### 55) עבודה זרה טו:
והאמר רב נחמן אמר רבה בר אבוה: כדרך שאמרו אסור למכור לישראל החשוד למכור לעובד כוכבים, כך אסור למכור לישראל החשוד למכור לעובד כוכבים ... א"ר דימי בר אבא: כדרך שאסור למכור לעובד כוכבים, אסור למכור ללסטים ישראל.

### 56) רמב"ם, הלכות עבודת כוכבים ט:ח
כשם שאין מוכרין לעובד כוכבים דברים שמחזיקין בהן ידיהן לעבודת כוכבים כך אין מוכרין להם דבר שיש בו נזק לרבים כגון דובים ואריות וכלי זיין וכבלים ושלשלאות ואין משחיזין להם את הזיין, וכל שאסור למוכרו לעובד כוכבים אסור למכור לישראל החשוד למכור לעובד כוכבים, וכן אסור למכור כלי זין לישראל ליסטם.

### 57) ויקרא יז:יג ופירושי מזרחי וגור אריה (על רש"י)
ואיש איש מבני ישראל ומן הגר הגר בתוכם אשר יצוד ציד חיה או עוף אשר יאכל ושפך את דמו וכסהו בעפר:

### 58) פירושי מזרחי וגור אריה (על רש"י) על ויקרא יז:יג
אשר יצוד – אין לי אלא ציד, אווזין ותרנגולין מניין, תלמוד לומר, "ציד". בתורת כהנים ומייתי לה בפרק כסוי הדם, "תנו רבנן, 'אשר יצוד' אין לי אלא 'אשר יצוד', צודין ועומדין מאליהן, כגון אווזין ותרנגולין מניין, תלמוד לומר, 'ציד' מכל מקום" אפילו יהיה צד ועומד בלתי שיצודו אותו, כגון אווזין ותרנגולין. ור"ל כן מה תלמוד לומר 'אשר יצוד', למדה תורה דרך ארץ, שלא יאכל בשר אלא בהזמנה הזאת". פרש"י, "כאילו הוא צד, שאינה מזומנת לו, כלומר לא יאכל בשר תדיר, שלא יעני":

תלמוד לומר ציד. פירוש, כי "ציד" נקרא אף על גב שהוא כבר נצוד ועומד, אפילו כי נקרא "ציד", שהרי הוא בביתו נצוד:

### 59) משנה ביצה ג:א-ב
אין צדין דגים מן הביברין ביום טוב, ואין נותנין לפניהם מזונות. אבל צדין חיה ועוף מן הביברין, ונותנין לפניהם מזונות. רבן שמעון בן גמליאל אומר, לא כל הביברין שוין. זה הכלל, כל המחוסר צידה אסור, ושאינו מחוסר צידה מותר: מצודות חיה ועוף ודגים שעשאן מערב יום טוב, לא יטול מהן ביום טוב, אלא אם כן יודע שנצודו מערב יום טוב. ומעשה בנכרי אחד, שהביא דגים לרבן גמליאל, ואמר, מותרין הן, אלא שאין רצוני לקבל הימנו:

כ' ד' ודבר באזני זקני העיר ההיא את דבריו, ולא
ששוו דבריהם לדבריו, וכן עיר שאין בה זקנים אינה
קולטת שנ' זקני העיר ההיא. השגת הראב"ד עיר
מקלט שיש בה רוצחים. א"א שיש בה רוב רוצחים.

### 45) מכות י.
ואין מוכרין בהן (בעיר מקלט) לא כלי זיין ולא כלי
מצודה, דברי רבי נחמיה, וחכמים מתירין ושין,
שאין פורסין בתוכן מצודות, ואין מפשילין לתוכן
חבלים, כדי שלא תהא רגל גואל הדם מצויה שם.

### 46) שיח יצחק על מכות
ושין שאין פורסין מצודות ואין מפשילין לתוכן
חבלים נראה שאין הטעם אף דחכמ' מתירין למכור כלי
זיין משום דלא חייש' שיהרוג אותו גוה"ד שהרי אם
הרגו בתוך העיר מקלטו נהרג עליו וא"כ לא יהרגנו.
רק חייש' שיזדמן לו הרוצח לגוה"ד אצל המצודות
הפרוסין, וישליך אותו להמצודה ויאמר שנהרג
מאליו או לתוך החבלים ויאמר שנחנק מאליו ע"י
איזה מכשול ובזה הכול מודין וז"פ:

### 47) בבא קמא עט: ורש"י שם
משנה: ... אין מגדלין חזירין בכל מקום. לא יגדל
אדם את הכלב אלא אם כן היה קשור בשלשלת ...
גמרא: ...אין מגדלין בהמה דקה בארץ ישראל, אבל
מגדלין במדבר שביהודה ובמדבר שבספר עכו. ואף
על פי שאמרו אין מגדלין בהמה דקה, אבל מגדלין
בהמה גסה, לפי שאין גוזרין גזרה על הצבור אלא אם
כן רוב צבור יכולין לעמוד בה ... כשם שאמרו אין
מגדלין בהמה דקה, כך אמרו אין מגדלין חיה דקה
ר' ישמעאל אומר: מגדלין כלבים כופרין, וחתולים,
וקופין, וחולדות סנאים, מפני שעשויים לנקר את
הבית.
**את הכלב** – מפני שנושך ומנבח ומפלת אשה מיראתו.
**כלבים כופריים** – קטנים וננסים הם ל"א כלבים
גדולים של ציידים ואין מזיקין.
**לנקר את הבית**- מן העכברים.

### 48) בבא קמא פג.
לא יגדל אדם את הכלב אא"כ קשור בשלשלאות כו'.
תנו רבנן: לא יגדל אדם את הכלב אלא אם כן קשור
בשלשלת, אבל מגדל הוא בעיר הסמוכה לספר,
וקושרו ביום ומתירו בלילה. תניא, רבי אליעזר
הגדול אומר: המגדל כלבים כמגדל חזירים ...
והיתה אשה מעוברת ביניהם וראויה להשלים, ונבח
בה כלב והפילה ...

### 49) שולחן ערוך, חושן משפט תט:א, ג
אין מגדלים בהמה דקה בארץ ישראל מפני שדרכם
לרעות בשדות של אחרים והיזקם מצוי, אבל מגדלים
בסוריא ובמדברות שבארץ ישראל, והאידנא שאין
מצוי שיהיו לישראל בארץ ישראל שדות, נראה דשרי.

---

אסור לגדל כלב רע, אלא אם כן הוא אסור
בשלשלאות של ברזל וקשור בהם, ובעיר הסמוכה
לספר מותר לגדלו, וקושרו ביום ומתירו בלילה.
**הגה:ויש** אומרים דהשתא שאנו שרויין בין העכו"ם
ואומות בכל ענין שרי, ופוק חזי מאי עמא דבר
(הגהת אלפסי החדשים), מיהו נראה אם הוא כלב
רע שיש לחוש שיזיק בני אדם דאסור לגדלו, אלא אם
כן קשור בשלשלאות של ברזל.

### 50) שו"ת פנים מאירות ב:קלג
וכל כי האי מילתא לימרי משמאי בשוקי ובבראי
דכסוי מהני לאצולי משום בזיון כמו שמהני במזוזה
לענין היתר תשמיש לכסות השם ה"נ דכוותי'. מה
שכתב מכ"ת שדברי רש"י בכ"ק דף פ"ה ע"א ד"ה
בכל שם המדינה כו' ואשמועינן דרב נחמן דהואיל
ויש בעל יישוב קבוע וישראל הרבה מותר לגדל
כלבים בעיר הסמוכה לספר כאלו היא מא"י ...
וממילא ידעינן דכל עיר הסמוכה לספר מותר לגדל
אלא ע"כ דהתנא דברייתא לא דיבר אלא בא"י משום
דרוב ישראל שם וצריכין שמירה מאויבי' אבל בשאר
ארצות לא התירו בשביל מעט ישראל הדרים בה
אפילו בסמוכה לספר וקמ"ל ר"נ בבל כעיר הסמוכה
לספר ותרגומה נהרדעי אשמועינן ר"נ הואיל ויש
בבבל יישוב קבוע וישראל הרבה מותר לגדל כלבים
בעיר הסמוכה לספר כאלו היא מא"י דמותר לגדל
בשביל שמירת רוב ישראל ה"נ בנהרדעי כן הן
דברי רש"י וק"ל וה"י זה שלום ממני אהובו נאמנו
מאיר.

### 51) שו"ת שאלת יעב"ץ א:יז
... ומספקא עלך מילתא אי הני בני מלאכה נינהו,
מסתברא דחשיבי נמי בני מלאכה קצת. דהחתול
מלאכתו מרובה לצוד העכברים. ובהדיא חשיב ליה
תלמודא לבעל מלאכה בהשאול (צ"ז) גבי ההוא
שונרא דחבור עליה עכברי ואכלוהו. דדיינינן ליה
כמה מחמת מלאכה וכן הכלב עבודתו גדולה. עבד
נאמן לאדוניו לשמור הבית מאריא וגנבי ביום
ובלילה. ואף על פי שאינו עושה מעשה ... שהמגדל
כלבים כמגדל חזירים למיקם עלה בארור. ולא
חילקו הפוסקים בין כלב לכלב. דלא קיי"ל כמאן
דשרי בכופרים. דיחידאה הוא. ושכיחא נמי סכנתא
בכולהו כמו שאירע כמה פעמים ר"ל וכל סכנתא
לחומרא. ואפי' מאן דפליג בכופרים. נ"ל דאפ"ה לא
שרי טפי מחד. לנטורי ביתא בלחוד.

### 52) שו"ת עטרת פז א:ג חושן משפט סימן ח
בדבר שאלתך שאלת חכם אם מותר לאנשי מקומכם
הי"ו לגדל כלב בחצר הבית, וזאת בעיקר מטעמי
שמירה ובטחון כיון שמקום מושבכם הוא סמוך
לכפרים הערבים אבו גוש וכפר עין נקובה, ומפני
חשש של נפש ורכוש ח"ו רוצים לגדל כלב לשמירה
אם מותר?

המקצר על המאריך.

כי חרבך הנפת עליה ותחלליה – ותעשה אותו מזבח חולין לפני, וחללת הקדושה שבו כי איני חפץ בשום דבר היזק:

### 32) ישעיהו ב:ד

וְשָׁפַט בֵּין הַגּוֹיִם וְהוֹכִיחַ לְעַמִּים רַבִּים וְכִתְּתוּ חַרְבוֹתָם לְאִתִּים וַחֲנִיתוֹתֵיהֶם לְמַזְמֵרוֹת לֹא־יִשָּׂא גוֹי אֶל־גּוֹי חֶרֶב וְלֹא־יִלְמְדוּ עוֹד מִלְחָמָה:

### 33) סנהדרין פב.

מיכן שאין נכנסין בכלי זיין לבית המדרש.

### 34) בית יוסף על טור, אורח חיים קנא

כתוב בארחות חיים (הל' ביהכ"נ אות ז) בשם הר"מ (תשב"ץ קטן סי' רב) שאסור ליכנס לבית הכנסת בסכין ארוך לפי שהתפלה מארכת ימיו של אדם והסכין מקצרם וליכנס בכיסו נמי אסור כדאמרינן (ברכות נד.) שלא יכנס להר הבית באפונדתו והגיה עליו ה"ר פרץ (שם) מיהו אין לחוש כי אם בגילוי הראש ע"כ. ובמסכת סופרים (פי"ד הט"ו) כתוב מי שראשו מגולה לא יוציא הזכרה מפיו עכ"ל:

### 35) שולחן ערוך, אורח חיים קנא:ו

מותר ליכנס בבהכ"נ במקלו ובתרמילו ובאפונדתו (פי' מיני כיסים תרגום ובילקוט ובתרמיליה). ויש אוסרים ליכנס בו סכין ארוך או בראש מגולה:

### 36) משנה שבת ו:ד

לא יצא האיש (בשבת) לא בסייף ולא בקשת, ולא בתריס, ולא באלה, ולא ברומח, ואם יצא חייב חטאת. רבי אליעזר אומר: תכשיטין הן לו, וחכמים אומרים: אינן אלא לגנאי, שנאמר: (ישעיהו ב) וכתתו חרבותם לאתים וחניתותיהם למזמרות ולא ישא גוי אל גוי חרב ולא ילמדו עוד מלחמה.

### 37) שולחן ערוך, אורח חיים שא:ז

... הלכך לא יצא איש לא בסייף ולא בקשת ולא בתריס (פי' מגן) ולא באלה ולא ברומח ולא בכלים שאינם תכשיט, ואם יצא חייב.

### 38) שבת סג.

ואמרי לה אמר רבי אבא אמר רבי שמעון בן לקיש: כל המגדל כלב רע בתוך ביתו מונע חסד מתוך ביתו

### 39) פירוש מהרש"א על שבת סג.

כל המגדל כלב רע בתוך ביתו מונע כו'. כבר אמרו במס' ב"ק אסור לאדם לגדל כלב רע שנאמר לא תשים דמים בביתך אבל הכא הוסיף דאל יגדל כלב אפי' הוא ידוע בו שאינו כלב רע ומשום דמונע חסד גו' דהאורחים והעניים לא ידעו בו שאינו רע וסוברים שהוא רע ויראים ממנו מלבא לביתו וכדמיתי הך

---

עובדא דלא היה היה הכלב רע ולא היה יכול להזיק ומתוך שהיתה סבורה שהוא רע הפילה ...

### 40) שו"ת יחוה דעת ה:יח

**שאלה:** חייל המצווייד בנשק, האם רשאי להיכנס לבית הכנסת עם הרובה או האקדח שעליו?

**תשובה:** ... בסיכום: נכון ורצוי מאוד שהחייל הנכנס לבית הכנסת להתפלל יכסה את נשקו תחת בגדיו, ולא יראה החוצה. ואם אי אפשר לו לכסותו, כגון רובה וכדומה, ויש צורך שישא נשקו עמו בגלל סיבה בטחונית וכיוצא בזה, יש להקל להיכנס עם הנשק לבית הכנסת לתפלה.

### 41) משנה בבא קמא א:ד

הזאב והארי והדוב והנמר והברדלס והנחש. הרי אלו מועדין. רבי אליעזר אומר בזמן שהן בני תרבות. אינן מועדין. והנחש מועד לעולם.

### 42) רמב"ם, הלכות נזקי ממון א:ו, שולחן ערוך, חושן משפט שפט:ח

חמשה מיני בהמה מועדין מתחלת ברייתן להזיק ואפילו הן תרבות, לפיכך אם הזיקו או המיתו בנגיחה או בנשיכה ודריסה וכיוצא בהן חייב נזק שלם, ואלו הן: הזאב והארי והדוב והנמר והברדלס, וכן הנחש שנשך הרי זה מועד ואפילו היה בן תרבות. חמשה מיני חיה מועדים מתחלת ברייתן להזיק אפילו אם הם בני תרבות, לפיכך אם הזיקו או המיתו בנגיחה או בנשיכה ודריסה וכיוצא בהם חייב נזק שלם, ואלו הם: הזאב, והארי, והדוב, והנמר, והברדלס, וכן הנחש שנשך, הרי זה מועד ואפילו היה בן תרבות, ויש אומרים דוקא נחש מועד לכל מיני היזק, אבל האחרים אינן מועדין אלא מה שדרכן בכך, כגון ארי לדרוס וזאב לטרוף, אבל לא איפכא

### 43) במדבר לה:ט-יג

וַיְדַבֵּר ד' אֶל־מֹשֶׁה לֵּאמֹר: דַּבֵּר אֶל־בְּנֵי יִשְׂרָאֵל וְאָמַרְתָּ אֲלֵהֶם כִּי אַתֶּם עֹבְרִים אֶת־הַיַּרְדֵּן אַרְצָה כְּנָעַן: וְהִקְרִיתֶם לָכֶם עָרִים עָרֵי מִקְלָט תִּהְיֶינָה לָכֶם וְנָס שָׁמָּה רֹצֵחַ מַכֵּה־נֶפֶשׁ בִּשְׁגָגָה: וְהָיוּ לָכֶם הֶעָרִים לְמִקְלָט מִגֹּאֵל וְלֹא יָמוּת הָרֹצֵחַ עַד־עָמְדוֹ לִפְנֵי הָעֵדָה לַמִּשְׁפָּט: וְהֶעָרִים אֲשֶׁר תִּתֵּנוּ שֵׁשׁ־עָרֵי מִקְלָט תִּהְיֶינָה לָכֶם:

### 44) רמב"ם, הלכות רוצח ז:ד-ו

שאר הלוים השוכנים בערי מקלט כשימות אחד מהן אינו נקבר בעיר ולא בתוך התחום, שנ' (במדבר לה:ג) "ומגרשיהם יהיו לבהמתם ולרכושם ולכל חיתם", לחיים ניתנו ולא לקבורה. רוצח שהרג בשגגה בעיר מקלטו גולה משכונה לשכונה ואינו יוצא מן העיר, ובן לוי שהרג במדינתו גולה למדינה אחרת מערי הלוים, אם הרג חוץ מערי הלוים וברח לעירו הרי זה קולטו. עיר מקלט שרובה רצחנים אינה קולטת, שנ' (יהושע

---

**17) יומא פה:**
והתורה אמרה: בא להרגך השכם להרגו.

**18) במדבר כה:טז-יח**
וַיְדַבֵּר ד' אֶל-מֹשֶׁה לֵּאמֹר: צָרוֹר אֶת-הַמִּדְיָנִים וְהִכִּיתֶם אוֹתָם: כִּי-צֹרְרִים הֵם לָכֶם בְּנִכְלֵיהֶם אֲשֶׁר-נִכְּלוּ לָכֶם עַל-דְּבַר פְּעוֹר וְעַל-דְּבַר כָּזְבִּי בַת-נְשִׂיא מִדְיָן אֲחֹתָם הַמֻּכָּה בְיוֹם-הַמַּגֵּפָה עַל-דְּבַר פְּעוֹר:

**19) מדרש תנחומא, פנחס ג**
וידבר ה' וגו' צרור את המדינים וגו' למה כי צוררים הם לכם מכאן ארז"ל אם בא להרגך השכם להרגו

**20) שמות כב:ב**
אִם-זָרְחָה הַשֶּׁמֶשׁ עָלָיו דָּמִים לוֹ שַׁלֵּם יְשַׁלֵּם אִם-אֵין לוֹ וְנִמְכַּר בִּגְנֵבָתוֹ:

**21) סנהדרין עב.**
תנו רבנן אין לו דמים אם זרחה השמש עליו וכי השמש עליו בלבד זרחה אלא אם ברור לך הדבר כשמש שאין לו שלום עמך הרגהו ואם לאו אל תהרגהו ... לא קשיא, כאן באב על הבן, כאן בבן על האב.

**22) מדרש מכילתא, משפטים נזיקין ו**
אם זרחה השמש עליו וכי השמש בלבד עליו זרחה והלא על כל העולם זרחה אלא מה שמש זה שלום בעולם אף זה אם ידוע בו שבשלום הרי זה חייב.

**23) רמב"ם, הלכות גניבה ט:י'-י"א**
היה הדבר ברור לבעל הבית שזה הגנב בא עליו אינו הורגו ולא בא אלא על עסקי ממון אסור להרגו, ואם הרגו הרי זה הורג נפש, שנ' שמות כ"ב ב' אם זרחה השמש עליו, אם ברור לך הדבר כשמש שיש לו שלום עמך אל תהרגהו, לפיכך אב הבא במחתרת על בנו אינו נהרג שודאי שאינו הורגו, אבל הבן הבא על אביו נהרג. וכן הגנב שגנב ויצא או שלא גנב ומצאו יוצא מן המחתרת הואיל ופנה עורף ואינו רודף יש לו דמים, וכן אם הקיפוהו עדים או בני אדם אע"פ שעדיין הוא ברשות זה שבא עליו אינו נהרג, ואין צריך לומר אם בא לבית דין שאינו נהרג

**24) בראשית ג:כד**
וַיְגָרֶשׁ אֶת-הָאָדָם וַיַּשְׁכֵּן מִקֶּדֶם לְגַן עֵדֶן אֶת-הַכְּרֻבִים וְאֵת לַהַט הַחֶרֶב הַמִּתְהַפֶּכֶת לִשְׁמֹר אֶת דֶּרֶךְ עֵץ הַחַיִּים:

**25) בראשית ד:כב ופירוש רש"י**
וְצִלָּה גַם-הִוא יָלְדָה אֶת-תּוּבַל קַיִן לֹטֵשׁ כָּל-חֹרֵשׁ נְחֹשֶׁת וּבַרְזֶל וַאֲחוֹת תּוּבַל קַיִן נַעֲמָה:
תובל קין – תובל אומנתו של קין. תובל לשון

תבלין תיבל והתקין אומנתו של קין לעשות כלי זיין לרוצחים:

**26) פירוש רמב"ן על בראשית ד:כג**
... אבל הנראה בעיני, כי היה למך איש חכם מאד בכל מלאכת מחשבת, ולמד לבנו הבכור ענין המרעה כפי טבעי הבהמות, ולמד את השני חכמת הנגון, ולמד את השלישי ללטוש ולעשות חרבות ורמחים וחניתות וכל כלי המלחמה והיו נשיו מתפחדות שלא יענש, כי הביא החרב והרציחה בעולם, והנה הוא תופש מעשה אבותיו בידו, כי הוא בן המרצח הראשון, וברא משחית לחבל והוא אמר להן אני לא הרגתי איש לפצעים ולא ילד לחבורות כאשר עשה קין, ולא יענישני השם, אבל ישמרני מן ההריגה יותר ממנו והזכיר כן לומר, כי לא בחרב וחנית יכול אדם להרוג בפצעים וחבורות, שימית במיתה רעה יותר מן החרב, ואין החרב גורם הרציחה, ואין על העושו חטא:

**27) שמות יג:יח**
וַיַּסֵּב אֱלֹקים | אֶת-הָעָם דֶּרֶךְ הַמִּדְבָּר יַם-סוּף וַחֲמֻשִׁים עָלוּ בְנֵי-יִשְׂרָאֵל מֵאֶרֶץ מִצְרָיִם:

**28) פירושי אבן עזרא, רשב"ם, רבינו בחיי על שמות יג:יח**
אבן עזרא: ... כי ביד רמה יצאו בכלי מלחמה. ולא כמו עבדים בורחים:
רשב"ם: וחמושים – בכלי זיין שהיו הולכים לירש את ארץ כנען כמו שכתוב למעלה ואומר אעלה אתכם מעני מצרים אל ארץ הכנעני וגו'. וכן תעברו חמושים דיהושע:
רבינו בחיי: וחמושים עלו בני ישראל. על דרך הפשט יצאו ישראל ממצרים חלוצים כאנשי צבא היוצאים למלחמה, ואף על פי שאין צבא ישראל כשר העמים שיהיו צריכים להזדיין כנגד האויבים, דרך התורה לצוות שיתנהג אדם במקצת בדרך הטבע והמקרה ואחרי כן יפעל הנס

**29) שמואל ב' כב:לה**
מְלַמֵּד יָדַי לַמִּלְחָמָה וְנִחַת קֶשֶׁת-נְחוּשָׁה זְרֹעֹתָי:

**30) שמות כ:כא-כב**
מִזְבַּח אֲדָמָה תַּעֲשֶׂה-לִּי וְזָבַחְתָּ עָלָיו אֶת-עֹלֹתֶיךָ וְאֶת-שְׁלָמֶיךָ אֶת-צֹאנְךָ וְאֶת-בְּקָרֶךָ בְּכָל-הַמָּקוֹם אֲשֶׁר אַזְכִּיר אֶת-שְׁמִי אָבוֹא אֵלֶיךָ וּבֵרַכְתִּיךָ: וְאִם-מִזְבַּח אֲבָנִים תַּעֲשֶׂה-לִּי לֹא-תִבְנֶה אֶתְהֶן גָּזִית כִּי חַרְבְּךָ הֵנַפְתָּ עָלֶיהָ וַתְּחַלְלֶהָ:

**31) פירושי רש"י ובכור שור על שמות כ:כב**
ותחללה – הא למדת שאם הנפת עליה ברזל חללת (פ"ג דמדות) שהמזבח נברא להאריך ימיו של אדם והברזל נברא לקצר ימיו של אדם אין זה בדין שיונף

**1) דברים ד:ט**

רַק הִשָּׁמֶר לְךָ וּשְׁמֹר נַפְשְׁךָ מְאֹד פֶּן תִּשְׁכַּח אֶת הַדְּבָרִים אֲשֶׁר רָאוּ עֵינֶיךָ וּפֶן יָסוּרוּ מִלְּבָבְךָ כָּל יְמֵי חַיֶּיךָ וְהוֹדַעְתָּם לְבָנֶיךָ וְלִבְנֵי בָנֶיךָ:

**2) דברים ד:טו**

וְנִשְׁמַרְתֶּם מְאֹד לְנַפְשֹׁתֵיכֶם כִּי לֹא רְאִיתֶם כָּל תְּמוּנָה בְּיוֹם דִּבֶּר ד' אֲלֵיכֶם בְּחֹרֵב מִתּוֹךְ הָאֵשׁ:

**3) חולין י.**

ש"מ: חמירא סכנתא מאיסורא, ש"מ.

**4) שולחן ערוך, אורח חיים קעג:ב**

... וחמירא סכנתא מאיסורא

**5) תהילים קכא:ז**

ד' יִשְׁמָרְךָ מִכָּל רָע יִשְׁמֹר אֶת נַפְשֶׁךָ:

**6) דברים כב:ח**

כִּי תִבְנֶה בַּיִת חָדָשׁ וְעָשִׂיתָ מַעֲקֶה לְגַגֶּךָ וְלֹא תָשִׂים דָּמִים בְּבֵיתֶךָ כִּי יִפֹּל הַנֹּפֵל מִמֶּנּוּ:

**7) פירוש רש"י על דברים כב:ח**

מעקה - גדר סביב לגג ואונקלוס תרגם תיקא כגון תיק שמשמר מה שבתוכו:
**כי יפול הנופל** - ראוי זה ליפול ואעפ"כ לא תתגלגל מיתתו על ידך שמגלגלין זכות ע"י זכאי וחובה ע"י חייב:

**8) פירוש רבינו בחיי על דברים כב:ח**

רבינו בחיי: **ועשית מעקה לגגך** - על דרך הפשט יזהיר שישתמר האדם מן הסכנה, כענין שכתוב (דברים ד, ט) השמר לך ושמור נפשך מאד, ולכך יצוה כי כשיבנה ביתו שיעשה מעקה לגגו ולא יניח ברשותו נזק ומכשול להכשל בו בני אדם, ולא ישים דמים בביתו, וכענין זה המגדל כלב רע או המעמיד סולם רעוע בתוך ביתו וכן הזכירו ז"ל. כי יפול הנופל, שמא יפול:

**9) שולחן ערוך, חושן משפט תכז:ו-ח, י**

כל המניח גגו בלא מעקה ביטל מצות עשה ועבר על לא תעשה, שנאמר (שם) ולא תשים דמים בביתך.
אחד הגג ואחד כל דבר שיש בו סכנה וראוי שיכשול בה אדם וימות, כגון שהיתה לו באר או בור בחצירו, בין שיש בו מים בין שאין בו מים, חייב לעשות חוליא גבוה י' טפחים או לעשות לה כיסוי, כדי שלא יפול בה אדם וימות.

---

וכן כל מכשול שיש בו סכנת נפשות, מצות עשה להסירו ולהשמר ממנו ולהזהר בדבר יפה, שנאמר (דברים ב:ט) "השמר לך ושמור נפשך", ואם לא הסיר והניח המכשולות המביאים לידי סכנה, ביטל מצות עשה ועובר בלא תשים דמים.
כל העובר על דברים אלו וכיוצא בהם, ואמר הריני מסכן בעצמי ומה לאחרים עלי בכך או איני מקפיד בכך מכין אותו מכת מרדות, והנזהר מהם תבא עליו ברכת טוב.

**10) בבא קמא טו:**

דתניא, ר' נתן אומר: מנין שלא יגדל אדם כלב רע בתוך ביתו, ולא יעמיד סולם רעוע בתוך ביתו? שנאמר (דברים כ"ב) "ולא תשים דמים בביתך".

**11) ויקרא יט:יד**

לֹא תְקַלֵּל חֵרֵשׁ וְלִפְנֵי עִוֵּר לֹא תִתֵּן מִכְשֹׁל וְיָרֵאתָ מֵּאֱלֹקֶיךָ אֲנִי ד':

**12) גיטין נט:**

כל התורה כולה נמי מפני דרכי שלום היא, דכתי': (משלי ג') "דרכיה דרכי נועם וכל נתיבותיה שלום".

**13) רמב"ם, ספר המצות, מצות לא תעשה רצב**

שהזהירנו מהרוג מחוייבי מיתה כשנראה שכבר עשה חטא שנתחייב עליו הריגה קודם הגיעו לבית דין אבל נביאהו לבית דין בהכרח ונעיד עליו בעדים לפניהם ... ואפילו היה בית דין הגדול הם שראוהו הורג והם כלם עדות תבא העדות אצל בית דין אחר ואחר ידינוהו.

**14) שמות כב:א**

אִם בַּמַּחְתֶּרֶת יִמָּצֵא הַגַּנָּב וְהֻכָּה וָמֵת אֵין לוֹ דָּמִים:

**15) פירוש רש"י על שמות כב:א**

**אין לו דמים** - אין זו רציחה, הרי הוא כמת מעיקרו. כאן למדתך תורה, אם בא להרגך השכם להרגו, וזה להרגך בא, שהרי יודע הוא שאין אדם מעמיד עצמו וראוה שנוטלין ממונו בפניו ושותק, לפיכך, על מנת כן בא, שאם יעמוד בעל הממון כנגדו, יהרגנו (סנהדרין עב:):

**16) סנהדרין עב.**

אמר רבא מאי טעמא דמחתרת חזקה אין אדם מעמיד עצמו על ממונו והאי מימר אמר אי אזילנא קאי לאפאי ולא שביק לי ואי קאי לאפאי קטילנא ליה והתורה אמרה אם בא להרגך השכם להורגו

היצירה משא"כ בקלטות.

ב אסור לצרוב דיסקים של תוכנות בלא רשות בעלי היצירה המקורית.

ג בתוכנות מחשב שעלותם גבוהה גם מה שמעתיק לצורך עצמו נחשב כמעתיק לצורך מסחר ואסור להעתיק גם אם סוברים שאין זכויות יוצרים מן התורה הואיל ויש איסור מצד דינא דמלכותא או מצד המנהג ואין הבדל אם בעלי היצירה יהודים או שאינם יהודים, ויש הסובר שגם באופן זה אין איסור אם מעתיק למטרה עצמית שאינה מסחרית.

ד ויש מי שמתיר להעתיק תוכנה שנפרצה לגמרי וכל אחד מעתיקה וכבר לא שייך שהבעלים ימכרו תוכנות חדשות דיש בזה יאוש ומותר אפ' למטרה מסחרית, ויש מי שאוסר בזה, דס"ל שיאוש שייך רק מה שתחת בעלות אדם פרטי ולא כששייך לחברה שיש לה סניפים.

ה לכו"ע אסור לקנות תקליטורים מעותקים מאלו המוכרים סחורה גנובה או גזולה או שהעתיקה באיסור וכן אסור לקבל בחובו או בעד טובה שעשה להנותן או לעשות טובה בשביל המתנה משום דמסייע ידי עוברי עבירה.

ו וכשאסור להעתיק תקליטור ותוכנה האיסור הוא גם על גירסא ישנה, ויש מי שכתב שיש להתיר את הגירסא ישנה שאין משווקים אותה יותר.

ז לפצח תוכנה לשבור קודים המקצועיים והגנות של תוכנות או להכניס וירוסים לכו"ע אסור.

ח תוכנת פונטים דהיינו סוגי אותיות סדר נקרא יצירה לכל דבר (וע"ע בפרק ה' סעי' כז)

ט ויש מי שאומר שהסיכונה מחשב ובתוך הדיסק קשיח יש תוכנות מועתקות מותר לקונה להשתמש בהם ברם לכתחילה יש לברר אם יש בהם תוכנות יקרות או רק משחקי מחשב שאז דינם כקלטות מוזיקה ונראה שלפי הסוברים שיש זכויות יוצרים ובעלות על הכמוה יש לו למחוק את התוכנות המועתקות ולא להשתמש בהם ועוד נראה שגם לדעות האוסרות להפר זכויות יוצרים מדין השגת גבול יש למוחקם וזאת באם נאמר שחרמות הוי איסור חפצא וכ"ש באם המוכר מוחזק למעתיק.

י אדם פרטי שהעתיק או שקיבל יצירה מועתקת ממי שאינו מוחזק למעתיק לדעות האוסרות רק משום השגת גבול הדין יהיה תלוי רק באם נאמר שחרמות הוי איסור חפצא והמיקל באופן שבעלי הזכויות הם אינם יהודים יש לו על מי לסמוך.

יא כל חברה המוכרת תקליטורים וכדומה ומודיעה על גבי התקליטור שאינה מוכרת את המוצר אלא רק זכות שימוש בו בלבד ואסור להעתיקו הן לעצמו והן לאחרים אפי' שלא לצרכי מסחר הרי יש לזה תוקף הלכתי לכל הדעות ואסור להעתיקו הן לעצמו והן לאחרים אפי' שלא לצרכי מסחר, וכן אסור לקנות מן המעתיקים והמעתיקים מן המעתיקים לעולם וכל הקונה מהם הרי הוא בגדר מסייע לידי עוברי עבירה.

---

יב בכח בעלי היצירה להגביל את השימוש רק למחשב אחד אף שבבעלותו שני מחשבים.

**59) משנת זכות היוצר, פרק יח, פסקי הרב אלישיב** פסקי דינים ותשובות ממרן הגרי"ש אלישיב שליט"א

1. היוצר יצירה האם יש לו בעלות על היצירה ומה המקור לזה?

תשובה: יש לו בעלות, וזהו סברא מוצקת מאד דבר שהשכל מחייבו (יעיין תשובת השו"מ חלק א' ס מד ובברכת שלמה חו"מ ס' כ"ד, כ"ה) ולכן הפוגע בזכותו עובר על גזל דאורייתא מההסכמות שניתנו לזמן מוגבל אין להוכיח שאין זכויות יוצרים כיון שניתנו לספרים של מו"ל ולא של מחבר

2. האם יש לבעל יצירה זכויות יוצרים מורחב יותר ממה שהחוק והמנהג נותן (דהיינו 50 שנה אחר מות המחבר?)
תשובה: כן

3. האם יש הבדל אם בעל זכות היצירה הוא יהודי או אינו יהודי או מומר?
תשובה: אין הבדל ואסור להעתיק מיהו מותר להעתיק תוכנות של אינו יהודי באם מוסכם בדעתו שאם יבוא הנכרי ויתבע אותו שישלם לו דחמס של יהודי איסורו מלא תחמוד בית רעך ואינו יהודי אינו רעך (עיין מנ"ח בהוצאת מכון ירושלים מצוה לח ובהערות למטה) ואם בקלות יכול לשלם לגוי חייב להשתדל להחזיר לו וכן אסור לו אח"כ להפקיע הלואתו של הגוי דכל שהעתיק ע"מ לשלם ואח"כ מפקיע את החוב הוי כהעתיק ע"מ שלא לשלם שהוי גזל מדאורייתא אבל אם בדעתו לשלם מותר אף שידע שהאינו יהודי לא יתבענו וזה הטעם שמותר לקנות חפצים שהם חיקויים מחברה אחרת שאינם יהודים אם דעתו לשלם לבעל היצירה באם יתבענו.

5. באופן שכל העולם מעתיקים ללא רשות היצירה מהבעלים או את החכמה כמו בקלטות משום שעדיין אין שינים לחוק האם מותר להעתיק באופן שההקלטה לצורך עצמי ולא מסחרי?
תשובה: אסור לכל יצירה שנעשתה למטרת רווח וכתב "כל הזכויות" אומדנא הוא שמשייר לעצמו את זכויות העתקה והו"ל כאילו שייר בפירוש, ולא אמרינן שהוי כ"זוטו של ים" שהריהיצירה אינה אבודה מכל אדם גם לא נחשב לאבידה מדעת שהרי נותנו רק תמורת תשלום ועל דעת שלא יעתיקו את יצירתו

6. אולי כתב כן כדי שאנשים ישרים המבינים שאין מן הראוי להעתיק קלטת שאחר טרח ועשה דבר מתוקן יקנו ממנו?
תשובה: א"כ הם שהם ישרים קובעים את המנהג אע"פ שהם מיעוט ולא האנשים שאינם ישרים קובעים את המנהג ואע"פ שהם רוב העולם

8. כשכותבים "כל הזכויות שמורות" ודעתו במילים אלו שזה תנאי ושיור בקנין האם זה אסור מפני שהוי כאילו התנה ושייר?
תשובה: ודאי שכן.

כיון שאמר זה ברבים שכל אחד יכול להעתיק על
טייפ אין לו שום רשות למנוע מלעשות טייפס, אם
לא כשאמר לכל אלו שבאו לשמוע שאינו אומר אלא
כשהשביחו לו שלא יעשו טייפס מזה מאיזה טעם
שאינו רוצה לפרסם דאף שלא שייך איסור גזל על
זה איכא עכ"פ איסור מלעבור על דעתו אף כשיודעין
השומעין שאינו רוצה גם בלא התנה וכ"ש בהתנה
שאסור שהרי הטריחוהו באופן שאמר שאינו רוצה
והוי כעשו מלאכה באחד בעל כרחו. ואף שהוא דברי
תורה שחייב הרב להשמיע יש הרבה שאינו ראוי
לפרסם משום שאין למסור אותם לכו"ע ויש שאין
מורין כן וכדאשכחן בגמ' טובא, ולפעמים מחמת
שלא ברור להרב אם דבריו נכונים ובדעתו שעוד
יעיין בדבר אם הם ראוין, ויש נמי רשות להרב לאסור
בשביל זה שלא יעשו טייפס דשמא יראה אח"כ הרב
שאין דבריו נכונים ויתבייש, אף שמסתבר דאין לו
רשות לאסור על התלמידים דבר כדי שלא ישכחו
וכדי שיוכלו לחזור עליהן דהא זהו ג"כ מצורכי
הלמוד לתלמידים הוא אך שיצום שלא יפרסמו עד
שיאמר להם שהוא ראוי גם לפרסם, אבל על טייפ
שהוא נעשה על זמן רב וליתן גם לאחרים יכול לעכב
שלא יעשו כלל, אבל עכ"פ הוא ענין איסור אחר ולא
איסור גזלה, אבל לעשות טייפ אחר מטייפ אחד שלא
ברשותו הוא איסור גזל.

**56) משנת זכות היוצר, פרק יג**

א בעל יצירה ששייר את זכות העתקה בקנינו או
עשה תנאי עם משפסי התנאים שלא להעתיק לכו"ע
בהעתקה שלא ברשות עוברים על איסור גזל מן
התורה בין למוכר ובין לקונה ' ואסור להשתמש
בקלטת המועתקת גם למטרה שאינה מסחרית (כנ"ל
פרק ו' סעי' א' ב') וכן הדין במי שגזל קלטת והעתיקה
(עיין לעיל פרק י' סעי' ה').

ג לדעה הסוברת שיש לאדם על יצירתו מן התורה
זכויות יוצרים ובעלות על החכמה אם בעל היצירה
קריאה למטרת רווחים אסור להעתיק גם כשלמו"ל
יהיה הפסד קטן גם בדברים שאינם של מצוה מוזיקה
והרצאות שאינם דברי תורה ויש המחלק בין קלטת
של רבנים שאם יעתיקו אפ' לצורך פרטי יהיה למו"ל
הפסד גדול, לבין קלטת של זמרים שאין הפסד גדול
כשמעתיקים לצורך עצמי, ואילו לדעה הסוברת
שאין מן התורה זכויות יוצרים ובעלות על חכמה –
האיסור הוא רק כשיש הפסד למו"ל (עיין לעיל פרק
ח' סע' כא ובפרק ו' סע' ט').

ד האיסור הוא גם ליחיד המעוניין להעתיק רק לעצמו
ולא למטרה מסחרית ויש להקל רק במעתיק חלקים
או באיכות ירודה מהיצירה המקורית, ויש שמקילים
במעתיק לעצמו גם כשהאיכות אינה ירודה וגם את
כל היצירה, מיהו לדעה הסוברת שיש לו מן התורה
בעלות על החכמה האיסור הוא בכל מקרה.

ה המעתיק מקלטת למטרה עצמית לא לשם מסחר
אם מעתיק בכמויות מסחריות אפשר שלכו"ע דינו

---

כמעתיק לשם מסחר.

ו המקליט מקלטת העומדת להמכר בלא שנטלה
[וכן את החזן עצמו בלא רשותו באופן שיש לו
התמעטות הכנסה – כנ"ל פרק ט' סעי' ט'] חייב
לשלם דמי הנהנה אבל אין בזה משום גזל דאין גזל
בקול ויש לעיין אם אפשר לחייבו באופן שהחזן מחה
גם כשאין החזן חסר.

ט לסוברים שיש לו מן התורה בעלות על החכמה
הוי גזל גם אם מעתיק מקלטת לא מקורית למטרה
עצמית, וחייב לשלם מה שנהנה ולסוברים שמן
התורה אין לו בעלות לא הוי גזל, וכן באופן שאין
השגת גבול ובדבר שהראשון לא טרח מותר להעתיק
וי"א שיכולים להקל בזה כיון שאינו משתמש בגוף
הדבר של בעל היצירה, ואסור להעתיק רק אם המו"ל
טרח להוציאו ועדיין לא הוציא את הרווחים שהרי
מפסידו, אבל אם כבר הוציא רווחיו מעיקר הדין אין
איסור להעתיק למטרה עצמית עם כל זה אין זה משנת
חסידים ומידי ריח גזל לא פלט שמסייע למעתיקים
או שעכ"פ מפסיד בפועל את המו"ל, ויש לדונו כנבל
ברשות התורה וי"א שאע"פ שאינו נקרא גזלן מ"מ
יכולים לחייבו מדין נהנה כדין זה נהנה וזה חסר.

יא אסור להעתיק מקלטת לא מקורית ולמכור
כשהממציא הראשון טרח להוציאו לאור ואם יש
אחרים שכבר מוכרים באיסור יש מקום להקל וכדאי
להחמיר ואם רוב המסחר בידי המוכרים באיסור
מותר לו למכור, מיהו לדעה הסוברת שיש בעלות
על החכמה האיסור הוא מן התורה בכל מקרה.

**57) ירחון המחשבים ה:1 לבית היהודי, כסלו תשנ"ט,
עמוד 27**

הרינו לאשר בזה שכל חברה המוכרת תקליטורים
וכדומה, ומודיע על גבי התקליטור "שאינה מוכרת
את המוצר אלא רק זכות שימוש בו בלבד ואסור
להעתיקו הן לעצמו והן לאחרים אפילו שלא לצרכי
מסחר" הרי יש לזה תוקף הלכתי לכל הדעות, ואסור
להעתיקו הן לעצמו והן לאחרים אפילו שלא לצרכי
מסחר, וכן אסור לקנות מן המעתיקים והמעתיקים
מן המעתיקים לעולם, וכל הקונה מהם הרי הוא
בגדר מסייע לידי עוברי עבירה, וע"ז באנו עה"ה,
משה שאול קליין, יהודה סילמן.

**58) משנת זכות היוצר, פרק יד**

א בעל יצירה ששייר את זכות העתקה בקנינו או
עשה תנאי עם משפט יהתנאים שלא להעתיק לכו"ע
בהעתקה שלא ברשות עוברים על איסור גזל מן
התורה בין למוכר ובין לקונה ואסור להשתמש
בקלטת המועתקת גם למטרה שאינה מסחרית דיני
העתקת תוכנה דומים מאוד לדינים של העתקת
קלטת המבוארים בפרק הקודם קחם משם אך
לעניין גיבוי תוכנה מותר כי בדרך כלל בעלי יצירת
התוכנות מרשים לעשות גיבוי לתוכנה כדי שיוכל
לתקן את התקליטור המקורי בלא להטריח את בעלי

א ע

**49) משנת זכות היוצר, פרק יח**

פסקי דינים ותשובות ממרן הגרש"ז אויערבאך זצ"ל
מהו מקור איסור הפרת זכויות יוצרים?

**תשובה:** האיסור הוא מדין השגת גבול ויורד
לאומנותו של חבירו

**הערה:** שמעתי שכך סוברים מרן החזו"א זצ"ל,
הגר"ש ואזנר שליט"א והר"ג קרליץ שליט"א, והנה
הגר"ש ואזנר בשנת תשס"ג בהסכמתו לספר עמק
המשפט חלק ד, גילה דעתו בדין העתקה ואף
למטרה עצמית, כי "ודאי דעת תורה נוטה, דאיכא
איסור גזל וכו' המה שחברו המציא לגמרי מחדש, הן
בספר הלכה וכיוצא בהן והן בשאר דברים. וכן הוא
בדינא דמלכותא בכל מקום בעולם" עכ"ל עייש.

**50) דברים ו:יח**

וְעָשִׂיתָ הַיָּשָׁר וְהַטּוֹב בְּעֵינֵי ד' לְמַעַן יִיטַב לָךְ וּבָאתָ
וְיָרַשְׁתָּ אֶת־הָאָרֶץ הַטֹּבָה אֲשֶׁר־נִשְׁבַּע ד' לַאֲבֹתֶיךָ:

**51) שו"ת הרי"ף קלג**

**שאלה.** אחד מן התלמידים גנב ספרי פרושין לחבירו
וכשנתבעו ממנו נשבע שבועה חמורה שלא יחזירם
לו עד שיעתיק אותם ויש מי שהורה שמותר לגנבן.
**תשובה.** הגונב והמורה כלם טעו שלא כדין עשו שזה
שהורה שמותר לעשות כן דומה לו משום שמתלמד
דברי תורה שהיא מצוה היא וטעה משום שאמר לולב
הגזול והיבש פסול ואתמר מה עלה משום דמצוה הבאה
בעבירה המקום שונאה שנאמר כי ה' אוהב משפט
שונא גזל בעולה וגו' הילכך הורה לו זה בהוראותו
חוטא ומחטיא והגונב יש עליו ג' לאוין אחד משום
גונב ואחד משום שנשבע שלא יחזיר אותם והו"ל על
דברי תורה נשבע שהיא גזלה ואחד משום גזל לפי
שהוא גוזל שלא מדעת ואף על פי שהגזלה בכלל
הגניבה היא אלא שנסתר בלקיחתו משום שאמר אל
תגנוב את שלך מאחרי הגנב שלא תראה עליו כגנב
ואם אסור בשלו כל שכן באחרים ואף אותה מצוה
שנתכוון לה לא עלתה בידו כמו שכתבו לולב הגזול
והיבש פסול שלא עלתה בידו מצותו.

**52) רמ"א, שולחן ערוך, חושן משפט רצב:כ**

**הגה:** וכמו שאסור לקרות ממנו כך אסור להעתיק
ממנו אות אחת, והני מילי בעם הארץ, אבל תלמיד
חכם שאין לו ספר כיוצא בזה מותר לקרות ולהעתיק
ממנו כי ודאי אדעתא דהכי הפקידו אצלו (מרדכי
ס"פ המקפיד). ובמקום ביטול תורה שאין ספרים
נמצאים יכולין בית דין לכוף לאחד להשאיל ספריו
ללמוד מהן, ובלבד שישלמו לו מה שיתקלקלו
הספרים (תשו' הרא"ש כלל צג סימן ג).

**53) שו"ת בית יצחק, יורה דעה ה:עב**

**השאלה.** מי שהניח כתבי חידושי תורה אם מותר
לאחר להעתיק מהם ולהדפיסם שלא ברשות היורשים
אף אם העתיק בחיי המחבר או יש בו משום גזל.

---

**תשובה:** הנה כת"ה דימה זכות הדפסה לטובת הנאה
דמבואר בסימן רע"ו ברמ"א דטובת הנאה אינה
בירושה ולפי דברי הש"ך אם הדבר ביד היורשים
זכו היורשים וגם טובת הנאה בירושה והבא והביא
דברי הקצה"ח שהוא מחלוקת בין הש"ה והש"ך
וה"ה הכא הכתבים ביד היורשים תליא במחלוקת...
ועל כן אין הספק רק אם העתיק הכתבים שלא בידיעת
היורשים או בחיי המחבר אם מותר להדפיסם ובזה
בהשקפת ראשונה לא אדע הפר בין אם שמע בע"פ
חידושי תורה או ראה בכתב והגע עצמך הרי שמע
מאחד חידושי תורה או שלמד אצלו הכי אין מותר
ללמד לאחרים ולפרסם חידוש תורה שלו בשם
אומרו ואפילו לאלפי אלפים תלמידים המקשיבים
לקולו ולמה ראה בכתבים לא יוכל לפרסם בשם
אומרו... והנני חוזר לגוף הדין הנה נראה דאף אם
הרשה המחבר בחייו להעתיק מקצת מהמכתבים
מ"מ אסור להדפיס בלי רשות היורשים...

**54) שו"ת שבט הלוי, חלק ד, חושן משפט רב**

... שאל בבית ספר שמלמדים יהדות ומלמדים זה
מכמה ספרים ואין לכל הבנות כל אלה הספרים
ומצלמים מאמר א' מספר פלוני ומאמר אחר מספר
אחר ונתעורר בכ' אם זה מותר שלא יהא נקרא נכנס
באומנת חברו דאם לא יצלמו כזה יה מוכרחים לקחת
הספרים, ולאידך גיסא קשה לכולם לקחת כל אחד
מהספרים שמכל ספר לא נצרך אלא מאמר א' בודד
או שתים.

אשיב בבקשתי כי קשה לי לרדת לענין יורד
לאומנותו של חבירו אבל מסברא כל זמן שלא לקח
המו"ל הסכמה וחרם שאסור להדפיס אפילו חלק
קטן מספר שמו"ל לרבים אין איסור לעשות כזאת,
דגם על עצם ההסכמות על ספרים נדפסים נתווכחו
גאוני עולם ונהי דאנן נקטינן כדעת מרן החתם סופר
חו"מ ס' מא ... מ"מ לחזור ולהדפיס מאמר בודד
ומכ"ש כנ"ל שאין מדפיס כלל להפיצו ברבים אלא
בין תלמידי בית ספר שקשה להם לקנות כמה וכמה
ספרים שמכל ספר לא נצרכו אלא לדברים אחדים
א"כ בכה"ג אדרבה מצוה יש בדבר להקל ... משא"כ
בנ"ד שעושים רק עלים בודדים לא בצורת ספר כלל
אינני מוצא מקום לנכון לאסור כזאת וכמובן אין להפיץ
הקונטרסים רק במסגרת פנים בבית ספר.

**55) שו"ת אגרות משה, אורח חיים, חלק ד, מ:יט**

מי שעושה טייפ מד"ת ואוסר להעתיקו בדבר אחד
שעושה טייפ מדברי תורה וכותב שאוסר לעשות
מטייפ שלו עוד טייפס ודאי אסור כי הוא ענין שוה
כסף ועשה הטייפ להרויח מזה שאחרים שירצו
יצטרכו לשלם לו שא"כ ליכא משום מדת סדום,
וממילא כיון שהוא חפצו אין רשאין ליקח אותו
להשתמש בו שלא ברשות, ואף כשלא שמעו ממנו
שאינו נותן רשות אסור להעתיק ממנו בסתמא כל
זמן שלא הרשה בפירוש, ואדרבא בעל הדברי תורה

שינויו כדי שיקנהו שכל העושה דברים אלו וכיוצא
בהן מחזק ידי עוברי עבירה ועובר על ויקרא י"ט י"ד
ולפני עור לא תתן מכשול. ב. אסור ליהנות בדבר
הגזול ואפילו לאחר יאוש ...

**38) שו"ת חתם סופר חלק ה, חושן משפט סימן מא**

... דלע"ד אין לגזור על זאת מכמה טעמים א' מאחר
שכעת הזכות ואחריות הדפוס הוא מחקי המלך
וזכיותיו בכמה דברים וא"כ מי יגזור לעכב על זכות
המלך וחקו ב' לא מצינו כיוצא בזה שזכה הראשון
דין לעכב על הבא אחריו ובפרט כי לא חדש
הוא ואין זה חלקו רק עמלו שמטריח מעט ונוטל
שכרו מאת מכרו ובמה שאינו מן הדין אין לשום רב
ומורה לגזור במדינתו מה שנוגע למדינה אחרת ...
אבל ראו קדמונינו בכל תפוצת ישראל מיום החל
הדפוס לגזור בגזירת עירין על כל המשיג גבול
למען לא יהי' שלוחי מצוה ניזוקי' ... אבל הכא א"א
להדפיס בלי שיוציא הוצאות הרבה ויבוא מי שיבוא
אחריו ויפסדנו קרנו ועמלו ומטעם זה אסר רמ"א
ספרי רמב"ם של המדפיס השני כמ"ש בתשובתו ...
ומ"ש הדרת מרנא נ"י דמפסיד חק המלכות לא הבנתי
מה זה ענין לחק המלכות אם ידפיסו המדפיסי' ס' זה
או אחר רק שישלמו לו מס שלו שנה שנה והאמת
אגיד כי זה ירחים הגיעני מכתב ממו"ח הגאון נ"י
וסיפר לי כי רב א' סמוך לגלילותיו מאן דהוא הוציא
דף בדפוס ושם נאמר משם עצמו שהדבר ידוע שאין
חרם מועיל והותר הרצועה ע"י חכמי ישראל וכעס
מו"ח הגאון נ"י ...

**39) שו"ת פרשת מרדכי, חושן משפט ז-ח**

... המחזורים החדשים שהוציאן לאור עולם החכם
השלם מו"ה וואלף רעדעלהיים נ"י ויש אתו הסכמות
מגאוני ארץ וגדולי הדור שלא ישיגו אחרים גבולו
משך כ"ה שנים ... ואחרי שנתבאר דבנ"ד ליכא
משום גזל לא מדיבריהם ולא מדרכי שלום גם בשם
רשע לא יקרא ...
... וממילא האידנא דרוב המדפיסים אינם ישראלים
שאינם מחייבים לשמע גזירת חרם שלנו וגם רבו
ישראלים הפורצים גדר החרם ושבועה א"כ הירא
יפסיד דעליו יחול החרם כשאחר מדפיס ...

**40) שולחן ערוך, אורח חיים נה:יא, חושן משפט
שסח:ז, רמ"א, יורה דעה קסה:א, חושן משפט רז:טו,
רלו:ט**

דינא דמלכותא דינא

**41) דברים יט:יד**

לֹא תַסִּיג גְּבוּל רֵעֲךָ אֲשֶׁר גָּבְלוּ רִאשֹׁנִים בְּנַחֲלָתְךָ אֲשֶׁר
תִּנְחַל בָּאָרֶץ אֲשֶׁר ד' אֱלֹקֶיךָ נֹתֵן לְךָ לְרִשְׁתָּהּ:

**42) שו"ת חתם סופר חלק ה, חושן משפט סימן עט**

... וירד לאומנו' שהוא גזל דאורייתא ויבואר לקמן

---

בסמוך אי"ה. פסיק השם הרביעי, יורד לאומנתו
לכאורה נראה כל הנוגע בענין זה אסור מדאורי' וגזל
גמור הוא מן התורה ...

**43) רמ"א, חושן משפט לז:כב**

הגה: כל דבר התלוי במנהג בני העיר אין אומרים בו
תרי כמאה אלא אזלינן ביה בתר הרוב וכן כל כיוצא
בזה שאין אנו צריכים עדות ממש. וכן לא אמרינן
בכיוצא בזה לא ראינו אינו ראיה אלא הוי ראיה
(מהרי"ק שורש קע"ג) ודנין בחזקת הישוב וכדומה
לזה מצרכי העיר אפילו על פי עד מפי עד מפי
הקבלה דהרי בלאו הכי כולן נוגעין בדבר (תשובת
מיימוני הל' עדות סי' י"ג) וע"ל סי' קנ"ו וקס"ג
מדינין אלו טובי הקהל הממונים לעסוק בצרכי רבים
או יחידים הרי הן כדיינים ואסורים להושיב ביניהם
מי שפסול לדון משום רשעה.

**44) תחומין, כרך ז, דפים 369-381 "תנאי ושיור
בהסכמים"**

**45) בבא מציעא עח.**

רבי מאיר היא, דאמר: כל המעביר על דעת של בעל
הבית נקרא גזלן

**46) שולחן ערוך, חושן משפט רי:ד:ח**

המוכר בית לחבירו על מנת שדיוטא עליונה שלי,
הרי זה שלו

**47) שולחן ערוך, חושן משפט ריב:ג**

אבל אם מכר לאחד בית ואילן וחורבה וחצר, ושייר
לעצמו דירת הבית ואכילת הפירות ואויר החורבה
ואויר החצר, מהני דהוי כאילו פירש ששייר לעצמו
מקום, ואפילו לא הזכיר שיור בחצר כלל אלא מכר לו
בית ואמר לו על מנת שדיוטא העליונה שלי, אמרינן
ששייר לו מקום בחצר להוציא זיזין מהדיוטא לחצר.

**48) משנת זכות היוצר, פרק ה**

גם לדעה השניה המצאתו ממנו זכות זה (1) מכח דינא
דמלכותא דינא באם קיבל רשיון וזכיון מהמלכות
על המצאתו (2) מי שאומנותו בכך, מצד המנהג,
במקום שהאומנין תיקנו תקנות בינם לבין עצמם או
מנהג שנהגו בני העיר מעצמם אפי' שלא התכנסו
כולן לקבוע אותו אלא אלא כך נהגו דינו כתנאי בי"ד.
פרטי הדין של יורד לאומנתו של הבירו הם דינא
דאורייתא וגזל דאורייתא

"The source of the prohibition of violating copy-
rights is based on the prohibitions of *Hasagas
Gvul* (Infringement of person's livelihood),
(where applicable), *Minhag Benai Ha-ir* (Accepted Practice) and *Dina Demalchusa Dina*
(Government Laws and Regulations)

אולם ביצירות חולין בקלטות תובנות וכדו' דעת כל
האחרונים הנ"ל שיש ליוצר בעלות גמורה

### 26) שו"ת שואל ומשיב, א:מ

ואמרתי לבאר ואכתוב בזה מה שהשבתי להרב
החריף מוה' שמואל וואלדבערג ... ובא כעת לבאר
טעמו ... וכאן המחבר עצמו אין לו כח וזכות מאחר
שבהדפסה ראשונה שנת תקצ"ו לא נזכר שום איסור
ואם היה נזכר איסור אפשר לדון שיש איסור עד
כלות זמן שגבל ואף לאחר שנמכר הספרים, אבל אם
לא נזכר שום זמן, אין מקום לאיסור כלל ... והנה
כל דבריו תמוהים דזה ודאי שספר חדש שמדפיס
מחבר וזכה שדבריו מתקבלים ע"פ תבל פשיטא שיש
לו זכות בזה לעולם והרי בלא"ה אם מדפיסים או
מחדשים איזה מלאכה אינו רשאי אחר לעשות בלא
רשותו ... וגם במדינתינו יש חק בהדפסה מבלי
להדפיס מצד חוקי הממשלה ... ומצד הדין ד"ת
אסור להשיג הגבול ...

### 27) בבא מציעא כא:

יאוש שלא מדעת, אביי אמר: לא הוי יאוש, ורבא
אמר: הוי יאוש.

### 28) רמב"ם, הלכות גזילה ואבדה יד:ה

יאוש שלא מדעת אפילו בדבר שאין בו סימן אינו
יאוש, כיצד, נפל ממנו דינר ולא ידע בו שנפל אע"פ
שכשידע בו שנפל יתיאש הרי זה אינו יאוש עתה עד
שידעו הבעלים שנפל

### 29) ביאור הלכה על שולחן ערוך, אורח חיים תרצט

... ואף דיתיאש לבסוף כשיודע לו הוי יאוש שלא
מדעת ולא הוי יאוש ...

### 30) רמב"ם, הלכות גנבה א:א-ג

כל הגונב ממון משוה פרוטה ומעלה עובר על לא
תעשה שנ' " לא תגנבו" ...
אסור לגנוב כל שהוא דין תורה, ואסור לגנוב דרך
שחוק, או לגנוב על מנת להחזיר, או לגנוב על מנת
לשלם, הכל אסור שלא ירגיל עצמו בכך
איזה הוא גנב, זה הלוקח ממון אדם בסתר ואין
הבעלים יודעין ...

### 31) טור, חושן משפט שנט:א

אסור לגזול אפי' כל שהוא לא שנא מישראל ול"ש
מעכו"ם שגזל העכו"ם אסור:
וכל הגוזל את חבירו שוה פרוטה כאילו נוטל
נפשו:
ואסור לגזול אפילו ע"מ לשלם

### 32) סמ"ע על טור, חושן משפט שנט:ט

וכל הגוזל את חבירו אפילו שוה פרוטה כאילו נוטל
נפשו- שנאמר "וְקָבַע אֶת קֹבְעֵיהֶם נָפֶשׁ" ולעיל

---

בסימן שמ"ח ושל"ט כתבתי דיש פלוגתא בזה אם
נפשו של גזלן או נפשו של נגזל דאמר.

### 33) סנהדרין קח.

אמר רבי יוחנן: בא וראה כמה כחה גדול של חמס,
שהרי דור המבול עברו על הכל ולא נחתם עליהם
גזר דינם עד שפשטו ידיהם בגזל, שנאמר (בראשית
ו') כי מלאה הארץ חמס מפניהם והנני משחיתם את
הארץ.

### 34) משלי א:יט ופירוש רבינו יונה

כֵּן אָרְחוֹת כָּל בֹּצֵעַ בָּצַע אֶת נֶפֶשׁ בְּעָלָיו יִקָּח:

### 35) פירוש רבינו יונה על משלי א:יט ובבא קמא קיט.

כן ארחות כל בוצע בוצע וגו' – רואה הנאת הבצע ושוכח הדין
והשילום, והנה הבצע את נפש בעליו יקח, כי יענש עליו
פעמים מיתה בידי שמים לפי הצער והנזק שיגיע בו
הנגזל, ואע"פ שלא נתפרש העונש הזה בתורה, וכתיב
"כי מה תקות חנף כי יבצע כי ישל אלוה נפשו (איוב
כז, ח), ואז"ל נפשו של גזלן (ב"ק קיט, ע"א). ועוד
אז"ל דור המבול שלא נחתם גזר דינם אלא על הגזל
(סנהדרין קח, ע"א). וי"מ לדמם היורבו, הרשעים
האורבים לדם וצופנים לנקי לדם עצמם יארובו
רב חסדא הוה ליה ההוא אריסא דהוה תקיל ויהיב
תקיל ושקיל, סליקה, קרא אנפשיה: (משלי י"ג)
וצפון לצדיק חיל חוטא. (איוב כ"ז) כי מה תקות חנף
כי יבצע כי ישל אלוה נפשו רב הונא ורב חסדא, חד
אמר: נפשו דנגזל, וח"א: נפשו של גזלן. מ"ד נפשו של
נגזל, דכתיב: (משלי א') כן ארחות כל בוצע בצע את
נפש בעליו יקח מ"ד נפשו של גזלן (משלי
כ"ב): אל תגזל דל כי דל הוא ואל תדכא עני בשער,
כי ה' יריב ריבם וקבע את קובעיהם נפש. ואידך נמי
הכתיב: נפש בעליו יקח מאי בעליו? בעליו דהשתא.
ואידך נמי הכתיב: וקבע את קובעיהם נפש מה טעם
קאמר, מה טעם וקבע את קובעיהם? משום דקבעי
נפש. א"ר יוחנן: כל הגוזל את חבירו שוה פרוטה
כאילו נוטל נשמתו ממנו, שנאמר: כן ארחות כל
בוצע בצע את נפש בעליו יקח,

### 36) רמב"ם, הלכות גזילה א:א-ג

איזה הוא גזול, זה הלוקח ממון האדם בחזקה, כגון
שחטף מטלטלין מידו, או שנכנס לרשותו שלא
ברצון הבעלים ונטל כלים משם, או שתקף בעבדיו
ובבהמתו ונשתמש בהן, או שירד לתוך שדהו ואכל
פירותיה, וכל כיוצא בזה הוא הגזול, כענין שנ'
שמואל ב' כ"ג כ"א ויגזול את החנית מיד המצרי.
כל הגוזל את חבירו שוה פרוטה עובר בלא תעשה
שנ' "לא תגזול" ... ואסור לגזול כל שהוא דין תורה,
אפילו גוי עובד עבודה זרה אסור לגזלו ...

### 37) רמב"ם, הלכות גזלה ה:א-ב

אסור לקנות דבר הגזול מן הגזלן ואסור לסעדו על

הפנים ולא רצו ללמד. שלחו חכמים והביאו אומנין
מאלכסנדריא של מצרים, והיו יודעין לאפות כמותן
ולא היו יודעין לרדות כמותן. שהללו מסיקין מבחוץ
ואופין מבחוץ, והללו מסיקין מבפנים ואופין מבפנים.
הללו פיתן מתעפשת, והללו אין פיתן מתעפשת.
כששמעו חכמים בדבר אמרו: כל מה שברא הקדוש
ברוך הוא לכבודו ברא, שנאמר (ישעיה מג) כל
הנקרא בשמי ולכבודי בראתיו, וחזרו בית גרמו
למקומן. שלחו להם חכמים ולא באו. כפלו להם
שכרן ובאו. בכל יום היו נוטלין שנים עשר מנה, והיום
עשרים וארבעה. רבי יהודה אומר: בכל יום עשרים
וארבעה, והיום ארבעים ושמונה. אמרו להם חכמים:
מה ראיתם שלא ללמד? אמרו להם: יודעין היו של
בית אבא שבית זה עתיד ליחרב, שמא ילמד אדם
שאינו מהוגן וילך ויעבוד עבודה זרה בכך.

### 18) ירמיהו ט:כב-כג

כֹּה אָמַר ד' אַל־יִתְהַלֵּל חָכָם בְּחָכְמָתוֹ וְאַל־יִתְהַלֵּל
הַגִּבּוֹר בִּגְבוּרָתוֹ אַל־יִתְהַלֵּל עָשִׁיר בְּעָשְׁרוֹ: כִּי אִם־
בְּזֹאת יִתְהַלֵּל הַמִּתְהַלֵּל הַשְׂכֵּל וְיָדֹעַ אוֹתִי כִּי אֲנִי ד'
עֹשֶׂה חֶסֶד מִשְׁפָּט וּצְדָקָה בָּאָרֶץ כִּי־בְאֵלֶּה חָפַצְתִּי
נְאֻם־ד':

### 19) משנה אבות ו:ו

שכל האומר דבר בשם אומרו. מביא גאולה לעולם.
שנאמר (אסתר ב). "ותאמר אסתר למלך בשם
מרדכי":

### 20) אסתר ב:כב

וַיִּוָּדַע הַדָּבָר לְמָרְדֳּכַי וַיַּגֵּד לְאֶסְתֵּר הַמַּלְכָּה וַתֹּאמֶר
אֶסְתֵּר לַמֶּלֶךְ בְּשֵׁם מָרְדֳּכָי:

### 21) מגן אברהם, אורח חיים קנו:ב

כל שאינו אומר דבר בשם אומרו עובר בלאו
[נדרים פ"ק]

### 22) תוספתא, בבא קמא ז:ג

אבל המתגנב מאחר חבר והולך ושונה פרקו אע"פ
שנקרא גנב זוכה לעצמו שנא' (משלי ו:ל) "לא יבוזו
לגנב כי יגנוב וגו'":

### 23) שו"ת הרמ"א סימן י

... הוא ה"ה הגאון מהר"ר מאיר מפאדוואה. והנה
שם מגמותי רעיוני ומחשבותי והשתתף עם אחד
מאנשי ארצו ומגדוליה דהיינו יענטילומרלו והוא
אחד מן מדפיסי הספרי'סלח והסכימו יחדיו להדפיס
החיבור הגדול משנה תורה, אשר חבר הרב הכולל
האמתי רבינו משה בן הרב המובהק הדיין רבינו
מיימון. וכאשר חשב כן החלו לעשות בעז"ה עד
שלע"עלט נגמר הדבר. והגיה אותו בשכלו הזך עד
אשר לא נשאר בתוך הבר תבן, וסלק המסלה עד
לא נשאר בה אבן. והנה קם אחד גם כן יענטילומר

---

מעשירי הארץ נגדומא ואמר אעשה גם אנכי לביתי
ואדפיס אנכי גם אני, וכן עשה. והעיקר הוא מאתו
שעושה דבר זה על מה שלא נשתתף עמו הגאון הנ"ל,
ועושה דבר זה להכעיס ממון הגאון הנ"ל ח"ו.
כי ידוע אם לא ימכור הגאון ספריו שיכבד עליו המשא
מנשוא. והנני לדון בדיני ישראל, אם היו שני אנשים
ישראלים על פי תורתנו הקדושה, ונוכיח שזכה הגאון
הנ"ל בדינו. ונפרד מזה ונהיה לארבעה ראשים, ועל
אלו הארבעה יסודות נרכיב הדבר ועניינו. ואומר,
שדין הוא עם הגאון שהוא ימכור ספריו ראשונה.
והואיל ובעונותינו שרבו אין ידנו תקיפה לעשות כפי
תורתנו, מ"מ לא נניח את שלנו ולומר שכל ישראל
ומי שבשם ישראל יכונה לא יקנה שום ספר מיימוני
החדשים רק מאותן היוצאים מתחת יד הגאון הנ"ל או
באי כחו, והוא מארבעה טעמים ...

### 24) מגילה יט: קול אליהו על אגדות ש"ס

... מלמד שהראהו הקדוש ברוך הוא למשה דקדוקי
תורה ודקדוקי סופרים, ומה שהסופרים עתידים
לחדש

... אמנם יתבאר דידוי הוא מה שכתבו כי התורה
שבכתב כבר נתנה השי"ת לנו וכתיבא וקיימא,
אך התורה שבעל פה הגם כי כולה כלולה ורמוזה
בהתורה שבכתב והכל נמסר למשה בסיני גם מה
שתלמיד ותיק עתיד לחדש בכל דור ודור עד עת
קץ על ידי פלפולו וליבון ובירור שמעתתא אליבא
דהלכתא אם כיוון האמת ...

### 25) עמק המשפט, חלק ד

בכלל יש לאמר שלדעת רבים מגדולי האחרונים
השואל ומשיב והההפלאה המחנה חיים והמהר"ם שיק
הנצי"ב המלבי"ם הנחל יצחק הבית יצחק הצפנת
פענח השדי חמד העמודי אש ... החפץ חיים הגר"ש
שקופ ... גם השך שהבאתי בסימן לט אות ה ע"ש
יש לאדם בעלות ממונית גמורה על חידושיו ויצירותיו
ורק בחידושי תורה ישנם במה מהאחרונים הנ"ל
הסוברים שבעלותו פעמה במקצת כפי שנבאר פרטי
הדינים והשיטות בפנים סימן יב ע"ש היטב וכאן
אתמצת רק שלכאו'

ישנם ארבע שיטות בדין בעלות של המחדש חידושי
תורה א) דעת השואל ומשיב וההפץ חיים שיש
בעלות לעולם ב) דעת הבית יצחק שבעלותו מוגבלת
עד תום מכירת המהדורה הראשונה ג) הצמח צדק
וההתעוררות תשובה סוברים שיש רק טובת הנאה
בחידושי תורה והזכות להרוויח מהטובת הנאה
מוגבלת ומצומצמת לשיעור מסוים וזוהי כנראה
גם דעת הגר"א רויטנברג תלמיד השו"מ ד) השערי
דעה שכתב שאין למחדש שום "דררא דממונא" לכאו'
כוונתו אפילו לא טובת הנאה ויש לפלפל שאולי
הוא מודה שיש למחדש טובת הנאה וילע' ובנוסף
לארבע שיטות אלו ישנה שיטה חמישית הסוברת שאין
כלל בעלות על יצירה גם לא יצירת חולין ובדבסמוך

# SOURCES ON DOWNLOADING FILMS AND SONGS, COPYING SOFTWARE: COPYRIGHT IN JUDAISM

**1) תהילים כד:א**
לְדָוִד מִזְמוֹר לַד' הָאָרֶץ וּמְלוֹאָהּ תֵּבֵל וְיֹשְׁבֵי בָהּ:

**2) שמות יט:ה**
וְעַתָּה אִם שָׁמוֹעַ תִּשְׁמְעוּ בְּקֹלִי וּשְׁמַרְתֶּם אֶת בְּרִיתִי וִהְיִיתֶם לִי סְגֻלָּה מִכָּל הָעַמִּים כִּי לִי כָּל הָאָרֶץ:

**3) ויקרא כה:כג**
וְהָאָרֶץ לֹא תִמָּכֵר לִצְמִתֻת כִּי לִי הָאָרֶץ כִּי גֵרִים וְתוֹשָׁבִים אַתֶּם עִמָּדִי:

**4) ויקרא יט:יא**
לֹא תִּגְנֹבוּ וְלֹא תְכַחֲשׁוּ וְלֹא תְשַׁקְּרוּ אִישׁ בַּעֲמִיתוֹ:

**5) דברי הימים א' כט:יד**
וְכִי מִי אֲנִי וּמִי עַמִּי כִּי נַעְצֹר כֹּחַ לְהִתְנַדֵּב כָּזֹאת כִּי מִמְּךָ הַכֹּל וּמִיָּדְךָ נָתַנּוּ לָךְ:

**6) משנה אבות ג:ז**
רַבִּי אֶלְעָזָר אִישׁ בַּרְתּוֹתָא אוֹמֵר, תֶּן לוֹ מִשֶּׁלּוֹ, שֶׁאַתָּה וְשֶׁלְּךָ שֶׁלּוֹ. וְכֵן בְּדָוִד הוּא אוֹמֵר (דברי הימים א כט) כִּי מִמְּךָ הַכֹּל וּמִיָּדְךָ נָתַנּוּ

**7) פירושי רע"ב ותפארת ישראל על**
**תן לו משלו** – לא תמנע מלהתעסק בחפצי שמים בין בגופך בין בממונך שאינך נותן משלו לא מגופך ולא מממונך. שאתה וממונך שלו:
**שאתה ושלך שלו** – נ"ל דלאו דוקא בצדקה מיירי, אלא ה"ק אם חננך ה' שום מעלה או כח, כעושר, גבורה, חכמה, זכרון, קול נעים, וכדומה, הקריבהו לה', להשתמש בו בקודש:

**8) סוטה יד**
ואמר רבי חמא ברבי חנינא, מאי דכתיב: (דברים יג) אחרי ה' אלקיכם תלכו? וכי אפשר לו לאדם להלך אחר שכינה? והלא כבר נאמר: (דברים ד) כי ה' אלקיך אש אוכלה הוא אלא להלך אחר מדותיו של הקב"ה, מה הוא מלביש ערומים, דכתיב: (בראשית ג) ויעש ה' אלהים לאדם ולאשתו כתנות עור וילבישם, אף אתה הלבש ערומים הקב"ה ביקר חולים, דכתיב: (בראשית יח) וירא אליו ה' באלוני ממרא, אף אתה בקר חולים

**9) בראשית א:א**
בְּרֵאשִׁית בָּרָא אֱלֹקִים אֵת הַשָּׁמַיִם וְאֵת הָאָרֶץ:

**10) מתוך תפילת שחרית, ברכות קריאת שמע**
בָּרוּךְ אַתָּה ד' אֱלֹקֵינוּ מֶלֶךְ הָעוֹלָם. יוֹצֵר אוֹר וּבוֹרֵא חֹשֶׁךְ. עֹשֶׂה שָׁלוֹם וּבוֹרֵא אֶת הַכֹּל:

**11) בראשית ב:ב, שמות כ:י, שמות לו:ד-ה**
וַיְכַל אֱלֹקִים בַּיּוֹם הַשְּׁבִיעִי מְלַאכְתּוֹ אֲשֶׁר עָשָׂה וַיִּשְׁבֹּת בַּיּוֹם הַשְּׁבִיעִי מִכָּל מְלַאכְתּוֹ אֲשֶׁר עָשָׂה:
וְיוֹם הַשְּׁבִיעִי שַׁבָּת לַד' אֱלֹקֶיךָ לֹא תַעֲשֶׂה כָל מְלָאכָה אַתָּה | וּבִנְךָ וּבִתֶּךָ עַבְדְּךָ וַאֲמָתְךָ וּבְהֶמְתֶּךָ וְגֵרְךָ אֲשֶׁר בִּשְׁעָרֶיךָ:
וַיָּבֹאוּ כָּל הַחֲכָמִים הָעֹשִׂים אֵת כָּל מְלֶאכֶת הַקֹּדֶשׁ אִישׁ אִישׁ מִמְּלַאכְתּוֹ אֲשֶׁר הֵמָּה עֹשִׂים: וַיֹּאמְרוּ אֶל מֹשֶׁה לֵּאמֹר מַרְבִּים הָעָם לְהָבִיא מִדֵּי הָעֲבֹדָה לַמְּלָאכָה אֲשֶׁר צִוָּה ד' לַעֲשֹׂת אֹתָהּ:

**12) שמות כ:ט**
שֵׁשֶׁת יָמִים תַּעֲבֹד וְעָשִׂיתָ כָּל מְלַאכְתֶּךָ:

**13) בראשית א:כז**
וַיִּבְרָא אֱלֹקִים אֶת הָאָדָם בְּצַלְמוֹ בְּצֶלֶם אֱלֹקִים בָּרָא אֹתוֹ זָכָר וּנְקֵבָה בָּרָא אֹתָם:

**14) נפש החיים א:ג**
זהו ויברא אלקים את האדם בצלמו בצלם אלקים גו'. כי בצלם אלקים עשה וגו'. שכמו שהוא ית' שמו הוא האלקים בעל הכחות הנמצאים בכל העולמות כולם. ומסדרם ומנהיגם כל רגע כרצונו. כן השליט רצונו יתברך את האדם שיהא הוא הפותח והסוגר של כמה אלפי רבואות כחות ועולמות.

**15) בראשית א:ג-ה**
וַיֹּאמֶר אֱלֹקִים יְהִי אוֹר וַיְהִי אוֹר: וַיַּרְא אֱלֹקִים אֶת הָאוֹר כִּי טוֹב וַיַּבְדֵּל אֱלֹקִים בֵּין הָאוֹר וּבֵין הַחֹשֶׁךְ: וַיִּקְרָא אֱלֹקִים לָאוֹר יוֹם וְלַחֹשֶׁךְ קָרָא לָיְלָה וַיְהִי עֶרֶב וַיְהִי בֹקֶר יוֹם אֶחָד:

**16) משנה יומא ג:יא**
משנה. ואלו לגנאי: של בית גרמו לא רצו ללמד על מעשה לחם הפנים, של בית אבטינס לא רצו ללמד על מעשה הקטורת, הוגרס בן לוי היה יודע פרק בשיר ולא רצה ללמד, בן קמצר לא רצה ללמד על מעשה הכתב. על הראשונים נאמר (משלי י) זכר צדיק לברכה, ועל אלו נאמר (משלי י) ושם רשעים ירקב

**17) יומא לח.**
גמרא. תנו רבנן: בית גרמו היו בקיאין במעשה לחם

דברי כהד"ג נ"י. ע"ד הנדון אם יוצאין מצוות ביקור
חולים בדיבור עם החולה ע"י הטעליפון /טלפון/.

... (י) ומה שנוגע לענין טעליוויישען /טלויזיה/,
שכ' כת"ה, זה פשיטא דהוי רק כמו בבואה במראה
מלוטש, דבודאי לא עלה על דעת שום אדם דיחייב
בברכה ברואה מלך בטעליוויישען, ועיין בת' בי"צ
(חא"ע ח"ב במפתחות סי' י"ג), דכתב שם, דאם
יצא אל הפועל מכונת טעלעפאט או טעלעסקאפ /
טלסקופ/, אשר יוכל לראות גם צורת המדבר עפ"י
פאטאגראפיע, /צלום/ אז יהיה ביותר ניקל, להתיר
עשיית שליח לקבלה ע"י המכונה הנ"ל עכ"ל, הרי
אז כבר דברו מחדשות הטעלעוויישען /הטלויזיה/,
ודייק שליח לקבלה, משום דשליח לקבלה מהני אף
שלא בפניו, עיין שם בגוף התשובה (אות ה') אולם

בנוגע לנד"ד שפיר צדקו דברי כת"ה, דאם יתפתח
הטעליוויישען לשימוש יחידים כמו הטעליפון /
הטלפון/ כהיום ויהי' יכולת לראות החולה ולספר
עמו, כידבר איש אל רעהו פנים בפנים, בודאי אין
צריכים שיראה כל דבר על שיערו האמיתי, ואין
נפ"מ אם הוי לי' כל דין ראיה, ומה מאד נכון הכרעת
כת"ה למעשה, דבפעם הראשונה, בודאי צריכים
לבקר בעצמו את החולה, שלא על ידי תליפון, /
טלפון/ דבדיבור ע"י התליפון, /הטלפון/ הוא ממשש
באפילה ולפעמים דיבורו עוד עליו למעמסה, ורק
אחרי שראהו פא"פ ובקי במצב החולה, אז כלפי מה
שאמרו רז"ל אפילו מאה פעמים ביום, אז בכל פעם
שחוקר ע"י תליפון /טלפון/ להתודע מצב החולה,
מקיים בזה מצות ביקור חולים.

מבקר כאילו שופך דמים.

אין מבקרין את החולה אלא מיום שלישי והלאה, ואם קפץ עליו החולי והכביד מבקרין אותו מיד, ואין מבקרין את החולה לא בשלש שעות ראשונות ביום, ולא בשלש אחרונות, מפני שהן מתעסקין בצרכי החולה, ואין מבקרין לא חולי מעיים ולא חולי העין, ולא מחושי הראש, מפני שהבקור קשה להן.

א מצוה לבקר חולים הקרובים והחברים נכנסים מיד והרחוקים אחר ג' ימים ואם קפץ עליו החולי אלו ואלו נכנסים מיד. (טור בקיצור מס' ת"ל להרמב"ן) : ב אפי' הגדול ילך לבקר הקטן ואפילו כמה פעמים ביום ואפילו בן גילו וכל המוסיף ה"ז משובח ובלבד שלא יטריח לו: הגה י"א דשונא יכול לילך לבקר חולה (מהרי"ל קצ"ז) ולא נראה לי אלא לא יבקר חולה ולא ינחם אבל שהוא שונא שלא יחשב ששמח לאידו ואינו לו אלא צער (ש"ס פ' כ"ג) : ד אין מבקרין החולה בג' שעות ראשונות של יום מפני שכל חולה מיקל עליו חליו בבקר ולא יחוש לבקש עליו רחמים ולא בג' שעות אחרונות של יום שאז מכביד עליו חליו ויתייאש מלבקש עליו רחמים (וכל שביקר ולא ביקש עליו רחמים לא קיים המצוה) (ב"י בשם הרמב"ן) :

**73) רמב"ם, הלכות אבל ח:ד, יד:יב, שולחן ערוך, יורה דעה שלה:ט**

וכן יראה לי שנוהגין עם גרי תושב בדרך ארץ וגמילות חסדים כישראל, שהרי אנו מצווין להחיותן שנאמר לגר אשר בשעריך תתננה ואכלה, וזה שאמרו חכמים אין כופלין להן שלום בעכו"ם לא בגר תושב, אפילו העכו"ם צוו חכמים לבקר חוליהם, ולקבור מתיהם עם מתי ישראל, ולפרנס ענייהם בכלל עניי ישראל, מפני דרכי שלום, הרי נאמר טוב ה' לכל ורחמיו על כל מעשיו, ונאמר דרכיה דרכי נועם וכל נתיבותיה שלום.

קוברין מתי עכו"ם ומנחמין אביליהם ומבקרין חוליהם מפני דרכי שלום:
מבקרין חולי עובדי כוכבים מפני דרכי שלום:

**74) שולחן ערוך, יורה דעה שלה:ה-ו**

כשמבקש עליו רחמים אם מבקש לפניו יכול לבקש בכל לשון שירצה ואם מבקש שלא בפניו לא יבקש אלא בלשון הקדש:
יכלול אותו בתוך חולי ישראל שיאמר המקום ירחם עליך בתוך חולי ישראל ובשבת אומר שבת היא מלזעוק ורפואה קרובה לבא:

**75) שו"ת אגרות משה, יורה דעה א:רכג**

ובדבר בק"ח על ידי שאלה בטעלעפאן ... הנה פשוט לע"ד שאף שמקיים מצוה דבק"ח אבל אינו שייך לומר שיצא י"ח כיון שחסר בבקור זה ענינים האחרים שיש בבק"ח. ורק יצא מזה שאם א"א לו לקיים בהליכה לשם לא נפטר לגמרי אלא צריך

---

לבקרו במה שאפשר לו לכה"פ ענין אחד או שנים שהוא גם ע"י הטעלעפאן ... ומה שהביא כתר"ה מס' העיקרים בטעם שמשה לא שבר את הלוחות תיכף כשאמר לו ה' שעשאו את העגל שהוא משום דראיה מעוררת יותר....

**76) שו"ת יחוה דעת ג:פג**

שאלה: האם יוצאים ידי חובת מצות ביקור חולים על ידי ששואל בשלום החולה דרך הטלפון, ומברך אותו בברכת רפואה שלמה, או שצריך דוקא ללכת ולבקר בעצמו אצל החולה?

תשובה: מצות ביקור חולים סמכוה חז"ל (בבבא מציעא ל' ע"ב) על הפסוק והודעת להם את הדרך ילכו בה, זו ביקור חולים ... ועוד, שעל ידי ביקורו באופן אישי את החולה, הוא מתרשם ומתפעל יותר ממצב החולה, שאינה דומה שמיעה לראיה, ומתעורר לבקש עליו רחמים בכל לב, וכן אמרו בנדרים (מ' ע"א), כל המבקר את החולה מבקש עליו רחמים שיחיה, וכל מי שאינו מבקר אינו מבקש עליו רחמים. כלומר, שעל ידי ביקורו מתעורר לבקש עליו רחמים שהשי"ת ישלח דברו הטוב וירפאהו ... לפיכך נראה שאם יכול ללכת לבקר החולה בעצמו, אינו יוצא ידי חובת המצוה בשלימותה על ידי הטלפון או על ידי מכתב ... ורק אם אינו יכול לבקר החולה בעצמו, מוטב לטלפן או לשלוח אליו מכתב ולעודדו ולחזקו בדברים.

**77) שו"ת חלקת יעקב, יורה דעה ב:קפח**

בדבר שאלתו אם יוצאין מצות ביקור חולים בדיבור עם החולה ע"י תלפון, וגם אי יוצאין בכתב להחולה או גם ע"י שליחו – וכת"ה האריך בזה בחריפות ובקיאות נפלא כיד ד' הטובה עליו – וענותנו תרבינו לידע גם חוות דעתי בזה.... ולפע"ד נראה ברור דעיקר מצוה אין יוצאין רק כשהולכין לבקר החולה בפניו ... וכאמרו דזה עיקר מצוה דביבקור חולים, ודאי דצריך לכנס לחדרו במקום שהשכינה למעלה מראשותיו,

**78) נדרים לח:**

מתני'. המודר הנאה מחבירו ונכנס לבקרו עומד אבל לא יושב, ומרפאו רפואת נפש אבל לא רפואת ממון. גמ'.... מיתיבי: חלה הוא נכנס לבקרו, חלה בנו שואלו בשוק.

**79) שו"ת מנחת יצחק ב:פד:י**

ב"ה, יום ה' ראה ה' תשט"ז לפ"ק, מנשסתער יצ"ו שוכט"ס לכבוד ידידי הגה"צ מפורסם לשבח ולתהלה חו"פ וכו', מוה"ר יחזקאל שרגא רבין הלברשטאם שליט"א, האדמו"ר מציעשינוב יצ"ו. אחדשה"ה באה"ר, את יקרת מכתבו הגיעני בצירוף קונטרסו הגדול בחו"ב בענין ביקור חולים, ובקש ממני לעיין בכל פרטי הדברים, ולעשות רצונות חפצתי וקיימתי

recovery from physical illness (F = 3.796, df = 1/146, p < .05). These findings have many useful implications for the medical social workers in Nigeria and in other parts of the world. Hence, it was recommended that the medical social workers have to give adequate attentions to the psycho-social needs of the patients. They have to assist the poor and helpless patients to overcome their financial, emotional, social and material problems in order to experience rapid recovery.

*Joint Commission on Quality and Safety*, Volume 9, no. 12 (December 2003). "Addressing Patients' Emotional and Spiritual Needs", Paul Alexander Clark, M.P.A., Maxwell Drain, M.A., Mary P. Malone, M.S., J.D

**Background**: A comprehensive, systematic literature review and original research were conducted to ascertain whether patients' emotional and spiritual needs are important, whether hospitals are effective in addressing these needs, and what strategies should guide improvement. **Methods**: The literature review was conducted in August 2002. Patient satisfaction data were derived from the Press Ganey Associates' 2001 National Inpatient Database; survey data were collected from 1,732,562 patients between January 2001 and December 2001. **Results**: Data analysis revealed a strong relationship between the "degree to which staff addressed emotional/spiritual needs" and overall patient satisfaction. Three measures most highly correlated with this measure of emotional/spiritual care were (1) staff response to concerns/complaints, (2) staff effort to include patients in decisions about treatment, and (3) staff sensitivity to the inconvenience that health problems and hospitalization can cause.

**(64) נדרים מ.**

בתלמיד אחד מתתלמידי ר' עקיבא שחלה, לא נכנסו חכמים לבקרו, ונכנס ר' עקיבא לבקרו, ובשביל שכיבדו וריבצו לפניו חיה, א"ל: רבי, החייתני יצא ר' עקיבא ודרש. כל מי שאין מבקר חולים כאילו שופך דמים. כי אתא רב דימי אמר: כל המבקר את החולה גורם לו שיחיה, וכל שאינו מבקר את החולה גורם לו שימות.

**(65) מדרש שוחר טוב תהילים מא**

א"ר הקפר מי שהוא מבקר את החולה מתיש ממנו אחד חמישים מחוליו ומי שאינו מבקרו מוסיף אחד חמישים לחליו.

**(66) רמב"ם, הלכות אבל יד:ד**

בקור חולים מצוה על הכל, אפילו גדול מבקר את הקטן, ומבקרין הרבה פעמים ביום, וכל המוסיף משובח ובלבד שלא יטריח, **וכל המבקר את החולה כאילו נטל חלק מחליו והקל מעליו, וכל שאינו מבקר כאילו שופך דמים.**

**(67) נדרים מא., רמב"ם, הלכות אבל יד:ה, טור ושולחן ערוך יורה דעה שלה:ח**

... ואין מבקרין לא חולי מעיים ולא חולי העין, ולא מחושי הראש, מפני שהבקור קשה להן.

**(68) ערוך השולחן, יורה דעה שלה:ג**

עיקר מצות ביקור חולים הוא לעיין בצרכי החולה ולעשות לו מה שצריך ...

**(69) מועד קטן כו:, רמב"ם, הלכות אבל ח:ד**

וחולה שמת לו מת אין מקרעין לו ולא מודיעין לו שלא תטרף עליו דעתו,

**(70) ערוך השולחן, יורה דעה שלה:ד**

יש ליזהר בביקור חולים שלא יהיה המבקר למשא על החולה דלפעמים יש שקשה עליו הדיבור ומפני כבוד המבקר מוכרח לדבר וגם יש שצריך לצרכיו והוא בוש לומר לו ולכן צריך להיות זהיר וחכם ומבין בזה ומטעם זה אמרו חז"ל [שם מ"א [אין מבקרין לא לחולי מעיים ולא לחולי העין ולא לחולי הראש דהדיבור קשה להן וחולי מעיים משום שמא יבוש לומר שצריך לצרכיו וכיצד יעשו נכנסים בבית החיצון לא בהחדר שהחולה שוכב שם ושואלים ודורשים מבני הבית אולי צריך דבר מה ושומעין צערו ומבקשים רחמים ומתפללים עליו:

**(71) רמב"ם, הלכות אבל יד:ו, שולחן ערוך, יורה דעה שלה:ג**

הנכנס לבקר את החולה לא ישב לא על גבי מטה ולא על גבי כסא, ולא על גבי ספסל, ולא על גבי מקום גבוה, ולא למעלה ממראשותיו, אלא מתעטף ויושב למטה ממראשותיו ומבקש עליו רחמים ויוצא. המבקר את החולה לא ישב ע"ג מטה ולא ע"ג כסא ולא ע"ג ספסל אלא מתעטף ויושב לפניו שהשכינה למעלה ממראשותיו: הגה ודוקא כשהחולה שוכב על הארץ דהיושב גבוה ממנו אבל כשכשוכב על המטה מותר לישב על כסא וספסל (ב"י בשם הר"ן והגהות מיימוני ותוס' והג"א) וכן נוהגין:

**(72) רמב"ם, הלכות אבל יד:ד-ה, שולחן ערוך, יורה דעה שלה**

בקור חולים מצוה על הכל, אפילו גדול מבקר את הקטן, ומבקרין הרבה פעמים ביום, וכל המוסיף משובח ובלבד שלא יטריח, וכל המבקר את החולה כאילו נטל חלק מחליו והקל מעליו, וכל שאינו

בעריסתן ובני אדם מבקרים אותן, מה הבריות אומרים? לא ה' שלחני לזה. דרש רבא: (במדבר טז) אם בריאה יברא ה' אם בריאה גיהנם מוטב תהיה, אם לאו יברא ה'.

**54) אבות דרבי נתן ל:א**

הוא היה אומר תנחומי אבלים וביקור חולים וגמ"ח מביאין טובה לעולם.

**55) ספר מצוות גדולות, מצות עשה ח**

מצות עשה ללכת בדרכיו הטובים והישרים שנאמר והלכת בדרכיו ואומר אחרי ה' אלקיכם תלכו ומפרש בפ"ק דסוטה (יד, א) אחרי מדותיו תלכו מה הוא מלביש ערומים שנאמר (בראשית ג, כא) ויעש ה' לאדם ולאשתו כתנות עור וילבישם, ומבקר חולים שנאמר (בראשית יח, א) וירא אליו ה' באלני ממרא,

**56) רמב"ם, ספר המצוות, שורש א, ב**

וכן מאה ברכות בכל יום ונחום אבלים ובקור חולים וקבורת מתים והלבשת ערומים וחשוב תקופות ושמנה עשר ימים לגמור בהן את ההלל והשתכל ממי שישמע לשונם נאמרו לו למשה בסיני

**57) רמב"ם, הלכות אבל יד:א**

מצות עשה של דבריהם לבקר חולים ... ואלו הן גמילות חסדים שבגופו שאין להם שיעור, אע"פ שכל מצות אלו מדבריהם הרי הן בכלל ואהבת לרעך כמוך, כל הדברים שאתה רוצה שיעשו אותם לך אחרים, עשה אתה אותן לאחיך בתורה ובמצות.

**58) טור, יורה דעה שלה**

א"ר יצחק בריה דרב יהודה לעולם יבקש אדם שלא יחלה שאם חלה אומרים לו הבא זכות והפטר וכיון שחלה האדם מצוה על כל אדם לבקרו שכן מצינו בהקב"ה שמבקר חולים כמו שדרשו בפסוק וירא אליו ה' באלוני ממרא מלמד שבא אליו לבקר החולה וסמכוה אקרא והודעת להם את הדרך ילכו בה ומצוה גדולה היא לבקר שמתוך כך יבקש עליו רחמים ונמצא כאילו מחיה אותו

**59) נדרים מ.**

אמר רב: כל המבקר את החולה ניצול מדינה של גיהנם ... ואם ביקר מה שכרו? מה שכרו? כדאמר: ניצול מדינה של גיהנם אלא מה שכרו בעוה"ז? (תהלים מא) ד' ישמרהו ויחייהו ואושר בארץ ואל תתנהו בנפש אויביו, יי' ישמרהו מיצר הרע, ויחייהו מן היסורין, ואושר בארץ שיהו הכל מתכבדין בו, ואל תתנהו בנפש אויביו שיזדמנו לו ריעים כנעמן שריפו את צרעתו, ואל יזדמנו לו ריעים כרחבעם שחילקו את מלכותו.

**60) שבת קכז. (ובסידור בברכות שחרית)**

אמר רב יהודה בר שילא אמר רבי אסי אמר רבי יוחנן: ששה דברים אדם אוכל פירותיהן בעולם הזה, והקרן קיימת לו לעולם הבא. ואלו הן: הכנסת אורחין, וביקור חולים, ועיון תפלה, והשכמת בית המדרש, והמגדל בניו לתלמוד תורה, והדן את חברו לכף זכות.

**61) בבא מציעא ל:**

... לא נצרכה אלא לבן גילו. דאמר מר: בן גילו נוטל אחד מששים בחליו

**62) נדרים לט:**

תניא: ביקור חולים אין לה שיעור. מאי אין לה שיעור? סבר רב יוסף למימר: אין שיעור למתן שכרה, אמר ליה אביי: וכל מצות מי יש שיעור למתן שכרן? והא תנן: הוי זהיר במצוה קלה כבחמורה, שאין אתה יודע מתן שכרן של מצות אלא אמר אביי: אפי' גדול אצל קטן. רבא אמר: אפי' מאה פעמים ביום. אמר רבי אחא בר חנינא: כל המבקר חולה נוטל אחד מששים בצערו. אמרי ליה: אם כן, ליעלון שיתין ולוקמוהָ אמר ליה: כעישורייתא דבי רבי, ובבן גילו דתניא, רבי אומר: בת הניזונית מנכסי אחין נוטלת עישור נכסים, אמרו לו לרבי: לדבריך, מי שיש לו עשר בנות ובן, אין לו לבן במקום בנות כלום אמר להן: ראשונה נוטלת עישור נכסים, שניה במה ששיירה, שלישית במה ששיירה, וחוזרות וחולקות בשוה.

**63) Impact of Emotional Reactions on Patients' Recovery from Physical Illness: Implications for the Medical Social Workers," J. K. Mojoyinola, Department of Social Work, Faculty of Education, University of Ibadan, Ibadan, Nigeria**

The study examined the impact of emotional reactions on recovery of patients from physical illness.

It also examined their implications for the medical social workers. The study was carried out among 147 physically ill patients in six selected government-owned hospitals in Oyo State, Nigeria. A single questionnaire tagged "Emotional Reactions and Recovery Assessment Questionnaire (ERARAQ) was developed and used for the study. Two hypotheses were formulated and tested; using analysis of variance (ANOVA). The hypotheses were tested at 0.05 level of significance. The study established that happiness has significant impact on recovery from physical illness ($F = 11.589$, $df = 1/146$, $p < .05$). It also established that anxiety and depression have significant impact on

## 39) דברי הימים ב' לב:כד

בַּיָּמִים הָהֵם חָלָה יְחִזְקִיָּהוּ עַד־לָמוּת וַיִּתְפַּלֵּל אֶל־ד' וַיֹּאמֶר לוֹ וּמוֹפֵת נָתַן לוֹ:

## 40) שבת לב.

אמר רב יצחק בריה דרב יהודה: לעולם יבקש אדם רחמים שלא יחלה, שאם יחלה אומרים לו: הבא זכות והפטר.... אדם יוצא לשוק יהי דומה בעיניו כמי שנמסר לסרדיוט, חש בראשו יהי דומה בעיניו כמי שנתנוהו בקולר, עלה למטה ונפל יהי דומה בעיניו כמו שהעלוהו לגרדום לידון דכל העולה לגרדום לידון, אם יש לו פרקליטין גדולים ניצול, ואם לאו אינו ניצול. ואלו הן פרקליטין של אדם תשובה ומעשים טובים. ואפילו תשע מאות ותשעים ותשעה מלמדים עליו חובה, ואחד מלמד עליו זכות ניצול, שנאמר (איוב לג) אם יש עליו מלאך מליץ אחד מני אלף להגיד לאדם ישרו ויחננו ויאמר פדעהו מרדת שחת וגו'

## 41) עירובין כט:

ומעשה ברבי חנינא שאכל חצי בצל וחצי נחש שבו, וחלה ונטה למות, ובקשו חביריו רחמים עליו וחיה, מפני שהשעה צריכה לו.

## 42) ברכות לב:

אמר רבי אלעזר: גדולה תפלה יותר ממעשים טובים. שאין לך גדול במעשים טובים יותר ממשה רבינו, אף על פי כן לא נענה אלא בתפלה, שנאמר: (דברים ג') אל תוסף דבר אלי, וסמיך ליה, עלה ראש הפסגה.

## 43) ברכות לד:

אמרו עליו על רבי חנינא בן דוסא, שהיה מתפלל על החולים ואומר, זה חי וזה מת. אמרו לו: מנין אתה יודע? אמר להם: אם שגורה תפלתי בפי יודע אני שהוא מקובל, ואם לאו אני יודע שהוא מטורף.

## 44) רמב"ם, הלכות אבל יד:ו

הנכנס לבקר את החולה לא ישב לא על גבי מטה ולא על גבי כסא, ולא על גבי ספסל, ולא על גבי מקום גבוה, ולא למעלה ממראשותיו, אלא מתעטף ויושב למטה ממראשותיו ומבקש עליו רחמים ויוצא.

## 45) רמ"א שולחן ערוך, יורה דעה שלה:ד

... וכו' שביקר ולא ביקש עליו רחמים לא קיים המצוה

## 46) שו"ת אגרות משה, יורה דעה ד:נא

... וגם הא עיקר מצוות בקור חולים הוא כדי שיתפלל כשיראהו שהשי"ת ישלח לו רפואה, ... ומפורש בנדרים דף מ' ע"א, כי אתא ר' דימי אמר כל המבקר את החולה גורם לו שיחיה, ופי' בגמ' שהוא בזה שמבקש עליו רחמים שיחיה. ......וכל

---

שביקר ולא ביקש עליו רחמים לא קיים המצוה ... וכ"ש כשהוא חכם, שאיתא בב"ב דף קט"ז ע"א, דרש ר' פנחס בן חמא כל מי שיש לו חולה בתוך ביתו ילך אצל חכם ויבקש עליו רחמים, ודריש זה מקרא דכתיב (משלי ט"ז י"א) חמת מלך מלאכי מות ואיש חכם יכפרנה, שקאי על מי שבאה צער מחמת מלך – הקדוש ברוך הוא, אף שהוא באופן גדול כהא דמלאכי מות – היינו חולה שנוטה למות, מועילה תפילת חכם ...

## 47) בראשית א:כז

וַיִּבְרָא אֱלֹקִים אֶת־הָאָדָם בְּצַלְמוֹ בְּצֶלֶם אֱלֹקִים בָּרָא אֹתוֹ זָכָר וּנְקֵבָה בָּרָא אֹתָם:

## 48) דברים כח:ט

יְקִימְךָ ד' לוֹ לְעַם קָדוֹשׁ כַּאֲשֶׁר נִשְׁבַּע־לָךְ כִּי תִשְׁמֹר אֶת־מִצְוֹת ד' אֱלֹקֶיךָ וְהָלַכְתָּ בִּדְרָכָיו:

## 49) דברים יג:ה

אַחֲרֵי ד' אֱלֹקֵיכֶם תֵּלֵכוּ וְאֹתוֹ תִירָאוּ וְאֶת־מִצְוֹתָיו תִּשְׁמֹרוּ וּבְקֹלוֹ תִשְׁמָעוּ וְאֹתוֹ תַעֲבֹדוּ וּבוֹ תִדְבָּקוּן:

## 50) סוטה יד.

ואמר רבי חמא ברבי חנינא, מאי דכתיב: (דברים יג) אחרי ה' אלקיכם תלכו? וכי אפשר לו לאדם להלך אחר שכינה? והלא כבר נאמר: (דברים ד) כי ה' אלקיך אש אוכלה הוא אלא להלך אחר מדותיו של הקב"ה, מה הוא מלביש ערומים, דכתיב: (בראשית ג) ויעש ה' אלהים לאדם ולאשתו כתנות עור וילבישם, אף אתה הלבש ערומים הקב"ה ביקר חולים, דכתיב: (בראשית יח) וירא אליו ה' באלוני ממרא, אף אתה בקר חולים

## 51) בבא מציעא ל:

דתני רב יוסף: (שמות יח) והודעת להם זה בית חייהם, את הדרך זו גמילות חסדים, (אשר) ילכו זה ביקור חולים, בה זו קבורה, ואת המעשה זה הדין, אשר יעשון זו לפנים משורת הדין.

## 52) מכילתא דרבי ישמעאל, מסכתא דעמלק ב

והודעת להם את הדרך- זו תלמוד תורה. ואת המעשה אשר יעשון זה מעשה הטוב דברי ר' יהושע ר' אליעזר המודעי אומר והודעת להם הודע להם בית חייהם ... את הדרך זו בקור חולים ... "והודעת להם" זה בית חייהם, "את הדרך" זו גמילות חסדים, "(אשר) ילכו" זה ביקור חולים ...

## 53) נדרים לט:

אמר ריש לקיש: רמז לביקור חולין מן התורה מנין? שנאמר: (במדבר טז) אם כמות כל האדם ימותון אלה ופקדת כל אדם וגו'. מאי משמע? אמר רבא: אם כמות כל האדם ימותון אלה, שהן חולים ומוטלים

**23) פירושי רש"י ותוספות יום טוב על משנה קידושין ד:יד**

טוב שברופאים לגיהנם – אינו ירא מן החולי ומאכלו מאכל בריאים ואינו משבר לבו למקום ופעמים שהורג נפשות ויש בידו לרפאות העני ואינו מרפא.

**24) פירוש רבינו ניסים על משנה קידושין ד:יד**

טוב שברופאים לגיהנם הם אותם שאינן משגיחין ומעיינין ברפואתם בפשיעה

**25) פירוש בניהו בן יהוידע על משנה קידושין ד:יד**

טוב שברופאים לגיהנם. נ"ל בס"ד, הרופא שאינו פקח ומומחה לא יסמוך על דעתו לתת סמים חריפים ותקיפים אלא יתן סמים קלים פשוטים, אשר אם לא יועילו ודאי לא יזיקו, ואם כן אין תקלה יוצאה מסיבתו, ואם יכבד חליו של חולה מאליו יכבד ולא יגיע לו נזק מן הסמים שנותן לו לשתות, אבל רופא שהוא בקי ומומחה סומך על דעתו, ונותן סמים חריפים ותקיפים לעשות בהם מלחמה עם החולי של החולה לגרשו בעל כרחו, ולפעמים ישגה לתת סם שיעור יותר ממה שצריך לחולה לפי מזגו וכוחו, ומחמת חריפות ותוקף הסם יזיק לו, ועוד לפעמים ישגה בעיקר החולי, ויתן סמים דלא שייכי לאותו החולי של החולה, ואז יזיק הסם אליו, ויהיה סיבה למיתתו בר מינן, ולזה אמר טוב שברופאים קרוב הוא לירד לגיהנם, בעבור שפיכות דמים של החולים אשר תסובב על ידו:

**26) שולחן ערוך, חושן משפט תכז:י'**

כל העובר על דברים אלו וכיוצא בהם, ואמר הריני מסכן בעצמי ומה לאחרים עלי בכך או אני מקפיד בכך מכין אותו מכת מרדות, והנזהר מהם עליו תבא ברכת טוב.

**27) יומא פג:**

דתניא: מי שנשכו נחש קורין לו רופא ממקום למקום ...

**28) עבודה זרה כח:**

אמר רב זוטרא בר טוביה אמר רב: עין שמרדה מותר לכוחלה בשבת.

**29) בבא מציעא פה:**

שמואל ירחינאה אסייה דרבי הוה, חלש רבי בעיניה. אמר ליה: אימלי לך סמא. אמר ליה: לא יכילנא. אשטר לך משטר? [אמר ליה]: לא יכילנא. הוה מותיב ליה בגובתא דסמני תותי בי סדייה, ואיתסי.

**30) סנהדרין יז:**

כל עיר שאין בה עשרה דברים הללו אין תלמיד חכם רשאי לדור בתוכה: בית דין מכין ועונשין, וקופה

---

של צדקה נגבית בשנים ומתחלקת בשלשה, ובית הכנסת, ובית המרחץ, ובית הכסא, רופא, ואומן, ולבלר, (וטבח), ומלמד תינוקות.

**31) רמב"ם, הלכות דעות ד:כג**

כל עיר שאין בה עשרה דברים האלו אין תלמיד חכם רשאי לדור בתוכה, ואלו הן: רופא, ואומן, ובית המרחץ, ובית הכסא, ומים מצויין כגון נהר ומעין, ובית הכנסת, ומלמד תינוקות, ולבלר, וגבאי צדקה, ובית דין מכים וחובשים.

**32) רמב"ם, הלכות דעות ג:ג**

המנהיג עצמו על פי הרפואה, אם שם על לבו שיהיה כל גופו ואבריו שלמים בלבד ושיהיו לו בנים עושין מלאכתו ועמלין לצורכו אין זו דרך טובה, אלא ישים על לבו שיהא גופו שלם וחזק כדי שתהיה נפשו ישרה לדעת את ה', שאי אפשר שיבין וישתכל בחכמות והוא רעב וחולה או אחד מאיבריו כואב ... ולא יוכל לעבוד את ה' והוא חולה.

**33) שולחן ערוך, חושן משפט תכ:כא**

אמר הנחבל תן לי שכר הרופא ואני ארפא את עצמי, יכול החובל לומר לו שמא לא תרפא עצמך יפה ויקראו אותי מזיק לעולם.

**34) שו"ץ ציץ אליעזר יא:מא, ס"ק ג**

... ועוד יותר מזה דמצוה וחיוב נמי איכא בדבר כיון דלפי מעשה האדם חיותו תלוי בכך או מכיון שבני האדם התחילו להתרפאות שוב הניחם טוב על הטבעים כדברי הרמב"ן שם, ומכיון שכן שוב מצוה כבר איכא להתרפאות משום סכנה יעו"ש.

**35) ברכות י'.**

כך מקובלני מבית אבי אבא אפילו חרב חדה מונחת על צוארו של אדם אל ימנע עצמו מן הרחמים.

**36) בראשית כ:ו-ז**

וַיֹּאמֶר אֵלָיו הָאֱלֹהִים בַּחֲלֹם גַּם אָנֹכִי יָדַעְתִּי כִּי בְתָם־לְבָבְךָ עָשִׂיתָ זֹּאת וָאֶחְשֹׂךְ גַּם־אָנֹכִי אוֹתְךָ מֵחֲטוֹ־לִי עַל־כֵּן לֹא־נְתַתִּיךָ לִנְגֹּעַ אֵלֶיהָ: וְעַתָּה הָשֵׁב אֵשֶׁת־הָאִישׁ כִּי־נָבִיא הוּא וְיִתְפַּלֵּל בַּעַדְךָ וֶחְיֵה וְאִם־אֵינְךָ מֵשִׁיב דַּע כִּי־מוֹת תָּמוּת אַתָּה וְכָל־אֲשֶׁר־לָךְ:

**37) שמואל ב' יב:טו-טז**

וַיֵּלֶךְ נָתָן אֶל־בֵּיתוֹ וַיִּגֹּף ד' אֶת־הַיֶּלֶד אֲשֶׁר יָלְדָה אֵשֶׁת־אוּרִיָּה לְדָוִד וַיֵּאָנַשׁ: וַיְבַקֵּשׁ דָּוִד אֶת־הָאֱלֹהִים בְּעַד הַנָּעַר וַיָּצָם דָּוִד צוֹם וּבָא וְלָן וְשָׁכַב אָרְצָה:

**38) מלכים ב' ד:לב-לג**

וַיָּבֹא אֱלִישָׁע הַבָּיְתָה וְהִנֵּה הַנַּעַר מֵת מֻשְׁכָּב עַל־מִטָּתוֹ: וַיָּבֹא וַיִּסְגֹּר הַדֶּלֶת בְּעַד שְׁנֵיהֶם וַיִּתְפַּלֵּל אֶל־ד':

**15) רמב"ם, פירוש המשניות, נדרים ד:ד**

רוצה לומר חיוב הרופא מן התורה לרפאות חולי ישראל, וזה נכלל בפירוש מה שאמר הפסוק (דברים כב), והשבותו לו, לרפאות את גופו שהוא כשרואה אתו מסוכן ויכול להצילו או בגופו או בממונו או בחכמתו:

**16) שולחן ערוך, יורה דעה שלו:א**

א נתנה התורה רשות לרופא לרפאות ומצוה היא ובכלל פיקוח נפש הוא ואם מונע עצמו הרי זה שופך דמים

**17) ט"ז על שולחן ערוך, יורה דעה שלו ס"ק א**

נתנה תורה רשות כו' ומצוה היא כו'. קשה כיון דבאמת מצוה היא למה קרי לה תחלה רשות ונראה דהכי הוא כוונת הענין זה דרפואה האמיתית היא ע"פ בקשת רחמים דמשמיא יש לו רפואה כמ"ש מחצתי ואני ארפא אלא שאין האדם זוכה לכך אלא צריך לעשות רפואה על פי טבע העולם והוא יתברך הסכים על זה ונתן הרפואה ע"י טבע הרפואות וזהו נתינת רשות של הקדוש ב"ה וכיון שכבר בא האדם לידי כך יש חיוב על הרופא לעשות רפואתו ...

**18) שולחן ערוך, יורה דעה שלו:א-ב**

א ... ומיהו לא יתעסק ברפואה אא"כ הוא בקי ולא יהא שם גדול ממנו שאם כן הרי זה שופך דמים ואם ריפא שלא ברשות בית דין חייב בתשלומין אפי' אם הוא בקי ואם ריפא ברשות ב"ד וטעה והזיק פטור מדיני אדם וחייב בדיני שמים ואם המית ונודע לו ששגג גולה על ידו:

ב הרופא אסור ליטול שכר החכמה והלימוד אבל שכר הטורח והבטלה מותר:

**19) שולחן ערוך, אורח חיים שא:כו**

נאמן לומר הרופא על עצמו שהוא מומחה:

**20) רמב"ם, הלכות חובל ומזיק ב:יח, שולחן ערוך, חושן משפט תכ:כא**

אמר לו המזיק אני ארפא אותך או יש לי רופא שמרפא בחנם, אין שומעין לו אלא מביא רופא אומן ומרפאו בשכר.

**21) משנה קידושין ד:יד**

טוב שברופאים לגיהנם

**22) משנה סנהדרין ד:ה**

שכל המאבד נפש אחת מישראל, מעלה עליו הכתוב כאילו אבד עולם מלא. וכל המקים נפש אחת מישראל, מעלה עליו הכתוב כאילו קים עולם מלא.

**11) פירושי עקידת יצחק, וישלח שער כו**

... ומכל זה דחייה עצומה למה שכתב הרמב"ן ז"ל, שאם נתנה רשות לרופא לרפאת דכתיב (שמות כא) ורפא ירפא, שלא נתנה רשות לחולה לקבל רפאותו, אלא שיקוה אל ה', השם מחלה בקרבו, כי הוא יהיה רופא כשיושלם עונו וכו', כמו שכתב שם פרשה אם בחקותי, כי מי ישמע אליו כל הדבר הזה, והלא כל אדם חייב להראות עצמו מהבינונים, אשר השתדלותם תועיל להם ... וראיתיו מאמרו (דברי הימים ב טז) וגם בחליו לא דרש את ה' כי ברופאים, אינה ראיה, שכבר אמרנו שאין לאדם לסמוך על השתדלותו בלי בקשת רחמי שמים, והראוי ומחוייב להקדים הבקשה והדרישה מאליו, וכמוהו בשאול וימת שאול במעלו וכו', וגם לשאול באוב לדרוש ולא דרש בה' וימיתהו (שם א י) כמו שכתב בפרשת קדושים תהיו, ולזה אין לפקפק כי אשר כתבנו הוא הראוי והנכון לנהוג בו:

**12) שו"ת אגרות משה, אורח חיים ג:צ**

הא דדרשת ר' ישמעאל שניתן רשות לרופא לרפאות הוא דוקא מדתנא ביה קרא ורפא ירפא מה שלא שמעינן מרפא לחודיה דהו"א ה"מ מכה דבידי אדם אבל חולי הבא ביד"ש כשמרפא נראה כסותר גזירת המלך קמ"ל דשרי, וא"כ אפשר שמה שהתורה חייבה וגם רשות לרפא אינו משום דקמ"ל דלא הוי כסותר גזירת המלך, מטעם דאמרינן דגזירת המלך היתה רק שיחלה עד שימצאו את הרופא והרפואה שיצטרך ושיהיה לו פחד שמא לא יתרפא ואם עולה הרפואה להוצאת ממון הוא גם להפסידו בממון יחד עם צער הגוף, אלא שאף שהוא בעצם כסותר גזירת המלך התירה תורה לרפאותו וגם חייבה, וכמו שמותר וגם חייבין להתפלל לבטל גזירת המלך כדמצינו בכל התפלות שבקראי, ואף במקום שלא גילה השי"ת דעתו שיתפלל אף בלשון הניחה לי, כמו כן התירה תורה לרפאות בכל מיני סמים לבטל גזירתו

**13) ויקרא יט:טז, דברים כב:ב**

לֹא־תֵלֵךְ רָכִיל בְּעַמֶּיךָ לֹא תַעֲמֹד עַל־דַּם רֵעֶךָ אֲנִי ד׳: וְאִם־לֹא קָרוֹב אָחִיךָ אֵלֶיךָ וְלֹא יְדַעְתּוֹ וַאֲסַפְתּוֹ אֶל־תּוֹךְ בֵּיתֶךָ וְהָיָה עִמְּךָ עַד דְּרֹשׁ אָחִיךָ אֹתוֹ וַהֲשֵׁבֹתוֹ לוֹ:

**14) שולחן ערוך, חושן משפט תכו:א**

הרואה את חבירו טובע בים או ליסטים באין עליו או חיה רעה באה עליו, ויכול להצילו הוא בעצמו או שישכור אחרים להציל ולא הציל, או ששמע עכו"ם או מוסרים מחשבים עליו רעה או טומנים לו פח ולא גילה אוזן חבירו והודיעו, או שידע בעכו"ם או באנס שהוא בא על חבירו ויכול לפייסו בגלל חבירו ולהסיר מה שבלבו ולא פייסו וכיוצא בדברים אלו, עובר על "לא תעמוד על דם רעך".

# SOURCES ON DOCTORS AND VISITING THE SICK –
## THE JEWISH VIEW

### 1) שמות טו:כו
וַיֹּאמֶר אִם־שָׁמוֹעַ תִּשְׁמַע לְקוֹל | ד' אֱלֹקֶיךָ וְהַיָּשָׁר בְּעֵינָיו תַּעֲשֶׂה וְהַאֲזַנְתָּ לְמִצְוֹתָיו וְשָׁמַרְתָּ כָּל־חֻקָּיו כָּל־הַמַּחֲלָה אֲשֶׁר־שַׂמְתִּי בְמִצְרַיִם לֹא־אָשִׂים עָלֶיךָ כִּי אֲנִי ד' רֹפְאֶךָ:

### 2) תהילים מא:ב-ג
אַשְׁרֵי מַשְׂכִּיל אֶל־דָּל בְּיוֹם רָעָה יְמַלְּטֵהוּ ד': ד' יִשְׁמְרֵהוּ וִיחַיֵּהוּ וְאֻשַּׁר בָּאָרֶץ וְאַל־תִּתְּנֵהוּ בְּנֶפֶשׁ אֹיְבָיו:

### 3) ברכה #8 של שמונה עשרה
רְפָאֵנוּ ד' וְנֵרָפֵא. הוֹשִׁיעֵנוּ וְנִוָּשֵׁעָה כִּי תְהִלָּתֵנוּ אָתָּה. וְהַעֲלֵה רְפוּאָה שְׁלֵמָה לְכָל מַכּוֹתֵינוּ. כִּי קֵל מֶלֶךְ רוֹפֵא נֶאֱמָן וְרַחֲמָן אָתָּה. בָּרוּךְ אַתָּה ד'. רוֹפֵא חוֹלֵי עַמּוֹ יִשְׂרָאֵל

### 4) שמות כא:יט, ברכות ס.
אִם־יָקוּם וְהִתְהַלֵּךְ בַּחוּץ עַל־מִשְׁעַנְתּוֹ וְנִקָּה הַמַּכֶּה רַק שִׁבְתּוֹ יִתֵּן וְרַפֹּא יְרַפֵּא:
"ורפא ירפא" מכאן שניתנה רשות לרופא לרפאות.

### 5) חובות הלבבות, שער רביעי, פרק ד
... וכן נאמר בענין הבריאות והחולי, כי על האדם לבטוח בבורא בזה ולהשתדל בהתמדת הבריאות בסיבות אשר מטבעו זה, ולדחות המדוה במה שנהגו לדחותו, כמו שציוה הבורא, יתעלה (שמות כא יט): ורפא ירפא, מבלי שיבטח על סיבות הבריאות והחולי, שהן מועילות או מזיקות אלא ברשות הבורא. וכאשר יבטח בבורא, ירפאהו מחליו בסיבה ובלתי סיבה, כמו שנאמר (תהלים קז כ): ישלח דברו וירפאם.

### 6) פירוש רמב"ן על ויקרא כו:יא
... והכלל כי בהיות ישראל שלמים והם רבים, לא יתנהג ענינם בטבע כלל, לא בגופם, ולא בארצם, לא בכללם, ולא ביחיד מהם, כי יברך השם לחמם ומימם, ויסיר מחלה מקרבם, עד שלא יצטרכו לרופא ולהשתמר בדרך מדרכי הרפואות כלל, כמו שאמר (שמות טו כו) כי אני ה' רופאך. וכן היו הצדיקים עושים בזמן הנבואה, גם כי יקרם עון שיחלו לא ידרשו ברופאים רק בנביאים, כענין חזקיהו בחלותו ...
... אבל הדורש השם בנביא לא ידרוש ברופאים ...
וזו היא כוונתם באמרם (שם) ורפא ירפא מכאן שניתנה רשות לרופא לרפאות, לא אמרו שניתנה רשות לחולה להתרפאות, אלא כיון שחלה החולה ובא להתרפאות כי נהג ברפואות והוא לא היה מעדת השם שחלקם

---

### 7) ט"ז על שולחן ערוך, יורה דעה שלו ס"ק א
... ונראה דהכי הוא כוונת הענין דזה דרפואה האמיתית היא ע"פ בקשת רחמים דמשמיא יש לו רפואה כמ"ש מחצתי ואני ארפא אלא שאין האדם זוכה לכך אלא צריך לעשות רפואה על פי טבע העולם והוא יתברך הסכים על זה ונתן הרפואה ע"י טבע הרפואות וזהו נתינת רשות של הקדוש ב"ה וכיון שכבר בא לידי האדם כך יש חיוב על הרופא לעשות רפואתו ...

### 8) שו"ת ציץ אליעזר יא:מא, ס"ק ג
והפתרון להבנת דברי הרמב"ן עה"ת הוא לדעתי כפי שכתבתי לבאר בספרי רמת רחל סי' ב' דדברי הרמב"ן נאמרים ביסוד עיקרי הדברים בשרשן בזמן שאין שום גורמים חיצוניים מפריעים אבל מכיון שלפי מציאות הדברים דכמעט רובא דרובא דבני אדם אינם זכאים לכך שתבוא רפואתם ע"י נס מן השמים והתורה בעצמה לא תסמוך דיני' על הנסים, כפי שכתב הרמב"ן בעצמו בסוף דבריו שם א"כ שוב כלול גם לחולה ...

### 9) פירושים אבן עזרא ורבינו בחיי על שמות כא:יט
ורפא ירפא – לאות שנתן רשות לרופאים לרפא המכות והפצעים שיראו בחוץ. רק כל חלי שהוא בפנים בגוף ביד השם לרפאתו.
... ומה שאמרו חז"ל (בבא קמא פה.) ורפא ירפא מכאן שניתנה רשות לרופא לרפאות לא אמרו אלא במכה שבחוץ שהכתוב מדבר בה אבל חולי מבפנים אין זה תלוי ביד הרופא אלא ביד הרופא כל בשר אשר בידו נפש כל חי:

### 10) תוספות על בבא קמא פה. ד"ה "שניתנה"
שניתנה רשות לרופא לרפאות – וא"ת והא מרפא לחודיה שמעינן ליה וי"ל דה"א ה"מ מכה בידי אדם אבל חולי הבא בידי שמים כשמרפא נראה כסותר גזירת המלך קמ"ל דשרי:

---

בחיים, אין לרופא לאסור עצמו מרפואתו, לא מפני חשש שמא ימות בידו, אחרי שהוא בקי במלאכה ההיא, ולא בעבור שיאמר כי השם לבדו הוא רופא כל בשר, שכבר נהגו ועל כן האנשים הנצים שהכו זה את זה באבן או באגרוף (שמות כא יח) יש על המכה תשלומי הרפואה, כי התורה לא תסמוך דיניה על הנסים, כאשר אמרה (דברים טו יא) כי לא יחדל אביון מקרב הארץ, מדעתו שכן יהיה אבל ברצות השם דרכי איש אין לו עסק ברופאים:

תָּבֹא עַד־מְלֹאת יְמֵי טָהֳרָהּ: וְאִם־נְקֵבָה תֵלֵד וְטָמְאָה שְׁבֻעַיִם כְּנִדָּתָהּ וְשִׁשִּׁים יוֹם וְשֵׁשֶׁת יָמִים תֵּשֵׁב עַל־דְּמֵי טָהֳרָה:

### 42) רמב"ם, הלכות אבות הטומאות א:ב

אחד בהמה וחיה בין המותרין באכילה בין האסורין אם מתו כולן בשרן מטמא בכזית, ושחיטת הבהמה טהורה וחיה טהורה מטהרתו בכ"מ, ואפילו שחט חולין בעזרה וקדשים בחוץ הרי אלו טהורין, ואם אירע פיסול בשחיטה הרי זו נבילה ומטמאה במשא כמו שביארנו בהלכות שחיטה.

### 43) ויקרא יב:ו-ז

וּבִמְלֹאת יְמֵי טָהֳרָהּ לְבֵן אוֹ לְבַת תָּבִיא כֶּבֶשׂ בֶּן־שְׁנָתוֹ לְעֹלָה וּבֶן־יוֹנָה אוֹ־תֹר לְחַטָּאת אֶל־פֶּתַח אֹהֶל־מוֹעֵד אֶל־הַכֹּהֵן: וְהִקְרִיבוֹ לִפְנֵי ד' וְכִפֶּר עָלֶיהָ וְטָהֲרָה מִמְּקֹר דָּמֶיהָ זֹאת תּוֹרַת הַיֹּלֶדֶת לַזָּכָר אוֹ לַנְּקֵבָה:

### 44) פירוש רבינו בחיי על ויקרא יב:ו-ז

וכפר עליה. אין לשון כפרה נופל כי אם על החטא, ולפיכך קרבן זה של יולדת מחודש כקרבן הנזיר, כי מה חטאה בזמן הלידה שתצריכנה התורה קרבן, ואם זה הקרבן הוא על שבאה בסכנה וניצלה מהמיתה, היה ראוי לה שתביא תודה, ולמה תביא עולה וחטאת: ויתכן לפרש שאין זה הקרבן הזה מצד חטא של עצמה רק מצד אמה שהיא היתה אם כל חי, כי לולא החטא

ההוא היה האדם מוליד עם אשתו שלא בדרך תאוה וחשק אלא בדרך הטבע הגמור, כטבע האילן המוציא פירותיו בכל שנה שלא בתאוה, והיולדת הזו כאמה בתה במעשה החטא, כי הענפים הם מקולקלים בקלקול השורש, ועל כן יצריכנה הכתוב קרבן לכפר על החטא הקדמוני ...

### 45) בראשית ג:טז

אֶל־הָאִשָּׁה אָמַר הַרְבָּה אַרְבֶּה עִצְּבוֹנֵךְ וְהֵרֹנֵךְ בְּעֶצֶב תֵּלְדִי בָנִים וְאֶל־אִישֵׁךְ תְּשׁוּקָתֵךְ וְהוּא יִמְשָׁל־בָּךְ:

### 46) ויקרא א:ב

דַּבֵּר אֶל־בְּנֵי יִשְׂרָאֵל וְאָמַרְתָּ אֲלֵהֶם אָדָם כִּי־יַקְרִיב מִכֶּם קָרְבָּן לַד' מִן־הַבְּהֵמָה מִן־הַבָּקָר וּמִן־הַצֹּאן תַּקְרִיבוּ אֶת־קָרְבַּנְכֶם:

### 47) Rabbi Jonathan Sacks, Chief Rabbi of England, Covenant and Conversation, Vayikra 5771

### 48) תלמוד ירושלמי, נדה י'.

רבי יסא בשם רבי יוחנן כולו אדם ופניו בהמה אינו וולד כולו בהמה ופניו אדם וולד הוא כולו אדם ופניו בהמה עומד וקורא בתורה אומרים לו בא לשחטך כולו בהמה ופניו אדם עומד וחורש בשדה אומרים לו בא וחלוץ או ייבם

אישיו ומה שישיגם מטוב או רע נמשך אחר הדין, כמו שאמר, "כי כל דרכיו משפט"; אבל שאר בעלי החיים, וכל שכן הצמחים וזולתם, דעתי בהם דעת אריסטו, לא אאמין כלל שזה העלה נפל בהשגחה בו, ולא שזה העכביש טרף זה הזבוב בגזרה מאת האלוה ורצונו באישי עתה, ולא שהירוק אשר רקק אותו ראובן התנועע עד שנפל על זה היתוש במקום מיוחד והרגו בגזרת האלוה, ולא שזה הדג חטף ובלע זאת התולעת מעל פני המים ברצון אלוהי אישי – אבל אלה כולם אצלי במקרה גמור ... שיש לאלוה השגחה באיש מאישי בעלי החיים, כי אם בבני אדם לבד ... כי (בעלי חיים) אלה כולם – השגחה מינית, לא אישית, וכאילו הוא מספר פעולותיו ית' בהכינו לכל מין מזונו ההכרחי וחומר עמידתו.

### 31) רמב"ם הלכות תשובה ח:א

הטובה הצפונה לצדיקים היא חיי העולם הבא והיא החיים שאין עמהן מות והטובה שאין עמה רעה, הוא שכתוב בתורה למען ייטב לך והארכת ימים, מפי השמועה למדו למען ייטב לך לעולם שכולו טוב והארכת ימים לעולם שכולו ארוך, וזהו הוא העולם הבא, שכר הצדיקים הוא שיזכו לנועם זה ויהיו בטובה זו, ופרעון הרשעים הוא שלא יזכו לחיים אלו אלא יכרתו וימותו, וכל מי שאינו זוכה לחיים אלו הוא המת שאינו חי לעולם אלא **נכרת ברשעו ואבד כבהמה**, וזהו כרת הכתובה בתורה ...

### 32) ספר חסידים תתשלא

לפי שנשמת האדם המדברת אינה מתה, לפיכך יחלום החי מן המת, אבל הבהמה שמתה אין לה נשמת החכמה, לפיכך לא יחלום אדם מבהמה שמתה או נשחטה:

### 33) רש"י על קהלת ג:כא

מי יודע – כמו (יואל ב) מי יודע ישוב מי הוא אשר מבין ונותן לב שרוח בני אדם היא העולה למעלה ועומדת בדין ורוח הבהמה היא היורדת למטה לארץ ואין לה ליתן דין וחשבון צריך שלא להתנהג כבהמה שאינה מקפדת על מעשיה:

### 34) מדרש, תנא דבי אליהו זוטא כד:א

בהמה שמתה יש לה מנוחה אבל בני אדם שעוברין על מצותיו של הקב"ה ומכעיסין אותו ובמעשיהן שאינם הגונין ומתו בלא תשובה מעמידין אותן לדין ומאירין להם כל מעשיהם בפניהם ודנין אותם על כל מעשיהם:

### 35) מהר"ל, דרוש על התורה דף יא

כל מה שראוי שיהיה בהם נמצא בם מיד כשנבראו. ולכך נקראת היותר עצמות שבהם בהמה, כי מה שראוי שימצא בה הרי הוא מתחלה בה. שאם נברא השור לחרוש והחמור לישא משא הרי נמצא בהם בהבראם, ואין דבר בה בכח שיצא שיצא אחר

---

כך אל הפעל. אבל האדם לא נקרא רק שיהיה הוא מוציא שלימותו אל הפעל, בבחינת האדמה הזאת אשר ממנה נוצר וכל זמן שלא הוציא שלימותו אל הפעל נחשב אדמה בכח בלבד.

### 36) מהר"ל, תפארת ישראל ג

הרי בשביל שלא הוציא שלימות שלו אל הפעל הוא כמו האדמה שלא עשתה פירות ולא הוציאה דבר אל הפעל ונשאר שמו בכח, ולפיכך שמו נקרא בשם אדם על שם אדמה נאה לו והוא נאה לשמו. והבהמה נקראת בשם בהמה על שם ב"ה מ"ה רצה לומר כי שלימות דבר שנברא עליו נמצא בה אף על גב שאינו שלמות גמור מכל מקום דבר זה נמצא עמה וזהו כי כי דבר מה נמצא עמה, הרי שכל אחד יורה שמו עליו.

### 37) בראשית א:כה

וַיַּעַשׂ אֱלֹקִים אֶת־חַיַּת הָאָרֶץ לְמִינָהּ וְאֶת־הַבְּהֵמָה לְמִינָהּ וְאֵת כָּל־רֶמֶשׂ הָאֲדָמָה לְמִינֵהוּ וַיַּרְא אֱלֹקִים כִּי־טוֹב: וַיֹּאמֶר אֱלֹקִים נַעֲשֶׂה אָדָם בְּצַלְמֵנוּ כִּדְמוּתֵנוּ וְיִרְדּוּ בִדְגַת הַיָּם וּבְעוֹף הַשָּׁמַיִם וּבַבְּהֵמָה וּבְכָל־הָאָרֶץ וּבְכָל־הָרֶמֶשׂ הָרֹמֵשׂ עַל־הָאָרֶץ: וַיִּבְרָא אֱלֹקִים אֶת־הָאָדָם בְּצַלְמוֹ בְּצֶלֶם אֱלֹקִים בָּרָא אֹתוֹ זָכָר וּנְקֵבָה בָּרָא אֹתָם

### 38) בראשית א:לא

... וַיַּרְא אֱלֹקִים אֶת־כָּל־אֲשֶׁר עָשָׂה וְהִנֵּה־טוֹב מְאֹד וַיְהִי־עֶרֶב וַיְהִי־בֹקֶר יוֹם הַשִּׁשִּׁי:

### 39) בראשית א:כו-כז

וַיֹּאמֶר אֱלֹקִים נַעֲשֶׂה אָדָם בְּצַלְמֵנוּ כִּדְמוּתֵנוּ וְיִרְדּוּ בִדְגַת הַיָּם וּבְעוֹף הַשָּׁמַיִם וּבַבְּהֵמָה וּבְכָל־הָאָרֶץ וּבְכָל־הָרֶמֶשׂ הָרֹמֵשׂ עַל־הָאָרֶץ: וַיִּבְרָא אֱלֹקִים אֶת־הָאָדָם בְּצַלְמוֹ בְּצֶלֶם אֱלֹקִים בָּרָא אֹתוֹ זָכָר וּנְקֵבָה בָּרָא אֹתָם:

### 40) ויקרא יא:כד-כו, לא, לט

וּלְאֵלֶּה תִּטַּמָּאוּ כָּל־הַנֹּגֵעַ בְּנִבְלָתָם יִטְמָא עַד־הָעָרֶב: וְכָל־הַנֹּשֵׂא מִנִּבְלָתָם יְכַבֵּס בְּגָדָיו וְטָמֵא עַד־הָעָרֶב: לְכָל־הַבְּהֵמָה אֲשֶׁר הִוא מַפְרֶסֶת פַּרְסָה וְשֶׁסַע אֵינֶנָּה שֹׁסַעַת וְגֵרָה אֵינֶנָּה מַעֲלָה טְמֵאִים הֵם לָכֶם כָּל־הַנֹּגֵעַ בָּהֶם יִטְמָא: וְכֹל הוֹלֵךְ עַל־כַּפָּיו בְּכָל־הַחַיָּה הַהֹלֶכֶת עַל־אַרְבַּע טְמֵאִים הֵם לָכֶם כָּל־הַנֹּגֵעַ בְּנִבְלָתָם יִטְמָא עַד־הָעָרֶב: אֵלֶּה הַטְּמֵאִים לָכֶם בְּכָל־הַשָּׁרֶץ כָּל־הַנֹּגֵעַ בָּהֶם בְּמֹתָם יִטְמָא עַד־הָעָרֶב: וְכִי יָמוּת מִן־הַבְּהֵמָה אֲשֶׁר־הִיא לָכֶם לְאָכְלָה הַנֹּגֵעַ בְּנִבְלָתָהּ יִטְמָא עַד־הָעָרֶב:

### 41) ויקרא יב:ב-ה

דַּבֵּר אֶל־בְּנֵי יִשְׂרָאֵל לֵאמֹר אִשָּׁה כִּי תַזְרִיעַ וְיָלְדָה זָכָר וְטָמְאָה שִׁבְעַת יָמִים כִּימֵי נִדַּת דְּוֹתָהּ תִּטְמָא: וּבַיּוֹם הַשְּׁמִינִי יִמּוֹל בְּשַׂר עָרְלָתוֹ: וּשְׁלֹשִׁים יוֹם וּשְׁלֹשֶׁת יָמִים תֵּשֵׁב בִּדְמֵי טָהֳרָה בְּכָל־קֹדֶשׁ לֹא־תִגָּע וְאֶל־הַמִּקְדָּשׁ לֹא

## 15) אוצר המדרשים, "מעשים" ט

גם פרשו חכמים אדם מתבייש בהמה אינו מתביישת
וזהו פירוש אין, ואלמלא תקנה שתיקן הקב"ה
שמתבייש האדם זה מזה היו נעשין כבהמות

## 16) פירוש אונקלוס על בראשית ב:ז

וַיִּיצֶר ד' אֱלֹקִים אֶת־הָאָדָם עָפָר מִן־הָאֲדָמָה וַיִּפַּח
בְּאַפָּיו נִשְׁמַת חַיִּים וַיְהִי הָאָדָם לְנֶפֶשׁ חַיָּה:
וּבְרָא ד' אֱלֹקִים יָת אָדָם עַפְרָא מִן אֲדַמְתָּא וּנְפַח
בְּאַנְפּוֹהִי נִשְׁמְתָא דְחַיֵּי וַהֲוַת בְּאָדָם לְרוּחַ מְמַלְלָא:

## 17) חגיגה טז., מדרש תנחומא, אמור טו, אוצר
## המדרשים, "מעשים" ט

ששה דברים נאמרו בבני אדם, שלשה כמלאכי
השרת, שלשה כבהמה. שלשה כמלאכי השרת: יש
להם דעת כמלאכי השרת, ומהלכין בקומה זקופה
כמלאכי השרת, ומספרים בלשון הקדש כמלאכי
השרת.

ומותר האדם מן הבהמה אין, מהו שהוא מדבר
והיא אינה מדברת, ועוד יש באדם דעה והבהמה אין
בה דעת והאדם יודע בין טוב לרע והבהמה אינה
יודעת כלום, ועוד האדם נוטל שכר על מעשיו
ובהמה אינה נוטלת שכר על מעשיה,
פירשו חז"ל ומותר האדם מן הבהמה אין, מה הוא
אין זה הקבר, וי"א זהו דיבור, שזה מדבר ונקבר וזה
אינו מדבר ואינו נקבר.

## 18) דברים ל:טו-יט

רְאֵה נָתַתִּי לְפָנֶיךָ הַיּוֹם אֶת־הַחַיִּים וְאֶת־הַטּוֹב וְאֶת־
הַמָּוֶת וְאֶת־הָרָע: אֲשֶׁר אָנֹכִי מְצַוְּךָ הַיּוֹם לְאַהֲבָה
אֶת־ד' אֱלֹקֶיךָ לָלֶכֶת בִּדְרָכָיו וְלִשְׁמֹר מִצְוֹתָיו
וְחֻקֹּתָיו וּמִשְׁפָּטָיו וְחָיִיתָ וְרָבִיתָ וּבֵרַכְךָ ד' אֱלֹקֶיךָ
בָּאָרֶץ אֲשֶׁר־אַתָּה בָא שָׁמָּה לְרִשְׁתָּהּ: וְאִם־יִפְנֶה
לְבָבְךָ וְלֹא תִשְׁמָע וְנִדַּחְתָּ וְהִשְׁתַּחֲוִיתָ לֵאלֹקִים
אֲחֵרִים וַעֲבַדְתָּם: הִגַּדְתִּי לָכֶם הַיּוֹם כִּי אָבֹד תֹּאבֵדוּן
לֹא־תַאֲרִיכֻן יָמִים עַל־הָאֲדָמָה אֲשֶׁר אַתָּה עֹבֵר אֶת־
הַיַּרְדֵּן לָבוֹא שָׁמָּה לְרִשְׁתָּהּ: הַעִדֹתִי בָכֶם הַיּוֹם
אֶת־הַשָּׁמַיִם וְאֶת־הָאָרֶץ הַחַיִּים וְהַמָּוֶת נָתַתִּי לְפָנֶיךָ
הַבְּרָכָה וְהַקְּלָלָה וּבָחַרְתָּ בַּחַיִּים לְמַעַן תִּחְיֶה אַתָּה
וְזַרְעֶךָ:

## 19) רמב"ם, הלכות תשובה ה:א

רשות לכל אדם נתונה אם רצה להטות עצמו לדרך
טובה ולהיות צדיק הרשות בידו, ואם רצה להטות
עצמו לדרך רעה ולהיות רשע הרשות בידו, הוא
שכתוב בתורה הן האדם היה כאחד ממנו לדעת טוב
ורע, כלומר הן מין זה של אדם היה יחיד בעולם
ואין מין שני דומה לו בזה הענין שיהא הוא מעצמו
בדעתו ובמחשבתו יודע הטוב והרע ועושה כל מה
שהוא חפץ ואין מי שיעכב בידו מלעשות הטוב או
הרע וכיון שכן הוא פן ישלח ידו.

## 20) תהילים מט:כא

אָדָם בִּיקָר וְלֹא יָבִין נִמְשַׁל כַּבְּהֵמוֹת נִדְמוּ:

## 21) ברכות יט.

תא שמע: גדול כבוד הבריות שדוחה [את] לא תעשה
שבתורה.

## 22) רמב"ם הלכות שבת כו:כג

גדול כבוד הבריות שדוחה [את] לא תעשה שבתורה.

## 23) שולחן ערוך, אורח חיים יג:ג

אם נודע לו בשבת כשהוא בכרמלית שהטלית שעליו
פסול לא יסירנו מעליו עד שיגיע לביתו דגדול כבוד
הבריות:

## 24) בבא קמא ג.

אי לרב, דאמר מבעה זה אדם,

## 25) שמות כ:ט-י

שֵׁשֶׁת יָמִים תַּעֲבֹד וְעָשִׂיתָ כָּל־מְלַאכְתֶּךָ: וְיוֹם הַשְּׁבִיעִי
שַׁבָּת לַד' אֱלֹקֶיךָ לֹא־תַעֲשֶׂה כָל־מְלָאכָה ...

## 26) מדרש בראשית רבה ח:יא

עומד כמלאכי השרת מדבר כמלאכי השרת יש בו
דעת כמלאכי השרת ורואה כמלאכי השרת ובהמה
אינו רואה אתמהא אלא זה מצדד

## 27) נפש החיים, שער א, ג

כן בדמיון זה כביכול ברא הוא יתברך את האדם
והשליטו על רבי רבבון כחות ועולמות אין מספר.
ומסרם בידו שיהא הוא המדבר והמנהיג אותם עפ"י
כל פרטי תנועות מעשיו ודבוריו ומחשבותיו וכל
סדרי הנהגותיו הן לטוב או להיפך ח"ו, כי במעשיו
ודבוריו ומחשבותיו הטובים הוא מקיים ונותן כח
בכמה כחות ועולמות עליונים הקדושים

## 28) דברים יא:יג תענית ב.

וְהָיָה אִם־שָׁמֹעַ תִּשְׁמְעוּ אֶל־מִצְוֹתַי אֲשֶׁר אָנֹכִי מְצַוֶּה
אֶתְכֶם הַיּוֹם לְאַהֲבָה אֶת־ד' אֱלֹקֵיכֶם וּלְעָבְדוֹ בְּכָל־
לְבַבְכֶם וּבְכָל־נַפְשְׁכֶם: דתניא: (דברים י"א) "לאהבה
את ה' אלקיכם ולעבדו בכל לבבכם", איזו היא
עבודה שהיא בלב הוי אומר זו תפלה.

## 29) עיקר י' מי"ג עיקרים בסידור

אֲנִי מַאֲמִין בֶּאֱמוּנָה שְׁלֵמָה. שֶׁהַבּוֹרֵא יִתְבָּרַךְ שְׁמוֹ
יוֹדֵעַ כָּל מַעֲשֵׂה בְנֵי אָדָם וְכָל מַחְשְׁבוֹתָם. שֶׁנֶּאֱמַר.
הַיֹּצֵר יַחַד לִבָּם הַמֵּבִין אֶל כָּל מַעֲשֵׂיהֶם:

## 30) רמב"ם, מורה נבוכים ג:יז

... שֶׁהַהַשְׁגָּחָה הָאֱלֹקִית אָמְנָם הִיא בָזֶה הָעוֹלָם
הַתַּחְתּוֹן – רְצוֹנִי לוֹמַר, מִתַּחַת גַּלְגַּל הַיָּרֵחַ – בְּאִישֵׁי
מִין הָאָדָם לְבַד, וְזֶה הַמִּין לְבַדּוֹ הוּא אֲשֶׁר כָּל עִנְיְנֵי

### 1) קהלת ג:יט

כִּי מִקְרֶה בְנֵי־הָאָדָם וּמִקְרֶה הַבְּהֵמָה וּמִקְרֶה אֶחָד לָהֶם כְּמוֹת זֶה כֵּן מוֹת זֶה וְרוּחַ אֶחָד לַכֹּל וּמוֹתַר הָאָדָם מִן־הַבְּהֵמָה אָיִן כִּי הַכֹּל הָבֶל:

### 2) חגיגה טז.

שלשה כבהמה: אוכלין ושותין כבהמה, ופרין ורבין כבהמה, ומוציאין רעי כבהמה.

### 3) מדרש בראשית רבה ח:יא

אוכל ושותה כבהמה פרה ורבה כבהמה ומטיל גללים כבהמה ומת כבהמה

### 4) חזון איש, אמונה ובטחון א:ז

בעלי החיים משתוים עם האדם במבנה הגוף ובחינתיו וסגולותיו, חומר גופו בשר ודם, גיד עצם וקרמה, והם בעלי נפש חיונית, בעלי חושים כמו האדם, נזונים כבני אדם, בעלי שני מינים זכר ונקבה ...

### 5) פירוש רמב"ן על בראשית א:כט

... מפני שבעלי נפש התנועה יש להם קצת מעלה בנפשם, נדמו בה לבעלי הנפש המשכלת, ויש להם בחירה בטובתם ומזוניהם, ויברחו מן הצער והמיתה.

### 6) שולחן ערוך, יורה דעה ב:יא

שחיטת קוף, פסול

### 7) בראשית א:כז

וַיִּבְרָא אֱלֹקִים אֶת־הָאָדָם בְּצַלְמוֹ בְּצֶלֶם אֱלֹקִים בָּרָא אֹתוֹ זָכָר וּנְקֵבָה בָּרָא אֹתָם:

### 8) בראשית ב:ז

וַיִּיצֶר ד' אֱלֹקִים אֶת־הָאָדָם עָפָר מִן־הָאֲדָמָה וַיִּפַּח בְּאַפָּיו נִשְׁמַת חַיִּים וַיְהִי הָאָדָם לְנֶפֶשׁ חַיָּה:

### 9) בראשית א:כד-כז

וַיֹּאמֶר אֱלֹקִים תּוֹצֵא הָאָרֶץ נֶפֶשׁ חַיָּה לְמִינָהּ בְּהֵמָה וָרֶמֶשׂ וְחַיְתוֹ־אֶרֶץ לְמִינָהּ וַיְהִי־כֵן: וַיַּעַשׂ אֱלֹקִים אֶת־חַיַּת הָאָרֶץ לְמִינָהּ וְאֶת־הַבְּהֵמָה לְמִינָהּ וְאֵת כָּל־רֶמֶשׂ הָאֲדָמָה לְמִינֵהוּ וַיַּרְא אֱלֹקִים כִּי־טוֹב: וַיֹּאמֶר אֱלֹקִים נַעֲשֶׂה אָדָם בְּצַלְמֵנוּ כִּדְמוּתֵנוּ וְיִרְדּוּ בִדְגַת הַיָּם וּבְעוֹף הַשָּׁמַיִם וּבַבְּהֵמָה וּבְכָל־הָאָרֶץ וּבְכָל־הָרֶמֶשׂ הָרֹמֵשׂ עַל־הָאָרֶץ: וַיִּבְרָא אֱלֹקִים אֶת־הָאָדָם בְּצַלְמוֹ בְּצֶלֶם אֱלֹקִים בָּרָא אֹתוֹ זָכָר וּנְקֵבָה בָּרָא אֹתָם:

### 10) בראשית ב:ד-ח

אֵלֶּה תוֹלְדוֹת הַשָּׁמַיִם וְהָאָרֶץ בְּהִבָּרְאָם בְּיוֹם עֲשׂוֹת ד' אֱלֹקִים אֶרֶץ וְשָׁמָיִם: וְכֹל שִׂיחַ הַשָּׂדֶה טֶרֶם יִהְיֶה בָאָרֶץ וְכָל־עֵשֶׂב הַשָּׂדֶה טֶרֶם יִצְמָח כִּי לֹא הִמְטִיר ד' אֱלֹקִים עַל־הָאָרֶץ וְאָדָם אַיִן לַעֲבֹד אֶת־הָאֲדָמָה: וְאֵד יַעֲלֶה מִן־הָאָרֶץ וְהִשְׁקָה אֶת־כָּל־פְּנֵי הָאֲדָמָה: וַיִּיצֶר ד' אֱלֹקִים אֶת־הָאָדָם עָפָר מִן־הָאֲדָמָה וַיִּפַּח בְּאַפָּיו נִשְׁמַת חַיִּים וַיְהִי הָאָדָם לְנֶפֶשׁ חַיָּה: וַיִּטַּע ד' אֱלֹקִים גַּן־בְּעֵדֶן מִקֶּדֶם וַיָּשֶׂם שָׁם אֶת־הָאָדָם אֲשֶׁר יָצָר:

### 11) תהילים ח:ה-י

מָה־אֱנוֹשׁ כִּי־תִזְכְּרֶנּוּ וּבֶן־אָדָם כִּי תִפְקְדֶנּוּ: וַתְּחַסְּרֵהוּ מְּעַט מֵאֱלֹהִים וְכָבוֹד וְהָדָר תְּעַטְּרֵהוּ: תַּמְשִׁילֵהוּ בְּמַעֲשֵׂי יָדֶיךָ כֹּל שַׁתָּה תַחַת־רַגְלָיו: צֹנֶה וַאֲלָפִים כֻּלָּם וְגַם בַּהֲמוֹת שָׂדָי: צִפּוֹר שָׁמַיִם וּדְגֵי הַיָּם עֹבֵר אָרְחוֹת יַמִּים: ד' אֲדֹנֵינוּ מָה־אַדִּיר שִׁמְךָ בְּכָל־הָאָרֶץ:

### 12) מדרש ויקרא רבה יד:א

הה"ד (תהלים קלט) אחור וקדם צרתני ... אמר ר"ל אחור זה יום האחרון וקדם זה יום הראשון על דעתיה דר"ל דכתיב (שם ) ורוח אלהים מרחפת על פני המים זה רוחו של מלך המשיח אם זכה אדם אומרים לו אתה קדמת לכל מעשה בראשית ואם לאו אומרי' לו יתוש קדמך שלשול קדמך

### 13) דרך השם ג:ב

... האדם מורכב מב' הפכים דהיינו מנשמה שכלית וזכה וגוף ארציי ועבור שבל אחד מהם יטה נטע לצדו דהיינו הגוף לחומריות והנשמה לשכליות ותמצא ביניהם מלחמה באופן שאם תגבר הנשמה תתעלה היא ותעלה הגוף עמה ויהי' אותו האדם המשתלם כשלימות המעותד ואם יניח האדם שינצח בו החומר הגה ישפל הגוף ותשפל נשמתו עמו ויהי' אותו האדם בלתי הגון לשלימות ונדחה ממנו ח"ו ולאדם הזה יכולת להשפיל חומרו לפני שכלו ונשמתו ולקנות שלימותו כמ"ש

### 14) בראשית ב:כה, ג:ו-ז

וַיִּהְיוּ שְׁנֵיהֶם עֲרוּמִּים הָאָדָם וְאִשְׁתּוֹ וְלֹא יִתְבֹּשָׁשׁוּ: וַתֵּרֶא הָאִשָּׁה כִּי טוֹב הָעֵץ לְמַאֲכָל וְכִי תַאֲוָה־הוּא לָעֵינַיִם וְנֶחְמָד הָעֵץ לְהַשְׂכִּיל וַתִּקַּח מִפִּרְיוֹ וַתֹּאכַל וַתִּתֵּן גַּם־לְאִישָׁהּ עִמָּהּ וַיֹּאכַל: וַתִּפָּקַחְנָה עֵינֵי שְׁנֵיהֶם וַיֵּדְעוּ כִּי עֵירֻמִּם הֵם וַיִּתְפְּרוּ עֲלֵה תְאֵנָה וַיַּעֲשׂוּ לָהֶם חֲגֹרֹת:

**Testimony of Rabbi Moshe David Tendler to National Bioethics Advisory Commission, Stem Cell Research and Therapy: A Judeo-Biblical Perspective Ethical Issues in Human Stem Cell Research, Volume III: Religious Perspectives, September 1999, p.H-4.** (37

"In stem cell research and therapy, the moral obligation to save human life, the paramount ethical principle in biblical law, supersedes any concern for lowering the barrier to abortion by making the sin less heinous. Likewise, the expressed concern that this research facilitates human cloning is without merit. First, no reputable research facility is interested in cloning a human, which is not even a distant goal, despite the pluripotency of stem cells. Second, those on the leading edge of stem cell research know that the greater contribution to human welfare will come from replacement of damaged cells and organs by fresh stem cell products, not from cloning. Financial reward and acclaim from the scientific community will come from such therapeutic successes, not from cloning."

**ligious Perspectives, September 1999, p.H-4.**
"The Judeo-biblical tradition does not grant moral status to an embryo before forty days of gestation. Such an embryo has the same moral status as male and female gametes, and its destruction prior to implantation is of the same moral import as the 'wasting of human seed.' After forty days-the time of 'quickening' recognized in common law-the implanted embryo is considered to have humanhood, and its destruction is considered an act of homicide. Thus, there are two prerequisites for the moral status of the embryo as a human being: implantation and forty days of gestational development. The proposition that humanhood begins at zygote formation, even in vitro, is without basis in biblical moral theology." Testimony of Rabbi Moshe Dovid Tendler, Ph.D, *Stem Cell Research and Therapy: A Judeo-Biblical Perspective,* Ethical Issues in Human Stem Cell Research, Volume III: Religious Perspectives, September 1999, p.H-3.

save and heal human lives is an integral part of valuing human life from the traditional Jewish perspective. Moreover, our rabbinic authorities inform us that an isolated fertilized egg does not enjoy the full status of person-hood and its attendant protections. Thus, if embryonic stem cell research can help us preserve and heal humans with greater success, and does not require or encourage the destruction of life in the process, it ought to be pursued. Nevertheless, we must emphasize, that research on embryonic stem cells must be conducted under careful guidelines. Critical elements of these guidelines. from our perspective, relate to where the embryonic stem cells to be researched upon are taken from. We believe it is entirely appropriate to utilize for this research existing embryos, such as those created for IVF purposes that would otherwise be discarded but for this research. We think it another matter to create embryos ab initio for the sole purpose of conducting this form of research. Because of the ethical concerns presented by embryonic stem cell research and the reports of potentially garnering similar benefits from research on adult stem cells, we would urge you to simultaneously increase funding for adult stem cell research. Other elements of an ethically sensitive oversight regime would include a rigorous informed consent process from future IVF procedure participants, a fully funded and empowered oversight body comprised of scientists and bio-ethicists, and periodic reviews by relevant Executive branch agencies and congressional committees. We hope these views are useful to you in your deliberations over this critical issue of public policy. We wish you the paramount blessing for political leaders that the Jewish tradition offers – wisdom.

Sincerely,

Harvey Blitz, President, UOJCA
Nathan Diament,
Director of Public Policy, UOJCA
Rabbi Herschel Billet President, RCA
Rabbi Steven Dworken
Executive Vice President, RCA

**Testimony of Rabbi Moshe David Tendler to National Bioethics Advisory Commission, Stem Cell Research and Therapy: A Judeo-Biblical Perspective Ethical Issues in Human Stem Cell Research, Volume III: Re-** (36

**Personal communication, January 9, 2001 with Dr. A. Steinberg, as quoted by Fred Rosner, M.D. in "Embryonic Stem Cell Research In Jewish Law" in the Journal of Halacha and Contemporary Society, vol. 43, page 58, footnote 18** (34

**Letter of Orthodox Union about Stem Cell Research, July 6, 2001** (35

The OU–RCA letter
UNION of ORTHODOX JEWISH
CONGREGATIONS OF AMERICA
Eleven Broadway
New York, New York 10004
212-613-8159

RABBINICAL COUNCIL OF AMERICA
305 Seventh Avenue
New York, New York 10001
212-807-7888
July 26, 2001 6 Av, 5761

President George W. Bush
The White House
Washington. DC 20500

Dear President Bush:
We write to you on behalf of this nation's largest Orthodox Jewish synagogue umbrella organization and Orthodox Jewish rabbinical organization with regard to a serious matter you are currently considering – whether to permit federal funds to support embryonic stem cell research. On the basis of consultations with leading rabbinic authorities in our community as well as with scientists sensitive to traditional Jewish values, we write to express our support for federal funding for embryonic stem cell research to be conducted under carefully crafted and well-monitored guidelines. As you no doubt appreciate, the decision you face is one with complex moral dimensions. On the one hand scientific research indicates that there is great life-saving potential in embryonic stem cell research, potential that warrants federal support. On the other hand, we must be vigilant against any erosion of the value that American society affords to human life, including potential human life. Our Torah tradition places great value upon human life; we are taught in the opening chapters of Genesis that each human was created in G-d's very image. The potential to

לא קא משמע לן. ואיכא דסבירא ליה דאין מחללין משום נפלים אלא עוברה שהריחה חששא דמיתה דידה היא שכל המפלת בחזקת סכנה היא. וטעמא דיושבת על המשבר שמתה טעמא אחרינא הוא הרי הוא כילוד דתו לאו על ירך אמו הוא דלאו בדידה תליא אלא הוא ודלת נעולה בפניו וליכא חששא אלא דלא ה״ל חזקה דחיותא וספק נפשות להקל. ולא ידעתי מה צורך לכל אלו הדקדוקים דלא משכחת סכנת עובר בלא סכנת עוברה ולא סכנת עוברה בלא סכנת עובר. דהמפלת בחזקת הסכנה היא וכן פרש״י דאם אינה אוכלת שניהם מסוכנים:

### 28) שולחן ערוך, אורח חיים של:ה

היושבת על המשבר ומתה מביאין סכין בשבת אפילו דרך רה״ר וקורעים בטנה ומוציאים הולד שמא ימצא חי:

### 29) ערוך השולחן אורח חיים, תרי:א

האמנם עוברה שהריחה ריח מאכל דהעובר מריח והיא מתאוה לזה ואם אינה אוכלת שניהן ... אך המעוברת נאמנת גם בלא השתנות הפנים מפני שזה מצוי במעוברת:

### 30) שו״ת ציץ אליעזר יא:מג

אם מותר לחלל שבת עבור פקוח נפש של עובר גם במקום שלא נשקפת כל סכנה לאם ... וא״כ לכאורה נלמד מהאמור בפשיטות שמחללין את השבת עבור הצלת עובר, ולא רק כשההצלה ודאית כי אם גם אפילו מספיקה ...

### 31) שו״ת שרידי אש ג:קכז

מיהו יש מקום לומר דקודם מ׳ יום אין איסור להרוג את העובר, דקודם מ׳ יום הוא מיא בעלמא ואין עליו שם עובר כלל, כמבואר ביבמות ס״ט ע״ב. דבת כהן שנשאת לישראל ומת בו ביומסותרת לאכול תרומה דאי לא מיעברא הא לא מיעברא ואי מיעברא עד ארבעים מיא בעלמא היא ולא נחשב כלל לעובר. והא דמותר לחלל עליו את השבת לפי בה״ג יש לומר שהתורה התירה חילול שבת בשביל צמיחת החיים העתידים כמש״כ הרמב״ן שגם קודם מ׳ יום יש לומר חלל עליו שבת אחת כדי שישמור שבתות הרבה היינו שמחללין שבת בשביל שמירת שבת העתידה לבוא לאחר שיולד ויתקיים בחיים ... היוצא מכל השו״ט להלכה באשה שחלתה בשעת הריונה במחלת אדמת, שלפי״ד הרופאים עלול הולד להיות מחוסר אבר או מחוסר דעת קודם מ׳ יום להריונה מותר להפיל את העובר שקודם מ׳ יום הוא מיא בעלמא כמפורש ביבמות ס״ט ואינו חשוב עובר. וכן תפסו כל גדולי האחרונים. עי׳ בש״ך חו״מ סי׳ רי״ו ס״ק ב׳ דמזכה לעובר קודם ארבעים יום לא קנה מיא בעלמא הוא, כדאסרינן ביבמות ...

### 32) שו״ת תורת חסד, אבן העזר מב:לג

... דאפילו לפי דעת הסוברים דעובר אסור להמיתו מה״ת י״ל דזה דוקא לאחר מ׳ לקליטתו ... ובתוך ארבעים לקליטתה נ״ל דגם ב״נ אין נהרג ... הרי דהמכילתא ממעט איש דאין נהרגין על העוברין א״כ ע״כ הך דרשא דאדם קאי על ב״נ דוקא ולא על ישראל ... והנה הרמב״ם ז״ל הנפל אע״פ שעדיין לא נתקשרו איבריו בגידין מטמא כו׳כי שנאמר הנוגע במת לכל נפש אדם. וכתב המל״מ נראה דבבציר מן מ׳ יום אינו מטמא. והכי תנן בפ׳ בתרא דאהלות כמה ישהה בתוכה ויהי׳ צריך בדיקה מ׳ יום עכ״ל א״כ נשמע מזה דקודם ארבעים לקליטה אינו בכלל נפש אדם.... א״כ לפ״ז אחר דהא דהא דאסרין לישראל בעובר הוא משום מי איכא מידי דב״נ נהרג מ׳ אחר לישראל שרי הוא דוקא לאחר מ׳ ולא קודם. א״כ כ״ש דאין דאין איסור דאורייתא לאשה להשחית זרע בעלה שבא אחר תשמיש.

### 33) שו״ת שבט הלוי ה:מז

... לזוג אשר תחילת קליטת הזרע היתה אפשרית ביניהם ועשו תחילת הקליטה בחוץ (באופן שיהי׳ מותר עפ״י הלכה) בתנאי המבחנה ואח״כ הוכנסו בהקלטם התאים חזרה לגוף האם והשאלה אם בתנאים מוקדמים אלה יש צורך לחלל שבת כדי להמשיך התפתחותם אם מותר והספק בזה וגם אם בכה״ג אמר הב״ה׳ג דמחללין על העוברין ומטעם שישמור שבתות הרבה וכסברתו דגם לפני מ׳ יום אע״פ דכמיא בעלמא נחשב מכ״מ מחללין וכמבואר ברמב״ן ור״ן לדעת בה״ג אי דלמא דוקא שכבר הם בגוף האם אע״פ שעדיין לפני מ׳ יום וכו׳ משא״כ הכא עדין חסר מעשה להביא הא לגוף האם אתו י״ל מעל״ד והאריך קצת. לדעתי ברור דגם לבה״ג אסור לחלל שבת בזה דע לא התיר בה״ג לחלל שבת בעל העוברין אפילו לפני מ׳ יום אע״ג דמיא בעלמא הוא אלא בעובר תוך מעי האם דאע״ג דטעם "וחי בהם" עדין ליכא מכ״מ הא דפסקינן עליו שמותר לחלל שבת גם זה נבנה על היסוד שיהי׳ עכ״פ אח״כ בני קיימא ע״י שרוב ולדות בני קיימא הם ורק מיעוט מפילות ... דהני "וחי בהם" עכשיו ליכא עדין בגדר זה וגם ישראל אינו מצווה על העוברין מכ״מ כן דנתברר מדין רוב שיהי׳ בן מצוות גם לחלל עליו שבת מותר. משא״כ זרע זה שבתוך המבחנה שאינו נכלל בכלל ברוב זה דרור העוברין בני קיימא הם דבוחנים רק מבחוץ איך יהי׳ התפתחות הדברים ... משא״כ בן בן דעדין אינו בגדר תחילת עיבור ... (וגם אם יתפתח אולי עד שיהי׳ אחוז גדול מצליח בנסיון הנ״ל מ״מ הדעת נוטה כנ״ל) ... אבל הכא דלא הול חזקת חיותא אימא דלא קמ״ל הרי מבואר חילוק הנ״ל ... מבואר בפוסקים דשאני התם דהעיבור כבר נגמר או דעכ״פ שם עיבור ולד עליו משא״כ כנ״ל.

פק"נ חוץ לדרך הטבע ... דכיון שאפשר לה לחכות
אין להקדים,

**17) שו"ת אגרות משה, חושן משפט ב:סט**

... ולכן לדינא בין לתוס' בין להרמב"ם ואף לרש"י
איכא איסור רציחה מלא תרצח גם על עובר ורק
שפטור ההורגו ממיתה, ואסור להורגו אף לפ"נ
=לפקוח נפש= דכל אינשי ורק להצלת אמו שלא
תמות בלידתו הוא ההיתר ולא בשביל שום צורך
דהאם שזה אסור בפשיטות ... ולכן לדינא בין לתוס'
בין להרמב"ם ואף לרש"י איכא איסור רציחה מלא
תרצח גם על עובר ורק שפטור ההורגו ממיתה,
ואסור להורגו אף לפ"נ =לפקוח נפש= דכל אינשי
ורק להצלת אמו שלא תמות בלידתו הוא ההיתר
ולא בשביל שום צורך דהאם שזה אסור בפשיטות.
שו"ת אגרות משה ... אבל אם תשובה זו אמת נראה
לי נכון מש"כ הגרא"י אונטערמן שם דהיה זה קודם
ארבעים יום וחמור ישראל מבן נח בקודם ארבעים
יום שאף לישראל אסור ... אבל לע"ד אין זה ענין
אבריייהו אלא רציחה אך שלא חייבה עליו מיתה ...

**18) יבמות לה:**

הכנוס את יבמתו, ונמצאת מעוברת וילדה ...
וחייבין בקרבן.

**19) שו"ת יעב"ץ א:מג**

ששאלת אם יש איסור לקלקל עובר בבטן אמו
שזינתה. בין פנויה בין אשת איש
תשובה בס' חות יאיר (אחר סי' ל"א) מצאתי שנשאל
הרב בעל הס' על אשת איש הרה לזנונים. ואחר
המעשה נתחרטה כו' אם רשאה דבר מאבקת
רוכל לשלשל זרע המקולל אשר בקרבה, וז"ל הרב
בעל התשובה ואחשבה כי תכונת השאלה בא"א דבר
בדוי הוא לא הי' כו' כי כאשר בתשובתי על השאלה
אין חילוק בין היות המעוברת נשואה וכשירה
בנשים, או ממזר מא"א שהרי לא נפלאת היא דדין
ממזר לכל דבר כישראל כשר וכו' עכ"ל ... אמנם
נדון השאול בא"א שזנתה שאלה הגונה היא. וקרוב
בעיני להתירה אם הייתי כדאי. כי נ"ל שיש מקום
להקל כיון שניאפה זאת ודם בידיה. מעתה בת קטלא
היא מדין תורה ... וא"כ לדברינו ודאי בעלמא (ר"ל
בעובר כשר) איסורא איכא להשחית עובר ... דלא
נחית לפלוגי בין א"א לכשרה.

**20) מנחת חינוך, מצוה א**

... זהו מצוה הבאה בעבירה ... נהי דהמצוה של
הבנים באה ע"י עבירה דביאת איסור, מ"מ המצות
עשה היינו הבנים,
והבעילה היא רק הכשר מצוה דאי אפשר

**21) קידושין ל:**

שלשה שותפין הן באדם: הקב"ה, ואביו, ואמו

**22) הרב בקשי-דורון, תחומין טו, דף 311**

הנחת יסוד היא שאין כל היתר להפסיק הריון
מתקדם של אישה נשואה ולהפיל את עוברה. זאת
גם אם האישה הרתה לשם כך, וגם אם מדובר בצורך
חשוב ביותר ... כל התהליך של ההריון ושל הלידה
כרוך בסיכון בחייה של היולדת ... ההיתר להיכנס
לתוךסכנה זו נובע הן משום המצוה שבדבר (פרו
ורבו, לשבת יצרה) והן משום שדרך כל הארץ
ו"שומר פתאים ד'". אישה הנכנסת לתהליך של הריון
כדי שלא לקיים את המצוה וגם לא כדרך על הארץ,
מי התיר לה להיכנס למצב של סכנת נפשות? מה
עוד, שבשלה ההפלה היא נוטלת על עצמה סיכון
נוסף? האפשרות שבכך עשויה היא להקלת החיים
על אביה, עדיין אינה מתירה להכניס את עצמה
לסכנה ...

**23) שו"ת חכם צבי צג**

... דהכי דייק קרא בראשית ט:ו (אף שיש בו דרשות
אחרות) (עיין סנהדרין נז:) "שופך דם האדם באדם
דמו ישפך "דוקא אדם הנוצר תוך אדם דהיינו עובר
הנוצר במעי אמו הוא דחייב עליה משום שפיכת
דמים, יצא ההוא גברא דברא רבא דבר שלא נעשה
במעי אשה ...

**24) יבמות סט:**

בת כהן שנישאת לישראל ומת טובלת ואוכלת
בתרומה לערב אמר רב חסדא: טובלת ואוכלת
עד ארבעים, דאי לא מיעברא הא לא מיעברא, ואי
מיעברא עד ארבעים מיא בעלמא היא.

**25) רמב"ם, הלכות איסורי ביאה י':א**

ואין צורת הולד נגמרת לפחות מארבעים יום אחד
הזכר ואחד הנקבה.

**26) ספר הלכות גדולות יג**

... ואמרינן גבי עוברה (כריתות יג א) התירו לה
לעוברה לאכול פחות מכשיעור מפני הסכנה, היכי
דמי, אי דאיכא סכנה, אפילו כשיעור נמי, אלא אימא
פחות מכשיעור ואפילו טובא נמי.

**27) רא"ש על יומא ח:יג**

וכתב הרמב"ן ז"ל משמע מתוך דברי בעל הלכות
דמשום סכנת וולד לחודיה מחללין אפילו ליכא
למיחש לידה. דהיינו דגרסינן בשילהי פרק קמא
דערכין (דף ז.) האשה שישבה על המשבר ומתה
בשבת מביאין סכין וקורעין כריסה ומוציאין את
הוולד. פשיטא מאי עביד מחתך בבשר בעלמא הוא.
אמר רבא מאי לא נצרכה אלא להביא סכין דרך רשות
הרבים. מאי קא משמע לן דעל ספיקא מחללין שבת.
תניא ספק ספק חי ספק מת ספק נכרי ספק ישראל מחללין מפקחין.
מהו דתימא ספק התם הוא דהוה ליה חזקה דחיותא אבל
הכא דלא הוה ליה חזקה דחיותא דמעיקרא אימא

# SOURCES ON CONCEIVING TO ABORT FOR STEM CELLS AND OTHER STEM CELL ISSUES

**9) ערכין ז.**

מתני׳- האשה שיצאה ליהרג אין ממתינין לה עד
שתלד. גמ׳ – ... אמר רב יהודה אמר שמואל: האשה
היוצאה ליהרג, מכין אותה כנגד בית הריון כדי
שימות הוולד תחילה, כדי שלא תבא לידי ניוול.

**10) ערכין ז:**

א״ר נחמן אמר שמואל: האשה שישבה על המשבר
ומתה בשבת, מביאין סכין ומקרעים את כריסה
ומוציאין את הוולד ... מהו דתימא: התם הוא דהוה
ליה חזקה דחיותא, אבל הכא דלא הוה ליה חזקה
דחיותא מעיקרא אימא לא, קמ״ל.

**11) משנה אוהלות ז:ו**

האשה שהיא מקשה לילד.מחתכין את הולד במעיה
ומוציאין אותו אברים אברים. מפני שחייה קודמין
לחייו. יצא רובו. אין נוגעין בו. שאין דוחין נפש
מפני נפש:

**12) תוספות על נידה מד., ד״ה "איהו"**

וי״ל דמכל מקום משום פקוח נפש מחללין עליו את
השבת אף ע״ג דמותר להרגו ...

**13) בראשית א:כח, ישעיה מה:יח**

וַיְבָרֶךְ אֹתָם אֱלֹקִים וַיֹּאמֶר לָהֶם אֱלֹקִים פְּרוּ וּרְבוּ
וּמִלְאוּ אֶת־הָאָרֶץ וְכִבְשֻׁהָ וּרְדוּ בִּדְגַת הַיָּם וּבְעוֹף
הַשָּׁמַיִם וּבְכָל־חַיָּה הָרֹמֶשֶׂת עַל־הָאָרֶץ:
כִּי־כֹה אָמַר־ד׳ בּוֹרֵא הַשָּׁמַיִם הוּא הָאֱלֹקִים יֹצֵר הָאָרֶץ
וְעֹשָׂהּ הוּא כוֹנְנָהּ לֹא־תֹהוּ בְרָאָהּ לָשֶׁבֶת יְצָרָהּ אֲנִי ד׳
וְאֵין עוֹד:

**14) שו״ת אגרות משה אבן העזר א:עא**

... אסור מטעם הוצאת זרע לבטלה שאסור לאדם
להוציא זרע שלא ע״י ביאה באשתו, ואף שאין זרעו
ראוי להוליד אין זה היתר להוציא הזרע שלא במעי
אשתו אף ע״י התחבולות וגרמא ...

**15) שו״ת אגרות משה, חושן משפט ב:סט**

הרי מפורש בתוס׳ סנהדרין שישראל נאסרו ג״כ
בהריגת עוברים באיסור דרציחה.

**16) שו״ת אגרות משה, יורה דעה ב:עד**

... הרופא שמיעץ לאשה שחשבה שכלו לה החדשים
לקבוע שעה להקדים הלידה ע״י תחבולות שכתר״ה
מצדד לאסור. הנה אני לא שמעתי שאפשר לעשות
כן בלידה דרך הרחם ... דאין להביא את האשה לידי

**1) רמב״ם, הלכות יסודי התורה ה:א-ב**

... כיצד כשיעמוד עובד כוכבים ויאנוס את ישראל
לעבור על אחת מכל מצות האמורות בתורה או
יהרגנו יעבור ואל יהרג שנאמר במצות אשר יעשה
אותם האדם וחי בהם, וחי בהם ולא שימות בהם,
ואם מת ולא עבר הרי זה מתחייב בנפשו. ב במה
דברים אמורים בשאר מצות חוץ מעבודת כוכבים
וגלוי עריות ושפיכת דמים, אבל שלש עבירות אלו
אם יאמר לו עבור על אחת מהן או תהרג, יהרג ואל
יעבור ...

**2) ויקרא יח:ה**

וּשְׁמַרְתֶּם אֶת־חֻקֹּתַי וְאֶת־מִשְׁפָּטַי אֲשֶׁר יַעֲשֶׂה אֹתָם
הָאָדָם וָחַי בָּהֶם אֲנִי ד׳:

**3) יומא פה:**

רבי שמעון בן מנסיא אומר: (שמות לא) ושמרו בני
ישראל את השבת, אמרה תורה: חלל עליו שבת
אחת, כדי שישמור שבתות הרבה. אמר רבי יהודה
אמר שמואל: אי הואי התם הוה אמינא: דידי עדיפא
מדידהו, (ויקרא יח) וחי בהם ולא שימות בהם.

**4) סוכה ל.**

(לולב הגזול פסול) משום דהוה ליה מצוה הבאה
בעבירה

**5) משנה ברורה על שולחן ערוך, אורלח חיים י׳:לא
לעשותן – ר״ל (אסור) להטיל הציצית אלו (גנובים)**
בבגדו משום מצוה הבאה בעבירה ועיין בבה״ל:

**6) שמות כא:כב**

וְכִי־יִנָּצוּ אֲנָשִׁים וְנָגְפוּ אִשָּׁה הָרָה וְיָצְאוּ יְלָדֶיהָ וְלֹא
יִהְיֶה אָסוֹן עָנוֹשׁ יֵעָנֵשׁ כַּאֲשֶׁר יָשִׁית עָלָיו בַּעַל הָאִשָּׁה
וְנָתַן בִּפְלִלִים:

**7) סנהדרין מ:**

אמר רב יהודה: דאמר קרא (בראשית ט׳) "אך את
דמכם לנפשתיכם אדרש" ... משום רבי ישמעאל
אמרו אף על העוברין. מאי טעמיה דרבי ישמעאל?
דכתיב (בראשית ט׳) "שפך דם האדם באדם דמו
ישפך", איזהו אדם שהוא באדם הוי אומר זה עובר
שבמעי אמו.

**8) רמב״ם, הלכות מלכים א:ד**

בן נח שהרג נפש אפילו עובר במעי אמו נהרג עליו

אבל אחרי שגמר הדין ואמר איש פלוני אתה זכאי
איש פלוני אתה חייב אינו רשאי לעשות פשרה
ביניהן אלא יקוב הדין את ההר.

רשאי לעשות פשרה ביניהם שלא במושב דין הקבוע
למשפט

### 78) שולחן ערוך, חושן משפט יב:ב

מצוה לומר לבעלי דינים בתחילה הדין אתם רוצים
או הפשרה אם רצו בפשרה עושים ביניהם פשרה
וכשם שמוזהר שלא להטות הדין כך מוזהר שלא יטה
הפשרה לאחד יותר מחבירו וכל בית דין שעושה
פשרה תמיד הרי זה משובח במה דברים אמורים
קודם גמר דין אע"פ ששמע דבריהם ויודע להיכן
הדין נוטה מצוה לבצוע אבל אחר שגמר הדין ואמר
איש פלוני אתה זכאי איש פלוני אתה חייב אינו
רשאי לעשות פשרה ביניהם אבל אחר שאינו דיין

### 79) סנהדרין לב:, רמב"ם, הלכות רוצח יג:יב, שולחן ערוך, חושן משפט רעב:יד

שתי ספינות עוברות בנהר ופגעו זה בזה, אם עוברות
שתיהן שתיהן טובעות, בזה אחר זה שתיהן עוברות.
וכן שני גמלים שהיו עולים במעלות בית חורון ופגעו
זה בזה, אם עלו שניהן שניהן נופלין, בזה אחר זה
שניהן עולין. הא כיצד? טעונה ושאינה טעונה
תידחה שאינה טעונה מפני טעונה. קרובה ושאינה
קורבה תידחה קרובה מפני שאינה קרובה. היו
שתיהן קרובות, שתיהן רחוקות הטל פשרה ביניהן,
ומעלות שכר זו לזו.

בדבר מועט שלא יבואו לידי תחרות וקנאה כאחי
יוסף עם יוסף

### 69) פלא יועץ, ערך "נצוח"

אהבת הנצוח מדה זו לשנואי ישראל ידכה ישוח
ומעכבת ביאת משיח היא הגורמת קטיגוריא בין
ת"ח וכל מחלוקת ושנאה ותחרות ומצה ומריבה
שיש בעולם הכל הוא לאהבת הנצוח הלא תראה
שאם ילך אדם אצל חכם לדרוש אלקי"ם על דיני
איסור והתר יקבל עליו את הדין תכף באהבה אפי' אם
יצטרך להפסיד אלף אלפים דינרי זהב ולא יהא פוצה
פה ומצפצף רק יאמר נא ישראל ברוך שנתן לנו תורת
אמת אשריהם ישראל וכי יהיה ריב בין אנשים אפי' על
שוה פרוטה ונגשו אל המשפט ושפטום היוצא חייב
בדין ירבה במחלוקת ואיבה ישית עם השופט ועם
בעל דינו וכמה ממון וכמה נפשות נשקעים על עסקי
דבה ונעשים כתות כתות אגודות אגודות עד שאש
להבת המחלוקת עולה ואין מכבה מתוך
שכל כת מתנשא לאמר דידן נצח ולמה אשפיל עצמי
ואשאר תחת חברי ולו חכמו ישכילו כי מה יתן ומה
יוסיף היות נוצח או מנוצח האמת יורה דרכו ומודים
דרבנן היינו שבחיינו ורז"ל הקדושים היו אומר' בפני
קהל עדת ישראל דברים שאמרתי בפניכם טעות הם
בידי ואף אם יראה בעיניו לפי תומו שהאמת אתו
וחביריו תועים מדרך השכל לא יהא תוקע עצמו ברוב
עז ותעצומות להקים את דברו ויהא טוב ויותר טוב
עצמו ויהא מנוצח כדי לבקש שלום וכדי להרבות
שלום ולזה יקרא נוצח אמיתי שנוצח את יצרו וכובש
את רוחו ומה לו לנצח אדם שכמותו להבל דמה יותר
טוב וגבור יקרא שנוצח מלך שנוצח ותקיף הוא
שטן הוא יצה"ר אשר בתחבולות והבלים אלו עושה
עמו מלחמה להפילו בבאר שחת ואם ינצח את יצרו
בענין זה זהו כבודו ויזכה לכבוד גדול לפום צערא
אגרא הוא יעלה מעלה מעלה:

### 70) מסילת ישרים, פרק כ

רְאֵה, פָּשׁוּט הוּא שֶׁרָאוּי לְכָל אָדָם לִהְיוֹת מַקְדִּים וְרָץ
לִדְבַר מִצְוָה וּלְהִשְׁתַּדֵּל לִהְיוֹת מִן הָעוֹסְקִים בָּהּ, אַךְ
הִנֵּה לִפְעָמִים יָכוֹל לְהִגַּיַע מְזֶה מְרִיבָה, שֶׁיּוֹתֵר תִּתְכַּבֶּה
הַמִּצְוָה וְיִתְחַלֵּל בָּהּ שֵׁם שָׁמַיִם מִמַּה שֶׁיִּתְכַּבֵּד, בְּכַיּוֹצֵא
בָזֶה וַדַּאי שֶׁחַיָּב הֶחָסִיד לְהָנִיחַ אֶת הַמִּצְוָה וְלֹא לִרְדֹּף
אַחֲרֶיהָ. וְכֵן אָמְרוּ ז"ל בְּעִנְיָן הַלֵּוִיִּים ז"ל (בְּמִדְבַּר רַבָּה
פֶּה), "מִפְּנֵי שֶׁהַיּוּ יוֹדְעִים שֶׁכָּל מִי שֶׁטּוֹעֵן בָּאָרוֹן שְׂכָרוֹ
מְרֻבֶּה, וְהָיוּ מַנִּיחִין אֶת הַשֻּׁלְחָן וְהַמְּנוֹרָה וְהַמִּזְבְּחוֹת
וְכֻלָּן רָצִים לָאָרוֹן לִטֹּל שָׂכָר, וּמִתּוֹךְ כָּךְ הָיָה זֶה מֵרִיב
וְאוֹמֵר, אֲנִי טוֹעֵן כָּאן, וְזֶה מֵרִיב וְאוֹמֵר, אֲנִי טוֹעֵן
כָּאן, וּמִתּוֹךְ כָּךְ הָיוּ נוֹהֲגִין קַלּוּת רֹאשׁ, וְהָיְתָה הַשְּׁכִינָה
פּוֹגַעַת בָּהֶם." וְכוּ'.

### 71) ספר אמונה ובטחון לחזון איש ב:ה

ואכן מדת הבטחון קנין הלב, ומטבע הבוטח באמת
בהצנע לכת ולא ישמע מפיו כי הוא מן הבוטחים, וגם

---

בלבו הוא נאנח על חסרון בטחונו ומיעוט שלימותו
בזה, ורק למעשה תלוה עמו בטחון ועצמה בו ית',
לא יחת אם רעהו פותח חנות, ישתדל עוד לעזור
לרעהו, לתקנו בעצה טובה, לעשות עבורו, ולשקוד
על תקנתו, וכמה מן הקדושה מוסיף בעולם לראות
איש עושה חסד עם המתעתד להתחרות עמו, ומוסיף
תהלה ליראיו, אשריו ואשרי דורו ...

### 72) סנהדרין ו:

רבי אליעזר בנו של רבי יוסי הגלילי אומר: אסור
לבצוע, וכל הבוצע הרי זה חוטא, וכל המברך את
הבוצע הרי זה מנאץ, ועל זה נאמר (תהלים י')
בצע ברך נאץ ה', אלא: יקוב הדין את ההר, שנאמר
(דברים א') כי המשפט לאלקים הוא, וכן משה היה
אומר יקוב הדין את ההר, אבל אהרן אוהב שלום
ורודף שלום, ומשים שלום בין אדם לחבירו

### 73) פירוש רש"י על סנהדרין ו:

אבל אהרן אוהב שלום ורודף שלום – וכיון שהיה
שומע מחלוקת ביניהם, קודם שיבואו לפניו לדין היה
רודף אחריהן, ומטיל שלום ביניהן.

### 74) ברכות מג.

אמר רבי יוחנן: הלכה כדברי המכריע:

### 75) חולין קלז.

והאמר מר: אין הכרעה שלישית מכרעת

### 76) מהר"ל, דרך חיים, א:יב

... ובודאי מה שאמר הלל אוהב שלום ורודף שלום,
בודאי בעל המדה הזאת אינו עומד על מדותיו שאם
היה עומד על מדותיו איך יהיה רודף שלום, שכל
ענין מה שהוא רודף שלום שיאמר לחבירו שיהיה
מוותר מה שעשה לו חבירו ולא יעמוד על מדותיו,
וזה היה בודאי מדת הלל שלא היה קפדן ומדתו
לוותר. ולכך בא שמאי ואמר כי אמת היא שמדה
הזאת שלא לעמוד על מדותיו היא מדה טובה, ודבר
זה שייך במילי דעלמא אבל שיהיה האדם נוטה
לגמרי אל מדה זאת שלא יהיה מעמיד מדותיו כלל,
ורצה להנהיג הכל על דרך שלא לעמוד במדותיו,
דבר זה אינו טוב ...

### 77) רמב"ם, הלכות סנהדרין כב:ד

מצוה לומר לבעלי דינים בתחילה הדין אתם רוצים
או בפשרה, אם רצו בפשרה עושין ביניהן פשרה, וכל
בית דין שעושין פשרה תמיד הרי זה משובח ועליו
נאמר משפט שלום שפטו בשעריכם אי זהו משפט
שיש עמו שלום הוי אומר זה ביצוע, וכן דוד הוא
אומר ויהי דוד עושה משפט וצדקה לכל עמו איזהו
משפט שיש עמו צדקה הוי אומר זהו ביצוע והיא
הפשרה, במה דברים אמורים קודם גמר דין אע"פ
ששמע דבריהם וידע להיכן הדין נוטה מצוה לבצוע

להיות כמותם, ומפני הקנאה מרבה על חכמתו
וטורח ומוסיף לעשות טובה וללכת בדרך ישרה,
אך יותר שוה אם בלא קנאה חפץ באלה כי נאם
ה' הם וזאת היא מלאכת האדם, וזהו שאמר שלמה
ע"ה (קהלת ד, ד), "וראיתי אני את כל עמל ואת
כל כשרון המעשה כי היא קנאת איש מרעהו גם זה
הבל ורעות רוח" ... כי עושה הראוי מנדבת לבו
הולך באמת ובלבב שלם וחשוב מן העושהו מקנאת
אדם כי תעלה על לב, ואם מזה או מזה המעשה
יעשה ...

## 52) מדרש תהילים, מזמור לז

... אמר הקב"ה, קנא לי, שאילולי הקנאה אין העולם
מתקיים. לפי שאין אדם נושא אשה ובונה בית.

## 53) אורחות צדיקים, שער הקנאה

... לכל שנאה יש תקוה, שאם ישנא חבירו עבור
שגזלו, תסור השנאה כשישיב לו אותו דבר. וכן כל
שנאה התלויה בדבר אחר, כשיתוקן הדבר ההוא
תיבטל השנאה, חוץ מן השנאה מחמת קנאה ...

## 54) תנא דבי אליהו רבה יט:ב

בא וממוצאן שיושבין קהלין קהלין ועסוקין בתורה,
עליהן הוא אומר קנאת סופרים תרבה עליו חכמה,
זה סימן טוב לישראל

## 55) בבא בתרא כא.

ואמר רבא: האי מקרי ינוקי דגריס, ואיכא אחרינא
דגריס טפי מיניה לא מסלקינן ליה, דלמא אתי
לאיתרשולי. רב דימי מנהרדעא אמר: כ"ש דגריס
טפי, קנאת סופרים תרבה חכמה.

## 56) תענית ז.

אמר רבי חמא (אמר רבי) (מסורת הש"ס: ברבי)
חנינא: מאי דכתיב (משלי כ"ז) ברזל בברזל יחד,
לומר לך: מה ברזל זה, אחד מחדד את חבירו אף שני
תלמידי חכמים מחדדין זה את זה בהלכה.

## 57) משלי כז:יז

בַּרְזֶל בְּבַרְזֶל יָחַד וְאִישׁ יַחַד פְּנֵי־רֵעֵהוּ׃

## 58) בבא בתרא כב.

אמר רב יוסף: ומודי רב הונא במקרי דרדקי דלא
מצי מעכב, דאמר מר: (עזרא תיקן להן לישראל
שיהו מושיבין סופר בצד סופר. וניחוש דילמא אתי
לאיתרשולי. א"ל): קנאת סופרים תרבה חכמה

## 59) פלא יועץ, ערך "חברותא"

צריך חברותא שמחדדין זה לזה בהלכה וידוע
מארז"ל על פסוק חרב אל הבדים ונואלו רחמנא
ליצלן ולישבזן אך צריך לבחור חברים טובים
שנוחים זה לזה בהלכה ומודים על האמת לא כן

---

כשאינם טובים שמנגחים ז"לז בדברי קינטורים ודבה
קטיגוריה ושנאה ותחרות כל כי הא ההעדר טוב ...

## 60) יבמות יד.

ת"ש: אע"פ שאלו אוסרים ואלו מתירים, לא נמנעו
ב"ש מלישא נשים מב"ה ...

## 61) בתי מדרשות חלק ב, תמורה השלם ה

תמורה עשרים ושש ועת לשנא כנגד הודו לאל
השמים שהיהודייה גדולה מבקשין ישראל להודות
להקב"ה שהטיל ביניהם ובין אומות העולם שנאה
ותחרות שאילולי כן היו מתערבין בגוים ולמדים
ממעשיהם כמו שנאמר (תהלים קו לה) ויתערבו
בגוים וילמדו מעשיהם לפיכך הודו לאל השמים כי
לעולם חסדו:

## 62) מגילה ו.

קסרי וירושלים, אם יאמר לך אדם: חרבו שתיהן אל
תאמן, ישבו שתיהן אל תאמן. חרבה קסרי וישבה
ירושלים, חרבה ירושלים וישבה קסרי תאמן.

## 63) בבא בתרא כא:

עושה אדם חנות בצד חנותו של חבירו, ומרחץ בצד
מרחצו של חבירו, ואינו יכול למחות בידו, מפני
שיכול לומר לו: אתה עושה בתוך שלך ואני עושה
בתוך שלי

## 64) בבא מציעא ס.

רבי יהודה אומר: לא יחלק החנוני קליות ואגוזין
לתינוקות, מפני שהוא מרגילן לבא אצלו. וחכמים
מתירין. ולא יפחות את השער, וחכמים אומרים: זכור
לטוב.

## 65) רש"י על בבא מציעא ס.

זכור לטוב – שמתוך כך אוצרי פירות מוכרין בזול.

## 66) שולחן ערוך, חושן משפט רכח:יח

מותר לחנוני לחלק קליות ואגוזים לתינוקות כדי
להרגילם שיקנו ממנו, וכן יכול למכור בזול יותר
מהשער כדי שיקנו ממנו, ואין בני השוק יכולים
לעכב עליו

## 67) אבות דרבי נתן כח:ג

רשב"ג אומר כל המשים שלום בתוך ביתו מעלה
עליו הכתוב כאילו משים שלום בישראל על כל אחד
ואחד. וכל המטיל קנאה ותחרות בתוך ביתו מעלה
עליו הכתוב כאילו מטיל קנאה ותחרות בישראל לפי
שכל אחד ואחד מלך בתוך ביתו שנא' (אסתר א)
להיות כל איש שורר בביתו

## 68) רמב"ם, הלכות נחלות ו:יג

צוו חכמים שלא ישנה אדם בין הבנים בחייו אפילו

לפרוש. וכן הוא אומר "יעזוב רשע דרכו, ואיש און מחשבותיו" (ישעיהו נה, ז):

### 43) פירוש רבינו בחיי על שמות ד:כד

... לפי דעתי בלשון נתקנאו כי המלאכים אין ביניהם קנאה לפי שהקנאה ממדות יצר הרע והמלאכים אין להם יצר הרע, וכן אמרו (חגיגה טו.) אין למעלה לא ישיבה ולא עמידה ולא קנאה ולא תחרות, ומפני שכולן נסכמים לדעת אחת והיא השגת הבורא יתברך, וההשגה הזאת היא מזונם וקיומם של מלאכי השרת, וכשם שהאדם נמשך אחר מזון הגוף שהוא קיומו כך המלאכים נמשכים אחר מזונם שהוא השגתו יתברך והוא קיומם, וכיון שאין להם אלא רצון אחד ודעת אחת מן הנמנע שתהיה הקנאה מצויה בהם, ומן הידוע עוד כי הקנאה המצויה במין האנושי איננה נמצאת כי אם באותם הקרובים במעלה ...

### 44) מדרש ויקרא רבה ט:ט

בר קפרא אמר חורי גדול שלום מה אם העליונים שאין להם לא קנאה ולא שנאה ולא תחרות ולא מצות וריבות ולא מחלוקת ולא עין רעה צריכין שלום הה"ד (איוב כה) עושה שלום במרומיו התחתונים שיש בהם כל המדות הללו עאכ"ו

### 45) פירוש רבינו בחיי על דברים טז:יח

... וכך דרשו חז"ל (בראשית רבה יב, ח), המשל הזה מיכאל, ופחד זה גבריאל, והקב"ה עושה שלום ביניהם, והלא דברים קל וחומר ומה במקום שאין איבה ותחרות צריכין שלום, במקום שיש איבה ותחרות לא כל שכן. והענין כי לשון עושה שלום במרומיו הוא כולל שלום השמים בעצמם, הנבראים והמיוסדים מאש ומים, וכולל גם כן המלאכים שבמרומיו שעליהם רמז המשל ופחד, וקרא למיכאל המשל מפני שהוא השר הגדול הממונה והמושל לבקש רחמים על ישראל. ואין צריך לומר החיים שאפילו המתים צריכין שלום, שנאמר (בראשית טו, טו) ואתה תבא אל אבותיך בשלום. מדת השלום ניתנה לאהרן, ועמה זכה להיות לו החיים והשלום (מלאכי ב, ה), וזכה זרעו לכהונת עולם לברך את ישראל שנאמר (במדבר ו, כו) וישם לך שלום. הא למדת שהשלום קיום העולם:

### 46) יערות דבש א:א

בברכת שים שלום, יש להתפלל על השלום, כי אין כלי מחזיק ברכה אלא השלום, [סוף עוקצין] כי הוא קשר הנחמד, והוא אחדות גמור של ישראל, וכאשר יתפלל על השלום, יתפלל שלא תהיה מחלוקת בישראל, ולא יהיה קנאה ושנאה ותחרות, כי כולם יהיו אהובים אחוזים ואחודים בתכלית היחוד ואהבה ואחוה וריעות, ויהיו כל ישראל נפש אחת. ויכוין לקיים ואהבת לרעך כמוך, שהוא כלל כל התורה, וזה יהיה בתכלית התפלה, שהוא כלל כל התפלה,

---

ויתפלל שלא תהיה בו מדת כעס כי אם עניו לכל, והוא במדרגת שלום, כי במקום שהכעס מצוי אין שלום.

### 47) ברכות יז.

[לא כעולם הזה העולם הבא] העולם הבא אין בו לא אכילה ולא שתיה ולא פריה ורביה ולא משא ומתן ולא קנאה ולא שנאה ולא תחרות אלא צדיקים יושבין ועטרותיהם בראשיהם ונהנים מזיו השכינה שנאמר ויחזו את האלקים ויאכלו וישתו:

### 48) רמב"ם, הלכות מלכים יב:ד-ה

לא נתאוו החכמים והנביאים ימות המשיח לא כדי שישלטו על כל העולם ולא כדי שירדו בעכו"ם ולא כדי שינשאו אותם העמים ולא כדי לאכול ולשתות ולשמוח אלא כדי שיהיו פנויין בתורה וחכמתה ולא יהיה להם נוגש ומבטל כדי שיזכו לחיי העולם הבא כמו שביארנו בהלכות תשובה:
ובאותו הזמן לא יהיה שם לא רעב ולא מלחמה ולא קנאה ותחרות שהטובה תהיה מושפעת הרבה וכל המעדנים מצויין כעפר ולא יהיה עסק כל העולם אלא לדעת את ה' בלבד ולפיכך יהיו ישראל חכמים גדולים ויודעים דברים הסתומים וישיגו דעת בוראם כפי כח האדם שנאמר כי מלאה הארץ דעה את ה' כמים לים מכסים:

### 49) משנה יומא ב:א

בראשונה, כל מי שרוצה לתרום את המזבח, תורם. ובזמן שהן מרובין, רצין ועולין בכבש, וכל הקודם את חברו בארבע אמות זכה. ואם היו שניהם שוין, הממונה אומר להם הצביעו. ומה הן מוציאין, אחת או שתים, ואין מוציאין אגודל במקדש:

### 50) משנה בכורים ג:ז-ח

ז בראשונה, כל מי שיודע לקרות, קורא. וכל מי שאינו יודע לקרות, מקרין אותו. נמנעו מלהביא. התקינו שיהו מקרין את מי שיודע ואת מי שאינו יודע:
ח העשירים מביאים בכוריהם בקלתות של כסף ושל זהב. והעניים מביאים אותם בסלי נצרים של ערבה קלופה. והסלים והבכורים נתנין לכהנים:

### 51) פירוש רבינו יונה למשנה אבות ד:כא

בענין הקנאה יש שני דרכים ... הדרך האחד מקנא בטובה והוא הדרך הרע. והענין הראשון, כי יראה חבירו טוב, ורע בעיניו. וכאשר יעסוק בתורה ובמצות והולך בדרך טובה מקנא בו כי הוא שונא אוהבי השם ית' ועושה רצונו, המדה הזאת מוציאתו מן העולם והיא הרעה הגדולה ... ויש דרך טובה בקנאה, ואם אחרת טובה ממנה, מה שאמרו חכמים ז"ל (ב"ב כא, א), קנאת סופרים תרבה חכמה, כי על ידי שרואה חבירו קדושים וחכמים גם הוא חפץ

32) פירוש רש"י על במדבר ז:יט

הקריב נתנאל בן צוער – ... מהו הקריב הקריב שני פעמים, שבשביל שני דברים זכה להקריב שני לשבטים, אחת שהיו יודעים בתורה שנאמר ומבני יששכר יודעי בינה לעתים (דברי הימים א יב, לג.), ואחת שהם נתנו עצה לנשיאים להתנדב קרבנות הללו, וביסודו של רבי משה הדרשן מצאתי, אמר רבי פנחס בן יאיר, נתנאל בן צוער השיאן עצה זו:

33) במדבר ז:ג

וַיָּבִיאוּ אֶת קָרְבָּנָם לִפְנֵי ד' שֵׁשׁ עֶגְלֹת צָב וּשְׁנֵי עָשָׂר בָּקָר עֲגָלָה עַל שְׁנֵי הַנְּשִׂאִים וְשׁוֹר לְאֶחָד וַיַּקְרִיבוּ אוֹתָם לִפְנֵי הַמִּשְׁכָּן:

34) ספר אמונה ובטחון לחזון איש ה:א

והשכל איש ריבו אוהב את הבחינה השכלית, מחבר את המאזנים, חומד את משפטי החשבון, חושק את חקי המחקר:

טבע בן אדם לאהוב את ההתחרות, אם שנים – אחד מתחרה את רעהו, אם עדה – את חברתה, או אם דורות הראשונים מתחרים עם דורות האחרונים, גם זה מושך את הלב, וההתאבקות שלהם נעימה לראות עין, ולשמע אוזן:

35) מדרש שיר השירים רבה ח:יז

... ותנו דעתכם שלא תשנאו זה את זה ולא תקנאו זה את זה ולא תחרחרו זה עם זה ולא תביישו זה לזה שלא יאמרו מלאכי השרת לפני רבש"ע תורה שנתת להם לישראל אינם עוסקין בה והרי איבה וקנאה ושנאה ותחרות ביניהם ואתם מקיימים אותה בשלום בר קפרא אמר למה קרא למלאכי השרת חברים לפי שאין ביניהם איבה וקנאה ושנאה ותחרות ומינות ופלוגת דברים:

36) פירוש רש"י על שבת קנב

מי שיש לו קנאה – ותחרות על חברו

37) ספר העיקרים ב:כח

ודע כי המלאכים להיותם נבדלים מחומר ואי אפשר שישיגום המקרים הנמשכים לבעלי החומר כקנאה ושנאה ותחרות כי הם נקיים מכל רע ואין בהם לא גאוה ולא בחירה אל הרע ואל החטא כלל אבל בחירתם תמיד אל הטוב ...

38) שמות טו:כה, מדרש מכילתא, משפטים נזיקין א

וַיִּצְעַק אֶל ד' וַיּוֹרֵהוּ ד' עֵץ וַיַּשְׁלֵךְ אֶל הַמַּיִם וַיִּמְתְּקוּ הַמָּיִם שָׁם שָׂם לוֹ חֹק וּמִשְׁפָּט וְשָׁם נִסָּהוּ:
רבי שמעון אומר מה ראו דינין לקדום לכל מצות שבתורה שכשהדין בין אדם לחבירו תחרות ביניהם נפסק הדין נעשה שלום ביניהם. וכן יתרו אומר (שם י"ח) אם את הדבר הזה תעשה וגו':

39) ספר החינוך, מצוה תקא

שלא ירבה לו המלך נשים הרבה. ועל זה נאמר (דברים יז יז) וְלֹא יַרְבֶּה לּוֹ נָשִׁים. וְטַעַם הַמִּצְוָה מְבֹאָר בַּכָּתוּב, כִּי הַנָּשִׁים מְסִירוֹת לֵב בַּעֲלֵיהֶן, כְּלוֹמַר שֶׁמְּפַתּוֹת אוֹתָם לַעֲשׂוֹת מַה שֶּׁאֵינוֹ רָאוּי בְּהַתְמַדָתָן עֲלֵיהֶם, תַּחֲרוּת, וְרִבּוּי דְּבָרִים, וַהֲקַלְקָלוֹת.

40) מועד קטן כז.

תנו רבנן: בראשונה היו מוליכין בבית האבל, עשירים בקלתות של כסף ושל זהב, ועניים בסלי נצרים של ערבה קלופה. והיו עניים מתביישים, התקינו שיהו הכל מביאין בסלי נצרים של ערבה קלופה, מפני כבודן של עניים. תנו רבנן: בראשונה היו משקין בבית האבל, עשירים בזכוכית לבנה, ועניים בזכוכית צבועה, והיו עניים מתביישין. התקינו שיהו הכל משקין בזכוכית צבועה, מפני כבודן של עניים. בראשונה היו מגלין פני עשירים ומכסין פני עניים, מפני שהיו מושחרין פניהן מפני בצורת, והיו עניים מתביישין. התקינו שיהו מכסין פני הכל, מפני כבודן של עניים. בראשונה היו מוציאין עשירים בדרגש, ועניים בכליכה, והיו עניים מתביישין, התקינו שיהו הכל מוציאין בכליכה, מפני כבודן של עניים. בראשונה היו מניחין את המוגמר תחת חולי מעים מתים, והיו חולי מעים חיים מתביישין, התקינו שיהו מניחין תחת הכל, מפני כבודן של חולי מעים חיים. בראשונה היו מטבילין את הכלים על גבי נדות מתות, והיו נדות חיות מתביישות, התקינו שיהו מטבילין על גבי כל הנשים, מפני כבודן של נדות חיות. בראשונה מטבילין על גבי זבין מתים, והיו זבין חיים מתביישין. התקינו שיהו מטבילין על גבי זבין חיים, מפני כבודן של זבין חיים. בראשונה היתה הוצאת המת קשה לקרוביו יותר ממיתתו, עד שהיו קרוביו מניחין אותו ובורחין. עד שבא רבן גמליאל ונהג קלות בעצמו ויצא בכלי פשתן, ונהגו העם אחריו לצאת בכלי פשתן.

41) תלמוד ירושלמי ברכות כה.

א"ר חנינא בראשונה היו משפחות עומדות ואבלים עוברין משרבה תחרות בציפורין התקין ר"י בן חלפתא שיהו המשפחות עוברות והאבלים עומדים א"ר שמעון דתוספתא חזרו הדברים ליושנן

42) רמב"ם, הלכות תשובה ז:ג

ואל תאמר שאין תשובה אלא מעבירות שיש בהן מעשה, כגון זנות וגזל וגניבה. כשם שצריך אדם לשוב מאלו, כך הוא צריך לחפש בדעות רעות שיש לו ולשוב מהן, מן הכעס, ומן האיבה, ומן הקנאה, ומן התחרות, ומן ההתל, ומרדיפת הממון והכבוד, ומרדיפת המאכלות, וכיוצא בהן – מן הכול צריך לחזור בתשובה. ואלו העוונות, קשין מאותן שיש בהן מעשה, שבזמן שאדם נשקע באלו, קשה הוא

וראך ושמח בלבו – לא כשאתה סבור שיהא מקפיד עליך שאתה עולה לגדולה, ומשם זכה אהרן לעדי החשן הנתנן על הלב:

וראך ושמח בלבו – לא היו מתקנאים במעלתם זה על זה, זהו שאמר הכתוב (תהלים קלג, א) הנה מה טוב ומה נעים שבת אחים גם יחד. ושמח בפיו לא נאמר אלא בלבו אמר רבי שמעון בן יוחai הלב ששמח בגדולת אחיו ילבש אורים ותומים שנאמר (שמות כח, ל) והיו על לב אהרן (תנחומא שמות כז):

### 22) מדרש תנחומא ויקהל ד, שמות רבה א:יז

אהרן כהן גדול משה מלך ויהי בישרון מלך, ומה שכר נטלה מרים חכמה
... בתי כהונה ולויה ממשה ואהרן בתי מלכות ממרים ...

### 23) דברים כד:ט, מדרש ספרי, כי תצא סה

זָכוֹר אֵת אֲשֶׁר־עָשָׂה ד' אֱלֹקֶיךָ לְמִרְיָם בַּדֶּרֶךְ בְּצֵאתְכֶם מִמִּצְרָיִם:

בצאתכם ממצרים – בשעת גאולתכם אלא שתלה הכתוב הכל ללמדך שכל זמן שהיו הדגלים נוסעים לא היו הולכים עד שמרים מקדמת לפניהם. וכן הוא אומר (מיכה ו) ואשלח לפניו את משה אהרן ומרים:

### 24) במדבר יב:א-ג, ט-יג, טו

וַתְּדַבֵּר מִרְיָם וְאַהֲרֹן בְּמֹשֶׁה עַל־אֹדוֹת הָאִשָּׁה הַכֻּשִׁית אֲשֶׁר לָקָח כִּי־אִשָּׁה כֻשִׁית לָקָח: וַיֹּאמְרוּ הֲרַק אַךְ־ בְּמֹשֶׁה דִּבֶּר ד' הֲלֹא גַּם־בָּנוּ דִבֵּר וַיִּשְׁמַע ד': וְהָאִישׁ מֹשֶׁה עָנָו [עֲנָיו] מְאֹד מִכֹּל הָאָדָם אֲשֶׁר עַל־פְּנֵי הָאֲדָמָה:

וַיִּחַר־אַף ד' בָּם וַיֵּלַךְ: וְהֶעָנָן סָר מֵעַל הָאֹהֶל וְהִנֵּה מִרְיָם מְצֹרַעַת כַּשָּׁלֶג וַיִּפֶן אַהֲרֹן אֶל־מִרְיָם וְהִנֵּה מְצֹרָעַת: וַיֹּאמֶר אַהֲרֹן אֶל־מֹשֶׁה בִּי אֲדֹנִי אַל־נָא תָשֵׁת עָלֵינוּ חַטָּאת אֲשֶׁר נוֹאַלְנוּ וַאֲשֶׁר חָטָאנוּ: אַל־נָא תְהִי כַּמֵּת אֲשֶׁר בְּצֵאתוֹ מֵרֶחֶם אִמּוֹ וַיֵּאָכֵל חֲצִי בְשָׂרוֹ: וַיִּצְעַק מֹשֶׁה אֶל־ד' לֵאמֹר אֵ-ל נָא רְפָא נָא לָהּ: וַתִּסָּגֵר מִרְיָם מִחוּץ לַמַּחֲנֶה שִׁבְעַת יָמִים וְהָעָם לֹא נָסַע עַד־הֵאָסֵף מִרְיָם:

### 25) פירוש רש"י על במדבר ז:ג

ויקריבו אותם לפני המשכן – שלא קבל משה מידם עד שנאמר לו ק מפי המקום. אמר רבי נתן, מה ראו הנשיאים להתנדב כאן בתחלה ובמלאכת המשכן לא התנדבו תחלה, אלא כך אמרו הנשיאים, יתנדבו צבור מה שיתנדבו ומה שמחסרין אנו משלימין, כיון שראו שהשלימו צבור את הכל, שנאמר והמלאכה היתה דַיָּם (שמות לו, ז), אמרו מעתה מה לנו לעשות, הביאו את אבני השוהם והמלואים לאפוד ולחשן, לכך התנדבו כאן תחלה:

### 26) שמות לו:ה-ז

וַיֹּאמְרוּ אֶל־מֹשֶׁה לֵּאמֹר מַרְבִּים הָעָם לְהָבִיא מִדֵּי

---

הָעֲבֹדָה לַמְּלָאכָה אֲשֶׁר־צִוָּה ד' לַעֲשֹׂת אֹתָהּ: וַיְצַו מֹשֶׁה וַיַּעֲבִירוּ קוֹל בַּמַּחֲנֶה לֵאמֹר אִישׁ וְאִשָּׁה אַל־יַעֲשׂוּ־ עוֹד מְלָאכָה לִתְרוּמַת הַקֹּדֶשׁ וַיִּכָּלֵא הָעָם מֵהָבִיא: וְהַמְּלָאכָה הָיְתָה דַיָּם לְכָל־הַמְּלָאכָה לַעֲשׂוֹת אֹתָהּ וְהוֹתֵר:

### 27) במדבר ז:יב-יז

וַיְהִי הַמַּקְרִיב בַּיּוֹם הָרִאשׁוֹן אֶת־קָרְבָּנוֹ נַחְשׁוֹן בֶּן־ עַמִּינָדָב לְמַטֵּה יְהוּדָה: וְקָרְבָּנוֹ קַעֲרַת־כֶּסֶף אַחַת שְׁלֹשִׁים וּמֵאָה מִשְׁקָלָהּ מִזְרָק אֶחָד כֶּסֶף שִׁבְעִים שֶׁקֶל בְּשֶׁקֶל הַקֹּדֶשׁ שְׁנֵיהֶם | מְלֵאִים סֹלֶת בְּלוּלָה בַשֶּׁמֶן לְמִנְחָה: כַּף אַחַת עֲשָׂרָה זָהָב מְלֵאָה קְטֹרֶת: פַּר אֶחָד בֶּן־בָּקָר אַיִל אֶחָד כֶּבֶשׂ־אֶחָד בֶּן־שְׁנָתוֹ לְעֹלָה: שְׂעִיר עִזִּים אֶחָד לְחַטָּאת: וּלְזֶבַח הַשְּׁלָמִים בָּקָר שְׁנַיִם אֵילִם חֲמִשָּׁה עַתּוּדִים חֲמִשָּׁה כְּבָשִׂים בְּנֵי־שָׁנָה חֲמִשָּׁה זֶה קָרְבַּן נַחְשׁוֹן בֶּן־עַמִּינָדָב:

### 28) מדרש תנחומא נשא יד

"ויקריבו נשיאי ישראל" אמרו הרי השעה שנקריב קרבנות בשמחה שֹשרתה שכינה בינותינו כיון שראו שנעשה המשכן ולא היה חסר בו כלום אמרו מה יש לנו להביא הלכו והביאו עגלות שיהיו נושאין עליהן את המשכן ומי נתן את העצה הזו שבטו של יששכר שהיו חכמים וגבורים בתורה שנאמר (ד"ה א יב) ומבני יששכר יודעי בינה לעתים לפיכך זכו להקריב ביום השני שנאמר ביום השני הקריב נתנאל בן צוער נשיא יששכר למה נאמר בכל הנשיאים קרבנו קערת כסף אחת וכאן נאמר הקריב את קרבנו שע"פ הדבור הקריב שבקשו שאר השבטים להקריב תחלה לפי שהיו גדולים ממנו והכריעו אותן מן השמים ונצטוה שבט יששכר להקריב קרבן המזבח ולהקריב קרבנו תדע לך שכן כתיב הקרב חסר שהיה רחוק ונתקרב לבא על כל כך למה על שהיו יודעים בתורה שנאמר (שם) ומבני יששכר יודעי בינה לעתים לדעת מה יעשה ישראל ראשיהם מאתים אלו ראשי סנהדראות וכל אחיהם על פיהם ללמדך שכולם מסכימים הלכה על פיהם:

### 29) מדרש בראשית רבה עב:ה

... ביום השני הקריב נתנאל בן צוער נשיא יששכר מפני מה מפני שהיה בן תורה הה"ד (ד"ה א יב) ומבני יששכר יודעי בינה לעתים מה לעתים

### 30) פירוש בעל הטורים על במדבר ז:יח

ביום השני הקריב – בגימטריא נתן להם עצה:

### 31) במדבר ז:יח-יט

בַּיּוֹם הַשֵּׁנִי הִקְרִיב נְתַנְאֵל בֶּן־צוּעָר נְשִׂיא יִשָּׂשכָר: הִקְרִב אֶת־קָרְבָּנוֹ קַעֲרַת־כֶּסֶף אַחַת שְׁלֹשִׁים וּמֵאָה מִשְׁקָלָהּ מִזְרָק אֶחָד כֶּסֶף שִׁבְעִים שֶׁקֶל בְּשֶׁקֶל הַקֹּדֶשׁ שְׁנֵיהֶם מְלֵאִים סֹלֶת בְּלוּלָה בַשֶּׁמֶן לְמִנְחָה:

חמשת שקלים לגלגלת, אמר משה: כיצד אעשה להן
לישראל? אם אומר לו תן לי פדיונך וצא יאמר לי:
כבר פדאני בן לוי. מה עשה? הביא עשרים ושנים
אלפים פיתקין, וכתב עליהן בן לוי, ועל שלשה
ושבעים ומאתים כתב עליהן חמשה שקלים, בללן
ונתנן בקלפי. אמר להן: טלו פיתקיכם. מי שעלה
בידו בן לוי אמר לו: כבר פדאך בן לוי. מי שעלה
בידו חמשת שקלים, אמר לו: תן פדיונך וצא.

### 16) מדרש, במדבר רבה ה:א, ט

... מפני שהיו יודעין שכל מי שטוען בארון שכרו
מרובה והיו מניחין את השלחן והמנורה והמזבחות
וכולן רצין לארון ליטול שכר ומתוך כך היה מריב
ואומר אני טוען כאן וזה מריב ואומר אני טוען כאן
ומתוך כך היו נוהגין בקלות ראש והיתה השכינה
פוגעת בהם אמר האלהים למשה עשה להם תקנה
כדי שלא יתכלו מן העולם אל תכריתו וגו' אלא
יסדרו אותם על עבודתם ועל משאם שלא יריבו זה
עם זה

"אהרן ובניו יבאו ושמו אותם וגו'" מיכן היה ר'
שמואל ברבי נחמן אומר מפני שהיו בני קהת יודעין
שכל מי שטוען בארון שכרו מרובה והיו מניחין
השלחן והמנורה והמזבחות וכו' [כמו שכתוב
למעלה] עד אהרן ובניו יבאו וגו' ולא יבאו לראות
כבלע וגו'

### 17) במדבר ד:טו, יז-כ

וְכִלָּה אַהֲרֹן וּבָנָיו לְכַסֹּת אֶת־הַקֹּדֶשׁ וְאֶת־כָּל־כְּלֵי
הַקֹּדֶשׁ בִּנְסֹעַ הַמַּחֲנֶה וְאַחֲרֵי־כֵן יָבֹאוּ בְנֵי־קְהָת לָשֵׂאת
וְלֹא־יִגְּעוּ אֶל־הַקֹּדֶשׁ וָמֵתוּ אֵלֶּה מַשָּׂא בְנֵי־קְהָת בְּאֹהֶל
מוֹעֵד
וַיְדַבֵּר ד' אֶל־מֹשֶׁה וְאֶל־אַהֲרֹן לֵאמֹר: אַל־תַּכְרִיתוּ אֶת־
שֵׁבֶט מִשְׁפְּחֹת הַקְּהָתִי מִתּוֹךְ הַלְוִיִּם: וְזֹאת עֲשׂוּ לָהֶם
וְחָיוּ וְלֹא יָמֻתוּ בְּגִשְׁתָּם אֶת־קֹדֶשׁ הַקֳּדָשִׁים אַהֲרֹן וּבָנָיו
יָבֹאוּ וְשָׂמוּ אוֹתָם אִישׁ אִישׁ עַל־עֲבֹדָתוֹ וְאֶל־מַשָּׂאוֹ
וְלֹא־יָבֹאוּ לִרְאוֹת כְּבַלַּע אֶת־הַקֹּדֶשׁ וָמֵתוּ:

### 18) במדבר טז:א-ג ופירוש רש"י

וַיִּקַּח קֹרַח בֶּן־יִצְהָר בֶּן־קְהָת בֶּן־לֵוִי וְדָתָן וַאֲבִירָם בְּנֵי
אֱלִיאָב וְאוֹן בֶּן־פֶּלֶת בְּנֵי רְאוּבֵן: וַיָּקֻמוּ לִפְנֵי מֹשֶׁה
וַאֲנָשִׁים מִבְּנֵי־יִשְׂרָאֵל חֲמִשִּׁים וּמָאתָיִם נְשִׂיאֵי עֵדָה
קְרִאֵי מוֹעֵד אַנְשֵׁי־שֵׁם: וַיִּקָּהֲלוּ עַל־מֹשֶׁה וְעַל־אַהֲרֹן
וַיֹּאמְרוּ אֲלֵהֶם רַב־לָכֶם כִּי כָל־הָעֵדָה כֻּלָּם קְדֹשִׁים
וּבְתוֹכָם ד' וּמַדּוּעַ תִּתְנַשְּׂאוּ עַל־קְהַל ד':
ודתן ואבירם – בשביל שהיה שבט ראובן שרוי
בחנייתם תימנה שכן לקהת ובניו החונים תימנה
נשתתפו עם קרח במחלוקתו אוי לרשע אוי לשכנו.
ומה ראה קרח לחלוק עם משה נתקנא על נשיאותו
של אליצפן בן עוזיאל (תנחומא) שמינהו משה נשיא
על בני קהת על פי הדבור. אמר קרח אחי אבא
ארבעה היו שנא' (שמות ו) ובני קהת וגו' הבכור
נטלו שני בניו גדולה אחד מלך ואחד כהן

---

גדול מי ראוי ליטול את השניה לא אני שאני בן יצהר
שהוא שני לעמרם והוא מנה נשיא את בן אחיו הקטן
מכולם הריני חולק עליו ומבטל את דבריו. מה עשה
עמד וכנס ר"ן ראשי סנהדראות רובן משבט ראובן
שכניו והם אליצור בן שדיאור וחביריו וכיוצא בו
שנאמר נשיאי עדה קריאי מועד ...

### 19) ספר התודעה, פרק יא

צר היה להם לראות בשכנותם ממלכה קטנה, ממלכת
יהודה, שאף כי היא כבושה בידם, הרי היא שוכנת
לה לבדד, ובכל תורת יון וחכמתה לא תתחשב, והיא
בוזה בלבה לעטרת כבודה ואינה נותנת לרוח היונית
שתתדור אליה: לא התחרות של כח היתה שם, שכן
היתה היהודה למס עובד לכובשיה. אלא התחרות של
רוח. בהתחרות של כח היתה יד יון על העליונה,
ובהתחרות של רוח – ידה של יהודה היתה על
העליונה, למורת רוחם של שליטי העמים:

### 20) שמות א:טו-כ ופירוש רש"י, ב:א-ז, טו, טז-כ-כא

וַיֹּאמֶר מֶלֶךְ מִצְרַיִם לַמְיַלְּדֹת הָעִבְרִיֹּת אֲשֶׁר שֵׁם
הָאַחַת שִׁפְרָה וְשֵׁם הַשֵּׁנִית פּוּעָה: וַיֹּאמֶר בְּיַלֶּדְכֶן אֶת־
הָעִבְרִיּוֹת וּרְאִיתֶן עַל־הָאָבְנָיִם אִם־בֵּן הוּא וַהֲמִתֶּן אֹתוֹ
וְאִם־בַּת הִוא וָחָיָה: וַתִּירֶאןָ הַמְיַלְּדֹת אֶת־הָאֱלֹקִים
וְלֹא עָשׂוּ כַּאֲשֶׁר דִּבֶּר אֲלֵיהֶן מֶלֶךְ מִצְרָיִם וַתְּחַיֶּיןָ
אֶת־הַיְלָדִים: וַיִּקְרָא מֶלֶךְ־מִצְרַיִם לַמְיַלְּדֹת וַיֹּאמֶר לָהֶן
מַדּוּעַ עֲשִׂיתֶן הַדָּבָר הַזֶּה וַתְּחַיֶּיןָ אֶת־הַיְלָדִים: וַתֹּאמַרְןָ
הַמְיַלְּדֹת אֶל־פַּרְעֹה כִּי לֹא כַנָּשִׁים הַמִּצְרִיֹּת הָעִבְרִיֹּת
כִּי־חָיוֹת הֵנָּה בְּטֶרֶם תָּבוֹא אֲלֵהֶן הַמְיַלֶּדֶת וְיָלָדוּ: וַיֵּיטֶב
אֱלֹקִים לַמְיַלְּדֹת וַיִּרֶב הָעָם וַיַּעַצְמוּ מְאֹד:
שפרה – זו יוכבד, על שם שמשפרת את הולד:
פועה – זו מרים,
וַיֵּלֶךְ אִישׁ מִבֵּית לֵוִי וַיִּקַּח אֶת־בַּת־לֵוִי: וַתַּהַר הָאִשָּׁה
וַתֵּלֶד בֵּן וַתֵּרֶא אֹתוֹ כִּי־טוֹב הוּא וַתִּצְפְּנֵהוּ שְׁלֹשָׁה
יְרָחִים: וְלֹא־יָכְלָה עוֹד הַצְּפִינוֹ וַתִּקַּח־לוֹ תֵּבַת גֹּמֶא
וַתַּחְמְרָה בַחֵמָר וּבַזָּפֶת וַתָּשֶׂם בָּהּ אֶת־הַיֶּלֶד וַתָּשֶׂם
בַּסּוּף עַל־שְׂפַת הַיְאֹר: וַתֵּתַצַּב אֲחֹתוֹ מֵרָחֹק לְדֵעָה מַה־
יֵּעָשֶׂה לוֹ: וַתֵּרֶד בַּת־פַּרְעֹה לִרְחֹץ עַל־הַיְאֹר וְנַעֲרֹתֶיהָ
הֹלְכֹת עַל־יַד הַיְאֹר וַתֵּרֶא אֶת־הַתֵּבָה בְּתוֹךְ הַסּוּף
וַתִּשְׁלַח אֶת־אֲמָתָהּ וַתִּקָּחֶהָ: וַתִּפְתַּח וַתִּרְאֵהוּ אֶת־הַיֶּלֶד
וְהִנֵּה־נַעַר בֹּכֶה וַתַּחְמֹל עָלָיו וַתֹּאמֶר מִיַּלְדֵי הָעִבְרִים
זֶה: וַתֹּאמֶר אֲחֹתוֹ אֶל־בַּת־פַּרְעֹה הַאֵלֵךְ וְקָרָאתִי לָךְ
אִשָּׁה מֵינֶקֶת מִן הָעִבְרִיֹּת וְתֵינִק לָךְ אֶת־הַיָּלֶד:
וַתִּקַּח מִרְיָם הַנְּבִיאָה אֲחוֹת אַהֲרֹן אֶת־הַתֹּף בְּיָדָהּ
וַתֵּצֶאןָ כָל־הַנָּשִׁים אַחֲרֶיהָ בְּתֻפִּים וּבִמְחֹלֹת: וַתַּעַן לָהֶם
מִרְיָם שִׁירוּ לַד' כִּי גָאֹה גָּאָה סוּס וְרֹכְבוֹ רָמָה בַיָּם:

### 21) שמות ד:יד-טו, ופירושי רש"י ורבינו בחיי

וַיִּחַר־אַף ד' בְּמֹשֶׁה וַיֹּאמֶר הֲלֹא אַהֲרֹן אָחִיךָ הַלֵּוִי
יָדַעְתִּי כִּי־דַבֵּר יְדַבֵּר הוּא וְגַם הִנֵּה־הוּא יֹצֵא לִקְרָאתֶךָ
וְרָאֲךָ וְשָׂמַח בְּלִבּוֹ: וְדִבַּרְתָּ אֵלָיו וְשַׂמְתָּ אֶת־הַדְּבָרִים
בְּפִיו וְאָנֹכִי אֶהְיֶה עִם־פִּיךָ וְעִם־פִּיהוּ וְהוֹרֵיתִי אֶתְכֶם
אֵת אֲשֶׁר תַּעֲשׂוּן:.

ולא יָכְלוּ לָשֶׁבֶת יַחְדָּו: וַיְהִי־רִיב בֵּין רֹעֵי מִקְנֵה־אַבְרָם
וּבֵין רֹעֵי מִקְנֵה־לוֹט וְהַכְּנַעֲנִי וְהַפְּרִזִּי אָז יֹשֵׁב בָּאָרֶץ:
וַיֹּאמֶר אַבְרָם אֶל־לוֹט אַל־נָא תְהִי מְרִיבָה בֵּינִי וּבֵינֶיךָ
וּבֵין רֹעַי וּבֵין רֹעֶיךָ כִּי־אֲנָשִׁים אַחִים אֲנָחְנוּ: הֲלֹא כָל־
הָאָרֶץ לְפָנֶיךָ הִפָּרֶד נָא מֵעָלָי אִם־הַשְּׂמֹאל וְאֵימִנָה
וְאִם־הַיָּמִין וְאַשְׂמְאִילָה: וַיִּשָּׂא־לוֹט אֶת־עֵינָיו וַיַּרְא אֶת־
כָּל־כִּכַּר הַיַּרְדֵּן כִּי כֻלָּהּ מַשְׁקֶה לִפְנֵי | שַׁחֵת ד' אֶת־סְדֹם
וְאֶת־עֲמֹרָה כְּגַן־ד' כְּאֶרֶץ מִצְרַיִם בֹּאֲכָה צֹעַר: וַיִּבְחַר־
לוֹ לוֹט אֵת כָּל־כִּכַּר הַיַּרְדֵּן וַיִּסַּע לוֹט מִקֶּדֶם וַיִּפָּרְדוּ
אִישׁ מֵעַל אָחִיו:

א"ר עזריה כשם שהיתה תחרות בין הרועים כך היתה
תחרות בין אברם ללוט מנין שכן כתיב אל נא תהי
מריב ביני וביניך

## 9) בראשית כא:ח-יב
וַיִּגְדַּל הַיֶּלֶד וַיִּגָּמַל וַיַּעַשׂ אַבְרָהָם מִשְׁתֶּה גָדוֹל בְּיוֹם
הִגָּמֵל אֶת־יִצְחָק: וַתֵּרֶא שָׂרָה אֶת־בֶּן־הָגָר הַמִּצְרִית
אֲשֶׁר־יָלְדָה לְאַבְרָהָם מְצַחֵק: וַתֹּאמֶר לְאַבְרָהָם גָּרֵשׁ
הָאָמָה הַזֹּאת וְאֶת־בְּנָהּ כִּי לֹא יִירַשׁ בֶּן־הָאָמָה הַזֹּאת
עִם־בְּנִי עִם־יִצְחָק: וַיֵּרַע הַדָּבָר מְאֹד בְּעֵינֵי אַבְרָהָם עַל
אוֹדֹת בְּנוֹ: וַיֹּאמֶר אֱלֹקִים אֶל־אַבְרָהָם אַל־יֵרַע בְּעֵינֶיךָ
עַל־הַנַּעַר וְעַל־אֲמָתֶךָ כֹּל אֲשֶׁר תֹּאמַר אֵלֶיךָ שָׂרָה שְׁמַע
בְּקֹלָהּ כִּי בְיִצְחָק יִקָּרֵא לְךָ זָרַע:

## 10) זהר, חלק ב, לב, מדרש ילקוט שמעוני ו:מה
ארבע מאה שנין קיימא ההוא ממנא דבני ישמעאל,
ובעא קמי קודשא בריך הוא, אמר ליה מאן דאתגזר
אית ליה חולקא בשמך, אמר ליה אין, אמר ליה והא
ישמעאל דאתגזר (ולא עוד אלא דאתגזר בר תליסר
שנין) אמאי לית ליה חולקא בך כמו יצחק, אמר ליה
דא אתגזר כדקא יאות וכתיקונוי ודא לאו הכי, ולא
עוד אלא דאלין מתדבקין בי כדקא יאות לתמניא
יומין, ואלין רחיקין מני עד כמה ימים, אמר ליה ועם
כל דא כיון דאתגזר לא יהא ליה אגר טב בגיניה. ווי
על ההוא זמנא דאתיליד ישמעאל בעלמא ואתגזר,
מה עבד קודשא בריך הוא, ארחיק לון לבני ישמעאל
מדבקותא דלעילא, ויהב להו חולקא לתתא בארעא
קדישא, בגין ההוא גזירו דבהון, וזמינין בני ישמעאל
למשלט בארעא קדישא כד איהו ריקניא מכלא זמנא
סגי, כמה דגזירו דלהון בריקניא בלא שלימו, ואינון
יעכבון להון לבני ישראל לאתבא לדוכתייהו, עד
דישתלים ההוא זכותא דבני ישמעאל.

ששה נקראו בשמותם עד שלא נולדו ואלו הן
ישמעאל ויצחק ומשה ושלמה ויאשיהו ומלך
המשיח. ישמעאל מנין שנאמר הנך הרה וילדת בן
וגו' (נד) ולמה נקרא שמו ישמעאל שעתיד הקב"ה
לשמוע באנקת העם ממה שבני ישמעאל עושין להם
באחרית הימים.

## 11) מדרש פרקי דרבי אליעזר ל
בן שלשים ושבע שנה היה יצחק בלכתו אל הר
המוריה וישמעאל בן חמשים שנה נכנס תחרות

בין אליעזר וישמעאל אמ' ישמעאל לאליעזר עכשו
אברהם הקריב את יצחק בנו מוקדה על המזבח ואני
בכורו יורש אברהם אמ' לו אליעזר כבר גרשך כאשה
שהיא מגורשת מבעלה ושלחך למדבר אבל אני
עבדו משרת אותו ביום ובלילה ואני הוא היורש את
אברהם ורוח הקדש משיבה אותם ואומרת להם לא
זה יורש ולא זה יורש

## 12) סנהדרין יז.
תנו רבנן: (במדבר י"א) וישארו שני אנשים במחנה יש
אומרים בקלפי נשתיירו. שבשעה שאמר לו הקדוש
ברוך הוא למשה אספה לי שבעים איש מזקני ישראל
אמר משה: כיצד אעשה? אברור ששה מכל שבט
ושבט נמצאו שנים יתירים, אברור חמשה מכל
שבט ושבט נמצאו עשרה חסרים, אברור ששה
משבט זה וחמשה משבט זה הריני מטיל קנאה בין
השבטים? בירר ששה ששה, והביא שבעים
ושנים פיתקין, על שבעים כתב זקן ושנים הניח חלק,
בלל ונתנן בקלפי. אמר להם: בואו וטלו פיתקיכם
כל מי שעלה בידו זקן אמר: כבר קידשך שמים, מי
שעלה בידו חלק אמר: המקום לא חפץ בך, אני מה
אעשה לך?

## 13) במדבר כו:נה-נו, ומדרש ילקוט שמעוני על בראשית כב:צח
אַךְ־בְּגוֹרָל יֵחָלֵק אֶת־הָאָרֶץ לִשְׁמוֹת מַטּוֹת־אֲבֹתָם
יִנְחָלוּ: עַל־פִּי הַגּוֹרָל תֵּחָלֵק נַחֲלָתוֹ בֵּין רַב לִמְעָט:
על פי הגורל – שהיה הגורל כורז ואני גורלו של פלוני
לשמו עליתי, למה כן, רבי לוי בשם רבי חנינא אומר
בשביל שלא תהא תחרות בין השבטים שלא יאמרו
מה שבקש אלעזר עשה.

## 14) במדבר ג:יא-יג, מד-נא
וַיְדַבֵּר ד' אֶל־מֹשֶׁה לֵּאמֹר: וַאֲנִי הִנֵּה לָקַחְתִּי אֶת־הַלְוִיִּם
מִתּוֹךְ בְּנֵי יִשְׂרָאֵל תַּחַת כָּל־בְּכוֹר פֶּטֶר רֶחֶם מִבְּנֵי
יִשְׂרָאֵל וְהָיוּ לִי הַלְוִיִּם: כִּי לִי כָּל־בְּכוֹר בְּיוֹם הַכֹּתִי כָל־
בְּכוֹר בְּאֶרֶץ מִצְרַיִם הִקְדַּשְׁתִּי לִי כָל־בְּכוֹר בְּיִשְׂרָאֵל
מֵאָדָם עַד־בְּהֵמָה לִי יִהְיוּ אֲנִי ד':
וַיְדַבֵּר ד' אֶל־מֹשֶׁה לֵּאמֹר: קַח אֶת־הַלְוִיִּם תַּחַת כָּל־
בְּכוֹר בִּבְנֵי יִשְׂרָאֵל וְאֶת־בֶּהֱמַת הַלְוִיִּם תַּחַת בְּהֶמְתָּם
וְהָיוּ־לִי הַלְוִיִּם אֲנִי ד': וְאֵת פְּדוּיֵי הַשְּׁלֹשָׁה וְהַשִּׁבְעִים
וְהַמָּאתָיִם הָעֹדְפִים עַל־הַלְוִיִּם מִבְּכוֹר בְּנֵי יִשְׂרָאֵל:
וְלָקַחְתָּ חֲמֵשֶׁת חֲמֵשֶׁת שְׁקָלִים לַגֻּלְגֹּלֶת בְּשֶׁקֶל הַקֹּדֶשׁ
תִּקָּח עֶשְׂרִים גֵּרָה הַשָּׁקֶל: וְנָתַתָּה הַכֶּסֶף לְאַהֲרֹן וּלְבָנָיו
פְּדוּיֵי הָעֹדְפִים בָּהֶם: וַיִּקַּח מֹשֶׁה אֵת כֶּסֶף הַפִּדְיוֹם מֵאֵת
הָעֹדְפִים עַל פְּדוּיֵי הַלְוִיִּם: מֵאֵת בְּכוֹר בְּנֵי יִשְׂרָאֵל לָקַח
אֶת־הַכָּסֶף חֲמִשָּׁה וְשִׁשִּׁים וּשְׁלֹשׁ מֵאוֹת וָאֶלֶף בְּשֶׁקֶל
הַקֹּדֶשׁ: וַיִּתֵּן מֹשֶׁה אֶת־כֶּסֶף הַפְּדֻיִם לְאַהֲרֹן וּלְבָנָיו עַל־
פִּי ד' כַּאֲשֶׁר צִוָּה ד' אֶת־מֹשֶׁה:

## 15) סנהדרין יז.
כיוצא בדבר אתה אומר: (במדבר ג') ולקחת חמשת

## 1) בראשית א:טז ופירוש רש"י

וַיַּעַשׂ אֱלֹקִים אֶת־שְׁנֵי הַמְּאֹרֹת הַגְּדֹלִים אֶת־הַמָּאוֹר הַגָּדֹל לְמֶמְשֶׁלֶת הַיּוֹם וְאֶת־הַמָּאוֹר הַקָּטֹן לְמֶמְשֶׁלֶת הַלַּיְלָה וְאֵת הַכּוֹכָבִים:

**המאורת הגדולים** – שוים נבראו, ונתמעטה הלבנה, על שקטרגה ואמרה אי אפשר לשני מלכים שישתמשו בכתר אחד:

**הכוכבים** – על ידי שמיעט את הלבנה, הרבה צבאיה להפיס דעתה:

## 2) מדרש, פרקי דרבי אליעזר ה

ברביעי חבר שני מאורות, ולא זה גדול מזה, שוין בגובהן ובתארן ובאורן, שנ' ויעש אלהים את שני המאורות, נכנס תחרות ביניהן, זה אומ' לזה אני גדול ממך, וזה אומ' לזה אני גדול ממך, מה עשה הב"ה הקב"ה ליתן שלום ביניהם, הגדיל אחד והקטין האחר, שנ' את המאור הגדול לממשלת ביום ואת המאור הקטן לממשלת בלילה

## 3) מדרש, פרקי דרבי אליעזר ג

... שנ' זאת עולת חדש בחדשו, ר' זכריה אומ' אחר עולת החדש מה כתיב ושעיר עזים אחד לחטאת לה', החטאת למה, כשברא הב"ה את עולמו ברא שני מאורות גדולות, שנ' ויברא אלהים את שני המאורות הגדולים, הגדול אחד והקטן אחד, והקשה הירח את ערפו שלא לעשות רצון בוראו שלא רצה להיות קטן, לפי' מקריבים עליו שעיר חטאת למעלה לעולת ראש חדש, שנ' ושעיר עזים אחד לחטאת לה', החַטָּאת אמ' הב"ה השעיר הזה יהיה כפ'ר עלי על שמעטתי את הירח

## 4) מדרש, בראשית רבה כה:ה

ר' אחא אמר לו הקב"ה אני עשיתיך מלך על הבהמה ועל החיה ואתה לא בקשת אני עשיתיך שתהא מהלך קוממיות כאדם ואתה לא בקשת על גחונך תלך אני עשיתיך שתהא אוכל מאכלות כאדם ואתה לא בקשת ועפר תאכל כל ימי חייך אתה בקשת להרוג את האדם ולישא את חוה ואיבה אשית בינך ובין האשה ...

## 5) יערות דבש א:א

כללו של דבר, עיקר העון שאדם נענש על עבירתו, מחמת הנחש שהוא נגד הטבע עפר ואדמה, גאוה חמדה קנאה ותחרות, כעס לשון הרע ורכילות, וזה מן הנחש הכרוך בעקביו של אדם, כדכתיב [בראשית שם] ואתה תשופנו עקב ...

## 6) פירוש אברבנל על בראשית ד:א-ח

והנה הביא קין גם כן מנחה לה', לא להודות לו על הצלחתם באומנותם, אלא לפי שנתחדשה ביניהם קטטה. שהיה קין אומר שמלאכתו ואומנותו היתה יותר טובה ונרצית לפניו יתברך, להיותו עובד אדמה נותן לחם לכל בשר, שכל זולתו יצטרך אליו והוא לא יצטרך אליהם, והיא מעלה גדולה. גם שהיו בעבודתו מינים רבים – מהפירות וירק עשב, שהוא ע.רבות רב. ומלבד זה היה גם כן מפרי האדמה מוציא הפשתן, שבו יכסה האדם ערומיו. ולרמוז לזה אמרו זכרונם לברכה (תנחומא בראשית, ט) שזרע פשתן הקריב. גם שהיו הקנינים דברים הכרחיים לחיות האדם, והחיות הכרחי להשגת שלמותו. ולא היתה כן מלאכת הבל, כי היא כולה בדברים מדומים, את כל אלה ישא רוח. והבל היה אומר להפך זה, שאומנותו יותר נכבדת מאומנות קין, שהוא החי המרגיש, ומלאכת קין היה צומח. כל שכן שהאדמה נתקללה בעבור אדם וקוץ ודרדר תצמיח, אבל לא נתקלל מרעה הצאן. ולכן הביא מבכורות צאנו ומחלביהן, להגיד על שלמותם וברכתם. עם שהיה בהם דברים טובים למאכל מלבד הבשר, רוצה לומר חמאה וחלב, ומגז כבשים יתחמם. ומלבד זה היה זה ענין ההנהגה והכבוד טוב בעצמו, עד שנקרא הקדוש ברוך הוא:

## 7) מדרש בראשית רבה כב:ז

ויאמר קין אל הבל אחיו ויהי בהיותם וגו' – על מה היו מדינים אמרו בואו ונחלוק את העולם אחד נטל הקרקעות ואחד נטל את המטלטלין דין אמר ארעא דאת קאים עליה דידי ודין אמר מה דאת לביש דידי דין אמר חלוץ ודין אמר פרח מתוך כך ויקם קין אל הבל אחיו ויהרגהו רבי יהושע דסכנין בשם רבי לוי אמר שניהם נטלו את הקרקעות ושניהן נטלו את המטלטלין ועל מה היו מדינין אלא זה אומר בתחומי בהמ"ק נבנה וזה אומר בתחומי בהמ"ק נבנה שנא' ויהי בהיותם בשדה ואין שדה אלא בהמ"ק היך מה דאת אמר (מיכה ג) ציון שדה תחרש ומתוך כך (בראשית ד) ויקם קין אל הבל אחיו וגו' ר' יהודה בר אמי אמר על חוה הראשונה היו מדינין אמר רבי איבו חוה הראשונה חזרה לעפרה לעפרה מה מדינין אמר רבי הונא תאומה יתירה נולדה עם הבל זה אומר אני נוטלה שאני בכור וזה אומר אני נוטלה שנולדה עמי ומתוך כך ויקם קין:

## 8) בראשית יג:ה-יא, מדרש פסיקתא רבתי ג

וְגַם־לְלוֹט הַהֹלֵךְ אֶת־אַבְרָם הָיָה צֹאן־וּבָקָר וְאֹהָלִים:
וְלֹא־נָשָׂא אֹתָם הָאָרֶץ לָשֶׁבֶת יַחְדָּו כִּי־הָיָה רְכוּשָׁם רָב

Kotler and Rav Moshe Feinstein that the rule of *Dina Demalchuta Dina* (the obligation to honor the laws of the land in which we reside) applies to the law as it is applied, not as it is written. For example, Rav Kotler permitted driving sixty-two miles per hour in a fifty five mile per hour zone, since police did not issue a ticket for travelling less than sixty three miles per hour."

חרב לולי השבועה, מפני שכרתו להם ברית, והרי הוא אומר לא תכרות להם ברית, אלא היה דינם שיהיו למס עבדים, והואיל ובטעות נשבעו להן בדין היה שיהרגו על שהטעום לולי חלול השם.

**"Gray Matter", Volume 3, Rabbi Chaim Jachter, 2008, page 217, footnote no. 7** (44

"This is similar to the idea I heard Rav Mordecahi Willig cite in the name of Rav Ahron

אפשרות לדקדק בדבר. ויש לברר אם פעולה מעין זו יכולה להחשב כפעולה מלחמתית

### Rabbi J. David Bleich, "Preemptive (36
### War in Jewish Law", Contemporary Halakhic Problems 3:276–277

"... war almost inevitably results in civilian casualties as well as the loss of combatants ... However, not only does one search in vain for a ruling prohibiting military activity likely to result in the death of civilians, but, to this writer's knowledge, there exists no discussion in classical rabbinical sources that takes cognizance of the likelihood of causing civilian casualties in the course of hostilities ..."

### 37) הרב דב ליאור, תחומין ד:קפו

יש מקום לרחמנות על האויב בעת קרב. והרי כאן מטעים הרמב"ן את החיוב לפתוח הנצור את הפתח הרביעי, שבזה נלמד להתנהג בחמלה אפילו עם אויבינו בעת מלחמה (השמטות לספר המצוות מצוה ה). אולם רחמנות זו אינה נכתבת לנו ע"י רגשותינו. התורה היא שמצוה אותנו עליה. רחמנות הנובעת מתוך רגש בלבד, יש והיא הופכת לאכזריות, כגון במלחמת שאול ועמלק. במלחמותינו עיתים שהשפכה הרחמנות על אויב לאכזריות כלפי חיילינו, שנפלו בקרב כאשר נמנעו מפגיעה באוכלוסייה אזרחית שהסתירה מאחורי גבה כוחות צבא של אויב. מובן שכל זאת בשעת מלחמה. שלא בשעת מלחמה אין כל הצדקה לפגיעות שכאלו. אך בשעת מלחמה קיים ושריר הבסיס ההלכתי לכל פעולה הנעשית על מנת שלא יפגע ח"ו חייל אחד משלנו.

### 38) הרב אהרן לכטנשטיין, תחומין ד:קפה

מדוד המלך נמנע לבנות את בית הבחירה משום שדמים רבים שפך ארצה (דהי"א כב ח) אף שהיה זה במלחמות מצוה. אפילו חרב ששימשה במלחמות מצוה אינה ראויה לסייע כבניין המזבח, וכמו שנאמר במכילתא עה"פ (שמות כ כב) "כי חרבך הנפת עליה ותחללה". כאשר באים להצדיק מלחמה יש לקחת בחשבון את כל מרכיבי המחיר שהזכרנו. יש להתחשב בנתונים ובעובדות.

### Tradition (39:4:25–26), Rabbi Yitzcahk (39
### Blau "Biblical Narratives and the Status of Enemy Civilians in Wartime," pages 25–26

The corruption of a society that comes in wartime receives eloquent expression in our sources. Part of avoiding this corruption entails not treating war as a time of ethical anarchy. We have seen that many of our traditional sources were concerned that we attempt to spare enemy

innocents. We have found sources that teach this principle directly without even mentioning broader ethical commandments such as imitatio Dei or the desire to avoid *Chillul HaShem*. I will not be so presumptuous as to try to demarcate the exact lines as to the precise degree that this concern factors into our wartime strategy. However, I am convinced that it must be a factor.

### 40) בבא קמא צב. ורש"י שם

אמר ליה רבא לרבה בר מרי, מנא הא מילתא דאמרי אינשי: בהדי הוצא לקי כרבא? א"ל, דכתיב: (ירמיהו ב') למה תריבו אלי כלכם פשעתם בי נאם ה'.
בהדי הוצא לקי כרבא – קוץ הגדל אצל הכרוב כשבא לעקרו פעמים שנעקר הכרוב עמו ונמצא לוקה בשבילו כלומר שכיני רשע לוקין עמו.

### 41) שבועות לה: ותוספות שם

דאמר שמואל: מלכותא דקטלא חד משיתא בעלמא לא מיענשא
דקטלא חד משיתא בעלמא כו'. בהוצאת למלחמת הרשות קאמר

### 42) יהושע ט:ג-יח

וְיֹשְׁבֵי גִבְעוֹן שָׁמְעוּ אֵת אֲשֶׁר עָשָׂה יְהוֹשֻׁעַ לִירִיחוֹ וְלָעָי: וַיַּעֲשׂוּ גַם-הֵמָּה בְּעָרְמָה וַיֵּלְכוּ וַיִּצְטַיָּרוּ וַיִּקְחוּ שַׂקִּים בָּלִים לַחֲמוֹרֵיהֶם וְנֹאדוֹת יַיִן בָּלִים וּמְבֻקָּעִים וּמְצֹרָרִים: וּנְעָלוֹת בָּלוֹת וּמְטֻלָּאוֹת בְּרַגְלֵיהֶם וּשְׂלָמוֹת בָּלוֹת עֲלֵיהֶם וְכֹל לֶחֶם צֵידָם יָבֵשׁ הָיָה נִקֻּדִים: וַיֵּלְכוּ אֶל-יְהוֹשֻׁעַ אֶל-הַמַּחֲנֶה הַגִּלְגָּל וַיֹּאמְרוּ אֵלָיו וְאֶל-אִישׁ יִשְׂרָאֵל מֵאֶרֶץ רְחוֹקָה בָּאנוּ וְעַתָּה כִּרְתוּ-לָנוּ בְרִית: וַיֹּאמֶר [וַיֹּאמְרוּ] אִישׁ-יִשְׂרָאֵל אֶל-הַחִוִּי אוּלַי בְּקִרְבִּי אַתָּה יוֹשֵׁב וְאֵיךְ אֶכְרוֹת [אֶכְרָת] -לְךָ בְרִית: וַיֹּאמְרוּ אֶל-יְהוֹשֻׁעַ עֲבָדֶיךָ אֲנָחְנוּ וַיֹּאמֶר אֲלֵהֶם יְהוֹשֻׁעַ מִי אַתֶּם וּמֵאַיִן תָּבֹאוּ: וַיֹּאמְרוּ אֵלָיו מֵאֶרֶץ רְחוֹקָה מְאֹד בָּאוּ עֲבָדֶיךָ לְשֵׁם ד' אֱלֹקֶיךָ כִּי-שָׁמַעְנוּ שָׁמְעוֹ וְאֵת כָּל-אֲשֶׁר עָשָׂה בְּמִצְרָיִם: וְאֵת כָּל-אֲשֶׁר עָשָׂה לִשְׁנֵי מַלְכֵי הָאֱמֹרִי אֲשֶׁר בְּעֵבֶר הַיַּרְדֵּן לְסִיחוֹן מֶלֶךְ חֶשְׁבּוֹן וּלְעוֹג מֶלֶךְ-הַבָּשָׁן אֲשֶׁר בְּעַשְׁתָּרוֹת: וַיֹּאמְרוּ אֵלֵינוּ זְקֵינֵינוּ וְכָל-יֹשְׁבֵי אַרְצֵנוּ לֵאמֹר קְחוּ בְיֶדְכֶם צֵידָה לַדֶּרֶךְ וּלְכוּ לִקְרָאתָם וַאֲמַרְתֶּם אֲלֵיהֶם עַבְדֵיכֶם אֲנַחְנוּ וְעַתָּה כִּרְתוּ-לָנוּ בְרִית: זֶה לַחְמֵנוּ חָם הִצְטַיַּדְנוּ אֹתוֹ מִבָּתֵּינוּ בְּיוֹם צֵאתֵנוּ וַיִּשָּׁבְעוּ לָהֶם נְשִׂיאֵי הָעֵדָה: וַיְהִי מִקְצֵה שְׁלֹשֶׁת יָמִים אַחֲרֵי אֲשֶׁר-כָּרְתוּ לָהֶם בְּרִית וַיִּשְׁמְעוּ כִּי-קְרֹבִים הֵם אֵלָיו וּבְקִרְבּוֹ הֵם יֹשְׁבִים: וַיִּסְעוּ בְנֵי-יִשְׂרָאֵל וַיָּבֹאוּ אֶל-עָרֵיהֶם בַּיּוֹם הַשְּׁלִישִׁי וְעָרֵיהֶם גִּבְעוֹן וְהַכְּפִירָה וּבְאֵרוֹת וְקִרְיַת יְעָרִים: וְלֹא הִכּוּם בְּנֵי יִשְׂרָאֵל כִּי-נִשְׁבְּעוּ לָהֶם נְשִׂיאֵי הָעֵדָה בַּד' אֱלֹקֵי יִשְׂרָאֵל וַיִּלֹּנוּ כָל-הָעֵדָה עַל-הַנְּשִׂיאִים:

### 43) רמב"ם, הלכות מלכים ו:ה

ולמה קשה הדבר לנשיאים וראו שראוי להכותם לפי

... וכבר פירשתי (לעיל לד יג) כי יעקב קצף על
שמעון ולוי בהרגם אנשי העיר בעבור שעשו חמס,
כי הם לא חטאו להם כלל ובאו בברית ונמולו ...

### 30) פירוש גור אריה על בראשית לד:יג

... אך קשה אם שכם חטא כל העיר מה חטאו
להרוג, ותירץ הרמב"ם (הלכות מלכים פ"ט הי"ד)
דבני נח מצווים על הדינין, ועבירה אחת שעובר –
נהרג על ידי, וכאן ראו המעשה הרע הזה ולא דנוהו,
לכך היו חייבין מיתה שלא היו דנין אותם. ובאמת
דבר תימה הם אלו הדברים, כי איך אפשר להם לדון
את בן נשיא הארץ (פסוק ב), כי היו יראים מהם,
ואף על גב שנצטוו על הדינין – היינו כשיוכלו לדון,
אבל אונס רחמנא פטריה (ב"ק כח ע"ב), ואיך אפשר
להם לדון אותם: ונראה דלא קשיא מידי, משום
דלא דמי שני אומות, כגון בני ישראל וכנעניים,
שהם שני אומות, כדכתיב (פסוק טז) "והיינו לעם
אחד" – ומתחלה לא נחשבו לעם אחד, ולפיכך
הותר להם ללחום כדין אומה שבא ללחום על אומה
אחרת, שהתירה התורה. ואף על גב דאמרה התורה
(דברים כ, י) "כי תקרב אל עיר להלחם עליה וקראת
אליה לשלום", היינו היכי דלא עשו לישראל דבר,
אבל היכי דעשו לישראל דבר, כגון זה שפרצו בהם
לעשות להם נבלה, אף על גב דלא עשה רק אחד
מהם – כיון דמכלל העם הוא, כיון שפרצו להם
תחלה – מותרים ליקח נקמתם מהם. והכי נמי כל
המלחמות שהם נמצאים כגון "צרור את המדינים
וגו'" (במדבר כה, יז), אף על גב דהיו הרבה שלא
עשו – אין זה חילוק, כיון שהיו באותה אומה שעשה
רע להם – מותרין לבא עליהם למלחמה, וכן הם כל
המלחמות:

### 31) פירוש אוזנים לתורה על בראשית לד:כה

ויהרגו כל זכר – המפרשים עמלו למצוא היתר
להריגת כל אנשי שכם ... אך זה היה עול בין עם
לעם ... אין זה חטא נגד יחיד, אך נגד עם ישראל
... וכן עשו בני יעקב, הם עלו למלחמה על שכם,
אלא שהשתדלו מקודם להחליש את האויב (ע"י
מילה) כנהוג במלחמה. וגם יעקב לא דרש משמעון
ולוי תשכפת דמי אנשי שכם, מכיוון שהרגום
במלחמה, אלא שגער בהם על שנסתבכו בלי ידעתו,
במלחמה, ...

### 32) שו"ת עמוד הימיני (ר' שאול ישראלי) טז:ב

... א"כ לפי הנ"ל י"ל שבזה תלוי' מחלוקת הרמב"ם
והרמב"ן, לפי שהרמב"ן הולך בשיטת התוס' מותר
לקיימם ומ"מ אין איסור גם שכתב שדמם כמים
והרמב"ם הולך השיטת תוספות השניה שמה"ת
איסור יש להרגם למרות
שהם עובדים ע"ז ע"ז לא הי' יכול לפרש שדמם
הותר מצד ע"ז וגי"ע והי' מוכרח למצוא נימוק אחר

---

### 33) עקבי הצאן (ר' צבי שכטר), לב:ג

ונראה דאף דאין שמה חיילים ערבים היורים
בתותחים ואין אווירונים הזורקים פצצות מכ"מ עפ"י
הלכה מדינת ישראל היום היא במצב של מלחמה
עם הערבים ... שמדינת ישראל עומדת היא במצב
של מלחמה וכל הפרעות והמהומות שבזמנו דינם
עפ"י הלכה כהמשך מהמלחמה הראשונה מלחמת
השחרור שהרי הערבים טוענים בפירוש ובפה מלא
שהם רוצים את ירושלים ואת תל אביב ואת חיפה
וכו' וכו' וממילא צריכים אנשי צה"ל לנהוג עם כל
המשתתפים באלו הפרעות כמו שנוהגים בשעת
מלחמה ממש שאם יש צורך בכך שיירא בהם ע"מ
להרוג ואם יש צורך בכך כי לפעמים מן הנמנע
לברר מי הם המחבלים והטרוריסטים המארגנים את
הפרעות ואת המהומות רשאים וחייבים צה"ל להכות
ואף להרוג כפי הדרוש לנצח במלחמה אף אחרים
מאותה האומה שהם חפים מפשע וכמבואר בגור
אריה למהר"ל מפראג לפ' וישלח וכן נראה נמי לומר
דהואיל והמצב כעת בארץ הוא מצב של מלחמה
שאין להתחשב בסכנ"פ של היחידים וכאשר הבאנו
מדברי המנח"ח והנצי"ב ומדברי שאר המחברים

### 34) הרב אברהם שפירא, תחומין ד:קפב

שאלה: מה דינה של אוכלוסית אויב אזרחית בעת
מלחמה, האם יש מצד הדין היתר לפגוע בה על מנת
למנוע פגיעה אפשרית בחיילי ישראל?
תשובה: כל עוד אין סכנה ממשית לחיילינו אין היתר
לפגוע בנפש ואף לא ברכוש. אולם כאשר הסכנה
היא מוחשית, הרי יש לזכור שעל כף המאזניים
אין עומדת רק היחידה הלוחמת מול האוכלוסיה
האזרחית, איבודה של יחידה אחת או חלק ממנה
עלול לפגוע במערכת המלחמה כולה. על כן כאשר
נידרש וכאשר הסכנה גלויה לעין, אין מקום למדוד
את מספר החיילים שלנו העלולים להיפגע חלילה
כנגד מספר אזרחי מדינת האויב משונאי ישראל,
שעלולים לשלם את מחיר המלחמה. יש בזה הלכה
ברורה ברמב"ם בהלכות מלחמה וחייבין להציל את
חייו של כל חייל יהודי.

### 35) שו"ת עמוד הימיני (ר' שאול ישראלי) טז:ה:א

דנו עד כה על הענין מבחינת פעולה במסגרת חיי
יום יום. אכן קיימת עוד גישה לנידון והיא: לראות
זאת כפעולה מלחמתית. שהרי ההלכה מתירה
מלחמה עם הנכרים ואז בהכרח יורד איסור זה של
פגיעה בנפשות ולא מצינו במלחמה גם חובה לדקדק
ולהבדיל בין דם לדם. ואעפ"י שלאחרשכבש עיר
של שונא אסור להרוג את הטף והנשים
כמו שכתב הרמב"ם (פ"ו ממלכים ה"ד) ואין הורגים
לא אישה ולא קטן כשכאשר נשים והטף. מ"מ ברור
שדין זה אמור רק לאחר שכבשום ונמצאים תחת
ידינו, אבל במהלך המלחמה כשצרים על העיר
וכיו"ב אין שום חובה ואין גם

כל היכול להציל באבר מאיבריו ולא טרח בכך אלא הציל בנפשו של רודף והרגו ה רי זה שופך דמים וחייב מיתה אבל אין בית דין ממיתין אותו:

### 20) רמב"ם, הלכות רוצח א:ו

... אבל הרודף אחר חבירו להרגו אפילו היה הרודף קטן הרי כל ישראל מצווין להציל הנרדף מיד הרודף ואפילו בנפשו של רודף:

### 21) שולחן ערוך, חושן משפט תכה:א

הרודף אחר חבירו להרגו והזהירוהו והרי הוא רודף אחריו, אפילו היה הרודף קטן הרי כל ישראל מצווין להצילו באבר מאברי הרודף, ואם אינם יכולים לכוין ולא להצילו אלא אם כן יהרגו לרודף, הרי אלו הורגים אותו אע"פ שעדיין לא הרג

### 22) שו"ת עמוד הימיני (ר' שאול ישראלי) טז:ד

לאחר שהסקנו שהאוכלוסיה כולה אם היא תומכת בכנופיות יש עליה תורת רודף וניתן להציל בנפשם מתעוררת השאלה כשבתוך האוכלוסיה נמצאת גם נקיים מפשע זה כגון קטנים וכיו"ב אלא שהפעולה כשנעשית אינה יכולה להבחין ובהכרח שיש גם קרבנות נקיים האם מותרת פעולה זו בכללה או שנאמר מכיון שלא ימלט שלא יפגעו בנקיים אסור לעשות פעולה זו בכלל.
כיוצא בזה מצינו במלחמת עמלק (שמואל א' ט"ו) שהוזהר הקיני לסור מתוך עמלקי "פן אוספך עמו" וזה סובן מאליו שאם ישנה אפשרות להזהיר את הנקיים מפשע שיסתלקו מהמקום שיש לעשות זאת ... והנה זה נראה פשוט לכאורה שאם נאמר שפעולה זו נמצא שקטנים אלה מסייעים לרודפים שעל ידם הרודף יכול להוציא זממו לפועל והרי הם ג"כ כרודפים לפ"מ שהעלינו לעיל שכל המסייע לרודף וגורם לרציחתה הרי הוא בדין רודף אלא שיש בזה הוא שלא מדעתם ולא הם העושים זאת אלא הרודפים הם שמסתייעים על ידם ... אולם לאחר עיון יש מקום לומר שבמקרה דנן דבר זה במחלוקת תלוי בין הרמב"ם והראב"ד.
ב הרמב"ם סוף ה' חו"מ כ' שספינה שחישבה להשבר מרוב כיבד המשא ובא א' מהאנשים וזרק מן המשא שהי' כספינה פטור שהמשא שבה כמו רודף אחריהם להרגם ומצוה רבה עשה שהשליך והושיעם, והראב"ד השיגו אין כאן לא מלה ולא תבלין שאין כאן דין רודף כלל ואין זה דומה למעשה דחמרא דפ' הגזל ...

### 23) רמב"ם, הלכות חובל ומזיק ח:טו

ספינה שחשבה להשבר מכובד המשוי ועמד אחד מהן והקל ממשאה והשליך בים פטור, שהמשא א שבה כמו רודף אחריהם להרגם ומצוה רבה עשה שהשליך והושיעם

---

### 24) שו"ת עמוד הימיני (ר' שאול ישראלי) טז:ד

... הרמב"ם סוף ה' חו"מ כ' שספינה שחישבה להשבר מרוב כיבד המשא ובא א' מהאנשים וזרק מן המשא שהי' כספינה פטור שהמשא שבה כמו רודף אחריהם להרגם ומצוה רבה עשה שהשליך והושיעם, והראב"ד השיגו אין כאן לא מלה ולא תבלין שאין כאן דין רודף כלל ואין זה דומה למעשה דחמרא דפ' הגזל ...

### 25) רמב"ם, הלכות חובל ומזיק ח:טו

... השגת הראב"ד: ספינה שחישבה וכו' שהמשא שבה כמו רודף אחריהם להרגם. א"א אין כאן לא מלה ולא תבלין שאין כאן דין רודף כלל

### 26) רמב"ם, הלכות מלכים ט:יד

וכיצד מצווים הן על הדינין חייבין להושיב דיינין ושופטים בכל פלך ופלך לדון בשש מצות אלו ולהזהיר את העם ובן נח שעבר על אחת משבע מצות אלו יהרג בסייף ומפני זה נתחייבו כל בעלי שכם הריגה שהרי שכם גזל והם ראו וידעו ולא דנוהו ...

### 27) בראשית ט:ה ופירוש העמק דבר

וְאַךְ אֶת דִּמְכֶם לְנַפְשֹׁתֵיכֶם אֶדְרֹשׁ מִיַּד כָּל חַיָּה אֶדְרְשֶׁנּוּ וּמִיַּד הָאָדָם מִיַּד אִישׁ אָחִיו אֶדְרֹשׁ אֶת נֶפֶשׁ הָאָדָם – פירש הקב"ה אימתי האדם נענש בשעה שראוי לנהוג באחוה. משא"כ בשעת מלחמה ועת לשנוא אז עת להרוג ואין עונש ע"ז כלל ...

### 28) קהלת ג:ח

עֵת לֶאֱהֹב וְעֵת לִשְׂנֹא עֵת מִלְחָמָה וְעֵת שָׁלוֹם:

### 29) פירוש רמב"ן על בראשית לד:יג, מט:ה

... ויתכן שהיה הכעס ליעקב שארר אפם על שהרגו אנשי העיר אשר לא חטאו לו, והראוי להם שיהרגו שכם לבדו. וזהו מה שאמר הכתוב ויענו בני יעקב את שכם ואת חמור אביו במרמה ... ורבים ישאלו, ואיך עשו בני יעקב הצדיקים המעשה הזה לשפוך דם נקי. והרב השיב בספר שופטים (רמב"ם הלכות מלכים פי"ד ה"ט) ואמר שבני נח מצווים על הדינים, והוא להושיב דיינין בכל פלך ופלך לדון בשש מצות שלהן, ובן נח שעבר על אחת מהן הוא נהרג בסייף, ראה אחד שעבר על אחת מהן ולא דנוהו להרגו הרי זה הרואה יהרג בסייף. ומפני זה נתחייבו כל בעלי שכם הריגה שהרי שכם גזל, והם ראו וידעו ולא דנוהו: ואין דברים הללו נכונים בעיני, שאם כן היה יעקב אבינו חייב להיות קודם וזוכה במיתתם, ואם פחד מהם למה כעס על בניו וארר אפם אחר כמה זמנים, וענש אותם וחלקם והפיצם, והלא הם זכו ועשו מצוה ובטחו באלהים והצילום: ... ומה יבקש בהן הרב חיוב, וכי אנשי שכם ומגלה עריות ועושים כל תועבות השם היו ...

---

אֲשֶׁר ד' אֱלֹקֶיךָ נֹתֵן לְךָ נַחֲלָה לֹא תְחַיֶּה כָּל נְשָׁמָה:

**11) דברי הימים א' כב:ח ופירוש רד"ק**

וַיְהִי עָלַי דְּבַר ד' לֵאמֹר דָּם לָרֹב שָׁפַכְתָּ וּמִלְחָמוֹת גְדֹלוֹת עָשִׂיתָ לֹא תִבְנֶה בַיִת לִשְׁמִי כִּי דָּמִים רַבִּים שָׁפַכְתָּ אַרְצָה לְפָנָי:

... כי דם נקיים היה בדמים אשר שפך כי דם אוריה וזה לפני. גם בדמי הכהנים היה היא הסיבה ... גם בדמי הגויים אשר שפך אותם שלא היו בני מלחמתו אפשר שהיה בהם אנשים טובים וחסידים אעפ"י כן לא נענש עליהם כי כוונתו לכלות הרשעים שלא יפרצו בישראל, ולהציל את עצמו כשהיה בארץ פלשתים לא יחיה איש ואשה. אבל כיוון שנזדמן לו שפיכות דמים לרוב, מנעו מלבנות בית המקדש שהוא לשלום ולכפרת עון ולעטרת תפילה. כמו שמנעו להניף ברזל במזבח ובבית המקדש לפי שהברזל עושים ממנו כלי הריגה לא יעשו ממנו כלי שלום ברוב:

**12) מנחת אשר (ר' אשר וייס), דברים לב:ו**

ולמדנו אף מדבריו (של הרד"ק) דמעיקר הדין אין להמנע מהריגת הרוצחים אף אם החפים מפשע נהרגים עמהם ומשום כך לא נענש דוד על דם רב ששפך אלא שמ"מ מנעו הקב"ה מלבנות את בית הבחירה דמ"מ יש בזה פגם מסוים של שפיכות דמים וגם מדבריו יש להבין כפי שנתבאר לעיל דבודאי יש להשתדל במניעת הריגתם של אלה שלא פשעו ולא חטאו אך כשאי אפשר גם הם נספים עם אלה שבקרבם שמצוה להרגם ודו"ק בכל זה.

שו"ר בספרי (שופטים אות קצ"ט) "כי תקרב אל עיר להלחם עליה" ולא להרעיבה ולא להצמיאה ולא להמיתה

מיתת תחלואים" ומכאן שנטעונו על רחמים במלחמה" ושם ש"ב באות כ' אמרו דבמלחמת מצוה "אף להרעיבה ואף להצמיאה ואף להמיתה במיתת תחלואים" עי"ש.

**13) מדרש ספרי, שופטים נו, נז**

כי תקרב אל עיר. במלחמת הרשות הכתוב מדבר.. להלחם עליה. ולא להרעיבה ולא להצמיאה ולא להמית מיתת תחלואי':

אם לא תשלים עמך ועשתה עמך מלחמה. הכתוב מבשרך שאם אינ' משלמת עמך לסוף שהוא עוש' עמך מלחמה: וצרת עליה: אף להרעיבה אף להצמיאה אף להמית במיתת תחלואים. ונתנה ה' אלקיך בידך. אם עשית את כל האמור בענין לסוף שה' אלקיך נתנה בידך:

והכית את כל זכורה. שומע אני אף הקטנים שבתוכה ת"ל רק הנשים והטף והבהמה. או אינו אלא טף של נקבות. אמרת ומה מדין שהמית את הנקבות הגדולות החיה את הקטנות כאן שהחיה את הגדולות אינו דין שיחיה את הקטנות הא אינו אומר כאן טף

אלא טף של זכרים:

**14) רמב"ם, הלכות מלכים ו:ה**

כשצרין על עיר לתפשה, אין מקיפין אותה מארבע רוחותיה אלא משלש רוחותיה, ומניחין מקום לבורח ולכל מי שירצה להמלט על נפשו, שנאמר ויצבאו על מדין כאשר צוה ה' את משה מפי השמועה למדו שבכך צוהו.

**15) רמב"ם, הלכות מלכים ו:ז**

שלשה כתבים שלח יהושע עד שלא נכנס לארץ, הראשון שלח להם מי שרוצה לברוח יברח, וחזר ושלח מי שרוצה להשלים ישלים, וחזר ושלח מי שרוצה לעשות מלחמה יעשה, אם כן מ פני מה הערימו יושבי גבעון, לפי ששלח להם בכלל ולא קבלו, ולא ידעו משפט ישראל ו דימו שאין פותחין להם לשלום:

**16) רמב"ם, הלכות מלכים ו:ד**

ואין הורגין אישה ולא קטן ...

**17) דברים יג:יג-יז ופירוש רמב"ן על דברים יג:טז**

כִּי תִשְׁמַע בְּאַחַת עָרֶיךָ אֲשֶׁר ד' אֱלֹקֶיךָ נֹתֵן לְךָ לָשֶׁבֶת שָׁם לֵאמֹר: יָצְאוּ אֲנָשִׁים בְּנֵי בְלִיַּעַל מִקִּרְבֶּךָ וַיַּדִּיחוּ אֶת יֹשְׁבֵי עִירָם לֵאמֹר נֵלְכָה וְנַעַבְדָה אֱלֹהִים אֲחֵרִים אֲשֶׁר לֹא יְדַעְתֶּם: וְדָרַשְׁתָּ וְחָקַרְתָּ וְשָׁאַלְתָּ הֵיטֵב וְהִנֵּה אֱמֶת נָכוֹן הַדָּבָר נֶעֶשְׂתָה הַתּוֹעֵבָה הַזֹּאת בְּקִרְבֶּךָ: הַכֵּה תַכֶּה אֶת יֹשְׁבֵי הָעִיר הַהוּא לְפִי חָרֶב הַחֲרֵם אֹתָהּ וְאֶת כָּל אֲשֶׁר בָּהּ וְאֶת בְּהֶמְתָּהּ לְפִי חָרֶב: וְאֶת כָּל שְׁלָלָהּ תִּקְבֹּץ אֶל תּוֹךְ רְחֹבָהּ וְשָׂרַפְתָּ בָאֵשׁ אֶת הָעִיר וְאֶת כָּל שְׁלָלָהּ כָּלִיל לַד' אֱלֹקֶיךָ וְהָיְתָה תֵּל עוֹלָם לֹא תִבָּנֶה עוֹד:

החרם אתה ואת כל אשר בה אותה – הם האנשים הנדחים, ואת כל אשר בה, הנשים הנגררות אחר האנשים אבל הטף שהם קטנים בזכרים ובנקבות אין ממיתין אותן, וכן אמרו בספרי, חנן אומר לא יומתו אבות על בנים וגו', בעיר הנדחת הכתוב מדבר אבל בתוספתא של מסכת סנהדרין (פ"ד ה"א) נחלקו בה, קטני בני אנשי עיר הנדחת שהודחו עמה אין נהרגין, רבי אליעזר אומר נהרגין

**18) סנהדרין עד.**

רודף שהיה רודף אחר חבירו להורגו, ויכול להצילו באחד מאבריו ולא הציל נהרג עליו.

**19) רמב"ם, הלכות רוצח א:ז, יג**

... ואם יכולים להצילו באבר מאיברי הרודף כגון שיכו אותו בחץ או באבן או בסייף ויקטעו את ידו או ישברו את רגלו או יסמו את עינו עושין, ואם אינ יכולין לכו ין ולא להצילו אלא אם כן הרגוהו לרודף הרי אלו הורגין אותו ואע"פ שעדיין לא הרג שנאמר (דברים כ"ה י"ב) וקצותה את כפה לא תחוס עינך.

# SOURCES ON COLLATERAL DAMAGE:
## UNAVOIDABLE CIVILIAN CAUSALITIES

### 1) בראשית טו:א ופירוש רש"י שם

אַחַר הַדְּבָרִים הָאֵלֶּה הָיָה דְבַר־ד' אֶל־אַבְרָם בַּמַּחֲזֶה לֵאמֹר אַל־תִּירָא אַבְרָם אָנֹכִי מָגֵן לָךְ שְׂכָרְךָ הַרְבֵּה מְאֹד: **אחר הדברים האלה** – כל מקום שנאמר אחר, סמוך. אחרי, מופלג (ב"ר מד, ה,). אחר הדברים האלה, אחר שנעשה לו נס זה שהרג את המלכים, והיה דואג ואומר שמא קבלתי שכר על כל צדקותי, לכך אמר לו המקום אל תירא אברם אנכי מגן לך. מן העונש, שלא תענש על כל אותן נפשות שהרגת, ומה שאתה דואג על קבול שכרך, שכרך הרבה מאד:

### 2) מדרש, בראשית רבה מד:ד

אנכי מגן לך רבי לוי אמר תרתין ורבנן אמרי חדא ר' לוי אמר לפי שהיה אבינו אברהם מתפחד ואומר תאמר אותן אוכלסין שהרגתי שהיה בהם צדיק אחד וירא שמים משל לאחד שהי' עובר לפני פרדסו של מלך ראה חבילה של קוצים וירד ונטלה והציץ המלך וראה אותו התחיל מטמין מפניו א"ל מפני מה אתה מטמין כמה פועלים הייתי צריך שיקושש אותה עכשיו שקששת אותה בא וטול שכר כך אמר הקב"ה לאברהם אותן אוכלסין שהרגת קוצים כסוחים היו הדא הוא דכתיב (ישעיה לג) והיו עמים משרפות סיד קוצים כסוחים ...

### 3) פירוש לבוש אורה על רש"י, בראשית טו:א

... וכי תימה ומ"ט לא היה אברם דואג על העונש אומר אני שאין זו קושיא כי אברם חשב ואמר הרי ודאי ידעתי שהיו בהם רשעים הרבה ובאבוד רשעים רנה ויש לי לקבל שכר על שבערתי הקוצים מן הכרם מה יש לי לומר שמא היה בהם ג"כ קצת טובים ובעבורם יש לי לדאוג עליהם. על זה העונש אני מייאש לומר לי שכרי כנגד עונשי ולא אקבל עונש על ההריגה ולא שכר על ביער הקוצים כי יצא שכרי בהפסדי ...

### 4) בראשית לב:ז ורש"י שם

וַיִּירָא יַעֲקֹב מְאֹד וַיֵּצֶר לוֹ וַיַּחַץ אֶת־הָעָם אֲשֶׁר־אִתּוֹ וְאֶת־הַצֹּאן וְאֶת־הַבָּקָר וְהַגְּמַלִּים לִשְׁנֵי מַחֲנוֹת: **ויירא ויצר** – וירא שמא יהרג, ויצר לו, אם יהרוג הוא את אחרים (מדרש תנחומא וישלח ד).

### 5) פירוש שפתי חכמים על רש"י בראשית לב:ז

... אי נמי יש לומר דיעקב ודאי לא היה ירא שמא יהרוג את עשיו דיעקב 'הבא להרגך השכם והרגו.' אלא דיעקב היה מתירא שמא יהרוג הוא אנשיו של עשיו ואולי הם לא באו להרוג את יעקב ... ויעקב

---

היה ירא שמא יהרוג אותן מכח בלבול המלחמה ... :

### 6) שמואל א' טו:ה-ו

וַיָּבֹא אוּל עַד־עִיר עֲמָלֵק וַיָּרֶב בַּנָּחַל: וַיֹּאמֶר אוּל אֶל־הַ קֵּינִי לְכוּ סֻּרוּ רְדוּ מִתּוֹךְ עֲמָלֵקִי פֶּן־אֹסִפְךָ עִמּוֹ וְאַתָּה עָשִׂיתָה חֶסֶד עִם־כָּל־בְּנֵי יִשְׂרָאֵל בַּעֲלוֹתָם מִמִּצְרָיִם וַיָּסַר קֵינִי מִתּוֹךְ עֲמָלֵק:

### 7) במדבר כא:כא-כג ופיורש רש" שם

וַיִּשְׁלַח יִשְׂרָאֵל מַלְאָכִים אֶל־סִיחֹן מֶלֶךְ הָאֱמֹרִי לֵאמֹר: אֶעְבְּרָה בְאַרְצֶךָ לֹא נִטֶּה בְּשָׂדֶה וּבְכֶרֶם לֹא נִשְׁתֶּה מֵי בְאֵר בְּדֶרֶךְ הַמֶּלֶךְ נֵלֵךְ עַד אֲשֶׁר־נַעֲבֹר גְּבֻלֶךָ: וְלֹא־נָתַן סִיחֹן אֶת־יִשְׂרָאֵל עֲבֹר בִּגְבֻלוֹ וַיֶּאֱסֹף סִיחֹן אֶת־כָּל־עַמּוֹ וַיֵּצֵא לִקְרַאת יִשְׂרָאֵל הַמִּדְבָּרָה וַיָּבֹא יָהְצָה וַיִּלָּחֶם בְּיִשְׂרָאֵל: **אעברה בארצך** – אע"פ שלא נצטוו לפתוח להם בשלום בקשו מהם שלום:

### 8) דברים ב:כו-כז ופירוש רש"י שם

וָאֶשְׁלַח מַלְאָכִים מִמִּדְבַּר קְדֵמוֹת אֶל־סִיחוֹן מֶלֶךְ חֶשְׁבּוֹן דִּבְרֵי שָׁלוֹם לֵאמֹר: אֶעְבְּרָה בְאַרְצֶךָ בַּדֶּרֶךְ בַּדֶּרֶךְ אֵלֵךְ לֹא אָסוּר יָמִין וּשְׂמֹאול: **ממדבר קדמות** – אע"פ שלא צוני המקום לקרוא לסיחון לשלום

### 9) מדרש תנחומא צו ג

... ומי שלא חטא אלא בשלום אני בא עליהם שנא' (שם דברים ב) ואשלח מלאכים ממדבר קדמות דברי שלום אעברה בארצך, כיון שראה שלא בא לשלום הכהו שנא' "ויכו אותו ואת בניו ואת כל עמו", אמר הקב"ה אני אמרתי כי החרם תחרימם ואתה לא עשית כן חייך כשם שאמרת כך אני עושה שנא' (שם דברים כ) "כי תקרב אל עיר להלחם עליה וקראת אליה לשלום" לכך נאמר (משלי ג) דרכיה דרכי נועם וכל נתיבותיה שלום.

### 10) דברים כ:י-טז

כִּי־תִקְרַב אֶל־עִיר לְהִלָּחֵם עָלֶיהָ וְקָרָאתָ אֵלֶיהָ לְשָׁלוֹם: וְהָיָה אִם־שָׁלוֹם תַּעַנְךָ וּפָתְחָה לָךְ וְהָיָה כָּל־הָעָם הַנִּמְצָא־בָהּ יִהְיוּ לְךָ לָמַס וַעֲבָדוּךָ: וְאִם־לֹא תַשְׁלִים עִמָּךְ וְעָשְׂתָה עִמְּךָ מִלְחָמָה וְצַרְתָּ עָלֶיהָ: וּנְתָנָהּ ד' אֱלֹקֶיךָ בְּיָדֶךָ וְהִכִּיתָ אֶת־כָּל־זְכוּרָהּ לְפִי־חָרֶב: רַק הַנָּשִׁים וְהַטַּף וְהַבְּהֵמָה וְכֹל אֲשֶׁר יִהְיֶה בָעִיר כָּל־שְׁלָלָהּ תָּבֹז לָךְ וְאָכַלְתָּ אֶת־שְׁלַל אֹיְבֶיךָ אֲשֶׁר נָתַן ד' אֱלֹקֶיךָ לָךְ: כֵּן תַּעֲשֶׂה לְכָל־הֶעָרִים הָרְחֹקֹת מִמְּךָ מְאֹד אֲשֶׁר לֹא־מֵעָרֵי הַגּוֹיִם הָאֵלֶּה הֵנָּה: רַק מֵעָרֵי הָעַמִּים הָאֵלֶּה

descendant. Or show me a child whose survival depends on transplantation of bone marrow. I would advise cloning to save the child's life. A child produced for this purpose would then be doubly loved.

(Rabbi) M. D. TENDLER

reproduction. But the salient issue for me is under what circumstances cloning could be morally acceptable. Show me a young man who is sterile, whose family was obliterated by the Holocaust and who is the last in a genetic line. I would advise cloning him to create a

### 39) ספר החינוך, מצוה סב

וענין הכישוף הוא לפי דעתי כן, שהשם ברוך הוא שם בתחילת הבריאה לכל דבר ודבר מדברי העולם טבע לפעול פעולתו טובה וישרה לטובת בני העולם אשר ברא, וציוה כל אחד לפעול פעלו למינהו, כמו שכתוב בפרשת בראשית ...
ובמלאכת התערובות יש בה תערובות שלא הורשו בני אדם להשתמש בהן, כי יודע אלהים שסוף המעשה היוצא לבני אדם באותן צדדין רע להן ומפני זה מנעם מהם. וזהו אמרם זכרונם לברכה דרך כלל, כל שיש בו משום רפואה אין בו משום דרכי האמורי [שבת דף ס"ז ע"א], כלומר אין לאסור מפני צד כישוף, אחר שיש בו תועלת בו מצוי בנסיון באמת אין זה מן הצדדין האסורין

### 40) תענית ב.

אמר רבי יוחנן: שלשה מפתחות בידו של הקדוש ברוך הוא שלא נמסרו ביד שליח, ואלו הן: מפתח של גשמים, מפתח של חיה, ומפתח של תחיית המתים ... מפתח של תחיית המתים מנין דכתיב (יחזקאל לז) "וידעתם כי אני ה', בפתחי את קברותיכם."

### 41) מדרש בראשית רבה מו:ג, חגיגה יב.

רבי נתן ורבי אחא ורבי ברכיה בשם רבי יצחק אני אל שדי אני הוא שאמרתי לעולמי ולשמים די לארץ די שאלולי שאמרתי להם די עד עכשיו היו נמתחים והולכים,
מאי דכתיב (בראשית ל"ה) אני אל שדי אני הוא שאמרתי לעולם די. אמר ריש לקיש: בשעה שברא הקדוש ברוך הוא את הים היה מרחיב והולך, עד שגער בו הקדוש ברוך הוא ויבשו

### 42) רמב"ם, הלכות ממרים ב:ג, ה

במה דברים אמורים בדברים שלא אסרו אותן כדי לעשות סייג לתורה אלא כשאר דיני תורה, אבל דברים שראו בית דין לגזור ולאסרן לעשות סייג אם פשט איסורן בכל [ישראל] אין בית דין גדול אחר יכול לעקרן ולהתירן אפילו היה גדול מן הראשונים. כיצד בית דין שראו לחזק הדת ולעשות סייג כדי שלא יעברו העם על דברי תורה, מכין ועונשין שלא כדין אבל אין קובעין הדבר לדורות ואומרים שהלכה כך הוא, וכן אם ראו לפי שעה לבטל מצות עשה או לעבור על מצוה כדי להחזיר רבים לדת או להציל רבים מישראל מלהכשל בדברים אחרים עושין לפי מה שצריכה השעה, כשם שהרופא חותך ידו או רגלו של זה כדי שיחיה כולו כך בית דין מורים בזמן מן הזמנים לעבור על קצת מצות לפי שעה כדי שיתקיימו [כולם] כדרך שאמרו חכמים חלל עליו שבת אחת כדי שישמור שבתות הרבה.

### 43) "Cloning and Its Challenges" in the Torah U-Madda Journal, vol. 9, 200, page 195

### 44) משנה יבמות יב:ב ופירוש רש"י שם

משנה - הגיורת שנתגיירו בניה עמה לא חולצין ולא מייבמין, אפילו הורתן של ראשון שלא בקדושה ולידתו בקדושה, והשני הורתו ולידתו בקדושה. וכן שפחה שנשתחררו בניה עמה
לא חולצין כו' - דאחוה מן האב בעינן וגר אין לו שאר האב דרחמנא אפקרי' כזרע בהמה שנאמר (יחזקאל כג) וזרמת סוסים זרמתם.

Two people (like clones) who are considered siblings even tough not generically similar (they are not technically related to their mother who converted) – not related to each other, but have the same genes.

### 45) סוטה מו:

תניא: היא לוז שצובעין בה תכלת, היא לוז שבא סנחריב ולא בלבלה, נבוכדנצר ולא החריבה, ואף מלאך המות אין לו רשות לעבור בה, אלא זקנים שבה בזמן שדעתן קצה עליהן - יוצאין חוץ לחומה והן מתים

### 46) איוב יד:א, טו:יד, יומא עה:, נדה יג., מדרש ויקרא רבה יד:ב

אָדָם יְלוּד אִשָּׁה קְצַר יָמִים וּשְׂבַע־רֹגֶז:
מָה־אֱנוֹשׁ כִּי יִזְכֶּה וְכִי־יִצְדַּק יְלוּד אִשָּׁה:
אמרו: עתיד מן זה שתיפח במעיהם, כלום יש ילוד אשה שמכניס ואינו מוציא?
דקרי שמואל עליה: אין זה ילוד אשה.
א"ר הושעיא אשרי ילוד אשה שכך שומע מפי בוראו

### 47) בראשית ב:כד ופירוש רש"י

עַל־כֵּן יַעֲזָב־אִישׁ אֶת־אָבִיו וְאֶת־אִמּוֹ וְדָבַק בְּאִשְׁתּוֹ וְהָיוּ לְבָשָׂר אֶחָד:
לבשר אחד - הולד נוצר ע"י שניהם ושם נעשה בשרם אחד

### 48) פירוש בית הבחירה על סנהדרין סז:

אפילו ידעו לברא בריות יפות שלא מזווג המין כמו שנודע בספרי הטבע שאין הדבר נמנע רשאים לעשות שכל שהוא טבעי אינו בכלל הכשוף ודומה לזה שיש בו משום רפואה אין בו משום דרכי האמורי כמו שיתבאר במקומו כל שנאסר בדברים אלו שכתבנו לא נאסר אלא לעשות אבל להבין ולהורות הכל מותר

### 49) Letter to the Editor, by Rabbi Dr. Moses Tendler, New York Times, December 12, 1997

To the Editor:
As an Orthodox Jew and rabbi, I oppose "elective" or "autonomous" cloning on biblical grounds (Op-Ed, Dec. 5). As a professor of biology, I see it as a form of assisted sexual

אחר שכינה? והלא כבר נאמר: (דברים ד') "כי ה'
אלקיך אש אוכלה הוא" אלא להלך אחר מדותיו של
הקב"ה, מה הוא מלביש ערומים ... אף אתה הלבש
ערומים הקב"ה ביקר חולים ... אף אתה בקר חולים
הקב"ה ניחם אבלים ... אף אתה נחם אבלים הקב"ה
קבר מתים ... אף אתה קבור מתים.

**29) ישעיהו סה:יז, סו:כב**

כִּי־הִנְנִי בוֹרֵא שָׁמַיִם חֲדָשִׁים וָאָרֶץ חֲדָשָׁה וְלֹא תִזָּכַרְנָה
הָרִאשֹׁנוֹת וְלֹא תַעֲלֶינָה עַל־לֵב:
כִּי כַאֲשֶׁר הַשָּׁמַיִם הַחֲדָשִׁים וְהָאָרֶץ הַחֲדָשָׁה אֲשֶׁר אֲנִי
עֹשֶׂה עֹמְדִים לְפָנַי נְאֻם־ד' כֵּן יַעֲמֹד זַרְעֲכֶם וְשִׁמְכֶם:

**30) ישעיהו כו:יט**

יִחְיוּ מֵתֶיךָ נְבֵלָתִי יְקוּמוּן הָקִיצוּ וְרַנְּנוּ שֹׁכְנֵי עָפָר כִּי
טַל אוֹרֹת טַלֶּךָ וָאָרֶץ רְפָאִים תַּפִּיל:

**31) סנהדרין סה: ורש"י שם**

רבא ברא גברא, שדריה לקמיה דרבי זירא. הוה קא
משתעי בהדיה, ולא הוה קא מהדר ליה. אמר ליה:
מן חברייא את, הדר לעפריך. רב חנינא ורב אושעיא
הוו יתבי כל מעלי שבתא ועסקי בספר יצירה, ומיברו
להו עיגלא תילתא, ואכלי ליה.
ברא גברא – על ידי ספר יצירה שלמדו צרוף אותיות
של שם.
ולא היה מהדר ליה – שלא היה בו דבור.
עיגלא תילתא – גדול כאלו הגיע לשליש שניו וגמרה
גדילתו, דהכי שביחי ומעלי למיכל ...

**32) רש"י סנהדרין סז: ד"ה עסקי**

עסקי בהלכות יצירה – וממילא אברו להו עגלא
תילתא על ידי שהיו מצרפים אותיות השם שבהם
נברא העולם, ואין כאן משום מכשפות דמעשה
הקדוש ברוך הוא הן, על ידי שם קדושתו שלו הוא.

**33) רבינו בחיי, כד הקמח, ערך "רשות", פירוש על בראשית ב:ז**

... ולפי שפעולותיו של אדם נכללים בג' דברים והם
המחשבה והדבור והמעשה ...
וצריך אתה לדעת כי חכמי המחקר נחלקו בענין
הנפש ויסדו בזה ספרים אין קץ והאריכו והרחיבו
לשון בהם, יש מהם אומרים שהנפש אחת ויש בה
שלש כוחות, הכח המתאוה אשר לבעלי הנפש
הבהמית, והכח הצומח אשר לבעלי הנפש הצומחת,
והכח המשכיל היא נפש החכמה, ושלש כוחות אלו
הם נפש אחת, ויש מהם אומרים כי הם באדם שלש
נפשות שונות חלוקות זו מזו, הנפש החכמה לעצמה
הצומחת לעצמה והבהמית לעצמה, הנפש הבהמית
היא הנפש המתאוה המאכל והמשתה והמשגל
והשינה והכעס, בה ישתתף האדם עם הבהמות
והחיות וכל בעלי נפש התנועה ומשכנה בכבד והיא
הנקראת נפש ורוח ... הנפש הצומחת הוא הכח

המגדל באדם בה ישתתף עם האילנות והצמחים,
וענין הנפש הזאת שתגדל גוף הצמח והאילן ויגביהנו
וירחיבנו, וכן באדם ואין משכנה במקום מיוחד בגוף
רק בכולו והיא מתגברת עד זמן קצוב, הנפש החכמה
נמצאת באדם לבדו בה משתתף עם העליונים
הקדושים העומדים לעד לעולם בחכמה ושכל
ומשכנה במוח והיא הנקראת נשמה ... ולדעת אלה
החכמים הסוברים שיש באדם שלש נפשות חלוקות
מצינו ראיה לחז"ל ממה שאמרו (סנהדרין סה ע"ב)
רבא ברא גברא שדריה לקמיה דרבי זירא הוה
משתעי ליה ולא משתעי אמר דמן חבריא את תוב
לעפרך, המאמר זה יורה ששלושתם באדם נפשות
שונות חלוקות זו מזו כי רבא מתוך חכמתו הרחבה
שצפה והעמיק בחכמת ספר יצירה ברא האדם ההוא
והטיל בו נפש התנועה ולא היה לו כח לתת הדיבור
בו כי הדיבור מצד הנפש החכמה:

**34) רב יעקב אמדין, מגילת ספר, דף 4**

... עיין בס' תשובותיו של אבא מרי הגאון ז"ל (סי'
צג) דברא גברא, וספר ממנו מעשה כי הנוצר ההוא
היה בלי דבור והיה משמשו כעבד, וכראות הרב
שיצור כפיו הולך וחזק וגדול מאד, ע"י השם הכתוב
בנייר שדבקין במצחו, באופן שהיה מתירא ר"א בעל
שם שלא יזיק וישחית, נתחזק עליו מהרה וקרע
מעליו הגליון שהיה כתוב עליו השם ונתקו ממצחו
ונפל גוש עפר כשהיה, אבל הזיק לרבו כי סרט אותו
בפניו כשלקח הכתב ונתק השם מעליו ...

**35) פירוש מהרש"א על ברכות י'.**

גם שאמרו פרק ד' מיתות (סה) רבא ברא גברא
ור"ח ור"א מיברו להו עגלא תלתא ואכלי ליה והיינו
בשמותיו של הקב"ה כפירש"י שם מ"מ נשמה לא היו
יכולין להטיל ביה כדאמרינן התם שלא היה בו דבור
זה כח הדבור שהוא כח הנשמה שבאדם כדכתיב
לנפש חיה ומתרגם לרוח ממללא וז"ש ברכי נפשי
שהיא הנשמה שבה מובדל מנפש בהמה מה כל קרבי
ברכו שם קדשו שבראם מה שאין ב"ו הצר צורה יכול
ליוצרם וק"ל:

**36) בראשית ב:ז ותרגום אונקלוס**

וַיִּיצֶר ד' אֱלֹקִים אֶת־הָאָדָם עָפָר מִן־הָאֲדָמָה וַיִּפַּח
בְּאַפָּיו נִשְׁמַת חַיִּים וַיְהִי הָאָדָם לְנֶפֶשׁ חַיָּה:
בְּרָא יְיָ אֱלֹקִים יָת אָדָם עַפְרָא מִן אַדַמְתָּא וּנְפַח
בְּאַפּוֹהִי נִשְׁמְתָא דְחַיֵּי וַהֲוַת בְּאָדָם לְרוּחַ מְמַלְלָא:

**37) שמות כב:יז**

מְכַשֵּׁפָה לֹא תְחַיֶּה:

**38) סנהדרין סז:**

אמר רבי יוחנן: למה נקרא שמן כשפים שמכחישין
פמליא של מעלה.

**21) פירוש כתב וקבלה על שמות כ:י'**

... ושם מלאכה הונח על כל דבר מעשה המביא לידי תכלית ותועלת ויש בו תקון העולם, והם כלל ל"ט מלאכות שהוזכרו בדרז"ל, כמבואר היטב בדברי החכם רנ"ו בביאור שם מלאכה. והנה לכל מלאכת מעשה נצטרך לשתי כחות כלליות, הא' כח האדם לעשות מלאכתו כזריעה חרישה וכדומה, והשני הכח הטבעי שהוכן ממנו ית', לתת כח הטבעי בכל דבר מעשי האדם, לתת כח בזרעים ויבולי האדמה וכן בכל מלאכת מעשה, הנה שתי כחות אלה הן האדם וכח הטבעי הם כמו זוג זה עם זה לפעול ולהתפעל, וכל מה שנתחדש ונולד ע"י שתי כחות אלה, הוא הנקרא בן זוג ותולדותם; אמנם כל זה יתכן בששת ימי המעשה שבהם יש מקום לשתי כחות אלה, האדם בפעולותיו ואדמת הטבע בכחותי', וע"י הזדווגות כחות האלה יוכל להתחדש ולהולד מלאכה להיותה הנולד מן הזוג, והיא המלאכה שהוא העסק המביא לידי תכלית תקון וקיום העולם

**Rabbi Joseph Soloveitchik, "Confronta- (22 tion" Tradition, volume VI:2, p. 20**

The limited role we played until modern times in the great cosmic confrontation was not of our choosing. Heaven knows that we never encouraged the cruel relationship which the world displayed toward us. We have always considered ourselves an inseparable part of humanity and we were ever ready to accept the divine challenge "מלאו את הארץ וכבשה" "Fill the earth and subdue it," and the responsibility implicit in human existence. We have never proclaimed the philosophy of contemptus or odium seculi. We have steadily maintained that involvement in the creative scheme of things is mandatory. Involvement with the rest of mankind in the cosmic confrontation ... First, as we have mentioned previously, we, created in the image of God, are charged with responsibility for the great confrontation of man and the cosmos.

**Rabbi Joseph Soloveitchik, "Lonely (23 Man of Faith" Tradition, volume VI:2, p. 15**

Man reaching for the distant stars is acting in harmony with his nature which was created, willed, and directed by his Maker. It is a manifestation of obedience to rather than rebellion against God. nature which was created, willed, and directed by his Maker. It is a manifestation of obedience to rather than rebellion against God.

**24) שו"ת אגרות משה, אורח חיים ג:צ**

הא דדרשת ר' ישמעאל שניתן רשות לרופא לרפאות הוא דוקא מדתנא ביה קרא ורפא ירפא מכה דמה שלא שמעינן מרפא לחודיה דהו"א ה"מ מכה בידי אדם אבל חולי הבא ביד"ש כשמרפא נראה כסותר גזירת המלך קמ"ל דשרי, וא"כ אפשר שמה שהתורה התירה וגם חייבה לרפא אינו משום דקמ"ל דלא הוי כסותר גזירת המלך, מטעם דאמרינן דגזירת המלך היתה רק שיחלה לו פחד שמא לא יתרפא והרפואה שיצטרך ושיהיה לו להוציאת ממון הוא גם להפסידו בממון יחד עם צער הגוף, אלא שאף שהוא בעצם כסותר גזירת המלך התירה תורה לרפאותו וגם חייבה, וכמו שמותר וגם חייבין להתפלל לבטל גזירת המלך כדמצינו בכל התפלות שבקראי, ואף במקום שלא גילה השי"ת דעתו שיתפלל אף בלשון הניחה לי, כמו כן התירה תורה לרפאות בכל מיני סמים לבטל גזירתו

**25) שבת לא.**

אמר רבא: בשעה שמכניסין אדם לדין אומרים לו: נשאת ונתת באמונה, קבעת עתים לתורה, עסקת בפריה ורביה, צפית לישועה, פלפלת בחכמה, הבנת דבר מתוך דבר?

**26) זוהר חלק א קיז.**

ובשית מאה שנין לשתיתאה. יתפתחון תרעי דחכמתא לעילא. ומבועי דחכמתא לתתא. ויתתקן עלמא לאעלא בשביעאה. כבר נש דמתתקן ביומא שתיתאה מכי ערב שמשא לאעלא בשבתא. אוף הכי נמי. וסימניך (בראשית ז יא) "בשנת שש מאות שנה לחיי נח וגו' . נבקעו כל מעיינות תהום רבה."

**27) קל"ח פתחי חכמה של משה חיים לוצאטו, מבוא**

בזוה"ק וירא קיז ע"א ובשית מאה שנין לשתיתאה יתפתחון תרעי דחכמתא דלעילא ומבועי דחכמתא דלתתא ויתתקן עלמא לאעלא בשביעה וסימנך בשנת שש מאות שנה לחיי נח וגו' נבקעו כל מעיינות תהום רבה וארובות שמים נפתחו ומ"ש יתפתחון כו' ר"ל שניתנה רשות לכל המשתוקקים להדבק באלקים חיים ולהתעסק בחכמת האמת לכנס ולטול את השם כראוי וכל מי שיעמיק בזה ישכיל וימצא ולא היה כל זה קודם שנת ת"ר כי אז היה הדבר סתום וחתום אלא רק ליחידי סגולה לבד כן שמעתי בשם הגאון החסיד ר' ישראל סלאנטער ז"ל " ע"כ לשון ספר לש"ו על התנאים הנדרשים לאלה שרוצים לעסוק בחכמת האמת עי' בספר אור נערב לרמ"ק הק' חלק ג' פרק א-

**28) סוטה יד.**

ואמר רבי חמא ברבי חנינא, מאי דכתיב: (דברים יג) "אחרי ה' אלקיכם תלכו"? וכי אפשר לו לאדם להלך

## 11) סנהדרין לז.

לפיכך נברא אדם יחידי, ללמדך שכל המאבד נפש אחת מישראל מעלה עליו הכתוב כאילו איבד עולם מלא, וכל המקיים נפש אחת מישראל מעלה עליו הכתוב כאילו קיים עולם מלא ... ולהגיד גדולתו של הקדוש ברוך הוא, שאדם טובע כמה מטבעות בחותם אחד כולן דומין זה לזה, ומלך מלכי המלכים הקדוש ברוך הוא טבע כל אדם בחותמו של אדם הראשון ואין אחד מהן דומה לחבירו.

## 12) ישעיהו סה:יז, סו:כב

כִּי־הִנְנִי בוֹרֵא שָׁמַיִם חֲדָשִׁים וָאָרֶץ חֲדָשָׁה וְלֹא תִזָּכַרְנָה הָרִאשֹׁנוֹת וְלֹא תַעֲלֶינָה עַל־לֵב:
כִּי כַאֲשֶׁר הַשָּׁמַיִם הַחֲדָשִׁים וְהָאָרֶץ הַחֲדָשָׁה אֲשֶׁר אֲנִי עֹשֶׂה עֹמְדִים לְפָנַי נְאֻם־ד' כֵּן יַעֲמֹד זַרְעֲכֶם וְשִׁמְכֶם:

## 13) ישעיה כו:יט

יִחְיוּ מֵתֶיךָ נְבֵלָתִי יְקוּמוּן הָקִיצוּ וְרַנְּנוּ שֹׁכְנֵי עָפָר כִּי טַל אוֹרֹת טַלֶּךָ וָאָרֶץ רְפָאִים תַּפִּיל:

## 14) פסחים נד.

רבי יוסי אומר: שני דברים עלו במחשבה ליבראות בערב שבת ולא נבראו עד מוצאי שבת, ובמוצאי שבת נתן הקדוש ברוך הוא דיעה באדם הראשון מעין דוגמא של מעלה, והביא שני אבנים וטחנן זו בזו ויצא מהן אור. והביא שתי בהמות והרכיב זו בזו ויצא מהן פרד.

## 15) מהר"ל, באר הגולה לט

כי בששת ימי בראשית לא נבראו רק הדברים הטבעיים, אבל דברים שהוא על הטבע ועל ידי האדם היו בכח ועל ידי האדם שהוא שכלי והוא על הטבע היו יוצאים לפועל ... ומה שהם תמהים על הרכבת שני מינין, בודאי לפי התורה שנתן הקב"ה לישראל הדבר הוא אסור משום כלאים, אבל אדם הראשון היה עושה דבר זה, כי הדבר הזה ראוי שיהיה בעולם עד שיהיה נשלם העולם, ואף כי לפי התורה שנתן השם יתברך דבר זה אסור מפני שהוא כלאים, דרך התורה לבד. וכמה מינים שנבראו בעולם והתורה אסרם באכילה, ועם כל זה נבראו בעולם שבהם יושלם העולם ... וכבר אמרנו דרך התורה בלבד, והשלמת העולם לבד ... ויצא לפועל על ידי האדם שכל ראוי להיות ...

## 16) פירוש תפארת ישראל על משנה ידים ד:ג

שכל דבר שלא נדע טעם לאסרו מותר הוא בלי טעם דלא הזכירה התורה דברים המותרין כולן רק דברים האסורין.

## 17) ישעיה נט:ב

כִּי אִם־עֲוֹנֹתֵיכֶם הָיוּ מַבְדִּלִים בֵּינֵכֶם לְבֵין אֱלֹקֵיכֶם וְחַטֹּאותֵיכֶם הִסְתִּירוּ פָנִים מִכֶּם מִשְּׁמוֹעַ:

## 18) סנהדרין סה: ופירוש רש"י שם

אבל מה אעשה שעונותינו גרמו לנו שנאמר (ישעיהו נ"ט) כי [אם] עונותיכם היו מבדלים ביניכם לבין אלהיכם. אמר רבא: אי בעו צדיקי ברו עלמא, שנאמר כי עונותיכם היו מבדלים וגו'. רבא ברא גברא, שדריה לקמיה דרבי זירא. הוה קא משתעי בהדיה, ולא הוה קא מהדר ליה. אמר ליה: מן חבריא את, הדר לעפריך. רב חנינא ורב אושעיא הוו יתבי כל מעלי שבתא ועסקי בספר יצירה, ומיברו להו עיגלא תילתא, ואכלי ליה.

הוו ברו עלמא שנאמר כי אם עונותיכם היו מבדילים – הא אם לא היו בהם עונות אין כאן הבדלה.

## 19) שבת ל: ופירוש בית הלוי על בראשית יז:א

ותו יתיב רבן גמליאל וקא דריש: עתידה ארץ ישראל שתוציא גלוסקאות וכלי מילת, שנאמר (תהלים עב) יהי פסת בר בארץ.

... וכדרך משל בזרעים רואים אנחנו שהולך ונתתקן דבהתחלה יוצא מן השדה קש ואח"כ מהממעולה שבזרע נעשה למעלה שבולת ואח"כ נעשה בה המוץ שמונחה בו הקמח ואח"כ קרוב להגמרו נגדל בו הקמח, ואלמלא אמר די היה די הולך ונתתקן עוד דהמחטמה היה יוצא גלוסקא הראוי לאכילה ואמר לו די שיוותר לא יתוקן, יען כי כן גזרה חכמתו יתברך דסוף של התיקון וגמרו יהיה ע"י מעשה האדם וכן יהיה עד לבסוף, שלעתיד בימי התיקון אמרו עתידה ארץ ישראל שתוציא גלוסקאות וכלי מילת שיהיה עד לעתיד הניח להאדם עמל לגמרו. וזהו עתה כשנצוה אותו למול וכדי שלא יהיה קשה לאברהם אבינו כמו שהקשה טורנוסרופוס הרשע לר' עקיבא אם רצונו במולים מפני מה אין האדם נולד מהול (תנחומא תזריע סי' ה'), וזהו שאמר לו אני שאמרתי לעולמי די וכל הבריאה הנחתי להאדם שיגמרנה וכמו כן כן בריאת האדם ושלמה שלו הנחתי על האדם שימול את עצמו. שוב מצאתיו בספר תפארת יהונתן:

## 20) מדרש, בראשית רבה מו:ג

אמר אם חביבה היא המילה מפני מה לא נתנה לאדם הראשון

אמר לו הקדוש ב"ה לאברהם דייך אני ואתה בעולם ואם אין את מקבל עליך לימול די לעולמי עד כאן דייה לערלה עד כאן ודייה למילה שתהא עגומה עד כאן אמר עד שלא מלתי היו באים ומזדווגים לי תאמר משמלתי הן באין ומזדווגים לי אמר לו הקב"ה אברהם דייך שאני אלוהך דייך שאני פטרונך ולא לך לעצמך אלא דיי לעולמי שאני אלוהו דיי לעולמי שאני פטרונו רבי נתן ורבי אחא ורבי ברכיה בשם רבי יצחק אני אל שדי אני הוא שאמרתי לעולמי ולשלמים דיי לארץ דיי שאלולי שאמרתי להם דיי עד עכשיו היו נמתחים והולכים תני משום רבי אלעזר בן יעקב אני הוא שאין העולם ומלואו כדי לאלהותי תרגום עקילוס אכסיוס ואנקוס:

# SOURCES ON CLONING OF HUMAN BEINGS

**1) משנה אבות ה:כב**

בן בג בג אומר הפך בה והפך בה. דכולא בה.

**2) בראשית א:כז**

וַיִּבְרָא אֱלֹקִים אֶת־הָאָדָם בְּצַלְמוֹ בְּצֶלֶם אֱלֹקִים בָּרָא אֹתוֹ זָכָר וּנְקֵבָה בָּרָא אֹתָם:

**3) בראשית א:כח ופירוש רמב"ן**

וַיְבָרֶךְ אֹתָם אֱלֹקִים וַיֹּאמֶר לָהֶם אֱלֹקִים פְּרוּ וּרְבוּ וּמִלְאוּ אֶת־הָאָרֶץ וְכִבְשֻׁהָ וּרְדוּ בִּדְגַת הַיָּם וּבְעוֹף הַשָּׁמַיִם וּבְכָל־חַיָּה הָרֹמֶשֶׂת עַל־הָאָרֶץ:

וכבשוה – נתן להם כח וממשלה בארץ לעשות כרצונם בבהמות ובשרצים וכל זוחלי עפר, ולבנות, ולעקור נטוע, ומהרריה לחצוב נחשת, וכיוצא בזה.

**4) בראשית ב:ב-ג, שמות כ:ט-י', לא:ב-ג, לו:א**

וַיְכַל אֱלֹקִים בַּיּוֹם הַשְּׁבִיעִי מְלַאכְתּוֹ אֲשֶׁר עָשָׂה וַיִּשְׁבֹּת בַּיּוֹם הַשְּׁבִיעִי מִכָּל־מְלַאכְתּוֹ אֲשֶׁר עָשָׂה: וַיְבָרֶךְ אֱלֹקִים אֶת־יוֹם הַשְּׁבִיעִי וַיְקַדֵּשׁ אֹתוֹ כִּי בוֹ שָׁבַת מִכָּל־מְלַאכְתּוֹ אֲשֶׁר־בָּרָא אֱלֹקִים לַעֲשׂוֹת:

שֵׁשֶׁת יָמִים תַּעֲבֹד וְעָשִׂיתָ כָּל־מְלַאכְתֶּךָ: וְיוֹם הַשְּׁבִיעִי שַׁבָּת לַד' אֱלֹקֶיךָ לֹא־תַעֲשֶׂה כָל־מְלָאכָה אַתָּה וּבִנְךָ וּבִתֶּךָ עַבְדְּךָ וַאֲמָתְךָ וּבְהֶמְתֶּךָ וְגֵרְךָ אֲשֶׁר בִּשְׁעָרֶיךָ:

רְאֵה קָרָאתִי בְשֵׁם בְּצַלְאֵל בֶּן־אוּרִי בֶן־חוּר לְמַטֵּה יְהוּדָה: וָאֲמַלֵּא אֹתוֹ רוּחַ אֱלֹקִים בְּחָכְמָה וּבִתְבוּנָה וּבְדַעַת וּבְכָל־מְלָאכָה:

וְעָשָׂה בְצַלְאֵל וְאָהֳלִיאָב וְכֹל | אִישׁ חֲכַם־לֵב אֲשֶׁר נָתַן ד' חָכְמָה וּתְבוּנָה בָּהֵמָּה לָדַעַת לַעֲשֹׂת אֶת־כָּל־מְלֶאכֶת עֲבֹדַת הַקֹּדֶשׁ לְכֹל אֲשֶׁר־צִוָּה ד':

**5) תהילים קטו:טז**

הַשָּׁמַיִם שָׁמַיִם לַד' וְהָאָרֶץ נָתַן לִבְנֵי־אָדָם:

**6) בראשית יא:ג-ד, ח**

וַיֹּאמְרוּ אִישׁ אֶל־רֵעֵהוּ הָבָה נִלְבְּנָה לְבֵנִים וְנִשְׂרְפָה לִשְׂרֵפָה וַתְּהִי לָהֶם הַלְּבֵנָה לְאָבֶן וְהַחֵמָר הָיָה לָהֶם לַחֹמֶר: וַיֹּאמְרוּ הָבָה נִבְנֶה־לָּנוּ עִיר וּמִגְדָּל וְרֹאשׁוֹ בַשָּׁמַיִם וְנַעֲשֶׂה־לָּנוּ שֵׁם פֶּן־נָפוּץ עַל־פְּנֵי כָל־הָאָרֶץ: וַיָּפֶץ ד' אֹתָם מִשָּׁם עַל־פְּנֵי כָל־הָאָרֶץ וַיַּחְדְּלוּ לִבְנֹת הָעִיר: עַל־כֵּן קָרָא שְׁמָהּ בָּבֶל כִּי־שָׁם בָּלַל ד' שְׂפַת כָּל־הָאָרֶץ וּמִשָּׁם הֱפִיצָם ד' עַל־פְּנֵי כָּל־הָאָרֶץ:

**7) ויקרא יט:יט**

אֶת־חֻקֹּתַי תִּשְׁמֹרוּ בְּהֶמְתְּךָ לֹא־תַרְבִּיעַ כִּלְאַיִם שָׂדְךָ לֹא־תִזְרַע כִּלְאָיִם וּבֶגֶד כִּלְאַיִם שַׁעַטְנֵז לֹא יַעֲלֶה עָלֶיךָ:

---

**8) פירושי רמב"ן ואבן עזרא על ויקרא יט:יט**

רמב"ן – ... חקים אלו גזרות מלך שאין טעם לדבר, לשון רש"י ... והטעם בכלאים, כי השם ברא המינים בעולם, בכל בעלי הנפשות בצמחים ובבעלי נפש התנועה, ונתן בהם כח התולדה שיתקיימו המינים בהם לעד כל זמן שירצה הוא יתברך בקיום העולם. וצוה בכחם שיוציאו למיניהם ולא ישתנו לעד לעולם ... זו עם זו לקיום המינין כאשר יבואו האנשים על הנשים לפריה ורביה. והמרכיב שני מינין, משנה ומכחיש במעשה בראשית, כאילו יחשוב שלא השלים הקב"ה בעולמו כל הצורך ויחפוץ הוא לעזור בבריאתו של עולם להוסיף בו בריות.

אבן עזרא – ... לא תעשה לבהמה לשנות מעשה השם על כן כתוב את חקתי תשמרו לשמור כל מין שלא יתערב מין עם מין:

**9) פירוש של שמשון רפאל הירש, ויקרא יט:יט**

If we consider the prohibitions classed together in the verse ... we find that כלאים and כלאי בהמה are actually interferences in the Law of Creation. Species of animals and plants which Nature has ordained "closed" to one another is forced unnaturally into union ... It is quite evident that already in כלאי זרעים the prohibition goes further than forbidding any interference in God's Laws of Nature regarding mating. It is rather to bring Man in his work of plant culture to the thought of the Creator's rule of למינהו ... And Man, too, has been given the Law for his own mating, and is to be reminded of it especially at the time of his wearing human clothing ... Expressed symbolically – taking the צמר as cloth-material to represent the animal, and פש-תים the vegetative element in the human being – in animals, צמר ופשתים are יחדיו. But in man, the animal element, mind and will power, is not to incline towards the vegetative one, is not to be closely connected with the urges of the stomach and of sexual life. In man, צמר and פשתים are to be separated, each one to be kept contained in his own separate realm. Not downwards towards vegetative sensuality, upwards towards the pinnacle of Mankind.

**10) קידושין ל:**

ת"ר, שלשה שותפין הן באדם: הקב"ה, ואביו, ואמו

מהמלכות שידונו היהודים לעצמם בדיני התורה,
ומ"מ לא היה נמצא כמעט בכל הדורות רוצחים
ביהודים מפני חומר האיסור ומפני מה שנתחנכו
ע"י התורה וע"י עונשי התורה להבין חומר האיסור
... וכל זה הוא כשלא הופקר איסור הרציחה אלא
שבשביל איזה תאוה גדולה או איזה מריבה על טענת
ממון וכבוד עשה זה, אבל מי שהורג נפשות מחמת
שהופקר אצלו איסור הרציחה והוא אכזרי ביותר,
וכן כשנתרבו רוצחים ועושי רשעה היה דין למיגדר
מלתא למנוע מעשה רציחה שהוא הצלת המדינה.

**Tradition 38:1 2004.** **(24**
**"Judaism and the Death Penalty: Of Two**
**Minds but One Heart", page 78, Letter from**
**Rabbi Ahron Soloveitchik to David Luchins**
**at the Orthodox Union, 1970's**
[I]t is irresponsible and unfair to submit a statement in favor of capital punishment in the name
of Orthodox Jewry. In my humble opinion,
from a Halachik point of view, every Jew should
be opposed to capital punishment. It is true ...
that the Torah recognizes capital punishment.
However, the Torah delegates the authority to
mete out capital punishment only to Sanhedrin,
not to anyone else. Even Sanhedrin are [sic] not
able to mete out capital punishment if there is
no Beis Hamikdash.

**22) תשובות הרא"ש יז:ח**
ותמהתי מאד בבאי הלום, איך היו דנין דיני נפשות
בלא סנהדרין, ואמרו לי כי הורמנא דמלכא הוא.
וגם העדה שופטים להציל, כי כמה דמים היו
נשפכים יותר אם היו נדו נים ע"י הערבים, והנחתיה
להם כמנהגם, אבל מעולם לא הסכמתי עמהם על
איבוד נפש.

**23) שו"ת אגרות משה, חושן משפט ב:סח**
עתה אשיב בקצרה, כי בעצם נאמרו בתורה עונשי
מיתה לעבירות החמורות מאד כרציחת נפש אדם,
ומיני גניבת אדם, ומיני עריות, ועל אחד שעובד
עבודה זרה ... יש הדגשה על חשיבותו של כל נפש,
ועוד חשבונות, ולכן נצטוינו שלדון דיני נפשות
אינם כשרים אלא על פי סנהדרין שנסמכו לזה ואין
סומכין לזה אלא אלא לגדולים ביותר בחכמת התורה
וגם גדולים בשאר חכמות, ויהיו ענוים מאד ויראי
השם יתברך ושונאי ממון ואוהבי האמת ואהובים
לבריות בזה שהם בעלי טובה ונפש שפלה וחברתן
טובה ודבורן ומשאן בנחת עם הבריות ולא יהא שום
גנאי ולא שם רע עליהם ורחמנים ביותר. ומטעם זה
אין מעמידין זקן מופלג בשנים שכבר נשכח ממנו
קצת צער גדול בנים ולא מי שאין לו בנים שאולי
חסר לו קצת רחמנות ויכעוס על העוברים יותר מדי
... וגם לא אפשר לדון דיני נפשות אלא כשביהמ"ק
=כשבית המקדש= היה קיים וישבו סנהדרין של ע"א
שהם עוד יותר גדולים בלשכת הגזית בביהמ"ק,
שלכן לא דנו דיני נפשות אף במדינות שהיה רשות

**13) רמב"ם, הלכות סנהדרין כד:ד**

יש לבית דין ... להרוג מי שאינו מחוייב מיתה ולא לעבור על דברי תורה אלא לעשות סייג לתורה, וכיון שרואים בית דין שפרצו העם בדבר יש להן לגדור ולחזק הדבר כפי מה שיראה להם הכל הוראת שעה לא שיקבע הלכה לדורות.... ומעשה באחד שרכב על סוס בשבת בימי יוונים

**14) רמב"ם, הלכות סנהדרין ב:ד**

וכל אלו הרצחנים וכיוצא בהן שאינן מחוייבים מיתת בית דין אם רצה מלך ישראל להרגם בדין המלכות ותקנת העולם הרשות בידו, וכן אם ראו בית דין להרוג אותן בהוראת שעה אם היתה השעה צריכה לכך הרי יש להם רשות כפי מה שיראו.

**15) תשובות רב נטרונאי גאון, חושן משפט סימן שעה**

מי שנתחייב מיתת בית דין – כגון שהרג את הנפש או שבא על אשת איש או על הזכר – בזמן הזה, במה דנין אותו.

כך הראונו מן השמים: אין מלקין אותו, מפני שמחוייבי מיתת בית דין אין מלקין אותן ... ועוד, מלקות דודאי דאורייתא ליכא בידן האידנא, דמלקות דודאי דאורייתא איכא אומדנא דבית דין ... אבל שלא לפוטרו לגמרי ושלא יהא הדבר כהיתר, מנדין אותו ומיסרין אותו ומבדילין אותו מן הקהל, ומכין אותו מכת מרדות מדרבנן ...

**16) רב שרירא גאון, תקנות הגאונים (טיקוצינסקי), פרק יב**

ההורג את הנפש בזמן הזה אין בידינו לעשות לו מאומה לא להורגו ולא לחובטו ולא להגלותו אלא לימנע ממנו שלא להתערב עמו ואסור להתפלל עמו ולהסתכל בדמותו ופסול לכל עדות שבעולם

**17) תקנות הגאונים (טיקוצינסקי), פרק יב (דף 106)**

בתקופה מאוחרת יותר ביצעו היהודים עונש מות בהסכמת השלטונות אבל לא משום דין תורה אלא משום דרישת תנאי הזמן גם בארצות אחרות חשבו כנראה להרוג כשאפשר את המוסרים למלכות בגלל הסכנה שבהם בר"י אור זרוע מוצאים רמז על נוהג זה בארצות שהיתה ליהודים זכות שיפוט עצמאי בדיני עונשין.

**18) שו"ת הרשב"א סימן שמט**

שאלת בארצנו יש תנאים בין הקהלות שכל יהודי שיהרוג יהודי יהרג. יהודי הרג יהודי מחל לו ההריגה על מנת שנצוה עליו לעשות כל הדברים שיש לו לעשות מנדוי ומגלות ומכיוצא בזה, הודיענו מה לעשות.

תשובה דבר תורה עכשיו אין דנין דיני נפשות, דכתיב "אשר יגידו לך מן המקום ההוא" מלמד שהמקום גורם, וכל שסנהדרין יושבין בלשכה דנין דיני נפשות

---

בכל מקום אין סנהדרין יושבין בלשכה אין דנין דיני נפשות ... אבל כל שראו הקהלות לדון ולגדור בפני הדור הפורץ, כגון לחתוך אחד מאבריו הרשות בידם, וכמו שאמרו ... שמעתי שב"ד מכין ועונשין שלא מן התורה ולא לעבור על דברי תורה אלא כדי לעשות סייג לתורה ... אתם יכולין לעשות לו מה שיראה בעיניכם ... אלמא אם ירצו ינקרו את עיניו. ואם ירצו יגזרו עליו מלקיות או גלות, הכל לפי מה שהוא אדם ראוי להחמיר עליו. או ראו לכנוס אותו לכיפה ולהאכילו לחם צר ומים לחץ ... ואעפ"י שאי אפשר לדונו בהן ולהורגו ממש ...

**19) רמב"ם, פירוש המשניות על חולין א:ב**

וכבר יצא מזה הלכה למעשה ... וגם כן מן המקובל בידינו והמפורסם לעשות על פיו שהאיש עושה עבירה שחייב עליה מיתת ב"ד הואיל ואין אנו יכולין לדון היום דיני נפשות היו מחרימים אותן חרם עולם בספרי תורות אחר שמלקין אותו ואין מתירים אותו לעולם

**20) רמב"ם, הלכות רוצח ד:ח-ט**

ההורג נפשות ולא היו שני העדים רואין אותו כאחת אלא ראהו האחד אחר האחד, או שהרג בפני שני עדים בלא התראה, או שהוכחשו העדים בבדיקות ולא הוכחשו בחקירות, כל אלו הרצחנים כונסין אותן לכיפה ומאכילין אותן לחם צר ומים לחץ עד שיצרו מיעיהן ואחר כך מאכילים אותן שעורים עד שכריסם נבקעת מכובד החולי.

ואין עושין דבר זה לשאר מחוייבי מיתת בית דין אלא אם נתחייב מיתה ממיתין אותו ואם אינו חייב מיתה פוטרין אותו, שאע"פ שיש עונות חמורין משפיכות דמים אין בהן השחתת ישובו של עולם כשפיכות דמים, אפילו ע"ז ואין צריך לומר עריות או חילול שבת אינן כשפיכות דמים, שאלו העונות הן מעבירות שבין אדם להקב"ה אבל שפיכות דמים מעבירות שבינו לבין חבירו, וכל מי שיש בידו עון זה הרי הוא רשע גמור ואין כל המצות שעשה כל ימיו שקולין כנגד עון זה ולא יצילו אותו מן הדין שנ' אדם עשוק בדם נפש וגו'.

**21) רמב"ם, ספר המצוות, לא תעשה רצ**

שהזהירנו שלא לחתוך הגדרים באומד הדעת החזק ואפילו היה קרוב לאמת כגון שיהיה אדם ירדפהו שונאו להרגו ולהנצל ממנו יכנס בבית אחד ויכנס הרודף ההוא אחריו ונכנס אנחנו אחריהם ונמצא הנרדף הרוג והוא מפרפר ושונאו שהיה רודפו עומד עליו והסכין בידו ושניהם מלוכלכים בדם מזה הרודף לא יהרגוהו הסנהדרין ... וכאשר חתכנו הגדרים בדמים ובאומד הנה פעמים נהרוג נקי כי יום אחד ולזכות אלף חוטאים יותר טוב ונכסף מהרוג זכאי יום אחד ...

**1) בראשית ט:ו**

שֹׁפֵךְ דַּם הָאָדָם בָּאָדָם דָּמוֹ יִשָּׁפֵךְ כִּי בְּצֶלֶם אֱלֹקִים עָשָׂה אֶת־הָאָדָם:

**2) שמות כא:יב, טו-יז, כב:יח, לא:יד, ויקרא כ:ב, י', יג, כד:טז**

מַכֵּה אִישׁ וָמֵת מוֹת יוּמָת:

וּמַכֵּה אָבִיו וְאִמּוֹ מוֹת יוּמָת: וְגֹנֵב אִישׁ וּמְכָרוֹ וְנִמְצָא בְיָדוֹ מוֹת יוּמָת: וּמְקַלֵּל אָבִיו וְאִמּוֹ מוֹת יוּמָת:

כָּל־שֹׁכֵב עִם־בְּהֵמָה מוֹת יוּמָת:

וּשְׁמַרְתֶּם אֶת־הַשַּׁבָּת כִּי קֹדֶשׁ הִוא לָכֶם מְחַלְלֶיהָ מוֹת יוּמָת כִּי כָּל־הָעֹשֶׂה בָהּ מְלָאכָה וְנִכְרְתָה הַנֶּפֶשׁ הַהִוא מִקֶּרֶב עַמֶּיהָ:

וְאֶל־בְּנֵי יִשְׂרָאֵל תֹּאמַר אִישׁ אִישׁ מִבְּנֵי יִשְׂרָאֵל וּמִן־הַגֵּר הַגֵּר בְּיִשְׂרָאֵל אֲשֶׁר יִתֵּן מִזַּרְעוֹ לַמֹּלֶךְ מוֹת יוּמָת עַם הָאָרֶץ יִרְגְּמֻהוּ בָאָבֶן:

וְאִישׁ אֲשֶׁר יִנְאַף אֶת־אֵשֶׁת אִישׁ אֲשֶׁר יִנְאַף אֶת־אֵשֶׁת רֵעֵהוּ מוֹת־יוּמַת הַנֹּאֵף וְהַנֹּאָפֶת:

וְאִישׁ אֲשֶׁר יִשְׁכַּב אֶת־זָכָר מִשְׁכְּבֵי אִשָּׁה תּוֹעֵבָה עָשׂוּ שְׁנֵיהֶם מוֹת יוּמָתוּ דְּמֵיהֶם בָּם:

וְנֹקֵב שֵׁם־ד' מוֹת יוּמָת רָגוֹם יִרְגְּמוּ־בוֹ כָּל־הָעֵדָה כַּגֵּר כָּאֶזְרָח בְּנָקְבוֹ־שֵׁם יוּמָת:

**3) דברים יז:ו**

עַל־פִּי שְׁנַיִם עֵדִים אוֹ שְׁלֹשָׁה עֵדִים יוּמַת הַמֵּת לֹא יוּמַת עַל־פִּי עֵד אֶחָד:

**4) משנה מכות א:י'**

סנהדרין ההורגת אחד בשבוע – נקראת חובלנית ... רבי אליעזר בן עזריה אומר: אחד לשבעים שנה. רבי טרפון ורבי עקיבא אומרים: אילו היינו בסנהדרין – לא נהרג אדם מעולם ... רשב"ג אומר: אף הן מרבין שופכי דמים בישראל.

**5) מדרש ספרי שופטים מד**

"ולא תחוס עינך עליו ובערת דם הנקי" (דברים יט:יג). שמא תאמר הואיל ונהרג זה למה אנו באים לחוב בדמו של זה ת"ל לא תחוס עינך עליו:

**6) משנה, הוריות א:ד ופירוש תוספות יום טוב רמב"ם על פירוש המשניות**

הורו בית דין וידע אחד מהן שטעו ... או זקן שלא ראה לו בנים. הרי אלו פטורין שנאמר כאן עדה. ונאמר להלן עדה. מה עדה האמור להל. עד שיהיו כולם ראויים להוראה. אף עדה האמורה כאן עד שיהיו כולם ראויים להוראה.

או זקן שלא ראה לו בנים – וכן העתיק הר"ב גם

הרמב"ם בפירושו. אבל בחבורו (פי"ג הלכה א' מה"ש) כתב או זקן או שלא ראה בנים וכן בברייתא פרק ד'דסנהדרין דף ל"ו. אין מושיבין בסנהדרין זקן וסריס. ומי שאין לו בנים. והעתיקה הרמב"ם בפ"ב [הלכה ג'] מהלכות סנהדרין. וכתב זקן מופלג בשנים. ובפירוש רש"י זקן ששכח כבר צער גידול בנים ואינו רחמני:

... וזקן שלא ראה בנים אינו כשר לדיני נפשות לפי שהוא אכזרי ולא ירחם על בני אדם לפי שאינו יודע אהבת הבנים

**7) רמב"ם, הלכות סנהדרין ב:ג**

אין מעמידין בכל הסנהדרין לא זקן מופלג בשנים ... מפני שיש בהן אכזריות ולא מי שאין לו בנים כדי שיהא רחמן:

**8) שמות כא:יד**

וְכִי־יָזִד אִישׁ עַל־רֵעֵהוּ לְהָרְגוֹ בְעָרְמָה מֵעִם מִזְבְּחִי תִּקָּחֶנּוּ לָמוּת:

**9) מדרש מכילתא על שמות כא:יד**

מעם מזבחי תקחנו למות. נמצינו למדין שהסנהדרין בצד המזבח.

**10) עבודה זרה ח:**

מ' שנה עד לא חרב הבית – גלתה סנהדרין וישבה לה בחנות. למאי הלכתא ... שלא דנו דיני נפשות. מ"ט כיון דחזו דנפישי להו רוצחנית ולא יכלי למידן, אמרו: מוטב נגל י ממקום למקום כי היכי דלא ליחייבו, דכתיב: (דברים יז) ועשית על פי הדבר אשר יג ידו לך מן המקום ההוא, מלמד שהמקום גורם.

**11) סנהדרין נב:**

אימרתא בת טלי בת כהן שזינתה הואי, אקפה רב חמא בר טוביה חבילי זמורות ושרפה. א מר רב יוסף: טעה בתרתי, טעה בדרב מתנה, וטעה בדתניא: (דברים י"ז) ובאת אל הכהן ם הלוים ואל השפט אשר יהיה בימים ההם, בזמן שיש כהן – יש משפט, בזמן שאין כהן – אין משפט.

**12) סנהדרין מו.**

תניא רבי אליעזר בן יעקב אומר: שמעתי שבית דין מכין ועונשין שלא מן התורה, ולא לעבור על דברי תורה, אלא כדי לעשות סייג לתורה. ומעשה באחד שרכב על סוס בשבת בימי יונים, והביאוהו לבית דין וסקלוהו. לא מפני שראוי לכך, אלא שהשעה צריכה לכך.

זימנא להוי תדיר בגריעותא ומסכנוסה וכו' – ובנ"ד כל המשתדל באורייתא בטול מינא חיובא דכוכבים ומזלות וכו' ועכ"פ ישתדל באורייתא יומא חד. כי מסוגל היום הזה לבטל ממנו כל גזירות רעות עי' ירושלמי ר"ה יט ע"ד שלה במהרה אדם נופל ביום גנוסיא שלו, נמצא שיום הזה הוא יום הצלחה ומזל.

## 71) ספר הקטן והלכותיו, פרק פד, ס"ק א

... ובשו"ת גנזי יוסף סי' ד' מביא מאנשי מעשה שבכל שנה ביום הולדת מהדרין לברך שהחיינו על פרי או בגד חדש ובשו"ת כתב סופר יו"ד סי' קמ"ח כתב שהיה עושה סיום על איזה מסכתא ביום שנולד בו וכן הובא בקונטרס אוהל לאה שנדפס בכתב סופר על התורה ועי"ש שהביא מעשה מתלמיד אחד שנכנס לרבו הכתב סופר והשתומם על המראה כי מצא את רבו גועה בבכי ושאל לו מדוע רבינו בוכה ויאמר לו דע תלמידי חביבי היום הזה הוא יום שבו נולדתי והרי אני כבן נ"ד שנים וד"ן אני את עצמי במה עסקתי כל אותם השנים הללו ומצאתים בלא תכלית הרבה אין בי לא תורה ולא חכמה ולא צדקות ולמה לא אבכה על בילוי ימי אשר אינם חוזרים ויש לי לבכות מאין הפוגות וע"ש בשו"ת אפרקסתא דעניא סי' קכ"א וראיתי מביאים שהתפארת ישראל כתב בצוואתו שמצוה לבניו ולבנותיו שביום הלידה ושל כל אחד יכתבו לו אחיו ואחיותיו ברכה מזל טוב וראה בירושלמי פ"ג ה"ח בר"ה דאיתא שעמלק בשלחם עם ישראל בחר אנשים שהיה אז יום הולדתם כדמפרש בקרבן עדה שם שביום הולדתו המזל שולט וכן הביא החיד"א בספרו חומת אנך

---

איוב רס"י ג' בשם המקובלים שהיום שנולד בו המזל חזק ובספר צדקה לחיים להגר"ח פאלג'י זצ"ל כתב שביים שנולד בו יהיה מרבה בצדקה כפי יכולתו ובפרט ביום שנכנס לשנת כ"א דהיינו בנשלם כ' שנה ביום זה צריך להזהר ביותר דהובא בספר חוקה על משלי ובדרשות אבן שועיב דבאותו מידה שנהג באותו יום לא תסור ממנו עד יום מותו ... ובקונטרס "אוצר החתר קרן שמואל" הביא שיהודי ירושלים עשו לרבם הגאון רבי שמואל סלנט זצ"ל יום חג בהגיעו לגיל שבעים ושמונים והיה שולח לצדקה מטבעות כמנין שנותיו וכן ערכו יום חג להגרי"ח זוננפלד זצ"ל כמסופר בספר מרא דארעא דישראל ח"ג. וראה בחות יאיר סי' ע' שכתב דבים שהחיינו בן שבעים שנה צריך לברך שהחיינו ויש לעשות סעודה וי"ל דהוי סעודת מצוה ...

## 72) ספר המנהגים של חב"ד, ענינים שונים, דף 81

להודיענו אודות יום ההולדת שלו בטח ינהג כמנהג אנ"ש בזמן האחרת ביום ההולדת בעליה לתורה ביום זה עצמו אם הוא יום הקריאה או בשבת שלפניו באם אינו יום הקריאה, נתינה לצדקה קודם תפלת שחרית ומנחה. ואם חל בש"ק או ביום טוב אזי ביום שלפניו. ולימודו שיעור נוסף בתורת הנגלה ובתורת החסידות נוסף על שיעוריו הקבועים ועל שלשת השיעורים השוים לכל נפש מתקנת כ"ק מו"ח אדמו"ר זצוקללה"ה נבג"ם זי"ע בחת"ת (חומש תהלים תניא) הידועים ללמדם ביום זה ביום ההולדת על האדם להתבודד ולהעלות זכרונותיו ולהתבונן בהם. והצריכים תקון תשובה ישוב ויתקנם.

**65) מנהגי חתם סופר ז:יד**

ביום ז' תשרי השלים החומש עם התלמידים על שם
שהיה יום זה יום לידתו ...

**66) שו"ת קנין תורה בהלכה, חלק ג:כא**

... ובשו"ת ערוה"ב (או"ח סי' רע"ז) תשובה חדשה
שכ' דכל מי שעושה חג יובל שבעים שנה וכ"ב
בודקין אחריו שמא מקטני אמונה הוא וכו' "ולשמחה
מה זו עושה" ... כשהשכמתי בבוקר מצאתיו יושב
ואומר תהלים בבכיות גדולות וכשראה עלי סיני
תמיה אמר לי אשר לא לסיבה חולשתי ל"ע אני בוכה
כן רק זה ביום זה היו לאמו ע"ה לחינם חבלי לידה
עכ"ל והי' זה ביום שנת השמונים לחייו נ"ע וכן לא
נזכר דבר זה בשום אחד מן הראשונים לעשות איזהו
חג ביום ... כי על כל אדם להודות ולהלל להש"ית
כל ימי חייו על כל נשימה ונשימה ולהתפלל על
העתיד במקביל אם עושה הודאה בחג מיוחד
ליום השבעים בסעודה וקריאת מוזמנים לו יהא עם
מצות סיום מסכת מה שבזולת אינו רגיל לעשות
בשום פעם יש לחוש פן תהי' חגיגת ההודאה יותר
גדולה מן התפילה על העתיד ואז יש לחוש שזה
יגרום לו ח"ו שלא יומשך לו הטובה הזאת ומטע"ז
ג"כ די שלא לעשות חדשות מה שלא ראינו אצל
אבותינו ורבותינו נ"ע ...

**67) לקט הקמח קלא**

וכן שמעתי לספר מצדיק בדורנו אשר אנשי שלומיו
חוגגים יום לידתם בכל שנה הס' גנזי יוסף שווארץ
בסי' ד' כתב שיודע מאנשים מעשה שבים הולדת
בכל שנה היו מהדרים לברך שהחיינו על איזה פרי
או בגד חדש ובעל ישרי לב עשה כן בהגיע לשבעים
ולעשות סעודה של ת"ח ביום הלידה מאותה שנה
ואילך וס' יפה ללב כתב משם והלאה יאמר בכל יום
מזמור ק"ג.

**68) חוות יאיר ע**

... או סעודת בן שבעים שיש להסתפק אם זה הבן
שבעים מברך שהחיינו כי כך נראה לי. מכל מקום לא
יחויב שיהיה סעודות מצוה לכן ראוי לדרוש בהם ...

**69) בן איש חי, פרשת ראש יז**

כשיגיע לגיל ששים או שבעים נכון ללבוש בגד חדש
או יקח פרי הדש ויברך עליו שהחיינו ויכוין גם על
שנותיו ויש עושים סעודה כשיגיעו לגיל שבעים

**70) שו"ת הלל אומר קלט**

... ומצוה הבאה לידו אל תחמיצנה, לכן היום
הראשון של כל שנה מימי חייו, הוא יום הולדת,
מחויב בר נש לקיים מחשבתו ורצונו של הקב"ה
ולהקדישו כולו, ולא רובו מתוך כולו, שיהיה קודש
לה'. ומקורו בנסתר בזוהר: אית זמנין דסיתרא ההיא
בפגימו ושריא בדינא וכו' ומאן דאתיליד ההוא

---

לע"ז שלהם נאסור אנו על עצמנו להתפלל לאלקינו
... אבל אלה החוגגים יום הולדת בשבח והודיה
בסעודה של מצוה ודברי תורה ודאי שיש בזה גם
משום שמחת מצוה כי אדם המאריך ימים ומשלים
שנותיו זבות היא לו וראוי להודות עליה לה' ...

**60) שו"ת יביע אומר, אורח חיים, חלק ו:כט**

... ואפי' בסתם יום הולדת אם אומרים שם ד"ת הוי
סעודת מצוה. וע' ובן איש חי (פר' ראה אות יז) שכ',
יש נוהגים לעשות את יום הלידה ליו"ט בכל שנה
ושנה, וסימן יפה הוא וכן נוהגים בביתנו ... והגאון
הראש"ל ח"ד בדרא ר' דוד חזן ז"ל בעל הנדיב לב
נהג לחוג את יום הולדתו מגיל שבעים והלאה מדי
שנה בשנה, כמ"ש בישרי לב (מע' ברכת שהחיינו דף
ב' ע"ב). והובא בשו"ת אפרקסתא דעניא שם. ועכ"פ
בודאי שכשיש שם ד"ת ושירות ותשבחות להש"ית
דהוי סעודת מצוה ...

**61) שו"ת אגרות משה, אורח חיים חלק א:ק"ד,
חלק ד:לו**

... ורק אם רוצה האב לעשות איזה שמחה בביתו
רשאי אבל אין זה שום ענין וסמך להחשיב זה דבר
מצוה וסעודת מצוה, כי הוא רק כשמחה של יום
הולדת בעלמא.
בדבר עצם חגיגת בת מצוה אין בזה ענין סעודת
מצוה אלא הוא כשמחה של יום הולדת בעלמא
שהוא רשות ולכן אין לעשות בביהכ"נ שסעודות
הרשות אין להתיר בביהכ"נ ...

**62) ספר ישיבת חכמי לובלין, דף קא=קב**

בשנת תרצ"א הגישו התלמידים לרבנו מגילת קלף
מעשה אומן בדברי ברכה ליום הולדתו ועליו חתמו
כל תלמידי הישיבה ... גם הנהלת הישיבה וידידי
רבנו היתה נוהגת לקבוע ארועים וכינוסים למען
הישיבה בז' אדר מתוך כוונה שקיומם ביום זה בו
מתעוררים רגשי ההוקרה לרבנו יועיל למטרות
הכינוסים ... מסורת זו של התכנסות ביום הולדת
רבינו נמשכה גם נשמרת גם פטירת רבנו ...

**63) מנהגי חתם סופר ז:יד**

ביום ז' תשרי השלים החומש עם התלמידים על שם
שהיה יום זה יום לידתו ...

**64) שמות כג:כה-כו ופירוש כתב סופר**

וַעֲבַדְתֶּם אֵת ד' אֱלֹקֵיכֶם וּבֵרַךְ אֶת-לַחְמְךָ וְאֶת-מֵימֶיךָ
וַהֲסִרֹתִי מַחֲלָה מִקִּרְבֶּךָ: לֹא תִהְיֶה מְשַׁכֵּלָה וַעֲקָרָה
בְּאַרְצֶךָ אֶת-מִסְפַּר יָמֶיךָ אֲמַלֵּא:
וי"ל עוד, שצריך האדם למנות ימיו כמה עברו
כבר משנותיו כדי שיהיה זריז בעבודת ד' ולהכין
צדה לעוה"ב, ואף שאין הברכה שורה בדבר המנוי,
הבטיח ד' את מספר ימיך אמלא:

## 51) רבבות אפרים ד:רמ

... בכ"ה בכסלו נגמר המשכן ועמד מקופל וכו'
בחודש שבו נולד יצחק. ומ"כ פקודי הקב"ה נתכוון
להעמיד המשכן בחודש שנולד בו יצחק. וביפה
תואר שם לעולם יום הולדתו של יצחק הוא יום
שמחה לעולם (מגילה י"ג). בז' אדר נולד משה
וכתב רש"י כדאי הלידה שתכפר על המיתה. ועי'
תוס' נזיר י"ד ביום הולדתו של משה שמחו שמחה
גדולה ועי' נפש חי' סי' תק"פ ממדרש הבהיר בחר
ביהושע כדי שיבחר אנשים שנולדו באדר שני כמותו
ובזכות שנולדו בזמן הולדתו של משה בודאי תגן
זכותו עליהם במלחמה. וידוע דדוד נולד בשבועות.
מקדשים לבנה במוצאי ט"ב כי נולד בן דוד ומקדשים
ללבנה ולישראל שעתיד להתחדש. רשב"י נולד בל"ג
כעומר עי' בני יששכר חודש אדר מאמר ל"ג בעומר.
הרי רואים שיש ליחס יום הולדת ליום שמחה ובשו"ת
כתב סופר יו"ד סי' קמ"ה כתב שעשה שהחיינו
לכשהגיע לנ' שנה ובגמ' מבואר בבן ס' עשו יו"ט (עי'
מו"ק כ"ח) ובשבת ע'. עיין בחות יאיר שמנהג לעשות
אז סעודה א"כ רואים שגדולים חגגו ביום הולדתם
ועוד מקורות וקצרתי בזה ...

## 52) רב צדוק הכהן, ישראל קדושים, אות ח

והנה ביום הלידה אינו יודע עוד מה יהיה ואין
שמשו זורח מכל מקום כבר קדושתו העתיד
להתגלות אחר כך בו שופעת ומאירה לפניה מיד
מיום הולדו ...

## 53) עירובין יג:

תנו רבנן: שתי שנים ומחצה נחלקו בית שמאי ובית
הלל, הללו אומרים: נוח לו לאדם שלא נברא יותר
משנברא, והללו אומרים: נוח לו לאדם שנברא יותר
משלא נברא. נמנו וגמרו: נוח לו לאדם שלא נברא
יותר משנברא, עכשיו שנברא יפשפש במעשיו.

## 54) אוצר כל מנהגי ישורון, דף 60

... היונים והרומים חגגו רק את יום הולדת של
החיים אלא גם יום הולדת של האנשים שכבר
מתו ולא מצינו לא בחכמי התלמוד ולא בגאונים
הראשונים ולא מצינו בחכמי התלמוד ולא כגאונים
הראשונים שחגגו יום הלידה ...

## 55) ספר הקטן והלכותיו, פרק פד, ס"ק א

וראיתי מובא מספר דברי תורה ח"ה אות פ"ח שכתב
שאין נוהגים לעשות סעודה בכל יום הולדת משום
דבאמת טוב לו שלא נברא משנברא וע"כ לשמחה זו
מה עושה אמנם אצל אומות העולם שאין להם אלא
רק ז' מצוות לא שייך לומר דטוב שלא נברא כיון
שכל הטעם דטוב שלא נברא הוא משום שרבים הם
המצוות אך זה לא שייך באומות העולם שיש להם
רק ז' מצוות ...

## 56) אוצר כל מנהגי ישורון, דף 60

... בקאוונא עיר מולדתי בשנת תרמ"ט (1889)
למספרם רצו אוהבי הרה"ג ר' יצחק אלחנן לחוג
חג יובלו למלאות חמשים שנה לרבנותו גם זה מאן
בדבר ועצור בעדם מלהפיק זממם. ולראובן לבנו, בני
ישראל אחינו, האוהבים לחקות כל מעשה שכניהם
כקוף המחקה בלי דעת בין טוב לרע עושים חג
כשמחת קציר ליום הולדת, ושמחה מה עושה?

## 57) הגאון האדר"ת "תפילת דוד" דף רד

אכן בכל לבי כעסתי על המברכים לברכני ליום
הולדתי ולשמחני בו ומרגלא בפי מעודי שלא
מצאנו שמחת יום הולדת בספרינו הקדושים רק
בלידת פרעה לבד ודבר זה אינו לרוח עם קדוש
המקובל אצלינו ונוח לו שלא נברא משנברא ואם
כן למה נשמח ביום הולדתינו בטרם ידענו שהועלנו
בבריאתנו רק צדיקים יכולים לשמוח כדברי התוס'
ע"ז ה. ד"ה שאלמלא וכו' ...

## 58) מדרש, שמות רבה מח.

... ויום המות מיום הולדו מיתתו יום ליום גדול
מיום לידתו למה שביום שנולד בו אין אדם יודע מה
מעשיו אבל כשמת מודיע מעשיו לבריות הוי יום
המות מיום הולדו אמר ר' לוי משל לשתי ספינות
שהיו פורשות לים הגדול אחת יוצאת מן הלמין
ואחת נכנסת ללמין זו שיוצאת היו הכל שמחין בה
זו שנכנסת לא היו הכל שמחין בה פקח אחד היה שם
אמר חלופי הדברים אני רואה כאן זו שהיא יוצאת
מן הלמין לא היו הכל צריכין לשמוח שאינן יודעין
באיזה פרק היא עומדת ומה ימים מזדווגין לה ומה
רוחות מזדווגות לה וזו שנכנסת ללמין היו הכל
צריכין לשמוח לפי שהם יודעים שנכנסת בשלום
ויוצאה בשלום מן הים כך אדם נולד מונין לו למיתה
מת מונין לו לחיים ועליו אמר שלמה (קהלת ז) ויום
המות מיום הולדו ...

## 59) עשה לך רב, חלק ד:כו

אלא שכל זה נהוג ע"י אותם עמים עובדי עבודה
זרה תוך כדי הקרבת קרבנות לאליליהם ... כמבואר
שם במשנה ונפסק להלכה ברמב"ם ושו"ע כידוע
וכל כוונתנו היתה ללמוד מזה מקור לחגיגות יום
הולדת ... אין נראה לי שום איסור לחוג כיום ימי
הולדת בחוג המשפחה שכן עצם החגיגה היא דבר
מובן והגיוני שכל שנת חיים נוספת שזוכה בה אדם
מעניקה לו ולמקורביו שמחת הלב העמים הקדמונים
ביטאו שמחה זאת בדרכם שלהם בקרבנות לע"ז אבל
אם ירצה אדם מישראל לבטא שמחה זאת בסעודה
הודיה לה' על שזיכהו לשנת חיים נוספת או אדם
חילוני בסתם שמחה הרי שאין כאן שום סרך עבודה
זרה שכן כאמור אין חגיגת יום ההולדת לע"ז ולמה יאסר
לנו לחוג בדרכנו שלנו וכי מפני שהם מתפללים

**40) שמות יב:ב ופירוש רמב"ן**

הַחֹדֶשׁ הַזֶּה לָכֶם רֹאשׁ חֳדָשִׁים רִאשׁוֹן הוּא לָכֶם לְחָדְשֵׁי הַשָּׁנָה:

... וטעם החדש הזה לכם ראש חדשים, שימנו אותו ישראל חדש הראשון, וממנו ימנו כל החדשים שני ושלישי עד תשלום השנה בשנים עשר חדש, כדי שיהיה זה זכרון בנס הגדול, כי בכל עת שנזכיר החדשים יהיה הנס נזכר, ועל כן אין לחדשים שם בתורה, אלא יאמר בחדש השלישי ...

**41) פירוש העמק דבר על שמות יב:ב**

והפי' לכם דוקא החדשה הזה מובחר בשנה כמו שחודש תשרי הוא המובחר במה שנוגע לצרכי העולם משום שבו נברא העולם. וכלל הוא שבאותו יום שנברא אותו דבר מסוגל זה היום גם לדורות להתחזק יותר משום הטעם טבע האש במוש"ק רותח יותר משום שאז נברא וכ"כ הרשב"א בשו"ת סי' תי"ג. ומש"ה בחודש תשרי עיקר דינו של אדם על כל השנה משום שבו ביום נידון אדה"ר כמש"כ הר"ן במס' ר"ה ...

**42) הושע ז:ה ופירוש מצודת דוד**

יוֹם מַלְכֵּנוּ הֶחֱלוּ שָׂרִים חֲמַת מִיָּיִן מָשַׁךְ יָדוֹ אֶת לֹצְצִים:

**יום מלכנו** – ר"ל ביום שמחת מלך ישראל כיום הלידה או יום המלכתו אז נעשו השרים חולים בעבור נאדות מהיין כי הרבו למלאותם לשתיה ונעשו חולים מרבוי השכרות

**43) יחזקאל טז:ד ופירוש מלבי"ם**

וּמוֹלְדוֹתַיִךְ בְּיוֹם הוּלֶּדֶת אֹתָךְ לֹא כָרַּת שָׁרֵּךְ וּבְמַיִם לֹא רֻחַצְתְּ לְמִשְׁעִי וְהָמְלֵחַ לֹא הֻמְלַחַתְּ וְהָחְתֵּל לֹא חֻתָּלְתְּ:

**ומולדותיך** – עתה צייר איך נולדה, שעז"א ומולדותיך, ומה נעשה עמה ביום לדתה, שעז"א ביום הולדת אתך לא כרת שרך – המנהג לעשות להנולד ארבעה תקונים א] שכורתים הטבור, שעד עתה ינק מזונותיו דרך הטבור והיה במדרגות הצומח שינוק מזונו דרך שרשו, וכשנולד כורתים הטבור וקושרים אותו כי מעתה יקח המזון דרך פיו, וכשלא נכרת טבורו הוא עדיין במדרגתו הראשונה, והנמשל שהאומה כאשר תולד להיות גוי מיוחד צריך שתתפרד מן האומה שבאה משם והיתה דבוקה שם בשרשה, אבל את לא כרת שרך – כי עדן היית דבוקה בשורש מעשה הכנענים. ב] אח"כ רוחצים אותו במים להסיר הדמים והגיעול, ובנמשל של האומה, שחכמי לב ירחצו מדותיהם הנשחתות ע"י מי החכמה והדעת שיקבעו בינהם נמוסים טובים ומשפטים ישרים, ואת במים לא רחצת – ג] אחר כך מולחים אותו לחזק הבשר, ד] וחותלים אותו לישר האיברים, כי במעי אמו היה הבשר ספוגי, והאברים כפופים ראשו בין ברכיו. ובנמשל האומה, שישתדלו לחזק האישים הפרטיים בגבורה ואומץ הלב, ולישר

---

את הכלל לשום עליהם ראשים שופטים ושוטרים, עד שיהיה כגוף נצב הקומה אמיץ וחזק ואיבריו מיושרים. וכ"ז לא נעשה לך:

**44) רב צדוק הכהן, פרי צדיק, עת האוכל אות יד**

... ויציאת מצרים נקרא לידה ביחזקאל ומולדותיך ביום הולדת וגו', וכן עד"ה עיין בפרי עץ חיים. וכן אמרו גוי מקרב גוי כעובר במעי אמו ואמרו ז"ל שירת מצרים לשון נקיבה מה שאין כן לעתיד.

**45) ראש השנה יא.**

מאן דאמר בניסן נולדו בניסן מתו. מאן דאמר בתשרי נולדו בתשרי מתו. שנאמר (דברים לא) ויאמר אלהם בן מאה ועשרים שנה אנכי היום. שאין תלמוד לומר היום, ומה תלמוד לומר היום היום מלאו ימי ושנותי, ללמדך שהקדוש ברוך הוא יושב וממלא שנותיהם של צדיקים מיום ליום מחדש לחדש, שנאמר (שמות כג) את מספר ימיך אמלא.

**46) שערי תשובה, אורח חיים תצד**

לפי שדוד המלך ע"ה מת בעצרת והקב"ה ממלא שנותיהם כו', ובודאי בעצרת נולד ומגילת רות נכתבה ליחס דוד

**47) פרי צדיק ל"ג בעומר, אות א**

ולכן קבעו ההלולא ביום פטירת ר' שמעון ב"ר יוחאי שהיה בו תרומות מתרוממות מדרותיו של רבי עקיבא, ומהס"ת נולד ר' שמעון ב"ר יוחאי גם כן ביום זה כמו שהוכיחו בגמרא (קידושין לח.) ומנין שבז' באדר נולד משה כו' שהקדוש ברוך הוא יושב וממלא שנותיהן של צדיקים מיום ליום ...

**48) תהילים ב:ז-ח ופירוש הרה"ק מאפטא זיע"א (הרב אברהם יהושע העשיל)**

אֲסַפְּרָה אֶל חֹק ד' אָמַר אֵלַי בְּנִי אַתָּה אֲנִי הַיּוֹם יְלִדְתִּיךָ: אֲסַפְּרָה אֶל חֹק ד' אָמַר אֵלַי בְּנִי אַתָּה אֲנִי הַיּוֹם יְלִדְתִּיךָ: שְׁאַל מִמֶּנִּי וְאֶתְּנָה גוֹיִם נַחֲלָתֶךָ וַאֲחֻזָּתְךָ אַפְסֵי אָרֶץ:

על הפסוק בתהילים "אני היום ילדתיך שאל ממני ואתנה" מובא משמם של צדיקים כי ביום הולדתו יכול אדם לבקש כל משאלות לבו והקב"ה מבטיחו שיענה להן. ... אך רוב גדולי ישראל המליצו על יום זה כיום של חשבון הנפש ותשובה

**49) ספר חומת אנך (חיד"א) קהלת י', איוב ג**

... דהנה עת הלידה הוא מזל בריא וחזק מאד ... יאבד ויום הולד בו וכו' – אפשר במ"ש המקובלים שהיום שנולד בו האדם מזלו בריא וחזק בכל ...

**50) מדרש שכל טוב מ:כ**

ורוב בני אדם מחבבים תשלום שנתו שהוא כנגד אותו היום שנולד בו ומשמחין בו משתה יום ועושין בו משתה

---

שנותיו של אדם ולא חטא שוב אינו חוטא,

### The Lore of Birthdays (New York, 1952) (30
### by Ralph and Adelin Linton

"The Greeks believed that everyone had a protective spirit or daemon who attended his birth and watched over him in life. This spirit had a mystic relation with the god on whose birthday the individual was born. The Romans also subscribed to this idea.... This notion was carried down in human belief and is reflected in the guardian angel, the fairy godmother and the patron saint.... The custom of lighted candles on the cakes started with the Greeks.... Honey cakes round as the moon and lit with tapers were placed on the temple altars of [Artemis] (moon god) ... Birthday candles, in folk belief, are endowed with special magic for granting wishes.... Lighted tapers and sacrificial fires have had a special mystic significance ever since man first set up altars to his gods. The birthday candles are thus an honor and tribute to the birthday child and bring good fortune"

31) ויקרא יח:ג

כְּמַעֲשֵׂה אֶרֶץ־מִצְרַיִם אֲשֶׁר יְשַׁבְתֶּם־בָּהּ לֹא תַעֲשׂוּ וּכְמַעֲשֵׂה אֶרֶץ־כְּנַעַן אֲשֶׁר אֲנִי מֵבִיא אֶתְכֶם שָׁמָּה לֹא תַעֲשׂוּ וּבְחֻקֹּתֵיהֶם לֹא תֵלֵכוּ:

32) עבודה זרה ח. ופירוש רש"י ורבינו חננאל

משנה: ואלו אידיהן של עובדי כוכבים: קלנדא, וסטרנורא, וקרטיסים, ויום גנוסיא של מלכיהם, ויום הלידה... ויום גנוסיא של מלכיהם, ויום שהומלך בו מלך לפניו אסור, אחריו מותר

ויום הלידה – של מלך עושין כל בני מלכותו יום איד משנה לשנה ומקריבין זבחים.

[יום] גינוסיא של מלכיהם פי' גנוסיא בלשון יון יום הלידה ב) ואוקימ' אלא מאי יום גנוסיא יום שמעמידין בו את המלך

33) שולחן ערוך, יורה דעה קעח

אין הולכין בחוקות העובדי כוכבים (ולא מדמין להם) ולא ילבש מלבוש המיוחד להם ולא יגדל ציצת ראשו כמו ציצת ראשם ולא יגלח מהצדדין ויניח השער באמצע ולא יגלח השער מכנגד פניו מאוזן לאוזן ויניח הפרע ולא יבנה מקומות כבנין היכלות של עבודת כוכבים כדי שיכנסו בהם רבים כמו שהם עושים: הגה אלא יהא מובדל מהם במלבושיו ובשאר מעשיו (שם) וכל זה אינו אסור אלא בדבר שנהגו בו העובדי כוכבים לשם פריצות ... או בדבר שנהגו למנהג ולחוק ואין טעם בדבר דאיכא למיחש ביה משום דרכי האמורי ושיש בו

שמץ עבודת כוכבים מאבותיהם אבל דבר שנהגו לתועלת כגון שדרכן שכל מי שהוא רופא מומחה יש לו מלבוש מיוחד שניכר בו שהוא רופא אומן מותר ללובשו וכן שעושין משום כבוד או טעם אחר מותר ...

### The Laws of Pesach 2002, Rabbi (34
### Avrohom Blumenkrantz, page 206

"We should stop this custom among our children. Make birthday cakes and cookies but do not use candles."

35) כף החיים (פלאגי) לא:כה, משלי כ:כז

אחר ההבדלה כשיכבה זה הנר לא יכבנו בפיו דהמכבה נר בפיו דמו בראשו

נֵר ד' נִשְׁמַת אָדָם חֹפֵשׂ כָּל־חַדְרֵי־בָטֶן:

36) ברכות נז: ותפילה בבוקר

שינה אחד מששים למיתה

מוֹדֶה אֲנִי לְפָנֶיךָ מֶלֶךְ חַי וְקַיָּם. שֶׁהֶחֱזַרְתָּ בִּי נִשְׁמָתִי בְּחֶמְלָה. רַבָּה אֱמוּנָתֶךָ.

אֱלֹקַי. נְשָׁמָה שֶׁנָּתַתָּ בִּי טְהוֹרָה הִיא.

37) פירוש אברבנאל על שמות יב:ב, שולחן ערוך, אורח חיים תקצ"ב:א, מחזור ראש השנה, סדר תקיעת שופר

... ועשתה התחלת השנה בתקופת תשרי, להיות הזמן ההוא התחלת הריון העולם וזריעת ההויות. ולכן נאמר (לקמן כג, טז) "וחג האסיף בצאת השנה", לפי שאז תצא שנה אחת ותכנס שנה אחרת. ולזה תקנו לומר אז: היום הרת עולם. ונהגו לומר כל פעם אחר שתקעו: היום הרת עולם. הַיּוֹם הֲרַת עוֹלָם, הַיּוֹם יַעֲמִיד בַּמִּשְׁפָּט כָּל יְצוּרֵי עוֹלָמִים ...

38) מדרש דברים רבה א:יג

א"ר אלעזר בכ"ה באלול נברא העולם, נמצא אדם הראשון נברא בר"ה שבא ביום הששי.

39) ראש השנה י':

תניא, רבי אליעזר אומר: בתשרי נברא העולם, בתשרי נולדו אבות, בתשרי מתו אבות, בפסח נולד יצחק, בראש השנה נפקדה שרה רחל וחנה, בראש השנה יצא יוסף מבית האסורין, בניסן נגאלו, בתשרי עתידין ליגאל. רבי יהושע אומר: בניסן נברא העולם, בניסן נולדו אבות, בניסן מתו אבות, בפסח נולד יצחק, בראש השנה נפקדה שרה רחל וחנה, בראש השנה יצא יוסף מבית האסורין, בראש השנה בטלה עבודה מאבותינו במצרים, בניסן נגאלו, בניסן עתידין ליגאל.

אדם נופל ביום גינוסיא שלו.

ר' יהושע אומר כשפן גדול היה עמלק, ומה היה
עושה היה מעמדי בני אדם נופל ביום גינוסיא שלו לומר
(ה) לא במהרה אדם נופל ביום גינוסיא שלו,

### 15) מגילה יג:

תנא: כיון שנפל פור בחדש אדר שמח שמחה גדולה,
אמר: נפל לי פור בירח שמת בו משה. ולא היה יודע
שבשבעה באדר מת ובשבעה באדר נולד.

### 16) שבת קנו.

רבי יוחנן אמר: אין מזל לישראל.

### 17) ברכות כח. ופירוש בו יהוידע

ההוא יומא בר תמני סרי שני הוה, אתרחיש ליה ניסא
ואהדרו ליה תמני סרי דרי חיורתא. היינו דקאמר
רבי אלעזר בן עזריה: הרי אני כבן שבעים שנה, ולא
בן שבעים שנה.

שם ההוא יומא בר תמני סרי שני הוה. נראה לי
בס"ד דקדק לומר ההוא יומא ולא אמר ההוא זמנא,
דאפשר אותו היום היה יום הלידה שלו, והיה לו י"ח
שנה שלמים, ולכך הצליח לעשות לו נס זה, דידוע
שיום הלידה יהיה המזל של האדם חזק בו ומוצלח, על
כן נהוגים שכל אדם יעשה יום הלידה יום טוב לעצמו,
והא דנעשה לו בנס שמנה עשר דארי חיוורתא כנגד
שנותיו, להורות שהוא צדיק גמור, שכל י"ח שנותיו
הם טובים בצדקות, והוא איש חי על דרך מה שכתוב
[שמואל ב' כ"ג כ'] ובניהו בן יהוידע בן איש חי,
קרינן חיל וכתיב חי:

### 18) מדרש תנחומא פקודי יא

ר' חנינא אומר בא' באדר היה נגמרה מלאכת
המשכן, למה שהמלאכה שנעשית בקיץ ביום אחד
נעשית בחורף בשני ימים, וכדברי רבי שמואל בר
נחמני שאמר שנעשה המשכן בג' חדשים למה לא
עמד מיד אלא מפני שחשב הקב"ה לערב שמחת
המשכן בשמחת היום שנולד בו יצחק אבינו, לפי
שבאחד בניסן נולד יצחק

### 19) מדרש פסיקתא רבתי ו:ד

... והאלקים שחשב לערב שמחת בית המקדש
בחודש שנולד בו אברהם בירח האתנים (שם מלכים
א' ח' ב') זה חודש תשרי ...

### 20) שבת קנו.

האי מאן דבכוכב יהי גבר נהיר וחכים, משום דספרא
דחמה הוא. האי מאן דבלבנה יהי גבר סביל מרעין,
בנאי וסתיר, סתיר ובנאי, אכיל דלא דיליה ושתי
דלא דיליה, ורזוהי כסיין, אם גנב מצלח. האי מאן
דבשבתאי יהי גבר מחשבתיה בטלין, ואית דאמרי:
כל דמחשבין עליה בטלין. האי מאן דבצדק יהי גבר
צדקן, אמר רבי נחמן בר יצחק: וצדקן במצות. האי

מאן דבמאדים יהי גבר אשיד דמא. אמר רבי אשי:
אי אומנא, אי גנבא, אי טבחא, אי מוהלא. אמר רבה:
אנא במאדים הואי אמר אביי מר נמי עניש וקטיל.
איתמר, רבי חנינא אומר: מזל מחכים, מזל מעשיר,
ויש מזל לישראל. רבי יוחנן אמר: אין מזל לישראל.

### 21) קידושין עב:

כשמת ר' עקיבא נולד רבי, כשמת רבי נולד רב
יהודה, כשמת רב יהודה נולד רבא, כשמת רבא נולד
רב אשי, ללמדך, שאין צדיק נפטר מן העולם עד
שנברא צדיק כמותו
אמר רבי יוחנן: אין צדיק נפטר מן העולם עד שנברא
צדיק כמותו, שנאמר (קהלת א) וזרח השמש ובא
השמש

### 22) מדרש אגדת בראשית סח

... שביום שהחריב נבוכדנצר את הבית נולד
המשיח ...

### 23) מדרש אסתר רבה פתיחא יא

אף ההיא אינה צרה אלא שמחה שבו ביום נולד מנחם

### 24) איכה א:טו

סִלָּה כָל־אַבִּירַי אֲדֹנָי בְּקִרְבִּי קָרָא עָלַי מוֹעֵד לִשְׁבֹּר
בַּחוּרָי גַּת דָּרַךְ אֲדֹנָי לִבְתוּלַת בַּת־יְהוּדָה:

### 25) בית יוסף על טור, אורח חיים תקנד

אך מנהג קדום שהנשים רוחצות ראשון מן המנחה
ולמעלה ביום תשעה באב וזקנים הראשונים הנהיגו
זה ועשו סמך לדבר על מה שאמרו באגדה (פתיחה
לאסתר רבה אות יא ירושלמי ברכות פ"ב ה"ד) כי
המשיח נולד ביום תשעה באב וצריך לעשות זכר
לגואל ולמנחם כדי שלא יתיאשו מן הגאולה

### 26) רמ"א, שולחן ערוך יורה דעה קעט:ב

ולכן נהגו ג"כ להתחיל ללמוד בר"ח כי אע"פ שאין
ניחוש יש סימן במה שהוא יודע שאדם כנגד המזל
לא יעשה ולא יסמוך על הנס אלא שאין לחקור אחר
זה משום תמים תהיה (תשובת רמב"ן סימן רפ"ו)
כמו שנתבאר:

### 27) מועד קטן כח.

רב יוסף, כי הוה בר שיתין עבד להו יומא טבא
לרבנן. אמר: נפקי לי מכרת.

### 28) יומא לח:

רבי חייא בר אבא אמר רבי יוחנן: כיון שיצאו רוב
שנותיו של אדם ולא חטא שוב אינו חוטא,

### 29) נזיר מב., שולחן ערוך, יורה דעה צה:ב

רובא ככולו
רבי חייא בר אבא אמר רבי יוחנן: כיון שיצאו רוב

# SOURCES ON BIRTHDAYS IN JUDAISM

**1) בראשית מ:כ**

וַיְהִי בַּיּוֹם הַשְּׁלִישִׁי יוֹם הֻלֶּדֶת אֶת־פַּרְעֹה וַיַּעַשׂ מִשְׁתֶּה לְכָל־עֲבָדָיו וַיִּשָּׂא אֶת־רֹאשׁ שַׂר הַמַּשְׁקִים וְאֶת־רֹאשׁ שַׂר הָאֹפִים בְּתוֹךְ עֲבָדָיו:

**2) פירוש רש"י על בראשית מ:כ**

יום הלדת את פרעה – יום לידתו וקורין לו יום גינוסיא ולשון הולדת לפי שאין הולד נולד אלא ע"י אחרים שהחיה מילדת את האשה ועל כן החיה נקראת מילדת וכן (יחזקאל טז) ומולדותיך ביום הולדת אותך וכן (ויקרא יג) אחרי הוכבס את הנגע שכיבוסו על ידי אחרים:

**3) פירוש העמק דבר על בראשית מ:כ**

יום הולדת את פרעה – עת שמחת לבו ולעשות לו עונג בכל האפשר:

**4) פירוש אבן עזרא על בראשית מ:יב**

... ויתכן יום הלדת את פרעה כמו היום שנולד בו. כי הנה היום יש מלכים שיעשו משתה ביום תקופת שנתם ויקראו לכל עבדיהם ויתנו להם מתנות ...

**5) פירוש רש"י על שמות ל:טז ופירוש שפתי חכמים**

ונתת אותו על עבודת אהל מועד – ... תשובה לדבר אצל שנות האנשים בשנה אחת נמנו אבל למנין יציאת מצרים היו שתי שנים לפי שליציאת מצרים מונין מניסן כמו ששנינו במסכת ראש השנה ונבנה המשכן בראשונה והוקם בשנייה שנתחדשה שנה באחד בניסן אבל שנות האנשים מניין למנין שנות עולם המתחילין מתשרי נמצאו שני המונים בשנה אחת המנין הראשון היה בתשרי לאחר יום הכפורים שנתרצה המקום לישראל לסלוח להם ונצטוו על המשכן והשני באחד באייר:

ואין יכולים לבוא לכלל שנה אלא עד ראש השנה, וגם אותן שנולדו קודם ראש השנה כשבא ראש השנה באין לכלל שנה:

**6) שמות לח:כו, במדבר ב:לב**

בֶּקַע לַגֻּלְגֹּלֶת מַחֲצִית הַשֶּׁקֶל בְּשֶׁקֶל הַקֹּדֶשׁ לְכֹל הָעֹבֵר עַל־הַפְּקֻדִים מִבֶּן עֶשְׂרִים שָׁנָה וָמַעְלָה לְשֵׁשׁ־מֵאוֹת אֶלֶף וּשְׁלֹשֶׁת אֲלָפִים וַחֲמֵשׁ מֵאוֹת וַחֲמִשִּׁים:
אֵלֶּה פְּקוּדֵי בְנֵי־יִשְׂרָאֵל לְבֵית אֲבֹתָם כָּל־פְּקוּדֵי הַמַּחֲנֹת לְצִבְאֹתָם שֵׁשׁ־מֵאוֹת אֶלֶף וּשְׁלֹשֶׁת אֲלָפִים וַחֲמֵשׁ מֵאוֹת וַחֲמִשִּׁים:

**7) יחזקאל טז:ד**

וּמוֹלְדוֹתַיִךְ בְּיוֹם הוּלֶּדֶת אֹתָךְ לֹא־כָרַּת שָׁרֵּךְ וּבְמַיִם

---

לֹא־רֻחַצְתְּ לְמִשְׁעִי וְהָמְלֵחַ לֹא הֻמְלַחַתְּ וְהָחְתֵּל לֹא חֻתָּלְתְּ:

**8) תהילים ב:ז**

אֲסַפְּרָה אֶל חֹק ד' אָמַר אֵלַי בְּנִי אַתָּה אֲנִי הַיּוֹם יְלִדְתִּיךָ:

**9) ירמיהו כ:יד, איוב ג:א**

אָרוּר הַיּוֹם אֲשֶׁר יֻלַּדְתִּי בּוֹ יוֹם אֲשֶׁר־יְלָדַתְנִי אִמִּי אַל־יְהִי בָרוּךְ:
אַחֲרֵי־כֵן פָּתַח אִיּוֹב אֶת־פִּיהוּ וַיְקַלֵּל אֶת־יוֹמוֹ:

**10) קהלת ז:א**

טוֹב שֵׁם מִשֶּׁמֶן טוֹב וְיוֹם הַמָּוֶת מִיּוֹם הִוָּלְדוֹ:

**11) מדרש שמות רבה מח:א**

"וְיוֹם הַמָּוֶת מִיּוֹם הִוָּלְדוֹ" יוֹם מיתתו של אדם גדול מיום לידתו למה שביום שנולד בו אין אדם יודע מה מעשיו אבל כשמת מודיע מעשיו לבריות הוי יום המות מיום הולדו אמר ר' לוי משל לשתי ספינות שהיו פורשות לים האחת יוצאת מן הלמין ואחת נכנסת ללמין זו שיוצאת היו הכל שמחין בה זו שנכנסת לא היו הכל שמחין בה פקח אחד היה שם אמר חלופי הדברים אני רואה כאן זו שהיא יוצאת מן הלמין לא היו הכל צריכין לשמוח שאינן יודעין באיזה פרק היא עומדת ומה ימים מזדווגין לה ומה רוחות מזדווגות לה וזו שנכנסת ללמין היו הכל צריכין לשמוח לפי שהם יודעים שנכנסת בשלום ויצאה בשלום מן הים כך אדם נולד מונין לו למיתה מת מונין לו לחיים ועליו אמר שלמה (קהלת ז) "ויום המות מיום הולדו"

**12) משנה אבות ה:כא**

הוא היה אומר בן חמש שנים למקרא. בן עשר למשנה. בן שלש עשרה למצות. בן חמש עשרה לתלמוד. בן שמונה עשרה לחופה. בן עשרים לרדוף. בן שלשים לכח. בן ארבעים לבינה. בן חמשים לעצה. בן ששים לזקנה. בן שבעים לשיבה. בן שמונים לגבורה. בן תשעים לשוח.

**13) קהלת ג:ב**

עֵת לָלֶדֶת וְעֵת לָמוּת עֵת לָטַעַת וְעֵת לַעֲקוֹר נָטוּעַ:

**14) ירושלמי, ראש השנה יז:, ילקוט שמעוני חבקוק רמז:תקסד**

ריב"ל אמר עמלק כושפן היה מה היה עושה היה מעמיד בני אדם ביום גינוסיא שלו לומר לא במהרה

## 70) רמב"ם, הלכות דעות ב:ג

ויש דעות שאסור לו לאדם לנהוג בהן בבינונית אלא
יתרחק מן הקצה האחד עד הקצה האחר ... וכן
הכעס מדה רעה היא עד למאד וראוי לאדם שיתרחק
ממנה עד הקצה האחר, וילמד עצמו שלא יכעוס
ואפילו על דבר שראוי לכעוס עליו ...

## 71) של"ה הקדוש, שער האותיות אות ר

מדה רעה וגרועה מדת הכעס, אין רעה בעולם
כרעה זו

## 68) ספר החינוך, מצוה שלח

ואם אולי יכריחנו מחרף מבני אדם להשיב על דבריו,
ראוי לחכם שישיב לו דרך סלסול ונעימות ולא יכעס
הרבה, כי כעס בחיק כסילים ינוח, וינצל עצמו אל
השומעים מחירופיו וישליך המשא על המחרף, זהו
דרך הטובים שבבני אדם:

## 69) אבות ה:יא

ארבע מדות בדעות. נוח לכעוס ונוח לרצות. יצא
שכרו בהפסדו. קשה לכעוס וקשה לרצות. יצא
הפסדו בשכרו קשה לכעוס ונוח לרצות חסיד. נוח
לכעוס וקשה לרצות רשע:

אתקדש ממש. (ס"א אמאי והא אתדכי ואתקדיש)
א"ל תא חזי בשעתא דאיהו עקר קדושה דנפשיה
ושריא באתריה ההוא אל זר דאקרי טמא אסתאב בר
נש וסאיב למאן דקריב בהדיה והיא קדושה עקרת
מניה וכיון דעקרת מניה זמנא חדא כמה דעביד בר
נש עוד לא תיתוב לאתרהא.

### 60) קהלת ט:יז
דִּבְרֵי חֲכָמִים בְּנַחַת נִשְׁמָעִים מִזַּעֲקַת מוֹשֵׁל בַּכְּסִילִים:

### 61) רמב"ם, הלכות דעות ה:ז
תלמיד חכם לא יהא צועק וצווח בשעת דבורו
כבהמות וחיות, ולא יגביה קולו ביותר אלא דבורו
בנחת עם כל הבריות, וכשידבר בנחת שלא
יתרחק עד שיראה כדברי גסי הרוח ...

### 62) תענית ד. ורש"י שם
ואמר רבא: האי צורבא מרבנן דרתח אורייתא הוא
דקא מרתחא ליה, שנאמר (ירמיהו כ"ג) "הלוא כה
דברי כאש נאם ה'" ... אפילו הכי, מיבעי ליה לאיניש
למילף נפשיה בניחותא,
אורייתא מרתחא ליה – שיש לו רוחב לב מתוך
תורתו, ומשים ללבו יותר משאר בני אדם, וקא
משמע לן דחייבין לדונו לכף זכות.

### 63) ספר התניא, אגרות הקודש, פרק כה
והטעם מובן ליודעי בינה לפי שבעת כעסו נסתלקה
ממנו האמונה כי אילו היה מאמין שמאת ה' היתה
זאת לו לא היה בכעס כלל ואף שכן אדם שהוא בעל
בחירה מקללו או מכהו או מזיק בממונו ומתחייב
בדיני אדם ובדיני שמים לרוע בחירתו אעפי"כ על
הניזק כבר נגזר מן השמים והרבה שלוחים למקום

### 64) מדרש ספרי, מטות ה, מדרש ויקרא רבה יג
משה רבינו לפי שהיה בכלל כעס בא לכלל טעות. ר'
אלעזר אומר בג' מקומות בא לכלל כעס ובא לכלל
טעות. כיוצא בו אתה אומר (שם י) ויקצוף על אלעזר
ועל איתמר בני אהרן הנותרים לאמר קודש הוא לכם
מהו אומר מדוע לא אכלתם את החטאת וגו'. כיוצא
בו אתה אומר (במדבר כ) ויאמר אליהם שמעו נא
המורים המן הסלע הזה נוציא לכם מים מהו אומר
וירם משה את ידו ויך את הסלע במטהו פעמים. אף
כאן אתה אומר ויקצוף משה על פקודי החיל שרי
האלפים ושרי המאות הבאים מצבא המלחמה מה
אומר ויאמר אלעזר אל אנשי הצבא הבאים למלחמה.
משה רבינו לפי שבא לכלל כעס בא לכלל טעות.
ויקצוף על אלעזר ועל איתמר וכיון שכעס נתעלמה
ממנו הלכה א"ר הונא בשלשה מקומות כעס משה
ונתעלמה ממנו הלכה ואלו הן בשבת ובכלי מתכות
ואונן בשבת

---

### 65) אורחות צדיקים, שער יב, הכעס
כָּל כַּעֲסָן לֹא יִהְיֶה חָכָם גָּדוֹל, כִּי הַכַּעַס מַבְרִיחַ מִלִּבּוֹ
חָכְמָתוֹ,

### 66) ר' חיים ויטאל, שער רוח הקודש ח:
גם מדת הכעס, מלבד מה שמונעת ההשגה לגמרי,
וכמו שמצינו על פסוק ויקצף משה על אלעזר
ועל איתמר (ויקרא י') וארז"ל כל (הכועס) [אדם
שכועס] אם נביא הוא נבואתו מסתלקת ממנו וכו'
האמנם יתר רעה יש לו מדבר הנז' כמו שנתבאר,
והנה מורי ז"ל היה מקפיד בענין הכעס, יותר מכל
שאר העבירות, אפי' כשהוא כועס בשביל מצוה,
וענין משה כנז"ל, והיה נותן טעם לזה ואומר, כי
הלא כל שאר העבירות אינם פוגמים אלא כל עבירה
ועבירה פוגמת אבר אחד, אבל מדת הכעס פוגמת
כל הנשמה כלה, ומחליף אותה לגמרי, והענין הוא,
כי כאשר יתכעס האדם, הנה הנשמה הקדושה
מסתלקת ממנו לגמרי, ונכנסת במקומה נפש מצד
הקלי' וז"ס מש"ה טורף נפשו באפו וגו' (איוב י"ח)
כי ממש טורף נפשו הקדושה, ועושה אותה טריפה
וממית אותה בעת אפו וכעס, וכמבואר בזוהר בפ'
תצוה דף קפ"ב ע"ב וע"ש כמה מגזים ענין הכעס, עד
שאומר, כי מאן דמשתעי עם הכועס, כאלו משתעי
עם ע"ז עצמה, וע"ש, ואעפ"י שעושה האדם תקונים
לנפשו ותשובה מעולה על כל עונותיו, ומצות רבות
וגדולות, הכל נאבדים ממנו לגמרי, לפי שהרי אותה
הנשמה הקדושה, שעשתה כל המעשים הטובים,
נתחלפה בטמאה, והלכה לה, ... וצריך שיחזור פעם
אחרת, לחזור ולתקן כל התקונים הראשונים שעשה
בתחלה, וכן הוא בכל פעם ופעם שהוא כועס נמצא
כי בעל הכעס אין לו תקנה כלל, כי תמיד הוא ככלב
שב על קיאו, וגם גורם היזק גדול אחר לעצמו, ...
כי מי שהוא בעל כעס, אי אפשר לו, כל ימי היותו
בעל מדה זו, להשיג שום השגה, ואפילו אם יהיה
צדיק בכל שאר דרכיו, לפי שהוא בונה, וסותר כל
מה שבנה, בכל עת שכועס, ... ולא די זה אלא אפי'
כשהייתי מלמד את אחי יצ"ו, ולא היה יודע כפי
רצוני, והייתי מתכעס עמו על הדבר הזה, וגם על
הדבר הזה הזהירני והוכיחני מורי ז"ל במאד מאד ...

### 67) יומא פו
אביי אמר: כדתניא, (דברים ו) ואהבת את ה' אלקיך
שיהא שם שמים מתאהב על ידך, שיהא קורא ושונה
ומשמש תלמידי חכמים, ויהא משאו ומתנו בנחת
עם הבריות, מה הבריות אומרות עליו אשרי אביו
שלמדו תורה, אשרי רבו שלמדו תורה. אוי להם
לבריות שלא למדו תורה, פלוני שלמדו תורה ראו
כמה נאים דרכיו, כמה מתוקנים מעשיו, עליו הכתוב
אומר (ישעיהו מט) ויאמר לי עבדי אתה ישראל אשר
בך אתפאר

## 47) אורחות צדיקים, שער יב, הכעס

לֹא הַקַּפְּדָן מְלַמֵּד (אבות פ״ב מ״ה), כִּי מֵרֹב כַּעֲסוֹ הַתַּלְמִידִים יְרֵאִים מִמֶּנּוּ לִשְׁאֹל סְפֵקוֹתֵיהֶם פֶּן יִכְעַס עֲלֵיהֶם, וַאֲפִלּוּ אִם שׁוֹאֲלִים, אֵין לוֹ לֵב לְפָרֵשׁ לַתַּלְמִידִים כָּל הַצֹּרֶךְ. וְגַם יָשִׁיב לָהֶם דֶּרֶךְ כַּעַס, וּמִתּוֹךְ כָּךְ לֹא יָבִינוּ. וְהַתַּלְמִידִים אֲפִלּוּ שֶׁרַבָּן כּוֹעֵס עֲלֵיהֶם יִשְׁאֲלוּ וִידַקְדְּקוּ וְלֹא יָחוּשׁוּ עַל הַכַּעַס וְלֹא יָרִיבוּ עִם רַבָּן, וַעֲלֵיהֶם דָּרְשׁוּ רַבּוֹתֵינוּ, "וּמֵיץ אַפַּיִם יוֹצִיא רִיב" (משלי ל, לג) – כָּל הַכּוֹעֵס עָלָיו רַבּוֹ פַּעַם אַחַת וּשְׁתַּיִם וְשׁוֹתֵק, זוֹכֶה לְהַבְחִין בֵּין דִּינֵי מָמוֹנוֹת וְדִינֵי נְפָשׁוֹת, וְאָמַר מַר, אֵין לְךָ קָשֶׁה יוֹתֵר מִדִּינֵי מָמוֹנוֹת וְדִינֵי נְפָשׁוֹת (ברכות סג, ב):

## 48) ברכות סג:

כל תלמיד שכועס עליו רבו פעם ראשונה ושניה ושותק זוכה להבחין בין דיני ממונות לדיני נפשות. דתנן, רבי ישמעאל אומר: הרוצה שיתחכם יעסוק בדיני ממונות, שאין לך מקצוע בתורה יותר מהן, שהן כמעין נובע.

## 49) עירובין יג:

מפני מה זכו בית הלל לקבוע הלכה כמותן מפני שנוחין ועלובין היו

## 50) שבת לא.

שוב מעשה בנכרי אחד שבא לפני שמאי, אמר לו: גיירני על מנת שתלמדני כל התורה כולה כשאני עומד על רגל אחת. דחפו באמת הבנין שבידו. בא לפני הלל, גייריה. אמר לו: דעלך סני לחברך לא תעביד זו היא כל התורה כולה, ואידך פירושה הוא, זיל גמור.

## 51) נתיבות עולם, נתיב כעס פרק א

ובפרק קמא דעירובין (י״ג, ב׳) מפני מה זכו בית הילל לקבוע הלכה כמותן מפני שנוחין הן ועלובין הן ... כי אשר הוא בעל הנחה אינו יוצא מן היושר כלל ... שלא היו כבית שמאי שהיו קפדנין, וידוע כי הקפדן מפני גודל כעסו יוצא מן השווי לגמרי, וההלכה הוא הדרך שאינו יוצא לימין ולשמאל כלל רק הולך בשווי ... וזהו מדת ב״ה שהיה להם מדה זאת בכל הנהגתם שלא היו יוצאים מן השווי שהיו נוחים. ואל תאמר כי ב״ש לא היו חכמים, כי אדרבא היו חכמים גדולים וחריפים היו, רק לענין הלכה שהוא הדרך הישר הוא לב״ה מפני שהיו בעלי הנחה מבלי שיצאו מן הסדר. וכן במה שהיו עלובין שונים דבריהם ודברי חבריהם, וכל זה עניני הנחה לגמרי, כי שאר בני אדם כאשר יאמר לו דבר ממהר לכעוס ועולב מי שהעליב אותו, ואילו אצל ב״ה היו בעלי הנחה ולא היו עולבין אף אם העליב אותן. ... ואינם מכת המתגברים על חבריהם והם מכת המנצחים, ואף כי לפי ענין הפלפול הוא בעל טוב מ״מ הוא יוצא מן הסדר, ולענין ההלכה צריך שלא יצא מן הסדר והשווי כלל ...

## 52) ברכות כט:

אמר ליה אליהו לרב יהודה אחוה דרב סלא חסידא: לא תרתח ולא תחטי,

## 53) פסחים קיג:

שלשה הקדוש ברוך הוא אוהבן: מי שאינו כועס ומי שאינו משתכר, ומי שאינו מעמיד על מדותיו.

## 54) שבת פח:

תנו רבנן: עלובין ואינן עולבין, שומעין חרפתן ואינן משיבין, עושין מאהבה ושמחין ביסורין עליהן הכתוב אומר (שופטים ה) ואהביו כצאת השמש בגברתו.

## 55) פסחים קיג:

תנו רבנן: שלשה חייהן אינם חיים: הרחמנין, והרתחנין, ואניני הדעת.

## 56) אורחות צדיקים, שער יב, הכעס

הַכַּעַס מוֹנֵעַ מִמֶּנּוּ מוּסָרִים וְתוֹכָחוֹת, כִּי אֵין אָדָם רַשַּׁאי לְגַלּוֹת לוֹ טָעֻיּוֹתָיו וּדְרָכָיו הַמְכֹעָרִים, כִּי כָּל אָדָם יִפְחַד מִמֶּנּוּ לְהַגִּיד לוֹ עִנְיָנָיו, כִּי הוּא יִרְגַּז עֲלֵיהֶם; וַאֲפִלּוּ אִם יוֹכִיחַ אוֹתוֹ שׁוּם אָדָם, לֹא יְקַבֵּל מִמֶּנּוּ מִתּוֹךְ הַכַּעַס. כְּלָלוֹ שֶׁל דָּבָר, אֵין הַכַּעֲסָן מְקַבֵּל שׁוּם מִדָּה טוֹב אִם לֹא יָסִיר מִלִּבּוֹ הַכַּעַס:

## 57) אורחות צדיקים, שער יב, הכעס

הַכַּעַס מֵבִיא אָדָם לִידֵי מַחֲלֹקֶת. כְּשֶׁהוּא כּוֹעֵס עִם חֲבֵרָיו, יָרִיבוּ עִמּוֹ וְהוּא עִמָּהֶם. וּכְשֶׁיֵּשׁ מַחֲלֹקֶת, יֵשׁ קִנְאָה וְשִׂנְאָה.

## 58) אורחות צדיקים, שער יב, הכעס

הַכַּעֲסָן אֵין לוֹ חֵן בְּעֵינֵי הַבְּרִיּוֹת וְהוּא שָׂנוּא בְּעֵינֵיהֶם, וּמִתּוֹךְ כָּךְ אֵין מַעֲשָׂיו מְקֻבָּלִים בְּעֵינֵי הַבְּרִיּוֹת; וַאֲפִלּוּ אִם יֵשׁ בְּיָדוֹ תּוֹרָה וּמַעֲשִׂים טוֹבִים, אֵין הָעוֹלָם לְמֵדִין מִמֶּנּוּ.

## 59) זוהר, חלק ב, קפב:

ואי תימא הא רוגזא דרבנן. רוגזא דרבנן טב איהו לכל סטרין דהא תנינן דאורייתא אשא איהי ואורייתא קא מרתחא ליה דכתיב (ירמיה כג) הלא כה דברי כאש נאם יי׳. רוגזא דרבנן במלי דאורייתא. רוגזא דרבנן למיהב יקרא לאורייתא וכלא לפולחנא דקב״ה הוי לכך נאמר (דברים ד) כי יי׳ אלקיך אש אוכלה הוא אל קנא. אבל אי במלין אחרנין לאו פולחנא דקב״ה האי בגין דבכל חטאים דקא עביד בר נש לאו איהו כו״ס ממש כהאי ואסיר לקרבא בהדיה דהאי. ואיתימא הא לשעתא הוה דעבר והדר אהדר. לאו הכי דכיון דאעקר דאעקר קדושה דנפשיה מניה ומאתריה וההוא אל זר מקפח ההוא אתר אתתקף ביה ולא שביק ליה. בר כד אתדכי בר נש מכל וכל ועקר ליה לעלמין ולבתר אשתדל לאתקדשא ולאמשכא קדושה עליה. כדין ולוואי דאתקדש. א״ל רבי יוסי

לייסרם ותהיה דעתו מיושבת בינו לבין עצמו כאדם
שהוא מדמה כועס בשעת כעסו והוא אינו כועס ...

### 35) רמב"ם, הלכות דעות ב:ג

ויש דעות שאסור לו לאדם לנהוג בהן בבינונית אלא
יתרחק מן הקצה האחד עד הקצה האחר, והוא גובה
לב, שאין דרך הטובה שיהיה אדם עניו בלבד אלא
שיהיה שפל רוח ותהיה רוחו נמוכה למאד, ולפיכך
נאמר במשה רבינו ענו מאד ולא נאמר ענו בלבד,
ולפיכך צוו חכמים מאד מאד הוי שפל רוח, ועוד
אמרו שכל המגביה לבו כפר בעיקר שנאמר ורם
לבבך ושכחת את ה' אלקיך, ועוד אמרו בשמתא מאן
דאית ביה גסות הרוח ואפילו מקצתה, וכן הכעס
מדה רעה היא עד למאד וראוי לאדם שיתרחק ממנה
עד הקצה האחר, וילמד עצמו שלא יכעוס ואפילו על
דבר שראוי לכעוס עליו ... אמרו חכמים הראשונים
כל הכועס כאילו עובד עבודת כוכבים, ואמרו שכל
הכועס אם חכם הוא חכמתו מסתלקת ממנו ואם נביא
הוא נבואתו מסתלקת ממנו, ובעלי כעס אין חייהם
חיים, לפיכך צוו להתרחק מן הכעס עד שינהיג עצמו
שלא ירגיש אפילו לדברים המכעיסים וזו היא הדרך
הטובה,

### 36) שבת נד:

כל מי שאפשר למחות לאנשי ביתו ולא מיחה נתפס
על אנשי ביתו, באנשי עירו נתפס על אנשי עירו, בכל
העולם כולו נתפס על כל העולם כולו.

### 37) שבת נה.

אמר לו הקדוש ברוך הוא לגבריאל: לך ורשום על
מצחן של צדיקים תיו של דיו, שלא ישלטו בהם
מלאכי חבלה. ועל מצחם של רשעים תיו של דם,
כדי שישלטו בהן מלאכי חבלה. אמרה מדת הדין
לפני הקדוש ברוך הוא: רבונו של עולם, מה נשתנו
אלו מאלו? אמר לה: הללו צדיקים גמורים, והללו
רשעים גמורים. אמרה לפניו: רבונו של עולם, היה
בידם למחות ולא מיחו אמר לה: גלוי וידוע לפני,
שאם מיחו בהם לא יקבלו מהם. (אמר) (מסורת
הש"ס: [אמרה]) לפניו: רבונו של עולם, אם לפניך
גלוי להם מי גלוי?

### 38) זוהר, חלק ב, קפב.

ואי תימא הא רוגזא דרבנן. רוגזא דרבנן טב איהו
לכל סטרין דהא תנינן דאורייתא אשא איהי ואורייתא
קא מרתחא ליה דכתיב (ירמיה כג) הלא כה כה דברי
כאש נאם יי'. רוגזא דרבנן במלי דאורייתא. רוגזא
דרבנן למיהב יקרא לאורייתא וכלא לפולחנא דקב"ה
הוי לכך נאמר (דברים ד) כי יי' אלקיך אש אוכלה
הוא אל קנא. אבל אי במלין אחרנין לאו פולחנא
דקב"ה האי בגין דבכל חטאים דקא עביד בר נש לאו
איהו כו"ס ממש כהאי ואסיר לקרבא בהדיה דהאי.
ואיתימא הא לשעתא הוה דעבר והדר אהדר. לאו

---

הכי דכיון דאעקר קדושה דנפשיה מניה ומאתריה
וההוא אל זר מקפח ההוא אתר אתתקף ביה ולא
שביק ליה. בר כד אתדכי בר נש מכל וכל ועקר
ליה לעלמין ולבתר אשתדל לאתקדשא ולאמשכא
קדושה עליה. כדין ולואי דאתקדש. א"ל רבי יוסי
אתקדש ממש. (ס"א אמאי והא אתדכי ואתקדש)
א"ל תא חזי בשעתא דאיהו עקר קדושה דנפשיה
ושריא באתריה ההוא אל זר דאקרי טמא אסתאב בר
נש וסאיב למאן דקריב בהדיה וההיא קדושה עקרת
מניה וכיון דעקרת מניה זמנא חדא כמה דיעביד בר
נש עוד לא תיתוב לאתרהא

### 39) ויקרא יט:יז ופירוש רמב"ן

לֹא־תִשְׂנָא אֶת־אָחִיךָ בִּלְבָבֶךָ הוֹכֵחַ תּוֹכִיחַ אֶת־עֲמִיתֶךָ
וְלֹא־תִשָּׂא עָלָיו חֵטְא:

### 40) רמב"ם, הלכות דעות א:ד

... כיצד לא יהא בעל חמה נוח לכעוס ולא כמת
שאינו מרגיש אלא בינוני, לא יכעוס אלא על דבר
גדול שראוי לכעוס עליו כדי שלא יעשה כיוצא בו
פעם אחרת ...

### 41) מסכת דרך ארץ זוטה, פרק ג

והוי שפל רוח בפני כל האדם לאנשי ביתך יותר מכל
אדם ואם תתרעם ותלחם עם ביתך סופך גיהנם

### 42) מסכת כלה רבתי, פרק חמישי

והוי ... עלוב לכל אדם ועם נשי ביתך יותר
מכל אדם ...

### 43) גיטין ז.

א"ר אבהו: לעולם אל יטיל אדם אימה יתירה בתוך
ביתו, שהרי אדם גדול הטיל אימה יתירה בתוך ביתו
והאכילוהו דבר גדול ... אלא בקשו להאכילו דבר
גדול, ומאי ניהו? אבר מן החי.

### 44) אורחות צדיקים, שער יב, הכעס

הַכַּעֲסָן הוּא כָּבֵד עַל בָּנָיו – בֵּיתוֹ, הַשּׁוֹמְעִין תָּמִיד
כַּעֲסוֹ וְתִלְנָתוֹ, וְקָרוֹב הַדָּבָר לוֹ לָבוֹא לִידֵי תַּקָּלָה,
מִפְּנֵי שֶׁמַּטִּיל אֵימָה יְתֵרָה בְּתוֹךְ בֵּיתוֹ, כְּמוֹ הַהוּא
מַעֲשֶׂה דְּרַבִּי חֲנִינָא בֶּן גַּמְלִיאֵל, אֲשֶׁר בִּקְשׁוּ בְּנֵי
בֵיתוֹ לְהַאֲכִילוֹ אֵיבָר מִן הַחַי (גיטין ז, א). הַכַּעֲסָן אֵינוֹ
מַעֲבִיר עַל מִדּוֹתָיו וְאֵינוֹ מוֹחֵל, אַךְ הוּא נוֹקֵם וְנוֹטֵר
תָּמִיד:

### 45) אבות ב:ה

... ולא הקפדן מלמד ....

### 46) מסכת כלה רבתי, פרק חמישי

אמר אבא אליהו זכור לטוב לעולם אין תורה
מתפרשת אלא למי שאינו קפדן אף אני איני נגלה
אלא למי שאינו קפדן

עליהם? אם אתה מחזיר האהל למקומו מוטב, ואם
לאו יהושע בן נון תלמידך משרת תחתיך. והיינו
דכתיב ושב אל המחנה.

### (28) דברים כט:כג-כז

וְאָמְרוּ כָּל הַגּוֹיִם עַל מֶה עָשָׂה ד' כָּכָה לָאָרֶץ הַזֹּאת
מֶה חֳרִי הָאַף הַגָּדוֹל הַזֶּה: וְאָמְרוּ עַל אֲשֶׁר עָזְבוּ אֶת
בְּרִית ד' אֱלֹקֵי אֲבֹתָם אֲשֶׁר כָּרַת עִמָּם בְּהוֹצִיאוֹ אֹתָם
מֵאֶרֶץ מִצְרָיִם: וַיֵּלְכוּ וַיַּעַבְדוּ אֱלֹהִים אֲחֵרִים וַיִּשְׁתַּחֲווּ
לָהֶם אֱלֹהִים אֲשֶׁר לֹא יְדָעוּם וְלֹא חָלַק לָהֶם: וַיִּחַר אַף
ד' בָּאָרֶץ הַהִוא לְהָבִיא עָלֶיהָ אֶת כָּל הַקְּלָלָה הַכְּתוּבָה
בַּסֵּפֶר הַזֶּה: וַיִּתְּשֵׁם ד' מֵעַל אַדְמָתָם בְּאַף וּבְחֵמָה
וּבְקֶצֶף גָּדוֹל וַיַּשְׁלִכֵם אֶל אֶרֶץ אַחֶרֶת כַּיּוֹם הַזֶּה:

### (29) Time Magazine, December 15, 2010, "The Bright Side of Anger — It Motivates Others"

### (30) משנה שבת יג:ג

הקורע בחמתו ועל מתו. וכל המקלקלין. פטורין.
והמקלקל על מנת לתקן. שעורו כמתקן:

### (31) שבת קה:

הקורע בחמתו ובאבלו ועל מתו חייב ... אלא חמתו
אחמתו קשיא חמתו אחמתו נמי לא קשיא, הא רבי
יהודה. הא רבי שמעון. הא רבי יהודה, דאמר מלאכה
שאין צריכה לגופה חייב עליה, הא רבי שמעון,
דאמר מלאכה שאין צריכה לגופה פטור עליה. אימר
דשמעת ליה לרבי יהודה במתקן, במקלקל מי שמעת
ליה? אמר רבי אבין: **האי נמי מתקן הוא, דקעביד נחת
רוח ליצרו. וכהאי גוונא מי שרי?** והתניא, רבי שמעון
בן אלעזר אומר משום חילפא בר אגרא, שאמר
משום רבי יוחנן בן נורי: **המקרע בגדיו בחמתו,
והמשבר כלי בחמתו, והמפזר מעותיו בחמתו יהא
בעיניך כעובד עבודה זרה** שכך אומנתו של יצר הרע,
היום אומר לו עשה כך ולמחר אומר לו עשה כך. עד
שאומר לו עבוד עבודה זרה והולך ועובד ... זה יצר
הרע. לא צריכא, **דקא עביד למירמא אימתא אאינשי
ביתיה.**

### (32) רמב"ם, הלכות שבת ח:ח

... אבל החובל בחבירו אף על פי שנתכוון להזיק
חייב מפני נחת רוח יצרו שהרי נתקררה דעתו ושככה
חמתו והרי הוא כמתקן ...

### (33) פירוש רש"י על שבת קה:

מי שרי והא תניא כו' – אלמא לאו מתקן הוא, שמלמד
ומרגיל את יצרו לבא עליו.

### (34) רמב"ם, הלכות דעות ב:ג

... ואם רצה להטיל אימה על בניו ובני ביתו או
על הציבור אם היה פרנס ורצה לכעוס עליהן כדי
שיחזרו למוטב יראה עצמו בפניהם שהוא כועס כדי

---

אֶל מֹשֶׁה רָאִיתִי אֶת הָעָם הַזֶּה וְהִנֵּה עַם קְשֵׁה עֹרֶף
הוּא: וְעַתָּה הַנִּיחָה לִּי וְיִחַר אַפִּי בָהֶם וַאֲכַלֵּם וְאֶעֱשֶׂה
אוֹתְךָ לְגוֹי גָּדוֹל: וַיְחַל מֹשֶׁה אֶת פְּנֵי ד' אֱלֹקָיו וַיֹּאמֶר
לָמָה ד' יֶחֱרֶה אַפְּךָ בְּעַמֶּךָ אֲשֶׁר הוֹצֵאתָ מֵאֶרֶץ מִצְרַיִם
בְּכֹחַ גָּדוֹל וּבְיָד חֲזָקָה:

### (23) דברים יד:א, תפילת שחרית, ברכות לפני שמע

בָּנִים אַתֶּם לַד' אֱלֹקֵיכֶם לֹא תִתְגֹּדְדוּ וְלֹא תָשִׂימוּ
קָרְחָה בֵּין עֵינֵיכֶם לָמֵת:
... אָבִינוּ אָב הָרַחֲמָן. הַמְרַחֵם. רַחֵם עָלֵינוּ. וְתֵן בְּלִבֵּנוּ
בִּינָה לְהָבִין ...

### (24) שמות לב:ז, יט-כ

וַיְהִי כַּאֲשֶׁר קָרַב אֶל הַמַּחֲנֶה וַיַּרְא אֶת הָעֵגֶל וּמְחֹלֹת
וַיִּחַר אַף מֹשֶׁה וַיַּשְׁלֵךְ מִיָּדָו אֶת הַלֻּחֹת וַיְשַׁבֵּר אֹתָם
תַּחַת הָהָר: וַיִּקַּח אֶת הָעֵגֶל אֲשֶׁר עָשׂוּ וַיִּשְׂרֹף בָּאֵשׁ
וַיִּטְחַן עַד אֲשֶׁר דָּק וַיִּזֶר עַל פְּנֵי הַמַּיִם וַיַּשְׁקְ אֶת בְּנֵי
יִשְׂרָאֵל:

### (25) שמות לב:ז-יא

וַיְדַבֵּר ד' אֶל מֹשֶׁה לֶךְ רֵד כִּי שִׁחֵת עַמְּךָ אֲשֶׁר הֶעֱלֵיתָ
מֵאֶרֶץ מִצְרָיִם: סָרוּ מַהֵר מִן הַדֶּרֶךְ אֲשֶׁר צִוִּיתִם עָשׂוּ
לָהֶם עֵגֶל מַסֵּכָה וַיִּשְׁתַּחֲווּ לוֹ וַיִּזְבְּחוּ לוֹ וַיֹּאמְרוּ אֵלֶּה
אֱלֹקֶיךָ יִשְׂרָאֵל אֲשֶׁר הֶעֱלוּךָ מֵאֶרֶץ מִצְרָיִם: וַיֹּאמֶר ד'
אֶל מֹשֶׁה רָאִיתִי אֶת הָעָם הַזֶּה וְהִנֵּה עַם קְשֵׁה עֹרֶף
הוּא: וְעַתָּה הַנִּיחָה לִּי וְיִחַר אַפִּי בָהֶם וַאֲכַלֵּם וְאֶעֱשֶׂה
אוֹתְךָ לְגוֹי גָּדוֹל: וַיְחַל מֹשֶׁה אֶת פְּנֵי ד' אֱלֹקָיו וַיֹּאמֶר
לָמָה ד' יֶחֱרֶה אַפְּךָ בְּעַמֶּךָ אֲשֶׁר הוֹצֵאתָ מֵאֶרֶץ מִצְרַיִם
בְּכֹחַ גָּדוֹל וּבְיָד חֲזָקָה:

### (26) ברכות סג:

(שמות ל"ג) וְדִבֶּר ה' אֶל מֹשֶׁה פָּנִים אֶל פָּנִים. אמר
רבי יצחק: אמר לו הקדוש ברוך הוא למשה: משה,
אני ואתה נסביר פנים בהלכה. איכא דאמרי, כך אמר
לו הקדוש ברוך הוא למשה: כשם שאני הסברתי לך
פנים כך אתה הסבר פנים לישראל, והחזר האהל
למקומו. (שמות ל"ג) ושב אל המחנה וגו'. אמר
רבי אבהו, אמר לו הקדוש ברוך הוא למשה: עכשיו
יאמרו הרב בכעס ותלמיד בכעס, ישראל מה תהא
עליהם? אם אתה מחזיר האהל למקומו מוטב, ואם
לאו יהושע בן נון תלמידך משרת תחתיך. והיינו
דכתיב ושב אל המחנה.

### (27) רמב"ם, הקדמה לשמונה פרקים, פרק ד

(שמות ל"ג) וְדִבֶּר ה' אֶל מֹשֶׁה פָּנִים אֶל פָּנִים. אמר
רבי יצחק: אמר לו הקדוש ברוך הוא למשה: משה,
אני ואתה נסביר פנים בהלכה. איכא דאמרי, כך אמר
לו הקדוש ברוך הוא למשה: כשם שאני הסברתי לך
פנים כך אתה הסבר פנים לישראל, והחזר האהל
למקומו. (שמות ל"ג) ושב אל המחנה וגו'. אמר
רבי אבהו, אמר לו הקדוש ברוך הוא למשה: עכשיו
יאמרו הרב בכעס ותלמיד בכעס, ישראל מה תהא

**12) אבות ה:יא**

ארבע מדות בדעות. נוח לכעוס ונוח לרצות. יצא שכרו בהפסדו. קשה לכעוס וקשה לרצות. יצא הפסדו בשכרו קשה לכעוס ונוח לרצות חסיד. נוח לכעוס וקשה לרצות רשע:

**13) רמב"ם, הקדמה לשמונה פרקים, פרק ד**

... וחטאו, עליו השלום, הוא שנטה לצד אחד מקצוות ממעלות המדות, והוא הסבלנות, כאשר נטה לצד הרגזנות באמרו (במדבר כ' י'), "שמעו נא המורים", דקדק עליו השם יתברך, שיהיה אדם כמוהו כועס לפני עדת ישראל במקום שאין ראוי בו הכעס ...

**14) עירובין סה:**

אמר רבי אילעאי: בשלשה דברים אדם ניכר: בכוסו, ובכיסו, ובכעסו.

**15) אורחות צדיקים, שער יב, הכעס**

הכעס גורם עזות לאדם, ומחמת הכעס לא יכנע וגם לא יודה על האמת.

**16) גיטין לו:**

תנו רבנן: הנעלבין ואינן עולבים, שומעין חרפתן ואין משיבין, עושין מאהבה ושמחין ביסורין, עליהן הכתוב אומר: (שופטים ה') ואוהביו כצאת השמש בגבורתו.

**17) סנהדרין ז**

אמר רב הונא: האי תיגרא דמיא לצינורא דבידקא דמיא, כיון דרווח רווח. אביי קשישא אמר: דמי לגודא דגמלא, כיון דקם קם.... טוביה דשמע ואדיש, חלפוה בישתיה מאה.

**18) מסילת ישרים, פרק יא**

הנה יש הרגזן שאמרו עליו, "כל הכועס כאילו עובד עבודה זרה", והוא הנכעס על כל דבר שיעשה נגד רצונו ומתמלא חמה, עד שכבר לבו בל עמו ועצתו נבערה, והנה איש כזה כדאי להחריב עולם מלא אם יהיה יכולת בידו, כי אין השכל שולט בו כלל, והוא סר טעם ממש ככל החיות הטורפות, ועליו נאמר (איוב יח), "טורף נפשו באפו הלמענך תעזב ארץ", והוא קל ודאי לעבור כל מיני עברות שבעולם ... ויש כעסן רחוק מזה, והוא שלא על כל דבר אשר יבואהו שלא כרצונו אם קטן ואם גדול יבער אפו, אך בהגיעו להרגיז – ירגז ויכעס כעס גדול, והוא שקראוהו חז"ל (אבות ה), "קשה לכעוס וקשה לרצות", וגם זה רע ודאי, כי כבר יכולה לצאת תקלה רבה מתחת ידו בזמן הכעס, ואחר כך לא יוכל לתקן את אשר עותו.

ויש כעסן פחות מזה שלא יכעס על נקלה, ואפילו כשיגיע לכעוס יהיה כעסו קטן ולא יסור מדרכי

---

השכל, אך עודנו ישמר עברתו, והנה זה ההפסד יותר מהראשונים שזכרנו, ואף גם זאת ודאי שלא הגיע להיות נקי, כי אפילו זהיר איננו עדיין, כי עד שהכעס עושה בו רשם, לא יצא מכלל כעסן. ויש עוד פחות מזה, והוא, שקשה לכעס וכעסו לא להשחית ולא לכלה, אלא כעס מועט, וכמה זמנו? – רגע ולא יותר, דהיינו, משעה שהכעס מתעורר בו בטבע עד שגם התבונה תתעורר כנגדו, והוא מה שאמרו חז"ל (שם) "קשה לכעוס ונוח לרצות". הנה זה חלק טוב ודאי, כי טבע האדם מתעורר לכעס, ואם הוא מתגבר עליו שאפילו בשעת הכעס עצמו לא יבער הרבה, ומתגבר עליו שאפילו הכעס הקל לא יעמוד בו זמן גדול אלא יעבר וילך, ודאי שראוי לשבח הוא, ואמרו ז"ל (חולין פט), "תולה ארץ על בלימה" (איוב כו) – "אין העולם מתקיים אלא בשביל מי שבולם את עצמו בשעת מריבה", והיינו שכבר נתעורר טבעו בכעס והוא בהתגברותו בולם פיו. אמנם מדתו של הלל הזקן עולה על כל אלה, שכבר לא היה מקפיד על שום דבר ואפילו התעוררות של כעס לא נעשה בו, זהו ודאי הנקי מן הכעס מכל וכל. והנה אפילו לדבר מצוה הזהירונו ז"ל שלא לכעס, אפילו הרב עם תלמידו והאב עם בנו ולא שלא ייסרם, אלא ייסרם ויסרם, אך מבלי כעס, כי אם להדריך אותם בדרך הישרה, והכעס שיראה להם, יהיה כעס הפנים ולא כעס הלב (שבת קה). ואמר שלמה (קהלת ז), "אל תבהל ברוחך לכעוס" וגו'. ואומר (איוב ה), "כי לאויל יהרג כעש". ואמרו ז"ל (עירובין סה), "בשלשה דברים האדם נכר – בכוסו בכיסו בכעסו":

**19) של"ה הקדוש, שער האותיות אות ר**

מדה רעה וגרועה מדת הכעס, אין רעה בעולם כרעה זו:

**20) בראשית ד:ה**

ואל-קין ואל-מנחתו לא שעה ויחר לקין מאד ויפלו פניו:

**21) מדרש בראשית רבה לא:ב**

דבר אחר קץ כל בשר, כתיב (איוב לה) מרוב עשוקים יזעיקו ישוע מזרוע רבים, מרוב עשוקים יזעיקו, אלו הנעשקים, ישועו מזרוע רבים, אלו העושקים, אלו רבים על אלו, ואלו רבים על אלו, אלו רבים על אלו בחימוס ממון ואלו רבים על אלו בחימוס דברים, עד שנתחתם גזר דינם ולפי שהיו שטופים בגזל נימוחו מן העולם.

**22) שמות לב:ז-יא**

וידבר ד' אל-משה לך-רד כי שחת עמך אשר העלית מארץ מצרים: סרו מהר מן-הדרך אשר צויתם עשו להם עגל מסכה וישתחוו-לו ויזבחו-לו ויאמרו אלה אלהיך ישראל אשר העלוך מארץ מצרים: ויאמר ד'

# SOURCES ON ANGER IN JUDAISM

## 1) משנה אבות ב:י'
רבי אליעזר אומר ... ואל תהי נוח לכעוס.

## 2) רבינו יונה על
ואל תהי נוח לכעוס – ידוע כי מדת הכעס היא רעה עד מאד, אך טבע בני אדם להיות נמשך אחריה, על כן אמר, אחר שעל כרחך פעמים תכעוס, תזהר שלא תהא נוח לכעוס ...

## 3) נדרים כב:
אמר רבה בר רב הונא: כל הכועס אפי' שכינה אינה חשובה כנגדו ... ר' ירמיה מדיפתי אמר: משכח תלמודו ומוסיף טיפשות ... רב נחמן בר יצחק אמר: בידוע שעוונתיו מרובין מזכיותיו....

## 4) שבת קה:
שאמר משום רבי יוחנן בן נורי: המקרע בגדיו בחמתו, והמשבר כליו בחמתו, והמפזר מעותיו בחמתו יהא בעיניך כעובד עבודה זרה שכך אומנתו של יצר הרע, היום אומר לו עשה כך ולמחר אומר לו עשה כך. עד שאומר לו עבוד עבודה זרה והולך ועובד.

## 5) מסילת ישרים, פרק יא
"כָּל הַכּוֹעֵס כְּאִלּוּ עוֹבֵד עֲבוֹדָה זָרָה", וְהוּא הַנִּכְעָס עַל כָּל דָּבָר שֶׁיֵּעָשֶׂה נֶגֶד רְצוֹנוֹ וּמִתְמַלֵּא חֵמָה, עַד שֶׁכְּבָר לִבּוֹ בַּל עִמּוֹ וַעֲצָתוֹ נִבְעָרָה, וְהִנֵּה אִישׁ כָּזֶה כְּדַאי לְהַחֲרִיב עוֹלָם מָלֵא אִם יִהְיֶה אִם יְכֹלֶת בְּיָדוֹ, כִּי אֵין הַשֵּׂכֶל שׁוֹלֵט בּוֹ ...

## 6) שבת קה:
אמר רבי אבין: מאי קראה (תהילים פא) לא יהיה בך אל זר ולא תשתחוה לאל נכר, איזהו אל זר שיש בגופו של אדם הוי אומר זה יצר הרע.

## 7) סוכה נב.
אתא ההוא סבא, תנא ליה: כל הגדול מחבירו יצרו גדול הימנו.

## 8) זוהר, חלק ב קפב.
ברוגזיה ממש ידע ליה בר נש וישתמודע מאן איהו אי ההיא נשמתא קדישא נטר בשעתא דרוגזוי (אתי עליה) דלא יעקר לה מאתרהא בגין למשרי תחותה ההוא אל זר דא איהו בר נש דקא יאות. דא איהו עבדא דמאריה דא איהו גבר שלים. ואי ההוא בר נש לא נטיר לה ואיהו עקר קדושה דא עלאה מאתריה למשרי באתריה סטרא אחרא ודai דא איהו בר נש דמריד במאריה ואסיר לקרבא בהדיה ולאתחברא

עמיה ודא איהו (איוב יח) טורף נפשו באפו. איהו טריף ועקר נפשיה בגין רוגזיה ואשרי בגויה אל זר ועל דא כתיב חדלו לכם מן האדם אשר נשמה באפו דההיא נשמתא קדישא טריף לה וסאיב לה בגין אפו. אשר נשמה אחלף באפו. כי במה נחשב הוא. כו"ס אתחשיב ההוא בר נש. ומאן דאתחבר עמיה ומאן דאשתעי (ס"א דאשתתף) בהדיה כמאן אתחבר בכו"ס ממש מאי טעמא בגין דכו"ס ממש שמש שארי בגויה. ולא עוד אלא דעקר קדושה עלאה כו"ס אל זר. מה אל זר כתיב ביה (ויקרא יט) אל תפנו אל האלילים כגוונא דא אסיר לאסתכלא באנפוי ...

## 9) ספר חסידים תתשכו
בשעה שאדם כועס אל יתסכל אדם בו, כי עם ראיית עינים מלאך רע עומד וממהר לנקום על צרור, ועוד קשה לשכחה שמשכח תלמודו

## 10) רמב"ם, הלכות דעות ב:ג
אמרו חכמים הראשונים כל הכועס כאילו עובד עבודת כוכבים, ואמרו שכל הכועס אם חכם הוא חכמתו מסתלקת ממנו ואם נביא הוא נבואתו מסתלקת ממנו, ובעלי כעס אין חייהם חיים, לפיכך צוו להתרחק מן הכעס עד שינהיג עצמו שלא ירגיש אפילו לדברים המכעיסים וזו היא הדרך הטובה, ודרך הצדיקים הן עלובין ואינן עולבין שומעים חרפתם ואינם משיבין עושין מאהבה ושמחים ביסורים, ועליהם הכתוב אומר ואוהביו כצאת השמש בגבורתו.

## 11) ויקרא יט:יז ופירוש רמב"ן
לֹא־תִשְׂנָא אֶת־אָחִיךָ בִּלְבָבֶךָ הוֹכֵחַ תּוֹכִיחַ אֶת־עֲמִיתֶךָ וְלֹא־תִשָּׂא עָלָיו חֵטְא:
לא תשנא את אחיך בלבב – בעבור שדרך השונאים לכסות את שנאתם בלבם כמו שאמר (משלי כו כד) בשפתיו ינכר שונא, הזכיר הכתוב בהווה:
ואמר הוכח תוכיח את עמיתך – ... והנכון בעיני, כי "הוכח תוכיח", כמו והוכיח אברהם את אבימלך (בן אשית כא כה) ויאמר הכתוב, אל תשנא את אחיך בלבב בעשותו לך שלא כרצונך, אבל תוכיחנו מדוע ככה עשית עמדי, ולא תשא עליו חטא לכסות שנאתו בלבו ולא תגיד לו, כי בהוכיחך אותו יתנצל לך, או ישוב ויתודה על חטאו ותכפר לו ואחרי כן יזהיר שלא תנקום ממנו ולא תטור בלבב מה שעשה לך, כי יתכן שלא ישנא אותו אבל יזכור החטא בלבו, ולפיכך יזהירנו שימחה פשע אחיו וחטאתו מלבו ואחרי כן יצוה שיאהב לו כמוהו:

רוחו העגום, שאין ספק שהוא חלק נכבד ברפואת
המחלות, מכ"מ כיון שלעצם המחלה אין רפואה
בכך אין להתיר איסורים, ור' מתיא בהא עצמו חולק
והתיר מפני שחושב עליו שהוא רפואה אף על פי
שבאמת אינו רפואה כלל, מכ"מ הא גופא שחושב
עליו שהוא רפואה מקיל לו קצת ומש"ה התיר ר'
מתיא, ... והנה לדבריו הקדושים שכ' דלא התירה
תורה היא כהלכתא בלא טעמא דהיכן מצינו זה
דלא התירה תורה, דכיון דרפואות האלה רפואות
גמורות הם ומועילות לחולה זה ומותר להתרפאות
ע"י א"כ מנ"ל דפקו"נ כזה אינו דוחה איסור תורה,
אבל לשון הרמב"ם בפיה"מ שם וז"ל וחכמים סוברים
כי אין עוברים על המצוות אלא ברפואה בלבד ר"ל
בדברים המרפאים בטבע, והוא דבר אמתי הוציאו
הדעת והנסיון הקרוב לאמת, אבל להרפאות בדברים
המרפאין בסגולתן אסור כי כוחם חלוש אינו מצד
הדעת ונסיונו רחוק והיא טענה חלושה מן הטועה
(בתוי"ט מן הטוען) הנה אמר לנו רבינו מילתא
בטעמא, שכללי רפואה גמורה הם שתים שהוציאו

הדעת ור"ל שעצם חכמת הרפואה ולמוד הרפואה
צריך שיקבע שהגיון הלב והדעת קובע שכח רפואה
זו מועילה למחלה זאת, שנית שנסיון התרופה תהי'
אמיתית ור"ל שיש הרבה תרופות שכללי המדע
אומרים שהם מרפאים אבל הנסיון במציאות נותן
תמונה אחרת וזה כמה פעמים מצד המקבלים כי אין
הגופים מקבלים תרופות כאלה, אבל שני כללים אלה
יתכנו בדרך כלל ברפואות טבעיות.
אבל ברפואות סגוליות היות שמצד כללי המדע אין
יכולים לקבוע כוחם הרב ברפואה ורק באומדן דעת
סגולי ע"כ הם בגדר כוחם חלוש כלשון הרמב"ם,
ושנית שנסיונו רחוק והיא טענה חלושה מן הטוען
שכן הם מרפאים, כי בדרך כלל דברים אלה שהם
סגולים הגם שלפעמים מרפאים מכ"מ לא נעשה
מהם רציפות של נסיון וע"ז אין הנסיון אמיתי, ונהי
דמותר לרפואות בהם מכ"מ בכזה לא הותר לדחות
איסור תורה, א"כ אין זה כהלכתא בלא טעמא ואולי
גם הכפו"ת כיוון לזה אלא שקיצר במובן ...

שהוא דרך טבע אבל בדבר שהוא דרך סגולה לא.
והראיה דתנן בשלהי יומא מי שנשכו כלב שוטה אין
מאכילין אותו מחצר כבד שלו ור' מתיא בן חרש
מתיר וכתב הרמב"ם בפירוש המשנה ואין הלכה
כר' מתיא ו' חדש במה שהתיר להאכיל לאדם ביום
צום הכפורים מחצר כבד כלב שוטה הנשוך שזה
אינו מועיל אלא בדרך סגולה וחכמים סוברין שאין
עוברין על המצות אלא ברפואה לבד ר"ל בדברים
המרפאים דרך טבע וכו' עכ"ל ומשמע דאע"ג אין
ספק בסגולה זו שכבר הוחזקה שוודאי תועיל אפ"ה
כל שאינו רפואה דרך טבע אסרו חכמים לעבור על
דת משום רפואה בדרך סגולה וא"כ דון מינה לנ"ד כי
האף נימא דמילתא כדנא אתמחי שזה הכותב לנ"ד זו מננא
ומצלא מסמא דמותא אף מ"מ כיון שהוא בדרך סגולה
אין לכותבה בשבת ולחלל שבת במלאכה גמורה

ואע"ג דאשכחן דהתירו לצאת בקמיעא מומחה
וביצת התרנגול וכיוצא שכל אלו סגולות מ"מ
לא התידו איסור תורה שכל אלו אין בהן איסור
דתבנן שאינו מוציא כדרך המוציאין וכמו שביאר
יפה בתשובותיו חדשות מעתה בלשונות הרמב"ם
סימן קנ"ג העלב הרדב"ז דעת הרמב"ם הרפואות
הסגולות אינם רפואה ואפילו ספק רפואה אין בהם
לחלל שבת באיסור תורה או לאכול האסורים מן
התורה ע"ש באודך וא"כ בנ"ד לא שרי לכתוב סגולה
זו להציל ממות אשר סם לו

... אכן ראיתי להרב אדמת קדש ח"א י"ד סי' ו'
שכתב בנידונו אי שרי להאכיל תרנגולת נבילה שהוא
סגולה לשוטה והוכיח שם דהרמב"ן והרשב"א פליגי
על הרמב"ם ולא שאני להו בין כשהרפואה בדרך
סגולה לכשהיא בדרך רפואה בטבע וכתב דהלכתא
כוותייהו והיתיר בנ"ד. וכן ראיתי להרב אחיו בספר
פרי הארץ ח"ג סי' נ' מי"ד כתיבת יד שגם הוא התיר
בנדון זה והעד העיד דרבני שאלוניקי עובדא להתיר
וא"כ לכאורה נראה דשרי בנ"ד כיון דכבר אתמחי
בסגולה זו וכבר מפורסם דכמה נפשות ניצולו מן
המיתה בזה דצריך לעמוד בזה יפה ולברר דעת הרשב"א
והרמב"ן.

### 75) שו"ת חתם סופר חלק ב יורה דעה סימן שלט

ע"ד כהן שיש לו חולי נכפה ר"ל מסוכן מאוד לפעמים
נופל באחת הפחתים ובא באש ובמים ונמצא בספר
שיתן ידו ליד ערל מת ויאמר לחש קח ממני החולי
שאינו מזיק לך ולי אתה מטיבו וכבר ניסה א' רפואה
זו ונתרפא ועתה נפשו בשאלתו אם הכהן מותר
לסמוך לטמא עצמו במגע על מת ערל.

הנה כיון שיש סכנת נפשות בהחולי אם הי' הרפואה
בדוקה ואתמחי גברא וקמיעא פשוט שאין לך דבר
שעומד בפני פקו"נ =פקוח נפש= אך מסתפק מעלתו
שנראה לו שאין הרפואה בדוקה כ"כ אי יש לסמוך
על הספק.

לכאורה אין אי' דאוריי' על הספק ... הדרן להנ"ל
אם יארע יום שמת עליו מת ישראל בשכונתו באופן

---

שנטמא באותו יום ושוב יש לסמוך ארש"י ור"ת
ורא"ם וראב"ד ומצורף לזה אידך דרא"מ דעכו"ם אין
בו איסור מגע ויכול לסמוך במקום ס' סכנה ...

### 76) שו"ת ובחרת בחיים פז (ר' שלמה קלוגר)

הנה הציקתני רותי לא אוכל ארמה על חיול שבת
אשר משפטה כאש בוער בקרב' על הוראה רעה
ומקולקלת אשר נעשה בקהלתכם בשבת העבר אשר
הירה מורה אחר לחלל שנת בחלול אחר חלול לכתוב
בשבת קויטל וש'ס'ע יהודי עתר מג' פרסאות שהוא
דאורייתא ובסוס'ם של יהורדם אשר בדעתם היה למעט
בכמה מלאכות ולשלוח ע"י נכרי והוסיף עוד חטא
על פשע ששלח שני אנשים יהודים לשני מקומות
עם פדיוניות והנה האמת הוראה הזה מקולקלת
מתחילתו מאוד מאוד כי אף דבדין זה פשוט פקוח
נפש דוחה שבת אך לא היתר רק כרפואה שבדרך
הטבע ואף בזה שיהיה מומחה ידוע בדוק ומנוסה
אגל בדרך נסי ותפלה לא היתר בשום אופן אפילו
יהיה המתפלל כרחכ"ר לא ניתן שבת לדחות עבור
זה אפילו במלאכה דרבנן וכ"ש דאורייתא

... סוף דבר המורה הזה חילל שבת בכמה דברים
וכהן אם יחזור המורה לרעה הזה מהוראתו ויתודה
ברבים ששגגה

היה בידו ולא יוסיף כן, הרי טוב. ואם לאו ידעו שכל
הוראותיו המה מקולקלים והמה כתחיכה דאיסורא
ממש ואל יסמכו עליו בשום הוראה ונא להודיעני מי
המורה הזה אשר ראה על ככה כי לא אחשה ולא אתן
שינה לעיני ותנומה לעפעפי עד אפרסם קלונו בפני
כל המדינה. והשם יודע כי לא לכבודי אני מדבר ולא
לכבוד בית אבא ...

### 77) שו"ת שואל ומשיב תליתאה א:קצד

בדיעבד אפשר לשלוח טלגרף בשבת ע"י עכו"ם
שצדיק יתפלל

### 78) שו"ת שבט הלוי ה:נה

... עיקר שאלתו בענין כשרותם של התרופות
ההומיאופתיות לימות השנה ולימי הפסח.

הנה היסוד בהלכה זו אם זו תרופה טבעית או
סגולית, ואם היא סגוליות אם גם בתרופות סגוליות
יש הכלל של פקו"נ שדוחה כל האיסורים בודאן
וכמ"ש בספקין, ידוע משנתינו דיומא פ"ג ע"א מי
שנשכו כלב שוטה אין מאכילין אותו מחצר כבד
שלו ור' מתיא בן חרש מתיר, ופליגי אבות העולם
רש"י ורמב"ם דדעת רש"י דמחלוקתם אם היא
רפואה גמורה דלדעת ת"ק אינו רפואה גמורה אף
על פי שהרופאים רגילים לתתו, ולר' מתיא רפואה
גמורה היא ...

מבואר מדברי המאירי שהאיסור לת"ק מפני שבאמת
אינו רפואה כלל, אף על פי שהההמון נהגו בו, פי'
ועי"ז משקיט קצת פחד החולה ומשפיע גם על מצב

### 70) תפארת ישראל על יומא משנה ח:ו, שדי חמד

מחצר כבד שלו – דאין רפואה זו בדוקה, ואע"ג דכל ספק נפשות להקל היינו במרפא בטבע אבל זו רק רפואה בסגולה היא, כמ"ש בפי' משניות לרמב"ם ולהכי כל שאינו ברור רפואתו אסור:

### 71) רמ"א, שולחן ערוך, יורה דעה, קנה:ג, מגן אברהם על שולחן ערוך, אורח חיים שכח

מותר לשרוף שרץ או שאר דבר איסור ולאכלו לרפואה אפילו חולה שאין בו סכנה ... וכל חולה שמאכילין איסור צריכים שתהא הרפואה ידועה או על פי מומחה (שם כלל נ"ט) ואין מתירין שום דבר איסור לחולה אם יוכל לעשות הרפואה בהיתר כמו באיסור

... דבעינן שתהא הרפואה ידועה או ע"פ מומחה

### 72) שו"ת הרשב"א ד:רמה

יכול אדם לצאת בקמיע בשבת, בין בצוארו בין בזרועו אחד חולה שיש בו סכנה, ואחד חולה שאין בו סכנה. כך שמעתי מפי ה"ר אהרן ז"ל. ועוד אמר: שכותבין כל קמיע, אפי' בשבת, לחולה שיש בו סכנה, או ליולדת, היכא דאינהו תבעי, ליתובי דעתייהו. אף על פי שאין אנו יודעים אם הוא מומחה, אם לאו. אבל אם אינם תובעים, אלא שאמר חכם אחד: יש לי קמיע א', שמועיל לאותו חולי. אפשר שאין כותבין אותו בשבת מספק, אא"כ ידע דאמחי קמיע, או אמחי גברא, שרוצה לכתוב אותו קמיע..

### 73) פרי מגדים על שולחן ערוך, אורח חיים שכח

ומה שכבת שהרפואה ידועה צ"ע נמי ספק פיקוח נפש להקל ... י"ל דמיירי בחולה שאין סכנה ...

### 74) שו"ת ברכי יוסף אורח חיים שא:ו (חיים יוסף דוד אזולאי)

מעשה באיש אחד שמצא סגולה אחת בספר כ"י מאדם גדול מהראשונים למי ששתה סם המות לכתוב לו ותכף מקיא האדם וחוזר לבריאותו ואירע כמה פעמים שאיזה נער או מר נפש בכעסו שתה סם המות וזה האיש כתב קמיעא זו ועשה והצליח שהקיאו אותו הבריאו ויהי היום ליל ש"ק אירע שנערה ישראלית שתתה סם המות והתחילו לה דבקי מיתה ובאו אצל האיש הלז בליל שבת וקם וכתב הקמיעא לנערה ותכף הקיאה ועמדה על בוריה וביום השבת נודע בעיר כל אשר נעשה ולעזה עליו מדינה שחילל שבת בשאט נפש וכתב ונתן בידה, והוא השיב דפיקוח נפש דוחה שבת ואת"ל שחטא אי עבר אדאורייתא או אדרבנן.

והנה לפום ריהטא היה נראה דלא שפיר עבד דאע"ג דהלכה רווחא דמחללין השבת בשביל חולה שיש בו סכנה לעשות לו רפואה מ"מ היינו דווקא ברפואה

הגוים בהא ק"ל כיון דיש בה משום רפואה אין בה משום דרכי האמורי ושריא אבל רפואה דהיא דרך סגולה ויש בה איסור דאורייתא מצד כגון אכילת בהמה טמאה בכה"ג ק"ל להתרפאות ברפואה שהיא דרך סגולה כיון באכילתה איסור דאורייתא זה נ"ל ליישב דברי הרמב"ם.

### 68) פירוש המשניות של הרמב"ם על משנה ח:ו

ואין הלכה כרבי מתיא בן חרש בזה שהוא מתיר להאכיל לאדם הכבד של כלב שוטה כשנשך, כי זה אינו מועיל אלא בדרך סגולה. וחכמים סוברים כי אין עוברין על המצות אלא ברפואה בלבד, ר"ל בדברים המרפאין בטבע והוא דבר אמיתי הוציאו הדעת והנסיון הקרוב לאמת. אבל להתרפאות בדברים שהם מרפאים בסגולתן אסור, כי כחם חלוש אינו מצד הדעת ונסיונו רחוק והיא טענה חלושה מן הטועה, וזה העיקר דעהו וזכרהו כי הוא עיקר גדול.

### 69) שו"ת רדב"ז ה:קנג

...ועיקר דברי הרב צל"ע דכיון שהוא מודה שמרפא בסגולה אמאי אין מאכילין ליתובי דעתיה כדאמרינן גבי סומא יולדת שחברותיה מדליקין לה את הנר בשבת אפי' על ידי ספק ספקא של פקוח נפש דוחין כל המצות דכתיב "וחי בהם" ולא שימות בהם ובשלמא לפירש"י ז"ל שכתב ואף על פי שנהגו ברפואה זו אינה רפואה גמורה להתיר לו איסור בהמה טמאה על כך איכא למימר דאע"ג דהתירו ספק נפשות הנ"מ בדבר שרפואתו ידועה ודאי דכיון שהדבר ידוע שדבר זה מועיל לחולי זה מאכילין אותו אפי' שהחולי הוא ספק נפשות דספק נפשות דוחה אבל לא ספק תרופה והטעם שאם היו מתירין ספק רפואה היו באין לחלל שבת בדברים שלא יועילו ולא יצילו כהבלי הנשים והטפשים וכן לענין להאכיל דברים הטמאים. אבל לדברי הרב קשה שנראה מלשונו שהם מרפאים אלא שרפואתם בסגולה והיה אפשר לומר שמפני טעם זה השמיט אותו מהפסק שלא ראינו שכתב דין מי שנשכו כלב שוטה לא בהלכות יום הכפורים ולא בהלכות מאכלות אסורות ... וליכא למימר דס"ל דנשיכת כלב שוטה לא הוי סכנתא כאשר כתב ר"ת ... ויש לתרץ דעת הרב ז"ל דס"ל דרפואות הסגולות אינם רפואה כלל ואפי' ספק רפואה אין בהם לחלל בהם שבת באיסור תורה או לאכול דברים האסורים מן התורה וכן יש לדקדק ממה שכתב פרק י"ט מהלכות שבת יוצאין בכל דבר שתולין אותו משום רפואה והוא שיאמרו הרופאים שהוא מועיל ולא כתב שהוא מרפא ... הרי שאין הרב מסכים לרפואות הסגולות ומש"ה דעתיה ואי משום יתוב דעתיה של נשוך מה נשתנה דין הכלב שהוא בשר הכלב ליכא יישוב דעת /ואם יודע/ אדרבא נפשו קצה בו ויוסיף בחולי כנ"ל:

הַיּוֹם וּבְכָל יוֹם וָיוֹם מֵעַזֵּי פָנִים. וּמֵעַזּוּת פָּנִים. מֵאָדָם
רָע. מֵיֵצֶר רָע. מֵחָבֵר רָע. מִשָּׁכֵן רָע. מִפֶּגַע רָע. מֵעַיִן
הָרָע. וּמִלָּשׁוֹן הָרָע. מִדִּין קָשֶׁה. וּמִבַּעַל דִּין קָשֶׁה. בֵּין
שֶׁהוּא בֶן בְּרִית. וּבֵין שֶׁאֵינוֹ בֶן בְּרִית

### 60) שולחן ערוך, אורח חיים קמא:ו ומשנה ברורה שם

יכולים לקרות ב' אחים זה אחר זה והם אחר האב
ואין מניחים אלא בשביל עין הרע ואפי' אם א' הוא
השביעי וא' הוא המפטיר לא יקראו השני בשמו
משום עין הרע (מהרי"ל):

(יח) יכולים לקרות וכו'. פירוש מן הדין אין שום
חשש איסור (יז) וע"כ אם קראוהו וכבר עלה לא ירד
אך לכתחלה אין מניחים לקרות משום עין הרע: (יט)
בשביל עין הרע. אין נ"מ בין אחים מן האב (יח)
או מן האם ואפילו אומרים שאין מקפידים על עין
הרע שמחמירין אפילו על עם בנו בנו משום עינא
בישא (יט) ובמקום הצורך יש להתיר עם בן בנו:

### 61) פתחי תשובה יורה דעה קט"ז

...ועיין תשובת אדוני פז ס' כ"ה ס' ל"ד שכתב דיכול
לקרות שני בנים בשם אחד בין מת אחד או שניהם
חיים ושם במשמעות כתב דמ"ל יש לחוש משום עין
הרע ...

### 62) שולחן ערוך, אורח חיים סב:ג

אם יש שני חתנים יחד מברכים ברכת חתנים אחת
לשניהם: הגה ואפי' לא היו החתנים ביחד אלא שהיה
דעתו על שניהם כמו שנתבאר בי"ד סי' רס"ה לענין
מילה וי"א דאין לברך לב' חתנים ביחד משום עין
הרע (הגהות מיי' פ"י דאישות) וכן נוהגין לעשות
לכל א' חופה בפני עצמו ולברך לכל א' אבל לאחר
הסעודה מברכין להרבה חתנים ביחד אם אכלו יחד:

### 63) שו"ת יביע אומר חלק ד, אבן העזר סימן י

נשאלתי מבחור בן תורה מישיבת פורת יוסף פעה"ק
ירושלים ת"ו, בענין צוואת ר"י החסיד ששני אחים
לא ישאו ב' אחיות, ובהיות שהוצע לו שידוך כזה
שהוא מתאים מכל הבחינות, נפשו לשאול הגיעה אם
יש מקום להקל בזה.

... בספר חסידים (סי' תעז), שני אחים הנשואים
שתי אחיות, אחד מהם ימות, או לא יצליחו, לכך
לא ישא, ואם נעשה הדבר כך אחד מהם יגרש את
אשתו. והנוב"ת (אה"ע סי' עט) הקשה ע"ז מברכות
(מד), עיר אחת היתה בא"י וגופנית שמה שהיו בה
שמונים זוגות אחים כהנים נשואים לשמונים זוגות
אחיות כהנות. ע"ש.
וסיים, שהוא"ל וגם רב חסדא ורמי בר חמא ומר
עוקבא בר חמא עשו מעשה כן (וכמ"ש בברכות
מד), בודאי שאין לחוש. ע"ש. ובכנה"ג אה"ע (סי'
סב הגב"י אות ד) כ' שראינו רבים רבים ב' אחים נשואים ב'
אחיות, שלא עלה זיווגם יפה. והביאו החיד"א בשו"ת
יוסף אומץ (סי' לז אות ב). ע"ש. ובספרו ברית עולם

---

(סי' תעז) כתב, שאע"פ שבברכות מד מוכח שלא
היו חוששים לכך, י"ל דשאני בזה"ז שגברה הסטרא
אחרא של עין הרע, כשם שנמצא להיפך שבזמן הש"ס
היה סכנה בזוגות ובזה"ז אין קפידא בדבר כלל.
ע"ש. ולפע"ד אדרבה בזה"ז יש להקל מבזמן הש"ס,
וכמו שמצינו בכמה עניני רוח רעה שבטלו בזה"ז,
וכמ"ש התוס' חולין (קז:) גבי רוח רעה דשיבתא. וכן
במרדכי (פ' המוציא יין). ובס' ים של שלמה (פרק כל
הבשר). וה"נ לענין עין הרע שאין לחוש כ"כ בזה"ז,
ודלא קפיד לא קפדי בהדיה.... מ"מ ראה בעיר אחת
שלא הקפידו ע"ז, וחכם העיר לא מיחה, ואף הוא
אמר דלא קפיד לא קפדי בהדיה. ע"ש.

### 64) שו"ת אגרות משה, אבן העזר חלק ג:כו

... בענין עין הרע ודאי יש לחוש אבל אין להקפיד
הרבה כי בדברים כאלו הכלל מאן דלא קפיד לא
קפדין בהדיה, כהא דמצינו בזוגות בפסחים דף ק"י.

### 65) משנה יומא ח:ו

... מי שנשכו כלב שוטה, אין מאכילין אותו מחצר
כבד שלו, ורבי מתיא בן חרש מתיר ...

### 66) פירוש רש"י על משנה ח:ו

מי שאחזו בולמוס – חולי האוחז מחמת רעבון, עיניו
כהות והוא מסוכן למות, וכשמראיתו חוזרת בידוע
שנתרפא. אין מאכילין מחצר כבד שלו – ואף על פי
שנוהגין הרופאים ברפואה זו אינה רפואה גמורה
להתיר לו איסור בהמה טמאה על כך.
ורבי מתיא בן חרש מתיר – קסבר רפואה גמורה היא.

### 67) מהר"ם בן חביב, תוספת יום הכיפורים, יומא פג.

מי שנשכו כלב שוטה כו' – ופרש"י ואף על פי
שנוהגין הרופאים כו'. וק"ל מ"ש רש"י בטעמא
דרבנן דסברי דאינה רפואה גמורה דמשמעות דברים
הללו רצה לומר דרפואה זו לפעמים מעלה ארוכה
ולפעמים אינה מעלה ארוכה נמצא דאינה רפואה
גמורה ולפיכך אסרוה חכמים וזה תימה בעיני
רכינן דיש פעמים דמעלה ארוכה למה לא נאכיל
אותו משום ספק והלא קיימא לן ספק נפשות דוחה
שבת החמורה כ"ש בשאר האיסורין ... ומשמע לי
דכל רפואה טבעית שרגילין לעשות אע"פ שהיא
ספק רפואה יכולים להאכיל לחולה אף שהוא דבר
איסור או שצריכין לחלל שבת לעשות אותה רפואה
מחללים עליו השבת דספק נפשות להקל ... ומכל
זה נראה דמתרפאים גם ברפואות שהם מרפאין דרך
סגולה וזה סותר למה שפסק כחכמים ראין מאכילין
למי שנשכו כלב שוטה מחצר כבד שלו לפי שהיא
רפואה דרך סגולה ואינה טבעית וכיוצא בזה הקשה
מרי חמי בעץ החיים יע"ש ויראה דיש לחלק בין
רפואה לרפואה דסגולה דלית בה איסור מן
התורה כההנו דספ' דשבת דליכא למיחש בה משום
איסורא דאורייתא שצד עצמה אלא משום חוקות

### 45) שו"ת הרשב"א חלק א' סימן קסז

ולענין מה שבא בשאלותיך אם מותר לעשות צורת אריה בלא לשון חרותה על טס של כסף או של זהב לרפואה? ... אני אומר על חשש ראשון דאין דין איסור עשייה בזה.... ואי משום דרכי האמורי האמת כמו שאמרת. שכל שיש בו משום רפואה וידוע לרופאים שהוא כן אין בו משום דרכי האמורי. ויתר מזה נראה שכל שלא נאסר בגמרא באותן המנויין בדרכי האמורי אין לנו לאסרן.

### 46) רמב"ם, הלכות תפילין ה:ד

מנהג פשוט שכותבים על המזוזה מבחוץ כנגד הריוח שבין פרשה לפרשה שדי ואין בזה הפסד לפי שהוא מבחוץ, אבל אלו שכותבין מבפנים שמות המלאכים או שמות קדושים או פסוק או חותמות הרי הן בכלל מי שאין להם חלק לעולם הבא, שאלו הטפשים לא די להם שבטלו המצוה אלא שעשו מצוה גדולה שהיא יחוד השם של הקב"ה ואהבתו ועבודתו כאילו הוא קמיע של הניית עצמן כמו שעלה על לבם הסכל שזהו דבר המהנה בהבלי העולם.

### 47) שבת סא.

איזהו קמיע מומחה? כל שריפא, ושנה, ושלש. אחד קמיע של כתב, ואחד קמיע של עיקרין. אחד חולה שיש בו סכנה ואחד חולה שאין בו סכנה,

### 48) רמב"ם, הלכות שבת יט:יד

יוצאה האשה באבן תקומה ובמשקל אבן תקומה שנתכוין ושקלו לרפואה ולא אשה עוברה בלבד אלא אפילו שאר הנשים שמא תתעבר ותפיל ויוצאין בקמיע מומחה ואי זה הוא קמיע מומחה זה שריפא לשלשה בני אדם או שעשהו אדם שריפא שלשה בני אדם בקמיעין אחרים ואם יצא בקמיע שאינו מומחה פטור מפני שהוציאו דרך מלבוש וכן היוצא בתפילין פטור:

### 49) שולחן ערוך, יורה דעה קעט:יב

מותר להתרפאות בקמי"ע אפי' יש בהם שמות וכן מותר לישא קמיעין שיש בהם פסוקי' ודוקא להגן שלא יחלה אבל לא להתרפאות בהם מי שיש לו מכה או חולי אבל לכתוב פסוקים בקמיעים אסור:

### 50) בראשית מב:ה ורש"י שם

וַיָּבֹאוּ בְּנֵי יִשְׂרָאֵל לִשְׁבֹּר בְּתוֹךְ הַבָּאִים כִּי־הָיָה הָרָעָב בְּאֶרֶץ כְּנָעַן:

בתוך הבאים – מטמינין עצמן שלא יכירום, לפי שצוה להם אביהם שלא יתראו כולם בפתח אחד, אלא שיכנס כל אחד בפתחו, כדי שלא תשלוט בהם עין הרע שכולם נאים וכולם גבורים:

### 51) מדרש, בראשית רבה צא:ו

ויאמר לבניו למה תתראו אמר יעקב לבניו אתם

---

גבורים אתם נאים אל תכנסו בשער אחד ואל תעמדו במקום אחד שלא תשלוט בכם עין הרע

### 52) במדבר כד:ב ופירוש רש"י

וַיִּשָּׂא בִלְעָם אֶת־עֵינָיו וַיַּרְא אֶת־יִשְׂרָאֵל שֹׁכֵן לִשְׁבָטָיו וַתְּהִי עָלָיו רוּחַ אֱלֹקִים:

וישא בלעם את עיניו – בקש להכניס בהם עין רעה.

### 53) זוהר, חלק א, סח:

מה כתיב בבלעם. (במדבר כד ד) "ונאם הגבר שתום העין". דעינא בישא הוה ליה. ובכל אתר דהוה מסתכל ביה הוה אמשיך עליה רוח מחבלא.

### 54) משנה אבות ב:יא

רבי יהושע אומר עין הרע. ויצר הרע. ושנאת הבריות. מוציאין את האדם מן העולם:

### 55) פירוש רבינו יונה על משנה אבות ב:יא

ר' יהושע אומר, עין הרע. פירושו מי שאינו שמח בחלקו ועויין את חברו העשיר ממנו, מתי יעשר עושר גדול כמוהו והוא גורם רע לעצמו ולחברו. כאשר אמרו חכמי הטבע, החומד מכל אשר לרעהו אויר עולה מן המחשבה ההיא ושורף את הדברים שעויין בהם בעינו הרע, גם קרבו ישרף אחר שמתאוה לדברים שאין יכולת להיות מצוי בידו, והמחשבה ההיא מקללקלת גופו כי יתקצר רוחו ומוציאתו מן העולם. וזהו עין הרע שאמר ר' יהושע. וראיה לזה הפי' על שאמר כאן עין הרע בלשון זכר שזהו העוין הרע. ולמעלה אמר, עין רעה שפירשונה על מדת הכילות שלא כדברי מקצת המפרשים. ויצר הרע ושנאת הבריות. כמשמעו. מוציאין את האדם מן העולם:

### 56) בבא בתרא ב: ורש"י שם

אסור לאדם לעמוד בשדה חבירו בשעה שהיא עומדת בקמותיה.
אסור לאדם שיעמוד כו' – שלא יזיקנו בעין רעה.

### 57) בבא בתרא קיח.

התם עצה טובה קא משמע לן, דאיבעי ליה לאיניש לאיזדהורי מעינא בישא. והיינו דקאמר להו יהושע, דכתיב: (יהושע י"ז) ויאמר אליהם יהושע אם עם רב אתה עלה לך היערה, אמר להו: לכו והחבאו עצמכם ביערים שלא תשלוט בכם עין רע,

### 58) פסחים נ:

המשתכר בקנים ובקנקנים אינו רואה סימן ברכה לעולם. מאי טעמא? כיון דנפיש אפחזייהו שלטא בהו עינא.

### 59) סידור עדות מזרח, תפילת השחר

יְהִי רָצוֹן מִלְּפָנֶיךָ ד' אֱלֹקַי וֵאלֹקֵי אֲבוֹתַי שֶׁתַּצִּילֵנִי

ולבוא מתוכם לכפירה גמורה, שיחשוב כל טובתו ורעתו וכל אשר יקרהו שהוא דבר מקרי, לא בהשגחה מאת בוראו, ונמצא יוצא בכך מכל עקרי הדת. על כן, כי חפץ השם בטובתנו, ציונו להסיר מלבנו מחשבה זו ולקבוע בלבבינו כי כל הרעות והטוב מפי עליון תצאנה לפי מעשה האדם אם טוב ואם רע,

**31) שולחן ערוך, יורה דעה קעט:ג**

האומר פתי נפלה מפי או מקלי מידי או בני קורא לי מאחורי או שצבי הפסיקו בדרך או שעבר נחש מימינו או שועל משמאלו ולמי שאירע לו אחד מאלו עושה ניחוש ממנו שלא לצאת לדרך או שלא להתחיל במלאכה וכן המנחשים בחולדה ובעופות ובכוכבים וכן האומר אל תתחיל לגבות ממני שחרית הוא מוצאי שבת הוא מוצאי ר"ח הוא וכן האומר שחוט תרנגול שקרא כעורב ותרנגולת זו שקראה כתרנגול אסור: הגה י"א אם אינו אומר הטעם למה מצוה לשחוט התרנגולת אלא אומר סתם שחטו תרנגולת זו מותר לשחטה כשקראה כתרנגול (ב"י בשם הר"א והוא בתשו' מהרי"ל סימן קי"ח) וכן הוא המנהג:

**32) שולחן ערוך, יורה דעה קעט:ו**

מי שנשכו עקרב מותר ללחוש עליו ואפילו בשבת ואע"פ שאין הדבר מועיל כלום הואיל ומסוכן הוא התירו כדי שלא תטרף דעתו עליו:

**33) שולחן ערוך, יורה דעה קעט:ח**

הלוחש על המכה או על החולה ורוקק ואחר כך קורא פסוק מן התורה אין לו חלק לעוה"ב ואם אינו רוקק איסורא מיהא איכא ואם יש בו סכנת נפשות הכל מותר: הגה וי"א דכל זה אינו אסור אלא כשקורא הפסוק בלשון הקדש אבל בלשון לעז לא (רש"י בשם רבו) ומיהא ברוקק טוב ליזהר בכל ענין בפרט אם מזכירין השם שאין לו חלק לעוה"ב (כן משמע מהטור לדעת ר"י) :

**34) שולחן ערוך, יורה דעה קעט:ט**

תינוק שנפגע אין קורין עליו פסוק ואין מניחין עליו ס"ת:

**35) במדבר יז:ט-יד**

וַיְדַבֵּר ד' אֶל־מֹשֶׁה לֵּאמֹר: הֵרֹמּוּ מִתּוֹךְ הָעֵדָה הַזֹּאת וַאֲכַלֶּה אֹתָם כְּרָגַע וַיִּפְּלוּ עַל־פְּנֵיהֶם: וַיֹּאמֶר מֹשֶׁה אֶל־אַהֲרֹן קַח אֶת־הַמַּחְתָּה וְתֶן־עָלֶיהָ אֵשׁ מֵעַל הַמִּזְבֵּחַ וְשִׂים קְטֹרֶת וְהוֹלֵךְ מְהֵרָה אֶל־הָעֵדָה וְכַפֵּר עֲלֵיהֶם כִּי־יָצָא הַקֶּצֶף מִלִּפְנֵי ד' הֵחֵל הַנָּגֶף: וַיִּקַּח אַהֲרֹן כַּאֲשֶׁר דִּבֶּר מֹשֶׁה וַיָּרָץ אֶל־תּוֹךְ הַקָּהָל וְהִנֵּה הֵחֵל הַנֶּגֶף בָּעָם וַיִּתֵּן אֶת־הַקְּטֹרֶת וַיְכַפֵּר עַל־הָעָם: וַיַּעֲמֹד בֵּין־הַמֵּתִים וּבֵין הַחַיִּים וַתֵּעָצַר הַמַּגֵּפָה: וַיִּהְיוּ הַמֵּתִים בַּמַּגֵּפָה אַרְבָּעָה עָשָׂר אֶלֶף וּשְׁבַע מֵאוֹת מִלְּבַד הַמֵּתִים עַל־דְּבַר־קֹרַח:

---

**36) משנה שבת ו:י'**

משנה. יוצאין בביצת החרגול. ובשן של שועל. ובמסמר מן הצלוב. משום רפואה. דברי רבי מאיר. וחכמים אומרים אף בחול אסור. משום דרכי האמורי:

**37) שבת סז.**

כל דבר שיש בו משום רפואה אין בו משום דרכי האמורי. הא אין בו משום רפואה יש בו משום דרכי האמורי

**38) שבת סז.**

כולהו אית בהו משום דרכי האמורי, לבר מהני: מי שיש לו עצם בגרונו מביא מאותו המין ומניח ליה על קדקדו, ולימא הכי: חד חד נחית בלע, בלע נחית חד חד אין בו משום דרכי האמורי.

**39) מורה נבוכים ג:לז**

ואל יקשה עליך מה שהתירו מהם, כ"מסמר הצלוב ושן השועל", כי הדברים ההם בזמן ההוא היו חושבים בהם שהוציא אותם הנסיון והיו 'משום רפואה'

**40) שבת סא.**

אחד קמיע של כתב, ואחד קמיע של עיקרין

**41) תוספתא שבת ד:ט**

איזה קמיע מומחה כל שרפא ושנה ושלש אחד קמיע של כתב ואחד קמיע של עקרין יוצאין בו ואצ"ל שנכפה אלא אפי' שלא יכפה אין צריך לומר דבר שיש בו סכנה אלא אפי' דבר שאין בו סכנה [וקושרו] ומתירו בשבת ובלבד שלא יתננו לתוך השיר או לתוך הטבעת ויצא בו מפני מראית העין קמיע שאין מומחה אע"פ שאין יוצאין בו בשבת מטלטלין אותו בשבת:

**42) שבת סא.**

קושר ומתיר אפילו ברשות הרבים, ובלבד שלא יקשרנו בשיר ובטבעת ויצא בו ברשות הרבים משום מראית העין.

**43) ירושלמי, שבת לו.**

יוצאין בקמיע מומחה בין בכתב בין בעשבים. ובלבד שלא יתננו לא בשיר ולא בטבעת.

**44) שבת סא:**

איבעיא להו: קמיעין יש בהן משום קדושה או דילמא: אין בהן משום קדושה? למאי הילכתא אילימא לאצולינהו מפני הדליקה תא שמע: הברכות והקמיעין, אף על פי שיש בהן אותיות ומעניינות הרבה שבתורה אין מצילין אותן מפני הדליקה, ונשרפים במקומם.

### 23) שמות כב:יז, ויקרא כ:כז, דברים יח:ט-יב

מְכַשֵּׁפָה לֹא תְחַיֶּה:

וְאִישׁ אוֹ-אִשָּׁה כִּי-יִהְיֶה בָהֶם אוֹב אוֹ יִדְּעֹנִי מוֹת יוּמָתוּ בָּאֶבֶן יִרְגְּמוּ אֹתָם דְּמֵיהֶם בָּם:

כִּי אַתָּה בָּא אֶל-הָאָרֶץ אֲשֶׁר- ד' אֱלֹקֶיךָ נֹתֵן לָךְ לֹא-תִלְמַד לַעֲשׂוֹת כְּתוֹעֲבֹת הַגּוֹיִם הָהֵם: לֹא-יִמָּצֵא בְךָ מַעֲבִיר בְּנוֹ-וּבִתּוֹ בָּאֵשׁ קֹסֵם קְסָמִים מְעוֹנֵן וּמְנַחֵשׁ וּמְכַשֵּׁף: וְחֹבֵר חָבֶר וְשֹׁאֵל אוֹב וְיִדְּעֹנִי וְדֹרֵשׁ אֶל-הַמֵּתִים: כִּי-תוֹעֲבַת ד' כָּל-עֹשֵׂה אֵלֶּה וּבִגְלַל הַתּוֹעֵבֹת הָאֵלֶּה ד' אֱלֹקֶיךָ מוֹרִישׁ אוֹתָם מִפָּנֶיךָ:

### 24) סנהדרין סה: ורש"י שם

תנו רבנן: מעונן, רבי שמעון אומר: זה המעביר שבעה מיני זכור על העין. וחכמים אומרים: זה האוחז את העינים. רבי עקיבא אומר: זה המחשב עתים ושעות, ואומר: היום יפה לצאת, למחר יפה ליקח, לימודי ערבי שביעיות חיטין יפות, עיקורי קטניות מהיות רעות

אוחז את העינים – אוחז וסוגר עיני הבריות ומראה להם כאילו עושה דברים של פלא, והוא אינו עושה כלום.

### 25) סנהדרין סז:

אמר אביי: דקפיד אמנא שד, דלא קפיד אמנא כשפים. אמר אביי: הלכות כשפים כהלכות שבת, יש מהן בסקילה, ויש מהן פטור אבל אסור, ויש מהן מותר לכתחלה. העושה מעשה בסקילה, האוחז את העינים פטור אבל אסור, מותר לכתחלה כדרב חנינא ורב אושעיא. כל מעלי שבתא הוו עסקי בהלכות יצירה, ומיברי להו עיגלא תילתא ואכלי ליה.

### 26) משנה, סנהדרין ז:ז

... בעל אוב זה פיתום המדבר משחיו, וידעוני זה המדבר בפיו, הרי אלו בסקילה, והנשאל בהם באזהרה:

### 27) סנהדרין סה:

תנו רבנן: בעל אוב זה המדבר בין הפרקים ומבין אצילי ידיו. ידעוני זה המניח עצם ידוע בפיו, והוא מדבר מאליו. מיתיבי (ישעיהו כ"ט) והיה כאוב מארץ קולך, מאי לאו דמשתעי כי אורחיה? לא, דסליק ויתיב בין הפרקים ומשתעי. תא שמע: (שמואל א' כ"ח) ותאמר האשה אל שאול אלהים ראיתי עלים מן הארץ, מאי לאו דמשתעי כי אורחיה? לא, דיתיב בין הפרקים ומשתעי. שואל אוב היינו ודורש אל המתים למתים כדתניא: (דברים י"ח) ודורש אל המתים זה המרעיב עצמו והולך ולן בבית הקברות כדי שתשרה עליו רוח טומאה. וכשהיה רבי עקיבא מגיע למקרא זה היה בוכה, ומה המרעיב עצמו כדי שתשרה עליו רוח טומאה שורה עליו רוח טומאה, המרעיב עצמו כדי שתשרה עליו רוח טהרה על אחת כמה וכמה....

תנו רבנן: מעונן, רבי שמעון אומר: זה המעביר שבעה מיני זכור על העין. וחכמים אומרים: זה האוחז את העינים. רבי עקיבא אומר: זה המחשב עתים ושעות, ואומר: היום יפה לצאת, למחר יפה ליקח, לימודי ערבי שביעיות חיטין יפות, עיקורי קטניות מהיות רעות.... תנו רבנן: מנחש זה האומר פתו נפלה מפיו מקלו נפלה מידו. בנו קורא לו מאחריו. עורב קורא לו, צבי הפסיקו בדרך, נחש מימינו ושועל משמאלו. אל תתחיל בי, שחרית הוא, ראש חודש הוא מוצאי שבת הוא. תנו רבנן: (ויקרא י"ט) לא תנחשו ולא תעוננו כגון אלו המנחשים בחולדה בעופות ובדגים.

### 28) סוכה נג.

אמר רבי יוחנן: בשעה שכרה דוד שיתין, קפא תהומא ובעי למשטפא עלמא, אמר דוד חמש עשרה מעלות והורידן. אי הכי, חמש עשרה מעלות מעלין מיבעי ליה אמר ליה: הואיל ואדכרתן (מלתא), הכי אתמר: בשעה שכרה דוד שיתין קפא תהומא ובעא למשטפא עלמא, אמר דוד: מי איכא דידע אי שרי למכתב שם אחספא ונשדיה בתהומא ומנח? ליכא דקאמר ליה מידי. אמר דוד: כל דידע למימר ואינו אומר יחנק בגרונו. נשא אחיתופל קל וחומר בעצמו: ומה לעשות שלום בין איש לאשתו, אמרה תורה: שמי שנכתב בקדושה ימחה על המים, לעשות שלום לכל העולם כולו על אחת כמה וכמה. אמר ליה: שרי. כתב שם אחספא, ושדי לתהומא, ונחית תהומא שיתסר אלפי גרמידי.

### 29) רמב"ם, הלכות עובדי כוכבים יא:טז

ודברים האלו כולן דברי שקר וכזב הן והם שהטעו בהן עובדי כוכבים הקדמונים לגויי הארצות כדי שינהגו אחריהן, ואין ראוי לישראל שהם חכמים מחוכמים להמשך בהבלים אלו ולא להעלות על לב שיש תועלת בהן, שנאמר "כי לא נחש ביעקב ולא קסם בישראל", ונאמר "כי הגוים האלה אשר אתה יורש אותם אל מעוננים ואל קוסמים ישמעו ואתה לא כן וגו'", כל המאמין בדברים האלו וכיוצא בהן ומחשב בלבו שהן אמת ודבר חכמה אבל התורה אסרתן אינן אלא מן הסכלים ומחסרי הדעת ובכלל הנשים והקטנים שאין דעתן שלימה, אבל בעלי החכמה ותמימי הדעת ידעו בראיות ברורות שכל אלו הדברים שאסרה תורה אינם דברי חכמה אלא תהו והבל שנמשכו בהן חסרי הדעת ונטשו כל דרכי האמת בגללן, ומפני זה אמרה תורה כשהזהירה על כל אלו ההבלים תמים תהיה עם ה' אלקיך.

### 30) ספר החינוך, מצוות רמט, רן

רמט) משרשי המצוה, לפי שעניינים אלה הם דברי שגעון וסכלות גמורה, ולעם קדוש אשר בחר האל לא יאות להם שישעו בדברי שקר. ועוד שהם סבה להדיח האדם מאמונת השם ומתורתו הקדושה,

רפואות ומדבריו משמע בפירוש ורפא ירפא כמ"ש. אך יש לי מקום עיון במה שכתב שם שאין מעשה רפואות בבית הצדיקים וכן אמרו כל כ"ב שנה דמלך רבה אפילו אומנא לביתיה לא קרא עכ"ל משמע דמפרש שלא הוצרך לרפואה ובגמרא משמע דהוא הלך לבית האומן רק שלא נהג כבוד בעצמו לקרוא אותו לביתו. שוב ראיתי בסוף הוריות מביא גם כן אגדה זאת ומביא בעל עין יעקב שם פירוש גאון דהכי קאמר הזכות של ענוה של רב יוסף גרמה שלא הוצרך כלל לאומן ולזה כוון גם הרמב"ן:

### 11) ויקרא יט:טז, דברים כב:א-ב
לֹא־תֵלֵךְ רָכִיל בְּעַמֶּיךָ לֹא תַעֲמֹד עַל־דַּם רֵעֶךָ אֲנִי ד':
לֹא־תִרְאֶה אֶת־שׁוֹר אָחִיךָ אוֹ אֶת־שֵׂיוֹ נִדָּחִים וְהִתְעַלַּמְתָּ מֵהֶם הָשֵׁב תְּשִׁיבֵם לְאָחִיךָ: וְאִם־לֹא קָרוֹב אָחִיךָ אֵלֶיךָ וְלֹא יְדַעְתּוֹ וַאֲסַפְתּוֹ אֶל־תּוֹךְ בֵּיתֶךָ וְהָיָה עִמְּךָ עַד דְּרֹשׁ אָחִיךָ אֹתוֹ וַהֲשֵׁבֹתוֹ לוֹ:

### 12) רמב"ן, תורת האדם ו
וי"ל כיון שנתנה תורה רשות לרופא לרפאות, ומצוה נמי היא דרמנא רחמנא עליה אין לו לחוש כלום, שאם מתנהג ברפואות כשורה לפי דעתו, אין לו בהן אלא מצוה, דרחמנא פקדי' לרפויי, וליביה אנסיה למטעא.

### 13) יומא פג:
תניא: מי שנשכו נחש קורין לו רופא ממקום למקום

### 14) שולחן ערוך, יורה דעה שלו:א
נתנה התורה רשות לרופא לרפאות ומצוה היא ובכלל פיקוח נפש הוא ואם מונע עצמו הרי זה שופך דמים ואפי' יש לו מי שירפאנו שלא מן הכל אדם זוכה להתרפאות

### 15) שולחן ערוך, יורה דעה שלו:א
ומיהו לא יתעסק ברפואה אא"כ הוא בקי ולא יהא שם גדול ממנו שאם לא כן הרי זה שופך דמים ואם ריפא שלא ברשות בית דין חייב בתשלומין אפי' אם הוא בקי ואם ריפא ברשות ב"ד וטעה והזיק פטור מדיני אדם וחייב בדיני שמים ואם המית ונודע לו ששגג גולה על ידו:

### 16) שו"ת ריב"ש תמז
שאין לנו, לדון בדיני תורתנו ומצותיה, על פי חכמי הטבע והרפואה. שאם נאמין לדבריהם, אין תורה מן השמים, חלילה! כי כן הניחו הם, במופתיהם הכוזבים. ואם תדין בדיני הטרפות, על פי חכמי הרפואה; שכר הרבה תטול מן הקצבים ... כמוזכר בפרק המפלת (נידה ל':): "אני מביא ראיה מן התורה, ואתם מביאים ראיה מן השוטים?" ובכמה ענינים, בסוד היצירה, הם חולקים על דברי רז"ל. כמו צורת יצירת הולד לארבעים יום ...

### 17) שו"ת חתם סופר חלק ב (יורה דעה) מה
והנסיון הוא עד נאמן יותר מכל הסברות הבנויות על ראיות

### 18) דברים כו:ג, ראש השנה כה:
וּבָאתָ אֶל־הַכֹּהֵן אֲשֶׁר יִהְיֶה בַּיָּמִים הָהֵם וְאָמַרְתָּ אֵלָיו הִגַּדְתִּי הַיּוֹם לַד' אֱלֹהֶיךָ כִּי־בָאתִי אֶל־הָאָרֶץ אֲשֶׁר נִשְׁבַּע ד' לַאֲבֹתֵינוּ לָתֶת לָנוּ:
"ובאת אל הכהנים הלוים ואל השפט אשר יהיה בימים ההם" וכי תעלה על דעתך שאדם הולך אצל הדיין שלא היה בימיו? הא אין לך לילך אלא אצל שופט שבימיו

### 19) הרב אברהם יצחק הכהן קוק, עולת ראיה א:שצ
ומי הוא האדם שיוכל להתפאר ולומר שיודע הוא את כוחות הגוף והנפש, ואת יחושם גם כן את כוחות העולם הכללי אשר מסביב

### 20) שו"ת רדב"ז, חלק ד:סו, משלי יד:י
שאם אמר צריך אני לאכול אפילו שאמר הרופא שהמאכל יזיקהו שומעין לחולה דלב יודע מרת נפשו.
לֵב יוֹדֵעַ מָרַת נַפְשׁוֹ וּבְשִׂמְחָתוֹ לֹא־יִתְעָרַב זָר:

### 21) רמב"ם, הלכות שביתת העשור ב:ח, שולחן ערוך, אורח חיים תריח:ג ומגן אברהם שם
חולה שיש בו סכנה ששאל לאכול ביום הכפורים אע"פ שהרופאים הבקיאין אומרים אינו צריך מאכילין אותו על פי עצמו עד שיאמר די
ואם החולה (ביום כיפור) אומר צריך אני (לאכול) אפילו מאה רופאים אומרים א"צ שומעים לחולה:
צריך אני – אפילו הרופאים אומרים שהמאכל יזיקהו שומעין לחולה

### 22) שולחן ערוך, אורח חיים שכח:י'-י"א
י כל חולי שהרופאים אומרים שהוא סכנה אע"פ שהוא על הבשר מבחוץ מחללין עליו את השבת ואם רופא אחד אומר צריך ורופא אחד אומר א"צ מחללין ויש מי שאומר שאין צריך מומחה דכל בני אדם חשובים מומחין קצת וספק נפשות להקל: הגה וי"א דוקא ישראלים אבל סתם א"י שאינו רופאין לא מחזיקין אותם כבקיאים (איסור והיתר הארוך). מי שרוצים לאנסו לעבור עבירה גדולה אין מחללין עליו השבת כדי להצילו (ע"ל סימן ש"ו) (ב"י בשם הרשב"א) :

יא חולה שיש בו סכנה שאמדוהו ביום שבת שצריך לעשות לו רפואה ידועה שיש בה מלאכת חילול שבת שמונה ימים אין אומרים נמתין עד הלילה ונמצא שלא לחלל עליו אלא שבת אחת אלא יעשו מיד אע"פ שמחללין עליו שתי שבתות ולכבות הנר בשביל שיישן ע"ל סי' רע"ח:

# SOURCES ON ALTERNATIVE MEDICINE IN JUDAISM

**1) דברים ד:טו, סנהדרין לז.**
וְנִשְׁמַרְתֶּם מְאֹד לְנַפְשֹׁתֵיכֶם כִּי לֹא רְאִיתֶם כָּל־תְּמוּנָה בְּיוֹם דִּבֶּר ד' אֲלֵיכֶם בְּחֹרֵב מִתּוֹךְ הָאֵשׁ:
... ללמדך שכל המאבד נפש אחת מישראל (מעלה) עליו הכתוב כאילו איבד עולם מלא, וכל המקיים נפש אחת (מישראל) מעלה עליו הכתוב כאילו קיים עולם מלא.

**2) בבא קמא מו:**
הא למה לי קרא? סברא הוא, דכאיב ליה כאיבא אזיל לבי אסיא ...

**3) שמות כא:יט**
אִם־יָקוּם וְהִתְהַלֵּךְ בַּחוּץ עַל־מִשְׁעַנְתּוֹ וְנִקָּה הַמַּכֶּה רַק שִׁבְתּוֹ יִתֵּן וְרַפֹּא יְרַפֵּא:

**4) רמב"ן, פירוש המשניות על נדרים ד:ד**
... ורפואת נפשו הוא שירפא לגופו ורפואת ממון שירפא בהמתו, ומותר לו להגיד מה שיועיל לבהמתו, ואמנם אסור לו לרפאותה בידיו, ואין זה אסור לחולה עצמו, לפי שהוא מצוה, רוצה לומר חיוב הרופא מן התורה לרפאות חולי ישראל, וזה נכלל בפירוש מה שאמר הפסוק (דברים כב), והשבותו לו, לרפאות את גופו שהוא כשראאה אתו מסוכן ויכול להצילו או בגופו או בממונו או בחכמתו

**5) רמב"ם, הלכות דעות ג:ג, ד:כג**
המנהיג עצמו על פי הרפואה, אם שם על לבו שיהיה כל גופו ואבריו שלמים בלבד ושיהיו לו בנים עושין מלאכתו ועמלין לצורכו אין זו דרך טובה, אלא ישים על לבו שיהיה גופו שלם וחזק כדי שתהיה נפשו ישרה לדעת את ה', שאי אפשר שיבין וישתכל בחכמות והוא רעב וחולה או אחד מאיבריו כואב.
כל עיר שאין בה עשרה דברים האלו אין תלמיד חכם רשאי לדור בתוכה, ואלו הן: רופא, ואומן, ובית המרחץ, ובית הכסא, ומים מצויין כגון נהר ומעין, ובית הכנסת, ומלמד תינוקות, ולבלר, וגבאי צדקה, ובית דין מכים וחובשים.

**6) שמות טו:כו**
וַיֹּאמֶר אִם־שָׁמוֹעַ תִּשְׁמַע לְקוֹל ד' אֱלֹהֶיךָ וְהַיָּשָׁר בְּעֵינָיו תַּעֲשֶׂה וְהַאֲזַנְתָּ לְמִצְוֹתָיו וְשָׁמַרְתָּ כָּל־חֻקָּיו כָּל־הַמַּחֲלָה אֲשֶׁר־שַׂמְתִּי בְמִצְרַיִם לֹא־אָשִׂים עָלֶיךָ כִּי אֲנִי ד' רֹפְאֶךָ:

**7) שמונה עשרה לחול, ברכה #10**
רְפָאֵנוּ ד' וְנֵרָפֵא. הוֹשִׁיעֵנוּ וְנִוָּשֵׁעָה כִּי תְהִלָּתֵנוּ אָתָּה.

---

וְהַעֲלֵה רְפוּאָה שְׁלֵמָה לְכָל מַכּוֹתֵינוּ. כִּי אֵל מֶלֶךְ רוֹפֵא נֶאֱמָן וְרַחֲמָן אָתָּה. בָּרוּךְ אַתָּה ד'. רוֹפֵא חוֹלֵי עַמּוֹ יִשְׂרָאֵל:

**8) בבא קמא פה.**
תניא, דבי ר' ישמעאל אומר: (שמות כ"א) ורפא ירפא מכאן שניתנה רשות לרופא לרפאות.

**9) שמות כא:יט**
אִם־יָקוּם וְהִתְהַלֵּךְ בַּחוּץ עַל־מִשְׁעַנְתּוֹ וְנִקָּה הַמַּכֶּה רַק שִׁבְתּוֹ יִתֵּן וְרַפֹּא יְרַפֵּא:

**10) טורי זהב א על שולחן ערוך, יורה דעה של**
נתנה תורה רשות כו' ומצוה היא כו' - קשה כיון דבאמת מצוה היא למה קרי לה תחלה רשות ונראה דהכי הוא כוונת הענין זה דרפואה האמיתית היא ע"פ בקשת רחמים דמשמיא יש לו רפואה כמ"ש מחצתי ואני ארפא אלא שאין האדם זוכה לכך אלא צריך לעשות רפואה על פי טבע העולם והוא יתברך הסכים על זה ונתן הרפואה ע"י טבע הרפואות וזהו נתינת רשות של הקדוש ב"ה וכיון שכבר בא האדם לידי כך יש חיוב על הרופא לעשות רפואתו וזה מבואר בגמרא פרק הרואה (דף ס"ב) דאמר רב אחא הנכנס להקיז דם אומר יהי רצון מלפניך שיהא עסק זה לי לרפואה ותרפאני כי א"ל רופא נאמן אתה ורפואתך אמת לפי שאין דרכן של בני אדם לרפאות פירש"י כלומר לא היה להם לעסוק ברפואות אלא לבקש רחמים אמר אביי לא לימא אינש הכי דתנא דבי רבי ישמעאל ורפא ירפא מכאן שניתנה רשות לרופא לרפא והאי לישנא שכן אין דרכן של בני אדם בנוסח התפלה שאומר המקיז דם דהיינו שהוא מתנצל למה מבקש רפואה על ידי ההקזה שהוא לפי הטבע אף שאינו מן הראוי לעשות כן אלא לבקש רחמים להנצל ע"י רחמים של מעלה מ"מ מאחר שכבר נהגו לעשות רפואה ע"י הטבע גם אני עושה כן ועל כל פנים אני מודה שהכל בא על ידך כי א"ל רופא נאמן אתה ועל זה חולק אביי דלא לימא שכן נהגו דגם התורה הסכימה על זה שיהא רפואה ע"פ הטבע כי ירידה תורה לסוף דעת האדם שלא יהיה זכאי כל כך שתבא רפואתו ע"י נס מן השמים וע"כ אין שייך לומר דהאי קרא דרפא ירפא מצוה דאלו האדם זכאי אינו צריך לכך ואדרבה היה צריך דוקא רפואה ע"י שמים אלא דלפי דרכו של אדם רשות הוא לו וע"כ הוה האידנא חיוב לדבר ומצוה היא כיון דלפי מעשה האדם חיותו תלוי בכך כן נ"ל נכון ועיין ברמב"ן פ' בחקותי האריך בענין זה של

# SOURCES FOR INTRODUCTION

**1) משנה, אבות ה:כב**
בן בג בג אומר, הפך בה והפך בה, דכולא בה.

**2) אבן שלמה א:ב**
עיקר חיות האדם הוא להתחזק תמיד בשבירת
המידות, ואם לאו למה לו חיים?

**3) תהילים יט:ח**
תּוֹרַת ד' תְּמִימָה מְשִׁיבַת נָפֶשׁ עֵדוּת ד' נֶאֱמָנָה
מַחְכִּימַת פֶּתִי:

**4) מגילה יג.**
כל דבריך אחד הם

**5) תהילים לד:ט**
טַעֲמוּ וּרְאוּ כִּי־טוֹב ד' אַשְׁרֵי הַגֶּבֶר יֶחֱסֶה־בּוֹ:

**6) מדרש ספרי, האזינו א**
ד"א היה ר' יהודה או' לעולם הוי כונס דברי תורה
כללים ומוציאם כללים שנאמר יערוף כמטר לקחי
ואין יערף אלא לשון כנעני משל איך אדם או' לחבירו
פרוט לי סלע זו אלא ערוף לי סלע זו כך הוי כונס
דברי תורה כללים ופורט ומוציאם כטיפים הללו של
טל ולא כטיפי הללו של מטר גדולות אלא כטיפים
הללו של טל שהם קטנים

**7) משלי ג:ו**
בְּכָל־דְּרָכֶיךָ דָעֵהוּ וְהוּא יְיַשֵּׁר אֹרְחֹתֶיךָ:

**8) רמב"ם, הלכות דעות ג:ב**
צריך האדם שיכוון לבו וכל מעשיו כולם לידע את
השם ברוך הוא בלבד, ויהיה שבתו וקומו ודבורו הכל
לעומת זה הדבר, כיצד כשישא ויתן או יעשה מלאכה
ליטול שכר, לא יהיה בלבו לקבוץ ממון בלבד אלא
יעשה דברים האלו כדי שימצא דברים שהגוף צריך
להם מאכילה ושתיה וישיבת בית ונשיאת אשה,
וכן כשיאכל וישתה ויבעול לא ישים בלבו לעשות
דברים האלו כדי ליהנות בלבד עד שנמצא שאינו
אוכל ושותה אלא המתוק לחיך ויבעול כדי ליהנות,
אלא ישים על לבו שיאכל וישתה כדי להברות גופו
ואיבריו בלבד ...

**9) מהר"ל, דרך חיים, פרק א, דף כה**
מה שהאדם הוא טוב עד שאומרים עליו כמה בריאה
זו טובה, היינו כשהוא טוב בעצמו ור"ל בצד בחינת
עצמו יש בו הטוב, וזהו בחינה אחת שאומרים עליו
הבריאה הזאת יש לה מעלה והיא טובה מצד עצמה,
הבחינה השנית שראוי שיהיה טוב לשמים הוא הש"י

---

אשר ברא את האדם ויהיה אליו עובד עושה רצונו,
הג' שראוי שיהיה טוב אל זולתו מבני אדם אשר הם
נמצאים עמו, כי אין האדם נמצא בלבד רק הוא נמצא
עם בני אדם זולתו. וצריך שיהיה האדם טוב בכל
מיני בחינות אשר יבחן האדם, אם בערך עצמו צריך
שיהיה טוב שהרי תיכף ומיד במעשה בראשית נאמר
בכל בריאה כי טוב, שמזה תראה שהבריאה בעצמה
צריך שיהיה בה הטוב, ואם בערך העלה שהוא נמצא
ממנו וצריך שיהיה ג"כ טוב בערך זולתו מבני אדם,
כלל הדבר צריך שיהיה הטוב כאשר יבחן בכל החלקים
כי אין זה כזה ובהקדמה ביארנו אלו ג' דברים ג"כ.

**10) תפילה לפני ברכת ציצית, אושפיזין בסוכות,
הקדמה לארבע מינים**
וּתְהֵא חֲשׁוּבָה מִצְוַת צִיצַת לְפְנֵי הַקָּדוֹשׁ בָּרוּךְ הוּא
כְּאִלּוּ קִיַּמְתִּיהָ בְּכָל פְּרָטֶיהָ וְדִקְדּוּקֶיהָ וְכַוָּנוֹתֶיהָ
וְתַרְי"ג מִצְוֹת הַתְּלוּיִם בָּהּ.
וּתְהֵא חֲשׁוּבָה מִצְוַת סֻכָּה זוֹ שֶׁאֲנִי מְקַיֵּם כְּאִלּוּ
קִיַּמְתִּיהָ בְּכָל פְּרָטֶיהָ וְדִקְדּוּקֶיהָ וּתְנָאֶיהָ וְכָל מִצְוֹת
הַתְּלוּיִם בָּהּ ...
וּתְהֵא חֲשׁוּבָה לְפָנֶיךָ מִצְוַת אַרְבָּעָה מִינִים אֵלּוּ,
כְּאִלּוּ קִיַּמְתִּיהָ בְּכָל פְּרָטוֹתֶיהָ וְשָׁרָשֶׁיהָ וְתַרְי"ג מִצְוֹת
הַתְּלוּיִם בָּהּ ...

**11) ברכת התורה בברכות השחר של תפילת שחרית**
בָּרוּךְ אַתָּה ד' אֱלֹקֵינוּ מֶלֶךְ הָעוֹלָם אֲשֶׁר קִדְּשָׁנוּ
בְּמִצְוֹתָיו וְצִוָּנוּ לַעֲסוֹק בְּדִבְרֵי תוֹרָה:

**12) שמות יט:ח, כד:ג, כד, ז**
וַיַּעֲנוּ כָל־הָעָם יַחְדָּו וַיֹּאמְרוּ כֹּל אֲשֶׁר־דִּבֶּר ד' נַעֲשֶׂה
וַיָּשֶׁב מֹשֶׁה אֶת־דִּבְרֵי הָעָם אֶל־ד':
וַיָּבֹא מֹשֶׁה וַיְסַפֵּר לָעָם אֵת כָּל־דִּבְרֵי ד' וְאֵת כָּל־
הַמִּשְׁפָּטִים וַיַּעַן כָּל־הָעָם קוֹל אֶחָד וַיֹּאמְרוּ כָּל־הַדְּבָרִים
אֲשֶׁר־דִּבֶּר ד' נַעֲשֶׂה:
וַיִּקַּח סֵפֶר הַבְּרִית וַיִּקְרָא בְּאָזְנֵי הָעָם וַיֹּאמְרוּ כֹּל אֲשֶׁר־
דִּבֶּר ד' נַעֲשֶׂה וְנִשְׁמָע:

**13) פירוש המשניות לרמב"ם, סנהדרין י':ג**
כבר הזכרנו לך כמה פעמים שכל מחלוקת שתהיה
בין החכמים ואינה תלויה במעשה אלא קביעת סברא
בלבד אין מקום לפסוק הלכה כאחד מהם

**14) חגיגה טו.**
למה נמשלו תלמידי חכמים לאגוז? לומר לך: מה
אגוז זה, אף על פי שמלוכלך בטיט ובצואה אין מה
שבתוכו נמאס, אף תלמיד חכם, אף על פי שסרח אין
תורתו נמאסת.